MW01041039

40th
SA RUGBY ANNUAL 2011

Edited by Duane Heath & Eddie Grieb

Statistics: Paul Dobson, Eddie Grieb, Piet Landman & Kobus Smit
Production Editor: Alison Ward
Designer: Ryan Manning
Text by the Editors or as credited
Photographs by Gallo Images or as credited

© 2010 – SARU & MWP Media (Pty) Ltd
Printed & bound by Creda Communications, Eliot Ave, Eppindust II, Cape Town
ISBN 978-0-620-48386-5 2011 SA Rugby Annual

The Editors welcome suggestions and notification of any errors or omissions. Email duane@mwp.co.za; fax 086 684 7068;
write to PO Box 22643 Fish Hoek 7974 or Email eddieg@sarugby.co.za; fax 086 559 0744; write to PO Box 989 Olifantsfontein 1665.

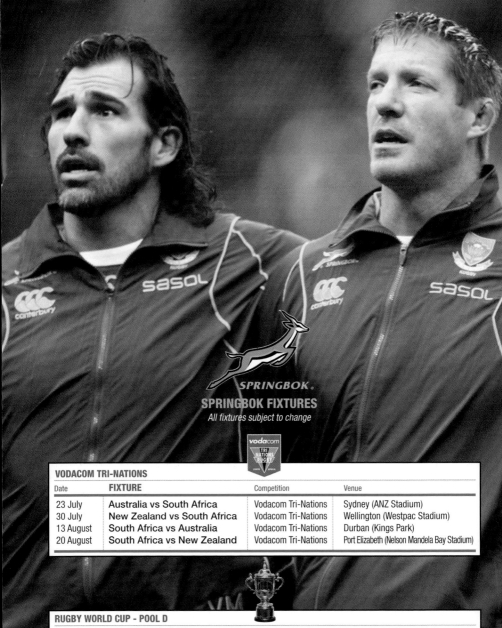

SPRINGBOK FIXTURES

All fixtures subject to change

VODACOM TRI-NATIONS

Date	FIXTURE	Competition	Venue
23 July	Australia vs South Africa	Vodacom Tri-Nations	Sydney (ANZ Stadium)
30 July	New Zealand vs South Africa	Vodacom Tri-Nations	Wellington (Westpac Stadium)
13 August	South Africa vs Australia	Vodacom Tri-Nations	Durban (Kings Park)
20 August	South Africa vs New Zealand	Vodacom Tri-Nations	Port Elizabeth (Nelson Mandela Bay Stadium)

RUGBY WORLD CUP - POOL D

Date	FIXTURE	Venue
11 September	South Africa vs Wales	Wellington (Regional Stadium)
17 September	South Africa vs Fiji	Wellington (Regional Stadium)
22 September	South Africa vs Namibia	Albany (North Harbour Stadium)
30 September	South Africa vs Samoa	Albany (North Harbour Stadium)

2010 – A year of ups and downs

SOUTH African rugby supporters are some of the most passionate you'll find anywhere on the planet. They love the Springboks and our other national teams dearly – as well as their preferred provincial and club sides – and none of us take defeat lightly. That is why the season that has just passed has been a difficult one for all of us involved in the game in South Africa – from coaches, players and administrators to the fans themselves. Yes, there were quite a number of remarkable achievements and milestones, but unfortunately we could not reproduce the results that made 2009 such an astonishing year.

The South African Rugby Union started the year with our Champion Tour – a trip of 6000km around South Africa in a 22-metre-long vehicle filled to the brim with the trophies won by our teams over the past few seasons. It was in the far corners of the country – places such as Robertson, Springbok, Peddie, Polokwane and Ermelo – that we witnessed the passion for rugby. What a privilege to share our successes with the people of our beautiful land.

The Vodacom Bulls and Vodacom Stormers dominated the final Vodacom Super 14 by reaching a historic final at the Orlando Stadium in Soweto – the first game of such magnitude played in this sprawling township south-west of Johannesburg. By winning their third title in four years, the Bulls underlined why they were the best team in the five years of Super 14 rugby and made all of us proud. To underline the depth in Pretoria, the Vodacom Blue Bulls won a thrilling Vodacom Cup final by beating the Vodacom Free State Cheetahs with a drop goal after the siren had sounded. It was a magnificent advertisement for the riches of young players we have in South Africa.

The Springboks started the international season on a good note, beating Wales in Cardiff before crushing France, the Six Nations champions, in Cape Town. Italy followed in Witbank – the first-ever Test played in Mpumalanga – and East London, setting Peter de Villiers and his team up for the defence of their Vodacom Tri-Nations title. The rejuvenated All Blacks and Wallabies were too good for the Boks in New Zealand and Australia. It didn't go much better at home, with last-minute defeats in Soweto and Bloemfontein while the Boks managed to beat the Wallabies with a great come-from-behind performance in Pretoria.

The Soweto Test against the All Blacks was a very special occasion. Our long-standing captain, John Smit, ran out for South Africa for the 100th time and the biggest official crowd to witness a Bok Test turned out at a packed FNB Stadium.

A week later Victor Matfield followed Smit by becoming only the third Bok to reach 100 Tests – in front of his home crowd at Loftus Versfeld. We are privileged to have players like John and Victor in the Springbok set-up – for a decade now they've been superb ambassadors for South Africa and are respected the world over.

Our Springbok Sevens team fought gallantly in an attempt to reclaim their IRB Sevens World Series title, but after losing a number of experienced players to the fifteen-man code, coach Paul Treu and his side struggled.

The Sharks and Vodacom Western Province showed that our domestic game is in great shape with an epic Absa Currie Cup final in Durban, where the home team won the coveted golden cup for the second time in three years. And wasn't it good to see the rugby revival in Port Elizabeth, where the Eastern Province Kings showed their intention to be ready when they take the step up to Super Rugby level in 2013 as the anchor province in the Southern Kings franchise. The Kings won the Absa Currie Cup First Division, but were pipped at the post in their quest to win promotion to the Premier Division.

Unfortunately the Boks could not achieve the Grand Slam in November, but under difficult circumstances and in trying conditions showed we have some excellent young players coming through – depth should not be a problem at the Rugby World Cup in New Zealand in 2011. With less than a year to go before the Boks head down to the Land of the Long White Cloud to defend the Webb Ellis Cup, we'll be doing everything in our power to help them achieve success.

It's going to take a lot of hard work, but we're confident we have the players and coaches to turn things around in 2011. There is much to be optimistic about and as we get ready for RWC 2011, we urge everyone to Unite behind the Boks.

OREGAN HOSKINS
President
South African Rugby Union

Victor Matfield receives his golden 100-Test cap from SARU President Oregan Hoskins after the Springboks had beaten Australia at Loftus Versfeld.

CONTENTS

SA RUGBY ANNUAL 2011

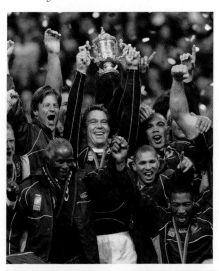

NOTES & ABBREVIATIONS

NOTES

1. All records are correct as at 1 January 2011, unless otherwise stated.

2. All teams listed are in the order of fullback (15) to loosehead prop (1).

3. For record purposes, team names at the time of the establishment of the record have been used.

4. Union names and the names of their senior teams in 2009 are as follows:

Blue Bulls Rugby Union (formerly Northern Transvaal) – playing as Vodacom Blue Bulls.

Boland Rugby Union – playing as Boland Cavaliers.

Border Rugby Union – playing as Border Bulldogs.

Eastern Province Rugby Football Union – playing as Eastern Province Kings.

Free State Rugby Union (formerly Orange Free State) – playing as Vodacom Free State Cheetahs.

Golden Lions Rugby Union (formerly Transvaal and Gauteng Lions) – playing as Xerox Lions.

Griffons Rugby Union (formerly Northern Free State) – playing as the Griffons.

Griqualand West Rugby Union – playing as GWK Griquas.

Leopards Rugby Union (formerly Western Transvaal & North West) – playing as Platinum Leopards.

Mpumalanga Rugby Union (formerly South Eastern Transvaal) – playing as the Pumas.

KwaZulu-Natal Rugby Union (formerly Natal) – playing as the Sharks.

South Western Districts Rugby Football Union – playing as SWD Eagles.

Valke Rugby Union (formerly Eastern Transvaal, Gauteng Falcons & Falcons) – playing as the Valke.

Western Province Rugby Football Union – playing as Vodacom Western Province.

5. Definition of a 'first-class match' and 'first-class appearance':

i) To qualify as a first-class match, it must be played strictly according to the Laws of the game (no more than seven players on the bench).

ii) The following categories of matches qualify for first-class status if point i) is fulfilled:

a) All matches featuring the South African national team (Springboks);

b) All matches in senior competitions sanctioned by SARU;

c) All matches against touring international teams;

d) All matches between senior provincial teams and touring teams of the same or a higher status;

e) All matches between senior provincial teams outside of SARU competitions where the strongest possible teams are fielded;

f) All matches played by senior teams carrying the name of a South African national team;

g) All matches played by senior composite teams in IRB approved competitions.

iii) Any player appearing in one of the above matches (either in the starting XV or as a replacement – blood replacements and yellow-card replacements included) will be deemed to have made a first-class appearance.

TEAM ABBREVIATIONS

SOUTH AFRICAN TEAMS: BB – Blue Bulls, Bol – Boland, Bor – Border, EP – Eastern Province, ETvl – Eastern Transvaal, F – Falcons (if province), FS – Free State, GF – Gauteng Falcons, GL – Golden Lions, GW – Griqualand West, Mpu – Mpumalanga, NEC – North Eastern Cape, NED – North Eastern Districts, NNtl – Northern Natal, NOFS – Northern Orange Free State, NTvl – Northern Transvaal, OFS – Orange Free State, SWD – South Western Districts, Tvl – Transvaal, WP – Western Province, WTvl – Western Transvaal.

MAJOR INTERNATIONAL TEAMS: A – Australia, Arg – Argentina, BI – British Isles, E – England, F – France (if opponent), I – Ireland, It – Italy, NZ – New Zealand, S – Scotland, W – Wales.

OTHER TEAMS: Bots – Botswana, C – Canada, Cam – Cameroon, Fj – Fiji, G – Georgia, Gulf – Gulf States, IC – Ivory Coast, J – Japan, Ken – Kenya, Mad – Madagascar, Mor – Morocco, Nam – Namibia, Neth – Netherlands, Nor – Norway, NZC – New Zealand Cavaliers (1986), P – Portugal, PI – Pacific Islanders, R – Romania, Russ – Russia, Sam – Samoa, SAm – South America, SETvl – South Eastern Transvaal, Sp – Spain, SWA – South West Africa, Swazi – Swaziland, T – Tonga, Tan – Tanzania, Tun – Tunisia, U – Uruguay, Ug – Uganda, WS – Western Samoa, WT – World XV, Z – Zimbabwe, Zam – Zambia

Preface

SOUTH Africans, it seems, are never short of old-fashioned guts and *gees* whenever a unique challenge presents itself.

Like so many Springbok sides who have prevailed against the odds down the years, this 40th anniversary edition of the *SA Rugby Annual* would simply not have seen the light of day without an almighty team effort.

Rugby teaches one to dig deep – no matter on which side of the famed 'four white lines' you find yourself – and it's thanks to the determination of everyone involved, from the journalists, photographers and statisticians to the printers, marketers and distributors that the *SA Rugby Annual 2011* is once again available for players, fans, grannies, aunts, wives and girlfriends to find on the bookshelves before Christmas.

The 2010 edition was the first to break with the tradition of a New Year release when it came off the presses just two weeks after the final match of the season. For the 2011 edition the margins were even tighter because of the Springboks' December fixture against the Barbarians.

Cue the guts and *gees*. Within hours of the final whistle, the book you are holding was ready to be transformed from an unassuming electronic file into a vibrant, physical record of an historic year in South African rugby.

Without the unrivalled statistics that are found between its covers, the *Annual* would not be nearly as definitive a record of the South African season as is the case. For their tireless efforts once again, my co-editor Eddie Grieb and his team of Kobus Smit, Piet Landman, Paul Dobson, Heinrich Schulze, Gideon Nieman, Ashley Berry, Frikkie van Rensburg and Jean de Witt can't be thanked enough for their determination to deliver on deadline.

Thanks also to Herman le Roux and Johan Botes, and to our overseas friends – John Griffiths (IRB statistician), Geoff Miller (NZRU statistician), Matthew Alvarez (ARU statistician), Stuart Farmer (Stuart Farmer Media Services Ltd, England) and Lee Ashton (New Zealand).

The Annual is, as always, also a showcase for fine sports photography, thanks to Paul Sales and his team of lensmen at Gallo Images – Duif du Toit, Lee Warren, Steve Haag, Carl Fourie, Tertius Pickard, Charles Lombard, Dominic Barnardt, Michael Sheehan, Louis Botha, Johan Pretorius, Anesh Debiky, Shaun Roy and Wessel Oosthuizen.

On the journalism side, I am grateful to the many writers whose unique way with words has once again made the *2011 Annual* not only an entertaining read but also a respected document of record.

In alphabetical order they are: John Bishop, Ken Bor-land, Marco Botha, Ruan Bruwer, Jon Cardinelli, Jonathan Cook, Piet de Jager, Louis de Villiers, Paul Dobson, Michael Green, JJ Harmse, Rob Houwing, Pieter Jordaan, Brian McLean, Stephen Nell, Gideon Nieman, Craig Ray, Dan Retief and Heinrich Schulze.

Rayaan Adriaanse, De Jongh Borchardt and Yusuf Jackson of the SARU communications department also deserve thanks for contributing to the final product, while special thanks goes to the Annual's long-time editor and now SARU strategic communications manager, Andy Colquhoun, for his unwavering support and input – despite having so many other matters else to deal with on a daily basis.

Our friends at the provincial unions must again be thanked for answering our calls with enthusiasm – Saartjie Olivier (Blue Bulls), Loret Hechter (Golden Lions), Piet Strydom (KZN), Marius van Rensburg (Mpumalanga), Emil Oelrich (Valke), Revenne Maritz (WP), Hendrik Snyders (Boland), Lewies van Zyl (SWD), Karen Crafford (Leopards), Leah van Wyk (Griffons), Debbie Ellis (EP), Lizette Viviers & Frikkie van Rensburg (Free State) and Human Kriek (Griquas).

Speaking of administrators, thanks as always must go to the South African Rugby Union for their ongoing support of a publication that has been called the best yearbook in world rugby. Without their vision and funding, the Annual would simply cease to exist – and rugby would be the poorer for it.

I would also like to acknowledge the tremendous support given by production editor Alison Ward of MWP, who co-publish the Annual together with SARU; Lesley Ackermann and Linda Kay of printers Creda Communications, whose enthusiasm and professionalism were greatly appreciated; and Mark Hackney, Neille Wrigley and Natasha Store at Blue Weaver.

Finally, very special thanks go once again to Eddie Grieb and designer Ryan Manning, whose creativity and attention to detail can be seen on every page, as well as to Kobus Smit and Stephen Nell for their willingness to go beyond the call of duty.

And, as always, on behalf of them I must thank our long-suffering family members who made the late nights more bearable with their patience and coffee-making skills – Alida Grieb and Lee & Edrich; Vanessa Manning and Hannah & Joshua; Miranda Smit; and, finally, to my wife Aisling and our son Kian.

Duane Heath
Cape Town, December 2010

SOUTH AFRICAN RUGBY UNION

SA RUGBY

ADDRESS:
Fifth Floor, Sports Science
Institute of SA Building,
Boundary Rd, Newlands, 7700,
Cape Town.
TELEPHONE:
+27 21 659 6700 or 6900
EMAIL:
info@sarugby.co.za

SARU OFFICE BEARERS

| Oregan Hoskins | Mark Alexander | James Stoffberg |
| (President) | (Deputy President) | (Vice-President) |

MEMBERS OF THE EXECUTIVE COUNCIL
Dr Jan Marais (Chairman)
Mark Alexander
Boet Fick
Dawie Groenewald
Basil Haddad (CFO)
Oregan Hoskins
Dr Ismail Jakoet (Company secretary)
*Jurie Roux (CEO)
James Stoffberg
Mike Stofile
Monde Tabata

Replaced Johan Prinsloo as CEO on 1 October 2010

STAFF (as at 1 December 2010)
Zeenat Abdullah, Allie Abrahams, Ethelwyn Adams, Hilton Adonis, Rayaan Adriaanse, Maria Ananias, Anna Andreas, Margareth Arendse, Chumani Bembe, Justine Blacker, De Jongh Borchardt, Louise Bradbury, Andy Colquhoun, Aletta Coetzee, Lois Coetzee, Nelda Cozyn, Peter de Villiers, Patricia Dlakavu, Dana Eitzen, Michele English, Tanya Everson, Christo Ferreira, JJ Fredericks, John Gallard, Fred Geduldt, Philicia George, Arnold Gertse, Valda Gertse, Sumantha Gounden, Mervin Green, Debra Griffiths, Ronel Groenewald, Basil Haddad, Neville Heilbron, Danielle Isaacs, Yusuf Jackson, Dr Ismail Jakoet, Craig Joubert, Jonathan Kaplan, Kolisa Kongo, Xhanti Lamani, Mark Lawrence, Nomini Malungisa, Ingrid Mangcu, Willie Maree, Andy Marinos, Ziada Martin, Herman Masimla, Khaya Mayedwa, Annelee Murray, Mveleli Ncula, Karen Nell, Irven October, Zolile Peni, Andrea Pharaoh, Johan Prinsloo, Mahlubi Puzi, Martha Qabo, Clint Readhead, Juanita Roodman, Steven Roos, Jurie Roux, Sesi Sekhosana, Eric Sofisa, Hazel Solomon, Unathi Sompondo, Paul Treu, Carla van der Merwe, Frikkie van Eeden, Mingon van Rooyen, Dr. Wayne Viljoen, Andre Watson, Jenny Wentzel, Christine Williams, Sarah Williams, Marvin Wymers, Coris Zietsman.

EXECUTIVE COUNCIL OF THE SOUTH AFRICAN RUGBY UNION IN 2010
BACK ROW (L to R): Basil Haddad, Dawie Groenewald, Jurie Roux (CEO), Piet Heymans (Sarpa),
Mike Stofile, Dr Ismail Jakoet (Company Secretary), Monde Tabata.
FRONT ROW (L to R): James Stoffberg (Vice-president), Dr Jan Marais (Chairman), Oregan Hoskins (President),
Mark Alexander (Deputy-president), Boet Fick.

SECTION 1
COMMENT & AWARDS

Notes by the Editor

HISTORY AND HINDSIGHT

THE 2010 season may not be remembered as the greatest year in Springbok history but away from the cauldron of the international game, and its associated fine lines between winning and losing, there was much about South African rugby to be positive about as the game entered a World Cup year.

The headlines and the history books will show that Peter de Villiers' world champion Springboks managed just eight wins from their 15 appearances, including five defeats in the Vodacom Tri-Nations and a failed attempt at the grand slam during their November tour to Europe that reached its nadir with defeat against Scotland.

But history, as they say, has a funny way of repeating itself, and as the year wound down and the players caught their collective breath after another non-stop 11 months spent travelling the globe, the general feeling, as it was at the corresponding time in 2006 under Jake White, was that there was no reason why the Boks could not steady the ship and challenge strongly for the Webb Ellis Cup, their off-colour performances in 2010 notwithstanding.

De Villiers' troops tasted defeat in six Tests as well as against the Barbarians, while White had a similar record of seven losses in 12 Tests in the year before the World Cup.

In both instances, however, the Springboks began the task of rebuilding their self-confidence with a morale-boosting season-ending victory over England at Twickenham.

Only time will tell whether the Boks' 2010 win will provide a similar springboard to World Cup glory for De Villiers as it did for White four years previously. The lure of becoming the first team to successfully defend their title is sure to guarantee stiff competition for places in the final 30, made all the more interesting by the return in 2011 of the likes of John Smit, Fourie du Preez, Schalk Burger, Jaque Fourie, JP Pietersen, Juan de Jongh and Gurthrö Steenkamp.

Also weighted heavily in the Boks' favour is that World Cups have a knockout component that suits South Africans to a tee. As the All Blacks have found out in five successive tournaments dating back to 1991, it's one thing to start as favourites, but quite another to navigate through a draw that could very easily put the form sides on a collision course long before the final.

The Springboks, thanks to the Absa Currie Cup, have honed their hunger for knockout rugby over many decades and it's this deeply ingrained ability to scrap out wins – as they did against England – which should serve them better than any grand slam.

WHEN IN SOWETO…

THE FIFA World Cup left a lasting sporting legacy in 2010 in the form of world-class stadiums, but what was completely unexpected was how the world's biggest sporting event helped rugby to enter new territory and make new friends.

With Loftus Versfeld off limits to the Vodacom Bulls as they entered the Vodacom Super 14 knockout rounds, the Blue Bulls Rugby Union took a decision to play their semi-final, and later the final, at the Orlando Stadium in Soweto. The result, clear to see in the pages of this book, was a vibrant mix of dyed-in-the-wool Bulls fans mixing with rugby's newest converts – and sharing the experience in shebeens across the township. The Bulls benefited greatly from the positive publicity generated from the two matches, and few would be surprised if Victor Matfield's men don't revisit the scene of their third Super 14 triumph in the not-too-distant future.

ALL BLACK HEARTACHE

THE Golden Lions Rugby Union, under their new president Kevin de Klerk, weren't about to be outdone by their northern neighbours and promptly moved the Springboks vs All Blacks Vodacom Tri-Nations clash from Coca-Cola Park to the FNB Stadium just a month after the massive stadium hosted the FIFA World Cup final.

It was also the occasion of Springbok captain John Smit's 100th Test appearance, although his evening ended in heartbreak in front of the biggest crowd to watch a Test in South Africa since 1955 when he missed a tackle in injury time that allowed the All Blacks to snatch a come-from-behind victory.

MATFIELD MILESTONE

SMIT wasn't the only player to pass the magical three-figure mark in 2010. Bulls captain and Smit's long-time dep-

uty, Victor Matfield, celebrated his century on his home ground a week later when the Boks beat the Wallabies in a high-scoring thriller. With Smit missing the end-of-year tour with a neck injury, Matfield assumed the captaincy with aplomb and demonstrated just how well South African rugby is served in the leadership department by stepping into Smit's considerable boots without fuss.

KINGS FIND THEIR CROWN

AWAY from the international scene, 2010 will be remembered as the year that Eastern Province rugby rose from the ashes. Under former Springbok assistant coach Alan Solomons, the team, renamed the EP Kings, won the Currie Cup First Division title but lost a hard-fought promotion/relegation battle against the Pumas. The defeat came as a massive setback for rugby in the Eastern Cape, given their Super Rugby ambitions, but with Solomons at the helm it is surely only a matter of time until EP rugby returns to its former glory.

SAFETY FIRST

SARU's mission to make the game as safe as possible, through its excellent BokSmart National Rugby Safety Programme, took another bold step forward when they announced that, as from 1 January 2011, no referee would be allowed to handle a SARU-sanctioned game without being BokSmart Certified.

BokSmart had already educated 17,000 coaches and referees countrywide by the end of 2010, having conducted more than 737 rugby safety workshops across the 14 provinces. Dan Lombard, a C4/5 Quadriplegic, recorded a notable landmark when he became the first quadriplegic rugby coach to attend a BokSmart safety course, hosted by the Blue Bulls Rugby Union at Loftus Versfeld.

"Hopefully with the BokSmart programme, we can ensure that few players have to experience what Dan has at such a young age," said BokSmart's Project Manager Wayne Viljoen. "However, it is really good to see that Dan is still actively involved in the game and playing such a positive role. Dan and all the players catastrophically injured on the rugby fields before him, are the reason why BokSmart has come about, and if everyone involved in the game performs their role properly we can make a meaningful difference in curtailing these kinds of injuries."

FUND TURNS 30

THE Chris Burger Petro Jackson Players' Fund commemorated its 30th anniversary in 2010 and continues to go from strength to strength under the chairmanship of founder and former Springbok captain Morné du Plessis. The Fund, which was established in 1980 after Du Plessis' Western Province teammate Chris Burger died after breaking his neck in a Currie Cup match against Free State in Bloemfontein, cares for over 100 former players who were all catastrophically injured playing the game they loved.

However, thanks to their partnership with BokSmart, Du Plessis believes that the rate of serious injuries, especially amongst schoolboys, can be slowed through proper education. The rugby public once again showed their generosity when nearly R1-million was raised at the Fund's annual banquet and telethon held at Montecasino in Johannesburg.

NEEDLE IN A HAYSTACK

SOUTH African rugby was dragged into the larger sports doping debate after Springboks Chiliboy Ralepelle and Bjorn Basson in November became the latest athletes worldwide to fall foul of the stimulant methylhexaneamine.

The sport may not yet be ready to admit it, but these

days everyone from size-obsessed schoolboys to prominent Springboks use a cocktail of supplements freely available in pharmacies and health shops in the often mistaken belief that the substances will make them better rugby players.

The supplement industry has however moved on from the days of sugar-laden 'weight-gainers' and amino acid tablets: today's aspiring schoolboy stars, obsessed with being as big as the steroid-fuelled bodybuilders in their local gym, are now seduced by 'pre-workout boosters' that they have begun to take before practices and matches as well.

It's in these "explosive energy drinks" that manufacturers are resorting to inserting substances such as methylhexaneamine, in order to hook customers with the "kick" they believe will allow them to make the big hit or score the winning try.

Anabolic steroid abuse in SA rugby remains a concern, especially at schoolboy level, but ironically it took a relatively innocuous stimulant like methylhexaneamine to provide a wake-up call for the sport.

VARSITY CUP FEVER
STUDENT rugby continued its revival in 2010 thanks to the highly successful Varsity Cup tournament, which was won for the third time in a row by the Maties of Stellenbosch. Since its inception in 2008, the Varsity Cup has not only managed to breathe new life into a once vibrant student game, but also served as an additional shop window for professional coaches on the lookout for talented players who, for some reason or other, had slipped through the Craven Week net. At the time of writing, organisers had planned to expand the competition to include a number of second-tier universities such as Fort Hare and the University of the Western Cape – a move that can only help the tournament grow from strength to strength.

2010 SARU Award Winners:

SARU Player of the Year –
Gurthrö Steenkamp (Vodacom Blue Bulls)

Players' Player of the Year –
Gio Aplon (Vodacom Western Province)

SARU Young Player of the Year –
Elton Jantjies (Xerox Lions)

SARU Team of the Year –
Vodacom Bulls

Absa Coach of the Year –
Allister Coetzee

Vodacom Super 14 Player of the Year –
Andries Bekker (Vodacom Stormers)

Absa Curie Cup Premier Division Player of the Year –
Bjorn Basson (GWK Griquas)

Absa Curie Cup First Division Player of the Year –
Norman Nelson (Eastern Province Kings)

SuperSport Try of the Year –
Jaque Fourie (Vodacom Stormers v Crusaders)

Sasol Sevens Player of the Year –
Kyle Brown

SA Under-20 Player of the Year –
Elton Jantjies (Xerox Lions)

Vodacom Cup Player of the Year –
Francois Brummer (Vodacom Blue Bulls)

SAA Club Champs Player of the Year –
Lourens Adriaanse (Maties)

SARU Women's Rugby Achiever of the Year –
Dolly Mavungwana

Marriott Refereeing Achievement of the Year –
Craig Joubert

Coca-Cola Craven Week Player of the Tournament –
Johan Goosen (Free State)

SARU PLAYER OF THE YEAR
GURTHRÖ STEENKAMP
(Vodacom Blue Bulls & South Africa)

IN the life and professional rugby career of Gurthrö Steenkamp, 6 November 2009 will remain forever his personal D-Day. It was on that day that, at 28 years of age, he was written off as a has-been after taking heavy strain during the Springboks' midweek defeat to the Leicester Tigers.

Italy's Martin Castrogiovanni – one of the best tight-head props on the planet – scrummed Steenkamp into the ground. He was replaced shortly after half-time and did not play again on the end-of-year tour, returning to South Africa injured and shamed.

Now fast-forward a few months, to 19 June 2010. Steenkamp was up against Castrogiovanni again, this time after helping the Vodacom Bulls to their third Vodacom Super 14 title in four years. He was playing superb rugby and getting through heaps of work all around the park.

This time, on the hard turf of the Puma Stadium in Witbank, the shoe was literally on the other foot. Castrogiovanni left the field in the 19th minute, the much-vaunted Italian scrum spent most of the afternoon in reverse, and even though the Boks' victory was not convincing, the man wearing No 1 on his back felt vindicated.

Add to this the demolition of France's tighthead Nicolas Mas a week earlier at Newlands, and a second scrumming lesson handed to the Azzurri on 26 June, and it became clear that Steenkamp was back to his brilliant best – a mere seven months after he was told he would never play for South Africa again.

Speaking after the Vodacom Tri-Nations, during which he started in every one of the Boks' six Tests and scored three tries, Steenkamp admitted he was a shattered man at the end of 2009.

"Beast (Tendai Mtawarira) played very well against the British & Irish Lions and the tour at the end of 2009 did not work out well for me," he said. "But I made the decision to get back to my best and I think I achieved that. All the games that I played for the Boks were a lovely bonus."

The secret to his success? Good old-fashioned hard work. Steenkamp slogged away tirelessly during the Bulls' notorious annual training camp in George and did not let up when the season started. He played in 14 of the champions' 15 games and emerged as one of the leaders of a powerful pack that stood back for no one.

Playing a crucial role for the Bulls in their title-winning campaign gave Steenkamp the confidence he needed to excel at international level once more. His Super 14 form, coupled with Mtawarira's passport issues, meant Springbok coach Peter de Villiers was not going to look around too much when writing down the name of his loosehead prop.

This product of Paarl Boys' High who played for Free State before moving to Pretoria in 2005, has an impressive record in green and gold. Of his 31 Tests, Steenkamp has left the field on the winning side 23 times.

Steenkamp needs just one try to become the top-scoring Springbok prop of all time – and if one takes into consideration his ability to cross the whitewash with regularity, especially in 2010, it becomes clear just how integral a part he played in the Boks' season. Yes, perhaps it wasn't the greatest year for the team, but that should not detract from what Steenkamp the individual achieved in 2010.

He was fated to miss the Grand Slam tour through injury, but with a proper rest break Gurthrö Steenkamp will be back in 2011 – and this time not just to make up the numbers.

PLAYER OF THE YEAR

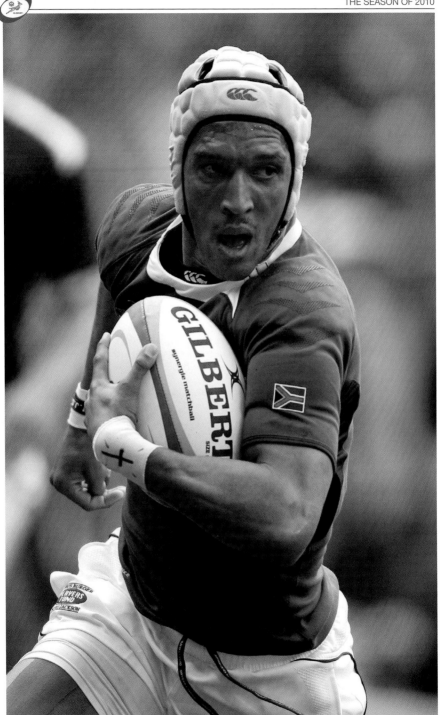

PLAYER OF THE YEAR FINALIST

GIO APLON

(Vodacom Western Province & South Africa)

"**E**VERYBODY'S always asking me about my size," says an exasperated Gio Aplon. "Every week I have to prove people wrong. I hope that the topic won't come up again, but that's wishful thinking, isn't it? I know that I'm going to have to go out there next week and prove people wrong all over again."

Aplon doesn't believe in the tale of the underdog. He doesn't deal in clichés, which is ironic considering every Aplon success is succeeded by the media's favourite platitude: 'Size Doesn't Matter'. He's fighting popular perception every week, deflecting questions about his 1.75m, 75kg frame. For Aplon, size isn't an issue. He doesn't want to hear about David and Goliath. For him, the metaphor simply doesn't apply. Full stop. Move on.

Perseverance and bravery are qualities admired in men big and small, and Aplon's rise to the top has been characterised by a refusal to give in and a hope that, some day, the top coaches would acknowledge his talent.

He proved an invaluable member of the South African Sevens team that captured their inaugural IRB title in 2009. Most believed Aplon's switch to the shorter version of the game would be permanent, but a bold declaration to the contrary marked his return to fifteens ahead of the 2010 Vodacom Super 14. He said that Super Rugby was his ultimate focus and that he was determined to take the opportunity presented by a long-term injury to Vodacom Stormers fullback Conrad Jantjes.

Aplon made good on his word and emerged as one of the players of the tournament, those gliding, counter-attacking runs matched only by some gutsy defence. He also showcased his hard edge, getting up from a vicious Bakkies Botha cleanout in the final league game of the season in Cape Town. That brutal transgression resulted in a four-week suspension for Botha and, at the time, the Newlands crowd feared for Aplon's safety.

"Some people think that because I'm small, I must be brave, but I've chosen to play this sport and I know the risks," he says. "I'm no braver than anyone else out there. If you want to play rugby with the big dogs, you really have to be up for it."

Injuries to JP Pietersen, Jongi Nokwe and Lionel Mapoe presented Aplon with another opportunity as coach Peter de Villiers, as he is wont to do, ignored the critics and picked the small man for the Springboks. Aplon was solid on debut in Cardiff against Wales and captured the man-of-the-match accolade in the subsequent win over France thanks to a stirring, two-try display.

His limited appearances in the Vodacom Tri-Nations were equally encouraging. Like the Australasians Israel Dagg and James O'Connor, Aplon's a player who lends the attack an unpredictable edge. In the modern game, where

defensive lines are so well organised, you need somebody with that uncoachable, line-breaking quality.

While some members of the public may need further convincing, Gio Aplon's got the South African coaching staff, and indeed his peers, to buy into a new mantra: if you're good enough, you're big enough.

PLAYER OF THE YEAR FINALIST

PLAYER OF THE YEAR FINALIST
SCHALK BURGER
(Vodacom Western Province & South Africa)

IF Schalk Burger was a cartoon character, he'd have been Bam Bam Rubble.

Blonde hair, easygoing smile and the impression he leaves on a rugby field. Bam! Bam! Bambambambambam!

His form in 2010 didn't surprise those who remember the tearaway under-20 flank that enjoyed the whoosh every bit as much as he enjoyed the bam; what surprised them was that it took him so long to rediscover the joy of space.

But you will recall that the carefree under-20 flank didn't get much chance for carefree under-20 rugby.

A blistering start to his Vodacom Western Province career saw Burger hurried into a beleaguered Bok side on the eve of its disastrous 2003 Rugby World Cup campaign, just in time for Kamp Staaldraad.

Burger had to box his captain and childhood hero, Corné Krige, in what was one of the low points in one of the low points of Springbok history, both players flattening each other once.

But with the horrors of 2003 behind him, Burger was at the forefront of a Bok renaissance the following year, earning the IRB World Player Of The Year award after just his first full international season.

It was a season that found him at the coalface, in the unfamiliar role of having to play to the ball. A role that involves a lot of bamming and bamming; a role that easily turns a big man into a yello-carded penitent. Breakaway flankers live on the edge of rugby's murky laws and if you're the biggest, blondest man at the point of breakdown, chances are you're going to get nailed.

Burger did, but at the breakdown and on defence he wreaked enough havoc that the risk of losing him for 10 minutes was easily outweighed by the advantage of having him around for the other 70.

He was pivotal in the generation of 2004 that reversed Springbok rugby's slide for the first time since '98, but it hasn't been all beer and skittles along the way since.

Every tiny slump in form has been jumped on by critics as evidence of a decline, but an openside flank depends on a solid performance from his tight five and Burger's all-action style can seem rash in a lost cause.

In 2006, he left the field against Scotland in PE in the first half, drawing concerned gasps from everywhere: what does it take to get Schalk Burger off the field? Cracked vertebrae, as it turned out, requiring cervical fusion surgery.

Of course, it made no difference to his approach – six months later he was back at it, bamming away through the Vodacom Super 14 and playing a key role in the Boks winning the 2007 Rugby World Cup, despite serving a two-match suspension for a high tackle against Samoa.

Disaster struck again against the British & Irish Lions two seasons later, when a stray Burger hand appeared to be seeking Luke Fitzgerald's eye. The Bok himself was shocked upon viewing the incident. Carelessly rough his rugby might get, but dirty Burger isn't.

And while serving his eight-week ban, his Springbok jersey was convincingly usurped by one Heinrich Brüssow of Free State.

How would Burger react in 2010?

Simple: by playing his best rugby for six years, by rediscovering his joy at sprinting into space and offloading to his threequarters. By leading the Vodacom Stormers to their first Super 14 final, where an early onslaught from the Vodacom Bulls put paid to their dreams. By leading Vodacom Western Province to their first Absa Currie Cup final in a decade, where the Sharks repeated the treatment.

This suggests Burger has work to do on his team talk, but his leadership has been exemplary and the never-say-die attitude his outgunned sides displayed on both occasions suggests a bright future.

If you see Burger around, chances are he's smiling. He's earned it – been there, done that and got the 55 Test jerseys. There'll be more.

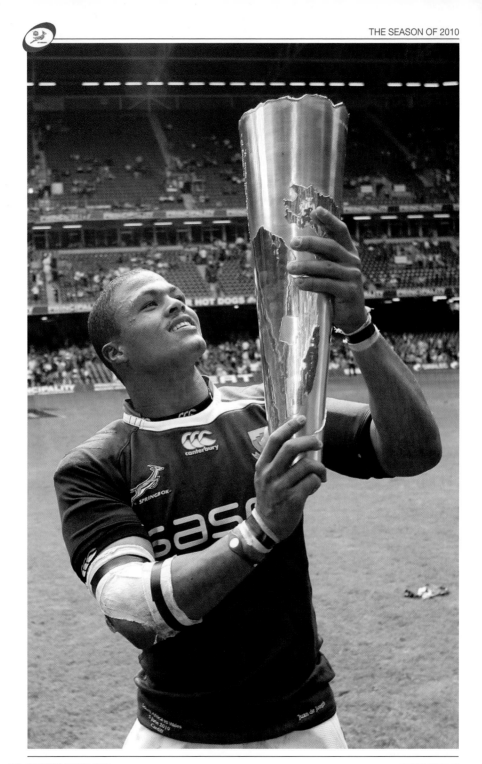

PLAYER OF THE YEAR FINALIST
JUAN DE JONGH
(Vodacom Western Province & South Africa)

HE might have sidestepped his way into the Springbok team, but Juan de Jongh didn't fight his way to the front of the international centre queue simply by cutting corners.

De Jongh was capped on the Boks' 2009 European tour but announced himself on the international stage in grand style when his trademark jink and inside step bamboozled Wales in Cardiff in South Africa's first Test of 2010.

It was almost a carbon copy of the solo effort that broke the back of the Waratahs in the Vodacom Super 14 semi-final a few weeks earlier – and the moment that the former Wellington schoolboy had some long-time mentors knowingly nodding their heads in agreement.

Shy and well-mannered, the muscular centre's rise to prominence didn't surprise Chean Roux, who coached De Jongh when he turned out for Stellenbosch in the 2008 and 2009 FNB Varsity Cups. "Juan went to the same school as I did (Hugenote), and ever since I first saw him play there I thought he was a very down-to-earth person and a clever rugby player," said Roux, who, having coached Maties to their third straight student title in 2010, certainly knows his duds from his diamonds.

"So many players let fame go to their heads, especially when they think they've made it to the top easily, but not Juan. The attributes that made him stand out as a schoolboy are still there. He's got explosive pace and ruthless defence. I remember all the boys he played against were petrified of him in midfield."

De Jongh's quiet demeanour as he felt his way into the Springbok ranks ahead of his first home Test, against France at Newlands, was in stark contrast to his forceful on-field personality. "It's just awesome to be in the set-up," he said. "I grew up watching my teammates on TV and now I'm playing with them. It's such a cliché but it really is a dream come true for me."

Players at this level are past masters in PR-speak, coached to deliver banalities to quote-hungry journalists. De Jongh's words may sound like a variation on that theme, but they also carry a straightforward honesty borne of a level-headed upbringing and a genuine appreciation not only of his talents, but also where they have taken him.

"I'm not a guy who thinks too far ahead but when I made my (Bok) debut last year, I thought I had a chance to go far. This year I set the goal of breaking into the starting line-up, but I'm not going to get ahead of myself. If you do that, what happens is that you only end up losing focus on what's really important."

Born in Paarl, De Jongh's talents at junior level saw him represent Boland at the 2006 Craven Week and SA Schools in 2007, followed by a spell with Paul Treu's Springbok sevens team. At the time, De Jongh was studying sports management at Stellenbosch, but rugby commitments forced him to put those on hold.

Such was De Jongh's form in 2010 that he finished the year as one of the shoe-ins for a place in the 2011 World Cup squad – despite injuring himself in the Absa Currie Cup final and therefore being unable, together with teammate Jaque Fourie, to take part in the Boks' end-of-year grand slam attempt.

Barring further injury or an inexplicable loss of form, De Jongh, Fourie and Jean de Villiers look set to slug it out in the 2011 Vodacom Super 15 for the two starting spots in the Stormers and Bok midfield – a scenario which would have been mere wishful thinking a year ago.

Roux sums it up well: "Juan's got everything required to go all the way – I mean, he's already there," he said. "Now he just needs to keep learning."

BY DAN RETIEF,
Editor: Springbok Opus

PLAYER OF THE YEAR FINALIST

FRANCOIS HOUGAARD
(*Vodacom Blue Bulls & South Africa*)

A TINY entry in the Who's Who section in one of the more recent SA Rugby Annuals should provide a source of inspiration for any young player who feels he has been given a raw deal.

What it says, probably to the embarrassment of Vodacom Western Province's recruiters, is: FC debut: 2007. Prov career: WP 2007 3-0-0-0-0-0. It's the first listing after the name of Hougaard, Francois (Paul Roos Gym).

Two years later, said Hougaard, Francois was handed his first Springbok cap when he went on the end-of-year tour to the UK; a cap richly deserved after his heroics for the Vodacom Blue Bulls while playing away from his favourite position of scrumhalf.

Francois Hougaard is the man Western Province allowed to get away and the Blue Bulls are the happy beneficiaries. Earmarked as Fourie du Preez's understudy, coach Frans Ludeke realised the powerful youngster from Stellenbosch was the kind of player he wanted on the field – anywhere on the field.

So the decision was made to field Hougaard on the wing – which says something about his exceptional pace – and he responded by scoring a try in the 2009 Absa Currie Cup final as well as the try that clinched their Vodacom Super 14 triumph over the Stormers at the Orlando Stadium.

Hougaard thus established his credentials as a sparkling diamond in the rich pipe of talent available in South Africa and perhaps the biggest compliment to his abilities is when striking a comparison with his mentor Du Preez.

When Du Preez was injured the general response was: "What are the Boks going to do without him?" But after some outstanding displays amid the dross of the Boks' performances in the Vodacom Tri-Nations people were saying: "Why were we worried?"

Hougaard had set himself the task to learn from Du Preez, and he was clearly a good pupil, but he recalls his first mission at Loftus Versfeld was to disavow an all too easily made association.

"Everyone thought I was Derick Hougaard's brother," he laughs. "Uncle Hugh Bladen even said it on TV. But funnily enough even though we're from the same area (Derick Hougaard hails from Piketberg and attended Boland Landbou) we know of no family connection. If we are at all related it must only be very distant."

Francois Hougaard is a product of good rugby lineage. He says he has been told his father, Wickus, was a good player who should have made more of his rugby and that his maternal grandfather, Church de Klerk, was highly rated.

"And going to Paul Roos means you can't help but get caught up in rugby culture. The school carries the name of the man who first called us Springboks, it is right alongside the Maties and we play in the same maroon jersey, white shorts, maroon socks with gold trim," he explained. "I was also very fortunate to have had a coach, Dawie Snyman, not the Dawie Snyman of the Springboks and Stellenbosch, who made us work very hard at improving and honing our skills."

A natural sportsman, Hougaard was a provincial-class swimmer at school but he was besotted with rugby. "I found swimming too lonely a sport, and much preferred a team game like rugby," he said.

Hougaard's big rival was none other than a boy from Paul Roos's big rivals Paarl Gym; a kid by the name of Dewaldt Duvenage. Duvenage got the Craven Week nod ahead of him but they were both selected for the SA Under-20 side that went to Wales in 2008.

They alternated in the No9 jersey but crucially the youngster with the funny haircut attracted the attention of Blue Bull scouts and the rest, as they say, is history.

PREVIOUS PLAYERS OF THE YEAR

2009: Fourie du Preez (Player of the Year, Blue Bulls), Heinrich Brüssow (Free State), Victor Matfield (Blue Bulls), John Smit (Sharks), Morné Steyn (Blue Bulls).

2008: Jean de Villiers (Player of the Year, Western Province); Tendai Mtawarira, Bismarck du Plessis, Ryan Kankowski, Adrian Jacobs (all KwaZulu Natal).

2007: Bryan Habana (Player of the Year, Blue Bulls), Fourie du Preez (Blue Bulls), Victor Matfield (Blue Bulls), Percy Montgomery (Natal), Juan Smith (Free State).

2006: Fourie du Preez (Player of the Year, Blue Bulls), Os du Randt (Free State), Victor Matfield (Blue Bulls), Pierre Spies (Blue Bulls), Luke Watson (Western Province).

2005: Bryan Habana (Player of the Year, Blue Bulls), Bakkies Botha, Victor Matfield (both Blue Bulls), Jean de Villiers (WP), Ricky Januarie (Lions).

2004: Schalk Burger (Player of the Year, WP), Os du Randt (Free State), De Wet Barry, Marius Joubert (WP), Bakkies Botha (Blue Bulls).

2003: Ashwin Willemse (Player of the Year, Lions), Juan Smith (Free State), Richard Bands, Bakkies Botha (Blue Bulls), Joe van Niekerk (Lions).

2002: Joe van Niekerk (Player of the Year), Jannes Labuschagne, André Pretorius, Lawrence Sephaka (all Lions), Werner Greeff (WP).

2001: André Vos (Player of the Year, Lions), Braam van Straaten (WP), Victor Matfield (Blue Bulls), Lukas van Biljon (Natal), Conrad Jantjes (Lions).

2000: Breyton Paulse (Player of the Year, WP), Thinus Delport, Rassie Erasmus (both Lions), Kennedy Tsimba (Free State), Corné Krige (WP).

1999: André Venter (Player of the Year, Free State), Breyton Paulse, Cobus Visagie (both WP), Joost van der Westhuizen (Blue Bulls), Hennie le Roux (Lions).

1998: Gary Teichmann (Player of the Year, Natal), Joost van der Westhuizen, Krynauw Otto (Blue Bulls), Gaffie du Toit (Griqualand West), Bobby Skinstad (WP).

1997: Os du Randt (Player of the Year, Free State), Pieter Rossouw, Percy Montgomery, Dick Muir (all WP), Johan Roux (Lions).

1996: André Joubert (Player of the Year), Henry Honiball, Gary Teichmann (both Natal), Ruben Kruger, Joost van der Westhuizen (both NTvl).

1995: Ruben Kruger (Player of the Year), Joost van der Westhuizen (both NTvl), Francois Pienaar (Tvl), Joel Stransky (WP), André Joubert (Natal).

1994: Chester Williams (Player of the Year, WP), Mark Andrews, André Joubert (both Natal), Ruben Kruger, Joost van der Westhuizen (both NTvl).

1993: Gavin Johnson (Player of the Year), Francois Pienaar (both Tvl), James Small (Natal), Tiaan Strauss (WP), Joost van der Westhuizen (NTvl).

1992: Tiaan Strauss (Player of the Year), Danie Gerber (both WP), Jacques Olivier, Naas Botha, Adriaan Richter (all NTvl).

1991: Uli Schmidt (Player of the Year), Naas Botha, Gerbrand Grobler (all NTvl), André Joubert (OFS), Wahl Bartmann (Natal).

1990: Uli Schmidt (Player of the Year), Robert du Preez (both NTvl), Wahl Bartmann, Joel Stransky (both Natal), Tiaan Strauss (WP).

1989: Johan Heunis (Player of the Year), Robert du Preez, Burger Geldenhuys (all NTvl), André Joubert (OFS), Carel du Plessis (WP).

1988: Calla Scholtz (Player of the Year), Tiaan Strauss (both WP), Naas Botha, Adolf Malan (both NTvl), Gerhard Mans (SWA).

1987: Naas Botha (Player of the Year), Adri Geldenhuys (both NTvl), Gysie Pienaar (OFS), John Robbie, Jannie Breedt (both Tvl).

1986: Jannie Breedt (Player of the Year), Wahl Bartmann (both Tvl), Carel du Plessis (WP), Uli Schmidt (NTvl), Garth Wright (EP).

1985: Naas Botha (Player of the Year, NTvl), Jannie Breedt (Tvl), Schalk (SWP) Burger (WP), Danie Gerber (EP), Gerrie Sonnekus (OFS).

1984: Danie Gerber (Player of the Year, EP), Rob Louw, Calla Scholtz (both WP), Ray Mordt (NTvl), Errol Tobias (Boland).

1983: Hennie Bekker (Player of the Year), Divan Serfontein, Carel du Plessis (all WP), Liaan Kirkham (Tvl), Ray Mordt (NTvl).

1982: Divan Serfontein (Player of the Year), Colin Beck, Hennie Bekker (all WP), Naas Botha, Johan Heunis (both NTvl).

1981: Naas Botha (Player of the Year), Johan Heunis (both NTvl), Ray Mordt (Tvl), Divan Serfontein, De Villiers Visser (both WP).

1980: Gysie Pienaar (Player of the Year, OFS), Naas Botha, Louis Moolman (both NTvl), Morné du Plessis (WP), Gerrie Germishuys (Tvl).

1979: Naas Botha (Player of the Year), Louis Moolman (both NTvl), Morné du Plessis, Rob Louw, De Villiers Visser (all WP).

1978: Thys Lourens (Player of the Year), Tommy du Plessis, Pierre Edwards (all NTvl), De Wet Ras (OFS), Ian Robertson (Rhodesia).

1977: Moaner van Heerden (Player of the Year), Thys Lourens (both NTvl), Morné du Plessis (WP), Hermanus Potgieter, Theuns Stofberg (both OFS).

***1976:** Morné du Plessis (WP), Moaner van Heerden (NTvl), Bryan Williams, Sid Going, Peter Whiting (all NZ).

***1975:** Gerald Bosch (Tvl), Gerrie Germishuys (OFS), Pierre Spies, Thys Lourens (both NTvl), Johan Oosthuizen (WP).

***1974:** Gareth Edwards, Willie John McBride, JPR Williams (all British Lions), Willem Stapelberg, John Williams (both NTvl).

***1973:** Gerald Bosch (Tvl), Dirk de Vos, Moaner van Heerden, Pierre Spies (all NTvl), Johan Oosthuizen (WP).

***1972:** Kevin de Klerk (Tvl), Sam Doble (England), Jan Ellis (SWA), Carel Fourie (North East Cape) John Pullin (England).

***1971:** Benoit Dauga (France), Frik du Preez (NTvl), Jan Ellis (SWA), Hannes Marais (EP), Hannes Viljoen (Natal).

***1970:** Piet Greyling (Tvl), Joggie Jansen (OFS), Ian McCallum (WP), Alan Sutherland, Bryan Williams (both NZ).

Before 1977, no single player of the year was named

YOUNG PLAYER OF THE YEAR

Lion Jantjies leads new pack

JUST a few years ago South Africans were still clutching at any old straw as they desperately sought a successor for King Henry Honiball's flyhalf throne. Not only do the Springboks now possess a dependable No 10 in Morné Steyn, but they also have two bright youngsters in **Elton Jantjies** and **Patrick Lambie** coming through the ranks.

Both were nominated for the young player of the year award, alongside **Bjorn Basson**, **Juan de Jongh** and **Francois Hougaard**.

To choose a winner from such a list is no easy task, but **Jantjies** ultimately got the nod based on a superb Absa Currie Cup campaign for the Xerox Lions. He was also named SA Under-20 Player of the Year.

The youngster's generalship of the Johannesburg-based side was so impressive that it led to a call-up for the Springbok tour of the United Kingdom and Ireland.

While it was all about introducing him to the culture rather than exposing him to the rough and tumble of Test rugby – the plan was always for him to only play against the Barbarians – Jantjies certainly made an impression in the environment.

While fringe players are sometimes known to tire from carrying tackle bags on tour, Jantjies' attitude and work ethic certainly made a good impression.

"Elton showed so much promise this year. If we had an injury concern at flyhalf prior to the match against England, I could have started him with full confidence," said Springbok coach Peter de Villiers. "He surprised me on tour. His

contribution in the team environment was particularly surprising. Elton is one of the few players in the years I have spent with the team that is prepared to challenge senior players on certain things in their team talks. That does not happen easily in the Springbok environment.

"Elton is very confident and backs his knowledge of the game. That is what really surprised me about him."

Jantjies also owes his rise to some astute man-management by Lions coach John Mitchell. The former All Black coach initially took a softly-softly approach to blooding the youngster in Currie Cup rugby.

Jantjies played a combined total of just 29 minutes in the Lions' first three matches, as a substitute for veteran Herkie Kruger in the domestic competition, before being thrust into the pressure situation of starting a home match against the Vodacom Blue Bulls.

In his third start, he was the man of the match as the Lions found their feet with an inspired 30-26 win over the Vodacom Free State Cheetahs. He repeated that feat in their 46-28 win over Vodacom Western Province in Johannesburg, notching 31 points against the eventual finalists in the process.

The Lions had lost 32-0 to WP at Newlands earlier in the season and Jantjies played just 22 minutes in a lost cause that day. However, the side underwent an incredible transformation, and Jantjies was one of the exciting youngsters that emerged in a Lions side that was clearly responding positively to Mitchell's mentorship.

Jantjies ended up a regular in the side and started 10 of the Lions' Currie Cup matches. His two tries, 25 conversions and 27 penalties placed him sixth among the competition's leading points scorers.

While his boot proved an effective weapon for the Lions, he was clearly also benefiting from working under former All Black flyhalf Carlos Spencer, who is one of Mitchell's assistants at the Lions.

Mitchell was not too keen on the idea of Jantjies being rushed into the Bok side and said he would have preferred that the player's ankle injury heal properly.

However, his trip to the northern hemisphere was all about getting him used to the Bok culture while the recovery from his injury could also take place under the watchful eye of the national team's medical staff.

Whilst it appears a fait accompli that Jantjies will make his Test debut in the next year or two, he still has a long road to travel. There is still Super Rugby that needs conquering on a consistent basis before he can be considered the genuine article.

It is, after all, a competition that places fierce physical demands on players and measures them against the best in the southern hemisphere.

However, with sensible management of his career – both the Lions and Springboks have thus far been astute in that regard – this is a challenge that should not prove beyond him. The lad certainly has a superb temperament to go with his undoubted talent – a potentially winning combination for Lions and Springbok rugby.

Perhaps in the not too distant future our southern hemisphere rivals will also start glancing enviously at the depth of South Africa's flyhalf talent.

PREVIOUS YOUNG PLAYERS OF THE YEAR

2009: Heinrich Brüssow (Young Player of the Year, Free State), Juan de Jongh (WP), Francois Hougaard (Blue Bulls), Lionel Mapoe (Free State), Frans Steyn (Sharks).

2008: Robert Ebersohn (Young Player of the Year, Free State), Heinrich Brüssow (Free State), Nick Koster (WP), Tendai Mtawarira, Bismarck du Plessis (both KZN).

2007: Francois Steyn (Young player of the Year), JP Pietersen, Ryan Kankowski (all KwaZulu-Natal), Heinke van der Merwe (Lions), Richardt Strauss (Free State).

2006: Pierre Spies (Young Player of the Year, Blue Bulls), JP Pietersen, Keegan Daniel (KwaZulu-Natal), Hilton Lobberts (Blue Buls), Gio Aplon (Western Province).

2005: Jongi Nokwe (Young Player of the Year, Boland), Wynand Olivier, Morné Steyn (Blue Bulls), Ruan Pienaar, JP Pietersen (KwaZulu-Natal).

2004: Bryan Habana (Young Player of the Year, Lions), Schalk Burger (WP), Schalk Brits (Lions), Fourie du Preez (Blue Bulls), Luke Watson (Natal).

2003: Ashwin Willemse (Young Player of the Year, Lions), Schalk Burger (WP), John Mametsa (Blue Bulls), Jaque Fourie (Lions), Fourie du Preez (Blue Bulls).

2002: Pedrie Wannenburg (Young Player of the Year, Blue Bulls), Brent Russell (Pumas), Hanyani Shimange (Free State), Jaque Fourie (Lions), Derick Hougaard (Blue Bulls).

2001: Conrad Jantjes (Young Player of the Year), Gcobani Bobo, Joe van Niekerk (all Lions), Adi Jacobs (Falcons), Wylie Human (Free State).

2000: Marius Joubert (Boland), Conrad Jantjes (Lions), De Wet Barry, Adri Badenhorst (both WP), Wylie Human (Free State).

1999: John Smit (Natal), Kaya Malotana (Border), Jannes Labuschagne (Lions), Wayne Julies (Boland), Torros Pretorius (Pumas).

1998: Lourens Venter, Robert Markram (both Griquas), Grant Esterhuizen, Nicky van der Walt (both Blue Bulls), André Vos (Golden Lions).

1997: Thinus Delport (Gauteng Lions), Breyton Paulse, Louis Koen, Bobby Skinstad (all WP), Jan-Harm van Wyk (Free State).

1996: Dawie du Toit, Hannes Venter (both NTvl), Marius Goosen (Boland), MJ Smith (Free State), André Vos (EP).

1995: Stephen Brink, Jorrie Kruger (both OFS), Robbie Kempson (Natal), Danie van Schalkwyk, Joggie Viljoen (both NTvl).

1994: Frikkie Bosman (ETvl), Braam Els (OFS), Harold Karele (EP), André Snyman (NTvl), Justin Swart (WP).

1993: Krynauw Otto, FP Naude (both NTvl), Ryno Oppermann (OFS), Johan Roux (Tvl), Christiaan Scholtz (WP).

1992: Jannie de Beer, Hentie Martens, Brendan Venter, André Venter (all OFS), Joost van der Westhuizen (NTvl).

1991: Pieter Hendriks (Tvl), Hennie le Roux (EP), Pieter Müller (OFS), Johan Nel, Jacques Olivier (both NTvl).

1990: Andrew Aitken (Natal), Jannie Claassens, Theo van Rensburg (both NTvl), Bernard Fourie (WTvl), Ian Macdonald (Tvl).

1989: Stompie Fourie (OFS), Pieter Nel, Verwoerd Roodt (both NTvl), Joel Stransky, Jeremy Thomson (both Natal).

1988: Kobus Burger, Christian Stewart (WP), Jacques du Plessis (EP), André Joubert (OFS), JJ van der Walt (NTvl).

1987: Chris Badenhorst (OFS), Robert du Preez (WTvl), Jan Lock, Charles Rossouw (both NTvl), Andrew Paterson (EP).

1986: Keith Andrews, Tiaan Strauss (both WP), Martin Knoetze (WTvl), Hendrik Kruger (NTvl), Frans Wessels (OFS).

1985: Schalk (SW) Burger, Faffa Knoetze (both WP), Deon Coetzee (Tvl), Christo Ferreira (OFS), Giepie Nel (NTvl).

1984: Paul Botes, Uli Schmidt (both NTvl), Niel Burger (WP), Wessel Lightfoot, Helgard Müller (both OFS).

1983: Wahl Bartmann (Tvl), Jannie Dreyer, Adolf Malan (both NTvl), Calla Scholtz (WP), Gert Smal (WTvl).

1982: Wilfred Cupido (South African Rugby Federation), Michael du Plessis (WP), Liaan Kirkham (Tvl), Piet Kruger (NTvl), Rudie Visagie (OFS).

1981: Harry Viljoen, Jannie Breedt, André Skinner (all NTvl), Jan du Toit, Ernest Viljoen (both OFS).

1980: Colin Beck (WP), Cliffie Brown (Natal), Johan Marais (NTvl), Chris Rogers (Zimbabwe), Japie Wessels (OFS).

1979: Darius Botha (NTvl), Willie du Plessis (WP), Doug Jeffrey (OFS), André Markgraaff (WTvl), Gawie Visagie (Griquas).

1978: Burger Geldenhuys, Okkie Oosthuizen (both NTvl), Eben Jansen (OFS), Ray Mordt, David Smith (both Rhodesia).

1977: Naas Botha, Thys Burger (both NTvl), Agie Koch, Flippie van der Merwe (both WP), Gysie Pienaar (OFS).

1976: Dirk Froneman, Wouter Hugo (both OFS), Divan Serfontein, Nick Mallet (both WP), LM Rossouw (NTvl).

1975: Tommy du Plessis, Christo Wagenaar (both NTvl), Corrie Pypers (Tvl), Hermanus Potgieter, De Wet Ras (both OFS).

1974: Gavin Cowley (EP), Peter Kirsten (WP), John Knox, Louis Moolman (both NTvl), Johan Strauss (Tvl).

1973: Dave Frederickson (Tvl), Wilhelm Landman (WP), Martiens le Roux (OFS), Keith Thoresson (Natal), Barry Wolmarans (Boland).

1972: Paul Bayvel, Gerald Bosch (both Tvl), Pikkie du Toit (OFS), Dugald Macdonald (WP), Jackie Snyman (OFS).

1971: Kevin de Klerk, Gert Schutte (both Tvl), Piet du Plessis (NTvl), Buddy Swartz (Griquas), Johan Wagenaar (OFS).

1970: Francois de Villiers, Johan Walters (both WP), Peter Cronje (Tvl), Jannie van Aswegen (Griquas), John Williams (NTvl).

YOUNG PLAYER OF THE YEAR

SECTION 2
THE SEASON IN 2010

THE SEASON IN 2010

AGGREGATE FIRST-CLASS TEAM RECORDS *Ranked by winning percentage*

TEAM	Played	Won	Drawn	Lost	Points For	Points Against	Tries For	Tries Against	% Position
Sharks Invitational XV	1	1	0	0	80	3	12	0	100.0%
Vodacom Bulls (S14)	15	12	0	3	500	386	51	37	80.0%
Vodacom Blue Bulls	25	19	0	6	781	564	91	55	76.0%
KwaZulu-Natal Sharks	16	12	0	4	538	322	66	31	75.0%
Vodacom Free State Cheetahs	26	18	0	8	816	576	96	58	69.2%
Vodacom Western Province	25	17	0	8	767	481	85	49	68.0%
Sharks XV (Vodacom Cup)	9	6	0	3	245	188	26	20	66.7%
Vodacom Stormers (S14)	15	10	0	5	407	202	39	18	66.7%
Golden Lions (Vodacom Cup)	8	5	0	3	265	155	33	15	62.5%
Eastern Province Kings	21	12	2	7	571	517	65	58	57.1%
Boland Cavaliers	20	11	0	9	634	538	82	55	55.0%
SWD Eagles	22	12	0	10	603	580	73	74	54.5%
Sharks (S14)	13	7	0	6	297	299	23	27	53.8%
Springboks (Tests & tour)	15	8	0	7	417	370	42	39	53.3%
GWK Griquas	23	12	0	11	814	720	111	89	52.2%
Golden Lions	14	7	0	7	401	407	45	46	50.0%
Pampas XV	7	3	3	1	220	151	29	16	42.9%
Pumas	23	9	1	13	651	800	89	102	39.1%
Vodacom Cheetahs (S14)	13	5	1	7	316	393	34	50	38.5%
Griffons	19	7	0	12	566	617	73	85	36.8%
Leopards	24	5	0	19	598	902	72	127	20.8%
Border Bulldogs	18	3	0	15	386	766	45	109	16.7%
Welwitchias	7	1	0	6	194	300	23	42	14.3%
Valke	18	1	0	17	395	936	54	138	5.6%
Xerox Lions (S14)	13	0	0	13	270	585	32	72	0.0%

MATCH FEATURES

Seventy-five points by a team
80	Sharks Inv XV vs. Valke	Compulsory friendly
78	Free State Cheetahs vs. Leopards	Absa Currie Cup

Ten tries by a team
12	Sharks Inv XV vs. Valke	Compulsory Friendly
10	Sharks XV vs. Border	Vodacom Cup
10	Griffons vs. Valke	Absa Currie Cup

Won by 50 points
77	Sharks Inv XV vs. Valke (80-3)	Compulsory Friendly
71	Free State Cheetahs vs. Leopards (78-07)	Absa Currie Cup
61	Sharks XV vs. Border (69-08)	Vodacom Cup
57	Free State Cheetahs vs. Leopards	Absa Currie Cup
57	Sharks vs. Leopards (63-06)	Absa Currie Cup
52	Pumas vs. Griffons (66-14)	Vodacom Cup
51	Leopards vs. Valke (59-08)	Vodacom Cup

Twenty-five points by a player
31	ET Jantjies (Golden Lions vs. WP)	Absa Currie Cup
31	LA Basson (Border vs. Valke)	Absa Currie Cup
28	P Lambie (Sharks vs. Golden Lions)	Absa Currie Cup
27	EG Watts (Pumas vs. Leopards)	Absa Currie Cup
27	J-L Potgieter (Blue Bulls vs. Golden Lions)	Absa Currie Cup
25	P Lambie (Sharks vs. WP)	Absa Currie Cup

Three tries by a player
5	NT Nelson (EP Kings vs. Valke)	Absa Currie Cup
4	BA Basson (Griquas vs. Sharks)	Absa Currie Cup
3	WG Mjekevu (Lions vs Chiefs)	Super 14
3	CV Oosthuizen (FS Cheetahs vs Griquas)	Absa Currie Cup*
3	KR Daniel (Sharks vs. Pumas)	Absa Currie Cup

3	LJ Botes (Sharks Inv XV vs. Valke)	Compulsory Friendly
3	EG Watts (Pumas vs. Leopards)	Absa Currie Cup
3	JJ Engelbrecht (WP vs. Griquas)	Absa Currie Cup
3	L Karemaker (Griquas vs. Valke)	Vodacom Cup
3	BA Basson (Griquas vs. Blue Bulls)	Absa Currie Cup
3	BA Basson (Griquas vs. WP)	Absa Currie Cup
3	HG Noble (Border vs. Valke)	Absa Currie Cup
3	ER Fredericks (Griffons vs. Valke)	Absa Currie Cup
3	JW Jonker (Griffons vs. Valke)	Absa Currie Cup
3	CF Cronje (Valke vs. SWD Eagles)	Absa Currie Cup
3	CF Cronje (Valke vs. Border)	Absa Currie Cup
3	WJ le Roux (Boland vs Valke)	Absa Currie Cup
3	C Hendricks (Boland vs. Border)	Absa Currie Cup
3	BJH McBean (SWD vs. Valke)	Absa Currie Cup

* First hat-trick by a prop in Currie Cup history

Seven conversions
8	G Dumond	Sharks XV vs. Border	Vodacom Cup
8	R Croy	Pumas vs. Griffons	Vodacom Cup
7	IP Olivier	Griquas vs Pumas	Absa Currie Cup

Seven penalties
7	M Steyn	Blue Bulls vs. WP	Absa Currie Cup

Two drop goals
2	F Brummer	Blue Bulls vs. Free State Cheetahs	Vodacom Cup
2	M Steyn	Bulls vs. Crusaders	Super 14

Scored in all four ways
18pts   IP Olivier [1T, 2C, 2P, 1DG]
        Griquas vs. Free State Cheetahs   Absa Currie Cup

THE SEASON IN 2010

LEADING PLAYERS IN 2010

100 POINTS OR MORE

PLAYER	Team/s	Matches	Tries	Conversions	Penalties	Drop Goals	Points
M Steyn	Bulls/Blue Bulls/SA	29	8	67	96	3	471
IP Olivier	Griquas/Cheetahs	27	4	63	46	3	293
W de Waal	Stormers/WP	26	1	45	62	0	281
LI Strydom	FS Cheetahs	24	0	42	56	0	252
P Lambie	KZN/SA	29	7	37	36	0	217
G Dumond	KZN/EP	24	1	36	38	2	197
J-L Potgieter	Blue Bulls/Bulls	28	3	31	37	0	188
J Jansen	Boland	20	5	42	21	0	172
BA Basson	Griquas/SA	25	34	0	0	0	170
AR Barendse	SWD	18	2	28	30	1	159
ET Jantjies	Golden Lions	15	2	26	28	0	146
PJ Grant	Stormers	14	1	20	32	0	141
C Durand	Leopards	17	0	27	29	0	141
R Pienaar	KZN/SA	24	3	22	24	1	134
J Peach	EP Kings	10	5	15	23	0	124
HC Kruger	Lions/Golden Lions	12	1	20	26	0	123
EG Watts	Pumas	22	10	17	9	0	111
C Botha	Welwitchias/Valke	18	8	16	12	0	108
LA Basson	Griquas/Border	13	5	21	13	0	106
F Brummer	Blue Bulls/Bulls	15	1	13	17	6	100

Ten tries

BA Basson	Griquas/Cheetahs	34
LN Mvovo	Sharks/SA	14
GJ van den Heever	Blue Bulls/Bulls	13
OM Ndungane	KZN/SA	12
ER Fredericks	Griffons	12
GG Aplon	WP/SA	12
S Watermeyer	Blue Bulls	11
PAB Snyman	FS Cheetahs	11
NT Nelson	EP Kings	11
WJ le Roux	Boland	11
BJH McBean	SWD	11
PJ Louw	Stormers/WP	11
EG Watts	Pumas	10
D Scholtz	Leopards	10
C Hendricks	Boland	10
S Raubenheimer	SWD	10
KR Daniel	KZN/SA	10
AF Johnson	Cheetahs/FS	10
M Killian	Lions/Golden Lions	10
BG Habana	Stormers/WP/SA	10

30 Appearances

GG Aplon	SA/WP/Stormers	39
Z Kirchner	SA/BB/Bulls	33
PR van der Merwe	SA/BB/Bulls	33
A van Zyl	Stormers/WP/Barbarians	33
L-FP Louw	Stormers/WP/SA	32

J Harris	Stormers/WP	32
DJ Vermeulen	Stormers/WP	32
DO Duvenage	Stormers/WP	31
DA Fourie	Stormers/WP	30
JN du Plessis	SA/KZN	30

Players who recorded a 100th appearance for their province in 2010

EJ (Elroy) Ligman	EP Kings vs. Sharks XV	Apr 9
SJ (Sarel) Louw	Griffons vs. EP Kings	Sep 3
H (Henry) Grimes	SWD vs. Griffons	Oct 8

Youngest and oldest first-class players in 2010

JJ Taute	Golden Lions vs. Griffons, March 19	
	18 years 11 months 29 days	
W Stoltz	EP Kings vs Pumas, Oct 29	
	35 years 8 months 26 days	

Tallest, shortest, heaviest and lightest players in 2010

A Bekker	WP/Stormers	2.08m
W Stoltz	EP Kings	2.08m
HJ Adams	Blue Bulls	1.68m
AS Buys	Pumas	130kg
PR Uys	Pumas	130kg
HJ Adams	Blue Bulls	67kg

CAREER LEADERS IN 2010

500 POINTS OR MORE

PLAYER	Province	Matches	Tries	Conversions	Penalties	Drop Goals	Points
M Steyn	Blue Bulls	196	43	370	306	33	1972
W de Waal	Western Province	177	23	323	346	18	1853
LJ Koen	Boland	151	22	346	316	17	1801
AS Pretorius	Golden Lions	167	26	279	224	37	1471
J Peach	Boland	178	40	266	242	0	1458
LI Strydom	Free State	165	14	244	248	8	1326
IP Olivier	Griquas	118	30	252	177	4	1197
CS Terblanche	KZN	311	151	10	19	6	850

Fifty tries*

CS Terblanche	KZN	151
BG Habana	WP	115
J Fourie	WP	86
ER Fredericks	WP	83
BF Welsh	WP	78
AA Jacobs	KZN	73
DB Coeries	Griffons	71
J De Villiers	WP	66

Two hundred and fifty appearances*

V Matfield	Blue Bulls	322
CS Terblanche	KZN	311
JW Smit	KZN	308
DJ Rossouw	Blue Bulls	262

* only in South Africa

THE SEASON IN 2010

SOUTH AFRICANS ABROAD

South Africans appearing for leading clubs overseas at some point in 2010.
* Springbok   + Overseas international

A

+	NJ (Nick) Abendanon	Bath	England
	HJ (Heini) Adams	Bordeaux-Begles	France
	C (Chad) Alcock	New South Wales	Australia
	RD (Rob) Andrew	Pau	France
	DZ (Zane) Ansell	Padova	Italy

B

	AJ (Adri) Badenhorst	Agen	France
	P (Paul) Barker	Esher	England
	C (Conrad) Barnard	Agen	France
	PC (Pat) Barnard	Brive	France
	BM (Brad) Barritt	Saracens	England
	CJ (Coenie) Basson	Bourgoin	France
	S (Stefan) Basson	Rovigo	Italy
	R (Roland) Bernard	Grenoble	France
	N (Naude) Beukes	Oyonnax	France
*	G (Gcobani) Bobo	Newcastle	England
	L (Lorenzo) Bocchini	L'Aquila	Italy
	JF (Jake) Boer	Gloucester	England
		Cinderford	England
	AT (Andy) Borgen	Moseley	England
	JdB (Jannie) Bornman	Dax	France
		Castres	France
	WT (Tobie) Botes	Treviso	Italy

*	BJ (BJ) Botha	Ulster	Ireland
	E (Evan) Botha	Pau	France
	J (Jacques) Botha	Lannemezan	France
	MJ (Mouritz) Botha	Saracens	England
	MF (Maso) Bowles	Westcombe Park	England
	R (Rudi) Brits	Cornish Pirates	England
*	SB (Schalk) Brits	Saracens	England
*	GJJ (Gerrie) Britz	Perpignan	France
	JL (Lodie) Britz	Mont-de-Marsan	France
	RG (Raynn) Bruce	Worthing	England
	AM (Albertus) Buckle	Bourgoin	France
	PB (Philip) Burger	Perpignan	France

C

*	PD (Deon) Carstens	Saracens	England
+	MJ (Mike) Catt	London Irish	England
	D (Dario) Chistolini	Padova	Italy
	AD (Antonie) Claassen	Brive	France
	E (Errie) Claassens	London Welsh	England
*	M (Michael) Claassens	Bath	England
	AM (Ashley) Clarke	Racing Club	France
	A (Arno) Coetzee	Aurillac	France
*	D (Danie) Coetzee	London Irish	England
	EL (Eduard) Coetzee	Biarritz	France
	ML (Michael) Coetzee	Castres	France

Schalk Brits is now plying his rugby skills under Brendan Venter at English club Saracens.

Hendré Fourie won his first test cap against New Zealnd on their end-of-tour clash against England at Twickenham.

R (Rudi) Coetzee	Bourgoin	France
C (Cilliers) Coetzer	Tarbes	France
RJ (Ronnie) Cooke	Brive	France
* J (Jacques) Cronje	Racing Club	France
D		
D (Danie) de Beer	Grenoble	France
	Pays d'Aix	France
+ B (Benjamin) de Jager	Treviso	Italy
RCA (Ryan) de la Harpe	Moseley	England
G (Gert) de Kock	Canterbury	England
* NA (Neil) de Kock	Saracens	England
MRD (Marc) de Marigny	Llandovery	Wales
+ RJ (Roland) de Marigny	Gran Parma	Italy
* J (Jean) de Villiers	Munster	Ireland
JJ (Jacques) Deen	Bayonne	France
	Dax	France
+ CA (Carlo) del Fava	Viadana	Italy
	Aironi	Italy
* GM (Thinus) Delport	Stourbridge	England
S (Stephane) Delpuech	Albi	France
D (Danwel) Demas	Aironi	Italy
D (Dylan) des Fountain	Aironi	Italy
W (Willem) de Waal	Treviso	Italy
RJE (Robbie) Diack	Ulster	Ireland
H (Hanno) Dirksen	Ospreys	Wales
PJ (Pieter) Dixon	Bath	England
RH (Regardt) Dreyer	Northampton	England
D (Daniel) du Plessis	Agen	France
NA (Nico) du Plessis	Gran Parma	Italy
PVW (Petrus) du Plessis	Nottingham	England
	Saracens	England
R (Ruaan) du Preez	Bourgoin	France
* WH (Wian) du Preez	Munster	Ireland
JJ (Jaco) du Toit	L'Aquila	Italy
JJ (Jaco) du Toit	Pau	France
J (Jaco) du Toit	Westcombe Park	England
	Cambridge	England
R (Rory) Duncan	Yamaha Jubilo	Japan
E		
C (Christiaan) Els	Lannemezan	France
+ J (Jaco) Erasmus	Viadana	Italy
	Aironi	Italy
+ I (Ian) Evans	Ospreys	Wales
M (Matt) Evans	Cornish Pirates	England
	Ealing	England
F		
CH (Hendré) Fourie	Leeds	England
JL (Jeandre) Fourie	Narbonne	France
JJ (Josh) Fowles	Macclesfield	England
G		
+ Q (Quintin) Geldenhuys	Viadana	Italy
	Aironi	Italy
D (Durandt) Gerber	Gran Parma	Italy

R (Rayno) Gerber	Stade Francais	France
SC (Sam) Gerber	Bayonne	France
SE (Stephan) Gerber	Aurillac	France
B (Brett) Gillespie	Toyota Verblitz	Japan
G (Greg) Goosen	Racing Club	France
WM (Marius) Goosen	Treviso	Italy
* PJ (Peter) Grant	Kobe Steelers	Japan
JA (Cobus) Grobler	La Rochelle	France
P (Piet) Grobler	Mont-de-Marsan	France
H		
G (Guthrie) Hall	Ealing	England
TM (Trevor) Hall	Biarritz	France
H (Drikus) Hancke	Montpellier	France
RL (Robbie) Harris	Leicester	England
	Saint Ettienne	France
DS (Dane) Haylett-Petty	Biarritz	France
TW (Tom) Hayman	Westcombe Park	England
	Richmond	England
RW (Rob) Herring	Blackheath	England
	London Irish	England
WAJ (Willem) Heymans	Gran Parma	Italy
CO (Cliffie) Hodgson	Rotherham	England
T (Tyrone) Holmes	Cornish Pirates	England
* DJ (Derick) Hougaard	Saracens	England
A (Andre) Hough	Pau	France
A (Alten) Hulme	Begles	France
	Grenoble	France
* DCF (Daan) Human	Toulouse	France
PG (Gerhard) Human	Ricoh Black Rams	Japan

WA (Wylie) Human	Grenoble	France	
G (Gavin) Hume	Perpignan	France	
I			
JA (Braam) Immelman	Rovigo	Italy	
J			
NBS (Nick) Jackson	Cornish Pirates	England	
* AD (Butch) James	Bath	England	
EA (Rassie) Jansen van Vuuren	Aurillac	France	
ER (Ricky) Januarie	Ospreys	Wales	
EW (Wessel) Jooste	Bourgoin	France	
E (Ernst) Joubert	Saracens	England	
ED (Eben) Joubert	Otago	New Zealand	
* MC (Marius) Joubert	Clermont	France	
* W (Wayne) Julies	Pays d'Aix	France	
K			
JB (Kobus) Kemp	Aurillac	France	
R (Robin) Kitching	Hull	England	
DM (Dan) Kotze	Aurillac	France	
GE (Gareth) Krause	Viadana	Italy	
	Aironi	Italy	
PJJ (Juandre) Kruger	Northampton	England	
L			
RA (Rod) Labuschagne	Cornish Pirates	England	
+ G (Gideon) Lensing	Castres	France	
B (Bernard) le Roux	Racing Club	France	
M (Matthew) Lewis	Llandovery	Wales	
+ B (Brian) Liebenberg	Stade Francais	France	
S (Stef) Liebenberg	Cambridge	England	
	Old Albanians	England	
PL (Vickus) Liebenberg	Aironi	Italy	
RF (Robin) Linde	Bayonne	France	
TP (Thomas Pieter) Loftus	Tarbes	France	
W (Werner) Loftus	Tarbes	France	
* FH (Hottie) Louw	Ricoh Black Rams	Japan	
A (Alistair) Lyon	Richmond	England	
M			
S (Scott) Mathie	Leeds	England	
+ AP (Andrew) Mehrtens	Racing Club	France	
RJG (Justin) Melck	Saracens	England	
SD (Steve) Meyer	Perpignan	France	
CI (Chris) Micklewood	Newcastle	England	
W (Wouter) Moore	Prato	Italy	
* BV (Brian) Mujati	Northampton	England	
AJ (Bertus) Mulder	Manawatu	New Zealand	
GH (Gert) Muller	Agen	France	
* GJ (Johann) Muller	Ulster	Ireland	
PH (Piet) Myburgh	Pays d'Aix	France	
J (Jeandre) Mynhardt	Narbonne	France	
JP (JP) Nel	NTT Shining Arcs	Japan	
N			
RD (Duncan) Naude	Lannemezan	France	
	Aurillac	France	
DP (Darron) Nell	Castres	France	
+ J (Jacques) Nieuwenhuis	Aurillac	France	
O			
NH (Noel) Oelschig	Stade Francais	France	
L (Len) Olivier	Montauban	France	
P			
S (Shaun) Pammenter	Cornish Pirates	England	
BJM (Ben) Pienaar	Nottingham	England	
	Leicester	England	
* R (Ruan) Pienaar	Ulster	Ireland	
JC (Joe) Pietersen	Bayonne	France	
+ DW (David) Pocock	Western Force	Australia	
D (Delkeith) Pottas	Narbonne	France	
A (Andries) Pretorius	Cardiff Blues	Wales	
N (Nico) Pretorius	Biarritz	France	
	Dax	France	
N (Naude) Pretorius	Blaydon	England	
R			
* SJ (Faan) Rautenbach	London Irish	England	
+ GP (Greg) Rawlinson	Worcester Warriors	England	
G (Grant) Rees	Montpellier	France	
B (Bryan) Rennie	Exeter Chiefs	England	
E (Ethienne) Reynecke	Saracens	England	
R (Riccardo) Robuschi	Parma	Italy	
HL (Hendrik) Roodt	New South Wales	Australia	
* G (Gideon) Roux	Westcombe Park	England	
* RB (Brent) Russell	Clermont	France	
SA (Shaun) Ruwers	Stourbridge	England	
	London Wasps	England	
S			
DS (Danie) Saayman	Castres	France	
D (Donovan) Sanders	Jersey	England	
JJ (Jared) Saunders	Barking	England	
	Saracens	England	
H (Handre) Schmidt	Bedford	England	
JC (Jacques) Schutte	Montpellier	France	
DM (Dewald) Senekal	Toulon	France	
BC (Brett) Sharman	Northampton	England	
RC (Ross) Skeate	Toulon	France	
AJ (Bertus) Smit	Pays d'Aix	France	
* RS (Shaun) Sowerby	Toulouse	France	
SL (Scott) Spedding	Brive	France	
* FPL (Frans) Steyn	Racing Club	France	
CR (Richardt) Strauss	Leinster	Ireland	
N (Nic) Strauss	Narbonne	France	
M (Mark) Swanepoel	Western Force	Australia	
T			
PD (PD) Terblanche	Tarbes	France	
D (Danie) Thiart	Montpellier	France	
+ RM (Rhys) Thomas	Llanelli	Wales	
	Scarlets	Wales	
K (Kyle) Tonetti	Leinster	Ireland	
	Sale	England	
MD (Mathew) Turner	Bristol	England	
U			
R (Retief) Uys	Brive	France	
V			
* CJ (CJ) van der Linde	Leinster	Ireland	
+ DTH (DTH) van der Merwe	Glasgow	Scotland	
FC (Francois) van der Merwe	Racing Club	France	

* HS (Heinke) van der Merwe	Leinster	Ireland
PW (Pieter) van der Merwe	North Otago	New Zealand
SM (Schalk) van der Merwe	Rovigo	Italy
J (Joe) van der Molem	Southend	England
C (Crisjean) van der Westhuizen	Albi	France
J (Jannie) van Deventer	Waterloo	England
* JL (Wikus) van Heerden	Saracens	England
W (Wayne) van Heerden	Suntory Sungoliath	Japan
* JC (Joe) van Niekerk	Toulon	France
HJ (Henjo) van Niekerk	Venezia	Italy
R (Ruahan) van Jaarsveld	Venezia	Italy
	Lazio	Italy
T (Thomas) van Rooyen	Huddersfield	England
F (Francois) van Schalkwyk	Richmond	England
HJ (Jaco) van Schalkwyk	Bordeaux-Begles	France
E (Eugene) van Staden	Montpellier	France
D (Donovan) van Vuuren	Huddersfield	England
C (Corniel) van Zyl	Treviso	Italy
+ WP (Piet) van Zyl	Bourgoin	France

H (Henno) Venter	Coventry	England
	Jersey	England
BS (Bian) Vermaak	Treviso	Italy
+ DJ (Dan) Vickerman	Northampton	England
R (Rudi) Vogt	Oyonnax	France
JF (Vleis) Volschenk	Oyonnax	France
I (Ian) Voortman	Kendal	England
G (Gerhard) Vosloo	Brive	France

W

LR (Lorne) Ward	London Welsh	England
* PJ (Pedrie) Wannenberg	Ulster	Ireland
JG (Johan) Wasserman	Montpellier	France
* LA (Luke) Watson	Bath	England
* MvZ (Marco) Wentzel	Leeds	England
FW (Willie) Wepener	Clermont	France
B (Brett) Wilkinson	Connacht	Ireland
+ AW (Andy) Wilson	Ayr	Scotland
WA (Willem) Wium	Venezia	Italy

Marco Wentzel and Luke Watson both captain their respective clubs, Leeds and Bath, in the English Premiership.

WHO'S WHO IN 2010

A complete list of all 709 players who appeared in a first-class match in South Africa in 2010.

A

Adams, Benjamin (Bennie) (Zandvliet HS) b 16/08/82, Tygerberg. 1.86m. 82kg. Flank. FC DEBUT: 2002. PROV CAREER: WP 2002-04 7-0-0-0-0-0. Leopards 2006-10 74-3-0-0-0-15. REP HONOURS: SA Sevens 2004. SA U21 2003 5-1-0-0-0-5. FC RECORD: 86-4-0-0-0-20. RECORD IN 2010: (Leopards) 3-0-0-0-0-0.

Adams, Heinrich Jaco (Heinie) (Esselen Park SS) b 29/05/80, Worcester. 1.68m. 67kg. Scrumhalf. FC DEBUT: 2003. PROV CAREER: Eagles 2003-04 35-3-0-0-0-15. Bulls 2005-10 48-7-0-0-0-35. SUPER 14: Bulls 2005-10 36-3-0-0-0-15. REP HONOURS: SA Tour 2009 2-0-0-0-0-0. SA 'A' 2004 1-0-0-0-0-0. Emerging Springboks 2007,09 3-0-0-0-0-0. FC RECORD: 125-13-0-0-0-65. RECORD IN 2010: (Bulls, Blue Bulls) 8-0-0-0-0-0.

Adriaanse, Jacobus Petrus (Jacobie). Prop. FC DEBUT: 2008. PROV CAREER: Boland 2008-09 23-0-0-0-0-0. Griquas 2010 21-1-0-0-0-5. REP HONOURS: Emerging Springboks 2008 1-0-0-0-0-0. FC RECORD: 45-1-0-0-0-5. RECORD IN 2010: (Griquas) 21-1-0-0-0-5.

Alberts, Willem Schalk (Monument HS) b 05/11/84, Pretoria. 1.91m. 106kg. Lock. ›› FC debut: 2005. Prov career: Lions 2005 & 07-09 35-7-0-0-0-35. Lions XV 2007-08 2-1-0-0-0-5. Young Lions 2005 3-0-0-0-0-0. KZN 2010 13-2-0-0-0-10. Super 14: Lions 2007-09 37-4-0-0-0-20. Sharks 2010 12-0-0-0-0-0. Rep honours: SA 2010 Tests: 3-3-0-0-0-15. SA Tour 2010 1-0-0-0-0-0. Total: 4-3-0-0-0-15. FC record: 103-16-0-0-0-80. RECORD IN 2010 (SA, Sharks, KZN) 29-5-0-0-0-25.

Amill, Herzon Chacido Hans (Harmony Sport Academy) b 09/03/1988, George. 1.78m. 107kg. Prop. FC DEBUT: 2010. PROV CAREER: Eagles 2010 3-0-0-0-0-0. FC RECORD: 3-0-0-0-0-0. RECORD IN 2010: (Eagles) 3-0-0-0-0-0.

Anderson, Deon (AHS, Pretoria) b 25/05/1987, Pretoria. 1.77m. 87kg. Flyhalf. FC DEBUT: 2010. PROV CAREER: Valke 2010 7-1-3-4-0-23. FC RECORD: 7-1-3-4-0-23. RECORD IN 2010 (Valke) 7-1-3-4-0-23.

Annandale, Gavin Barnard (Brandwag HS) b 27/04/89, Welkom. 1.94m. 112kg. Lock. FC DEBUT: 2009. PROV CAREER: Valke 2009 5-0-0-0-0-0. Griffons 2010 3-0-0-0-0-0. FC RECORD: 8-0-0-0-0-0. RECORD IN 2010: (Griffons) 3-0-0-0-0-0.

Aplon, Gio Giaan (Hawston High School) b 06/10/82, Hermanus. 1.75m. 70kg. Fullback. ›› FC debut: 2005. Prov career: WP 2005-10 70-27-2-0-0-139. Super 14: Stormers 2007-08 & 10 30-1-0-0-0-5. Rep honours: SA 2010 Tests: 13-3-0-0-0-15. SA Tour: 1-0-0-0-0-0. Total: 14-3-0-0-0-15. Sevens 2006-07. WP XV 2006 1-2-0-0-0-10. Misc info: Try of the Year 2006 (WP vs. Bulls). PoY nominee 2010. FC record: 115-33-2-0-0-169. RECORD IN 2010: (SA, Stormers, WP) 38-12-0-0-0-60.

April, Brendon Terence (Bergrivier HS) b 20/12/83, Paarl. 1.80m. 75kgs. Wing. FC DEBUT: 2005. PROV CAREER: Valke 2005-06 32-12-0-0-0-60. Griffons 2007 2-0-0-0-0-0. Boland 2010 7-2-0-0-0-10. FC RECORD: 41-14-0-0-0-70. RECORD IN 2010: (Boland) 7-2-0-0-0-10.

Astle, John-Charles (Pionier HS & UOFS) b 30/08/1990, Queenstown. 1.98m. 92kg. Lock. FC DEBUT: 2010. PROV CAREER: Cheetahs 2010 3-0-0-0-0-0. FC RECORD: 3-0-0-0-0-0. RECORD IN 2010: (Cheetahs) 3-0-0-0-0-0.

B

Badenhorst, Rudolf Scheepers (Skipper) (AHS, Pretoria) b 01/12/78, Oudtshoorn. 1.84m. 102kg. Hooker. FC DEBUT: 2000. PROV CAREER: Valke 2000-02 52-4-0-0-0-20. Pumas 2003-04 33-4-0-0-0-20. KZN 2005-09 54-3-0-0-0-15. Sharks XV 2005-09 19-0-0-0-0-0. Sharks Inv XV 2009 1-0-0-0-0-0. Cheetahs 2010 16-4-0-0-0-20. Cheetahs XV 2010 1-0-0-0-0-0. SUPER 14: Stormers 2003 2-0-0-0-0-0. Sharks 2004-06 & 08-09 20-0-0-0-0-0. Cheetahs 2010 3-0-0-0-0-0. REP HONOURS: SA 'A' 2004 1-1-0-0-0-5. SA U23s 2001 1-0-0-0-0-0; SA U21s 1999 5-1-0-0-0-5. FC RECORD: 206-17-0-0-0-85. RECORD IN 2010: (Cheetahs S14, Cheetahs, Cheetahs XV) 20-4-0-0-0-20.

Ball, Donovan Rossouw (Sand du Plessis HS) b 15/01/1989, Bloemfontein. 1.97m. 94kg. Flanker. FC DEBUT: 2010. PROV CAREER: Griffons 2010 4-0-0-0-0-0. FC RECORD: 4-0-0-0-0-0. RECORD IN 2010: (Griffons) 4-0-0-0-0-0.

Bantjes, Henri James b 6/3/88, Pretoria. 1.85m. 106kg. Hooker. FC DEBUT: 2008. PROV CAREER: Blue Bulls 2008-10 14-0-0-0-0-0. FC RECORD: 14-0-0-0-0-0. RECORD IN 2010: (Blue Bulls) 2-0-0-0-0-0.

Barends, Ambrose Regan (Bros) (Diazville High) b 09/08/80, Saldanha. 1.86m. 83kg. Fullback. FC DEBUT: 2002. PROV CAREER: Cavaliers 2002 8-0-0-3-0-9. Eagles 2006-08 & 10 72-12-89-73-2-463. FC RECORD: 80-12-89-76-2-472. RECORD IN 2010: (Eagles) 18-2-28-30-1-159.

Barnes, Ryno Joseph (Paarl Gymnasium) b 05/11/81, Cape Town. 1.86m. 110kg. Hooker. FC DEBUT: 2006. PROV CAREER: WP 2006 13-0-0-0-0-0. Valke 2007-08 41-5-0-0-0-25. Griquas 2009-10 39-6-0-0-0-30. Cheetahs XV 2010 1-0-0-0-0-0. SUPER 14: Cheetahs 2010 8-0-0-0-0-0. REP HONOURS: Royal XV 2009 1-1-0-0-0-5. FC RECORD: 103-12-0-0-0-60. RECORD IN 2010: (Cheetahs S14, Griquas, Cheetahs XV) 25-3-0-0-0-15.

Barry, De Wet (Paarl Gym) b 24/06/78, Ceres. 1.88m. 91kgs. Centre. FC DEBUT: 1997. PROV CAREER: WP 1999-02&04-07 78-16-0-0-0-80. EP Kings 2009-10 27-7-0-0-0-35. EP Inv XV 2010 1-0-0-0-0-0. SUPER 14: Stormers 2000-07 78-13-0-0-0-65. Bulls 2010 1-0-0-0-0-0. REP HONOURS: SA 2000-06 Tests 39-3-0-0-0-15, Tour 2-1-0-0-0-5, Total 41-4-0-0-0-20; Springbok XV 2006. SA U23s 2000 3-1-0-0-0-5; SA Tech 1997; SA U21s 1998-99 8-1-0-0-0-5. British Barbarians 2003. S/Kings 2009 1-0-0-0-0-0. MISC INFO: YPoY nominee 2000. PoY nominee 2004. FC RECORD: 240-42-0-0-0-210. RECORD IN 2010: (Bulls, EP Kings, EP Inv XV) 21-3-0-0-0-15.

Bashiya, Yves Mulengi Tshiumbi (Capricorn HS) b 13/02/87, Kinshasa. 1.87m. 97kg. Flanker. FC DEBUT: 2009. PROV CAREER: Valke 2009-10 14-2-0-0-0-10. EP Kings 2009-10 12-1-0-0-0-5. EP Inv XV 2010 1-0-0-0-0-0. FC RECORD: 27-3-0-0-0-15. RECORD IN 2010: (EP Kings, Valke, EP Inv XV) 10-1-0-0-0-5.

Basson, Bjorn Alberic (Dale College) b 11/02/87, King Williams Town. 1.87m. 82kg. Wing/Fullback. FC DEBUT: 2008. PROV CAREER: Griquas 2008-10 56-47-0-0-0-235. SUPER 14: Cheetahs 2009-10 9-6-0-0-0-30. REP HONOURS: SA 2010 Tests: 4-0-0-0-0-0. Emerging Springboks 2008-09 4-1-0-0-0-5. Royal XV 2009 1-0-0-0-0-0. MISC INFO: Holder of record for most Currie Cup tries in a season (21). ACC PoY 2010, YPoY nominee 2010. FC RECORD: 74-54-0-0-0-270. RECORD IN 2010: (SA, Cheetahs S14, Griquas) 29-34-0-0-0-170.

Basson, Logan Andrew (Dale Coll.) b 09/03/1989, Kingwilliamstown. 1.91m. 77kg. Flyhalf. FC DEBUT: 2010. PROV CAREER: Bulldogs 2010 10-5-13-12-0-87. Griquas 2010 3-0-8-1-0-19. FC RECORD: 13-5-21-13-0-106. RECORD IN 2010: (Bulldogs, Griquas) 13-5-21-13-0-106.

Bax, Liam (Tiger) b 10/04/1988, East London. 1.83m. 80kg. FC DEBUT: 2009. PROV CAREER: WP 2009-

10 5-1-0-0-0-5. SUPER 14: Stormers 2009 1-0-0-0-0-0. FC RECORD: 6-1-0-0-0-5. RECORD IN 2010: (WP) 1-0-0-0-0-0.

Becker, Raynor Le Roux (Oakdale Agric. HS) b 08/06/1990, Stilbaai. 1.78m. 76kg. Wing. FC DEBUT: 2010. PROV CAREER: Eagles 2010 1-0-0-0-0-0. FC RECORD: 1-0-0-0-0-0. RECORD IN 2010: (Eagles) 1-0-0-0-0-0.

Bekker, Andries (Paul Roos Gym) b 05/12/83, Cape Town. 2.08m. 120kg. Lock. FC DEBUT: 2003. PROV CAREER: WP 2004-09 37-11-0-0-0-55. SUPER 14: Stormers 2005-10 62-9-0-0-0-45. REP HONOURS: SA 2008-10 Tests 24-1-0-0-0-5 Tour: 2009 2-0-0-0-0-0. Totals 26-1-0-0-0-5. SA U21 2003-04 7-1-0-0-0-5. FC RECORD: 132-22-0-0-0-110. MISC INFO: S14 PoY 2010, Son of HJ (Hennie) Bekker, SA (1981). RECORD IN 2010: (SA, Stormers) 18-3-0-0-0-15.

Bekker, Beyers (Outeniqua HS) b 22/01/1987, Vanderbijlpark. 1.84m. 115kg. Prop. FC DEBUT: 2010. PROV CAREER: Eagles 2010 7-0-0-0-0-0. FC RECORD: 7-0-0-0-0-0. RECORD IN 2010: (Eagles) 7-0-0-0-0-0.

Bekker, Jacobus Christiaan (Jaco) (Gill Coll.) b 17/05/83. 1.83m. 90kg. Centre. FC DEBUT: 2004. PROV CAREER: Leopards 2004-05 5-0-0-0-0-0. Griquas 2006-09 42-3-0-0-0-15. EP Kings 2010 12-0-0-0-0-0. EP Inv XV 2010 1-0-0-0-0-0. REP HONOURS: SA U21 2004 1-0-0-0-0-0. FC RECORD: 61-3-0-0-0-15. RECORD IN 2010: (EP Kings, EP Inv XV) 13-0-0-0-0-0.

Bekker, Theodore b 17/03/80. 1.90m. 96kg. Flanker. FC DEBUT: 2004. PROV CAREER: Valke 2004 & 09-10 16-1-0-0-0-5. FC RECORD: 16-1-0-0-0-5. RECORD IN 2010 (Valke) 9-0-0-0-0-0.

Bennett, Wayne Anthony (Grey HS, Port Elizabeth) b 25/07/78. 1.82m. 102kg. Hooker. FC DEBUT: 2001. PROV CAREER: Elephants 2001-06 70-6-0-0-0-30. Eagles 2007-10 50-9-0-0-0-45. FC RECORD: 120-15-0-0-0-75. RECORD IN 2010: (Eagles) 8-5-0-0-0-25.

Bester, Alwyn (Boland Agric) b 15/04/87, Vredendal. 1.93m. 105kg. Eightman. FC DEBUT: 2009. PROV CAREER: Boland 2009 18-2-0-0-0-10. Pumas 2010 7-1-0-0-0-5. FC RECORD: 25-3-0-0-0-15. RECORD IN 2010: (Pumas) 7-1-0-0-0-5.

Bezuidenhout, Carl (Union HS) b 10/02/86, Grahamstown. 1.90m. 90kg. Fullback. FC DEBUT: 2006. PROV CAREER: KZN 2006 1-1-0-0-0-5. Sharks XV 2006 & 08-09 10-1-0-0-0-5. Elephants 2009 8-2-8-7-0-47. Pumas 2010 11-1-7-2-25. FC RECORD: 30-5-15-9-0-82. RECORD IN 2010: (Pumas) 11-1-7-2-0-25.

Bezuidenhout, Martin Johannes (Klerksdorp HS & UJ)

b 21/08/1989, Orkney. 1.82m. 102kg. Hooker. FC DE-BUT: 2010. PROV CAREER: Golden Lions 2010 14-0-0-0-0-0. Young Lions 2010 7-0-0-0-0-0. FC RECORD: 21-0-0-0-0-0. RECORD IN 2010: (Golden Lions, Young Lions) 21-0-0-0-0-0.

Birkholtz, Brad (Graeme Coll.) b 28/07/1988, King-williamstown. 1.81m. 87kg. Wing. FC DEBUT: 2010. PROV CAREER: Bulldogs 2010 6-0-0-0-0-0. FC RECORD: 6-0-0-0-0-0. RECORD IN 2010: (Bulldogs) 6-0-0-0-0-0.

Blaauw, Johannes Lodewicus (Wicus) (Upington HS) b 08/04/86, Windhoek. 1.90m. 125kg. Prop. FC DE-BUT: 2007. PROV CAREER: Leopards 2007 10-1-0-0-0-5. WP 2008-10 41-0-0-0-0-0. SUPER 14: Stormers 2009-10 19-0-0-0-0-0. FC RECORD: 70-1-0-0-0-5. RECORD IN 2010: (Stormers, WP) 17-0-0-0-0-0.

Blignaut, Hendrik Nikolai (Boysville HS) b 10/01/1985, East London. 1.95m. 101kg. Lock. FC DEBUT: 2005. PROV CAREER: KZN 2005-09 16-1-0-0-0-5. Sharks XV 24-2-0-0-0-10. KZN XV 2007 1-0-0-0-0-0. Boland 2010 14-1-0-0-0-5. REP HON-OURS: Emerging Springboks 2007 2-0-0-0-0-0. SA U21 2005-06 10-0-0-0-0-0. FC RECORD: 67-4-0-0-0-20. RECORD IN 2010: (Leopards) 14-1-0-0-0-5.

Blom, Jandré (Riebeeckstad HS) b 24/12/84, Vredendal. 1.74m. 75kg. Scrumhalf. FC DEBUT: 2005. PROV CA-REER: Cheetahs 2005-09 46-9-37-39-1-239. Griffons 2008 8-1-3-1-2-20. Eagles 2009-10 33-4-26-23-0-141. REP HONOURS: SA Sevens 2005-07. FC RECORD: 87-14-66-63-3-400. RECORD IN 2010: (Eagles) 21-1-15-10-0-65.

Bondesio, Michael (Lichtenburg HS) b 10/03/85, Mid-delburg. 1.76m. 84kg. Scrumhalf. FC DEBUT: 2008. PROV CAREER: Leopards 2008-10 52-13-0-0-0-65. FC RECORD: 52-13-0-0-0-65. RECORD IN 2010: (Leopards) 17-8-0-0-0-40.

Booi, Ayabonga Ludwe (Pretoria THS & Univ. Fort Hare) b 14/05/1987, Butterworth. 1.79m. 90kg. Wing. FC DEBUT: 2010. PROV CAREER: Bulldogs 2010 2-0-0-0-0-0. FC RECORD: 2-0-0-0-0-0. RECORD IN 2010: (Bulldogs) 2-0-0-0-0-0.

Booi, Chumani Nande (Union HS, Graaff-Reinet) b 15/02/80, Sada, Whittlesea. 1.75m. 75kgs. Fullback. FC DEBUT: 2001. PROV CAREER: Border 2001-03 & 09-10 64-17-14-7-0-134. Pumas 2003 14-6-0-0-0-30. Griquas 2004-06 23-8-2-0-0-44. WP 2006 5-0-0-0-0-0. SUPER 14: Sharks 2004 5-0-0-0-0-0. Cats 2005 10-1-0-0-0-5. Stormers 2006 5-0-0-0-0-0. REP HONOURS: SA 'A' 2004 2-1-0-0-0-5. WP XV 2006 1-0-0-0-0-0. SA U21s 2001 4-3-0-0-0-15; CW Elephants 1997-98. FC

RECORD: 133-36-16-7-0-233. RECORD IN 2010: (Bulldogs) 12-2-7-5-0-39.

Booysen, Franco (Brakpan HS) b 26/03/87, Welkom. 1.83m. 90kg. Centre. FC DEBUT: 2008. PROV CA-REER: Valke 2008-10 21-4-0-0-0-20. FC RECORD: 21-4-0-0-0-20. RECORD IN 2010: (Valke) 7-1-0-0-0-5.

Bosch, Paul Wilhelm (Ellisras HS) b 24/09/84, Preto-ria. 1.88m. 86kg. Utility back. FC DEBUT: 2006. PROV CAREER: Leopards 2006-08 8-1-0-0-0-5. WP 2009-10 28-3-0-0-0-15. REP HONOURS: SA Students 2007-09 3-0-0-0-0-0. FC RECORD: 39-4-0-0-0-20. RECORD IN 2010 (WP) 18-2-0-0-0-10.

Boshoff, Jan Hendrik (Jannie) (Maritzburg College) b 13/01/86, Newcastle. 1.78m. 87kg. Centre. FC DEBUT: 2006. PROV CAREER: Golden Lions 2006-10 31-9-0-0-0-45. Lions XV 2007 1-1-0-0-0-5. Young Lions 2006-10 8-2-0-0-0-10. SUPER 14: Lions 2007-09 23-3-0-0-0-15. FC RECORD: 63-15-0-0-0-75. RECORD IN 2010: (Golden Lions, Young Lions) 13-3-0-0-0-15.

Boshoff, Marnitz Louis (Nelspruit HS & TUKS) b 11/01/89, Nelspruit. 1.76m. 78kg. Flyhalf. FC DEBUT: 2009. PROV CAREER: Blue Bulls 2009-10 9-2-11-0-1-35. FC RECORD: 9-2-11-0-1-35. RECORD IN 2010: (Blue Bulls) 8-2-9-0-1-31.

Boshoff, Ruan Jopie (Nelspruit HS) b 22/02/87, Nel-spruit. 1.80m. 80kg. Flyhalf. FC DEBUT: 2007. PROV CAREER: Blue Bulls 2007-09 28-2-5-6-0-38. Blue Bulls XV 2007 1-0-2-1-0-7. Lions 2009 8-1-5-0-0-15. Young Lions 2010 3-0-1-1-0-5. FC RECORD: 40-3-13-8-0-65. RECORD IN 2010: (Young Lions) 3-0-1-1-0-5.

Bosman, Hendrik Meyer (Oakdale Agric. HS & Free State Univ.) b 19/04/85, Bethlehem. 1.91m. 94kg. Util-ity back. FC DEBUT: 2005. PROV CAREER: Cheetahs 2005-10 59-10-21-9-0-119. SUPER 14: Cheetahs 2006-10 61-4-27-38-0-188. REP HONOURS: SA Tests: 2005-06 3-0-2-1-0-7. Tour: 2006,2009 3-0-0-0-0-0, Total: 6-0-2-1-0-7. Emerging Springboks 2007 2-0-0-0-0-0. FC RECORD: 128-14-50-48-0-314. RECORD IN 2010: (Cheetahs S14, Cheetahs) 27-4-13-9-0-73.

Botes, Louis Jacques (Jacques) (Potchefstroom Gym) b 12/04/80, Nelspruit. 1.81m. 97kg. Eighthman. FC DEBUT: 2002. PROV CAREER: Pumas 2002-04 41-5-0-0-0-25. KZN 2005-10 86-27-0-0-0-135. Sharks XV 1-0-0-0-0-0. Sharks Inv XV 2009-10 2-5-1-0-0-27. SUPER 14: Sharks 2005-10 74-22-0-0-0-110. REP HONOURS: Emerging Springboks 2009 1-0-0-0-0-0. FC RECORD: 205-59-1-0-0-297. RECORD IN 2010: (Sharks, KZN, Sharks Inv XV) 30-8-1-0-0-42.

Botha, Andries Hendrik (Nylstroom HS) b 08/05/1990, Nylstroom. 1.80m. 80kg. Centre. FC DE-

BUT: 2010. PROV CAREER: Leopards 2010 1-0-0-0-0-0. FC RECORD: 1-0-0-0-0-0. RECORD IN 2010: (Leopards) 1-0-0-0-0-0.

Botha, Bêrend Johannes (Berries) (Klerksdorp HS) b 11/03/88, Springs. 1.96m. 118kg. Lock. FC DEBUT: 2008. PROV CAREER: Blue Bulls 2009-10 13-0-0-0-0-0. REP HONOURS: Emerging Springboks 2008 2-0-0-0-0-0. FC RECORD: 15-0-0-0-0-0. RECORD IN 2010: (Blue Bulls) 8-0-0-0-0-0.

Botha, Bernardo Carl (Florida HS) b 04/07/88, Oudtshoorn. 1.81m. 86kg. Wing. FC DEBUT: 2009. PROV CAREER: Young Lions 2009-10 8-4-0-0-0-20. SUPER 14: Lions 2010 2-0-0-0-0-0. FC RECORD: 10-4-0-0-0-20. RECORD IN 2010: (Lions S14, Young Lions) 3-0-0-0-0-0.

Botha, Brendon James (BJ) (DHS) b 04/01/80, Durban. 1.82m. 110kg. Prop. FC DEBUT: 2001. PROV CAREER: KZN 2001-06 & 08 64-3-0-0-0-15. SUPER 14: Sharks 2003-08 56-3-0-0-0-15. REP HONOURS: SA 2006-10 Tests: 25-1-0-0-0-5. Tour: 2007 1-0-0-0-0-0. Total: 26-1-0-0-0-5. SA 'A' 2004. SA U21s 2001 4-2-0-0-0-10. British Barbarians 2009 1-0-0-0-0-0. MISC INFO: St Helens (Eng) 2000-01. FC RECORD: 151-9-0-0-0-45. RECORD IN 2010: (SA) 6-1-0-0-0-5.

Botha, Chrysander Antonio (Walvis Bay HS) b 13/07/1988, Walvis Bay. 1.88m. 72kg. Fullback. SA FC DEBUT: 2010. PROV CAREER: Valke 2010 11-3-0-3-0-24. SA FC RECORD: 11-3-0-3-0-24. REP HONOURS: Welwitschias 2010. RECORD IN 2010: (Valke) 11-3-0-3-0-24.

Botha, Gary van Ginkel (Overkruin HS/Waterkloof HS & Pretoria Tech. Inst of Rugby) b 12/10/81, Pretoria. 1.81m. 108kgs. Hooker. FC DEBUT: 2001. PROV CAREER: Blue Bulls 2002-06 & 10 83-12-0-0-0-60. SUPER 14: Sharks 2003 10-1-0-0-0-5; Bulls 2004-07 & 10 63-7-0-0-0-35. REP HONOURS: SA 2005-07 Tests: 12-0-0-0-0-0. Tour: 2007 1-0-0-0-0-0. Total: 13-0-0-0-0-0. Springbok XV 2006. SA XV 2006 1-0-0-0-0-0. SA U21s 2001-02 9-2-0-0-0-10; British Barbarians 2004. SA Schools 1998-99; Blue Bulls CW 1998-99. MISC INFO: SA RL 1997-98. FC RECORD: 181-22-0-0-0-110. RECORD IN 2010: (Bulls, Blue Bulls) 22-2-0-0-0-10.

Botha, Jean (Paul Roos Gym) b 23/07/85, Cape Town. 1.79m. 106kg. Prop. FC DEBUT: 2007. PROV CAREER: WP 2007 7-0-0-0-0-0. Boland 2008 20-1-0-0-0-5. Cheetahs 2009-10 7-0-0-0-0-0. Griquas 2010 10-1-0-0-0-5. SUPER 14: Cheetahs 2009 2-0-0-0-0-0. FC RECORD: 46-2-0-0-0-10. RECORD IN 2010: (Cheetahs, Griquas) 12-1-0-0-0-5.

Botha, John Philip (Bakkies) (Vereeniging THS/Mid-delburg THS) b 22/09/79, Newcastle. 2.02m. 118kg. Lock. FC DEBUT: 1999. Prov career: Valke 1999-2000 22-2-1-0-0-12. Blue Bulls 2001-02 & 04-05 & 09-10 53-10-0-0-0-50. Super 14: Bulls 2002-10 86-9-0-0-0-45. Rep honours: SA 2002-05 & 07-10 Tests: 72-7-0-0-0-35. SA Tour 2010: 1-1-0-0-0-5. Total: 73-8-0-0-0-40. SA 'A' 2001-03 6-1-0-0-0-5; SA U23s 2001 3-1-0-0-0-5; SA Schools 1998 (captain); CW Pumas 1997. British Barbarians 2008 1-0-0-0-0-0. Misc info: PoY nominee 2003, 2004, 2005. Locked together with Victor Matfield in 60 tests (world record). FC record: 244-31-1-0-0-157. RECORD IN 2010: (SA, Bulls, B Bulls) 13-1-0-0-0-5.

Botha, Jovan Lamprect (THS Ligbron) b 22/02/85, Hillbrow. 1.79m. 90kg. Centre. FC DEBUT: 2006. PROV CAREER: Pumas 2006-10 42-7-0-0-0-35. FC RECORD: 42-7-0-0-0-35. RECORD IN 2010: (Pumas) 5-0-0-0-0-0.

Botha, Shaun (Welkom Gym.) b 09/04/75. 1.90m. 94kg. Eighthman. FC DEBUT: 2003. PROV CAREER: Griffons 2003-05 & 08-10 54-2-0-0-0-10. FC RECORD: 54-2-0-0-0-10. Record in 2010: (Griffons) 7-0-0-0-0-0.

Botha, Zane Dawid (Grey Coll.) b 03/02/1989, Bloemfontein. 1.79m. 96kg. Hooker. FC DEBUT: 2010. PROV CAREER: Blue Bulls 2010 8-2-0-0-0-10. FC RECORD: 8-2-0-0-0-10. RECORD IN 2010: (Blue Bulls) 8-2-0-0-0-10.

Bothma, Renaldo (Volkskool Heidelberg) b 18/09/1989, Alberton. 1.87m. 100kg. Flanker. FC DEBUT: 2010. PROV CAREER: Golden Lions 2010 7-2-0-0-0-10. FC RECORD: 7-2-0-0-0-10. RECORD IN 2010: (Golden Lions) 7-2-0-0-0-10.

Bouwer, Willem Sterrenberg Jacobus Marais (Jaco) (Waterkloof HS) b 04/09/85, Kempton Park, 1.84m. 97kg. Flank. FC DEBUT: 2007. PROV CAREER: Leopards 2007-08 34-8-0-0-0-40. Pumas 2009-10 37-12-0-0-0-60. FC RECORD: 71-20-0-0-0-100. RECORD IN 2010: (Pumas) 21-8-0-0-0-40.

Bowles, Jovan Jacques (Marist Brothers) b 27/06/83, Durban. 1.87m. 94kg. Centre. FC DEBUT: 2004. PROV CAREER: KZN 2004 12-1-0-0-0-5. Valke 2006 7-2-0-0-0-10. Bulldogs 2008 16-0-0-0-0-0. Leopards 2009-10 41-13-0-0-0-65. FC RECORD: 76-16-0-0-0-80. RECORD IN 2010: (Leopards) 21-5-0-0-0-25.

Brache, Marcel Girard (Rondebosch Boys HS & UCT) b 15/10/1987, Los Angeles. 1.90m. 88kg. Centre. FC DEBUT: 2010. PROV CAREER: WP 2010 2-0-0-0-0-0. FC RECORD: 2-0-0-0-0-0. RECORD IN 2010: (WP) 2-0-0-0-0-0.

Bratz, Ronald Denzil (Morester HS) b 01/11/1983, Oudtshoorn. 1.85m. 100kg. Flanker. FC DEBUT:

2010. PROV CAREER: Eagles 2010 5-0-0-0-0-0. FC RECORD: 5-0-0-0-0-0. RECORD IN 2010: (Eagles) 5-0-0-0-0-0.

Breedt, Nico (Kearsney Coll. & UNISA) b 23/03/79, Johannesburg. 1.96m. 110kg. Eighthman. FC DEBUT: 2001. PROV CAREER: Eagles 2001-02 41-10-0-0-0-50. Cheetahs 2003 & 08-09 45-11-0-0-0-55. KZN 2004-06 48-7-0-0-0-35. Cheetahs XV 2010 1-0-0-0-0-0. SUPER 14: Cats 1-0-0-0-0-0; Sharks 2004-05 12-1-0-0-0-5. Cheetahs 2009-10 20-1-0-0-0-5. REP HONOURS: SA Schools 1998; CW KZN 1997-98. MISC INFO: Toulon (Fra) 2006-07. FC RECORD: 168-30-0-0-0-150. RECORD IN 2010: (Cheetahs S14, Cheetahs XV) 10-0-0-0-0-0. OTHER FC: Toulon, France 2007-08 14-2-0-0-0-10.

Bresler, Anton (Durban HS) b 16/02/1988, Windhoek. 1.97m. 106kg. Lock. FC DEBUT: 2010. PROV CA-REER: KZN 2010 4-0-0-0-0-0. Sharks XV 2010 9-0-0-0-0-0. Sharks In XV 2010 1-0-0-0-0-0. FC RECORD: 14-0-0-0-0-0. RECORD IN 2010: (KZN, Sharks XV, Sharks Inv XV) 14-0-0-0-0-0.

Breytenbach, Johannes Christiaan (Joe) (Ben Vorster HS) b 17/11/83, Tzaneen. 1.80m. 95kg. Centre. FC DEBUT: 2009. PROV CAREER: Eagles 2009-10 36-7-0-0-0-35. FC RECORD: 36-7-0-0-0-35. RECORD IN 2010: (Eagles) 21-6-0-0-0-30.

Briedenhann, Jannie Gysbert (Gys) (Jim Fouche HS) b 14/05/85, Kempton Park. 1.97m. 111kg. Lock. FC DEBUT: 2007. PROV CAREER: Griffons 2007-09 28-3-0-0-0-15. Leopards 2010 8-0-0-0-0-0. MISC INFO: Brother of Marnus Briedenhann. FC RECORD: 36-3-0-0-0-15. RECORD IN 2010: (Leopards) 8-0-0-0-0-0.

Briedenhann, Marnus (Jim Fouche HS) b 24/08/87, Kempton Park. 1.92m. 106kg. Lock. FC DEBUT: 2008. PROV CAREER: Cheetahs 2008-09 15-1-0-0-0-5. Griffons 2009-10 26-2-0-0-0-10. MISC INFO: Brother of Gys Briedenhann. FC RECORD: 41-3-0-0-0-15. RECORD IN 2010: (Griffons) 15-2-0-0-0-10.

Brinkhuys, Angelo (Breërivier HS, Worcester) b 04/06/82, Worcester. 1.79m. 90kg. Lock. FC DEBUT: 2003. PROV CAREER: Boland 2003-10 84-8-0-0-0-40. FC RECORD: 84-8-0-0-0-40. RECORD IN 2010: (Boland) 1-0-0-0-0-0.

Brits, Schalk Burger (Paul Roos & Stellenbosch Univ.) b 16/05/81, Empangeni. 1.82m. 98kg. Hooker. FC DE-BUT: 2002. PROV CAREER: WP 2002-03 & 06-08 39-6-0-0-0-30. Lions 2004-05 35-11-0-0-0-55. SUPER 14: Cats 2005 11-0-0-0-0-0. Stormers 2006-09 51-4-0-0-0-20. REP HONOURS: SA 2008 Tests: 3-0-0-0-0-0. Emerging Springboks 2007 3-2-0-0-0-10. SA 'A'

2004 3-2-0-0-0-10. WP XV 2006. British Barbarians 2007,09,10 3-0-0-0-0-0. SA Schools 1999. MISC INFO: YPoY nominee 2004. FC RECORD: 149-25-0-0-0-125. RECORD IN 2010: (British Barbarians) 1-0-0-0-0-0.

Britz, Willem Stephanus (Willie) (Diamantveld HS & UFS) b 31/08/88, Cape Town. 1.91m. 98kg. FC DE-BUT: 2009. PROV CAREER: Cheetahs 2009 1-0-0-0-0-0. Griffons 2010 8-2-0-0-0-10. FC RECORD: 9-2-0-0-0-10. RECORD IN 2010: (Griffons) 8-2-0-0-0-10.

Brown, Ryan Clifford (Uitenhage HS) b 10/02/87, Uitenhage. 1.81m. 72kg. Fullback. FC DEBUT: 2008. PROV CAREER: EP Kings 2008-10 30-4-26-19-0-129. E/Cape XV 2008 2-0-0-7-0-21. Bulldogs 2010 4-0-0-0-0-0. EP Inv XV 2010 1-0-0-0-0-0. FC RECORD: 37-4-26-26-0-150. RECORD IN 2010: (EP Kings, Bulldogs, EP Inv XV) 9-0-0-0-0-0.

Brüssow, Heinrich Wilhelm (Grey Coll., Bloemfontein) b 21/07/86, Bloemfontein. 1.81m. 101kg. Flank. FC DE-BUT: 2006. PROV CAREER: Cheetahs 2006-09 52-24-0-0-0-120. Cheetahs XV 2010 1-0-0-0-0-0. SUPER 14: Cheetahs 2007-10 33-5-0-0-0-25. REP HONOURS: SA 2008-09 Tests: 13-1-0-0-0-5. SA Sevens 2006, SA Schools 2004. MISC INFO: YPoY nominee 2008, POY Nominee 2009. FC RECORD: 99-30-0-0-0-150. RECORD IN 2010: (Cheetahs S14, Cheetahs XV) 5-1-0-0-0-5.

Brummer, Francois (Waterkloof HS) b 17/05/1989, Pretoria. 1.82m. 90kg. Flyhalf. FC DEBUT: 2008. PROV CAREER: Blue Bulls 2008-10 38-6-54-73-14-399. SU-PER 14: Bulls 2010 1-0-1-0-0-2. MISC INFO: Voda-com Cup PoY 2010. FC RECORD: 39-6-55-73-14-401. RECORD IN 2010: (Bulls, Blue Bulls) 16-1-13-17-6-100.

Buckle, Albertus Marthinus (Boland Agric) b 09/09/83, Paarl. 1.80m. 122kg. Hooker. FC DEBUT: 2007. PROV CAREER: Griquas 2007-10 62-15-0-0-0-75. REP HONOURS: Royal XV 2009 1-0-0-0-0-0. FC RECORD: 63-15-0-0-0-75. RECORD IN 2010: (Gri-quas) 12-6-0-0-0-30.

Bullbring, David James (Alexander Road HS & UJ) b 12/09//89, Port Elizabeth. 1.98m. 104kg. Lock. FC DEBUT: 2009. PROV CAREER: Golden Lions 2010 7-0-0-0-0-0. Young Lions 2009-10 12-2-0-0-0-10. SU-PER 14: Lions 2010 1-0-0-0-0-0. FC RECORD: 20-2-0-0-0-10. RECORD IN 2010: (Lions S14, Golden Lions, Young Lions) 15-1-0-0-0-5.

Burch, Jody David (SACS & ETA) b 06/10/82, Cape Town. 1.88m. 112kg. FC DEBUT: 2009. PROV CA-REER: Eagles 2009 10-0-0-0-0-0. WP 2009-10 13-4-0-0-0-20. FC RECORD: 23-4-0-0-0-20. RECORD IN

2010: (WP) 6-0-0-0-0-0.

Burden, Craig Bruce (Maritzburg College) b 13/05/85, Durban. Hooker. FC DEBUT: 2005. PROV CAREER: KZN 2005-10 48-18-0-0-0-90. Sharks XV 2005-10 22-9-0-0-0-45. Sharks Inv XV 2007 & 09-10 3-1-0-0-0-5. SUPER 14: Sharks 2006 & 08 &10 21-1-0-0-0-5. FC RECORD: 94-29-0-0-0-145. RECORD IN 2010: (Sharks, KZN, Sharks XV, Sharks Inv XV) 23-4-0-0-0-20.

Burger, Schalk Willem Petrus (Paarl Gym) b 13/04/83, Port Elizabeth. 1.93m. 110kg. Flank. FC DEBUT: 2002. PROV CAREER: WP 2003-05 & 08-10 30-7-0-0-0-35. SUPER 14: Stormers 2004-10 74-4-0-0-0-20. REP HONOURS: SA 2003-10 Tests: 63-13-0-0-0-65; SA U21 2002-03 8-4-0-0-0-20; British Barbarians 2004 & 08,09 3-0-0-0-0-0. S Hemisphere XV 2005 1-1-0-0-0-5. MISC INFO: SA PoY 2004. IRB PoY 2004. IRPA PoY & YPoY 2004. SA YPoY nominee 2003, 2004. SA PoY nominee 2010; Son of 1984-86 Springbok SWP (Schalk) Burger. FC RECORD: 170-27-0-0-0-135. RECORD IN 2010: (Stormers, WP): 16-2-0-0-0-10.

Buys, Ashley Schutte (George HS) b 01/06/79, Blanco. 1.80m. 112kg. Prop. FC DEBUT: 2005. PROV CAREER: Eagles 2005-08 58-3-0-0-0-15. Pumas 2009-10 44-0-0-0-0-0. FC RECORD: 102-3-0-0-0-15. RECORD IN 2010: (Pumas) 23-0-0-0-0-0.

Buys, Hendrik Cornelius Wian (Paarl Boys HS & UJ) b 04/01/1989, Klerksdorp. 1.85m. 85kg. Fullback. FC DEBUT: 2010. PROV CAREER: Young Lions 2010 5-1-0-0-0-5. FC RECORD: 5-1-0-0-0-5. RECORD IN 2010: (Young Lions) 5-1-0-0-0-5.

Buys, Kevin (Dr E G Jansen HS) b 26/04/86, Benoni. 1.91m. 120kgs. Eightman. FC DEBUT: 2007. PROV CAREER: Blue Bulls 2007 6-0-0-0-0-0. Blue Bulls XV 2007 1-0-0-0-0-0. Golden Lions 2009-10 19-0-0-0-0-0. Young Lions 2010 1-0-0-0-0-0. SUPER 14: Lions 2010 5-0-0-0-0-0. FC RECORD: 32-0-0-0-0-0. RECORD IN 2010 (Lions S14, Golden Lions, Young Lions) 11-0-0-0-0-0.

C

Calldo, Jacobus Gerber (Cobus) (Oakdale Agric.) b 30/04/81, Caledon. 1.94m. 120kg. Prop. FC DEBUT: 2002. PROV CAREER: Wildebeest 2002 2-0-0-0-0-0. Blue Bulls 2003 7-1-0-0-0-5. Cheetahs 2006-10 70-1-0-0-0-5. Griffons 2009 1-0-0-0-0-0. SUPER 14: Cheetahs 2008-10 19-0-0-0-0-0. FC RECORD: 99-2-0-0-0-10. RECORD IN 2010: (Cheetahs S14, Cheetahs) 19-1-0-0-0-5.

Campher, Rowan Keenan (Nico Malan HS) b 31/08/1986, Humansdorp. 1.85m. 87kg. Wing. FC DE-

BUT: 2010. PROV CAREER: Valke 2010 3-0-0-0-0-0. FC RECORD: 3-0-0-0-0-0. RECORD IN 2010: (Valke) 3-0-0-0-0-0.

Carse, Tertius Gerard (Bellville HS, Paul Roos) b 13/02/83, Brackenfell. 1.87m. 87kg. Scrumhalf. FC DEBUT: 2003. PROV CAREER: WP 2003-05 25-3-0-0-0-15. Griquas 2006-07 41-16-1-0-0-82. Eagles 2008 8-1-0-0-0-5. Cheetahs 2009-10 32-4-0-0-0-20. SUPER 14: Cheetahs 2007 & 10 2-0-0-0-0-0. FC RECORD: 118-24-1-0-0-122. RECORD IN 2010: (Cheetahs S14, Cheetahs) 21-3-0-0-0-15. OTHER FC: Aurillac, France 2007-08 11-0-0-0-0-0.

Carstens, Pieter Deon (Boland HS) b 03/06/79, Goodwood. 1.84m. 116kg. Prop. FC DEBUT: 2000. PROV CAREER: KZN 2001-06 & 08-09 86-9-0-0-0-45. Sharks XV 2001-09 8-1-0-0-0-5. SUPER 14: Sharks 2001-10 84-4-0-0-0-20. REP HONOURS: SA 2002 & 06-07&09 Tests: 9-0-0-0-0-0. Springbok XV 2006. SA 'A' 2001 2-0-0-0-0-0; SA XV 2006 1-0-0-0-0-0. SA U23s 2001 5-0-0-0-0-0; SA U21s 2000 2-0-0-0-0-0; SA U19s 1998; SA Schools 1997; CW WP 1997. FC RECORD: 199-14-0-0-0-70. RECORD IN 2010: (Sharks) 3-0-0-0-0-0.

Chadwick, Dale Michael (Westville Boys HS) b 20/06/89, Westville. 1.83m. 105kg. Prop. FC DEBUT: 2009. PROV CAREER: KZN 2009 1-0-0-0-0-0. Sharks XV 2010 4-0-0-0-0-0. Sharks Inv XV 2009 1-0-0-0-0-0. FC RECORD: 6-0-0-0-0-0. RECORD IN 2010: (Sharks XV) 4-0-0-0-0-0.

Chavhanga, Tonderai (Prince Edward, Harare) b 24/12/83, Masvingo, Zimbabwe. 1.84m. 86kg. Wing. FC DEBUT: 2003. PROV CAREER: Cheetahs 2003-04 3-1-0-0-0-5. WP 2005 & 07-09 40-16-0-0-0-80. Golden Lions 2010 1-0-0-0-0-0. Young Lions 2010 1-0-0-0-0-0. SUPER 14: Stormers 2004-06 & 08-09 37-14-0-0-0-70. Lions 2010 11-2-0-0-0-10. REP HONOURS: SA Tests: 2005 & 07-08 4-6-0-0-0-30. Emerging Springboks 2007 2-2-0-0-0-10. SA Sevens 2003. SA U21 2003 3-2-0-0-0-10. Zimbabwe CW 2000-01. FC RECORD: 102-43-0-0-0-215. RECORD IN 2010: (Lions S14, Golden Lions, Young Lions) 13-2-0-0-0-10.

Christians, Marvin (Bishops HS) b 13/09/1987, Cape Town. 1.85m. 93kg. Fullback. FC DEBUT: 2010. PROV CAREER: WP 2010 4-0-0-0-0-0. FC RECORD: 4-0-0-0-0-0. RECORD IN 2010: (WP) 4-0-0-0-0-0.

Cilliers, Patric Michael (Michaelhouse HS) b 03/03/87, Pietermaritzburg. 1.85m. 101kg. Prop. FC DEBUT: 2007. PROV CAREER: KZN 2007-10 34-5-0-0-0-25. Sharks XV 2007-10 18-3-0-0-0-15. Sharks Inv XV 2009-10 2-0-0-0-0-0. SUPER 14: Sharks 2007 & 09-

10 3-0-0-0-0-0. REP HONOURS: Emerging Spring-
boks 2009 1-0-0-0-0-0. FC RECORD: 58-8-0-0-0-40.
RECORD IN 2010: (Sharks, KZN, Sharks XV, Sharks
Inv XV) 20-5-0-0-0-25.
Claasen, Nicolaas (Nick) (Marais Viljoen HS) b
01/04/88, Vereeniging. 1.89m. 85kg. Wing. FC DEBUT:
2009. PROV CAREER: Sharks XV 2009 8-1-0-0-0-5.
Valke 2010 5-1-0-0-0-5. FC RECORD: 13-2-0-0-0-10.
RECORD IN 2010: (Valke) 5-1-0-0-0-5.
Clark, Nolan. Lock. FC DEBUT: 2007. PROV CA-
REER: Sharks XV 2008-09 10-0-0-0-0-0. Sharks Inv
XV 2007 1-1-0-0-0-5. Griquas 2009 6-0-0-0-0-0. EP
Kings 2009-10 16-0-0-0-0-0. EP Inv XV 2010 1-0-0-0-
0-0. FC RECORD: 34-1-0-0-0-5. RECORD IN 2010:
(EP Kings, EP Inv XV) 16-0-0-0-0-0.
Clever, Todd b 16/01/1983, Palm Springs, California,
1.90m. 97kg. Flank, SA FC DEBUT: 2009. PROV
CAREER: Lions 2009 11-0-0-0-0-0. SUPER 14: Lions
2009-10 21-3-0-0-0-15. REP HONOURS: USA RWC
2007. FC record SA: 32-3-0-0-0-15. RECORD IN 2010:
(Lions S14) 9-2-0-0-0-10.
Cloete, Rouaan Francois (AHS, Pretoria) b 10/03/84,
Pretoria. 1.84m. 94kg. Centre. FC DEBUT: 2007. PROV
CAREER: Valke 2007-08 21-5-0-0-0-25. Lions 2009
3-0-0-0-0-0. Young Lions 2009-10 8-1-0-0-0-5. FC
RECORD: 32-6-0-0-0-30. RECORD IN 2010: (Young
Lions) 6-1-0-0-0-5.
Coeries, Darryl Brenten (Parkdene HS) b 26/02/76,
George. 1.75m. 75kg. Wing. FC DEBUT: 1998. PROV
CAREER: Eagles 1998-05 118-53-0-0-0-265. Pumas
2006 16-6-0-0-0-30. Griquas 2007-08 14-7-0-0-0-35.
Griffons 2008-10 32-6-0-0-0-30. Super 12: Bulls 2000
1-0-0-0-0-0. REP HONOURS: SA Sevens 2002-03.
CW Eagles 1995. MISC INFO: Holds Eagles record for
most tries in a career (53). FC RECORD: 182-72-0-0-0-
360. RECORD IN 2010: (Griffons) 6-1-0-0-0-5.
Coetzee, Eric Meyer (Pietersburg HS) b 04/05/87,
Pretoria. 1.82m. 118kg. FC DEBUT: 2009. PROV CA-
REER: WP 2009 2-0-0-0-0-0. Griquas 2009 1-0-0-0-0-
0. Leopards 2010 6-0-0-0-0-0. FC RECORD: 9-0-0-0-0-
0. RECORD IN 2010: (Leopards) 6-0-0-0-0-0.
Coetzee, Jacques (Volkskool HS) b 22/10/83, Bethal.
1.77m. 78kg. Scrumhalf. FC DEBUT: 2007. PROV CA-
REER: Pumas 2007-10 71-16-14-5-0-123. SUPER 14:
Lions 2010 10-0-0-0-0-0. REP HONOURS: Royal XV
2009 1-0-0-0-0-0. FC RECORD: 82-16-14-5-0-123.
RECORD IN 2010: (Lions S14, Pumas) 21-1-0-0-0-5.
Coetzee, Jacques (Florida HS) b 29/10/81. 1.83m.
121kgs. Prop. FC DEBUT: 2003. PROV CAREER:
Valke 2003 & 10 14-1-0-0-0-5. Griffons 2004 2-0-0-0-0-

0. FC RECORD: 16-1-0-0-0-5. Record in 2010: (Valke)
1-0-0-0-0-0
Coetzee, Johannes Jurie (Hanno) (Wittedrift HS, Plet-
tenberg Bay & Stellenbosch Univ.) b 02/05/79, Pletten-
berg Bay. 1.88m. 93kg. Centre. FC DEBUT: 2002. PROV
CAREER: WP 2002 2-0-0-0-0-0. Pumas 2003-04 17-1-
0-0-0-5. Valke 2005-08 63-8-0-0-0-40. Griquas 2009-10
13-2-0-0-0-10. SUPER 14: Cheetahs 2009 3-0-0-0-0-0.
REP HONOURS: Royal XV 2009 1-0-0-0-0-0. FC
RECORD: 98-11-0-0-0-55. MISC INFO: SA Schools
decathlete. RECORD IN 2010: (Griquas) 3-0-0-0-0-0.
Coetzee, Johan Voges (Boland Agric. Coll.) b
14/03/1988, Windhoek. 1.87m. 122kg. Prop. FC DE-
BUT: 2010. PROV CAREER: Leopards 2010 11-0-0-0-
0-0. FC RECORD: 11-0-0-0-0-0. RECORD IN 2010:
(Leopards) 11-0-0-0-0-0.
Coetzer, Marius (Waterkloof HS) b 04/04/84, Pretoria.
2.00m. 104kg. Lock. FC DEBUT: 2005. PROV CA-
REER: Blue Bulls 2005 1-0-0-0-0-0. WP 2006 5-0-0-0-
0-0. Valke 2007-08 26-0-0-0-0-0. Pumas 2009-10 36-5-
0-0-0-25. FC RECORD: 68-5-0-0-0-25. RECORD IN
2010: (Pumas) 20-2-0-0-0-10.
Combrink, Ruan Jacobus (Michaelhouse HS) b
10/05/1990, Vryheid. 1.83m. 96kg. Wing. FC DEBUT:
2010. PROV CAREER: WP 2010 1-0-0-0-0-0. FC
RECORD: 1-0-0-0-0-0. RECORD IN 2010: (WP)
1-0-0-0-0-0.
Conradie, Johannes Haindly Joseph (Bolla) (Kasselsvlei SS) b 24/02/78, Cape Town. 1.69m. 75kg. Scrumhalf.
FC DEBUT: 1998. PROV CAREER: WP 2001-09 79-
16-0-0-0-80. Boland 2010 14-3-0-0-0-15. SUPER 14:
Stormers 2002-09 77-10-0-0-1-53. REP HONOURS:
SA 2002 & 04-05 & 08 Tests 18-2-0-0-1-13. SA 'A' 2001
& 03 6-0-0-0-0-0; SA U23s 2001 5-0-0-0-0-0; SA U21s
1998 3-0-0-0-0-0; SA Sevens 1999-00; SA Schools
1996-97; CW WP 1996-97. FC RECORD: 202-31-0-
0-2-161. RECORD IN 2010: (Boland) 14-3-0-0-0-15.
Constant, Ashton (Voortrekker HS, Cape Town, UWC)
b 28/09/83, Cape Town. 1.82m. 110kg. Hooker. FC
DEBUT: 2004. PROV CAREER: WP 2004-05 5-0-0-
0-0-0. Pumas 2006-08 47-6-0-0-0-30. Eagles 2009 11-1-
0-0-0-5. Boland 2010 13-0-0-0-0-0. REP HONOURS:
Emerging Springboks 2007 3-1-0-0-0-5. SA U21 2004
5-1-0-0-0-5. FC RECORD: 84-9-0-0-0-45. RECORD
IN 2010: (Boland) 13-0-0-0-0-0.
Cooper, Kyle Lorran (Glenwood HS) b 10/02/1989,
Johannesburg. 1.77m. 107kg. Hooker. FC DEBUT: 2010.
PROV CAREER: KZN 2010 8-0-0-0-0-0. Sharks XV
2010 9-1-0-0-0-5. Sharks Inv XV 2010 1-1-0-0-0-5. FC
RECORD: 18-2-0-0-0-10. RECORD IN 2010: (KZN,

Sharks XV, Sharks Inv XV) 18-2-0-0-0-10.

Cornelius, Lionel Curtis (Hermanus HS) b 29/10/86, Hermanus. 1.75m. 91kg. Fullback. FC DEBUT: 2007. PROV CAREER: Boland 2007-10 56-9-15-18-0-129. FC RECORD: 56-9-15-18-0-129. RECORD IN 2010: (Boland) 15-4-1-2-0-28.

Cronje, Coert Frederick (Jeugland HS & UJ) b 11/05/1988, Vereeniging. 1.82m. 86kg. Centre. FC DEBUT: 2010. PROV CAREER: Valke 2010 11-9-0-0-0-45. FC RECORD: 11-9-0-0-0-45. RECORD IN 2010: (Valke) 11-9-0-0-0-45.

Cronje, Lionel (Queens Coll. & UOFS) b 25/05/1989, Bloemfontein. 1.84m. 90kg. Flyhalf. FC DEBUT: 2010. PROV CAREER: WP 2010 14-2-9-0-0-28. SUPER 14: Stormers 2010 2-0-0-0-0-0. FC RECORD: 16-2-9-0-0-28. RECORD IN 2010: (Stormers, WP) 16-2-9-0-0-28.

Cronje, Ross (Michaelhouse) b 26/7/89, Johannesburg. 1.81m. 79kg. Scrumhalf. FC DEBUT: 2009. PROV CAREER: KZN 2009 4-0-0-0-0-0. Sharks XV 2009-10 13-1-11-1-0-30. SUPER 14: Sharks 2009 1-0-0-0-0-0. MISC INFO: Twin brother of Guy Cronje. FC RECORD: 18-1-11-1-0-30. RECORD IN 2010: (Sharks XV) 9-1-1-0-0-7.

Crous, Daniel Johannes (Grey Coll.) b 24/03/87, Bethlehem. 1.81m. 101kgs. FC DEBUT: 2009. PROV CAREER: Blue Bulls 2009 1-0-0-0-0-0. Leopards 2010 6-0-0-0-0-0. FC RECORD: 7-0-0-0-0-0. RECORD IN 2010: (Leopards) 6-0-0-0-0-0.

Croy, Ricardo (Paarl Gymnasium) b 07/12/86, Belville. 1.72m. 77kg. Flyhalf. FC DEBUT: 2006. PROV CAREER: WP 2006 & 08 14-2-14-6-0-56. Eagles 2008-09 22-4-37-31-2-193. Pumas 2010 19-1-22-14-2-97. REP HONOURS: SA U19 2005. MISC INFO: Son of former WP scrumhalf Richard Croy. FC RECORD: 55-7-73-51-4-346. RECORD IN 2010: (Pumas) 19-1-22-14-2-97.

D

Dames, Hendrik Daniel Petrus (Danie) (Duineveld HS) b 07/02/86, Pretoria. 1.90m. 84kg. Utility back. FC DEBUT: 2008. PROV CAREER: Sharks XV 2008-09 12-0-0-0-0-0. Leopards 2009-10 24-6-0-0-0-30. FC RECORD: 36-6-0-0-0-30. RECORD IN 2010: (Leopards) 13-2-0-0-0-10.

Daniel, Keegan Rhys (Dale Coll.) b 05/03/85, Humansdorp. 1.85m. 89kg. Flank. ›› FC debut: 2006. Prov career: KZN 2006-10 69-27-0-0-0-135. Sharks XV 2006-09 9-4-0-0-0-20. Sharks Inv XV 2009-10 2-2-1-0-0-12. Super 14: Sharks 2006-10 48-5-0-0-0-25. Rep honours: SA 2010 Tests: 1-0-0-0-0-0. SA Tour 2010: 1-0-0-0-0-0. Total: 2-0-0-0-0-0. SA U21 2006 5-3-0-0-0-15.

Misc info: U21 PoY 2006, VC PoY 2006, YPoY nominee 2006, IRB YPoY nominee 2006. FC record: 135-41-1-0-0-207. RECORD IN 2010: (SA, Sharks, KZN, Sharks Inv XV) 26-10-1-0-0-52.

Daniels, Earl Allister (Jan Kriel HS) b 20/01/1987, Cape Town. 1.97m. 107kg. Flanker. FC DEBUT: 2010. PROV CAREER: Griffons 2010 3-0-0-0-0-0. FC RECORD: 3-0-0-0-0-0. RECORD IN 2010: (Griffons) 3-0-0-0-0-0.

Daniller, Hendrick Joseph (Hennie) (Paarl Gym) b 05/04/84, Cape Town. 1.95m. 95kg. Fullback. FC DEBUT: 2003. PROV CAREER: Blue Bulls 2003 & 05-06 19-1-0-0-0-5. Boland 2006-07 19-1-0-0-0-5. Cheetahs 2008-10 36-6-0-0-0-30. Griffons 2008 5-0-0-0-0-0. Cheetahs XV 2010 1-0-0-0-0-0. SUPER 14: Bulls 2004 7-0-0-0-0-0. Cheetahs 2008-10 37-4-0-0-0-20. REP HONOURS: SA U21 2004-05 9-3-0-0-0-15. SA U19 2003. SA Schools 2002. FC RECORD: 133-15-0-0-0-75. RECORD IN 2010: (Cheetahs S14, Cheetahs, Cheetahs XV) 27-6-0-0-0-30.

Daniller, Tertius (Paarl Gym.) b 04/08/1989, Paarl. 1.94m. 88kg. Eightman. FC DEBUT: 2010. PROV CAREER: WP 2010 1-0-0-0-0-0. FC RECORD: 1-0-0-0-0-0. RECORD IN 2010: (WP) 1-0-0-0-0-0.

De Beer, Jan Fourie (Jandre) (Pietersburg HS) b 19/09/1988, Pietersburg. 1.81m. 100kg. Hooker. FC DEBUT: 2010. PROV CAREER: Eagles 2010 14-0-0-0-0-0. FC RECORD: 14-0-0-0-0-0. RECORD IN 2010: (Eagles) 14-0-0-0-0-0.

De Bruin, Johann (Kempton Park HS)b 23/07/86, Kempton Park. 1.98m. 95kg. Lock. FC DEBUT: 2008. PROV CAREER: Valke 2008-10 25-2-0-0-0-10. FC RECORD: 25-2-0-0-0-10. RECORD IN 2010: (Valke) 13-1-0-0-0-5.

De Bruin, Zandre (Afrikaans HS) b 19/03/1990, Pongola. 1.80m. 91kg. Centre. FC DEBUT: 2010. PROV CAREER: Cheetahs 2010 1-0-0-0-0-0. FC RECORD: 1-0-0-0-0-0. RECORD IN 2010: (Cheetahs) 1-0-0-0-0-0.

De Bruyn, Mattheus Johannes (Tewis) (Grey Coll., Bloemfontein) b 05/08/82, Hoopstad. 1.73m. 81kg. Scrumhalf. FC DEBUT: 2002. PROV CAREER: Leopards 2002-03 23-2-16-3-1-54. Eagles 2004-06 51-6-10-7-1-74. Boland 2006-07 14-0-12-4-0-36. Cheetahs 2007-10 51-10-29-1-0-111. Cheetahs XV 2010 1-0-1-2-0-8. SUPER 14: Cheetahs 2008-10 32-2-2-1-0-17. FC RECORD: 172-20-70-18-2-300. RECORD IN 2010: (Cheetahs S14, Cheetahs, Cheetahs XV) 26-2-1-2-0-18.

De Doncker, Basil (Booysen Park SSS) b 12/06/83, Port Elizabeth. 1.73m. 80kg. Centre. FC DEBUT: 2004. PROV CAREER: Lions 2004 1-1-0-0-0-5. Elephants 2004-07

54-6-0-0-0-30. Leopards 2008-10 36-6-0-0-0-30. REP HONOURS: SA U19 2002. FC RECORD: 91-14-0-0-0-70. RECORD IN 2010: (Leopards) 5-0-0-0-0-0.

De Jongh, Juan Leon (Hugenot HS) b 15/04/88, Paarl. 1.77m. 84kg. Centre. FC DEBUT: 2009. PROV CAREER: WP 2009-10 25-9-0-0-0-45. SUPER 14: Stormers 2010 13-1-0-0-0-5. REP HONOURS: SA 2009-10 Tests: 6-1-0-0-0-5. Tour 2009 2-1-0-0-0-5. Total: 8-2-0-0-0-10. MISC INFO: YPOY Nominee 2009,2010. Poy nominee 2010. FC RECORD: 44-11-0-0-0-55. RECORD IN 2010: (SA, Stormers, WP) 28-6-0-0-0-30.

De Klerk, Pieter Rossouw (Paarl Gym.) b 21/08/89. Vredenburg. 1.86m. 110kg. Prop. FC DEBUT: 2009. PROV CAREER: Blue Bulls 2009-10 18-0-0-0-0-0. SUPER 14: Bulls 2010 1-0-0-0-0-0. FC RECORD: 19-0-0-0-0-0. RECORD IN 2010: (Bulls, Blue Bulls) 15-0-0-0-0-0.

De Kock, Tiaan (Paarl Boys HS) b 13/03/85, Bellville. 1.97m. 111kg. Prop. FC DEBUT: 2006. PROV CAREER: Eagles 2006-10 56-0-0-0-0-0. FC RECORD: 56-0-0-0-0-0. RECORD IN 2010: (Eagles) 1-0-0-0-0-0.

De la Port, Dieter Carl (Dr EG Jansen) b 18/11/87, Phalaborwa. 1.92m. 92kg. FC DEBUT: 2009. PROV CAREER: Valke 2009-10 10-2-0-0-0-10. FC RECORD: 10-2-0-0-0-10. RECORD IN 2010: (Valke) 6-1-0-0-0-5.

De Neuily-Rice, Michael Vincent (Mike) (Grey HS) b 14/04/87, Cape Town. 1.83m. 111kg. Prop. FC DEBUT: 2008. PROV CAREER: WP 2008-10 16-1-0-0-0-5. Boland 2009 5-0-0-0-0-0. EP Kings 2010 7-0-0-0-0-0. FC RECORD: 28-1-0-0-0-5. RECORD IN 2010: (EP Kings, WP) 11-0-0-0-0-0.

De Villiers, David Jacobus (Empangeni HS) b 20/09/80, Johannesburg. 1.99m 108kg. Lock/flank. FC DEBUT: 2002. PROV CAREER: WP 2002 2-0-0-0-0-0. Boland 2004-07 44-4-0-0-0-20. Cheetahs 2007-10 46-3-0-0-0-15. Griffons 2010 5-0-0-0-0-0. Cheetahs XV 2010 1-0-0-0-0-0. SUPER 14: Cheetahs 2008-10 29-2-0-0-0-10. FC RECORD: 127-9-0-0-0-45. RECORD IN 2010: (Cheetahs S14, Cheetahs, Griffons, Cheetahs XV) 14-0-0-0-0-0.

De Villiers, Jean (Paarl Gym.) b 24/02/81, Paarl. 1.90m. 100kg. Centre. FC DEBUT: 2001. PROV CAREER: WP 2001-05 & 08 & 10 44-28-0-0-0-140. SUPER 14: Stormers 2005-09 53-18-0-0-0-90. REP HONOURS: SA 2002 & 2004-10 Tests: 67-19-0-0-0-95. SA XV 2006 1-0-0-0-0-0. SA Sevens 2002. SA U21s 2001-02 9-7-0-0-0-35; SA U19 2000. SA Schools 1999; CW WP Academy 1999. British Barbarians 2008 1-0-0-0-0-0. MISC INFO: SA Rugby PoY 2008. PoY nominee 2005. Holds SA Record for most tests as a centre - 43. Son of former

WP lock André de Villiers. FC RECORD: 175-72-0-0-0-360. RECORD IN 2010: (SA, WP) 19-4-0-0-0-20.

De Waal, Willem (Boland Agric. HS) b 17/02/78, Paarl. 1.89m. 93kg. Flyhalf. FC DEBUT: 2002. PROV CAREER: Leopards 2002-03 32-7-69-54-1-338. Cheetahs 2004-07 66-9-152-161-14-874. WP 2008-10 32-2-62-99-1-434. REP HONOURS: SA 'A' 2004 3-0-4-0-0-8. Emerging Springboks 2009 1-0-1-0-0-2. SUPER 14: Bulls 2004 10-1-10-2-0-31. Cats 2005 4-0-0-0-0-0. Cheetahs 2006-07 15-2-18-20-1-109. Stormers 2009-10 15-2-8-10-1-59. MISC INFO: CC PoY 2007. PPoY 2007. Leading CC points scorer in 2004, 2005, 2006, 2007. FC RECORD: 178-23-324-346-18-1855. RECORD IN 2010: (Stormers, WP) 26-1-45-62-0-281. OTHER FC: Narbonne, France 2007-2008 24-2-21-48-0-196.

Delport, Marius (Swartkop HS) b 06/03/85, Pretoria. 1.93m. 90kg. Wing/fullback. FC DEBUT: 2004. PROV CAREER: Blue Bulls 2004-09 82-35-0-0-0-175. Golden Lions 2010 8-1-0-0-0-5. Young Lions 2010 4-3-0-0-0-15. SUPER 14: Bulls 2007-09 9-0-0-0-0-0. Lions 2010 5-0-0-0-0-0. REP HONOURS: Emerging Springboks 2007 2-3-0-0-0-15. SA U21 2004-06 12-7-0-0-0-35. SA U19s 2003-2004. SA Schools 2003. CW Blue Bulls 2002-2003. FC RECORD: 122-49-0-0-0-245. RECORD IN 2010: (Lions S14, Golden Lions, Young Lions) 17-4-0-0-0-20.

Demas, Danwel (New Orleans HS) b 15/10/81, Paarl. 1.86m. 79kg. Wing. FC DEBUT: 2004. PROV CAREER: Pumas 2004 11-2-0-0-0-10. Blue Bulls 2005-08 27-8-0-0-0-40. Boland 2008 7-5-0-0-0-25. Cheetahs 2009 12-3-0-0-0-15. Cheetahs XV 2010 1-0-0-0-0-0. SUPER 14: Bulls 2006 & 08 4-0-0-0-0-0. Cheetahs 2009-10 21-2-0-0-0-10. REP HONOURS: Emerging Springboks 2009 1-1-0-0-0-5. SA Sevens 2003-06. FC RECORD: 84-21-0-0-0-105. RECORD IN 2010: (Cheetahs S14, Cheetahs XV) 11-0-0-0-0-0.

Dercksen, Theunis (Brandwag HS) b 06/07/1990, Boksburg. 1.93m. 93kg. Flanker. FC DEBUT: 2010. PROV CAREER: Eagles 2010 3-0-0-0-0-0. FC RECORD: 3-0-0-0-0-0. RECORD IN 2010: (Eagles) 3-0-0-0-0-0.

Des Fountain, Dylan (Paarl Gym) b 07/06/85. 1.87m. 84kg. Centre. FC DEBUT: 2004. PROV CAREER: Blue Bulls 2004 1-0-0-0-0-0. WP 2007-10 24-4-0-0-0-20. SUPER 14: Stormers 2007-09 18-3-0-0-0-15. FC RECORD: 43-7-0-0-0-35. RECORD IN 2010 (WP) 8-2-0-0-0-10.

Deysel, Jean Roy (Hentie Cilliers HS) b 05/03/85, Virginia. 1.92m. 103kg. Flank. FC DEBUT: 2005. PROV CAREER: Lions 2005-07 21-1-0-0-0-5. KZN 2007-10 30-1-0-0-0-5. Sharks XV 2007-08 3-0-0-0-0-0. Sharks Inv XV 2007,09 2-3-0-0-0-15. SUPER 14: Sharks

2008-10 28-0-0-0-0-0. REP HONOURS: SA Tests 1-0-0-0-0-0. Tour: 2009 2-0-0-0-0-0. Total: 3-0-0-0-0-0. Emerging Springboks 2009 1-0-0-0-0-0. SA Students 2007 1-0-0-0-0-0. MISC INFO: Absa CC PoY 2008. FC RECORD: 89-5-0-0-0-25. RECORD IN 2010: (Sharks, KZN) 15-0-0-0-0-0.

Dinkelman, Ernst Heinrich (Grey Coll.) b 26/04/1990, Ermelo. 1.84m. 94kg. Centre. FC DEBUT: 2010. PROV CAREER: Blue Bulls 2010 6-1-0-0-0-5. FC RECORD: 6-1-0-0-0-5. RECORD IN 2010: (Blue Bulls) 6-1-0-0-0-5.

Dippenaar, Stephanus Christiaan (Stephan) (Paul Roos Gymasium) b 03/01/88, Moorreesburg. 1.88m. 88kg. Centre. FC DEBUT: 2008. PROV CAREER: Blue Bulls 2008-10 25-4-0-0-0-20. SUPER 14: Bulls 2008 & 10 13-1-0-0-0-5. FC RECORD: 38-5-0-0-0-25. RECORD IN 2010: (Bulls, Blue Bulls) 20-2-0-0-0-10.

Doneghan, Ross (Daniel Stewarts HS, Melville) b 08/10/88, Edinburgh. 1.88m. 98kg. FC DEBUT: 2009. PROV CAREER: Bulldogs 2009-10 14-2-0-0-0-10. FC RECORD: 14-2-0-0-0-10. RECORD IN 2010: (Bulldogs) 13-2-0-0-0-10.

Dorfling, Tiaan Arno (Framesby HS & North West Univ.) b 26/07/1990, Port Elizabeth. 1.75m. 80kg. Scrumhalf. FC DEBUT: 2010. PROV CAREER: Leopards 2010 2-0-0-0-0-0. FC RECORD: 2-0-0-0-0-0. RECORD IN 2010: (Leopards) 2-0-0-0-0-0.

Downey, Justin (Northwood HS) b 11/11/86, Johannesburg. 1.93m. 102kg. Flank. FC DEBUT: 2008. PROV CAREER: KZN 2009 3-0-0-0-0-0. Sharks XV 2008-10 18-3-0-0-0-15. Sharks Inv XV 2009-10 2-0-0-0-0-0. Griquas 2010 6-1-0-0-0-5. FC RECORD: 29-4-0-0-0-20. RECORD IN 2010: (Griquas, Sharks XV, Sharks Inv XV) 16-2-0-0-0-10.

Dreyer, Ruan Martin (Monument HS) b 16/09/1990, Carletonville. 1.86m. 113kg. Prop. FC DEBUT: 2010. PROV CAREER: Young Lions 2010 3-0-0-0-0-0. FC RECORD: 3-0-0-0-0-0. RECORD IN 2010: (Young Lions) 3-0-0-0-0-0.

Dry, Christopher Adriaan (Grey Coll. & Central Univ. of Tech.) b 13/02/88, Cape Town. 1.91m. 95kg. FC DEBUT: 2009. PROV CAREER: Cheetahs 2009-10 5-0-0-0-0-0. FC RECORD: 5-0-0-0-0-0. RECORD IN 2010: (Cheetahs) 4-0-0-0-0-0.

Du Plessis, Bismarck Wilhelm (Grey Coll., Bloemfontein & UFS) b 22/05/1984, Bethlehem. 1.89m. 105kg. Hooker. FC DEBUT: 2003. PROV CAREER: Cheetahs 2003 2-0-0-0-0-0. KZN 2005-10 33-10-0-0-0-50. Sharks XV 2005-08 3-2-0-0-0-10. SUPER 14: Sharks 2005-10 66-7-0-0-0-35. REP HONOURS: SA 2007-10 Tests: 36-5-0-0-0-25. Tour: 2007 2-0-0-0-0-0. Total:

38-5-0-0-0-25. SA U21 2005 1-1-0-0-0-5. British Barbs. 2009 1-0-0-0-0-0. MISC INFO: PoY nominee 2008. Brother of FS Cheetah prop Jannie du Plessis. Son of former EOFS prop Francois du Plessis. FC RECORD: 144-25-0-0-0-125. RECORD IN 2010: (SA, Sharks, KZN) 22-2-0-0-0-10.

Du Plessis, Charl Francois (Monument HS) b 08/04/87, Cape Town. 1.87m. 113kg. Prop. FC DEBUT: 2008. PROV CAREER: Young Lions 2008-10 7-0-0-0-0-0. Valke 2009 9-0-0-0-0-0. Boland 2010 8-0-0-0-0-0. FC RECORD: 24-0-0-0-0-0. RECORD IN 2010: (Young Lions, Boland) 10-0-0-0-0-0.

Du Plessis, Christo John (George HS) b 02/06/1989, George. 1.86m. 92kg. Flanker. FC DEBUT: 2010. PROV CAREER: Eagles 2010 9-1-0-0-0-5. FC RECORD: 9-1-0-0-0-5. RECORD IN 2010: (Eagles) 9-1-0-0-0-5.

Du Plessis, Jan Nathaniël (Jannie) (Grey Coll., Bloemfontein) b 16/11/82, Bethlehem. 1.87m.113kg. Prop. FC DEBUT: 2003. PROV CAREER: Cheetahs 2003-07 69-3-0-0-0-15. KZN 2008-10 27-3-0-0-0-15. SUPER 14: Cheetahs 2006-07 26-0-0-0-0-0. Sharks 2008-10 39-0-0-0-0-0. REP HONOURS: SA 2007-10 Tests: 24-1-0-0-0-5. Tour: 2007, 09 2-0-0-0-0-0. Total: 26-1-0-0-0-5. SA U21 2003 4-0-0-0-0-0. MISC INFO: Brother of Natal Sharks hooker Bismarck du Plessis. Son of former EOFS prop Francois du Plessis. FC RECORD: 191-7-0-0-0-35. REP HONOURS: CW Free State 2000. RECORD IN 2010: (SA, Sharks, KZN) 30-3-0-0-0-15.

Du Preez, Petrus Fourie (AHS, Pretoria) b 24/03/82, Pretoria. 1.83m. 88kg. Scrumhalf. FC DEBUT: 2001. PROV CAREER: Blue Bulls 2001-05 & 08-09 52-19-0-0-0-95. SUPER 14: Bulls 2003-10 99-19-0-0-0-95. REP HONOURS: SA 2004-09 55-13-0-0-0-65. SA U21 2002-03 9-1-0-0-0-5. SA U19 2001. British Barbarians 2008,09 2-0-0-0-0-0. MISC INFO: YPoY nominee 2003, 2004, PoY 2006 PoY nominee 2007. S14 PoY 2007. SA Rugby POY 2009. IRB Rugby POY Nominee 2009. Son of former Northern Transvaal No. 8 Fourie du Preez (Snr) FC RECORD: 217-52-0-0-0-260. RECORD IN 2010: (Bulls) 14-2-0-0-0-10.

Du Preez, Ruaan (Outeniqua HS) b 20/03/84, Port Elizabeth. 1.86m. 111kg. Prop. FC DEBUT: 2005. PROV CAREER: Boland 2005-07 34-0-0-0-0-0. WP 2008 8-0-0-0-0-0. Griquas 2008-10 31-1-0-0-0-5. FC RECORD: 73-1-0-0-0-5. RECORD IN 2010: (Griquas) 2-0-0-0-0-0.

Du Preez, Vernon (Stoffberg HS) b 23/04/1986, Springs. 1.75m. 108kg. Hooker. FC DEBUT: 2010. PROV CAREER: Valke 2010 2-0-0-0-0-0. FC RECORD: 2-0-0-0-0-0. RECORD IN 2010: (Valke)

2-0-0-0-0-0.

Du Preez, Wian Hunter (Grey Coll., Bloemfontein) b 30/10/82, Bloemfontein. 1.85m. 113kg. Prop. FC DEBUT: 2003. PROV CAREER: Cheetahs 2003-09 105-7-0-0-0-35. SUPER 14: Sharks 2005 2-0-0-0-0-0. Cheetahs 2006-10 59-0-0-0-0-0. REP HONOURS: Tests SA Tests: 2009 1-0-0-0-0-0. Tour 2009 1-0-0-0-0-0. Total: 2-0-0-0-0-0. Emerging Springboks 2009 1-0-0-0-0-0. FC RECORD: 169-7-0-0-0-35. RECORD IN 2010: (Cheetahs S14) 13-0-0-0-0-0.

Du Toit, Andre Jeremy (Groenberg HS) b 22/02/80, Grabouw. 1.86m. 98kg. Flank. FC DEBUT: 2008. PROV CAREER: Pumas 2008 8-0-0-0-0-0. Boland 2009-10 11-0-0-0-0-0. FC RECORD: 19-0-0-0-0-0. RECORD IN 2010: (Boland) 4-0-0-0-0-0.

Du Toit, Marcel (Gill College & UOFS) b 14/05/84, Potchefstroom. 1.76m. 79kgs. Flyhalf. FC DEBUT: 2007. PROV CAREER: Griffons 2007 10-0-1-0-0-2. Cheetahs 2007 4-1-0-0-0-5. Leopards 2010 2-0-5-0-0-10. FC RECORD: 16-1-6-0-0-17. RECORD IN 2010: (Leopards) 2-0-5-0-0-10.

Dubase, Onke Sydwell (Hudson HS) b 06/08/1989, East London. 1.82m. 89kg. Lock. FC DEBUT: 2010. PROV CAREER: Bulldogs 2010 1-0-0-0-0-0. FC RECORD: 1-0-0-0-0-0. RECORD IN 2010: (Bulldogs) 1-0-0-0-0-0.

Dukisa, Ntabeni (Loyolo HS) b 25/07/1988. Wing. FC DEBUT: 2010. PROV CAREER: Bulldogs 2010 1-0-0-0-0-0. FC RECORD: 1-0-0-0-0-0. RECORD IN 2010: (Bulldogs) 1-0-0-0-0-0.

Dumond, Cecil (Orkney HS) b 08/04/87, Klerksdorp. 1.82m. 84kgs. Flyhalf. FC DEBUT: 2007. PROV CAREER: Leopards 2007 & 09-10 24-2-18-29-2-139. FC RECORD: 24-2-18-29-1-139. RECORD IN 2010: (Leopards) 12-1-4-11-1-49.

Dumond, Godfried (Monty) (Orkney HS) b 20/08/82, Klerksdorp. 1.82m. 87kg. Fullback. FC DEBUT: 2003. PROV CAREER: KZN 2003,07-10 34-7-22-15-0-124. Sharks XV 2003,07-10 18-2-29-42-1-197. Leopards 2004 4-1-7-5-0-34. KZN Inv XV 2007,10 2-0-11-0-0-22. EP Kings 2010 7-0-15-18-1-87. SUPER 14: Sharks 2009-10 6-0-0-0-0-0. FC RECORD: 71-10-84-80-2-464. RECORD IN 2010: (Sharks, KZN, Sharks XV, Sharks Inv XV, EP Kings) 25-1-36-38-2-197. OTHER FC: Oyonnax, France 2007-2008 6-1-0-4-0-17.

Duncan, Rory (Grey High School, PE) b 26/07/7, Durban. 1.88m. 105kg. Lock. FC DEBUT: 1999. PROV CAREER: KZN 1999-01 11-1-0-0-0-5. EP Kings 2001-03&05 & 10 54-5-0-0-0-25. Cheetahs 2006-07 31-3-0-0-0-15. Super 14; Cheetahs 2007-08 19-2-0-0-0-10.

MISC INFO: Son of former Natal prop Paul Duncan. FC RECORD: 115-11-0-0-0-55. RECORD IN 2010: (EP Kings) 9-0-0-0-0-0.

Durand, Clayton (Vereeniging THS) b 15/06/84, Vereeniging. 1.83m. 83kg. Flyhalf. FC DEBUT: 2005. PROV CAREER: Lions 2005 7-1-7-16-0-67. Leopards 2006-10 72-2-119-115-5-608. Valke 2007 1-0-0-0-0-0. FC RECORD: 80-3-126-131-5-675. RECORD IN 2010: (Leopards) 17-0-27-29-0-141.

Dutton, Billy (Cambridge HS) b 09/06/1989, Transkai. 1.85m. 93kg. Flanker. FC DEBUT: 2010. PROV CAREER: Bulldogs 2010 1-0-0-0-0-0. FC RECORD: 1-0-0-0-0-0. RECORD IN 2010: (Bulldogs) 1-0-0-0-0-0.

Duvenage, CJ (Stoffel) (Potchefstroom Univ.) b 05/06/86. 1.76m. 92kg. Hooker. FC DEBUT: 2009. PROV CAREER: Leopards 2010 2-0-0-0-0-0. REP HONOURS: SA Students 2009 2-0-0-0-0-0. FC RECORD: 4-0-0-0-0-0. RECORD IN 2010: (Leopards) 2-0-0-0-0-0.

Duvenage, Dewaldt Otto (Paarl Gym.) b 22/05/88, Bellville. 1.76m. 75kg. Scrumhalf. FC DEBUT: 2007. PROV CAREER: Boland 2007-08 24-3-0-0-0-15. WP 2008-10 37-1-0-0-0-5. SUPER 14: Stormers 2009-10 25-2-0-0-0-10. FC RECORD: 86-6-0-0-0-30. RECORD IN 2010: (Stormers, WP) 31-2-0-0-0-10.

Dyer, Robert James (Otto du Plessis HS) b 04/12/86, Port Elizabeth. 1.82m. 103kg. FC DEBUT: 2008. PROV CAREER: EP Kings 2008-10 25-2-0-0-0-10. EP Inv XV 2010 1-0-0-0-0-0. FC RECORD: 26-2-0-0-0-10. RECORD IN 2010: (EP Kings, EP Inv XV) 12-0-0-0-0-0.

E

Earle, George (Westville Boys HS) b 09/01/87, Durban. 1.96m. 108kg. Lock. FC DEBUT: 2008. PROV CAREER: WP 2008-09 12-0-0-0-0-0. Boland 2009 8-0-0-0-0-0. Golden Lions 2010 12-1-0-0-0-5. SUPER 14: Lions 2010 6-0-0-0-0-0. FC RECORD: 38-1-0-0-0-5. RECORD IN 2010: (Lions S14, Golden Lions) 18-1-0-0-0-5.

Ebersohn, Josias Mathiem (Sias) (Grey Coll.) b 23/02/89, Bloemfontein. 1.75m. 81kg. Flyhalf. FC DEBUT: 2008. PROV CAREER: Cheetahs 2008-10 30-1-17-5-2-60. Cheetahs XV 2010 1-0-0-0-0-0. SUPER 14: Cheetahs 2010 2-0-0-0-0-0. MISC INFO: Twin brother of Robert Ebersohn. FC RECORD: 33-1-17-5-2-60. RECORD IN 2010: (Cheetahs S14, Cheetahs, Cheetahs XV) 25-0-13-4-1-41.

Ebersohn, Robert Thompson (Grey Coll.) b 23/02/89, Bloemfontein. 1.80m. 82kg. Centre. FC DEBUT: 2008. PROV CAREER: Cheetahs 2008-10 37-8-0-0-0-40. SUPER 14: Cheetahs 2010 10-0-0-0-0-0. MISC INFO:

YPoY 2008. Sasol u 20 PoY 2008. Twin brother of Sias Ebersohn. REP HONOURS: SA Sevens 2008. FC RECORD: 47-8-0-0-0-40. RECORD IN 2010: (Cheetahs S14, Cheetahs) 27-4-0-0-0-20.

Ehlers, Chris Erich (Wesvalia HS) b 22/05/1988, Kroonstad. 1.99m. 95kg. Lock. FC DEBUT: 2010. PROV CAREER: Valke 2010 13-0-0-0-0-0. FC RECORD: 13-0-0-0-0-0. RECORD IN 2010: (Valke) 13-0-0-0-0-0.

Eksteen, Hendrik Oostewald (Henk) (Oakdale HS) b 29/02/80, Mossel Bay. 2.00m. 115kgs. Lock. FC DEBUT: 2001. PROV CAREER: Boland 2001-05 82-5-0-0-0-25. Eagles 2010 7-0-0-0-0-0. SUPER 14: Stormers 2006 6-0-0-0-0-0. MISC INFO: Son of former SWD lock Ossie Eksteen. Narbonne (Fra) 2006-07. FC RECORD: 95-5-0-0-0-25. RECORD IN 2010: (Eagles) 7-0-0-0-0-0.

Els, Jarrid Wayde (Hudsen Park HS) b 16/10/1988, King William's Town. 1.92m. 102kg. Flanker. FC DEBUT: 2010. PROV CAREER: Bulldogs 2010 4-0-0-0-0-0. FC RECORD: 4-0-0-0-0-0. RECORD IN 2010: (Bulldogs) 4-0-0-0-0-0.

Elstadt, Rynhardt (Montagu HS) b 02/12/1989, Johannesburg. 1.98m. 112kg. Lock. FC DEBUT: 2010. PROV CAREER: WP 2010 13-0-0-0-0-0. FC RECORD: 13-0-0-0-0-0. RECORD IN 2010: (WP) 13-0-0-0-0-0.

Emslie, Charles (Monument HS) b 14/06/1988, Randfontein. 1.89m. 100kg. Hooker. FC DEBUT: 2010. PROV CAREER: Young Lions 2010 3-1-0-0-0-5. SUPER 14: Lions 2010 10-0-0-0-0-0. FC RECORD: 13-1-0-0-0-5. RECORD IN 2010: (Lions S14, Young Lions) 13-1-0-0-0-5.

Engelbrecht, Gabriel Joubert (Upington HS) b 27/06/1989, Kimberley. 1.89m. 90kg. Centre. FC DEBUT: 2010. PROV CAREER: Leopards 2010 1-0-0-0-0-0. FC RECORD: 1-0-0-0-0-0. RECORD IN 2010: (Leopards) 1-0-0-0-0-0.

Engelbrecht, Jacques Jacobus (JJ) (Monument HS) b 10/06/85, Cape Town. 1.94m. 105kg. Flank. FC DEBUT: 2007. PROV CAREER: WP 2007-10 15-8-0-0-0-40. Eagles 2008-10 48-3-0-0-0-15. FC RECORD: 63-11-0-0-0-55. RECORD IN 2010: (Eagles, WP) 30-9-0-0-0-45.

Engelbrecht, Nicolaas Johannes Els (Oos Moot HS) b 02/11/1988, Klerksdorp. 1.91m. 108kg. Prop. FC DEBUT: 2010. PROV CAREER: Valke 2010 10-1-0-0-0-5. FC RECORD: 10-1-0-0-0-5. RECORD IN 2010: (Valke) 10-1-0-0-0-5.

Engelbrecht, Pieter (Paul Roos Gym.) b 14/03/86, Bloemfontein. 1.83m. 100kg. Centre. FC DEBUT: 2009. PROV CAREER: Golden Lions 2009-10 11-1-0-0-0-5.

Young Lions 2010 7-2-0-0-0-10. FC RECORD: 18-3-0-0-0-15. RECORD IN 2010: (Golden Lions, Young Lions) 9-2-0-0-0-10.

Engels, Jaco (Volkskool, Potchefstroom) b 17/12/80, Oranjemundt. 1.85m. 118kg. Prop. FC DEBUT: 2003. PROV CAREER: Leopards 2003-04 40-6-0-0-0-30. Boland 2005 22-4-0-0-0-20. Blue Bulls 2006-10 67-6-0-0-0-30. SUPER 14: Bulls 2006-10 40-2-0-0-0-10. REP HONOURS: S/Kings 2009 1-0-0-0-0-0. FC RECORD: 170-18-0-0-0-90. RECORD IN 2010: (Bulls, Blue Bulls) 17-1-0-0-0-5.

Erasmus, Danwill (Zwaanswyk HS) b 05/02/1987, Hermanus. 1.78m. 78kg. Centre. FC DEBUT: 2010. PROV CAREER: Griquas 2010 1-0-0-0-0-0. FC RECORD: 1-0-0-0-0-0. RECORD IN 2010: (Griquas) 1-0-0-0-0-0.

Espag, Ivann b 08/09/87. Prop. FC DEBUT: 2008. PROV CAREER: Blue Bulls 2008 & 10 8-0-0-0-0-0. Boland 2009 6-0-0-0-0-0. Griquas 2010 2-0-0-0-0-0. FC RECORD: 16-0-0-0-0-0. RECORD IN 2010: (Blue Bulls, Griquas) 9-0-0-0-0-0.

Ewerts, Charlton Dean (Brighton HS) b 18/11/1989, Oudtshoorn. 1.61m. 64kg. Wing. FC DEBUT: 2010. PROV CAREER: Eagles 2010 3-1-0-0-0-5. FC RECORD: 3-1-0-0-0-5. RECORD IN 2010: (Eagles) 3-1-0-0-0-5.

F

Faasen, Daniel Cornelius (Danie) (Afrikaans HS) b 11/11/1989, Middelburg. 1.74m. 70kg. Scrumhalf. FC DEBUT: 2010. PROV CAREER: Blue Bulls 2010 7-1-0-0-0-5. FC RECORD: 7-1-0-0-0-5. RECORD IN 2010 (Blue Bulls) 7-1-0-0-0-5.

Fenner, Anthony (Shenley Brook End HS) b 12/12/1989, London. 1.80m. 85kg. Fullback. SA FC DEBUT: 2010. PROV CAREER: EP Kings 2010 3-0-0-0-0-0. FC RECORD: 3-0-0-0-0-0. RECORD IN 2010: (EP Kings) 3-0-0-0-0-0.

Ferreira, Piet Louis (Pietie) (Nico Malan HS, Humansdorp) b 22/04/76, Humansdorp. 1.92m. 100kgs. Flanker. FC DEBUT: 1998. PROV CAREER: WP 1998-03 79-24-0-0-0-120. Lions 2005-06 29-5-0-0-0-25. EP Kings 2010 11-3-0-0-0-15. Super 12: Stormers 2000-02, 05 8-1-0-0-0-5. Cats 2004 11-2-0-0-0-10. REP HONOURS: SA 'A' 2004. SA Barbs 1999. WP XV 2006. FC RECORD: 142-35-1-0-0-177. RECORD IN 2010: (EP Kings) 11-3-0-0-0-15.

Fick, Johan Tian (Homeschool & Varsity Coll.) 2.03m. 103kg. Lock. FC DEBUT: 2009. PROV CAREER: Valke 2009 6-0-0-0-0-0. FC RECORD: 6-0-0-0-0-0. RECORD IN 2009: (Valke) 6-0-0-0-0-0.

Fihlani, Lwazi Samora(Lumnko HS) b 14/05/85, East London. 1.98m. 104kg. Lock. FC DEBUT: 2008. PROV CAREER: Bulldogs 2008-10 35-2-0-0-0-10. FC RECORD: 35-2-0-0-0-10. RECORD IN 2010: (Bulldogs) 18-1-0-0-0-5.

Floors, Lucas (Kabamba) (Morestêr SS) b 15/11/80, Oudtshoorn. 1.75m. 84kg. Flank. FC DEBUT: 2003. PROV CAREER: Eagles 2003-04 33-18-0-0-0-90. Cheetahs 2005-10 91-24-0-0-0-120. SUPER 14: Cheetahs 2006-10 44-10-0-0-0-50. REP HONOURS: SA 2006 Tests: 1-0-0-0-0-0. SA 'A' 2004. Emerging Springboks 2007 3-2-0-0-0-10. SA Sevens 2003-06. MISC INFO: Holds Eagles record for most tries in a CC season (14) and shares record for most in all matches in a season (18). PPoY 2006. CC PoY 2006. FC RECORD: 173-54-0-0-0-270. RECORD IN 2010: (Cheetahs S14, Cheetahs) 22-5-0-0-0-25.

Fondse, Adriaan (AHS, Pretoria) b 09/06/83, Pretoria. 1.96m. 108kg. Lock/Flank. FC DEBUT: 2004. PROV CAREER: Blue Bulls 2005-07 44-6-0-0-0-30. WP 2008-10 34-6-0-0-0-30. SUPER 14: Bulls 2007 1-0-0-0-0-0. Stormers 2008-10 30-0-0-0-0-0. REP HONOURS: SA U21 2004 5-1-0-0-0-5. FC RECORD: 114-13-0-0-0-65. RECORD IN 2010: (Stormers, WP) 27-4-0-0-0-20.

Fortuin, Bevin André (George SS) b 06/02/79, George. 1.79m. 91kg. Fullback. FC DEBUT: 2000. PROV CAREER: Eagles 2000-05,09-10 122-29-7-4-2-177. Cheetahs 2005-09 57-12-7-0-0-74. SUPER 14: Cheetahs 2006-08 22-4-1-0-1-25. REP HONOURS: SA 2006-07 Tests: 2-0-0-0-0-0. Springbok XV 2006. Emerging Springboks 2007 3-0-0-0-0-0. S/Kings 2009 1-0-0-0-0-0. SA U21s 2000 2-1-0-0-0-5; SA Sevens 2001. FC RECORD: 210-46-15-4-3-281. RECORD IN 2010: (Eagles) 22-4-0-0-0-20.

Fortuin, Bradley b 03/12/82. 1.90m. 101kg. Flanker. FC DEBUT: 2009. PROV CAREER: Valke 2009-10 14-3-0-0-0-15. WP 2010 3-1-0-0-0-5. FC RECORD: 17-4-0-0-0-20. RECORD IN 2010: (Valke, WP) 12-4-0-0-0-20.

Fourie, Armon (George Randall HS) b 07/01/80, East London. 1.89m. 132kg. Prop. FC DEBUT: 2003. PROV CAREER: Bulldogs 2003,07-08 & 10 18-0-0-0-0-0. FC RECORD: 18-0-0-0-0-0. RECORD IN 2010: (Bulldogs) 13-0-0-0-0-0.

Fourie, Corne (Waterkloof HS) b 02/09/1988, Roodepoort. 1.87m. 116kg. Prop. FC DEBUT: 2010. PROV CAREER: Blue Bulls 2010 1-0-0-0-0-0. FC RECORD: 1-0-0-0-0-0. RECORD IN 2010: (Blue Bulls) 1-0-0-0-0-0.

Fourie, Deon André (Pietersburg HS) b 25/09/86, Pretoria. 1.76m. 97kg. Hooker. FC DEBUT: 2006. PROV CAREER: WP 2006-10 55-9-0-0-0-45. SUPER 14:

Stormers 2008-10 24-3-0-0-0-15. REP HONOURS: SA Sevens 2007. FC RECORD: 79-12-0-0-0-60. RECORD IN 2010: (Stormers, WP) 30-5-0-0-0-25.

Fourie, Jaco (Grey Coll.) b 19/04/1988, Bloemfontein. 1.81m. 98kg. Hooker. FC DEBUT: 2010. PROV CAREER: Blue Bulls 2010 1-0-0-0-0-0. EP Kings 2010 10-1-0-0-0-5. FC RECORD: 1-0-0-0-0-0. RECORD IN 2010: (Blue Bulls) 1-0-0-0-0-0.

Fourie, Jaque (Monument HS, RAU) b 04/03/83, Carletonville. 1.88m. 96kg. Fullback. FC DEBUT: 2002. PROV CAREER: Lions 2002-05 & 08 43-25-0-0-0-125. WP 2010 1-0-0-0-0-0. SUPER 14: Cats 2003-06 44-15-0-0-0-75. Lions 2007-09 24-9-0-0-0-45. Stormers 2010 15-7-0-0-0-35. REP HONOURS: SA 2003-10 Tests: 62-30-0-0-0-150. Tour: 2007 2-0-0-0-0-0. Total: 64-30-0-0-0-150. S Hemisphere XV 2005 1-1-0-0-0-5. SA XV 2006 1-0-0-0-0-0. British Barbs. 2009 1-0-0-0-0-0. MISC INFO: YPoY nominee 2002, 2003. Supersport Try of the Year 2010. FC RECORD: 194-86-0-0-0-430. RECORD IN 2010: (SA, Stormers, WP) 24-9-0-0-0-45.

Fourie, John b 06/01/74. Utility forward. FC DEBUT: 2006. PROV CAREER: Griffons 2006-07,09-10 33-3-0-0-0-15. FC RECORD: 33-3-0-0-0-15. RECORD IN 2010: (Griffons) 4-0-0-0-0-0.

Fourie, Giovano Etienne (Hentie Cilliers HS) b 30/12/86, Port Elizabeth. 1.68m. 101kg. Hooker. FC DEBUT: 2009. PROV CAREER: Elephants 2009-10 7-1-0-0-0-5. FC RECORD: 7-1-0-0-0-5. RECORD IN 2010: (EP Kings) 3-1-0-0-0-5.

Francis, Burton Kenvin (Klein Nederburg HS) b 02/01/87, Paarl. 1.84m. 85kg. Flyhalf. FC DEBUT: 2008. PROV CAREER: Blue Bulls 2008-09 28-3-42-30-7-210. Golden Lions 2010 6-1-4-3-0-22. SUPER 14: Bulls 2008-09 9-1-3-1-0-14. Lions 2010 5-0-5-5-0-25. FC RECORD: 48-5-54-39-7-271. RECORD IN 2010: (Lions S14, Golden Lions) 11-1-9-8-0-47.

Franklin, Johannes (Hannes) (Bekker HS) b 06/10/81, Randfontein. 1.82m. 99kg. Hooker. FC DEBUT: 2003. PROV CAREER: Valke 2003-04 22-1-0-0-0-5. Pumas 2005,09-10 53-12-0-0-0-60. Eagles 2006-08 58-18-0-0-0-90. SUPER 14: Lions 2010 12-2-0-0-0-10. FC RECORD: 145-33-0-0-0-165. RECORD IN 2010: (Lions S14, Pumas) 28-2-0-0-0-10.

Fredericks, Edrick Reginald (Eddie) (Cloetesville HS) b 31/12/77, Stellenbosch. 1.80m. 80kg. Wing. FC DEBUT: 1997. PROV CAREER: WP 1998 4-1-0-0-0-5; Leopards 1999 17-0-0-0-0-0; Griffons 2000,09-10 33-18-0-0-0-90; Cheetahs 2001-09 105-50-0-0-0-250. SUPER 14: Bulls 2003-04 20-6-0-0-0-30. Cats 2005 3-0-0-0-0-0. Cheetahs 2006-08 33-7-0-0-0-35. REP

HONOURS: SA Sevens 1999-00. SA 'A' 2003-04 2-1-0-0-0-5. SA U21s 1997 1-0-0-0-0-0. FC RECORD: 218-83-0-0-0-415. RECORD IN 2010: (Griffons) 16-12-0-0-0-60.

Frolick, Shandré (Worcester Gym) b 01/02/86, Graaff-Reinet. 1.80m. 84kgs. Fullback. FC DEBUT: 2005. PROV CAREER: WP 2005-06 4-1-0-0-0-5. Lions 2009 2-1-0-0-0-5. Young Lions 2010 4-1-0-0-0-5. Cheetahs 2010 1-0-0-0-0-0. SUPER 14: Lions 2009 6-1-0-0-0-5. FC RECORD: 17-4-0-0-0-20. REP HONOURS: SA Sevens 2005; SA U19s 2005. RECORD IN 2010: (Young Lions, Cheetahs) 5-1-0-0-0-5.

G

Gagiano, Jonathan Richard (JJ) (Bishops HS & UCT) b 14/08/1985, Cape Town. 1.91m. 103kg. Eightman. FC DEBUT: 2010. PROV CAREER: EP Kings 2010 9-1-0-0-0-5. MISC INFO: USA international. FC RECORD: 9-1-0-0-0-5. RECORD IN 2010: (EP Kings) 9-1-0-0-0-5.

Ganto, Sinovuyo (Winterberg Agric. HS) b 24/07/1987, Alice. 1.80m. 85kg. Wing. FC DEBUT: 2010. PROV CAREER: Bulldogs 2010 9-1-0-0-0-5. FC RECORD: 9-1-0-0-0-5. RECORD IN 2010: (Bulldogs) 9-1-0-0-0-5.

Gauche, Eddie. Lock. FC DEBUT: 2010. PROV CAREER: Valke 2010 18-4-0-0-0-20. FC RECORD: 18-4-0-0-0-20. RECORD IN 2010: (Valke) 18-4-0-0-0-20.

Gawie, Clayton (Hillside SS) b 28/05/83, Port Elizabeth. 1.64m. 72kg. Scrumhalf. FC DEBUT: 2004. PROV CAREER: EP Kings 2004-08 & 10 56-3-2-0-0-19. Griffons 2009 1-0-0-0-0-0. FC RECORD: 57-3-2-0-0-19. RECORD IN 2010: (EP Kings) 7-0-0-0-0-0.

Geel, Albertus Daniel (Barry) (FH Odendaal HS) b 30/04/82, Springs. 1.83m. 87kg. Centre. FC DEBUT: 2002. PROV CAREER: Leopards 2002-06 91-21-0-0-0-105. Griquas 2007-10 68-23-0-0-0-115. Cheetahs XV 2010 1-0-0-0-0-0. SUPER 14: Cheetahs 2010 1-0-0-0-0-0. FC RECORD: 161-44-0-0-0-220. RECORD IN 2010: (Cheetahs S14, Griquas, Cheetahs XV) 21-3-0-0-0-15.

Geldenhuys, Johannes Petrus (JP) (Boland Agric. HS & UOFS) b 18/03/1986, Paarl. 1.85m. 105kg. Prop. FC DEBUT: 2010. PROV CAREER: Bulldogs 2010 9-0-0-0-0-0. FC RECORD: 9-0-0-0-0-0. RECORD IN 2010: (Bulldogs) 9-0-0-0-0-0.

Geldenhuys, Ross (St. Andrews Coll.) b 19/04/83, Cape Town. 1.89m. 122kg. Prop. FC DEBUT: 2005. PROV CAREER: Bulldogs 2005 3-0-0-0-0-0. Pumas 2007 17-2-0-0-0-10. Lions 2008-10 22-1-0-0-0-5. Young Lions 2009 3-0-0-0-0-0. SUPER 14: Lions 2008 & 10 19-0-0-0-0-0. FC RECORD: 64-3-0-0-0-15. RECORD IN 2010 (Lions S14, Golden Lions) 22-0-0-0-0-0.

George, Jacques Nicolas (Alexander Road HS & Damelin) b 29/07/80, Port Elizabeth. 1.88m. 116kg. Prop. FC DEBUT: 2009. PROV CAREER: Young Lions 2009 7-0-0-0-0-0. Valke 2009-10 26-1-8-5-0-36. FC RECORD: 33-1-8-5-0-36. RECORD IN 2010: (Valke) 17-1-8-5-0-36.

Gerber, Danre (Middelburg HS) b 20/12/88, Port Elizabeth. 1.89m. 97kg. FC DEBUT: 2009. PROV CAREER: Boland 2009-10 10-2-4-7-0-39. RECORD IN 2010: (Boland) 6-1-1-2-0-13.

Gerber, Reinhardt (Monument) b 15/04/80, Johannesburg. 1.86m 97kgs. Flyhalf. FC DEBUT: 2002. PROV CAREER: Leopards 2002 1-0-0-0-0-0. Lions 2004 5-3-0-0-0-15. Bulldogs 2004-07,09-10 73-4-116-116-2-606. REP HONOURS: CW Lions 1988. FC RECORD: 79-7-116-116-2-621. RECORD IN 2010: (Bulldogs) 1-0-0-4-0-12.

Goode, Andrew James. Flyhalf. SA FC DEBUT: 2010. SUPER 14: Sharks 2010 9-0-2-11-1-40. REP HONOURS: England. SA FC RECORD: 9-0-2-11-1-40. RECORD IN 2010: (Sharks) 9-0-2-11-1-40.

Goodes, Barry (Grey Coll., Bloemfontein) b 03/04/82, Welkom. 1.84m. 95kgs. Centre. FC DEBUT: 2002. PROV CAREER: Cheetahs 2002-05,07,10 46-5-0-0-0-25. Lions 2009 1-0-0-0-0-0. Young Lions 2009 4-1-0-0-0-5. Griffons 2010 2-0-2-0-0-4. SUPER 14: Cats 2005 4-1-0-0-0-5. Cheetahs 2006 10-1-0-0-0-5. Lions 2009 2-0-0-0-0-0. FC RECORD: 69-8-2-0-0-44. RECORD IN 2010: (Cheetahs, Griffons) 12-1-2-0-0-9.

Gouws, Pieter Willem (Grey Coll.) b 23/03/86, Bloemfontein. 1.94m. 100kgs. Lock. FC DEBUT: 2008. PROV CAREER: Cheetahs 2008 & 10 11-1-0-0-0-5. FC RECORD: 11-1-0-0-0-5. RECORD IN 2010: (Cheetahs) 3-0-0-0-0-0.

Gqobo, Andisa (Hudson Park HS) b 02/06/86, East London. 1.72m. 83kg. Flyhalf. FC DEBUT: 2008. PROV CAREER: Bulldogs 2008-10 22-5-7-6-0-57. FC RECORD: 22-5-7-6-0-57. RECORD IN 2010: (Bulldogs) 5-2-2-1-0-17.

Grant, Dean (Rondebosch HS & Stellenbosch Univ.) b 18/03/1989, Gauteng. 1.80m. 87kg. Flyhalf. FC DEBUT: 2010. PROV CAREER: Boland 2010 4-1-9-7-0-44. FC RECORD: 4-1-9-7-0-44. RECORD IN 2010: (Boland) 4-1-9-7-0-44.

Grant, Peter John (Maritzburg Coll.) b 15/08/84, Durban. 1.88m. 90kg. Flyhalf. FC DEBUT: 2004. PROV CAREER: WP 2004-09 55-9-52-43-1-281. SUPER 14: Stormers 2006-10 62-8-85-109-0-533. REP HON-

OURS: SA 2007-08 Tests: 5-0-0-0-0-0. Emerging Springboks 2007 3-0-10-8-0-44. WP XV 2006 1-0-2-0-0-4. British Barbarians 2007 1-0-0-0-0-0. SA U19 2003. SA Schools 2002. CW KZN 2002. FC RECORD: 127-17-149-160-1-862. RECORD IN 2010: (Stormers) 14-1-19-34-0-141.

Greeff, Stephan (Gill Coll.) b 24/12/1989, Cape Town. 1.98m. 103kg. Lock. FC DEBUT: 2010. PROV CAREER: WP 2010 4-0-0-0-0-0. FC RECORD: 4-0-0-0-0-0. RECORD IN 2010: (WP) 4-0-0-0-0-0.

Grey, Siyanda (Hlumani HS) b 16/08/1989, Komga. 1.79m. 79kg. Centre. FC DEBUT: 2010. PROV CAREER: EP Kings 2010 4-2-0-0-0-10. FC RECORD: 4-2-0-0-0-10. RECORD IN 2010: (EP Kings) 4-2-0-0-0-10.

Greyling, Gert Johannes (Sand du Plessis HS) b 07/03/85, Bloemfontein. 1.84m. 118kg. Prop. FC DEBUT: 2007. PROV CAREER: Griffons 2007-10 53-0-0-0-0-0. FC RECORD: 53-0-0-0-0-0. RECORD IN 2010: (Griffons) 9-0-0-0-0-0.

Greyling, MacGuyver Dean (AHS, Pretoria) b 01/01/86, Potgietersrus. 1.92m, 115kg. Prop. FC DEBUT: 2005. PROV CAREER: Blue Bulls 2005,07-10 47-5-0-0-0-25. SUPER 14: Bulls 2008 & 10 3-0-0-0-0-0. REP HONOURS: S/Kings 2009 1-0-0-0-0-0. FC RECORD: 51-5-0-0-0-25. RECORD IN 2010 (Bulls, Blue Bulls) 22-5-0-0-0-25.

Griesel, Werner (Welkom Gym.) b 01/07/86, Welkom. 1.80m. 90kg. Centre. FC DEBUT: 2008. PROV CAREER: Griffons 2008-10 53-13-0-0-0-65. FC RECORD: 53-13-0-0-0-65. RECORD IN 2010: (Griffons) 19-6-0-0-0-30.

Grimes, Henry (Montana HS) b 25/01/80, Pretoria. 2.00m. 114kg. Lock. FC DEBUT: 2005. PROV CAREER: Eagles 2006-10 103-11-0-0-0-55. REP HONOURS: SA Students 2005 1-0-0-0-0-0. FC RECORD: 104-11-0-0-0-55. RECORD IN 2010: (Eagles) 21-1-0-0-0-5.

Grobbelaar, Leon (Sand du Plessis HS & UOFS) b 23/05/1985, De Aar. 1.98m. 110kg. Lock. FC DEBUT: 2010. PROV CAREER: Griffons 2010 6-1-0-0-0-5. FC RECORD: 6-1-0-0-0-5. RECORD IN 2010: (Griffons) 6-1-0-0-0-5.

Grobbelaar, Petrus Jacobus Johannes (Cobus) (Jan Viljoen HS) b 27/05/81, Randfontein. 1.84m. 100kg. Flank. FC DEBUT: 2003. PROV CAREER: Lions 2003-09 90-13-0-0-0-65. Young Lions 2003-08 15-3-0-0-0-15. SUPER 14: Cats 2004-06 24-0-0-0-0-0. Lions 2007-10 45-5-0-0-0-25. REP HONOURS: SA 'A' 2004 2-0-0-0-0-0. FC RECORD: 176-21-0-0-0-105. RECORD IN 2010: (Lions S14) 12-2-0-0-0-10.

Grobler, Johannes Hermanus (Hans) (Paarl Gym. & UOFS) b 11/12/1986, Bloemfontein. 1.82m. 108kg. Hooker. FC DEBUT: 2010. PROV CAREER: Cheetahs 2010 1-0-0-0-0-0. Eagles 2010 12-1-0-0-0-5. FC RECORD: 13-1-0-0-0-5. RECORD IN 2010: (Cheetahs, Eagles) 13-1-0-0-0-5.

Groenewald, Lambert Smith (Paul Roos Gym.) b 01/02/1989, Worcester. 1.89m. 106kg. Flanker. FC DEBUT: 2010. PROV CAREER: Sharks XV 2010 6-1-0-0-0-5. FC RECORD: 6-1-0-0-0-5. RECORD IN 2010: (Sharks XV) 6-1-0-0-0-5.

Groenewald, Wilmar Romano (Hentie Cilliers HS) b 30/04/1990, George. 1.84m. 81kg. Flanker. FC DEBUT: 2010. PROV CAREER: Griffons 2010 1-0-0-0-0-0. FC RECORD: 1-0-0-0-0-0. RECORD IN 2010: (Griffons) 1-0-0-0-0-0.

Groepes, Hayden Gareth (Paarl Vallei HS) b 04/11/87, Stellenbosch. 1.80m. 85kg. Fullback/Flyhalf. FC DEBUT: 2006. PROV CAREER: WP 2006-09 18-4-0-0-0-20. Boland 2009 6-0-0-0-0-0. Blue Bulls 2010 6-1-0-0-0-5. FC RECORD: 30-5-0-0-0-25. RECORD IN 2010: (Blue Bulls) 6-1-0-0-0-5.

Gronum, Anthonie Johannes (Oakdale Agricultural HS) b 15/06/85, Knysna. 2.02m. 112kg. Lock. FC DEBUT: 2006. PROV CAREER: Blue Bulls 2006 2-0-0-0-0-0. Leopards 2007-10 55-2-0-0-0-10. FC RECORD: 57-2-0-0-0-10. RECORD IN 2010: (Leopards) 21-1-0-0-0-5.

Guinazu, Eusebio (ICE & Univ. of Mendoza) b 15/01/1982, Mendoza. 1.81m. 114kg. Prop. SA FC DEBUT: 2010. PROV CAREER: Boland 2010 12-1-0-0-0-5. SUPER 14: Stormers 2010 7-0-0-0-0-0. SA FC RECORD: 19-1-0-0-0-5. RECORD IN 2010: (Stormers, Boland) 19-1-0-0-0-5.

Gwavu, Lubabalo Vincent (Daniel Pienaar HTS) b 04/09/87, Port Elizabeth. 1.84m. 99kg. Flank. FC DEBUT: 2008. PROV CAREER: Blue Bulls 2008-10 22-2-0-0-0-10. Eagles 2009 2-1-0-0-0-5. FC RECORD: 24-3-0-0-0-15. RECORD IN 2010: (Blue Bulls) 5-1-0-0-0-5.

Gysman, Bronwin Fernando (Hentie Cilliers HS) b 03/08/87, Port Elizabeth. 1.65m. 65kg. Scrumhalf. FC DEBUT: 2008. PROV CAREER: Griffons 2008-10 15-0-0-0-0-0. FC RECORD: 15-0-0-0-0-0. RECORD IN 2010: (Griffons) 2-0-0-0-0-0.

H

Habana, Bryan Gary (KES & RAU) b 12/06/83, Johannesburg. 1.79m. 92kg. Wing. FC DEBUT: 2003. PROV CAREER: Lions 2003-04 21-17-0-0-0-85. Blue Bulls 2005 & 08-09 14-9-0-0-0-45. WP 2010 3-1-0-0-0-5. SUPER 14: Bulls 2005-09 61-37-0-0-0-185. Stormers 2010 14-7-0-0-0-35. REP HONOURS: SA Tests: 2004-10 68-38-0-0-0-190. Tour: 2007 2-0-0-0-0-0. Total: 70-38-0-0-0-190. SA Sevens 2004. SA U21 2004 3-3-0-0-0-15. British Barbarians 2008,09 2-3-0-0-0-15. MISC INFO: PoY 2005, 2007. YPoY 2004, S12 PoY 2005. IRB PoY 2007. IRB PoY nominee 2005. IRPA YPoY 2005. Leading FC try-scorer 2004, 2005, 2007. Holds SA record for most tries in a season (13 in 2007). FC RECORD: 188-115-0-0-0-575. RECORD IN 2010: (SA, Stormers, WP) 28-10-0-0-0-50.

Halangahu, Antonio (Daramalan Coll.) b 02/03/1981, Sydney. Hooker. SA FC DEBUT: 2010. PROV CAREER: EP Kings 2010 11-0-0-0-0-0. FC RECORD: 11-0-0-0-0-0. RECORD IN 2010: (EP Kings) 11-0-0-0-0-0.

Hall, Trevor Manning (Kearsney Coll.) b 02/10/78, Johannesburg. 1.95m. 112kgs. Lock. FC DEBUT: 2000. PROV CAREER: Eagles 2000-02 35-2-0-0-0-10. Lions 2003-05,10 33-2-0-0-0-10. Young Lions 2003-05 10-0-0-0-0-0. SUPER 14: Cats 2005-06 13-0-0-0-0-0. MISC INFO: Biarritz (Fra) 2006-07. FC RECORD: 91-4-0-0-0-20. RECORD IN 2010: (Golden Lions) 7-0-0-0-0-0.

Halvorsen, Thorleif (Boland Agric. HS) b09/05/1988, Cape Town. 1.93m. 107kg. Eighthman. FC DEBUT: 2010. PROV CAREER: Boland 2010 6-0-0-0-0-0. FC RECORD: 6-0-0-0-0-0. RECORD IN 2010: (Boland) 6-0-0-0-0-0.

Hancke, Shane (Welkom HTS) b 20/02/83, Welkom. 1.75m. 85kg. Utility Back. FC DEBUT: 2005. PROV CAREER: Griffons 2005,08-10 35-8-0-0-0-40. FC RECORD: 35-8-0-0-0-40. Record in 2010 (Griffons) 4-2-0-0-0-10.

Hanekom, Morne (Boland Agric. & Stellenbosch Univ.) b 15/02/88, Malmesbury. 1.94m. 112kg. FC DEBUT: 2009. PROV CAREER: WP 2009 1-0-0-0-0-0. EP Kings 2010 2-0-0-0-0-0. FC RECORD: 3-0-0-0-0-0. RECORD IN 2010: (EP Kings) 2-0-0-0-0-0.

Hargreaves, Alistair John (Durban HS) b 29/04/86, Durban. 2.00m. 102kg. Lock. ›› FC debut: 2006. Prov career: KZN 2006-10 36-1-0-0-0-5. Sharks XV 2006-08,10 19-2-0-0-0-10. Sharks Inv XV 2010 1-0-0-0-0-0. Super 14: Sharks 2009-10 14-0-0-0-0-0. Rep honours: SA 2009-10 Tests: 2-0-0-0-0-0. Tour: 2009,10: 3-0-0-0-0-0. Total: 5-0-0-0-0-0. SA U21 2006 5-0-0-0-0-0. SA U19 2004-05. FC record: 80-3-0-0-0-15. RECORD IN 2010: (SA, Sharks, KZN, Sharks XV, Sharks Inv XV) 29-2-0-0-0-10.

Harmse, Willem Johannes (Wicus) (PW Botha HS) b 19/11/84. 1.76m. 110kg. Prop. FC DEBUT: 2005. PROV CAREER: Eagles 2005-10 68-3-0-0-0-15. FC

RECORD: 68-3-0-0-0-15. RECORD IN 2010: (Eagles) 13-1-0-0-0-5.

Harris, Juan (Brok) (Bastion HS) b 22/02/85, Roodepoort. 1.83m. 113kg. Prop. FC DEBUT: 2006. PROV CAREER: WP 2006-10 68-10-0-0-0-50. SUPER 14: Stormers 2007-10 45-2-0-0-0-10. FC RECORD: 113-12-0-0-0-60. RECORD IN 2010: (Stormers, WP) 32-3-0-0-0-15.

Hartnick, Lyndon Lee (Kairos HS) b 08/07/86, Heidelberg. 1.90m. 97kgs. Flanker. FC DEBUT: 2008. PROV CAREER: Bulldogs 2008 6-0-0-0-0-0. Eagles 2010 13-1-0-0-0-5. FC RECORD: 19-1-0-0-0-5. RECORD IN 2010: (Eagles) 13-1-0-0-0-5.

Hartzenberg, Yaasir (Paarl Boys HS & Boland Coll.) b 06/01/89, Cape Town. 1.94m. 109kg. FC DEBUT: 2009. PROV CAREER: WP 2009-10 17-5-0-0-0-25. FC RECORD: 17-5-0-0-0-25. RECORD IN 2010: (WP) 11-5-0-0-0-25.

Harwood, Derek John (Oakdale HS) b10/03/88, Kareedouw. 1.83m. 110kg. Hooker. FC DEBUT: 2009. PROV CAREER: Lions 2009 9-0-0-0-0-0. Young Lions 2009-10 7-0-0-0-0-0. FC RECORD: 16-0-0-0-0-0. RECORD IN 2010: (Young Lions) 1-0-0-0-0-0.

Havenga, Wayne Raymond (Weston Coll.) b 29/11/1985, Johannesburg. 1.98m. 89kg. Flanker. FC DEBUT: 2010. PROV CAREER: Valke 2010 3-0-0-0-0-0. FC RECORD: 3-0-0-0-0-0. RECORD IN 2010: (Valke) 3-0-0-0-0-0.

Hefer, Andries Christo (BB) (President HS) b 22/12/86, Johannesburg. 1.80m. 108kg. Hooker. FC DEBUT: 2008. PROV CAREER: Lions 2008 2-0-0-0-0-0. Valke 2009-10 26-2-0-0-0-10. FC RECORD: 28-2-0-0-0-10. RECORD IN 2010: (Valke) 16-1-0-0-0-5.

Helberg, Gideon Gerhardus (Middelburg THS) b 27/09/1989, Lichtenburg. 1.87m. 91kg. Wing. FC DEBUT: 2010. PROV CAREER: Blue Bulls 2010 10-4-0-0-0-20. SUPER 14: Bulls 2010 1-0-0-0-0-0. MISC INFO: SA Sevens. FC RECORD: 11-4-0-0-0-20. RECORD IN 2010: (Bulls, Blue Bulls) 11-4-0-0-0-20.

Hellmuth, Johannes Urbanus (Dougie) (Grey Coll., Bloemfontein) b 23/03/85, Douglas. 1.78m. 89kg. Scrumhalf. FC DEBUT: 2006. PROV CAREER: Cheetahs 2006 12-3-0-0-0-15. Griffons 2007 11-4-0-0-0-20. Griquas 2008-09 26-2-0-0-0-10. Eagles 2009-10 29-4-0-0-0-20. FC RECORD: 78-13-0-0-0-65. RECORD IN 2010: (Eagles) 22-2-0-0-0-10.

Hendricks, Carlyle (Kyle) (Excelsior HS) b 12/12/86, Cape Town. 1.74m. 70kg. Wing. FC DEBUT: 2009. PROV CAREER: Valke 2009-10 15-9-0-0-0-45. FC RECORD: 15-9-0-0-0-45. RECORD IN 2010: (Valke)

WHO'S WHO IN 2010

13-9-0-0-0-45.

Hendricks, Cornal (Berg River HS) b 18/04/88, Paarl. 1.88m. 85kg. Wing. FC DEBUT: 2008. PROV CAREER: Boland 2008-10 35-11-0-0-0-55. FC RECORD: 35-11-0-0-0-55. RECORD IN 2010 (Boland) 20-10-0-0-0-50.

Hendricks, David Joseph (Vesbrank HS, Malmesbury) b 10/12/79, Malmesbury. 1.85m. 104kg. Flank. FC DEBUT: 2001 PROV CAREER: Boland 2001-03 & 08-10 45-11-0-0-0-55. WP 2004-08 44-9-0-0-0-45. SUPER 14: Stormers 2005-06 6-0-0-0-0-0. FC RECORD: 95-20-0-0-0-100. RECORD IN 2010: (Boland) 1-0-0-0-0-0.

Hendrikz, Ryno Steve (Marais Viljoen HS) b 05/02/88, Marymount. 1.76m. 80kg. Scrumhalf. FC DEBUT: 2009. PROV CAREER: Valke 2009-10 7-0-0-0-0-0. FC RECORD: 7-0-0-0-0-0. RECORD IN 2010: (Valke) 3-0-0-0-0-0.

Herbst, Wiehahn Jovan (Klerksdorp HS & Unisa) b 05/07/88, Klerksdorp. 1.80m. 110kg. Prop. FC DEBUT: 2009. PROV CAREER: KZN 2009-10 15-0-0-0-0-0. Sharks XV 2009-10 11-0-0-0-0-0. Sharks Inv XV 2009-10 2-0-0-0-0-0. SUPER 14: Sharks 2010 1-0-0-0-0-0. FC RECORD: 29-0-0-0-0-0. RECORD IN 2010: (Sharks, KZN, Sharks XV, Sharks Inv XV) 17-0-0-0-0-0.

Hess, Cornell Norman (Afrikaans HS) b 01/03/1989, Wynberg. 2.0m. 106kg. Lock. FC DEBUT: 2010. PROV CAREER: Blue Bulls 2010 10-0-0-0-0-0. FC RECORD: 10-0-0-0-0-0. RECORD IN 2010: (Blue Bulls) 10-0-0-0-0-0.

Hewitt, Edwin Westley (Afrikaans HS) b 28/03/1988, Pretoria. 1.94m. 115kg. Lock. FC DEBUT: 2010. PROV CAREER: Griquas 2010 6-0-0-0-0-0. FC RECORD: 6-0-0-0-0-0. RECORD IN 2010: (Griquas) 6-0-0-0-0-0.

Heyneke, Graeme Athol (Marlow HS & UOFS) b 23/07/1988, Port Elizabeth. 1.74m. 98kg. Hooker. FC DEBUT: 2010. PROV CAREER: Griffons 2010 4-0-0-0-0-0. FC RECORD: 4-0-0-0-0-0. RECORD IN 2010: (Griffons) 4-0-0-0-0-0.

Hilpert, Sebastian Lester (Port Alfred HS) b 04/07/82, Port Alfred. 1.89m. 90kg. Flank. FC DEBUT: 2003. PROV CAREER: EP Kings 2003-05,07-08,10 74-8-0-0-0-40. Boland 2006 8-3-0-0-0-15. Bulldogs 2009 8-0-0-0-0-0. E/Cape XV 2008 2-0-0-0-0-0. FC RECORD: 92-11-0-0-0-55. RECORD IN 2010: (EP Kings) 1-0-0-0-0-0.

Hoffmann, Conrad Fritz (Paarl Boys HS) b 09/11/87, Worcester. 1.81m. 79kg. Scrumhalf. FC DEBUT: 2007. PROV CAREER: WP 2007,09-10 44-7-4-8-0-67. SUPER 14: Stormers 2008 1-0-0-0-0-0. FC RECORD: 45-7-4-8-0-67. RECORD IN 2010: (WP) 21-2-4-8-0-42.

Hollenbach, Alwyn Wilhelm Cornelius Johannes (Grey Coll., Bloemfontein) b 14/06/85, Johannesburg. 1.90m. 95kg. Wing. FC DEBUT: 2005. PROV CAREER: Cheetahs 2005-07,09 41-11-0-0-0-55. Griquas 2008 2-0-0-0-0-0. Lions 2009 12-4-0-0-0-20. Young Lions 2010 1-0-0-0-0-0. SUPER 14: Cheetahs 2007 2-0-0-0-0-0. FC RECORD: 58-15-0-0-0-75. RECORD IN 2010: (Young Lions) 1-0-0-0-0-0.

Horn, Gido (Kempton Park HS) b 15/01/88, Kempton Park. 1.79m. 90kg. Flyhalf. FC DEBUT: 2009. PROV CAREER: Valke 2009-10 17-2-11-5-0-47. FC RECORD: 17-2-11-5-0-47. RECORD IN 2010: (Valke) 8-1-5-2-0-21.

Horn, Joubert Prinsloo (Burgersdorp HS & Grey Coll. & UOFS) b 08/10/1988, Welkom. 1.95m. 100kg. Lock. FC DEBUT: 2010. PROV CAREER: Griffons 2010 6-0-0-0-0-0. FC RECORD: 6-0-0-0-0-0. RECORD IN 2010: (Griffons) 6-0-0-0-0-0.

Hougaard, Francois (Paul Roos Gym.) b 06/04/88, Paarl. 1.79m. 86kg. Scrumhalf. ›› FC debut: 2007. Prov career: WP 2007 3-0-0-0-0-0. Blue Bulls 2008-10 36-11-0-0-0-55. Super 14: Bulls 2008-10 16-7-0-0-0-35. Rep honours: SA 2009-10 Tests: 8-0-0-0-0-0. Tour: 2009,2010: 3-0-0-0-0-0. Total: 11-0-0-0-0-0. S/Kings 2009 1-0-0-0-0-0. Misc info: YPOY Nominee 2009, 2010. SA PoY nominee 2010. FC record: 67-18-0-0-0-90. RECORD IN 2010: (SA, Bulls, Blue Bulls) 28-9-0-0-0-45.

Hugo, Abraham Pieter Marnus (Paarl Gymnasium) b 24/09/86, Paarl. 1.70m. 84kg. Scrumhalf. FC DEBUT: 2006. PROV CAREER: Boland 2006 & 08-09 26-4-0-0-0-20. Griquas 2010 14-0-0-0-0-0. SUPER 14: Cheetahs 2010 2-0-0-0-0-0. FC RECORD: 42-4-0-0-0-20. RECORD IN 2010: (Cheetahs S14, Griquas) 16-0-0-0-0-0.

Human, Petrus Gerhardus (Pote) (Grey HS, Port Elizabeth) b 12/01/86, Port Elizabeth. 1.91m. 101kg. Flank. FC DEBUT: 2006. PROV CAREER: Blue Bulls 2006-07 23-1-0-0-0-5. Lions 2008 3-0-0-0-0-0. Cheetahs 2010 5-0-0-0-0-0. Griquas 2010 8-0-0-0-0-0. FC RECORD: 39-1-0-0-0-5. RECORD IN 2010: (Cheetahs, Griquas) 13-0-0-0-0-0.

Hyman, Morne (Kempton Park HS) b 18/11/1987, Kempton Park. 1.85m. 104kg. Hooker. FC DEBUT: 2010. PROV CAREER: Valke 2010 2-0-0-0-0-0. FC RECORD: 2-0-0-0-0-0. RECORD IN 2010: (Valke) 2-0-0-0-0-0.

I

Immelman, Jacobus Abraham (Braam) (Paul Roos Gym) b 26/10/81, Victoria West. 1.94m. 101kgs. Flanker.

FC DEBUT: 2003. PROV CAREER: WP 2003-04 11-2-0-0-0-10. KZN 2005-06 15-6-0-0-0-30. Boland 2010 11-4-0-0-0-20. SUPER 14: Sharks 2005-06 9-0-0-0-0-0. REP HONOURS: SA 7s 2002. MISC INFO: Mountauban (Fra) 2006-07. FC RECORD: 46-12-0-0-0-60. RECORD IN 2010: (Boland) 11-4-0-0-0-20.

J

Jack, Sinethemba (Ndzondelelo HS) b 15/07/86, Uitenhage. 1.57m. 70kg. Scrumhalf. FC DEBUT: 2008. PROV CAREER: Elephants 2008-09 12-0-0-0-0-0. E/Cape XV 2008 2-0-0-0-0-0. EP Inv XV 2010 1-0-0-0-0-0. FC RECORD: 15-0-0-0-0-0. RECORD IN 2010: (EP Inv XV) 1-0-0-0-0-0.

Jackson, Johan (Rustenburg HS) b 24/01/87, Rustenburg. 1.81m. 96kg. Centre. FC DEBUT: 2007. PROV CAREER: Valke 2008 7-3-0-0-0-15. Blue Bulls 2008 4-2-0-0-0-10. Blue Bulls XV 2007 1-0-0-0-0-0. Lions 2009 12-4-0-0-0-20. Pumas 2010 7-2-0-0-0-10. Young Lions 2010 1-0-0-0-0-0. FC RECORD: 32-11-0-0-0-55. RECORD IN 2010: (Pumas, Young Lions) 8-2-0-0-0-10.

Jacobs, Adrian Abraham (Adi) (Scotsville SS) b 14/08/80, Kraaifontein. 1.70m. 87kg. Centre. ›› FC debut: 2000. Prov career: Valke 2000-03 46-20-29-5-0-173. KZN 2004-10 61-22-3-0-0-116. Sharks XV 2008 1-0-0-0-0-0. Super 14: Bulls 2001-02 21-9-0-0-0-45; Cats 2003 4-1-0-0-0-5. Sharks 2004-10 74-11-0-0-0-55. Rep honours: SA 2001-02 & 08-10 Tests 32-7-0-0-0-35. SA Tour 2010 1-0-0-0-0-0. Total: 33-7-0-0-0-35; SA Sevens 2000; SA U21s 2000 4-0-0-0-0-0; SA U23s 2000 3-1-0-0-0-5; SA 'A' 2004 3-2-0-0-0-10. SA U19s 1998; SA Schools 1998; CW WP 1998. Misc info: PoY nominee 2008. YPoY nominee 2001; FC record: 250-73-32-5-0-444. RECORD IN 2010: (SA, Sharks, KZN) 11-3-0-0-0-15.

Jacobs, Neil (Newton Tech. HS) b 02/12/84, Port Elizabeth 1.84m. 103kg. Hooker. FC DEBUT: 2007. PROV CAREER: EP Kings 2007-10 36-0-0-0-0-0. E/Cape XV 2008 1-0-0-0-0-0. EP Inv XV 2010 1-0-0-0-0-0. FC RECORD: 38-0-0-0-0-0. RECORD IN 2010: (EP Kings, EP Inv XV) 3-0-0-0-0-0.

Jacobs, Neill (Afrikaans HS) b 30/06/88, Pretoria. 1.83m. 91kg. Flyhalf. FC DEBUT: 2009. PROV CAREER: Leopards 2009-10 13-0-6-5-1-30. FC RECORD: 13-0-6-5-1-30. RECORD IN 2010: (Leopards) 11-0-5-5-1-28.

Jansen, Jaquin (Bergrivier HS) b 27/05/86, Paarl. 1.75m. 83kg. Flyhalf. FC DEBUT: 2008. PROV CAREER: Boland 2008-10 25-6-43-21-0-179. FC RECORD: 25-6-43-21-0-179. RECORD IN 2010: (Boland) 20-5-42-21-0-172.

Jansen, Rocco Reginald (Queens College) b 21/07/86, Queenstown. 1.79m. 88kg. Wing. FC DEBUT: 2007. PROV CAREER: Blue Bulls 2007-09 28-22-0-0-0-110. Blue Bulls XV 2007 1-1-0-0-0-5. Elephants 2009 5-6-0-0-0-30. Sharks Inv XV 2009 1-0-0-0-0-0. Griquas 2010 16-4-0-0-0-20. REP HONOURS: Emerging Springboks 2008 3-1-0-0-0-5. FC RECORD: 54-34-0-0-0-170. RECORD IN 2010: (Griquas) 16-4-0-0-0-20.

Jantjes, Conrad Alcon (CBC Boksburg) b 24/03/80, Boksburg. 1.84m. 90kg. Fullback. FC DEBUT: 1998. PROV CAREER: Lions 2000-05 62-15-0-1-1-81. WP 2007-08 & 10 36-4-1-0-0-22. SUPER 14: Cats 2001-06 41-9-0-0-0-45. Stormers 2007-09 27-4-0-0-0-20. REP HONOURS: SA 2001 & 05,07-08 Tests 24-4-1-0-0-22; Tour: 1-0-0-0-0-0. Total: 25-4-1-0-0-22. SA 'A' 2003-04 4-1-0-0-0-5. SA U23s 2000 6-7-23-2-0-87; SA U21s 2000-01 6-1-0-0-0-5; SA Sevens 1999-03; SA U19s 1998; SA Schools 1997; CW Valke 1997. British Barbarians 2003. MISC INFO: PoY nominee 2001; YPoY 2001; YPoY nominee 2000; SA Schools & SA U19s cricketer 1996; Plascon National Cricket Academy 1998; Easterns Cricket Union 1998; SA U19 & U17s soccer. FC RECORD: 208-45-25-3-1-287. RECORD IN 2010: (WP) 17-2-0-0-0-10.

Jantjies, Elton Thomas (Florida HS & UJ) b 01/08/1990, Graaff Reinet. 1.76m. 84kg. Flyhalf. >> FC debut: 2010. Prov career: Golden Lions 2010 13-2-25-27-0-141. Young Lions 2010 1-0-0-0-0-0. Misc Info: SA YPoY 2010, SA u/20 PoY 2010. Rep honours: SA Tour: 2010: 1-0-1-1-0-5. FC record: 15-2-26-28-0-146. RECORD IN 2010: (SA, Golden Lions, Young Lions) 15-2-26-28-0-146.

Januarie, Enrico Ricardo (Ricky) (Weston SS) b 01/02/82, Hopefield. 1.70m. 80kg. Scrumhalf. FC DEBUT: 2002. PROV CAREER: Boland 2002 16-4-0-0-0-20. Lions 2003-06 40-5-0-0-0-25. WP 2008-10 11-3-0-0-0-15. SUPER 14: Cats 2003-04;06 31-2-0-0-0-10. Lions 2007 12-0-0-0-0-0. Stormers 2008-10 40-3-0-0-0-15. REP HONOURS: SA 2005-10 Tests: 47-5-0-0-0-25. Tour: 3-0-0-0-0-0. Total: 50-5-0-0-0-25. SA XV 2006 1-0-0-0-0-0. SA U21 2002-03 11-1-0-0-0-5. SA U19 2001. SA Schools 2000. CW Boland 2000. MISC INFO: PoY Nominee 2005. FC RECORD: 212-23-0-0-0-115. RECORD IN 2010: (SA, Stormers, WP) 24-0-0-0-0-0.

Jeacocks, Russell (Selborne Coll.) b 09/02/84. 1.82m. 82kg. Fullback. FC DEBUT: 2004. PROV CAREER: Bulldogs 2004,07-08 33-10-1-0-0-52. Leopards 2009-10 25-9-0-0-0-45. REP HONOURS: Royal XV 2009 1-0-0-0-0-0. FC RECORD: 59-19-1-0-0-97. RECORD IN

2010 (Leopards) 9-2-0-0-0-10.

Jenner, Dwayne (Dr. EG Jansen HS) b 17/11/1990, Benoni. 1.83m. 99kg. Wing. FC DEBUT: 2010. PROV CAREER: Sharks Inv XV 2010 1-1-0-0-0-5. FC RECORD: 1-1-0-0-0-5. RECORD IN 2010: (Sharks Inv XV) 1-1-0-0-0-5.

Jinka, Dustin (Bishops HS) b 28/04/1986, Cape Town. 1.76m. 82kg. Scrumhalf. FC DEBUT: 2010. PROV CAREER: Blue Bulls 2010 4-0-0-0-0-0. WP 2010 5-1-1-0-0-7. FC RECORD: 9-1-1-0-0-7. RECORD IN 2010: (WP, Blue Bulls) 9-1-1-0-0-7.

Johnson, Ashley Francois (Paarl Gymnasium) b 16/05/86, Wynberg. 1.86m. 101kg. Eighthman. FC DEBUT: 2006. PROV CAREER: Cheetahs 2007-10 55-18-0-0-0-90. Griffons 2008-09 19-3-0-0-0-15. Cheetahs XV 2010 1-0-0-0-0-0. SUPER 14: Cheetahs 2010 4-1-0-0-0-5. REP HONOURS: SA Tour: 2009 2-0-0-0-0-0. Emerging Springboks 2008 3-0-0-0-0-0. SA U21 2006 3-0-0-0-0-0. MISC INFO: Brother of Hercholl Johnson. FC RECORD: 87-22-0-0-0-110. RECORD IN 2010: (Cheetahs S14, Cheetahs, Cheetahs XV) 27-10-0-0-0-50.

Johnson, Hercholl Jacques (Paarl Gym. & UFS) b 09/07/87, Wynberg. 1.90m. 108kg. FC DEBUT: 2009. PROV CAREER: Griffons 2009-10 22-0-0-0-0-0. MISC INFO: Brother of Ashley Johnson. FC RECORD: 22-0-0-0-0-0. RECORD IN 2010: (Griffons) 6-0-0-0-0-0.

Johnson, Sean Garth (Rand Park HS) b 19/08/80, Port Elizabeth. 1.82m. 113kg. Prop. FC DEBUT: 2005. PROV CAREER: Pumas 2005-09 46-4-0-0-0-20. Valke 2009-10 16-0-0-0-0-0. FC RECORD: 62-4-0-0-0-20. RECORD IN 2010: (Valke) 13-0-0-0-0-0.

Jonck, Chris (Otto Du Plessis HS & UPE) b 16/06/80, Port Elizabeth. 1.77m. 83kg. Scrumhalf. FC DEBUT: 2001. PROV CAREER: Elephants 2001-07 121-18-85-54-1-425. Lions 2008-10 20-2-2-2-0-20. Lions XV 2008 1-0-0-0-0-0. Young Lions 2010 6-1-4-0-0-13. SUPER 14: Lions 2008-10 20-1-1-2-0-13. FC RECORD: 168-22-92-58-1-471. RECORD IN 2010: (Lions S14, Golden Lions, Young Lions) 11-1-4-0-0-13.

Jonker, Jacobus Willem (JW) (Grey Coll., Bloemfontein) b 19/03/87, Bloemfontein. 1.81m. 85kg. Centre. FC DEBUT: 2006. PROV CAREER: Cheetahs 2006-10 65-18-0-0-0-90. Griffons 2010 4-6-0-0-0-30. SUPER 14: Cheetahs 2008-09 16-6-0-0-0-30. REP HONOURS: SA Students 2007 1-0-0-0-0-0. FC RECORD: 86-30-0-0-0-150. RECORD IN 2010: (Cheetahs, Griffons) 13-6-0-0-0-30.

Jordaan, Chris Malan (Paarl Gym.) b 10/07/86, Worcester. 1.85m. 87kg. Fullback. FC DEBUT: 2008. PROV CA-

REER: KZN 2008-09 15-4-0-0-0-20. Sharks XV 2008-10 13-6-0-0-0-30. Sharks Inv XV 2009 1-1-0-0-0-5. SUPER 14: Sharks 2009 2-1-0-0-0-5. FC RECORD: 31-12-0-0-0-60. RECORD IN 2010: (Sharks XV) 6-2-0-0-0-10.

Jordaan, Zandre (Paarl Boys HS) b 24/09/87, Empangeni. 1.91m. 93kg. FC DEBUT: 2009. PROV CAREER: Boland 2009-10 22-7-0-0-0-35. WP 2009 4-2-0-0-0-10. FC RECORD: 26-9-0-0-0-45. RECORD IN 2010: (Boland) 18-5-0-0-0-25.

Joubert, Jean-Pierre (JP) (Framesby HS & PE Tech.) b 27/02/78, Port Elizabeth. 1.78m. 85kg. Scrumhalf. FC DEBUT: 2000. PROV CAREER: Eagles 2000 4-0-0-0-0-0. Griffons 2002-05 52-12-1-0-0-62. Griquas 2005-06 23-4-0-0-0-20. Boland 2007 2-0-0-0-0-0. Blue Bulls 2007-09 35-3-0-0-1-18. Cheetahs 2009 14-1-0-0-0-5. Golden Lions 2010 6-0-0-0-0-0. SUPER 14: Stormers 2007 11-0-0-0-0-0. Lions 2010 6-1-0-0-0-5. FC RECORD: 153-21-1-0-1-110. RECORD IN 2010: (Lions S14, Golden Lions) 12-1-0-0-0-5.

Joubert, Marthinus Godfrey (Bobby) (Grey Coll., Bloemfontein) b 05/05/82, Nelspruit. 1.82m. 80kg. Fullback. FC DEBUT: 2003. PROV CAREER: Griquas 2003-07 73-21-3-3-0-120. Eagles 2008-10 50-16-0-0-0-80. MISC INFO: Son of former SE-Tvl wing Bokkie Joubert. FC RECORD: 123-37-3-3-0-200. RECORD IN 2010: (Eagles) 19-5-0-0-0-25.

Joubert, Victor Hugo (Afrikaans HS) b 29/05/86, Vereeniging. 1.82m. 97kg. Flank. FC DEBUT: 2008. PROV CAREER: Eagles 200809 36-2-0-0-0-10. Leopards 2010 9-0-0-0-0-0. FC RECORD: 45-2-0-0-0-10. RECORD IN 2010: (Leopards) 9-0-0-0-0-0.

Juries, Christopher (Kingswood College) b 11/03/88, Grahamstown. 1.80m. 76kgs. Wing. FC DEBUT: 2006. PROV CAREER: Elephants 2006 1-1-0-0-0-5. EP Inv XV 2010 1-0-0-0-0-0. MISC INFO: Brother of EP & SA Sevens player, Fabian. FC RECORD: 2-1-0-0-0-5. RECORD IN 2010: (Elephants) 1-0-0-0-0-0.

Juries, Fabian Mark (Mary Waters High School & Kingswood Coll.) b 28/02/79, Grahamstown. 1.73m. 70kg. Wing. FC DEBUT: 2000. PROV CAREER: Elephants 2001-05,07 62-46-1-0-1-235. Cheetahs 2007-09 15-7-0-0-0-35. Griffons 2008-09 8-5-0-0-0-25. WP 2010 9-0-0-0-0-0. SUPER 14: Bulls 2003 7-3-0-0-0-15. Cheetahs 2009 12-0-0-0-0-0. REP HONOURS: SA U23s 2001 1-1-0-0-0-5; SA U21s 2000 2-5-0-0-0-25; SA Sevens 2000-05; SA U19s 1997-98; CW Elephants 1996. Misc. info: Shares EP record for most tries in a CC season (14) 2003; leading try-scorer U21s champs. 2000 (10). FC RECORD: 116-67-1-0-1-340. RECORD IN 2010: (WP) 9-0-0-0-0-0.

K

Kankowski, Ryan (St Andrew's College) b 14/10/85, Port Elizabeth. 1.93m. 103kg. Eighthman. ›› FC debut: 2006. Prov career: KZN 2006-10 52-14-0-0-0-70. Sharks XV 2009 1-0-0-0-0-0. Super 14: Sharks 2007-10 51-13-0-0-0-65. Rep honours: SA 2007-10 Tests: 17-1-0-0-0-5. Tour 2007,2010: 2-0-0-0-0-0. Total: 19-1-0-0-0-5. SA Sevens 2006. Misc info: PoY nominee 2008. YPoY nominee 2008. Son of former EP & Griquas wing Tino Kankowski. FC record: 123-28-0-0-0-140. RECORD IN 2010: (SA, Sharks, KZN) 26-5-0-0-0-25.

Karemaker, Leon (Bellville HS) b 18/05/85, Cape Town. 1.92m. 98kgs. Centre. FC DEBUT: 2004. PROV CAREER: WP 2005-06 14-5-0-0-0-25. Griquas 2010 14-5-0-0-0-25. REP HONOURS: SA U21 2004 2-0-0-0-0-0. SA U19s 2003-2004. SA Schools 2002-03. CW WP 2003. FC RECORD: 30-10-0-0-0-50. RECORD IN 2010: (Griquas) 14-5-0-0-0-25.

Kayser, Clinton (Groenberg HS) b 26/01/84, Grabouw. 1.89m. 93kg. Centre. FC DEBUT: 2009. PROV CAREER: Valke 2009-10 16-0-0-0-0-0. FC RECORD: 16-0-0-0-0-0. RECORD IN 2010: (Valke) 9-0-0-0-0-0.

Kebe, Ntando Lucky (Thubalethu HS & Univ. Fort Hare) b 19/08/1988, East London. 1.79m. 80kg. Scrumhalf. FC DEBUT: 2010. PROV CAREER: Bulldogs 2010 16-0-0-0-0-0. FC RECORD: 16-0-0-0-0-0. RECORD IN 2010: (Bulldogs) 16-0-0-0-0-0.

Keil, Rudolf Reginald (Rudi) (KES) b 08/12/77, Johannesburg. 1.85m. 90kgs. Centre. FC DEBUT: 1998. PROV CAREER: Lions 1998-99 20-3-7-3-0-38; Eagles 2000 21-3-9-6-0-51; Boland 2001 10-1-0-0-0-5. KZN 2002-05 38-7-0-0-0-35. EP Kings 2010 2-0-0-0-0-0. Super 12: Sharks 2002-03&05 28-2-0-0-0-10. REP HONOURS: SA U21s 1998 4-0-0-0-0-0; CW Lions 1996. Misc. info: Worcester (Eng) 2000-01. FC RECORD: 123-16-16-9-0-139. RECORD IN 2010: (EP Kings) 2-0-0-0-0-0.

Kember, Reginald (RW) (Daniel Pienaar THS) b 15/04/83, Adelaide. 1.87m. 105kg. Eighthman. FC DEBUT: 2006. PROV CAREER: Elephants 2006-07 30-5-0-0-0-25. Leopards 2008-10 49-7-0-0-0-35. Lions 2008 6-0-0-0-0-0. SUPER 14: Lions 2008 1-0-0-0-0-0. REP HONOURS: Royal XV 2009 1-0-0-0-0-0. FC RECORD: 87-12-0-0-0-60. RECORD IN 2010: (Leopards) 21-3-0-0-0-15.

Kemp, Cecil-John (Landbou HS) b 14/03/81, Robertson. 1.98m. 125kg. Lock. FC DEBUT: 2008. PROV CAREER: Boland 2008 18-0-0-0-0-0. Griquas 2009-10 33-3-0-0-0-15. FC RECORD: 51-3-0-0-0-15. RECORD IN 2010: (Griquas) 21-2-0-0-0-10.

Kennedy, Charl Emile (De Vos HS) b 23/09/1965, King Williams Town. 90kg. Wing. FC DEBUT: 2010. PROV CAREER: Bulldogs 2010 9-0-0-0-0-0. FC RECORD: 9-0-0-0-0-0. RECORD IN 2010: (Bulldogs) 9-0-0-0-0-0.

Kennedy, Royden Danilo (Dale Coll.) b 17/10/87, King Williams Town. 1.75m. 87kg. FC DEBUT: 2009. PROV CAREER: Bulldogs 2009-10 16-2-0-0-0-10. FC RECORD: 16-2-0-0-0-10. RECORD IN 2010: (Bulldogs) 11-2-0-0-0-10.

Kettledas, Allister (Humansdorp HS) b 02/03/82, Port Elizabeth. 1.87m. 94kg. Wing. FC DEBUT: 2004. PROV CAREER: Lions 2004 1-0-0-0-0-0. Eagles 2006-08 41-21-0-0-0-105. Pumas 2009-10 40-33-0-0-0-165. FC RECORD: 82-54-0-0-0-270. RECORD IN 2010: (Pumas) 19-94-0-0-0-45.

Killian, Michael (Muir Coll., Uitenhage) b 22/11/83, Uitenhage. 1.82m. 84kg. Flyhalf. FC DEBUT: 2004. Prov career; Elephants 2004-07 58-22-0-0-0-110. Lions 2008-10 30-11-0-0-0-55. Young Lions 2008-09 10-3-0-0-1-18. Lions XV 2008. SUPER 14: Lions S14 2009-10 15-7-0-0-0-35.REP HONOURS: SA Students 2005,07 2-0-0-0-0-0. FC RECORD: 116-43-0-0-1-218. RECORD IN 2010: (Lions S14, Golden Lions) 25-10-0-0-0-50.

Killian, Zane Jonathan (Huguenot HS, Springs) b 11/07/81, Springs. 1.78m. 105kg. Fullback. FC DEBUT: 2003. PROV CAREER: Pumas 2003-04 11-1-0-0-0-5. Valke 2004-09 69-1-0-0-0-5. Griquas 2009-10 6-0-0-0-0-0. FC RECORD: 86-2-0-0-0-10. RECORD IN 2010: (Griquas) 1-0-0-0-0-0.

King, Charles (Charlie) (Robertson HS) b 03/05/83, Robertson. 1.75m. 80kg. Scrumhalf. FC DEBUT: 2003. PROV CAREER: Leopards 2003-04 & 10 22-3-0-0-0-15. WP 2008-09 5-0-0-0-0-0. Boland 2009 5-0-0-0-0-0. FC RECORD: 32-3-0-0-0-15. Record in 2010: (Leopards) 3-0-0-0-0-0.

Kirchner, Zane (PW Botha Coll.) b 16/06/84, George. 1.84m. 92kg. Fullback. FC DEBUT: 2003. PROV CAREER: Griquas 2003-04 & 06-07 58-9-32-22-0-175. Blue Bulls 2008-10 31-5-2-0-0-29. SUPER 14: Bulls 2008-10 40-11-0-0-0-55. REP HONOURS: SA 2009-10 Tests: 14-1-0-0-0-5. Emerging Springboks 2009 1-0-0-0-0-0. CW SWD 2002. MISC INFO: VC PoY 2007. FC RECORD: 144-26-34-22-0-264. RECORD IN 2010: (SA, Bulls, Blue Bulls) 33-6-1-0-0-32.

Kirsten, Frederick Barend Christoffel (Frik) (Afrikaans Boys HS) b 18/08/88, Sandton. 1.93m. 118kg. Prop. FC DEBUT: 2008. PROV CAREER: Blue Bulls 2008-10 24-0-0-0-0-0. SUPER 14: Bulls 2009 2-0-0-0-0-0. FC RECORD: 26-0-0-0-0-0. RECORD IN 2010:

WHO'S WHO IN 2010

(Blue Bulls) 3-0-0-0-0-0.

Kitshoff, Rohan (Drostdy THS) b 13/09/85, Windhoek. 1.81m. 95kg. Flank. FC DEBUT: 2007. PROV CAREER: Griquas 2007-10 59-12-0-0-0-60. FC RECORD: 59-12-0-0-0-60. RECORD IN 2010: (Griquas) 14-2-0-0-0-10.

Klonaridis, Andonis Emanuel (Anthony) (Vereeniging HTS) b 19/06/88, Vereeniging. 1.89m. 98kg. Centre. FC DEBUT: 2009. PROV CAREER: Valke 2009-10 12-3-0-0-0-15. FC RECORD: 12-3-0-0-0-15. RECORD IN 2010: (Valke) 9-1-0-0-0-5.

Kloppers, Pieter Hugo (Worcester Gym.) b 14/10/1988, Worcester. 1.97m. 99kg. Lock. FC DEBUT: 2010. PROV CAREER: WP 2010 4-0-0-0-0-0. FC RECORD: 4-0-0-0-0-0. RECORD IN 2010: (WP) 4-0-0-0-0-0.

Kobokana, Suvuyile (Mzontsundu HS) b 27/09/81, Port Elizabeth. 1.82m. 95kg. Flank. FC DEBUT: 2006. PROV CAREER: EP Kings 2006 & 08-10 33-5-0-0-0-25. E/Cape XV 2008 2-0-0-0-0-0. EP Inv XV 2010 1-0-0-0-0-0. FC RECORD: 36-5-0-0-0-25. RECORD IN 2010: (EP Kings, EP Inv XV) 3-0-0-0-0-0.

Kock, Alexander Hendrik (Alex) (Monument HS) b 03/04/1988, Pietermaritzburg. 1.80m. 85kg. Scrumhalf. FC DEBUT: 2009. PROV CAREER: Sharks XV 2009 1-1-0-0-0-5. Young Lions 2010 3-0-0-0-0-0. Boland 2010 8-5-0-0-0-25. FC RECORD: 12-6-0-0-0-30. RECORD IN 2010: (Boland, Young Lions) 11-5-0-0-0-25.

Koch, Wilhelm Johannes (Swartland HS) b 29/04/83. 1.88m. 95kg. Loose Forward. FC DEBUT: 2006. PROV CAREER: Leopards 2006-07,09-10 56-6-0-0-1-33. Lions 2007-08 17-0-0-0-0-0. Lions XV 2007-08 2-2-0-0-0-10. SUPER 14: Lions 2008 4-0-0-0-0-0. REP HONOURS: Royal XV 2009 1-1-0-0-0-5. FC RECORD: 80-9-0-0-1-48. RECORD IN 2010: (Leopards) 22-4-0-0-0-20.

Kockott, Rory Michael (Selborne College) b 25/06/86, East London. 1.79m. 85kg. Scrumhalf. FC DEBUT: 2006. PROV CAREER: Lions 2006 3-1-1-0-0-7. KZN 2007-10 47-3-40-50-1-248. Sharks Inv XV 2009-10 2-0-10-2-0-26. SUPER 14: Sharks 2007-10 50-3-46-42-1-236. FC RECORD: 102-7-97-94-2-517. RECORD IN 2010: (Sharks, KZN, Sharks Inv XV) 27-3-10-16-0-83.

Koen, Louis Johannes (Paarl Gym & Univ. of Stellenbosch) b 07/07/75, Cape Town. 1.80m. 80kgs. Flyhalf. FC DEBUT: 1996. PROV CAREER: WP 1996-99 46-11-123-92-0-577; Lions 2000-02 28-5-87-60-4-391. Boland 2010 1-0-3-2-0-12. Super 12: Stormers 1998-99 12-2-20-11-1-86; Cats 2000-02 28-3-42-74-3-330. Bulls 2003 11-0-17-28-7-139. REP HONOURS: SA 2000 & 03 Tests 15-0-23-31-2-145; Emerging Springboks 1998 1-0-2-2-0-10; SA 'A' 1996 7-1-29-13-0-102; SA U21s 1996 1-0-1-3-

0-11; SA Schools and WP Craven Week 1993-94. Misc. info: YPoY nominee 1997; Shares Spriongbok record for most penalties in a match (6); Holds S12 record for most drop goals in a season (7) and shares record for most in a match (3); Holds Cats record for most points in a S12 season (157) and a S12 career (330); Holds CC record for most conversions in a season (62); Holds WP record for most points in a CC match (32); Top S12 scorer in 2001 (157 pts). FC RECORD: 151-22-346-316-17-1801. Record in 2010: (Boland) 1-0-3-2-0-12.

Koster, Ralph Nicholas (Nick) (Bishops Coll.) b 22/02/90, Robertson. 1.90m 102kg. Flank. FC DEBUT: 2008. PROV CAREER: WP 2008 & 10 18-4-0-0-0-20. SUPER 14: Stormers 2009 4-0-0-0-0-0. REP HONOURS: British Barbarians 2008 1-0-0-0-0-0. MISC INFO: YPoy nominee 2008. FC RECORD: 23-4-0-0-0-20. RECORD IN 2010: (WP) 11-2-0-0-0-10.

Kotze, Divan (Welkom HS) b 28/06/80, Welkom. 1.90m. 125kg. Prop. FC DEBUT: 2008. PROV CAREER: Leopards 2008-10 41-0-0-0-0-0. FC RECORD: 41-0-0-0-0-0. RECORD IN 2010: (Leopards) 11-0-0-0-0-0.

Kotze, Marco (Marais Viljoen HS) b 25/08/86, Germiston. 1.93m. 109kgs. Flanker. FC DEBUT: 2006. PROV CAREER: Lions 2006 5-0-0-0-0-0. Valke 2010 9-2-0-0-0-10. FC RECORD: 14-2-0-0-0-10. RECORD IN 2010: (Valke) 9-2-0-0-0-10.

Kotze, Theuns Andries Willem (Upington HS & NWU) b 16/07/1987, Karasburg. 1.81m. 88kg. Scrumhalf. FC DEBUT: 2010. PROV CAREER: Leopards 2010 3-0-0-0-0-0. FC RECORD: 3-0-0-0-0-0. RECORD IN 2010: (Leopards) 3-0-0-0-0-0.

Kotze, Wesley (Marais Viljoen HS) b 07/10/1988, Johannesburg. 1.93m. 108kg. Flanker. FC DEBUT: 2010. PROV CAREER: Boland 2010 5-0-0-0-0-0. FC RECORD: 5-0-0-0-0-0. RECORD IN 2010: (Boland) 5-0-0-0-0-0.

Kotzee, Gerhardus Dirk (Volkskool, Heidelberg) b 22/08/89, Vereeniging. 1.80m. 85kg. Wing. FC DEBUT: 2009. PROV CAREER: Valke 2009-10 12-0-0-0-0-0. FC RECORD: 12-0-0-0-0-0. RECORD IN 2010: (Valke) 5-0-0-0-0-0.

Kriel, Jacobus Albertus (Jaco) (Standerton HS & UJ) b 21/08/1989, Standerton. 1.83m. 86kg. Flanker. FC DEBUT: 2010. PROV CAREER: Golden Lions 2010 1-0-0-0-0-0. Young Lions 2010 8-3-0-0-0-15. FC RECORD: 9-3-0-0-0-15. RECORD IN 2010: (Golden Lions, Young Lions) 9-3-0-0-0-15.

Kritzinger, Johan Chris (JC) (Stellenberg HS) b 04/12/87, Humansdorp. 1.82m. 116kg. Prop. FC DE-

BUT: 2008. PROV CAREER: WP 2008-10 29-1-0-0-0-5. SUPER 14: Stormers 2010 10-0-0-0-0-0. FC RECORD: 39-1-0-0-0-5. RECORD IN 2010: (Stormers) 22-0-0-0-0-0.

Kritzinger, Nicky (Dundee HS) b 16/06/84, Krugersdorp. 1.80m. 80kg. Wing. FC DEBUT: 2007. PROV CAREER: Valke 2007-08 12-6-0-0-0-30. Leopards 2009 7-3-0-0-0-15. Pumas 2010 12-4-0-0-0-20. FC RECORD: 31-13-0-0-0-65. RECORD IN 2010: (Pumas) 12-4-0-0-0-20.

Kruger, Andries Gerhardus (AHS, Pretoria) b 19/06/84, Witbank. 1.98m. 101kg. Lock. FC DEBUT: 2005. PROV CAREER: Valke 2005-06 17-0-0-0-0-0. Bulldogs 2007-09 41-3-0-0-0-15. Pumas 2010 11-1-0-0-0-5. FC RECORD: 69-4-0-0-0-20. RECORD IN 2010: (Pumas) 11-1-0-0-0-15.

Kruger, Andries Marthinus (Hentie Cilliers HS) b 10/12/84, Virginia. 1.82m. 106kg. Hooker. FC DEBUT: 2006. PROV CAREER: Griffons 2006-09 37-3-0-0-0-15. Griquas 2009-10 18-2-0-0-0-10. Boland 2010 5-0-0-0-0-0. FC RECORD: 60-5-0-0-0-25. RECORD IN 2010: (Boland, Griquas) 11-2-0-0-0-10.

Kruger, Hercules Christiaan (Herkie) (Grey Coll., Bloemfontein) b 21/3/79, Kempton Park. 1.83m. 82kg. Flyhalf. FC DEBUT: 2000. PROV CAREER: KZN 2000-02 & 05 33-5-69-52-1-322. Griquas 2006-08 28-4-1-2-0-28. Lions 2009-10 16-0-33-37-0-177. Young Lions 2010 3-0-7-10-0-44. SUPER 14: Sharks 2001-02&05 13-0-5-7-2-37. Cheetahs 2007 9-2-0-1-2-19. Lions 2010 6-1-8-10-0-51. REP HONOURS: SA U23s 2001 1-0-0-1-0-3; SA Academy 1998; CW Cheetahs 1997. MISC INFO: Served two-year suspension for doping offence 2003-04. Calvisano (Italy) 2005-06. FC RECORD: 109-12-123-120-5-681. RECORD IN 2010: (Lions S14, Golden Lions, Young Lions): 12-1-20-26-0-123.

Kruger, Jan Ernest (Ernie) (Oudtshoorn HS) b 18/12/85, Pretoria. 1.84m. 92kg. Centre. FC DEBUT: 2007. PROV CAREER: Valke 2007-08 & 10 26-12-0-0-0-60. Boland 2009 13-1-0-0-0-5. FC RECORD: 39-13-0-0-0-65. RECORD IN 2010: (Valke) 6-0-0-0-0-0.

Kruger, Ockert Cornelius (AHS, Pretoria) b 12/01/87, Empangeni. 1.87m. 97kg. Eighthman. FC DEBUT: 2007. PROV CAREER: Blue Bulls 2007-10 36-10-0-0-0-50. Blue Bulls XV 2007 1-0-0-0-0-0. SUPER 14: Bulls 2010 1-0-0-0-0-0. FC RECORD: 38-10-0-0-0-50. RECORD IN 2010: (Bulls, Blue Bulls) 17-4-0-0-0-20.

Kruger, Petrus Johannes Juandre (Juandre) (Paul Roos Gym.) b 06/09/85, Cape Town. 1.97m. 107kg. Lock. FC DEBUT: 2007. PROV CAREER: WP 2007 6-2-0-0-0-10. Blue Bulls 2008 & 10 30-3-0-0-0-15. FC RECORD:

36-5-0-0-0-25. RECORD IN 2010: (Blue Bulls) 11-1-0-0-0-5.

Kruger, Robert Albertus (Standerton HS & Potch Univ.) b 28/04/1988, Johannesburg. 1.94m. 106kg. FC DEBUT: 2009. PROV CAREER: Lions 2009-10 4-0-0-0-0-0. Young Lions 2009-10 4-1-0-0-0-5. SUPER 14: Lions 2009-10 9-0-0-0-0-0. FC RECORD: 17-1-0-0-0-5. RECORD IN 2010: (Lions S14, Golden Lions, Young Lions) 6-0-0-0-0-0.

Kruger, Rossouw (Boland Agric. HS) b 03/05/1989, Cape Town. 121kg. Prop. FC DEBUT: 2010. PROV CAREER: Boland 2010 11-0-0-0-0-0. FC RECORD: 11-0-0-0-0-0. RECORD IN 2010: (Boland) 11-0-0-0-0-0.

Kruger, Werner (Kempton Park HS) b 23/01/85, Kempton Park. 1.90m. 107kg. Prop. ›› FC debut: 2003. Prov career: Blue Bulls 2003 & 05-07-10 83-5-0-0-0-25. Blue Bulls XV 2007 1-0-0-0-0-0. Super 14: Bulls 2008-10 42-3-0-0-0-15. Rep honours: SA Tour 2010: 1-0-0-0-0-0. Emerging Springboks 2009 1-0-0-0-0-0. SA U21 2005-06 6-0-0-0-0-0. FC record: 134-8-0-0-0-40. RECORD IN 2010: (SA, Bulls, Blue Bulls) 27-0-0-0-0-0.

Kuün, Gabriel Willem Frederick (Derick) (AHS, Pretoria) b 08/06/84, Johannesburg. 1.84m. 92kg. Flank. FC DEBUT: 2004. PROV CAREER: Blue Bulls 2004-10 95-33-0-0-0-165. SUPER 14: Bulls 2007-10 56-8-0-0-0-40. REP HONOURS: S/Kings 2009 1-0-0-0-0-0. SA Sevens 2005. SA U21 2004-05 10-8-0-0-0-40. SA U19 2003. SA Schools 2002. CW Blue Bulls 2001-02. MISC INFO: IRB U21 PoY nominee 2005. FC RECORD: 157-43-0-0-0-215. RECORD IN 2010: (Bulls, Blue Bulls) 29-6-0-0-0-30.

L

Labuschagne, Jan Johannes (Jannes) (Schweizer Reinecke HS & RAU) b 16/04/76, Bloemhof. 1.96m. 115kg. Lock. FC DEBUT: 1997. PROV CAREER: Lions 1997, 1999-04 & 08 106-13-1-0-0-67. Young Lions 2010 2-0-0-0-0-0. SUPER 14: Cats 2000-06 44-2-0-0-0-10. Lions 2009 8-0-0-0-0-0. REP HONOURS: SA 2000 & 2002 Tests 11-0-0-0-0-0; SA 'A' 2001 2-2-0-0-0-10; SA Barbs. 2001 1-0-0-0-0-0; CW Stellaland 1992-94. MISC INFO: YPoY nominee 1999. FC RECORD: 174-17-1-0-0-87. RECORD IN 2010: (Young Lions) 2-0-0-0-0-0.

Labuschagne Anthony (Rod) (Hilton Coll.) b 21/09/79, Durban. 1.98m. 108kgs. Lock. FC DEBUT: 2002. PROV CAREER: KZN 2002-03 15-0-0-0-0-0. Boland 2010 6-0-0-0-0-0. FC RECORD: 21-0-0-0-0-0. RECORD IN 2010: (Boland) 6-0-0-0-0-0.

La Grange, Gideon (Doppies) (Port Natal HS & RAU) b 01/12/81, Sasolburg. 1.82m. 93kg. Centre. FC DEBUT:

2003. PROV CAREER: Lions 2003-04 & 06-10 80-24-0-0-0-120. Young Lions 2003-08 10-3-0-0-0-15. SUPER 14: Cats 2003-04 7-1-0-0-0-5. Lions 2007-10 34-2-0-0-0-10. FC RECORD: 131-30-0-0-0-150. RECORD IN 2010: (Lions S14, Golden Lions) 19-2-0-0-0-10.

Lambie, Patrick (Michaelhouse) b 17/10/90, Durban. 1.77m. 86kg. Flyhalf. FC DEBUT: 2009. Prov career: KZN 2009-10 17-5-36-36-0-205. Sharks Inv XV 2009 1-0-1-1-0-5. Super 14: Sharks 2010 8-2-0-0-0-10. Rep honours: SA 2010 Tests: 4-0-1-0-0-2. SA 2010 Tour: 1-0-0-0-0-0. Total: 5-0-1-0-0-2. Misc info: YPoY nominee 2010. FC record: 31-7-38-37-0-222. RECORD IN 2010: (SA, Sharks, KZN) 29-7-37-36-0-217.

Lamprecht, Ruan (Hentie Cilliers HS) b 25/08/83, Virginia. 1.82m. 86kg. Fullback/Wing. FC DEBUT: 2007. PROV CAREER: Pumas 2007-09 34-8-0-0-0-40. Griffons 2010 10-2-0-0-0-10. FC RECORD: 44-10-0-0-0-50. RECORD IN 2010: (Griffons) 10-2-0-0-0-10.

Landman, Barry (Merensky HS & UOFS) b 14/03/1988, Pietersburg. 1.95m. 112kg. Flanker. FC DEBUT: 2010. PROV CAREER: Eagles 2010 2-0-0-0-0-0. FC RECORD: 2-0-0-0-0-0. RECORD IN 2010: (Eagles) 2-0-0-0-0-0.

Landman, Rynard Jaco (Despatch HS) b 24/07/86, East London. 1.97m. 114kg. Lock. FC DEBUT: 2008. PROV CAREER: Leopards 2008-10 39-2-0-0-0-10. SUPER 14: Lions 2009 2-0-0-0-0-0. REP HONOURS: Royal XV 2009 1-0-0-0-0-0. FC RECORD: 42-2-0-0-0-10. RECORD IN 2010: (Leopards) 12-2-0-0-0-10.

Larson, Raoul Jonathan (Grey Coll., Bloemfontein) b 14/05/84, Katima Mulilo. 1.85m. 120kgs. Prop. FC DEBUT: 2006. PROV CAREER: Cheetahs 2006-07 16-0-0-0-0-0. Griffons 2007 9-0-0-0-0-0. Elephants 2009 9-0-0-0-0-0. Boland 2010 7-0-0-0-0-0. FC RECORD: 41-0-0-0-0-0. RECORD IN 2010: (Boland) 7-0-0-0-0-0.

Lawson, Richard James (Wynberg Boys HS) b 20/10/86, Johannesburg. 1.83m. 87kg. Fullback. FC DEBUT: 2006. PROV CAREER: WP 2006-08 16-3-0-0-0-15. Griquas 2009-10 19-5-0-0-0-25. REP HONOURS: Emerging Springboks 2008 3-0-0-0-0-0. FC RECORD: 38-8-0-0-0-40. RECORD IN 2010: (Griquas) 10-1-0-0-0-5.

Le Roux, Abraham Jacobus (AJ) (Overkruin HS) b 12/12/1990, Pretoria. 1.80m. 108kg. Hooker. FC DEBUT: 2010. PROV CAREER: Blue Bulls 2010 2-0-0-0-0-0. FC RECORD: 2-0-0-0-0-0. RECORD IN 2010: (Blue Bulls) 2-0-0-0-0-0.

Le Roux, Christo (Oakdale Agri. HS) b 28/03/85, Bloemfontein. 1.91m. 108kg. Eighthman. FC DEBUT: 2008. PROV CAREER: Eagles 2008 15-3-0-0-0-15. Pumas 2009-10 43-8-0-0-0-40. FC RECORD: 58-11-0-0-0-55.

RECORD IN 2010: (Pumas) 23-5-0-0-0-25.

Le Roux, Grant (Flippie) (Vereeniging THS & Potch Univ.) b 13/01/86, Sasolburg. 1.97m. 110kg. FC DEBUT: 2009. PROV CAREER: Boland 2009-10 22-0-0-0-0-0. FC RECORD: 22-0-0-0-0-0. RECORD IN 2010: (Boland) 19-0-0-0-0-0.

Le Roux, Willem Jacobus (Paul Roos Gym.) b 18/08/1989, Cape Town. 1.86m. 88kg. Flyhalf. FC DEBUT: 2010. PROV CAREER: Boland 2010 18-11-0-0-2-61. FC RECORD: 18-11-0-0-2-61. RECORD IN 2010: (Boland) 18-11-0-0-2-61.

Lemmer, Phillip (Hans Moore HS) b 30/06/83, Benoni. 1.83m. 98kg. Prop. FC DEBUT: 2005. PROV CAREER: Lions 2005 3-0-0-0-0-0. Valke 2006-07 20-0-0-0-0-0. Cheetahs 2008 15-0-0-0-0-0. Leopards 2009-10 21-1-0-0-0-5. REP HONOURS: Emerging Springboks 2008 3-0-0-0-0-0. FC RECORD: 62-1-0-0-0-5. RECORD IN 2010: (Leopards) 7-1-0-0-0-5.

Lewis, Clement (Boland Agricultural HS) b 10/10/83. 1.75m. 90kg. Flank. FC DEBUT: 2006. PROV CAREER: Boland 2006-10 61-1-0-0-0-5. FC RECORD: 61-1-0-0-0-5. RECORD IN 2010: (Boland) 19-1-0-0-0-5.

Lewis, Marlon Shaun (Bertram HS) b 07/10/87, Port Elizabeth. 1.65m. 73kg. Scrumhalf. FC DEBUT: 2008. PROV CAREER: EP Kings 2008-10 39-5-0-0-1-28. E/ Cape XV 2008 1-0-0-0-0-0. EP Inv XV 2010 1-0-0-0-0-0. FC RECORD: 41-5-0-0-1-28. RECORD IN 2010: (EP Kings, EP Inv XV) 9-1-0-0-0-5.

Liebenberg, Christiaan Rudolph (Tiaan) (Grey Coll., Bloemfontein) b 18/12/81, Kimberley. 1.85m. 107kg. Hooker. FC DEBUT: 2002. PROV CAREER: KZN 2002 2-0-0-0-0-0. Griquas 2003-06 64-4-1-0-0-22. WP 2006-07,09-10 40-2-0-0-0-10. SUPER 14: Cheetahs 13-1-0-0-0-5. Stormers 2007-10 38-2-0-0-0-10. REP HONOURS: SA 2007 Tour: 1-0-0-0-0-0. Emerging Springboks 2009 1-0-0-0-0-0. MISC INFO: Brother of FS hooker Hercu. Son of former GW & FS flyhalf & fullback Henning Liebenberg. FC RECORD: 159-9-1-0-0-47. RECORD IN 2010: (Stormers, WP) 23-1-0-0-0-5.

Liebenberg, Herculaas Johannes (Hercu) (Grey Coll., Bloemfontein) b 16/05/86, Bloemfontein. 1.78m. 104kg. Hooker. FC DEBUT: 2006. PROV CAREER: Cheetahs 2006-08 & 10 26-0-0-0-0-0. Elephants 2009 11-1-0-0-0-5. MISC INFO: Brother of GW & WP hooker Tiaan. Son of former GW & FS flyhalf & fullback Henning Liebenberg. FC RECORD: 37-1-0-0-0-5. RECORD IN 2010: (Cheetahs) 4-0-0-0-0-0.

Liebenberg, Philipus Lodevickus (Vickus) (Upington HS & Varsity Coll.) b 20/02/85, Upington. 1.98m. 121kg. FC DEBUT: 2009. PROV CAREER: Eagles

2009-10 20-0-0-0-0-0. FC RECORD: 20-0-0-0-0-0. RECORD IN 2010: (Eagles) 6-0-0-0-0-0.

Ligman, Elroy John (Scottsdene SS & Kasselsvlei HS) b 14/01/82, Pearston. 1.78m. 82kg. Flank. FC DEBUT: 2001. PROV CAREER: EP Kings 2001 & 03-10 101-17-0-0-0-85. REP HONOURS: SA U19 2001. FC RECORD: 101-17-0-0-0-85. RECORD IN 2010: (EP Kings) 3-0-0-0-0-0.

Linde, Edrich (Overkruin HS) b 09/10/82, Empangeni. 2.04m. 98kg. Lock. FC DEBUT: 2003. PROV CAREER: Bulldogs 2003 15-0-0-0-0-0. Leopards 2005-10 83-2-0-0-0-10. FC RECORD: 98-2-0-0-0-10. RECORD IN 2010: (Leopards) 13-0-0-0-0-0.

Lindeque, Petrus Johannes (Piet) (Grey Coll.) b 31/01/1991, Winburg. 1.82m. 88kg. Centre. FC DEBUT: 2010. PROV CAREER: Sharks Inv XV 2010 1-0-0-0-0-0. FC RECORD: 1-0-0-0-0-0. RECORD IN 2010: (Sharks Inv XV) 1-0-0-0-0-0.

Lloyd, Colin Randell (Gordon HS, Strand) b 04/03/81, Strand. 1.74m. 80kg. Wing. FC DEBUT: 2002. PROV CAREER: WP 2002 7-2-0-0-0-10. Griquas 2003 17-2-0-0-0-10. Leopards 2004-10 90-48-14-11-0-301. Lions 2007-08 13-2-9-4-0-40. Lions XV 2007 1-0-0-0-0-0. SUPER 14: Lions 2007 1-0-0-0-0-0. FC RECORD: 129-54-23-15-0-361. RECORD IN 2010: (Leopards) 3-0-0-0-0-0.

Lobberts, Hilton (New Orleans SS) b 11/06/86, Paarl. 1.90m. 102kg. Flank. FC DEBUT: 2005. PROV CAREER: Blue Bulls 2006-08 37-5-0-0-0-25. Boland 2009-10 17-0-0-0-0-0. WP 2009 4-0-0-0-0-0. SUPER 14: Bulls 2007-08 7-0-0-0-0-0. Stormers 2009 5-0-0-0-0-0. REP HONOURS: SA 2006-07 Tests: 2-0-0-0-0-0. Tour: 1-0-0-0-0-0. Total: 3-0-0-0-0-0. Emerging Springboks 2007 1-0-0-0-0-0. Springbok XV 2006. SA U21 2005-06 10-1-0-0-0-5. SA U19s 2004-05. FC RECORD: 85-6-0-0-0-30. RECORD IN 2010: (Boland) 12-0-0-0-0-0.

Lombaard, Jacques (Elsburg HS) b 06/12/78. 2.03m. 110kg. Lock. FC DEBUT: 2004. PROV CAREER: Valke 2004-05 26-3-0-0-0-15. Pumas 2006-07 28-6-0-0-0-30. Griquas 2008-09 35-2-0-0-0-10. Young Lions 2010 2-1-0-0-0-5. SUPER 14: Lions 2010 7-1-0-0-0-5. REP HONOURS: Royal XV 2009 1-0-0-0-0-0. CW Lions 1996. FC RECORD: 99-13-0-0-0-65. RECORD IN 2010: (Lions S14, Young Lions) 9-2-0-0-0-10.

Lombard, Gerhardus Johannes (Nardus) b 09/01/85. Prop. FC DEBUT: 2007. PROV CAREER: Leopards 2007-10 51-0-0-0-0-0. FC RECORD: 51-0-0-0-0-0. RECORD IN 2010: (Leopards) 7-0-0-0-0-0.

Lourens, Vogan Jean Pierre (Outeniqua HS) b

13/01/1990, George. 1.68m. 77kg. Wing. FC DEBUT: 2010. PROV CAREER: Eagles 2010 1-0-0-0-0-0. FC RECORD: 1-0-0-0-0-0. RECORD IN 2010: (Eagles) 1-0-0-0-0-0.

Louw, Francois Hermanus (Hottie) (Boland Agric. HS & Cape Tech.) b 02/03/76, Paarl. 1.99m. 118kgs. Lock. FC DEBUT: 1996. PROV CAREER: WP 1996-03 92-9-0-0-0-45. Blue Bulls 2006-07 28-1-0-0-0-5. Boland 2010 19-2-0-0-0-10. Super 12: Stormers 1998-03 61-2-0-0-0-10. REP HONOURS: SA 2000 & 2002 Tests: 3-0-0-0-0-0. Tour 4-0-0-0-0-0. Total: 7-0-0-0-0-0; SA Trials 1998 1-0-0-0-0-0; SA 'A' 1996 8-2-0-0-0-10; SA Barbs. 1996 & 2000 2-0-0-0-0-0; British Barbarians 2003,06 5-0-0-0-0-0. WP XV 2006. SA U21s 1996-97 4-0-0-0-0-0; SA Schools and Craven Week WP 1994. MISC INFO: Clermont Ferrand (Fra) 2003-05, Llanelli (Wal) 2005-06, Bath (Eng) 2006-07. FC RECORD: 229-16-0-0-0-80. RECORD IN 2010: (Boland) 19-2-0-0-0-10.

Louw, Louis-Francois Pickard (Francois) (Bishops) b 15/06/85, Cape Town. 1.90m. 110kg. Flank. FC DEBUT: 2006. PROV CAREER: WP 2006-10 65-13-0-0-0-65. SUPER 14: Stormers 2008-10 35-3-0-0-0-15. REP HONOURS: SA 2010 Tests: 7-2-0-0-0-10. FC RECORD: 107-18-0-0-0-90. RECORD IN 2010: (SA, Stormers, WP) 32-9-0-0-0-45.

Louw, Pieter Johannes (Paarl Boys' High) b 24/01/85, Cape Town. 1.90m. 98kg. Eighthman. FC DEBUT: 2005. PROV CAREER: WP 2005-10 64-17-0-0-0-85. SUPER 14: Stormers 2009-10 17-3-0-0-0-15. REP HONOURS: SA U21 2005-06 7-1-0-0-0-5. SA U19 2003-04. FC RECORD: 88-21-0-0-0-105. RECORD IN 2010: (Stormers, WP) 25-11-0-0-0-55.

Louw, Sarel (Goudveld HS) b 27/04/78, Odendaalsrus. 1.87m. 108kg. Prop. FC DEBUT: 2001. PROV CAREER: Griffons 2001-04,07-10 104-11-0-0-0-55. FC RECORD: 104-11-0-0-0-55. RECORD IN 2010: (Griffons) 19-1-0-0-0-5.

Louw, Wilmaure Derrick (Carlton van Heerden HS) b 02/02/87, Upington. 1.83m. 86kg. Centre. FC DEBUT: 2009. PROV CAREER: Griquas 2009-10 30-2-0-0-0-10. SUPER 14: Cheetahs 2010 3-0-0-0-0-0. FC RECORD: 33-2-0-0-0-10. RECORD IN 2010: (Cheetahs S14, Griquas) 22-0-0-0-0-0.

Luckan, Ghafoer (Rylands HS) b 18/12/85, Cape Town. 1.78m. 85kg. Wing. FC DEBUT: 2009. PROV CAREER: Bulldogs 2009 11-3-0-0-0-15. Leopards 2010 2-0-0-0-0-0. FC RECORD: 13-3-0-0-0-15. RECORD IN 2010: (Leopards) 2-0-0-0-0-0.

Ludik, Louis (Dr EG Jansen) b 08/10/86, Kempton

Park. 1.82m. 92kg. Wing. FC DEBUT: 2006. PROV CAREER: Lions 2006-09 45-12-0-0-0-60. Lions XV 2008 1-1-0-0-0-5. Young Lions 2006-08 12-4-0-0-0-20. KZN 2010 13-3-0-0-0-15. Sharks XV 2010 3-1-0-0-0-5. Sharks Inv XV 2010 1-0-0-0-0-0. SUPER 14: Lions 2007-09 36-4-0-0-0-20. REP HONOURS: Emerging Springboks 2007 1-0-0-0-0-0. FC RECORD: 112-25-0-0-0-125. RECORD IN 2010: (KZN, Sharks XV, Sharks Inv XV) 17-4-0-0-0-20.

Lusaseni, Luvuyiso (Selborne Coll. & Ethekwini Coll.) b 16/12/88, East London. 1.96m. 102kg. FC DEBUT: 2009. PROV CAREER: Sharks XV 2009-10 11-1-0-0-0-5. Griquas 2010 3-0-0-0-0-0. FC RECORD: 14-1-0-0-0-5. RECORD IN 2010: (Griquas, Sharks XV) 11-1-0-0-0-5.

Luus, Nicolaas Johannes (Nico) (Birchleigh HS) b 31/03/77, Klerksdorp. 2.00m. 112kg. Lock. FC DEBUT: 2001. PROV CAREER: Valke 2001-09 134-24-0-0-0-120. Lions 2009 14-0-0-0-0-0. Young Lions 2010 4-0-0-0-0-0. SUPER 14: Lions 2010 7-0-0-0-0-0. FC RECORD: 159-24-0-0-0-120. RECORD IN 2010: (Lions S14, Young Lions) 11-0-0-0-0-0.

M

Maarman, Tertius (Hentie Cilliers HS) b 14/04/87, Port Elizabeth. 1.69m. 79kg. Utility back. FC DEBUT: 2008. PROV CAREER: Griffons 2008-10 28-4-0-0-0-20. FC RECORD: 28-4-0-0-0-20. RECORD IN 2010: (Griffons) 14-2-0-0-0-10.

Maart, Alvandre Graham (Breidbach Sen. Sec. & Dale Coll.) b 09/11/85, King Williams Town. 1.79m. 80kg. Scrumhalf. FC DEBUT: 2009. PROV CAREER: Valke 2009-10 12-1-0-0-0-5. FC RECORD: 12-1-0-0-0-5. RECORD IN 2010: (Valke) 3-0-0-0-0-0.

Mabeta, Mthunzi Karl (Fudge) (Pretoria Boys HS) b 13/06/87, Boston. 1.99m. 102kg. Lock. FC DEBUT: 2007. PROV CAREER: Blue Bulls 2007-10 45-2-0-0-0-10. Blue Bulls XV 2007 1-0-0-0-0-0. SUPER 14: Bulls 2010 2-0-0-0-0-0. FC RECORD: 48-2-0-0-0-10. RECORD IN 2010: (Bulls, Blue Bulls) 20-0-0-0-0-0.

Mafumo, Glen Piet (Ben Vorster HS) b 09/07/1988, Namakgale. 1.90m. 93kg. Flanker. FC DEBUT: 2010. PROV CAREER: Griffons 2010 5-1-0-0-0-5. FC RECORD: 5-1-0-0-0-5. RECORD IN 2010: (Griffons) 5-1-0-0-0-5.

Magaba, Siwiwe Wilmot (Ithembelihle Comp HS) b 30/10/84, Port Elizabeth. 1.76m. 87kg. Centre. FC DEBUT: 2006. PROV CAREER: Elephants 2006,09 27-2-0-0-0-10. Griquas 2007-09 13-0-0-0-0-0. Pumas 2010 13-0-0-0-0-0. FC RECORD: 53-2-0-0-0-10. RECORD IN 2010: (Pumas) 13-0-0-0-0-0.

Maku, Bandise Grey (Dale College) b 24/06/86, King William's Town. 1.87m. 111kg. Hooker. FC DEBUT: 2006. Prov career: Blue Bulls 2006-10 61-3-0-0-0-15. Super 14: Bulls 2008 & 10 19-0-0-0-0-0. Rep honours: SA 2010 Tests: 1-0-0-0-0-0. Tour: 2009,2010 3-1-0-0-0-5. Total: 4-1-0-0-0-5. Emerging Springboks 2007,09 2-0-0-0-0-0. SA U21 2006 3-0-0-0-0-0. FC record: 87-4-0-0-0-20. RECORD IN 2010: (SA, Bulls, Blue Bulls) 24-2-0-0-0-10.

Malgas, Warren Amselm Dimitri (PW Botha HS) b 10/01/86, Oudtshoorn. 1.73m. 65kg. Scrumhalf. FC DEBUT: 2005. PROV CAREER: Eagles 2005-09 43-3-0-0-0-15. Griquas 2010 7-1-1-0-0-7. REP HONOURS: Emerging Springboks 2008 2-0-0-0-0-0. SA U21 2006 5-1-0-0-0-5. SAU19s 2005. FC RECORD: 57-5-1-0-0-27. RECORD IN 2010: (Griquas) 7-1-1-0-0-7.

Mametsa, Sello John (Capricorn HS & Pretoria Tech.) b 10/03/81, Pietersburg. 1.73m. 77kg. Wing. FC DEBUT: 2002. PROV CAREER: Blue Bulls 2002-10 136-71-0-0-0-355. SUPER 14: Bulls 2008 & 10 6-1-0-0-0-5. MISC INFO: ABSA Currie Cup PoY 2003; YPoY nominee 2003. FC RECORD: 142-72-0-0-0-360. RECORD IN 2010: (Bulls, Blue Bulls) 15-7-0-0-0-35.

Mangweni, Siyabonga (Tiger) (Ntsonkotha SS) b 20/06/80, Nxaruni. 1.87m. 80kg. Fullback. FC DEBUT: 2001. PROV CAREER: Bulldogs 2001-05 63-17-29-20-0-203. Griquas 2005-07 22-3-2-3-0-28. Blue Bulls 2008-10 46-15-0-0-1-78. EP Kings 2010 10-2-0-0-0-10. SUPER 14: Stormers 2005 2-0-0-0-0-0. Cheetahs 2007 7-1-0-0-0-5. Bulls 2010 1-0-0-0-0-0. REP HONOURS: SA 'A' 2004 2-0-0-0-0-0. S/Kings 2009 1-0-0-0-0-0. FC RECORD: 154-38-31-23-1-324. RECORD IN 2010: (Bulls, Blue Bulls, EP Kings) 21-5-0-0-0-25.

Manuel, Denzil Bryan John (Waveren SS) b 02/02/78, Tulbagh. 1.87m. 79kgs. Flank. FC DEBUT: 2000. PROV CAREER: Boland 2000 1-0-0-0-0-0; Pumas 2001 & 04-07 95-4-0-0-0-20. Leopards 2002-03 38-7-0-0-0-35. Eagles 2009-10 23-3-0-0-0-15. REP HONOURS: SA U21s 1999. FC RECORD: 157-14-0-0-0-70. RECORD IN 2010: (Eagles) 16-2-0-0-0-10.

Mapoe, Lionel Granton (Fichardtpark HS) b 13/07/88, Port Elizabeth. 1.82m. 84kg. Wing. FC DEBUT: 2008. PROV CAREER: Cheetahs 2008-09 12-6-0-0-0-30. Cheetahs XV 2010 1-0-0-0-0-0. SUPER 14: Cheetahs 2010 5-1-0-0-0-5. MISC INFO: YPOY Nominee 2009. FC RECORD: 18-7-0-0-0-35. RECORD IN 2010: (Cheetahs S14, Cheetahs XV) 6-1-0-0-0-5.

Marais, Conrad (Fish Hoek HS) b 26/04/1989, Walvis Bay. 1.94m. 100kg. Wing. FC DEBUT: 2010. PROV CAREER: Pumas 2010 2-0-0-0-0-0. WP 2010 1-1-0-

0-0-5. FC RECORD: 3-1-0-0-0-5. RECORD IN 2010: (Pumas, WP) 3-1-0-0-0-5.

Marais, Charles Maclean (Paarl Boys HS & UOFS) b 29/08/1988, Paarl. 1.91m. 114kg. Prop. FC DEBUT: 2010. PROV CAREER: Cheetahs 2010 5-0-0-0-0-0. FC RECORD: 5-0-0-0-0-0. RECORD IN 2010: (Cheetahs) 5-0-0-0-0-0.

Marais, Jan Andre (Jandre) (Welkom Gym.) b 14/06/89. 1.97m. 115kg. Lock. FC DEBUT: 2009. PROV CAREER: Sharks XV 2009-10 14-0-0-0-0-0. Sharks Inv XV 2009 1-0-0-0-0-0. FC RECORD: 15-0-0-0-0-0. RECORD IN 2010: (Sharks XV) 8-0-0-0-0-0.

Marais, Sarel Petrus (Paarl Boys HS) b 16/03/1989. 1.84m. 80kg. Wing. PROV CAREER: Leopards 2010 2-3-1-0-0-17. FC RECORD: 2-3-1-0-0-17. RECORD IN 2010: (Leopards) 2-3-1-0-0-17.

Marutlulle, Edgar (Potchefstroom HS) b 20/12/87, Boksburg. 1.77m. 91kg. Hooker. FC DEBUT: 2007. PROV CAREER: Golden Lions 2010 13-1-0-0-0-5. REP HONOURS: SA Students 2007-09 4-0-0-0-0-0. FC RECORD: 17-1-0-0-0-5. RECORD IN 2010: (Golden Lions) 13-1-0-0-0-5.

Marx, Tiaan (Nelspruit HS) b 17/03/86, Nelspruit. 1.86m. 82kg. Flyhalf. FC DEBUT: 2007. PROV CAREER: Leopards 2007 8-1-2-2-0-15. KZN 2008 6-2-6-2-1-31. Pumas 2008-10 40-12-7-8-1-101. FC RECORD: 54-15-15-12-2-147. RECORD IN 2010: (Pumas) 13-2-0-0-0-10.

Matfield, Victor (Pietersburg HS & Univ. of Pretoria) b 11/05/77, Pietersburg. 2.01m. 110kg. Lock. FC DEBUT: 1997. PROV CAREER: Blue Bulls 1998 & 2001-02 & 04-05 & 08-10 52-5-0-0-0-25; Griquas 1999-2000 36-8-0-0-0-40. Blue Bulls XV 1-0-0-0-0-0. SUPER 14: Cats 1999-2000 8-0-0-0-0-0; Bulls 2001-07 & 09-10 101-8-0-0-0-40. REP HONOURS: SA 2000-10 Tests 105-7-0-0-0-35, Tour 4-0-0-0-0-0, Total 109-7-0-0-0-35; SA U23s 2000 5-1-0-0-0-5; SA U21s 1997-98 8-1-0-0-0-5; SA 'A' 2002 1-0-0-0-0-0. S Hemisphere XV 2005 1-0-0-0-0-0. British Barbs. 2009 1-0-0-0-0-0. SA Academy 1995; CW Far North 1994-95. MISC INFO: PoY nominee 2005, 2006, 2007, 2009. IRB PoY nominee 2005, 2010. Holds SA career record for most Tests (105). Holds SA record for most tests as a lock - 105. Locked together with Bakkies Botha in 60 tests (world record). FC RECORD: 323-30-0-0-0-150. RECORD IN 2010: (SA, Bulls, Blue Bulls) 29-3-0-0-0-15. OTHER FC: Toulon, France 2007-08 15-1-0-0-0-5.

Mathee, Rudi (Otto du Plessis HS) b 25/02/86, Port Elizabeth. 1.95m. 108kg. Lock. FC DEBUT: 2006. PROV CAREER: Lions 2006-07 6-1-0-0-0-5. Leopards

2008-09 26-6-0-0-0-30. Cheetahs 2010 6-2-0-0-0-10. Griffons 2010 6-2-0-0-0-10. REP HONOURS: SA Students 2007 1-1-0-0-0-5. Royal XV 2009 1-0-0-0-0-0. FC RECORD: 46-12-0-0-0-60. RECORD IN 2010: (Cheetahs, Griffons) 12-4-0-0-0-20.

Matyeshana, Dumisani (Selborne Coll.) b 11/02/81, Mdansane. 1.85m. 86kg. Wing. FC DEBUT: 2004. PROV CAREER: Bulldogs 2004-06,09 44-13-0-0-0-65. Leopards 2007 & 10 31-13-0-0-0-65. KZN 2007-08 4-0-0-0-0-0. KZN XV 2007 1-0-0-0-0-0. FC RECORD: 80-26-0-0-0-130. RECORD IN 2010: (Leopards) 23-8-0-0-0-40.

Mayaba, Siphephelo (Pinetowen Boys HS & Unisa) b 31/05/87, Pietermaritzburg. 1.81m. 120kg. Prop. FC DEBUT: 2009. PROV CAREER: Sharks XV 2009 2-0-0-0-0-0. EP Kings 2010 2-0-0-0-0-0. FC RECORD: 4-0-0-0-0-0. RECORD IN 2010: (EP Kings) 2-0-0-0-0-0.

Mbiyozo, Mpho Mzukisi (Grey HS, Port Elizabeth & UCT) b 07/02/83, Lusikisiki. 1.82m. 94kg. Flank. FC DEBUT: 2005. PROV CAREER: WP 2005-06 18-2-0-0-0-10. Boland 2008 1-0-0-0-0-0. EP Kings 2010 4-0-0-0-0-0. REP HONOURS: S/Kings 2009 1-1-0-0-0-5. SA Sevens 2008. FC RECORD: 24-3-0-0-0-15. RECORD IN 2010: (EP Kings) 4-0-0-0-0-0.

Mboto, Vuyo . Wing. FC DEBUT: 2010. PROV CAREER: Bulldogs 2010 6-1-0-0-0-5. FC RECORD: 6-1-0-0-0-5. RECORD IN 2010: (Bulldogs) 6-1-0-0-0-5.

McBean, Baldwin (Cillié HS) b 08/03/82, Port Elizabeth 1.80m. 87kg. Wing. FC DEBUT: 2005. PROV CAREER: Elephants 2005-06 31-13-0-0-0-65. Griquas 2007 11-2-0-0-0-10. Eagles 2008-10 47-16-0-0-0-80. REP HONOURS: SA Sevens 2007. CW EP 2000. FC RECORD: 89-31-0-0-0-155. RECORD IN 2010: (Eagles) 21-11-0-0-0-55.

Mcguigan, Byron (Milnerton HS) b 20/08/1989, Walvis Bay. 1.85m. 85kg. Centre. FC DEBUT: 2010. PROV CAREER: Bulldogs 2010 7-1-0-0-0-5. FC RECORD: 7-1-0-0-0-5. RECORD IN 2010: (Bulldogs) 7-1-0-0-0-5.

McLeod, Charl (Wonderboom HS) b 05/08/83, Johannesburg. 1.79m. 82kg. Scrumhalf. ›› FC debut: 2005. Prov career: WP 2005-06 12-1-0-0-0-5. Lions 2007 6-3-0-0-0-15. Valke 2007 11-2-0-0-0-10. KZN 2008-10 31-7-0-0-0-35. Sharks XV 2008-10 19-7-0-0-0-35. Sharks Inv XV 2009-10 2-2-0-0-0-10. Lions XV 2007 1-0-0-0-0-0. Super 14: Sharks 2009-10 6-0-0-0-0-0. Rep honours: SA Tour 2010: 1-0-0-0-0-0. FC record: 89-22-0-0-0-110. RECORD IN 2010: (SA, Sharks, KZN, Sharks XV, Sharks Inv XV) 28-8-0-0-0-40.

Meier, Ashley (Selborne Coll.) b 26/11/1975. 1.80m. 102kg. Prop. FC DEBUT: 2010. PROV CAREER:

Bulldogs 2010 1-0-0-0-0-0. FC RECORD: 1-0-0-0-0-0. RECORD IN 2010: (Bulldogs) 1-0-0-0-0-0.

Mellet, Morne Melvin (Dr. EG Jansen HS) b 02/10/1988, Boksburg. 1.87m. 115kg. Prop. FC DEBUT: 2010. PROV CAREER: Blue Bulls 2010 5-1-0-0-0-5. FC RECORD: 5-1-0-0-0-5. RECORD IN 2010: (Blue Bulls) 5-1-0-0-0-5.

Mentz, Hendrik (Henno) (Ermelo HS) b 25/09/79, Ermelo. 1.85m. 88kg. Wing. FC DEBUT: 2001. PROV CAREER: Leopards 2001-03 33-22-0-0-0-110. KZN 2003-05,07-08 65-31-0-0-0-155. Lions 2009 5-1-0-0-0-5. Young Lions 2010 7-3-0-0-0-15. SUPER 14: Sharks 2004-06 & 08 27-9-0-0-0-45. Lions 2009 10-6-0-0-0-30. REP HONOURS: SA Tests: 2004 2-0-0-0-0-0. MISC INFO: Shares Leopards record for most tries in a CC match (3). Brother of Griquas wing MJ Mentz. Son of former SE-Tvl wing and current Pumas President Hein Mentz. Grandson of Moolman Mentz (E-Tvl & N-Tvl). FC RECORD: 149-72-0-0-0-360. RECORD IN 2010: (Young Lions) 7-3-0-0-0-15.

Meslane, Dumisane Kelvin (Ithembelhle HS) b 11/05/85, Port Elizabeth. 1.86m. 92kg. Flanker. FC DEBUT: 2008. PROV CAREER: Bulldogs 2008-10 42-7-0-0-0-35. FC RECORD: 42-7-0-0-0-35. RECORD IN 2010: (Bulldogs) 15-3-0-0-0-15.

Methula, Mbuso Petros (Glenwood HS) b 10/10/83, Durban. 1.80m. 110kg. Prop. FC DEBUT: 2004. PROV CAREER: Elephants 2007-08 39-1-0-0-0-5. Griffons 2009-10 19-0-0-0-0-0. REP HONOURS: SA U21 2004 3-0-0-0-0-0. FC RECORD: 61-1-0-0-0-5. RECORD IN 2010: (Griffons) 6-0-0-0-0-0.

Meyer, Jaco (Jan Fouche HS) b 01/03/1985, Bloemfontein. 1.76m. 83kg. Wing. FC DEBUT: 2010. PROV CAREER: Griffons 2010 10-2-0-0-0-10. FC RECORD: 10-2-0-0-0-10. RECORD IN 2010: (Griffons) 10-2-0-0-0-10.

Meyer, Pieter Gideon Joubert (Waterkloof HS) b 04/09/87, Newcastle. 1.85m. 98kg. Flank. FC DEBUT: 2007. PROV CAREER: Blue Bulls 2007-08 8-0-0-0-0-0. Blue Bulls XV 2007 1-0-0-0-0-0. Pumas 2009-10 10-1-0-0-0-5. FC RECORD: 19-1-0-0-0-5. RECORD IN 2010: (Pumas) 2-0-0-0-0-0.

Meyer, Steve (Kearsney Coll.) b 21/03/84, Durban. 1.81m. 84kgs. Flyhalf. FC DEBUT: 2004. PROV CAREER: KZN 2004-06 & 10 6-1-4-1-0-16. Sharks XV 2004-06 & 10 19-3-34-14-0-125. Sharks Inv XV 2010 1-0-0-0-0-0. MISC INFO: Perpignan (Fra) 2006-07. FC RECORD: 26-4-38-15-0-141. RECORD IN 2010: (KZN, Sharks Inv XV) 5-1-0-0-0-5.

Meyer, Tian Carel (Westville HS) b 20/09/1988, Pi-

etermaritzburg. 1.76m. 71kg. Scrumhalf/Centre. FC DEBUT: 2010. PROV CAREER: Pumas 2010 19-6-0-0-0-30. FC RECORD: 19-6-0-0-0-30. RECORD IN 2010: (Pumas) 19-6-0-0-0-30.

Mhlanga, Alec. (Ben Vorster HS) b 24/04/1989, Tzaneen. 1.82m. 80kg. Wing. FC DEBUT: 2010. PROV CAREER: Cheetahs 2010 5-1-0-0-0-5. FC RECORD: 5-1-0-0-0-5. RECORD IN 2010: (Cheetahs) 5-1-0-0-0-5.

Mhlobiso, Luvuyo (Daniel Pienaar HS, Uitenhage) b 05/06/86, Port Elizabeth. 1.80m. 95kg. Wing. FC DEBUT: 2006. PROV CAREER: Blue Bulls 2006-08 10-2-0-0-0-10. Elephants 2009 3-0-0-0-0-0. Bulldogs 2010 6-1-0-0-0-5. EP Inv XV 2010 1-0-0-0-0-0. REP HONOURS: SA U19 2005 FC RECORD: 20-3-0-0-0-15. RECORD IN 2010: (Bulldogs, EP Inv XV) 7-1-0-0-0-5.

Micklewood, Christopher Ian (Westville Boys HS & Varsity Coll.) b 14/03/1987, Durban. 1.86m. 90kg. Fullback. FC DEBUT: 2010. PROV CAREER: Boland 2010 4-0-2-0-0-4. FC RECORD: 4-0-2-0-0-4. RECORD IN 2010: (Boland) 4-0-2-0-0-4.

Minnie, Derick Johannes (Marais Viljoen) b 29/10/86, Alberton. 1.86m. 95kg. Flank. FC DEBUT: 2006. PROV CAREER: Golden Lions 2006-10 31-9-0-0-0-45. Young Lions 2006-09 20-4-0-0-0-20. Lions XV 2007 1-0-0-0-0-0. SUPER 14: Lions 2010 13-2-0-0-0-10. FC RECORD: 65-15-0-0-0-75. RECORD IN 2010: (Lions S14, Golden Lions) 26-5-0-0-0-25.

Mjekevu, Wandile Gabada (KES & UJ) b 07/01/1991, Houghton. 1.90m. 87kg. Wing. FC DEBUT: 2010. PROV CAREER:. SUPER 14: Lions 2010 10-4-0-0-0-20. FC RECORD: 10-4-0-0-0-20. RECORD IN 2010: (Lions S14) 10-4-0-0-0-20.

Mkaza, Yongama (Ebenezer Majombozi HS) b 09/05/75, East London. 1.78m. 82kg. Scrumhalf. FC DEBUT: 2003. PROV CAREER: Bulldogs 2003 & 06-10 62-5-0-0-0-25. Elephants 2005 7-0-0-0-0-0. FC RECORD: 69-5-0-0-0-25. RECORD IN 2010: (Bulldogs) 15-2-0-0-0-10.

Mkhafu, Khwezilokusa (Kwezi) (Lebogang HS) b 17/06/1988, Engcobo. 1.77m. 97kg. Hooker. FC DEBUT: 2010. PROV CAREER: Bulldogs 2010 14-0-0-0-0-0. FC RECORD: 14-0-0-0-0-0. RECORD IN 2010: (Bulldogs) 14-0-0-0-0-0.

Mkokeli, Thembani Moeren (Msobumvu SSS) b 12/03/84, East London. 1.78m. 74kg. Flyhalf. FC DEBUT: 2003. PROV CAREER: Bulldogs 2003-06 & 08-10 64-12-0-1-0-63. REP HONOURS: SA U19 2003. SA Schools 2001-02. CW Border 2001-02. FC RECORD: 64-12-0-1-0-63. RECORD IN 2010: (Bulldogs) 18-6-0-0-0-30.

Mkona, Sokahana (Dale Coll.) b 08/04/86, King Williams Town. 1.86m. 98kg. Flank. FC DEBUT: 2007. PROV CAREER: Bulldogs 2008-10 23-1-0-0-0-5. REP HONOURS: SA Students 2007-09 3-1-0-0-0-5. FC RECORD: 26-2-0-0-0-10. RECORD IN 2010: (Bulldogs) 7-0-0-0-0-0.

Mntunjani, Bonga (Hlumani HS) b 07/04/83, Komga. 1.92m. 92kgs. Flank. FC DEBUT: 2006. PROV CAREER: Bulldogs 2006,09-10 30-4-0-0-0-20. FC RECORD: 30-4-0-0-0-20. RECORD IN 2010: (Bulldogs) 17-4-0-0-0-20.

Mockford, Bradley Peter (Capricorn HS) b 24/11/83, Polokwane. 2.03m. 115kg. Lock. FC DEBUT: 2008. PROV CAREER: Boland 2008 13-1-0-0-0-5. Lions 2009 1-0-0-0-0-0. Leopards 2009-10 16-0-0-0-0-0. FC RECORD: 30-1-0-0-0-5. RECORD IN 2010: (Leopards) 12-0-0-0-0-0.

Mofu, Zolani (Jongile Nompondo HS, Stutterheim) b 25/01/81, Stutterheim. 1.78m. 89kg. Flank. FC DEBUT: 2002. Prov career : Bulldogs 2002-06 60-8-0-0-0-40. Boland 2007-09 50-3-0-0-0-15. EP Kings 2010 10-0-0-0-0-0. EP Inv XV 2010 1-0-0-0-0-0. REP HONOURS: Emerging Springboks 2008 3-0-0-0-0-0. SA Sevens 2005-06. SA 'A' 2004 3-0-0-0-0-0. FC RECORD: 127-11-0-0-0-55. RECORD IN 2010: (EP Kings, EP Inv XV) 11-0-0-0-0-0.

Mokuena, Jonathan (Voortrekker HS, Kenilworth & Cape Tech.) b 29/05/81, Cape Town. 1.87m. 98kg. Flank. FC DEBUT: 2001. PROV CAREER: WP 2002-03 5-0-0-0-0-0. Leopards 2004-06 55-19-0-0-0-95. Cheetahs 2007 8-2-0-0-0-10. Griffons 2008 13-0-0-0-0-0. Griquas 2009 24-1-0-0-0-5. Golden Lions 2010 2-0-0-0-0-0. Young Lions 2010 5-0-0-0-0-0. SUPER 14: Lions 2010 3-0-0-0-0-0. REP HONOURS: Emerging Springboks 2007 3-0-0-0-0-0. Royal XV 2009 1-0-0-0-0-0. SA Sevens 2005-07. SA U21s 2001 3-0-0-0-0-0. SA U19 2000. MISC INFO: VC PoY 2005. Vodacom Cup POY 2009. FC RECORD: 123-22-0-0-0-110. RECORD IN 2010: (Lions S14, Golden Lions, Young Lions) 10-0-0-0-0-0.

Molefe, Thabang (Kimberley Boys' HS & Tshwane Univ. of Technology) b 06/06/1984, Taung. 1.80m. 96kg. Centre. FC DEBUT: 2005. PROV CAREER: Blue Bulls 2005 5-1-0-0-0-5. Lions 2006-08 20-2-0-0-0-10. Lions XV 2007 1-0-0-0-0-0. Griffons 2009-10 22-5-0-0-0-25. Griquas 2009 2-0-0-0-0-0. REP HONOURS: SA U21 2005 4-0-0-0-0-0. SA Students 2005 1-0-0-0-0-0. MISC INFO: IRB U21 PoY nominee 2005. FC RECORD: 55-8-0-0-0-40. RECORD IN 2010: (Griffons) 13-2-0-0-0-10.

Moller, Jan Daniel (JD) (Paarl BHS, Stellenbosch University) b 22/10/82, Carnarvon. 1.88m. 115kg. Prop. FC DEBUT: 2003. PROV CAREER: WP 2003-07,09-10 80-3-0-0-0-15. SUPER 14: Stormers 2005-10 53-0-0-0-0-0. REP HONOURS: SA U21 2003 1-0-0-0-0-0. WP XV 2006. SA Schools 2000. CW WP 2000. FC RECORD: 135-3-0-0-0-15. RECORD IN 2010: (Stormers, WP) 24-0-0-0-0-0.

Moore, Wouter (Despatch SS) b 15/05/84, Despatch. 2.04m. 109kg. Lock. FC DEBUT: 2004. PROV CAREER: KZN 2006-07 16-3-0-0-0-15. Valke 2008 13-0-0-0-0-0. Blue Bulls 2008 1-0-0-0-0-0. Lions 2009 5-0-0-0-0-0. Young Lions 2010 7-1-0-0-0-5. SUPER 14: Lions 2010 1-0-0-0-0-0. REP HONOURS: SA U21 2004 4-0-0-0-0-0. SA U19 2003. CW EP 2002. MISC INFO: Son of former EP lock **Frans Moore**. FC RECORD: 47-4-0-0-0-20. RECORD IN 2010: (Lions S14, Young Lions) 8-1-0-0-0-5.

Morrison, Randall Anthony (Grens HS) b 12/02/1984, East London. 1.86m. 88kg. Lock. FC DEBUT: 2010. PROV CAREER: Young Lions 2010 1-0-0-0-0-0. FC RECORD: 1-0-0-0-0-0. RECORD IN 2010: (Young Lions) 1-0-0-0-0-0.

Mostert, Gerhard (Rustenburg HS & PUK) b 04/10/84, Rustenburg. 1.99m. 103kg. Lock. FC DEBUT: 2004. PROV CAREER: Leopards 2004-05 11-0-0-0-0-0. Lions 2006 & 08 14-0-0-0-0-0. Lions XV 2008 1-0-0-0-0-0. KZN 2010 2-0-0-0-0-0. SUPER 14: Cats 2006 3-0-0-0-0-0. Lions 2008-09 23-0-0-0-0-0. Sharks 2010 1-0-0-0-0-0. REP HONOURS: SA U21 2005 5-0-0-0-0-0. SA Students 2005 1-0-0-0-0-0. FC RECORD: 61-0-0-0-0-0. RECORD IN 2010: (Sharks, KZN) 3-0-0-0-0-0.

Mostert, Nicol (Waterkloof HS) b 05/02/85, Roodepoort. 1.94m. 105kg. Lock. FC DEBUT: 2008. PROV CAREER: Pumas 2008-10 26-2-0-0-0-10. FC RECORD: 26-2-0-0-0-10. RECORD IN 2010: (Pumas) 2-0-0-0-0-0.

Mostert, Sybrand Jacobus (Grey Coll.) b 26/08/88, Duiwelskloof. 1.87m. 96kgs. Lock. FC DEBUT: 2008. PROV CAREER: Cheetahs 2008 1-0-0-0-0-0. Griffons 2010 5-0-0-0-0-0. FC RECORD: 6-0-0-0-0-0. RECORD IN 2010: (Griffons) 5-0-0-0-0-0.

Mtawarira, Tendai (Beast) (Peterhouse) b 01/07/85, Harare. 1.88m. 112kg. Prop. ›› FC debut: 2006. Prov career: KZN 2006-10 31-2-0-0-0-10. Sharks XV 2006-08 7-0-0-0-0-0. Sharks Inv XV 2010 1-1-0-0-0-5. Super 14: Sharks 2007-10 50-0-0-0-0-0. Rep honours: SA 2008-10 Tests 26-1-0-0-0-5. SA Tour 2010: 1-0-0-0-0-0. Total: 27-1-0-0-0-5. British Barbs. 2009 1-0-0-0-0-0.

Misc info: PoY nominee 2008. YPoY nominee 2008. FC record:117-4-0-0-0-20. RECORD IN 2010: (SA, Sharks, KZN, Sharks Inv XV) 27-2-0-0-0-10.

Mtimka, Lonwabo Lwethu Jackson (Black) (Dale Coll.) b 27/06/81, Zwelitsha, King Williams Town. 1.80m. 108kg. Prop. FC DEBUT: 2001. PROV CAREER: Bulldogs 2001-10 109-3-0-0-0-15. E/Cape XV 2008 1-0-0-0-0-0. REP HONOURS: SA U19 2000. SA Schools 1999. FC RECORD: 110-3-0-0-0-15. RECORD IN 2010: (Bulldogs) 9-0-0-0-0-0.

Mtyanda, Lubabalo (Cowan HS) b 19/03/86, Port Elizabeth. 1.99m. 116kgs. Lock. FC DEBUT: 2006. PROV CAREER: Elephants 2006 13-0-0-0-0-0. Lions 2007 4-0-0-0-0-0. Eagles 2010 31-4-0-0-0-20. FC RECORD: 48-4-0-0-0-20. RECORD IN 2010: (Eagles) 16-3-0-0-0-15.

Mulamba, Patrick (Bracken HS) b 03/05/82, Kinshasha. 1.82m. 105kg. Prop. FC DEBUT: 2008. PROV CAREER: Bulldogs 2008-09 27-3-0-0-0-15. EP Inv XV 2010 1-0-0-0-0-0. FC RECORD: 28-3-0-0-0-15. RECORD IN 2010: (EP Inv XV) 1-0-0-0-0-0.

Muller, Gert Hendrik (Gert) (THS Vereeniging) b 05/02/86, Alberton. 1.86m. 110kg. Prop. FC DEBUT: 2006. PROV CAREER: Lions 2006 & 08-09 19-1-0-0-0-5. Young Lions 2006 & 08 & 10 19-3-0-0-0-15. Lions XV 2008 1-0-0-0-0-0. SUPER 14: Lions 2009-10 17-0-0-0-0-0. FC RECORD: 56-4-0-0-0-20. RECORD IN 2010: (Lions S14, Young Lions) 9-1-0-0-0-5.

Muller, Gysbert Johannes (Johann) (Oakdale) b 06/01/80, Mossel Bay. 2.00m. 106kg. Lock. FC DEBUT: 2001. PROV CAREER: KZN 2001-06 & 08-09 65-0-0-0-0-0. Sharks XV 2001-08 19-1-0-0-0-5. SUPER 14: Sharks 2002-10 82-2-0-0-0-10. REP HONOURS: SA 2006-07 & 09 Tests: 23-0-0-0-0-0. Tour: 2007 2-0-0-0-0-0. Total: 25-0-0-0-0-0. SA XV 2006 1-0-0-0-0-0. British Barbarians 2008 1-0-0-0-0-0. FC RECORD: 194-3-0-0-0-15. RECORD IN 2010: (Sharks) 8-0-0-0-0-0.

Muller, Martin Dirk (Bishops HS, Cape Town Univ.) b 23/03/1988, Cape Town. 1.98m. 105kg. Lock. FC DEBUT: 2009. PROV CAREER: WP 2009-10 22-1-0-0-0-5. SUPER 14: Stormers 2009 3-0-0-0-0-0. REP HONOURS: SA Students 2009 2-0-0-0-0-0. FC RECORD: 27-1-0-0-0-5. RECORD IN 2010: (WP) 12-0-0-0-0-0.

Muller, Reg-Hack (Marais Viljoen HS) b 06/03/86, Johannesburg. 1.89m. 104kg. Eighthman. FC DEBUT: 2007. PROV CAREER: KZN 2007 3-0-0-0-0-0. Valke 2008-10 40-13-0-0-0-65. FC RECORD: 43-13-0-0-0-65. RECORD IN 2010: (Valke) 12-2-0-0-0-10.

Murray, Waylon Michael (Westville Boys' High) b 27/04/86, Durban. 1.90m. 105kg. Centre. FC DEBUT: 2005. PROV CAREER: KZN 2005-09 52-18-0-0-0-90.

Sharks XV 2005-10 8-0-0-0-0-0. Golden Lions 2010 14-4-0-0-0-20. SUPER 14: Sharks 2006-10 41-5-0-0-0-25. REP HONOURS: SA Tests: 2007 3-0-0-0-0-0. Tour: 1-0-0-0-0-0. Total: 4-0-0-0-0-0. SA U21 2006 5-3-0-0-0-15. FC RECORD: 124-30-0-0-0-150. RECORD IN 2010: (Sharks, Sharks XV, Golden Lions) 23-4-0-0-0-20.

Mvovo, Lwazi Ncedo (Maria Louw HS) b 03/06/86, Unthatha. 1.81m. 84kg. Wing. FC DEBUT: 2007. Prov career: KZN 2007-10 30-15-0-0-0-75. Sharks XV 2007-10 20-9-0-0-0-45. Sharks Inv XV 2009 1-0-0-0-0-0. Super 14: Sharks 2010 5-1-0-0-0-5. Rep honours: SA 2010 Tests: 2-1-0-0-0-5. SA Tour 2010: 1-0-0-0-0-0. Total: 3-1-0-0-0-5. FC record: 59-26-0-0-0-130. RECORD IN 2010: (SA, Sharks, KZN, Sharks XV) 25-14-0-0-0-70.

Mxoli, Sangoni Mpumelelo (DHS & Univ. of KZN) b 08/01/85, Durban. 1.83m. 110kg. Prop. FC DEBUT: 2004. PROV CAREER: KZN 2005-07 21-0-0-0-0-0. Valke 2007 8-0-0-0-0-0. Blue Bulls 2008-09 8-0-0-0-0-0. EP Kings 2009-10 21-2-0-0-0-10. EP Inv XV 2010 1-0-0-0-0-0. REP HONOURS: Emerging Springboks 2007-08 3-0-0-0-0-0. SA U21 2004-06 15-4-0-0-0-20. SA U19 2003-04. SA Schools 2002-03. CW KZN 2002-03. FC RECORD: 77-6-0-0-0-30. RECORD IN 2010: (EP Kings, EP Inv XV) 13-1-0-0-0-5.

Mxunyelwa, Buhle (Stirling HS) b 25/06/86, East London. 1.87m. 129kg. Prop. FC DEBUT: 2008. PROV CAREER: Bulldogs 2008-09 19-2-0-0-0-10. E/Cape XV 2008 1-0-0-0-0-0. WP 2010 8-0-0-0-0-0. MISC INFO: Brother of Siya Mxunyelwa. FC RECORD: 28-2-0-0-0-10. RECORD IN 2010: (WP) 8-0-0-0-0-0.

Myburgh, Johan Christoffel (Grens HS) b 19/07/87, Elliot. 1.90m. 92kg.Flyhalf. FC DEBUT: 2007. PROV CAREER: Griffons 2007 & 10 12-0-28-15-0-101. Cheetahs 2008 7-0-16-11-1-68. FC RECORD: 19-0-44-26-1-169. RECORD IN 2010: (Griffons) 11-0-27-14-0-96.

Myburgh, Pieter Abraham (Paul Roos Gym) b 10/01/86, Windhoek. 1.88m. 96kg. Flanker. FC DEBUT: 2005. PROV CAREER: WP 2005,07-10 42-6-0-0-0-30. SUPER 14: Stormers 2008 5-0-0-0-0-0. REP HONOURS: SA U19s 2005. FC RECORD: 47-6-0-0-0-30. RECORD IN 2010 (WP) 13-3-0-0-0-15.

Myburgh, Pieter Stephanus (Hopetown HS) b 21/05/1988, Bloemfontein. 1.82m. 86kg. Flyhalf. FC DEBUT: 2010. PROV CAREER: Griffons 2010 2-0-1-3-0-11. FC RECORD: 2-0-1-3-0-11. RECORD IN 2010: (Griffons) 2-0-1-3-0-11.

N

Naqelevuki, Sireli (Lelean Memorial HS) b 30/09/80, Suva, Fiji. 1.91m. 113kg. Utility Back. FC DEBUT: 2006. PROV CAREER: WP 2006-09 29-19-0-0-0-95. SUPER

14: Stormers 2008-10 36-11-0-0-0-55. REP HONOURS: Fiji Sevens (2005-06). SA FC RECORD: 65-30-0-0-0-150. RECORD IN 2010: (Stormers) 11-3-0-0-0-15.

Naude, Jacob Johannes (Japie) (Diamantveld HS) b 02/03/88, Kimberley. 1.74m. 85kg. Flyhalf. FC DEBUT: 2009. PROV CAREER: Bulldogs 2009 1-0-0-0-0-0. Valke 2010 7-0-5-1-0-13. FC RECORD: 8-0-5-1-0-13. RECORD IN 2010: (Valke) 7-0-5-1-0-13.

Ndlovu, Sikholiwe (Northwood Boys HS) b 13/02/85. 1.80m. 90kg. Flank. FC DEBUT: 2007. PROV CAREER: KZN 2007-10 12-1-0-0-0-5. Sharks XV 2007-10 15-3-0-0-0-15. KZN XV 2007 1-0-0-0-0-0. SUPER 14: Sharks 2009 5-0-0-0-0-0. FC RECORD: 33-4-0-0-0-20. RECORD IN 2010: (KZN, Sharks XV) 11-1-0-0-0-5.

Ndungane, Akona Zilindlovu (Hudson Park HS, East London) b 20/02/81, Umtata. 1.83m. 86kg. Wing. FC DEBUT: 2003. PROV CAREER: Elephants 2003 13-6-0-0-0-30. Bulldogs 2004-05 17-14-0-0-0-70. Blue Bulls 2005-06 & 08-10 26-15-0-0-0-75. SUPER 14: Bulls 2005-09 64-24-0-0-0-120. REP HONOURS: SA 2006-07 Tests: 11-1-0-0-0-5. Tour: 2007 2-0-0-0-0-0. Total: 13-1-0-0-0-5. SA 'A' 2004 1-3-0-0-0-15. SA Sevens 2004. MISC INFO: Holds Border record for most CC tries in a season (10). Twin Brother of Natal Sharks wing Odwa Ndungane. FC RECORD: 134-63-0-0-0-315. RECORD IN 2010: (Blue Bulls) 1-1-0-0-0-5.

Ndungane, Odwa Mzuzo (Hudson Park HS & Eastern Cape Tech.) b 20/02/81, Umtata. 1.83m. 85kg. Wing. ›› FC debut: 2000. Prov career: Bulldogs 2000-03 49-25-0-0-0-125. Blue Bulls 2004 2-0-0-0-0-0. KZN 2005-10 53-19-1-0-0-97. Sharks XV 2005-08 2-0-0-0-0-0. Super 14: Bulls 2004 10-3-0-0-0-15. Sharks 2005-10 63-19-0-0-0-95. Rep honours: SA 2008-10 Tests: 7-2-0-0-0-10. Tour: 2009,2010 3-1-0-0-0-5. Total: 10-3-0-0-0-15. SA 'A' 2004 2-2-0-0-0-10. Emerging Springboks 2007 2-0-0-0-0-0. SA U21 2002 1-0-0-0-0-0. Misc info: Twin brother of Springbok and Blue Bulls wing Akona Ndungane. FC record: 193-71-1-0-0-357. RECORD IN 2010: (SA, Sharks, KZN) 25-12-0-0-0-60.

Ndungane, Sibulele (Hudson HS) b 16/02/1985. 1.82m. 85kg. Wing. FC DEBUT: 2010. PROV CAREER: Bulldogs 2010 5-0-0-0-0-0. FC RECORD: 5-0-0-0-0-0. RECORD IN 2010: (Bulldogs) 5-0-0-0-0-0.

Nel, Brett Anthony (Port Rex HS) b 03/12/86, East London. 1.81m. 113kg. Prop. FC DEBUT: 2007. PROV CAREER: Bulldogs 2007-08 24-1-0-0-0-5. Pumas 2009-10 7-1-0-0-0-5. FC RECORD: 31-2-0-0-0-10. RECORD IN 2010: (Pumas) 3-0-0-0-0-0.

Nel, Japie (Goudveld HS) b 20/11/82, Welkom. 1.90m. 105kg. Wing. FC DEBUT: 2005. PROV CAREER:

Griffons 2005-07 34-8-0-0-0-40. Leopards 2008-10 35-4-0-0-0-20. FC RECORD: 69-12-0-0-0-60. RECORD IN 2010: (Leopards) 5-0-0-0-0-0.

Nel, Willem Petrus (Drostdy THS, Worcester) b 30/04/86, Loeriesfontein. 1.80m. 92kg. Prop. FC DEBUT: 2008. PROV CAREER: WP 2008 4-0-0-0-0-0. Boland 2008 11-1-0-0-0-5. Cheetahs 2009-10 40-10-0-0-0-50. Cheetahs XV 2010 1-0-0-0-0-0. SUPER 14: Cheetahs 2009-10 15-2-0-0-0-10. REP HONOURS: British Barbs. 2009 1-0-0-0-0-0. FC RECORD: 72-13-0-0-0-65. RECORD IN 2010: (Cheetahs S14, Cheetahs, Cheetahs XV) 28-6-0-0-0-30.

Nell, Darron Paul (Muir Coll.) b 08/03/80, Uitenhage. 1.94m. 108kg. Eighthman. FC DEBUT: 2002. PROV CAREER: Cheetahs 2002-08 66-11-0-0-0-55. EP Kings 2010 9-3-0-0-0-15. SUPER 14: Cheetahs 2007-08 10-2-0-0-0-10. REP HONOURS: S/Kings 2009 1-0-0-0-0-0. FC RECORD: 86-16-0-0-0-80. RECORD IN 2010: (EP Kings) 9-3-0-0-0-15.

Nelson, Norman Tsimba (Patensie HS) b 10/08/83, Patensie. 1.75m. 81kg. Wing. FC DEBUT: 2006. PROV CAREER: EP Kings 2006-08 & 10 68-41-0-0-0-205. E/Cape XV 2008 1-0-0-0-0-0. Eagles 2009 20-15-1-0-0-77. MISC INFO: ACC First Division PoY 2010, FC RECORD: 89-56-1-0-0-282. RECORD IN 2010: (EP Kings) 20-11-0-0-0-55.

Nepgen, Jaco b 03/01/86. 1.98m. 103kg. Lock. FC DEBUT: 2008. Prov caree: Griquas 2010 8-0-0-0-0-0. REP HONOURS: SA Students 2008-09 3-1-0-0-0-5. FC RECORD: 11-1-0-0-0-5. RECORD IN 2010: (Griquas) 8-0-0-0-0-0.

Newman, Morgan Ram (Bishops) b 05/02/86, Cape Town. 1.79m. 90kg. Centre. FC DEBUT: 2006. PROV CAREER: WP 2006-10 59-11-11-5-0-92. SUPER 14: Stormers 2009 3-0-0-0-0-0. REP HONOURS: Emerging Springboks 2008-09 4-0-2-2-0-10. SA U21 2006 1-0-0-0-0-0. FC RECORD: 67-11-13-7-0-102. RECORD IN 2010: (WP) 7-0-0-0-0-0.

Ngidi, Thulani Sphamandla (Nhlanhlayethu HS) b 11/01/1986, Durban. 1.74m. 106kg. Prop. FC DEBUT: 2010. PROV CAREER: Valke 2010 11-0-0-0-0-0. FC RECORD: 11-0-0-0-0-0. RECORD IN 2010: (Valke) 11-0-0-0-0-0.

Nhlapo, Sabelo (Highlands North Boys HS) b 17/12/88, Johannesburg. 1.95m. 106kg. Prop. FC DEBUT: 2009. PROV CAREER: Sharks XV 2009-10 11-0-0-0-0-0. FC RECORD: 11-0-0-0-0-0. RECORD IN 2010: (Sharks XV) 4-0-0-0-0-0.

Noble, Dusty Clint (General Hertzog HS) b 30/04/84, Stellenbosch. 1.75m. 70kg. Wing. FC DEBUT: 2005.

PROV CAREER: KZN 2005-07 20-7-0-0-0-35. KZN XV 2007 1-2-0-0-0-10. Lions 2008-09 19-5-0-0-0-25. Young Lions 2009 7-2-0-0-0-10. SUPER 14: Sharks 2006 3-0-0-0-0-0. Lions 2008-10 16-1-0-0-0-5. REP HONOURS: SA Sevens 2006-07. MISC INFO: Son of former WP-League utility back Aubrey Noble. FC RECORD: 66-17-0-0-0-85. RECORD IN 2010: (Lions S14) 1-0-0-0-0-0.

Noble, Howard Gerald (Cloetesville HS) b 08/11/85, Cape Town. 1.79m. 82kg. Wing. FC DEBUT: 2007. PROV CAREER: KZN 2007 2-0-0-0-0-0. KZN XV 2007 1-2-0-0-0-10. Griffons 2008 11-7-0-0-0-35. Cheetahs 2008-09 12-3-0-0-0-15. EP Kings 2009-10 17-12-0-0-0-60. EP Inv XV 2010 1-0-0-0-0-0. Bulldogs 2010 4-4-0-0-0-20. REP HONOURS: Emerging Springboks 2007-08 3-2-0-0-0-10. SA Sevens 2007. FC RECORD: 51-30-0-0-0-150. RECORD IN 2010: (EP Kings, Bulldogs, EP Inv XV) 12-9-0-0-0-45.

Nodikida, Phumlani (Qaphelani HS) b 04/12/78, Port Elizabeth. 1.83m. 110kg. Prop. FC DEBUT: 2006. PROV CAREER: EP Kings 2006 & 08-10 72-2-0-0-0-10. E/Cape XV 2008 2-0-0-0-0-0. EP Inv XV 2010 1-0-0-0-0-0. Griquas 2007 3-0-0-0-0-0. FC RECORD: 78-2-0-0-0-10. RECORD IN 2010: (EP Kings, EP Inv XV) 16-1-0-0-0-5.

Nogampula, Ayanda Maxwell (Moses Mabhida HS) b 14/11/84, Kirkwood. 1.88m. 118kg. Prop. FC DEBUT: 2009. PROV CAREER: EP Kings 2009-10 14-0-0-0-0-0. FC RECORD: 14-0-0-0-0-0. RECORD IN 2010: (EP Kings) 5-0-0-0-0-0.

Nokwe, Jongikhaya Lutric (Jongi) (Kwamfundo SS) b 30/12/81, Ngxalawe, Ciskei. 1.82m. 80kg. Wing. FC DEBUT: 2003. PROV CAREER: Boland 2003-07 55-33-0-0-0-165. Cheetahs 2008-10 35-26-0-0-0-130. Cheetahs XV 2010 1-0-0-0-0-0. SUPER 14: Stormers 2006 6-2-0-0-0-10. Cheetahs 2008-10 30-15-0-0-0-75. REP HONOURS: SA 2008-09 Tests: 4-5-0-0-0-25. Tour: 2009 2-3-0-0-0-15. Total: 6-8-0-0-0-40. Springbok XV 2006. SA Sevens 2004-05. MISC INFO: YPoY 2005. FC RECORD: 134-81-0-0-0-405. RECORD IN 2010: (Cheetahs S14, Cheetahs, Cheetahs XV) 23-8-0-0-0-40.

Nqoro, Mlindazwe (St John's Coll.) b 16/12/1988, Queenstown. 1.77m. 85kg. Wing. FC DEBUT: 2010. PROV CAREER: EP Kings 2010 5-1-0-0-0-5. FC RECORD: 5-1-0-0-0-5. RECORD IN 2010: (EP Kings) 5-1-0-0-0-5.

Nyakane, Trevor Ntando (Ben Vorster HS) b 04/05/1989, Bushbuck Ridge. 1.78m. 109kg. Prop. FC DEBUT: 2010. PROV CAREER: Cheetahs 2010 5-2-0-0-0-10. FC RECORD: 5-2-0-0-0-10. RECORD IN 2010: (Cheetahs) 5-2-0-0-0-10.

Nyoka, Sinovuyo (Dale Coll.) b 07/08/1990, King Williamstown. 1.68m. 67kg. Scrumhalf. FC DEBUT: 2010. PROV CAREER: Bulldogs 2010 5-0-0-0-0-0. FC RECORD: 5-0-0-0-0-0. RECORD IN 2010: (Bulldogs) 5-0-0-0-0-0.

O

Oberholzer, Johan Christiaan (Jan Viljoen HS) b 14/11/1989, Krugersdorp. 1.78m. 92kg. Hooker. FC DEBUT: 2010. PROV CAREER: Leopards 2010 1-0-0-0-0-0. FC RECORD: 1-0-0-0-0-0. RECORD IN 2010: (Leopards) 1-0-0-0-0-0.

Odendaal, Gerrit Hendrik (Gerrie) (AHS, Pretoria) b 29/04/86, Standerton. 1.74m. 77kg. Scrumhalf. FC DEBUT: 2007. PROV CAREER: Blue Bulls 2007 4-0-0-0-0-0. Valke 2008 22-4-0-0-0-20. Blue Bulls XV 2007 1-0-0-0-0-0. Cheetahs 2009-10 8-0-0-0-0-0. Griffons 2009 7-2-0-0-0-10. EP Kings 2010 12-5-0-0-0-25. SUPER 14: Cheetahs 2009 1-0-0-0-0-0. FC RECORD: 55-11-0-0-0-55. RECORD IN 2010: (EP Kings, Cheetahs) 13-5-0-0-0-25.

Odendaal, Willem Adriaan (Eldoraigne HS) b 11/07/1990, Pretoria. 1.83m. 92kg. Scrumhalf. FC DEBUT: 2010. PROV CAREER: Valke 2010 9-0-0-0-0-0. FC RECORD: 9-0-0-0-0-0. RECORD IN 2010: (Valke) 9-0-0-0-0-0.

Olivier, Ignatius Petrus (Naas) (Potchefstroom THS) b 10/03/82, Klerksdorp. 1.80m. 77kg. Flyhalf. FC DEBUT: 2003. PROV CAREER: Leopards 2003-05 21-8-57-43-0-283. WP 2006-07 25-3-56-35-1-235. Griquas 2008-10 40-14-107-61-1-470. SUPER 14: Stormers 2006-07 17-3-7-12-0-65. Cheetahs 2009-10 16-1-25-26-2-139. REP HONOURS: SA Students 2005 1-1-0-0-0-5. Royal XV 2009 1-0-1-2-0-8. FC RECORD: 121-30-253-179-4-1205. RECORD IN 2010: (Cheetahs S14, Griquas) 27-4-63-46-3-293. OTHER FC: Auch, France 2007-08 7-0-2-8-1-31.

Olivier, Leonard (Len) (AHS, Pretoria) b 19/01/86, Pretoria. 1.80m. 86kg. Flyhalf. FC DEBUT: 2006. PROV CAREER: Blue Bulls 2006 12-1-16-12-1-76. Valke 2007-08 33-3-29-13-0-112. Sharks XV 2009 7-0-4-3-0-17. FC RECORD: 52-4-49-28-1-205. RECORD IN 2009: (Sharks XV) 7-0-4-3-0-17.

Olivier, Wynand (AHS, Pretoria) b 11/06/83, Welkom. 1.84m. 87kg. Centre. FC DEBUT: 2003. PROV CAREER: Blue Bulls 2003-06 & 08-10 63-25-0-0-0-125. SUPER 14: Bulls 2005-10 72-19-0-0-0-95. REP HONOURS: SA 2006-07 & 09-10 Tests: 32-1-0-0-0-5. Tour: 4-0-0-0-0-0. Total: 36-1-0-0-0-5. SA XV 2006 1-0-0-0-0-0. SA U21 2004 5-2-0-0-0-10. MISC INFO: YPoY nominee 2005. FC RECORD: 177-47-0-0-0-235. RECORD IN 2010: (SA, Bulls, Blue Bulls) 23-7-0-0-0-35.

Oosthuizen, Coenraad Victor (Grey Coll.) b 22/03/89, Potchefstroom. 1.83m. 125kg. Prop. >> FC debut: 2008. Prov career: Cheetahs 2008-10 39-8-0-0-0-40. Cheetahs XV 2010 1-0-0-0-0-0. Super 14: Cheetahs 2010 13-1-0-0-0-5. Rep honours SA Tour 2010 1-0-0-0-0-0. FC record: 54-9-0-0-0-45. RECORD IN 2010: (SA, Cheetahs S14, Cheetahs, Cheetahs XV) 31-9-0-0-0-45.

Oosthuizen, Devin Andre (HTS John Vorster) b 28/05/1988. 1.94m. 104kg. Flanker. FC DEBUT: 2010. PROV CAREER: Blue Bulls 2010 10-1-0-0-0-5. EP Kings 2010 5-1-0-0-0-5. FC RECORD: 15-2-0-0-0-10. RECORD IN 2010: (Blue Bulls, EP Kings) 15-2-0-0-0-10.

Oosthuizen, Josephus (Sewes) (Grey Coll.) b 10/01/87, Bethlehem. 1.81m. 115kg. Prop. FC DEBUT: 2009. PROV CAREER: Griffons 2009-10 23-4-0-0-0-20. FC RECORD: 23-4-0-0-0-20. RECORD IN 2010: (Griffons) 12-0-0-0-0-0.

P

Paige, Rudy (Bastion HS) b 02/08/1989, Riversdal. 1.67m. 70kg. Scrumhalf. FC DEBUT: 2010. PROV CAREER: Young Lions 2010 5-0-0-0-0-0. FC RECORD: 5-0-0-0-0-0. RECORD IN 2010: (Young Lions) 5-0-0-0-0-0.

Palm, Juan (Zwartkop HS & Univ. Pretoria) b 04/03/1988, Roodepoort. 1.89m. 98kg. Flanker. FC DEBUT: 2010. PROV CAREER: Valke 2010 2-1-0-0-0-5. FC RECORD: 2-1-0-0-0-5. RECORD IN 2010: (Valke) 2-1-0-0-0-5.

Papier, Neil (Robinvale SS) b 22/07/77, Malmesbury. 1.77m. 76kg. Scrumhalf. FC DEBUT: 2000. PROV CAREER: Boland 2000-02 & 04-10 126-11-0-0-0-55. Valke 2003 21-1-0-0-0-5. FC RECORD: 147-12-0-0-0-60. RECORD IN 2010: (Boland) 18-0-0-0-0-0.

Parsons, Albert James (Kroonstad HS) b 20/03/86, Kroonstad. 1.89m. 97kg. Flank. FC DEBUT: 2008. PROV CAREER: Griffons 2008-10 33-8-0-0-0-40. Cheetahs 2008 9-3-0-0-0-15. FC RECORD: 42-11-0-0-0-55. RECORD IN 2010: (Griffons) 11-4-0-0-0-20.

Passaportis, Michael John Richard (St. Johns Coll & UCT) b 30/06/86, Bulawayo. 1.98m. 108kg. Lock. FC DEBUT: 2009. PROV CAREER: Elephants 2009 1-0-0-0-0-0. Griquas 2010 11-0-0-0-0-0. FC RECORD: 12-0-0-0-0-0. RECORD IN 2010: (Griquas) 11-0-0-0-0-0.

Payi, Lungelo (Phillip Mtywakuss) b 22/05/81, Peelton. 1.92m. 115kg. Lock. FC DEBUT: 2006. PROV CAREER: WP 2006 3-1-0-0-0-5. Bulldogs 2006-07 24-1-0-0-0-5. Valke 2008 8-0-0-0-0-0. EP Kings 2010 11-0-0-0-0-0. FC RECORD: 46-2-0-0-0-10. RECORD IN 2010:

(EP Kings) 11-0-0-0-0-0.

Peach, Justin (Westview SS, Port Elizabeth) b 07/06/81, Durban. 1.80m. 72kg. Fullback. FC DEBUT: 2001. PROV CAREER: EP Kings 2001-05 & 10 94-23-162-170-0-949. Boland 2005-09 84-17-104-72-0-509. EP Inv XV 2010 1-0-0-3-0-9. FC RECORD: 179-40-266-245-0-1467. RECORD IN 2010: (EP Kings, EP Inv XV) 11-5-15-26-0-133.

Peacock, Johann (Strand HS) b 09/12/87, Gauteng. 1.95m. 115kgs. Lock. FC DEBUT: 2008. PROV CAREER: Boland 2008 & 10 7-0-0-0-0-0. FC RECORD: 7-0-0-0-0-0. RECORD IN 2010: (Boland) 6-0-0-0-0-0.

Pekeur, Wigan Marvin (Belville THS) b 24/11/87, Stellenbosch. 1.86m. 75kg. Wing. FC DEBUT: 2008. PROV CAREER: Young Lions 2008-10 6-1-0-0-0-5. Lions XV 2008. SUPER 14: Lions 2010 4-2-0-0-0-10. FC RECORD: 11-3-0-0-0-15. RECORD IN 2010: (Lions S14, Young Lions) 6-3-0-0-0-15.

Perez, Paul Lusi (New Plymouth HS) b 26/07/1986, Motootura. 1.82m. 102kg. Wing. FC DEBUT: 2010. PROV CAREER: EP Kings 2010 9-6-0-0-0-30. FC RECORD: 9-6-0-0-0-30. RECORD IN 2010: (EP Kings) 9-6-0-0-0-30.

Perkins, George (Monument HS) b 21/01/82, Johannesburg. 1.83m. 97kg. Centre. FC DEBUT: 2009. PROV CAREER: Valke 2009-10 6-0-0-0-0-0. FC RECORD: 6-0-0-0-0-0. RECORD IN 2010: (Valke) 2-0-0-0-0-0.

Perkins, Warren (President HS) b 27/07/84, Johannesburg. 1.91m. 101kg. Flanker. FC DEBUT: 2008. PROV CAREER: Valke 2008 & 10 35-3-0-0-0-15. Young Lions 2009 4-2-0-0-0-10. MISC INFO: Brother of Jeffrey and Reggie Perkins. FC RECORD: 39-5-0-0-0-25. RECORD IN 2010: (Valke) 17-2-0-0-0-10.

Pienaar, Ruan (Grey Coll., Bloemfontein) b 10/03/84, Bloemfontein. 1.86m. 84kg. Scrumhalf. FC DEBUT: 2004. PROV CAREER: Cheetahs 2004 9-2-1-0-0-12. KZN 2005-06 & 08-10 33-7-59-36-0-261. SUPER 14: Sharks 2005-10 67-10-35-42-2-252. REP HONOURS: SA 2006-10 Tests: 47-6-13-16-1-107. Tour 2006, 07, 09 5-0-1-7-0-23. Total: 52-6-14-23-1-130. SA XV 2006 1-0-0-1-0-3. SA U21 2004-05 10-1-3-0-0-11. SA U19 2003. SA Schools 2002. CW Free State 2002. MISC INFO: YPoY nominee 2005, Son of 1980-81 Springbok ZMJ Pienaar. FC RECORD: 171-26-112-102-2-666. RECORD IN 2010: (SA, Sharks, KZN) 25-3-22-24-1-134.

Pieterse, Barend Hermanus (Waterkloof HS & RAU) b 23/01/79, Virginia. 1.96m. 100kg. Lock. FC DEBUT: 2000. PROV CAREER: Lions 2001-04 49-4-0-0-0-20. Cheetahs 2004-08 & 10 75-7-0-0-0-35. SUPER 14: Cats 2005 11-1-0-0-0-5. Cheetahs 2006 & 08 & 10 33-2-0-

0-0-10. REP HONOURS: SA 2007 Tour: 1-1-0-0-0-5. SA 'A' 2004 1-0-0-0-0-0. SA U21s 2000 5-0-0-0-0-0. FC RECORD: 175-15-0-0-0-75. RECORD IN 2010: (Cheetahs S14, Cheetahs) 16-1-0-0-0-5.

Pietersen, Alfonso (Brandwag HS) b 27/05/83, Uitenhage. 1.89m. 95kg. Centre. FC DEBUT: 2009. PROV CAREER: EP Kings 2009-10 11-2-0-0-0-10. FC RECORD: 11-2-0-0-0-10. RECORD IN 2010: (EP Kings) 1-0-0-0-0-0.

Pietersen, Johan Christiaan (Joe) (Grey Coll., Bloemfontein) b 18/05/84, Vryheid. 1.78m. 78kg. Wing. FC DEBUT: 2004. PROV CAREER: WP 2004-09 57-21-45-50-5-360. SUPER 14: Stormers 2006 & 08-10 21-7-10-17-0-106. REP HONOURS: WP XV 2006. SA Sevens 2006. CW Free State 2002. FC RECORD: 79-28-55-67-5-466. RECORD IN 2010: (Stormers) 10-3-10-17-0-86.

Pietersen, Jon-Paul Roger (JP) (General Hertzog HS) b 12/07/86, Stellenbosch. 1.90m. 98kg. Wing/Fullback. FC DEBUT: 2005. PROV CAREER: KZN 2005-06 & 08-10 35-16-0-0-0-80. SUPER 14: Sharks 2006-10 56-21-0-0-0-105. REP HONOURS: SA 2006-10 Tests: 36-12-0-0-0-60. Tour: 2-0-0-0-0-0. Total: 38-12-0-0-0-60. SA U21 2006 5-2-0-0-0-10. Misc. info: YPoY nominee 2005, 2006. FC RECORD: 134-51-0-0-0-255. RECORD IN 2010: (SA, Sharks, KZN) 18-3-0-0-0-15.

Plaatjies, Jeremy John (Outeniqua HS, George) b 01/01/83, George. 1.80m. 72kg. Wing. FC DEBUT: 2001. PROV CAREER: Eagles 2001-07 91-42-0-0-0-210. Elephants 2008-09 6-1-0-0-0-5. Griquas 2008 8-1-0-0-0-5. Boland 2010 18-8-0-0-0-40. REP HONOURS: SA U21 2004 4-2-0-0-0-10. SA Schools 2001. CW SWD 2001. FC RECORD: 127-54-0-0-0-270. RECORD IN 2010: (Boland) 18-8-0-0-0-40.

Poolman, Daniel Johannes George (Paul Roos Gym.) b 10/03/1989, Pretoria. 1.89m. 92kg. Wing. FC DEBUT: 2010. PROV CAREER: WP 2010 3-0-0-0-0-0. FC RECORD: 3-0-0-0-0-0. RECORD IN 2010: (WP) 3-0-0-0-0-0.

Potgieter, Dewald Johan (Daniel Pienaar THS, Uitenhage) b 22/02/87, Port Elizabeth. 1.90m. 98kg. Eighthman. FC DEBUT: 2007. PROV CAREER: Blue Bulls 2007-10 45-9-0-0-0-45. SUPER 14: Bulls 2008-10 31-2-0-0-0-10. REP HONOURS: SA Tests: 2009-10 6-1-0-0-0-5. Tours: 2009 2-0-0-0-0-0. Total: 8-1-0-0-0-5. Emerging Springboks 2009 1-0-0-0-0-0. FC RECORD: 85-12-0-0-0-60. RECORD IN 2010: (SA, Bulls, Blue Bulls) 25-5-0-0-0-25.

Potgieter, Hein (DF Malherbe HS) b 20/09/82, Port Elizabeth. 2.03m. 103kgs. Utility forward. FC DEBUT:

2006. PROV CAREER: Elephants 2006 & 10 8-0-0-0-0-0. EP Inv XV 2010 1-0-0-0-0-0. Valke 2007 16-0-0-0-0-0. Eagles 2008-09 14-0-0-0-0-0. FC RECORD: 39-0-0-0-0-0. RECORD IN 2010: (EP Kings, EP Inv XV) 8-0-0-0-0-0.

Potgieter, Jacques-Louis (AHS, Pretoria) b 02/09/84, Pretoria. 1.98m. 86kg. Flyhalf. FC DEBUT: 2005. PROV CAREER: Blue Bulls 2005-07 & 10 55-7-86-81-4-462. Griffons 2008 5-2-9-17-0-79. Cheetahs 2008-09 26-4-57-32-5-245. SUPER 14: Bulls 2007 & 10 15-2-1-1-0-15. Cheetahs 2008-09 17-1-19-13-1-85. FC RECORD: 118-16-172-144-10-886. RECORD IN 2010: (Bulls, Blue Bulls) 28-3-31-37-0-188.

Potgieter, Johannes Izak (Ian) (Bothaville HS) b 20/11/1989, Bothaville. 1.95m. 135kg. Prop. FC DEBUT: 2010. PROV CAREER: Cheetahs 2010 2-0-0-0-0-0. FC RECORD: 2-0-0-0-0-0. RECORD IN 2010: (Cheetahs) 2-0-0-0-0-0.

Potgieter, Ulrich Jacques (Daniel Pienaar HTS) b 24/04/86, Port Elizabeth. 1.94m. 104kg. Lock. FC DEBUT: 2008. PROV CAREER: KZN 2008 2-0-0-0-0-0. EP Kings 2009-10 30-3-0-0-0-15. FC RECORD: 32-3-0-0-0-15. RECORD IN 2010: (EP Kings) 19-3-0-0-0-15.

Potts, Marchell Clide Lluwellyn (Pacallsdorp HS) b 19/08/1988, George. 1.74m. 77kg. Wing. FC DEBUT: 2010. PROV CAREER: Eagles 2010 8-2-0-0-0-10. FC RECORD: 8-2-0-0-0-10. RECORD IN 2010: (Eagles) 8-2-0-0-0-10.

Pretorius, André Stefan (Dinamika HS) b 29/12/78, Johannesburg. 1.76m. 90kgs. Flyhalf. FC DEBUT: 1998. PROV CAREER: Lions 1999-06,09 45-7-120-72-15-536. Young Lions 1-0-2-1-0-7. KZN 2010 8-0-6-0-0-12. SUPER 14: Cats 2002-06 47-10-74-95-5-498. Lions 2007 & 09 22-1-26-22-8-147. REP HONOURS: SA 2002-03& 05-07 Tests: 31-2-31-25-8-171. Tour: 2007 2-0-0-1-0-3. Total: 33-2-31-26-8-174. SA 'A' 2004 3-1-11-0-0-27. SA U23s 2001 2-2-2-0-0-14; SA Sevens 2000-01 (inc RWC 7s); SA U21s 1998 6-3-7-9-1-59; SA Barbarians 2001 1-0-0-0-0-0. MISC INFO: Holds Cats/Lions record for most career points (685), cons (101), pens (117), drop goals (13). SA 7s PoY 2001; Leading scorer U21s champs. 1999 (129 points) & 1998 (80 points). FC RECORD: 168-26-280-225-37-1479. RECORD IN 2010: (KZN) 8-0-6-0-0-12.

Pretorius, Braam (Wonderboom HS & TUT) b 28/05/84, Pretoria. 1.78m. 90kg. Wing. FC DEBUT: 2009. PROV CAREER: Pumas 2009-10 21-7-68-37-0-282. FC RECORD: 21-7-68-37-0-282. RECORD IN 2010: (Pumas) 7-4-12-3-0-53.

Pretorius, Dewald Petrus (Stilfontein HS) b 29/11/86,

Welkom. 1.86m. 96kg. Centre. FC DEBUT: 2007. PROV CAREER: Blue Bulls 2007 3-2-0-0-0-10. Valke 2008 14-4-0-0-0-20. Griquas 2009-10 20-10-0-0-0-50. FC RECORD: 37-16-0-0-0-80. RECORD IN 2010: (Griquas) 9-3-0-0-0-15.

Pretorius, Ettiene (Goudveld HS) b 14/01/81, Kimberley. 1.80m. 87kgs. Flyhalf. FC DEBUT: 2006. PROV CAREER: Griffons 2006 & 10 5-0-1-0-0-2. FC RECORD: 5-0-1-0-0-2. RECORD IN 2010: (Griffons) 3-0-1-0-0-2.

Pretorius, Jaco Christiaan (Randburg HS & RAU) b 10/12/79, Johannesburg. 1.82m. 88kg. Centre. FC DEBUT: 2001. PROV CAREER: Lions 2001-04 & 06-08 60-34-0-0-0-170. Blue Bulls 2009-10 27-7-0-0-0-35. SUPER 14: Lions 2007-08 18-0-0-0-0-0. Bulls 2009-10 19-1-0-0-0-5. REP HONOURS: SA 2006-07 Tests: 2-0-0-0-0-0. Springbok XV 2006. Emerging Springboks 2007 3-0-0-0-0-0. SA Sevens 2002-06. British Barbarians 2008 2-0-0-0-0-0. FC RECORD: 132-42-0-0-0-210. RECORD IN 2010: (Bulls, Blue Bulls) 17-3-0-0-0-15.

Pretorius, Jerome (Voortrekker HS) b 22/03/1988, Boksburg. 1.81m. 85kg. Centre. FC DEBUT: 2010. PROV CAREER: Sharks XV 2010 8-4-0-0-0-20. FC RECORD: 8-4-0-0-0-20. RECORD IN 2010: (Sharks XV) 8-4-0-0-0-20.

Pretorius, Johannes Hermanus (Herman) (Reitz HS/ Grey Coll., Bloemfontein) b 12/03/86, Sasolburg. 1.84m. 86kg. Centre. FC DEBUT: 2005. PROV CAREER: Cheetahs 2005-08 14-4-0-0-0-20. Griquas 2009-10 10-2-0-0-0-10. MISC INFO: Brother of Valke scrumhalf Sarel Pretorius. FC RECORD: 24-6-0-0-0-30. RECORD IN 2010: (Griquas) 3-1-0-0-0-5.

Pretorius, Sarel Johannes (Reitz HS) b 18/04/84, Reitz. 1.75m. 75kg. Scrumhalf. FC DEBUT: 2006. PROV CAREER: Valke 2006-07 37-16-0-0-0-80. Griquas 2007-10 57-22-0-0-0-110. Cheetahs XV 2010 1-0-0-0-0-0. SUPER 14: Cheetahs 2009-10 22-6-0-0-0-30. REP HONOURS: Emerging Springboks 2008 3-0-0-0-0-0. Royal XV 2009 1-0-0-0-0-0. MISC INFO: Brother of Cheetahs centre Herman Pretorius. FC RECORD: 121-44-0-0-0-220. RECORD IN 2010: (Cheetahs S14, Griquas, Cheetahs XV) 29-10-0-0-0-50.

Prinsloo, Johannes Gerhardus (Boom) (Grey Coll.) b 12/03/1989, Bloemfontein. 1.87m. 95kg. Flanker. FC DEBUT: 2010. PROV CAREER: Cheetahs 2010 7-1-0-0-0-5. FC RECORD: 7-1-0-0-0-5. RECORD IN 2010: (Cheetahs) 7-1-0-0-0-5.

R

Ralepelle, Mahlatse Chilliboy (Pretoria BHS) b 11/09/1986, Tzaneen. 1.78m. 95kg. Hooker. FC DEBUT: 2005. PROV CAREER: Blue Bulls 2006 & 08-

10 29-2-0-0-0-10. SUPER 14: Bulls 2006-07 & 09-10 19-1-0-0-0-5. Rep. honours: Tests: SA 2006 & 08-10 18-0-0-0-0-0. Tour: 2006, 09 2-0-0-0-0-0. Total: 20-0-0-0-0. SA U21 2005-06 9-0-0-0-0-0. SA U19 2004-05, SA Schools 2002-03. CW Blue Bulls. MISC INFO: IRB U19 PoY nominee 2005. FC RECORD: 77-3-0-0-0-15. RECORD IN 2010 (SA, Bulls, Blue Bulls) 24-1-0-0-0-5.

Ramashala, Rebaballetswe Makholokoe (Kholo) (Queens Coll.) b 22/05/1989, Aliwal North. 1.78m. 79kg. Wing. FC DEBUT: 2010. PROV CAREER: Cheetahs 2010 8-2-0-0-0-10. FC RECORD: 8-2-0-0-0-10. RECORD IN 2010: (Cheetahs) 8-2-0-0-0-10.

Raubenheimer, Davon (Pacaltsdorp SS) b 16/07/1984, Knysna. 1.94m. 92kg. Flank. FC DEBUT: 2005. PROV CAREER: Eagles 2005-08 60-5-0-0-0-25. Griquas 2009-10 40-1-0-0-0-5. SUPER 14: Cheetahs 2010 6-1-0-0-0-5. REP HONOURS: SA Tour: 2009 2-0-0-0-0-0. Emerging Springboks 2008 2-0-0-0-0-0. Royal XV 2009 1-0-0-0-0-0. SA U21 2005 3-0-0-0-0-0. FC RECORD: 114-7-0-0-0-35. RECORD IN 2010: (Cheetahs S14, Griquas) 22-1-0-0-0-5.

Raubenheimer, Shaun (George Hill HS) b 10/11/83, George. 1.80m. 94kg. Flanker. FC DEBUT: 2008. PROV CAREER: Bulldogs 2008 15-2-0-0-0-10. Eagles 2009-10 28-12-0-0-0-60. FC RECORD: 43-14-0-0-0-70. RECORD IN 2010: (Eagles) 20-10-0-0-0-50.

Rautenbach, Cornelius Johannes (Kempie) (Afrikaans HS) b 25/04/1988, Delmas. 1.87m. 96kg. Centre. FC DEBUT: 2010. PROV CAREER: Leopards 2010 9-0-0-0-0-0. FC RECORD: 9-0-0-0-0-0. RECORD IN 2010: (Leopards) 9-0-0-0-0-0.

Redelinghuys, Julian (Monument HS) b 11/09/89, Pretoria. 1.76m. 100kg. Prop. FC DEBUT: 2009. PROV CAREER: KZN 2009 1-0-0-0-0-0. Sharks XV 2010 7-0-0-0-0-0. FC RECORD: 8-0-0-0-0-0. RECORD IN 2010: (Sharks XV) 7-0-0-0-0-0.

Rens, Johan Herman (Hugenote HS) b 15/04/81, Springs. 1.75m. 90kg. FC DEBUT: 2009. PROV CAREER: Valke 2009-10 2-0-0-0-0-0. FC RECORD: 2-0-0-0-0-0. RECORD IN 2010: (Valke) 1-0-0-0-0-0.

Rhodes, Michael Kenworthy (Michaelhouse) b 19/12/87, Durban. 1.97m. 110kg. Lock. FC DEBUT: 2007. PROV CAREER: KZN 2009-10 19-1-0-0-0-5. Sharks XV 2008-10 18-5-0-0-0-25. Sharks Inv XV 2007 & 10 2-1-0-0-0-5. FC RECORD: 39-7-0-0-0-35. RECORD IN 2010: (KZN, Sharks XV, Sharks Inv XV) 19-2-0-0-0-10.

Rhodes, Theo Matthew (Sao Bras Sec.) b 18/02/83, Cape Town. 1.77m. 88kg. Centre. FC DEBUT: 2009. PROV CAREER: Valke 2009-10 21-2-0-0-0-10. FC

RECORD: 21-2-0-0-0-10. RECORD IN 2010: (Valke) 11-1-0-0-0-5.

Richards, Mark (Michaelhouse HS) b 09/09/1989, Springs. 1.75m. 81kg. Wing. FC DEBUT: 2010. PROV CAREER: Sharks XV 2010 9-0-0-0-0-0. Sharks Inv XV 2010 1-1-0-0-0-5. FC RECORD: 10-1-0-0-0-5. RECORD IN 2010: (Sharks XV, Sharks Inv XV) 10-1-0-0-0-5.

Riddles, Denzel Brain (Jan Kriel HS) b 10/08/88, Cape Town. 1.80m. 105kg. FC DEBUT: 2009. PROV CAREER: WP 2009-10 6-0-0-0-0-0. FC RECORD: 6-0-0-0-0-0. RECORD IN 2010: (WP) 2-0-0-0-0-0.

Roberts, Willem Andries Stephanus (Steph) (Grey Coll., Bloemfontein) b 20/03/85, Bloemfontein. 1.80m. 108kg. Prop. FC DEBUT: 2005. PROV CAREER: Cheetahs 2005-07 15-0-0-0-0-0. Griquas 2008-10 55-3-0-0-0-15. REP HONOURS:Royal XV 2009 1-0-0-0-0-0. SA Students 2007 1-0-0-0-0-0. FC RECORD: 72-3-0-0-0-15. RECORD IN 2010: (Griquas) 21-1-0-0-0-5.

Rhoode, Deroy Elizandro (Groot Brak HS) b 28/10/88. 1.6m. 64kg. FC DEBUT: 2009. PROV CAREER: Eagles 2009-10 9-0-2-1-0-7. FC RECORD: 9-0-2-1-0-7. RECORD IN 2010: (Eagles) 8-0-2-1-0-7.

Roodt, Hendrik Lambertus (Lichtenburg HS) b 06/11/1987, Lichtenburg. 1.98m. 121kg. Lock. FC DEBUT: 2007. PROV CAREER: Blue Bulls 2007-08 19-1-0-0-0-5. Blue Bulls XV 2007 1-0-0-0-0-0. Griquas 2010 2-0-0-0-0-0. REP HONOURS: Emerging Springboks 2008 3-0-0-0-0-0. FC RECORD: 25-1-0-0-0-5. RECORD IN 2010: (Griquas) 2-0-0-0-0-0.

Rose, Earl Enver (Strand HS) b 12/01/84, Strand. 1.80m. 77kg. Flyhalf. FC DEBUT: 2004. PROV CAREER: WP 2004-05 19-6-14-4-0-70. Lions 2006-09 46-10-72-36-1-305. Lions XV 2008 1-0-3-0-0-6. Young Lions 2010 3-0-6-8-1-39. SUPER 14: Cats 2006 11-2-5-5-0-35. Lions 2007-10 36-6-25-19-2-143. REP HONOURS: SA Tours: 2009 2-0-0-0-0-0. SA Emerging Springboks 2009 1-0-0-2-0-6. SA Sevens 2003-04. SA U21 2004-05 10-4-0-0-0-20. SA U19 2003. SA Schools 2002. CW WP 2002. MISC INFO: Brother of Lions flyhalf Jody Rose. Son of former WP-League wing Enver Rose. FC RECORD: 129-28-125-74-4-624. RECORD IN 2010: (Lions S14, Young Lions) 10-0-14-15-1-76.

Rosslee, Matthew Ryan (RBHS) b 24/02/87, Cape Town. 1.81m. 88kg. Flyhalf. FC DEBUT: 2008. PROV CAREER: WP 2008 2-0-0-0-0-0. Griquas 2010 7-1-0-0-0-5. REP HONOURS: SA Students 2009 2-0-0-0-0-0. FC RECORD: 11-1-0-0-0-5. RECORD IN 2010: (Griquas) 7-1-0-0-0-5.

Rossouw, Daniel Jacobus (Danie) (Rob Ferreira HS) b

05/06/78, Sabie. 1.97m. 118kg. Flank. FC DEBUT: 1999. PROV CAREER: Blue Bulls 1999-06 & 08-10 97-24-0-0-0-120. Blue Bulls XV 3-0-0-0-0-0. SUPER 14: Bulls 2002-10 102-5-0-0-0-25. REP HONOURS: SA 2003-10 Tests: 54-8-0-0-0-40; Tour: 2006, 07, 09 4-1-0-0-0-5. Total: 58-9-0-0-0-45. SA 'A' 2004. SA XV 2006 1-0-0-0-0-0. FC RECORD: 262-38-0-0-0-190. RECORD IN 2010: (SA, Bulls, Blue Bulls) 23-1-0-0-0-5.

Rossouw, Jean Jacques (Paarl Gym.) b 06/04/1988, George. 1.84m. 120kg. Prop. FC DEBUT: 2010. PROV CAREER: Boland 2010 3-0-0-0-0-0. FC RECORD: 3-0-0-0-0-0. RECORD IN 2010: (Boland) 3-0-0-0-0-0.

Roux, Jacobus Stephanus (Bees) (Marlow Agricultural, Cradock) b 09/12/81, Upington. 1.86m. 115kg. Forward. FC DEBUT: 2005. PROV CAREER: Leopards 2005-06 41-1-0-0-0-5. Griquas 2007-09 31-1-0-0-0-5. Blue Bulls 2010 7-0-0-0-0-0. SUPER 14: Cheetahs 2008-09 17-0-0-0-0-0. Bulls 2010 14-0-0-0-0-0. REP HONOURS: Royal XV 2009 1-0-0-0-0-0. FC RECORD: 111-2-0-0-0-10. RECORD IN 2010: (Bulls, Blue Bulls) 21-0-0-0-0-0.

Russell, Virgil (Hentie Cilliers HS) b 09/05/89, Port Elizabeth. 1.70m. 75kg. Wing. FC DEBUT: 2008. PROV CAREER: Griffons 2008-10 11-3-1-0-0-17. FC RECORD: 11-3-1-0-0-17. RECORD IN 2010: (Griffons) 4-1-1-0-0-7.

Ryland, Zhahier (Trafalgar HS) b 23/10/81, Cape Town. 1.79m. 74kg. Wing. FC DEBUT: 2004. PROV CAREER: WP 2004-08 56-21-0-0-0-105. WP XV 2006 1-2-0-0-0-10. Griquas 2010 7-3-0-0-0-15. FC RECORD: 64-26-0-0-0-130. RECORD IN 2010: (Griquas) 7-3-0-0-0-15.

S

Saayman, Johannes Izak Adolf (Brackenfell HS & Cape Tech.) b 01/10/80, Cape Town. 1.85m. 95kg. Centre. FC DEBUT: 2001. PROV CAREER: WP 2001 3-2-0-0-0-10. Leopards 2002-03 33-13-1-0-0-67. Eagles 2004-10 97-30-4-0-0-158. FC RECORD: 133-45-5-0-0-235. RECORD IN 2010: (Eagles) 2-1-0-0-0-5.

Sadie, Johann (Paarl Gym. & Univ. Stellenbosch) b 23/01/1989, Malmesbury. 1.88m. 88kg. Wing. FC DEBUT: 2010. PROV CAREER: WP 2010 5-2-0-0-0-10. FC RECORD: 5-2-0-0-0-10. RECORD IN 2010: (WP) 5-2-0-0-0-10.

Samaai, Muhammed Shuaib (Bom) (Rylands HS) b 06/05/85, Cape Town. 1.84m. 94kgs. Wing. FC DEBUT: 2007. PROV CAREER: Leopards 2007,09-10 40-17-0-0-0-85. FC RECORD: 40-17-0-0-0-85. RECORD IN 2010: (Leopards) 9-5-0-0-0-25.

Schlechter, Andre (Mariental HS) b 13/10/86, Otjiwarongo. 1.88m. 119kg. FC DEBUT: 2009. PROV

CAREER: WP 2009 8-0-0-0-0-0. EP Kings 2010 10-0-0-0-0-0. Griquas 2009 1-0-0-0-0-0. Cheetahs 2010 1-0-0-0-0-0. FC RECORD: 20-0-0-0-0-0. RECORD IN 2010: (EP Kings, Cheetahs) 11-0-0-0-0-0.

Schmidt, Byron Ruan (Grey HS) b b 30/07/86, Port Elizabeth. 1.85m. 105kgs. Prop. FC DEBUT: 2008. PROV CAREER: Bulldogs 2008 & 10 10-0-0-0-0-0. Elephants 2008 2-0-0-0-0-0. FC RECORD: 12-0-0-0-0-0. RECORD IN 2010: (Bulldogs) 9-0-0-0-0-0.

Schoeman, Danie Burger (Boland Agric. HS) b 26/09/1988, Paarl. 1.90m. 105kg. Eightman. FC DEBUT: 2010. PROV CAREER: Griquas 2010 13-3-0-0-0-15. FC RECORD: 13-3-0-0-0-15. RECORD IN 2010: (Griquas) 13-3-0-0-0-15.

Scholtz, Deon (Skurweberg HS) b 12/09/85, Ceres. 1.69m. 75kg. Wing/Centre. FC DEBUT: 2008. PROV CAREER: Boland 2008-09 27-8-0-0-0-40. Leopards 2010 21-10-0-0-0-50. FC RECORD: 48-18-0-0-0-90. RECORD IN 2010: (Leopards) 21-10-0-0-0-50.

Scholtz, Hendro (Voortrekker HS, Bethlehem) b 22/03/79, Bethlehem. 1.86m. 100kg. Flank. FC DEBUT: 1999. PROV CAREER: Cheetahs 1999-10 142-28-0-0-0-140. SUPER 14: Bulls 2001 2-0-0-0-0-0. Cats 2003-05 20-1-0-0-0-5. Cheetahs 2006-10 39-2-0-0-0-10. REP HONOURS: SA 2002-03 Tests: 5-1-0-0-0-5. SA 'A' 2001-02 5-1-0-0-0-5; SA U23s 2001 1-1-0-0-0-5; SA U21s 1999-00 10-1-0-0-0-5; SA Schools 1997. CW Griffons 1997. FC RECORD: 224-35-0-0-0-175. RECORD IN 2010: (Cheetahs S14, Cheetahs) 26-4-0-0-0-20.

Schreuder, Louis (Paarl Gym.) b 25/04/1990, Paarl. 1.84m. 82kg. Wing. FC DEBUT: 2010. PROV CAREER: WP 2010 4-0-0-0-0-0. FC RECORD: 4-0-0-0-0-0. RECORD IN 2010: (WP) 4-0-0-0-0-0.

Schultz, Theodor Noble Enrico (Kroonstad HS) b 08/04/88, Kroonstad. 1.74m. 80kg. FC DEBUT: 2009. PROV CAREER: Griffons 2009-10 22-6-2-0-0-34. FC RECORD: 22-6-2-0-0-34. RECORD IN 2010: (Griffons) 17-6-2-0-0-34.

Scott, Ashwin Robert (Parkdene HS) b 02/06/85. 1.74m. 80kg. Wing. FC DEBUT: 2004. PROV CAREER: Eagles 2004-08 39-11-0-0-1-58. Pumas 2009-10 27-3-0-0-0-15. REP HONOURS: SA Schools 2003. CW SWD 2003. FC RECORD: 66-14-0-0-1-73. RECORD IN 2010: (Pumas) 12-1-0-0-0-5.

Scott, Wenstley Shane (Florida HS) b 09/04/1988, George. 1.74m. 83kg. Centre. FC DEBUT: 2010. PROV CAREER: Eagles 2010 5-2-0-0-0-10. FC RECORD: 5-2-0-0-0-10. RECORD IN 2010: (Eagles) 5-2-0-0-0-10.

Sephaka, Lawrence Dumisani (Reiger Park SS, Springs THS & RAU) b 08/08/78, Johannesburg. 1.78m. 110kg.

Prop. FC DEBUT: 1998. PROV CAREER: Valke 2000 18-0-0-0-0-0; Lions 2001-02 & 04-09 63-2-0-0-0-10. Young Lions 2001-08 & 10 15-0-0-0-0-0. Leopards 2007 5-0-0-0-0-0. SUPER 14: Cats 2002-03 & 05-06 37-0-0-0-0-0. Sharks 2004 2-0-0-0-0-0. Lions 2007 & 09 14-0-0-0-0-0. REP HONOURS: SA 2000-03 & 05-06 Tests 24-0-0-0-0-0, Tour 4-0-0-0-0-0, Total 28-0-0-0-0-0; Springbok XV 2006. SA 'A' 2002 & 04 4-1-0-0-0-5. SA XV 2006 1-0-0-0-0-0. SA U23s 2000-01 8-0-0-0-0-0; SA U21s 1998-99 12-2-0-0-0-10; SA Barbs. 2001 1-0-0-0-0-0; Namibian XV 2004. CW Valke 1996. MISC INFO: PPoY 2002. FC RECORD: 209-5-0-0-0-25. RECORD IN 2010: (Young Lions) 7-0-0-0-0-0. OTHER FC: Toulon, France 2007-08 13-2-0-0-0-10.

September, Franzel Julio (Bergrivier HS) b 06/06/86, Paarl. 1.80m. 100kg. FC DEBUT: 2009. PROV CAREER: Eagles 2009 1-0-0-0-0-0. Boland 2010 18-7-0-0-0-35. FC RECORD: 19-7-0-0-0-35. RECORD IN 2010: (Boland) 18-7-0-0-0-35.

Serfontein, Paul. Hooker. FC DEBUT: 2005. PROV CAREER: Elephants 2005-08 55-0-0-0-0-0. Bulldogs 2010 1-0-0-0-0-0. ›› FC RECORD: 56-0-0-0-0-0. RECORD IN 2010: (Bulldogs) 1-0-0-0-0-0.

Serfontein, Willem Jacob (Framesby HS & Unisa) b 16/09/88, Port Elizabeth. 1.95m. 112kg. Lock. FC DEBUT: 2009. PROV CAREER: Blue Bulls 2009 8-1-0-0-0-5. Pumas 2010 23-1-0-0-0-5. FC RECORD: 31-2-0-0-0-10. RECORD IN 2010: (Pumas) 23-1-0-0-0-5.

Shimange, Masana Hanyani (Rondebosch BHS) b 17/04/78, Elim. 1.78m. 103kg. Hooker. FC DEBUT: 1999. PROV CAREER: KZN 2000-01 7-1-0-0-0-5. Cheetahs 2002-04 35-3-0-0-0-15. WP 2005-06 & 08-10 41-2-0-0-0-10. SUPER 14: Cats 2003-04 18-0-0-0-0-0. Stormers 2005-06 & 10 15-0-0-0-0-0. REP HONOURS: SA Tests: 2004-06 10-0-0-0-0-0. SA 'A' 2003 1-0-0-0-0-0. SA XV 2006 1-0-0-0-0-0. SA U23s 2000-01 7-4-0-0-0-20; SA U21s 1999 5-0-0-0-0-0. FC RECORD: 140-10-0-0-0-50. RECORD IN 2010: (Stormers, WP) 12-1-0-0-0-5.

Sithole, Sibusiso Camagu Thokazani (Varsity Coll.) b 14/06/1990, Queenstown. 1.78m. 90kg. Wing. FC DEBUT: 2010. PROV CAREER: Sharks XV 2010 3-0-0-0-0-0. FC RECORD: 3-0-0-0-0-0. RECORD IN 2010: (Sharks XV) 3-0-0-0-0-0.

Sithole, Simphiwe (Martin) (Kusaselethu SS) b 03/02/1984, Pietermaritzburg. 1.81m. 95kg. Flanker. FC DEBUT: 2005. Prov. career: Pumas 2008-10 33-6-0-0-0-30. Rep. honours: SA U21 2005 1-0-0-0-0-0. CW Pumas 2001-02. FC RECORD: 34-6-0-0-0-30. Record in 2010 (Pumas) 2-0-0-0-0-0.

Skeate, Ross Carson (SACS, UCT) b 02/08/82, Johannesburg. 2.00m. 110kg. Lock. FC DEBUT: 2003. PROV CAREER: WP 2003-08 55-6-0-0-0-30. KZN 2010 6-0-0-0-0-0. SUPER 14: Stormers 2005-08 35-1-0-0-0-5. REP HONOURS: Emerging Springboks 2007 2-0-0-0-0-0. S/Kings 2009 1-0-0-0-0-0. SA U21 2003 4-1-0-0-0-5. SA U19 2001. SA Schools 2000. CW WP 2000. British Barbarians 2008,10 3-0-0-0-0-0. FC RECORD: 104-8-0-0-0-40. RECORD IN 2010: (KZN, British Barbarians) 7-0-0-0-0-0.

Smart, Duwayne Enslin (George HS) b 08/09/87, George. 1.70m. 72kg. Wing. FC DEBUT: 2008. PROV CAREER: Eagles 2008 11-5-0-0-0-25. Pumas 2009-10 7-2-0-0-0-10. FC RECORD: 18-7-0-0-0-35. RECORD IN 2010: (Pumas) 2-0-0-0-0-0.

Smit, Adriaan Jacobus (Riaan) (THS Springs) b 28/04/84, Springs. 1.78m. 85kg. Fullback. FC DEBUT: 2006. PROV CAREER: Leopards 2006,09 7-2-7-6-0-42. Pumas 2007 15-5-14-12-0-89. Valke 2008 11-3-9-3-0-42. Griffons 2010 2-0-4-2-0-14. Cheetahs 2010 9-1-0-0-0-5. FC RECORD: 44-11-34-23-0-192. RECORD IN 2010: (Cheetahs, Griffons) 11-1-4-2-0-19.

Smit, Andries Adriaan (Nico Malan) b 27/08/82, Grahamstown. 1.96m. 115kg. Lock. FC DEBUT: 2006. PROV CAREER: EP Kings 2006-10 62-2-0-0-0-10. E/Cape XV 2008 1-0-0-0-0-0. EP Inv XV 2010 1-0-0-0-0-0. FC RECORD: 64-2-0-0-0-10. RECORD IN 2010: (EP Kings, EP Inv XV) 3-0-0-0-0-0.

Smit, John William (Pretoria BHS) b 03/04/78, Pietersburg. 1.88m. 116kg. Hooker. FC DEBUT: 1997. PROV CAREER: KZN 1997-06 & 08-09 61-13-0-0-0-65. Sharks XV 1997-08 11-2-0-0-0-10. SUPER 14: Sharks 1999-02 & 04-07 & 09-10 111-7-0-0-0-35. REP HONOURS: SA 2000-10 Tests 102-6-0-0-0-30, Tour 1-0-0-0-0-0, Total 94-6-0-0-0-30; SA 'A' 2003 1-0-0-0-0-0. SA U21s 1996-98 15-1-0-0-0-5; SA Barbs. 1999 1-0-0-0-0-0; S Hemisphere 2005 1-0-0-0-0-0. SA Schools and Blue Bulls CW 1996. British Barbarians 2008 1-0-0-0-0-0. MISC INFO: Most capped Springbok hooker (77 caps) and captain (66); captained SA to 2007 RWC title, 2004 T-N title; PPoY 2005; YPoY nominee 1999; captained SA U21s to 1999 SANZAR/UAR title. POY Nominee 2009. FC RECORD: 306-29-0-0-0-145. RECORD IN 2010: (SA, Sharks) 22-0-0-0-0-0. OTHER FC: Clermont, France 2007-08 16-1-0-0-0-5.

Smith, Jean-Pierre (Paarl Gym.) b 24/01/1990, Vryburg. 1.85m. 116kg. Prop. FC DEBUT: 2010. PROV CAREER: WP 2010 5-0-0-0-0-0. FC RECORD: 5-0-0-0-0-0. RECORD IN 2010: (WP) 5-0-0-0-0-0.

Smith, Juanne Hugo (Juan) (JBM Hertzog HS) b

30/07/81, Bloemfontein. 1.94m. 106kg. Eighthman/flank. ›› FC debut: 2002. Prov career: Cheetahs 2002 & 04-05 & 08 & 10 41-8-0-0-0-40. Cheetahs XV 2010 1-0-0-0-0-0. Super 14: Cats 2003-05 32-11-0-0-0-55. Cheetahs 2006-10 46-7-0-0-0-35. Rep honours: SA 2003 & 05-10 Tests: 69-12-0-0-0-60. Tour: 2-0-0-0-0-0. Total: 71-12-0-0-0-60. SA 'A' 2003 1-0-0-0-0-0. SA U21 2002 5-3-0-0-0-15. Misc info: PoY nominee 2003, 2007. FC record: 196-41-0-0-0-205. RECORD IN 2010: (SA, Cheetahs S14, Cheetahs, Cheetahs XV) 24-5-0-0-0-25.

Smith, Ruan-Henry (Paarl Gym.) b 24/01/1990, Vryburg. 1.87m. 125kg. Prop. FC DEBUT: 2010. PROV CAREER: WP 2010 1-0-0-0-0-0. FC RECORD: 1-0-0-0-0-0. RECORD IN 2010: (WP) 1-0-0-0-0-0.

Snyman, Brendon Michael (Pietersburg HS) b 21/08/84, Pietersburg. 122kg. Forward. FC DEBUT: 2005. PROV CAREER: Eagles 2005 16-1-0-0-0-5. Griquas 2006-09 67-9-0-0-0-45. EP Kings 2009-10 10-0-0-0-0-0. EP Inv XV 2010 1-0-0-0-0-0. FC RECORD: 94-10-0-0-0-50. RECORD IN 2010: (EP Kings, EP Inv XV) 10-0-0-0-0-0.

Snyman, Jacobus Phillipus (Jaco) (Schweizer Reneke HS) b 09/06/86, Schweizer Reneke. 1.75m. 78kg. Scrumhalf. FC DEBUT: 2007. PROV CAREER: Lions 2007-08 4-0-0-0-0-0. Valke 2009-10 12-3-0-0-0-15. FC RECORD: 16-3-0-0-0-15. RECORD IN 2010: (Valke) 9-3-0-0-0-15.

Snyman, Johan (Joe) (Outeniqua HS) b 09/07/86, Pretoria. 2.00m. 114kg. Lock. FC DEBUT: 2006. PROV CAREER: KZN 2006-07,09 2-1-0-0-0-5. Sharks XV 2006-09 9-0-0-0-0-0. Lions 2009-10 16-3-0-0-0-15. REP HONOURS: SA U19 2005. FC RECORD: 27-4-0-0-0-20. RECORD IN 2010: (Golden Lions) 7-2-0-0-0-10.

Snyman, Johannes Jurgens (Hannes) (Kroonstad Afrikaans HS) b 29/03/1989, Kroonstad. 1.86m. 90kg. Hooker. FC DEBUT: 2010. PROV CAREER: Sharks XV 3-0-0-0-0-0. FC RECORD: 3-0-0-0-0-0. RECORD IN 2010: (Sharks XV) 3-0-0-0-0-0.

Snyman, Phillipus Albertus Borman (Phillip) (Grey Coll.) b 26/03/87, Bloemfontein. 1.88m. 95kg. Centre. FC DEBUT: 2008. PROV CAREER: Griffons 2008-09 6-0-0-0-0-0. Cheetahs 2008-10 39-15-0-0-0-75. REP HONOURS: SA Sevens 2008. FC RECORD: 45-15-0-0-0-75. RECORD IN 2010: (Cheetahs) 25-11-0-0-0-55.

Snyman, Ruan (Afrikaans HS) b 09/03/87, Pretoria. 1.85m. 80kg. Scrumhalf. FC DEBUT: 2008. PROV CAREER: Blue Bulls 2008-10 37-5-0-0-0-25. SUPER 14: Bulls 2010 1-1-0-0-0-5. FC RECORD: 38-6-0-0-0-30. RECORD IN 2010: (Bulls, Blue Bulls) 21-6-0-0-0-30.

Specman, Rosko Shane (Mary Waters HS) b

28/04/1989, Grahamstown. 1.66m. 70kg. Wing. FC DEBUT: 2010. PROV CAREER: Sharks XV 2010 2-0-0-0-0-0. FC RECORD: 2-0-0-0-0-0. RECORD IN 2010: (Sharks XV) 2-0-0-0-0-0.

Spencer, Carlos b 14/10/1975, Levin. 1.84m. 95kg. Flyhalf. SA FC DEBUT: 2010. PROV CAREER: Golden Lions 2010 2-0-0-0-0-0. SUPER 14: Lions 2010 12-3-1-0-0-17. Auckland Blues 1996-2005. REP HONOURS: New Zealand 1997-2004. SA FC RECORD: 14-3-1-0-0-17. RECORD IN 2010: (Lions S14, Golden Lions) 14-3-1-0-0-17.

Spies, Frederik Albertus (Frikkie). (AHS, Kroonstad). b 08/02/85, Odendaalsrus. 1.96m. 109kg. Lock. FC DEBUT: 2005. PROV CAREER: Lions 2005,07 7-0-0-0-0-0. Cheetahs 2006 6-0-0-0-0-0. Boland 2008-09 22-0-0-0-0-0. Griquas 2010 16-3-0-0-0-15. FC RECORD: 51-3-0-0-0-15. RECORD IN 2010: (Griquas) 16-3-0-0-0-15.

Spies, Philippus. b 27/04/1982. 1.98m. 103kg. Lock. FC DEBUT: 2010. PROV CAREER: Eagles 2010 3-0-0-0-0-0. FC RECORD: 3-0-0-0-0-0. RECORD IN 2010: (Eagles) 3-0-0-0-0-0.

Spies, Pierre Johan (AHS Pretoria) b 08/06/1985, Pretoria. 1.95m. 106kg. Loose Forward, Wing. FC DEBUT: 2005. PROV CAREER: Blue Bulls 2005-06 & 08-10 17-4-0-0-0-20. SUPER 14: Bulls 2005-10 56-20-0-0-0-100. REP HONOURS: SA 2006-10 Tests: 40-7-0-0-0-35. SA U21 2006 4-3-0-0-0-15. SA Students 2005 1-1-0-0-0-5. MISC INFO: YPoY 2006. Son of former N-Tvl and Transvaal wing Pierre Spies. FC RECORD: 118-35-0-0-0-175. RECORD IN 2010: (SA, Bulls, Blue Bulls) 26-9-0-0-0-45.

Sprong, Gerrit (THS Port Rex) b 01/09/1984, Durban. 78kg. Fullback. FC DEBUT: 2010. PROV CAREER: Bulldogs 2010 1-0-0-0-0-0. FC RECORD: 1-0-0-0-0-0. RECORD IN 2010: (Bulldogs) 1-0-0-0-0-0.

St. Jerry, Justin (Monument HS) b 14/01/87, Grabouw. 1.82m. 80kg. Centre. FC DEBUT: 2007. PROV CAREER: Young Lions 2008-10 12-4-0-0-0-20. Lions XV 2007 1-0-0-0-0-0. SUPER 14: Lions 2008 1-0-0-0-0-0. REP HONOURS: Emerging Springboks 2008 2-0-0-0-0-0. FC RECORD: 16-4-0-0-0-20. RECORD IN 2010: (Young Lions) 5-2-0-0-0-10.

Stander, Christiaan Johan ((Oakdale Agric. HS & Univ. Pretoria) b 05/04/1990, George. 1.90m. 106kg. Loose Forward. FC DEBUT: 2010. PROV CAREER: Blue Bulls 2010 14-0-0-0-0-0. FC RECORD: 14-0-0-0-0-0. RECORD IN 2010: (Blue Bulls) 14-0-0-0-0-0.

Steenkamp, Cornelius Jacobus (Corné) (Ermelo HS) b 20/02/82, Ermelo. 1.80m. 94kg. Flank. FC DEBUT:

2005. PROV CAREER: Pumas 2005-10 98-15-0-0-0-75. FC RECORD: 98-15-0-0-0-75. RECORD IN 2010: (Pumas) 22-7-0-0-0-35.

Steenkamp, Gurthrö Garth (Paarl BHS & UFS) b 12/06/81, Paarl. 1.89m. 124kg. Prop. FC DEBUT: 2001. PROV CAREER: Cheetahs 2002-04 42-2-0-0-0-10. Blue Bulls 2005 & 08-10 24-5-0-0-0-25. SUPER 14: Cats 2004 10-1-0-0-0-5. Bulls 2005,07-10 56-1-0-0-0-5. REP HONOURS: SA Tests: 2004-05, 07-10 31-5-0-0-0-25. Tour: 2007, 09 2-0-0-0-0-0. Total: 33-5-0-0-0-25. SA U21s 2001-02 8-1-0-0-0-5; CW WP 1998-99. MISC INFO: SA Rugby PoY 2010. FC RECORD: 172-15-0-0-0-75. RECORD IN 2010: (SA, Bulls, Blue Bulls) 24-4-0-0-0-20.

Steenkamp, Jabez Wilhelmus (Wilhelm) (Paarl Boys HS) b 07/02/85, Calvinia. 2.00m. 104kg. Lock. FC DEBUT: 2006. PROV CAREER: Blue Bulls 2006-10 65-5-0-0-0-25. SUPER 14: Bulls 2008-09 18-0-0-0-0-0. Sharks 2010 5-0-0-0-0-0. REP HONOURS: Emerging Springboks 2007,09 4-0-0-0-0-0. SA U21 2006 5-2-0-0-0-10. Misc. info: Brother of De Kock Steenkamp. FC RECORD: 97-7-0-0-0-35. RECORD IN 2010: (Sharks, Blue Bulls) 14-0-0-0-0-0.

Steenkamp, Michiel de Kock (Paarl Boys HS & Stellenbosch Univ.) b 16/02/87, Calvinia. 1.97m. 106kg. FC DEBUT: 2009. PROV CAREER: WP 2009-10 24-0-0-0-0-0. SUPER 14: Stormers 2010 7-0-0-0-0-0. Misc. info: Brother of Wilhelm Steenkamp. FC RECORD: 31-0-0-0-0-0. RECORD IN 2010: (Stormers, WP) 19-0-0-0-0-0.

Stegmann, Gideon Johannes (Deon) (Grey Coll., Bloemfontein) b 22/03/86, Cradock. 1.81m. 99kg. Flank. FC DEBUT: 2007. PROV CAREER: Blue Bulls 2007-10 49-8-0-0-0-40. SUPER 14: Bulls 2008-10 39-1-0-0-0-5. REP HONOURS: SA 2010 Tests: 4-0-0-0-0-0. FC RECORD: 92-9-0-0-0-45. RECORD IN 2010: (SA, Bulls, Blue Bulls) 22-1-0-0-0-5.

Stemmet, Jean (Stellenbosch Univ.) b 06/06/86. 1.85m. 92kg. FC DEBUT: 2009. PROV CAREER: Sharks XV 2010 9-3-0-0-0-15. Griquas 2010 5-2-0-0-0-10. REP HONOURS: SA Students 2009 1-0-0-0-0-0. FC RECORD: 15-5-0-0-0-25. RECORD IN 2010: (Griquas, Sharks XV) 14-5-0-0-0-25.

Stevens, Donald Garth (Grey Coll. & Stellenbosch Univ.) b 10/06/87, Bethlehem. 1.71m. 82kg. Scrumhalf. FC DEBUT: 2009. PROV CAREER: Griquas 2009-10 7-0-6-1-0-15. EP Kings 2010 9-1-4-5-0-28. REP HONOURS: SA Students 2009 2-2-7-1-0-27. FC RECORD: 18-3-17-7-0-70. RECORD IN 2010: (EP Kings, Griquas) 14-1-10-6-0-43.

Stevens, Kevin Bruce (Grey Coll.) b 30/01/87, Virginia. 1.86m. 112kg. FC DEBUT: 2009. PROV CAREER: Cheetahs 2009 5-0-0-0-0-0. Griffons 2009-10 28-2-0-0-0-10. FC RECORD: 33-2-0-0-0-10. RECORD IN 2010: (Griffons) 18-2-0-0-0-10.

Stevens, Wayne. b 17/05/88. 1.85m. 86kg. Centre. FC DEBUT: 2008. PROV CAREER: Cheetahs 2009-10 10-1-0-0-0-5. EP Kings 2010 9-5-0-0-0-25. REP HONOURS: SA Students 2008 1-0-0-0-0-0. FC RECORD: 20-6-0-0-0-30. RECORD IN 2010: (EP Kings, Cheetahs) 12-5-0-0-0-25.

Steyn, Dawie (Afrikaans HS) b 05/01/84, Pretoria. 1.89m. 124kg. Prop. FC DEBUT: 2008. PROV CAREER: Pumas 2008-10 57-3-0-0-0-15. FC RECORD: 57-3-0-0-0-15. RECORD IN 2010: (Pumas) 21-1-0-0-0-5.

Steyn, Francois Philippus Lodewyk (Frans) (Grey Coll., Bloemfontein) b 14/05/87, Aliwal North. 1.91m. 100kg. Utility back. FC DEBUT: 2006. PROV CAREER: KZN 2006 & 08 18-4-12-6-1-65. SUPER 14: Sharks 2007-09 38-4-7-9-7-82. REP HONOURS: SA 2006-10 Tests: 42-6-5-16-3-97. Tour: 2-0-3-1-0-9. Total: 44-6-8-17-3-106. SA U19 2005-06. British Barbarians 2008 1-0-0-0-0-0. MISC INFO: YPoY 2007. U19 PoY 2006. YPOY Nominee 2009. IRB POY Nominee 2009. FC RECORD: 101-14-27-32-11-253. RECORD IN 2010: (SA) 6-1-0-2-0-11.

Steyn, Morné (Sand du Plessis HS) b 11/07/84, Bellville. 1.86m. 82kg. Flyhalf. FC DEBUT: 2003. PROV CAREER: Blue Bulls 2003-10 92-26-176-101-10-815. SUPER 14: Bulls 2005-10 73-10-139-126-17-757. REP HONOURS: SA 2009-10 Tests: 25-4-37-71-5-322. SA 'A' 2004 1-0-1-0-0-2. SA U21 2005 5-3-17-7-1-73. British Barbs. 2009 1-0-0-1-0-3. CW Free State 2001-2002. MISC INFO: YPoY nominee 2005. Leading FC points scorer 2005 (341). Holds SA record for most penalty goals by a player in a test (8 vs. New Zealand in 2009). Holds Bulls S14 record for most cons in a season (38) and a career (139). Holds Bulls record for most drop goals in a match (4), in a season (11) and a career (17). SA S14 POY 2009. POY Nominee 2009. FC RECORD: 197-43-370-306-33-1972. RECORD IN 2010: (SA, Bulls, Blue Bulls) 29-8-67-96-3-471.

Steyn, Nicolaas Phillips Jacobus (Nicky) (Welkom Gymnasium) b 02/08/85, Kroonstad. 1.90m. 101kg. Loose Forward. FC DEBUT: 2006. PROV CAREER: Cheetahs 2006-08 19-12-0-0-0-60. Griffons 2008-10 42-12-0-0-0-60. FC RECORD: 61-24-0-0-0-120. RECORD IN 2010: (Griffons) 14-5-0-0-0-25.

Steyn, Philippus Jacobus (Philip) (Fichardt Park HS) b 23/01/85, Bethlehem. 1.95m. 103kgs. Loose Forward.

FC DEBUT: 2007. PROV CAREER: Cheetahs 2007 & 10 11-0-0-0-0-0. Griffons 2007 10-2-0-0-0-10. FC RECORD: 21-2-0-0-0-10. RECORD IN 2010: (Cheetahs) 7-0-0-0-0-0.

Steyn, Roelof Petrus (Grey Coll. & UFS) b 09/02/87, Bloemfontein. 1.90m. 97kg. Wing. FC DEBUT: 2009. PROV CAREER: Griffons 2009 3-2-0-0-0-10. Pumas 2010 4-1-0-0-0-5. Eagles 2010 1-0-0-0-0-0. FC RECORD: 8-3-0-0-0-15. RECORD IN 2010: (Pumas, Eagles) 5-1-0-0-0-5.

Stick, Mzwandile (Newell HS) b 10/05/84, Port Elizabeth. 1.84m. 80kgs. Flyhalf. FC DEBUT: 2003. PROV CAREER: EP Kings 2003,07 & 10 15-0-4-2-0-14. KZN 2004-07 15-8-3-0-0-46. REP HONOURS: S/Kings 2009 1-0-0-0-0-0. SA U21 2005 5-0-0-0-0-0. SA Sevens 2004-06. FC RECORD: 36-8-7-2-0-60. RECORD IN 2010: (EP Kings) 9-0-4-2-0-14.

Stoltz, Willem (Vorentoe HS) b 3/02/75. 2.08m. 114kg. Lock. FC DEBUT: 1998. PROV CAREER: Lions 1998 & 2002-06 & 08-09 89-10-0-0-0-50; Young Lions 2002-08 & 10 10-0-0-0-0-0. Leopards 1999-2001 51-5-0-0-0-25. EP Kings 2010 7-0-0-0-0-0. SUPER 14: Cats 2002-03;06 28-2-0-0-0-10. Stormers 2004 8-0-0-0-0-0. Lions 2008 & 10 10-0-0-0-0-0. REP HONOURS: SA 'A' 2004 2-0-0-0-0-0. Quaggas 1999; Namibian XV 2004. MISC INFO: Agen (Fra) 2006-07. FC RECORD: 207-17-0-0-0-85. RECORD IN 2010: (Lions S14, EP Kings, Youn Lions) 16-0-0-0-0-0.

Strauss, Andries Jacobus (Grey Coll., Bloemfontein) b 05/03/84, Pretoria. 1.87m. 90kg. Centre. ›› FC debut: 2004. Prov career: Cheetahs 2004-05 8-2-0-0-0-10. KZN 2006-10 55-6-3-0-0-36. Sharks XV 2006-10 22-4-4-2-0-34. Sharks Inv XV 2007,09-10 3-2-0-0-0-10. Super 14: Sharks 2006 & 08-10 22-1-0-0-0-5. Rep honours: SA Tour 2010 1-0-0-0-0-0, SA Sevens 2007. SA U21 2004 2-0-0-0-0-0. SA U19 2004. SA Schools 2003. CW Free State 2003. Misc info: Brother of Cheetahs hooker Richardt Strauss and cousin of Cheetahs hooker Adriaan. FC record: 113-15-7-2-0-95. RECORD IN 2010: (SA, Sharks, KZN, Sharks XV, Sharks Inv XV) 29-1-0-0-0-5.

Strauss, Jan Adriaan (Grey Coll., Bloemfontein) b 18/11/85, Bloemfontein. 1.84m. 102kg. Hooker. FC DEBUT: 2005. Prov career: Blue Bulls 2005-06 23-3-0-0-0-15. Cheetahs 2007-10 40-7-0-0-0-35. Super 14: Bulls 2006 8-0-0-0-0-0. Cheetahs 2007-10 40-2-0-0-0-10. Rep honours: SA 2008-10 Tests: 9-0-0-0-0-0. Tour: 2-0-0-0-0-0. Total: 11-0-0-0-0-0. SA U21 2005-06 8-2-0-0-0-10. Misc info: Cousin of Andries and Richardt Strauss. FC record: 129-14-0-0-0-70. RECORD IN 2010: (SA, Cheetahs S14, Cheetahs) 24-6-0-0-0-30.

Strauss, Joshua Zac (Josh) (Paul Roos Gym.) B 23/10/86, Bellville. 1.92m. 103kgs. Lock. FC DEBUT: 2008. PROV CAREER: Boland 2008 5-1-0-0-0-5. Golden Lions 2010 8-2-0-0-0-10. FC RECORD: 13-3-0-0-0-15. RECORD IN 2010: (Golden Lions) 8-2-0-0-0-10.

Strydom, Louis Isias (Welkom THS) b 21/10/80, Welkom. 1.78m. 72kg. Flyhalf. FC DEBUT: 2001. PROV CAREER: Griffons 2001-03 26-5-25-45-0-210. Blue Bulls 2003-04 23-3-59-23-0-202. Valke 2005-06 42-3-70-83-6-422. Lions 2007-08 24-1-20-23-2-120. Lions XV 2007-08 2-1-5-0-0-15. Cheetahs 2009-10 37-1-60-56-0-293. SUPER 14: Lions 2007-08 12-0-4-18-0-62. Cheetahs 2010 1-0-1-0-0-2. FC RECORD: 167-14-244-248-8-1326. RECORD IN 2010: (Cheetahs S14, Cheetahs) 25-0-42-56-0-250.

Swanepoel, Jacobus Albertus Johannes (Riaan) (Grey Coll. & UOFS) b 13/04/85, Kroonstad. 1.87m. 97kg. Loose Forward. FC DEBUT: 2007. PROV CAREER: Griffons 2007 2-0-0-0-0-0. Leopards 2008-10 51-7-0-0-0-35. FC RECORD: 53-7-0-0-0-35. RECORD IN 2010: (Leopards) 21-0-0-0-0-0.

Swanepoel, Meyer (Paul Roos Gym.) b 07/05/1989, Belville. 1.96m. 101kg. Lock. FC DEBUT: 2010. PROV CAREER: Sharks XV 2010 3-0-0-0-0-0. FC RECORD: 3-0-0-0-0-0. RECORD IN 2010: (Sharks XV) 3-0-0-0-0-0.

Swanepoel, (Riaan) (Northern Cape HS) b 14/01/86, Cradock. 1.82m. 97kg. Centre. FC DEBUT: 2007. PROV CAREER: KZN 2007-10 30-3-1-0-1-20. Sharks XV 2007-09 12-1-0-1-0-8. SUPER 14: Sharks 2009-10 20-0-0-0-0-0. FC RECORD: 62-4-1-1-1-28. RECORD IN 2010: (Sharks, KZN) 22-0-0-0-0-0.

Swart, Johannes Jacobus (Jaco) (Oosterlig HS) b 06/11/1979, Benoni. 1.96m. 112kg. Lock. FC DEBUT: 2010. PROV CAREER: Valke 2010 3-0-0-0-0-0. FC RECORD: 3-0-0-0-0-0. RECORD IN 2010: (Valke) 3-0-0-0-0-0.

Swart, Wayne (Florida HS) b 10/03/86, Johannesburg. 1.86m. 106kg. Prop. FC DEBUT: 2008. PROV CAREER: Lions 2009-10 13-0-0-0-0-0. Young Lions 2008-10 13-0-0-0-0-0. FC RECORD: 26-0-0-0-0-0. RECORD IN 2010: (Golden Lions, Young Lions) 11-0-0-0-0-0.

Swartbooi, Dewey Floyd (Esselen Park & Worcester Gym) b 27/07/82, Sutherland. 1.79m. 84kg. Centre. FC DEBUT: 2001. PROV CAREER: Blue Bulls 2001-03 10-3-0-0-0-15. Cheetahs 2005 3-2-0-0-0-10. Lions 2005-06 15-3-0-0-0-15. Boland 2006-10 37-4-0-0-0-20. Super 12: Bulls 2003 9-0-0-0-0-0. Cats 2005 8-0-0-0-0-0. REP HONOURS: SA U21 2002-03 8-0-0-0-0-0.

SA U19s 2001; SA Schools 2000; CW Boland 2000. FC RECORD: 90-12-0-0-0-60. RECORD IN 2010: (Boland) 9-3-0-0-0-15.

Sykes, Steven Robert (Marlow HS) b 05/08/84, Middelburg, Cape. 1.97m. 106kg. Lock. FC DEBUT: 2005. PROV CAREER: KZN 2005-10 80-5-0-0-0-25. Sharks XV 2005-08 21-0-0-0-0-0. SUPER 14: Sharks 2007-10 37-5-0-0-0-25-. REP HONOURS: Emerging Springboks 2009 1-0-0-0-0-0. FC RECORD: 139-10-0-0-0-50. RECORD IN 2010: (Sharks. KZN) 29-0-0-0-0-0.

T

Taljaard, Matthew. Hooker. FC DEBUT: 2008. PROV CAREER: Bulldogs 2008-10 33-3-0-0-0-15. FC RECORD: 33-3-0-0-0-15. RECORD IN 2010: (Bulldogs) 15-2-0-0-0-10.

Taljard, Jeffrey John (Hudson Park HS) b 22/04/87, East London. 1.81m. 90kg. Utility back. FC DEBUT: 2008. PROV CAREER: Bulldogs 2008-10 33-6-23-28-0-160. E/Cape XV 2008 2-0-0-0-0-0. FC RECORD: 35-6-23-28-0-160. RECORD IN 2010: (Bulldogs) 12-1-9-11-0-56.

Taute, Jacob Johannes (Jaco) (Monument HS) b 21/03/91, Springs. 1.89m. 91kg. Flyhalf. FC DEBUT: 2009. PROV CAREER: Lions 2009-10 13-5-0-0-0-25. Young Lions 2010 3-0-2-0-0-4. SUPER 14: Lions 2010 3-0-0-0-0-0. FC RECORD: 19-5-2-0-0-29. RECORD IN 2010 (Lions S14, Golden Lions, Young Lions) 18-5-2-0-0-29.

Tayler-Smith, Mathew (Grey HS) b 22/04/1987, Port Elizabeth. 1.79m. 88kg. Flyhalf. FC DEBUT: 2010. PROV CAREER: EP Kings 2010 11-0-0-0-0-0. EP Inv XV 2010 1-0-0-0-0-0. FC RECORD: 12-0-0-0-0-0. RECORD IN 2010: (EP Kings, EP Inv XV) 12-0-0-0-0-0.

Taylor, Jarrod Edward (St. Benedicts HS, Bedfordview) b 20/12/85, Johannesburg. 1.78m. 100kg. Hooker. FC DEBUT: 2007. PROV CAREER: Bulldogs 2007-08 10-1-0-0-0-5. E/Cape XV 2008 2-0-0-0-0-0. Pumas 2010 2-0-0-0-0-0. FC RECORD: 14-1-0-0-0-5. RECORD IN 2010: (Pumas) 2-0-0-0-0-0.

Terblanche, Carl Stefan (Swellendam HS & Boland Teachers' Coll.) b 02/07/75, Mossel Bay. 1.87m. 95kg. Wing. FC DEBUT: 1994. PROV CAREER: Boland 1994-98 66-45-8-18-0-295; KZN 1999-02,07-10 88-38-2-1-5-212. Sharks Inv XV 2010 1-1-0-0-0-5. SUPER 14: Sharks 1998-03 & 08-10 105-32-0-0-1-163. REP HONOURS: SA 1998-2000 & 2002-03 Tests 37-19-0-0-0-95, Tour 4-4-0-0-0-20, Total 41-23-0-0-0-115; SA XV 1999 2-3-0-0-0-15; SA U 21s 1996 1-1-0-0-0-5; SA Barbarians 1996 1-1-0-0-0-5; Craven Week Eagles 1991-93. Misc. info: British Barbarians 2000-01& 04

WHO'S WHO IN 2010

3-2-0-0-0-10; Holds Sharks record for most tries in a S14 career (31) and shares Sharks record for most tries in a S12 match (4); Holds Boland records for most tries in a season (20) and in a CC season (14). FC RECORD: 311-150-10-19-6-845. RECORD IN 2010: (Sharks, KZN, Sharks Inv XV) 29-6-0-0-1-33. OTHER FC: Ospreys, Wales 2003-07 86-16-0-1-1-86.

Terblanche, De-Jay (Knysna HS) b 25/06/85, Knysna. 1.89m. 124kg. Prop. FC DEBUT: 2008. PROV CAREER: Pumas 2008-09 39-3-0-0-0-15. FC RECORD: 39-3-0-0-0-15. RECORD IN 2010: (Pumas) 16-0-0-0-0-0.

Terblanche, Jacobus Kruger (Jaco) b 04/03/81, Oudtshoorn. 1.86m. 115kg. Utility Forward. FC DEBUT: 2005. PROV CAREER: Eagles 2005-10 66-2-0-0-0-10. FC RECORD: 66-2-0-0-0-10. RECORD IN 2010: (Eagles) 18-2-0-0-0-10.

Theisinger, Bernd (Jim Fouche HS) b 03/02/87, Bloemfontein. 1.85m. 94kg. Centre. FC DEBUT: 2008. PROV CAREER: Cheetahs 2008 10-4-0-0-0-20. Griffons 2008 3-0-0-0-0-0. Leopards 2009-10 10-0-0-0-0-0. FC RECORD: 23-4-0-0-0-20. RECORD IN 2010: (Leopards) 2-0-0-0-0-0.

Thompson, Lee Ray (Pretoria Boys HS) b 09/12/1988, Port Elizabeth. 1.92m. 105kg. Lock. FC DEBUT: 2010. PROV CAREER: Sharks XV 2010 3-0-0-0-0-0. FC RECORD: 3-0-0-0-0-0. RECORD IN 2010: (Sharks XV) 3-0-0-0-0-0.

Thomsen, Martin (Hugenote HS) b 17/02/87, Springs. 1.74m. 90kg. Flyhalf. FC DEBUT: 2009. PROV CAREER: Valke 2009-10 8-2-20-2-0-56. FC RECORD: 8-2-20-2-0-56. RECORD IN 2010: (Valke) 6-1-16-2-0-41.

Thyse, Hyron Mario (Noorder Paarl SS, Huguenot HS & Tygerberg Coll.) b 06/10/78, Paarl. 1.82m. 88kg. Wing. FC DEBUT: 2000. PROV CAREER: Boland 2000-01 & 10 30-9-0-0-0-45. Griquas 2002-03 26-3-0-0-0-15. Pumas 2004-09 84-22-0-0-0-110. FC RECORD: 140-34-0-0-0-170. RECORD IN 2010: (Boland) 8-3-0-0-0-15.

Tiedt, Jean (Monument HS) b 28/03/83, Randfontein. 1.81m. 78kg. Scrumhalf. FC DEBUT: 2005. PROV CAREER: Leopards 2005-06,09-10 46-5-7-4-0-51. REP HONOURS: SA Students 2007-08 2-2-7-4-0-36. MISC INFO: Son of former W-Tvl, SWD & Tvl fullback Jannie Tiedt. FC RECORD: 48-7-14-8-0-87. RECORD IN 2010: (Leopards) 9-1-5-1-0-18.

Tobias, Sidney (Paul Roos Gym.) b 20/03/1989, Caledon. 1.75m. 93kg. Hooker. FC DEBUT: 2010. PROV CAREER: WP 2010 2-0-0-0-0-0. Mis info: son of Errol Tobias. FC RECORD: 2-0-0-0-0-0. RECORD IN 2010:

(WP) 2-0-0-0-0-0.

Tonga, Nomani (Tonga HS) b 16/05/83, Vava'u. 108kg. Lock. SA FC DEBUT: 2008. PROV CAREER: Bulldogs 2008-10 33-4-0-0-0-20. E/Cape XV 2008 2-0-0-0-0-0. SA FC RECORD: 35-4-0-0-0-20. RECORD IN 2010: (Bulldogs) 15-4-0-0-0-20.

Tshemese, Siyabonga (David Mama HS) b 20/11/1979, Mdantsane. 1.79m. 89kg. Eightman. FC DEBUT: 2010. PROV CAREER: Bulldogs 2010 4-1-0-0-0-5. FC RECORD: 4-1-0-0-0-5. RECORD IN 2010: (Bulldogs) 4-1-0-0-0-5.

Tyibilika, Solomzi (Solly) (Loyiso HS) b 23/06/79, Port Elizabeth. 1.88m. 95kg. Flanker. FC DEBUT: 2001. PROV CAREER: Griquas 2001-02 37-2-0-0-0-10. Lions 2003,07 6-1-0-0-0-5. KZN 2003-06 40-10-0-0-0-50. Bulldogs 2008-10 43-6-0-0-0-30. Lions XV 2007 1-0-0-0-0-0. E/Cape XV 2008 2-1-0-0-0-5. SUPER 14: Sharks 2004-06 16-1-0-0-0-5. REP HONOURS: SA Tests: 2004-06 8-3-0-0-0-15. SA 'A' 2004. Emerging Springboks 2007 3-0-0-0-0-0. S/Kings 2009 1-0-0-0-0-0. MISC INFO: SuperSport Club champs PoY 2003. FC RECORD: 158-24-0-0-0-120. RECORD IN 2010: (Bulldogs) 13-0-0-0-0-0.

U

Uys, BG. b 20/06/88. 1.90m. 113kg. Prop. FC DEBUT: 2008. PROV CAREER: Leopards 2010 10-0-0-0-0-0. REP HONOURS: SA Students 2008-09 3-1-0-0-0-5. FC RECORD: 13-1-0-0-0-5. RECORD IN 2010: (Leopards) 10-0-0-0-0-0.

Uys, Corné Janse (Bredasdorp HS) b 02/10/82, Alberton. 1.90m. 87kgs. Centre. FC DEBUT: 2004. PROV CAREER: WP 2004-07 48-16-0-0-0-80. Cheetahs 2009-10 27-5-0-0-0-25. Cheetahs XV 2010 1-0-0-0-0-0. SUPER 14: Stormers 2007 10-1-0-0-0-5. Cheetahs 2009-10 17-4-0-0-0-20. MISC INFO: Son of former SWD wing & Springbok Athlete Cornelis Uys. FC RECORD: 103-26-0-0-0-130. RECORD IN 2010: (Cheetahs S14, Cheetahs, Cheetahs XV) 19-5-0-0-0-25.

Uys, Francois Jacobus (Dr EG Jansen) b 12/03/86, Springs. 1.91m. 103kg. Flank. FC DEBUT: 2006. PROV CAREER: Lions 2006-08 24-5-0-0-0-25. Cheetahs 2009-10 30-5-0-0-0-25. Griffons 2008 & 10 10-0-0-0-0-0. Lions XV 2008 1-0-0-0-0-0. SUPER 14: Cheetahs 2009 2-0-0-0-0-0. REP HONOURS: SA U19 2005. FC RECORD: 67-10-0-0-0-50. RECORD IN 2010: (Cheetahs, Griffons) 20-3-0-0-0-15.

Uys, Philipus Rudolph (Ronnie) (FH Odendaal HS) b 19/04/79, Pretoria. 1.87m 130kg. Prop. FC DEBUT: 2005. PROV CAREER: Leopards 2005-07 42-8-0-0-0-40. KZN 2007 9-0-0-0-0-0. Cheetahs 2008 9-1-0-0-0-5.

Griffons 2008 6-0-0-0-0-0. Pumas 2009-10 32-4-0-0-0-20. KZN XV 2007 1-0-0-0-0-0. SUPER 14: Cheetahs 2008 2-0-0-0-0-0. FC RECORD: 101-13-0-0-0-65. RECORD IN 2010: (Pumas) 22-3-0-0-0-15.

V

Van Aswegen, Gary Jacques (Standerton HS & Univ. Stellenbosch) b 18/02/1990, Pretoria. 1.76m. 83kg. Fly-half. FC DEBUT: 2010. PROV CAREER: WP 2-0-4-0-0-8. FC RECORD: 2-0-4-0-0-8. RECORD IN 2010: (WP) 2-0-4-0-0-8.

Van den Berg, Willem Johannes (Kroonstad HS) b 13/03/1986, Frankfort. 1.74m. 81kg. Scrumhalf. FC DEBUT: 2010. PROV CAREER: Valke 2010 4-0-0-0-0-0. FC RECORD: 4-0-0-0-0-0. RECORD IN 2010: (Valke) 4-0-0-0-0-0.

Van den Heever, Gerhard Jacobus (Afrikaans HS) b 13/04/89, Bloemfontein. 1.90m. 93kg. Wing. FC DE-BUT: 2009. PROV CAREER: Blue Bulls 2009-10 33-18-0-0-0-90. SUPER 14: Bulls 2009-10 17-9-0-0-0-45. FC RECORD: 50-27-0-0-0-135. RECORD IN 2010 (Bulls, Blue Bulls) 28-13-0-0-0-65.

Van der Linde, Christoffel Johannes (CJ) (Grey Coll., Bloemfontein) b 27/08/80, Welkom. 1.90m. 122kg. Prop. FC DEBUT: 2000. Prov career: Cheetahs 2002-05 & 10 49-6-0-0-0-30. Super 14: Cats 2004-05 19-1-0-0-0-5. Cheetahs 2006-08 19-2-0-0-0-10. Rep honours: SA 2002 & 2004-10 Tests: 69-4-0-0-0-20. Tour: 2006, 07,09,10 5-0-0-0-0-0. Total: 74-4-0-0-0-20. SA U21s 2000-01 8-0-0-0-0-0; SA U19s 1999; SA Schools 1998; CW Cheetahs 1998. FC record: 169-13-0-0-0-65. RECORD IN 2010: (SA, Cheetahs) 16-0-0-0-0-0.

Van der Merwe, Daniel Joubert (Wilgerivier HS) b 24/01/1989, Frankfort. 1.83m. 119kg. Prop. FC DE-BUT: 2010. PROV CAREER: Young Lions 2010 1-0-0-0-0-0. FC RECORD: 1-0-0-0-0-0. RECORD IN 2010: (Young Lions) 1-0-0-0-0-0.

Van der Merwe, Franco (Hartswater HS) b 15/03/83, Paarl. 1.99m. 107kg. Lock/Flank. FC DEBUT: 2004. PROV CAREER: Leopards 2004-06 58-8-0-0-0-40. Lions 2006-10 65-8-0-0-0-40. Lions XV 2007-08 2-0-0-0-0-0. Young Lions 2009 2-0-0-0-0-0. SUPER 14: Lions 2007-10 44-4-0-0-0-20. REP HONOURS: Emerging Springboks 2009 1-0-0-0-0-0. SA U21 2004 3-0-0-0-0-0. FC RECORD: 175-20-0-0-0-100. RECORD IN 2010: (Lions S14, Golden Lions) 26-3-0-0-0-15.

Van der Merwe, Hendrik Schalk (Heinke) (Monument HS) b 03/05/85, Johannesburg. 1.82m. 110kg. Prop. FC DEBUT: 2005. PROV CAREER: Lions 2005-08 & 10 40-2-0-0-0-10. Young Lions 2005-10 8-0-0-0-0-0. SUPER 14: Sharks 2006 8-0-0-0-0-0. Lions 2007-10

45-0-0-0-0-0. Lions XV 2008 1-0-0-0-0-0. REP HON-OURS: SA 2007 Tests: 1-0-0-0-0-0. Tour: 2007,09 3-0-0-0-0-0. Total: 4-0-0-0-0-0. Emerging Springboks 2007 3-0-0-0-0-0. SA U21 2005-06 10-0-0-0-0-0. African Leopards 2005. MISC INFO: Son of former Tvl prop Schalk "Oupa" van der Merwe. FC RECORD: 120-2-0-0-0-10. RECORD IN 2010: (Lions S14, Young Lions) 12-0-0-0-0-0.

Van der Merwe, Louis Johannes (Noordelig HS) b 09/04/1981, Bothaville. 1.69m. 79kg. Scrumhalf. FC DEBUT: 2010. PROV CAREER: Valke 2010 2-0-0-0-0-0. FC RECORD: 2-0-0-0-0-0. RECORD IN 2010: (Valke) 2-0-0-0-0-0.

Van der Merwe, Phillip Rudolph (Flip) (Grey Coll., Bloemfontein) b 03/06/85, Potchefstroom. 1.99m. 117kg. Lock. FC DEBUT: 2006. Prov career: Cheetahs 2006-09 37-2-0-0-0-10. Griffons 2007 1-0-0-0-0-0. Blue Bulls 2009-10 23-3-0-0-0-15. Super 14: Cheetahs 2007-09 6-1-0-0-0-5. Bulls 2010 13-0-0-0-0-0. Rep honours: SA 2010 Tests: 10-1-0-0-0-5. SA Tour 2010: 1-0-0-0-0-0. SA Students 2007 1-0-0-0-0-0. Misc info: Son of Springbok Flippie van der Merwe. Brother of Francois van der Merwe (WP). FC record: 89-6-0-0-0-30. RECORD IN 2010: (SA, Bulls, Blue Bulls) 33-1-0-0-0-5.

Van der Nest, Andries Hendrik (Hendrik) (Wonderboom HS) b 27/11/81, Pretoria. 1.75m. 70kg. Scrumhalf. FC DEBUT: 2006. PROV CAREER: Eagles 2006-08 55-23-0-0-0-115. Pumas 2009-10 17-4-0-0-0-20. Griffons 2010 8-6-0-0-0-30. FC RECORD: 80-33-0-0-0-165. RECORD IN 2010: (Griffons) 8-6-0-0-0-30.

Van der Walt, Barend Christian (Volkskool, Heidelberg) b 07/03/82, Alberton. 1.86m. 127kg. Prop. FC DE-BUT: 2006. PROV CAREER: Pumas 2006 1-0-0-0-0-0. Elephants 2007-08 30-2-0-0-0-10. Leopards 2008-10 39-0-0-0-0-0. FC RECORD: 70-2-0-0-0-10. RECORD IN 2010: (Leopards) 19-0-0-0-0-0.

Van der Walt, Christoffel Philippus (Philip) (Adelaide Gym & UOFS) b 14/07/1989, Adelaide. 1.94m. 105kgs. Eightman. FC DEBUT: 2010. PROV CAREER: Cheetahs 2010 11-2-0-0-0-10. SUPER 14: Cheetahs 2010 5-1-0-0-0-5. FC RECORD: 16-3-0-0-0-15. RECORD IN 2010: (Cheetahs S14, Cheetahs) 16-3-0-0-0-15.

Van der Walt, Eduan Raymond (Zwartkop HS) b 20/03/87, Pretoria. 1.97m. 103kg. Lock. FC DEBUT: 2008. PROV CAREER: Blue Bulls 2008 2-0-0-0-0-0. Pumas 2008-10 36-6-0-0-0-30. FC RECORD: 38-6-0-0-0-30. RECORD IN 2010: (Pumas) 13-1-0-0-0-5.

Van der Walt, Hendrik Stefanus (Grey Coll. & UOFS) b 01/01/1990, Cape Town. 1.91m. 98kg. Eightman. FC DEBUT: 2010. PROV CAREER: Cheetahs 2010 2-0-0-

0-0-0. FC RECORD: 2-0-0-0-0-0. RECORD IN 2010: (Cheetahs) 2-0-0-0-0-0.

Van der Walt, Petrus Willem (Wimpie) (Nelspruit HS) b 06/01/1989, Brits. 1.87m. 102kg. Flanker. FC DEBUT: 2010. PROV CAREER: WP 2010 6-1-0-0-0-5. FC RECORD: 6-1-0-0-0-5. RECORD IN 2010: (WP) 6-1-0-0-0-5.

Van der Walt, Shöne (Springs THS) b 28/07/80, Springs. 1.78m. 100kg. Hooker. FC DEBUT: 2004. PROV CAREER: Falcons 2004,07-10 24-3-0-0-0-15. MISC INFO: Son of former Eastern Transvaal hooker Tjaart van der Walt. FC RECORD: 24-3-0-0-0-15. RECORD IN 2010 (Valke) 15-3-0-0-0-15.

Van der Westhuizen, Anton (Brood) (Patriot HS) b 03/05/75, Witbank. 1.87m. 123kgs. Prop. FC DEBUT: 2005. PROV CAREER: Elephants 2005-06 18-0-0-0-0-0. WP 2007 2-0-0-0-0-0. Eagles 2010 41-2-0-0-0-10. FC RECORD: 61-2-0-0-0-10. RECORD IN 2010: (Eagles) 20-1-0-0-0-5.

Van der Westhuizen, Izak Petrus (Diamandveldt HS) b 23/01/86, Kimberley. 1.96m. 108kg. Lock. FC DEBUT: 2007. PROV CAREER: Cheetahs 2007-10 46-1-0-0-0-5. Griffons 2008-09 14-0-0-0-0-0. SUPER 14: Cheetahs 2010 6-0-0-0-0-0. FC RECORD: 66-1-0-0-0-5. RECORD IN 2010: (Cheetahs S14, Cheetahs) 25-0-0-0-0-0.

Van der Westhuizen, Marthinus Riaan Stefanus (Pellow) (Middelburg THS) b 03/02/84, Uitenhage. 1.79m. 98kg. Hooker/Prop. FC DEBUT: 2004. PROV CAREER: Leopards 2005-10 85-7-0-0-0-35. KZN 2007 1-0-0-0-0-0. REP HONOURS: Royal XV 2009 1-0-0-0-0-0. SA U21 2004 5-0-0-0-0-0. SA Students 2005 1-0-0-0-0-0. SA U19 2003. FC RECORD: 93-7-0-0-0-35. RECORD IN 2010: (Leopards) 20-2-0-0-0-10.

Van der Westhuizen, Roche Rowland (Grey Coll.) b 09/02/88, Douglas. 1.82m. 111kg. Prop. FC DEBUT: 2008. PROV CAREER: Cheetahs 2008-09 14-0-0-0-0-0. Pumas 2010 1-0-0-0-0-0. FC RECORD: 15-0-0-0-0-0. RECORD IN 2010: (Pumas) 1-0-0-0-0-0.

Van der Westhuyzen, Jacobus Nicolaas Boshoff (Jaco) (Ben Viljoen HS & UNISA) b 06/04/78, Nelspruit. 1.78m. 86kgs. Flyhalf. FC DEBUT: 1997. PROV CAREER: KZN 1997-99 21-14-13-0-0-96. Pumas 2000 6-3-6-2-1-36. Blue Bulls 2001-03 & 06 & 10 48-20-50-26-1-281. SUPER 14: Bulls 2000 & 02-03 & 06-07 & 10 54-7-10-3-0-64. REP HONOURS: SA 2000-01 & 03-06 Tests 32-5-7-1-3-51. SA 'A' 2001 2-1-0-0-0-5. SA XV 2006 1-0-0-0-0-0. S/Kings 2009 1-0-0-1-0-3. SA U23s 2000-01 9-6-38-1-0-109. SA U21s 1998-99 8-5-6-4-0-49. SA Barbarians 2001 1-1-3-2-0-17. SA Schools 1996. CW Pumas 1995-96. MISC INFO: Leicester

(Eng) 2003-2004. NEC (Japan) 2004-07. FC RECORD: 178-62-133-40-5-711. RECORD IN 2010: (Bulls, Blue Bulls) 21-3-0-0-1-18.

Van Deventer, Johan Christiaan (Monument HS) b 05/04/88, Potgietersrus. 1.77m. 90kg. Flanker. FC DEBUT: 2008. PROV CAREER: Lions 2009 3-0-0-0-0-0. Young Lions 2008-10 14-5-0-0-0-25. Griquas 2010 6-1-0-0-0-5. SUPER 14: Lions 2009 3-1-0-0-0-5. FC RECORD: 26-7-0-0-0-35. RECORD IN 2010: (Griquas, Young Lions) 11-6-0-0-0-30.

Van Dyk, Hans Jacob (Middelburg THS) b 29/04/82, Bethal. 1.75m. 102kg. Hooker. FC DEBUT: 2005. PROV CAREER: Leopards 2005-06 43-3-0-0-0-15. Griquas 2007-08 37-6-0-0-0-30. Lions 2009 15-1-0-0-0-5. Young Lions 2010 5-1-0-0-0-5. Pumas 2010 5-1-0-0-0-5. SUPER 14: Cheetahs 2007 6-0-0-0-0-0. Lions 2009-10 15-0-0-0-0-0. MISC INFO: Brother of BW van Dyk. FC RECORD: 126-12-0-0-0-60. RECORD IN 2010: (Lions S14, Young Lions, Pumas) 13-2-0-0-0-10.

Van Eyk, Regardt (Daniel Pienaar HS) b 14/03/83, Port Elizabeth. 1.80m 83kgs. Flyhalf. FC DEBUT: 2003. PROV CAREER: EP Kings 2003-05 & 10 23-7-1-0-0-37. REP HONOURS: CW EP 2001. FC RECORD: 23-7-1-0-0-37. RECORD IN 2010: (EP Kings) 4-0-0-0-0-0.

Van Heerden, Derrick (Strand HS) b 15/02/1988. 1.78m. 103kg. Hooker. FC DEBUT: 2010. PROV CAREER: Griffons 2010 17-2-0-0-0-10. FC RECORD: 17-2-0-0-0-10. RECORD IN 2010: (Griffons) 17-2-0-0-10.

Van Heerden, Johannes Lodewikus (Wikus) (Waterkloof HS & RAU) b 25/02/79, Johannesburg. 1.95m. 104kg. Flank. FC DEBUT: 2000. PROV CAREER: Lions 2001-06 & 10 88-16-0-0-0-80. Young Lions 2001-06 & 10 4-4-0-0-0-20. Blue Bulls 2007-08 15-6-0-0-0-30. SUPER 14: Cats 2002, 2004-06 39-5-0-0-0-25. Bulls 2003,07-08 38-12-0-0-0-60. Lions 2010 6-0-0-0-0-0. REP HONOURS: SA 2003,07 Tests: 13-1-0-0-0-5. Tour: 2-1-0-0-0-5. Total: 16-2-0-0-0-10 SA 'A' 2004 4-0-0-0-0-0. SA U21s 2000 4-2-0-0-0-10; SA U19s 1998; CW Blue Bulls 1997. MISC INFO: Son of 1974-80 Springbok Moaner van Heerden. FC RECORD: 213-47-0-0-0-235. RECORD IN 2010: (Lions S14, Golden Lions, Young Lions) 12-1-0-0-0-5.

Van Heerden, Johannes Petrus (Hercules HS) b 09/12/86, Pretoria. 1.96m. 96kg. Lock. FC DEBUT: 2007. PROV CAREER: Pumas 2007-10 32-4-0-0-0-20. Griffons 2010 4-0-0-0-0-0. FC RECORD: 36-4-0-0-0-20. RECORD IN 2010: (Pumas, Griffons) 5-0-0-0-0-0.

Van Jaarsveld, Gregory John (Dirkie Uys HS) b 28/12/82, Pietersburg. 1.76m. 104kg. Hooker. FC DE-

BUT: 2007. PROV CAREER: Bulldogs 2007-10 47-0-0-0-0-0. REP HONOURS: Emerging Springboks 2008 1-0-0-0-0-0. FC RECORD: 48-0-0-0-0-0. RECORD IN 2010: (Bulldogs) 1-0-0-0-0-0.

Van Jaarsveld, Torsten George (Hendrik Verwoerd HS) b 30/06/87. 1.75m. 89kg. Hooker. FC DEBUT: 2008. PROV CAREER: Pumas 2008-10 34-5-0-0-0-25. FC RECORD: 34-5-0-0-0-25. RECORD IN 2010: (Pumas) 17-2-0-0-0-10.

Van Lill, Carel Philippus (Paarl Gym.) b 02/02/1987, Middelburg. 1.85m. 95kg. Wing. FC DEBUT: 2010. PROV CAREER: Valke 2010 7-1-0-0-0-5. FC RECORD: 7-1-0-0-0-5. RECORD IN 2010: (Valke) 7-1-0-0-0-5.

Van Niekerk, Christo (Kanonkop HS) b 23/01/81, Middelburg. 1.91m. 99kg. Loose Forward. FC DEBUT: 2004. PROV CAREER: Griffons 2004-07 67-12-0-0-0-60. Leopards 2008-10 39-5-0-0-0-25. FC RECORD: 106-17-0-0-0-85. RECORD IN 2010: (Leopards) 16-2-0-0-0-10.

Van Niekerk, Clint (Waterkloof HS) b 26/03/85, Pretoria. 1.83m. 117kgs. Prop. FC DEBUT: 2008. PROV CAREER: Young Lions 2008 & 10 4-0-0-0-0-0. FC RECORD: 4-0-0-0-0-0. RECORD IN 2010: (Young Lions) 1-0-0-0-0-0.

Van Niekerk, Johann Christiaan (Joe) (KES & RAU) b 14/05/80, Port Elizabeth. 1.92m. 106kg. Eighthman. FC DEBUT: 2000. PROV CAREER: Lions 2001-02 19-6-0-0-0-30. WP 2004-05,07 15-3-0-0-0-15. SUPER 14: Cats 2002-03 11-1-0-0-0-5. Stormers 2005-07 21-3-0-0-0-15.Lions 2008 12-1-0-0-0-5. REP HONOURS: SA 2001-06 & 08 & 10 Tests 52-10-0-0-0-50; SA XV 2006 1-0-0-0-0-0. SA U21s 2000-01 9-4-0-0-0-20; SA Sevens 2001; SA U19s 1998; SA Schools 1997-98; CW Lions 1997-98. MISC INFO: PoY 2002; PoY nominee 2003. IRB PoY nominee 2002. FC RECORD: 140-28-0-0-0-140. RECORD IN 2010: (SA) 1-0-0-0-0-0.

Van Niekerk, Johannes Lambrechts (Janru) (Paarl Boys HS) b 05/11/82, Worcester. 1.82m. 110kg. Prop. FC DEBUT: 2006. PROV CAREER: Boland 2006-10 92-5-0-0-0-25. REP HONOURS: Emerging Springboks 2008 3-0-0-0-0-0. FC RECORD: 95-5-0-0-0-25. RECORD IN 2010: (Boland) 18-1-0-0-0-5.

Van Rensburg, Andries Gideon (Deon) (Potch THS) b 24/01/82, Potchefstroom. 1.78m. 92kg. Centre. FC DEBUT: 2004. PROV CAREER: Leopards 2004-09 92-44-0-0-0-220. Golden Lions 2010 10-5-0-0-0-25. SUPER 14: Lions 2009-10 15-0-0-0-0-0. REP HONOURS: Emerging Springboks 2009 1-0-0-0-0-0. Royal XV 2009 1-0-0-0-0-0. FC RECORD: 119-49-0-0-0-

245. RECORD IN 2010: (Lions S14, Golden Lions) 18-5-0-0-0-25.

Van Rensburg, Jakobus Christo Janse (JC) (Oakdale HS) b 09/01/86, Prins Albert. 1.85m. 111kg. Prop. FC DEBUT: 2006. PROV CAREER: Lions 2006-10 43-0-0-0-0-0. Lions XV 2007-08 2-0-0-0-0-0. Young Lions 2006-09 8-1-0-0-0-5. SUPER 14: Lions 2008-10 24-1-0-0-0-5. REP HONOURS: SA U19 2005. FC RECORD: 77-2-0-0-0-10. RECORD IN 2010: (Lions S14, Golden Lions) 24-1-0-0-0-5.

Van Rooyen, Christiaan Stephanus (Windpomp) (Klerksdorp THS) b 29/04/81, Heidelberg. 2.04m. 112kg. Lock. FC DEBUT: 2002. PROV CAREER: Leopards 2002-03 10-0-0-0-0-0. Griquas 2004-06 47-5-0-0-0-25. Griffons 2007-10 56-1-0-0-0-5. Super 12: Cats 2005 1-0-0-0-0-0. REP HONOURS: SA U21 2002 5-0-0-0-0-0. FC RECORD: 119-6-0-0-0-30. RECORD IN 2010: (Griffons) 18-1-0-0-0-5.

Van Rooyen, Johannes Jacobus (Transvalia HS) b 08/11/1988, Vanderbijlpark. 1.80m. 82kg. Scrumhalf. FC DEBUT: 2010. PROV CAREER: Valke 2010 7-0-0-0-0-0. FC RECORD: 7-0-0-0-0-0. RECORD IN 2010: (Valke) 7-0-0-0-0-0.

Van Schalkwyk, Andries Johannes (Dries) (St Andrews HS) b 21/12/84, Bloemfontein. 1.92m. 105kg. Eighthman. FC DEBUT: 2006. PROV CAREER: Cheetahs 2006 4-1-0-0-0-5. Valke 2006 4-0-0-0-0-0. Boland 2007-08 31-7-0-0-0-35. Blue Bulls 2009-10 20-2-0-0-0-10. REP HONOURS: S/Kings 2009 1-0-0-0-0-0. FC RECORD: 60-10-0-0-0-50. RECORD IN 2010: (Blue Bulls) 4-2-0-0-0-10.

Van Schalkwyk, Hendrik Jacobus (Jaco) (Paarl BHS) b 13/09/79, Vanwyksvlei. 1.80m. 80kg. Fullback. FC DEBUT: 2001. PROV CAREER: WP 2001 12-4-0-0-0-20. Cheetahs 2002-05 49-8-2-0-0-44. Lions 2006-08 30-8-3-0-1-49. Lions XV 2008 1-0-0-0-0-0. EP Kings 2009-10 10-0-4-4-1-23. SUPER 14: Lions 2007-08 25-3-0-2-1-24 REP HONOURS: SA Sevens 2003-04. MISC INFO: Calvisano (Italy) 2005-06. FC RECORD: 127-23-9-6-3-160. RECORD IN 2010: (EP Kings) 7-0-4-4-1-23.

Van Schalkwyk, Robert (Voortrekker HS & UOFS) b 25/05/1990, Pietermaritzburg. 1.91m. 98kg. Wing. FC DEBUT: 2010. PROV CAREER: Cheetahs 2010 4-3-0-0-0-15. FC RECORD: 4-3-0-0-0-15. RECORD IN 2010: (Cheetahs) 4-3-0-0-0-15.

Van Staden, Eugene (Bredasdorp HS) b 16/12/80, Cradock. 1.81m. 120kgs. Prop. FC DEBUT: 2005. PROV CAREER: Elephants 2005 12-2-0-0-0-10. Griquas 2006-07 47-4-0-0-0-20. KZN 2010 15-2-0-0-0-10.

Sharks Inv XV 2010 1-0-0-0-0-0. FC RECORD: 75-8-0-0-0-40. RECORD IN 2010: (KZN, Sharks Inv XV) 16-2-0-0-0-10.

Van Staden, Justin (Merensky HS) b 03/06/1990, Tzaneen. 1.83m. 76kg. Centre. FC DEBUT: 2010. PROV CAREER: Blue Bulls 2010 1-0-0-0-0-0. FC RECORD: 1-0-0-0-0-0. RECORD IN 2010: (Blue Bulls) 1-0-0-0-0-0.

Van Tonder, Christoffel Johannes. b 05/05/1992. Wing. FC DEBUT: 2010. PROV CAREER: Valke 2010 2-0-0-0-0-0. FC RECORD: 2-0-0-0-0-0. RECORD IN 2010: (Valke) 2-0-0-0-0-0.

Van Velze, Gerrit-Jan (AHS, Pretoria) b 20/02/88, Secunda. 1.94m. 102kg. Eighthman. FC DEBUT: 2007. PROV CAREER: Blue Bulls 2008-10 40-8-0-0-0-40. Blue Bulls XV 2007 1-0-0-0-0-0. SUPER 14: Bulls 2010 1-0-0-0-0-0. FC RECORD: 42-8-0-0-0-40. RECORD IN 2010: (Bulls, Blue Bulls) 21-7-0-0-0-35.

Van Vuuren, Pieter-Willem (Grey Coll.) b 10/01/88, Cradock. 1.81m. 97kg. Hooker. FC DEBUT: 2008. PROV CAREER: Cheetahs 2008-10 20-2-0-0-0-10. Griffons 2010 8-0-0-0-0-0. FC RECORD: 28-2-0-0-0-10. RECORD IN 2010: (Cheetahs, Griffons) 20-1-0-0-0-5.

Van Wyk, Coenraad George (Paul Roos Gym.) b 08/01/88, Belville. 1.83m. 80kg. FC DEBUT: 2009. PROV CAREER: WP 2009 5-0-1-0-0-2. Griquas 2010 3-2-7-1-0-27. FC RECORD: 8-2-8-1-0-29. RECORD IN 2010: (Griquas) 3-2-7-1-0-27.

Van Wyk, Tiaan (Kroonstad HS) b 21/04/89, Kroonstad. 1.83m. 90kg. FC DEBUT: 2009. PROV CAREER: Griffons 2009-10 13-0-15-14-0-72. FC RECORD: 13-0-15-14-0-72. RECORD IN 2010: (Griffons) 10-0-13-14-0-68.

Van Wyk, Theo Clyde b 11/02/83. 1.79m. 80kg. Scrumhalf. FC DEBUT: 2004. PROV CAREER: Leopards 2004 & 06-10 81-9-0-0-0-45. FC RECORD: 81-9-0-0-0-45. RECORD IN 2010: (Leopards) 10-2-0-0-0-10.

Van Zyl, Anton (Rondebosch Boys HS) b 23/02/80, Cape Town. 1.97m. 108kg. Lock. ›› FC debut: 2002. Prov career: WP 2002,09-10 41-2-0-0-0-10. Lions 2006-08 45-3-0-0-0-15. Super 14: Lions 2007-09 30-1-0-0-0-5. Super 14: Stormers 2010 15-1-0-0-0-5. Misc info: Son of former Natal lock Mike van Zyl. FC record: 132-7-0-0-0-35. RECORD IN 2010: (Stormers, WP, Barbarians) 33-3-0-0-0-15.

Van Zyl, Arno Christiaan (Welkom Gym.) b 01/02/1989, Odendaalsrus. 1.78m. 89kg. Centre. FC DEBUT: 2010. PROV CAREER: Sharks XV 2010 3-0-0-0-0-0. FC RECORD: 3-0-0-0-0-0. RECORD IN 2010: (Sharks XV) 3-0-0-0-0-0.

Van Zyl, Divan (Noord-Kaap HS) b 14/10/88, Kuruman, 1.81m. 80kg. Flyhalf. FC DEBUT: 2008. PROV CAREER: Cheetahs 2008-09 11-1-0-0-0-5. Bulldogs 2010 9-0-0-0-0-0. Griquas 2010 6-0-1-0-0-2. FC RECORD: 26-1-1-0-0-7. RECORD IN 2010: (Griquas, Bulldogs) 15-0-1-0-0-2.

Van Zyl, Johannes Hermanus Albertus (Jan) (Paarl Gym.) b 23/01/85, Cape Town. 1.81m. 85kg. Fullback. FC DEBUT: 2007. PROV CAREER: Leopards 2007-10 53-23-0-0-0-115. FC RECORD: 53-23-0-0-0-115. RECORD IN 2010: (Leopards) 8-3-0-0-0-15.

Van Zyl, Petrus Erasmus (Pieter) (Grey Coll. & UOFS) b 14/09/1989, Pretoria. 1.74m. 81kg. Scrumhalf. FC DEBUT: 2010. PROV CAREER: Cheetahs 2010 9-2-0-0-0-10. FC RECORD: 9-2-0-0-0-10. RECORD IN 2010: (Cheetahs) 9-2-0-0-0-10.

Velthuizen, Johan Michiel (Luhan) (Middelburg THS) b 22/10/84, Middelburg. 1.96m. 117kg. Flank. FC DEBUT: 2008. PROV CAREER: Pumas 2008-10 30-1-0-0-0-5. FC RECORD: 30-1-0-0-0-5. RECORD IN 2010: (Pumas) 10-0-0-0-0-0.

Venter, Benjamin Christoffel Gerhardus (Ben) (Henneman HS) b 15/05/1987, Johannesburg. 1.97m. 116kg. Lock. FC DEBUT: 2010. PROV CAREER: Bulldogs 2010 9-1-0-0-0-5. Griquas 2010 1-0-0-0-0-0. FC RECORD: 10-1-0-0-0-5. RECORD IN 2010: (Bulldogs, Griquas) 10-1-0-0-0-5.

Venter, Christopher (Chris) (Waterkloof HS) b 18/04/82, Pretoria. 1.82m. 115kg. Hooker. FC DEBUT: 2005. PROV CAREER: Sharks XV 2005,09 10-0-0-0-0-0. Valke 2006 & 08 22-0-0-0-0-0. Griquas 2010 4-2-0-0-0-10. MISC INFO: Connacht (Ire) 2006-07. FC RECORD: 36-2-0-0-0-10. RECORD IN 2010: (Griquas) 4-2-0-0-0-10.

Venter, Jacques Landon (George Campbell HS & Univ. Pretoria) b 27/12/1983, Durban. 1.83m. 94kg. Flyhalf. FC DEBUT: 2010. PROV CAREER: Sharks XV 2010 6-0-1-4-0-14. FC RECORD: 6-0-1-4-0-14. RECORD IN 2010: (Sharks XV) 6-0-1-4-0-14.

Venter, Shaun (AHS, Pretoria) b 16/03/87, Witbank. 1.80m. 80kg. Scrumhalf. FC DEBUT: 2007. PROV CAREER: Pumas 2007-10 57-21-0-0-0-105. FC RECORD: 57-21-0-0-0-105. RECORD IN 2010: (Pumas) 15-8-0-0-0-40.

Venter, Walter (Monument HS) b 07/08/84, Virginia. 1.80m. 86kg. Centre. FC DEBUT: 2005. PROV CAREER: Lions 2005,07-09 18-7-0-0-0-35. Lions XV 2007-08 2-0-0-0-0-0. Young Lions 2005-09 13-5-0-0-0-25. Leopards 2006 & 10 13-4-0-0-0-20. Valke 2007 4-0-0-0-0-0. SUPER 14: Lions 2008-10 18-1-0-0-0-5. FC

RECORD: 68-17-0-0-0-85. RECORD IN 2010: (Lions S14, Leopards) 20-4-0-0-0-20.

Vermaak, Jano (THS Vereeniging) b 01/01/85, Graaff-Reinet. 1.75m. 77kg. Scrumhalf. FC DEBUT: 2005. PROV CAREER: Lions 2005-10 71-16-3-4-0-98. Young Lions 2005-08 & 10 6-1-0-0-0-5. SUPER 14: Cats 2006 11-1-0-0-0-5. Lions 2007-10 47-8-3-4-0-58. Lions XV 2008 1-0-0-0-0-0. REP HONOURS: Emerging Springboks 2007,09 4-2-0-0-0-10. SA U21 2006 5-2-0-0-0-10. SA Sevens 2005. MISC INFO: Son of former EP & NEC hooker Deon Vermaak. FC RECORD: 144-30-6-8-0-186. RECORD IN 2010: (Lions S14, Golden Lions, Young Lions) 24-5-0-0-0-25.

Vermaas, Cornelius Hermanus (Harry) (AHS, Pretoria & Tukkies) b 23/01/1984, Klerksdorp. 1.78m. 110kg. Prop. FC DEBUT: 2005. PROV CAREER: Blue Bulls 2005-06 22-4-0-0-0-20. Boland 2007-09 34-0-0-0-0-0. Pumas 2010 2-0-0-0-0-0. REP HONOURS: SA U21 2005 5-1-0-0-0-5. African Leopards 2005 1-0-0-0-0-0. MISC INFO: Leinster (Ire) 2006-07. FC RECORD: 64-5-0-0-0-25. RECORD IN 2010: (Pumas) 2-0-0-0-0-0.

Vermeulen, Daniel Johannes (Nelspruit HS) b 03/07/86, Nelspruit. 1.92m. 90kg. Flank. FC DEBUT: 2005. PROV CAREER: Pumas 2005-06 26-4-0-0-0-20. Cheetahs 2007-08 28-2-0-0-0-10. WP 2009-10 30-6-0-0-0-30. SUPER 14: Cheetahs 2007-08 20-3-0-0-0-15. Stormers 2009-10 28-2-0-0-0-10. REP HONOURS: Emerging Springboks 2009 1-0-0-0-0-0. FC RECORD: 133-17-0-0-0-85. RECORD IN 2010: (Stormers, WP) 32-6-0-0-0-30.

Vermeulen, Petrus Jacobus (PJ) (Northern Cape HS) b 03/03/87, De Aar. 1.82m. 86kg. Centre. FC DEBUT: 2007. PROV CAREER: WP 2007-09 26-6-0-0-0-30. Boland 2009-10 25-4-0-0-0-20. FC RECORD: 51-10-0-0-0-50. RECORD IN 2010: (Boland) 19-4-0-0-0-20.

Vermeulen, Riaan (Grey Coll., Bloemfontein) b 03/08/84, Middelburg. 1.84m. 122kg. Prop. FC DEBUT: 2003. PROV CAREER: Cheetahs 2003 & 10 10-1-0-0-0-5. WP 2006-07 15-0-0-0-0-0. EP Kings 2010 11-1-0-0-0-5. FC RECORD: 36-2-0-0-0-10. RECORD IN 2010: (EP Kings, Cheetahs) 18-2-0-0-0-10.

Vermeulen, Walt (UOVS) b 11/11/88. 1.99m. 108kg. Lock. FC DEBUT: 2008. PROV CAREER: Cheetahs 2009-10 22-0-0-0-0-0. Cheetahs XV 2010 1-0-0-0-0-0. SUPER 14: Cheetahs 2010 12-1-0-0-0-5. REP HONOURS: SA Students 2008 1-0-0-0-0-0. FC RECORD: 36-1-0-0-0-5. RECORD IN 2010: (Cheetahs S14, Cheetahs, Cheetahs XV) 27-1-0-0-0-5.

Victor, Grant (Marais Viljoen HS) b 16/07/88, Johannesburg. 1.83m. 92kg. Prop. FC DEBUT: 2009. PROV CAREER: Valke 2009-10 3-0-0-0-0-0. FC RECORD: 3-0-0-0-0-0. RECORD IN 2010: (Valke) 2-0-0-0-0-0.

Viljoen, Francis Jacobus Nicolas (Frans) (Grey Coll., Bloemfontein) b 22/10/82, Ficksburg. 1.89m. 104kg. Flank. FC DEBUT: 2002. PROV CAREER: Leopards 2002-04 40-16-0-0-0-80. Griquas 2005-08 60-14-0-0-0-70. Cheetahs 2009 20-8-0-0-0-40. Cheetahs XV 2010 1-0-0-0-0-0. SUPER 14: Cheetahs 2006 & 09-10 22-1-0-0-0-5. FC RECORD: 143-39-0-0-0-195. RECORD IN 2010: (Cheetahs S14, Cheetahs XV) 7-0-0-0-0-0.

Viljoen, Riaan (Klerksdorp HS) b 04/01/83, Carletonville. 1.81m. 86kg. Utility back. FC DEBUT: 2005. PROV CAREER: Valke 2005-07 57-17-32-18-5-218. Griquas 2008-10 60-11-42-41-6-280. Cheetahs XV 2010 1-0-0-0-0-0. SUPER 14: Cheetahs 2010 10-1-1-3-0-16. REP HONOURS: SA Tour: 2009 2-0-0-0-0-0. Royal XV 2009 1-0-1-0-0-2. FC RECORD: 131-29-76-62-11-516. RECORD IN 2010: (Cheetahs S14, Griquas, Cheetahs XV) 27-7-5-9-0-72.

Visagie, Callie-Theron (Paarl Boys HS & Univ. Stellenbosch) b 09/07/1988, Paarl. 1.89m. 103kg. Hooker. FC DEBUT: 2010. PROV CAREER: WP 2010 9-0-0-0-0-0. FC RECORD: 9-0-0-0-0-0. RECORD IN 2010: (WP) 9-0-0-0-0-0.

Visser, Juan (HTS Vereeniging) b 11/04/85, Pretoria. 1.73m. 85kg. Centre. FC DEBUT: 2009. PROV CAREER: Pumas 2009-10 12-1-0-0-0-5. FC RECORD: 12-1-0-0-0-5. RECORD IN 2010: (Pumas) 2-0-0-0-0-0.

Visser, Marius (Welkom THS) b 24/04/82. 1.90m. 130kgs. Prop. FC DEBUT: 2003. PROV CAREER: Griffons 2003-05 15-0-0-0-0-0. Bulldogs 2006-07,09-10 32-0-0-0-0-0. FC RECORD: 47-0-0-0-0-0. RECORD IN 2010: (Bulldogs) 16-0-0-0-0-0.

Visser, Petrus Jurgen (Paarl Gym.) b 13/09/89, Paarl. 1.91m. 88kg. Flyhalf. FC DEBUT: 2009. PROV CAREER: WP 2009-10 8-1-9-4-1-38. FC RECORD: 8-1-9-4-1-38. RECORD IN 2010: (WP) 7-1-1-2-1-16.

Viviers, Ashley (Daniel Pienaar THS) b 10/11/85, Port Elizabeth. 1.99m. 97kg. Lock. FC DEBUT: 2008. PROV CAREER: Elephants 2008-09 20-1-0-0-0-5. E/Cape XV 2008 2-0-0-0-0-0. Bulldogs 2010 6-0-0-0-0-0. FC RECORD: 28-1-0-0-0-5. RECORD IN 2010: (Bulldogs) 6-0-0-0-0-0.

Vogt, Rudi (Overberg HS) b 30/01/83, Paarl. 1.92m. 95kg. Centre. FC DEBUT: 2007. PROV CAREER: Pumas 2007-09 28-3-46-30-1-200. Griquas 2010 8-2-6-0-0-22. SUPER 14: Lions 2008 5-0-0-0-0-0. REP HONOURS: Emerging Springboks 2008 1-0-0-0-0-0. FC RECORD: 42-5-52-30-1-222. RECORD IN 2010: (Griquas) 8-2-6-0-0-22.

Volschenk, Jan Frederik (Oakdale HS) b 27/03/86, Ladysmith. 1.84m. 117kgs. Prop. FC DEBUT: 2006. PROV CAREER: Blue Bulls 2006 2-0-0-0-0-0. WP 2007 11-1-0-0-0-5. Eagles 2010 7-0-0-0-0-0. REP HONOURS: SA U19 2005. FC RECORD: 20-1-0-0-0-5. RECORD IN 2010: (Eagles) 7-0-0-0-0-0.

Vulindlu, Luzuko (Durban HS) b 14/11/87, Grahamstown. 1.83m. 98kg. Centre. FC DEBUT: 2008. PROV CAREER: KZN 2009-10 6-1-0-0-0-5. Sharks XV 2008-10 12-2-0-0-0-10. Sharks Inv XV 2009 1-0-0-0-0. SUPER 14: Sharks 2009 9-1-0-0-0-5. REP HONOURS: Emerging Springboks 2009 1-0-0-0-0-0. FC RECORD: 29-4-0-0-0-20. RECORD IN 2010: (KZN, Sharks XV) 8-1-0-0-0-5.

W

Waarts, Algernon Percival (Morestêr HS) b 22/04/85, Oudtshoorn. 1.90m. 103kg. Eighthman. FC DEBUT: 2006. PROV CAREER: Eagles 2006-10 34-0-0-0-0-0. FC RECORD: 34-0-0-0-0-0. RECORD IN 2010: (Eagles) 3-0-0-0-0-0.

Wagenaar, Wynand (Grens HS) b 16/10/1989, East London. 1.91m. 105kg. Lock. FC DEBUT: 2010. PROV CAREER: Bulldogs 2010 3-0-0-0-0-0. FC RECORD: 3-0-0-0-0-0. RECORD IN 2010: (Bulldogs) 3-0-0-0-0-0.

Wannenburg, Pedrie Johannes (Oakdale Agric. HS, Riversdale) b 02/01/81, Nelspruit. 1.95m. 112kg. Eighthman. FC DEBUT: 2001. PROV CAREER: KZN 2001 2-0-0-0-0-0. Blue Bulls 2002-09 80-22-0-0-0-110. SUPER 14: Bulls 2002-10 113-14-0-0-0-70. REP HONOURS: SA 2002-07 Tests: 20-3-0-0-0-15. SA 'A' 2003-04 4-1-0-0-0-5. SA XV 2006 1-0-0-0-0-0. SA U21s 2001-02 8-3-0-0-0-15. SA U19 2000. SA Schools 1999; CW SWD 1999. British Barbarians 2008 3-2-0-0-0-10. MISC INFO: Brother of Boland flank Callie Wannenburg. FC RECORD: 231-45-0-0-0-225. RECORD IN 2010: (Bulls) 15-1-0-0-0-5.

Watermeyer, Stefan (Waterkloof HS) b 03/06/88, Nelspruit. 1.85m. 95kg. FC DEBUT: 2007. PROV CAREER: Blue Bulls 2008-10 42-13-5-2-0-81. Blue Bulls XV 2007 1-0-0-0-0-0. SUPER 14: Bulls 2010 1-0-0-0-0-0. FC RECORD: 44-13-5-2-0-80. RECORD IN 2010: (Bulls, Blue Bulls) 23-11-5-2-0-71.

Watts, Elgar Graeme (Klein Nederberg HS) b 24/09/85, Paarl. 1.81m. 84kg. Flyhalf. FC DEBUT: 2008. PROV CAREER: Boland 2008-09 39-8-13-5-1-84. Pumas 2010 22-10-17-9-0-111. FC RECORD: 61-18-30-14-1-195. RECORD IN 2010: (Pumas) 22-10-17-9-0-111.

Weideman, Charl Francois Marais (Paul Roos Gym.) b 07/04/88, Bloemfontein. 1.89m. 87kgs. Centre. FC DEBUT: 2008. PROV CAREER: WP 2008 1-0-1-0-0-2.

Griffons 2010 11-1-0-0-0-5. FC RECORD: 12-1-1-0-0-7. RECORD IN 2010: (Griffons) 11-1-0-0-0-5.

Wells, Ashley David (Wynberg Boys HS) b 29/07/1985, Carltonville. 1.87m. 119kg. Prop. FC DEBUT: 2010. PROV CAREER: WP 2010 2-0-0-0-0-0. FC RECORD: 2-0-0-0-0-0. RECORD IN 2010: (WP) 2-0-0-0-0-0.

Welsh, Barend Frederik (Frikkie) (Kanonkop HS, Middelburg) b 26/10/78, Middelburg. 1.82m. 91kgs. Centre. FC DEBUT: 1998. PROV CAREER: KZN 1998-99 8-2-0-0-0-10; Pumas 2000-01 14-8-0-0-0-40; Blue Bulls 2001-04 & 06-07 65-25-0-0-0-125. WP 2009-10 26-6-0-0-0-30. SUPER 14: Bulls 1999-04 & 06-07 50-17-0-0-0-85. Stormers 2010 1-0-0-0-0-0. REP HONOURS: SA 'A' 2001 2-0-0-0-0-0; S/Kings 2009 1-0-0-0-0-0. SA U23s 2000-01 14-17-0-0-0-85; SA U21s 1998-99 9-4-0-0-0-20; CW Pumas 1996. SA Barbs. 2001 1-1-0-0-0-5. MISC INFO: Holds Bulls S12 record for most tries in a career (17). Bath (Eng) 2005-06. FC RECORD: 191-80-0-0-0-400. RECORD IN 2010: (Stormers, WP) 14-3-0-0-0-15.

Wessels, Petrus Johannes (Johan) (Afrikaans HS & UFS) b 29/11/88, Vereeniging. 1.85m. 98kg. FC DEBUT: 2009. PROV CAREER: Cheetahs 2009-10 24-4-0-0-0-20. Griffons 2010 8-0-0-0-0-0. FC RECORD: 32-4-0-0-0-20. RECORD IN 2010: (Cheetahs, Griffons) 16-0-0-0-0-0.

Westraadt, Simon (Grey HS) b 31/03/86, Port Elizabeth. 1.76m. 107kg. Hooker. FC DEBUT: 2007. PROV CAREER: WP 2007-08 6-0-0-0-0-0. Griquas 2009-10 25-5-0-0-0-25. FC RECORD: 31-5-0-0-0-25. RECORD IN 2010: (Griquas) 17-5-0-0-0-25.

Wheeler, Justin (Bastion HS) b 23/01/88, Krugersdorp. 1.87m. 98kg. Eighthman. FC DEBUT: 2008. PROV CAREER: Lions 2008 11-0-0-0-0-0. Young Lions 2009-10 9-3-0-0-0-15. Lions XV 2008 1-0-0-0-0-0. SUPER 14: Lions 2010 2-0-0-0-0-0. FC RECORD: 23-3-0-0-0-15. RECORD IN 2010: (Lions S14, Young Lions) 9-2-0-0-0-10.

Whitehead, George Alexander (Grey Coll.) b 17/03/89, Bloemfontein. 1.85m. 80kg. FC DEBUT: 2009. PROV CAREER: Cheetahs 2009-10 9-1-2-3-0-18. FC RECORD: 9-1-2-3-0-18. RECORD IN 2010: (Cheetahs) 8-1-2-3-0-18.

Whitehead, Tim (UCT) b30/05/88. 1.86m. 88kg. Centre. FC DEBUT: 2009. PROV CAREER: WP 2010 10-0-0-0-0-0. SUPER 14: Stormers 2010 10-0-0-0-0-0. REP HONOURS: SA Students 2009 2-1-0-0-0-5. FC RECORD: 22-1-0-0-0-5. RECORD IN 2010: (Stormers, WP) 20-0-0-0-0-0.

Whiteley, Warren Roger (Glenwood HS) b 18/09/87, Durban. 1.92m. 97kg. Flank. FC DEBUT: 2008. PROV CAREER: Sharks XV 2008-09 13-4-0-0-0-20. Elephants 2009 5-1-0-0-0-5. Golden Lions 2010 13-3-0-0-0-15. Young Lions 2010 4-0-0-0-0-0. FC RECORD: 35-8-0-0-0-40. RECORD IN 2010: (Golden Lions, Young Lions) 17-3-0-0-0-15.

Wilkins, Wesley A (US) b 15/07/85. 1.87m. 94kg. Flank. FC DEBUT: 2008. Prov caree: Griquas 2009-10 15-6-0-0-0-30. REP HONOURS: SA Students 2008-09 3-1-0-0-0-5. FC RECORD: 18-7-0-0-0-35. RECORD IN 2010: (Griquas) 13-6-0-0-0-30.

Williamson, Gavin (Outeniqua HS) b 05/08/83, George. 1.79m. 97kg. Hooker. FC DEBUT: 2002. PROV CAREER: Eagles 2002-06 38-2-0-0-0-10. Lions 2007-08 13-2-0-0-0-10. Lions XV 2007 1-0-0-0-0-0. Leopards 2007-10 67-2-0-0-0-10. SUPER 14: Lions 2008 1-0-0-0-0-0. FC RECORD: 120-6-0-0-0-30. RECORD IN 2010: (Leopards) 23-2-0-0-0-10.

Willis, Vainon Shanon (Waterkloof HS) b 11/10/1988, Cape Town. 1.83m. 85kg. Wing. FC DEBUT: 2009. PROV CAREER: Blue Bulls 2009-10 11-2-0-0-0-10. Pumas 2010 9-2-0-0-0-10. FC RECORD: 20-4-0-0-0-20. RECORD IN 2010: (Blue Bulls, Pumas) 19-4-0-0-0-20.

Winkler, Llewellyn Paul (Jan Mohr HS) b 07/09/1987, Windhoek. 1.76m. 82kg. Centre. FC DEBUT: 2010. PROV CAREER: Valke 2010 1-0-0-0-0-0. FC RECORD: 1-0-0-0-0-0. RECORD IN 2010: (Valke) 1-0-0-0-0-0.

Witbooi, Duncan Nasley (Florida HS & UJ) b 14/02/1988, Oudtshoorn. 1.67m. 84kg. Centre. FC DEBUT: 2010. PROV CAREER: Valke 2010 5-0-0-0-0-0. FC RECORD: 5-0-0-0-0-0. RECORD IN 2010: (Valke) 5-0-0-0-0-0.

Y

Yearsley, Christopher William (CBC Boksburg) b 07/05/1986, Kempton Park. 1.99m. 112kg. Lock. FC DEBUT: 2010. PROV CAREER: Valke 2010 9-0-0-0-0-0. FC RECORD: 9-0-0-0-0-0. RECORD IN 2010: (Valke) 9-0-0-0-0-0.

Yoyo, Kwezi (Itembelihle HS & Varsity Coll.) b 14/03/1979, Port Elizabeth. 1.85m. 114kg. Prop. FC DEBUT: 2010. PROV CAREER: EP Kings 2010 1-0-0-0-0-0. FC RECORD: 1-0-0-0-0-0. RECORD IN 2010: (EP Kings) 1-0-0-0-0-0.

Z

Zana, Eric Sydney (Outeniqua HS) b 25/03/1987, George. 1.76m. 70kg. Flyhalf. FC DEBUT: 2010. PROV CAREER: Eagles 2010 17-0-1-8-0-26. FC RECORD: 17-0-1-8-0-26. RECORD IN 2010: (Eagles) 17-0-1-8-0-26.

Zweni, Sinethemba (De Vos Malan HS) b 11/04/83, Port Elizabeth 1.75m. 88kg. Wing. FC DEBUT: 2005. PROV CAREER: Cheetahs 2005-06 9-0-0-0-0-0. Pumas 2005 12-5-0-0-0-25. Bulldogs 2007 17-4-0-0-0-20. Eagles 2008-10 34-4-0-0-0-20. SUPER 14: Cheetahs 2006 5-0-0-0-0-0. FC RECORD: 77-13-0-0-0-65. RECORD IN 2010: (Eagles) 18-4-0-0-0-20.

SECTION 3
SOUTH AFRICAN NATIONAL TEAMS

NOTE:
• For SA Women &
SA Schools, please
refer to Amateur
Teams section,
p366-71.

SPRINGBOKS IN 2010

Boks finish off low year on a high

ONE of my first spoken phrases was "kick 'n charge", a result of sitting on Dad's shoulders, aged two, watching Albertinia's first fifteen of '64 train.

Time and again the coach emphasised how rugby was that simple – often enough that the refrain of "kick and charge", to become a bane of my middle-aged existence, stuck to the toddler-tiny folds of my brain.

It provided no golden era for Albertinia then and nor did it in 2010 provide a year for the Springboks their fans would care to remember beyond say, wha... Oh yes. Springbok rugby, 2010.

Now, *there* was a babbelas after a lot of champagne.

A difficult win in Cardiff under trying circumstances, a simple series against Italy and a riot run against France promised much more, especially with two SA teams contesting the Vodacom Super 14 final.

But the Wallabies were more experienced this time, while the All Blacks, smarting from the humiliation of the previous season, had flyhalf Daniel Carter restored to their ranks and the Boks responded with... very much the same thing, only done poorly this time.

Whether the tactic of hoisting ceaseless up-and-unders on an increasingly nervous defence is truly dead and buried with new law interpretation tilted towards possession is a moot point, but their execution of Albertinia's 1964 tactics left a lot to be desired.

Playing with your pack to soften defence around the fringes is probably preferable these days. Most successful teams figured out that tackling all afternoon will win you some one-offs, but cannot possibly guarantee consistent success.

Without injured lynchpin Fourie du Preez to launch their bombs from scrumhalf, the Springboks' kicking and chasing was abysmal.

A year earlier, Bok chasers paced their runs properly and mowed down the catchers. This time around they contested in the air. Even on the odd occasion when they came off best, a waiting Kiwi or Aussie loose forward mostly gathered the loose ball gratefully.

With laws favouring possession, the aerial contest might have made sense – if Springbok backs were ever particularly good in the air.

They aren't – so why kick in the first place, especially if you have one of the planet's gnarliest packs of forwards to take it up? Tactical Kicking 2009 loaded unbearable pressure on defenders; Tactical Kicking 2010 merely alleviated it.

A single Bok win from six a season after winning five of

their Vodacom Tri-Nations fixtures makes for grim reading, a feeble defeat at Murrayfield in darkest November even more so.

The Tri-Nations delivered two good halves against Australia and 75 good minutes against New Zealand, but the November tour didn't bring many smiles either, with one good hour against Ireland, half a good hour against Wales and a fairly decent showing against England.

Yet the latter Test proved that it's far from sack cloth time on the eve of the World Cup – 2010 left the Boks in disarray, but there's history to be made for the first team to retain rugby's biggest prize.

The Springboks have the forwards and the place-kicker, half a dozen world stars returning to their ranks and this for a tournament that tests you at a one-off level, not for consistency and excellence over years.

So maybe we should write 2010 off and be sure not to repeat it in 2014. It'll be World Cup the year after.

RESULTS & SCORERS (Tests & tour matches)

Date	Venue	Opponent	Result	Score	Scorers
June 5	Cardiff	Wales	**WON**	34-31	T: OM Ndungane, Potgieter, De Jongh. C: Pienaar (2). P: Pienaar (4), FPL Steyn.
June 12	Cape Town	France	**WON**	42-17	T: Spies, Aplon (2), Steenkamp, Louw. C: M Steyn (3), Pienaar. P: M Steyn (3).
June 19	Witbank	Italy 1st	**WON**	29-13	T: Habana, Louw, M Steyn, Kirchner. C: M Steyn (3). P: M Steyn.
June 26	East London	Italy 2nd	**WON**	55-11	T: M Steyn (2), Spies, JN du Plessis, Habana, Van der Merwe, BJ Botha. C: M Steyn (5), Pienaar (2). P: M Steyn (2).
July 10	Auckland	New Zealand	Lost	12-32	P: M Steyn (4).
July 17	Wellington	New Zealand	Lost	17-31	T: Rossouw, Burger. C: M Steyn (2). P: M Steyn.
July 24	Brisbane	Australia	Lost	13-30	T: Fourie, Steenkamp. P: M Steyn.
Aug 21	Soweto	New Zealand	Lost	22-29	T: Burger. C: M Steyn. P: M Steyn (5).
Aug 28	Pretoria	Australia	**WON**	44-31	T: Smith, Steenkamp, Spies, FPL Steyn, Pietersen. C: M Steyn (4), James. P: M Steyn (2), FPL Steyn.
Sept 4	Bloemfontein	Australia	Lost	39-41	T: Fourie, Steenkamp, De Villiers. C: M Steyn (3). P: M Steyn (6).
Nov 6	Dublin	Ireland	**WON**	23-21	T: Smith, Aplon. C: M Steyn, Lambie. P: M Steyn (3).
Nov 13	Cardiff	Wales	**WON**	29-25	T: Alberts, Matfield. C: M Steyn (2). P: M Steyn (5).
Nov 20	Edinburgh	Scotland	Lost	17-21	T: Alberts. P: M Steyn (4).
Nov 27	London	England	**WON**	21-11	T: Alberts, Mvovo. C: M Steyn. P: M Steyn (3).
Dec 4	London	Barbarians	Lost	20-26	T: OM Ndungane, Botha, Maku. C: Jantjies. P: Jantjies.

Played	Won	Drawn	Lost	Points for	Points against	Tries for	Tries against
15	8	0	7	417	370	42	39

2010 SCORERS (Tests & tour matches)

PLAYER	Province	Apps	Tries	Conv	Pen	DG	Pts
M Steyn	Blue Bulls	13	3	25	40	–	185
R Pienaar	Kwazulu Natal	11	–	5	4	–	22
GG Steenkamp	Blue Bulls	9	4	–	–	–	20
PJ Spies	Blue Bulls	12	3	–	–	–	15
GG Aplon	Western Province	14	3	–	–	–	15
WS Alberts	Kwazulu Natal	4	3	–	–	–	15
FPL Steyn	Racing Metro, France	6	1	–	2	–	11
L-FP Louw	Western Province	7	2	–	–	–	10
BG Habana	Western Province	11	2	–	–	–	10
SWP Burger	Western Province	8	2	–	–	–	10
J Fourie	Western Province	8	2	–	–	–	10
JH Smith	Free State	8	2	–	–	–	10
OM Ndungane	Kwazulu Natal	2	2	–	–	–	10
BG Maku	Blue Bulls	2	1	–	–	–	5
ET Jantjies	Golden Lions	1	–	1	1	–	5
JP Botha	Blue Bulls	8	1	–	–	–	5
DJ Potgieter	Blue Bulls	5	1	–	–	–	5
JL de Jongh	Western Province	6	1	–	–	–	5
Z Kirchner	Blue Bulls	10	1	–	–	–	5
JN du Plessis	Kwazulu Natal	12	1	–	–	–	5
PR van der Merwe	Blue Bulls	11	1	–	–	–	5
BJ Botha	Ulster, Ireland	6	1	–	–	–	5
DJ Rossouw	Blue Bulls	8	1	–	–	–	5
J-PR Pietersen	Kwazulu Natal	3	1	–	–	–	5
J de Villiers	Western Province	12	1	–	–	–	5
V Matfield	Blue Bulls	13	1	–	–	–	5
LN Mvovo	Kwazulu Natal	3	1	–	–	–	5
AD James	Bath, England	5	–	1	–	–	2
P Lambie	Kwazulu Natal	5	–	1	–	–	2
		42	33	47	0		417

SPRINGBOK TEST APPEARANCES AND POINTS IN 2010

	Wales	France	Italy 1	Italy 2	New Zealand 1	New Zealand 2	Australia 1	New Zealand 3	Australia 2	Australia 3	Ireland	Wales	Scotland	England	Matches	Tries	Conversions	Penalties	Drop Goals	Points
FPL Steyn	15	–	–	–	–	–	–	–	15	15	–	13	13	13	6	1	0	2	0	11
GG Aplon	14	14	14	15	R	R	14	15	–	R	15	15	14	14	13	3	0	0	0	15
J Fourie	13	13	–	13	13	13	13	–	13	13	–	–	–	–	8	2	0	0	0	10
JL de Jongh	12	R	R	12	–	–	R	13	x	x	–	–	–	–	6	1	0	0	0	5
OM Ndungane	11	–	–	–	–	–	–	–	–	–	–	–	–	–	1	1	0	0	0	5
R Pienaar	10	R	R	R	R	R	9	–	–	–	9	9	R	9	11	0	5	4	0	22
ER Januarie	9	9	9	9	9	9	–	R	x	x	–	–	–	–	7	0	0	0	0	0
JC van Niekerk	8	–	–	–	–	–	–	–	–	–	–	–	–	–	1	0	0	0	0	0
DJ Potgieter	7	R	7	R	–	–	R	–	–	–	–	–	–	–	5	1	0	0	0	5
L-FP Louw	6	7	6	7	7	7	–	R	–	–	–	–	–	–	7	2	0	0	0	10
V Matfield	5	5	5*	–	5	5	5	5	5	5	5*	5*	5*	5*	13	1	0	0	0	5
DJ Rossouw	4	4	–	R	R	4	4	t+R	R	4	–	–	–	–	8	1	0	0	0	5
BJ Botha	3	3	–	R	R	R	3	–	–	–	–	–	–	–	6	1	0	0	0	5
JW Smit	2*	2*	–	2*	2*	2*	2*	2*	2*	2*	–	–	–	–	9	0	0	0	0	0
CJ van der Linde	1	–	R	–	–	3	t+R	R	R	R	R	R	R	R	11	0	0	0	0	0
MC Ralepelle	R	R	2	R	R	R	R	x	R	R	x	R	–	–	10	0	0	0	0	0
JN du Plessis	R	R	3	3	3	–	–	3	3	3	3	3	3	3	12	1	0	0	0	5
AJ Hargreaves	R	–	R	–	–	–	–	–	–	–	–	–	–	–	2	0	0	0	0	0
R Kankowski	R	–	R	–	–	R	7	–	x	R	–	–	8	–	8	0	0	0	0	0
Z Kirchner	R	15	15	–	15	15	15	–	–	–	13	R	15	15	10	1	0	0	0	5
BA Basson	R	–	R	–	–	–	–	–	–	–	14	14	–	–	4	0	0	0	0	0
HM Bosman	x	–	–	–	–	–	–	–	–	–	–	–	–	–	0	0	0	0	0	0
W Olivier	–	12	–	R	12	12	12	x	–	–	–	–	–	–	5	0	0	0	0	0
BG Habana	–	11	11	11	11	11	11	11	11	11	11	11	–	–	11	2	0	0	0	10
M Steyn	–	10	10	10	10	10	10	10	10	10	10	10	10	10	13	3	25	40	0	185
PJ Spies	–	8	8	8	8	8	8	8	8	8	8	8	–	8	12	3	0	0	0	15
SWP Burger	–	6	–	6	6	6	6	6	6	6	–	–	–	–	8	2	0	0	0	10
GG Steenkamp	–	1	1	1	1	1	1	1	1	1	–	–	–	–	9	4	0	0	0	20
J de Villiers	–	R	13	14	14	14	–	12	12	12	12	12	12	12	12	1	0	0	0	5
PR van der Merwe	–	R	–	R	–	–	R	4	4	R	R	R	R	R	10	1	0	0	0	5
AD James	–	–	12	R	R	x	R	x	R	–	–	–	–	–	5	0	1	0	0	2
JP Botha	–	–	4	4	4	–	–	–	–	–	4	4	4	4	7	0	0	0	0	0
BG Maku	–	–	R	–	–	–	–	–	–	–	–	–	–	–	1	0	0	0	0	0
A Bekker	–	–	–	5	R	R	–	–	–	–	–	–	–	–	3	0	0	0	0	0
F Hougaard	–	–	–	–	–	–	R	9	9	9	x	R	9	t	7	0	0	0	0	0
JH Smith	–	–	–	–	–	–	–	7	7	7	7	7	7	7	7	2	0	0	0	10
J-PR Pietersen	–	–	–	–	–	–	–	14	14	14	–	–	–	–	3	1	0	0	0	5
T Mtawarira	–	–	–	–	–	–	–	–	–	–	1	1	1	1	4	0	0	0	0	0
P Lambie	–	–	–	–	–	–	–	–	–	–	R	R	R	R	4	0	1	0	0	2
KR Daniel	–	–	–	–	–	–	–	–	–	–	R	–	–	–	1	0	0	0	0	0
BW du Plessis	–	–	–	–	–	–	–	–	–	–	2	2	2	2	4	0	0	0	0	0
AA Jacobs	–	–	–	–	–	–	–	–	–	–	R	–	x	R	2	0	0	0	0	0
GJ Stegmann	–	–	–	–	–	–	–	–	–	–	6	6	6	6	4	0	0	0	0	0
WS Alberts	–	–	–	–	–	–	–	–	–	–	–	R	t+R	R	3	3	0	0	0	15
LN Mvovo	–	–	–	–	–	–	–	–	–	–	–	–	11	11	2	1	0	0	0	5
JA Strauss	–	–	–	–	–	–	–	–	–	–	–	–	R	R	2	0	0	0	0	0
46 Players															39	32	46	0	397

*Captain

SPRINGBOKS IN 2010

SPRINGBOK REPRESENTATIVES IN 2010 (stats are Tests only)

	Province	Date of birth	Height	Weight	Career Tests	Tries	Conversions	Penalties	Drop Goals	Career Pts
WS Alberts	Kwazulu Natal	05/11/84	1.91	115	3	3	0	0	0	15
GG Aplon	Western Province	06/10/82	1.75	70	13	3	0	0	0	15
BA Basson	Griqualand West	11/02/87	1.87	82	4	0	0	0	0	0
A Bekker	Western Province	05/12/83	2.08	120	24	1	0	0	0	5
HM Bosman	Free State	19/04/85	1.91	94	3	0	2	1	0	7
BJ Botha	Ulster, Ireland	04/01/80	1.82	110	25	1	0	0	0	5
JP Botha	Blue Bulls	22/09/79	2.02	118	72	7	0	0	0	35
SWP Burger	Western Province	13/04/83	1.93	110	63	13	0	0	0	65
KR Daniel	Kwazulu Natal	05/03/85	1.85	89	1	0	0	0	0	0
JL de Jongh	Western Province	15/04/88	1.77	84	6	1	0	0	0	5
J de Villiers	Western Province	24/02/81	1.90	100	67	19	0	0	0	95
BW du Plessis	Kwazulu Natal	22/05/84	1.89	105	36	5	0	0	0	25
JN du Plessis	Kwazulu Natal	16/11/82	1.87	113	24	1	0	0	0	5
J Fourie	Western Province	04/03/83	1.88	96	62	30	0	0	0	150
BG Habana	Western Province	12/06/83	1.79	92	68	38	0	0	0	190
AJ Hargreaves	Kwazulu Natal	29/04/86	2.00	102	2	0	0	0	0	0
F Hougaard	Blue Bulls	06/04/88	1.79	86	8	0	0	0	0	0
AA Jacobs	Kwazulu Natal	14/08/80	1.70	87	32	7	0	0	0	35
AD James	Bath Rugby, England	08/01/79	1.84	98	40	3	26	26	1	148
ET Jantjies	Golden Lions	01/08/90	1.76	84	0	0	0	0	0	0
ER Januarie	Western Province	01/02/82	1.70	80	47	5	0	0	0	25
R Kankowski	Kwazulu Natal	14/10/85	1.93	103	17	1	0	0	0	5
Z Kirchner	Blue Bulls	16/06/84	1.84	92	14	1	0	0	0	5
W Kruger	Blue Bulls	23/01/85	1.90	120	0	0	0	0	0	0
P Lambie	Kwazulu Natal	17/10/90	1.77	86	4	0	1	0	0	2
L-FP Louw	Western Province	15/06/85	1.90	110	7	2	0	0	0	10
BG Maku	Blue Bulls	24/06/86	1.87	111	1	0	0	0	0	0
V Matfield	Blue Bulls	11/05/77	2.01	110	105	7	0	0	0	35
C McLeod	Kwazulu Natal	05/08/83	1.79	82	0	0	0	0	0	0
T Mtawarira	Kwazulu Natal	01/08/85	1.88	112	26	1	0	0	0	5
LN Mvovo	Kwazulu Natal	03/06/86	1.81	84	2	1	0	0	0	5
OM Ndungane	Kwazulu Natal	20/02/81	1.83	85	7	2	0	0	0	10
W Olivier	Blue Bulls	06/11/83	1.86	95	32	1	0	0	0	5
CV Oosthuizen	Free State	22/03/89	1.83	125	0	0	0	0	0	0
R Pienaar	Ulster, Ireland	10/03/84	1.86	84	47	6	13	17	0	107
J-PR Pietersen	Kwazulu Natal	12/07/86	1.84	102	36	12	0	0	0	60
DJ Potgieter	Blue Bulls	22/02/87	1.90	98	6	1	0	0	0	5
MC Ralepelle	Blue Bulls	11/09/86	1.78	95	18	0	0	0	0	0
DJ Rossouw	Blue Bulls	05/06/78	1.97	118	54	8	0	0	0	40
JW Smit	Kwazulu Natal	03/04/78	1.86	116	102	6	0	0	0	30
JH Smith	Free State	30/07/81	1.94	106	69	12	0	0	0	60
PJ Spies	Blue Bulls	08/06/85	1.95	106	40	7	0	0	0	35
GG Steenkamp	Blue Bulls	12/06/81	1.89	124	31	5	0	0	0	25
GJ Stegmann	Blue Bulls	22/03/86	1.81	99	4	0	0	0	0	0
FPL Steyn	Racing Metro, France	14/05/87	1.91	100	42	6	5	16	3	97
M Steyn	Blue Bulls	11/07/84	1.86	82	25	4	37	71	5	322
AJ Strauss	Free State	05/03/84	1.86	94	0	0	0	0	0	0
JA Strauss	Free State	18/11/85	1.84	102	9	0	0	0	0	0
CJ van der Linde	Free State	27/08/80	1.90	122	69	4	0	0	0	20
PR van der Merwe	Blue Bulls	03/06/85	1.99	117	10	1	0	0	0	5
JC van Niekerk	Toulon, France	14/05/80	1.93	108	52	10	0	0	0	50
					1429	235	84	131	9	1763

Bold letters denotes new Springbok

SPRINGBOKS IN 2010

Boks squeeze home in Cardiff

Wales 31 South Africa 34 *(halftime 16-14)*

June 5, Millennium Stadium, Cardiff (60 507). Referee: DA Lewis (Ireland)
WALES - TRIES: Hook, Prydie, A-W Jones. CONVERSIONS: SM Jones (2). PENALTY GOALS: SM Jones (3). DROP GOAL: Hook.
SOUTH AFRICA - TRIES: Ndungane, Potgieter, De Jongh. CONVERSIONS: Pienaar (2). PENALTY GOALS: Pienaar (4), Steyn.

SOUTH Africa's international season got off to a nailbiting start just a week after the Bulls beat the Stormers in the Vodacom Super 14 final, the Springboks hanging on for what would turn out to the first of two close shaves against Wales in 2010.

There would be just four points in it in their end-of-year tour fixture five months later, and things were just as close in the first match. What was vastly different was the composition of the Bok side, with just a handful of June selections making the November trip to the Millennium Stadium.

The Vodacom Stormers duo of flanker Francois Louw and winger Gio Aplon were among five players to make their Test debuts, but the man to make the most lasting impression on the day was their teammate, centre Juan de Jongh.

De Jongh, who enjoyed an excellent Super 14 season alongside the seasoned veteran Jaque Fourie, showed great promise alongside his provincial partner in his first international outing and capped it off with a typically jinking try that effectively broke the back of a dogged Welsh effort.

As in their November fixture, Wales galloped away to a big early lead, only to watch as the Boks reeled them in and then hung on for the win. Two Stephen Jones penal-

ties and a try and drop goal by James Hook gave the hosts a 16-3 lead after just 21 minutes, but Springbok flyhalf Ruan Pienaar was equal to the task, slotting three first-half penalties to keep the visitors in contention.

Winger Odwa Ndungane also scored in the corner in the 31st minute to allow the Boks to trail by just two points at halftime, a deficit they soon wiped out after the break when flanker Dewald Potgieter crashed over within three minutes of the restart.

A 56th-minute penalty by fullback Francois Steyn made it 24-19 after Jones had earlier kicked another penalty, before De Jongh announced himself on the Test stage in grand style when he took the ball on the Welsh 10-metre line in the 59th minute and proceeded to weave his way through the defence for an excellent try.

Pienaar's conversion made it 31-19, but Wales kept hammering away at the Bok line and were rewarded with tries to Tom Prydie and Alun-Wyn Jones, the latter being converted by Jones to bring Wales to within three points with three minutes to play.

But as they were to do in November, the Boks, drawing on old-fashioned guts, kept the Welsh at bay to hang on for the result.

SOUTH AFRICA TO WALES 2010

🦌 SPRINGBOK.	Date of birth	Height	Weight	Province	Wales	Matches	Tries	Conversions	Penalties	Drop Goals	Points
FPL Steyn	14/05/87	1.91	100	Racing Metro, France	15	1	0	0	1	0	3
GG Aplon	06/10/82	1.75	70	Western Province	14	1	0	0	0	0	0
J Fourie	04/03/83	1.88	96	Western Province	13	1	0	0	0	0	0
JL de Jongh	15/04/88	1.77	84	Western Province	12	1	1	0	0	0	5
OM Ndungane	20/02/81	1.83	85	Kwazulu Natal	11	1	1	0	0	0	5
R Pienaar	10/03/84	1.86	84	Kwazulu Natal	10	1	0	2	4	0	16
ER Januarie	01/02/82	1.70	80	Western Province	9	1	0	0	0	0	0
JC van Niekerk	14/05/80	1.93	108	Toulon, France	8	1	0	0	0	0	0
DJ Potgieter	22/02/87	1.90	98	Blue Bulls	7	1	1	0	0	0	5
L-FP Louw	15/06/85	1.90	110	Western Province	6	1	0	0	0	0	0
V Matfield	11/05/77	2.01	110	Blue Bulls	5	1	0	0	0	0	0
DJ Rossouw	05/06/78	1.97	118	Blue Bulls	4	1	0	0	0	0	0
BJ Botha	04/01/80	1.82	110	Ulster, Ireland	3	1	0	0	0	0	0
JW Smit*	03/04/78	1.86	116	Kwazulu Natal	2	1	0	0	0	0	0
CJ van der Linde	27/08/80	1.90	122	Leinster, Ireland	1	1	0	0	0	0	0
BA Basson	11/02/87	1.87	82	Griqualand West	R	1	0	0	0	0	0
R Kankowski	14/10/85	1.93	103	Kwazulu Natal	R	1	0	0	0	0	0
JN du Plessis	16/11/82	1.87	113	Kwazulu Natal	R	1	0	0	0	0	0
MC Ralepelle	11/09/86	1.78	95	Blue Bulls	R	1	0	0	0	0	0
AJ Hargreaves	29/04/86	2.00	102	Kwazulu Natal	R	1	0	0	0	0	0
Z Kirchner	16/06/84	1.84	92	Blue Bulls	R	1	0	0	0	0	0
HM Bosman	19/04/85	1.91	94	Free State	x	0	0	0	0	0	0
22 Players						3	2	5	0		34

*Captain

COACH: P de Villiers **ASSISTANT COACHES:** G Gold and DJ Muir

Min	Action	Score
09	SM Jones penalty	0-3
12	Hook drop goal	0-6
17	Pienaar penalty	3-6
19	SM Jones penalty	3-9
21	Hook try, SM Jones conversion	3-16
24	Pienaar penalty	6-16
31	Ndungane try,	
	Pienaar missed conversion	11-16
36	Pienaar penalty	14-16
43	Potgieter try, Pienaar conversion	21-16
46	SM Jones penalty	21-19
50	Pienaar missed drop goal	21-19
56	Steyn penalty	24-19
59	De Jongh try, Pienaar conversion	31-19
69	Phillips missed drop goal	31-19
73	Prydie try,	
	SM Jones missed conversion	31-24
75	Pienaar penalty	34-24
76	A-W Jones try, SM Jones conversion	34-31

WALES: LM Byrne; SL Halfpenny, JW Hook, JH Roberts, T Prydie; SM Jones, M Phillips; RP Jones (C), S Warburton (RJ McCusker, 77), J Thomas, DL Jones (A-W Jones, 58), BS Davies, AR Jones (J Yapp, 58), M Rees, P James. *Unused substitutes:* H Bennett, R Rees, DR Biggar and AM Bishop. TEST DEBUTANT: RJ McCusker.

SOUTH AFRICA: FPL Steyn (Z Kirchner, 75); GG Aplon, J Fourie, JL de Jongh, OM Ndungane (BA Basson, 34); R Pienaar, ER Januarie; JC van Niekerk, DJ Potgieter (R Kankowski, 56)*, L-FP Louw, V Matfield, DJ Rossouw (AJ Hargreaves, 75), BJ Botha (JN du Plessis, 58), JW Smit (C), CJ van der Linde (MC Ralepelle, 74). *Kankowski to #8; Van Niekerk to flank. *Unused substitute:* HM Bosman. TEST DEBUTANTS: GG Aplon, JL de Jongh, L-FP Louw, BA Basson and AJ Hargreaves.

Notes: *John Smit equalled the record of Percy Montgomery as most capped Springbok against Wales with 9 tests. Stephen Jones became the top point scorer for Wales against South Africa with 73 points in 9 tests. The previous record was held by Neil Jenkins with 72 points in 8 tests.*

MID-YEAR TESTS

World Cup vibe fails to inspire France

FRANCE arrived in South Africa on the eve of the country hosting the world's biggest sporting event, so it came as no surprise that their one-match, hit-and-run 'tour' was hardly a headline-hogger in the grand scheme of things.

Given that the tourists jetted into Cape Town for a Test scheduled to take place less than 24 hours after the FIFA football World Cup opening ceremony, it's fair to say that no touring team to this country has ever quite been allowed to plot a Springbok downfall as unobtrusively as Marc Lievremont's Six Nations champions.

France had not lost to South Africa for five years and, although rugby found itself temporarily shifted from its usual place on the back pages, for the players and coaches the Test at Newlands remained important, coming less than 15 months out from rugby's own World Cup.

The tourists went to great lengths to convince the local as well as travelling French media that they were physically and mentally up for the match, despite their domestic season finishing only a day before the team flew out. Not even the once-in-a-lifetime opportunity of watching their national soccer team play Uruguay in a World Cup opening match on the Friday night before the Test would be allowed to distract them from their mission.

"The football World Cup is huge and our national team is playing down the road, but none of the players chosen for the Test will be attending the match," team spokesman Lionel Rossigneux said. "We are here to play rugby."

Captain Thierry Dusautoir echoed those thoughts when he said: "It's the first time we've had our national football team play in the same country. It would be great to watch them but we have other things on our minds."

In the end, however, it was the Springboks who were allowed to canter to an easy victory as France, in typical French fashion, simply did not pitch for the game. It was only South Africa's third win in 10 meetings dating back to 2001, although with hindsight perhaps local supporters got a little too carried away with the margin of victory given that the same French team proceeded to suffer another heavy defeat against Argentina a week later.

Whatever the reasons for their poor form, the France tourists of 2010 were, sadly, Six Nations champions in name only.

FRANCE TO SOUTH AFRICA AND ARGENTINA 2010

	Date of birth	Height	Weight	Club	South Africa	Matches	Tries	Conversions	Penalties	Drop Goals	Points
C Poitrenaud	20/05/82	1.88	86	Toulouse	15	1	0	0	0	0	0
A Rougerie	29/09/80	1.94	93	Clermont Auvergne	14	1	1	0	0	0	5
D Marty	30/10/82	1.80	86	Perpignan	13	1	0	0	0	0	0
M Mermoz	28/07/86	1.80	90	Perpignan	12	1	0	0	0	0	0
V Clerc	07/05/81	1.78	88	Toulouse	11	1	0	0	0	0	0
F Trinh-Duc	11/11/86	1.84	82	Montpellier	10	1	0	0	0	0	0
M Parra	15/11/88	1.80	76	Clermont Auvergne	9	1	0	1	1	0	5
J Bonnaire	20/09/78	1.92	100	Clermont Auvergne	8	1	0	0	0	0	0
W Lauret	28/03/89	1.88	92	Biarritz	7	1	0	0	0	0	0
T Dusautoir*	18/11/81	1.88	95	Toulouse	6	1	0	0	0	0	0
R Millo-Chluski	20/04/83	1.94	99	Toulouse	5	1	0	0	0	0	0
L Nallet	14/09/76	1.95	115	Racing Metro	4	1	0	0	0	0	0
N Mas	25/05/80	1.80	110	Perpignan	3	1	0	0	0	0	0
D Szarzewski	26/01/83	1.80	100	Stade Francais	2	1	0	0	0	0	0
T Domingo	20/08/85	1.73	106	Clermont Auvergne	1	1	0	0	0	0	0
M Andreu	27/12/85	1.70	75	Castres	R	1	1	0	0	0	5
D Skrela	02/03/79	1.90	94	Toulouse	R	1	0	1	0	0	2
D Yachvili	19/09/80	1.82	81	Biarritz	R	1	0	0	0	0	0
G Guirado	17/06/86	1.80	99	Perpignan	R	1	0	0	0	0	0
J-B Poux	26/09/79	1.80	105	Toulouse	R	1	0	0	0	0	0
J Pierre	31/07/81	1.97	106	Clermont Auvergne	R	1	0	0	0	0	0
L Picamoles	05/02/86	1.92	106	Toulouse	R	1	0	0	0	0	0
J Porical	20/09/85	1.80	83	Perpignan	–	–	–	–	–	–	–
J Malzieu	03/05/83	1.93	92	Clermont Auvergne	–	–	–	–	–	–	–
M Bastareaud	17/09/88	1.83	111	Stade Francais	–	–	–	–	–	–	–
F Fritz	17/01/84	1.84	94	Toulouse	–	–	–	–	–	–	–
L Mazars	26/06/84	1.83	90	Bayonne	–	–	–	–	–	–	–
F Barcella	27/10/83	1.83	103	Biarritz	–	–	–	–	–	–	–
L Ducalcon	02/01/84	1.83	121	Castres	–	–	–	–	–	–	–
P Pape	05/12/80	1.96	115	Stade Francais	–	–	–	–	–	–	–
I Harinordoquy	20/02/80	1.92	102	Biarritz	–	–	–	–	–	–	–
31 Players							**2**	**2**	**1**	**0**	**17**

*Captain

COACH: M Lievremont **ASSISTANT COACHES:** E N'tamack, D Retiere, D Ellis & G Quesada **MANANGER:** J Maso

MID-YEAR TESTS

SOUTH AFRICA: Z Kirchner (J de Villiers, 61)*; GG Aplon, J Fourie (J de Villiers, 31-36), W Olivier (JL de Jongh, 61), BG Habana; M Steyn (R Pienaar, 66), ER Januarie; PJ Spies, L-FP Louw (DJ Potgieter, 51-57), SWP Burger (DJ Potgieter, 61), V Matfield, DJ Rossouw (PR van der Merwe, 61), BJ Botha (JN du Plessis, 57), JW Smit (C) (MC Ralepelle, H/T), GG Steenkamp. *De Villiers to right wing; Aplon to fullback. YELLOW CARD: PR van der Merwe, 69. TEST DEBUTANT: PR van der Merwe.

FRANCE: C Poitrenaud (M Andreu, 64); A Rougerie, D Marty (D Skrela, 72)**, M Mermoz, V Clerc; F Trinh-Duc, M Parra (D Yachvili, 67); J Bonnaire, W Lauret (L Picamoles, 53)*, T Dusautoir (C), R Millo-Chluski (J Pierre, 53), L Nallet, N Mas, D Szarzewski (G Guirado, 64), T Domingo (J-B Poux, H/T). *Picamoles to #8; Bonnaire to flank. **Skrela to flyhalf; Trinh-Duc to outside centre. YELLOW CARD: D Yachvili, 74. TEST DEBUTANT: W Lauret.

Notes: Six players in this Test are sons of Test-playing fathers: R Pienaar (ZMJ Pienaar - 1980-81), SWP Burger (SWP Burger Snr. - 1984-86), PR van der Merwe (PR van der Merwe Snr. - 1981-89), A Rougerie (J Rougerie - 1973), D Skrela (J-C Skrela - 1971-78) and D Yachvili (M Yachvili - 1968-75). Flip van der Merwe was only the second Springbok that was yellow-carded on test debut, the other being Bakkies Botha in 2002, also against France. The 42 points by the Springboks were the most against France at home in 21 tests since the first test at Newlands in 1958. It was also the biggest win against France on home soil and also the first win against France at this venue.

Aplon helps Boks bury France

South Africa 42 France 17 *(halftime 25-10)*

June 12, Newlands, Cape Town (46 885). Referee: BJ Lawrence (New Zealand)
SOUTH AFRICA - TRIES: Spies, Aplon (2), Steenkamp, Louw. **CONVERSIONS:** Steyn (3), Pienaar. **PENALTY GOALS:** Steyn (3).
FRANCE - TRIES: Rougerie, Andreu. **CONVERSIONS:** Parra, Skrela. **PENALTY GOAL:** Parra.

WING Gio Aplon scored two tries and flyhalf Morné Steyn kicked 15 points as South Africa crushed France at Newlands just a day after the FIFA World Cup kicked off a month-long, countrywide soccer celebration.

The diminutive Aplon celebrated his first Test on home soil with two superb solo tries that broke the Six Nations champions' resolve and earned him the man-of-the-match award.

The Springboks netted a further three tries through their forwards on a day when the visitors were outplayed up front and regularly harried off the ball at the breakdowns.

"It was an important week for us to get a result and they were a good team," said Springbok captain John Smit. "It was always going to be a very hyped-up game between the Tri-Nations and Six Nations champions and a week all about distractions and there were several of them."

The home side enjoyed a spectacular start, racing to a 14-0 lead after nine minutes and a 25-7 advantage with half an hour played.

Number eight Pierre Spies scored the first of three Springbok first-half tries when he dived over underneath the posts following a French mistake in the second minute. France centre David Marty threw a loose pass on halfway that was intercepted by winger Bryan Habana, who in turn fed centre Jaque Fourie. The veteran midfielder, playing his 56th Test, was quickly closed down but had the vision to feed an unmarked Spies on his left.

Aplon, who made his Test debut against Wales the weekend before, got onto the scoresheet in the eighth minute when he bumped off centre Maxime Mermoz, before rounding the cover defence. Steyn added the extra points before slotting two penalties to give his side a 20-0 lead.

France opened their account on the half hour when winger Aurelien Rougerie was freed down the right touchline for an easy run-in after the first sustained period of French pressure.

Scrumhalf Morgan Parra kicked the conversion and an injury-time penalty, but not before Springbok loosehead Gurthro Steenkamp scored his side's third try after Steyn floated a long pass to the unmarked prop forward standing on the tramlines.

Steyn extended the lead to 18 points soon after the restart when a French scrum infringement gifted the flyhalf three points from in front.

No sooner had play restarted than it was sevens star Aplon who brought the 46,885-strong crowd to their feet when he picked up a loose ball near his own line before sprinting away on a diagonal run for a length-of-the-field try.

The remainder of the half was characterised by numerous mistakes from both sides. The point-scoring drought was eventually ended when flanker Francois Louw barged over for his team's fifth try with five minutes remaining.

The visitors notched a consolation try through replacement winger Marc Andreu, converted by yet another substitute, David Skrela.

France coach Marc Lievremont lamented his team's poor start. "It's very difficult to find words to describe this match because we came with great intentions but things didn't go as planned," he said.

Min	Action	Score
2	Spies try, Steyn conversion	**7-0**
8	Aplon try, Steyn conversion	**14-0**
11	Steyn penalty	**17-0**
24	Steyn penalty	**20-0**
29	Rougerie try, Parra conversion	**20-7**
32	Steenkamp try,	
	Steyn missed conversion	**25-7**
44	Parra penalty	**25-10**
47	Steyn penalty	**28-10**
49	Aplon try, Steyn conversion	**35-10**
75	Louw try, Pienaar conversion	**42-10**
79	Andreu try, Skrela conversion	**42-17**

Mallett's men no match for Boks

THE fact that Nick Mallett had to shave his head after the first Test in Witbank told you everything you needed to know about South Africa's series against Italy.

In wrestling terms this would have been the Undertaker against a handpicked pipsqueak – the movement and guile of the latter might prove awkward for a few moments before he is eventually pounded into submission.

Mallett, a former Springbok coach who smashed the Azzurri by a century back in 1999, had promised the Italian players that his hair would go if they managed to lose by less than 20 points against the Springboks in Witbank.

Not only did they manage that with a 29-13 defeat, but they even achieved the morale-boosting feat of outscoring the word champions 10-7 in the second half. South Africa had led 22-3 at halftime and a decent thrashing seemed on the cards for the Italians.

But Italy under Mallett have mastered the art of being awkward opponents. And, with skipper Sergio Parisse leading the way, they really took the fight to the Boks in the second half.

Bok coach Peter de Villiers had said earlier in the year that he would use the two internationals against Italy to field separate 'north' and 'south' teams to trial players for the 2011 Rugby World Cup, but this plan did not materialise.

De Villiers, in fact, failed to heed a number of the warning signs that had already begun to appear during the series. The poor form of scrumhalf Ricky Januarie was simply overlooked and only acted against in the Tri-Nations, while centre Jean de Villiers was twice played out of position.

A trip to watch Bafana Bafana play a World Cup match in Pretoria whilst the Boks were based in Witbank also detracted from the team's focus.

De Villiers would complain about that the following week in East London and hopefully the potentially destructive effect of sideshows is a warning that will be heeded in future.

John Smit returned as captain for the second Test and brought with him a focus that was lacking in Witbank.

If the first Test was a morale-booster for the Italians, the second left no doubt about the mastery of the Boks. Francois Louw continued to build on his growing reputation as an international loose forward and, on the surface at least, the result was an impressive way of finishing off the first phase of the international season.

Sadly, this would not prove to be a pointer to Tri-Nations success.

ITALY TO SOUTH AFRICA 2010

	Date of birth	Height	Weight	Club	South Africa	South Africa	Matches	Tries	Conversions	Penalties	Drop Goals	Points
L McLean	29/06/87	1.88	95	Treviso	15	15	2	0	0	0	0	0
PK Robertson	29/10/80	1.78	78	Viadana	14	–	1	0	0	0	0	0
A Masi	30/03/81	1.85	92	Racing Metro	13	12	2	0	0	0	0	0
M Pratichetti	27/12/85	1.90	108	Viadana	12	x	1	0	0	0	0	0
Mirco Bergamasco	23/01/83	1.80	86	Stade Francais	11	11	2	0	1	4	0	14
C Gower	29/04/78	1.75	90	Bayonne	10	10	2	0	0	0	0	0
T Tebaldi	23/09/87	1.85	82	Gran Parma	9	R	2	0	0	0	0	0
S Parisse*	12/09/83	1.96	106	Stade Francais	8	8	2	1	0	0	0	5
A Zanni	31/01/84	1.93	100	Treviso	7	R	2	0	0	0	0	0
S Favaro	07/11/88	1.84	96	Rugby Parma	6	–	1	0	0	0	0	0
Q Geldenhuys	19/06/81	2.03	116	Viadana	5	R	2	0	0	0	0	0
V Bernabo	03/03/84	1.98	110	Rugby Roma	4	–	1	0	0	0	0	0
ML Castrogiovanni	21/10/81	1.88	118	Leicester Tigers	3	–	1	0	0	0	0	0
L Ghiraldini	26/12/84	1.83	99	Treviso	2	R	2	0	0	0	0	0
S Perugini	06/03/78	1.80	118	Bayonne	1	1	2	0	0	0	0	0
L Cittadini	17/12/82	1.88	116	Treviso	R	3	2	0	0	0	0	0
M Bortolami	12/06/80	1.98	112	Gloucester Rugby	R	5	2	0	0	0	0	0
F Ongaro	23/09/77	1.83	104	Saracens	R	2	2	0	0	0	0	0
G-J Canale	11/11/82	1.83	93	Clermont Auvergne	R	13	2	0	0	0	0	0
P Derbyshire	03/07/86	1.90	97	Padova	R	6	2	0	0	0	0	0
S Picone	26/09/82	1.80	88	Treviso	R	9	2	0	0	0	0	0
R Bocchino	03/03/88	1.80	80	Rovigo	x	R	1	0	0	0	0	0
M Sepe	08/10/86	1.83	87	Viadana	–	14	1	1	0	0	0	5
M Vosawai	12/08/83	1.88	110	Rugby Parma	–	7	1	0	0	0	0	0
C del Fava	01/07/81	1.98	115	Viadana	–	4	1	0	0	0	0	0
F Sbaraglini	03/12/82	1.79	103	Treviso	–	R	1	0	0	0	0	0
26 Players								**2**	**1**	**4**	**0**	**24**

*Captain

MANAGER: L Troiani **COACH:** NVH Mallett **ASSISTANT COACHES:** C Orlandi & A Troncon.

SPRINGBOK.

Struggling Boks still too strong for Italy

South Africa 29 Italy 13 *(halftime 22-3)*

June 19, Puma Stadium, Witbank (15 000). Referee: A Small (England)
SOUTH AFRICA - TRIES: Habana, Louw, Steyn, Kirchner. CONVERSIONS: Steyn (3). PENALTY GOAL: Steyn.
ITALY - TRY: Parisse. CONVERSION: Mirco Bergamasco. PENALTY GOALS: Mirco Bergamasco (2).

SOUTH Africa defeated Italy 29-13 despite a disjointed and lethargic performance at the Puma Stadium in Witbank. The Springboks appeared affected by the host of changes to the team that beat France the week before, although they still conjured four tries in the first of a two-Test series.

The visitors enjoyed greater territory and possession, especially in the opening quarter, but were too limited in their approach to seriously trouble the hosts.

Flyhalf Morné Steyn scored 14 points, while eight of Italy's points came from the boot of winger Mirco Bergamasco. Springbok captain Victor Matfield said he had been frustrated by his team's error-strewn display. "I don't think we played very well and we made too many basic errors," he said. "We'll work on that and next week will definitely be better. It's just the top three inches that we have to get right."

Bergamasco kicked a 13th-minute penalty to give Italy the lead for the first and only time but Steyn equalised two minutes later as his team mates shook off their rust.

Winger Bryan Habana put the Springboks in front in the 18th minute when a powerful drive by flanker Francois Louw produced quick ball for the backs.

Recalled centre Butch James made a well-timed pass to fullback Zane Kirchner, who grubbered through for Habana to run onto to score unopposed.

Louw, a late replacement for Schalk Burger, was in the action 10 minutes later when he barged over from a driving maul close to the Italian line.

Steyn was unable to convert but the flyhalf made amends on the stroke of halftime when he danced over for his side's third try and converted it for a 19-point lead.

Kirchner notched the fourth try nine minutes after the restart when Steyn probed the blindside from a ruck and found his Bulls teammate unmarked on the touchline.

The Springboks were later dealt a blow when James was yellow-carded, which gave Italy captain and man-of-the-match Sergio Parisse the space to dive over in the 63rd minute after a good break by scrumhalf Tito Tebaldi.

Bergamasco narrowed the gap to 13 points with his second penalty 11 minutes from time, but Italy could not convert a late rally into further points.

"I'm happy about the enthusiasm of my team, especially in the second half," Parisse said. "We're looking forward to the second test next week in East London."

SOUTH AFRICA: Z Kirchner (BA Basson, 75)**; GG Aplon, J de Villiers, AD James, BG Habana; M Steyn (JL de Jongh, 64)*, ER Januarie (R Pienaar, 64); PJ Spies, DJ Potgieter (R Kankowski, 75), L-FP Louw, V Matfield (C), JP Botha (AJ Hargreaves, 50), JN du Plessis (CJ van der Linde, 52), MC Ralepelle (BG Maku, 80), GG Steenkamp. *De Jongh to inside centre; James to flyhalf. **Basson to right wing; Aplon to fullback. TEST DEBUTANT: BG Maku.

ITALY: L McLean; PK Robertson, A Masi (G-J Canale, 58), M Pratichetti, Mirco Bergamasco; C Gower, T Tebaldi (S Piconi, 67); S Parisse (C), A Zanni, S Favaro (P Derbyshire, 64)*, Q Geldenhuys, V Bernabo (M Bortolami, 50), M-L Castrogiovanni (L Cittadini, 19), L Ghiraldini (F Ongaro, 58), S Perugini. *Derbyshire to #7 flank; Zanni to #6 flank. *Unused substitute: R Bocchino.*

Notes: Victor Matfield and Bakkies Botha extended their World record as a lock combination in the starting XV to 55 tests. Victor Matfield now shares the Springbok record with John Smit for the most capped forward (95). Victor Matfield played in his 28th consecutive test, a Springbok record for a lock. Bryan Habana increased his Springbok record for most tries in tests as a wing to 37. Jean de Villiers again became the most capped Springbok centre (46), a record he shared with Jaque Fourie before this test.

Min	Action	Score
13	Bergamasco penalty	0-3
15	Steyn penalty	3-3
18	Habana try, Steyn conversion	10-3
31	Louw try, Steyn missed conversion	15-3
37	Bergamasco missed penalty	15-3
39	Steyn try, Steyn conversion	22-3
49	Kirchner try, Steyn conversion	29-3
63	Parisse try, Bergamasco conversion	29-10
69	Bergamasco penalty	29-13

MID-YEAR TESTS

SOUTH AFRICA: GG Aplon; J de Villiers, J Fourie, JL de Jongh (W Olivier, 52), BG Habana (R Pienaar, 57)*; M Steyn (AD James, 61), ER Januarie; PJ Spies, L-FP Louw, SWP Burger (DJ Potgieter, 61), A Bekker, JP Botha (PR van der Merwe, 57), JN du Plessis (BJ Botha, 52), JW Smit (C) (MC Ralepelle, 63), GG Steenkamp. *Pienaar to fullback; Aplon to left wing.

ITALY: L McLean; M Sepe, G-J Canale, A Masi, Mirco Bergamasco; C Gower (R Bocchino, 61), S Piconi (T Tebaldi, 52); S Parisse (C), M Vosawai, P Derbyshire (A Zanni, 61), M Bortolami (Q Geldenhuys, 52), C-A Del Fava, L Cittadini (F Sbaraglini, 63), F Ongaro (L Ghiraldini, 52), S Perugini.

Steyn leads Boks to series win

South Africa 55 Italy 11 *(halftime 27-6)*
June 26, Buffalo City Stadium, East London (12 984). Referee: A Small (England)
SOUTH AFRICA - TRIES: Steyn (2), Spies, Du Plessis, Habana, Van der Merwe, BJ Botha. **CONVERSIONS:** Steyn (5), Pienaar (2).
PENALTY GOALS: Steyn (2).
ITALY - TRY: Sepe. **PENALTY GOALS:** Mirco Bergamasco (2).

FLYHALF Morné Steyn scored 26 points, including two tries, as South Africa beat Italy 55-11 at the Buffalo City Stadium. The win not only gave the Springboks a 2-0 series victory but also allowed them to gear up for the defence of their Vodacom Tri-Nations title.

"We needed to polish up a bit from last week and we were more clinical today," said Springbok captain John Smit. "We've still got lots to work on before the Tri-Nations starts but it was a step in the right direction. We've got a good group to pick from and we want to make the most of the talent we've got available."

The result of the match was never in doubt for the home side but the tenacious Italian defence forced numerous errors from the Springboks in a hard-fought first half.

Playing with a stiff southerly breeze at their backs, the hosts shook off a nervous opening quarter to run in three unanswered first-half tries before dominating after the break.

"The Springboks played very well today and we missed a lot of tackles," said Italy captain Sergio Parisse. "They were more aggressive than they were last week and it's not easy playing against the best team in the world."

Italy, who made 10 changes to the side that lost the first Test, were courageous on defence and combative at the breakdowns but had no answer to the pace of the Springboks.

Flyhalf Steyn and Italy wing Mirco Bergamasco traded early penalties before Steyn scored a solo try from close range in the 11th minute to make it 10-3.

Bergamasco cut the deficit to four points with a second penalty before Steyn stepped up with his second try on the half hour to make it 20-6.

Recalled lock Andries Bekker broke through the Italian midfield on the stroke of halftime before passing inside for eighth man Pierre Spies to score his team's third try.

The Springboks notched up another three tries in the third quarter, to prop Jannie du Plessis, winger Bryan Habana and replacement forward Flip van der Merwe, to lead 48-6.

Habana's try equalled the South African record of 38 held by former captain Joost van der Westhuizen – although few would have believed at the time that by the end of 2010 he would not have added to that figure.

Italy scored their only try in the 66th minute when winger Michele Sepe ran on to a Craig Gower grubber kick after a rare spell of sustained pressure by the visitors.

The Springboks had the final say when reserve prop BJ Botha crashed over on the hooter.

Notes: *This win was the Springboks' tenth consecutive win against Italy. Bryan Habana increased his Springbok record for most tries in tests as a wing to 38 and joins Joost van der Westhuizen as most prolific Springbok try scorer in tests. With Matfield not playing, John Smit is again the most capped forward with 96 tests. Jaque Fourie joined Jean de Villiers in first place for most capped Springbok centre (46).*

Min	Action	Score
01	Parisse missed drop goal	
05	Steyn penalty	3-0
09	Bergamasco penalty	3-3
11	Steyn try, Steyn conversion	10-3
15	Bergamasco penalty	10-6
20	Steyn penalty	13-6
31	Steyn try, Steyn conversion	20-6
37	Spies try, Steyn conversion	27-6
47	Parisse missed drop goal	27-6
52	Du Plessis try, Steyn conversion	34-6
57	Habana try, Steyn conversion	41-6
60	Van der Merwe try, Pienaar conversion	48-6
65	Sepe try, Bergamasco missed conversion	48-11
78	BJ Botha try, Pienaar conversion	55-11

MID-YEAR TESTS

VODACOM TRI-NATIONS

No silverware as Boks take wooden spoon

IF you had known beforehand that Morné Steyn would not miss a place-kick in the 2010 Vodacom Tri-Nations, you might well have only stiffened your belief as an optimistic South African that the Springboks would retain the crown.

After all, the flyhalf had been a hugely influential figure in the 2009 triumph, his 95 points topping the individual scoring list and his 77 this time – 29 unblemished shots at goal – again saw him rule that particular roost by 13 points from Matt Giteau and 14 from Dan Carter.

So for the Boks to nevertheless end rock-bottom of the standings would have come as a particularly nasty little counter-blow to that knowledge.

In the most violent form turnaround in the 15-year history of the competition, South Africa plummeted from five wins out of six last year to five defeats instead in 2010, being credited with a lone 44-31 triumph against second-placed Australia in Pretoria.

And even then the shaft of light was short-lived: the Boks duly crashed 41-39 in the crazily fluffy, helter-skelter follow-up (mercifully their final outing) against the Wallabies in Bloemfontein to seal the wooden spoon.

It will be remembered as the year when John Smit's side so unfathomably tossed away many of the key formulas for their 2009 success, the most glaring one being their famously suffocating, committed defence which had also so often translated into stealthy counter-strikes then.

Instead the floodgates haplessly opened – to the special delight of the powerfully resurgent All Blacks, who romped to a clean-sweep trio of victories over the old enemy en route to the title by a 16-point margin from the

Wallabies and 20-point chasm from the Boks.

South Africa, sorely missing for the entire campaign 2009 kingpins Fourie du Preez and Heinrich Brüssow, and with various stalwart personalities well off their known best levels, leaked all of 22 tries in their six matches whilst the fewest points they conceded in any one match was 29.

That came in a heartbreaking, seven-point reverse to New Zealand at FNB Stadium in Soweto, where a throbbing full house of 95,000 saw Smit's 100th appearance in a Bok jersey turn to nightmare as he botched a tackle on Ma'a Nonu that ultimately put substitute wing Israel Dagg away for the game-clinching try right on full time.

South Africa had earlier looked like bagging a morale-lifting victory, having led by five points until very deep in the final quarter, and the late sting by the visitors – even in supposedly disadvantageous Highveld conditions for them – only enhanced suspicions in some circles that certain Boks were becoming a tad too leaden-footed.

The writing was already on the wall for the defending champions after the upfront, winless away leg, in truth: South Africa incurred the debatable, pedantic wrath of a trio of different Irish referees, earning an unwanted first-quarter hat-trick of yellow cards.

They surrendered Bakkies Botha in this way in Auckland (13th minute), Danie Rossouw in Wellington (fourth minute) and Jaque Fourie in Brisbane (second minute).

It was demoralising, back-foot stuff, and somehow would help sum up their entire, ill-fated campaign.

2010 VODACOM TRI-NATIONS RESULTS

Date	Venue	Team 1	Score 1	Team 2	Score 2
July 10	Eden Park, Auckland	New Zealand	32	South Africa	12
July 17	Westpac Stadium, Wellington	New Zealand	31	South Africa	17
July 24	Suncorp Stadium, Brisbane	Australia	30	South Africa	13
July 31	Etihad Stadium, Melbourne	Australia	28	New Zealand	49
August 7	AMI Stadium, Christchurch	New Zealand	20	Australia	10
August 21	FNB Stadium, Soweto	South Africa	22	New Zealand	29
August 28	Loftus Versfeld, Pretoria	South Africa	44	Australia	31
September 4	Vodacom Park, Bloemfontein	South Africa	39	Australia	41
September 11	ANZ Stadium, Sydney	Australia	22	New Zealand	23

VODACOM TRI-NATIONS

Morné Steyn once again topped the scoring sheet with 77 points.

2010 VODACOM TRI-NATIONS LOG

Team	P	W	D	D	PF	PA	Diff	TF	TA	B4	B7	Pts
New Zealand	6	6	0	0	184	111	73	22	9	3	0	27
Australia	6	2	0	4	162	188	-26	17	21	2	1	11
South Africa	6	1	0	5	147	194	-47	13	22	1	2	7

2009 VODACOM TRI-NATIONS LEADING SCORERS

10 POINTS OR MORE

PLAYER	Country	Matches	Tries	Conversions	Penalties	Drop Goals	Points
M Steyn	South Africa	6	0	10	19	0	77
MJ Giteau	Australia	6	0	11	14	0	64
DW Carter	New Zealand	5	1	11	12	0	63
JD O'Connor	Australia	6	4	2	1	0	27
JM Muliaina	New Zealand	6	4	0	0	0	20
PAT Weepu	New Zealand	6	0	2	4	0	16
KJ Beale	Australia	5	2	0	2	0	16
DA Mitchell	Australia	5	3	0	0	0	15
GG Steenkamp	South Africa	6	3	0	0	0	15
RH McCaw	New Zealand	6	3	0	0	0	15
CG Smith	New Zealand	6	2	0	0	0	10
MA Nonu	New Zealand	6	2	0	0	0	10
SW Genia	Australia	6	2	0	0	0	10
TD Woodcock	New Zealand	6	2	0	0	0	10
J Fourie	South Africa	5	2	0	0	0	10
RD Elsom	Australia	6	2	0	0	0	10
SWP Burger	South Africa	6	2	0	0	0	10
IJA Dagg	New Zealand	4	2	0	0	0	10
A Ashley-Cooper	Australia	6	2	0	0	0	10
KJ Read	New Zealand	6	2	0	0	0	10

SPRINGBOK SQUAD - 2010 VODACOM TRI-NATIONS

	Date of birth	Height	Weight	Province	New Zealand	New Zealand	Australia	New Zealand	Australia	Australia	Matches	Tries	Conversions	Penalties	Drop Goals	Points
Z Kirchner	16/06/84	1.84	92	Blue Bulls	15	15	15	–	–	–	3	0	0	0	0	0
J de Villiers	24/02/81	1.90	100	Western Province	14	14	–	12	12	12	5	1	0	0	0	5
J Fourie	04/03/83	1.90	105	Golden Lions	13	13	13	–	13	13	5	2	0	0	0	10
W Olivier	06/11/83	1.86	95	Blue Bulls	12	12	12	x	–	–	3	0	0	0	0	0
BG Habana	12/06/83	1.79	92	Blue Bulls	11	11	11	11	11	11	6	0	0	0	0	0
M Steyn	11/07/84	1.84	90	Blue Bulls	10	10	10	10	10	10	6	0	10	19	0	77
ER Januarie	01/02/82	1.70	80	Western Province	9	9	–	R	x	x	3	0	0	0	0	0
PJ Spies	08/06/85	1.95	106	Blue Bulls	8	8	8	8	8	8	6	1	0	0	0	5
L-FP Louw	15/06/85	1.90	110	Western Province	7	7	–	R	–	–	3	0	0	0	0	0
SWP Burger	13/04/83	1.93	110	Western Province	6	6	6	6	6	6	6	2	0	0	0	10
V Matfield	11/05/77	2.01	110	Blue Bulls	5	5	5	5	5	5	6	0	0	0	0	0
JP Botha	22/09/79	2.02	118	Blue Bulls	4	–	–	–	–	–	1	0	0	0	0	0
JN du Plessis	16/11/82	1.87	113	Kwazulu–Natal	3	–	–	3	3	3	4	0	0	0	0	0
JW Smit	03/04/78	1.86	116	Kwazulu–Natal	2*	2*	2*	2*	2*	2*	6	0	0	0	0	0
GG Steenkamp	12/06/81	1.89	124	Blue Bulls	1	1	1	1	1	1	6	3	0	0	0	15
GG Aplon	06/10/82	1.75	70	Western Province	R	R	14	15	–	R	5	0	0	0	0	0
BJ Botha	04/01/80	1.82	110	Ulster, Ireland	R	R	3	–	–	–	3	0	0	0	0	0
R Pienaar	10/03/84	1.86	85	Kwazulu–Natal	R	R	9	–	–	–	3	0	0	0	0	0
AD James	08/01/79	1.84	98	Bath Rugby, England	R	x	R	x	R	–	3	0	1	0	0	2
DJ Rossouw	05/06/78	1.97	118	Blue Bulls	R	4	4	t+R	R	4	6	1	0	0	0	5
MC Ralepelle	11/09/86	1.78	105	Blue Bulls	R	R	R	x	R	R	5	0	0	0	0	0
A Bekker	05/12/83	2.08	120	Western Province	R	R	–	–	–	–	2	0	0	0	0	0
CJ van der Linde	27/08/80	1.90	122	Free State	–	3	t+R	R	R	R	5	0	0	0	0	0
R Kankowski	14/10/85	1.93	103	Kwazulu–Natal	–	R	7	–	x	R	3	0	0	0	0	0
JL de Jongh	15/04/88	1.77	84	Western Province	–	–	R	13	x	x	2	0	0	0	0	0
F Hougaard	06/04/88	1.79	86	Blue Bulls	–	–	R	9	9	9	4	0	0	0	0	0
DJ Potgieter	22/02/87	1.90	98	Blue Bulls	–	–	R	–	–	–	1	0	0	0	0	0
PR van der Merwe	03/06/85	1.99	118	Blue Bulls	–	–	R	4	4	R	4	0	0	0	0	0
J-PR Pietersen	12/07/86	1.84	102	Kwazulu–Natal	–	–	–	14	14	14	3	1	0	0	0	5
JH Smith	30/07/81	1.96	109	Free State	–	–	–	7	7	7	3	1	0	0	0	5
FPL Steyn	14/05/87	1.91	110	Racing Metro, France	–	–	–	–	15	15	2	1	0	1	0	8
T Mtawarira	01/07/85	1.88	112	Kwazulu–Natal	–	–	–	–	–	–	0	0	0	0	0	0
32 Players												**13**	**11**	**20**	**0**	**147**

VODACOM TRI-NATIONS

ALL BLACKS SQUAD - 2010 VODACOM TRI-NATIONS

ALL BLACKS	Date of birth	Height	Weight	Province	South Africa	South Africa	Australia	Australia	South Africa	Australia	Matches	Tries	Conversions	Penalties	Drop Goals	Points
JM Muliaina	31/07/80	1.83	85	Waikato	15	15	15	15	15	15	6	4	0	0	0	20
CS Jane	08/02/83	1.83	88	Wellington	14	14	14	14	14	14	6	1	0	0	0	5
CG Smith	12/10/81	1.86	95	Wellington	13	13	13	13	13	13	6	2	0	0	0	10
MA Nonu	21/05/82	1.82	104	Wellington	12	12	12	12	12	12	6	2	0	0	0	10
JT Rokocoko	06/06/83	1.89	98	Auckland	11	-	11	11	11	-	4	1	0	0	0	5
DW Carter	05/03/82	1.78	91	Canterbury	10	10	10	10	10	-	5	1	11	12	0	63
QJ Cowan	06/03/82	1.82	92	Southland	9	R	9	-	9	R	5	1	0	0	0	5
KJ Read	26/10/85	1.93	105	Canterbury	8	8	8	8	8	8	6	1	0	0	0	5
RH McCaw	31/12/80	1.87	106	Canterbury	7*	7*	7*	7*	7*	7*	6	3	0	0	0	15
J Kaino	06/04/83	1.96	105	Auckland	6	6	6	6	6	6	6	0	0	0	0	0
TJS Donnelly	01/10/81	2.00	113	Otago	5	5	5	5	5	5	6	0	0	0	0	0
BC Thorn	03/02/75	1.95	113	Canterbury	4	4	4	4	4	4	6	0	0	0	0	0
OT Franks	23/12/87	1.86	112	Canterbury	3	3	3	3	-	3	5	0	0	0	0	0
KF Mealamu	20/03/79	1.81	106	Auckland	2	2	2	2	2	2	6	0	0	0	0	0
TD Woodcock	27/01/81	1.84	118	North Harbour	1	1	1	1	1	1	6	2	0	0	0	10
RD Kahui	09/06/85	1.86	95	Waikato	R	-	-	-	-	-	1	0	0	0	0	0
LJ Messam	25/03/84	1.88	109	Waikato	R	R	-	-	-	-	2	0	0	0	0	0
BJ Franks	27/03/84	1.83	112	Tasman	R	R	R	R	3	-	5	0	0	0	0	0
PAT Weepu	07/09/83	1.78	94	Wellington	R	9	R	9	R	9	6	0	2	4	0	16
CR Flynn	05/01/81	1.84	106	Canterbury	R	R	R	R	x	R	5	1	0	0	0	5
SL Whitelock	12/10/88	2.02	102	Canterbury	R	R	R	R	R	-	5	0	0	0	0	0
AW Cruden	08/01/89	1.75	82	Manawatu	x	R	R	x	x	10	3	0	0	0	0	0
IJA Dagg	06/06/88	1.88	94	Hawke's Bay	-	R	R	-	R	11	4	2	0	0	0	10
RMN Ranger	30/09/86	1.82	97	Northland	-	11	-	-	-	R	2	1	0	0	0	5
VVJ Vito	27/03/87	1.92	109	Wellington	-	-	R	R	R	6	4	0	0	0	0	0
BJ Stanley	11/09/84	1.83	95	Auckland	-	-	-	x	-	-	0	0	0	0	0	0
A Mathewson	13/12/85	1.73	88	Wellington	-	-	-	-	R	-	1	0	0	0	0	0
IF Afoa	16/10/83	1.83	120	Auckland	-	-	-	-	R	R	2	0	0	0	0	0
AF Boric	27/12/83	2.00	110	North Harbour	-	-	-	-	-	R	1	0	0	0	0	0
CR Slade	10/10/87	1.83	87	Canterbury	-	-	-	-	-	R	1	0	0	0	0	0
30 Players												**22**	**13**	**16**	**0**	**184**

Australia 28 New Zealand 49 *(halftime 14-32)*
July 31, Etihad Stadium, Melbourne (51 409).
Referee: C Joubert (South Africa)
AUSTRALIA - TRIES: Mitchell, Ashley-Cooper, Elsom.
CONVERSIONS: Giteau (2). **PENALTY GOALS:** Giteau (3).
NEW ZEALAND - TRIES: Carter, Muliaina (2), McCaw, Jane, Rokocoko, Flynn. **CONVERSIONS:** Carter (4). **PENALTY GOALS:** Carter (2).
AUSTRALIA AP Ashley-Cooper; JD O'Connor, RG Horne (KJ Beale, 57); BS Barnes, DA Mitchell; MJ Giteau (AS Fainga'a, 77); SW Genia (L Burgess, 76); RN Brown, DW Pocock, RD Elsom (C), NC Sharpe (RA Simmons, 48); DW Mumm, RSL Ma'afu (JA Slipper, 60), ST Moore (SM Fainga'a, 48), BA Robinson. *Unused substitute: MJ Hodgson.* **YELLOW CARD:** DA Mitchell, 28. **RED CARD:** DA Mitchell, 44. **TRI-NATIONS DEBUTS:** KJ Beale and AS Fainga'a.
NEW ZEALAND JM Muliaina; CS Jane (IJA Dagg, 76); CG Smith, MA Nonu (AW Cruden, 72); JT Rokocoko; DW Carter, QJ Cowan (PAT Weepu, 34); KJ Read, RH McCaw (C), J Kaino, TJS Donnelly (VVJ Vito, 73); BC Thorn (SL Whitelock, 57), OT Franks (BJ Franks, 48), KF Mealamu (CR Flynn, 72), TD Woodcock. **YELLOW CARD:** OT Franks, 22. **TRI-NATIONS DEBUT:** VVJ Vito.
Notes: The two Fainga'a brothers became the third set of twins to play

for Australia. The other two being Mark and Glen Ella (1982-84) and Jim and Stewart Boyce (1962-65). Joe Rokocoko became the most capped All Black wing in his 64th test surpassing the two record holders, Jonah Lomu and John Kirwan.

New Zealand 20 Australia 10 *(halftime 17-10)*
August 7, AMI Stadium, Christchurch (39 000).
Referee: JI Kaplan (South Africa)
NEW ZEALAND - TRIES: Muliaina, Smith. **CONVERSIONS:** Carter (2).
PENALTY GOALS: Carter (2).
AUSTRALIA - TRY: Beale. **CONVERSION:** Giteau. **PENALTY GOAL:** Giteau.
NEW ZEALAND JM Muliaina; CS Jane, CG Smith, MA Nonu, JT Rokocoko; DW Carter, PAT Weepu (A Mathewson, 77); KJ Read, RH McCaw (C), J Kaino (VVJ Vito, 70), TJS Donnelly (SL Whitelock, 73); BC Thorn, OT Franks (BJ Franks, 43), KF Mealamu (CR Flynn, 77), TD Woodcock. *Unused substitutes: AW Cruden and BJ Stanley.* **TRI-NATIONS DEBUT:** A Mathewson.
AUSTRALIA KJ Beale; JD O'Connor, AP Ashley-Cooper, AS Fainga'a, DA Mitchell; MJ Giteau, SW Genia; RN Brown (MJ Hodgson, 56), DW Pocock, RD Elsom (C), NC Sharpe (RA Simmons, 65), DW Mumm, RSL Ma'afu (JA

AUSTRALIA SQUAD - 2010 VODACOM TRI-NATIONS

Wallabies	Date of birth	Height	Weight	Province	South Africa	New Zealand	New Zealand	South Africa	South Africa	New Zealand	Matches	Tries	Conversions	Penalties	Drop Goals	Points
AP Ashley–Cooper	27/03/84	1.82	98	ACT	15	15	13	13	13	13	6	2	0	0	0	10
JD O'Connor	05/07/90	1.80	80	Western Australia	14	14	14	14	14	14	6	4	2	1	0	27
RG Horne	15/08/89	1.86	88	New South Wales	13	13	-	-	-	-	2	0	0	0	0	0
MJ Giteau	29/09/82	1.78	85	ACT	12	10	10	12	12	12	6	0	11	14	0	64
DA Mitchell	26/03/84	1.82	92	New South Wales	11	11	11	11	11	-	5	3	0	0	0	15
QS Cooper	05/04/88	1.86	93	Queensland	10	-	-	10	10	10	4	0	0	0	0	0
SW Genia	17/01/88	1.82	85	Queensland	9	9	9	9	9	9	6	2	0	0	0	10
RN Brown	28/08/84	1.89	106	Western Australia	8	8	8	8	R	R	6	0	0	0	0	0
DW Pocock	23/04/88	1.81	101	Western Australia	7	7	7	7	7	7	6	0	0	0	0	0
RD Elsom	14/02/83	1.97	106	ACT	6*	6*	6*	6*	6*	6*	6	2	0	0	0	10
NC Sharpe	26/02/78	2.00	115	Western Australia	5	5	5	5	5	5	6	0	0	0	0	0
DW Mumm	05/03/84	1.96	109	New South Wales	4	4	4	4	R	R	6	1	0	0	0	5
SL Ma'afu	22/03/83	1.84	126	ACT	3	3	3	3	3	3	6	0	0	0	0	0
SM Fainga'a	02/02/87	1.87	100	Queensland	2	R	2	2	R	-	5	0	0	0	0	0
BA Robinson	19/07/84	1.83	113	New South Wales	1	1	1	1	1	1	6	0	0	0	0	0
BS Barnes	28/05/86	1.83	87	Queensland	R	12	x	x	R	t+R	4	0	0	0	0	0
BJ McCalman	18/03/88	1.92	106	Western Australia	R	-	-	R	8	8	4	0	0	0	0	0
RA Simmons	19/04/89	2.00	115	Queensland	R	R	R	R	-	-	4	0	0	0	0	0
ST Moore	20/01/83	1.86	112	ACT	R	2	x	t	2	2	5	1	0	0	0	5
JA Slipper	06/06/89	1.85	113	Queensland	R	R	R	R	R	R	6	0	0	0	0	0
KJ Beale	06/01/89	1.84	94	New South Wales	x	R	15	15	15	15	5	2	0	2	0	16
L Burgess	20/08/83	1.79	89	New South Wales	x	R	x	x	R	R	3	0	0	0	0	0
AS Fainga'a	02/02/87	1.78	88	Queensland	-	R	12	x	R	R	4	0	0	0	0	0
MJ Hodgson	25/06/81	1.84	100	Western Australia	-	x	R	-	-	-	1	0	0	0	0	0
CB Shepherd	30/03/84	1.89	97	Western Australia	-	-	x	-	-	-	0	0	0	0	0	0
MD Chisholm	19/09/81	1.97	112	ACT	-	-	-	-	4	4	2	0	0	0	0	0
LD Turner	11/05/87	1.89	88	New South Wales	-	-	-	-	-	11	1	0	0	0	0	0
H Edmonds	20/10/81	1.83	103	ACT	-	-	-	-	-	x	0	0	0	0	0	0
BP Daley	27/06/88	1.84	111	Queensland	-	-	-	-	-	-	0	0	0	0	0	0
DN Ioane	14/07/85	1.79	93	Queensland	-	-	-	-	-	-	0	0	0	0	0	0
S Higginbotham	05/09/86	1.94	112	Queensland	-	-	-	-	-	-	0	0	0	0	0	0
PJ Hynes	17/07/82	1.80	92	Queensland	-	-	-	-	-	-	0	0	0	0	0	0
32 Players											**17**	**13**	**17**		**0**	**162**

Slipper, 65), SM Fainga'a, BA Robinson. **TRI-NATIONS DEBUT:** MJ Hodgson.
Notes: Tony Woodcock became the most capped All Black prop in his 67th test surpassing Greg Somerville's 66 tests as prop. New Zealand equalled the record 9 consecutive wins against Australia set between 1936 and 1947. The current run started in 2008 at Eden Park, Auckland when the All Blacks won 39-10.

Australia 22 New Zealand 23 *(halftime 14-6)*
September 11, ANZ Stadium, Sydney (70 288). Referee: SM Lawrence (South Africa)
AUSTRALIA - TRIES: O'Connor, Ashley-Cooper. **PENALTY GOALS:** Giteau (3), Beale.
NEW ZEALAND - TRIES: McCaw, Read. **CONVERSIONS:** Weepu (2). **PENALTY GOALS:** Weepu (3).
AUSTRALIA KJ Beale; JD O'Connor, AP Ashley-Cooper (AS Fainga'a, 79), MJ Giteau, LD Turner; QS Cooper (BS Barnes, 69-74, 79), SW Genia (L Burgess, 72); BJ McCalman (RN Brown, 74), DW Pocock, RD Elsom (C), NC

Sharpe, MD Chisholm (DW Mumm, 56), RSL Ma'afu (JA Slipper, 53), ST Moore, BA Robinson. Unused substitute: H Edmonds.
NEW ZEALAND JM Muliaina; CS Jane (RMN Ranger, 69), CG Smith, MA Nonu, IJA Dagg; AW Cruden (CR Slade, 61), PAT Weepu (QJ Cowan, 79); KJ Read, RH McCaw (C), VVJ Vito (J Kaino, 49), TJS Donnelly (AF Boric, 61), BC Thorn, OT Franks (IF Afoa, 61), KF Mealamu (CR Flynn, 12), TD Woodcock.
TRI-NATIONS DEBUT: CR Slade.
Notes: Richie McCaw became New Zealand's most capped captain surpassing Shaun Fitzpatrick's record of 51 tests as captain. McCaw is also the most capped All Black captain in the Tri-Nations tournament with 25 caps as captain, three caps less than John Smit on 28. For the first time in the history of the tournament a team, New Zealand, went unbeaten in a season. New Zealand also set new records for most points in a Tri-Nation season (184) and most tries in a Tri-Nations season (22). This was New Zealand's 10th consecutive win against Australia improving their previous record of 9 consecutive wins set between 1936 and 1947.

NEW ZEALAND JM Muliaina; CS Jane, CG Smith, MA Nonu, JT Rokocoko (RD Kahui, 60); DW Carter, QJ Cowan (PAT Weepu, 55); KJ Read, RH McCaw (C), J Kaino (LJ Messam, 72), TJS Donnelly (SL Whitelock, 72), BC Thorn, OT Franks (BJ Franks, 65), KF Mealamu (CR Flynn, 79), TD Woodcock. *Unused substitute: AW Cruden.* **TRI-NATIONS DEBUTS:** TJS Donnelly, CR Flynn, BJ Franks, LJ Messam and SL Whitelock.

SOUTH AFRICA Z Kirchner; J de Villiers, J Fourie, W Olivier (GG Aplon, 72)*, BG Habana; M Steyn (AD James, 71), ER Januarie (R Pienaar, 76); PJ Spies, L-FP Louw (DJ Rossouw, 52), SWP Burger, V Matfield, JP Botha (A Bekker, 52), JN du Plessis (BJ Botha, 58), JW Smit (C) (MC Ralepelle, 72), GG Steenkamp. *Yellow card: JP Botha, 13.* **TRI-NATIONS DEBUTS:** Z Kirchner, GG Aplon and L-FP Louw.

Botha puts Boks on back foot

New Zealand 32 South Africa 12 *(halftime 20-3)*

July 10, Eden Park, Auckland (30 000). Referee: DA Lewis (Ireland)
NEW ZEALAND - TRIES: Smith, Nonu, Read, Woodcock. **CONVERSIONS:** Carter (3). **PENALTY GOALS:** Carter (2).
SOUTH AFRICA - PENALTY GOALS: Steyn (4).

THE controversial yellow-carding of Bakkies Botha and his subsequent banning for the most churlish of headbutts dominated the opening Vodacom Tri-Nations Test as the All Blacks began avenging the 3-0 whitewash by the Springboks the previous year.

Botha had been impeded by New Zealand scrumhalf Jimmy Cowan in the opening minute as the lock chased down Cowan's charged-down kick. When Botha then had Cowan in his grasp at the next phase, he headbutted him from behind – an incident replayed several times for the astonished Eden Park faithful.

Botha's lack of discipline came back to haunt him in the 14th minute when the Springboks, having repelled wave upon wave of All Black attacks, finally conceded their first ruck penalty in the red zone – only for referee Alan Lewis to reach for his yellow card to send their enforcer off the field.

The All Blacks scored 13 points while Botha was gone – fullback Mils Muliaina taking advantage of a disrupted defence that saw a flanker pack down at lock and a wing on the flank, to scythe through and set up centre Conrad

Smith for the opening try. Flyhalf Dan Carter added the conversion and two penalties.

But the major blow to the Springboks was that it allowed the All Blacks to emphatically seize all the momentum in the collisions, breakdowns and tackles. From then on, it was a case of trying to stop the hosts, who played with tremendous energy and intensity.

Centre Ma'a Nonu made the All Blacks' dominance count on the scoreboard when he scored just before halftime, having regathered his grubber after it bounced off Jean de Villiers and bursting through two tackles on the blindside of the subsequent ruck.

The Springboks did their best to mend the situation in the third quarter, flyhalf Morné Steyn kicking two further penalties, but there was a sense of injustice in the air when no All Black was yellow-carded despite several ruck offences inside their own 22.

Tremendous defence also managed to keep a lid on the Springboks' attacking aspirations, the locals' hunger and commitment fuelled by their ire over losing their last three Tests against their great rivals.

"That was a pretty special performance and a special day for this team and for All Black rugby," coach Graham Henry enthused afterwards. "I was very impressed with the set-pieces. The lineouts were excellent, the scrum was solid and the defence was superb. I think the edge was created by the results last year and everybody played well."

A pair of tries by eighthman Kieran Read and prop Tony Woodcock sealed a well-deserved bonus point for the All Blacks.

"If we had had the aggression they had, I would have been very happy. But they created their own luck," said Bok coach Peter de Villiers. "We allowed them too much and then, out of frustration, we tried to play too much rugby in our own half. If we allow them to compete with us physically and win the contests, then we will pay the price."

Min	Action	Score
03	Carter missed penalty	-
05	Steyn missed drop goal	-
08	Steyn penalty	0-3
14	Carter penalty	3-3
19	Smith try, Carter conversion	10-3
26	Carter penalty	13-3
35	Nonu try, Carter conversion	20-3
42	Steyn penalty	20-6
47	Steyn penalty	20-9
49	Steyn missed drop goal	20-9
57	Read try, Carter conversion	27-9
60	Steyn penalty	27-12
80	Woodcock try, Carter missed conversion	32-12

VODACOM TRI-NATIONS

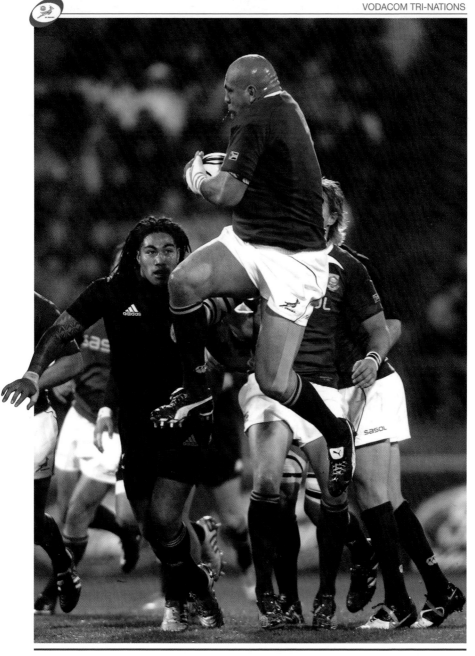

NEW ZEALAND JM Muliaina; CS Jane, CG Smith, MA Nonu (AW Cruden, 74), RMN Ranger (IJA Dagg, 63); DW Carter, PAT Weepu (QJ Cowan, 63); KJ Read, RH McCaw (C) (LJ Messam, 75), J Kaino, TJS Donnelly (SL Whitelock, 63), BC Thorn, OT Franks (BJ Franks, 70), KF Mealamu (CR Flynn, 75), TD Woodcock. **TRI-NATIONS DEBUTS:** AW Cruden, RMN Ranger and IJA Dagg.

SOUTH AFRICA Z Kirchner; J de Villiers (GG Aplon, H/T); J Fourie, W Olivier, BG Habana; M Steyn, ER Januarie (R Pienaar, 54); PJ Spies (R Kankowski, 70), L-FP Louw, SWP Burger, V Matfield, DJ Rossouw (A Bekker, 54), CJ van der Linde (BJ Botha, H/T), JW Smit (C) (MC Ralepelle, 75), GG Steenkamp. *Yellow card: DJ Rossouw, 04. Unused substitute: AD James.*

Boks build house of yellow cards

New Zealand 31 South Africa 17 *(halftime 13-7)*

July 17, Westpac Stadium, Wellington (35 000). Referee: AC Rolland (Ireland)

NEW ZEALAND - TRIES: Nonu, Muliaina, Ranger, Dagg. **CONVERSION:** Carter. **PENALTY GOALS:** Carter (2), Weepu.
SOUTH AFRICA - TRIES: Rossouw, Burger. **CONVERSIONS:** Steyn (2). **PENALTY GOAL:** Steyn .

UNBELIEVABLY, the Springboks were once again left chasing the game thanks to an early yellow card to Danie Rossouw – the suspended Bakkies Botha's replacement in the number-four jersey being sent to the sin-bin in the fourth minute for kicking out at All Black captain Richie McCaw on the ground.

New Zealand scored two tries while Rossouw was off the field to impose a stranglehold that an improved Springbok side never managed to break free from.

Rossouw's indiscretion overturned a penalty to the visitors and the All Blacks had the first try on the board just three minutes later. Eighthman Kieran Read ran from a Bryan Habana kick-ahead to set up the try for centre Ma'a Nonu, with wing Corey Jane, flanker McCaw and fullback Mils Muliaina all making their mark in a sweeping counter-attack.

The All Blacks' second try had a bit of good fortune about it, but the Springboks paid for their failure to secure the loose ball after Jaque Fourie had been tackled by centres Nonu and Conrad Smith. The bobbling ball eventually landed in the hands of scrumhalf Piri Weepu, who scooted clear to set up Muliaina.

The Springboks did cut the deficit to 13-7 shortly before halftime when wing Rene Ranger's obvious shoulder charge on fullback Zane Kirchner drew just a penalty and no yellow card. The lineout was set, scrumhalf Ricky Januarie was quick to spot a half-gap and his assured pass in the tackle saw centre Jean de Villiers running a great line that took him into the shadow of the posts. A ruck was formed, quick ball recycled and a pick-and-go by Rossouw saw him barge over.

The Springboks opened the second half in a similar vein, another top-class move off a lineout earning Morné Steyn a penalty which closed the gap to 13-10.

But just two minutes later, Kirchner lost his bearings under a Carter up-and-under and Ranger showed a keen nose for the line to score a try that perhaps should have been more closely examined by the TMO.

Carter missed the conversion, but one could sense the All Blacks had regained the initiative and another successful kick-and-chase by the home side saw Kirchner hunted down again, leading to a penalty by Weepu, who enjoyed an excellent game on his return to the starting line-up at his home ground.

Replacement wing Israel Dagg showed, in the 65th minute, why he is one of the most dangerous runners in world rugby as he jinked past four defenders for a superb individual try.

Carter bounced back to kick the conversion and a penalty to leave the All Blacks 31-10 up heading into the final 10 minutes.

The Springboks were also unhappy with the performance of referee Alain Rolland, his handling of the breakdowns being a particular bone of contention.

Coach Peter de Villiers aired his grievances after the Test: "I don't want to be as low as to prepare my guys to cheat, but sometimes it seems like that's the only way because loose play is now about 70% of the game," De Villiers said.

Min	Action	Score
06	Carter missed penalty	-
07	Nonu try, Carter missed penalty	5-0
12	Muliaina try, Carter missed conversion	10-0
31	Carter penalty	13-0
37	Rossouw try, Steyn conversion	13-7
41	Carter missed penalty	13-7
44	Steyn penalty	13-10
46	Ranger try, Carter missed conversion	18-10
52	Weepu penalty	21-10
65	Dagg try, Carter conversion	28-10
69	Carter penalty	31-10
75	Burger try, Steyn conversion	31-17

AUSTRALIA AP Ashley-Cooper; JD O'Connor, RG Horne, MJ Giteau (BS Barnes, 74), DA Mitchell; QS Cooper, SW Genia; RN Brown (BJ McCalman, 70), DW Pocock, RD Elsom (C), NC Sharpe, DW Mumm (RA Simmons, 68), RSL Ma'afu, SM Fainga'a (ST Moore, 54), BA Robinson (JA Slipper, 59). *Yellow card: Q Cooper, 54. Unused substitutes: L Burgess and KJ Beale.* **TRI-NATIONS DEBUTS:** RG Horne, QS Cooper, RA Simmons, RSL Ma'afu, SM Fainga'a, JA Slipper and BJ McCalman.

SOUTH AFRICA Z Kirchner; GG Aplon, J Fourie, W Olivier (JL de Jongh, 55), BG Habana; M Steyn (AD James, 55), R Pienaar (F Hougaard, 73); PJ Spies (CJ van der Linde, 49-56), R Kankowski (DJ Potgieter, 56), SWP Burger, V Matfield, DJ Rossouw (PR van der Merwe, 68), BJ Botha (CJ van der Linde, 68), JW Smit (C) (MC Ralepelle, 73), GG Steenkamp. *Yellow cards: J Fourie, 03; BJ Botha, 46.* **TRI-NATIONS DEBUTS:** JL de Jongh, F Hougaard, DJ Potgieter and PR van der Merwe.

Brisbane retains hoodoo status

Australia 30 South Africa 13 *(halftime 17-3)*

July 24, Suncorp Stadium, Brisbane (44 284). Referee: G Clancey (Ireland)
AUSTRALIA - TRIES: Mitchell, Genia. CONVERSION: O'Connor. PENALTY GOALS: Giteau (5), O'Connor.
SOUTH AFRICA - TRIES: Fourie, Steenkamp. PENALTY GOAL: Steyn.

FOR the third Test in succession, the Springboks wasted no time in giving the opposition a one-man advantage as centre Jaque Fourie was yellow-carded in the third minute for a tip-tackle.

Although the Wallabies failed to score while Fourie was off the field, it took some excellent scrambling defence to keep them out, and the expenditure of energy took its toll later in the game.

While the Springboks will linger over a turning point in the 35th minute, the Australians deserved their triumph for playing with more accuracy and purpose, and their outstanding defence put the South Africans' feeble first-time tackling to shame.

The Wallabies' match-winner was loose forward David Pocock, who constantly got his hands on their ball at the rucks and was allowed free rein by Irish referee George Clancy.

The first half-hour ebbed and flowed, with the home side having the edge as they got over the advantage line more regularly, Matt Giteau kicking four penalties to Morne Steyn's one.

Trailing 12-3 going into the last five minutes of the first half, the Springboks came face to face with how effective Pocock is in bending the rules. The Zimbabwean-born flanker bent over a ruck five metres from the Australian tryline and killed the ball from an offside position. Clancy only penalised him, the Springboks taking a scrum but then losing possession under the posts as centre Wynand Olivier was isolated and turned over.

The Wallabies then seized possession from a Springbok throw-in just outside their 22, with a juggling Drew Mitchell capitalising on a friendly defence to score and give the home team a 17-3 halftime lead, when it should have been 12-10.

Giteau kicked a fifth penalty soon after the restart to stretch the lead to 20-3, Clancy calling a maul but then penalising flanker Ryan Kankowski, who added a welcome degree of attacking verve, for playing the ball with his hands.

Clancy, a 33-year-old with limited experience in Tests between top-class teams, then raised more eyebrows by yellow-carding prop BJ Botha, who had fallen over a ruck inside the visitors' 22 but did not attempt to play the ball. Wing James O'Connor kicked the penalty and Australia led 23-3.

Wallaby flyhalf Quade Cooper was also yellow-carded, for a 54th-minute tip-tackle, and some marvellous handling by Pierre Spies allowed Fourie to force his way over for the Springboks' first try in Brisbane since 2002.

The South Africans were then trailing 23-8 but refused to lay down and die despite the odds so heavily stacked against them at a venue they have never enjoyed. Victor Matfield soared high to claim possession at a lineout and a secondary rolling maul allowed prop Gurthro Steenkamp to rumble over the line.

But with the Test going into the last five minutes, fullback Zane Kirchner was forced into touch on the corner flag and Australia set up a rolling maul, scrumhalf Will Genia sealing an impressive victory as he sniped over for a try from a subsequent ruck.

"Without a doubt, our defence has been the poorest facet of our game these last three weeks," said Bok captain John Smit.

Min	Action	Score
10	Steyn missed drop goal	-
15	Giteau penalty	3-0
18	Steyn penalty	3-3
20	Giteau penalty	6-3
24	Giteau penalty	9-3
32	Giteau penalty	12-3
40	Mitchell try, Giteau missed conversion	17-3
43	Giteau penalty	20-3
48	O'Connor penalty	23-3
62	Fourie try, Pienaar missed conversion	23-8
68	Giteau missed penalty	23-8
72	Steenkamp try, Pienaar missed conversion	23-13
75	Genia try, O'Connor conversion	30-13

VODACOM TRI-NATIONS

SOUTH AFRICA GG Aplon; JP-R Pietersen, JL de Jongh, J de Villiers, BG Habana; M Steyn, F Hougaard (ER Januarie, 76); PJ Spies, JH Smith (L-FP Louw, 59), SWP Burger, V Matfield, PR van der Merwe (DJ Rossouw, 26-37, 70), JN du Plessis (CJ van der Linde, 62), JW Smit (C), GG Steenkamp. *Unused substitutes: MC Ralepelle, AD James and W Olivier.*

NEW ZEALAND JM Muliaina; CS Jane, CG Smith, MA Nonu, JT Rokocoko (IJA Dagg, 58); DW Carter, QJ Cowan (PAT Weepu, 42); KJ Read, RH McCaw (C), J Kaino (VVJ Vito, 70), TJS Donnelly (SL Whitelock, 50), BC Thorn, BJ Franks (IF Afoa, 63), KF Mealamu, TD Woodcock. *Unused substitutes: CR Flynn and AW Cruden.*

Notes: New Zealand clinched their 10th Tri-Nations title out of 15 tournaments since 1996. Their 23 log-points equalled their own record set in 2006 with still one match to play against Australia in Sydney.

Dagg sours Soweto celebration

South Africa 22 New Zealand 29 *(halftime 16-14)*

August 21, FNB Stadium, Soweto (94 713). Referee: N Owens (Wales)
SOUTH AFRICA - TRY: Burger. CONVERSION: Steyn. PENALTY GOALS: Steyn (5).
NEW ZEALAND - TRIES: Woodcock, McCaw, Dagg. CONVERSION: Carter. PENALTY GOALS: Carter (4).

THE All Blacks snatched victory and the Vodacom Tri-Nations title with two tries in the final two minutes in a compelling first rugby Test to be played in Soweto, watched by a spellbound, record crowd of 94,700.

Coming just a month after the Soccer City stadium hosted the FIFA World Cup final and with John Smit playing his 100th Test, the occasion was highly emotional anyway, with a much-improved Springbok side being denied victory at the death in the cruellest fashion.

Smit was the defender as Ma'a Nonu powered through the midfield after superb counter-rucking by Richie McCaw and Keven Mealamu had turned over possession, the powerful All Black centre then flinging a long pass out to wing Israel Dagg for the match-winning try.

Smit said after the game that he blamed himself for the defeat, South Africa's first against New Zealand in Johannesburg for 13 years.

"At 22-22, the plan was to have a crack with ball in hand and get Morné Steyn into the pocket. But we suffered a turnover and I then missed a tackle and that was game over. I can't physically describe how it feels to lose your 100th game because of your own missed tackle," he said.

The Springbok defence was creaking badly in the last five minutes as the All Blacks, trailing 22-17, threw everything at the home side. McCaw eventually forced his way over in the right corner.

It was little wonder that the Springboks lost some of their edge in the second half as a flurry of New Zealand attacks meant they had to defend furiously, making 134 tackles to the All Blacks' 68, which eventually took its toll.

The All Blacks' dominance was not reflected on the scoreboard, however, partly due to the surprisingly uncertain goalkicking of flyhalf Dan Carter, who missed four of his nine attempts at goal, while Steyn succeeded with all six of his shots.

Francois Hougaard made an assured first Test start at scrumhalf and the returning Juan Smith showed how badly his class had been missed on the away leg, turning in a ferocious defensive display and also carrying the ball strongly.

Smith made his presence felt in the lineout, stealing All Black ball, which led to a ruck penalty, a quick tap and flank Schalk Burger forcing his way over.

Steyn converted to make the score 13-6, but Carter narrowed the gap with a 28th-minute penalty, before a delectable interchange between Hougaard and Smith led to another Steyn penalty.

Crucially, however, the Springbok defence cracked three minutes before halftime as the All Blacks tidied up loose ball in their own half, recycled possession and engineered a large overlap for prop Tony Woodcock to saunter over for the try.

Steyn kicked penalties in the 44th and 63rd minutes to extend the lead to 22-14, before Carter pulled the score back to 22-17 in the 68th, bringing the All Blacks back to within a try.

They were typically ruthless, though, and grabbed two.

"To come from behind at altitude against the world champions, who were right on the button mentally, was pretty significant. We were up against 94,700 people as well as the Springboks and I can't imagine too many of our wins rank up with this one," said All Black coach Graham Henry.

Min	Action	Score
06	Carter penalty	0-3
11	Steyn penalty	3-3
14	Steyn penalty	6-3
17	Carter missed penalty	6-3
21	Carter penalty	6-6
23	Steyn missed drop goal	6-6
25	Burger try, Steyn conversion.	13-6
28	Carter penalty	13-9
32	Steyn penalty	16-9
37	Woodcock try, Carter missed conversion	16-14
44	Steyn penalty	19-14
63	Steyn penalty	22-14
68	Carter penalty	22-17
74	Carter missed penalty	22-17
78	McCaw try, Carter missed conversion	22-22
80	Dagg try, Carter conversion	22-29

VODACOM TRI-NATIONS

SOUTH AFRICA FPL Steyn; J-PR Pietersen, J Fourie, J de Villiers, BG Habana; M Steyn (AD James, 65), F Hougaard; PJ Spies, JH Smith, SWP Burger, V Matfield, PR van der Merwe (DJ Rossouw, 49), JN du Plessis (CJ van der Linde, 54) (JW Smit, 80), JW Smit (C) (MC Ralepelle, 60), GG Steenkamp. *Unused substitutes: R Kankowski, ER Januarie and JL de Jongh.*

AUSTRALIA KJ Beale; JD O'Connor, AP Ashley-Cooper, MJ Giteau, DA Mitchell; QS Cooper, SW Genia; RN Brown (BJ McCalman, 58), DW Pocock, RD Elsom (C), NC Sharpe (RA Simmons, 65), DW Mumm, RSL Ma'afu (JA Slipper, 55), SM Fainga'a (ST Moore, 27-39), BA Robinson. *Unused substitutes: L Burgess, BS Barnes and AS Fainga'a.*

Matfield celebrates ton in style

South Africa 44 Australia 31 *(halftime 24-28)*

August 28, Loftus Versfeld, Pretoria (43 152). Referee: AC Rolland (Ireland)
SOUTH AFRICA - TRIES: Smith, Steenkamp, Spies, FPL Steyn, Pietersen. CONVERSIONS: M Steyn (4), James. PENALTY GOALS: M Steyn (2), FPL Steyn. **AUSTRALIA**: TRIES: Genia, O'Connor (2), Mumm. CONVERSIONS: Giteau (4). PENALTY GOAL: Giteau.

V ICTOR Matfield celebrated his 100th Test at his home ground and made a telling contribution to a thrilling Springbok victory, as his lineout steal inside his own 22 in the 69th minute repelled a period of fierce Australian pressure.

The quality of rugby might not have been of the highest class, but for sheer entertainment value, the match was spectacular, with five tries coming in the first 15 minutes.

The Springboks, who had not lost at altitude to the Wallabies in 11 Tests dating back to 1963, looked set to eat a helping of humble pie as the visitors raced into a 14-0 lead after six minutes.

Scrumhalf Will Genia began the try-spree when he slipped through Matfield's tackle to score in the second minute, and fullback Kurtley Beale set up wing James O' Connor's try four minutes later when he broke from his own 22 and found fine support from skipper Rocky Elsom, who was stopped just short of the line.

The Springboks were on the board in the ninth minute, with flanker Juan Smith scoring after he ran strongly onto scrumhalf Francois Hougaard's inside pass.

But Bryan Habana then dropped the kick-off, O'Connor pounced and went over from seven metres out.

The Springbok wing's confidence was clearly on the wane and he was also caught in possession under his own posts, leading to lock Dean Mumm's 26th-minute try that gave Australia a bonus point.

But the Wallabies also had telling fragilities in defence and prop Gurthro Steenkamp charged over after a lineout, before Hougaard sniped through a gap after concerted Springbok pressure to put eighthman Pierre Spies over for a try in the 32nd minute.

The Springbok comeback was greatly helped by the unerring kicking of flyhalf Morné Steyn, who kicked six out of six, including a 58-metre penalty in the 20th minute.

The home side trailed 28-24 at halftime, but a second Steyn penalty ate into the lead even further, after Wallaby hooker Saia Faingaa had crunched Hougaard with a high tackle.

Steyn did the same just two minutes later as he allowed flyhalf Matt Giteau to kick his only penalty, but the Bulls star made up for it when he produced an outrageous backflip pass in the tackle to allow fullback Francois Steyn to score in the corner, after a powerful run by centre Jaque Fourie had put the Springboks on attack.

Morné Steyn's touchline conversion gave the home team a 34-31 lead and they then withstood a long period of Wallaby pressure. The steely defence caused Beale to fall foul of referee Alain Rolland as he tried to run a kick back but was caught by the outstanding midfield duo of Jean de Villiers and Fourie, allowing Francois Steyn to kick a penalty from just inside his own half.

The Wallabies returned to the Springbok 22, however, and, in a thrilling conclusion, were stymied by Matfield and a great cover tackle by Hougaard on centre Adam Ashley-Cooper.

It gave the South Africans a turnover, Hougaard then sparked the counter-attack, Spies taking the ball up strongly and Matfield and De Villiers both handling, before wing JP Pietersen stepped inside the remaining defenders to score and seal the 2009 champions' first win of the tournament, allowing their veteran lock a happy ending.

Min	Action	Score
03	Genia try, Giteau conversion	**0-7**
05	O'Connor try, Giteau conversion	**0-14**
09	Smith try, M Steyn conversion	**7-14**
10	O'Connor try, Giteau conversion	**7-21**
14	Steenkamp try, M Steyn conversion	**14-21**
20	M Steyn penalty	**17-21**
22	Beale missed penalty	**17-21**
26	Mumm try, Giteau conversion	**17-28**
32	Spies try, M Steyn conversion	**24-28**
47	Steyn penalty	**27-28**
49	Giteau penalty	**27-31**
50	FPL Steyn try, M Steyn conversion	**34-31**
63	FPL Steyn missed drop goal	**34-31**
68	FPL Steyn penalty goal	**37-31**
79	Pietersen try, James conversion	**44-31**

VODACOM TRI-NATIONS

SOUTH AFRICA FPL Steyn; J-PR Pietersen, J Fourie, J de Villiers, BG Habana (GG Aplon, 51); M Steyn, F Hougaard; PJ Spies (R Kankowski, 65), JH Smith, SWP Burger, V Matfield, DJ Rossouw (PR van der Merwe, 61), JN du Plessis (CJ van der Linde, 55), JW Smit (C) (MC Ralepelle, 65), GG Steenkamp. *Unused substitutes: ER Januarie and JL de Jongh.*

AUSTRALIA KJ Beale; JD O'Connor, AP Ashley-Cooper, MJ Giteau (BS Barnes, 70), DA Mitchell (AS Fainga'a, 74)*; QS Cooper, SW Genia (L Burgess, 55); BJ McCalman (RN Brown, 71, ST Moore, 79-80), DW Pocock, RD Elsom (C), NC Sharpe, MD Chisholm (DW Mumm, 54), RSL Ma'afu (JA Slipper, 28), ST Moore (SM Fainga'a, 65, ST Moore, 80), BA Robinson. **Anthony Fainga'a to inside centre, Barnes to outside centre, Ashley-Cooper to fullback and Beale to left-wing. Yellow card: SM Fainga'a, 69.*

Notes: *John Smit ended the Tri-Nations season as most capped captain in the tournament's history with 28 caps as captain. Morné Steyn kicked 29 consecutive successful place-kicks in this season's tournament. It brought his record of total consecutive successful place kicks in the Tri-Nations to 37. In Test Rugby he has now kicked 38 consecutive successful place kicks which is a World Record. Jaque Fourie became the top try scorer for the Springboks in the Tri-Nations tournament with his ninth career try. Australia regained the Mandela Plate which they last won in 2008.*

Wallabies make highveld history

South Africa 39 Australia 41 *(halftime 13-31)*

September 4, Vodacom Park, Bloemfontein (38 523). Referee: W Barnes (England)

SOUTH AFRICA - TRIES: Fourie, Steenkamp, De Villiers. CONVERSIONS: M Steyn (3). PENALTY GOALS: M Steyn (6).

AUSTRALIA - TRIES: Beale, O'Connor, Moore, Elsom, Mitchell. CONVERSIONS: Giteau (4), O'Connor. PENALTY GOALS: Giteau, Beale.

THE Wallabies cut through the Springboks' defences with astonishing ease in the first half-hour of a historic Test, roaring into a 31-6 lead, but they had to rely on an heroic last-minute kick by 21-year-old fullback Kurtley Beale to register their first win on the highveld in 47 years.

Beale succeeded with the long-range penalty, his only kick of the game, seven metres in from touch and four metres from the halfway line, to deny a stirring comeback from the Springboks, who made up a deficit of 25 points to lead 36-31 with 11 minutes remaining.

Beale atoned for his previous mistakes, having earlier thrown a wild pass that went out touch-in-goal to give South Africa a five-metre scrum, from which centre Jean de Villiers scored. He then suffered the ignominy of slipping while he tried to field a kick, the ball rebounding off his head to Springbok centre Jaque Fourie, who sparked an attack that led to flyhalf Morné Steyn's 77th-minute penalty that gave the home team a 39-38 lead.

Matt Giteau and Steyn had traded penalties before Australia scored their first try in the eighth minute, Beale going over after centre Adam Ashley-Cooper had singed down the right touchline.

The Wallabies were able to get across the advantage line regularly and, with flyhalf Quade Cooper having the knack of finding the right men to pass to, wing James O'Connor stepped inside two defenders six minutes later to score the second try.

Hooker John Smit held on to possession well to earn the Springboks their second Steyn penalty in the 18th minute (6-17), but the defence continued to be poor, which one can ill-afford against such a slick attacking side as the Wallabies. Wing Drew Mitchell broke through in the 21st minute, before the forwards took over, driving the ball up for hooker Stephen Moore to score.

Giteau, who succeeded with all five of his kicks at goal, converted and the visitors seemed to have sealed victory when they scored their fourth try four minutes later (6-31).

With half-time beckoning, the Wallabies were once again teasing the Springbok line, earning a five-metre scrum as well as a shot at goal, which they turned down, but the home side earned a penalty to relieve the pressure and a marvellous piece of skill by lock Victor Matfield led to a try that lifted their spirits before the break.

Matfield galloped clear from a ruck and, without breaking stride, chipped over the advancing defence, regathered and quickly passed to Fourie for a superb try.

Steyn's conversion meant the Springboks were trailing 13-31 at the break and they raised the hopes of an angry crowd with a spectacular second-half comeback.

The Wallabies conceded 30 unanswered points because they continuously turned over possession via silly errors, but once they kept ball in hand for significant periods, they were able to snuff out the Springboks' hopes at the death.

The Bloemfontein crowd of over 38,000 jeered with one voice when Beale headed the ball into Fourie's hands to spark a Springbok attack that earned Steyn his ninth successful kick at goal, but it was the talented young fullback from New South Wales who was laughing loudest in the end.

Min	Action	Score
02	Giteau penalty	0-3
06	M Steyn penalty	3-3
08	Beale try, Giteau conversion	3-10
14	O'Connor try, Giteau conversion	3-17
18	M Steyn penalty	6-17
21	Moore try, Giteau conversion	6-24
25	Elsom try, Giteau conversion	6-31
41	Fourie try, M Steyn conversion.	13-31
46	Steenkamp try, M Steyn conversion	20-31
50	M Steyn penalty	23-31
54	De Villiers try, M Steyn conversion	30-31
61	M Steyn penalty	33-31
70	M Steyn penalty	36-31
72	Mitchell try, O'Connor conversion	36-38
77	M Steyn penalty	39-38
81	Beale penalty	39-41

END-OF-YEAR TOUR

Boks left to ponder what might've been

OH what might have been had it not been for one miserable week in Edinburgh!

It is indeed a pity that we have to reflect on the one major negative of the tour from the outset, but South Africa blew a golden opportunity for their first Grand Slam since 1960/61 by going down 21-17 to Scotland at a rain-soaked Murrayfield.

However, there were generally more positives than negatives to take from the end-of-season sojourn to the United Kingdom and Ireland, with three wins from four Tests going a long way towards restoring some confidence in Springbok rugby after a deeply disappointing Vodacom Tri-Nations campaign.

The highlight was undoubtedly the emphatic 21-11 win over England, with the success of the tour having hung in the balance after what had happened at Murrayfield. However, the Boks went purposefully about their business at Twickenham and demolished Martin Johnson's England side with a combination of brute force and superior tactical acumen.

It was by no means a flawless performance as the Boks were more than a little wasteful with all the try-scoring opportunities that came their way, but only winning will breed the confidence that will pave the way for more enterprise.

Consider also that South Africa were without a host of injured players. The injury list prior to the tour was 13 and Bryan Habana also broke his hand during the Tuesday training session in Edinburgh.

Earlier on tour, South Africa had already confounded their critics by edging Ireland 23-21. In truth, the winning margin did not do justice to the Boks' dominance.

While their performance against Wales was disappointing, they still managed to rally from 9-20 down to win 29-25, drawing on their world champion spirit to win a game that could easily have gone the other way.

It was Willem Alberts' try that kicked off a remarkable fightback at the Millennium Stadium and inspirational skipper Victor Matfield fittingly scored the decisive five-pointer, though the Boks had to defend their line desperately at the end to secure the win.

Prior to the tour the perception might well have been that the week in Edinburgh would be the easiest one, but it started with the bad news that Bjorn Basson and Chiliboy Ralepelle had returned positive tests for the use of the banned stimulant methylhexaneamine.

The shock news prompted the team to suspend the use of dietary supplements and send away a range of products for testing to ascertain the cause of the positive tests. Perhaps this traumatic episode proved a little unsettling.

But if there was big disappointment after the loss to Scotland, the joy of beating England certainly balanced the books. Once again the Springboks had been written off, but there was simply too much on the line for them to fail.

As far as the newcomers are concerned, Alberts was the biggest hit, scoring tries in all three his substitute appearances. Patrick Lambie was also eased into Test rugby and Lwazi Mvovo scored a terrific try at Twickenham.

Yet it was the established stars that played the biggest part. Matfield's captaincy was inspired, Bakkies Botha showed that he remains a potent force within the laws, Juan Smith was at his inspired best, Jannie du Plessis anchored the scrum brilliantly, and Bismarck du Plessis made a strong claim for the title of finest hooker in world rugby.

Jean de Villiers' love for the green and gold also came through in the manner he soldiered on with a groin injury. That about summed up the Springboks on this tour – wounded, but with plenty of courage under fire.

SPRINGBOK SQUAD APPEARANCES AND POINTS ON TOUR

	Date of birth	Height	Weight	Province	Ireland	Wales	Scotland	England	Barbarians	Matches	Tries	Conversions	Penalties	Drop Goals	Points
GG Aplon	06/10/82	1.75	70	Western Province	15	15	14	14	R	5	1	0	0	0	5
BA Basson	11/02/87	1.87	82	Griqualand West	14	14	–	–	–	2	0	0	0	0	0
Z Kirchner	16/06/84	1.84	92	Blue Bulls	13	R	15	15	–	4	0	0	0	0	0
J de Villiers	24/02/81	1.90	100	Western Province	12	12	13	12	–	4	0	0	0	0	0
BG Habana	12/06/83	1.79	92	Western Province	11	11	–	–	–	2	0	0	0	0	0
M Steyn	11/07/84	1.86	82	Blue Bulls	10	10	10	10	–	4	0	4	15	0	53
R Pienaar	10/03/84	1.86	84	Ulster, Ireland	9	9	R	9	–	4	0	0	0	0	0
PJ Spies	08/06/85	1.95	106	Blue Bulls	8	8	–	8	–	3	0	0	0	0	0
JH Smith	30/07/81	1.94	106	Free State	7	7	7	7	7*	5	1	0	0	0	5
GJ Stegmann	22/03/86	1.81	99	Blue Bulls	6	6	6	6	–	4	0	0	0	0	0
V Matfield	11/05/77	2.01	110	Blue Bulls	5*	5*	5*	5*	–	4	1	0	0	0	5
JP Botha	22/09/79	2.02	118	Blue Bulls	4	4	4	4	4	5	1	0	0	0	5
JN du Plessis	16/11/82	1.87	113	Kwazulu Natal	3	3	3	3	–	4	0	0	0	0	0
BW du Plessis	22/05/84	1.89	105	Kwazulu Natal	2	2	2	2	–	4	0	0	0	0	0
T Mtawarira	01/08/85	1.88	112	Kwazulu Natal	1	1	1	1	R	5	0	0	0	0	0
CJ van der Linde	27/08/80	1.90	122	Leinster, Ireland	R	R	R	R	3	5	0	0	0	0	0
PR van der Merwe	03/06/85	1.99	117	Blue Bulls	R	R	R	R	t+R	5	0	0	0	0	0
KR Daniel	05/03/85	1.85	89	Kwazulu Natal	R	–	–	–	R	2	0	0	0	0	0
P Lambie	17/10/90	1.77	86	Kwazulu Natal	R	R	R	R	15	5	0	1	0	0	2
AA Jacobs	14/08/80	1.70	87	Kwazulu Natal	R	–	x	R	13	3	0	0	0	0	0
MC Ralepelle	11/09/86	1.78	95	Blue Bulls	x	R	–	–	–	1	0	0	0	0	0
F Hougaard	06/04/88	1.79	86	Blue Bulls	x	R	9	t+R	9	4	0	0	0	0	0
FPL Steyn	14/05/87	1.91	100	Racing Metro, France	–	13	12	13	–	3	0	0	0	0	0
WS Alberts	05/11/84	1.91	115	Kwazulu Natal	–	R	t+R	R	6	4	3	0	0	0	15
LN Mvovo	03/06/86	1.81	84	Kwazulu Natal	–	–	11	11	11	3	1	0	0	0	5
R Kankowski	14/10/85	1.93	103	Kwazulu Natal	–	–	8	–	8	2	0	0	0	0	0
JA Strauss	18/11/85	1.84	102	Free State	–	–	R	R	2	3	0	0	0	0	0
AJ Hargreaves	29/04/86	2.00	102	Kwazulu Natal	–	–	–	–	5	1	0	0	0	0	0
CV Oosthuizen	22/03/89	1.83	125	Free State	–	–	–	–	1	1	0	0	0	0	0
ET Jantjies	01/08/90	1.76	84	Golden Lions	–	–	–	–	10	1	0	1	1	0	5
C McLeod	05/08/83	1.79	82	Kwazulu Natal	–	–	–	–	R	1	0	0	0	0	0
OM Ndungane	20/02/81	1.83	85	Kwazulu Natal	–	–	–	–	14	1	1	0	0	0	5
BG Maku	24/06/86	1.87	111	Blue Bulls	–	–	–	–	R	1	1	0	0	0	5
AJ Strauss	05/03/84	1.86	94	Free State	–	–	–	–	12	1	0	0	0	0	0
W Kruger	23/01/85	1.90	120	Blue Bulls	–	–	–	–	R	1	0	0	0	0	0
35 Players											**10**	**6**	**16**	**0**	**110**

*Captain

END-OF-YEAR TOUR

IRELAND: RDJ Kearney (KG Earls, 75); TJ Bowe, BG O'Driscoll (C), GM D'Arcy, L Fitzgerald; J Sexton (RJR O'Gara, 65), EG Reddan (PA Stringer, 65); JPR Heaslip, DP Wallace, SPH Ferris, MR O'Driscoll (D Ryan, 63), DP O'Callaghan, TD Buckley (TG Court, 51), R Best, CE Healy. *Unused substitutes: S Cronin and DP Leamy.*

SOUTH AFRICA: GG Aplon; BA Basson, Z Kirchner, J de Villiers (AA Jacobs, 67); BG Habana, M Steyn (P Lambie, 59), R Pienaar; PJ Spies, JH Smith, GJ Stegmann (KR Daniel, 65), V Matfield (C), JP Botha (PR van der Merwe, 70), JN du Plessis (CJ van der Linde, 70), BW du Plessis, T Mtawarira. *Unused substitutes: MC Ralepelle and F Hougaard.* YELLOW CARD: BG Habana, 75.

Notes: *Morné Steyn's magnificent run of consecutive successful place kicks ended early in the second half when he missed a penalty goal after kicking 41 consecutive place kicks. Victor Matfield and Bakkies Botha extended their record of most tests as a lock pairing in the starting line-up to 57. Victor Matfield joined Percy Montgomery and John Smit as the most capped Springboks of all time with 102 test caps.*

Makeshift Boks break Dublin hoodoo

Ireland 21 South Africa 23 *(halftime 6-13)*

November 6, AVIVA Stadium, Dublin (35 517). Referee: N Owens (Wales)
IRELAND - TRIES: Bowe, Kearney. CONVERSION: O'Gara. PENALTY GOALS: Sexton (3).
SOUTH AFRICA - TRIES: Smith, Aplon. CONVERSIONS: Steyn, Lambie. PENALTY GOALS: Steyn (3).

A conversion attempt from replacement Ireland flyhalf Ronan O'Gara five minutes from time hit the upright to give the Springboks their first victory in Dublin in a decade and help break a three-match losing streak against Brian O'Driscoll's men.

It was also South Africa's first win against Ireland since the second Test at Newlands in 2004, during coach Jake White's first series in charge.

Victor Matfield's makeshift side were given little chance of arresting a recent poor run of form against the Irish on the occasion of the grand reopening of the rebuilt Lansdowne Road. The Boks had arrived in the Emerald Isle just two days before the match and had to contend with a long injury list that necessitated some creative thinking among the selectors.

Bulls fullback Zane Kirchner, who was not even part of the 30-man squad picked a week before the tour, found himself starting at outside centre after earlier injuries to regulars Wynand Olivier, Jaque Fourie and Juan de Jongh.

It was the same story at openside flank, where uncapped Bulls backrower Deon Stegmann parachuted into the starting lineup from nowhere after incumbent Schalk Burger broke a rib playing for Western Province in the Absa Currie Cup final seven days earlier.

The scoreline in the end might have been a bit closer than coach Peter de Villiers would have wanted, but the coach was nevertheless able to reflect on a winning start to the four-Test tour and had the satisfaction of blooding rookies such as Stegmann, Pat Lambie and Keegan Daniel in the process.

Unfortunately for the latter trio, their first steps in Test rugby took place against the backdrop of swathes of empty seats as recession-hit Irish fans, who had regularly filled the 80,000-seater Croke Park in recent years while Lansdowne was being rebuilt, voted with their feet in protest at what they considered exorbitant ticket prices.

Those who did stay away – and it must be said that an evening kickoff in freezing weather didn't help matters – missed a match that was dominated by the visitors for an hour before the home side stormed back to almost snatch victory.

Flyhalf Morné Steyn opened the scoring in the sixth minute with a penalty before flanker Juan Smith intercepted from a wayward pass at a lineout to gallop 60 metres for his 11th try in Test rugby. Steyn added the extra points before he and opposite number Jonny Sexton traded penalties to give the Boks a 16-9 lead with 20 minutes remaining.

At this point, De Villiers introduced Lambie to Test rugby, with Steyn leaving the field. Four minutes later, the debutante's nerves showed as he hurried a straightforward penalty attempt from bang in front and 30 metres out. But the Sharks sensation shrugged off the early jitters to put his backline away in the 65th minute, which resulted in fullback Gio Aplon cutting in for a well-worked try that Lambie converted to make it 23-9.

At this point, Ireland looked dead and buried, but the introduction of veteran halfback pair Ronan O'Gara (in his 100th Test) and Peter Stringer turned the game on its head. O'Gara chipped ahead in the 69th minute for winger Tommy Bowe to run onto for a score that closed the gap to seven, before the flyhalf looped a long scoring pass to fullback Rob Kearney five minutes later to make it 23-21.

But the Munster general couldn't pot the touchline conversion that would in all likelihood have given his team a share of the spoils.

Min	Action	Score
03	Steyn missed drop goal	
06	Steyn penalty	0-3
17	Smith try, Steyn conversion	0-10
24	Sexton missed penalty	0-10
27	Sexton penalty	3-10
38	Steyn penalty	3-13
41	Sexton penalty	6-13
42	Steyn missed penalty	6-13
53	Steyn penalty	6-16
56	Sexton penalty	9-16
63	Lambie missed penalty	9-16
65	Aplon try, Lambie conversion	9-23
69	Bowe try, O'Gara conversion	16-23
74	Kearney try, O'Gara missed conversion	21-23

WALES: LM Byrne; G North, TGL Shanklin (AM Bishop, 39-46), JW Hook, SM Williams (CD Czekaj, H/T); SM Jones, WM Phillips (RS Rees, 70); J Thomas, ME Williams, A Powell (RP Jones, 60)*, A-W Jones (DL Jones, 74), BS Davies, AR Jones, M Rees (C) (H Bennett, 71), P James (J Yapp, 71). *Ryan Jones to #8; Jonathan Thomas to flank.

SOUTH AFRICA: GG Aplon; BA Basson, FPL Steyn, J de Villiers, BG Habana (Z Kirchner, 74)*; M Steyn (P Lambie, 65), R Pienaar (F Hougaard, 60); PJ Spies, JH Smith, GJ Stegmann (WS Alberts, 47), V Matfield (C), JP Botha (PR van der Merwe, 60), JN du Plessis (CJ van der Linde, 76), BW du Plessis (MC Ralepelle, 74), T Mtawarira. *Zane Kirchner to fullback; Gio Aplon to left wing.

Notes: *South Africa scored a record 12th consecutive win against Wales. Victor Matfield became the most capped Springbok in his 103rd test match and also equalled the records of Percy Montgomery and John Smit of most capped Springbok against Wales with 9 caps. Willem Alberts became the 80th Springbok to score a try on test debut. Jean de Villiers played in his 51st test as a centre, thereby equaling Jaque Fourie's record of most tests as a centre for South Africa. George North scored his first try after only 5 minutes of International rugby.*

Boks hang on to keep slam dream alive

Wales 25 South Africa 29 *(halftime 17-9)*

November 13, Millennium Stadium, Cardiff (73 143). Referee: SR Walsh (Australia)
WALES - TRIES: North (2), Hook. CONVERSIONS: SM Jones (2). PENALTY GOALS: SM Jones (2).
SOUTH AFRICA - TRIES: Alberts, Matfield. CONVERSIONS: M Steyn (2). PENALTY GOALS: M Steyn (5).

FOR the second week in a row, the Springboks hung on grimly against determined northern-hemisphere opponents to keep their grand slam tour alive.

But for long stretches of this match, however, it was Wales who had a firm grip on proceedings – so much so that most observers would have given South Africa no way back after they trailed 17-6 with less than half an hour played.

Very rarely can it be said that a Springbok side is all but dead and buried only 29 minutes into a Test match but such was the home team's dominance in the first half that the statement certainly seemed not all that far-fetched.

South Africa under Victor Matfield are however nothing if not resilient, and this they proved for the second week running as the team rallied to pull off an improbable victory.

A few well-timed second-half substitutions by coach Peter de Villiers was just what the doctor ordered after a first half in which Wales scored two tries to race into an 11-point lead – only for flyhalf Morné Steyn to kick his third penalty of the half in the 44th minute of actual playing time to keep the Boks in with a shout in a one-sided match.

Steyn opened the scoring in the second minute with his first penalty but Wales responded four minutes later when the 1.91m, 18-year-old debutant wing George North, who had been written up in the build-up as the "Welsh Jonah Lomu", lived up to the hype by going over near the posts.

Veteran flyhalf Stephen Jones kicked the extra points before centre and fellow Lion James Hook rounded off a superb counter-attack sparked by fullback Lee Byrne and winger Shane Williams to make it 14-3.

Steyn and Jones then traded penalties to give the home side a 20-12 lead after 50 minutes before two tries from the Boks turned the match on its head.

There are certain players who battle to take the step up to Test rugby while others take to it like a fish to water, and replacement flanker Willem Alberts undoubtedly showed that he belongs in the latter category.

No sooner had the strapping Sharks backrower galloped onto the field than he found himself diving over the line for a try that pulled the Boks back to within a point of the Welsh score.

Two minutes later, skipper Matfield, sensing the turning tide, sold a neat dummy to dive over near the posts for Steyn to convert. From nothing, the visitors were suddenly 26-20 ahead – although North's second try in the 57th minute suggested that Wales weren't about to go quietly into the Cardiff night.

South Africa held on to their one-point lead, which they extended to four thanks to Steyn's 65th-minute penalty, to force a tense final 10 minutes which saw Wales camped on the South African line.

But try as they might, Wales could find no way through a Springbok defence that underwent a dramatic second-half rejuvenation, leaving coach Warren Gatland to rue yet another missed opportunity against a southern-hemisphere team.

Min	Action	Score
02	M Steyn penalty	0-3
06	North try, SM Jones conversion	7-3
12	M Steyn missed penalty	7-3
17	Hook try, SM Jones conversion	14-3
20	M Steyn penalty	14-6
25	Hook missed penalty	14-6
29	SM Jones penalty	17-6
44	M Steyn penalty	17-9
43	SM Jones penalty	20-9
47	M Steyn penalty	20-12
51	Alberts try, M Steyn conversion	20-19
54	Matfield try, M Steyn conversion	20-26
57	North try, SM Jones missed conversion	25-26
65	M Steyn penalty	25-29

END-OF-YEAR TOUR

SCOTLAND: HFG Southwell; N Walker (CD Paterson, 74), J Ansbro, GA Morrison, SF Lamont; DA Parks, RGM Lawson (C); KDR Brown (RM Rennie, 79), JA Barclay, NJ Hines, SJ MacLeod (RJ Vernon, 35)*, RJ Gray, EA Murray (MJ Low, 69), RW Ford (DWH Hall, 69), AF Jacobsen. *Richie Vernon to flank; Nathan Hines to lock. Unused substitutes: GD Laidlaw and RJH Jackson.

SOUTH AFRICA: Z Kirchner; GG Aplon, J de Villiers, FPL Steyn, LN Mvovo; M Steyn (P Lambie, 64), F Hougaard (R Pienaar, 47); R Kankowski, JH Smith (WS Alberts, 20-27), GJ Stegmann (WS Alberts, 47), V Matfield (C), JP Botha (PR van der Merwe, 65), JN du Plessis, BW du Plessis (JA Strauss, 74), T Mtawarira (CJ van der Linde, 72). Unused substitute: AA Jacobs.

Notes: *Jean de Villiers became South Africa's most capped centre - 52 caps. Morné Steyn scored his 300th point in tests with the first penalty of the match. The fastest 300 points in Springbok test rugby - 24 Tests. He is also the new record holder for most penalties by a Springbok in a test season (37). Victor Matfield is now the most capped Springbok against Scotland - 8. The six penalties by Scotland is a new record in tests against South Africa, surpassing the 4 penalties in 1999 (Edinburgh) and 2003 (Johannesburg). Dan Parks' 21 points is a new record against South Africa, surpassing the previous 16 points by Kenny Logan scored in 1999 (Edinburgh) and his 6 penalties also surpassed the record held jointly by Kenny Logan and Chris Paterson.*

Scotland dash Slam dream

Scotland 21 South Africa 17 *(halftime 12-9)*
November 20, Murrayfield, Edinburgh (35 555). Referee: SJ Dickinson (Australia)
SCOTLAND - PENALTY GOALS: Parks (6). DROP GOAL: Parks.
SOUTH AFRICA - TRY: Alberts. PENALTY GOALS: M Steyn (4).

THIS wasn't a result that South African supporters would want to dwell on for any length of time but even the darkest days in the Springbok story must be recorded for posterity.

Who knows? Perhaps future generations will stumble upon these words and be forewarned as to the folly of underestimating the opposition – one of rugby's most easily-committed sins. But whether or not Victor Matfield's side did indeed take too lightly a Scotland team that had, just seven days earlier, been humiliated 49-3 by the All Blacks, is one for the speculators to argue about.

For what is certain is that a tumultuous week off the pitch played a not insignificant part in the Springboks' disjointed preparations for the third leg of their attempt at the Grand Slam – with the net result being that they played their poorest rugby of a season in which, it must be said, they rarely scaled the great heights of 2009.

The sending home of wing Bjorn Basson and reserve hooker Chiliboy Ralepelle on the Monday before the Test set the tone. The pair tested positive for the banned stimulant methylhexaneamine following the tour-opener against Ireland and were subsequently banned from all rugby until the results of their B samples could be determined.

To make matters worse, a team missing a number of

frontline stars suffered another blow when wing Bryan Habana broke a bone in his hand during training – although Habana's misfortune allowed uncapped Sharks winger Lwazi Mvovo, originally named as a substitute, to make a deserved Test debut at Murrayfield.

Habana might have been on the brink of claiming the Springbok try-scoring record but the 2007 world player of the year's form in 2010 was patchy, and compared to everything else going on around the Bok camp in the build-up, Habana's withdrawal did not attract nearly as many headlines as it might have done.

Coach Peter de Villiers largely stuck with the team that beat Wales, with scrumhalf Francois Hougaard replacing Ruan Pienaar and eighthman Ryan Kankowski getting a start ahead of Pierre Spies.

But the former selection, in particular, would prove to be debatable as the Springboks ran out in exactly the kind of cold and rainy conditions that would have suited Pienaar, who plays his club rugby for Ulster, perfectly.

In the end, the Boks scored the only try of the match, to in-form replacement flanker Willem Alberts in the 71st minute, but Scotland flyhalf Dan Parks produced an excellent kicking display to score all his team's points.

Morné Steyn gave the Boks a 6-0 lead inside 13 minutes but Parks responded with three penalties and a drop goal to make it 12-6 after half an hour. Steyn drew the Boks level in the 47th minute but Parks slotted another three penalties to give the hosts a 21-12 lead with 12 minutes remaining.

Alberts's try gave the visitors hope but given Matfield's ongoing frustration at the refereeing of Australian Stuart Dickinson one felt that this was a match in which the Boks would struggle to find their get-out-of-jail-free card – and so it proved.

Min	Action	Score
03	M Steyn penalty	0-3
07	M Steyn missed penalty	0-3
09	FPL Steyn missed penalty	0-3
13	M Steyn penalty	0-6
17	Parks penalty	3-6
20	Parks drop goal	6-6
25	Parks penalty	9-6
31	Parks penalty	12-6
37	M Steyn penalty	12-9
47	M Steyn penalty	12-12
54	Parks penalty	15-12
64	Parks penalty	18-12
68	Parks penalty	21-12
71	Alberts try, Lambie missed conversion	21-17

END-OF-YEAR TOUR

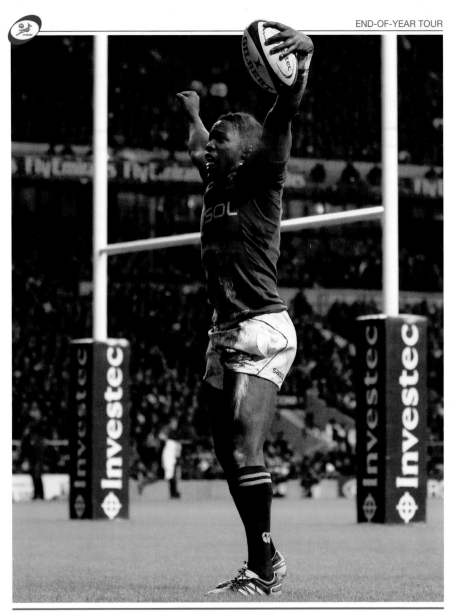

ENGLAND: BJ Foden; CJ Ashton (MA Banahan, 73), MJ Tindall, SE Hape, MJ Cueto; TGAL Flood (CC Hodgson, 34), BR Youngs (DS Care, 62); NJ Easter, LW Moody (C), TR Croft (CH Fourie, 22), TP Palmer, CL Lawes (SD Shaw, 68), DR Cole (DG Wilson, 68), DM Hartley (SG Thompson, 73), AJ Sheridan.

SOUTH AFRICA: Z Kirchner (AA Jacobs, 48)*; GG Aplon (F Hougaard, 60-68)** (P Lambie, 79)***, FPL Steyn, J de Villiers (F Hougaard, 68), LN Mvovo; M Steyn, R Pienaar; PJ Spies, JH Smith, GJ Stegmann (WS Alberts, 48), V Matfield (C), JP Botha (PR van der Merwe, 67), JN du Plessis (CJ van der Linde, 53), BW du Plessis (JA Strauss, 79), T Mtawarira. *Jacobs to outside centre, Frans Steyn to fullback. **Aplon to fullback on return, Frans Steyn back to centre. ***Lambie replaced Aplon at fullback.

Notes: This was the seventh consecutive win by the Springboks against England since November, 2006. Morné Steyn became the second highest point scorer in tests for the Springboks. He surpassed Naas Botha's career total of 312 with his first penalty goal. Victor Matfield and Bakkies Botha played in their World Record 60th test as a lock combination in the starting line-up. Bismarck and Jannie du Plessis have now played together in 14 tests. The most by any brother combination in Springbok Rugby.

Boks end low year on high

England 11 South Africa 21 *(halftime 6-6)*

November 27, Twickenham, London (80 793). Referee: G Clancy (Ireland)
ENGLAND - TRY: Foden. **PENALTY GOALS**: Flood (2).
SOUTH AFRICA - TRIES: Alberts, Mvovo. **CONVERSION**: M Steyn. **PENALTY GOALS**: M Steyn (3).

PETER de Villiers was forced to add 22 extra names to his Christmas card list after the under-fire Springboks bludgeoned England at Twickenham to finish a disappointing Test season on a high note.

The Boks might have kissed the grand slam goodbye when they lost to Scotland the week before, but their convincing 21-11 victory went a long way towards righting a listing Springbok ship just 10 months out from the defence of their Rugby World Cup title.

This was by no means a faultless performance but De Villiers and captain Victor Matfield were able to adopt a glass-half-full attitude going into the final week of the tour, which finished with a match against the Barbarians, also at Twickenham.

Going into the match, De Villiers and his selectors had been criticised for not giving exciting youngsters like Patrick Lambie the opportunity to show their worth at international level. But be that as it may, a number of players still managed to force their way into contention through sheer weight of performances.

There was no bigger winner than the strapping Sharks flanker Willem Alberts, who capped off a memorable first fortnight of Test rugby by scoring the first of two Springbok tries as the highly physical visitors, held to a 6-6 halftime

scoreline, pulled away in the second half after their forwards administered enough doses of slow poison to stop a herd of elephants.

For Alberts, Test rugby must seem like a walk in the park: it was the third week in a row that he came on as a second-half replacement to score a try and his 'super sub' impact has almost certainly pushed him near the front of the queue for one of the priceless 30 World Cup squad spots on offer.

Alberts' Sharks teammate Lwazi Mvovo, who made his Test debut against Scotland, was another who returned home with reputation enhanced. He scored South Africa's other try while flyhalf Morné Steyn passed the great Naas Botha's point-scoring mark with 11 points to seal an emphatic victory.

The Springboks' lack of incisiveness and creativity in their back play remains a concern, but against England it was about victory at all costs and the pack had no qualms taking the less scenic route to the finish line.

England flyhalf Toby Flood and Steyn traded early penalties before Alberts galloped over in the right-hand corner on the hour to open up a 14-6 lead. Mvovo's solo effort from 25 metres with 10 minutes remaining put the matter beyond doubt, with England fullback Ben Foden's last-minute try succeeding only to gloss over what had been a thoroughly comprehensive and one-sided contest.

Min	Action	Score
06	Flood penalty	3-0
11	M Steyn penalty	3-3
19	Flood penalty	6-3
24	M Steyn missed penalty	6-3
31	FPL Steyn missed penalty	6-3
36	M Steyn penalty	6-6
40	M Steyn missed drop goal	6-6
43	M Steyn penalty	6-9
54	FPL Steyn missed drop goal	6-9
59	Alberts try,	
	M Steyn missed conversion	6-14
70	Mvovo try, M Steyn conversion	6-21
75	FPL Steyn missed drop goal	6-21
79	Foden try, Tindall missed conversion	11-21

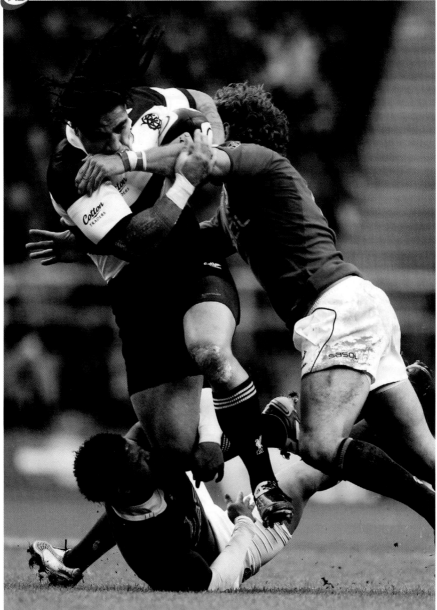

BARBARIANS: JD O'Connor; JT Rokocoko (S Rabeni, 64), AP Ashley-Cooper, MA Nonu (SR Donald, 64), DA Mitchell; MJ Giteau (C), SW Genia (AM Ellis, 49); C Bourke (D Braid, 22)*, ME Williams (Q Geldenhuys, 22-30), R So'oialo (Q Geldenhuys, 49), CR Jack, A van Zyl, NS Tialata (J Yapp, 64), ST Moore (KF Mealamu, H/T), S Perugini. *Braid to flank, So'oialo to No.8.

SOUTH AFRICA: P Lambie; OM Ndungane, AA Jacobs, AJ Strauss, LN Mvovo; ET Jantjies (GG Aplon, 73)**, F Hougaard (C McLeod, 64); R Kankowski (KR Daniel, 55)*, JH Smith (C), WS Alberts, AJ Hargreaves (PR van der Merwe, H/T), JP Botha (PR van der Merwe, 30-39), CJ van der Linde, JA Strauss (BG Maku, 60), CV Oosthuizen, (T Mtawarira, 46). *Daniel to flank, Alberts to No. 8. **Aplon to fullback, Lambie to flyhalf.

Boks no match for determined BaaBaas

Barbarians 26 South Africa 20 *(halftime 19-3)*

December 4, Twickenham, London (31 313). Referee: P Gauzere (France)
BARBARIANS -TRIES: Mitchell (2), O'Connor, Geldenhuys. **CONVERSIONS:** O'Connor (3)..
SOUTH AFRICA - TRIES: Ndungane, Botha, Maku.. **CONVERSION:** Jantjies. **PENALTY GOAL:** Jantjies.

THERE was little brotherly love on show at a bitterly cold Twickenham as a trio of South Africans conspired against their own countrymen to ensure the Springboks slumped to an uninspired defeat to the Barbarians to bring the curtain down on a largely forgettable international season.

For Nick Mallett, the current Italy coach who led the Springboks to a world record equalling 17 successive Test victories between 1997 and 1998, it was a case of sweet revenge as he masterminded a surprisingly one-sided victory over his old team, a full decade after relinquishing the Bok reins.

Despite a second defeat of what was marketed beforehand as a grand slam tour, Mallett's opposite number, Peter de Villiers was assured in the build-up that his job was safe just 10 months out from the Rugby World Cup.

However, there were bound to be renewed concerns about the Boks' play after an aimless and strangely lethargic display against a team who traditionally limit their pre-match preparations to the pub.

Of concern was that this was South Africa's 11th loss in their past 20 matches, and while De Villiers was quick to brush it off as inconsequential given the opposition, the inexperienced Springboks did look all at sea against what was admittedly a star-studded Barbarians lineup.

On paper, the Springbok teamsheet had a callow look about it and so it proved during the ensuing 80 minutes, as the South Africans made a bucketload of elementary mistakes that did not go unpunished.

The Barbarians outscored the tourists by four tries to three but as a contest the game was more heavily weighted in favour of the BaaBaas than the final scoreline suggested, replacement hooker Bandise Maku scoring after the hooter to add some degree of respectability to the scoreline.

Apart from Mallett, the main Bok tormentors on the day were the South African lock pairing of Quintin Geldenhuys, now of Italy, and Anton van Zyl, of Vodacom Western Province and the Stormers. Geldenhuys scored a crucial try in the 62nd minute that put his side 26-10 up, while Van Zyl's robust play earned him the man of the match award.

The Barbarians' other tries were scored by Wallaby wing Drew Mitchell, who netted a brace, and his countryman James O'Connor, who also kicked three conversions.

For the Springboks, Maku was joined on the scoresheet by wing Odwa Ndungane, who intercepted in the 44th minute to race clear, and lock Bakkies Botha, who flopped over from close range with 10 minutes remaining.

But any hopes of what would have been yet another gutsy if not commanding Springbok victory were dented by some wayward placekicking, with debutant flyhalf Elton Jantjies missing three and fullback Patrick Lambie also pushing wide a conversion attempt.

But to blame the two 20-year-olds for the defeat would be to ignore a generally lacklustre team display characterised by a plethora of handling errors and poor option-taking.

It was oh so different against England just seven days previously, but then a week, as they say, is a very long time in South African rugby.

Min	Action	Score
06	Mitchell try,	
	O'Connor missed conversion	**5-0**
10	Jantjies penalty	**5-3**
16	O'Connor try, O'Connor conversion	**12-3**
20	Jantjies missed penalty	**12-3**
21	Mitchell try, O'Connor conversion	**19-3**
38	O'Connor missed penalty	**19-3**
44	Ndungane try, Jantjies conversion	**19-10**
57	Jantjies missed penalty	**19-10**
62	Geldenhuys try, O'Connor conversion	**26-10**
70	Botha try, Jantjies missed conversion	**26-15**
81	Maku try, Lambie missed conversion	**26-20**

END-OF-YEAR TOUR

SPRINGBOK SEVENS

Title hangover for Sevens Boks

SAMOA stormed to their maiden IRB World Series title as champions South Africa not only tamely surrendered their crown but also most of their silverware during a disappointing title defence.

Paul Treu's Springboks won the Dubai, George and Adelaide events on their way to prising the 2008/09 title from New Zealand's grasp, only to end their series reign with a bare trophy cabinet.

Injuries to frontline players certainly hampered their campaign, but the Boks were also their own worst enemies as they failed on numerous occasions to win the tight matches that separate champions from also-rans.

One Cup final – a 19-14 defeat to bogey team Australia in London – was as close to a title as the Boks got in 2009/10, as the men in green, resplendent in their bright new uniforms, spent much of the year battling for Plate honours after habitually falling at the quarter-final hurdle.

South Africa contested six Plate deciders in all, with their only win coming in Las Vegas, where they squeezed home against Fiji in a low-scoring scrap. Three of their five losses – in Dubai, Wellington and Hong Kong – were inflicted by the up-and-coming Aussies, who proceeded to rub salt in the Springbok wounds by coming from behind at Twickenham to leave Treu and his men wondering what it would take to return to the winners' podium.

Despite their series disappointment, Treu remained upbeat as he looked ahead to the 2010 Commonwealth Games and the code's Olympic return. "Guys like Mzwandile Stick and Mpho Mbiyozo, who have been mainstays over the past few seasons, have opted to concentrate on their 15s careers while the likes of Gio Aplon are playing Test rugby," said Treu. "It just shows that our sevens programme is working. It's not difficult for me to con-

Mzwandile Stick and his team celebrate winning the Plate final at the IRB Sevens Tournament in Las Vegas.

vince some of the best young talent in the country to come and play sevens.

"They've seen the team on TV, they've seen them win a World Series and compete all over the world in front of packed stadia. And it's not just 20-year-olds that I'm looking at, it's kids leaving school this year or maybe even next, who could score the winning try in the 2016 Olympic final.

"Not only do they realise that sevens is a possible stepping stone to higher honours, they can see too how it is now a full-time profession, a sport in its own right."

IRB SEVENS SERIES TOURNAMENT PERFORMANCES AND LOG 2009/10

Team	Dub	Geo	NZL	USA	Aus	HK	Lon	Sco	Points
Samoa	20	6	20	24	24	30	16	24	164
New Zealand	24	24	16	20	12	25	12	16	149
Australia	12	6	12	16	16	16	24	20	122
Fiji	16	20	24	8	6	20	8	6	108
England	16	12	16	6	4	20	6	16	96
South Africa	8	8	8	12	8	10	20	6	80
Argentina	6	16	0	0	16	0	16	8	62
Kenya	6	16	6	16	0	8	0	0	52
Wales	4	4	4	6	6	0	6	4	34
United States	0	0	0	4	20	8	0	0	32
Canada	0	0	6	0	0	5	4	0	15
Scotland	0	0	0	0	0	0	0	12	12

SPRINGBOK SEVENS

2009/10 SERIES TOURNAMENT SUMMARY

Tournament 1:

Dubai, December 4-5, 2009

South Africa looked impressive against Australia in their last match of the day when they scored five tries to win 29-0. Earlier they were made to work hard by Wales in their opening match but managed to win 28-14. Fiji caused an upset by knocking the Springboks out in the quarter-finals after which Australia shocked the Boks in the Plate final. New Zealand won the Cup final 24-12 against Samoa.

SA RESULTS: bt Wales 28-14; bt Arabian Gulf 36-7; bt Australia 29-0; lost Fiji 0-14 (quarter-final); bt Kenya 19-14 (Plate semi-final); lost Australia 0-7 (Plate final).

Tournament 2:

George, South Africa, December 11-12, 2009

The Springboks suffered an early setback when Ryno Benjamin was withdrawn from the team for disciplinary reasons and replaced by Shaun Venter. Then Deon Helberg was involved in the SA Airlink emergency landing incident at George Airport but nonetheless performed well in the tournament. Kenya forced a 12-12 draw in the pool games after which SA lost another quarter-final to Fiji and ended up losing the plate final against England. New Zealand beat Fiji 21-12 to win the Cup final.

SA RESULTS: bt France 38-14; bt Zimbabwe 29-5; drew with Kenya 12-12; lost Fiji 17-21 (quarter final); bt Samoa 10-7 (Plate semi-final); lost 7-20 England (Plate final).

Tournament 3:

Wellington, New Zealand, February 5-6, 2010

Captain Paul Delport was ruled out of rugby for 10 weeks after the George tournament and Mzwandile Stick took over the captaincy. A number of new caps from the under-21 ranks were given an opportunity to display their skills. The results followed a similar pattern than those of the first two tournaments with Fiji being SA's nemesis in the quarter-finals and Australia pipping the Boks in the Plate final. Fiji won the Cup final against Samoa 19-14.

SA RESULTS: bt Niue 38-10; bt Wales 38-5; lost New Zealand 7-19; lost Fiji 5-21 (quarter-final); bt Canada 29-5 (Plate semi-final); Lost Australia 22-26 (Plate final).

Tournament 4:

Las Vegas, USA, February 13-14, 2010

At last some success! The Springboks enjoyed their best tournament this season by beating Fiji 12-7 in the Plate final. Fiji, again, forced South Africa out of contention for the Cup title by beating them 12-5 in the pool stages. This put them up against New Zealand and again they could not overcome their challenge. Samoa produced a superb display to beat New Zealand 33-12 and win the Cup final.

SA RESULTS: bt Canada 33-0; bt USA 33-12; lost Fiji 5-12; lost New Zealand 5-12 (quarter-finals); bt England 27-14 (Plate semi-final); beat Fiji 12-7 (Plate final).

Tournament 5:

Adelaide, Australia, March 19-21, 2010

The Springboks suffered a major blow when Mzwandile Stick sustained a knee injury prior to their departure for Adelaide. Kyle Brown took over the captaincy. Argentina knocked SA out of Cup contention by beating them 17-14 in the quarter-finals. Springbok debutant Sampie Mastriet scored nine tries in the tournament. The USA made huge strides to reach their first Cup final but lost against Samoa 38-10.

SA RESULTS: bt Japan 40-0; bt France 38-0; drew Samoa 12-12; lost Argentina (quarter-finals); bt Wales 29-0 (Plate semi-final); Lost to New Zealand 14-21 (Plate final).

Tournament 6:

Hong Kong, China, March 26-28, 2010

For the third time in the series, the South Africans were runners-up to Australia in the Plate final. Both sides lost their respective quarterfinals by narrow margins but recovered well to reach the Plate final. Samoa defeated New Zealand 24-21 to win the Cup final.

SA RESULTS: bt Zimbabwe 28-15; bt Korea 40-7; lost Kenya 7-21; lost Fiji 12-14 (quarter final); bt Kenya 19-12 (Plate semi-final); lost Australia 5-12 (Plate final).

Tournament 7:

London, United Kingdom, May 24-25, 2010

The Springboks got past the quarterfinal stages at last and ended up in the Cup final where they lost a close game to Australia, 14-19. The return of stalwarts Juries, Stick and Powell helped a lot in this tournament. On their way to the final they disposed of Fiji (draw), England and Samoa.

SA RESULTS: bt France 19-12; bt Canada 43-0; drew Fiji 21-21; bt England 17-12 (quarter final); bt Samoa 24-12 (semi-final); lost Australia 14-19 (Cup final).

Tournament 8:
Edinburgh, Scotland, May 31 – June 1, 2010

After the London tournament, Springbok supporters expected something better in Scotland but it turned out to be another disappointing tournament. New Zealand in the pool games and Samoa in the quarterfinals proved too good for the Springboks and they finished sixth in the series. Samoa won the Cup final and the series.

SA RESULTS: bt Italy 49-5; bt Russia 19-7; lost to New Zealand 17-24; lost to Samoa 0-19 (quarter final) lost to Scotland 14-19 (Plate semi-final).

Commonwealth Games,
Delhi, India October 11-12, 2010

With four new caps the Games was going to be a tough tournament as both Australia and New Zealand were using some of their top players from the 15-man game. With Fiji out of the Games due to political reasons the odds were slightly lowered. The Springboks (with the Bok badge on the sleeve) cruised through the pool matches to get to the play-off for third place. N They fought back from 5-14 down to beat England and claim the Bronze medal. New Zealand won their fourth successive Commonwealth Games gold medal by beating Australia 24-17 in the final.

SA RESULTS: bt Wales 21-5; bt Tonga 29-0; bt India 59-0; bt Scotland 10-7 (quarterfinals) lost to Australia 17-24 (semifinal); bt England 17-14 (Bronze medal play-off)

SA SEVENS PLAYERS 2009/10

Player	Province	Dub	Geo	Nzl	USA	Aus	HK	Lon	Sco	CG
Mbiyozo, MM (Mpho)	SARU Contracted	X	X	X	X	X	X	X	X	–
Minnaar, CD (Chase)	SARU Contracted	X	X	X	X	X	X	X	X	x
Horne, FH (Frankie)	SARU Contracted	X	X	X	X	X	X	X	X	–
Afrika, CS (Cecil)	SARU Contracted	X	X	x	X	X	X	X	X	X
Powell, JD (Neill)	SARU Contracted	X	–	–	–	–	–	X	X	X
Helberg, GG (Deon)	Blue Bulls	X	X	–	–	–	–	–	–	–
Brown, KG (Kyle)	SARU Contracted	X	X	X	X	X(c)	X(c)	–	–	–
Delport, P (Paul)	SARU Contracted	X(c)	X(c)	–	–	–	–	–	–	X(c)
Benjamin, RS (Ryno)	SARU Contracted	X	–	X	X	X	X	X	X	X
Jonker, J W (JW)	SARU Contracted	X	X	–	–	X	X	–	–	–
Stick, MW (Mzwandile)	SARU Contracted	X	X	X(c)	X(c)	–	–	X(c)	X(c)	–
Mentz, M J (MJ)	SARU Contracted	X	X	–	–	–	X	X	X	X
Schoeman, MW (Marius)	SARU Contracted	–	X	X	X	–	–	–	–	–
Venter, S (Shaun)	SARU Contracted	–	X	–	–	–	–	–	–	–
Van der Walt, CP (Phillip)	FS Cheetahs	–	–	X	X	–	–	–	–	–
Du Preez, BWN (Branco)	Blue Bulls	–	–	X	X	X	X	–	–	–
Maritz, H van H (Hoffman)	FS Cheetahs	–	–	X	X	X	X	X	X	–
Hunt, SM (Steven)	Western Province	–	–	X	X	X	–	–	–	–
Dry, CA (Chris)	SARU contracted	–	–	–	–	X	X	X	X	–
Mastriet, S (Sampie)	Blue Bulls	–	–	–	–	X	X	–	–	–
Dazel, RL (Renfred)	SARU Contracted	–	–	–	–	–	–	X	X	X
Juries, FM (Fabian)	Western Province	–	–	–	–	–	–	X	X	–
Prinsloo, JG (Boom)	FS Cheetahs	–	–	–	–	–	–	–	–	X
Kruger, OC (Okkie)	Blue Bulls	–	–	–	–	–	–	–	–	X
Mtembu, LS (Lubabalo)	Sharks	–	–	–	–	–	–	–	–	X
Sithole, SCT (Sibusiso)	Sharks	–	–	–	–	–	–	–	–	X
Botha, B. (Bernardo)	Golden Lions	–	–	–	–	–	–	–	–	X

SPRINGBOK SEVENS

SA UNDER-20

BY YUSUF JACKSON,
Team Media Liaison

Bronze again for Baby Boks

THE SA Under-20 team had to once again settle for bronze at the IRB Junior World Championship in Argentina following their 36-7 semi-final loss to eventual champions New Zealand at Rosario's Estadio El Coloso del Parque stadium.

It was the third consecutive year that the side, coached each time by Eric Sauls, failed to make the final of the annual tournament.

The Baby Boks hung on to beat England 27-22 in the third-place playoff match to snatch bronze, but the cold reality was that they were completely outplayed by their Kiwi opponents.

SA's only points in that match came thanks to some individual brilliance by centre Branco du Preez, who scored a try for fullback Patrick Lambie to convert.

New Zealand were physically stronger and their superior conditioning was painfully evident in every facet of play against the Baby Boks, resulting in four tries.

The South Africans qualified for the playoffs after finishing second in Pool C. The side, captained by Blue Bulls flanker CJ Stander, grinded out a 40-14 win over Tonga before outclassing Scotland 73-0 in Santa Fé. SA were however handed the task of taming the rampant Kiwis after losing 42-35 to eventual finalists Australia in a match that not only decided the pool but also the Baby Boks' fate.

Despite the team's failed campaign, the likes of Lambie (Sharks, right), Wandile Mjekevu, Elton Jantjies and Jaco Taute

(all Golden Lions) and skipper Stander showed promise and represented their provinces in the Currie Cup, as did vice-captain and scrumhalf Louis Schreuder, who ran out for Western Province.

Lambie racked up 25 points during the Tonga match and scored the decisive fourth try, which ensured that the South Africans collected maximum points from the encounter. Lambie also kicked four penalties and four conversions after further tries from wing Sampie Mastriet, centre Francois Venter and Stander.

It was one-way traffic for the Baby Boks in their second match, against Scotland, with 11 tries scored in the process. Sibusiso Sithole (2), Siyamthanda Kolisi (2), Jantjies (2), Mjekevu, Marcel van der Merwe, Brummer Badenhorst, Kene Okafor and Lambie, who kicked eight conversions, went over for tries.

It was another story against Australia, as David Shipperley ran in a hat-trick to go with tries by Edward Quirk and Robbie Coleman. The Baby Boks also scored five tries, through Mjekevu (2), Van der Merwe, Taute and Lambie, who added two penalties and two conversions.

After losing to New Zealand, the South Africans did however pick themselves up for their third-place playoff game against England. The result at least ensured that the team would return home with a medal, but the fact that it was a bronze and that Sauls' side had once again failed to reach the final, let alone win the title, made for yet another bittersweet campaign.

IRB UNDER-20 WORLD CHAMPIONSHIP LOG

Pool A	P	W	D	D	PF	PA	TF	TA	B	Pts
New Zealand	3	3	0	0	164	28	22	3	3	15
Wales	3	2	0	1	63	59	5	8	0	8
Fiji	3	1	0	2	29	87	3	8	0	4
Samoa	3	0	0	3	32	114	3	14	1	1
Pool B	P	W	D	D	PF	PA	TF	TA	B	Pts
England	3	3	0	0	101	52	9	5	1	13
France	3	2	0	1	65	62	5	5	1	9
Argentina	3	1	0	2	69	100	8	11	0	4
Ireland	3	0	0	3	64	85	5	6	2	2
Pool C	P	W	D	D	PF	PA	TF	TA	B	Pts
Australia	3	3	0	0	167	53	25	7	3	15
South Africa	3	2	0	1	148	56	20	6	4	12
Scotland	3	1	0	2	40	134	4	20	0	4
Tonga	3	0	0	3	22	134	2	18	0	0

FINAL STANDINGS

1 New Zealand
2 Australia
3 South Africa
4 England
5 France
6 Argentina
7 Wales
8 Fiji
9 Ireland
10 Scotland
11 Tonga
12 Samoa

SA UNDER-20

SA UNDER-20 MATCH RESULTS AND SCORERS

South Africa 40 Tonga 14
June 5. Club Atletico Estudiantes, Paranà.
Referee: Peter Allan (Scotland)
SOUTH AFRICA - TRIES: Mastriet, Stander, Venter, Lambie. CONS: Lambie (4). PENS: Lambie (4).
Lambie, Mastriet (Scheepers), Taute, Venter, Mjekevu, Jantjies, Schreuder (Du Preez), Stander (c), Van der Walt (Du Toit), Kolisi, De Chaves, Okafor (Marais), Van der Merwe (Dreyer), Hadebe, Badenhorst. Unused subs: Bali, Jacobs.
TONGA - TRY: G Moala. PENS: Toloke (3).
Charles Piutau, Jonnie Morath (Paki Falepapalangi), Etuate Lolohea, Sekope Tu'a (George Moala), Michael Toloke, James Naufahu (Manu Soatame), Villiame Sa, Topui Sekona (Langitoto Tongamoa), Kotoni Ale (Ofa Finau), Seilami Tuku'afu (c), Josh Fisi'iahi (Nili Moala), Alfred Pinomi, David Fe'ao, Pateleone Vi, Mone Latu. Unused sub: Sefo Sakalia.

South Africa 73 Scotland 00
June 9, Estadio CA Colon, Santa Fe.
Referee: Francisco Pastrana (Argentina)
SOUTH AFRICA - TRIES: Sithole (2), Kolisi (2), Jantjies (2), Mjekevu, Van der Merwe, Badenhorst, Lambie, Okafor. CONS: Lambie (8), Jantjies.
Lambie (Scheepers), Mjekevu, Du Preez, Venter, Sithole, Jantjies, Schreuder, Stander (c), Bali, Kolisi (Mtembu), De Chaves (Marais), Okafor, Van der Merwe (Dreyer), Hadebe (Du Toit), Badenhorst (Du Rand). Unused sub: Jacobs.
SCOTLAND - no points
Oliver Grove (Tom Brown), Michael Tait (Jonny Kennedy), Callum MacBurnie, James Johnstone, Dougie Fife, Matthew Scott, Alex Black (Russell Weir), Stuart McInally (c, Michael Maltman). Michael Fedo (Robert Harley), Callum Stidston-Nott, Grant Gilchrist, David Denton, Colin Phillips (George Hunter), Alun Walker (Nicky Little), Anthony Kent.

South Africa 35 Australia 42
June 13, Estadio CA Colon, Santa Fe.
Referee: Garratt Williamson (New Zealand)
SOUTH AFRICA - TRIES: Mjekevu (2), Lambie, Van der Merwe, Taute. CONS: Lambie (2). PENS: Lambie (2).
Lambie, Mastriet, Taute, Venter (Du Preez), Mjekevu, Jantjies, Schreuder, Stander (c), Van der Walt, Kolisi (Mtembu), De Chaves (Bali), Okafor, Van der Merwe (Dreyer), Hadebe (Du Toit), Badenhorst (Du Rand). Unused sub: Scheepers.

AUSTRALIA - TRIES: Shipperley (3), Coleman, Quirk. CONS: Toomua (4). PENS: Toomua (3).
Luke Morahan, Dominic Shipperley (Gregory Jeloudev), Kimami Sitauti, Robbie Coleman, Aidan Toua, Matt Toomua, Justin Turner (Nicholas White), Jake Schatz (c), Liam Gill, Edward Quirk, Gregory Peterson, Phoenix Battye (Luke Jones), Paul Alo-Emile, Siliva Siliva (Samuel Robertson), Salesi Manu. Unused subs: Cruze Ah-Nau, Lachlan McCaffrey, Jonathan Lance

South Africa 07 New Zealand 36 (Semi-Final)
June 17, Estadio El Coloso del Parque, Rosario.
Referee: John Lacey (Ireland)
SOUTH AFRICA - TRY: Du Preez. CON: Lambie.
Lambie, Scheepers, Taute, Du Preez (A Jacobs), Mjekevu (Sithole), Jantjies, Schreuder (L Jacobs), Stander (c), Van der Walt, Kolisi (Mtembu), De Chaves (Bali), Okafor, Van der Merwe, Hadebe (Du Toit), Badenhorst (Dreyer).
NEW ZEALAND - TRIES: Savea (2), Thomson, Grice. CONS: Bleyendaal (2). PENS: Bleyendaal (4).
Tom Marshall, Julian Savea, Star Timu (Jason Woodward), Charlie Ngatai (Hayden Parker), Telusa Veainu, Tyler Bleyendaal (c), Tawera Kerr-Barlow (Kayne Hammington), Rory Grice, Sean Polwart (Thomas Franklin), Luke Whitelock, Liaki Moli, Blade Thomson (Matt Graham), Jeff Allen (Willie Ioane-Afuvai), Liam Coltman (Paul Ngaumo), Angus Taavao-Matau.

South Africa 27 England 22 (3rd Place Play-Off)
June 21, Estadio El Coloso del Parque, Rosario.
Referee: Francisco Pastrana (Argentina).
SOUTH AFRICA - TRIES: Sithole (2), Scheepers, Lambie. CONS: Lambie (2). PENS: Lambie.
Lambie, Scheepers (Sithole), Taute, Venter, Mjekevu, Jantjies, Schreuder (L Jacobs), Stander (c), Van der Walt, Kolisi (Mtembu), De Chaves (Bali), Okafor, Van der Merwe, Hadebe, Du Rand (Dreyer). Unused sub: Du Toit.
ENGLAND - TRIES: Burns, Watson, Marler. CONS: Burns (2). PEN: Clegg.
Tom Homer, Christian Wade, Jonny May, Tom Cason (Rory Clegg), Marcus Watson, Freddie Burns (Sam Smith), Sam Harrison (Charlie Davies), Jamie Gibson, Jacon Rowan (c), Will Welch (Alex Gray), George Kruis (Charlie Matthews), Calum Green, Mako Vunipola (Shaun Knight), Jamie George (Rob Buchanan), Joe Marler.

RESULTS

June 5

South Africa	40	Tonga	14
Argentina	22	England	48
New Zealand	44	Fiji	11
France	25	Ireland	22
Australia	58	Scotland	13
Wales	22	Samoa	13

June 09

South Africa	73	Scotland	0
Argentina	23	France	31
New Zealand	77	Samoa	7
England	36	Ireland	21
Australia	67	Tonga	5
Wales	31	Fiji	3

June 13

South Africa	35	Australia	42
Argentina	24	Ireland	21
New Zealand	43	Wales	10
England	17	France	9
Scotland	27	Tonga	3
Fiji	15	Samoa	12

June 17 9th place Semi Final

Ireland	37	Samoa	10
Scotland	28	Tonga	8

5th place Semi Final

Wales	19	Argentina	19
France	44	Fiji	9

Semi Finals

Australia	28	England	16
New Zealand	36	South Africa	7

June 21

11th Place Play-Off

Samoa	3	Tonga	23

9th Place Play-Off

Ireland	53	Scotland	23

7th Place Play-Off

Wales	39	Fiji	15

5th Place Play-Off

Argentina	23	France	37

3rd Place Play-Off

South Africa	27	England	22

Final

New Zealand	62	Australia	17

LEADING POINTS SCORERS

Tyler Bleyendaal	New Zealand	82
Patrick Lambie	South Africa	75
Matthew Jarvis	Wales	61
Matt Toomua	Australia	54
Tom Homer	England	50
Gilles Bosch	France	46
Duncan Weir	Scotland	46
Julian Savea	New Zealand	40
James McKinney	Ireland	37
Noel Reid	Ireland	34
Freddie Burns	England	28
Santiago Mendez	Argentina	27
Ignacio Muedra	Argentina	26
Andrew Conway	Ireland	25
Jean Marc Doussain	France	25
Hayden Parker	New Zealand	25
Telusa Veainu	New Zealand	25
Josh Matavesi	Fiji	23
Nicholas White	Australia	23
Tomas de la Vega	Argentina	20

LEADING TRY SCORERS

Julian Savea	New Zealand	8
Andrew Conway	Ireland	5
Telusa Veainu	New Zealand	5
Tomas de la Vega	Argentina	4
Patrick Lambie	South Africa	4
Tom Marshall	New Zealand	4
Jonny May	England	4
Sibusiso Sithole	South Africa	4
Aidan Toua	Australia	4
Morgan Allen	Wales	3
Freddie Burns	England	3
Robbie Coleman	Australia	3
Antoine Erbani	France	3
Stuart McInally	Scotland	3
Wandile Mjekevu	South Africa	3
Luke Morahan	Australia	3
Dominic Shipperley	Australia	3
Blade Thomson	New Zealand	3
Nicholas White	Australia	3
Niall Annett	Ireland	2

IRB JUNIOR WORLD CHAMPIONSHIPS *

2008	New Zealand in Wales	3rd	Gerrit-Jan van Velze	Eric Sauls
2009	New Zealand in Japan	3rd	Robert Ebersohn	Eric Sauls
2010	New Zealand in Argentina	3rd	CJ Stander	Eric Sauls

This competition replaced the Under 19 Rugby World Championship and Under 21 Rugby World Championship.

SA UNDER-20

SA UNDER-20 SQUAD

BACKS	Position	Date of birth	Height	Weight	Province
P (Patrick) Lambie	Fullback	17/10/1990	1.77	86	Sharks
S (Sampie) Mastriet	Wing	03/08/1990	1.80	81	Blue Bulls
WG (Wandile) Mjekevu	Wing	07/01/1991	1.90	87	Golden Lions
JN (Nico) Scheepers	Wing	27/02/1990	1,.86	90	Free State
ST (Sibusiso) Sithole	Wing	14/06/1990	1.78	90	Sharks
JJ (Jaco) Taute	Centre	21/03/1991	1.87	95	Golden Lions
JF (Francois) Venter	Centre	19/04/1991	1.85	88	Blue Bulls
AJ (Adri) Jacobs	Centre	08/07/1990	1.80	80	Blue Bulls
BBN (Branco) du Preez	Centre	08/05/1990	1.66	72	Blue Bulls
ET (Elton) Jantjies	Flyhalf	01/08/1990	1.76	84	Golden Lions
L (Louis) Schreuder	Scrumhalf	25/04/1990	1.84	82	WP
FJ (Freddie) Muller	Scrumhalf	02/02/1990	1.70	73	WP
WJ (Lohan) Jacobs	Scrumhalf	23/04/1991	1.74	83	Blue Bulls
FORWARDS					
CJ (CJ) Stander	No 8	05/04/1990	1.90	106	Blue Bulls
HS (Fanie) van der Walt	Flanker	01/01/1990	1.91	98	Free State
S (Siya) Kolisi	Flanker	16/06/1991	1.86	96	WP
LS (Lubabalo) Mtembu	Flanker	09/12/1990	1.87	99	Sharks
K (Kene) Okafor	Lock	08/12/1990	1.96	103	Sharks
SJ (Sebastian) de Chaves	Lock	30/10/1990	2.01	105	Golden Lions
M (Mlungisi) Bali	Lock	01/06/1990	1.97	103	Blue Bulls
PC (Peet) Marais	Lock	31/10/1990	1.98	115	Sharks
M (Marcel) van der Merwe	Prop	24/10/1990	1.89	121	Free State
RM (Ruan) Dreyer	Prop	16/09/1990	1.86	113	Golden Lions
WHB (Brummer) Badenhorst	Prop	06/09/1990	1.88	110	WP
CW (Wessel) du Rand	Prop	23/05/1990	1.81	108	Golden Lions
MS (Monde) Hadebe	Hooker	09/12/1990	1.77	101	Sharks
F (Francois) du Toit	Hooker	17/08/1990	1.78	100	Golden Lions

27 Players

COACHES & MANAGEMENT

COACH Eric Sauls
ASSISTANT COACHES
Pine Pienaar & Nico Serfontein
VIDEO ANALYST Elliott Fana
MANAGER Willem Oliphant
CONDITIONING Graham Bentz
PHYSIO Wayne Hector
DOCTOR Arthur Williams
LOGISTICS Tim Dlulane
COMMUNICATIONS Yusuf Jackson

APPEARANCES AND POINTS IN CHAMPIONSHIP

	Tonga	Scottad	Australia	New Zealand	England	Matches	Tries	Conversions	Penalties	Drop Goals	Points
Patrick Lambie	15	15	15	15	15	5	4	17	9	–	75
Sampie Mastriet	14	–	14	–	–	2	1	–	–	–	5
Jaco Taute	13	–	13	13	13	4	1	–	–	–	5
Francois Venter	12	12	12	–	12	4	1	–	–	–	5
Wandile Mjekevu	11	14	11	11	11	5	3	–	–	–	15
Elton Jantjies	10	10	10	10	10	5	2	1	–	–	12
Louis Schreuder	9	9	9	9	9	5	–	–	–	–	0
CJ Stander	8c	8c	8c	8c	8c	5	1	–	–	–	5
Fanie van der Walt	7	–	7	7	7	4	–	–	–	–	0
Siya Kolisi	6	6	6	6	6	5	2	–	–	–	10
Sebastian de Chaves	5	5	5	5	5	5	–	–	–	–	0
Kenny Okafor	4	4	4	4	4	5	1	–	–	–	5
Marcel van der Merwe	3	3	3	3	3	5	2	–	–	–	10
Monde Hadebe	2	2	2	2	2	5	–	–	–	–	0
Brummer Badenhorst	1	1	1	1	–	4	1	–	–	–	5
Francois du Toit	7R	2R	2R	2R	x	4	–	–	–	–	0
Ruan Dreyer	3R	3R	3R	1R	1R	5	–	–	–	–	0
Peet Marais	4R	5R	–	–	–	2	–	–	–	–	0
Mlungisi Bali	x	7	5R	5R	5R	4	–	–	–	–	0
Branco du Preez	9R	13	12R	12	x	4	1	–	–	–	5
Adri Jacobs	x	x	–	12R	–	1	–	–	–	–	0
Nico Scheepers	14R	15R	x	14	14	4	1	–	–	–	5
Sibusiso Sithole	–	11	–	11R	14R	3	4	–	–	–	20
Wessel du Rand	–	3R	1R		1	3	–	–	–	–	0
Lubabalo Mtembu	–	8R	6R	6R	6R	4	–	–	–	–	0
Lohan Jacobs	–	–	–	9R	9R	2	–	–	–	–	0
Freddie Muller	–	–	–	–	–	0	–	–	–	–	0
27 players						**104**	**25**	**18**	**9**	**0**	**182**

SA UNDER-20

SECTION 4
VODACOM SUPER 14

VODACOM SUPER 14

Bulls ride the Soweto wave

THE saying goes that necessity is the mother of invention. And so, with apparently no place to go due to Loftus Versfeld temporarily being under the control of FIFA, the Vodacom Bulls found a temporary home in Soweto.

It proved a two-week period in which the franchise made plenty of new friends, lifted the country's collective spirit and secured their third Vodacom Super14 title in four years thanks to a 25-17 win over the Stormers.

The all-South African final bore testimony to the immense quality of depth at the country's disposal.

While the Vodacom Stormers made it to the final with a little help from the Bulls – the champions fielded a weakened side in their final league match at Newlands due to finding themselves in an unassailable position at the top of the log – it is fair to say that the two best teams contested the final.

The Sharks also recovered well from a horrendous start and ultimately won more games than they lost, while the Cheetahs brought some respectability to their campaign with a late surge that took in three straight victories, over the Blues, Western Force and Lions.

In fact, when one considers the facts, Springbok supporters will be completely gobsmacked as to how this did not translate into a better international season.

The only negative came in the form of the A&G Lions, who suffered the ignominy of losing all of their 13 league games – the worst performance in the history of the competition. Their extraordinary 72-65 home defeat to the Chiefs put their bizarre season, in which defence was very much an afterthought, into perspective.

However, there was an enormous amount to celebrate for South African rugby, not least the legacy left by the Bulls in Super 14 rugby. It was quite appropriate, therefore, that they would win the tournament in the last year before expansion.

The revival of the Stormers was equally pleasing. They produced some of the most compelling performances of the competition, including stunning victories over the Chiefs and Crusaders, as they became the first South African side to beat all five New Zealand teams in a single campaign.

All Blacks coach Graham Henry said during April that he thought the Stormers were the best side in the competition. There were indeed times that it looked that way, but the Bulls' experience and class told in the final, with the collective effort by their forwards and their outstanding tactical kicking game proving decisive.

Even if the Stormers had pinched a treasured asset in wing Bryan Habana from the champions, Francois Hougaard was outstanding in the Bulls' No 11 jersey and even scored a terrific try in the final.

Whereas Bulls fans will no doubt remember the game for Hougaard incisively slicing his way through the stingiest defence in the competition, just about every fan at the game will probably have a story to tell about the unique experience of rugby in Soweto.

The shebeens around Orlando Stadium did a roaring trade on successive weekends as the Bulls knocked over the Crusaders in the semifinal and then Schalk Burger's Capetonians a week later.

Not only was the Super 14 an uplifting experience for South African rugby, but also the country as a whole, with rugby again demonstrating its power as a nation-builder.

2010 VODACOM SUPER 14 LOG

Team	P	W	D	D	PF	PA	Diff	TF	TA	B4	B7	B	Pts
Vodacom Bulls	13	10	3	0	436	345	91	47	32	1	6	7	47
Vodacom Stormers	13	9	4	0	365	171	194	36	17	4	4	8	44
NSW Waratahs	13	9	4	0	385	288	97	45	31	1	6	7	43
Crusaders	13	8	4	1	388	295	93	43	24	1	6	7	41
Queensland Reds	13	8	5	0	366	308	58	43	38	2	5	7	39
ACT Brumbies	13	8	5	0	358	291	67	40	25	2	3	5	37
Blues	13	7	6	0	376	333	43	47	32	2	7	9	37
Hurricanes	13	7	5	1	358	323	35	40	37	2	5	7	37
Sharks	13	7	6	0	297	299	-2	23	27	4	1	5	33
Vodacom Cheetahs	13	5	7	1	316	393	-77	34	50	1	3	4	26
Chiefs	13	4	8	1	340	418	-78	40	48	4	4	8	26
Highlanders	13	3	10	0	297	397	-100	34	53	4	3	7	19
Western Force	13	4	9	0	258	364	-106	24	42	2	1	3	19
A & G Lions	13	0	13	0	270	585	-315	32	72	2	3	5	5

VODACOM SUPER 14

2010 VODACOM SUPER 14 LEADING SCORERS

50 POINTS OR MORE

PLAYER	TEAM	Tries	Conversions	Penalties	Drop Goals	Points
M Steyn	Bulls	5	38	51	3	263
QS Cooper	Reds	5	31	27	1	171
DW Carter	Crusaders	1	26	30	2	153
SA Brett	Blues	2	28	23	2	141
PJ Grant	Stormers	1	20	32	0	141
MJ Giteau	ACT Brumbies	1	25	26	1	136
SR Donald	Chiefs	2	22	25	0	129
R Pienaar	Sharks	3	17	20	1	112
IP Olivier	Cheetahs	1	19	21	2	112
IJA Dagg	Highlanders	5	16	18	0	111
JD O'Connor	Western Force	1	15	23	0	104
BS Barnes	NSW Waratahs	1	19	17	3	103
JC Pietersen	Stormers	3	10	17	0	86
DK Halangahu	NSW Waratahs	3	12	14	0	81
PAT Weepu	Hurricanes	1	12	16	0	77
WKN Ripia	Hurricanes	0	6	15	0	57
HC Kruger	Lions	1	8	10	0	51
RM Kockott	Sharks	1	0	15	0	50

2010 VODACOM SUPER 14 PLAY-OFF RESULTS

SEMI-FINAL: Bulls 39 Crusaders 24 (halftime 23-10)
Orlando Stadiium, Soweto, Saturday, May 22
Referee: Stuart Dickinson (Australia)
Bulls: TRIES: Spies, Du Preez, Kirchner. CONVERSIONS: Steyn (3). PENALTIES: Steyn (6).
Crusaders: TRIES: McCaw, S Whitelock, Maitland. CONVERSIONS: Carter (3). PENALTY: Carter.
SEMI-FINAL: Stormers 25 Waratahs 6 (halftime 13-6)
Newlands Stadium, Cape Town, Saturday, May 22
Referee: Mark Lawrence (SA)
Stormers: TRY: De Jongh. CONVERSION: Grant. PENALTIES: Grant (6).
Waratahs: PENALTY: Barnes. DROP GOAL: Barnes.

FINAL: Bulls 25 Stormers 17 (halftime 16-3)
Orlando Stadium, Soweto, Saturday, May 29
Referee: Craig Joubert (SA)
Bulls: TRY: Hougaard. CONVERSION: Steyn. PENALTIES: Steyn (6).
Stormers: TRIES: Habana, P Louw. CONVERSIONS: Grant (2). PENALTY: Grant.

FIVE TRIES OR MORE

DA Mitchell	NSW Waratahs	9
JT Rokocoko	Blues	9
GJ van den Heever	Bulls	8
BE Alexander	ACT Brumbies	7
J Fourie	Stormers	7
BG Habana	Stormers	7
F Hougaard	Bulls	7
SD Maitland	Crusaders	7
RMN Ranger	Blues	7
D Smith	Blues	7
ZR Guildford	Crusaders	6
M Killian	Lions	6
AS Mathewson	Blues	6
MA Nonu	Hurricanes	6
PJ Spies	Bulls	6
LD Turner	NSW Waratahs	6
BA Basson	Cheetahs	5
KJ Beale	NSW Waratahs	5
WJ Chambers	Reds	5
QS Cooper	Reds	5
IJA Dagg	Highlanders	5
R Davies	Reds	5
K Fotuaili'i	Crusaders	5
DN Ioane	Reds	5
RD Kahui	Chiefs	5
W Olivier	Bulls	5
M Steyn	Bulls	5
FM Vainikolo	Highlanders	5
RN Wulf	Blues	5

VODACOM SUPER RUGBY 1996 - 2010

LOG BY AVERAGE POSITION

TEAM	1996	1997	1998	1999	2000	2001	2002	2003	2004	2005	2006	2007	2008	2009	2010	Semi-finals	Finals	Total	Champions	Ave Position
Crusaders	12th	6th	2nd	4th	2nd	10th	1st	2nd	2nd	1st	1st	3rd	1st	4th	4th	12	9	21	7	3.66
ACT Brumbies	5th	2nd	10th	5th	1st	1st	3rd	4th	1st	5th	6th	5th	9th	7th	6th	6	5	11	2	4.66
Blues	2nd	1st	1st	9th	6th	11th	6th	1st	5th	7th	8th	4th	6th	9th	7th	5	4	9	3	5.53
Sharks/Natal	4th	4th	3rd	7th	12th	2nd	10th	11th	7th	12th	5th	1st	3rd	6th	9th	6	3	9	-	6.40
NSW Waratahs	7th	9th	6th	8th	9th	8th	2nd	5th	8th	2nd	3rd	13th	2nd	5th	3rd	5	2	7	-	6.00
Highlanders	8th	12th	4th	3rd	3rd	5th	4th	7th	9th	8th	9th	9th	11th	11th	12th	4	1	5	-	7.66
Hurricanes	9th	3rd	8th	10th	8th	9th	9th	3rd	11th	4th	2nd	8th	4th	3rd	8th	6	1	7	-	6.60
Queensland Reds	1st	10th	5th	1st	7th	4th	5th	8th	10th	10th	12th	14th	12th	13th	5th	3	-	3	-	7.80
Chiefs	6th	11th	7th	6th	10th	6th	8th	10th	4th	6th	7th	6th	7th	2nd	11th	2	1	3	-	7.13
Bulls / N Tvl	3rd	8th	11th	12th	11th	12th	12th	6th	6th	3rd	4th	2nd	10th	1st	1st	6	3	9	3	6.60
Stormers / WP	11th	-	9th	2nd	5th	7th	7th	9th	3rd	9th	11th	10th	5th	10th	2nd	3	1	4	-	7.14
Cheetahs/ Free State	-	7th	-	-	-	-	-	-	-	-	10th	11th	13th	14th	10th	-	-	0	-	10.83
Lions/Cats	10th	5th	12th	11th	4th	3rd	11th	12th	12th	11th	13th	12th	14th	12th	14th	2	-	2	-	10.40
Western Force	-	-	-	-	-	-	-	-	-	-	14th	7th	8th	8th	13th	-	-	0	-	10.00

Bold type indicates champion

LOG BY WINNING PERCENTAGE

TEAM	Played	Won	Lost	Drawn	Pts For	Pts Against	Difference	Tries For	Tries Against	Bonus Tries	Bonus >7	Points	% Win
Crusaders	196	131	59	6	5858	4435	1423	664	477	19	73	525	66.84%
Blues	184	111	70	3	5283	4405	878	659	476	27	76	515	60.33%
ACT Brumbies	186	112	72	2	5182	4120	1062	632	440	26	74	515	60.22%
NSW Waratahs	182	98	80	4	4646	4114	532	526	447	33	61	486	53.85%
Hurricanes	182	94	84	4	4671	4563	108	539	512	20	56	418	51.65%
Sharks	184	89	89	6	4571	4546	25	519	509	37	50	439	48.37%
Chiefs	178	83	91	4	4577	4724	-147	519	548	37	52	389	46.63%
Highlanders	180	81	97	2	4383	4602	-219	472	544	37	40	402	45.00%
Stormers	168	78	85	5	3888	4152	-264	419	462	31	40	384	46.43%
Queensland Reds	178	79	96	3	4101	4549	-448	446	518	38	41	400	44.38%
Bulls	184	84	93	7	4760	5173	-413	517	606	22	48	351	45.65%
Western Force	65	24	37	4	1332	1582	-250	146	189	14	14	132	36.92%
Lions	177	46	127	4	3907	5618	-1711	414	664	39	38	269	25.99%
Cheetahs	76	22	52	2	1622	2198	-576	183	263	18	15	125	28.95%
	2320	1132	1132	56	58781	58781	0	6655	6655	398	678	5350	

VODACOM SUPER 14

VODACOM BULLS

GROUND Loftus Versfeld **CAPACITY** 50 000
ADDRESS Kirkness Street, Sunnyside, Pretoria, 0002
TELEPHONE NUMBER 012 420 0700
WEBSITE www.bluebulls.co.za
COLOURS Navy fading from shoulders to waist, sky-blue collar, sleeves and socks. Navy shorts
COACH Frans Ludeke **CAPTAIN** Victor Matfield
CEO Barend van Graan **CHAIRMAN** Boet Fick

www.bluebulls.co.za

Bulls prove to be Super 14's dominant force

AFTER five years of Vodacom Super 14, before giving way to the radically redesigned Super 15 in 2011, the Bulls ended the cycle as the most dominant force in the southern hemisphere's major provincial competition by claiming their third title in four years.

A 25-17 victory over the Stormers in an historic final at the Orlando Stadium in Soweto earned the men from Pretoria a back-to-back title and ensured that only they and the Crusaders won the tournament in its 14-team format.

Captain Victor Matfield led from the front with his lineout dominance while scrumhalf Fourie du Preez was the fulcrum around which the entire Bulls gameplan revolved.

Flyhalf Morné Steyn continued to produce match-winning performances with his lethal boot and young wings Gerhard van den Heever and Francois Hougaard delivered the try-scoring touches many feared had been lost with the departure of Bryan Habana at the end of 2009.

Steyn, for a second time, finished as top scorer in the competition with a record 263 points. He scored 92 points more than the next man, the Queensland Reds' Quade Cooper, and his haul was five more than the Western Force

scored during the entire season.

The Bulls were so dominant in their run to the final that coach Frans Ludeke took the decision to rest most of his key players for the match against the Stormers in Cape Town. The Cape side duly secured a predictable 38-10 win but the Bulls were fresh for what they knew would be an epic contest against the Crusaders in Orlando.

Due to Loftus Versfeld being used as one of the venues for the FIFA World Cup, the Bulls were evicted from their home ground for the play-offs and the forward-thinking management decided to break new ground by taking the team and the fans out of their comfort zone to play at the 41,000-seater Orlando Stadium.

Initial scepticism gave way to curiosity and eventually to joyous scenes as thousands of Bulls fans descended on Vilikazi Street in Soweto. It was a sight no one would have believed 10 years earlier.

Despite a different ground the results were the same as first the Crusaders succumbed 39-24 before the Bulls secured their hat-trick against the Stormers in a north-south derby to bring down the curtain on Super 14 rugby.

RESULTS & SCORERS

Date	Venue	Referee	Opponent	Result	Score	Scorers
Feb 12	Bloemfontein	Jonathan Kaplan	CHEETAHS	WON	51-34	T: Pretorius, Steyn, Van den Heever, Kirchner, Olivier, Penalty try. C: Steyn (5), Potgieter. P: Steyn (3).
Feb 20	Pretoria	Mark Lawrence	BRUMBIES	WON	50-32	T: Steyn (2), Du Preez, Van den Heever, Olivier. C: Steyn (5). P: Steyn (5).
Feb 27	Pretoria	Marius Jonker	WARATAHS	WON	48-38	T: Hougaard (2), Van den Heever, J-L Potgieter, Dippenaar, Olivier. C: Steyn (6). P: Steyn (2).
Mar 13	Pretoria	Jonathan Kaplan	HIGHLANDERS	WON	50-35	T: Hougaard (2), Spies (2), Van den Heever, G Botha, Olivier. C: Steyn (6). P: Steyn.
Mar 19	Pretoria	Steve R Walsh	HURRICANES	WON	19-18	T: Kirchner. C: Steyn. P: Steyn (4).
Mar 27	Perth	Nathan Pearce	W FORCE	WON	28-15	T: Spies, Kirchner, Steyn. C: Steyn (2). P: Steyn (3).
April 3	Auckland	Craig Joubert	BLUES	LOST	17-32	T: Spies. P: Steyn (3). DG: Steyn.
April 9	Hamilton	Jonathan Kaplan	CHIEFS	WON	33-19	T: Spies, Van den Heever, D Potgieter, Botha. C: Steyn (2). P: Steyn (3).
April 17	Brisbane	Craig Joubert	REDS	LOST	12-19	T: Kuun, Wannenburg. P: Steyn.
April 24	Pretoria	Marius Jonker	LIONS	WON	51-11	T: Van den Heever (2), Kuun, Mametsa, Olivier, Steyn. C: Steyn (3). P: Steyn (5).
May 1	Pretoria	Jonathan Kaplan	SHARKS	WON	27-19	T: Van den Heever, J-L Potgieter. C: Steyn. P: Steyn (5).
May 7	Pretoria	Marius Jonker	CRUSADERS	WON	40-35	T: Hougaard (2), Matfield. C: Steyn (2). P: Steyn (5). DG: Steyn (2).
May 15	Cape Town	Jonathan Kaplan	STORMERS	LOST	10-38	T: Snyman. C: Brummer. P: J-L Potgieter.
SEMI-FINAL						
May 22	Soweto[1]	Stuart Dickinson	CRUSADERS	WON	39-24	T: Spies, Kirchner, Du Preez. C: Steyn (3). P: Steyn (6).
FINAL						
May 29	Soweto[1]	Craig Joubert	STORMERS	WON	25-17	T: Hougaard. C: Steyn. P: Steyn (6).

[1]Orlando Stadium

Played	Won	Drawn	Lost	Points for	Points against	Tries for	Tries against
15	**12**	**0**	**3**	**500**	**386**	**51**	**37**

COACHES AND MANAGEMENT

HEAD COACH Frans Ludeke **BACKLINE COACH** Pieter Rossouw **FORWARDS COACH** Johann van Graan **DEFENCE COACH** John McFarland **MANAGER** Wynie Strydom **KICKING COACH** Vlok Cilliers **STRENGTH AND CONDITIONING** Basil Carzis & Stephen Plummer **TEAM DOCTOR** Dr Org Strauss **PHYSIOTHERAPIST** Roneé Eksteen & Karabo Morokane **BAGGAGE MASTER** Andries Kabinde **MASSEUR** Lwazi Booi **MEDIA OFFICER** Ian Schwartz

APPEARANCES AND POINTS IN SUPER RUGBY

2010 SQUAD	Province	Debut	Matches	Tries	Conversions	Penalties	Drop Goals	Points
Heini Adams	Blue Bulls	2005	36	3	–	–	–	15
De Wet Barry	Eastern Province	2000	79	13	–	–	–	65
Francois Brummer	Blue Bulls	2010	1	–	1	–	–	2
Bakkies Botha	Blue Bulls	2002	86	9	–	–	–	45
Gary Botha	Blue Bulls	2003	73	8	–	–	–	40
Rossouw de Klerk	Blue Bulls	2010	1	–	–	–	–	0
Stephan Dippenaar	Blue Bulls	2008	13	1	–	–	–	5
Fourie du Preez	Blue Bulls	2003	99	19	–	–	–	95
Jaco Engels	Blue Bulls	2006	40	2	–	–	–	10
Dean Greyling	Blue Bulls	2008	3	–	–	–	–	0
Deon Helberg	Blue Bulls	2010	1	–	–	–	–	0
Francois Hougaard	Blue Bulls	2008	16	7	–	–	–	35
Zane Kirchner	Blue Bulls	2008	40	11	–	–	–	55
Okkie Kruger	Blue Bulls	2010	1	–	–	–	–	0
Werner Kruger	Blue Bulls	2008	42	3	–	–	–	15
Derick Kuün	Blue Bulls	2007	56	8	–	–	–	40
Fudge Mabeta	Blue Bulls	2010	2	–	–	–	–	0
Bandise Maku	Blue Bulls	2008	19	–	–	–	–	0
John Mametsa	Blue Bulls	2008	6	1	–	–	–	5
Tiger Mangweni	Blue Bulls	2005	10	–	–	–	–	0
Victor Matfield	Blue Bulls	1999	109	8	–	–	–	40
Wynand Olivier	Blue Bulls	2005	72	19	–	–	–	95
Dewald Potgieter	Blue Bulls	2008	31	2	–	–	–	10
Jacques-Louis Potgieter	Blue Bulls	2007	32	3	20	14	1	100
Jaco Pretorius	Blue Bulls	2007	37	1	–	–	–	5
Chillyboy Ralepelle	Blue Bulls	2006	19	1	–	–	–	5
Danie Rossouw	Blue Bulls	2002	102	5	–	–	–	25
Bees Roux	Blue Bulls	2008	31	–	–	–	–	0
Ruan Snyman	Blue Bulls	2010	1	1	–	–	–	5
Pierre Spies	Blue Bulls	2005	56	20	–	–	–	100
Gürthro Steenkamp	Blue Bulls	2004	66	2	–	–	–	10
Deon Stegmann	Blue Bulls	2008	39	1	–	–	–	5
Morné Steyn	Blue Bulls	2005	73	10	139	126	17	757
Gerhard van den Heever	Blue Bulls	2009	17	9	–	–	–	45
Flip van der Merwe	Blue Bulls	2007	19	1	–	–	–	5
Jaco van der Westhuyzen	Blue Bulls	1997	56	7	10	3	–	64
Gerrit-Jan Van Velze	Blue Bulls	2010	1	–	–	–	–	0
Pedrie Wannenburg	Blue Bulls	2002	113	14	–	–	–	70
Stefan Watermeyer	Blue Bulls	2010	1	–	–	–	–	0
Totals			**1499**	**189**	**170**	**143**	**18**	**1768**

VODACOM SUPER RUGBY FINAL LOG POSITIONS

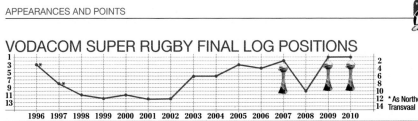

* As Northern Transvaal

1996 1997 1998 1999 2000 2001 2002 2003 2004 2005 2006 2007 2008 2009 2010

APPEARANCES AND POINTS IN 2010 SUPER 14

	Cheetahs	Brumbies	Waratahs	Highlanders	Hurricanes	W Force	Blues	Chiefs	Reds	Lions	Sharks	Crusaders	Stormers	Crusaders	Stormers	Matches	Tries	Conversions	Penalties	Drop Goals	Points
Z Kirchner	15	15	15	15	15	15	15	15	15	15	15	15	–	15	15	14	4	–	–	–	20
G van den Heever	14	14	14	14	14	14	14	14	14	14	14	14	–	–	14	13	8	–	–	–	40
J Pretorius	13	–	–	–	–	13	13	–	–	13	–	–	–	13	13	6	1	–	–	–	5
W Olivier	12	12	12	12	12	12	12	12	12	12	13	13	–	12	12	14	5	–	–	–	25
J Mametsa	11	11R	–	–	–	–	–	–	–	11	–	–	–	–	–	3	1	–	–	–	5
M Steyn	10	10	10	10	10	10	10	10	10	10	10	10	–	10	10	14	5	38	51	3	263
F du Preez	9	9	9	9	9	9	9	9	9	9R	9	9	–	9	9	14	2	–	–	–	10
P Spies	8	8	–	8	8	8	8	8	8	8	8	8	–	8	8	13	6	–	–	–	30
P Wannenburg	7	7	7	7R	7R	7R	7R	6R	7R	8R	7R	7R	8	7R	7R	15	1	–	–	–	5
D Stegmann	6	6	8R	6R	6	6	6	6	6R	6R	6	6	–	6	6	14	–	–	–	–	0
V Matfield	5c	5c	5c	5c	5c	5c	5c	5c	5c	5c	5c	5c	–	5c	5c	14	1	–	–	–	5
D Rossouw	4	–	8	4	4	4	4	4	4	4	4R	4	–	4	4	13	–	–	–	–	0
W Kruger	3	3	3	3	3	3	3	3	3	3	3	3	–	3	3	14	–	–	–	–	0
G Botha	2	2	2	2	2	2	2	2	2	2	2	2	–	2	2	14	2	–	–	–	10
G Steenkamp	1	1	1	1	1	1	1	1	1	1	1	1	–	1	1	14	–	–	–	–	0
B Maku	2R	2R	2R	2R	x	2R	2R	2R	x	2R	2R	2R	2	2R	2R	13	–	–	–	–	0
B Roux	3R	3R	3R	–	1R	3R	3R	3R	3R	1R	3R	3R	3	3R	3R	14	–	–	–	–	0
F van der Merwe	4R	4	4	4R	4R	4R	4R	4R	4R	4R	–	–	5	4R	4R	13	–	–	–	–	0
D Kuün	7R	7R	6	6	6R	6R	6R	–	6	6	6R	6R	6	6R	6R	14	2	–	–	–	10
H Adams	9R	9R	9R	–	–	–	–	9R	x	9	9R	–	9	–	–	7	–	–	–	–	0
J-L Potgieter	12R	10R	13R	13R	x	13R	13R	11R	13R	13R	12	12	10	12R	13R	14	2	1	1	–	15
S Dippenaar	13R	13	13	13	13	–	–	13	13	–	12R	12R	13	13R	–	11	1	–	–	–	5
F Hougaard	–	11	11	11	11	11	11	11	11	–	11	11	–	11	11	12	7	–	–	–	35
F Mabeta	–	8R	–	–	–	–	–	–	–	–	–	–	4R	–	–	2	–	–	–	–	0
D Potgieter	–	–	6R	7	7	7	7	7	7	7	7	7	–	7	7	12	1	–	–	–	5
J van der Westhuyzen	–	–	11R	14R	x	11R	14R	–	–	–	–	19R	14	14	14R	8	–	–	–	–	0
R de Klerk	–	–	–	1R	–	–	–	–	–	–	–	–	–	–	–	1	–	–	–	–	0
J Engels	–	–	–	–	–	–	1R	–	–	–	–	–	1	–	–	2	–	–	–	–	0
B Botha	–	–	–	–	–	–	–	–	–	4	4R	4c	–	–	–	3	–	–	–	–	0
T Mangweni	–	–	–	–	–	–	–	–	–	–	–	–	15	–	–	1	–	–	–	–	0
DW Barry	–	–	–	–	–	–	–	–	–	–	–	–	12	–	–	1	–	–	–	–	0
D Helberg	–	–	–	–	–	–	–	–	–	–	–	–	11	–	–	1	–	–	–	–	0
G-J Van Velze	–	–	–	–	–	–	–	–	–	–	–	–	7	–	–	1	–	–	–	–	0
C Ralepelle	–	–	–	–	–	–	–	–	–	–	–	–	2R	–	–	1	–	–	–	–	0
D Greyling	–	–	–	–	–	–	–	–	–	–	–	–	3R	–	–	1	–	–	–	–	0
O Kruger	–	–	–	–	–	–	–	–	–	–	–	–	7R	–	–	1	–	–	–	–	0
R Snyman	–	–	–	–	–	–	–	–	–	–	–	–	9R	–	–	1	1	–	–	–	5
F Brummer	–	–	–	–	–	–	–	–	–	–	–	–	10R	–	–	1	–	1	–	–	2
S Watermeyer	–	–	–	–	–	–	–	–	–	–	–	–	11R	–	–	1	–	–	–	–	0
Penalty try	–	–	–	–	–	–	–	–	–	–	–	–	–	–	–	0	1	–	–	–	5
39 players																**325**	**51**	**40**	**52**	**3**	**500**

VODACOM SUPER 14

VODACOM BULLS SUPER 14 SQUAD AND MANAGEMENT IN 2010

BACK ROW (L to R): Lwazi Booi, Stephen Plummer, Derick Kuun, Werner Kruger, Gerhard van den Heever, Pierre Spies, Flip van der Merwe, Dewald Potgieter, Gurthro Steenkamp, Bees Roux, Dr Org Strauss, Andries Kabinde. **MIDDLE ROW** (L to R): Vlok Cilliers, Ian Schwartz, Jaco van der Westhuyzen, Francois Hougaard, Jacques-Louis Potgieter, Deon Stegmann, Jaco Pretorius, Zane Kirchner, Bandise Maku, Gary Botha, Karabo Morokane, Ronee Eksteen, Basil Carzis. **FRONT ROW** (L to R): Barend van Graan (CEO), Morné Steyn, Pieter Rossouw, Pedrie Wannenburg, Frans Ludeke (Coach), Victor Matfield, Boet Fick (President), Fourie du Preez, Wynie Strydom (Manager), Danie Rossouw, Johann van Graan, Wynand Olivier, John McFarland.

VODACOM BULLS RECORDS

MATCH RECORDS

Biggest win	89	v Queensland Reds (92-3)	Pretoria	2007
Heaviest defeat	64	v ACT Brumbies (9-73)	Canberra	1999
Highest score	92	v Queensland Reds (92-3)	Pretoria	2007
Most points conceded	75	v Crusaders (25-75)	Christchurch	2000
Most tries	13	v Queensland Reds (92-3)	Pretoria	2007
Most tries conceded	11	v Crusaders (25-75)	Christchurch	2000
Most points by a player	39	JH Kruger (1t 5c 8p) v Highlanders	Pretoria	1996
Most tries by a player	3	AJ Richter v Blues	Pretoria	1997
	3	PF du Preez v Cats	Pretoria	2004
Most conversions by a player	11	DJ Hougaard v Queensland Reds	Pretoria	2007
Most penalties by a player	8	JH Kruger v Highlanders	Pretoria	1996
	8	DJ Hougaard v Crusaders	Pretoria	2007
Most drop goals by a player	4	M Steyn vs Crusaders	Pretoria	2009

SEASON RECORDS

Most team points	500	from 15 matches	2010
Most points by a player	263	M Steyn	2010
Most team tries	51	from 15 matches	2010
Most tries by a player	9	BG Habana	2005
Most conversions by a player	38	M Steyn	2010
Most penalties by a player	51	M Steyn	2010
Most drop goals by a player	11	M Steyn	2009

CAREER RECORDS

Most appearances	113
PJ Wannenburg	2002-2010
Most points	**757**
M Steyn	**2005-2010**
Most tries	37
BG Habana	2005-2009
Most conversions	139
M Steyn	2005-2010
Most penalties	126
M Steyn	2005-2010
Most drop goals	17
M Steyn	2005-2010

VODACOM SUPER 14

VODACOM CHEETAHS

GROUND Vodacom Park **CAPACITY** 46 000
ADDRESS Att Horak St, Bloemfontein **TELEPHONE** 051 407 1700
COLOURS White jersey with orange collar and turquoise & purple details. White shorts, navy socks
WEBSITE www.vodacomcheetahs.co.za
COACH Naka Drotské **CAPTAIN** Juan Smith
MANAGER Eugene van Wyk **CEO** Gerda von Solms
CHAIRMAN Harold Verster

Underpowered Cheetahs struggle again

THE Vodacom Cheetahs again flattered to deceive after a bright start to a Super 14 campaign that appeared to be heading towards a top-eight finish. But a lack of depth, which became apparent when injuries set in, eventually saw the Cheetahs claim a creditable but uninspiring 10th in the final standings.

Losing Springbok flank Heinrich Brüssow to a serious knee injury just four weeks into the season was a huge blow for Naka Drotské's side.

And things got worse when decorated Bok flank Juan Smith withdrew from the team prior to their overseas tour after news that his father, Giel, was in a critical condition following a bout of Rift Valley fever.

After recording sensational wins against the Sharks and Hurricanes in the first month of the competition, the Cheetahs, in the absence of Smith and Brüssow, slumped to four straight losses.

Smith snr's disease had been diagnosed while the Cheetahs were still at home, and the veteran delayed his tour departure date to as late as possible.

But 48 hours after he landed in Sydney, and just days before the Cheetahs were due to meet the Brumbies in round eight, Smith's father's condition deteriorated rapidly and he passed away. The devastated player returned home immediately.

Smith is the embodiment of all that is good about Cheetahs rugby – he is tough, honest, talented and hardworking – and his personal trials left the team shaken. In his absence, they faltered.

Later flank Kabamba Floors received a five-week suspension for a spear tackle on Brumbies fullback Julian Huxley while strapping loose forward Frans Viljoen was also ruled out for the season with a broken jaw before the team departed for Australasia.

These blows stretched the Cheetahs' limited resources to breaking point, and the dam wall broke in a 45-6 loss to the Crusaders in Christchurch in round nine.

But Smith responded to an SOS from his team and headed back across the Indian Ocean for a third time in a matter of weeks to lead the side in their last tour match against 2009 finalists the Chiefs.

The World Cup-winning blindsider was at his sensational best as his teammates responded to his lead-from-the-front style to force an incredible 25-25 draw against one of the pre-tournament favourites. It was the first time the Cheetahs had avoided defeat in New Zealand.

"Losing my dad was very tough. He lived for rugby, he lived for my rugby and going back to play was my last gift to him," Smith said after the match.

When they returned home with Smith at the helm once again, the Cheetahs recorded three straight wins over the Blues (36-32), Western Force (29-14) and Lions (59-10) to finish ahead of the Chiefs and Highlanders.

Considering they'd finished bottom the previous season, and had won five matches compared to just two in 2009, the 2010 campaign was a modest success.

RESULTS & SCORERS

Date	Venue	Referee	Opponent	Result	Score	Scorers
Feb 12	Bloemfontein	Jonathan Kaplan	BULLS	LOST	34-51	T: Mapoe, Smith, Nokwe. C: Olivier (2). P: Olivier (5).
Feb 19	Durban	Jonathan Kaplan (replaced by Pro Legoete)	SHARKS	WON	25-20	T: R Viljoen. C: Olivier. P: Olivier (3), R Viljoen (2). DG: Olivier.
Feb 27	Bloemfontein	Pro Legoete	HIGHLANDERS	LOST	24-31	T: Brussow, Smith. C: Olivier. P: Olivier (4).
Mar 6	Bloemfontein	Bryce Lawrence	HURRICANES	WON	28-12	T: Floors. C: Olivier. P: Bosman (4), Olivier (3).
Mar 20	Cape Town	Chris Pollock	STORMERS	LOST	08-21	T: Bosman. DG: Olivier.
Mar 26	Bloemfontein	Vinny Munro	REDS	LOST	10-31	T: Johnson. C: Olivier. P: Bosman.
April 3	Sydney	Keith Brown	WARATAHS	LOST	17-40	T: Nel, Uys. C: Olivier. P: Olivier.
April 10	Canberra	Bryce Lawrence	BRUMBIES	LOST	15-61	T: Strauss, Pretorius. C: R Viljoen. P: Olivier.
April 17	Christchurch	Jonathon White	CRUSADERS	LOST	06-45	P: R Viljoen, Bosman.
April 23	Hamilton	Bryce Lawrence	CHIEFS	DREW	25-25	T: Raubenheimer, Nel, Bosman. C: Olivier (2). P: Olivier (2).
May 1	Bloemfontein	Marius Jonker	BLUES	WON	36-32	T: Smith, Nokwe, Basson, Van der Walt, Vermeulen. C: Olivier (2), Bosman (2). P: Olivier.
May 8	Bloemfontein	Craig Joubert	W FORCE	WON	29-14	T: Basson (2), Olivier, Pretorius. C: Olivier (3). P: Olivier.
May 15	Welkom	Craig Joubert	LIONS	WON	59-10	T: Basson (2), Pretorius (2), Daniller (2), Pieterse, Oosthuizen, Uys. C: Olivier (6). P: Strydom.

Played	Won	Drawn	Lost	Points for	Points against	Tries for	Tries against
13	5	1	7	316	393	34	50

VODACOM SUPER 14

COACHES AND MANAGEMENT

HEAD COACH Naka Drotské **ASSISTANT COACHES** Hawies Fourie, David Maidza & Barend Pieterse
TRAINER Niel du Plessis **VIDEO ANALYST** Charl Strydom **MANAGER** Eugene van Wyk
DOCTOR Dr Ian Morris **PHYSIOTHERAPIST** JP du Toit **LOGISTICS** Cecil van Rooyen
MEDIA OFFICER Yolandi Beneke

APPEARANCES AND POINTS IN SUPER RUGBY

2010 SQUAD	Province	Debut	Matches	Tries	Conversions	Penalties	Drop Goals	Points
Skipper Badenhorst	Free State	2003	25	–	–	–	–	0
Ryno Barnes	Griquas	2010	8	–	–	–	–	0
Bjorn Basson	Griquas	2009	9	6	–	–	–	30
Meyer Bosman	Free State	2006	61	4	27	38	–	188
Nico Breedt	Free State	2003	33	2	–	–	–	10
Heinrich Brüssow	Free State	2007	33	5	–	–	–	25
Kobus Calldo	Free State	2008	19	–	–	–	–	0
Tertius Carse	Free State	2007	2	–	–	–	–	0
Hennie Daniller	Free State	2004	44	4	–	–	–	20
Danwel Demas	Free State	2006	25	2	–	–	–	10
Tewis de Bruyn	Free State	2008	32	2	2	1	–	17
David de Villiers	Free State	2008	29	2	–	–	–	10
Niel du Plessis	Free State	–	0	–	–	–	–	0
Wiaan du Preez	Free State	2005	61	–	–	–	–	0
Sias Ebersohn	Free State	2010	2	–	–	–	–	0
Robert Ebersohn	Free State	2010	10	–	–	–	–	0
Kabamba Floors	Free State	2006	44	10	–	–	–	50
Barry Geel	Griquas	2010	1	–	–	–	–	0
Marnus Hugo	Griquas	2010	2	–	–	–	–	0
Ashley Johnson	Free State	2010	4	1	–	–	–	5
Wilmaure Louw	Griquas	2010	3	–	–	–	–	0
Lionel Mapoe	Free State	2010	5	1	–	–	–	5
WP Nel	Free State	2009	15	2	–	–	–	10
Jongi Nokwe	Free State	2006	36	17	–	–	–	85
Coenie Oosthuizen	Free State	2010	13	1	–	–	–	5
Naas Olivier	Griquas	2006	33	4	32	38	2	204
Sarel Pretorius	Griquas	2009	22	6	–	–	–	30
Barend Pieterse	Free State	2005	44	3	–	–	–	15
Davon Raubenheimer	Griquas	2010	6	1	–	–	–	5
Hendro Scholtz	Free State	2001	61	2	–	–	–	15
Juan Smith	Free State	2003	78	18	–	–	–	90
Adriaan Strauss	Free State	2007	48	2	–	–	–	10
Louis Strydom	Free State	2007	13	–	5	18	–	64
Corné Uys	Free State	2007	27	5	–	–	–	25
Philip van der Walt	Free State	2010	5	1	–	–	–	5
Izak van der Westhuizen	Free State	2010	6	–	–	–	–	0
Waltie Vermeulen	Free State	2010	12	1	–	–	–	5
Frans Viljoen	Free State	2006	22	1	–	–	–	5
Riaan Viljoen	Griquas	2010	10	1	1	3	–	16
Totals			**870**	**104**	**67**	**98**	**2**	**959**

www.vodacomcheetahs.co.za

VODACOM SUPER RUGBY FINAL LOG POSITIONS

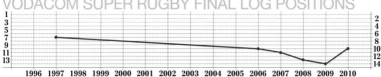

APPEARANCES AND POINTS IN 2010 SUPER 14

	Bulls	Sharks	Highlanders	Hurricanes	Stormers	Reds	Waratahs	Brumbies	Crusaders	Chiefs	Blues	W Force	Lions	Matches	Tries	Conversions	Penalties	Drop Goals	Points
Viljoen	15	15	15	x	–	15	10R	10R	10	x	10R	10R	15R	10	1	1	3	–	16
Mapoe	14	13	13	14	14	–	–	–	–	–	–	–	–	5	1	–	–	–	5
Uys	13	–	–	–	x	13R	11R	13	–	13	–	14	12	7	2	–	–	–	10
Bosman	12	12	12	12	12	12	12	12	10R	12	12	12	–	12	2	4	6	–	36
Nokwe	11	11	11	11	11	–	11	11	11	11	11	–	–	10	2	–	–	–	10
Olivier	10	10	10	10	10	10	10	10	–	10	10	10	10	12	1	19	21	2	112
de Bruyn	9	9	9	9R	9R	9R	9	9	x	9R	–	–	–	9	–	–	–	–	0
Johnson	8	x	8R	–	–	8	8	–	–	–	–	–	–	4	1	–	–	–	5
Smith	7c	7c	7c	7c	7c	–	–	–	7c	7c	7c	7c	–	9	3	–	–	–	15
Brüssow	6	6	6	6	–	–	–	–	–	–	–	–	–	4	1	–	–	–	5
de Villiers	5	5	5	4R	–	–	–	–	–	–	–	–	–	4	–	–	–	–	0
Breedt	4	4	4	4	4	4	4	4R	4R	x	–	–	–	9	–	–	–	–	0
Nel	3	3	3	3	3	3	3	3	3	3	–	3	3	12	2	–	–	–	10
Strauss	2	2	2	2	2	2c	2c	2c	2c	x	–	–	–	9	1	–	–	–	5
du Preez	1	1	1	1	1	1	1	1R	1R	1	1	1	1	13	–	–	–	–	0
Barnes	x	x	x	2R	x	–	2R	2R	2R	2	2	2R	2R	8	–	–	–	–	0
Oosthuizen	1R	1R	1R	1R	1R	1R	1R	1	1	1R	1R	1R	1R	13	1	–	–	–	5
Vermeulen	4R	4R	5R	5	5	5	5	5	5	–	4R	5R	5R	12	1	–	–	–	5
Viljoen	8R	8	8	8	8	–	–	–	–	–	8	–	–	6	–	–	–	–	0
Pretorius	9R	9R	9R	9	9	9	9R	9R	9	9	9	9	9	13	4	–	–	–	20
S Ebersohn	13R	x	10R	–	–	–	–	–	–	–	–	–	–	2	–	–	–	–	0
Demas	10R	14	14	x	14R	11	14	–	14	14	11R	12R	–	10	–	–	–	–	0
Daniller	–	15R	15R	15	15	–	15	15	15	15	15	15	15	11	2	–	–	–	10
R Ebersohn	–	–	–	13	13	13	13	14R	13	13R	13	13	13	10	–	–	–	–	0
Floors	–	–	–	8R	8R	6R	8R	8	–	–	–	–	–	5	1	–	–	–	5
Scholtz	–	–	–	–	6	6	6	6	6	6	6	6	6	9	–	–	–	–	0
Pieterse	–	–	–	–	6R	7	7	7	7	5	5	5	5	9	1	–	–	–	5
Basson	–	–	–	–	14	–	–	–	–	14	11	11	–	4	5	–	–	–	25
Badenhorst	–	–	–	–	x	–	–	–	–	–	2R	2	2	3	–	–	–	–	0
N du Plessis	–	–	–	–	x	–	–	–	–	–	–	–	–	0	–	–	–	–	0
Louw	–	–	–	–	x	–	–	14	13R	–	–	–	14	3	–	–	–	–	0
Raubenheimer	–	–	–	–	–	–	4R	5R	8	8	–	6R	8R	6	1	–	–	–	5
van der Westhuizen	–	–	–	–	–	–	–	4	4	4	4	4	4	6	–	–	–	–	0
Geel	–	–	–	–	–	–	–	12	–	–	–	–	–	1	–	–	–	–	0
van der Walt	–	–	–	–	–	–	–	8R	8R	8R	8	8	–	5	1	–	–	–	5
Calldo	–	–	–	–	–	–	–	–	–	–	3	–	–	1	–	–	–	–	0
Carse	–	–	–	–	–	–	–	–	–	–	9R	–	–	1	–	–	–	–	0
Hugo	–	–	–	–	–	–	–	–	–	–	–	9R	7R	2	–	–	–	–	0
Strydom	–	–	–	–	–	–	–	–	–	–	–	–	10R	1	–	1	–	–	2
39 players														**270**	**34**	**25**	**30**	**2**	**316**

VODACOM SUPER 14

VODACOM CHEETAHS RECORDS

MATCH RECORDS

Biggest win	49	vs. Lions (59-10)	Welkom	2010
Heaviest defeat	46	vs. Brumbies (15-61)	Canberra	2010
Highest score	59	vs. Lions (59-10)	Welkom	2010
Most points conceded	61	vs. Brumbies (15-61)	Canberra	2010
Most tries	9	vs. Lions (59-10)	Welkom	2010
Most tries conceded	9	vs. Brumbies (15-61)	Canberra	2010
Most points by a player	26	HM Bosman vs. Stormers	Cape Town	2006
Most tries by a player	2	C Badenhorst vs. Highlanders	Invercargill	1997
	2	C Badenhorst vs. Blue Bulls	Pretoria	1997
	2	AE Drotske vs. Highlanders	Invercargill	1997
	2	G Pieters vs. Sharks	Durban	2006
	2	BA Fortuin vs. Blues	Bloemfontein	2006
	2	DP Nell vs. Crusaders	Bloemfontein	2007
	2	JW Jonker vs. Bulls	Bloemfontein	2008
	2	JL Nokwe vs. Sharks	Bloemfontein	2009
	2	BA Basson vs. Force	Bloemfontein	2010
	2	BA Basson vs. Lions	Welkom	2010
	2	SJ Pretorius vs. Lions	Welkom	2010
	2	HJ Daniller vs. Lions	Welkom	2010
Most conversions by a player	7	JH de Beer vs. Highlanders	Invercargill	1997
Most penalties by a player	8	HM Bosman vs. Stormers	Cape Town	2006
Most drop goals by a player	1	By six players		

SEASON RECORDS

Most team points	316	in 13 games	2010
Most points by a player	112	IP Olivier	2010
Most team tries	34	in 13 games	2008
	34	in 13 games	2010
Most tries by a player	7	JL Nokwe	2008
Most conversions by a player	19	JH de Beer	1997
	19	IP Olivier	2010
Most penalties by a player	21	HM Bosman	2006
	21	IP Olivier	2010
Most drop goals by a player	2	IP Olivier	2010
	2	HC Kruger	2007

CAREER RECORDS

Most appearances	61	HM Bosman	2006-2010
Most points	188	HM Bosman	2006-2010
Most tries	**15**	**JL Nokwe**	**2008-2010**
Most conversions	27	HM Bosman	2006-2010
Most penalties	38	HM Bosman	2006-2010
Most drop goals	2	IP Olivier	2009-2010
	2	HC Kruger	2007

VODACOM SUPER 14

AUTO & GENERAL LIONS

GROUND Coca-Cola Park (previously Ellis Park) **CAPACITY** 62 300
ADDRESS South Office Block, Johannesburg Stadium, 124 Van Beek Street, Doornfontein 2094
TELEPHONE NUMBER 011 402 2960
COLOURS White and red trim jersey, black shorts and black socks
WEBSITE www.lionsrugby.co.za
COACH Dick Muir **CAPTAIN** Cobus Grobbelaar
CHAIRMAN Kevin de Klerk **CEO** Manie Reynecke

Leaky Lions set unwanted records

WHAT can one say about a Vodacom Super14 campaign in which a team set a new record by losing all 13 of its league matches? If the A&G Lions are truthful, they will reflect on this period as one in which they hit rock bottom. Just about the only positive spin one can put on this is that the only way from here is up.

They were left bereft of any sort of star quality after the contractual debacles that bled the Golden Lions Rugby Union and saw Jaque Fourie head off to the Stormers, and Willem Alberts and Louis Ludik to the Sharks.

The appointment of Dick Muir as coach was one that had the potential to inspire confidence, but rugby in Johannesburg has simply gone through too many turbulent times. In the space of one year from 2009, players could have been coached by Eugene Eloff, Hans Coetzee, Jake White (in his role as consultant) and then Muir.

To cap it all, former All Black coach John Mitchell arrived to take the reins before the Currie Cup, though this played a role in giving the team much-needed structure and he may well be the foil that Muir needs to repeat his success at the Sharks.

But, on reflection, the Super 14 campaign was awful and even when the team scored 65 points in a home match against the Chiefs, they ended up conceding 72!

Defence clearly was a major problem and they conceded 585 points at an average of 45 per game. The 270 they scored, at an average of 21 per game, was not the least in the competition – that rather dubious honour went to the

Western Force – but an average score of 21-45 against you provides a compelling argument to take stock.

Yes, the Lions could play a bit, too – their 32 tries scored was more than the 23 of the Sharks or 24 of the Western Force – and it was refreshing to see a youngster such as Wandile Mjekevu come through the ranks while quality players such as prop JC Janse van Rensburg, utility forward Franco van der Merwe and utility back Michael Killian appeared to come through it all unscathed.

But this was sadly a campaign that will be remembered for all the wrong reasons, as defence was an afterthought and the Lions' approach defied the old rugby truth that it is indeed defence that wins trophies.

It is true that the new interpretation of the breakdown laws encouraged attacking rugby, but the game still requires you to have an effective plan in place to stop what is coming. The Lions did not and conceded half-centuries against the Chiefs, Waratahs, Bulls, Blues and even the Cheetahs.

The closest they came to pulling off a win was at home against the Sharks, but they went down fighting 28-32. Perhaps it was all for the better, as a win might have put some form of gloss on an exercise that die-hard Lions fans will never want to see repeated.

Fortunately that does not appear to be on the cards, with the Lions having played some inspired rugby in patches in the Currie Cup. Mitchell will remain in charge for 2011, providing some much-needed continuity, the lack of which probably played its part in a disastrous Super 14 campaign.

RESULTS & SCORERS

Date	Venue	Referee	Opponent	Result	Score	Scorers
Feb 13	Johannesburg	Jaco Peyper	STORMERS	LOST	13-26	T: Killian. C: Rose. P: Rose (2).
Feb 19	Johannesburg	Marius Jonker	CHIEFS	LOST	65-72	T: Mjekevu (3), Clever, Spencer, La Grange, Grobbelaar, Chavhanga, Lombaard. C: Rose (5), Francis (2). P: Rose (2).
Feb 27	Wellington	Paul Marks	HURRICANES	LOST	18-33	T: Minnie, Clever. C: Rose. P: Rose (2).
Mar 5	Canberra	Steve R Walsh	BRUMBIES	LOST	13-24	T: Franklin. C: Francis. P: Francis (2).
Mar 12	Sydney	Vinny Munro	WARATAHS	LOST	12-73	T: Chavhanga, Janse van Rensburg. C: Francis.
Mar 20	Christchurch	Garratt Williamson	CRUSADERS	LOST	19-46	T: Franklin. C: Francis. P: Francis (3), Rose.
Mar 26	Dunedin	Stuart Dickinson	HIGHLANDERS	LOST	29-39	T: Pekeur (2), Grobbelaar, Joubert, Killian. C: Spencer, Rose.
Apr 10	Johannesburg	Mark Lawrence	REDS	LOST	26-41	T: Killian (2), F van der Merwe, H Kruger. C: H Kruger (3).
Apr 17	Johannesburg	Mark Lawrence	SHARKS	LOST	28-32	T: Minnie, F van der Merwe, Killian. C: H Kruger (2). P: H Kruger (3).
Apr 24	Pretoria	Marius Jonker	BULLS	LOST	11-51	T: Mjekevu. P: H Kruger (2).
May 1	Johannesburg	Craig Joubert	W FORCE	LOST	12-33	P: H Kruger (4).
May 8	Johannesburg	Mark Lawrence	BLUES	LOST	14-56	T: Spencer (2). C: H Kruger (2).
May 15	Welkom	Craig Joubert	CHEETAHS	LOST	10-59	T: Killian. C: H Kruger. P: H Kruger.

Played	Won	Drawn	Lost	Points for	Points against	Tries for	Tries against
13	**0**	**0**	**13**	**270**	**585**	**32**	**72**

COACHES AND MANAGEMENT

HEAD COACH Dick Muir **BACKLINE COACH** Hans Coetzee **FORWARDS COACH** Johan Ackermann
MANAGER Mustapha Boomgaard **ANALYST** JP Ferreira **STRENGTH & CONDITIONING** Wayne Taylor
DOCTOR Dr Rob Collins **PHYSIOTHERAPIST** Dave Leicher **ASSISTANT MANAGER** Johane Singwane
MEDIA OFFICER Krystle Geach

APPEARANCES AND POINTS IN SUPER RUGBY

2010 SQUAD	Province	Debut	Matches	Tries	Conversions	Penalties	Drop Goals	Points
Bernardo Botha	Golden Lions	2010	2	–	–	–	–	0
David Bulbring	Golden Lions	2010	1	–	–	–	–	0
Kevin Buys	Golden Lions	2010	5	–	–	–	–	0
Tonderai Chavanga	Golden Lions	2004	48	16	–	–	–	80
Todd Clever	Golden Lions	2009	21	3	–	–	–	15
Jacques Coetzee	Pumas	2010	10	–	–	–	–	0
Marius Delport	Golden Lions	2007	14	–	–	–	–	0
George Earle	Golden Lions	2010	6	–	–	–	–	0
Charles Emslie	Golden Lions	2010	10	–	–	–	–	0
Burton Francis	Golden Lions	2008	14	1	8	6		39
Hannes Franklin	Pumas	2010	12	2	–	–	–	10
Ross Geldenhuys	Golden Lions	2008	19	–	–	–	–	0
Cobus Grobbelaar	Golden Lions	2004	69	5	–	–	–	25
JC Janse van Rensburg	Golden Lions	2008	24	1	–	–	–	5
Chris Jonck	Golden Lions	2008	20	1	1	2	–	13
JP Joubert	Golden Lions	2007	17	1	–	–	–	5
Michael Killian	Golden Lions	2009	15	7	–	–	–	35
Herkie Kruger	Golden Lions	2001	28	3	13	18	4	107
Robert Kruger	Golden Lions	2009	9	–	–	–	–	0
Doppies la Grange	Golden Lions	2003	50	3	–	–	–	15
Jacques Lombaard	Golden Lions	2010	7	1	–	–	–	5
Nico Luus	Golden Lions	2010	7	–	–	–	–	0
Derick Minnie	Golden Lions	2010	13	2	–	–	–	10
Wandile Mjekevu	Golden Lions	2010	10	4	–	–	–	20
Jonathan Mokuena	Golden Lions	2010	3	–	–	–	–	0
Wouter Moore	Golden Lions	2010	1	–	–	–	–	0
Gert Muller	Golden Lions	2009	17	–	–	–	–	0
Dusty Noble	Golden Lions	2006	19	1	–	–	–	5
Wigan Pekeur	Golden Lions	2010	4	2	–	–	–	10
Earl Rose	Golden Lions	2006	47	8	30	24	2	178
Carlos Spencer	Golden Lions	1996	108	28	121	78	3	625
Willem Stoltz	Golden Lions	2002	44	2	–	–	–	10
Jaco Taute	Golden Lions	2010	3	–	–	–	–	0
Franco van der Merwe	Golden Lions	2007	44	4	–	–	–	20
Heinke van der Merwe	Golden Lions	2006	53	–	–	–	–	0
Hans van Dyk	Golden Lions	2008	21	–	–	–	–	0
Wikus van Heerden	Golden Lions	2002	83	15	–	–	–	75
Deon van Rensburg	Golden Lions	2009	15	–	–	–	–	0
Walter Venter	Golden Lions	2008	18	1	–	–	–	5
Jano Vermaak	Golden Lions	2006	58	9	3	–	–	63
Justin Wheeler	Golden Lions	2010	2	–	–	–	–	0
Totals			**971**	**120**	**176**	**128**	**9**	**1375**

www.lionsrugby.co.za

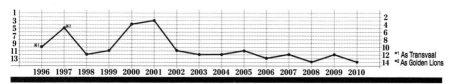

*1 As Transvaal
*2 As Golden Lions

APPEARANCES AND POINTS IN 2010 SUPER 14

	Stormers	Chiefs	Hurricanes	Brumbies	Waratahs	Crusaders	Highlanders	Reds	Sharks	Bulls	W Force	Blues	Cheetahs	Matches	Tries	Conversions	Penalties	Drop Goals	Points
Rose	15	15	15	11R	15	15	12R	–	–	–	–	–	–	7	–	8	7	–	37
Chavanga	14	14	14	14	14	–	11	–	11R	15R	14	14	14	11	2	–	–	–	10
van Rensburg	13	13	13	–	–	–	–	–	13R	13R	13	13	11	8	–	–	–	–	0
La Grange	12	12	12	12	12	12	12	12	12	–	–	–	–	9	1	–	–	–	5
Mjekevu	11	11	11	15R	11	11	11R	11	11	11	–	–	–	10	4	–	–	–	20
Spencer	10	10	10	–	10	10R	10	10	15	15	15	15	15	12	3	1	–	–	17
Joubert	9	9	9	9	9	–	9R	–	–	–	–	–	–	6	1	–	–	–	5
Mokuena	8	8R	–	–	–	–	–	–	–	–	–	–	6R	3	–	–	–	–	0
F van der Merwe	7	4	5	4R	4	5	5	5	5	5	–	5	7	12	2	–	–	–	10
Grobbelaar	6c	6c	6c	6c	6c	6c	6c	6c	6c	6c	6c	6c	–	12	2	–	–	–	10
Stoltz	5	5	–	5	5	8R	8R	4R	4R	–	–	–	–	8	–	–	–	–	0
Lombaard	4	5R	4R	5R	5R	4R	–	–	–	–	5R	–	–	7	1	–	–	–	5
Geldenhuys	3	3	3	–	–	3	3	–	–	–	3	3R	3	8	–	–	–	–	0
Franklin	2	2	2	2R	2	2	2	2	2R	2R	2R	–	2R	12	2	–	–	–	10
HS van der Merwe	1	1	1	3R	1	3R	3R	1	3R	–	3R	1R	–	11	–	–	–	–	0
Emslie	2R	2R	2R	2	2R	2R	2R	–	–	–	2	2	2	10	–	–	–	–	0
Janse van Rensburg	3R	–	–	1	3R	1	1	3R	1	1	1	1	1	11	1	–	–	–	5
Clever	8R	8	8	8	8	8	8	8	8R	8	–	–	–	9	2	–	–	–	10
Minnie	4R	7	7	7	7	7	7	8	8R	8	8	8	8	13	2	–	–	–	10
Coetzee	9R	9R	9R	9R	–	9R	–	11R	–	9R	9R	9R	9R	10	–	–	–	–	0
Francis	11R	10R	–	10	10R	10	–	–	–	–	–	–	–	5	–	5	5	–	25
Killian	10R	13R	13R	15	–	12R	15	15	14	14	11	11	11R	12	6	–	–	–	30
Buys	–	3R	3R	3	3	–	–	–	–	3R	–	–	–	5	–	–	–	–	0
Earle	–	–	4	4	–	4	–	–	–	–	5	4	4	6	–	–	–	–	0
Venter	–	–	10R	13	13	13	13	13	–	12	12	12	–	9	–	–	–	–	0
Kruger	–	–	8R	–	6R	–	4R	–	–	–	–	–	–	3	–	–	–	–	0
Noble	–	–	–	11	–	–	–	–	–	–	–	–	–	1	–	–	–	–	0
Vermaak	–	–	–	–	9R	9	9	9	9	9	9	9	9	9	–	–	–	–	0
Pekeur	–	–	–	–	14R	14	14	14	–	–	–	–	–	4	2	–	–	–	10
Luus	–	–	–	–	–	–	4	4	4	4	4	4R	5	7	–	–	–	–	0
van Heerden	–	–	–	–	–	–	–	7	7	7	7	7	6c	6	–	–	–	–	0
Muller	–	–	–	–	–	–	–	3	3	3	–	3	3R	5	–	–	–	–	0
Van Dyk	–	–	–	–	–	–	–	2R	2	2	–	–	–	3	–	–	–	–	0
Kruger	–	–	–	–	–	–	–	14R	10	10	10	10	10	6	1	8	10	–	51
Delport	–	–	–	–	–	–	–	13R	13	13	–	12R	13	5	–	–	–	–	0
Jonck	–	–	–	–	–	–	–	9R	–	–	–	–	–	1	–	–	–	–	0
Moore	–	–	–	–	–	–	–	–	5R	–	–	–	–	1	–	–	–	–	0
Wheeler	–	–	–	–	–	–	–	–	18R	x	7R	–	–	2	–	–	–	–	0
Taute	–	–	–	–	–	–	–	–	–	10R	2R	12		3	–	–	–	–	0
Botha	–	–	–	–	–	–	–	–	–	14R	–		15R	2	–	–	–	–	0
Bulbring	–	–	–	–	–	–	–	–	–	–	–		5R	1	–	–	–	–	0
41 players														**285**	**32**	**22**	**22**	**0**	**270**

BACK ROW (L to R): JP Ferreira (Analyst), Carlos Spencer, Justin Wheeler, Marius Delport, Robert Kruger, Nico Luus, David Bulbring, Jacques Lombaard, Wouter Moore, George Earle, Jaco Taute, Kevin Buys, Charles Emslie, Ross Geldenhuys, Gert Muller, Wayne Taylor (Conditioning Coach), **MIDDLE ROW** (L to R): Dr Rob Collins (Team Doctor), Jacques Coetzee, Chris Jonck, Tonderai Chavhanga, JP Joubert, Hannes Franklin, JC Janse Van Rensburg, Jonathan Mokuena, Burton Francis, Herkie Kruger, Dusty Noble, Wigan Pekeur, Michael Killian, Bernado Botha, Derick Minnie, Walter Venter, Deon van Rensburg, Hans van Dyk, Johane Singwane (Assistant Manager), **FRONT ROW** (L to R): Johan Ackermann (Assistant Coach), Jano Vermaak, Mac Hendricks (Pro Rugby Operations Manager), Heinke van der Merwe, Manie Reyneke (CEO), Wikus van Heerden, Kevin de Klerk (President), Cobus Grobbelaar (Captain), Dick Muir (Director of Coaching), Earl Rose, Mustapha Boomgaard (Team Manager), Franco van der Merwe, Dave Leicher (Physiotherapist), **ABSENT:** Willem Stoltz, Todd Clever, Hans Coetzee (Assistant Coach), Doppies la Grange.

AUTO & GENERAL LIONS RECORDS

MATCH RECORDS

Biggest win	50	vs. Chiefs (53-3)	Bloemfontein	2000
Heaviest defeat	64	vs. ACT Brumbies (0-64)	Canberra	2000
Highest score	65	vs. Chiefs (65-72)	Johannesburg	2010
Most points conceded	72	vs. Chiefs (65-72)	Johannesburg	2010
Most tries	9	vs Chiefs (65-72)	Johannesburg	2010
Most tries conceded	10	vs. ACT Brumbies (16-64)	Canberra	2002
Most points by a player	32	GK Johnson vs. Highlanders	Johannesburg	1997
Most tries by a player	3	JA van der Walt vs. Bulls	Pretoria	1998
	3	JA van der Walt vs. Stormers	Johannesburg	1998
	3	C Stoltz vs. Crusaders	Nelson	1999
	3	G Bobo vs. Bulls	Pretoria	2002
	3	GJJ Britz vs. Bulls	Pretoria	2004
	3	J Fourie vs. Blues	Johannesburg	2006
	3	H Mentz vs. Reds	Brisbane	2009
	3	**WG Mjekevu vs. Chiefs**	**Johannesburg**	**2010**
Most conversions by a player	7	CJN Fourie vs. Bulls	Pretoria	2004
Most penalties by a player	7	JH de Beer vs. Chiefs	Bloemfontein	1998
	7	J Engelbrecht vs. ACT Brumbies	Johannesburg	1999
Most drop goals by a player	2	GS du Toit vs. Stormers	Cape Town	1999
	2	AS Pretorius	Johannesburg	2009

SEASON RECORDS

Most team points	325	in 12 matches	2000
Most points by a player	157	LJ Koen	2001
Most team tries	37	in 11 matches	1999
Most tries by a player	9	JA van der Walt	1998
Most conversions by a player	22	AS Pretorius	2009
Most penalties by a player	36	LJ Koen	2001
Most drop goals by a player	6	AS Pretorius	2009

CAREER RECORDS

Most appearances	69	AS Pretorius	2002-2009
	69	PJJ Grobbelaar	2004-2010
Most points	645	AS Pretorius	2002-2009
Most tries	24	J Fourie	2003-2009
Most conversions	106	AS Pretorius	2002-2009
Most penalties	115	AS Pretorius	2002-2009
Most drop goals	11	AS Pretorius	2002-2009

VODACOM SUPER 14

THE SHARKS

THE SHARKS

GROUND ABSA Stadium
CAPACITY 54 000
ADDRESS Walter Gilbert Road, Durban
TELEPHONE NUMBER 031 308 8400
COLOURS Grey jersey with black and white trim, blacks shorts and socks
WEBSITE www.sharksrugby.co.za
COACH John Plumtree **CAPTAIN** John Smit
CEO Brian van Zyl **CHAIRMAN** John Swain

Sharks sunk by lack of bite

IT was one of those 'could have, should have, would have' seasons, said head coach John Plumtree as he reflected on the Sharks' failed 2010 Vodacom Super 14 campaign.

The Sharks began the competition with high hopes but without a flyhalf and, ultimately, it derailed their campaign.

The schizophrenic Sharks continued to bewilder their supporters. In 2009, they were steaming along as log leaders with seven wins (four away from home) from eight outings – only to lose four of their last five games to end sixth. In 2010, they lost their first five games but then won seven out of the next eight but still only finished ninth.

Plumtree, wondering might have been, was left praising the character of the players who stood up when all was already lost.

"We were written off, there was all that talk of the squad disintegrating and that we would finish last," he said. "The response and character of the players in turning the season around made me proud and was the highlight of the season."

There was a nightmare start to the campaign for Plumtree, who had planned to chase tries and bonus points with a high-tempo style that would pay off a few months later during a triumphant Currie Cup campaign. He had the tools, with Argentinian flyhalf Juan Hernandez partnering Ruan Pienaar at halfback and a back division that included Springboks JP Pietersen, Odwa Ndungane, Adi Jacobs, Waylon Murray and Stefan Terblanche.

But the Sharks never really made it out of the blocks. Hernandez left Durban with a back injury weeks before the tournament kicked off and replacement Steve Meyer quit rugby on the eve of the opening game, while injury and poor form disrupted the back division.

Plumtree meanwhile wanted to return Pienaar to his preferred position of scrumhalf and so the Sharks spent the opening fortnight frantically searching the rugby world for a quality No 10. They finally settled on journeyman England flyhalf Andy Goode before their five-match tour of New Zealand and Australia and he was solid without being spectacular.

The five opening games were lost but four were by five points or less. The Sharks battled to find any attacking rhythm but they also suffered from some marginal calls and Australian referee Paul Marks was even dropped from the panel after their controversial 25-21 loss to the Waratahs in Sydney.

Plumtree, without a penetrative, cohesive backline, finally had to find other ways to win and settled on using his big ball-carrying forwards – Jean Deysel, Willem Alberts, the Du Plessis brothers and John Smit – to create momentum and win territory and penalties.

The revamped scrum, with Smit switched from tight-head to loosehead, was a major factor in the Sharks' revival as the Highlanders, Hurricanes, Reds, Lions, Blues, Stormers and Force were beaten in the closing weeks, with their only defeat coming at Loftus to the Bulls (27-19).

Their lack of tries – just 23 in 13 games and the fewest in the competition – was a major concern.

"We were simply not threatening enough on attack," said Plumtree. Could have, would have, should have.

RESULTS & SCORERS

Date	Venue	Referee	Opponent	Result	Score	Scorers
Feb 13	Durban	Keith Brown	CHIEFS	LOST	18-19	P: Kockott (6).
Feb 19	Durban	Jonathan Kaplan	CHEETAHS	LOST	20-25	T: Kankowski. P: Kockott (5).
		(replaced by Pro Legoete)				
Feb 26	Christchurch	Chris Pollock	CRUSADERS	LOST	6-35	P: Kockott (2).
Mar 6	Sydney	Paul Marks	WARATAHS	LOST	21-25	T: Kankowski, Jacobs. C: Goode. P: Goode, Pienaar. DG: Goode.
Mar 13	Canberra	Garratt Williamson	BRUMBIES	LOST	22-24	T: Pienaar. C: Goode. P: Goode (5).
Mar 20	Dunedin	Jonathon White	HIGHLANDERS	WON	30-16	T: B du Plessis, Jacobs, Terblanche. C: Pienaar (3). P: Pienaar (3).
Mar 27	Wellington	Ian Smith	HURRICANES	WON	29-26	T: Pietersen, Lambie. C: Pienaar (2). P: Pienaar (5).
Apr 3	Durban	Chris Pollock	REDS	WON	30-28	T: Botes, Pietersen, Ndungane. C: Pienaar (3). P: Pienaar (3).
Apr 17	Johannesburg	Mark Lawrence	LIONS	WON	32-28	T: B du Plessis, Botes, Ndungane, Lambie. C: Pienaar (3). P: Pienaar (2).
Apr 24	Durban	Mark Lawrence	BLUES	WON	23-10	T: Pienaar. P: Pienaar (2), Kockott (2), Goode. DG: Pienaar.
May 1	Pretoria	Jonathan Kaplan	BULLS	LOST	19-27	T: Kockott. C: Pienaar. P: Goode (4).
May 8	Durban	Stuart Dickinson	STORMERS	WON	20-14	T: Ndungane, Pienaar. C: Pienaar (2). P: Pienaar (2).
May 14	Durban	Pro Legoete	W FORCE	WON	27-22	T: Mvovo, Kankowski, Botes. C: Pienaar (3). P: Pienaar (2).

Played	Won	Drawn	Lost	Points for	Points against	Tries for	Tries against
13	7	0	6	297	299	23	27

VODACOM SUPER 14

THE SHARKS

COACHES AND MANAGEMENT

COACH John Plumtree **ASSISTANT COACHES** Grant Bashford & Chris Boyd
TECHNICAL ANALYST Clinton Isaacs **MANAGER** Trevor Barnes **DOCTOR** Dr Craig Roberts
PHYSIOTHERAPIST Deane Macquet **CONDITIONING TRAINER** Mark Steele
ADMIN MANAGER Piet Strydom **MASSEUR** Robert Russell **MEDIA OFFICER** Megan Harris

APPEARANCES AND POINTS IN SUPER RUGBY

2010 SQUAD	Province	Debut	Matches	Tries	Conversions	Penalties	Drop Goals	Points
Willem Alberts	Sharks	2007	49	4	–	–	–	20
Craig Burden	Sharks	2006	21	1	–	–	–	5
Jacques Botes	Sharks	2005	74	22	–	–	–	110
Deon Carstens	Sharks	2001	83	4	–	–	–	20
Pat Cilliers	Sharks	2007	3	–	–	–	–	0
Keegan Daniel	Sharks	2006	48	5	–	–	–	25
Jean Deysel	Sharks	2008	28	–	–	–	–	0
Monty Dumond	Sharks	2009	6	–	–	–	–	0
Bismarck du Plessis	Sharks	2005	66	7	–	–	–	35
Jannie du Plessis	Sharks	2006	65	–	–	–	–	0
Andy Goode	Sharks	2010	9	–	2	11	1	40
Alistair Hargreaves	Sharks	2009	14	–	–	–	–	0
Wiehahn Herbst	Sharks	2010	1	–	–	–	–	0
Adrian Jacobs	Sharks	2001	99	21	–	–	–	105
Ryan Kankowski	Sharks	2007	51	13	–	–	–	65
Rory Kockott	Sharks	2007	50	3	46	42	1	236
Patrick Lambie	Sharks	2010	8	2	–	–	–	10
Charl McLeod	Sharks	2008	6	–	–	–	–	0
Gerhard Mostert	Sharks	2006	27	–	–	–	–	0
Tendai Mtawarira	Sharks	2007	50	–	–	–	–	0
Johann Muller	Sharks	2003	82	2	–	–	–	10
Waylon Murray	Sharks	2006	41	5	–	–	–	25
Lwazi Mvovo	Sharks	2010	5	1	–	–	–	5
Odwa Ndungane	Sharks	2004	73	22	–	–	–	110
Ruan Pienaar	Sharks	2005	67	10	35	42	2	252
JP Pietersen	Sharks	2006	56	21	–	–	–	105
Michael Rhodes	Sharks	–	0	–	–	–	–	0
John Smit	Sharks	1999	111	7	–	–	–	35
Wilhelm Steenkamp	Bulls	2008	23	–	–	–	–	0
Andries Strauss	Sharks	2006	22	1	–	–	–	5
Riaan Swanepoel	Sharks	2009	20	–	–	–	–	0
Steven Sykes	Sharks	2007	37	5	–	–	–	25
Stefan Terblanche	Sharks	1998	105	34	–	–	1	173
Total			**1400**	**190**	**83**	**95**	**5**	**1416**

VODACOM SUPER RUGBY FINAL LOG POSITIONS

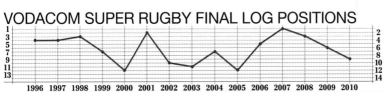

APPEARANCES AND POINTS IN 2010 SUPER 14

	Chiefs	Cheetahs	Crusaders	Waratahs	Brumbies	Highlanders	Hurricanes	Reds	Lions	Blues	Bulls	Stormers	W Force	Matches	Tries	Conversions	Penalties	Drop Goals	Points
Terblanche	15	15	15	15	15	14	14	13	13	13	13	13	13	13	1	–	–	–	5
Ndungane	14	14	14	14	14	–	12R	14	14	14	14	14	14	12	3	–	–	–	15
Murray	13	13	13	12R	14R	x	13R	–	–	–	–	–	–	6	–	–	–	–	0
Strauss	12	x	–	–	–	–	–	12R	12R	12	12R	13R	12R	7	–	–	–	–	0
Pietersen	11	11	11	11	11	11	11	11	11	11	–	–	–	10	2	–	–	–	10
Dumond	10	x	–	–	–	–	–	–	–	–	–	–	–	1	–	–	–	–	0
Kockott	9	9	9	10R	10R	10R	10R	x	10R	10R	10R	9	9	12	1	–	15	–	50
Kankowski	8	8	8	8	8	8	8	8	–	R7	8	8		11	3	–	–	–	15
Deysel	7	7	7R	5R	7R	7	7R	8R	7	7	7	6	7	13	–	–	–	–	0
Daniel	6	6R	6R	6	6R	6	–	–	–	–	8R	8R	8R	9	–	–	–	–	0
Muller	5	–	5	5	5	5	–	–	5	5	5	–	–	8	–	–	–	–	0
Sykes	4	4	4	4	4	4	4	4	4	4	4	4	4	13	–	–	–	–	0
Smit	3c	2c	3c	2c	3c	1c	1c	1c	1c	1c	2c	2c	2c	13	–	–	–	–	0
B du Plessis	2	3R	2	2R	2	2	2	2	2	2	–	–	–	10	2	–	–	–	10
Mtawarira	1	1	1	1R	1	–	1R	3R	3R	3R	1	1	1	12	–	–	–	–	0
Burden	6R	–	–	–	15R	x	–	x	8R	x	3R	3R	3R	6	–	–	–	–	0
J du Plessis	1R	3	3R	3	3R	3	3	3	3	3	3	3	3	13	–	–	–	–	0
Mostert	5R	–	–	–	–	–	–	–	–	–	–	–	–	1	–	–	–	–	0
Alberts	5R	7R	7	7	7	7R	7	7	8	8	8	7		12	–	–	–	–	0
Botes	7R	6	6	6R	6	6R	6	6	6	6	6	7R	6	13	3	–	–	–	15
Pienaar	10R	10	10	9	9	9	9	9	9	9	9	10	10	13	3	17	20	1	112
Jacobs	13R	12	12	13	13	13	13	–	–	–	–	–	–	7	2	–	–	–	10
Hargreaves	–	5	–	–	4R	5R	5	5	5R	5R	5R	5	5	10	–	–	–	–	0
Carstens	–	1R	1R	1	–	–	–	–	–	–	–	–	–	3	–	–	–	–	0
Steenkamp	–	4R	4R	4R	–	–	x	5R	x	–	–	x	5R	5	–	–	–	–	0
Goode	–	–	9R	10	10	10	10	10	10	10	10	x	x	9	–	2	11	1	40
Swanepoel	–	–	13R	12	12	12	12	12	12	12R	12	12	12	11	–	–	–	–	0
Lambie	–	–	–	–	–	15	15	15	15	15	15	15	15	8	2	–	–	–	10
Herbst	–	–	–	–	–	x	x	–	–	–	1R	–	–	1	–	–	–	–	0
Mvovo	–	–	–	–	–	–	–	x	11R	11R	11	11	11	5	1	–	–	–	5
Rhodes	–	–	–	–	–	–	–	–	x	–	–	–	–	0	–	–	–	–	0
Cilliers	–	–	–	–	–	–	–	–	–	–	–	x	1R	1	–	–	–	–	0
McLeod	–	–	–	–	–	–	–	–	–	–	–	–	9R	1	–	–	–	–	0
33 players														**269**	**23**	**19**	**46**	**2**	**297**

VODACOM SUPER 14

SHARKS SUPER 14 SQUAD AND MANAGEMENT IN 2010

BACK ROW (L to R): Waylon Murray, Jean Deysel, Willem Alberts, Steven Sykes, Wilhelm Steenkamp, Alistair Hargreaves, Ryan Kankowski, Jannie du Plessis, Bismarck du Plessis, Andries Strauss. **THIRD ROW** (L to R): Tendai Mtawarira, Clinton Isaacs (Technical), Deane Macquet (Physiotherapist), Grant Bashford (Assistant Coach), Jimmy Wright (Biokineticist), Chris Boyd (Assistant Coach), Patric Cilliers. **SECOND ROW** (L to R): Bob Russell (Masseur), Warren van Zyl (Mental Conditioning Coach), Wiehahn Herbst, Monty Dumond, Riaan Swanepoel, Craig Burden, Keegan Daniel, Lwazi Mvovo, Rory Kockott, Charl McLeod, Hugh-Reece Edwards (Assistant Coach), Mark Steele (Fitness). **FRONT ROW** JP Pietersen, Ruan Pienaar, Trevor Barnes (Manager), Adrian Jacobs, Deon Carstens, Brian van Zyl (CEO Sharks (Pty) Ltd), John Smit (Captain), John Swain (Chairman), Johann Muller, Stefan Terblanche, John Plumtree (Coach), Jacques Botes, Odwa Ndungane. **ABSENT:** Andrew Goode, Gerhard Mostert, Patrick Lambie.

THE SHARKS

SHARKS RECORDS

MATCH RECORDS

Biggest win	38	v Chiefs (63-25)	Durban	1996
Heaviest defeat	43	v Crusaders (34-77)	Christchurch	2005
Highest score	75	v Highlanders (75-43)	Durban	1997
Most points conceded	77	v Crusaders (34-77)	Christchurch	2005
Most tries	9	v Highlanders (75-43)	Durban	1997
Most tries conceded	11	v Crusaders (34-77)	Christchurch	2005
Most points by a player	50	GE Lawless (4t, 9c, 4p) v Highlanders	Durban	1997
Most tries by a player	4	GE Lawless v Highlanders	Durban	1997
	4	CS Terblanche v Chiefs	Port Elizabeth	1998
Most conversions by a player	9	GE Lawless v Highlanders	Durban	1997
Most penalties by a player	7	GE Lawless v NSW Waratahs	Durban	1997
Most drop goals by a player	2	FPL Steyn v Blues	Albany	2007

SEASON RECORDS

Most team points	453	in 13 matches	1996
Most points by a player	170	GE Lawless	1997
Most team tries	56	in 13 matches	1996
Most tries by a player	13	JT Small	1996
Most conversions by a player	26	RM Kockott	2009
Most penalties by a player	30	GE Lawless	1997
Most drop goals by a player	4	FPL Steyn	2007

CAREER RECORDS

Most appearances	111
JW Smit	1999-2008
Most points	390
AD James	2001-2007
Most tries	**34**
CS Terblanche	**1998-2009**
Most conversions	63
HW Honiball	1996-1999
AD James	2001-2007
Most penalties	74
AD James	2001-2007
Most drop goals	7
FPL Steyn	2007-2009

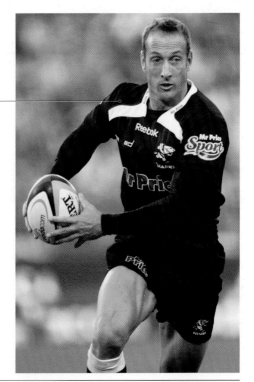

VODACOM STORMERS

GROUND Newlands
CAPACITY 49 000
ADDRESS 11 Boundary Road, Newlands, Cape Town, 7700
TELEPHONE NUMBER 021 659 4500
COLOURS Navy blue jersey, shorts and socks
WEBSITE www.iamastormer.com
COACH Allister Coetzee **CAPTAIN** Schalk Burger
CEO Rob Wagner **CHAIRMAN** Pat Kuhn

Stormers fall at final hurdle

IT all ended in disappointment against the Bulls in Soweto, but the Vodacom Stormers team of 2010 marked themselves as the most successful in the franchise's history by reaching the Vodacom Super14 final.

The closest the Stormers had previously come was in 1999, when they lost a home semifinal against the Highlanders at Newlands.

Their semifinal was a clinical 25-6 shutout of the New South Wales Waratahs at the same venue.

Whereas the '99 team was known for its attacking prowess, a mean defence was the outstanding feature of the class of 2010, conceding only 17 tries in 13 league games.

Not that the Stormers were ineffective on attack, mind you: Bryan Habana scored the try of the tournament following a sweeping counter-attack from deep in their own territory against the Chiefs in Hamilton.

However, they reserved their best performance for Newlands, thrashing a Crusaders team boasting All Black superstars Dan Carter and Richie McCaw 42-14.

Springbok flanker Schalk Burger had taken over the captaincy and the side seemed to respond particularly well to his easy-going leadership style. One genuinely got the impression that the Stormers were a team in the true sense of the word.

As far as the coaching of the team was concerned, Allister Coetzee coped with the pressures of the job better than his predecessor, Rassie Erasmus.

The latter, however, still played an important backroom role and pulled off the contracting masterstrokes that brought Habana and Bok centre Jaque Fourie to the Cape.

But for a player of the season one need not look any further than giant lock Andries Bekker. Not only did he become almost as effective as Victor Matfield in contesting lineouts, but he was immense with his work-rate around the field.

Peter Grant was also crucial at flyhalf and managed a goalkicking success ratio in excess of 80 percent, while outside of him Juan de Jongh had a breakthrough season at inside centre. Gio Aplon's form also provided a springboard into the Springbok side, while the likes of Vermeulen and hardworking tighthead prop Brok Harris could consider themselves unlucky that they were not rewarded with Springbok jerseys following their super seasons.

However, much of the Stormers' success was down to the coaching staff and squad knuckling down and doing the hard yards.

The scientific approach they took in studying referees prior to matches epitomised this and not a peep was heard in terms of complaints until after the final, when the Stormers were seething about the performance of Craig Joubert.

However, he was not to blame for the Stormers pack wilting under the onslaught and, on reflection, Coetzee will realise that too.

But while the campaign ended with a few tears, the Stormers can take a bow.

RESULTS & SCORERS

Date	Venue	Referee	Opponent	Result	Score	Scorers
Feb 13	Johannesburg	Jaco Peyper	LIONS	WON	26-13	T: Pietersen, J Fourie. C: Pietersen. P: Pietersen (4).
Feb 20	Cape Town	Keith Brown	WARATAHS	WON	27-6	T: Habana (2), F Louw. C: Pietersen (3). P: Pietersen (2).
Feb 26	Cape Town	Craig Joubert	BRUMBIES	LOST	17-19	T: P Louw. P: Pietersen (4).
Mar 6	Cape Town	Mark Lawrence	HIGHLANDERS	WON	33-0	T: D Fourie, Burger, P Louw, Habana. C: Pietersen, Grant. P: Pietersen (3).
Mar 13	Cape Town	Steve R Walsh	HURRICANES	WON	37-13	T: Harris, Vermeulen, J Fourie, Pietersen, Naqelevuki. C: Pietersen (3). P: Pietersen (2).
Mar 20	Cape Town	Chris Pollock	CHEETAHS	WON	21-8	T: Pietersen, J Fourie. C: Pietersen. P: Pietersen (2), De Waal.
Apr 2	Perth	Stuart Dickinson	W FORCE	LOST	15-16	P: Grant (5).
Apr 10	Auckland	Stuart Dickinson	BLUES	WON	33-21	T: Duvenage, J Fourie, Van Zyl. C: Grant (3). P: Grant (4).
Apr 16	Hamilton	Steve R Walsh	CHIEFS	WON	49-15	T: Bekker, Habana, D Fourie, Vermeulen, Naqelevuki, Liebenberg. C: Grant (4), De Waal. P: Grant (3).
Apr 23	Brisbane	Chris Pollock	REDS	LOST	13-16	T: Bekker. C: Grant. P: Grant (2).
Apr 30	Cape Town	Stuart Dickinson	CRUSADERS	WON	42-14	T: J Fourie (2), Naqelevuki. C: Grant (3). P: Grant (7).
May 8	Durban	Stuart Dickinson	SHARKS	LOST	14-20	T: Grant, F Louw. C: Grant (2).
May 15	Cape Town	Jonathan Kaplan	BULLS	WON	38-10	T: Habana (2), Bekker, J Fourie. C: Grant (3). P: Grant (4).
SEMI-FINAL						
May 22	Cape Town	Mark Lawrence	WARATAHS	WON	25-6	T: De Jongh. C: Grant. P: Grant (6).
FINAL						
May 29	Soweto[1]	Craig Joubert	BULLS	LOST	17-25	T: Habana, P Louw. C: Grant (2). P: Grant.

[1]*Orlando Stadium*

Played	Won	Drawn	Lost	Points for	Points against	Tries for	Tries against
15	**10**	**0**	**5**	**407**	**202**	**39**	**18**

VODACOM SUPER 14

COACHES AND MANAGEMENT

COACH Allister Coetzee **ASSISTANT COACH** Robbie Fleck & Matthew Proudfoot
DEFENCE COACH Jacques Nienaber **MANAGER** Chippie Solomon
DOCTOR Dr Ryan Kohler **FITNESS & CONDITIONING** Stephan du Toit & Greg Hechter
PHYSIOTHERAPIST Lize van Schalkwyk **TECHNICAL ANALYST** Southy Steenkamp
MASSEUR Greg Daniels **MEDIA OFFICER** Gavin Lewis

APPEARANCES AND POINTS IN SUPER RUGBY

2010 SQUAD	Province	Debut	Matches	Tries	Conversions	Penalties	Drop Goals	Points
Gio Aplon	Vodacom WP	2007	30	1	–	–	–	5
Andries Bekker	Vodacom WP	2005	62	9	–	–	–	45
Wicus Blaauw	Vodacom WP	2009	19	–	–	–	–	0
Schalk Burger	Vodacom WP	2004	74	4	–	–	–	20
Lionel Cronje	Vodacom WP	2010	2	–	–	–	–	0
Juan de Jongh	Vodacom WP	2010	13	1	–	–	–	5
Willem de Waal	Vodacom WP	2004	44	5	36	32	2	199
Dewaldt Duvenage	Vodacom WP	2009	25	2	–	–	–	10
Adriaan Fondse	Vodacom WP	2007	31	–	–	–	–	0
Deon Fourie	Vodacom WP	2008	24	3	–	–	–	15
Jaque Fourie	Vodacom WP	2003	83	31	–	–	–	155
Peter Grant	Vodacom WP	2006	62	8	86	107	0	533
Eusebio Guinazu	Vodacom WP	2010	7	–	–	–	–	0
Bryan Habana	Vodacom WP	2005	75	44	–	–	–	220
Brok Harris	Vodacom WP	2007	45	2	–	–	–	10
Ricky Januarie	Vodacom WP	2003	83	5	–	–	–	25
JC Kritzinger	Vodacom WP	2010	10	–	–	–	–	0
Tiaan Liebenberg	Vodacom WP	2006	51	3	–	–	–	15
Francois Louw	Vodacom WP	2008	35	3	–	–	–	15
Pieter Louw	Vodacom WP	2009	17	3	–	–	–	15
JD Moller	Vodacom WP	2005	53	–	–	–	–	0
Sireli Naqelevuki	Vodacom WP	2008	36	11	–	–	–	55
Joe Pietersen	Vodacom WP	2006	21	7	10	17	–	106
Hanyani Shimange	Vodacom WP	2003	33	–	–	–	–	0
De Kock Steenkamp	Vodacom WP	2010	7	–	–	–	–	0
Anton van Zyl	Vodacom WP	2007	45	2	–	–	–	10
Duane Vermeulen	Vodacom WP	2009	48	5	–	–	–	25
Frikkie Welsh	Vodacom WP	1999	51	17	–	–	–	85
Tim Whitehead	Vodacom WP	2010	10	–	–	–	–	0
Totals			**1097**	**166**	**131**	**158**	**2**	**1568**

VODACOM SUPER RUGBY FINAL LOG POSITIONS

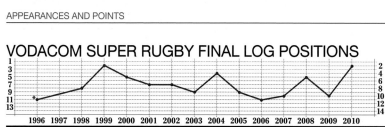

1996 1997 1998 1999 2000 2001 2002 2003 2004 2005 2006 2007 2008 2009 2010

* As Western Province

APPEARANCES AND POINTS IN 2010 SUPER 14

	Lions	Waratahs	Brumbies	Highlanders	Hurricanes	Cheetahs	W Force	Blues	Chiefs	Reds	Crusaders	Sharks	Bulls	Waratahs	Bulls	Matches	Tries	Conversions	Penalties	Drop Goals	Points
Pietersen	15	15	15	15	15	15	–	–	–	–	–	11R	15	15	15	10	3	10	17	–	86
Aplon	14	14	14	15R	11R	14	15	15	15	15	15	15	14	14	14	15	–	–	–	–	0
Fourie	13	13	13	13	13	13	13	13	13	13	13	13	13	13	13	15	7	–	–	–	35
de Jongh	12	12	12	12	12	–	–	12	12	12	12	12	12	12	12	13	1	–	–	–	5
Habana	11	11	11	11	11	11	11	11	11	11	11	–	11	11	11	14	7	–	–	–	35
Grant	10	10	10	10	10	–	10	10	10	10	10	10	10	10	10	14	1	21	32	–	141
Duvenage	9	9R	9R	9	9	9	9R	9	9	9	9	9	9	9	9	15	1	–	–	–	5
Vermeulen	8	8	8	8	8	8	8	8	8	8	8	8	8	8	8	15	2	–	–	–	10
L-FP Louw	7	7	7	7	7	7	7	7	7	7	7	7	7	7	7	15	2	–	–	–	10
Burger	6c	6c	–	6c	6c	6c	6c	6c	6c	6c	6c	6c	6c	6c	6c	14	1	–	–	–	5
Bekker	5	5	5c	5	5	5	5	5	5	5	5	5	5	5	5	15	3	–	–	–	15
Steenkamp	4	4	4	4R	4R	4R	4	–	–	–	–	–	–	–	–	7	–	–	–	–	0
Harris	3	3	3	3	3	3	3	3	3	3	3	3	3	3	3	15	1	–	–	–	5
Liebenberg	2	2	2	–	2	2	2	2	2	2	2	2	2	2	2	14	1	–	–	–	5
Blaauw	1	–	–	1	1	1	–	–	–	–	–	–	1	1	1	7	–	–	–	–	0
Fourie	2R	7R	x	2	2R	2R	2R	2R	2R	2R	2R	2R	6R	2R	2R	14	2	–	–	–	10
Kritzinger	1R	1	1	1R	1R	1R	1	–	1R	1	–	–	–	–	1R	10	–	–	–	–	0
Van Zyl	4R	4R	4R	4	4	4	4R	4R	4R	4R	5R	4R	5R	4R	4R	15	1	–	–	–	5
PJ Louw	7R	6R	6	6R	6R	7R	7R	7R	8R	x	7R	x	7R	6R	3R	13	3	–	–	–	15
Januarie	9R	9	9	9R	9R	x	9	9R	9R	9R	9R	9R	9R	9R	9R	14	–	–	–	–	0
Cronje	13R	x	x	13R	x	–	–	–	–	–	–	–	–	–	–	2	–	–	–	–	0
Naqelevuki	14R	14R	x	14	14	15R	14	14	14	14	14	–	–	–	–	11	3	–	–	–	15
Guinazu	–	3R	1R	–	–	–	1R	1R	–	–	1R	x	3R	1R	–	7	–	–	–	–	0
Myburgh	–	–	x	–	–	–	–	–	–	–	–	–	–	–	–	0	–	–	–	–	0
Shimange	–	–	–	2R	–	–	–	–	–	–	–	–	–	–	–	1	–	–	–	–	0
Whitehead	–	–	–	–	–	12	12	12R	12R	12R	11R	11	15R	11R	12R	10	–	–	–	–	0
De Waal	–	–	–	–	–	10	12R	x	10R	x	12R	x	13R	10R	x	6	–	1	1	–	5
Juries	–	–	–	–	–	x	–	–	–	–	–	–	–	–	–	0	–	–	–	–	0
Welsh	–	–	–	–	–	–	14R	–	–	–	–	–	–	–	–	1	–	–	–	–	0
Fondse	–	–	–	–	–	–	4	4	4	4	4	4	4	4	4	8	–	–	–	–	0
Moller	–	–	–	–	–	–	1	1	1R	1	1	–	–	–	–	5	–	–	–	–	0
31 players																**315**	**39**	**31**	**50**	**0**	**407**

VODACOM SUPER 14

VODACOM STORMERS SUPER 14 SQUAD AND MANAGEMENT IN 2010

VODACOM STORMERS RECORDS

MATCH RECORDS

Biggest win	38	vs. Lions (56-18)	Cape Town	2009
Heaviest defeat	61	vs. Bulls (14-75)	Pretoria	2005
Highest score	56	vs. Lions (56-18)	Cape Town	2009
Most points conceded	75	vs. Bulls (14-75)	Pretoria	2005
Most tries	8	vs. Blues (51-23)	Auckland	2004
	8	vs. Lions (56-18)	Cape Town	2009
Most tries conceded	11	vs. Blues (28-74)	Auckland	1998
Most points by a player	28	AJJ van Straaten (1t 4c 5p) vs. Hurricanes		
			Cape Town	2000
Most tries by a player	3	BJ Paulse vs. Bulls	Pretoria	2001
	3	PWG Rossouw vs. Chiefs	Hamilton	2002
Most conversions by a player	5	AJJ van Straaten vs. Crusaders	Cape Town	2001
	5	C Rossouw vs. Highlanders	Cape Town	2004
Most penalties by a player	7	JT Stransky vs. Transvaal	Johannesburg	1996
	7	AJJ van Straaten vs. Bulls	Pretoria	1999
	7	PJ Grant vs. Crusaders	Cape Town	2010
Most drop goals by a player	2	PC Montgomery vs. Cats	Johannesburg	2000

SEASON RECORDS

Most team points	407	in 15 matches	2010
Most points by a player	153	AJJ van Straaten	2001
Most team tries	39	in 15 matches	2010
Most tries by a player	11	PWG Rossouw	2002
Most conversions by a player	23	AJJ van Straaten	2000 & 2001
Most penalties by a player	34	AJJ van Straaten	1999 & 2001
Most drop goals by a player	2	PC Montgomery	2000

CAREER RECORDS

Most appearances	79	BJ Paulse	1998-2007
Most points	**533**	**PJ Grant**	**2006-2010**
Most tries	35	BJ Paulse	1998-2007
Most conversions	86	PJ Grant	2006-2010
Most penalties	107	PJ Grant	2006-2010
Most drop goals	2	PC Montgomery	1996-2002

VODACOM SUPER 14

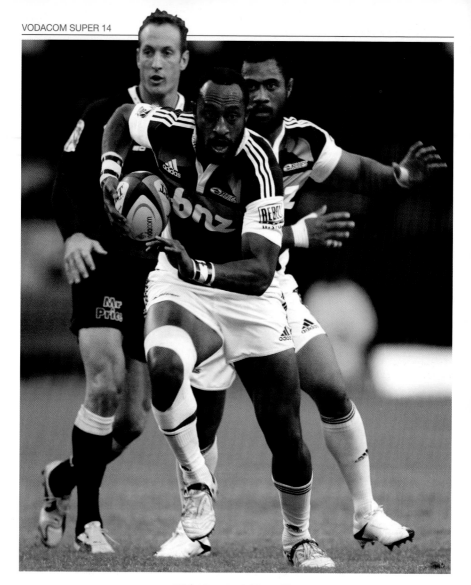

BLUES

GROUND Eden Park
CAPACITY 42 500
ADDRESS Walters Road, Mount Eden, Auckland
TELEPHONE NUMBER +64 9 815 4850
COLOURS Blue with navy sleeves and white piping, blue shorts and socks
WEBSITE www.theblues.co.nz
CAPTAIN Keven Mealamu
CEO Andy Dalton **CHAIRMAN** Greg Muir

BLUES RECORDS

MATCH RECORDS

Biggest win	53	vs. Hurricanes (60-7)	Wellington	2002
Heaviest defeat	38	vs. Queensland Reds (13-51)	Brisbane	1996
Highest score	74	vs. Stormers (74-28)	Auckland	1998
Most points conceded	63	vs. Chiefs (34-63)	Hamilton	2009
Most tries	11	vs. Stormers (74-28)	Auckland	1998
Most tries conceded	9	vs. Chiefs (34-63)	Hamilton	2009
Most points by a player	27	AR Cashmore (2t, 4c, 3p) vs. Highlanders	Auckland	1998
Most tries by a player	4	J Vidiri vs. Bulls	Auckland	2000
	4	DC Howlett vs. Hurricanes	Wellington	2002
	4	JM Muliaina vs. Bulls	Auckland	2002
Most conversions by a player	7	AR Cashmore vs. Stormers	Auckland	1998
	7	AR Cashmore vs. Bulls	Auckland	2000
	7	CJ Spencer vs. Bulls	Auckland	2002
Most penalties by a player	6	AR Cashmore vs. Chiefs	Auckland	1998
	6	AR Cashmore vs. Hurricanes	Auckland	1999
	6	JA Arlidge vs. Bulls	Auckland	2001
	6	SA Brett vs. Bulls	Auckland	2010
Most drop goals by a player	1	on nine occasions		

SEASON RECORDS

Most team points	513	in 13 matches	1997
Most points by a player	180	AR Cashmore	1998
Most team tries	70	in 13 matches	1996
Most tries by a player	12	DC Howlett	2003
Most conversions by a player	34	AR Cashmore	1998
Most penalties by a player	34	AR Cashmore	1999
Most drop goals by a player	2	O Ai'i	2000
	2	SA Brett	2010

CAREER RECORDS

Most appearances	**106**	**KF Mealamu**	**2000-2010**
Most points	619	AR Cashmore	1996-2000
Most tries	55	DC Howlett	1999-2007
Most conversions	120	CJ Spencer	1996-2005
Most penalties	114	AR Cashmore	1996-2000
Most drop goals	3	CJ Spencer	1996-2005

HONOURS
Champions
1996, 1997, 2003

RESULTS & SCORERS

Date	Venue	Referee	Opponent	Result	Score	Scorers
Feb 12	Albany	Stuart Dickinson	HURRICANES	LOST	20-34	T: Brett, Afoa. C: Brett (2). P: Brett (2).
Feb 19	Dunedin	Bryce Lawrence	HIGHLANDERS	WON	19-15	T: P Williams (2), Ranger. C: Brett (2).
Feb 26	Brisbane	Steve R Walsh	REDS	WON	27-18	T: Mathewson, Boric, Ranger, Wulf. C: Brett, Munro. P: Brett.
Mar 6	Christchurch	Keith Brown	CRUSADERS	LOST	20-33	T: Mathewson. P: Brett: (4). DG: Brett.
Mar 19	Auckland	Mark Lawrence	BRUMBIES	WON	39-34	T: Rokocoko (2), Stanley, Ranger, Toeava. C: Brett (4). P: Brett. DG: Brett.
Mar 27	Sydney	Garratt Williamson	WARATAHS	LOST	32-39	T: Ranger (2), Wulf, Toeava. C: Brett (3). P: Brett (2).
Apr 3	Auckland	Craig Joubert	BULLS	WON	32-17	T: Rokocoko, Toeava. C: Brett (2). P: Brett (6).
Apr 10	Auckland	Stuart Dickinson	STORMERS	LOST	21-33	T: Lilo, Mcalister, Rokocoko. C: Brett (3).
Apr 17	Auckland	Keith Brown	W FORCE	WON	38-17	T: Rokocoko (3), Wulf, Woodcock., Mathewson. C: McAlister (4).
Apr 24	Durban	Mark Lawrence	SHARKS	LOST	10-23	T: Saili. C: Brett. P: Brett.
May 1	Bloemfontein	Marius Jonker	CHEETAHS	LOST	32-36	T: Toeava, Ranger, Mathewson, Tuitavake. C: Brett: (3). P: Brett (2).
May 8	Johannesburg	Mark Lawrence	LIONS	WON	56-14	T: Rokocoko (2), P Williams, Ranger, Brett, Mathewson, McCartney. C: Brett (6). P: Brett (3).
May 15	Auckland	Paul Marks	CHIEFS	WON	30-20	T: Wulf (2), Mathewson, Stanley, P Williams. C: Brett. P: Brett.

Played	Won	Drawn	Lost	Points for	Points against	Tries for	Tries against
13	**7**	**0**	**6**	**376**	**333**	**47**	**32**

VODACOM SUPER 14

COACHES AND MANAGEMENT

HEAD COACH Pat Lam **ASSISTANT COACHES** Shane Howarth & Liam Barry **SCRUM COACH** Mike Casey
STRENGTH & CONDITIONING Mark Harvey **DOCTOR** Dr Stephen Kara **PHYSIOTHERAPIST** Mark Plummer
ANALYST Troy Webber **MANAGER** Ant Strachan **MEDIA OFFICER** Jo Coleman

APPEARANCES AND POINTS IN SUPER RUGBY

2010 SQUAD	Date of Birth	Height	Weight	Matches	Tries	Conversions	Penalties	Drop Goals	Points
John Afoa	16/10/1983	1.83	118	83	2	–	–	–	10
Anthony Boric	27/12/1983	2.01	108	44	3	–	–	–	15
Stephen Brett	23/11/1985	1.85	85	52	6	58	49	4	305
Tom Chamberlain	02/01/1987	1.91	101	7	–	–	–	–	0
Charlie Faumuina	24/12/1986	1.85	125	21	–	–	–	–	0
Kurtis Haiu	14/07/1984	1.95	104	46	5	–	–	–	25
Jerome Kaino	06/04/1983	1.95	103	67	4	–	–	–	20
Dan Kirkpatrick	28/08/1988	1.81	88	11	1	3	2	–	17
Serge Lilo	03/04/1985	1.83	95	35	4	–	–	–	20
Viliami Ma'afu	09/03/1982	1.88	107	13	–	–	–	–	0
Tevita Mailau	25/04/1985	1.85	115	13	–	–	–	–	0
Alby Mathewson	13/12/1985	1.73	86	49	10	–	–	–	50
Luke McAlister	29/08/1983	1.80	95	35	5	46	45	–	252
Tom McCartney	06/09/1985	1.83	101	19	1	–	–	–	5
Keven Mealamu	20/03/1978	1.80	104	117	8	–	–	–	40
Taniela Moa	11/03/1985	1.80	95	27	5	–	–	–	25
Lachie Munro	27/11/1986	1.80	85	2	–	1	–	–	2
Filo Paulo	06/11/1987	1.85	101	12	–	–	–	–	0
George Pisi	29/06/1986	1.85	98	18	–	–	–	–	0
René Ranger	30/09/1986	1.82	97	23	9	–	–	–	45
Mike Reid	22/10/1985	1.88	110	1	–	–	–	–	0
Joe Rokocoko	06/07/1983	1.88	96	78	37	–	–	–	185
Peter Saili	01/04/1988	1.92	112	21	3	–	–	–	15
Chris Smylie	22/03/1982	1.80	93	35	2	–	–	–	10
Benson Stanley	11/09/1984	1.83	95	26	3	–	–	–	15
Isaia Toeava	15/01/1986	1.80	92	63	20	3	–	–	106
Anthony Tuitavake	12/02/1982	1.83	88	55	16	–	–	–	80
Andrew van der Heijden	03/04/1984	1.98	110	4	–	–	–	–	0
Paul Williams	22/04/1983	1.88	96	43	9	–	6	–	63
Tony Woodcock	27/01/1981	1.85	116	95	5	–	–	–	25
Rudi Wulf	02/02/1984	1.83	89	43	18	–	–	–	90
Totals				**1158**	**176**	**111**	**102**	**4**	**1420**

www.theblues.co.nz

VODACOM SUPER RUGBY FINAL LOG POSITIONS

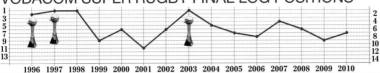

1996 1997 1998 1999 2000 2001 2002 2003 2004 2005 2006 2007 2008 2009 2010

APPEARANCES AND POINTS IN 2010 SUPER 14

	Hurricanes	Highlanders	Reds	Crusaders	Brumbies	Waratahs	Bulls	Stormers	W Force	Sharks	Cheetahs	Lions	Chiefs	Matches	Tries	Conversions	Penalties	Drop Goals	Points
RN Wulf	15	11	11	11	11	11	11	11	11	11	–	–	11	11	5	–	–	–	25
JT Rokocoko	14	14	14	14	14	14	14	14	14	14	11	14	14	13	9	–	–	–	45
I Toeava	13	13	–	–	15	15	15	15	15	15	13	15	–	10	4	–	–	–	20
BJW Stanley	12	12	12	12	12	12	12	–	13	13	12	12	12	12	2	–	–	–	10
RMN Ranger	11	13R	13	13	13	13	13	13	13R	12R	14	13	13	13	7	–	–	–	35
SA Brett	10	10	10	10	10	10	10	10	10	10	10	10	10	13	2	28	23	2	141
AS Mathewson	9	9	9	9	9	9	9	9	9	9	9	9	9	13	6	–	–	–	30
VS Ma'afu	8	8	7R	8	8	8	8	8	8	7R	8	6R	8	13	–	–	–	–	0
SF Lilo	7	7	7	7	7	7	7	7	–	7	–	7	7	11	1	–	–	–	5
J Kaino	6	6	6	6	6	6	6	6	6	6	6c	6c	–	12	–	–	–	–	0
AF Boric	5	5	5	5	5	5	5	5	–	–	4R	5	5	11	1	–	–	–	5
KT Haiu	4	4	4	4	4	4	4	4	4	4	4	4	4	13	–	–	–	–	0
IF Afoa	3	3	1	3	3	3	3	–	3	3	3	3	3	12	1	–	–	–	5
KF Mealamu	2c	2c	2c	2c	2c	2c	2c	2c	2c	2c	–	–	2c	11	–	–	–	–	0
TD Woodcock	1	1	3R	1	1	1	–	–	1	1	1	1	1	11	–	–	–	–	5
TR McCartney	x	x	x	2R	x	x	2R	x	2R	2R	2	2	2R	7	1	–	–	–	5
CC Faumuina	3R	1R	3	1R	1R	1R	1	3	–	1R	1R	3R	1R	12	–	–	–	–	0
TAM Paulo	5R	5R	4R	5R	5R	x	8R	4R	5	5	5	7R	5R	12	–	–	–	–	0
P Saili	7R	8R	8	–	7R	7R	7R	8R	7R	8	7R	8	6	12	1	–	–	–	5
CB Smylie	9R	9R	x	10R	9R	–	9R	9R	9R	x	9R	9R	9R	10	–	–	–	–	0
DPJ Kirkpatrick	10R	12R	x	14R	12R	10R	–	x	–	–	12R	12R	–	7	–	–	–	–	0
PB Williams	12R	15	15	15	15R	14R	15R	13R	15R	13R	15	11	15	13	4	–	–	–	20
LH Munro	–	–	15R	–	–	–	–	–	–	–	–	–	–	1	–	1	–	–	2
GT Pisi	–	–	–	12R	–	–	–	–	–	–	–	13R	14R	3	–	–	–	–	0
TD Chamberlain	–	–	–	6R	–	–	–	–	7	–	7	–	7R	4	–	–	–	–	0
T Moa	–	–	–	–	–	9R	–	–	–	–	–	–	–	1	–	–	–	–	0
TS Mailau	–	–	–	–	–	–	3R	1	3R	–	3R	1R	–	5	–	–	–	–	0
CL McAlister	–	–	–	–	–	–	12R	12	12	12	–	–	12R	5	1	4	–	–	13
M Reid	–	–	–	–	–	–	–	3R	–	–	–	–	–	1	–	–	–	–	0
ARD van der Heijden	–	–	–	–	–	–	–	–	4R	x	–	–	–	1	–	–	–	–	0
AT Tuitavake	–	–	–	–	–	–	–	–	–	13R	–	–	–	1	1	–	–	–	5
31 players														**274**	**47**	**33**	**23**	**2**	**376**

VODACOM SUPER 14

CHIEFS

GROUND Waikato Stadium **CAPACITY** 25 000
ADDRESS Seddon Road, Hamilton
TELEPHONE NUMBER +64 7 839 5675
COLOURS Black jersey with red and yellow panels. Black shorts and socks
WEBSITE www.chiefs.co.nz
COACH Ian Foster
CAPTAINS Mils Muliaina & Liam Messam **CEO** Gary Dawson
CHAIRMAN Graeme Elvin

CHIEFS RECORDS

MATCH RECORDS

Biggest win	38	vs. Transvaal (47-9)	Hamilton	1997
Heaviest defeat	50	vs. Cats (3-53)	Bloemfontein	2000
Highest score	72	vs. Lions (72-65)	Johannesburg	2010
Most points conceded	65	vs. Lions (72-65)	Johannesburg	2010
Most tries	9	vs. Western Force (64-36)	Hamilton	2007
	9	vs. Blues (63-34)	Hamilton	2009
	9	vs. Lions (72-65)	Johannesburg	2010
Most tries conceded	9	vs. Lions (72-65)	Johannesburg	2010
Most points by a player	32	SR Donald (1t, 9c, 3p) vs. Lions	Johannesburg	2010
Most tries by a player	4	SW Sivivatu vs. Blues	Hamilton	2009
Most conversions by a player	9	SR Donald vs. Lions	Johannesburg	2010
Most penalties by a player	6	GW Jackson vs. Queensland Reds	Rotorua	2001
	6	SR Donald vs. Crusaders	Christchurch	2007
Most drop goals by a player	1	on seven occasions		

SEASON RECORDS

Most team points	369	in 15 matches	2009
Most points by a player	164	SR Donald	2007
Most team tries	47	in 15 matches	2009
Most tries by a player	12	RQ Randle	2002
Most conversions by a player	36	SR Donald	2009
Most penalties by a player	34	SR Donald	2007
Most drop goals by a player	2	ID Foster	1996

CAREER RECORDS

Most appearances	82	MJ Collins	1999-2005
Most points	**738**	**SR Donald**	**2005-2010**
Most tries	37	SW Sivivatu	2003-2010
Most conversions	132	SR Donald	2005-2010
Most penalties	127	SR Donald	2005-2010
Most drop goals	2	ID Foster	1996-1998
	2	GW Jackson	1999-2004

RESULTS & SCORERS

Date	Venue	Referee	Opponent	Result	Score	Scorers
Feb 13	Durban	Keith Brown	SHARKS	WON	19-18	T: Willison. C: Donald. P: Donald (4).
Feb 19	Johannesburg	Marius Jonker	LIONS	WON	72-65	T: Kahui (3), Donald, Sivivatu, Messam, Poluleuligaga, Bruce, Leonard. C: Donald (9). P: Donald (3).
Feb 27	Perth	Jaco Peyper	W FORCE	WON	37-19	T: Bourke, Elliott, Masaga, Nanai-Williams. C: Donald (4). P: Donald (3).
Mar 5	Hamilton	Chris Pollock	REDS	LOST	18-23	T: Sivivatu, Taumololo, Masaga. P: Donald.
Mar 12	Hamilton	Mark Lawrence	CRUSADERS	LOST	19-26	T: Kahui. C: Donald. P: Donald (4).
Mar 26	Canberra	Jaco Peyper	BRUMBIES	LOST	23-30	T: Leonard, Kahui. C: Donald (2). P: Donald (3).
Apr 3	Mt Maunganui	Marius Jonker	HIGHLANDERS	WON	27-21	T: Taumololo, Lauaki, Donald. C: Donald (3). P: Donald (2).
Apr 9	Hamilton	Jonathan Kaplan	BULLS	LOST	19-33	T: Leonard. C: Donald. P: Donald (4).
Apr 16	Hamilton	Steve R Walsh	STORMERS	LOST	15-49	T: Latimer, Nanai-Williams. C: Donald. P: Donald.
Apr 23	Hamilton	Bryce Lawrence	CHEETAHS	DREW	25-25	T: Bourke, Sweeney, Elliott, Smith, Messam.
May 1	Wellington	Keith Brown	HURRICANES	LOST	27-33	T: Taumololo, Messam, Willison, Nanai-Williams. C: Bruce (2). P: Bruce.
May 8	Hamilton	Steve R Walsh	WARATAHS	LOST	19-46	T: Willison (2), Nanai-Williams. C: Bruce, Sweeney.
May 15	Auckland	Paul Marks	BLUES	LOST	20-30	T: Messam, Tokula. C: Renata (2). P: Renata (2).

Played	Won	Drawn	Lost	Points for	Points against	Tries for	Tries against
13	**4**	**1**	**8**	**340**	**418**	**40**	**48**

VODACOM SUPER 14

COACHES & MANAGEMENT

HEAD COACH Ian Foster **ASSISTANT COACH** Craig Stevenson **LINEOUT COACH** Keith Robinson
STRENGTH & CONDITIONING COACH Phil Healey **VIDEO ANALYST** Matt Toulson
MASSEUR Dale McClunie **DOCTOR** Dr Zig Khouri **PHYSIOTHERAPIST** Dennis Shepherd
MANAGER Stewart Williams **MEDIA OFFICER** Erin Andersen

APPEARANCES AND POINTS IN SUPER RUGBY

2010 SQUAD	Date of Birth	Height	Weight	Matches	Tries	Conversions	Penalties	Drop Goals	Points
Ben Afeaki	12/01/1988	1.93	128	11	–	–	–	–	0
Colin Bourke	15/10/1984	1.97	112	17	3	–	–	–	15
Luke Braid	05/10/1988	1.86	103	9	–	–	–	–	0
Callum Bruce	09/06/1983	1.80	90	57	8	4	3	1	60
Phil Burleigh	22/10/1986	1.83	92	2	–	–	–	–	0
Craig Clarke	01/08/1983	2.01	101	43	–	–	–	–	0
Mike Delany	15/06/1982	1.78	87	31	2	9	10	1	61
Aled de Malmanche	11/09/1984	1.85	107	46	2	–	–	–	10
Stephen Donald	03/12/1983	1.85	94	72	18	132	127	1	738
Hika Elliott	22/01/1986	1.85	114	39	5	–	–	–	25
Romana Graham	29/05/1986	2.02	116	4	–	–	–	–	0
Jarrad Hoeata	12/12/1982	1.98	112	5	–	–	–	–	0
Jason Hona	06/10/1986	1.89	102	4	–	–	–	–	0
Richard Kahui	09/06/1985	1.88	93	42	15	–	–	–	75
Vern Kamo	05/04/1986	1.83	104	5	–	–	–	–	0
Tanerau Latimer	06/05/1986	1.85	97	52	7	–	–	–	35
Sione Lauaki	22/06/1981	1.93	117	70	14	–	–	–	70
Brendon Leonard	16/04/1985	1.80	88	44	15	–	–	–	75
Lelia Masaga	30/08/1986	1.80	90	47	23	–	–	–	115
James McGougan	12/10/1984	1.83	122	16	–	–	–	–	0
Liam Messam	25/03/1984	1.90	104	63	14	–	–	–	70
Tim Mikkelson	13/08/1986	1.91	99	4	–	–	–	–	0
Tristan Moran	15/08/1983	1.80	109	1	–	–	–	–	0
Mils Muliaina	31/07/1980	1.83	92	92	28	1	–	–	142
Tim Nanai-Williams	12/06/1989	1.82	90	11	4	–	–	–	20
Kevin O'Neill	24/02/1982	2.01	110	45	0	–	–	–	0
Siale Piutau	13/10/1985	1.83	96	1	–	–	–	–	0
Junior Poluleuligaga	05/02/1981	1.84	93	21	2	–	–	–	10
Trent Renata	13/05/1988	1.80	90	2	–	2	2	–	1
Culum Retallick	05/08/1984	1.99	115	13	–	–	–	–	0
Sitiveni Sivivatu	19/04/1982	1.85	96	75	39	–	–	–	195
Toby Smith	10/10/1988	1.90	114	6	1	–	–	–	5
Dwayne Sweeney	08/08/1984	1.80	90	46	8	3	–	–	46
Sona Taumalolo	13/11/1981	1.85	110	24	4	–	–	–	20
Save Tokula	15/06/1985	1.87	96	2	1	–	–	–	5
Nathan White	04/09/1981	1.88	118	30	–	–	–	–	0
Jackson Willison	05/09/1988	1.83	94	16	5	–	–	–	25
Totals				**1066**	**218**	**151**	**142**	**3**	**1818**

VODACOM SUPER RUGBY FINAL LOG POSITIONS

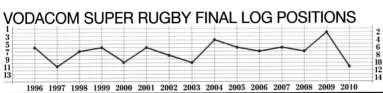

1996 1997 1998 1999 2000 2001 2002 2003 2004 2005 2006 2007 2008 2009 2010

APPEARANCES AND POINTS IN 2010 SUPER 14

	Sharks	Lions	W Force	Reds	Crusaders	Brumbies	Highlanders	Bulls	Stormers	Cheetahs	Hurricanes	Waratahs	Blues	Matches	Tries	Conversions	Penalties	Drop Goals	Points
MP Delany	15	15	15	12R	13R	11R	10	10	10	–	–	–	–	9	–	–	–	–	0
TT Nanai-Williams	14	15R	15R	–	–	11R	14R	15	15	15	15	15	15	11	4	–	–	–	20
RD Kahui	13	13	13	13	13	13	13	13	13	10R	13	13	–	12	5	–	–	–	25
JDK Willison	12	12R	14R	–	–	12	12R	x	13R	13	12	12	13	10	4	–	–	–	20
SW Sivivatu	11	11	–	11	11	11	–	–	–	11	–	–	–	6	2	–	–	–	10
SR Donald	10	10	10	10	10	10	12	12	12	10	–	–	–	10	2	22	25	–	129
BG Leonard	9	11R	9	9	9	9	9	9	9	9R	9R	9R	9	13	3	–	–	–	15
CR Bourke	8	–	8	8	8	–	8R	8R	8R	8	8	8	8	11	2	–	–	–	10
TD Latimer	7	9R	7	7	7	7	–	7	7	7	7	7	7	12	1	–	–	–	5
LJ Messam	6c	6	6c	6	6	6	6	6c	6c	6c	6c	6c	6c	13	4	–	–	–	20
KJ O'Neill	5	–	–	–	–	–	–	–	–	5R	5R	5	5R	5	–	–	–	–	0
CBJ Clarke	4	4	–	4	4	4	4	4	4	4	4	4	4	11	–	–	–	–	0
NJ White	3	3	3	3	3	3R	–	–	3R	3	3	3	–	10	–	–	–	–	0
AP de Malmanche	2	2	2R	2R	2	2	–	–	–	–	2R	2R	2	9	–	–	–	–	0
FKA Taumalolo	1	1	1	1	1	1	1	1	–	–	1	1	–	10	3	–	–	–	15
HTP Elliott	2R	2R	2	2	–	2R	2	2	2	2	2	2	2R	12	2	–	–	–	10
BTP Afeaki	3R	3R	3R	–	3R	3	3	3	3	–	3R	3R	3	11	–	–	–	–	0
JK McGougan	x	–	–	–	–	–	–	–	–	3R	–	–	–	1	–	–	–	–	0
CJ Retallick	5R	5	5	5	5R	5	5	5	5	5	5	4R	5	13	–	–	–	–	0
JMRA Hoeata	x	4R	4R	5R	–	5R	x	5R	–	–	–	–	–	5	–	–	–	–	0
AJ Poluleuligaga	9R	9	9R	9R	9R	9R	9R	x	9R	9	9	9	9R	12	1	–	–	–	5
JTA Hona	14R	–	–	–	–	–	–	–	–	x	11	11	11	4	–	–	–	–	0
DWH Sweeney	–	14	11	11R	12R	–	11	11	11	14	14	14	–	10	1	1	–	–	7
CA Bruce	–	12	12	12	12	–	–	10R	10R	12	10	10	–	9	1	3	1	–	14
ST Lauaki	–	8c	–	–	–	8	8	8	8	8R	–	–	–	6	1	–	–	–	5
LG Braid	–	7	8R	8R	6R	8R	7	–	–	–	8R	8R	8R	9	–	–	–	–	0
LCT Masaga	–	–	14	14	14	14	14	14	14	–	–	–	–	7	2	–	–	–	10
RJ Graham	–	–	4	4	5	–	–	–	5R	–	–	–	–	4	–	–	–	–	0
JM Muliaina	–	–	–	15c	15c	15c	15c	–	–	–	–	–	–	4	–	–	–	–	0
TJ Smith	–	–	–	3R	–	–	3R	1R	1	1	–	–	1	6	1	–	–	–	5
VA Kamo	–	–	–	–	2R	–	x	2R	2R	2R	–	–	–	4	–	–	–	–	0
TWK Renata	–	–	–	–	–	–	–	–	–	–	15R	–	10	2	–	2	2	–	10
PD Burleigh	–	–	–	–	–	–	–	–	–	–	x	13R	12	2	–	–	–	–	0
S Tokula	–	–	–	–	–	–	–	–	–	–	–	11R	14	2	1	–	–	–	5
TJ Mikkelson	–	–	–	–	–	–	–	–	–	–	–	–	12R	1	–	–	–	–	0
TF Moran	–	–	–	–	–	–	–	–	–	–	–	–	1R	1	–	–	–	–	0
S Piutau	–	–	–	–	–	–	–	–	–	–	–	–	11R	1	–	–	–	–	0
37 players														**278**	**40**	**28**	**28**	**0**	**340**

VODACOM SUPER 14

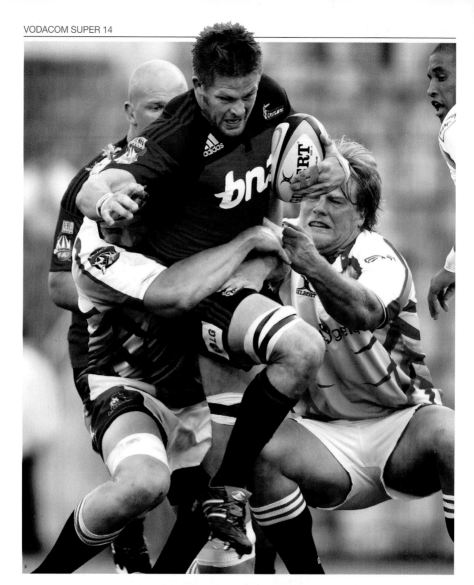

CRUSADERS

GROUND AMI Stadium **CAPACITY** 39 000
ADDRESS 30 Stevens Street, Christchurch
TELEPHONE + 64 3 379 8300
COLOURS Red jersey with black side panels. Black shorts and black socks
WEBSITE www.crusaders.co.nz
COACH Todd Blackadder **CAPTAIN** Richie McCaw
CEO Hamish Riach
CHAIRMAN Murray Ellis

CRUSADERS RECORDS

MATCH RECORDS

Biggest win	77	vs. NSW Waratahs (96-19)	Christchurch	2002
Heaviest defeat	36	vs. Queensland Reds (16-52)	Brisbane	1996
Highest score	96	vs. NSW Waratahs (96-19)	Christchurch	2002
Most points conceded	58	vs. Natal (26-58)	Durban	1996
Most tries	14	vs. NSW Waratahs (96-19)	Christchurch	2002
Most tries conceded	8	vs. Natal (26-58)	Durban	1996
Most points by a player	29	BA Blair (1t, 3c, 6p) vs. Bulls	Pretoria	2001
Most tries by a player	4	CS Ralph vs. NSW Waratahs	Christchurch	2002
Most conversions by a player	13	AP Mehrtens vs. NSW Waratahs	Christchurch	2002
Most penalties by a player	6	AP Mehrtens vs. Stormers	Christchurch	1998
	6	AP Mehrtens vs. Highlanders	Christchurch	2000
	6	BA Blair vs. Bulls	Pretoria	2001
	6	AP Mehrtens vs. Highlanders	Christchurch	2002
	6	AP Mehrtens vs. Blues	Christchurch	2002
Most drop goals by a player	3	AP Mehrtens vs. Highlanders	Christchurch	1998

SEASON RECORDS

Most team points	541	from 13 matches	2005
Most points by a player	221	DW Carter	2006
Most team tries	71	from 13 matches	2005
Most tries by a player	15	RL Gear	2005
Most conversions by a player	37	DW Carter	2005
Most penalties by a player	43	AP Mehrtens	1999
Most drop goals by a player	4	AP Mehrtens	1998, 1999, 2002

HONOURS

Champions
1998, 1999, 2000, 2002,
2005, 2006, 2008

CAREER RECORDS

Most appearances	129	RD Thorne	1996-2008
Most points	**1078**	**DW Carter**	**2003-2010**
Most tries	52	CS Ralph	1999-2008
Most conversions	183	DW Carter	2003-2010
Most penalties	202	AP Mehrtens	1996-2005
Most drop goals	17	AP Mehrtens	1996-2005

RESULTS & SCORERS

Date	Venue	Referee	Opponent	Result	Score	Scorers
Feb 13	Christchurch	Chris Pollock	HIGHLANDERS	WON	32-17	T: Ellis, Payne, Maitland, Guildford. C: Carter (3). P: Carter (2).
Feb 19	Brisbane	Craig Joubert	REDS	LOST	20-41	T: Ellis, Thorn. C: Carter (2). P: Carter (2).
Feb 26	Christchurch	Chris Pollock	SHARKS	WON	35-6	T: Guildford (2), MacDonald, A Whitelock. C: Carter (3). P: Carter (3).
Mar 06	Christchurch	Keith Brown	BLUES	WON	33-20	T: Crotty, Fruean, G Whitelock. C: Carter (3). P: Carter (4).
Mar 12	Hamilton	Mark Lawrence	CHIEFS	WON	26-19	T: Fotuali'i (2). C: Carter (2). P: Carter (4).
Mar 20	Christchurch	Garratt Williamson	LIONS	WON	46-19	T: Maitland (2), Poff, A Whitelock, Heinz. C: Slade (3). P: Slade (5).
Apr 02	Wellington	Jonathan Kaplan	HURRICANES	DREW	26-26	T: Guildford, G Whitelock, Paulo. C: Carter. P: Carter (3).
Apr 10	Christchurch	Craig Joubert	WARATAHS	WON	20-13	T: Fotuali'i. P: Carter (5).
Apr 17	Christchurch	Jonathon White	CHEETAHS	WON	45-6	T: Waldrom (2), B Franks, Fotuali'i, Crotty, Maitland, Guildford. C: Slade (5).
Apr 23	Perth	Jonathon White	W FORCE	LOST	16-24	T: Fotuali'i. C: Carter. P: Carter. DG: Fotuali'i, Carter.
Apr 30	Cape Town	Stuart Dickinson	STORMERS	LOST	14-42	T: Carter, Slade. C: Carter (2).
May 7	Pretoria	Marius Jonker	BULLS	LOST	35-40	T: Thorn, Ellis, Maitland, Paulo. C: Carter (3). P: Carter (2). DG: Carter.
May 14	Christchurch	Bryce Lawrence	BRUMBIES	WON	40-22	T: Maitland, Read, O Franks, McCaw, Guildford. C: Carter (3). P: Carter (3).
Semi-final						
May 22	Soweto [1]	Stuart Dickinson	BULLS	LOST	24-39	T: McCaw, S Whitelock, Maitland. C: Carter (3). P: Carter.

[1] Orlando Stadium

Played	Won	Drawn	Lost	Points for	Points against	Tries for	Tries against
14	**8**	**1**	**5**	**412**	**334**	**46**	**27**

VODACOM SUPER 14

COACHES & MANAGEMENT

HEAD COACH Todd Blackadder **ASSISTANT COACHES** Mark Hammett & Daryl Gibson
HIGH PERFORMANCE LEADER Steve Lancaster **ANALYST** Jamie Hamilton
PERFORMANCE CO-ORDINATOR Ashley Jones **LOGISTICS** John Miles
DOCTOR Dr Tony Page **PHYSIOTHERAPIST** Steve Muir
MANAGER Tony Thorpe **MEDIA OFFICER** Patrick McKendry

APPEARANCES AND POINTS IN SUPER RUGBY

2010 SQUAD	Date of Birth	Height	Weight	Matches	Tries	Conversions	Penalties	Drop Goals	Points
Tim Bateman	03/06/1987	1.83	85	35	4	–	–	–	20
Peter Borlase	22/05/1985	1.93	114	2	–	–	–	–	0
Daniel Bowden	01/04/1986	1.78	89	27	3	15	11	–	78
Dan Carter	05/03/1982	1.78	91	82	26	183	187	7	1078
Wyatt Crockett	24/01/1983	1.93	110	68	2	–	–	–	10
Ryan Crotty	23/09/1988	1.81	92	21	3	–	–	–	15
Andy Ellis	21/02/1984	1.83	88	58	10	–	–	2	56
Corey Flynn	15/01/1981	1.85	106	83	13	–	–	–	65
Kahn Fotuali'i	22/05/1982	1.83	94	28	6	–	–	1	33
Ben Franks	27/03/1984	1.83	110	48	1	–	–	–	5
Owen Franks	23/12/1987	1.86	112	24	2	–	–	–	10
Robert Fruean	17/07/1988	1.90	104	14	1	–	–	–	5
Zac Guildford	08/02/1989	1.83	93	32	14	–	–	–	70
Willi Heinz	24/11/1986	1.80	92	4	1	–	–	–	5
Chris Jack	05/09/1978	2.02	112	98	7	–	–	–	35
Quentin MacDonald	25/09/1988	1.80	101	2	1	–	–	–	5
Sean Maitland	14/09/1988	1.88	92	28	12	–	–	–	60
Richie McCaw	31/12/1980	1.88	104	103	24	–	–	–	120
Ti'i Paulo	13/01/1983	1.83	110	34	5	–	–	–	25
Jared Payne	13/10/1985	1.85	93	22	2	–	–	–	10
Dan Perrin	01/07/1983	1.81	104	8	1	–	–	–	5
Jonathan Poff	27/09/1983	1.86	102	8	1	–	–	–	5
Kieran Read	26/10/1985	1.93	103	55	8	–	–	–	40
Isaac Ross	27/10/1984	2.01	116	32	3	–	–	–	15
Colin Slade	10/10/1987	1.83	90	26	–	12	7	–	45
Brad Thorn	03/02/1975	1.95	111	77	11	–	–	–	55
Tu Umaga-Marshall	03/03/1983	1.91	101	1	–	–	–	–	0
Thomas Waldrom	28/04/1983	1.85	109	56	5	–	–	–	25
Joe Wheeler	12/12/1984	1.83	89	1	–	–	–	–	0
Adam Whitelock	17/04/1987	1.85	95	20	4	–	–	–	20
George Whitelock	27/03/1986	1.90	104	25	2	–	–	–	10
Sam Whitelock	10/12/1988	2.02	108	14	1	–	–	–	5
Totals				**1135**	**173**	**210**	**205**	**10**	**1930**

www.crusaders.co.nz

VODACOM SUPER RUGBY FINAL LOG POSITIONS

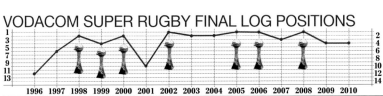

1996 1997 1998 1999 2000 2001 2002 2003 2004 2005 2006 2007 2008 2009 2010

APPEARANCES AND POINTS IN 2010 SUPER 14

	Highlanders	Reds	Sharks	Blues	Chiefs	Lions	Hurricanes	Waratahs	Cheetahs	W Force	Stormers	Bulls	Brumbies	Bulls	Matches	Tries	Conversions	Penalties	Drop Goals	Points
CR Slade	15	15	15R	14R	14R	10	15	15	15	15R	15	15	15	15	14	1	8	5	–	36
JB Payne	14	14	15	15	15	15	15R	x	14	–	x	15R	14R	15R	11	1	–	–	–	5
R Fruean	13	13	13	13	13	15R	13	13	–	13	13	13	13	13	13	1	–	–	–	5
TES Bateman	12	12	–	–	–	–	–	–	13	–	–	13R	13R	13R	6		–	–	–	0
ZR Guildford	11	11	11	11	11	11	11	11	14R	11	11	11	11	11	14	6	–	–	–	30
DW Carter	10	10	10	10	10	11R	10	10	–	10	10	10	10	10	13	1	26	30	2	153
AM Ellis	9	9	9	9	–	–	9	–	–	9R	9R	9	9	9	10	3	–	–	–	15
TR Waldrom	8	8	8	–	x	8	7R	7R	8	8	6R	6R	6R	6R	12	2	–	–	–	10
GB Whitelock	7	7	7	7	7	8R	7	7	6	8R	6	6	6	6	14	2	–	–	–	10
KJ Read	6c	6c	6c	8	8	–	8	8	–	6	8	8	8	8	12	1	–	–	–	5
IB Ross	5	5	–	5R	5	5	–	–	–	–	–	–	–	–	5		–	–	–	0
SL Whitelock	4	4	5	5	5R	4	5	4R	5	5R	5R	5R	5	5	14	1	–	–	–	5
OT Franks	3	3	3R	3	3	3	3	3	1R	3	3	1R	3	3	14	1	–	–	–	5
TT Paulo	2	2	2	2	2	2	2	2	2	2	2R	2	2	2	14	2	–	–	–	10
BJ Franks	1	1	3	–	3R	1	1R	3R	3	1	1R	3	1	1	13	1	–	–	–	5
QJRWJMacDonald	2R	x	2R	–	–	–	–	–	–	–	–	–	–	–	2	1	–	–	–	5
PW Borlase	3R	–	–	1R	–	–	–	–	–	–	–	–	–	–	2		–	–	–	0
BC Thorn	5R	4R	4	4	4	–	4	5	4R	4	4	4	4	4	13	2	–	–	–	10
JHM Poff	7R	8R	–	7R	–	7	–	–	7R	–	–	–	–	–	5	1	–	–	–	5
KF Fotuali'i	9R	x	9R	9R	9	9	9R	9	9	9	9	12R	–	9R	12	5	–	–	1	28
AJ Whitelock	x	12R	13R	12R	13R	13	x	13R	–	14	–	–	–	–	7	2	–	–	–	10
SD Maitland	14R	15R	14	14	14	14	14	14	11	15	14	14	14	14	14	7	–	–	–	35
WWW Crockett	–	3R	1	1	1	3R	1	1	1	3R	1	1	3R	3R	13		–	–	–	0
RS Crotty	–	–	12	12	12	12	12	12	12	12	12	–	–	–	9	2	–	–	–	10
JT Wheeler	–	–	4R	–	–	–	–	–	–	–	–	–	–	–	1		–	–	–	0
RH McCaw	–	–	6R	6c	6c	6c	6c	6c	7c	7c	7c	7c	7c	7c	12	2	–	–	–	10
CR Flynn	–	–	–	2R	2R	x	–	–	–	–	2	–	–	–	3		–	–	–	0
WA Heinz	–	–	–	–	9R	9R	–	x	9R	–	–	–	10R	–	4	1	–	–	–	5
CR Jack	–	–	–	–	–	5R	5R	4	4	5	5	5	4R	4R	9		–	–	–	0
DM Perrin	–	–	–	–	–	–	x	x	2R	x	–	x	2R	2R	3		–	–	–	0
DR Bowden	–	–	–	–	–	–	–	–	10	12R	13R	12	12	12	6		–	–	–	0
TP Umaga-Marshall	–	–	–	–	–	–	–	11R	–	–	–	–	–	–	1		–	–	–	0
32 players															**295**	**46**	**34**	**35**	**3**	**412**

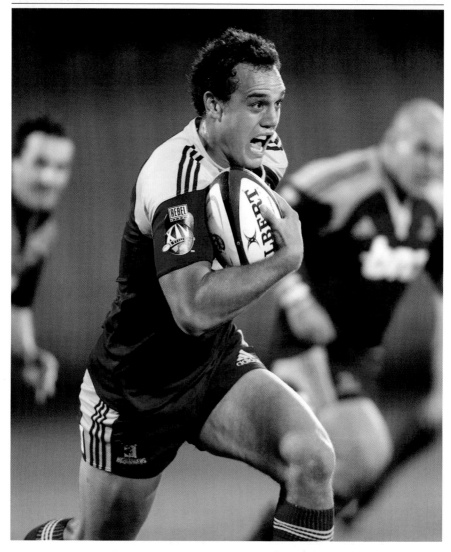

HIGHLANDERS

GROUND Carisbrook
CAPACITY 30 000
ADDRESS Burns Street, Dunedin
TELEPHONE NUMBER +64 3 446 4010
COLOURS Blue jersey with gold stripes. Blue shorts and socks
WEBSITE www.highlandersrugby.co.nz
CAPTAIN Jimmy Cowan
CEO Richard Reid **CHAIRMAN** Ross Laidlaw

HIGHLANDERS RECORDS

MATCH RECORDS

Biggest win	42	vs. Bulls (65-23)	Invercargill	1999
Heaviest defeat	44	vs. ACT Brumbies (26-70)	Canberra	1996
Highest score	65	vs. Bulls (65-23)	Invercargill	1999
Most points conceded	75	vs. Sharks (43-75)	Durban	1997
Most tries	9	vs. Bulls (65-23)	Invercargill	1999
Most tries conceded	9	vs. ACT Brumbies (26-70)	Canberra	1996
Most points by a player	28	BA Blair vs. Sharks	Durban	2005
Most tries by a player	3	TM Vaega vs. Western Province	Cape Town	1996
	3	DC Howlett vs. Chiefs	Hamilton	1997
	3	JW Wilson vs. Stormers	Cape Town	1998
	3	JC Stanley vs. Stormers	Cape Town	1998
	3	TR Nicholas vs. Bulls	Pretoria	2002
	3	BA Blair vs. Sharks	Durban	2005
	3	IJA Dagg vs. Bulls	Pretoria	2010
Most conversions by a player	7	TE Brown vs. Bulls	Invercargill	1999
Most penalties by a player	8	WC Walker vs. Chiefs	Hamilton	2003
Most drop goals by a player	1	on 16 occasions		

SEASON RECORDS

Most team points	374	from 12 matches	1998
Most points by a player	150	TE Brown	2000
Most team tries	40	from 12 matches	1998
Most tries by a player	10	JW Wilson	1998
Most conversions by a player	21	TE Brown	1999
Most penalties by a player	34	TE Brown	2000
Most drop goals by a player	2	SD Culhane	1996
	2	BJ Laney	1999
	2	NJ Evans	2005

CAREER RECORDS

Most appearances	127	AD Oliver	1996-2007
Most points	**817**	**TE Brown**	**1996-2004**
Most tries	35	JW Wilson	1996-2002
Most conversions	132	TE Brown	1996-2004
Most penalties	171	TE Brown	1996-2004
Most drop goals	5	TE Brown	1996-2004

RESULTS & SCORERS

Date	Venue	Referee	Opponent	Result	Score	Scorers
Feb 13	Christchurch	Chris Pollock	CRUSADERS	LOST	17-32	T: Hobbs (2). C: Hobbs (2). P: Hobbs.
Feb 19	Dunedin	Bryce Lawrence	BLUES	LOST	15-19	T: Hobbs, Dagg. C: Hobbs. P: Dagg.
Feb 27	Bloemfontein	Pro Legoete	CHEETAHS	WON	31-24	T: Vainikolo, Lynn, Hobbs. C: Hobbs, Dagg. P: Dagg (4).
Mar 6	Cape Town	Mark Lawrence	STORMERS	LOST	0-33	
Mar 13	Pretoria	Jonathan Kaplan	BULLS	LOST	35-50	T: Dagg (3), Boys, Robinson. C: Berquist (3), Dagg (2).
Mar 20	Dunedin	Jonathon White	SHARKS	LOST	16-30	T: Smith. C: Dagg. P: Dagg (3).
Mar 26	Dunedin	Stuart Dickinson	LIONS	WON	39-29	T: Triggs, Lynn, Penalty try. C: Dagg (3). P: Dagg (6).
Apr 3	Mt Maunganui	Marius Jonker	CHIEFS	LOST	21-27	T: Triggs, Vainikolo. C: Dagg. P: Dagg (2). DG: Robinson.
Apr 10	Queenstown	Marius Jonker	W FORCE	LOST	27-41	T: Setephano, King, Vainikolo. P: Berquist (4).
Apr 24	Dunedin	Vinny Munro	HURRICANES	LOST	31-33	T: Rutledge, Soakai, J Cowan, Smith, Murray. C: Dagg (3).
Apr 30	Invercargill	Bryce Lawrence	WARATAHS	WON	26-10	T: Thomson (2), Setephano. C: Dagg. P: Berquist (3).
May 8	Canberra	Chris Pollock	BRUMBIES	LOST	3-31	P: Dagg.
May 15	Brisbane	Steve R Walsh	REDS	LOST	36-38	T: Vainikolo (2), King, Dagg, Rutledge. C: Dagg (4). P: Dagg.

Played	Won	Drawn	Lost	Points for	Points against	Tries for	Tries against
13	**3**	**0**	**10**	**297**	**397**	**34**	**53**

VODACOM SUPER 14

COACHES & MANAGEMENT

HEAD COACH Glenn Moore **ASSISTANT COACHES** Peter Russell & Barry Matthews
SCRUM COACH Mike Cron **CONDITIONING COACH** Matt Dallow
PHYSIOTHERAPIST Karl McDonald **VIDEO ANALYST** Wayne Inch
DOCTOR Dr Sandy Webb **PHYSIOTHERAPIST** Karl McDonald
MANAGER Greg O'Brien **MEDIA OFFICER** Kate Shirtcliff

APPEARANCES AND POINTS IN SUPER RUGBY

2010 SQUAD	Date of Birth	Height	Weight	Matches	Tries	Conversions	Penalties	Drop Goals	Points
Josh Bekhuis	26/04/1986	2.00	111	26	1	–	–	–	5
Matthew Berquist	05/11/1983	1.82	88	18	1	13	15	–	76
Tim Boys	19/02/1984	1.88	92	34	1	–	–	–	5
Keith Cameron	2/3/78	1.88	110	9	–	–	–	–	0
Scott Cowan	19/06/1986	1.82	89	3	–	–	–	–	0
Jimmy Cowan	06/03/1982	1.85	93	79	8	–	–	–	40
Israel Dagg	06/06/1988	1.82	88	25	8	18	20	–	133
Tom Donnelly	01/10/1981	2.00	113	53	–	–	–	–	0
John Hardie	27/07/1988	1.83	97	11	–	–	–	–	0
Jayden Hayward	02/11/1987	1.82	88	9	–	–	–	–	0
Michael Hobbs	18/10/1987	1.87	90	17	5	5	1	–	38
Chris King	30/04/1981	1.85	114	70	6	–	–	–	30
Kenny Lynn	30/11/1982	1.82	88	18	3	–	–	–	15
Jason MacDonald	11/03/1980	1.80	106	52	3	–	–	–	15
Jamie MacKintosh	20/02/1985	1.93	127	31	–	–	–	–	0
Nasi Manu	15/08/1988	1.90	104	17	1	–	–	–	5
Peter Mirrielees	05/02/1983	1.80	108	0	–	–	–	–	0
Bronson Murray	06/11/1982	1.84	118	21	1	–	–	–	5
Clint Newland	26/03/1980	1.95	128	34	1	–	–	–	5
James Paterson	11/04/1987	1.85	98	11	–	–	–	–	0
Robbie Robinson	22/08/1989	1.81	84	9	1	–	–	1	8
Sean Romans	27/07/1985	1.76	84	11	–	–	–	–	0
Jason Rutledge	15/12/1977	1.75	100	27	4	–	–	–	20
Steven Setephano	15/08/1984	1.93	106	30	4	–	–	–	20
Jason Shoemark	02/05/1981	1.83	82	36	3	–	–	–	15
Ben Smith	01/06/1986	1.82	88	26	6	–	–	–	30
Alando Soakai	11/05/1983	1.83	101	43	2	–	–	–	10
Adam Thomson	23/03/1982	1.95	110	39	9	–	–	–	45
Hayden Triggs	22/02/1982	2.01	106	37	2	–	–	–	10
Joe Tuineau	18/08/1981	2.03	121	7	–	–	–	–	0
Fetu'u Vainikolo	30/01/1985	1.83	93	37	13	–	–	–	65
Totals				**824**	**83**	**36**	**36**	**1**	**595**

VODACOM SUPER RUGBY FINAL LOG POSITIONS

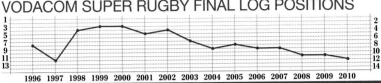

APPEARANCES AND POINTS IN 2010 SUPER 14

	Crusaders	Blues	Cheetahs	Stormers	Bulls	Sharks	Lions	Chiefs	W Force	Hurricanes	Waratahs	Brumbies	Reds	Matches	Tries	Conversions	Penalties	Drop Goals	Points
IJA Dagg	15	15	15	15	15	15	15	15	–	15	15	15	15	12	5	16	19	–	111
BR Smith	14	14	14	14	14	14	14	14	15	14	14	13	14	13	2	–	–	–	10
JL Shoemark	13	13	12	12	12	–	12R	12	12	12	12	12	12	12	–	–	–	–	0
J Hayward	12	12	–	–	–	12R	–	–	12R	–	–	14R	–	5	–	–	–	–	0
JD Paterson	11	11	11R	11R	11R	11	11	x	14	11R	13R	14	x	11	–	–	–	–	0
MW Berquist	10	–	13R	12R	10	–	–	10R	10	–	10	10	10	9	–	3	7	–	27
QJ Cowan	9c	9c	9c	9c	–	9c	9c	9c	9c	9c	9c	9c	9c	12	1	–	–	–	5
LT Manu	8	–	–	–	–	–	–	–	–	–	–	–	–	1	–	–	–	–	0
A Soakai	7	7	7	7	7	7	–	7	7	7	7	7	7	12	1	–	–	–	5
AJ Thomson	6	6	8	8	–	8	6	6	6	6	6	6	6	12	2	–	–	–	10
TJS Donnelly	5	5	5	5	5	–	–	–	–	–	–	–	–	5	–	–	–	–	0
JJG Bekhuis	4	4	4	4	4	4	4	4	4	4	4	4	4	13	–	–	–	–	0
CJ Newland	3	3	3	3	–	3	3	3	3	3	3	–	–	10	–	–	–	–	0
JK Rutledge	2	2	2	2	2R	2	2	2	2	2	2	2	2	13	2	–	–	–	10
JL MacKintosh	1	1	1	1	1c	1	1	–	–	–	–	–	3R	8	–	–	–	–	0
JM MacDonald	2R	x	x	2R	2	2R	2R	2R	2R	–	–	–	–	7	–	–	–	–	0
CC King	3R	3R	3R	–	3	3R	–	1	1	1	1	1	1	11	2	–	–	–	10
HS Triggs	4R	x	4R	5R	5R	5	5	5	5	5	5	5	5	12	2	–	–	–	10
JI Hardie	8R	8R	6	6	8R	6	7	–	–	8R	8R	8R	8R	11	–	–	–	–	0
ST Romans	9R	x	x	9R	9	x	9R	x	x	–	–	–	–	4	–	–	–	–	0
MJD Hobbs	10R	10	10	10	–	12	12	–	–	10	–	–	–	7	4	4	1	–	31
FM Vainikolo	11R	11R	11	11	11	11R	11R	11	11	11	11	11	11	13	5	–	–	–	25
SM Setephano	–	8	–	–	8	–	8	8	8	8	8	8	8	9	2	–	–	–	10
RB Robinson	–	10R	–	–	10R	10	10	10	14R	10R	10R	10R	x	9	1	–	–	1	8
KG Lynn	–	–	13	13	13	13	13	13	13	13	13	–	13	10	2	–	–	–	10
TP Boys	–	–	7R	6R	6	6R	8R	8R	8R	–	–	–	–	7	1	–	–	–	5
BI Murray	–	–	–	3R	3R	–	3R	3R	3R	3R	3R	3	3	9	1	–	–	–	5
SP Cowan	–	–	–	–	9R	–	–	–	–	x	x	x	9R	2	–	–	–	–	0
JML Tuineau	–	–	–	–	–	5R	7R	x	4R	5R	4R	4R	4R	7	–	–	–	–	0
P Mirrielees	–	–	–	–	–	–	–	–	–	x	x	x	x	0	–	–	–	–	0
KN Cameron	–	–	–	–	–	–	–	–	–	–	–	3R	–	1	–	–	–	–	0
Penalty try	–	–	–	–	–	–	–	–	–	–	–	–	–	0	1	–	–	–	5
31 players														**267**	**34**	**23**	**27**	**1**	**297**

VODACOM SUPER 14

HURRICANES

GROUND Westpac Stadium
CAPACITY 34 500
ADDRESS Waterloo Quay, Wellington
TELEPHONE NUMBER + 64 4 389 0020
COLOURS Yellow jersey with black piping, black shorts and socks
WEBSITE www.hurricanes.co.nz
COACH Colin Cooper **CAPTAIN** Andrew Hore
CEO Greg Peters **CHAIRMAN** Paul Collins

HURRICANES RECORDS

MATCH RECORDS

Biggest win	49	vs. ACT Brumbies (56-7)	Wellington	2009
Heaviest defeat	53	vs. Blues (7-60)	Wellington	2002
Highest score	64	vs. Northern Transvaal (64-32)	New Plymouth	1997
Most points conceded	60	vs. Blues (7-60)	Wellington	2002
Most tries	9	vs. Highlanders (60-34)	Wellington	1997
Most tries conceded	8	vs. Blues (7-60)	Wellington	2002
Most points by a player	30	DE Holwell (1t, 2c, 7p) vs. Highlanders	Napier	2001
Most tries by a player	3	JF Umaga vs. Northern Transvaal	New Plymouth	1997
	3	JF Umaga vs. Highlanders	Wellington	1997
	3	CM Cullen vs. Free State	Wellington	1997
	3	JD O'Halloran vs. Blues	Wellington	1998
	3	JF Umaga vs. Queensland Reds	New Plymouth	2000
	3	MA Nonu vs. ACT Brumbies	Wellington	2005
	3	HE Gear vs. Reds	Wellington	2010
	3	AK Hore vs. Chiefs	Wellington	2006
Most conversions by a player	6	CM Cullen vs. Highlanders	Wellington	1997
	6	JA Gopperth vs. Cats	Johannesburg	2005
Most penalties by a player	7	JB Cameron vs. Blues	Palmerston North	1996
	7	DE Holwell vs. Highlanders	Napier	2001
Most drop goals by a player	1	By three players		

SEASON RECORDS

Most team points	436	from 12 matches	1997
Most points by a player	152	JP Preston	1997
Most team tries	54	from 12 matches	1997
Most tries by a player	12	JF Umaga	1997
Most conversions by a player	28	JP Preston	1997
	28	DE Holwell	2003
Most penalties by a player	29	JP Preston	1997
Most drop goals by a player	1	By three players	

CAREER RECORDS

Most appearances	122	JF Umaga	1996-2007
Most points	676	DE Holwell	1998-2006
Most tries	**56**	**CM Cullen**	**1996-2003**
Most conversions	118	DE Holwell	1998-2006
Most penalties	135	DE Holwell	1998-2006
Most drop goals	1	By three players	

RESULTS & SCORERS

Date	Venue	Referee	Opponent	Result	Score	Scorers
Feb 12	Albany	Stuart Dickinson	BLUES	WON	34-20	T: Gear. C: Weepu. P: Ripia (5), Weepu (4).
Feb 20	Wellington	Vinny Munro	W FORCE	WON	47-22	T: D Smith (2), Jane, Nonu, Paterson, Tialata, Keats. C: Ripia, Weepu, Cruden. P: Ripia (2).
Feb 27	Wellington	Paul Marks	LIONS	WON	33-18	T: Hore, D Smith, Paterson, Weepu. C: Weepu, Ripia. P: Ripia (3).
Mar 6	Bloemfontein	Bryce Lawrence	CHEETAHS	LOST	12-28	T: D Smith, Jane. C: Ripia.
Mar 13	Cape Town	Steve R Walsh	STORMERS	LOST	13-37	T: D Smith, Keats. P: Ripia.
Mar 19	Pretoria	Steve R Walsh	BULLS	LOST	18-19	T: Lowe, Thrush. C: Ripia. P: Ripia (2).
Mar 27	Wellington	Ian Smith	SHARKS	LOST	26-29	T: Vito, Nonu. C: Weepu (2). P: Ripia (2), Weepu (2).
Apr 2	Wellington	Jonathan Kaplan	CRUSADERS	DREW	26-26	T: Nonu, Thrush. C: Ripia (2). P: Weepu (4).
Apr 16	Canberra	Jonathan Kaplan	BRUMBIES	WON	23-13	T: Vito, C Smith. C: Cruden (2). P: Cruden (3).
Apr 24	Dunedin	Vinny Munro	HIGHLANDERS	WON	33-31	T: Paterson, Lowe, Keats, Cruden, Nonu. C: Cruden (3), Weepu.
May 1	Wellington	Keith Brown	CHIEFS	WON	33-27	T: Nonu (2), Jane, Tialata. C: Cruden, Weepu. P: Cruden (2), Weepu.
May 7	Wellington	Bryce Lawrence	REDS	WON	44-21	T: Gear (3), Jane, T Ellison, D Smith. C: Weepu (4). P: Weepu (2).
May 14	Sydney	Chris Pollock	WARATAHS	LOST	16-32	T: D Smith. C: Weepu. P: Weepu (3).

Played	Won	Drawn	Lost	Points for	Points against	Tries for	Tries against
13	**7**	**1**	**5**	**358**	**323**	**40**	**37**

VODACOM SUPER 14

COACHES & MANAGEMENT

COACH: Colin Cooper **ASSISTANT COACH:** Jonathan Phillips **VIDEO ANALYSTS:** Doug Neilson
CONDITIONING COACHES: Andrew Beardmore & David Gray **DOCTOR:** Dr Ian Murphy
TECHNICAL ADVISORS: Alama Ieremia & Greg Feek **PHYSIOTHERAPIST:** Kev McQuoid
MANAGER: Tony Ward **OPERATIONS MANAGER:** Tony Bedford **MEDIA OFFICER:** Sam Rossiter-Stead

APPEARANCES AND POINTS IN SUPER RUGBY

2010 SQUAD	Date of Birth	Height	Weight	Matches	Tries	Conversions	Penalties	Drop Goals	Points
James Broadhurst	12/01/1987	2.03	112	2	–	–	–	–	0
Dane Coles	12/10/1986	1.84	103	18	1	–	–	–	5
Nick Crosswell	03/04/1986	1.95	110	9	–	–	–	–	0
Aaron Cruden	08/01/1989	1.78	79	13	1	7	5	–	34
Chris Eaton	29/03/1984	7.75	94	0	–	–	–	–	0
Jason Eaton	21/08/1982	2.03	108	49	8	–	–	–	40
Jacob Ellison	25/02/1985	1.88	103	30	–	–	–	–	0
Tamati Ellison	01/04/1983	1.85	93	54	7	–	–	–	35
Bryn Evans	28/10/1984	1.96	115	27	–	–	–	–	0
Hosea Gear	16/03/1984	1.88	100	58	20	–	–	–	100
Andrew Hore	13/09/1978	1.83	108	97	18	–	–	–	90
Cory Jane	08/02/1983	1.83	83	47	12	–	–	–	60
Jason Kawau	02/05/1981	1.75	98	21	3	–	–	–	15
Tyson Keats	06/06/1981	1.75	85	13	3	–	–	–	15
Alapati Leiua	21/09/1988	1.85	91	3	–	–	–	–	0
Karl Lowe	17/09/1984	1.81	109	23	2	–	–	–	10
Ma'a Nonu	21/05/1982	1.83	100	98	40	–	–	–	200
Michael Paterson	09/05/1985	1.95	96	35	3	–	–	–	15
Anthony Perenise	18/10/1982	1.82	118	16	–	–	–	–	0
William Ripia	20/08/1985	1.78	81	30	1	30	29	–	152
John Schwalger	28/09/1983	1.88	120	61	2	–	–	–	10
Conrad Smith	12/10/1981	1.85	93	59	9	–	–	–	45
David Smith	10/12/1985	1.86	90	41	14	–	–	–	70
Rodney So'oialo	03/10/1979	1.90	105	101	10	–	–	–	50
Andre Taylor	11/01/1988	1.78	85	5	–	–	–	–	0
Jeremy Thrush	19/04/1985	1.98	109	37	5	–	–	–	25
Neemiah Tialata	15/07/1982	1.88	116	86	3	–	–	–	15
Victor Vito	27/03/1987	1.93	109	19	3	–	–	–	15
Scott Waldrom	25/07/1980	1.80	98	31	3	–	–	–	15
Piri Weepu	07/09/1983	1.78	92	79	4	46	46	–	250
Totals				**1162**	**172**	**83**	**80**	**0**	**1266**

VODACOM SUPER RUGBY FINAL LOG POSITIONS

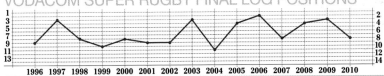

1996 1997 1998 1999 2000 2001 2002 2003 2004 2005 2006 2007 2008 2009 2010

APPEARANCES AND POINTS IN 2010 SUPER 14

	Blues	W Force	Lions	Cheetahs	Stormers	Bulls	Sharks	Crusaders	Brumbies	Highlanders	Chiefs	Reds	Waratahs	Matches	Tries	Conversions	Penalties	Drop Goals	Points
CS Jane	15	15	15	15	15	–	15	15	15	15	15	15	15	12	4	–	–	–	20
TE Ellison	14	14	14	–	14	14	14	–	14	14	14	14	14	11	1	–	–	–	5
CG Smith	13	13	13	–	13	13	13	13	13	13	13	–	13	11	1	–	–	–	5
MA Nonu	12	12	12	12	12	12	12	12	12	12	12	12	12	13	6	–	–	–	30
HE Gear	11	–	–	–	–	–	–	11	11	11	11	11	11	7	4	–	–	–	20
WKN Ripia	10	10	10	10R	10	10	10	10	x	–	–	10R	–	9	–	6	15	–	57
PAT Weepu	9	9	9	9	9	9R	9R	9	–	9R	9R	9	9	12	1	12	16	–	77
VVJ Vito	8	8	–	6	6	6	6	6	6	6	6	–	–	10	2	–	–	–	10
SL Waldrom	7	7	7R	7R	7	–	–	7R	–	–	–	7R	7R	8	–	–	–	–	0
NJ Crosswell	6	–	5R	–	–	6R	8R	–	7	8R	8R	6R	4R	9	–	–	–	–	0
JJ Eaton	5	–	5	–	–	–	–	–	–	–	–	–	–	2	–	–	–	–	0
MJS Paterson	4	6	6	5	5	5	5	5	5	5	5	6	6	13	3	–	–	–	15
NS Tialata	3	3	3	3	3	3	3	3	3	3	3	3	3	13	2	–	–	–	10
AK Hore	2c	2c	2c	2c	2c	2c	2c	2c	2c	2c	2c	2c	2c	13	1	–	–	–	5
JE Schwalger	1	1	1	1	3R	1	1	1	1	1	1	3R	1	13	–	–	–	–	0
DS Coles	x	2R	2R	x	2R	2R	x	x	2R	2R	2R	2R	2R	9	–	–	–	–	0
JO Ellison	3R	1R	3R	–	1	1R	1R	–	3R	1R	1R	1	1R	11	–	–	–	–	0
BR Evans	6R	4	4	4	4	4R	4R	8R	4R	4	4	5	5	13	–	–	–	–	0
KW Lowe	7R	7R	7	7	7R	7	7	7	–	7	7	7	7	12	2	–	–	–	10
TP Keats	x	9R	x	9R	9R	9	9	x	9	9	9	9R	10R	10	3	–	–	–	15
AW Cruden	10R	10R	10R	10	10R	10R	10R	10R	10	10	10	10	10	13	1	7	5	–	34
D Smith	11R	11	11	11	11	11R	14R	–	14R	14R	–	13R	14R	11	7	–	–	–	35
JP Broadhurst	–	5	–	–	–	–	–	–	7R	–	–	–	–	2	–	–	–	–	0
R So'oialo	–	5R	8	8	8	8	8	8	8	8	8	8	8	12	–	–	–	–	0
AS Taylor	–	15R	–	14	–	15	11	14	–	–	x	–	–	5	–	–	–	–	0
A Leiua	–	–	–	13	15R	11	–	–	–	–	–	–	–	3	–	–	–	–	0
JI Thrush	–	–	–	5R	4R	4	4	4	4	4R	4R	4	4	10	2	–	–	–	10
MJS Perenise	–	–	–	3R	–	–	–	1R	–	–	–	–	–	2	–	–	–	–	0
JM Kawau	–	–	–	–	–	–	x	–	12R	13R	13	18R		4	–	–	–	–	0
C Eaton	–	–	–	–	–	–	x	–	–	–	–	–	–	0	–	–	–	–	0
30 players														**273**	**40**	**25**	**36**	**0**	**358**

ACT BRUMBIES

GROUND Canberra Stadium **CAPACITY** 27 000
ADDRESS Battye St, Bruce ACT
TELEPHONE NUMBER +61 2 6260 8588
COLOURS Navy blue jersey with gold trim and white sides, navy shorts and socks
WEBSITE www.brumbies.com.au
COACH Andy Friend **CAPTAIN** Stephen Hoiles
CEO Andrew Fagan **CHAIRMAN** Sean Hammond

ACT BRUMBIES RECORDS

MATCH RECORDS

Biggest win	64	vs. Bulls (73-9)	Canberra	1999
	64	vs. Cats (64-0)	Canberra	2000
Heaviest defeat	49	vs. Hurricanes (07-56)	Wellington	2009
Highest score	73	vs. Bulls (73-9)	Canberra	1999
Most points conceded	56	vs. Hurricanes (07-56)	Wellington	2009
Most tries	10	vs. Bulls (73-9)	Canberra	1999
	10	vs. Cats (64-16)	Canberra	2002
	10	vs. Cats (68-28)	Canberra	2004
Most tries conceded	8	vs. Hurricanes (07-56)	Wellington	2009
Most points by a player	25	SA Mortlock (1t 4c 4p) vs. Stormers	Canberra	2001
	25	JWC Roff (1t 7c 2p) vs. Chiefs	Canberra	2003
Most tries by a player	4	JWC Roff vs. Sharks	Manuka	1996
Most conversions by a player	9	JWC Roff vs. Cats	Canberra	2004
Most penalties by a player	6	J Huxley vs. Highlanders	Canberra	2002
Most drop goals by a player	1	on 20 occasions		

SEASON RECORDS

Most team points	487	in 13 matches	2004
Most points by a player	194	SA Mortlock	2000
Most team tries	67	in 13 matches	2004
Most tries by a player	15	JWC Roff	1997
Most conversions by a player	51	JWC Roff	2004
Most penalties by a player	32	SA Mortlock	2000
Most drop goals by a player	2	GM Gregan	2001
	2	SJ Larkham	2001 & 2002
	2	CP Lealiifano	2009

CAREER RECORDS

Most appearances	136	GM Gregan	1996-2007
Most points	**1019**	**SA Mortlock**	**1998-2010**
Most tries	57	JWC Roff	1996-2004
Most conversions	161	SA Mortlock	1998-2010
Most penalties	144	SA Mortlock	1998-2010
Most drop goals	5	SJ Larkham	

HONOURS
Champions
2001, 2004

RESULTS & SCORERS

Date	Venue	Referee	Opponent	Result	Score	Scorers
Feb 12	Perth	Steve R Walsh	W FORCE	**WON**	24-15	T: Valentine, Moore, Edmonds. C: Mortlock 3. P: Mortlock.
Feb 20	Pretoria	Mark Lawrence	BULLS	LOST	32-50	T: G Smith, McCabe, Elsom. C: Mortlock. P: Mortlock (4). DG: Giteau
Feb 26	Cape Town	Craig Joubert	STORMERS	**WON**	19-17	T: G Smith. C: Giteau. P: Giteau (4)
Mar 5	Canberra	Steve R Walsh	LIONS	**WON**	24-13	T:Lealiifano, Moore, Penalty try. C: Giteau (3). P: Giteau.
Mar 13	Canberra	Garratt Williamson	SHARKS	**WON**	24-22	T: Alexander (2). C: Giteau. P: Giteau (4).
Mar 19	Auckland	Mark Lawrence	BLUES	LOST	34-39	T: Ma'afu, Edmonds, Phibbs. C: Giteau (2). P: Giteau (5).
Mar 26	Canberra	Jaco Peyper	CHIEFS	**WON**	30-23	T: Valentine, Toomua, Hooper. C: Giteau (3). P: Giteau (3).
Apr 10	Canberra	Bryce Lawrence	CHEETAHS	**WON**	61-15	T: Alexander (2), Elsom, Hoiles, Phibbs, Toomua, Ashley-Cooper, T Smith, Mafi. C: Giteau (6), Huxley (2).
Apr 16	Canberra	Jonathan Kaplan	HURRICANES	LOST	13-23	T: Giteau, Phibbs. P: Giteau.
Apr 24	Sydney	Steve R Walsh	WARATAHS	LOST	12-19	P: Giteau (4).
May 1	Canberra	Chris Pollock	REDS	**WON**	32-12	T: Alexander (2), Chisholm, Valentine. C: Giteau (3). P: Giteau (2).
May 8	Canberra	Chris Pollock	HIGHLANDERS	**WON**	31-3	T: Elsom, Ma'afu, Valentine, Toomua. C: Giteau (4). P: Giteau.
May 14	Christchurch	Bryce Lawrence	CRUSADERS	LOST	22-40	T: T Smith, Alexander, Edmonds. C: Giteau (2). P: Giteau.

Played	Won	Drawn	Lost	Points for	Points against	Tries for	Tries against
13	**8**	**0**	**5**	**358**	**291**	**40**	**25**

VODACOM SUPER 14

COACHES & MANAGEMENT
COACH Andy Friend **ASSISTANT COACH** Tony Rea **FORWARDS COACH** Owen Finegan **SCRUM COACH** Bill Young **KICKING COACH** Adam Friend **MANAGER** Rob McQuade **PERFORMANCE ANALYST** Daniel McFarlane **DOCTOR** Dr Angus Bathgate **PHYSIOTHERAPIST** Tim McGrath & Ed Hollis **HEAD STRENGTH & CONDITIONING** Rod Lindsell **STRENGTH & CONDITIONING** Marcus Kain **SOFT TISSUE THERAPISTS** Steve Reynolds, Richard Martensz, Casey Weber, Jodie Mills & Nicole Punch **ASSISTANT MANAGER** Garry Quinlivan **CAREER AND EDUCATION ADVISER** Sue Crawford **ADMINISTRATION ASSISTANT** Mary Robinson **MEDIA OFFICER** Nick Smith

APPEARANCES AND POINTS IN SUPER RUGBY

2010 SQUAD	Date of Birth	Height	Weight	Matches	Tries	Conversions	Penalties	Drop Goals	Points
Ben Alexander	14/11/1988	1.88	116	32	11	–	–	–	55
Adam Ashley-Cooper	28/03/1988	1.83	96	62	13	–	–	–	65
Mitchell Chapman	16/03/1987	1.98	108	58	4	–	–	–	20
Mark Chisholm	19/09/1985	1.98	110	89	17	–	–	–	85
Robbie Coleman	03/08/1990	1.79	83	1	–	–	–	–	0
Huia Edmonds	21/10/1985	1.83	105	39	4	–	–	–	20
Rocky Elsom	14/02/1983	1.95	104	78	13	–	–	–	65
Colby Faingaa	31/03/1991	1.82	95	6	–	–	–	–	0
Francis Fainifo	26/11/1987	1.90	97	39	5	–	–	–	25
Matt Giteau	29/09/1982	1.78	83	89	29	93	81	2	580
Ben Hand	24/04/1982	1.96	114	36	–	–	–	–	0
Justin Harrison	20/04/1974	2.01	113	96	1	–	–	–	5
Stephen Hoiles	14/10/1985	1.90	96	77	8	–	–	–	40
Michael Hooper	29/10/1990	1.82	97	5	1	–	–	–	5
Julian Huxley	04/08/1983	1.85	89	58	8	39	51	1	274
Brackin Karauria-Henry	31/07/1988	1.82	97	2	–	–	–	–	0
Christian Lealiifano	25/09/1991	1.80	89	28	7	–	–	2	41
Salesi Ma'afu	23/03/1987	1.83	122	42	3	–	–	–	15
Alfi Mafi	08/06/1988	1.85	86	16	1	–	–	–	5
Pat McCabe	21/03/1988	1.85	90	13	1	–	–	–	5
Stephen Moore	20/01/1983	1.90	112	72	4	–	–	–	20
Stirling Mortlock	21/05/1981	1.90	98	123	53	161	144	–	1019
Patrick Phibbs	17/10/1985	1.80	88	57	7	–	–	–	35
Guy Shepherdson	18/02/1986	1.85	115	70	–	–	–	–	0
Andrew Smith	10/01/1985	1.93	105	5	–	–	–	–	0
George Smith	15/07/1984	1.80	101	128	17	–	–	–	85
Tyrone Smith	13/05/1987	1.78	90	38	5	–	–	–	25
James Stannard	21/02/1983	1.73	82	12	1	–	–	–	5
Ed Stubbs	02/02/1989	1.84	97	3	–	–	–	–	0
Matt Toomua	03/01/1994	1.83	88	20	3	1	–	1	20
Josh Valentine	22/02/1983	1.76	78	74	9	–	–	–	45
Henry Vanderglas	09/05/1985	1.92	103	3	–	–	–	–	0
Jerry Yanuyanutawa	04/10/1985	1.83	114	4	–	–	–	–	0
Totals				1475	225	294	276	6	2559

VODACOM SUPER RUGBY FINAL LOG POSITIONS

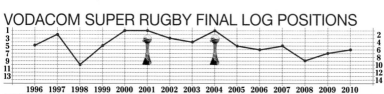

```
1                                                                    2
3                                                                    4
5                                                                    6
7                                                                    8
9                                                                    10
11                                                                   12
13                                                                   14
  1996 1997 1998 1999 2000 2001 2002 2003 2004 2005 2006 2007 2008 2009 2010
```

APPEARANCES AND POINTS IN 2010 SUPER 14

	W Force	Bulls	Stormers	Lions	Sharks	Blues	Chiefs	Cheetahs	Hurricanes	Waratahs	Reds	Highlanders	Crusaders	Matches	Tries	Conversions	Penalties	Drop Goals	Points
AP Ashley-Cooper	15	15	15	15	15	15	15	11	13	11	15	15	11	13	1	–	–	–	5
P McCabe	14	14	14	14	14	14	14	14	14	14	14	14	14	13	1	–	–	–	5
SA Mortlock	13	13	13	13	13	–	13	–	–	–	–	–	–	6	–	4	5	–	23
CP Lealiifano	12	12	12	12	12	12	–	–	–	–	–	–	–	6	1	–	–	–	5
FP Fainifo	11	11	11	11	11	11	11	–	–	–	–	–	–	7	–	–	–	–	0
MP Toomua	10	10R	x	x	x	12R	10	10	–	–	–	10	10	7	3	–	–	–	15
JJ Valentine	9	9	9	9	9	9	9	–	–	9	9	9	9	11	4	–	–	–	20
SA Hoiles	8c	8c	8c	8c	8c	8c	8c	8c	8c	8c	8c	8c	8c	13	1	–	–	–	5
GB Smith	7	7	7	7	7	7	–	–	–	–	–	7	7	8	2	–	–	–	10
MJ Chapman	6	5R	8R	6R	x	7R	4	4	–	4	4	4	4	11	–	–	–	–	0
MD Chisholm	5	5	5	5	5	5	5R	4R	5	5	5	5	5	13	1	–	–	–	5
JBG Harrison	4	4	4R	5R	x	5R	–	–	4R	–	–	–	–	6	–	–	–	–	0
GT Shepherdson	3	3R	x	3R	x	–	–	3R	x	x	–	–	–	4	–	–	–	–	0
ST Moore	2	2	2	2	2	2	2	2	2	2	2	2	2	13	2	–	–	–	10
BE Alexander	1	1	1	1	1	1	1	1	1	1	1	1	1	13	7	–	–	–	35
H Edmonds	2R	2R	2R	2R	2R	2R	2R	2R	2R	2R	2R	2R	2R	13	3	–	–	–	15
SL Ma'afu	3R	3	3	3	3	3	3	3	3	3	3	3	3	13	2	–	–	–	10
BT Hand	5R	4R	4	4	4	4	5	5	4	4R	5R	5R	5R	13	–	–	–	–	0
H Vanderglas	x	–	–	–	–	–	–	–	–	–	–	–	–	0	–	–	–	–	0
P Phibbs	9R	9R	9R	9R	x	9R	9R	9	9	9R	9R	9R	9R	12	3	–	–	–	15
TB Smith	11R	11R	x	11R	13R	13	13R	13	12	12	12	13	13	12	2	–	–	–	10
A Mafi	x	–	–	–	–	–	–	11	11	15R	–	–	–	3	1	–	–	–	5
MJ Giteau	–	10	10	10	10	10	12	12	10	10	10	12	12	12	1	25	26	1	136
RD Elsom	–	6	6	6	6	6	6	6	6	6	6	6	6	12	3	–	–	–	15
J Yanuyanutawa	–	–	–	–	–	3R	–	–	–	–	1R	3R	3R	4	–	–	–	–	0
A Smith	–	–	–	–	–	11R	–	–	x	13	13	11	15R	5	–	–	–	–	0
M Hooper	–	–	–	–	–	–	7	7	7	7R	7R	–	–	5	1	–	–	–	5
JL Huxley	–	–	–	–	–	–	11R	15	15	15	–	–	15	5	–	2	–	–	4
FP Faingaa	–	–	–	–	–	–	7R	7R	7R	7	7	7R	x	6	–	–	–	–	0
JM Stannard	–	–	–	–	–	–	–	10R	x	–	–	–	–	1	–	–	–	–	0
E Stubbs	–	–	–	–	–	–	12R	–	–	11R	12R	–	–	3	–	–	–	–	0
B Karauria-Henry	–	–	–	–	–	–	–	–	x	22R	11	x	x	2	–	–	–	–	0
RJ Coleman	–	–	–	–	–	–	–	–	–	–	15R	–	–	1	–	–	–	–	0
Penalty try	–	–	–	–	–	–	–	–	–	–	–	–	–	0	1	–	–	–	5
33 players														**266**	**40**	**31**	**31**	**1**	**358**

NSW WARATAHS

GROUND Sydney Football Stadium
CAPACITY 44 000
ADDRESS Driver Avenue, Moore Park
TELEPHONE NUMBER + 61 2 8354 3300
COLOURS Sky blue jersey with navy collar, navy shorts and sky blue socks
WEBSITE www.waratahs.com.au
COACH Chris Hickey **CAPTAIN** Phil Waugh
CEO Jim L'Estrange **CHAIRMAN** Edwin Zemancheff

NSW WARATAHS RECORDS

Biggest win	46	vs. Bulls (53-7)	Sydney	2001
	61	vs. Lions (73-12)	Sydney	2010
Heaviest defeat	77	vs. Crusaders (19-96)	Christchurch	2002
Highest score	53	vs. Bulls (53-7)	Sydney	2001
	73	vs. Lions (73-12)	Sydney	2010
Most points conceded	96	vs. Crusaders (19-96)	Christchurch	2002
Most tries	8	vs. Bulls (51-19)	Pretoria	2002
	11	vs. Lions (73-12)	Sydney	2010
Most tries conceded	14	vs. Crusaders (19-96)	Christchurch	2002
Most points by a player	34	PG Hewat (3t 2c 5p) vs. Bulls	Sydney	2005
	4	DA Mitchell vs. Lions	Sydney	2010
Most tries by a player	3	A Murdoch vs. Hurricanes	Sydney	1996
	3	MC Burke vs. Northern Transvaal	Sydney	1997
	3	S Taupeaafe vs. Sharks	Sydney	1998
	3	SNG Staniforth vs. Chiefs	Rotorua	2002
	3	PG Hewat vs. Bulls	Sydney	2005
Most conversions by a player	9	BS Barnes	Sydney	2010
Most penalties by a player	7	MC Burke vs. Blues	Sydney	2001
Most drop goals by a player	1	on eleven occasions		

SEASON RECORDS

Most team points	391	from 14 matches	2010
Most points by a player	191	PG Hewat	2006
Most team tries	45	from 14 matches	2010
Most tries by a player	10	PG Hewat	2005
Most conversions by a player	31	MC Burke	2002
Most penalties by a player	36	PG Hewat	2000
Most drop goals by a player	**3**	**BS Barnes**	**2010**

CAREER RECORDS

Most appearances	123	PR Waugh	2000-2010
Most points	959	MC Burke	1996-2004
Most tries	29	LD Tuqiri	2003-2009
Most conversions	160	MC Burke	1996-2004
Most penalties	173	MC Burke	1996-2004
Most drop goals	3	KJ Beale	2007-2010
	3	BS Barnes	2010

RESULTS & SCORERS

Date	Venue	Ref	Opponent	Result	Score	Scorers
Feb 13	Brisbane	Craig Joubert	REDS	WON	30-28	T: Sidey, Palu. C: Halangahu. P: Barnes (4), Halangahu. DG: Barnes.
Feb 20	Cape Town	Keith Brown	STORMERS	LOST	6-27	P: Barnes (2).
Feb 27	Pretoria	Marius Jonker	BULLS	LOST	38-48	T: Mowen, Mitchell, Turner, Polota-Nau. C: Barnes (2), Beale. P: Barnes (3). DG: Barnes.
Mar 6	Sydney	Paul Marks	SHARKS	WON	25-21	T: Halangahu, Polota-Nau, Carter. C: Barnes (2). P: Barnes (2).
Mar 12	Sydney	Vinny Munro	LIONS	WON	73-12	T: Mitchell (4), Turner (2), Holmes (2), Mumm, Carter, Palu. C: Barnes (9).
Mar 20	Perth	Jaco Peyper	W FORCE	WON	14-10	T: Mitchell. P: Halangahu (2), Barnes.
Mar 27	Sydney	Garratt Williamson	BLUES	WON	39-32	T: Halangahu (2), Polota-Nau, Mumm, Turner. C: Halangahu (4). P: Halangahu (2).
Apr 3	Sydney	Keith Brown	CHEETAHS	WON	40-17	T: Baxter, Robinson, Horne, Beale, Holmes. C: Halangahu (2), Barnes. P: Halangahu (3).
Apr 10	Christchurch	Craig Joubert	CRUSADERS	LOST	13-20	T: Horne. C: Halangahu. P: Halangahu, Barnes.
Apr 24	Sydney[1]	Steve R Walsh	BRUMBIES	WON	19-12	T: Turner. C: Halangahu. P: Halangahu (4).
Apr 30	Invercargill	Bryce Lawrence	HIGHLANDERS	LOST	10-26	T: Beale. C: Halangahu. P: Halangahu.
May 8	Hamilton	Steve R Walsh	CHIEFS	WON	46-19	T: Waugh, Mowen, Barnes, Mitchell, Turner, Beale, Fitzpatrick. C: Barnes (2), Halangahu (2).Barnes.
May 14	Sydney	Chris Pollock	HURRICANES	WON	32-16	T: Beale (2), Mitchell (2). C: Barnes (3). P: Barnes (2).
SEMI-FINAL						
May 22	Cape Town	Mark Lawrence	STORMERS	LOST	6-25	P: Barnes. DG: Barnes.

[1] ANZ Stadium

Played	Won	Drawn	Lost	Points for	Points against	Tries for	Tries against
14	**9**	**0**	**5**	**391**	**313**	**45**	**32**

VODACOM SUPER 14

WARATAHS

COACHES & MANAGEMENT

HEAD COACH Chris Hickey **ASSISTANT COACHES** Michael Foley & Scott Wisemantel
KICKING COACH Matt Burke **ANALYST** Anthony Wakeling **PERFORMANCE MANAGER** Peter McDonald
DOCTOR Dr Sharron Flahive **PHYSIOTHERAPIST** Keiran Cleary **STRENGTH & CONDITIONING** Tom Tomleson
MANAGER Chris Webb **ASSISTANT TEAM MANAGER** Nick Verhelst **MEDIA OFFICER** Brett Moore

APPEARANCES AND POINTS IN SUPER RUGBY

2010 SQUAD	Date of Birth	Height	Weight	Matches	Tries	Conversions	Penalties	Drop Goals	Points
Chris Alcock	24/06/1988	1.82	103	1	–	–	–	–	0
Sosene Anesi	03/06/1981	1.87	90	53	12	–	–	–	60
Berrick Barnes	28/05/1986	1.83	87	59	7	37	24	9	208
Al Baxter	21/01/1977	1.90	114	106	1	–	–	–	5
Kurtley Beale	06/01/1989	1.85	88	51	8	32	23	3	182
Luke Burgess	20/08/1983	1.80	83	42	3	–	–	–	15
Will Caldwell	17/08/1982	1.98	110	61	2	–	–	–	10
Tom Carter	25/02/1983	1.88	101	42	5	–	–	–	25
Dave Dennis	01/10/1986	1.92	104	14	–	–	–	–	0
Kane Douglas	01/06/1989	2.01	115	14	–	–	–	–	0
Damian Fitzpatrick	06/08/1989	1.82	104	15	1	–	–	–	5
Adam Freier	20/03/1980	1.75	99	88	12	–	–	–	60
Daniel Halangahu	06/03/1984	1.80	86	49	7	23	26	–	159
Josh Holmes	07/01/1987	1.87	91	43	7	–	–	–	35
Rob Horne	15/08/1989	1.85	83	30	6	–	–	–	30
Cam Jowitt	05/02/1983	2.01	113	1	–	–	–	–	0
Sekope Kepu	05/02/1986	1.88	115	20	–	–	–	–	0
Locky McCaffrey	17/03/1990	2.00	116	1	–	–	–	–	0
Patrick McCutcheon	24/06/1987	1.87	100	4	–	–	–	–	0
Drew Mitchell	26/03/1984	1.83	90	87	27	–	–	–	135
Ben Mowen	12/01/1984	1.95	106	28	3	–	–	–	15
Dean Mumm	05/03/1984	1.98	110	52	8	–	–	–	40
Dan Palmer	13/09/1988	1.80	103	13	–	–	–	–	0
Wycliff Palu	27/07/1982	1.93	118	62	10	–	–	–	50
Tatafu Polota-Nau	26/07/1985	1.80	110	66	8	–	–	–	40
Benn Robinson	19/07/1984	1.83	109	62	5	–	–	–	25
Hendrik Roodt	06/11/1987	2.00	121	1	–	–	–	–	0
Rory Sidey	04/07/1986	1.88	100	4	1	–	–	–	5
Chris Thomson	07/10/1985	2.04	117	11	–	–	–	–	0
Jeremy Tilse	06/02/1986	1.94	117	6	–	–	–	–	0
Lachie Turner	11/05/1987	1.88	88	50	21	–	–	–	105
Phil Waugh	22/09/1979	1.75	98	123	12	–	–	–	60
Totals				**1259**	**166**	**92**	**73**	**12**	**1269**

www.waratahs.com.au

VODACOM SUPER RUGBY FINAL LOG POSITIONS

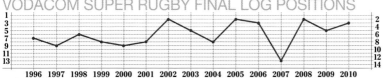

APPEARANCES AND POINTS IN 2010 SUPER 14

	Reds	Stormers	Bulls	Sharks	Lions	W Force	Blues	Cheetahs	Crusaders	Brumbies	Highlanders	Chiefs	Hurricanes	Stormers	Matches	Tries	Conversions	Penalties	Drop Goals	Points
SR Anesi	15	15	15	15	15	15	13R	14R	13R	10R	10R	10R	–	–	12	–	–	–	–	0
LD Turner	14	14	14	14	14	14	14	14	14	14	14	14	14	14	14	6	–	–	–	30
TJO Carter	13	13	13	13	13	13	12R	10R	10R	13	12	12	12	12	14	2	–	–	–	10
KJ Beale	12	12	14R	15R	15R	12R	15	15	15	15	15	15	15	15	14	5	1	–	–	27
DA Mitchell	11	11	11	11	11	11	11	11	11	11	11	11	11	11	14	9	–	–	–	45
BS Barnes	10	10	12	12	12	12	12	12	12	12	12	10	10	10	14	1	19	17	3	103
L Burgess	9	9	9	9	9	9	9	9	9	9R	9R	9	9	9	14	–	–	–	–	0
W Palu	8	8	8	8	8	–	8	–	8	–	–	–	–	–	7	2	–	–	–	10
PR Waugh	7c	7c	7c	7c	7c	7c	7c	–	7c	7c	7c	7c	7c	7c	13	1	–	–	–	5
DW Mumm	6	–	–	4	4	4	4	4c	4	4	4	4	4	4	12	2	–	–	–	10
CM Jowitt	5	–	–	–	–	–	–	–	–	–	–	–	–	–	1	–	–	–	–	0
WJB Caldwell	4	4	5R	5R	5R	x	7R	5R	5R	5R	–	–	–	–	9	–	–	–	–	0
AKE Baxter	3	3	3	3	3	–	3	3	3	3	3	3	3	3	13	1	–	–	–	5
SUT Polota-Nau	2	2	2	2	2	2	2	2	2	–	2	2	2	2	13	3	–	–	–	15
BA Robinson	1	1	1	1	1	1	1	1	1	–	–	1	–	–	10	1	–	–	–	5
DN Fitzpatrick	x	2R	2R	2R	2R	x	x	2R	2R	2R	2R	2R	3R	2R	11	1	–	–	–	5
SM Kepu	1R	1R	1R	1R	3R	3	3R	3R	1R	1	–	–	–	–	10	–	–	–	–	0
KP Douglas	4R	5	5	5	5	5	5	5	5	5	5	5	5	5	14	–	–	–	–	0
BSC Mowen	5R	6	6	6R	7R	8	8R	8	6	8	8	8	8	8	14	2	–	–	–	10
JM Holmes	9R	9R	x	9R	9R	9R	9R	9R	9R	9	9	9R	9R	9R	13	3	–	–	–	15
DK Halangahu	10R	11R	10	10	10	10	10	10	10	10	10	13R	10R	15R	14	3	12	14	–	81
RJ Sidey	11R	x	–	–	–	–	–	–	–	x	13R	–	11R	13R	4	1	–	–	–	5
HL Roodt	–	5R	–	–	–	–	–	–	–	–	–	–	–	–	1	–	–	–	–	0
DA Dennis	–	4R	4	6	6	6	6	6	8R	6	6	7R	8R	6R	13	–	–	–	–	0
LP McCaffrey	–	–	x	–	–	x	–	6R	–	–	–	–	–	–	1	–	–	–	–	0
RG Horne	–	–	10R	12R	13R	13R	13	13	13	–	–	13	13	13	10	2	–	–	–	10
DP Palmer	–	–	–	–	–	3R	–	–	–	3R	1	–	1	1	5	–	–	–	–	0
CS Alcock	–	–	–	–	–	–	–	7	–	x	–	–	–	–	1	–	–	–	–	0
AL Freier	–	–	–	–	–	–	–	–	–	2	–	–	–	–	1	–	–	–	–	0
JD Tilse	–	–	–	–	–	–	–	–	–	–	3R	1R	1R	1R	4	–	–	–	–	0
PJ McCutcheon	–	–	–	–	–	–	–	–	–	–	6R	6	6	6	4	–	–	–	–	0
CP Thomson	–	–	–	–	–	–	–	–	–	–	5R	4R	4R	x	3	–	–	–	–	0
32 players															**297**	**45**	**32**	**31**	**3**	**391**

QUEENSLAND REDS

GROUND Suncorp Stadium
ADDRESS Castlemaine Street, Milton
TELEPHONE + 61 7 3354 9333
CAPACITY 52 000
COLOURS Cardinal red jersey, socks and shorts
WEBSITE www.redsrugby.com.au
COACH Ewen McKenzie **CAPTAINS** James Horwill & Will Genia
CEO Jim Carmichael **CHAIRMAN** Rod McCall

QUEENSLAND REDS RECORDS

MATCH RECORDS

Biggest win	40	vs. Force (50-10)	Brisbane	2010
Heaviest defeat	89	vs. Bulls (3-92)	Pretoria	2007
Highest score	52	vs. Crusaders (52-16)	Brisbane	1996
Most points conceded	92	vs. Bulls (3-92)	Pretoria	2007
Most tries	7	vs. Blues (51-13)	Brisbane	1996
	7	vs. Bulls (48-12)	Brisbane	2002
	7	vs. Force (50-10)	Brisbane	2010
Most tries conceded	13	vs. Bulls (3-92)	Pretoria	2007
Most points by a player	31	QS Cooper (2t, 3c, 5p) vs Crusaders	Brisbane	2010
Most tries by a player	2	on 38 occasions - nine times by CE Latham		
Most conversions by a player	5	JA Eales on four occasions		
	5	EJ Flatley vs. Stormers	Brisbane	2002
	5	QS Cooper vs. Force	Brisbane	2010
Most penalties by a player	6	JA Eales vs. Northern Transvaal	Brisbane	1996
	6	NR Spooner vs. NSW Waratahs	Sydney	1999
	6	S Drahm vs. Cats	Bloemfontein	2000
	6	S Drahm vs. ACT Brumbies	Canberra	2000
Most drop goals by a player	2	BS Barnes	Canberra	2008

SEASON RECORDS

Most team points	366	from 13 matches	2010
Most points by a player	171	QS Cooper	2010
Most team tries	43	from 13 matches	2010
Most tries by a player	10	CE Latham	2002
Most conversions by a player	31	QS Cooper	2010
Most penalties by a player	40	NR Spooner	1999
Most drop goals by a player	4	BS Barnes	2008
			2006

CAREER RECORDS

Most appearances	123	SP Hardman	2000-2010
Most points	**629**	**EJ Flatley**	**1996-2006**
Most tries	41	CE Latham	1997-2008
Most conversions	92	EJ Flatley	1996-2006
Most penalties	130	EJ Flatley	1996-2006
Most drop goals	6	BS Barnes	2006-2009

RESULTS & SCORERS

Date	Venue	Referee	Opponent	Result	Score	Scorers
Feb 13	Brisbane	Craig Joubert	WARATAHS	LOST	28-30	T: Braid, Horwill, Penalty try. C: Cooper (2). P: Cooper (2). DG: Cooper.
Feb 19	Brisbane	Craig Joubert	CRUSADERS	WON	41-20	T: Cooper (2), Ioane, Davies. C: Cooper (3). P: Cooper (5).
Feb 27	Brisbane[1]	Steve R Walsh	BLUES	LOST	18-27	T: Genia, Weeks. C: Cooper. P: Cooper (2).
Mar 5	Hamilton	Chris Pollock	CHIEFS	WON	23-18	T: Morahan, Chambers. C: Cooper (2). P: Cooper (3).
Mar 14	Brisbane	Ian Smith	W FORCE	WON	50-10	T: A Faingaa (2), Ioane (2), Higginbotham (2), Morahan. C: Cooper (5), Lucas. P: Cooper.
Mar 26	Bloemfontein	Vinny Munro	CHEETAHS	WON	31-10	T: Genia, Ioane, Hynes. C: Cooper (2). P: Cooper (3), Genia.
Apr 3	Durban	Chris Pollock	SHARKS	LOST	28-30	T: Chambers (2), Cooper, Holmes. C: Cooper (4).
Apr 10	Johannesburg	Mark Lawrence	LIONS	WON	41-26	T: Davies (2), Taylor, Hynes, Cooper, S Faingaa. C: Cooper (4).
Apr 17	Brisbane	Craig Joubert	BULLS	WON	19-12	T: Higginbotham, Davies. P: Cooper (3).
Apr 23	Brisbane	Chris Pollock	STORMERS	WON	16-13	T: Chambers. C: Cooper. P: Cooper (3).
May 1	Canberra	Chris Pollock	BRUMBIES	LOST	12-32	P: Cooper (4).
May 7	Wellington	Bryce Lawrence	HURRICANES	LOST	21-44	T: Higginbotham, Davies, Chambers. C: Cooper (3).
May 15	Brisbane	Steve R Walsh	HIGHLANDERS	WON	38-36	T: Luafutu (2), Ioane, Hynes, Cooper, Samo. C: Cooper (4).

[1] Ballymore Stadium

Played	Won	Drawn	Lost	Points for	Points against	Tries for	Tries against
13	8	0	5	366	308	43	38

VODACOM SUPER 14

COACHES & MANAGEMENT

HEAD COACH Ewen McKenzie **ASSISTANT COACH** Jim McKay
DOCTOR Dr Greg Smith **PHYSIOTHERAPIST** Geoff Clark
PERFORMANCE COACH Damian Marsh **MANAGER** Lonnie Toia
MEDIA OFFICER Paul Reid

APPEARANCES AND POINTS IN SUPER RUGBY

2010 SQUAD	Date of Birth	Height	Weight	Matches	Tries	Conversions	Penalties	Drop Goals	Points
Daniel Braid	13/02/1981	1.86	96	78	17	–	–	–	85
Adam Byrnes	29/06/1981	2.01	116	19	1	–	–	–	5
Will Chambers	26/05/1988	1.86	100	12	5	–	–	–	25
Blair Connor	29/09/1988	1.83	82	7	1	–	–	–	5
Quade Cooper	05/04/1988	1.85	83	48	11	33	28	1	208
Ben Daley	27/06/1988	1.83	106	18	–	–	–	–	0
Rod Davies	18/05/1989	1.80	88	13	5	–	–	–	25
Anthony Faingaa	02/02/1987	1.78	88	25	3		–	–	15
Saia Faingaa	02/02/1987	1.87	100	51	2	–	–	–	10
Will Genia	17/01/1988	1.75	82	39	7	–	1	–	38
James Hanson	15/09/1988	1.80	100	1	–	–	–	–	0
Sean Hardman	06/05/1977	1.83	103	123	5	–	–	–	25
Scott Higginbotham	05/09/1986	1.95	102	31	6	–	–	–	30
Greg Holmes	11/06/1983	1.83	110	55	6	–	–	–	30
James Horwill	29/05/1985	2.01	113	48	4	–	–	–	20
Leroy Houston	10/11/1986	1.90	102	37	2	–	–	–	10
Van Humphries	08/01/1976	2.03	114	65	5	–	–	–	25
Peter Hynes	18/07/1982	1.83	87	75	19	–	–	–	95
Digby Ioane	14/07/1985	1.78	92	50	15	–	–	–	75
Jack Kennedy	28/07/1987	1.84	110	8	–	–	–	–	0
Richard Kingi	17/03/1989	1.76	80	5	–	–	–	–	0
Poutasi Luafutu	02/12/1987	1.86	111	16	2	–	–	–	10
Ben Lucas	30/12/1987	1.80	79	27	1	4	5	–	28
Luke Morahan	13/04/1990	1.87	93	8	2	–	–	–	10
Ed Quirk	28/08/1991	1.91	106	1	–	–	–	–	0
Radike Samo	09/07/1976	1.97	116	37	5	–	–	–	25
Jake Schatz	25/07/1990	1.90	104	9	–	–	–	–	0
Andrew Shaw	02/02/1989	1.91	100	4	–	–	–	–	0
James Slipper	06/06/1989	1.85	113	3	–	–	–	–	0
Rob Simmons	19/04/1989	2.00	118	13	–	–	–	–	0
Ben Tapuai	19/01/1989	1.78	95	4	1	–	–	–	5
Ezra Taylor	06/04/1983	1.93	111	23	1	–	–	–	5
Lei Tomiki	22/07/1983	1.83	100	1	–	–	–	–	0
Morgan Turinui	05/01/1982	1.88	102	76	24	–	–	–	120
Brandon Va'aulu	03/05/1987	1.78	92	35	3	–	–	–	15
Tim Walsh	10/04/1979	1.75	86	6	2	–	–	–	10
Laurie Weeks	05/04/1986	1.81	114	23	1	–	–	–	5
Totals				**1094**	**156**	**37**	**34**	**1**	**959**

VODACOM SUPER RUGBY FINAL LOG POSITIONS

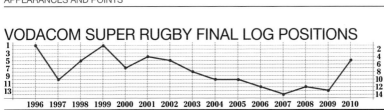

APPEARANCES AND POINTS IN 2010 SUPER 14

	Waratahs	Crusaders	Blues	Chiefs	W Force	Cheetahs	Sharks	Lions	Bulls	Stormers	Brumbies	Hurricanes	Highlanders	Matches	Tries	Conversions	Penalties	Drop Goals	Points
PJ Hynes	15	15	15	–	14	15	15	15	15	15	15	15	14	12	3	–	–	–	15
R Davies	14	14	14	–	–	11R	13R	14	14	–	–	14	–	8	5	–	–	–	25
M Turinui	13	13	13	13	13R	–	–	–	–	–	–	–	–	5	–	–	–	–	0
A Faingaa	12	12	12	12	12	12	12	12	12	12	12	12	–	12	2	–	–	–	10
DN Ioane	11	11	11	–	13	13	11	11	11	11	11	11	11	12	5	–	–	–	25
QS Cooper	10	10	10	10	10	10	10	10	10	10	10	10	10	13	5	31	27	1	171
SW Genia	9	9	9c	9c	9c	9c	9c	9c	9c	9c	9c	9c	9c	13	2	–	1	–	13
S Higginbotham	8	8	8	6	6	6	6	6	6	6	6	6	6	13	4	–	–	–	20
DJ Braid	7	7	7	7	7	–	7	7	7	7	7	–	–	10	1	–	–	–	5
JE Horwill	6c	5c	–	–	–	–	–	–	–	–	–	–	–	2	1	–	–	–	5
VC Humphries	5	–	5	5	5	5	5	5	5	–	–	5	5	10	–	–	–	–	0
A Byrnes	4	4	4	4	5R	x	4	–	–	5	5	–	–	8	–	–	–	–	0
LS Weeks	3	3	3	3	3	3	3	3	3	3	–	–	–	10	1	–	–	–	5
SP Hardman	2	–	2R	2R	2R	2R	2	2R	2R	x	2R	2R	2	11	–	–	–	–	0
BP Daley	1	1	1	1	1	1	1	1	1	1	1	1	1	12	–	–	–	–	0
S Faingaa	2R	2	2	2	2	2	2R	2	2	2	2	2	–	12	1	–	–	–	5
JA Slipper	3R	–	–	–	–	–	–	–	–	–	–	–	3R	3	–	–	–	–	0
EL Taylor	5R	–	–	–	8R	–	5R	4R	x	5R	4R	4R	–	7	1	–	–	–	5
AG Shaw	6R	–	–	–	–	–	–	–	–	–	7	–	–	2	–	–	–	–	0
RTI Kingi	9R	9R	x	–	–	–	–	–	–	–	–	–	12R	3	–	–	–	–	0
TM Walsh	x	10R	15R	–	–	–	–	–	–	–	–	–	–	2	–	–	–	–	0
WJ Chambers	14R	13R	14R	14	11R	x	13	13	13	13	13	13	13	12	5	–	–	–	25
JW Schatz	–	6	6	x	7R	7	8	8R	x	x	4R	8R	7	9	–	–	–	–	0
JE Hanson	–	2R	–	–	–	–	–	–	–	–	–	–	x	1	–	–	–	–	0
GS Holmes	–	3R	3R	3R	1R	1R	3R	3R	x	1R	3R	3	3	11	1	–	–	–	5
R Simmons	–	5R	4R	4	4	4R	4	4	4	4	–	–	–	10	–	–	–	–	0
LD Houston	–	6R	6R	8	8	8	8R	8	8	8	8	8	8	12	–	–	–	–	0
LJ Morahan	–	–	–	15	14	14	14	11R	–	x	14R	–	–	6	2	–	–	–	10
BWF Va'aulu	–	–	–	11	11	11	–	–	11R	14	14	14R	15R	8	–	–	–	–	0
B Connor	–	–	–	11R	–	–	–	–	–	–	–	–	–	1	–	–	–	–	0
BJ Lucas	–	–	–	14R	10R	x	x	15R	x	x	15R	12R	15	6	–	1	–	–	2
B Tapuai	–	–	–	x	–	–	–	12R	–	–	7R	–	12	3	–	–	–	–	0
JR Kennedy	–	–	–	–	–	x	–	3R	3R	3	–	–	x	3	–	–	–	–	0
R Samo	–	–	–	–	–	–	–	–	–	–	–	4	4	2	1	–	–	–	5
L Tomiki	–	–	–	–	–	–	–	–	–	–	–	7R	–	1	–	–	–	–	0
EC Quirk	–	–	–	–	–	–	–	–	–	–	–	–	6R	1	–	–	–	–	0
PVT Luafutu	–	–	–	–	–	–	–	–	–	–	–	–	8R	1	2	–	–	–	10
Penalty try	–	–	–	–	–	–	–	–	–	–	–	–	–	0	1	–	–	–	5
37 players														**267**	**43**	**32**	**28**	**1**	**366**

VODACOM SUPER 14

WESTERN FORCE

GROUND ME Bank Stadium
CAPACITY 30 000
ADDRESS 310 Pier Street, Perth, WA 6000
TELEPHONE NUMBER + 61 8 9422 1500
COLOURS Ocean blue jersey with black shorts and socks
WEBSITE www.rugbywa.com.au
COACH John Mitchell **CAPTAIN** Nathan Sharpe
CEO Vern Reid **CHAIRMAN** Geoff Stooke OAM

WESTERN FORCE RECORDS

MATCH RECORDS

Biggest win	41	vs. Lions (55-14)	Perth	2009
Heaviest defeat	53	vs. Crusaders (0-53)	Christchurch	2007
Highest score	55	vs. Lions (55-14)	Perth	2009
Most points conceded	53	vs. Crusaders (0-53)	Christchurch	2007
Most tries	8	vs. Lions (55-14)	Perth	2009
Most tries conceded	8	vs. Crusaders (0-53)	Christchurch	2007
Most points by a player	25	CB Shepherd vs. Bulls (2t, 3c, 3p)	Pretoria	2007
Most tries by a player	3	SNG Staniforth vs. Cats	Johannesburg	2006
	3	CB Shepherd vs. Brumbies	Canberra	2009
Most conversions by a player	6	MJ Giteau vs. Lions	Perth	2009
Most penalties by a player	5	CB Shepherd vs. Stormers	Cape Town	2007
	5	MJ Giteau vs. Sharks	Perth	2007
	5	JD O'Connor vs. Brumbies	Perth	2010
	5	JD O'Connor vs. Bulls	Perth	2010
Most drop goals by a player	1	MJ Giteau vs. Cheetahs	Perth	2009
	1	DW Hill vs. Stormers	Perth	2010

SEASON RECORDS

Most team points	328	from 13 matches	2009
Most points by a player	128	MJ Giteau	2009
Most team tries	42	from 13 matches	2009
Most tries by a player	9	SNG Staniforth	2006
Most conversions by a player	28	MJ Giteau	2009
Most penalties by a player	**23**	**JD O'Connor**	**2010**
Most drop goals by a player	1	MJ Giteau	2009
	1	DW Hill	2010

CAREER RECORDS

Most appearances	62	NC Sharpe	2006-2010
Most points	337	CB Shepherd	2006-2010
Most tries	26	CB Shepherd	2006-2010
Most conversions	55	MJ Giteau	2007-2009
Most penalties	51	CB Shepherd	2006-2009
Most drop goals	1	MJ Giteau	2007-2009
	1	DW Hill	2010

RESULTS & SCORERS

Date	Venue	Referee	Opponent	Result	Score	Scorers
Feb 12	Perth	Steve R Walsh	BRUMBIES	LOST	15-24	P: O'Connor (5).
Feb 20	Wellington	Vinny Munro	HURRICANES	LOST	22-47	T: Tatupu, Haylett-Petty, O'Young. C: O'Connor (2). P: O'Connor.
Feb 27	Perth	Jaco Peyper	CHIEFS	LOST	19-37	T: Cross. C: O'Connor. P: O'Connor (3), Sheehan.
Mar 14	Brisbane	Ian Smith	REDS	LOST	10-50	T: Cummins. C: O'Connor. P: O'Connor.
Mar 20	Perth	Jaco Peyper	WARATAHS	LOST	10-14	T: Staniforth. C: O'Connor. P: O'Connor.
Mar 27	Perth	Nathan Pearce	BULLS	LOST	15-28	P: O'Connor (5).
Apr 2	Perth	Stuart Dickinson	STORMERS	WON	16-15	T: Pocock. C: O'Connor. P: O'Connor (2). DG: Hill.
Apr 10	Queenstown	Marius Jonker	HIGHLANDERS	WON	41-27	T: Shepherd (2), Cross (2), O'Connor, Turner. C: O'Connor (4). P: O'Connor.
Apr 17	Auckland	Keith Brown	BLUES	LOST	17-38	T: Pocock, Penalty try. C: O'Connor (2). P: O'Connor.
Apr 23	Perth	Jonathan Kaplan	CRUSADERS	WON	24-16	T: Cowan, Whittaker, Hodgson. C: Hill (3). P: Hill.
May 1	Johannesburg	Craig Joubert	LIONS	WON	33-12	T: Staniforth, Bartholomeusz, Hill. C: Hill (3). P: Hill (4).
May 8	Bloemfontein	Craig Joubert	CHEETAHS	LOST	14-29	T: Cross, Hodgson. C: O'Connor (2).
May 14	Durban	Pro Legoete	SHARKS	LOST	22-27	T: Cummins. C: O'Connor. P: O'Connor (3). P: Sheehan (2).

Played	Won	Drawn	Lost	Points for	Points against	Tries for	Tries against
13	**4**	**0**	**9**	**258**	**364**	**24**	**42**

VODACOM SUPER 14

COACHES & MANAGEMENT

HEAD COACH John Mitchell **ASSISTANT COACH** Richard Graham **SKILLS COACH** Geoff Townsend
CONDITIONING COACH Haydn Masters **VIDEO ANALYST** Scott Anderson **DOCTOR** Dr Mark de Cruz
KICKING COACH Daryl Halligan **MEDIA OFFICER** Mark White **MANAGER** Mitch Hardy

APPEARANCES AND POINTS IN SUPER RUGBY

2010 SQUAD	Date of Birth	Height	Weight	Matches	Tries	Conversions	Penalties	Drop Goals	Points
Mark Bartholomeusz	30/06/1977	1.79	90	79	21	–	–	–	105
Richard Brown	28/08/1989	1.88	104	47	4	–	–	–	20
Nathan Charles	09/01/1989	1.83	103	7	–	–	–	–	0
Pekahou Cowan	02/06/1986	1.83	109	32	1	–	–	–	5
Ryan Cross	06/10/1979	1.90	97	49	15	–	–	–	75
Nick Cummins	05/10/1987	1.88	94	24	4	–	–	–	20
Matt Dunning	19/12/1978	1.82	115	101	2	–	–	1	13
Tim Fairbrother	12/03/1982	1.83	119	75	1	–	–	–	5
Sam Harris	30/01/1980	1.90	103	37	4	–	–	–	20
Dane Haylett-Petty	18/06/1989	1.89	95	9	1	–	–	–	5
Nic Henderson	01/05/1981	1.85	117	78	–	–	–	–	0
David Hill	31/07/1978	1.88	94	67	6	89	71	1	424
Tom Hockings	22/02/1986	1.98	106	32	2	–	–	–	10
Matthew Hodgson	25/06/1981	1.85	101	56	3	–	–	–	15
Stefano Hunt	11/08/1991	1.82	86	1	–	–	–	–	0
Mitch Inman	34/10/1988	1.91	102	13	–	–	–	–	0
Jono Jenkins	26/06/1986	1.86	100	1	–	–	–	–	0
Luke Jones	02/04/1991	2.01	108	2	–	–	–	–	0
Kieran Longbottom	20/12/1985	1.80	107	8	–	–	–	–	0
Ben McCalman	18/03/1988	1.92	106	13	–	–	–	–	0
James O'Connor	05/07/1990	1.80	79	25	7	16	23	–	136
Chris O'Young	03/03/1981	1.80	83	54	3	–	–	–	15
David Pocock	23/04/1988	1.83	101	46	3	–	–	–	15
Ted Postal	16/05/1991	1.90	96	1	–	–	–	–	0
Joelin Rapana	23/04/1986	1.88	98	1	–	–	–	–	0
Haig Sare	25/03/1982	1.83	90	33	7	–	–	–	20
Nathan Sharpe	26/02/1978	2.01	113	132	6	–	–	–	30
Brett Sheehan	16/09/1979	1.79	90	58	1	–	3	–	14
Cameron Shepherd	30/04/1984	1.88	98	67	32	27	51	–	367
Richard Stanford	25/04/1986	1.98	110	17	–	–	–	–	0
Scott Staniforth	12/12/1977	1.88	97	106	41	–	–	–	205
Mark Swanepoel	26/10/1990	1.80	92	1	–	–	–	–	0
Josh Tatupu	06/11/1986	1.85	100	13	3	–	–	–	15
Justin Turner	12/03/1990	1.80	93	7	1	–	–	–	5
Ryan Tyrrell	09/11/1983	1.89	113	4	–	–	–	–	0
Ben Whittaker	10/10/1989	1.89	111	12	1	–	–	–	5
Sam Wykes	25/04/1988	1.95	106	25	–	–	–	–	0
Totals				**1327**	**169**	**132**	**148**	**2**	**1544**

VODACOM SUPER RUGBY FINAL LOG POSITIONS

APPEARANCES AND POINTS IN 2010 SUPER 14

	Brumbies	Hurricanes	Chiefs	Reds	Waratahs	Bulls	Stormers	Highlanders	Blues	Crusaders	Lions	Cheetahs	Sharks	Matches	Tries	Conversions	Penalties	Drop Goals	Points
JD O'Connor	15	15	10	12	12	12	15	15	15	–	x	15	15	11	1	15	23	–	104
DS Haylett-Petty	14	14	11R	15	–	–	–	15R	–	–	–	–	x	5	1	–	–	–	5
RP Cross	13	–	13	13	13	13	12	12	12	12	12	12	12	12	4	–	–	–	20
JJ Tatupu	12	12	–	–	–	–	–	–	–	–	–	–	–	2	1	–	–	–	5
HW Sare	11	11	–	–	–	–	14R	–	–	x	–	–	–	3	–	–	–	–	0
SR Harris	10	10	x	15R	x	15R	x	13R	12R	x	13R	14R	13R	9	–	–	–	–	0
BR Sheehan	9	9	9	9	9	–	–	–	–	9	9	–	9	8	–	–	3	–	9
RN Brown	8	–	–	–	–	–	6R	8	8	8	8	8	8	8	–	–	–	–	0
DW Pocock	7	–	–	–	–	–	7	7	7	7	7	7	7	8	2	–	–	–	10
MJ Hodgson	6	7	7	7	7	7	8	6	6	6	6	6	6	13	2	–	–	–	10
NC Sharpe	5c	5c	5c	5c	5c	5c	5c	5c	5c	5c	5c	5c	5c	13	–	–	–	–	0
SL Wykes	4	8	8	4	4	–	–	5R	x	4R	4	5R	4R	10	–	–	–	–	0
MJ Dunning	3	1	3R	3R	–	–	1R	3R	1R	3R	3	1R	3R	11	–	–	–	–	0
PJM Cowan	2	2	2	2R	–	2R	1	1	–	1	1	–	1	10	1	–	–	–	5
NJ Henderson	1	1R	1	1	1	1	–	–	1	–	–	1	–	8	–	–	–	–	0
BJ Whittaker	x	–	–	–	2R	2	2	2	2R	2	2	2R	2	9	1	–	–	–	5
TJ Fairbrother	3R	3	3	3	3	3	3	3	3	3	–	3	3	12	–	–	–	–	0
RD Stanford	4R	4R	4R	8	8	8	x	–	–	–	–	–	–	6	–	–	–	–	0
BJ McCalman	8R	6	6	6	6	6	6	4R	4R	4	4R	4R	4	13	–	–	–	–	0
CM O'Young	9R	9R	9R	9R	9R	9	9	9	9	–	–	9R	–	10	1	–	–	–	5
MBW Inman	11R	13	12	4R*	14R	11R	13	13	13	13	13	13	13	13	–	–	–	–	0
SC Hunt	x	10R	–	–	–	–	–	–	–	–	–	–	–	1	–	–	–	–	0
TJ Hockings	–	4	4	8R	4R	4	4	4	4	x	8R	4	–	10	–	–	–	–	0
RS Tyrrell	–	2R	2R	2	2	–	–	–	–	–	–	–	–	4	–	–	–	–	0
EJP Rapana	–	14R	–	–	–	–	–	–	–	–	–	–	–	1	–	–	–	–	0
LM Jones	–	8R	x	–	x	4R	–	–	–	–	–	–	–	2	–	–	–	–	0
MA Bartholomeusz	–	–	15	–	15	15	11	14	14	15	15	10R	10	10	1	–	–	–	5
SNG Staniforth	–	–	14	14	14	14	14	–	–	–	14	–	–	6	2	–	–	–	10
NM Cummins	–	–	11	11	11	11	–	–	14R	14	11	14	14	9	2	–	–	–	10
DW Hill	–	–	–	10	10	10	10	10	10	10	10	10	–	9	1	6	5	1	35
JPM Jenkins	–	–	–	4R	–	–	–	–	–	–	–	–	–	1	–	–	–	–	0
KA Longbottom	–	–	–	–	1R	1R	–	–	–	–	1R	–	–	3	–	–	–	–	0
T Postal	–	–	–	–	–	8R	–	–	–	–	–	–	–	1	–	–	–	–	0
M Swanepoel	–	–	–	–	–	9R	–	–	–	–	–	–	–	1	–	–	–	–	0
NL Charles	–	–	–	–	–	–	2R	2R	2	2R	2R	2	2R	7	–	–	–	–	0
JS Turner	–	–	–	–	–	–	9R	9R	9R	9R	9R	9	9R	7	1	–	–	–	5
CB Shepherd	–	–	–	–	–	–	–	11	11	11	–	11	11	5	2	–	–	–	10
Penalty try	–	–	–	–	–	–	–	–	–	–	–	–	–	0	1	–	–	–	5
37 players														**271**	**24**	**21**	**31**	**1**	**258**

VODACOM SUPER 14

SECTION 5
DOMESTIC CHAMPIONSHIPS

Sharks surge to Currie Cup title

THE Sharks surged to their second Absa Currie Cup title in three years when they beat Vodacom Western Province 30-10 at the Absa Stadium in Durban to usher in what looks for all money like another golden age for the KZN team.

This was the 50th final in the competition's 118-year history but also one of the most one-sided, as coach John Plumtree not only added a second trophy to go with that won in 2008 against the Blue Bulls, but also won his tactical battle against his opposite number, Allister Coetzee, with astounding ease.

The match was also a personal triumph for Patrick Lambie, the 20-year-old flyhalf who came from absolutely nowhere to lead his team to the biggest prize in South African rugby.

Lambie, who began the year having made one Currie Cup appearance off the bench during 2009, scored two tries en route to a personal haul of 25 points in a performance so dominant that one cannot avoid making comparisons with a young Naas Botha.

Lambie's man-of-the-match performance also launched him into the international big time, and he duly made his Test debut against Ireland in Dublin just seven days after hoisting aloft Sir Donald Currie's iconic jug.

The Sharks' irresistible form in the final, and indeed during their 16-12 semifinal win over defending champions the Vodacom Blue Bulls, was not entirely unexpected – although perhaps the levels of ruthlessness were.

Plumtree's men, captained expertly by veteran centre Stefan Terblanche, finished the league stages four points clear at the top of the table, which provided them with the all-important home-ground advantage in the playoffs.

Western Province, meanwhile, began the tournament strongly, with six straight wins before coming unstuck against the selfsame Sharks in Durban. Coetzee's men however recovered well to finish second on the log and earn a home semi against the ever-dangerous Vodacom Free State Cheetahs.

The 31-7 scoreline in WP's favour set up a mouthwatering final, which pitted, simplistically it must be said, Province's star-studded backs against the Sharks' grizzled pack. In the end, however, WP just were never at the races in the game that mattered, scrumhalf Charl McLeod and Lambie striking with early tries to

The Sharks' victory in the Currie Cup final was also a personal triumph for coach John Plumtree (right) and 20-year-old flyhalf Pat Lambie, whose 25 points in the final earned him a Springbok call-up.

set the tone for the rest of the evening.

But the platform was laid up front, and it was here that Tendai Mtawarira and the Du Plessis brothers, Bismarck and Jannie, were immense against a WP forward pack that looked to have shaken off their 'soft-touch' reputations.

Sadly, there can be only one winner – and one was left with the surprising thought that the likes of WP captain Schalk Burger and centre Jean de Villiers, despite winning everything there is to win at international level, do not seem destined to lift the Currie Cup.

There were no such concerns for Jannie du Plessis, who reacquainted himself with a trophy he had won on four previous occasions – three of them as part of the Cheetahs set-up.

Elsewhere, the 2010 Currie Cup will be remembered for GWK Griquas wing Bjorn Basson breaking the season try-scoring record of 19 held jointly by Colin Lloyd and former Bok wing Carel du Plessis. Basson's brace in the team's final match, against the Blue Bulls, took him to 21 and booked him his ticket onto the Boks' end-of-year

tour, where he promptly slipped into the number 14 jersey against Ireland.

At the bottom of the table, the Pumas and Leopards finished in the relegation zone, but held off the challenges of the EP Kings – the First Division champions – and the SWD Eagles respectively in two-legged promotion/relegation battles to retain their Premier Division status for another year.

PREMIER DIVISION ABSA CURRIE CUP LOG 2010

PREMIER DIVISION

Team	P	W	D	L	PF	PA	Diff	TF	TA	BP	Pts
The Sharks	14	10	4	0	492	300	192	62	30	12	52
Vodacom WP	14	10	4	0	520	280	240	59	28	8	48
Vodacom FS Cheetahs	14	10	4	0	488	323	165	60	33	7	47
Vodacom Blue Bulls	14	9	5	0	437	374	63	47	39	11	47
Xerox Lions	14	7	7	0	401	407	-6	45	46	11	39
GWK Griquas	14	6	8	0	477	496	-19	60	60	13	37
Barloworld Toyota Pumas	14	4	10	0	329	573	-244	45	78	7	23
Platinum Leopards	14	0	14	0	263	654	-391	30	94	5	5

ABSA CURRIE CUP
PLAY-OFF RESULTS

SEMI-FINALS: Sharks bt Vodacom Blue Bulls **16-12** (Durban).
Vodacom Western Province bt Vodacom Free State Cheetahs **31-7** (Cape Town).

2010 ABSA CURRIE CUP FINAL
The Absa Stadium, Durban, Saturday, 30 October 2010. Referee: C Joubert . Crowd: 52 000
Sharks 30 (Tries: Lambie 2, McLeod. Conversions: Lambie 3. Penalties: Lambie 3)
Vodacom WP 10 (Try: Burger. Conversion: De Waal. Penalty: De Waal)
SHARKS: L Ludik (AS Pretorius, 79), OM Ndungane, CS Terblanche (c), AJ Strauss (R Swanepoel, 71), LN Mvovo, P Lambie, C McLeod (RM Kockott, 40), R Kankowski, WS Alberts, KR Daniel, AJ Hargreaves (LJ Botes, 68), SR Sykes (A Bresler, 79), JN du Plessis (E van Staden, 56), BW du Plessis (CB Burden, 79), T Mtawarira.
VODACOM WP: CA Jantjes, GG Aplon, JL de Jongh (PW Bosch, 30/LCronje, 68), J de Villiers, BG Habana, W de Waal, ER Januarie (DO Duvenage, 17), DJ Vermeulen, L-FP Louw, SWP Burger (c), A van Zyl, AR Fondse (MD Steenkamp, 56), J Harris, DA Fourie, JD Moller (JC Kritzinger, 40). *Unused replacements: HM Shimange, PJ Louw.*

ABSA CURRIE CUP

2010 PREMIER DIVISION LEADING SCORERS

100 POINTS OR MORE

PLAYER	Province	Tries	Conversions	Penalties	Drop Goals	Points
W de Waal	Vodacom WP	0	35	50	0	220
P Lambie	Sharks	5	36	36	0	205
IP Olivier	GWK Griquas	3	40	25	1	173
J-L Potgieter	Vodacom Blue Bulls	1	30	36	0	173
LI Strydom	Vodacom FS Cheetahs	0	31	28	0	173
ET Jantjies	Xerox Lions	2	25	27	0	141
BA Basson	GWK Griquas	21	0	0	0	105
EG Watts	Pumas	9	16	9	0	104

SEVEN TRIES

BA Basson	GWK Griquas	21	KR Daniel	Sharks		8
LN Mvovo	Sharks	12	AF Johnson	Vodacom FS Cheetahs		7
EG Watts	Pumas	9	OM Ndungane	Sharks		7
GG Aplon	Vodacom WP	9	S Venter	Pumas		7

FIRST DIVISION ABSA CURRIE CUP LOG 2010

FIRST DIVISION

Team	P	W	D	L	PF	PA	Diff	TF	TA	BP	Pts
SWD Eagles	10	8	2	0	342	243	99	41	29	7	39
EP Kings	10	8	2	0	306	204	102	37	20	5	37
Boland	10	5	5	0	359	305	54	48	36	9	29
Griffons	10	5	5	0	350	250	100	46	32	8	28
Border	10	3	7	0	264	396	-132	29	52	4	16
Valke	10	1	9	0	276	499	-223	39	71	7	11

2010 FIRST DIVISION LEADING SCORERS

45 POINTS OR MORE

PLAYER	Province	Tries	Conversions	Penalties	Drop Goals	Points
AR Barends	SWD	2	21	26	1	133
J Jansen	Boland	4	30	13	0	119
JC Myburgh	Griffons	0	27	14	0	96
LA Basson	Border	5	13	12	0	87
G Dumond	EP Kings	0	11	11	0	58
CF Cronje	Valke	9	0	0	0	45
NT Nelson	EP Kings	9	0	0	0	45
JJ Taljard	Border	1	8	8	0	45

SIX TRIES

CF Cronje	Valke	9	WJ le Roux	Boland	6
NT Nelson	EP Kings	9	JC Breytenbach	SWD	6
C Hendricks	Boland	8	W Griesel	Griffons	6
K Hendricks	Valke	7	JW Jonker	Griffons	6
BJH McBean	SWD	7	JJ Plaatjies	Boland	6

ABSA CURRIE CUP FIRST DIVISION PLAY-OFF RESULTS

SEMI-FINALS: SWD Eagles bt Griffons **32-30** (George). EP Kings bt Boland **26-25** (Port Elizabeth)

2010 ABSA CUP FINAL

Outeniqua Park, George, Friday, 15 October 2010. Referee: L Legoete . Crowd: 8600

SWD Eagles 12 (Penalties: Blom 2, Barends 2).

EP Kings 16 (Try: W Stevens. Conversion: Dumond. Penalties: Dumond 3)

SWD EAGLES: MG Joubert, BJH McBean, S Zweni, BA Fortuin (c) (JU Hellmuth, 26-31), JC Breytenbach, AR Barends, J Blom (JU Hellmuth, 53), JJ Engelbrecht, S Raubenheimer (CJ du Plessis, 2-4), LL Hartnick, H Grimes, HO Eksteen (L Mtyanda, 58), W Harmse (A van der Westhuizen, 29), JH Grobler, JK Terblanche. *Unused subs: JF de Beer, ES Zana, WS Scott.*

EP KINGS: MW Stick (c), PL Perez, IW Stevens, De W Barry, NT Nelson, G Dumond, GH Odendaal (DG Stevens, 61), JR Gagiano (DP Nell, 59), DA Oosthuizen, UJ Potgieter, W Stoltz (L Payi, 67), R Duncan, A Schlechter (R Vermeulen, 29-40), J Fourie (A Halangahu, 53), PE Nodikida. *Unused subs: A Fenner, M Nqoro.*

PROMOTION/RELEGATION LOG

Team	P	W	D	L	PF	PA	Diff	TF	TA	BP	Pts
Pumas	2	1	0	1	82	64	18	12	7	2	8
Leopards	2	1	1	0	65	54	11	7	9	2	6
SWD Eagles	2	1	1	0	54	65	-11	9	7	2	6
EP Kings	2	0	1	1	64	82	-18	7	12	1	3

2010 FIRST DIVISION LEADING SCORERS

45 POINTS OR MORE

PLAYER	Province	Tries	Conversions	Penalties	Drop Goals	Points
G Dumond	EP Kings	0	4	7	0	29
C Durand	Leopards	0	5	6	0	28
C Bezuidenhout	Pumas	0	7	2	0	20
SP Marais	Leopards	3	1	0	0	17

RESULTS

Pumas and EP Kings drew **36-36**, October 22, Puma Stadium, Witbank. Leopards beat SWD Eagles **37-22**, October 23, Olen Park, Potchefstroom. SWD Eagles beat Leopards **32-28**, October 29, Ouenqua Park, George. Pumas beat EP Kings **46-28**, October 29, Nelson Mandela Bay Stadium, PE.

ABSA CURRIE CUP

VODACOM CUP

Blue Bulls win dramatic final

ANOTHER trophy was added to what was an already full cabinet at Loftus Versfeld when the Vodacom Blue Bulls beat the Free State Cheetahs 31-29 in dramatic fashion to win the 2010 Vodacom Cup.

The hosts also scooped the R1-million prizemoney on offer and ensured that the Blue Bulls became the first union to hold the Vodacom Super 14, Absa Currie Cup and Vodacom Cup titles at the same time.

"We never plan to stumble along the way, especially when you work for the Bulls. You are not allowed to lose here," said coach Nico Serfontein after his side had recorded their 10th consecutive win in the 2010 competition.

"You are not allowed to lose finals and you are not allowed not to get into finals. That pressure is always going to be on us here. But it's probably something that our fans demand from us and that's probably why we are such a great union. We have structures that are in place and we never plan to fail."

Flyhalf Francois Brummer, who was later named player of the tournament at the annual SA Rugby awards, was the hero for the Blue Bulls after he kicked an injury-time drop goal for a personal haul of 16 points to steer his side to their third triumph in the competition's history.

Francois Brummer chipping ahead in the Blue Bulls' rain-soaked quarterfinal against Western Province

The Cheetahs had built a 16-8 halftime lead, but a spirited fightback by the hosts saw them score two quick tries after the break to lead 25-19 with 20 minutes remaining. However Riaan Vermeulen crashed his way over the line with four minutes left for Louis Strydom to convert and so hand Free State back the lead.

The two flyhalves then traded penalties to make it 29-28, before the Blue Bulls were awarded a penalty in the dying seconds. Keeping the ball in hand, the Bulls plugged away until they could free up Brummer for an after-the-hooter drop goal, which he nailed expertly.

"That kick, was magical. But I don't think you could say we didn't deserve to win this game as we have enjoyed a great season," said Serfontein.

The Bulls certainly did, finishing six points clear at the top of the North section as the competition's only unbeaten team.

Free State, in contrast, could finish only third in the South section yet wins over the Golden Lions in the quarterfinals and Boland Cavaliers in the semis saw them through.

The Bulls, by contrast accounted for Vodacom WP in the last eight, before they dismantled the Sharks XV 33-3 in Pretoria to set up what proved to be a memorable final.

VODACOM CUP PLAY-OFF RESULTS

QUARTER FINALS: Cavaliers beat Leopards **30-25** (Wellington), Sharks XV beat Griquas **28-24** (Durban) Free State beat Golden Lions **30-20** (Johannesburg), Blue Bulls beat WP **17-06** (Pretoria)

SEMI-FINALS: Free State beat Cavaliers **22-14** (Wellington), Blue Bulls beat Sharks XV **33-03** (Pretoria)

FINAL: Loftus Versfeld B-Field, Pretoria, Friday, May 7. Referee: Jason Jaftha

Vodacom Blue Bulls 31 (TRY: Van Velze, Helberg, Dinkelmann. **CONVERSION:** Brummer 2. **PENALTIES:** Brummer 2 **DROP GOAL:** Brummer 2)

Vodacom Free State 29 (TRY: Goodes, Vermeulen. **CONVERSIONS:** Strydom 2. **PENALTIES:** Strydom 5)

VODACOM BLUE BULLS: S Mangweni SJ Mametsa (EH Dinkelmann, 31), GH Helberg, S Watermeyer, VS Willis, F Brummer, R Snyman, G-J van Velze (c), DA Oosthuizen, OC Kruger, MK Mabeta, CN Hess, MD Greyling (PR de Klerk, 51), MC Ralepelle, J Engels (MM Mellett, 65). *Unused replacements: J Fourie, LV Gwavu, DC Faasen, ML Boshoff.*

FREE STATE CHEETAHS: GA Whitehead, JW Jonker (JMI Ebersohn, 70), PAB Snyman, B Goodes (c) (IW Stevens, 60), RM Ramashala, Ll Strydom, TG Carse (PE van Zyl, 53), AF Johnson, JG Prinsloo (HS van der Walt, 62), PJ Wessels, PJ Steyn (J-C Astle, 36), F Uys, JG Calldo, P-W van Vuuren (HJ Liebenberg, 62)), CM Marais (R Vermeulen, 70).

VODACOM CUP LOG 2010

NORTH SECTION

Team	P	W	D	L	PF	PA	Diff	TF	TA	BP	Pts
Blue Bulls	7	7	0	0	251	136	115	34	13	4	32
Golden Lions	7	5	2	0	245	125	120	30	13	6	26
Griquas	7	5	2	0	263	184	79	39	24	6	26
Leopards	7	4	3	0	245	164	81	33	20	5	21
Pumas	7	4	3	0	240	163	77	32	17	5	21
Griffons	7	2	5	0	181	306	-125	23	45	3	11
Welwitchias	7	1	6	0	194	300	-106	23	42	3	7
Valke	7	0	7	0	116	357	-241	15	55	2	2

SOUTH SECTION

Team	P	W	D	L	PF	PA	Diff	TF	TA	BA	Pts
Boland Cavaliers	7	5	2	0	206	160	46	26	14	4	24
Sharks XV	7	5	2	0	214	131	83	23	12	3	23
Free State	7	5	2	0	195	150	45	24	14	3	23
Western Province	7	5	2	0	171	142	29	18	15	2	22
Pampas XV	7	3	3	1	220	151	69	29	16	6	20
Eastern Province	7	2	4	1	159	194	-35	18	23	3	13
SWD Eagles	7	2	5	0	151	176	-25	17	26	4	12
Border	7	0	7	0	115	327	-212	15	50	3	3

2010 VODACOM CUP LEADING SCORERS

50 POINTS OR MORE

PLAYER	Province	Matches	Tries	Conversions	Penalties	Drop Goals	Points
G Dumond	Sharks XV	8	0	18	20	1	99
Ll Strydom	Free State	8	0	6	28	0	96
J Peach	Eastern Province	7	5	12	15	0	94
F Brummer	Blue Bulls	10	1	11	15	6	90
CA Botha	Welwitchias	7	5	16	9	0	84
M Rodrigues	Pampas XV	7	1	15	8	2	65
R Croy	Pumas	7	0	14	9	1	58
J Jansen	Boland Cavaliers	9	1	12	8	0	53

FIVE TRIES

8	WJ Bouwer	Pumas		5	M Bustos Moyano	Pampas XV
7	ER Fredericks	Griffons		5	AO Gosio	Pampas XV
6	BA Basson	Griquas		5	WJ le Roux	Cavaliers
6	A Kettledas	Pumas		5	HG Noble	Eastern Province
6	AM Buckle	Griquas		5	J Peach	Eastern Province
6	D Scholtz	Leopards		5	PAB Snyman	Free State
5	WA Bennett	SWD Eagles		5	JC van Deventer	Golden Lions
5	MS Samaai	Leopards		5	G-J van Velze	Blue Bulls
5	L Karemaker	Griquas		5	S Watermeyer	Blue Bulls
5	CA Botha	Welwitchias		5	S Westraadt	Griquas

ABSA UNDER-21 CHAMPIONSHIP

WP hammer old foes to take title

IT was not all doom and gloom for Western Province on the day of the Absa Currie Cup final in Durban.

The two curtain-raisers also happened to feature teams from the Cape and the Under-21 team, in particular, was clinical in taking the Blue Bulls apart. The final score of 43-32 did not quite tell the full story as the youngsters from Pretoria salvaged some pride with two tries inside the last three minutes.

Province had led by only 15-3 at the break and even fell behind early in the second half after Gerhard van den Heever scored for the Bulls. However, a spell of four tries inside 20 action-packed second-half minutes made all the difference.

If one had to single out a man of the match from the final it would probably be centre Johann Sadie. If they hone his creative abilities, WP may well have a player in the mould of Jean de Villiers coming through their ranks.

However, there were several other youngsters that also put up their hands, including wings Danie Poolman and JJ Engelbrecht, the halfback pairing of Louis Schreuder and Gary van Aswegen, flanker Yaya Hartzenberg and hooker Sidney Tobias. Flyhalf Van Aswegen was also prolific with the boot.

The Bulls, Sharks and Free State can also reflect on satisfying campaigns. In fact, WP were involved in three epic clashes with Free State throughout the under-21

It seems as if the major unions are taking the development of youth rugby seriously and see the national under-21 tournament as an avenue for dominance at senior level.

competition, with all of them being decided by the narrowest of margins.

First WP beat Free State 42-40 in Bloemfontein, then 40-39 in Cape Town and finally advanced by virtue of scoring more tries in their 49-49 semifinal draw at Newlands.

The Bulls advanced to the final courtesy of a 39-35 win over an impressive generation of Sharks youngsters in their semifinal. While the Bulls ended up playing second fiddle to WP, they can certainly take heart from talented youngsters such as flyhalf Marnitz Boshoff and loose forward CJ Stander, to name just a few.

The season was also not a failure for the Sharks. In fact, they inflicted WP's only defeat of the season and it was a heavy one at that – 41-14 in Durban.

If there was a negative to the tournament, it was some of the lopsided scorelines. Boland, for example, conceded centuries against the Sharks, Western Province and Free State.

However, the positive is that the major unions are clearly taking the development of youth rugby seriously and clearly see it as an avenue for dominance at senior level.

WP are in pole position for now, but there are a number of unions in hot pursuit. And the biggest beneficiary may ultimately be Springbok rugby.

UNDER-21 CHAMPIONSHIP

ABSA UNDER-21 LOGS

SECTION A

Team	P	W	L	D	PF	PA	Diff	TF	TA	BP	Pts
WP	12	11	1	0	533	264	269	69	30	7	51
Blue Bulls	12	9	3	0	474	326	148	62	33	12	48
Sharks	12	9	3	0	543	274	269	73	31	10	46
Free State	12	6	6	0	561	366	195	71	46	11	35
Leopards	12	4	8	0	370	406	-36	45	52	9	25
Xerox Lions U21	12	3	9	0	325	393	-68	43	51	6	18
Boland	12	0	12	0	105	882	-777	13	133	1	1

SECTION B

Team	P	W	L	D	PF	PA	Diff	TF	TA	BP	Pts
EP	6	5	0	1	241	134	107	32	14	4	26
Griffons	6	4	0	2	216	138	78	31	15	5	25
Valke	6	3	2	1	249	146	103	31	19	5	19
Mpumalanga	6	3	3	0	215	166	49	23	21	5	17
Griquas	6	2	4	0	152	199	-47	19	25	4	12
Border	6	1	5	0	110	273	-163	15	38	2	6
SWD	6	1	5	0	92	219	-127	12	31	0	4

2010 UNDER-21 LEADING SCORERS

85 POINTS OR MORE

PLAYER	Province	Tries	Conversions	Penalties	Drop Goals	Points
GJ van Aswegen	WP	1	44	37	1	207
ML Boshoff	Blue Bulls	5	39	20	1	166
LD van Z Fouche	Leopards	3	25	22	2	137
GA Whitehead	Free State	3	30	18	2	135
F du Toit	Free State	2	32	16	1	125
G Cronje	Sharks	3	27	14	0	111
N Jansen van Rensburg	Pumas	1	20	18	4	111
WNF du Plessis	Sharks	2	31	7	1	96
DJG Poolman	WP	17	0	0	0	85

SEVEN TRIES

DJG Poolman	WP	17	M Nienaber	Valke	9
M Schoeman	Blue Bulls	13	CL Jacobs	Free State	8
R Syphus	Valke	10	JG Prinsloo	Free State	8
M Richards	Sharks	10	SP Marais	Leopards	7
GD Janke	Griffons	9	JJ Engelbrecht	WP	7

ABSA UNDER-21 CUP
FINALS RESULTS
FINALS - SECTION A
The Absa Stadium, Durban, Saturday, 30 October. Referee: Tiaan Jonker
WP 43 (TRIES: Sadie 2, Van Aswegen, Schreuder. CONS: Van Aswegen 4. PEN: Van Aswegen 5).
Blue Bulls 32 (TRIES: Van den Heever 2, Montague, Mastriet. CONS: Boshoff 3. PEN: Boshoff 2).
WP: OM du Toit, DJG Poolman, J Sadie, BW Klaasen (NJ Hanekom, 57), JJ Engelbrecht, GJ van Aswegen, L Schreuder (c) (NJ Groom, 71), N Koster, Y Hartzenberg (T Daniller, 49), PW van der Walt (RB Johannes, 69), DP Hugo, Q Roux (S Greeff, 45), T Botha (R-H Smith, 64), S Tobias, R-H Smith (J-P Smith, 29). *Unused replacement: AJ de Swardt.*
BLUE BULLS: A Coetzee, S Mastriet, AJ Jacobs (J-C Roos, 80), S Mtimkulu (G Helberg, 75), G van den Heever, ML Boshoff (c), DC Faasen (W Moolman, 75), JM Ross (TA Chikukwa, 62), M Schoeman (WC Nel, 69), CJ Stander, CN Hess, F Mostert, P-R De Klerk, AJ le Roux (RL Coetzee, 62), MM Melllet (VP Koch, 40).

FINALS - SECTION B
Outeniqua Park, George, Friday, 15 October. Referee: Matt Kemp
Valke 53 (TRIES: Nienaber 2, Van Deventer, Syphus, Coetzee, Mtwa. CONS: Laubscher 4. PEN: Laubscher 5).
EP 36 (TRIES: Van Rooyen 2, Sias, Van Staden, Grey. CONS: Sias 4. PEN: Sias).
VALKE: PMR Syphus, P Moloi, JMJ Radebe (F Gondo, 79), R Coetzee, M Nienaber, DW Laubscher, MA Robbertse (G Venter, 73), AL Van Deventer, FNJ Kalp, JG van Niekerk (B Van der Merwe, 76), A Gower (S Mtwa, 31), P Lubbe(c) (S Mtwa, 5-16), B-CX Van Jaarsveld, B Muller, H Ludik (C Nolte, 79). *Unused replacements: A Nel, M Kotzee.*
EP: M Van Staden, Z Sodladla, S Grey, Y Stampu (c), GL Mdyozi, CI Sias, R Van Rooyen (K King, 45), A Manentsa, GF Rademan, ZN April (FA Gerber, 45), S Borsaah, CH Dicks (T Bholi, 40), TL Mngomezulu, W Lotter (D du P Grobler, 40), D Barnard. *Unused replacements: AP Lalla-Kooverjee, M Banda, V Dyantjies.*

UNDER-21 CHAMPIONSHIP

ABSA UNDER-19 CHAMPIONSHIP

Western Province juniors clean up

THOUGH neither the Stormers nor Western Province could win their respective grand finals, 2010 was a truly remarkable year for Province rugby as a whole.

This was emphasised when every one of WP's junior sides, from under-13B to under-21, played in the main fixtures or finals of their respective tournaments.

And, building on their Craven Week success of 2009, WP's U19 team won the A-section of the 2010 Absa national competition – beating the Blue Bulls three times in the process. The third victory was the one that really mattered, however: the final, played in Durban, which WP won 26-20.

Rick Schroeder, the Gregan-like scrumhalf who captained that 2009 Craven Week side, continued his good run at the helm with 10 wins from 12 league matches, with WP's only losses coming against the Leopards (36-37) and Sharks (32-36).

The Leopards defeat was avenged in emphatic fashion in the semifinals (49-13), and it was this form that WP took into the final. Well, at least for the first half.

Leading 20-6 at halftime, this match must have seemed just as easy as the two previous encounters against the Bulls, when WP won 22-7 and 29-8 respectively.

But two quick tries after the break by Arno Botha and JJ Breet put the Bulls back in the game. Thankfully for WP, however, the boot of flyhalf William van Wyk saw them home.

Western Province lost only two matches all year, one of them being a 36-32 defeat at the hands of the Sharks. But they won the matches that mattered to claim the national title in 2010.

Ironically, Van Wyk's lack of kicking form in 2009 attracted a lot of criticism after he was included in the SA Schools side. Practice, it seems, made perfect in the end.

Looking to the future, Van Wyk, Schroeder as well as loose forwards Jakobus Porter, Nizaam Carr and Siya Kolisi impressed all year. Kolisi, an eighthman who also represented the U21 side at times, in particular looks to be the real deal. It would also come as no surprise if he was drafted into the Springbok sevens team sooner rather than later.

Still sticking to the A section, but turning to the opposite side of the coin, Free State endured a terrible year. Champions in 2009, the young Cheetahs only managed to win three of their 12 matches. Considering that many of these players would have run for Grey College in 2009, the poor return does pose some questions to Free State's decision-makers regarding the collapse of their youth sides, especially as the U21 team, also defending champions, could win only 50 percent of their matches in 2010.

In the B section, SWD's Young Eagles at least made sure that the trophy stayed in the Western Cape after Boland won it the year before. In the final, the Eagles beat the Valke 27-20 – this in a year where boardroom politics nearly brought the George-based union to its knees.

UNDER-19 CHAMPIONSHIP

ABSA UNDER-19 LOGS

SECTION A

Team	P	W	D	L	PF	PA	Diff	TF	TA	BP	Pts
Western Province	12	10	2	0	426	214	212	50	25	9	49
Blue Bulls	12	9	3	0	472	239	233	64	25	10	46
Sharks	12	8	4	0	387	245	142	50	26	10	42
Leopards	12	7	5	0	364	334	30	47	46	8	36
Lions	12	4	7	1	332	419	-87	39	49	6	24
Free State	12	3	9	0	300	424	-124	32	47	5	17
Griffons	12	0	11	1	198	604	-406	23	87	5	7

SECTION B

Team	P	W	D	L	PF	PA	Diff	TF	TA	BP	Pts
Eastern Province	6	6	0	0	214	92	122	31	14	5	29
Pumas	6	3	3	0	175	130	45	24	16	5	17
SWD	6	4	2	0	121	118	3	16	15	1	17
Valke	6	2	3	1	156	137	19	23	18	5	15
Griquas	6	2	3	1	141	129	12	22	17	3	13
Boland	6	2	4	0	157	165	-8	23	24	5	13
Border	6	1	5	0	56	249	-193	5	40	0	4

2010 UNDER-19 LEADING SCORERS

65 POINTS OR MORE

PLAYER	Province	Tries	Conversions	Penalties	Drop Goals	Points
U Beyers	WP	1	42	29	0	176
P van der Walt	Blue Bulls	3	36	24	0	159
JN Lourens	Leopards	3	33	23	0	150
AA Olivier	Sharks	1	25	15	1	103
LV Moos	Griffons	2	16	15	0	87
W van Wyk	WP	8	5	5	5	80
D Sabbagh	Lions	0	17	15	0	79
CF Schoeman	Pumas	1	23	6	0	69

SEVEN TRIES

CD Skosan	Blue Bulls	9	J-J Breet	Blue Bulls	7
W van Wyk	WP	8	FG Fouche	Leopards	7
RJ de Bruyn	Lions	8	S Kolisi	WP	7
P Lindeque	Sharks	7	MG van der Spuy	WP	7
WJ Jacobs	Blue Bulls	7			

ABSA UNDER-19 CUP
FINALS RESULTS

FINALS - SECTION A
The Absa Stadium, Durban, Saturday, 30 October. Referee: Rasta Rasivhenge
WP 26 (TRIES: Schroeder, Ntubeni. CONS: Van Wyk 2. PEN: Van Wyk 2. DG: Van Wyk 2).
Blue Bulls 20 (TRIES: Botha, Breet. CONS: Van der Walt 2. PEN: Van der Walt 2).

WP: U Beyers, CT Khumalo, MG van der Spuy, ST Lane, S Maseko (P-S de Wet, 57), W van Wyk, R Schroeder (c),
S Kolisi, N Carr, JAH Porter, W van der Sluys, E Etzebeth, J Malherbe, S Ntubeni (N Rautenbach, 35), A Botha (AJ Kotze,
68). *Unused subs: C Lindsay, JT Reyneke, GJ Jordaan, D de Allende.*
BLUE BULLS: P van der Walt, CD Skosan, BJ Moolman, JF Venter (GCF Maritz, 56), CM Lombaard, A Jantjies, WJ Jacobs
(R van Rooyen, 56), AF Botha (c), J-P le Grange, L Schwartz, JR Julies (J-J Breet, 36), S van Heerden, SJP Pretorius,
CJ Momberg (M Mbonambi, 52), JL Schoeman. *Unused subs: D van der Westhuizen, GF Bondesio, PG Oosthuizen.*

FINALS - SECTION B
Outeniqua Park, George, Friday, 15 October. Referee: Francois Veldsman
SWD 27 (TRIES: Eksteen 2, Jansen, Schuld. CONS: Moos 2 PEN: Moos).
VALKE 20 (TRIES: Greyling, Kotze. CONS: Poley 2. PEN: Poley 2).

SWD: AP Poley, TT Marobela, JC Greyling, M Kotzee, TM Manaka, DA-N Pekeur (HR Smith, 64), A Richter, A Nel, SJ van
Staden, M Erasmus, PFJ van Vuuren (c), J Alberts, P Groenewald, K Ngwenya (W Coetzer, 67), Z Grobler (TG Mabaso,
61). *Unused subs: JM Behrens, EG Crow, M Mongia, J-P Bezuidenhout.*
VALKE: G Smith, CS Afrika, K-H Schuld (CC Crowley, 55), G Jansen, C-TJ Moos (GJ de Jager, 69), DC Roberts, EN Tem-
perman (c), FR Eksteen, C da Silva (A Erasmus, 58), L Kiewiet, HM Leslie (S de Klerk, 56), W Fourie, FH Langenhoven,
C Esterhuizen (L Maxeke, 63), LJ Steytler (RJ van Deventer, 63). *Unused sub: R Agent..*

UNDER-19 CHAMPIONSHIP

SECTION 6
THE PROVINCES

BLUE BULLS RUGBY UNION

FOUNDED 1938 (as Northern Transvaal) **GROUND** Loftus Versfeld
CAPACITY 50 000 **ADDRESS** Kirkness Street, Sunnyside, Pretoria, 0002
POSTAL ADDRESS PO Box 28680, Sunnyside, Pretoria, 0132
TELEPHONE NUMBER 012 420 0700 **WEBSITE** www.bluebulls.co.za
COLOURS Sky blue jersey and socks, navy shorts
CURRIE CUP COACH Frans Ludeke **VODACOM CUP COACH** Nico Serfontein
CAPTAIN Victor Matfield **PRESIDENT** Boet Fick **COMPANY CEO** Barend van
Graan **UNION GENERAL MANAGER** Johan Schoeman

Blue Bulls suffer 2010 blues

WITH the two other major rugby trophies already nestled in the Loftus Versfeld cabinet, it was almost a given that the Absa Currie Cup should join the Vodacom Super 14 and Vodacom Cup trophies to round off a fantastic 2010 season for the Pretoria boys.

Oops, not to be, as the Sharks stung the Blue Bulls in Durban and in so doing caused them to miss only their second final since 2002.

The only other time the Blue Bulls failed to get past their semifinal opponents since then was in 2007, when they were deprived of a dozen Springboks playing in the World Cup in France.

The introduction of the Springboks a week before the semifinals this time around probably cost the Blue Bulls more than the other unions, but even they failed to ignite their teammates, who were stop-start all year.

Even the most diehard of Blue Bulls fans must have felt uncomfortable with the erratic way the 2009 champions were going about defending their title and this time even their reliable internationals could not push them all the way.

Even at Fortress Loftus, the Blue Bulls looked vulnerable without their experienced core and not only lost to the Free State Cheetahs at home in the early rounds, but had to hang on desperately to beat the lowly Leopards and Griquas, with the latter only losing because Naas Olivier missed a straightforward conversion at the death.

There were better shows at home against the resurgent Lions, Sharks and Western Province, but a shock loss against the Pumas in Nelspruit cost the Bulls dearly.

Taking nothing away from a wonderful debut for the home side at their new Mbombela Stadium, but the 'Bees Roux incident' certainly rocked the Blue Bulls to their core, after the prop was arrested for murder on the morning of the match.

Despite their inability to put in a decent 80 minutes all season, there were some good individual performances from the likes of Juandré Kruger, Dean Greyling, Stefan Watermeyer and Fudge Mabeta.

Greyling, Werner Kruger and Deon Stegmann all received call-ups to the wider Springbok training group at the end of the season, while Flip van der Merwe was pulled out of Currie Cup action to join the Springboks on their Tri-Nations tour in Australasia.

There was also a solid introduction to senior rugby for the likes of CJ Stander, the national under-20 captain, and coach Frans Ludeke highlighted the growth of depth as the one plus from the season.

Jacques-Louis Potgieter (173) was the main point-scorer for the Blue Bulls, but even he failed to reach the lofty heights as a match-winning pivot in the same way as he had done at the Cheetahs a year earlier.

Watermeyer, Greyling and Kruger probably were the main contenders for player of the season, with Watermeyer's six tries the most scored by any player. Only two players, Gerhard van den Heever and Derick Kuün, started in all the matches.

Kuün and Gary Botha shared most of the captaincy duties, but the latter had a stop-start season due to knee and ankle injuries.

Gerhard van den Heever was one of only two players to appear in every Currie Cup game

BLUE BULLS LOG POSITIONS

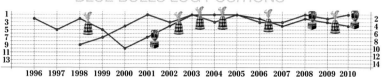

1996 1997 1998 1999 2000 2001 2002 2003 2004 2005 2006 2007 2008 2009 2010

BLUE BULLS RESULTS AND SCORERS IN 2010

Played	Won	Drawn	Lost	Points for	Points against	Tries for	Tries against	Winning %
25	**19**	**0**	**6**	**781**	**564**	**91**	**55**	**76%**

VODACOM CUP Played **10** Won **10** Drawn **0** Lost **0** Points for **332** Points against **174** Tries for **42** Tries against **15**

Date	Venue	Opponent	Result	Score	Scorers
Feb 26	Kimberley	GRIQUAS	WON	22-17	T: Snyman, Kruger. P: Brummer (2). DG: Brummer, Boshoff.
Mar 5	Pretoria	PUMAS	WON	29-15	T: Helberg, Watermeyer, Kruger, Z Botha. C: Brummer (2), Boshoff. P: Brummer.
Mar 13	Raiders RC	LIONS	WON	27-22	T: Van Schalkwyk (2), Oosthuizen. C: Brummer (3). P: Brummer (2).
Mar 19	Pretoria	LEOPARDS	WON	25-15	T: Mametsa, Botha, Greyling. C: Brummer (2). P: Brummer. D: Brummer.
Mar 27	Kempton Park	VALKE	WON	50-7	T: Willis (2), Mangweni, Helberg, Watermeyer, Boshoff, Snyman, Van Velze. C: Boshoff (5).
April 10	Windhoek	WELWITCHIAS	WON	58-34	T: Watermeyer (2), Mametsa, Ndungane, Brummer, Snyman, Mellett, Gwavu, Faasen. C: Boshoff (3), Watermeyer (2). P: Watermeyer.
April 17	Atteridgeville	GRIFFONS	WON	40-26	T: Mangweni, Helberg, Boshoff, Kruger, Watermeyer. C: Watermeyer (3). P: Brummer (2), Watermeyer.
Quarter final					
April 24	Pretoria	WP	WON	17-6	T: Van Velze. P: Brummer (3). D: Brummer.
Semi-final					
May 1	Pretoria	SHARKS XV	WON	33-3	T: Van Velze (2), Mangweni, Ralepelle. C: Brummer (2). P: Brummer (2). D: Brummer.
Final					
May 7	Pretoria	FREE STATE	WON	31-29	T: Helberg, Van Velze, Dinkelmann. C: Brummer (2). P: Brummer (2). DG: Brummer (2).

ABSA Currie Cup Played **15** Won **9** Lost **6** Drawn **0** Points for **449** Points against **390** Tries for **49** Tries against **40**

Date	Venue	Opponent	Result	Score	Scorers
July 9	Pretoria	PUMAS	WON	38-15	T: Mametsa (2), Dippenaar, Watermeyer, Stegmann, Greyling. C: Potgieter (3), Brummer.
July 17	Durban	SHARKS	LOST	28-34	T: Van den Heever, Van Velze, Greyling. C: Potgieter (2). P: Potgieter (3).
July 24	Pretoria	CHEETAHS	LOST	23-25	T: Watermeyer, Kuun. C: Potgieter (2). P: Potgieter (3).
July 31	Johannesburg	GOLDEN LIONS	WON	32-18	T: Van den Heever, J-L Potgieter. C: Potgieter (2). P: Potgieter (6).
Aug 6	Pretoria	LEOPARDS	WON	43-38	T: Van den Heever (2), Watermeyer, Hougaard, D Potgieter, Kuun. C: J-L Potgieter (5). P: Potgieter.
Aug 14	Cape Town	WP	LOST	12-15	P: Potgieter (4).
Aug 20	Pretoria	GRIQUAS	WON	39-38	T: Mametsa (2), Snyman, Maku, Greyling. C: Potgieter (4). P: Potgieter (2).
Aug 27	Nelspruit	PUMAS	LOST	21-22	T: D Potgieter, Greyling. C: J-L Potgieter. P: Brummer (2), J-L Potgieter.
Sept 4	Pretoria	SHARKS	WON	40-34	T: Olivier, Snyman, J Kruger, Engels. C: J-L Potgieter (3), Kirchner. P: Potgieter (4).
Sept 11	Bloemfontein	CHEETAHS	LOST	14-20	T: Van der Westhuyzen. P: J-L Potgieter (3).
Sept 18	Pretoria	GOLDEN LIONS	WON	24-21	T: Watermeyer, Van Velze. C: J-L Potgieter. P: Potgieter (4).
Sept 25	Potchefstroom	LEOPARDS	WON	39-26	T: Pretorius, Watermeyer, Van der Westhuyzen, Hougaard, Kuun, Groepes. C: J-L Potgieter (3). P: Potgieter.
Oct 2	Pretoria	WP	WON	36-32	T: Kirchner, Watermeyer, O Kruger. C: J-L Potgieter (3). P: Potgieter (4). D: Van der Westhuyzen.
Oct 9	Kimberley	GRIQUAS	WON	48-36	T: Van den Heever, Pretorius, Olivier, D Potgieter, Van der Westhuyzen, Kuun, Matfield. C: Steyn (4), J-L Potgieter. P: Steyn.
Semi-final					
Oct 16	Durban	SHARKS	LOST	12-16	P: Steyn (4).

APPEARANCES AND POINTS FOR BLUE BULLS IN 2010 — CAREER

PLAYER	Appearances	Tries	Conversions	Penalties	Drop Goals	Points	Career Matches	Career Tries	Conversions	Penalties	Drop Goals	Points
HJ (Heinie) Adams	1	–	–	–	–	0	48	7	–	–	–	35
HJ (Henri) Bantjes	2	–	–	–	–	0	14	–	–	–	–	0
ML (Marnitz) Boshoff	8	2	9	–	1	31	9	2	11	–	1	35
BJ (Berend) Botha	8	–	–	–	–	0	13	–	–	–	–	0
G van G (Gary) Botha	8	–	–	–	–	0	85	12	–	–	–	60
JP (Bakkies) Botha	2	–	–	–	–	0	52	10	–	–	–	50
ZD (Zane) Botha	8	2	–	–	–	10	8	2	–	–	–	10
F (Francois) Brummer	15	1	12	17	6	98	38	6	54	73	14	399
PR (Rossouw) de Klerk	14	–	–	–	–	0	18	–	–	–	–	0
EH (Ernst) Dinkelman	6	1	–	–	–	5	6	1	–	–	–	5
SC (Stefan) Dippenaar	9	1	–	–	–	5	25	4	–	–	–	20
J (Jaco) Engels	15	1	–	–	–	5	67	6	–	–	–	30
I (Ivann) Espag	7	–	–	–	–	0	8	–	–	–	–	0
DG (Danie) Faasen	7	1	–	–	–	5	7	1	–	–	–	5
C (Corne) Fourie	1	–	–	–	–	0	1	–	–	–	–	0
J (Jaco) Fourie	1	–	–	–	–	0	1	–	–	–	–	0
MD (Dean) Greyling	21	5	–	–	–	25	47	5	–	–	–	25
HG (Hayden) Groepes	6	1	–	–	–	5	6	1	–	–	–	5
LV (Lubabalo) Gwavu	5	1	–	–	–	5	22	2	–	–	–	10
GG (Deon) Helberg	10	4	–	–	–	20	10	4	–	–	–	20
CN (Cornell) Hess	10	–	–	–	–	0	10	–	–	–	–	0
F (Francois) Hougaard	8	2	–	–	–	10	36	11	–	–	–	55
D (Dustin) Jinka	4	–	–	–	–	0	4	–	–	–	–	0
Z (Zane) Kirchner	9	1	1	–	–	7	31	5	2	–	–	29
FBC (Frik) Kirsten	3	–	–	–	–	0	24	–	–	–	–	0
OC (Ockie) Kruger	16	4	–	–	–	20	36	10	–	–	–	50
PJJ (Juandre) Kruger	11	1	–	–	–	5	30	3	–	–	–	15
W (Werner) Kruger	13	–	–	–	–	0	83	5	–	–	–	25
GWF (Derick) Kuun	15	4	–	–	–	20	95	33	–	–	–	165
AJ (AJ) le Roux	2	–	–	–	–	0	2	–	–	–	–	0
MK (Fudge) Mabeta	18	–	–	–	–	0	46	2	–	–	–	10
BG (Bandise) Maku	9	1	–	–	–	5	61	3	–	–	–	15
SJ (John) Mametsa	12	6	–	–	–	30	136	71	–	–	–	355
S (Tiger) Mangweni	10	3	–	–	–	15	46	15	–	–	1	78
V (Victor) Matfield	2	1	–	–	–	5	52	5	–	–	–	25
MM (Morne) Mellet	5	1	–	–	–	5	5	1	–	–	–	5
AZ (Akona) Ndungane	1	1	–	–	–	5	26	15	–	–	–	75
W (Wynand) Olivier	4	2	–	–	–	10	62	25	–	–	–	125
DA (Devin) Oosthuizen	10	1	–	–	–	5	10	1	–	–	–	5
DJ (Dewald) Potgieter	8	3	–	–	–	15	45	9	–	–	–	45
J-L (Jacques-Louis) Potgieter	14	1	30	36	–	173	55	7	86	81	4	462
JC (Jaco) Pretorius	11	2	–	–	–	10	27	7	–	–	–	35
MC (Chiliboy) Ralepelle	13	1	–	–	–	5	29	2	–	–	–	10
DJ (Danie) Rossouw	2	–	–	–	–	0	97	24	–	–	–	120
JS (Bees) Roux	7	–	–	–	–	0	7	–	–	–	–	0
R (Ruan) Snyman	20	5	–	–	–	25	37	5	–	–	–	25
PJ (Pierre) Spies	1	–	–	–	–	0	17	4	–	–	–	20
CJ (CJ) Stander	14	–	–	–	–	0	14	–	–	–	–	0
GG (Gurthro) Steenkamp	1	–	–	–	–	0	24	5	–	–	–	25
JWA (Wilhelm) Steenkamp	9	–	–	–	–	0	65	5	–	–	–	25
GJ (Gideon) Stegmann	4	1	–	–	–	5	49	8	–	–	–	40
M (Morne) Steyn	2	–	4	5	–	23	93	26	176	101	10	815
GJ (Gerhard) van den Heever	15	5	–	–	–	25	34	18	–	–	–	90
PR (Flip) van der Merwe	9	–	–	–	–	0	23	3	–	–	–	15
JNB (Jaco) van der Westhuyzen	13	3	–	–	1	18	48	20	50	26	1	281
AJ (Dries) van Schalkwyk	4	2	–	–	–	10	20	2	–	–	–	10
J (Justin) van Staden	1	–	–	–	–	0	1	–	–	–	–	0
G-J (Gerrit-Jan) van Velze	20	7	–	–	–	35	40	8	–	–	–	40
S (Stefan) Watermeyer	22	11	5	2	–	71	42	13	5	2	–	81
VS (Vainon) Willis	10	2	–	–	–	10	11	2	–	–	–	10
61 Players	**516**	**91**	**61**	**60**	**8**	**781**	**2058**	**436**	**384**	**283**	**31**	**3890**

PROVINCIAL ROUND-UP

APPEARANCES AND POINTS IN VODACOM CUP 2010

	Griquas	Pumas	Golden Lions	Leopards	Valke	Welwitchias	Griffons	WP	Sharks XV	Free State	Matches	Tries	Conversions	Penalties	Drop Goals	Points
Tiger Mangweni	15	15	15c	15	15	15	15	15	15	15	10	3	–	–	–	15
Deon Helberg	14	13	13	13	14	13	14	14	13	13	10	4	–	–	–	20
Ernst Dinkelman	13	12R	–	–	13	–	13	x	12R	14R	6	1	–	–	–	5
Stefan Watermeyer	12	12	12	12	12	12	10R	12	12	12	10	5	5	2	–	41
Vainon Willis	11	11	11	11	11	14R	11	11	11	11	10	2	–	–	–	10
Francois Brummer	10	10	10	10	10R	10	12	10	10	10	10	1	11	15	6	90
Ruan Snyman	9	9	9R	9	9	9	9	9	9	9	10	3	–	–	–	15
Gerrit-Jan van Velze	8c	8c	–	8c	8c	8c	8c	8c	8c	8c	9	5	–	–	–	25
Okkie Kruger	7	7	7	6	6	6	6	6	6	6	10	3	–	–	–	15
Dries van Schalkwyk	6	6	8	7	–	–	–	–	–	–	4	2	–	–	–	10
Fudge Mabeta	5	5	5	5	–	–	–	5	5	5	7	–	–	–	–	0
Berend Botha	4	5R	5R	4R	4	4	4	–	–	–	7	–	–	–	–	0
Rossouw de Klerk	3	3	–	3	3R	3	3	3R	3R	3R	9	–	–	–	–	0
Henri Bantjes	2	–	–	–	–	–	–	–	–	–	1	–	–	–	–	0
Dean Greyling	1	1	3	1	1	1	–	3	3	3	9	1	–	–	–	5
Zane Botha	2R	2	2	2	2	2R	2	x	2R	–	8	2	–	–	–	10
Jaco Engels	1R	–	1	1R	–	–	–	1	1	1	6	–	–	–	–	0
Ivann Espach	3R	3R	3R	3R	3	1R	3R	–	–	–	7	–	–	–	–	0
Cornell Hess	4R	4	4	4	5	5	5	4	4	4	10	–	–	–	–	0
Danie Faasen	x	9R	–	9R	9R	9R	9R	x	9R	x	6	1	–	–	–	5
Marnitz Boshoff	12R	10R	10R	10R	10	12R	10	x	15R	x	8	2	9	–	1	31
Devin Oosthuizen	6R	6R	6	7R	7	7	7R	7	7	7	10	1	–	–	–	5
John Mametsa	–	14	14	14	–	14	–	–	14	14	6	2	–	–	–	10
AJ le Roux	–	2R	x	2R	–	–	–	–	–	–	2	–	–	–	–	0
Heinie Adams	–	–	9	–	–	–	–	–	–	–	1	–	–	–	–	0
Morne Mellet	–	–	x	–	1R	3R	1	x	1R	1R	5	1	–	–	–	5
CJ Stander	–	–	x	–	6R	–	–	–	–	–	1	–	–	–	–	0
Chiliboy Ralepelle	–	–	–	–	2R	2	–	2	2	2	5	1	–	–	–	5
Vincent Gwavu	–	–	–	–	7R	6R	7	7R	7R	x	5	1	–	–	–	5
Akona Ndungane	–	–	–	–	–	11	–	–	–	–	1	1	–	–	–	5
Jaco Fourie	–	–	–	–	–	–	4R	–	–	x	1	–	–	–	–	0
Corne Fourie	–	–	–	–	–	–	1R	–	–	–	1	–	–	–	–	0
Justin van Staden	–	–	–	–	–	–	13R	–	–	–	1	–	–	–	–	0
Stephan Dippenaar	–	–	–	–	–	–	–	13	–	–	1	–	–	–	–	0
34 Players											**207**	**42**	**25**	**17**	**7**	**332**

APPEARANCES AND POINTS IN ABSA CURRIE CUP 2010

	Pumas	Sharks	Cheetahs	Golden Lions	Leopards	WP	Griquas	Pumas	Sharks	Cheetahs	Golden Lions	Leopards	WP	Griquas	Sharks	Matches	Tries	Conversions	Penalties	Drop Goals	Points
van der Westhuyzen	15	15	15	15	15	x	15	x	11	11	11	11	11	11	11	13	3	–	–	1	18
van den Heever	14	14	14	14	14	14	14	14	14	14	14	14	14	14	14	15	5	–	–	–	25
Dippenaar	13	13	13	13	11R	–	13R	–	–	12R	13R	–	x	–	–	8	1	–	–	–	5
Watermeyer	12	12	12	12	12	12	12	–	10R	12	12	12	12	–	–	12	6	–	–	–	30
Mametsa	11	11	11	11	–	11	11	–	–	–	–	–	–	–	–	6	4	–	–	–	20
J-L Potgieter	10	10	10	10	10	10	10	10R	10	10	10	10	10	10R	x	14	1	30	36	–	173
Snyman	9	9	9	9R	–	9	9	9R	9	–	–	9R	x	9R	x	10	2	–	–	–	10
van Velze	8	8	8	8	8	8	8	–	8	8	8	8	–	–	–	11	2	–	–	–	10
Kuun	7	7	7	6	6c	6	6c	6c	6c	6c	6c	6	6c	6	6	15	4	–	–	–	20
Stegmann	6	6	6	–	–	–	–	–	–	–	–	–	–	–	6R	4	1	–	–	–	5
Mabeta	5	5	5	5R	4R	6R	5	5R	5	–	–	5	5	–	–	11	–	–	–	–	–
van der Merwe	4	–	–	4	4	–	–	–	–	4	4	4	4	4R	4R	9	–	–	–	–	–
Kruger	3	3	3	3	–	3	3	3	–	3	3	3	3	3	3	13	–	–	–	–	–
Botha	2c	2c	2c	2c	–	2c	–	–	–	2R	2R	2c	–	–	–	8	–	–	–	–	–
Greyling	1	1	1	–	–	1	1	1	1	1	1	1	–	1	1	12	4	–	–	–	20
Maku	2R	2R	x	–	2R	2R	2	2	2	–	–	–	6R	2R	x	9	1	–	–	–	5
Roux	3R	3R	1R	1R	3	3R	3R	–	–	–	–	–	–	–	–	7	–	–	–	–	–
Kruger	5R	–	4R	5	5	4	4	5	4	5	5	7	–	–	–	11	1	–	–	–	5
CJ Stander	8R	8R	6R	8R	8R	7R	7	7	7R	7	7	–	8	5R	–	13	–	–	–	–	–
Faasen	9R	x	x	–	–	–	–	–	–	–	–	–	–	–	–	1	–	–	–	–	–
Brummer	10R	x	10R	10R	12R	–	–	10	–	–	–	–	x	–	–	5	–	1	2	–	8
Groepes	15R	11R	x	11R	11	–	–	11	–	–	–	11R	–	–	–	6	1	–	–	–	5
Steenkamp	–	4	4	–	–	5	5R	4	5R	4R	x	4R	5R	–	–	9	–	–	–	–	–
Botha	–	4R	–	–	–	–	–	–	–	–	–	–	–	–	–	1	–	–	–	–	–
Hougaard	–	–	9	9	–	–	–	–	9	9	9	9	9	9	9	8	2	–	–	–	10
Potgieter	–	–	7	7	7	7	–	8	7	–	–	–	8R	7	7	8	3	–	–	–	15
Engels	–	–	1	1	1R	1R	–	1R	1R	1R	1R	–	1R	–	–	9	1	–	–	–	5
Ralepelle	–	–	–	2R	2	–	–	–	–	2	2	2R	2	2	2	8	–	–	–	–	–
Pretorius	–	–	–	13	13	13	13	13	13	13	13	13	13	13	13	11	2	–	–	–	10
Kirsten	–	–	–	3R	–	–	3R	3	–	–	–	–	–	–	–	3	–	–	–	–	–
Jinka	–	–	–	9R	x	x	9	9R	x	9R	–	–	–	–	–	4	–	–	–	–	–
Kirchner	–	–	–	–	15	15	15	15	15	15	15	15	15	15	15	9	1	1	–	–	7
Bantjies	–	–	–	–	–	x	x	6R	–	–	–	–	–	–	–	1	–	–	–	–	–
Kruger	–	–	–	–	–	8R	7R	–	6R	7R	7R	7	–	–	–	6	1	–	–	–	5
Olivier	–	–	–	–	–	12	12	–	–	–	–	–	12	12	–	4	2	–	–	–	10
de Klerk	–	–	–	–	–	–	3R	3R	x	3R	1R	3R	x	–	–	5	–	–	–	–	–
Steenkamp	–	–	–	–	–	–	–	–	–	–	–	1	–	–	–	1	–	–	–	–	–
Steyn	–	–	–	–	–	–	–	–	–	–	–	–	10	10	–	2	–	4	5	–	23
Matfield	–	–	–	–	–	–	–	–	–	–	–	–	5c	5c	–	2	1	–	–	–	5
Rossouw	–	–	–	–	–	–	–	–	–	–	–	–	8	8	–	2	–	–	–	–	–
Botha	–	–	–	–	–	–	–	–	–	–	–	–	4	4	–	2	–	–	–	–	–
Spies	–	–	–	–	–	–	–	–	–	–	–	–	–	–	8R	1	–	–	–	–	–
42 Players																**309**	**49**	**36**	**43**	**1**	**449**

PROVINCIAL ROUND-UP

Marnitz Boshoff taking on the Western Province defence in an under-21 clash at Newlands.

ABSA UNDER-21 CHAMPIONSHIP (Runner-up, 2nd, Section A)

Played	Won	Drawn	Lost	Points for	Points against	Tries for	Tries against	Winning %
14	10	0	4	545	404	71	41	71.00%

RESULTS: Bt Boland (a) 43-18. Bt Sharks (a) 20-16. Lost Free State (h) 32-34. Bt Lions (a) 35-26. Bt Leopards (h) 43-30. Lost WP (a) 16-27. Bt Boland (h) 87-10. Bt Sharks (h) 51-31. Bt Free State (a) 36-35. Bt Lions (h) 32-21. Bt Leopards (a) 41-36. Lost WP (h) 38-42. SEMI FINAL Bt Sharks (h) 39-35. FINAL Lost WP (a) 32-43.

SCORERS: 166 Marnitz Boshoff (5t,39c,20p,1d); 65 Marnus Schoeman (13t); 28 Francois Brummer (2t,9c); 25 Sampie Mastriet (5t); 22 Juan-Claude Roos (5c,4p); 20 Tendayi Chikukwa, Simphiwe Mtimkulu, Danie Faasen, Deon Helberg, Jonathan Ross (4t each); 19 Justin van Staden (2t,3c,1d); 15 Willem Nel (3t); 10 Abraham le Roux, Clayton Blommetjies, Whestley Moolman, Adri Jacobs, Petrus Vorster, Andries Ferreira, Gerhard van den Heever (2t each); 5 Ernst Dinkelmann, Morne Mellett, Rossouw de Klerk, Juan-Philip Pike, Dalton Davis, Frans Mostert, Christiaan Stander (1t each).

ABSA U19 CHAMPIONSHIP (Runner-up, 2nd, Section A)

Played	Won	Drawn	Lost	Points for	Points against	Tries for	Tries against	Winning %
14	10	0	4	516	286	68	31	71.00%

RESULTS: Bt Griffons (h) 71-5. Bt Sharks (a) 25-15. Bt Free State (h) 35-28. Bt Lions (a) 38-20. Bt Leopards (h) 33-10. Lost WP (a) 17-22. Bt Griffons (a) 85-12. Lost Sharks (h) 15-19. Bt Free State (a) 49-21. Bt Lions (h) 56-27. Bt Leopards (a) 40-31. Lost WP (h) 8-29. SEMI FINAL Bt Sharks (h) 24-21. FINAL Lost WP (a) 20-26.

SCORERS: 161 Pieter van der Walt (3t,37c,24p); 56 Willem Jacobs (8t,5c,2p); 45 Courtnall Skosan (9t); 35 Jan-Jacobus Breet (7t); 30 Christiaan Lombaard (6t); 25 Arnold Botha (5t); 22 Gert Maritz (4t,1c); 20 Bradley Moolman (4t), Antonio Jantjies (2t,2c,2p); 10 Pieter Oosthuizen, Lean Schwartz, Abednego Mamushi, Juan Schoeman, Craig Pheiffer (2t each); 7 Jacobus Venter (1t,1c); 5 Mbongeni Mbonambi, Willem Redelinghuys, Giacomo Bendesio, Hagan Mumba, Louwrens van Heerden, Rudi van Rooyen, Jose Julies, Dandre van der Westhuizen, Penalty try (1t each).

AMATEUR CHAMPIONSHIP

Assupol Blue Bulls (2nd, North Section)

Played	Won	Drawn	Lost	Points for	Points against	Tries for	Tries against
5	3	0	2	217	139	28	17

RESULTS: Lost Leopards (h) 30-34. Bt Lowveld (a) 68-19. Bt Lions (h) 44-12. Bt Pumas (h) 41-18. Lost Valke (a) 34-56. Bt Limpopo (a) 51-18.

Blue Bulls Limpopo (3rd, North Section)

Played	Won	Drawn	Lost	Points for	Points against	Tries for	Tries against
5	3	0	2	189	171	26	22

RESULTS: Lost Pumas (a) 38-53. Bt Lions (h) 38-23. Lost Leopards (a) 47-49. Bt Lowveld (h) 40-22. Bt Valke (a) 26-24. Lost Blue Bulls (h) 18-51.

BLUE BULLS RECORDS

MATCH RECORDS

Biggest win	147-8	vs. South Western Districts (CC) (Currie Cup Record)		
			Polokwane	1996
Heaviest defeat	13-57	vs. Transvaal (CC)	Johannesburg	1994
Highest score	147	vs. South Western Districts (147-8, CC)	Polokwane	1996
Most points conceded	64	vs. Wellington Hurricanes (32-64)	New Plymouth	1997
Most tries	23	vs. South Western Districts (147-8, CC) (Currie Cup Record)		
			Polokwane	1996
Most points by a player	40	CP Steyn vs. SWD Eagles (CC)	Pretoria	2000
Most tries by a player	7	J Olivier vs. SWD (CC) (Currie Cup Record)	Polokwane	1996
Most conversions by a player	14	LR Sherrell vs. SWD (CC) (Currie Cup Record)		
			Polokwane	1996
Most penalties by a player	9	JH Kruger vs. Western Province (CC) (SA Record)		
			Pretoria	1996
	9	DJ Hougaard vs. Western Province (CC) (SA Record)		
			Pretoria	2002
Most drop goals by a player	5	HE Botha vs. Natal (CC Record)	Pretoria	1992

SEASON RECORDS

Most team points	1193	28 matches	1996
Most team points in Currie Cup	783	13 matches	1997
Most points by a player	361	CP Steyn	1999
Most Currie Cup points	268	JW Heunis (Currie Cup Record)	1989
Most team tries	142	28 matches	2004
Most tries by a player	25	PJ Spies	1975
Most Currie Cup tries by a player	18	E Botha	2004

CAREER RECORDS

Most appearances	184	SB Geldenhuys	1977-1989
Most points	2511	HE Botha (179 matches)	1977-1992
Most tries	85	DE Oosthuysen (140 matches)	1986-1994

HONOURS

ABSA Currie Cup	1946, 1956, 1968, 1969, 1971 (shared), 1973, 1974, 1975, 1977, 1978, 1979 (shared), 1980, 1981, 1987, 1988, 1989 (shared), 1991, 1998, 2002, 2003, 2004, 2006 (shared), 2009.
Lion Cup	1985, 1990, 1991
Bankfin Cup	2000
Vodacom Cup	2001, 2009, 2010

PROVINCIAL ROUND-UP

BOLAND RUGBY UNION

FOUNDED 1939 **GROUND** Boland Stadium
CAPACITY 10 000 **ADDRESS** Fontein Street, Wellington
POSTAL ADDRESS PO Box 127, Wellington, 7654
TELEPHONE NUMBER 021 873 2317 **WEBSITE** www.bolandrugby.com
COLOURS Old gold and black & white jersey, black shorts
CURRIE CUP COACH Eugene Eloff
VODACOM CUP COACH Eugene Eloff
CAPTAIN Bolla Conradie **PRESIDENT** Francois Davids **CEO** Piet Bergh

Boland change – and stay the same

A NEW coach, two semifinals, investors, a lot of excitement and expectations. And yet the Boland Cavaliers still have nothing to show for it.

After a hellish 2009, the Wellington-based union can at least reflect on a year with more good news than bad. It started with former Lions coach Eugene Eloff turning down a few lucrative European offers to take up the challenge of getting the Cavaliers out of the doldrums.

Eloff took up the job as director of rugby at the end of 2009, and took his senior side to the semifinals of both the 2010 Vodacom Cup and Currie Cup First Division. This followed Boland's relegation from the Premier League the previous year.

More good news was that a company called Game Plan obtained a stake of just under 50% in Boland Rugby for R5-million. Of particular interest were the individuals involved in the consortium: Springbok coach Peter de Villiers, Springbok lock Victor Matfield, entertainer Kurt Darren, and Renier Swart, the Pretoria businessman of the year in 2001.

There were immediately reports of conflicts of interest. This soon died down, but so did the excitement of having investors, with Game Plan unable to secure a new team sponsor before the start of the Currie Cup, or, for that matter, even by the end of the season.

This meant that Eloff could not lure the high-profile players that might have helped the Cavaliers regain their Premier League status for 2011. Instead he had to settle for former Springboks such as Bolla Conradie and Hottie Louw, but it was only by the second round of First Division matches that they did justice to their Bok tags. After a run of four consecutive defeats, they lifted their game and Conradie, in particular, stepped up as the captain Boland needed at the time.

However, Boland lost their Vodacom Cup and First Division semifinals – to Free State (22-14) and the Eastern Province Kings (26-25). More crucially, Boland also finished outside of the top two and therefore missed out on the promotion-relegation fixtures.

Conradie was paid a salary that would be considered very reasonable even at a bigger union. When one reflects on the year, the business sense behind that decision can be questioned.

That being said, Boland did produce a few exciting future prospects – players such as flyhalf Willie le Roux, fullback Jacquin Jansen (who later trained with the Springbok sevens squad), former UJ scrumhalf Alex Kock, and flanker Franzel September.

But without a team sponsor and consequently a few big names in their ranks, Boland aren't going places beyond where they found themselves at the end of 2010.

Promises of a rugby academy for under-19-players were made by president Francois Davids and while it was a better year for him and his union, words will have to translate into deeds if he is to justify the support he enjoys among the greater Boland rugby community.

Boland Cavaliers fullback Jacquin Jansen impressed on the field and was later called up for a Springbok Sevens training squad.

PROVINCIAL ROUND-UP

BOLAND CAVALIERS LOG POSITIONS

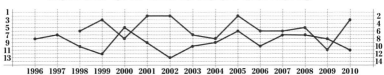

1996 1997 1998 1999 2000 2001 2002 2003 2004 2005 2006 2007 2008 2009 2010

BOLAND CAVALIERS RESULTS AND SCORERS IN 2010

Played	Won	Drawn	Lost	Points for	Points against	Tries for	Tries against
20	11	0	9	634	538	82	55

VODACOM CUP PLAYED **9** WON **6** DRAWN **0** LOST **3** POINTS FOR **250** POINTS AGAINST **207** TRIES FOR **31** TRIES AGAINST **17** WINNING PERCENTAGE **67%**

Date	Venue	Referee	Opponent	Result	Score	Scorers
Feb 27	Bredasdorp	Archie Sehlako	WESTERN PROVINCE	WON	37-28	T: September (2), Grant, Louw, Jordaan. C: Grant (3). P: Grant (2).
Mar 6	Bloemfontein	Joey Salmans	FREE STATE	LOST	29-37	T: Jansen, Vermeulen. C: Grant (2). P: Grant (5).
Mar 13	Saldanha	Lourens van der Merwe	SWD EAGLES	WON	25-24	T: Thyse, W Le Roux, Jordaan. C: Jansen (2). P: Jansen (2).
Mar 19	Wellington	Jason Jaftha	PAMPAS XV	WON	26-13	T: Thyse, Plaatjies, W le Roux, September. C: Grant (3).
Mar 26	Pietermaritzburg	Joey Salmans	SHARKS XV	LOST	20-35	T: Gerber, W le Roux. C: Gerber, Grant. P: Gerber (2).
April 10	East London[1]	Francois Groenewald	BULLDOGS	WON	33-13	T: Jordaan (2). Cornelius, W le Roux, September. C: Jansen (4).
April 17	Piketberg	Matt Kemp	EASTERN PROVINCE	WON	36-10	T: C Hendricks (2), Thyse, Plaatjies, Cornelius. C: Jansen (4). P: Jansen.

Quarter-final

April 24	Wellington	Mlungiselele Mdasha	LEOPARDS	WON	30-25	T: Swartbooi, Van Niekerk, Cornelius, Blignaut. C: Jansen (2). P: Jansen (2).

Semi-final

May 1	Wellington	Ben Crouse	FREE STATE	LOST	14-22	T: W le Roux. P: Jansen (3).

[1] Sisa Dukashe Stadium

ABSA CURRIE CUP First Division: PLAYED **11** WON **5** LOST **6** DREW **0** PF **384** PA **331** TF **51** TA **38** WINNING PERCENTAGE **45%**

Date	Venue	Referee	Opponent	Result	Score	Scorers
July 24	Kempton Park	Joey Salmans	VALKE	WON	53-10	T: W le Roux (3), Jansen (2), Conradie, Swartbooi, Louw, Plaatjies. C: Micklewood (2), Jansen (2).
July 31	Wellington	Jaco Peyper	EP KINGS	LOST	22-33	T: Hendricks, Plaatjies, Vermeulen. C: Jansen (2). DG: W le Roux.
August 6	George	Marius Jonker	SWD EAGLES	LOST	36-45	T: Immelman, Swartbooi, September, Plaatjies, Vermeulen. C: Jansen (4). P: Jansen.
Aug 13	Wellington	Jason Jaftha	BORDER	LOST	46-50	T: Hendricks (3), September, Plaatjies, Cornelius. C: Jansen (4), Cornelius. P: Cornelius (2).
Aug 20	Welkom	Sandile Mayende	GRIFFONS	LOST	13-52	T: Lewis, Hendricks. P: Jansen.
Sep 3	Wellington	Joey Salmans	VALKE	WON	41-21	T: Kock (2), Hendricks, Plaatjies, Vermeulen. C: Koen (3), Jansen (2). P: Koen (2).
Sep 10	Port Elizabeth	Marius Jonker	EP Kings	LOST	16-23	T: Immelman. C: Jansen. P: Jansen (3).
Sep 17	Wellington	Mark Lawrence	SWD EAGLES	WON	38-33	T: Kock, Immelman, Jansen, W le Roux. C: Jansen (3). P: Jansen (3). DG: W le Roux.
Sep 24	East London	Lourens van der Merwe	BORDER	WON	54-13	T: Conradie (2), Immelman, Hendricks, Guinazu, September, Plaatjies. C: Jansen (5). P: Jansen (3).
Oct 1	Wellington	Joey Salmans	GRIFFONS	WON	40-25	T: W le Roux (2), Kock, April, Hendricks, Jordaan. C: Jansen (5).

Semi-final

Oct 9	Port Elizabeth	Jaco Peyper	EP KINGS	LOST	25-26	T: Kock, April, Jansen. C: Jansen (2). P: Jansen (2).

APPEARANCES AND POINTS FOR BOLAND IN 2010   CAREER

PLAYER	Appearances	Tries	Conversions	Penalties	Drop Goals	Points	Career Matches	Career Tries	Conversions	Penalties	Drop Goals	Points
BT (Brendon) April	7	2	–	–	–	10	7	2	–	–	–	10
NS (Nikolai) Blignaut	14	1	–	–	–	5	14	1	–	–	–	5
A (Angelo) Brinkhuys	1	–	–	–	–	0	84	8	–	–	–	40
JHJ (Bolla) Conradie	14	3	–	–	–	15	14	3	–	–	–	15
A (Ashton) Constant	13	–	–	–	–	0	13	–	–	–	–	0
LC (Lionel) Cornelius	15	4	1	2	–	28	56	9	15	18	–	129
CF (Charl) du Plessis	8	–	–	–	–	0	8	–	–	–	–	0
AJ (André) du Toit	4	–	–	–	–	0	11	–	–	–	–	0
D (Danré) Gerber	6	1	1	2	–	13	10	2	4	7	–	39
D (Dean) Grant	4	1	9	7	–	44	4	1	9	7	–	44
E (Eusebio) Guinazu	12	1	–	–	–	5	12	1	–	–	–	5
T (Thor) Halvorsen	6	–	–	–	–	0	6	–	–	–	–	0
C (Cornal) Hendricks	20	10	–	–	–	50	35	11	–	–	–	55
DJ (David) Hendricks	1	–	–	–	–	0	45	11	–	–	–	55
JA (Braam) Immelman	11	4	–	–	–	20	11	4	–	–	–	20
J (Jacquin) Jansen	20	5	42	21	–	172	25	6	43	21	–	179
Z (Zandré) Jordaan	18	5	–	–	–	25	22	7	–	–	–	35
AH (Alex) Kock	8	5	–	–	–	25	8	5	–	–	–	25
LJ (Louis) Koen	1	–	3	2	–	12	1	–	3	2	–	12
W (Wesley) Kotze	5	–	–	–	–	0	5	–	–	–	–	0
AM (Andries) Kruger	5	–	–	–	–	0	5	–	–	–	–	0
R (Rossouw) Kruger	11	–	–	–	–	0	11	–	–	–	–	0
R (Rod) Labuschagne	6	–	–	–	–	0	6	–	–	–	–	0
RJ (Raoul) Larson	7	–	–	–	–	0	7	–	–	–	–	0
C (Clemen) Lewis	19	1	–	–	–	5	61	1	–	–	–	5
G (Grant) Le Roux	19	–	–	–	–	0	22	–	–	–	–	0
WJ (Willie) le Roux	18	11	–	–	2	61	18	11	–	–	2	61
H (Hilton) Lobberts	12	–	–	–	–	0	17	–	–	–	–	0
FH (Hottie) Louw	19	2	–	–	–	10	19	2	–	–	–	10
CI (Christopher) Micklewood	4	–	2	–	–	4	4	–	2	–	–	4
N (Neil) Papier	18	–	–	–	–	0	126	11	–	–	–	55
J (Johann) Peacock	7	–	–	–	–	0	6	–	–	–	–	0
JJ (Jeremy) Plaatjies	18	8	–	–	–	40	18	8	–	–	–	40
JJ (Jean) Rossouw	3	–	–	–	–	0	3	–	–	–	–	0
FJ (Franzel) September	18	7	–	–	–	35	18	7	–	–	–	35
DF (Dewey) Swartbooi	9	3	–	–	–	15	37	4	–	–	–	20
HM (Hyron) Thyse	8	3	–	–	–	15	30	9	–	–	–	45
JL (Janru) van Niekerk	18	1	–	–	–	5	92	5	–	–	–	25
PJ (PJ) Vermeulen	19	4	–	–	–	20	25	4	–	–	–	20
39 players	**425**	**82**	**58**	**34**	**2**	**634**	**1176**	**152**	**137**	**98**	**1**	**1331**

PROVINCIAL ROUND-UP

APPEARANCES AND POINTS IN VODACOM CUP 2010

	WP	Free State	SWD Eagles	Pampas XV	Sharks XV	Bulldogs	Elephants	Leopards	Free State	Matches	Tries	Conversions	Penalties	Drop Goals	Points
Jaquin Jansen	15	15	15	15	15R	15	15	15	15	9	1	12	8	–	53
Hyron Thyse	14	14	14	14	14R	–	11R	11R	11	8	3	–	–	–	15
PJ Vermeulen	13	13	13	13	13	13	13	13	13	9	1	–	–	–	5
Lionel Cornelius	12	12	12	12	12	12	10	10	10	9	3	–	–	–	15
Jeremy Plaatjies	11	11	11	11	11	11	11	11	–	8	2	–	–	–	10
Dean Grant	10	10	–	10	12R	–	–	–	–	4	1	9	7	–	44
Bolla Conradie	9c	–	–	–	–	–	9c	9c	–	3	–	–	–	–	0
Zandré Jordaan	8	8	8	8	8	8	8	8	8	9	4	–	–	–	20
Hilton Lobberts	7	7	7	7	7	7	7	7	7	9	–	–	–	–	0
Franzel September	6	6	6	6	6	6	6	–	6	8	4	–	–	–	20
Hottie Louw	5	5c	5c	5c	5c	5c	5	5	5c	9	1	–	–	–	5
Grant le Roux	4	4	4	4	4R	4	4	4	4	9	–	–	–	–	0
Rossouw Kruger	3	3	3R	–	–	1R	3R	3R	3R	7	–	–	–	–	0
Ashton Constant	2	2	2	2	2	2	2	2	2	9	–	–	–	–	0
Janro van Niekerk	1	1	1	1	1	–	1	1	1	8	1	–	–	–	5
Clemen Lewis	2R	2R	x	2R	2R	2R	2R	2R	2R	8	–	–	–	–	0
Raoul Larson	3R	–	–	3	3	3	3	3	3	7	–	–	–	–	0
Johann Peacock	4R	4R	4R	4R	4	5R	–	–	–	6	–	–	–	–	0
David Hendricks	7R	–	–	–	–	–	–	–	–	1	–	–	–	–	0
Neil Papier	9R	9	9	9	9	9	9R	9R	9	9	–	–	–	–	0
Willie le Roux	15R	12R	10	12R	10	10	–	–	10R	7	5	–	–	–	25
Cornal Hendricks	13R	14R	14R	14R	14	14	14	14	14	9	2	–	–	–	10
Danré Gerber	–	x	9R	–	15	15R	10R	12R	11R	6	1	1	2	–	13
Eusebio Guinazu	–	3R	3	–	–	–	–	–	–	2	–	–	–	–	0
Nikolai Blignaut	–	8R	7R	6R	7R	4R	4R	4R	4R	8	1	–	–	–	5
Wesley Kotze	–	–	8R	–	–	–	–	6R	8R	3	–	–	–	–	0
Jean Rossouw	–	–	–	1R	3R	1	–	–	–	3	–	–	–	–	0
Angelo Brinkhuys	–	–	–	7R	–	–	–	–	–	1	–	–	–	–	0
Dewey Swartbooi	–	–	–	–	–	12R	12	12	12	4	1	–	–	–	5
André du Toit	–	–	–	–	–	6R	6R	6	6R	4	–	–	–	–	0
30 players										**196**	**31**	**22**	**17**	**0**	**250**

APPEARANCES AND POINTS IN ABSA CURRIE CUP 2010

	Valke	EP Kings	SWD Eagles	Border	Griffons	Valke	EP Kings	SWD Eagles	Border	Griffons	SWD Eagles	Matches	Tries	Conversions	Penalties	Drop Goals	Points
Jacquin Jansen	15	15	15	15	15	14	15	15	15	15	15	11	4	30	13	–	119
Cornal Hendricks	14	14	14	14	14	13	14	13	14	14	14	11	8	–	–	–	40
PJ Vermeulen	13	13	13	13	13	15R	13	–	13	13	13	10	3	–	–	–	15
Dewey Swartbooi	12	12	12	12	12	–	–	–	–	–	–	5	2	–	–	–	10
Jeremy Plaatjies	11	11	11	11	11	11	11	11	11	11	–	10	6	–	–	–	30
Willie le Roux	10	10	10	10	10	10R	10	10	10	10	10	11	6	–	–	2	36
Bolla Conradie	9c	9c	9c	9c	9c	9c	9c	9c	9c	9c	9c	11	3	–	–	–	15
Zandré Jordaan	8	8	–	8	8	7R	–	8	8	8	8	9	1	–	–	–	5
Braam Immelman	7	7	7	7	7	8	8	7	7	7	7	11	4	–	–	–	20
Franzel September	6	6	6	6	6	6	6	–	6	6	6	10	3	–	–	–	15
Hottie Louw	5	5		5	5	5	5	5	5	5	5	10	1	–	–	–	5
Rod Labuschagne	4	4R	4	4R	4R	–	–	–	8R	–	–	6	–	–	–	–	0
Eusebio Guinazu	3	3	3	3	3	–	3	3	3	3	3	10	1	–	–	–	5
Clemen Lewis	2	2	2	2	2	2	2	2	5R	2	2	11	1	–	–	–	5
Janru van Niekerk	1	1	1	1	–	1	1	1	1	1	1	10	–	–	–	–	0
Ashton Constant	2R	2R	x	x	2R	–	–	2R	–	–	x	4	–	–	–	–	0
Charl du Plessis	3R	3R	x	3R	1	3	–	–	1R	1R	3R	8	–	–	–	–	0
Grant le Roux	4R	4	5	4	4	–	2R	7R	4	5R	4R	10	–	–	–	–	0
Nikolai Blignaut	7R	–	–	–	–	4R	4	4	–	4	4	6	–	–	–	–	0
Neil Papier	14R	11R	x	9R	9R		x	9R	9R	9R	9R	9	–	–	–	–	0
Alex Kock	12R	12R	–	–	–	12	12	12	12	12	12	8	5	–	–	–	25
Christopher Micklewood	11R	10R	x	–	–	15	–	8R	–	–	–	4	–	2	–	–	4
Wesley Kotze	8R	x	–	–	–	–	–	7R	–	–	2	–	–	–	–	0	
Thor Halvorsen	–	–	8	–	8R	7	7R	6	–	8R	x	6	–	–	–	–	0
André du Toit	–	–	x	–	–	–	–	–	–	–	–	0	–	–	–	–	0
Brendon April	–	–	x	13R	13R	–	13R	14	11R	11R	11	7	2	–	–	–	10
Hilton Lobberts	–	–	–	8R	–	4	7	–	–	–	–	3	–	–	–	–	0
Lionel Cornelius	–	–	–	15R	12R	12R	x	12R	12R	12R	x	6	1	1	2	–	13
Rossouw Kruger	–	–	–	–	3R	1R	3R	3R	–	–	–	4	–	–	–	–	0
Louis Koen	–	–	–	–	–	10	–	–	–	–	–	1	–	3	2	–	12
Andries Kruger	–	–	–	–	–	2R	6R	4R	2	2R	x	5	–	–	–	–	0
31 players												**229**	**51**	**36**	**17**	**2**	**384**

Paul Perez during the Absa Currie Cup First Division semi-final match between EP Kings and Boland at Nelson Mandela Bay Stadium.

ABSA UNDER-21 CHAMPIONSHIP (7th, Section A)

Played	Won	Drawn	Lost	Points for	Points against	Tries for	Tries against	Winning %
12	0	0	12	105	882	12	133	0.00%

RESULTS Lost Blue Bulls (h) 18-43. Lost KZN (a) 03-106. Lost Leopards (a) 24-46. Lost Golden Lions (h) 06-40. Lost Leopards (h) 18-34. Lost WP (a) 00-54. Lost Blue Bulls (a) 10-87. Lost KZN (h) 05-85. Lost Free State (h) 10-110. Lost Golden Lions (a) 11-57. Lost WP (h) 00-111. Lost Free State (a) 00-109.

SCORERS 29 Brynn Gericke (4c, 7p). 15 Percival Williams (3t). 10 Dual Erasmus (2t). 8 Ryan Jordaan (1c, 2p). 5 Gavern Skippers (1c, 1p), Francois Geduld (1t), Kenwinn Wiener (1t), Jan Hugo (1t), Donovan Arendse (1t), Lee Becker (1t), Izak Swiegers (1t), Justin Morgan (1t). 3 Yazeed Johnson (1dg).

ABSA UNDER-19 CHAMPIONSHIP (6th, Section B)

Played	Won	Drawn	Lost	Points for	Points against	Tries for	Tries against	Winning %
6	2	0	4	157	165	23	24	33.00%

RESULTS Bt Griquas (h) 27-22. Lost Valke (a) 24-29. Lost EP (h) 18-44. Lost SWD (a) 28-34. Bt Border (h) 32-00. Lost Mpumalanga (a) 28-36.

SCORERS 30 Leroy Bitterhout (4t, 2c, 2p). 29 Morné Hugo (1t, 6c, 4p). 15 Dugald Williams, Ruan van Rooy, Jason Engledoe (3t each). 10 Brandon Bailing, Frederick Marang, Hirchel Grové (2t each). 8 Lance Ruthford (4c). 5 Gerrit Visagie, Cornell Pekeur, Geoffrey Allies (1t each).

AMATEUR CHAMPIONSHIP (2nd, South Section)

Played	Won	Drawn	Lost	Points for	Points against	Tries for	Tries against	Winning %
7	6	0	1	301	179	43	21	86.00%

RESULTS Bt SWD (a) 56-30. Lost WP (a) 20-30. Bt Border (h) 59-19. Bt EP (a) 32-29. Bt Griquas Rural (a) 30-27. Bt EP Rural (h) 49-30. Bt Border Rural (a) 55-14.

BOLAND CAVALIERS RECORDS

MATCH RECORDS

Biggest win	96-5	vs Zimbabwe	1996
Biggest win (Currie Cup)	65-5	vs. Mpumalanga	2007
Heaviest defeat	8-96	vs Western Province	1993
	3-91	vs Free State Cheetahs (Currie Cup)	2007
Highest score	96	vs Zimbabwe (96-5)	1996
Highest score (Currie Cup)	75	vs Northern Free State	1997
Moist points conceded	96	vs Western Province (8-96)	1993
Moist points conceded (Currie Cup)	91	vs Free State Cheetahs	2007
Most tries	15	vs Zimbabwe	1996
Most tries (Currie Cup)	11	vs Northern Free State	1997
Most points by a player	34	F Horn vs South Western Districts	1996
Most points by a player (Currie Cup)	25	P O'Neill vs Northern Free State	1997
Most tries by a player (Currie Cup)	6	FP Marais vs North Eastern Districts	1952

SEASON RECORDS

Most team points	956	24 matches	2001
Most team points (Currie Cup)	536	18 matches	2003
Most points by a player	355	F Horn	1996
Most points by a player (Currie Cup)	164	G Goosen	2004
Most team tries	137	24 matches	2001
Most team tries (Currie Cup)	70	18 matches	2003
Most tries by a player	20	CS Terblanche	1997
Most tries by a player (Currie Cup)	**16**		
RS Benjamin			**2006**

CAREER RECORDS

Most appearances	144	WP van Zyl	2001-2008
Most points	524	P O'Neill	1996-2002
Most tries	82	JI Daniels	1998-2008

HONOURS

Currie Cup First Division	2001, 2003, 2004, 2006
Vodacom Shield	2004

PROVINCIAL ROUND-UP

BORDER RUGBY FOOTBALL UNION

FOUNDED 1891 **GROUND** Border Rugby Stadium (formerly the Basil Kenyon Stadium)
CAPACITY 15 000 **ADDRESS** Recreation Road, East London, 5201
POSTAL ADDRESS PO Box 75, East London, 5200
TELEPHONE NUMBER 043-743 5998 **WEBSITE** www.borderbulldogs.co.za
COLOURS Green jersey with white sleeves and red and brown piping, white shorts, green socks
CURRIE CUP COACH David Thobela
VODACOM CUP COACH David Maidza **CAPTAIN** Yongama Mkaza
PRESIDENT Buntu Ondala **UNION CEO** Leon Botha

Beleaguered Border at a crossroads

THEY tried hard and played their hearts out, but it was another season of heartbreak for the Border Bulldogs.

With no extra income to secure high-profile players, the Bulldogs squad in 2010 were young and inexperienced, apart from flank Solly Tyibilika, centre Chumani Booi, scrumhalf Yongama Mkaza, tighthead prop Marius Visser and lock Nomani Tonga.

So it was not surprising that their Vodacom Cup campaign proved to be a painful experience. In losing all seven of their matches, Border were only able to garner three points but, on the positive side, they suffered few injuries.

The Bulldogs received a setback when head coach David Maidza announced he was to link up with neighbours the Eastern Province Kings, and he was replaced by David Dobela for the Bulldogs' Currie Cup First Division campaign.

The Bulldogs, bolstered by players loaned from Griquas – lock Ben Venter, prop Johannes Venter and centre Divan van Zyl – won three matches but it should have been more. They lost 25-24 to the bottom-placed Valke at home, but beat them away in their last match of the season.

To their credit, the Bulldogs had away wins against the Griffons and Boland but inexperience and a lack of depth counted against them. If they stick together as a squad, this Bulldogs side, with one or two extra experienced forwards and the proper incentive, should have a far more successful campaign in 2011.

Both the Border U21 and U19 teams struggled, only winning one match from six while the Border Rural side failed to win a match. However, the Border Urban side capped a fine season by finishing fourth on the table, having won four from seven.

On the club scene, East London Police won the Premier League and Old Selbornians the Aloe Cup. Because of a High Court order instigated by Fort Hare University,

Police were not allowed to officially represent their province at the annual SAA National Club Championships in Stellenbosch, but ended up playing anyway, as guests of the South African Rugby Union.

They promptly astounded all and sundry by making it through to the Plate final, which was televised live. This was by far the best achievement by any Border club side at the club champs.

Good news for Border fans was that they were able

The Bulldogs lost 25-24 to the bottom-placed Valke at home, but then made up for it by beating them away in their final match.

to watch the second Test between the Springboks and Italy in East London but even then there was controversy when the Buffalo City Municipality argued over whether they would pay the R2-million guarantee to SARU.

Rugby on the Border is now at a crossroads. They have no outside sponsor, there was a walkout at the annual meeting, which has split the union in two, and there's every chance Buffalo City won't renew the Buffalo City Stadium lease.

If a compromise is not reached, Border Rugby stands to lose its home.

Perhaps Border Rugby Football Union CEO Leon Botha got out at just the right time when he resigned at the end of September after accepting a package.

BORDER BULLDOGS LOG POSITIONS

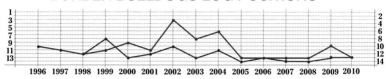

1996 1997 1998 1999 2000 2001 2002 2003 2004 2005 2006 2007 2008 2009 2010

BORDER RESULTS AND SCORERS IN 2010

Played	Won	Drawn	Lost	Points for	Points against	Tries for	Tries against	Winning %
18	3	0	15	386	766	45	109	16%

VODACOM CUP PLAYED 7 WON 0 DRAWN 0 LOST 7 POINTS FOR 115 POINTS AGAINST 327 TRIES FOR 15 TRIES AGAINST 50

Date	Venue	Opponent	Result	Score	Scorers
Feb 26	Durban	SHARKS XV	LOST	08-69	T: Meslane. P: Booi.
Mar 6	Queenstown¹	ELEPHANTS	LOST	32-34	T: Gqobo (2), Mkokeli, Tshemese.. C: Booi (3). P: Booi (2).
Mar 13	Cape Town	PAMPAS XV	LOST	14-73	T: Mntunjani, Fihlani. C: Booi (2).
Mar 20	Cape Town	WP	LOST	00-29	
Mar 27	East London²	FREE STATE	LOST	18-50	T: Mcguigan, Mntunjani, Doneghan. P: Taljard.
Apr 10	East London³	CAVALIERS	LOST	13-33	T: Taljaard. C: Taljard. P: Taljard (2).
Apr 17	Beaufort West	EAGLES	LOST	30-39	T: Mkokeli (2), Mboto, Booi. C: Booi (2). P: Booi (2).

¹Queens College, ²Sisa Dukashe Stadium, ³Saisa Dukashe Stadium.

ABSA CURRIE CUP PLAYED 10 WON 3 DRAWN 0 LOST 7 POINTS FOR 264 POINTS AGAINST 396 TRIES FOR 29 TRIES AGAINST 52

Date	Venue	Opponent	Result	Score	Scorers
July 16	East London	EP KINGS	LOST	28-42	T: R Kennedy, Mkokeli, Mkaza. C: Gqobo, Basson. P: Basson (2), Gqobo.
July 23	George	EAGLES	LOST	12-33	P: Gerber (4).
Aug 6	East London	GRIFFONS	WON	22-20	T: Mkokeli, Ganto, Tonga. C: Taljard (2). P: Taljard.
Aug 13	Wellington	CAVALIERS	WON	50-46	T: Basson, Mntunjani, Venter, Doneghan, Taljaard, Mhlobiso. C: Taljard (2), Basson (2). P: Basson (3), Taljard.
Aug 20	East London	VALKE	LOST	37-38	T: Basson (2), R Kennedy, Tonga, Taljard. C: Basson (3). P: Basson (2).
Aug 27	Port Elizabeth	EP KINGS	LOST	6-49	P: Basson (2).
Sept 3	East London	EAGLES	LOST	7-17	T: Mkaza. C: Taljard.
Sept 18	Welkom	GRIFFONS	LOST	33-48	T: Noble, Mkokeli, Meslane. C: Taljard (3). P: Taljard (4).
Sept 24	East London	CAVALIERS	LOST	13-54	T: Tonga. C: Basson. P: Taljard (2).
Oct 2	Kempton Park	VALKE	WON	56-49	T: Noble (3), Basson (2), C Booi, Mntunjani. C: Basson (6). P: Basson (3).

COMPULSORY FRIENDLY

July 3	East London	Cheetahs	LOST	7-43	T: Meslane. C: Gqobo.

Team: Andisa Gqobo, Sino Ganto, Chumani Booi (c), Divan van Zyl, Royden Kennedy, Thembani Mkokeli, Yongama Mkaza, Bonga Mtunjani, Dumisane Meslane, Nomani Tonga, Samora Fihlani, Ben Venter, Marius Visser, Matthew Taljaard, Lonwabo Mtimka. RESERVES: Khwezi Mkhafu, Armon Fourie, Sokhana Mkona, Ross Doneghan, Ntando Kebe, Logan Basson, Charl Kennedy.

APPEARANCES AND POINTS FOR BORDER IN 2010　　　　CAREER

PLAYER	Appearances	Tries	Conversions	Penalties	Drop Goals	Points	Career Matches	Career Tries	Conversions	Penalties	Drop Goals	Points
LA (Logan) Basson	10	5	13	12	–	87	10	5	13	12	–	87
B (Brad) Birkholtz	6	–	–	–	–	0	6	–	–	–	–	0
AL (Ludwe) Booi	2	–	–	–	–	0	2	–	–	–	–	0
CN (Chumani) Booi	12	2	7	5	–	39	64	17	14	7	–	134
RC (Ryan) Brown	4	–	–	–	–	0	4	–	–	–	–	0
R (Ross) Doneghan	13	2	–	–	–	10	14	2	–	–	–	10
OS (Onke) Dubase	1	–	–	–	–	0	1	–	–	–	–	0
N (Ntabeni) Dukisa	1	–	–	–	–	0	1	–	–	–	–	0
B (Billy) Dutton	1	–	–	–	–	0	1	–	–	–	–	0
JW (Jarrid) Els	4	–	–	–	–	0	4	–	–	–	–	0
LS (Samorai) Fihlani	18	1	–	–	–	5	35	2	–	–	–	10
A (Armon) Fourie	13	–	–	–	–	0	18	–	–	–	–	0
S (Sinovuyo) Ganto	9	1	–	–	–	5	9	1	–	–	–	5
JP (JP) Geldenhuys	9	–	–	–	–	0	9	–	–	–	–	0
R (Reinhard) Gerber	1	–	–	4	–	12	73	4	116	116	2	606
A (Andisa) Gqobo	5	2	2	1	–	17	22	5	7	6	–	57
NL (Ntando) Kebe	16	–	–	–	–	0	16	–	–	–	–	0
CE (Charl) Kennedy	9	–	–	–	–	0	9	–	–	–	–	0
RD (Royden) Kennedy	11	2	–	–	–	10	16	2	–	–	–	10
V (Vuyo) Mboto	6	1	–	–	–	5	6	1	–	–	–	5
B (Byron) Mcguigan	7	1	–	–	–	5	7	1	–	–	–	5
A (Ashley) Meier	1	–	–	–	–	0	1	–	–	–	–	0
DK (Dumza) Meslane	15	3	–	–	–	15	42	7	–	–	–	35
L (Luvuyo) Mhlobiso	6	1	–	–	–	5	6	1	–	–	–	5
K (Kwezi) Mkhafu	14	–	–	–	–	0	14	–	–	–	–	0
Y (Yongama) Mkaza	15	2	–	–	–	10	62	5	–	–	–	25
T (Thembani) Mkokeli	18	6	–	–	–	30	64	12	–	1	–	63
S (Sokhona) Mkona	7	–	–	–	–	0	23	1	–	–	–	5
B (Bonga) Mntunjani	17	4	–	–	–	20	30	4	–	–	–	20
LJJ (Black) Mtimka	9	–	–	–	–	0	109	3	–	–	–	15
S (Sibulele) Ndungane	5	–	–	–	–	0	5	–	–	–	–	0
HG (Howard) Noble	4	4	–	–	–	20	4	4	–	–	–	20
S (Sinovuyo) Nyoka	5	–	–	–	–	0	5	–	–	–	–	0
B (Byron) Schmidt	9	–	–	–	–	0	10	–	–	–	–	0
P (Paul) Serfontein	1	–	–	–	–	0	1	–	–	–	–	0
G (Gerrit) Sprong	1	–	–	–	–	0	1	–	–	–	–	0
M (Matthew) Taljaard	15	2	–	–	–	10	33	3	–	–	–	15
JJ (Jeff) Taljard	12	1	9	11	–	56	33	6	23	28	0	157
N (Norman) Tonga	15	3	–	–	–	15	33	4	–	–	–	20
S (Siyabonga) Tshemese	4	1	–	–	–	5	4	1	–	–	–	5
S (Solly) Tyibilika	13	–	–	–	–	0	43	6	–	–	–	30
GJ (Greg) van Jaarsveld	1	–	–	–	–	0	47	–	–	–	–	0
D (Divan) van Zyl	9	–	–	–	–	0	9	–	–	–	–	0
BCG (Ben) Venter	9	1	–	–	–	5	9	1	–	–	–	5
M (Marius) Visser	16	–	–	–	–	0	32	–	–	–	–	0
A (Ashley) Viviers	6	–	–	–	–	0	6	–	–	–	–	0
W (Wynand) Wagenaar	3	–	–	–	–	0	3	–	–	–	–	0
47 players	**388**	**45**	**31**	**33**	**0**	**386**	**956**	**98**	**173**	**170**	**2**	**1349**

PROVINCIAL ROUND-UP

APPEARANCES AND POINTS IN VODACOM CUP 2010

	Sharks XV	EP Kings	Pampas XV	WP	Free State	Cavaliers	SWD Eagles	Matches	Tries	Conversions	Penalties	Drop Goals	Points
Gerrit Sprong	15	–	–	–	–	–	–	1	–	–	–	–	0
Vuyo Mboto	14	14	10R	12R	–	14	11	6	1	–	–	–	5
Byron Mcguigan	13	13	13	14	14	–	12R	6	1	–	–	–	5
Chumani Booi	12	12	12	13	13	13c	13c	7	1	7	5	–	34
Brad Birkholtz	11	11	11	11	11	11	–	6	–	–	–	–	0
Thembani Mkokeli	10	15	15	10	15R	15	10	7	3	–	–	–	15
Ntando Kebe	9	9R	–	–	9R	9R	14R	5	–	–	–	–	0
Siyabonga Tshemese	8	8	8	–	–	R 6	–	4	1	–	–	–	5
Solly Tyibilika	7c	7c	7c	7c	7c	–	6R	6	–	–	–	–	0
Dumisani Meslane	6	6R	8R	6	–	7	7	6	1	–	–	–	5
Ashley Viviers	5	5	5	–	5	–	5R	5	–	–	–	–	0
Samora Fihlani	4	4	4	4	6	5	5	7	1	–	–	–	5
Marius Visser	3	3	3	1	1	1	1	7	–	–	–	–	0
Greg van Jaarsveld	2	–	–	–	–	–	–	1	–	–	–	–	0
Lonwabo Mtimka	1	1	1	3R	1R	1R	–	6	–	–	–	–	0
Matthew Taljaard	2R	2	2	2	–	R 2	R 2	6	1	–	–	–	5
Armon Fourie	3R	3R	3R	3	3	3	3	7	–	–	–	–	0
Ashley Meier	1R	–	–	–	–	–	–	1	–	–	–	–	0
Sokhana Mkona	5R	–	–	–	–	7R	7R	3	–	–	–	–	0
Billy Dutton	6R	–	–	–	–	–	–	1	–	–	–	–	0
Sinovuyo Nyoka	9R	–	9R	9	–	–	–	3	–	–	–	–	0
Charl Kennedy	14R	10R	11R	–	10R	10	12	6	–	–	–	–	0
Andisa Gqobo	–	10	10	–	10	–	–	3	2	–	–	–	10
Yongama Mkaza	–	9	9	9R	9	9	9	6	–	–	–	–	0
Bonga Mntunjani	–	6	6	8	8	8	8	6	2	–	–	–	10
Kwezi Mkhafu	–	x	2R	2R	2	2	2	5	–	–	–	–	0
Wynand Wagenaar	–	x	5R	5	7R	–	–	3	–	–	–	–	0
Royden Kennedy	–	14R	14	15	15	–	15	5	–	–	–	–	0
Jeff Taljard	–	–	–	12	12	12	–	3	–	1	3	–	11
Nomani Tonga	–	–	–	6R	4	4	4	4	–	–	–	–	0
Ross Doneghan	–	–	–	5R	5R	6	6	4	1	–	–	–	5
Sibulele Ndungane	–	–	–	11R	–	10R	14	3	–	–	–	–	0
Paul Serfontein	–	–	–	–	2R	–	–	1	–	–	–	–	0
Byron Schmidt	–	–	–	–	–	3R	3R	2	–	–	–	–	0
34 Players								**152**	**15**	**8**	**8**	**0**	**115**

APPEARANCES AND POINTS IN ABSA CURRIE CUP 2010

	EP Kings	SWD Eagles	Griffons	Cavaliers	Valke	EP Kings	SWD Eagles	Griffons	Cavaliers	Valke	Matches	Tries	Conversions	Penalties	Drop Goals	Points
Andisa Gqobo	15	–	–	–	–	–	–	–	–	–	1	–	1	1	–	5
Sinovuyo Ganto	14	11	11	11	11	11	–	11	11	x	8	1	–	–	–	5
Chumani Booi	13	–	–	–	–	–	–	15	13	13	4	1	–	–	–	5
Divan van Zyl	12	13	13	13	12	13R	13	–	11R	–	8	–	–	–	–	0
Royden Kennedy	11	14	–	–	14	14	14	–	–	–	5	2	–	–	–	10
Thembani Mkokeli	10	10	15	15	15	15	15	10	10	10	10	3	–	–	–	15
Yongama Mkaza	9c	9c	9c	9c	9c	9c	9c	–	9c	–	8	2	–	–	–	10
Bonga Mntunjani	8	8	8	8	8	8	6R	8R	5R	8	10	2	–	–	–	10
Dumisani Meslane	7	7	6R	6R	7	–	5R	6R	6R	–	8	1	–	–	–	5
Solly Tyibilika	6	6	–	–	6R	6R	8	8	8	–	7	–	–	–	–	0
Samora Fihlani	5	5	5	5	5	5	5	5	5	5	10	–	–	–	–	0
Ben Venter	4	4	7	4	–	4	4	4	4	–	8	1	–	–	–	5
Marius Visser	3	1	3	–	3	3	3	3c	–	3c	8	–	–	–	–	0
Khwezi Mkhafu	2	2	–	2R	–	2R	2R	2R	2R	2	8	–	–	–	–	0
Lonwabo Mtimka	1	–	–	–	–	–	–	–	3R	–	2	–	–	–	–	0
Armon Fourie	1R	3	1R	3	3R	–	–	–	–	–	5	–	–	–	–	0
Johan Geldenhuys	x	3R	1	1	1	1	1	1R	3	1	9	–	–	–	–	0
Norman Tonga	4R	7R	4	7	4	7	7	7	7	7	10	3	–	–	–	15
Sokhana Mkona	x	8R	–	–	–	–	–	4R	–	8R	3	–	–	–	–	0
Ntando Kebe	9R	9R	9R	9R	9R	9R	11R	9	9R	9	10	–	–	–	–	0
Jeffrey Taljard	13R	12	12	12	12R	12	12	12	12	–	9	1	8	8	–	45
Logan Basson	15R	10R	10	10	10	10	10	–	15	15	9	5	13	12	–	87
Reinhard Gerber	–	15	–	–	–	–	–	–	–	–	1	–	–	4	–	12
Ludwe Booi	–	x	–	–	11R	10R	–	–	–	–	2	–	–	–	–	0
Byron McGuigan	–	14R	–	–	–	–	–	–	–	–	1	–	–	–	–	0
Sibulele Ndungane	–	–	14	14	–	–	–	–	–	–	2	–	–	–	–	0
Ross Doneghan	–	–	6	6	6	8R	6	6	6	6	8	1	–	–	–	5
Matthew Taljaard	–	–	2	2	2	2	2	2	2	2R	8	1	–	–	–	5
Byron Schmidt	–	–	x	3R	1R	3R	1R	1	1	1R	7	–	–	–	–	0
Jarrid Els	–	–	7R	4R	7R	6	–	–	–	–	4	–	–	–	–	0
Luvuyo Mhlobiso	–	–	x	14R	13	13	–	13	12R	12	6	1	–	–	–	5
Ryan Brown	–	–	10R	13R	11R	–	11	–	–	–	4	–	–	–	–	0
Howard Noble	–	–	–	–	–	–	14R	14	14	14	4	4	–	–	–	20
Charl Kennedy	–	–	–	–	–	–	13R	–	11	–	2	–	–	–	–	0
Sinovuyo Nyoka	–	–	–	–	–	–	9R	–	9R	–	2	–	–	–	–	0
Ashley Viviers	–	–	–	–	–	–	–	–	–	4	1	–	–	–	–	0
Onke Dubase	–	–	–	–	–	–	–	–	–	4R	1	–	–	–	–	0
Nobeni Dukisa	–	–	–	–	–	–	–	–	–	14R	1	–	–	–	–	0
38 Players											**214**	**29**	**22**	**25**	**0**	**264**

PROVINCIAL ROUND-UP

Thembani Mkokeli of Border beats Nico Engelbrecht during the Absa First Division match against the Valke.

ABSA UNDER-21 CHAMPIONSHIP (6th, Section B)

Played	Won	Drawn	Lost	Points for	Points against	Tries for	Tries against	Winning %
6	1	0	5	111	273	15	38	16.00%

RESULTS: Bt Griquas (h) 15-11. Lost EP (a) 18-35. Lost SWD (h) 11-18. Lost Griffons (a) 27-73. Lost Pumas (h) 28-53. Lost Valke (a) 12-83.

SCORERS: 30 Byron Mcguigan (1t,2c,7p); 15 Sinovuyo Nyoka (3t); 11 Justin Kopke (4c,1p); 10 Lukhanyo Siyobo, Kyle EdwardsSinithenbile Calwe (2t each); 5 Saneliso Ngoma, Brett Allam, Kyle Theron, Luzuko Nyabaza, Billy Dutton (1t each).

ABSA U19 CHAMPIONSHIP (7th, Section B)

Played	Won	Drawn	Lost	Points for	Points against	Tries for	Tries against	Winning %
6	1	0	5	56	249	5	40	16.00%

RESULTS: Lost Griquas (h) 10-45. Lost EP (a) 0-50. Bt SWD (h) 16-8. Lost Boland (a) 0-32. Lost Pumas (h) 9-61. Lost Valke (a) 21-53.

SCORERS: 26 Athenkosi Gxotiwe (1c,8p); 13 Grant Collett (2t,1p); 10 Oliver Zono (2t); 5 Roallan Webb (1t); 2 Alwin Adonis (1c).

AMATEUR CHAMPIONSHIP

BORDER (4th, South Section)

Played	Won	Drawn	Lost	Points for	Points against	Tries for	Tries against	Winning %
7	4	0	3	183	239	22	33	57%

RESULTS: Bt Border Rural (h) 29-11. Bt SWD (h) 50-37. Lost Boland (a) 19-59. Lost WP (a) 0-69. Lost EP (h) 25-30. Bt Griquas Rural (a) 41-18. Bt EP Rural (h) 19-15.

BORDER RURAL (8th, South Section)

Played	Won	Drawn	Lost	Points for	Points against	Tries for	Tries against	Winning %
7	0	0	7	95	305	11	42	0%

RESULTS: Lost Bulldogs (a) 11-29. Lost Elephants (a) 6-65. Lost Griquas Rural (h) 14-24. Lost EP Rural (a) 23-38. Lost WP (h) 20-57. Lost SWD (a) 7-37. Lost Boland (h) 14-55.

www.borderbulldogs.co.za

BORDER BULLDOGS RECORDS

MATCH RECORDS

Biggest win	85-3	vs. Zimbabwe	1996
Biggest Currie Cup win	56-23	vs. Northern Free State	1997
Heaviest defeat	14-87	vs. Griqualand West (Currie Cup)	1998
Highest score	85	vs. Zimbabwe (85-3)	1996
Most points conceded	87	vs. Griqualand West (14-87)	1998
Most tries	15	vs. Zimbabwe (85-3)	1996
Most Currie Cup tries	8	vs. Northern Free State (56-23)	1997
Most points by a player	28	M Flutey vs. North East Cape	1995
Most Currie Cup points by player	25	GJT Wright vs. Mighty Elephants	2002
Most tries by a player	4	A Stephenson vs. Far North	1976
	4	RG Bennett vs. Zimbabwe	1996

SEASON RECORDS

Most team points	778	27 matches	1996
Most Currie Cup points by team	332	12 matches	2004
Most points by a player	31	LA Basson vs. Valke	2010
Most Currie Cup points by player	31	LA Basson vs. Valke	2010
Most team tries	101	27 matches	1996
Most Currie Cup tries by team	39	12 matches	2004
Most tries by a player	20	RG Bennett	1996
Most Currie Cup tries by a player	10	A Ndungane	2004

CAREER RECORDS

Most appearances	183	W Weyer	1988-2000
Most points	672	GK Miller	1996-2001
Most tries	44	A Alexander	

HONOURS

ABSA Currie Cup	1932 (shared), 1934 (shared)
Vodacom Shield	2003

Logan Basson scored 31 points against the Valke in their ABSA Currie First Division encounter, the most by a Border player in a single match.

PROVINCIAL ROUND-UP

BY MICHAEL GREEN,
Sport24

EASTERN PROVINCE RUGBY FOOTBALL UNION

MIGHTY ELEPHANTS

FOUNDED 1888 **GROUND** Nelson Mandela Bay Stadium, EPRFU Stadium
CAPACITY 35 000 **ADDRESS** La Roche Drive, Humewood, Port Elizabeth, 6001
POSTAL ADDRESS PO Box 13111, Humewood, 6013
TELEPHONE NUMBER 041 508 7700 **EMAIL** eprugby@intekom.co.za
COLOURS Red and black hooped jersey, black shorts, red and black socks
CURRIE CUP COACH Alan Solomons **VODACOM CUP COACH** Corné Korff
CAPTAIN De Wet Barry **PRESIDENT** Cheeky Watson
COMPANY CEO Anele Pamba

Premier heartbreak for Kings

2010 will be remembered as the year in which the Eastern Province Rugby Union used the slogan 'EP Rugby on the rise' – which is indeed what happened.

The professional team changed its name from the Mighty Elephants to the Eastern Province Kings and the side duly went on to win the First Division. Unfortunately the Kings also lost to the Pumas in a tough promotion/relegation series and will compete again in the First Division in 2011.

The year started of with Corné Korff and Ryan Felix in charge of the Mighty Elephants for the Vodacom Cup. The Elephants were highly competitive and were unlucky to only win two of their seven matches. Still, one had the feeling that the Elephants weren't really playing to their potential and really should have done better.

Players who performed consistently were fullback Justin Peach, wing Howard Noble and loose forward Jacques Potgieter.

Things changed dramatically in the second half of the season. Alan Solomons arrived to take over the coaching and he appointed Adrian Kennedy and David Maidza as his assistants.

It was then that the Elephants transformed into the Kings and at times they lived up to the name. Solomons brought in a lot of new faces and at first this didn't help the team's momentum at all. Although he changed his sides quite a lot, the Kings started to win and the people started to flock to the matches. It was not unusual to see anything between 10,000 and 15,000 spectators at the Nelson Mandela Bay stadium, which is not bad at all for the First Division.

The Kings lost only two matches – the same as the South Western Districts Eagles – but the Eagles ended at top of the log by way of more bonus points.

This meant the Eagles had the easier promotion/relegation matches against the Leopards while the Kings had to face the tough Pumas.

But before those matches, the Kings had to play against the Boland Cavaliers in the semifinal of the First Division.

They beat the Cavaliers and then travelled to George where they beat the Eagles 16-12 in a thrilling encounter. It was the first trophy for the EP Rugby Union since 2002's now defunct Vodacom Shield.

The Kings next travelled to Witbank for the first of their promotion/relegation matches against the Pumas and surprised many people by drawing 36-36.

The last match on their home ground proved one too many for the battle-weary Kings, who by this time were struggling to get a fit side onto the field. They lost 46-28 in front of 45,000 rugby-crazed fans who did their best to cheer their team all the way to the Premier Division.

There were many players who at times shone for the Kings, but it must be said that tough flanker Potgieter and speedy wing Norman Nelson, who was named First Division player of the year in November, really gave their all in every match. Whenever he was fit to play, the veteran lock Rory Duncan also made a huge difference.

Norman Nelson capped off a marvellous year by being named First Division player of the year.

EASTERN PROVINCE KINGS LOG POSITIONS

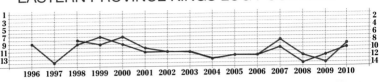

EASTERN PROVINCE RESULTS AND SCORERS IN 2010

Played	Won	Lost	Drawn	Points for	Points against	Tries for	Tries against	Winning %
21	12	7	2	571	517	65	58	62%

VODACOM CUP Played **7** Won **2** Lost **4** Drawn **1** Points For **159** Points Against **194** Tries For **18** Tries Against **23**

Date	Venue	Opponent	Result	Score	Scorers
Feb 26	Port Elizabeth[1]	PAMPAS XV	DREW	27-27	T: Noble, Penalty try. C: Peach. P: Peach (5).
Mar 06	Queenstown[2]	BULLDOGS	WON	34-32	T: Noble (2), Peach, Nodikita, Lewis. C: Peach (3). P: Peach.
Mar 12	Port Elizabeth	WP	LOST	23-28	T: Peach, Grey, Bashiya. C: Peach. P: Peach (2).
Mar 19	Bloemfontein[3]	FREE STATE	LOST	16-25	T: Peach. C: Peach. P: Peach (3).
Mar 26	Port Elizabeth	EAGLES	WON	24-19	T: Nelson, Grey, Noble. C: Peach (3). P: Peach.
April 09	Port Elizabeth	SHARKS XV	LOST	25-27	T: Peach (2), Noble. C: Peach (2). P: Peach (2).
April 17	Piketberg	CAVALIERS	LOST	10-36	T: Fourie. C: Peach. P: Peach.

[1] Nelson Mandela Bay Stadium, [2] Queens College, [3] Shimla Park.

ABSA CURRIE CUP Played **14** Won **10** Lost **3** Drawn **1** Points For **412** Points Against **323** Tries For **47** Tries Against **35**

Date	Venue	Opponent	Result	Score	Scorers
July 16	East London	BULLDOGS	WON	42-28	T: Mangweni, W Stevens, D Stevens, Nelson, Potgieter. C: D Stevens (2), Peach (2). P: Peach (2), D Stevens.
July 23	Port Elizabeth	GRIFFONS	WON	26-25	T: Nelson, Fourie, Mxoli. C: D Stevens. P: Peach (3).
July 31	Wellington	CAVALIERS	WON	33-22	T: Nell (2), W Stevens, Vermeulen. C: Peach, Stick. P: Peach (3).
Aug 7	Port Elizabeth	VALKE	WON	38-3	T: Ferreira (2), Barry, Nell, Odendaal. C: Stick (2). P: Stick (2). D: Van Schalkwyk.
Aug 20	George	EAGLES	WON	19-17	T: Nelson. C: D Stevens. P: Stevens (4).
Aug 27	Port Elizabeth	BULLDOGS	WON	49-6	T: Potgieter (2), Mangweni, Perez, Nqoro, Odendaal. C: Van Schalkwyk (4), Stick. P: Van Schalkwyk (3).
Sep 3	Welkom	GRIFFONS	LOST	18-27	T: Odendaal (2), Ferreira. P: Van Schalkwyk.
Sep 10	Port Elizabeth	CAVALIERS	WON	23-16	T: Perez (2). C: Dumond (2). P: Dumond (3).
Sep 17	Kempton Park	VALKE	WON	50-35	T: Nelson (5), Barry, Perez. C: Dumond (6). P: Dumond.
Oct 1	Port Elizabeth	EAGLES	LOST	8-25	T: Perez. P: Dumond.
Semi-Final					
Oct 8	Port Elizabeth	CAVALIERS	WON	26-25	T:Nelson, Odendaal. C: Dumond (2). P: Dumond (3). D: Dumond.
Final					
Oct 15	George	EAGLES	WON	16-12	T: W Stevens. C: Dumond. P: Dumond (3).
PROMOTION/RELEGATION					
Oct 22	Witbank	PUMAS	DREW	36-36	T: Perez, Barry, Nelson, Oosthuizen. C: Dumond (2). P: Dumond (4).
Oct 29	Port Elizabeth	PUMAS	LOST	28-46	T: W Stevens (2), Gagiano. C: Dumond (2). P: Dumond (3).

eprugby@intekom.co.za

APPEARANCES AND POINTS FOR EP KINGS IN 2010   CAREER

PLAYER	Appearances	Tries	Conversions	Penalties	Drop Goals	Points	Career Matches	Career Tries	Conversions	Penalties	Drop Goals	Points
De W (De Wet) Barry	19	3	–	–	–	15	27	7	–	–	–	35
YMY (Yves) Bashiya	7	1	–	–	–	5	12	1	–	–	–	5
JC (Jaco) Bekker	12	–	–	–	–	0	12	–	–	–	–	0
RC (Ryan) Brown	4	–	–	–	–	0	30	4	26	19	–	129
N (Nolan) Clark	15	–	–	–	–	0	16	–	–	–	–	0
MV (Mike) de Neuilly-Rice	7	–	–	–	–	0	7	–	–	–	–	0
G (Monty) Dumond	7	–	15	18	1	87	7	–	15	18	1	87
R (Rory) Duncan	9	–	–	–	–	0	54	5	–	–	–	25
RJ (Robert) Dyer	11	–	–	–	–	0	25	2	–	–	–	10
A (Anthony) Fenner	3	–	–	–	–	0	3	–	–	–	–	0
PL (Pietie) Ferreira	11	3	–	–	–	15	11	3	–	–	–	15
GE (Giovano) Fourie	3	1	–	–	–	5	7	1	–	–	–	5
J (Jaco) Fourie	10	1	–	–	–	5	10	1	–	–	–	5
JR (Jonathan) Gagiano	9	1	–	–	–	5	9	1	–	–	–	5
CL (Clayton) Gawie	7	–	–	–	–	0	56	3	2	–	–	19
S (Siyanda) Grey	4	2	–	–	–	10	4	2	–	–	–	10
A (Antonio) Halangahu	11	–	–	–	–	0	11	–	–	–	–	0
M (Morne) Hanekom	2	–	–	–	–	0	2	–	–	–	–	0
SL (Sebastian) Hilpert	1	–	–	–	–	0	74	8	–	–	–	40
N (Neil) Jacobs	2	–	–	–	–	0	36	–	–	–	–	0
R (Rudi) Keil	2	–	–	–	–	0	2	–	–	–	–	0
S (Sivuyile) Kobokana	1	–	–	–	–	0	33	5	–	–	–	25
MS (Marlon) Lewis	8	1	–	–	–	5	39	5	–	–	–	25
EJ (Elroy) Ligman	3	–	–	–	–	0	101	17	–	–	–	85
S (Tiger) Mangweni	10	2	–	–	–	10	10	2	–	–	–	10
S (Sphephelo) Mayaba	2	–	–	–	–	0	2	–	–	–	–	0
MM (Mpho) Mbiyozo	4	–	–	–	–	0	4	–	–	–	–	0
Z (Zolani) Mofu	10	–	–	–	–	0	10	–	–	–	–	0
SM (Sangoni) Mxoli	12	1	–	–	–	5	21	2	–	–	–	10
DP (Darron) Nell	9	3	–	–	–	15	9	3	–	–	–	15
NT (Norman) Nelson	20	11	–	–	–	55	68	41	–	–	–	205
HG (Howard) Noble	7	5	–	–	–	25	17	12	–	–	–	60
PE (Pumlani) Nodikida	15	1	–	–	–	5	72	2	–	–	–	10
AM (Ayanda) Nogampula	5	–	–	–	–	0	14	–	–	–	–	0
M (Mlindazwe) Nqoro	5	1	–	–	–	5	5	1	–	–	–	5
GH (Gerrie) Odendaal	12	5	–	–	–	25	12	5	–	–	–	25
DA (Devin) Oosthuizen	5	1	–	–	–	5	5	1	–	–	–	5
L (Lungelo) Payi	11	–	–	–	–	0	11	–	–	–	–	0
J (Justin) Peach	10	5	15	23	–	124	94	23	162	170	0	949
PL (Paul) Perez	9	6	–	–	–	30	9	6	–	–	–	30
A (Alfonso) Pietersen	1	–	–	–	–	0	11	2	–	–	–	10
H (Hein) Potgieter	7	–	–	–	–	0	8	–	–	–	–	0
UJ (Ulrich) Potgieter	19	3	–	–	–	15	30	3	–	–	–	15
A (Andre) Schlechter	10	–	–	–	–	0	10	–	–	–	–	0
AA (Andries) Smit	2	–	–	–	–	0	62	2	–	–	–	10
BM (Brendon) Snyman	9	–	–	–	–	0	10	–	–	–	–	0
DG (Donald) Stevens	9	1	4	5	–	28	9	1	4	5	–	28
IW (Wayne) Stevens	9	5	–	–	–	25	9	5	–	–	–	25
M (Mzwandile) Stick	9	–	4	2	–	14	15	–	4	2	–	14
W (Willem) Stoltz	7	–	–	–	–	0	7	–	–	–	–	0
M (Matthew) Tayler-Smith	11	–	–	–	–	0	11	–	–	–	–	0
R (Regardt) van Eyk	4	–	–	–	–	0	23	7	1	–	–	37
HJ (Jaco) van Schalkwyk	7	–	4	4	1	23	10	–	4	4	1	23
R (Riaan) Vermeulen	11	1	–	–	–	5	11	1	–	–	–	5
K (Kwezi) Yoyo	1	–	–	–	–	0	1	–	–	–	–	0
Penalty try	–	1	–	–	–	5	–	–	–	–	–	–
55 players												

APPEARANCES AND POINTS IN VODACOM CUP 2010

	Pampas XV	Bulldogs	WP	Free State	Eagles	Sharks XV	Cavaliers	Matches	Tries	Conversions	Penalties	Drop Goals	Points
Justin Peach	15	15	15	15	15	15	15	7	5	12	15	–	94
Norman Nelson	14	14	14	14	14	14	14	7	1	–	–	–	5
Jaco Bekker	13	–	–	13R	13R	13R	13	5	–	–	–	–	0
De Wet Barry	12c	12c	12c	12c	12c	12c	12c	7	–	–	–	–	0
Howard Noble	11	11	11	11	11	11	11	7	5	–	–	–	25
Matthew Tayler-Smith	10	10	x	x	10	10	10	5	–	–	–	–	0
Marlon Lewis	9	9R	9R	9	9R	9R	9R	7	1	–	–	–	5
Sivuyile Kobokana	8	–	–	–	–	–	–	1	–	–	–	–	0
Jacques Potgieter	7	8R	8	8	8	8	–	6	–	–	–	–	0
Zolani Mofu	6	6	6	6	–	6R	7R	6	–	–	–	–	0
Hein Potgieter	5	5	–	5R	5	5	5	6	–	–	–	–	0
Brendon Snyman	4	5R	5	5	–	–	–	4	–	–	–	–	0
Sangoni Mxoli	3	–	3	3	3	3R	3R	6	–	–	–	–	0
Bobby Dyer	2	2	2	2	2R	–	–	5	–	–	–	–	0
Phumlani Nodikida	1	1	1	1	1	1	1	7	1	–	–	–	5
Giovano Fourie	x	x	x	x	2	2	2	3	1	–	–	–	5
Ayanda Nogampula	3R	3	7R	3R	3R	–	–	5	–	–	–	–	0
Nolan Clark	5R	4	4	4	4	4	4	7	–	–	–	–	0
Yves Bashiya	7R	7	7	7	7	7	7	7	1	–	–	–	5
Clayton Gawie	9R	9	9	9R	9	9	9	7	–	–	–	–	0
Regardt van Eyk	10R	10R	10	10	–	–	–	4	–	–	–	–	0
Ryan Brown	15R	x	15R	–	–	15R	10R	4	–	–	–	–	0
Sebastian Hilpert	–	8	–	–	–	–	–	1	–	–	–	–	0
Kwezi Yoyo	–	3R	–	–	–	–	–	1	–	–	–	–	0
Alfonso Pietersen	–	13	–	–	–	–	–	1	–	–	–	–	0
Siyanda Grey	–	–	13	13	13	13	x	4	2	–	–	–	10
Andries Smit	–	–	x	–	5R	x	5R	2	–	–	–	–	0
Pietie Ferreira	–	–	6R	6R	6R	–	8	4	–	–	–	–	0
Elroy Ligman	–	–	–	–	6	6	6	3	–	–	–	–	0
Curtis Sias	–	–	–	–	x	–	–	0	–	–	–	–	0
Sphephelo Mayaba	–	–	–	–	–	3	3	2	–	–	–	–	0
Neil Jacobs	–	–	–	–	–	2R	2R	2	–	–	–	–	0
Penalty try	–	–	–	–	–	–	–	0	1	–	–	–	5
33 Players								**143**	**18**	**12**	**15**	**0**	**159**

eprugby@intekom.co.za

APPEARANCES AND POINTS IN ABSA CURRIE CUP 2010*

	Bulldogs	Griffons	Cavaliers	Valke	Eagles	Bulldogs	Griffons	Cavaliers	Valke	Eagles	Cavaliers	Eagles	Pumas	Pumas	Matches	Tries	Conversions	Penalties	Drop Goals	Points
Tiger Mangweni	15	15	15	15	15	15	15	15	15	15	–	–	–	–	10	2	–	–	–	10
Norman Nelson	14	14	14	14	14	–	11	11	11	11	14	11	11	11	13	10	–	–	–	50
Wayne Stevens	13	13	13	–	13	12c	–	–	–	–	12	13	13	13	9	5	–	–	–	25
De Wet Barry	12c	12c	12c	12c	12c	–	12c	12c	12c	12c	–	12	12	12c	12	3	–	–	–	15
Justin Peach	11	11	11	–	–	–	–	–	–	–	–	–	–	–	3	–	3	8	–	30
Jaco van Schalkwyk	10	10	10	15R	10	10	10	x	–	–	–	–	–	–	7	–	4	4	1	23
Donald Stevens	9	9	9	–	9	x	9	–	9R	9R	x	9R	x	9R	9	1	4	5	–	28
Darron Nell	8	8	8	8	8	–	–	–	–	8	–	8R	8R	8R	9	3	–	–	–	15
Zolani Mofu	7	7	–	–	–	7R	8R	x	–	–	–	–	–	–	4	–	–	–	–	–
Jacques Potgieter	6	6	6	6	6	6	6	–	6	6	6	6	6	6	13	3	–	–	–	15
Lungelo Payi	5	5	5	5	5	–	–	5	5	5	–	5R	5R	5R	11	–	–	–	–	–
Rory Duncan	4	4	4	4	4	–	–	–	–	–	5R	4	4	4	9	–	–	–	–	–
Riaan Vermeulen	3	3	3	3	–	3R	1R	3R	–	3R	1R	3R	x	6R	11	1	–	–	–	5
Robert Dyer	2	2	–	–	–	2R	2R	–	2R	2R	–	–	–	–	6	–	–	–	–	–
Pumlani Nodikita	1	1	1	3R	–	–	–	–	–	–	1	1	1	1	8	–	–	–	–	–
Jaco Fourie	2R	2R	2R	2R	x	–	–	R 2	2	–	2	2	2	2	10	1	–	–	–	5
Sangoni Mxoli	1R	1R	1R	1	1R	–	–	–	1R	–	–	–	–	–	6	1	–	–	–	5
Nolan Clark	5R	5R	–	–	–	4	4	4R	4R	4R	5	–	–	–	8	–	–	–	–	–
Morne Hanekom	x	7R	7R	–	–	–	–	–	–	–	–	–	–	–	2	–	–	–	–	–
Gerrie Odendaal	x	9R	9R	9	x	9	9R	9	9	9	9	9	9	9	12	5	–	–	–	25
Matthew Tayler-Smith	10R	10R	10R	10R	–	12R	10R	x	x	–	–	–	–	–	6	–	–	–	–	–
Mzwandile Stick	x	x	11R	10	x	10R	15R	–	15R	15R	15c	15c	15c	–	9	–	4	2	–	14
Pietie Ferreira	–	–	7	7	7	–	7	6	8	8R	x	–	–	–	7	3	–	–	–	15
Antonio Halangahu	–	–	2	2	2	2	2	2	–	2	2R	2R	2R	2R	11	–	–	–	–	–
Brendon Snyman	–	–	5R	5R	4R	5	5	–	–	–	–	–	–	–	5	–	–	–	–	–
Jaco Bekker	–	–	–	13	11R	13	13	13	13	13	–	–	x	x	7	–	–	–	–	–
Mlindazwe Nqoro	–	–	–	11	11	11	–	–	–	–	11	x	–	11R	5	1	–	–	–	5
Marlon Lewis	–	–	–	9R	–	–	–	x	–	–	–	–	–	–	1	–	–	–	–	–
Jonathan Gagiano	–	–	–	8R	x	8	8	8	7R	–	8	8	8	8	9	1	–	–	–	5
Andre Schlechter	–	–	–	–	3	3	3	3	3	3	3	3	3	3	10	–	–	–	–	–
Michael de Neuilly-Rice	–	–	–	–	1	1	1	1	1	1	1	–	–	–	7	–	–	–	–	–
Paul Perez	–	–	–	–	–	14	14	14	14	14	13	14	14	14	9	6	–	–	–	30
Mpho Mbiyozo	–	–	–	–	–	7	–	7	7	7	–	–	–	–	4	–	–	–	–	–
Hein Potgieter	–	–	–	–	–	5R	–	–	–	–	–	–	–	–	1	–	–	–	–	–
Devin Oosthuizen	–	–	–	–	–	–	5R	–	–	–	7	7	7	7	5	1	–	–	–	5
Monty Dumond	–	–	–	–	–	–	10	10	10	10	10	10	10	10	7	–	15	18	1	87
Willem Stoltz	–	–	–	–	–	–	4	4	4	4	5	5	5	–	7	–	–	–	–	–
Rudi Keil	–	–	–	–	–	–	–	–	13R	11R	–	–	–	–	2	–	–	–	–	–
Anthony Fenner	–	–	–	–	–	–	–	–	–	14R	x	–	15R	15	3	–	–	–	–	–
39 Players															**287**	**47**	**30**	**37**	**2**	**412**

* Totals include performances in promotion/relegation play-offs

PROVINCIAL ROUND-UP

The EP Kings players celebrate their First Division title win over the SWD Eagles.

ABSA U21 CHAMPIONSHIP (Runner-up, 1st, Section B)

Played	Won	Drawn	Lost	Points for	Points against	Tries for	Tries against	Winning %
8	6	1	1	320	207	43	22	81.00%

RESULTS: Bt Pumas (h) 23-21. Bt (h) Border 35-18. Drew Griffons (a) 36-36. Bt Valke (a) 26-22. Bt Griquas (a) 48-25. Bt SWD (h) 73-12. SEMI FINAL Bt Pumas (h) 43-20. FINAL Lost Valke (h) 35-53.

SCORERS: 68 Curis Sias (2t,11c,12p); 36 Masixola Banda (3t,6c,3p); 33 Morne van Staden (3t,9c); 25 Athenkosi Manentsa (5t); 20 Yondela Stampu, Samuel Borsaah, Gladman Mdzayi (4t each); 15 Kalvano Kingt (3t); 10 Vusumzi Dyantjies, Thembelani Bholi, Zwelakhe Sadladla, Dewald Barnard, Siyanda Grey, Reynier van Rooyen (2t each); 7 Werner Kapp (1t,1c); 6 Carl van Niekerk (2p); 5 Thabiso Mngomezulu, Penalty try (1t each).

ABSA U19 CHAMPIONSHIP (1st, Section B)

Played	Won	Drawn	Lost	Points for	Points against	Tries for	Tries against	Winning %
7	6	1	0	250	128	37	20	93.00%

RESULTS: Bt Pumas (h) 25-5. Bt Border (h) 50-0. Bt Boland (a) 44-18. Bt Valke (a) 37-34. Bt Griquas (a) 29-20. Bt SWD (h) 29-15. SEMI FINAL Drew Valke (h) 36-36.

SCORERS: 38 Andile Witbooi (5t,5c,1p); 33 Lorenzo Baatjies (9c,5p); 30 Roche Killian (6t); 28 Shane Gates (5t,1p); 20 Denzil Lindoor (4t); 15 Elandre van Eck, Phaphama Hoyi (3t each); 14 Jonathan Mudrovcic (4c,2p); 10 Darren van Winkel (2t); 7 Scott McCarthy (1t,1c); 5 Kayle van Zyl, Nico Steenkamp, Jan-Frederik Enslin, Keegan Ehret, Marquz Maarman, Brenden Olivier, Jason Potgieter, Rynier Bernardo (1t each).

AMATEUR CHAMPIONSHIP

Eastern Province (3rd, South Section)

Played	Won	Drawn	Lost	Points for	Points against	Tries for	Tries against
7	5	0	2	298	159	40	22

RESULTS: Bt EP Rural (a) 56-16. Bt Border Rural (h) 65-6. Bt SWD (h) 63-8. Lost Boland (a) 29-32. Bt Border (a) 30-25. Lost WP (a) 7-41. Bt Griffons Rural (h) 48-31. *SEMI FINAL Bt Blue Bulls (h) 22-19. FINAL Lost Griquas (a) 31-38.

EP Rural (6th, South Section)

Played	Won	Drawn	Lost	Points for	Points against	Tries for	Tries against
7	2	0	5	170	236	22	33

RESULTS: Lost EP (h) 16-56. Lost Griquas Rural (a) 17-20. Lost WP (h) 18-52. BT Border Rural (h) 38-23. Bt SWD (h) 36-17. Lost Boland (a) 30-49. Lost Border (a) 15-19. *

eprugby@intekom.co.za

EASTERN PROVINCE RECORDS

MATCH RECORDS

Biggest win	110-17	vs. Welwitschias (Namibia)	2001
Biggest Currie Cup win	50-0	vs. Orange Free State	1993
Heaviest defeat	12-80	vs. Griqualand West	1998
Heaviest Currie Cup defeat	3-65	vs. Northern Transvaal	1984
Highest score	110	vs. Welwitschias (Namibia) (110-17)	2001
Most points conceded	80	vs. Griqualand West (12-80)	1998
Most tries	16	vs. Welwitschias (Namibia) (110-17)	2001
Most Currie Cup tries	10	vs. North West (64-15)	1998
Most points by a player	38	HP le Roux vs. Eastern Transvaal	1991
Most Currie Cup points by a player	29	AP Kruger vs. North West	1996
Most tries by a player	5	FW Knoetze vs. Stellaland	1991
	5	FG Crous vs. Western Transvaal	1994
Most tries by a player	5	FW Knoetze vs. Stellaland	1991
	5	FG Crous vs. Western Transvaal	1994
	5	N Nelson vs. Valke (Currie Cup, First Div.)	2010

SEASON RECORDS

Most team points	776	24 matches	2003
Most Currie Cup points by team	364	13 matches	2005
Most points by a player	282	AP Kruger	1996
Most Currie Cup points by a player	153	B Hennessey	2002
Most team tries	103	24 matches	2003
Most Currie Cup tries by team	51	11 matches	2000
Most tries by a player	14	M van Vuuren	1994
	14	H Pedro	1998
	14	FM Juries	2003
Most Currie Cup tries by a player	13	H Pedro	1998

CAREER RECORDS

Most appearances	173	BC Pinnock 1993-2002
Most points	1126	GC van Zyl 1981-1988
Most Currie Cup points	755	GC van Zyl 1981-1988
Most tries	48	DM Gerber 1978-1990

HONOURS

Vodacom Shield	2002
First Division	**2010**

FREE STATE RUGBY UNION

FOUNDED 1895 (as Orange Free State) **GROUND** Vodacom Park, Bloemfontein
CAPACITY 46 000 **ADDRESS** Att Horak St, Bloemfontein, 9300
POSTAL ADDRESS Att Horak St, Bloemfontein, 9301
TELEPHONE NUMBER 051 407 1700 **WEBSITE** www.fscheetahs.co.za
COLOURS White jersey with orange stripes, black shorts
CURRIE CUP COACH Naka Drotské
VODACOM CUP COACH Pine Pienaar **CAPTAIN** Juan Smith
PRESIDENT Harold Verster **COMPANY & UNION CEO** Gerda von Solms

Consistent Cheetahs go close again

JUST how they manage to pull it off with clockwork regularity remains a closely guarded secret, but the Free State Cheetahs again shrugged off the kind of challenges that would hamstring most other top professional teams' ambitions by renewing their membership of the 'Big Four' club for another year.

Given their budget and player resources, the Cheetahs should really be a top-six Premier Division team who see it as a bonus whenever they reach the Absa Currie Cup playoffs.

Perhaps it's indeed something in the Bloemfontein water, but whatever the reason, the union sets itself lofty goals and, year after year, either achieves them or comes naggingly close.

2010 was one of those 'could-have, should-have' seasons, with coach Naka Drotské's side finishing third on the Currie Cup log, just one point adrift of a home semifinal, after winning 10 of their 14 round-robin matches.

A quick flip through the record books reveals their amazing consistency in the competition: you have to go back to the 2003 season for the last time they missed the semi-finals. Since then, apart from three titles in 2005, 2006 and 2007, the Cheetahs have topped the log twice and finished third on three occasions.

In the end, however, that one vital log point cost them dear. The Cheetahs travelled to Newlands hoping to repeat their semifinal heroics of 2009, when they beat the Sharks in Durban, but Western Province weren't in charitable mood and ran out convincing 31-7 winners to dash hopes of a fourth title in six years.

Despite the heavy defeat, Drotské, his skippers Adriaan Strauss and Juan Smith, and the other 27 players used during the campaign can hold their heads high. Eighthman Ashley Johnson capped a fine year, scoring the most tries (7) and being chosen as the team's player of the year,

while flyhalf Louis Strydom topped the point-scoring charts with 146. In fact, perhaps the secret to the Cheetahs' consistency is consistency: no fewer than 18 players appeared in 13 or more of the team's 15 matches, with half of those not missing a single match.

Off the field, the Cheetahs also made headlines in 2010 thanks to the long-running contract saga of Lionel Mapoe. The promising wing, who was desperately unlucky not to win his Springbok colours on the 2009 end-of-year tour, became embroiled in a much publicised and at times ugly spat between the Free State and KwaZulu Natal rugby unions over the validity of his Cheetahs contract.

Free State president Harold Verster, who had watched helplessly as scores of players were lured across the Drakensberg to Durban over the years, decided enough was enough and took a stand with Mapoe. The player, meanwhile, had had already begun training with the Sharks in defiance of a court order for him to return to Bloemfontein.

At the time of writing, Mapoe, who didn't make it near the field of play in the Currie Cup, had reportedly signed for the Golden Lions. At his best, Mapoe is a potential Test wing but one can't help get the feeling that he missed the boat in 2010 and will struggle to reclaim the substantial ground he lost to the likes of Sharks flyer Lwazi Mvovo, who played himself into the Springbok team for their grand slam tour on the back of Natal's Currie Cup title.

There was better news for Coenie Oosthuizen, the massive front-ranker whose consistent season earned him a Bok call-up. Oosthuizen's reward was a metaphor for the entire Free State union itself – despite having only a fraction of the money available to bigger teams, the region continues to churn out talented youngsters with the physical and mental ingredients necessary to play Test rugby.

FREE STATE LOG POSITIONS

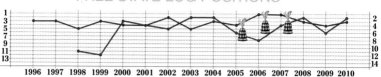

FREE STATE RESULTS AND SCORERS IN 2010

Played	Won	Drawn	Lost	Points for	Points against	Tries for	Tries against
26	18	0	8	816	576	96	58

VODACOM CUP PLAYED 10 WON 7 DRAWN 0 LOST 3 POINTS FOR 276 POINTS AGAINST 215 TRIES FOR 29 TRIES AGAINST 21 WINNING PERCENTAGE 70%

Date	Venue	Referee	Opponent	Result	Score	Scorers
Feb 27	George[1]	Francois Veldsman	SWD EAGLES	WON	22-13	T: Snyman (2), van Zyl, Floors. C: Whitehead
Mar 6	Bloemfontein	Joey Salmans	BOLAND	WON	37-29	T: Badenhorst (2), Johnson, Mathee. C: Whitehead. P: Whitehead (3), Strydom (2).
Mar 13	Empangeni	Matt Kemp	SHARKS XV	LOST	17-26	T: Whitehead. P: Strydom (4).
Mar 19	Bloemfontein[2]	Pieter de Villiers	EASTERN PROVINCE	WON	25-16	T: Mhlanga, Johnson, Snyman. C: S Ebersohn (2). P: S Ebersohn. DG: S Ebersohn
Mar 27	East London[3]	Sandile Mayende	BORDER	WON	50-18	T: Van Schalkwyk (3), Nyakane (2), Snyman, Ramashala, Smit. C: S Ebersohn (2), P: S Ebersohn (2).
April 10	Parow	Lusanda Jam	PAMPAS XV	LOST	24-36	T: Van Vuuren, Mathee, Carse. C: Strydom (2), S Ebersohn. P: Strydom.
April 17	Petrusburg	Luke Burger	WESTERN PROVINCE	WON	20-12	T: Prinsloo. P: Strydom (5).
Quarter-final						
April 23	Johannesburg[4]	Francois Veldsman	GOLDEN LIONS	WON	30-20	T: Snyman, Ramashala. C: Strydom. P: Strydom (6)
Semi-Final						
May 1	Wellington	Ben Crouse	BOLAND	WON	22-14	T: Van Zyl. C: Strydom. P: Strydom (5).
Final						
May 7	Pretoria[5]	Jason Jaftha	BLUE BULLS	LOST	29-31	T: Goodes, Vermeulen. C: Strydom (2). P: Strydom (5).

1 Saasveld, 2 Shimlapark, 3 Sisa Dukashe Stadium, 4 Johannesburg Stadium, 5 Loftus Versfeld B-Field

ABSA CURRIE CUP PLAYED 15 WON 10 LOST 5 DREW 0 POINTS FOR 495 POINTS AGAINST 354 TRIES FOR 60 TRIES AGAINST 36 WINNING PERCENTAGE 67%

Date	Venue	Referee	Opponent	Result	Score	Scorers
July 10	Bloemfontein	Marius Jonker	WESTERN PROVINCE	LOST	11-25	T: De Bruyn. P: Strydom (2).
July 16	Bloemfontein	Mark Lawrence	GRIQUAS	WON	33-26	T: Oosthuizen (3), Nokwe, R Ebersohn. C: Strydom (4)
July 24	Pretoria	Pro Legoete	BLUE BULLS	WON	25-23	T: Badenhorst. C: S Ebersohn. P: Strydom (5), S Ebersohn.
July 31	Bloemfontein	Mark Lawrence	SHARKS	LOST	13-25	T: De Bruyn. C: Strydom. P: Strydom (2).
Aug 7	Witbank	Mark Lawrence	PUMAS	WON	45-30	T: Oosthuizen, Scholtz, Daniller, Nokwe, Bosman, R Ebersohn. C: Strydom (4), S Ebersohn (2). P: Strydom.
Aug 14	Johannesburg	Sandile Mayende	GOLDEN LIONS	LOST	26-30	T: Johnson, Calldo. C: Strydom. P: Strydom (4).
Aug 20	Bloemfontein	Jason Jaftha	LEOPARDS	WON	57-00	T: Snyman (2), Strauss, Van der Walt, Oosthuizen, F Uys, Scholtz, R Ebersohn, Nel. C: Bosman (6).
Aug 27	Cape Town	Pro Legoete	WESTERN PROVINCE	WON	29-24	T: Nokwe, Floors. C: Strydom (2). P: Strydom (5).
Sep 3	Kimberley	Sandile Mayende	GRIQUAS	WON	33-28	T: Nokwe (2), Johnson. C: Strydom (3. P: Strydom (3), Bosman.
Sep 11	Bloemfontein	Jason Jaftha	BLUE BULLS	WON	20-14	T: Van der Walt, Scholtz. C: Strydom (2). P: Strydom (2).
Sep 18	Durban	Pro Legoete	SHARKS	LOST	16-30	T: F Uys. C: Strydom. P: Strydom (2), Bosman.
Sep 24	Bloemfontein	Joey Salmans	PUMAS	WON	59-24	T: Johnson, Strauss (2), Nel (2), R Ebersohn, Badenhorst, C Uys. C: Strydom (5), Bosman (2).
Oct 2	Bloemfontein	Stuart Berry	GOLDEN LIONS	WON	43-37	T: Johnson (2), Daniller, Strauss, Nel, Snyman. C: Strydom (2). P: Strydom (2).
Oct 8	Phokeng	Marius Jonker	LEOPARDS	WON	78-07	T: C Uys (2), Daniller (2), Snyman (2), Strauss, Johnson, Oosthuizen, Scholtz, Bosman, Carse. C: Strydom (6), S Ebersohn (3).
Semi-Final						
Oct 16	Cape Town	Mark Lawrence	WESTERN PROVINCE	LOST	07-31	T: Snyman. C: S Ebersohn

OTHER FIRST CLASS MATCHES

Date	Venue	Referee	Opponent	Result	Score	Scorers
July 3	East London	Sandile Mayende	BORDER BULLDOGS	WON	43-07	T: Floors (2), Oosthuizen (2), F Uys, Nokwe, Carse. C: Strydom (4), S Ebersohn.

Team: H Daniller, JW Jonker, R Ebersohn (C Uys), M Bosman, J Nokwe (S Frolick), L Strydom (S Ebersohn), T Carse (T de Bruyn), A Johnson (K Floors), F Uys, H Scholtz , W Vermeulen (D de Villiers), I van der Westhuizen, K Calldo, PW van Vuuren (H Grobler),

APPEARANCES AND POINTS FOR FREE STATE IN 2010   CAREER

PLAYER	Appearances	Tries	Conversions	Penalties	Drop Goals	Points	Career Matches	Career Tries	Conversions	Penalties	Drop Goals	Points
J-C (JC) Astle	3	–	–	–	–	0	3	–	–	–	–	0
RS (Skipper) Badenhorst	16	4	–	–	–	20	16	4	–	–	–	20
HM (Meyer) Bosman	15	2	9	3	–	37	59	10	21	9	–	119
J (Jean) Botha	2	–	–	–	–	0	7	–	–	–	–	0
JG (Kobus) Calldo	18	1	–	–	–	5	70	1	–	–	–	5
TG (Tersius) Carse	20	3	–	–	–	15	32	4	–	–	–	20
HJ (Hennie) Daniller	15	4	–	–	–	20	36	6	–	–	–	30
Z (Zandre) de Bruin	1	–	–	–	–	0	1	–	–	–	–	0
MJ (Tewis) de Bruyn	16	2	–	–	–	10	51	10	29	1	–	111
DJ (David) de Villiers	4	–	–	–	–	0	46	3	–	–	–	15
FC (Franna) du Toit	0	–	–	–	–	0	0	–	–	–	–	0
CA (Chris) Dry	4	–	–	–	–	0	5	–	–	–	–	0
RT (Robert) Ebersohn	17	4	–	–	–	20	37	8	–	–	–	40
JM (Sias) Ebersohn	22	–	13	4	1	41	30	1	17	5	2	60
L (Kabamba) Floors	17	4	–	–	–	20	91	24	–	–	–	120
S (Shandre) Frolick	1	–	–	–	–	0	1	–	–	–	–	0
B (Barry) Goodes	10	1	–	–	–	5	46	5	–	–	–	25
PW (Pieter) Gouws	3	–	–	–	–	0	11	1	–	–	–	5
JH (Hans) Grobler	1	–	–	–	–	0	1	–	–	–	–	0
PG (Gerhard) Human	5	–	–	–	–	0	5	–	–	–	–	0
AF (Ashley) Johnson	22	9	–	–	–	45	55	18	–	–	–	90
JW (JW) Jonker	9	–	–	–	–	0	65	18	–	–	–	90
HJ (Hercu) Liebenberg	4	–	–	–	–	0	26	–	–	–	–	0
CM (Charles) Marais	5	–	–	–	–	0	5	–	–	–	–	0
R (Rudi) Mathee	6	2	–	–	–	10	6	2	–	–	–	10
A (Alec) Mhlanga	5	1	–	–	–	5	5	1	–	–	–	5
TN (Trevor) Nyakane	5	2	–	–	–	10	5	2	–	–	–	10
WP (WP) Nel	15	4	–	–	–	20	40	10	–	–	–	50
JL (Jongi) Nokwe	12	6	–	–	–	30	35	26	–	–	–	130
GH (Gerrie) Odendaal	1	–	–	–	–	0	8	–	–	–	–	0
CV (Coenie) Oosthuizen	16	8	–	–	–	40	39	8	–	–	–	40
BH (Barend) Pieterse	7	–	–	–	–	0	75	7	–	–	–	35
JI (Ian) Potgieter	2	–	–	–	–	0	2	–	–	–	–	0
JG (Boom) Prinsloo	7	1	–	–	–	5	7	1	–	–	–	5
RM (Kholo) Ramashala	8	2	–	–	–	10	8	2	–	–	–	10
A (Andre) Schlechter	1	–	–	–	–	0	1	–	–	–	–	0
H (Hendro) Scholtz	17	4	–	–	–	20	140	29	–	–	–	145
AJ (Riaan) Smit	9	1	–	–	–	5	9	1	–	–	–	5
JH (Juan) Smith	6	–	–	–	–	0	41	8	–	–	–	40
PAB (Philip) Snyman	25	11	–	–	–	55	39	15	–	–	–	75
IW (Wayne) Stevens	3	–	–	–	–	0	10	1	–	–	–	5
PJ (Philip) Steyn	7	–	–	–	–	0	11	–	–	–	–	0
JA (Adriaan) Strauss	13	5	–	–	–	25	40	7	–	–	–	35
LI (Louis) Strydom	24	–	41	56	–	250	37	1	60	56	–	293
CJ (Corné) Uys	11	3	–	–	–	15	27	5	–	–	–	25
F (Francois) Uys	19	3	–	–	–	15	30	5	–	–	–	25
CJ (CJ) van der Linde	4	–	–	–	–	0	49	6	–	–	–	30
CP (Philip) van der Walt	11	2	–	–	–	10	11	2	–	–	–	10
HS (Fanie) van der Walt	2	–	–	–	–	0	2	–	–	–	–	0
IP (Izak) van der Westhuizen	19	–	–	–	–	0	46	1	–	–	–	5
J-P (Juan-Pierre) van Rooyen	0	–	–	–	–	0	0	–	–	–	–	0
R (Robbie) van Schalkwyk	4	3	–	–	–	15	4	3	–	–	–	15
P-W (PW) van Vuuren	12	1	–	–	–	5	20	2	–	–	–	10
PE (Pieter) van Zyl	9	2	–	–	–	10	9	2	–	–	–	10
P V (Waltie) Vermeulen	14	–	–	–	–	0	22	–	–	–	–	0
R (Riaan) Vermeulen	7	1	–	–	–	5	10	1	–	–	–	5
PJ (Johan) Wessels	8	–	–	–	–	0	24	4	–	–	–	20
GA (George) Whitehead	8	1	2	3	–	18	9	1	2	3	–	18
58 players	**547**	**97**	**65**	**66**	**1**	**816**	**1474**	**320**	**165**	**79**	**7**	**2188**

PROVINCIAL ROUND-UP

APPEARANCES AND POINTS IN VODACOM CUP 2010

	SWD Eagles	Boland	Sharks XV	EP	Border	Pampas XV	WP	Golden Lions	Boland	Blue Bulls	Matches	Tries	Conversions	Penalties	Drop Goals	Points
George Whitehead	15	15	11	15	–	–	15	15	15	15	8	1	2	3	–	18
Alec Mhlanga	14	14	14	14	–	14	–	–	–	–	5	1	–	–	–	5
Philip Snyman	13	13	13	13	13	13	13	13	13	13	10	5	–	–	–	25
Robert Ebersohn	12	–	–	–	–	–	–	–	–	–	1	–	–	–	–	0
Kholo Ramashala	11	11	–	11	11	–	11	11	11	11	8	2	–	–	–	10
Barry Goodes	10c	12c	12c	12c	12c	12c	12c	12c	12c	12c	10	1	–	–	–	5
Pieter van Zyl	9	9	9	9R	9	9	–	9R	9	9R	9	2	–	–	–	10
Kabamba Floors	8	–	–	–	–	–	–	–	–	–	1	1	–	–	–	5
Pieter Gouws	7	7	7	–	–	–	–	–	–	–	3	–	–	–	–	0
Hendro Scholtz	6	–	–	–	–	–	–	–	–	–	1	–	–	–	–	0
Barend Pieterse	5	5	5	–	–	–	–	–	–	–	3	–	–	–	–	0
Izak van der Westhuizen	4	4	4	5	5	–	–	–	–	–	5	–	–	–	–	0
Kobus Calldo	3	3	3	3	3	–	–	–	–	3	6	–	–	–	–	0
PW van Vuuren	2	2R	2R	2R	2	2R	2R	2R	2	2	10	1	–	–	–	5
Trevor Nyakane	1	1	1	1	1	–	–	–	–	–	5	2	–	–	–	10
Hercu Liebenberg	2R	–	–	–	2R	–	–	–	2R	2R	4	–	–	–	–	0
Jean Botha	3R	–	3R	–	–	–	–	–	–	–	2	–	–	–	–	0
Rudi Mathee	5R	5R	4R	4	4	4	–	–	–	–	6	2	–	–	–	10
Gerhard Human	6R	6	6	7R	–	x	5R	–	–	–	5	–	–	–	–	0
Tertius Carse	12R	9R	9R	9	–	9R	9	9	–	9	8	1	–	–	–	5
Franna du Toit	x	–	–	–	–	–	–	–	–	–	0	–	–	–	–	0
Robbie van Schalkwyk	14R	x	15R	x	14	11	–	–	–	–	4	3	–	–	–	15
Sias Ebersohn	–	10	10	10	10	10	x	x	11R	14R	7	–	5	3	1	22
Ashley Johnson	–	8	8	8	–	–	–	8	8	8	6	2	–	–	–	10
Skipper Badenhorst	–	2	2	2	–	2	2	2	–	–	6	2	–	–	–	10
Louis Strydom	–	10R	15	–	15	15	10	10	10	10	8	–	6	28	–	96
Riaan Vermeulen	–	3R	–	x	3R	3	3R	3	3	1R	7	1	–	–	–	5
Boom Prinsloo	–	7R	–	–	6R	8	8	6R	6R	7	7	1	–	–	–	5
Johan Wessels	–	–	6R	6	6	6	6	6	6	6	8	–	–	–	–	0
Philip van der Walt	–	–	7R	7	7	–	–	–	–	–	3	–	–	–	–	0
Philip Steyn	–	–	–	5R	4R	5	5	5	5	5	7	–	–	–	–	0
Riaan Smit	–	–	–	15R	11R	15R	–	–	–	–	3	1	–	–	–	5
Fanie van der Walt	–	–	–	–	8	–	–	–	–	7R	2	–	–	–	–	0
Gerrie Odendaal	–	–	–	–	9R	–	x	–	x	–	1	–	–	–	–	0
Zandré de Bruin	–	–	–	–	12R	–	–	–	–	–	1	–	–	–	–	0
Francois Uys	–	–	–	–	–	7	4	4	4	4	5	–	–	–	–	0
Charles Marais	–	–	–	–	–	1	1	1	1	1	5	–	–	–	–	0
JW Jonker	–	–	–	–	–	14R	14	14	14	14	5	–	–	–	–	0
Ian Potgieter	–	–	–	–	–	3R	3	–	–	–	2	–	–	–	–	0
Chris Dry	–	–	–	–	–	7R	7	7	7	–	4	–	–	–	–	0
Wayne Stevens	–	–	–	–	–	–	12R	x	15R	12R	3	–	–	–	–	0
John-Charles Astle	–	–	–	–	–	–	4R	x	7R	5R	3	–	–	–	–	0
Juan-Pierre van Rooyen	–	–	–	–	–	–	x	–	–	–	0	–	–	–	–	0
Andre Schlechter	–	–	–	–	–	–	–	–	3R	–	1	–	–	–	–	0
44 players											**208**	**29**	**13**	**34**	**1**	**276**

www.fscheetahs.co.za

APPEARANCES AND POINTS IN ABSA CURRIE CUP 2010

Player	WP	Griquas	Blue Bulls	Sharks	Pumas	Lions	Leopards	WP	Griquas	Blue Bulls	Sharks	Pumas	Lions	Leopards	WP	Matches	Tries	Conversions	Penalties	Drop Goals	Points
Hennie Daniller	15	15	15	15	15	15	15	15	15	15	15	–	15	15	15	14	4	–	–	–	20
Phillip Snyman	14	14	14	14	14	14	14	14	14	14	14	14	11	14	14	15	6	–	–	–	30
Robert Ebersohn	13	13	13	13	13	13	13	13	13	13	13	13	13	13	13	15	4	–	–	–	20
Meyer Bosman	12	12	–	12R	12	12	12	12	12	12	12	12	12	12	12	14	2	9	3	–	37
Jongi Nokwe	11	11	11	11	11	–	11	11	11	11	11	11	–	–	–	11	5	–	–	–	25
Louis Strydom	10	10	10	10	10	10	10R	10	10	10	10	10	10	10	10	15	–	31	28	–	146
Tewis de Bruyn	9	9	9	9	9	9	9	9	9	9	9	9	9	9	9	15	2	–	–	–	10
Ashley Johnson	8	8	8	8	8	8	8	8	8	8	8	8	8	8	8	15	7	–	–	–	35
Francois Uys	7	4	–	–	7	7	4	4	4	4	4	4	4	4	4	13	2	–	–	–	10
Hendro Scholtz	6c	6	6	6	6	6	6	6	6	6	6	11R	6	6	6	15	4	–	–	–	20
Waltie Vermeulen	5	5	5R	7R	5R	5	5	5	5	5	–	–	5	5	5	13	–	–	–	–	0
Izak van der Westhuizen	4	–	4	4	4	4	–	4R	4R	5R	4R	5R	7R	12R	4R	13	–	–	–	–	0
WP Nel	3	3	3	3	3	3	3R	3R	3R	3R	3R	3	3	3	3	15	4	–	–	–	20
Skipper Badenhorst	2	2	2R	5R	2R	x	2R	x	x	x	2R	2R	x	2R	2R	10	2	–	–	–	10
Coenie Oosthuizen	1	1	1	1	1	1	1	1	1	1	1	1	1	1	1	15	6	–	–	–	30
PW van Vuuren	x	2R	–	–	–	–	–	–	–	–	–	–	–	–	–	1	–	–	–	–	0
Kobus Calldo	3R	3R	3R	–	–	3R	3	3	3	3	3	3R	3R	–	–	11	1	–	–	–	5
Juan Smith	4R	7c	7c	7c	–	–	–	–	–	–	–	–	7	7c	–	6	–	–	–	–	0
Kabamba Floors	8R	6R	6R	6R	6R	6R	6R	6R	6R	6R	6R	6	6R	8R	6R	15	1	–	–	–	5
Tertius Carse	9R	9R	9R	9R	9R	11R	9R	x	x	x	9R	15R	x	9R	9R	11	1	–	–	–	5
Corné Uys	13R	12R	12	12	–	–	–	–	–	13R	13R	13R	14	11	11	10	3	–	–	–	15
Sias Ebersohn	10R	10R	10R	10R	10R	10R	10	x	10R	10R	10R	10R	10R	10R	10R	14	–	7	1	–	17
Barend Pieterse	–	5R	5	5	5	–	–	–	–	–	–	–	–	–	–	4	–	–	–	–	0
Adriaan Strauss	–	–	2	2	2c	2c	2c	2c	2c	2c	2c	2c	2c	2c	2	13	5	–	–	–	25
Jonker, JW	–	–	14R	–	13R	11	–	–	–	–	–	–	–	–	–	3	–	–	–	–	0
CJ van der Linde	–	–	–	3R	3R	–	–	–	–	–	–	–	3R	3R	–	4	–	–	–	–	0
Philip van der Walt	–	–	–	–	–	4R	7	7	7	7	7	7	7	–	–	8	2	–	–	–	10
Riaan Smit	–	–	–	–	–	13R	15R	x	x	–	–	15	11R	15R	11R	6	–	–	–	–	0
David de Villiers	–	–	–	–	–	–	4R	–	–	–	5	5	–	–	–	3	–	–	–	–	0
29 players																**317**	**61**	**47**	**32**	**0**	**495**

PROVINCIAL ROUND-UP

Coenie Oosthuizen dives over for one of his three tries scored against GWK Griquas in the ABSA Currie Cup.

ABSA UNDER-21 CHAMPIONSHIP (4th, Section A)

Played	Won	Drawn	Lost	Points for	Points against	Tries for	Tries against	Winning %
13	6	1	6	610	415	75	52	46.00%

RESULTS Lost WP (h) 40-42. Bt Blue Bulls (a) 34-32. Lost KZN (h) 23-27. Bt Golden Lions (a) 43-17. Bt Leopards (h) 30-24. Lost WP (a) 39-40. Bt Boland (a) 110-10. Lost Blue Bulls (h) 35-36. Lost KZN (a) 25-51. Bt Boland (h) 109-00. Bt Golden Lions (h) 53-25. Lost Leopards (a) 20-62. SEMI-FINAL Drew WP (a) 49-49.

SCORERS 135 George Whitehead (3t, 30c, 18p, 2dg). 125 Franna du Toit (2t, 32c, 16p, 1dg). 40 Johan Prinsloo, Cameron Jacobs (8t each). 35 Mayibuye Ndwandwa (7t). 30 Marcel van der Merwe (6t each). 25 Frank Herne (5t). 20 Jamba Ulengo (4t). 15 Hoffman Maritz, Robert van Schalkwyk, Pieter van Zyl, Brendon Groenewald, Lappies Labuschagne (3t each). 10 Hanno Pieterse, Nico Scheepers, Martin Ferreira, Schalk van der Merwe, Trevor Nyakane, Kholo Ramashala, Earl Snyman, Inus Kritzinger (2t each). 5 Teboho Mohoje (1t).

ABSA UNDER-19 CHAMPIONSHIP (6th Section A)

Played	Won	Drawn	Lost	Points for	Points against	Tries for	Tries against	Winning %
12	3	0	9	300	424	35	47	25.00%

RESULTS Lost WP (h) 27-31. Bt Griffons (a) 40-35. Lost Blue Bulls (a) 28-35. Lost KZN (h) 13-33. Lost Golden Lions (a) 24-33. Lost Leopards (h) 22-31. Lost WP (a) 13-35. Lost Blue Bulls (h) 21-49. Lost KZN (a) 28-37. Bt Griffons (h) 33-28. Bt Golden Lions (h) 28-27. Lost Leopards (a) 23-50. PROMOTION-RELEGATION

SCORERS 64 Hanro Louw (1t, 10c, 13p). 30 Johann Goosen (6c, 6p). 25 Adriaan Britz (5t). 23 Lucien Ruiters (2t, 2c, 2p, 1dg). 19 Danie Marais (2c, 5p). 15 Egbert Ras, Martin Keyser (3t each). 14 Frederick Ras (2t, 2c). 10 Nicolaas Steenkamp, Brendon Groenewald, Leon van Straaten, Pieter Coetzee, Pieter Rademan (2t each). 5 Wilhelm van Zyl, Danie Cronjé, Carl Wegner, Stephan Kotze, Barend Koortzen, Jean Cook, Johan Meintjies, Heinrich Douglas, Michael van Vuuren (1t each).

AMATEUR PROVINCIAL CHAMPIONSHIP

Free State (1st , Central Section)

Played	Won	Drawn	Lost	Points for	Points against	Tries for	Tries against	Winning %
7	6	0	1	361	167	48	15	71.0%

RESULTS Bt Griffons Rural (h) 40-20. Bt Free State Rural (a) 52-16. Bt KZN Rural (a) 48-24. Bt Griquas (h) 76-12. Bt Valke Rural (a) 62-20. Bt Griffons (h) 44-27. SEMI-FINAL Lost WP (a) 39-48.

Free State Rural (6th, Central Section)

Played	Won	Drawn	Lost	Points for	Points against	Tries for	Tries against	Winning %
6	1	0	5	171	275	24	42	17.00%

RESULTS Lost Free State (h) 16-52. Lost Griquas (a) 31-45. Lost Griffons (a) 24-53. Lost Griffons Rural (a) 29-54. Lost KZN Rural (h) 17-57. Bt Valke Rural (h) 54-14.

FREE STATE RECORDS

MATCH RECORDS

Biggest win	132-3	vs. Eastern Orange Free State	1977
Biggest Currie Cup win	106-0	vs. Northern Free State	1997
Heaviest defeat	0-50	vs. Eastern Province (Currie Cup)	1993
Highest score	132	vs. Eastern Orange Free State (132-3)	1977
Highest Currie Cup score	113	vs. South Western Districts (113-11)	1996
Most points conceded	64	vs. Griqualand West (17-64)	1998
Most tries	23	vs. Eastern Orange Free State (132-3)	1977
Most Currie Cup tries	17	vs. South Western Districts (113-11)	1996
Most points by a player	48	WJdeW Ras vs. Eastern Orange Free State	1977
Most Currie Cup points by player	46	JH de Beer vs. Northern Free State	1977
Most tries by a player	6	HL Potgieter vs. Eastern Orange Free State	1977
Most Currie Cup tries by a player	4	On six occasions	
Most conversions by a player	20	WJdeW Ras vs. Eastern Orange Free State (SA Record)	1977
Most Currie Cup conversions	14	JH de Beer vs. Northern Free State	1977
Most penalties by a player	8	AF Fourie vs. Griqualand West (Currie Cup)	1997

SEASON RECORDS

Most team points	1434	31 matches (SA Record)	1996
Most Currie Cup points by team	703	15 matches	1997
Most points by a player	460	MJ Smith	1996
Most Currie Cup points by player	230	K Tsimba	2003
Most team tries	191	31 matches (SA Record)	1996
Most Currie Cup tries by team	91	15 matches	1997
Most tries by a player	**24**	**J-H van Wyk**	**1996**
Most Currie Cup tries by a player	**16**	**J-H van Wyk**	**1997**

CAREER RECORDS

Most appearances	245	HL Müller	1983-1998
Most Currie Cup appearances	142	HL Müller (SA Record)	1983-1998
Most points	1707	WJdeW Ras	1974-1986
Most Currie Cup points	1101	WJdeW Ras	1974-1986
Most tries	136	C Badenhorst	1986-1999
Most Currie Cup tries	65	C Badenhorst	1986-1999

HONOURS

ABSA Currie Cup	1976, 2005, 2006 (shared), 2007
Lion Cup	1983
Bankfin Nite Series	1996
Vodacom Cup	2000

PROVINCIAL ROUND-UP

GOLDEN LIONS RUGBY UNION

FOUNDED 1889 **GROUND** Coca-Cola Park (previously Ellis Park) **CAPACITY** 60 000
ADDRESS South Office Block, Johannesburg Stadium, 124 Van Beek Street, Doornfontein 2094
POSTAL ADDRESS PO Box 15724, Doornfontein, 2028
TELEPHONE NUMBER 011-402 2960 **WEBSITE** www.lionsrugby.co.za
COLOURS White and red trim jersey, black shorts and black socks
CURRIE CUP COACH John Mitchell **VODACOM CUP COACH** Timmy Goodwin
CAPTAIN Franco van der Merwe **PRESIDENT** Kevin de Klerk
COMPANY CEO Manie Reynecke

Mitchell repairs Lions' rudder

IT'S not often that a team finishing fifth in the Absa Currie Cup can reflect on a hugely satisfying campaign, but the Lions deserve credit for putting it to good use.

John Mitchell was appointed as coach for the Currie Cup and the biggest compliment one can pay him is that it actually appeared for once as if the team was being coached.

And, with nothing to lose and plenty of pride to regain in the wake of a disastrous Vodacom Super 14 campaign, the Lions recovered from a shaky start to regain some self-respect.

In the process a new generation of talented young players was unearthed. Flyhalf Elton Jantjies was the biggest gem of the lot and was brilliantly polished by Mitchell's astute man-management.

The youngster also flourished under the tutelage of former All Black flyhalf Carlos Spencer and by mid-campaign was already being spoken about as a Springbok tour contender.

Perhaps some of the hype was premature, but Lions fans were looking for reasons to believe that a better future was around the corner, and found it in the coaching of Mitchell, the composure of a young flyhalf, and the energy of other talented hopefuls such as fullback Jaco Taute, No 8 Warren Whiteley, flanker Josh Strauss and lock George Earle.

The Currie Cup also provided a platform for talented Springbok centre Waylon Murray to revive his career.

When you add the more established players, such as scrumhalf Jano Vermaak, wing Michael Killian, lock Franco van der Merwe, loose forwards Wikus van Heerden and Cobus Grobbelaar, and prop JC Janse van Rensburg into the mix, you realise that Mitchell has the makings of a side that can potentially be competitive in Super Rugby as opposed to perennial whipping boys.

The turnaround was best captured by the stunning 46-28 win over Western Province at Coca-Cola Park in mid-season. Consider that WP had beaten the Lions 32-0 at Newlands in the second round and you realise just how well the Lions had recovered.

It looked all over for their semifinal hopes towards the end of September when they lost to the Blue Bulls, but the Lions stubbornly refused to give up hope and snatched a stunning late 22-20 win over the Sharks courtesy of Van der Merwe's late try.

However, they came back down to earth with a 43-37 defeat to Free State in Bloemfontein before an upset loss to the Pumas finally scuppered the mathematical thread by which they were still holding on and robbed the revival of some of its gloss.

Why then should we be happy? Well, if the Currie Cup is about developing talent, the Lions managed to do that.

Notwithstanding the upset by the Pumas, they are back on the map and South African rugby will be stronger for that.

There has also been investment in the union, with businessmen Robert Gumede and Ivor Ichikowitz acquiring a 49.9% stake and undertaking to aggressively develop the franchise. Money, of course, offers no magic cure, but their Currie Cup campaign proved that the Lions are a union on the up, and importantly, Mitchell is staying.

New Lions coach and former All-Blacks trainer John Mitchell instilled discipline and a fierce work ethic at the Gauteng union.

PROVINCIAL ROUND-UP

GOLDEN LIONS LOG POSITIONS

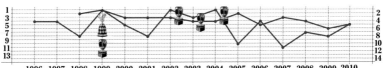

1996 1997 1998 1999 2000 2001 2002 2003 2004 2005 2006 2007 2008 2009 2010

GOLDEN LIONS RESULTS AND SCORERS IN 2010

VODACOM CUP Played **8** Won **5** Drawn **0** Lost **3** Points for **265** Points against **155** Tries for **33** Tries against **15**

Date	Venue	Opponent	Result	Score	Scorers
Feb 27	Johannesburg[1]	LEOPARDS	**WON**	27-22	T: Delport, St. Jerry, Van Deventer. C: Kruger (3). P: Kruger (2).
Mar 6	Nigel	VALKE	**WON**	34-13	T: Pekeur, Wheeler, Van Deventer, J Boshoff, Jonck. C: Jonck (2), R Boshoff. P: R Boshoff.
Mar 13	Johannesburg[2]	BLUE BULLS	LOST	22-27	T: Van Dyk. C: Kruger. P: Kruger (5).
Mar 19	Welkom	GRIFFONS	**WON**	48-16	T: Kriel (2), Van Deventer (2), Buys, Delport, St. Jerry, Bullbring. C: Jonck (2), Taute (2).
Mar 26	Johannesburg[1]	GRIQUAS	**WON**	45-05	T: Delport, Engelbrecht, Van Heerden, Kriel, Muller, Cloete. C: Kruger (3). P: Kruger (3).
April 9	Secunda	PUMAS	LOST	18-22	P: Rose (6).
April 17	Johannesburg[1]	WELWITCHIAS	**WON**	51-20	T: Engelbrecht, Mentz, Wheeler, Lombaard, Moore, Emslie, Frolick. C: Rose (5). P: Rose. DG: Rose.

Quarter-final

Date	Venue	Opponent	Result	Score	Scorers
April 23	Johannesburg[1]	Free State	LOST	20-30	T: Mentz (2), Van Deventer. C: Rose. P: Rose.

[1]Johannesburg Stadium, [2]Bill Jardine Stadium, Raiders RC

GOLDEN LIONS RESULTS AND SCORERS

Played	Won	Drawn	Lost	Points for	Points against	Tries for	Tries against	Winning %
14	7	0	7	401	407	45	46	50.00%

ABSA CURRIE CUP Played **14** Won **7** Drawn **0** Lost **7** Points for **401** Points against **407** Tries for **45** Tries against **46**.

Date	Venue	Opponent	Result	Score	Scorers
July 9	Rustenburg	LEOPARDS	**WON**	43-13	T: Vermaak (2), Taute, Delport, Murray. C: Kruger (3). P: Kruger (4).
July 17	Cape Town	WP	LOST	0-32	
July 24	Kimberley	GRIQUAS	LOST	20-26	T: Vermaak, Earle. C: Kruger (2). P: Kruger (2).
July 31	Johannesburg	BLUE BULLS	LOST	18-32	T: Van Rensburg, Whiteley. C: Jantjies. P: Jantjies (2).
Aug 7	Durban	SHARKS	LOST	19-48	T: Van Rensburg. C: Jantjies. P: Jantjies (4).
Aug 14	Johannesburg	CHEETAHS	**WON**	30-26	T: Van Rensburg, Jantjies, Boshoff. C: Jantjies (3). P: Jantjies (3).
Aug 20	Witbank	PUMAS	**WON**	33-30	T: Van Rensburg, Taute, Vermaak, Minnie. C: Francis (2). P: Francis (3).
Aug 27	Johannesburg	LEOPARDS	**WON**	45-22	T: Bothma (2), Snyman (2), Killian, Vermaak, Whiteley. C: Jantjies (2), Francis (2).
Sep 3	Johannesburg	WP	**WON**	46-28	T: Killian (2), Jantjies, Minnie. C: Jantjies (4). P: Jantjies (6).
Sep 11	Johannesburg	GRIQUAS	**WON**	40-29	T: Taute (2), Boshoff, Strauss. C: Jantjies (4). P: Jantjies (4).
Sep 18	Pretoria	BLUE BULLS	LOST	21-24	T: Murray, La Grange. C: Jantjies. P: Jantjies (3).
Sep 25	Johannesburg	SHARKS	**WON**	22-20	T: Taute, Murray, Van der Merwe. C: Jantjies (2). P: Jantjies.
Oct 2	Bloemfontein	CHEETAHS	LOST	37-43	T: Killian, Strauss, Marutlulle, Francis. C: Jantjies (4). P: Jantjies (3).
Oct 8	Johannesburg	PUMAS	LOST	27-34	T: Murray, Van Rensburg, Whiteley, Minnie. C: Jantjies (2). P: Jantjies.

APPEARANCES AND POINTS FOR GOLDEN LIONS IN 2010 CAREER

PLAYER	Appearances	Tries	Conversions	Penalties	Drop Goals	Points	Career Matches	Career Tries	Conversions	Penalties	Drop Goals	Points
MJ (Martin) Bezuidenhout	14	–	–	–	–	0	14	–	–	–	–	0
JH (Jannie) Boshoff	9	2	–	–	–	10	31	9	–	–	–	45
R (Renaldo) Bothma	7	2	–	–	–	10	7	2	–	–	–	10
DJ (David) Bullbring	7	–	–	–	–	0	7	–	–	–	–	0
K (Kevin) Buys	5	–	–	–	–	0	19	–	–	–	–	0
T (Tonderai) Chavhanga	1	–	–	–	–	0	1	–	–	–	–	0
M (Marius) Delport	8	1	–	–	–	5	8	1	–	–	–	5
G (George) Earle	12	1	–	–	–	5	12	1	–	–	–	5
P (Pieter) Engelbrecht	2	–	–	–	–	0	11	1	–	–	–	5
BK (Burton) Francis	6	1	4	3	–	22	6	1	4	3	–	22
R (Ross) Geldenhuys	14	–	–	–	–	0	22	1	–	–	–	5
TM (Trevor) Hall	7	–	–	–	–	0	33	2	–	–	–	10
ET (Elton) Jantjies	13	2	25	27	–	141	13	2	25	27	–	141
C (Chris) Jonck	4	–	–	–	–	0	20	2	2	2	–	20
JP (JP) Joubert	6	–	–	–	–	0	6	–	–	–	–	0
M (Michael) Killian	13	4	–	–	–	20	30	11	–	–	–	55
JA (Jaco) Kriel	1	–	–	–	–	0	1	–	–	–	–	0
HC (Herkie) Kruger	3	–	5	6	–	28	16	–	33	37	–	177
RA (Robert) Kruger	1	–	–	–	–	0	4	–	–	–	–	0
G (Doppies) la Grange	10	1	–	–	–	5	80	24	–	–	–	120
E (Edgar) Marutlulle	13	1	–	–	–	5	13	1	–	–	–	5
DJ (Derick) Minnie	13	3	–	–	–	15	31	9	–	–	–	45
J (Jonathan) Mokuena	2	–	–	–	–	0	2	–	–	–	–	0
WM (Waylon) Murray	14	4	–	–	–	20	14	4	–	–	–	20
J (Joe) Snyman	7	2	–	–	–	10	16	3	–	–	–	15
CJ (Carlos) Spencer	2	–	–	–	–	0	2	–	–	–	–	0
JZ (Josh) Strauss	8	2	–	–	–	10	8	2	–	–	–	10
W (Wayne) Swart	8	–	–	–	–	0	13	–	–	–	–	0
JJ (Jaco) Taute	12	5	–	–	–	25	13	5	–	–	–	25
F (Franco) van der Merwe	14	1	–	–	–	5	65	8	–	–	–	40
JL (Wikus) van Heerden	5	–	–	–	–	0	88	16	–	–	–	80
AG (Deon) van Rensburg	10	5	–	–	–	25	10	5	–	–	–	25
JCJ (JC) van Rensburg	13	–	–	–	–	0	43	–	–	–	–	0
J (Jano) Vermaak	14	5	–	–	–	25	71	16	3	4	–	98
WR (Warren) Whiteley	13	3	–	–	–	15	13	3	–	–	–	15
35 Players	**291**	**45**	**34**	**36**	**0**	**401**	**743**	**129**	**67**	**73**	**0**	**998**

PROVINCIAL ROUND-UP

APPEARANCES AND POINTS FOR XEROX LIONS IN ABSA CURRIE CUP 2010

	Leopards	WP	Griquas	Blue Bulls	Sharks	Cheetahs	Pumas	Leopards	WP	Griquas	Blue Bulls	Sharks	Cheetahs	Pumas	Matches	Tries	Conversions	Penalties	Drop Goals	Points
Jaco Taute	15	15	15	15	15	15	15	15	15	15	15	15	–	–	12	5	–	–	–	25
Tonderai Chavhanga	14	–	–	–	–	–	–	–	–	–	–	–	–	–	1	–	–	–	–	–
Marius Delport	13	13	13	x	15R	–	–	–	11R	10R	x	–	14R	13	8	1	–	–	–	5
Waylon Murray	12	12	12	13	13	13	13	13	13	13	13	13	13	12	14	4	–	–	–	20
Michael Killian	11	11	11	11	11	11	11	11	11	11	11	11	15	–	13	4	–	–	–	20
Herkie Kruger	10	10	10	–	–	–	–	–	–	–	–	–	–	–	3	–	5	6	–	28
Jano Vermaak	9	9	9	9	9	9	9	9	9	9	9	9	9	9	14	5	–	–	–	25
Jonathan Mokuena	8	–	8R	–	–	–	–	–	–	–	–	–	–	–	2	–	–	–	–	–
Franco van der Merwe	7c	7c	7c	5c	5c	5c	5c	5c	5c	5c	5c	5c	5c	5c	14	1	–	–	–	5
Derick Minnie	6	6	6	6	6	7	7	x	6	6	6	6	6	6	13	3	–	–	–	15
David Bullbring	5	5	5	4R	7R	–	–	4R	4R	–	–	–	–	–	7	–	–	–	–	–
George Earle	4	4	4	4	4	4	4	5R	4	–	4	4	4	–	12	1	–	–	–	5
Ross Geldenhuys	3	3	3	3R	3R	3	3	3	3	3	3	3	3	3	14	–	–	–	–	–
Martin Bezuidenhout	2	2	2	2	2	2R	2R	2	2	2	2	2	2	2	14	–	–	–	–	–
JC Janse van Rensburg	1	1	–	1	1	1	1	1	1	1	1	1	1	1	13	–	–	–	–	–
Francois du Toit	x	–	–	–	–	–	–	–	–	–	–	–	–	–	0	–	–	–	–	–
Kevin Buys	3R	3R	1	3	3	–	–	–	–	–	–	–	–	–	5	–	–	–	–	–
Robert Kruger	4R	–	–	–	–	–	–	–	–	–	–	–	–	–	1	–	–	–	–	–
Warren Whiteley	8R	8	8	8	8	8	8	8	8	8	8	–	7R	8	13	3	–	–	–	15
Chris Jonck	9R	9R	9R	x	9R	–	–	–	–	–	–	–	–	–	4	–	–	–	–	–
Elton Jantjies	10R	10R	10R	10	10	10	x	10	10	10	10	10	10	10	13	2	25	27	–	141
Deon van Rensburg	14R	14	14	14	14	14	14	–	–	–	–	15R	11	14	10	5	–	–	–	25
Edgar Marutlulle	–	2R	2R	2R	2R	2	2	2R	2R	2R	2R	2R	2R	2R	13	1	–	–	–	5
Trevor Hall	–	5R	5R	7	7	–	–	–	–	–	–	7R	4R	4	7	–	–	–	–	–
Wikus van Heerden	–	8R	–	–	–	–	–	–	–	8R	7	7	7	5	–	–	–	–	–
Pieter Engelbrecht	–	11R	–	–	–	–	–	13R	–	x	–	–	–	x	2	–	–	–	–	–
Wayne Swart	–	–	3R	–	–	1R	1R	3R	x	1R	x	3R	3R	3R	8	–	–	–	–	–
Doppies la Grange	–	–	14R	12	12	12	12	12	12	–	12	12	12	–	10	1	–	–	–	5
Jaco Kriel	–	–	–	6R	–	–	–	–	–	–	–	–	–	–	1	–	–	–	–	–
Carlos Spencer	–	–	–	10R	10R	–	–	–	–	–	–	–	–	–	2	–	–	–	–	–
Renaldo Bothma	–	–	–	–	4R	6	6	6	7R	7R	–	–	–	6R	7	2	–	–	–	10
Jannie Boshoff	–	–	–	–	–	14R	14R	14	14	14	14	14	14	11	9	2	–	–	–	10
Joe Snyman	–	–	–	–	–	4R	4R	4	–	4	4R	4R	–	4R	7	2	–	–	–	10
Josh Strauss	–	–	–	–	–	6R	6R	7	7	7	7	8	8	–	8	2	–	–	–	10
JP Joubert	–	–	–	–	–	9R	15R	9R	9R	x	x	x	9R	9R	6	–	–	–	–	–
Burton Francis	–	–	–	–	–	x	10	10R	12R	12	x	x	12R	15	6	1	4	3	–	22
Wandile Mjekevu	–	–	–	–	–	–	–	–	–	–	–	–	–	x	0	–	–	–	–	–
37 Players															**291**	**45**	**34**	**36**	**0**	**401**

ABSA UNDER-21 CHAMPIONSHIP (6th Section A)

Played 12 Won 3 Lost 9 Drawn 0 Points for 325 Points against 393 Tries for 42 Tries against 50 Winning percentage 25%

RESULTS: Lost Leopards (a) 16-36. Lost WP (a) 8-33. Bt Boland (a) 40-6. Lost Blue Bulls (h) 26-35. Lost Sharks (a) 25-49. Lost Free State (h) 17-43. Bt Leopards (h) 33-14. Lost WP 37-55 (h). Bt Boland (h) 57-11. Lost Blue Bulls (a) 21-32. Lost Sharks (h) 20-26. Lost Free State (a) 25-53.

SCORERS: 65 Heinrich Cronje (4t,12c,7p); 56 Dewald Nel (8c,13p); 20 Marnitz Jacobs (4t); 17 Luan Steenkamp (3t,1c); 15 Jaco Kriel (3t); 12 Christopher Janse van Rensburg (2t,1c); 11 Justin Botha (1c,3p); 10 Rudy Paige, Francois du Toit, Shane Kirkwood, Riaan Arends, Jacques Erasmus, Blake Mecuur, Caylib Oosthuizen, Renaldo Bothma (2t each); 5 Divan Ferguson, Heinrich Terblanche, Sebastian de Chaves, Jacques Pretorius, Wian Buys, Hendrik la Grange, Winston Williams, Christiaan du Rand, David Bullbring, Mark Hennig (1t each).

PLAYER	FOR YOUNG LIONS IN 2010 VODACOM CUP						CAREER					
	Appearances	Tries	Conversions	Penalties	Drop Goals	Points	Career Matches	Career Tries	Conversions	Penalties	Drop Goals	Points
MJ (Martin) Bezuidenhout	7	–	–	–	–	0	7	–	–	–	–	0
JH (Jannie) Boshoff	4	1	–	–	–	5	8	2	–	–	–	10
RJ (Ruan) Boshoff	3	–	1	1	–	5	3	–	1	1	–	5
BC (Bernardo) Botha	1	–	–	–	–	0	8	4	–	–	–	20
DJ (David) Bullbring	7	1	–	–	–	5	12	2	–	–	–	10
K (Kevin) Buys	1	–	–	–	–	0	1	–	–	–	–	0
HCW (Wian) Buys	5	1	–	–	–	5	5	1	–	–	–	5
T (Tonderai) Chavhanga	1	–	–	–	–	0	1	–	–	–	–	0
RF (Rouaan) Cloete	6	1	–	–	–	5	8	1	–	–	–	5
M (Marius) Delport	4	3	–	–	–	15	4	3	–	–	–	15
RM (Ruan) Dreyer	3	–	–	–	–	0	3	–	–	–	–	0
CF (Charl) du Plessis	2	–	–	–	–	0	7	–	–	–	–	0
C (Charles) Emslie	3	1	–	–	–	5	3	1	–	–	–	5
P (Pieter) Engelbrecht	7	2	–	–	–	10	7	2	–	–	–	10
S (Shandre) Frolick	4	1	–	–	–	5	10	2	–	–	–	10
DJ (Derek) Harwood	1	–	–	–	–	0	7	–	–	–	–	0
AWCJ (Alwyn) Hollenbach	1	–	–	–	–	0	1	–	–	–	–	0
J (Johan) Jackson	1	–	–	–	–	0	1	–	–	–	–	0
ET (Elton) Jantjies	1	–	–	–	–	0	1	–	–	–	–	0
C (Chris) Jonck	6	1	4	–	–	13	6	1	4	–	–	13
AH (Alex) Kock	3	–	–	–	–	0	3	–	–	–	–	0
JA (Jaco) Kriel	8	3	–	–	–	15	8	3	–	–	–	15
HC (Herkie) Kruger	3	–	7	10	–	44	3	–	7	10	–	44
RA (Robert) Kruger	2	–	–	–	–	0	4	1	–	–	–	5
JJ (Jannes) Labuschagne	2	–	–	–	–	0	2	–	–	–	–	0
J (Jacques) Lombard	2	1	–	–	–	5	2	1	–	–	–	5
N (Nico) Luus	4	–	–	–	–	0	4	–	–	–	–	0
H (Henno) Mentz	7	3	–	–	–	15	7	3	–	–	–	15
J (Jonathan) Mokuena	5	–	–	–	–	0	5	–	–	–	–	0
W (Wouter) Moore	7	1	–	–	–	5	7	1	–	–	–	5
RA (Randall) Morrison	1	–	–	–	–	0	1	–	–	–	–	0
GH (Gert) Muller	4	1	–	–	–	5	19	3	–	–	–	15
R (Rudy) Paige	5	–	–	–	–	0	5	–	–	–	–	0
WM (Wigan) Pekeur	2	1	–	–	–	5	6	1	–	–	–	5
EE (Earl) Rose	3	–	6	8	1	39	3	–	6	8	1	39
L (Lawrence) Sephaka	7	–	–	–	–	0	15	–	–	–	–	0
J (Justin) St. Jerry	5	2	–	–	–	10	12	4	–	–	–	20
W (Willem) Stoltz	1	–	–	–	–	0	10	–	–	–	–	0
W (Wayne) Swart	3	–	–	–	–	0	13	–	–	–	–	0
JJ (Jaco) Taute	3	–	2	–	–	4	3	–	2	–	–	4
DJ (Daniel) van der Merwe	1	–	–	–	–	0	1	–	–	–	–	0
HS (Heinke) van der Merwe	1	–	–	–	–	0	8	–	–	–	–	0
JC (Johan) van Deventer	5	5	–	–	–	25	14	5	–	–	–	25
HJ (Hans) van Dyk	5	1	–	–	–	5	5	1	–	–	–	5
JL (Wikus) van Heerden	1	1	–	–	–	5	4	4	–	–	–	20
C (Clint) van Niekerk	1	–	–	–	–	0	4	–	–	–	–	0
J (Jano) Vermaak	1	–	–	–	–	0	6	1	–	–	–	5
J (Justin) Wheeler	7	2	–	–	–	10	9	3	–	–	–	15
WR (Warren) Whiteley	4	–	–	–	–	0	4	–	–	–	–	0
49 players	**171**	**33**	**20**	**19**	**1**	**265**	**290**	**50**	**20**	**19**	**1**	**350**

PROVINCIAL ROUND-UP

APPEARANCES AND POINTS IN VODACOM CUP 2010 (YOUNG LIONS XV)

	Leopards	Valke	Blue Bulls	Griffons	Griquas	Pumas	Welwitchias	Free State	Matches	Tries	Conversions	Penalties	Drop Goals	Points
Shandre Frolick	15	15	15	–	–	–	11R	–	4	1	–	–	–	5
Marius Delport	14	–	14	14	14	–	–	–	4	3	–	–	–	15
Jannie Boshoff	13	13R	13	–	13	–	–	–	4	1	–	–	–	5
Justin St. Jerry	12	10R	12	12	–	x	13R	–	5	2	–	–	–	10
Henno Mentz	11	–	11	11	11	11	11	11	7	3	–	–	–	15
Herkie Kruger	10c	–	10c	–	10c	–	–	–	3	–	7	10	–	44
Chris Jonck	9	9R	9	9	9	9	–	–	6	1	4	–	–	13
Justin Wheeler	8	8	8	8	8	8	8c	–	7	2	–	–	–	10
Jonathan Mokuena	7	7	–	–	–	6R	6R	8c	5	–	–	–	–	0
Johan van Deventer	6	6	6	6	–	–	–	6R	5	5	–	–	–	25
Nico Luus	5	5c	5	5c	–	–	–	–	4	–	–	–	–	0
Wouter Moore	4	4R	4	4	4R	5	4	–	7	1	–	–	–	5
Gert Muller	3	3	3	–	3	–	–	–	4	1	–	–	–	5
Hans van Dyk	2	2	2	2	2	–	–	–	5	1	–	–	–	5
Wayne Swart	1	3R	1	–	–	–	–	–	3	–	–	–	–	0
Derek Harwood	2R	–	–	–	–	–	–	–	1	–	–	–	–	0
Lawrence Sephaka	1R	1	1R	1	1	1	–	1	7	–	–	–	–	0
David Bullbring	4R	4	4R	4R	5	4R	–	4	7	1	–	–	–	5
Jaco Kriel	6R	7R	7	7	6	6	6	6	8	3	–	–	–	15
Alex Kock	9R	–	–	–	–	–	9R	9R	3	–	–	–	–	0
Ruan Boshoff	22R	10	x	10	–	–	–	–	3	–	1	1	–	5
Alwyn Hollenbach	15R	–	–	–	–	–	–	–	1	–	–	–	–	0
Wigan Pekeur	–	14	–	–	–	–	–	14	2	1	–	–	–	5
Rouan Cloete	–	13	–	13	13R	13	13	13	6	1	–	–	–	5
Pieter Engelbrecht	–	12	11R	13R	12	12	12	12	7	2	–	–	–	10
Johan Jackson	–	11	–	–	–	–	–	–	1	–	–	–	–	0
Jano Vermaak	–	9	–	–	–	–	–	–	1	–	–	–	–	0
Martin Bezuidenhout	–	1R	2R	2R	2R	2R	2R	2R	7	–	–	–	–	0
Randall Morrison	–	–	6R	–	–	–	–	–	1	–	–	–	–	0
Rudy Paige	–	–	9R	9R	9R	x	9	9	5	–	–	–	–	0
Wian Buys	–	–	–	15	15	15	15	15	5	1	–	–	–	5
Jaco Taute	–	–	–	10R	14R	–	–	11R	3	–	2	–	–	4
Ruan Dreyer	–	–	–	3	3R	–	3R	–	3	–	–	–	–	0
Daniel van der Merwe	–	–	–	3R	–	–	–	–	1	–	–	–	–	0
Warren Whiteley	–	–	–	8R	8R	–	8R	7	4	–	–	–	–	0
Wikus van Heerden	–	–	–	–	7	–	–	–	1	1	–	–	–	5
Jannes Labuschagne	–	–	–	–	4	4c	–	–	2	–	–	–	–	0
Earl Rose	–	–	–	–	–	10	10	10	3	–	6	8	1	39
Tonderai Chavhanga	–	–	–	–	–	14	–	–	1	–	–	–	–	0
Robert Kruger	–	–	–	–	–	7	7	–	2	–	–	–	–	0
Kevin Buys	–	–	–	–	–	3	–	–	1	–	–	–	–	0
Charles Emslie	–	–	–	–	–	2	2	2	3	1	–	–	–	5
Charl du Plessis	–	–	–	–	–	3R	1	x	2	–	–	–	–	0
Bernardo Botha	–	–	–	–	–	x	14	–	1	–	–	–	–	0
Jacques Lombard	–	–	–	–	–	–	5	5R	2	1	–	–	–	5
Clint van Niekerk	–	–	–	–	–	–	3	–	1	–	–	–	–	0
Willem Stoltz	–	–	–	–	–	–	–	5	1	–	–	–	–	0
Heinke van der Merwe	–	–	–	–	–	–	–	3	1	–	–	–	–	0
Elton Jantjies	–	–	–	–	–	–	–	10R	1	–	–	–	–	0
49 Players									171	33	20	19	1	265

GOLDEN LIONS RECORDS

MATCH RECORDS

Biggest win	116-10	vs. South Eastern Transvaal	1993
Biggest Currie Cup win	99-9	vs. Far North	1973
	104-14	vs. Vodacom Eagles	2003
Heaviest defeat	10-74	vs. British Lions	2009
Heaviest Currie Cup defeat	5-59	vs. Free State	2006
Highest score	116	vs. South Eastern Transvaal (116-10)	1993
Most points conceded	74	vs. British Lions (10-74)	2009
Most tries	18	vs. Madrid XV (96-6)	1979
Most Currie Cup tries	16	vs. Far North (99-9)	1973
Most points by a player	40	L Barnard vs. North East Cape	1979
Most Currie Cup points by a player	36	GR Bosch vs. Far North	1973
Most tries by a player	6	SA Smit vs. Orange Free State	1941
Most Currie Cup tries by a player	4	On seven occasions (most recently by GM Delport vs. Griffons 1997)	
Most conversions by a player	16	L Barnard vs. North East Cape	1979
Most Currie Cup conversions	13	GR Bosch vs. Far North	1973
Most penalties by a player	7	On four occasions in Currie Cup	
Most drop goals by a player in CC	3	GR Bosch vs. Eastern Transvaal	1972
	3	GR Bosch vs. Western Province	1974
	3	AS Pretorius vs. Griquas	2005
Most drop goals by a player	3	JC Robbie vs. Eastern Province	1987

SEASON RECORDS

Most team points	1390	33 matches	1999
Most team points in Currie Cup	580	14 matches	1997
Most points by a player	414	J Engelbrecht	1999
Most Currie Cup points by a player	263	GE Lawless	1996
Most team tries	181	33 matches	1999
Most team tries in Currie Cup	74	14 matches	1997
Most tries by a player	23	P Hendriks	1994
Most Currie Cup tries by a player	14	JA van der Walt	1996

CAREER RECORDS

Most appearances	153	HP le Roux	1992-2000
Most Currie Cup appearances	91	A Maritz	1977-1985
Most points	896	GR Bosch	1972-1978
Most Currie Cup points	521	GR Bosch	1972-1978
Most tries	89	P Hendriks	1990-1997
Most Currie Cup tries	38	P Hendriks	1990-1997

HONOURS

ABSA Currie Cup	1922, 1939, 1950, 1952, 1971 (shared), 1972, 1993, 1994, 1999
Lion Cup	1986, 1987, 1992, 1993, 1994
Super 10	1993
Vodacom Cup	1999, 2002, 2003, 2004

ABSA UNDER-19 CHAMPIONSHIP (5th in Section A)
Played 12 Won 4 Lost 7 Drawn 1 Points for 332 Points against 419 Tries for 41 Tries against 52 Winning percentage 38%
RESULTS: Bt Leopards (a) 25-22. Lost WP (a) 7-45. Lost Blue Bulls (h) 20-38. Bt Sharks (a) 26-24. Bt Free State (h) 33-24. Bt Griffons (a) 59-25. Lost Leopards (h) 36-37. Lost WP (h) 23-47. Lost Blue Bulls (a) 27-56. Lost Sharks (h) 15-39. Lost Free State (a) 27-28. Drew Griffons (h) 34-34.
Scorers: 91 Dale Sabbagh (17c,19p); 40 Robert de Bruyn (8t); 33 Francois de Klerk (1t,8c,4p); 25 John-Ronald Esterhuizen, Andries Oosthuizen (5t each); 20 Morne du Plessis (4t); 10 Tiaan Radyn, Janus Jonker, Pierre Lombaard, Brian Skosana, David Antonites (2t each); 8 Nico Kruger (1t,1p); 5 Jimmy Hughes, Nico van der Hoogt, Jacques Qnade, Sean Pretorius, Ulrich van Schalkwyk, Siyanda Yaka, Vincent Jobo (1t each); 5 David Schmidt (1c,1p).
PROVINCIAL AMATEUR CHAMPIONSHIP (5th, Northern Section)
Played 6 Won 3 Lost 3 Drawn 0 Points for 224 Points against 200 Tries for 27 Tries against 27 Winning percentage 50%
RESULTS: Lost Valke (a) 36-41. Lost Limpopo (a) 23-38. Bt Lowveld (h) 64-23. Bt Pumas (h) 42-19. Lost Blue Bulls (a) 12-44. Bt Leopards (h) 47-35. *

PROVINCIAL ROUND-UP

GRIFFONS RUGBY UNION

GRIFFONS

RUGBY

FOUNDED 1968 (as Northern Free State) **GROUND** North West Stadium, Welkom
CAPACITY 8 500 **ADDRESS** Rugby Street, Welkom
POSTAL ADDRESS PO Box 631, Welkom 9460
TELEPHONE NUMBER 057 352 6482 **EMAIL** rugbybond@icon.co.za
COLOURS Purple and yellow jersey, white shorts
CURRIE CUP COACH Oersond Gorgonzola
VODACOM CUP COACH Oersond Gorgonzola **CAPTAIN** Werner Griesel
PRESIDENT Randal September **COMPANY CEO** Eugene van Wyk

Griffons lack a fifth gear

THE Griffons will have to put their dreams of playing in the Absa Currie Cup Premier Division on hold for another season after the Welkom-based union finished well out of the running for the two playoff lifelines available to teams from the First Division.

The Northern Free Staters, with just five wins from their 10 round-robin matches, ended fourth on the log – their worst placing since 2006.

Coach Oersond Gorgonzola and captain Werner Griesel – who enjoyed a fine season in the midfield – would have been hoping for more from their men in the Currie Cup after enduring a Vodacom Cup campaign that delivered just two victories, against Namibia and the Valke. In the end, however, things just never came together for the former Purple People Eaters and they had to settle once more for the booby prize of a place in the First Division semifinals.

The Griffons' 28 log points was nine less than the 37 accumulated by the second-placed Eastern Province Kings, who themselves finished two points adrift of league winners the South Western Districts Eagles.

But while the Eagles and Kings could use the First Division semifinals as preparation for their promotion/relegation battles against the Leopards and Pumas respectively, frustratingly for the Griffons there was only pride left to play for.

In retrospect, they will look back on their last-four clash in George against SWD as yet another game that got away from them.

The Eagles opened up a 10-0 lead and looked to be cruising, only for the Griffons to rack up 27 unanswered points to threaten what would have been, given the respective form of the sides, a shock victory away from the familiarity of their North West Stadium home.

But the Eagles summoned a remarkable come-from-behind effort to run out 32-30 winners after the Griffons could manage only one score – a 67th-minute penalty to flyhalf Jannie Myburgh – in the second half.

Close games became a familiar theme for Griesel's charges during 2010 but unfortunately the history books do not award points for gutsy effort in losing causes. As the dust settled on their season, the Griffons were left ruing a two-week period between 23 July and 6 August during which they lost to the Kings in Port Elizabeth by a single point, to the Eagles in Welkom by four, and to the Border Bulldogs in East London by two – the equivalent of one converted try!

But such is the fine line between contenders and also-rans – and it would be pointless to go back over the tapes, wishing a penalty went over here, or a try-scoring pass went to hand there.

The Griffons played a total of 19 first-class matches in 2010, winning seven and losing 12, including a compulsory home friendly in July against Western Province.

Flyhalf Myburgh finished as his team's top point-scorer in the Currie Cup with 96 points, while skipper Griesel, wing JW Jonker and scrumhalf Hendrik van der Nest all finished with six tries apiece. The team scored 380 points while conceding only 282, including 49 tries to their opponents' 36. And yet they somehow managed to win only 45% of their matches.

It's a throwaway line at the best of times, but, given the numbers, perhaps all the Griffons were short of was a bit of old-fashioned luck.

The Griffons played a total of 19 first-class matches in 2010, winning seven and losing 12, including a friendly against WP.

PROVINCIAL ROUND-UP

GRIFFONS LOG POSITIONS

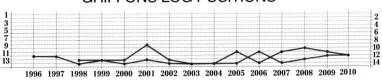

1996 1997 1998 1999 2000 2001 2002 2003 2004 2005 2006 2007 2008 2009 2010

GRIFFONS RESULTS AND SCORERS IN 2010

Played	Won	Drawn	Lost	Points for	Points against	Tries for	Tries against	Winning %
19	7	12	0	566	617	73	85	42.00%

VODACOM CUP Played 7 Won 2 Drawn 0 Lost 5 Points For 181 Points Against 306 Tries For 23 Tries Against 45 Winning Pecentage 29%

Date	Venue	Referee	Opponent	Result	Score	Scorers
Feb 27	Windhoek	Luke Burger	WELWITCHIAS	WON	45-26	T: Fredericks (3), Grobbelaar, Schultz. C: Van Wyk (4). P: Van Wyk (4).
Mar 5	Welkom	Jonathan Kaplan	GRIQUAS	LOST	31-59	T: Steyn (2), Parsons, Coeries. C: Van Wyk (4). P: Van Wyk.
Mar 12	Witbank	Stuart Berry	PUMAS	LOST	14-66	T: Mafumo, Molefe. C: Van Wyk, Russel.
Mar 19	Welkom	Mlungiseleli Mdashe	GOLDEN LIONS	LOST	16-48	T: Fredericks, C: Van Wyk. P: Van Wyk (3).
Mar 26	Potch	Archie Sehlako	LEOPARDS	LOST	13-43	T: Fredericks, Briedenhann. P: Van Wyk.
April 9	Welkom	Bongani Maloni	VALKE	WON	36-24	T: Maarman (2), Fredericks, Steyn, Louw, Schultz. C: Schultz (2), Pretorius.
Apr 17	Atteridgeville	Pieter de Villiers	BLUE BULLS	LOST	26-40	T: Fredericks, Meyer, Russell. C: Myburgh. P: Myburgh (3).

ABSA CURRIE CUP Played 11 Won 5 Lost 6 Drawn 0 Points For 380 Points Against 282 Tries For 49 Tries Against 36 Winning Percentage 45%

Date	Venue	Referee	Opponent	Result	Score	Scorers
July 17	Welkom	Jonathan Kaplan	VALKE	WON	43-08	T: Van Heerden (2), Van der Nest (2), Jonker, Lamprecht. C: Myburgh (5). P: Myburgh.
July 23	Port Elizabeth	Mark Lawrence	EP KINGS	LOST	25-26	T: Van der Nest, Meyer, Mathee. C: Myburgh (2). P: Myburgh (2).
July 31	Welkom	Sandile Mayende	SWD EAGLES	LOST	14-18	T: Griesel, Britz. C: Smit (2).
Aug 6	East London	Pro Legoete	BORDER	LOST	20-22	T: Fredericks (2). C: Smit (2). P: Smit (2).
Aug 20	Welkom	Sandile Mayende	BOLAND	WON	52-13	T: Jonker (2), Van der Nest, Briedenhann, Steyn, Mathee, Britz. C: Myburgh (4). P: Myburgh (3).
Aug 28	Kempton Park	Joey Salmans	VALKE	WON	69-30	T: Jonker (3), Griesel (2), Fredericks, Van der Nest, Stevens, Molefe, Schultz. C: Myburgh (6), Goodes (2). P: Myburgh
Sep 3	Welkom	Stuart Berry	EP KINGS	WON	27-18	T: Van der Nest, Griesel. C: Myburgh. P: Myburgh (3), Van Wyk (2).
Sep 10	George	Stuart Berry	SWD EAGLES	LOST	27-42	T: Schultz, Lamprecht, Penalty try. C: Van Wyk (3). P: Van Wyk (2).
Sep 18	Welkom	Jaco Peyper	BORDER	WON	48-33	T: Parsons (3), Fredericks, Schultz, Hancke, Griesel. C: Myburgh (5). P: Myburgh.
Oct 1	Wellington	Joey Salmans	BOLAND	LOST	25-40	T: Hancke, Griesel, Fredericks, Van Rooyen. C: Myburgh. P: Van Wyk.
Semi-final						
Oct 8	George	Sandile Mayende	SWD EAGLES	LOST	30-32	T: Stevens, Steyn, Weideman. C: Myburgh (3), P: Myburgh (3).

COMPULSORY FRIENDLY

Date	Venue	Referee	Opponent	Result	Score	Scorers
July 2	Welkom	Lourens van der Merwe	WP	LOST	05-29	T: Schultz

Team: R Lamprecht, J Meyer (T Maarman), W Griesel (C Weideman), T Molefe, E Fredericks, J Myburgh, E Schultz, N Steyn (c) (H Johnson), M Briedenhann, J Wessels (W Britz), J Horn (W van Rooyen), R Mathee, S Louw (S Oosthuizen), D van Heerden, P Methula (K Stevens).

rugbybond@icon.co.za

GRIFFONS
RUGBY

APPEARANCES AND POINTS FOR GRIFFONS IN 2010   CAREER

PLAYER	Appearances	Tries	Conversions	Penalties	Drop Goals	Points	Career Matches	Career Tries	Conversions	Penalties	Drop Goals	Points
GB (Gavin) Annandale	3	–	–	–	–	0	3	–	–	–	–	0
DR (Donovan) Ball	4	–	–	–	–	0	4	–	–	–	–	0
S (Shaun) Botha	7	–	–	–	–	0	54	2	–	–	–	10
M (Marnus) Briedenhann	15	2	–	–	–	10	26	2	–	–	–	10
WS (Willie) Britz	8	2	–	–	–	10	8	2	–	–	–	10
DB (Darryl) Coeries	6	1	–	–	–	5	32	6	–	–	–	30
EA (Earl) Daniels	3	–	–	–	–	0	3	–	–	–	–	0
DJ (David) de Villiers	5	–	–	–	–	0	5	–	–	–	–	0
JJ (Johnnie) Fourie	4	–	–	–	–	0	33	3	–	–	–	15
ER (Eddie) Fredericks	16	12	–	–	–	60	33	18	–	–	–	90
B (Barry) Goodes	2	–	2	–	–	4	2	–	2	–	–	4
GJ (Gert) Greyling	9	–	–	–	–	0	53	–	–	–	–	0
W (Werner) Griesel	19	6	–	–	–	30	53	13	–	–	–	65
L (Leon) Grobbelaar	6	1	–	–	–	5	6	1	–	–	–	5
WR (Wilmar) Groenewald	1	–	–	–	–	0	1	–	–	–	–	0
BF (Bronwin) Gysman	2	–	–	–	–	0	15	–	–	–	–	0
S (Shane) Hancke	4	2	–	–	–	10	35	8	–	–	–	40
GA (Graeme) Heyneke	4	–	–	–	–	0	4	–	–	–	–	0
JP (Joubert) Horn	6	–	–	–	–	0	6	–	–	–	–	0
GD (Grant) Janke	0	–	–	–	–	0	0	–	–	–	–	0
HJ (Hercholl) Johnson	6	–	–	–	–	0	22	–	–	–	–	0
JW (JW) Jonker	4	6	–	–	–	30	4	6	–	–	–	30
R (Ruan) Lamprecht	10	2	–	–	–	10	10	2	–	–	–	10
SJ (Sarel) Louw	19	1	–	–	–	5	104	11	–	–	–	55
T (Tertius) Maarman	14	2	–	–	–	10	28	4	–	–	–	20
GP (Glen) Mafumo	5	1	–	–	–	5	5	1	–	–	–	5
R (Rudi) Mathee	6	2	–	–	–	10	6	2	–	–	–	10
M (Petros) Methula	6	–	–	–	–	0	19	–	–	–	–	0
J (Jaco) Meyer	10	2	–	–	–	10	10	2	–	–	–	10
T (Thabang) Molefe	13	2	–	–	–	10	22	5	–	–	–	25
SJ (Sybrand) Mostert	5	–	–	–	–	0	5	–	–	–	–	0
JC (Jannie) Myburgh	11	–	27	14	–	96	11	–	27	14	–	96
PH (Pieter) Myburgh	2	–	1	3	–	11	3	–	1	3	–	11
O (Oshwill) Nortje	0	–	–	–	–	0	0	–	–	–	–	0
J (Sewes) Oosthuizen	12	–	–	–	–	0	23	4	–	–	–	20
AJ (Albert) Parsons	11	4	–	–	–	20	33	8	–	–	–	40
E (Ettienne) Pretorius	3	–	1	–	–	2	3	–	1	–	–	2
V (Virgill) Russell	4	1	1	–	–	7	11	1	1	–	–	7
TNE (Enrico) Schultz	17	6	2	–	–	34	22	6	2	–	–	34
AJ (Riaan) Smit	2	–	4	2	–	14	2	–	4	2	–	14
KB (Kevin) Stevens	18	2	–	–	–	10	28	2	–	–	–	10
NPJ (Nicky) Steyn	14	5	–	–	–	25	42	12	–	–	–	60
F (Francois) Uys	1	–	–	–	–	0	1	–	–	–	–	0
AH (Hendrik) van der Nest	8	6	–	–	–	30	8	6	–	–	–	30
D (Derrick) van Heerden	17	2	–	–	–	10	17	2	–	–	–	10
JP (Johan) van Heerden	4	–	–	–	–	0	4	–	–	–	–	0
CS (Windpomp) van Rooyen	18	1	–	–	–	5	56	1	–	–	–	5
P-W (PW) van Vuuren	8	–	–	–	–	0	8	–	–	–	–	0
T (Tiaan) van Wyk	10	–	13	14	–	68	13	–	15	14	–	72
PJ (Johan) Wessels	8	–	–	–	–	0	8	–	–	–	–	0
CFM (Charl) Weideman	11	1	–	–	–	5	11	1	–	–	–	5
Penalty try	–	1	–	–	–	5	–	1	–	–	–	5
51 players	**401**	**73**	**51**	**33**	**0**	**566**	**915**	**132**	**53**	**33**	**0**	**865**

PROVINCIAL ROUND-UP

APPEARANCES AND POINTS IN VODACOM CUP 2010

	Welwitchias	Griquas	Pumas	Golden Lions	Leopards	Valke	Blue Bulls	Matches	Tries	Conversions	Penalties	Drop Goals	Points
Tertius Maarman	15	15	15	15	15	15	15	7	2	–	–	–	10
Eddie Fredericks	14	–	14	14	13	14	14	6	7	–	–	–	35
Werner Griesel	13	13	13	13	12	13	13	7	–	–	–	–	0
Thabang Molefe	12	12	12	12	–	12	12	6	1	–	–	–	5
Darryl Coeries	11	11	11	11	11	–	–	5	1	–	–	–	5
Tiaan van Wyk	10	10	10	10	10	–	–	5	–	10	9	–	47
Enrico Schultz	9	9	9	9	9	9	9	7	2	2	–	–	14
Nicky Steyn	8c	8c	8c	8c	8c	8c	8c	7	3	–	–	–	15
Albert Parsons	7	6	6	6	6	6	–	6	1	–	–	–	5
Johnnie Fourie	6	–	7	7	–	–	7	4	–	–	–	–	0
Windpomp van Rooyen	5	4	4	4	4	4	4	7	–	–	–	–	0
Marnus Briedenhann	4	7	–	5	7	5	5	6	1	–	–	–	5
Gert Greyling	3	3	–	1R	1R	3R	3R	6	–	–	–	–	0
Derrick van Heerden	2	2	2	2	2	2	2	7	–	–	–	–	0
Sarel Louw	1	1	1	3	3	3	3	7	1	–	–	–	5
Graeme Heyneke	2R	2R	2R	2R	–	–	–	4	–	–	–	–	0
Kevin Stevens	3R	1R	1R	1	1	1	1R	7	–	–	–	–	0
Sewes Oosthuizen	1R	3R	3	–	–	–	–	3	–	–	–	–	0
Leon Grobbelaar	7R	5	5	7R	5R	–	–	5	1	–	–	–	5
Donovan Ball	6R	8R	6R	–	8R	–	–	4	–	–	–	–	0
Bronwin Gysman	9R	–	9R	–	–	–	–	2	–	–	–	–	0
Virgil Russel	x	–	15R	–	11R	11	11	4	1	1	–	–	7
Glen Mafumo	–	14	11R	15R	14	–	–	4	1	–	–	–	5
Earl Daniels	–	7R	5R	7R	–	–	–	3	–	–	–	–	0
Oshwill Nortje	–	x	–	–	–	–	–	0	–	–	–	–	0
Grant Janke	–	x	–	–	–	–	–	0	–	–	–	–	0
Petros Methula	–	–	–	3R	3R	–	1	3	–	–	–	–	0
Ettiene Pretorius	–	–	–	x	10R	10	9R	3	–	1	–	–	2
Gavin Annandale	–	–	–	–	5	6R	7R	3	–	–	–	–	0
Hercholl Johnson	–	–	–	–	2R	2R	2R	3	–	–	–	–	0
Willie Britz	–	–	–	–	–	7	–	1	–	–	–	–	0
Pieter Myburgh	–	–	–	–	–	9R	10	2	–	1	3	–	11
Shaun Botha	–	–	–	–	–	7R	6	2	–	–	–	–	0
Jaco Meyer	–	–	–	–	–	11R	11R	2	1	–	–	–	5
Wilmar Groenewald	–	–	–	–	–	x	6R	1	–	–	–	–	0
35 players								**149**	**23**	**15**	**12**	**0**	**181**

rugbybond@icon.co.za

GRIFFONS
RUGBY

APPEARANCES AND POINTS IN ABSA CURRIE CUP 2010

	Valke	EP Kings	SWD Eagles	Border	Boland	Valke	EP Kings	SWD Eagles	Border	Boland	SWD Eagles	Matches	Tries	Conversions	Penalties	Drop Goals	Points
Ruan Lamprecht	15	15	15	15	15	15	15	15	15	–	–	9	2	–	–	–	10
Eddie Fredericks	14	–	14	14	14	14	–	14	14	14	14	9	5	–	–	–	25
Werner Griesel	13	13c	13c	13c	13c	13c	13c	13c	13c	13c	13c	11	6	–	–	–	30
Thabang Molefe	12c	–	–	12	12	12	12	–	–	–	12R	6	1	–	–	–	5
JW Jonker	11	–	11	–	11	11	–	–	–	–	–	4	6	–	–	–	30
Jannie Myburgh	10	10	10	10R	10	10	10	–	10	10	10	10	–	27	14	–	96
Enrico Schultz	9	9R	–	9R	9R	9R	x	9R	9	9	9	9	3	–	–	–	15
Willie Britz	8	8	8	–	8	8	8	–	–	–	–	6	2	–	–	–	10
Rudi Mathee	7	7	7	7	6	–	–	–	–	–	–	5	2	–	–	–	10
Johan Wessels	6	6	6	6	–	6	6	6	–	–	–	7	–	–	–	–	0
Windpomp van Rooyen	5	5	5	5	5	4	5	5	–	5	5	10	1	–	–	–	5
Joubert Horn	4	4R	4R		4	4R	–	–	–	–	–	5	–	–	–	–	0
Sarel Louw	3	3	3R	3R	3	3	3	3	3	3R	3	11	–	–	–	–	0
Derick van Heerden	2	x	2R	2	2R	2R	8R	7R	2	8R	x	9	2	–	–	–	10
Petros Methula	1	1	–	–	–	–	–	–	–	–	x	2	–	–	–	–	0
Hercholl Johnson	2R	–	–	x	–	–	–	–	2R	–	–	2	–	–	–	–	0
Gert Greyling	3R	3R	–	–	3R	–	–	–	–	–	–	3	–	–	–	–	0
David de Villiers	4R	4	–	4	–	5	4	–	–	–	–	5	–	–	–	–	0
Sybrand Mostert	5R	–	–	6R	–	–	–	–	7	7	8R	5	–	–	–	–	0
Hendrik van der Nest	9R	9	9	9	9	9	9	9	–	–	–	8	6	–	–	–	30
Charl Weideman	12R	12	12	15R	12R	–	14	12	12	12	12	10	1	–	–	–	5
Jaco Meyer	11R	14	12R	11	–	–	11	11R	14R	x	x	7	1	–	–	–	5
Darryl Coeries	–	11	–	–	–	–	–	–	–	–	–	1	–	–	–	–	0
PW van Vuuren	–	2	2	–	2	2	2	2	–	2	2	8	–	–	–	–	0
Kevin Stevens	–	1R	1	1	1	1	1	1	1	1	1	10	2	–	–	–	10
Marnus Briedenhann	–	5R	6R	8	7	7	7	4	–	–	7	8	1	–	–	–	5
Tertius Maarman	–	x	15R	–	15R	14R	x	11	15R	15	x	6	–	–	–	–	0
Francois Uys	–	–	4	–	–	–	–	–	–	–	–	1	–	–	–	–	0
Sewes Oosthuizen	–	–	3	3	–	3R	1R	3R	3R	3	3R	8	–	–	–	–	0
Riaan Smit	–	–	10R	10	–	–	–	–	–	–	–	2	–	4	2	–	14
Shaun Botha	–	–	–	x	7R	7R	–	6R	5	7R	–	5	–	–	–	–	0
Nicky Steyn	–	–	–	–	8R	–	7R	8	8	8	8	6	2	–	–	–	10
Barry Goodes	–	–	–	–	–	10R	–	–	–	15R	–	2	–	2	–	–	4
Van Wyk, Tiaan	–	–	–	–	–	–	10R	10	10R	10R	15	5	–	3	5	–	21
Parsons, Albert	–	–	–	–	–	–	6R	7	6	6	6	5	3	–	–	–	15
Van Heerden, Johan	–	–	–	–	–	–	4R	4	4	4	4	4	–	–	–	–	0
Hancke, Shane	–	–	–	–	–	–	15R	11	11	11	11	4	2	–	–	–	10
Leon Grobbelaar	–	–	–	–	–	–	–	–	5R	x	–	1	–	–	–	–	0
Glen Mafumo	–	–	–	–	–	–	–	–	7R	–	–	1	–	–	–	–	0
Penalty try	–	–	–	–	–	–	–	–	–	–	–	0	1	–	–	–	5
39 players												**230**	**49**	**36**	**21**	**0**	**380**

PROVINCIAL ROUND-UP

Shane Hanke of the Griffons during the ABSA Currie Cup First Division semi-final against the SWD Eagles.

ABSA UNDER-21 CHAMPIONSHIP (2nd, Section B)

Played	Won	Drawn	Lost	Points for	Points against	Tries for	Tries against	Winning %
7	4	2	1	238	174	35	20	57.00%

RESULTS Bt Griquas (h) 29-10. Drew Valke (a) 25-25. Drew EP (h) 36-36. Bt SWD (a) 20-12. Bt Border (h) 73-27. Bt Mpumalanga (a) 33-28. SEMI-FINAL Lost Valke (h) 22-36.

SCORERS 45 Grant Janke (9t). 35 Tiaan van Wyk (7c, 7p). 29 Leon Krüger (1t, 12c). 20 Divandré Strydom (4t), Donavan Ball (4t). 15 Willmar Groenewald (3t). 10 Arno Visagie, Hendrik Prinsloo (2t each). 7 Christiano Swarts (1t, 1c). 5 Herbert Burger, Heinrich Roelfse, Juan-Leonard Wilson, Wesley Botes, Danie Viljoen, Jan Oosthuizen, Johan Matthysen, Petrus Cronjé, Virgil Russel (1t each). 2 Jacques Wilson (1c).

ABSA U19 CHAMPIONSHIP (7th, Section A)

Played	Won	Drawn	Lost	Points for	Points against	Tries for	Tries against	Winning %
13	0	1	12	219	628	25	91	8.00%

RESULTS Lost Leopards (a) 03-42. Lost Blue Bulls (a) 05-71. Lost Free State (h) 35-40. Lost KZN (a) 06-73. Lost WP (h) 03-63. Lost Golden Lions (h) 25-59. Lost Blue Bulls (h) 12-85. Lost Leopards (h) 29-47. Lost KZN (h) 11-28. Lost WP (a) 07-29. Lost Free State (a) 28-33. Drew Golden Lions (a) 34-34. PROMOTION RELEGATION Lost SWD (h) 21-24.

SCORERS 98 Leegan Moos (2t, 17c, 18p). 25 Mario Noordman (5t). 20 Dean Swart (4t). 15 Juhandry Pieterse, Clint Parnell (3t each). 6 Colin Herbert (2p). 5 Wayne Kahn, Buran Parks, Keenan Abrahams, Ashley Meyer, Siyasanga Mkunku, Siyavuya Ketshengana, Algarvon Ouman, Kirsten Heyns (1t each).

AMATEUR CHAMPIONSHIP

Griffons (3rd, Central Section)

Played	Won	Drawn	Lost	Points for	Points against	Tries for	Tries against	Winning %
6	4	0	2	206	174	28	24	67.00%

RESULTS Lost Griffons Rural (a) 08-27. Bt KZN Rural (h) 34-24. Bt Valke Rural (a) 25-21. Bt FS Rural (h) 53-24. Bt Griquas (h) 59-34. Lost Free State (a) 27-44.

Griffons Rural (2nd, Central Section)

Played	Won	Drawn	Lost	Points for	Points against	Tries for	Tries against	Winning %
6	5	0	1	239	133	35	19	83.00%

RESULTS Bt Griffons (h) 27-08. Lost Free State (a) 20-40. Bt KZN Rural (a) 27-19. Bt Valke Rural (h) 62-22. Bt Free State Rural (h) 54-29. Bt Griquas (a) 49-15.

rugbybond@icon.co.za

GRIFFONS
RUGBY

GRIFFONS RECORDS

MATCH RECORDS

Biggest win	72-12	vs Stellaland	1992
Biggest win (Currie Cup)	74-06	vs Eastern Orange Free State	1988
Heaviest defeat	8-91	vs Free State	1995
Heaviest defeat (Currie Cup)	0-106	vs Free State Cheetahs	1997
Highest score	72	vs Stellaland (72-12)	1992
Highest score (Currie Cup)	74	vs Eastern Orange Free State (74-6)	1988
Moist points conceded	91	vs Free State	1995
Moist points conceded (Currie Cup)	106	vs Free State Cheetahs (0-106)	1997
Most tries	11	vs Stellaland (72-12)	1992
Most tries (Currie Cup)	12	vs Eastern Orange Free State (74-6)	1988
Most points by a player	36	E Herbert vs Stellaland	1992
Most points by a player (Currie Cup)	36	E Herbert vs Falcons	1997
Most tries by a player (Currie Cup)	5	P Maritz vs SE Tvl	1982
Most conversions by a player	11	E Herbert vs Stellaland	1992
Most conversions by a player (Currie Cup)	10	E Herbert vs EOFS	1988
Most penalties by a player	9	E Herbert vs Pumas	2001
Most penalties by a player (Currie Cup)	9	E Herbert vs Falcons	1997
Most drop goals by a player (Currie Cup)	3	E Herbert vs FS Cheetahs	2000

SEASON RECORDS

Most team points	657	24 matches	2001
Most team points (Currie Cup)	344	13 matches	1997
Most points by a player	263	E Herbert	2001
Most points by a player (Currie Cup)	195	E Herbert	1988
Most team tries	83	28 matches	1999
Most team tries (Currie Cup)	41	13 matches	1999
Most tries by a player	14	O Damons	2004
Most tries by a player (Currie Cup)	8	GA Passens	1999
	8	MP Goosen	2005
	8	CS Afrika	2008
Most conversions by a player	43	E Herbert	2001
Most penalties by a player	56	E Herbert	2001
Most drop goals by a player	10	E Herbert	1988

CAREER RECORDS

Most appearances	205	E Herbert	1986-2001
Most consecutive games	102	A Gerber	1979-1985
Most matches as captain	95	JJ Jerling	1989-1997
Most points	2608	E Herbert	1986-2001
Most tries	36	CS Afrika	2006-2009
Most conversions by a player	331	E Herbert	1986-2001
Most penalties by a player	544	E Herbert	1986-2001
Most drop goals by a player	66	E Herbert	1986-2001

HONOURS

Paul Roos Trophy	1970
Vodacom Shield	2001
Bankfin Cup	2008

PROVINCIAL ROUND-UP

GRIQUALAND WEST RUGBY UNION

FOUNDED 1886 **GROUND** GWK Park, Kimberley **CAPACITY** 11 000
ADDRESS Resevoir Road, New Park, Kimberley
POSTAL ADDRESS PO Box 110825, Hadison Park, Kimberley 8306
TELEPHONE NUMBER 053 832 8773 **WEBSITE** www.griquas.co.za
COLOURS Peacock blue and white hooped jersey, black shorts
CURRIE CUP COACH Dawie Theron **VODACOM CUP COACH** Dawie Theron
CAPTAIN Naas Olivier **PRESIDENT** Dawie Groenewald (resigned and replaced by
Hennie van der Merwe **COMPANY CEO** Arni van Rooyen

Nearly-men miss out again

AS they had done the previous season, GWK Griquas once again come close to reaching the semifinals of the Absa Currie Cup – but once more it proved to be a bridge too far.

Although they were still in the running for a top-four spot by the penultimate round of the league phase, one always felt they were short of an away win over a big team. Griquas never achieved that, although they came very close against the Blue Bulls.

The record books will say they lost 39-38, but what it won't say is that Naas Olivier, the team's flyhalf and captain, missed an easy final-minute conversion to win the match.

Griquas eventually had to settle for the sixth place on the log – the fifth consecutive season that they managed to steer clear of the promotion-relegation zone.

The team's biggest problem throughout was their inability to play to their potential. A long injury list didn't help matters, and at no point could coach Dawie Theron pick the same starting XV on consecutive weekends.

Up to six players from other unions had to be borrowed to cover for the walking wounded. Of those, centre Jean Stemmet has been awarded a contract for 2011.

A big positive Griquas can take out of the 2010 Currie Cup season is that they never got humiliated in an away fixture. The heaviest defeat they suffered was an 18-point loss against the Sharks.

Griquas picked up bonus points in all their matches on the road and ended the league phase with 13 bonus points – the most by any team. In fact, they only missed out against Western Province when they suffered a 50-3 loss – their biggest home defeat since 2004.

Before the semi-final phase, the Peacock Blues scored 60 tries (joint second), but crucially conceded the same amount, with only the Pumas and Leopards leaking more.

Their try-scoring ability was mostly thanks to Springbok wing Bjorn Basson, fullback Riaan Viljoen, scrumhalf Sarel Pretorius and Olivier, who together formed one of the most dangerous backline combinations in the competition.

Basson scored a record-breaking 21 tries, which not only erased the long-standing Currie Cup record of 19 held by Bok great Carel du Plessis, but also broke a host of provincial records.

Basson also become Griquas' 71st Springbok when he made his Test debut against Wales in Cardiff. Sadly, yet inevitably, he left the union at the end of the 2010 season to join the Blue Bulls. Another loss was front-ranker Jacobie Adriaanse's departure to the Lions.

The rest of the squad has been retained, with new singings that include Springbok Earl Rose from the Lions, Fabian Juries (wing/fullback, WP), Lourens Adriaanse (prop, Maties), Ivann Espag (prop, Blue Bulls), Matt Dobson (hooker, Maties), Martin Muller (lock, WP) and Logan Basson (flyhalf, Border).

Off the field, GWK Park received a facelift with brand-new floodlights and a new surface thanks to Uruguay using the ground as their training base during the FIFA World Cup.

But perhaps the team's inability to break into the Currie Cup semifinals (or, conversely, their ability to punch above their weight) is best summed up by the fact that money was so tight that the union could not even afford to appoint a full-time doctor or physio.

Bjorn Basson had a season to remember, breaking the Currie Cup try-scoring record en-route to Bok colours.

GRIQUAS LOG POSITIONS

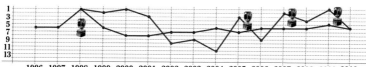

GRIQUAS RESULTS AND SCORERS IN 2010

Played	Won	Drawn	Lost	Points for	Points against	Tries for	Tries against
23	12	0	11	814	720	111	89

VODACOM CUP Played **8** Won **5** Drawn **0** Lost **3** Points For **287** Points Against **212** Tries For **43** Tries Against **27** Winning Percentage **63%**

Date	Venue	Referee	Opponent	Result	Score	Scorers
Feb 26	Kimberley[1]	Tiaan Jonker	BLUE BULLS	LOST	17-22	T: Buckle, Van Wyk. C: Van Wyk (2). P: Van Wyk.
Mar 5	Welkom	Jonathan Kaplan	GRIFFONS	WON	59-31	T: Buckle (2), Westraadt (2), Ryland (2), Van Wyk, H Pretorius, Wilkins. C: Van Wyk (5), Stevens (2).
Mar 13	Windhoek	Joey Salmans	WELWITCHIAS	WON	29-27	T: B Basson (2). Schoeman, Geel C: Stevens (2), Van Zyl. P: Stevens.
Mar 19	Kimberley[1]	Matt Kemp	PUMAS	WON	42-26	T: B Basson (2). F Venter (2), Kitshoff. C: Viljoen (4). P: Viljoen (3).
Mar 26	Johannesburg[2]	Stuart Berry	GOLDEN LIONS	LOST	05-45	T: D Pretorius.
April 9	Kimberley[1]	Tiaan Jonker	LEOPARDS	WON	51-21	T: Buckle (2), D Pretorius (2), Karemaker (2), B Basson. Westraadt. C: L Basson (4). P: L Bassson.
April 17	Kempton Park	Archie Sehlako	VALKE	WON	60-12	T: Karemaker (3), Kruger (2), Kitshoff, Buckle, B Basson, Jansen, Wilkins. . C: L Basson (4), Malgas.

Quarter-final

| April 24 | Durban | Jason Jaftha | SHARKS XV | LOST | 24-28 | T: Westraadt (2), Wilkins, Ryland. C: Stevens (2). |

[1] AR Abass Stadium, [2] Johannesburg Stadium

CURRIE CUP Played **14** Won **6** Drawn **0** Lost **8** Points For **477** Points Against **496** Tries For **60** Tries Against **60** Winning Percentage **43%**

Date	Venue	Referee	Opponent	Result	Score	Scorers
Jul 10	Kimberley	Jaco Peyper	SHARKS	WON	40-34	T: Basson (2), Barnes, Roberts, Wilkins. C: Olivier (3). P: Olivier (3).
Jul 16	Bloemfontein	Mark Lawrence	FREE STATE	LOST	26-33	T: Basson, S Pretorius. C: Olivier (2). P: Olivier (3), Viljoen.
Jul 24	Kimberley	Lourens van der Merwe	LIONS	WON	26-20	T: Basson, Adriaanse. C: Olivier (2). P: Olivier (4).
Jul 30	Potchefstroom	Jason Jaftha	LEOPARDS	WON	41-27	T: Basson (2), Olivier, S Pretorius, Spies. C: Olivier (5). P: Olivier (2).
Aug 7	Kimberley	Sandile Mayende	WESTERN PROVINCE	LOST	03-50	P: Olivier.
Aug 13	Kimberley	Lourens van der Merwe	PUMAS	WON	58-25	T: Viljoen (2), S Pretorius (2), Kemp, Spies, Jansen, Vogt. C: Olivier (6). P: Olivier (2).
Aug 20	Pretoria	Mark Lawrence	BLUE BULLS	LOST	38-39	T: Basson (3), Lawson. C: Olivier (3). P: Olivier (4).
Aug 27	Durban	Jonathan Kaplan	SHARKS	LOST	30-48	T: Basson (4). C: Olivier (2). P: Olivier, Viljoen.
Sep 3	Kimberley	Sandile Mayende	FREE STATE	LOST	28-33	T: Kemp, Schoeman, Olivier. C: Olivier (2). P: Olivier (2). DG: Olivier.
Sep 11	Johannesburg	Jaco Peyper	LIONS	LOST	29-40	T: Basson, Botha, Jansen, Vogt. C: Olivier (2), Vogt. P: Olivier.
Sep 17	Kimberley	Jason Jaftha	LEOPARDS	WON	29-20	T: Viljoen (2), Van Deventer, Downey. C: Olivier (3). P: Olivier.
Sep 24	Cape Town	Marius Jonker	WESTERN PROVINCE	LOST	32-48	T: Basson (3), Schoeman, Stemmett. C: Olivier, Vogt. P: Olivier.
Oct 2	Witbank	Jonathan Kaplan	PUMAS	WON	61-31	T: Basson (2), Geel, Olivier, Viljoen, Jansen, Barnes, S Pretorius, Wilkins. C: Olivier (7), Vogt.
Oct 9	Kimberley	Jonathan Kaplan	BLUE BULLS	LOST	36-48	T: Basson (2), Geel, Stemmett, S Pretorius. C: Olivier (2), Vogt (2). P: Viljoen.

COMPULSORY FRIENDLY

| July 2 | Oudtshoorn | Stuart Berry | SWD EAGLES | WON | 50-12 | T: Basson (2), Spies, Rosslee, Viljoen, Barnes, Malgas, Wilkins. C: Olivier (4), Vogt. |

Team: R Viljoen, D Pretorius (R Lawson), W Louw, M Rosslee, B Basson, N Olivier (c), S Pretorius (W Malgas/R Vogt), L Karemaker (G Human), D Raubenheimer, W Wilkins, C Kemp, H Roodt (F Spies), A Buckle (J Adriaanse), R Barnes (S Westraadt), S Roberts.

www.griquas.co.za

APPEARANCES AND POINTS FOR GRIQUAS IN 2010 — CAREER

PLAYER	Appearances	Tries	Conversions	Penalties	Drop Goals	Points	Career Matches	Career Tries	Conversions	Penalties	Drop Goals	Points
JP (Jacobie) Adriaanse	21	1	–	–	–	5	21	1	–	–	–	5
RJ (Ryno) Barnes	16	3	–	–	–	15	39	6	–	–	–	30
BA (Bjorn) Basson	21	29	–	–	–	145	56	47	–	–	–	235
LA (Logan) Basson	3	–	8	1	–	19	3	–	8	1	–	19
J (Jean) Botha	10	1	–	–	–	5	10	1	–	–	–	5
AM (Albertus) Buckle	12	6	–	–	–	30	62	15	–	–	–	75
JJ (Hanno) Coetzee	3	–	–	–	–	0	12	2	–	–	–	10
J (Justin) Downey	6	1	–	–	–	5	6	1	–	–	–	5
R (Ruaan) du Preez	2	–	–	–	–	0	31	1	–	–	–	5
D (Danwill) Erasmus	1	–	–	–	–	0	1	–	–	–	–	0
I (Ivann) Espag	2	–	–	–	–	0	2	–	–	–	–	0
AD (Barry) Geel	19	3	–	–	–	15	62	23	–	–	–	115
EW (Edwin) Hewitt	6	–	–	–	–	0	6	–	–	–	–	0
APM (Marnus) Hugo	14	–	–	–	–	0	14	–	–	–	–	0
PG (Gerhard) Human	8	–	–	–	–	0	8	–	–	–	–	0
RR (Rocco) Jansen	16	4	–	–	–	20	16	4	–	–	–	20
L (Leon) Karemaker	14	5	–	–	–	25	14	5	–	–	–	25
C-J (Cecil) Kemp	21	2	–	–	–	10	33	3	–	–	–	15
ZJ (Zane) Kilian	1	–	–	–	–	0	6	–	–	–	–	0
R (Rohan) Kitshoff	14	2	–	–	–	10	59	12	–	–	–	60
AM (Andries) Kruger	6	2	–	–	–	10	18	2	–	–	–	10
RJ (Richard) Lawson	10	1	–	–	–	5	19	5	–	–	–	25
WD (Wilmaure) Louw	19	–	–	–	–	0	30	2	–	–	–	10
L (Luvuyiso) Lusaseni	3	–	–	–	–	0	3	–	–	–	–	0
AWD (Warren) Malgas	7	1	1	–	–	7	7	1	1	–	–	7
J (Jaco) Nepgen	8	–	–	–	–	0	8	–	–	–	–	0
IP (Naas) Olivier	15	3	44	25	1	181	40	14	107	61	1	470
MJR (Michael) Passaportis	11	–	–	–	–	0	11	–	–	–	–	0
DP (Dewald) Pretorius	9	3	–	–	–	15	20	10	–	–	–	50
JH (Herman) Pretorius	3	1	–	–	–	5	10	2	–	–	–	10
SJ (Sarel) Pretorius	15	6	–	–	–	30	57	22	–	–	–	110
D (Davon) Raubenheimer	16	–	–	–	–	0	40	1	–	–	–	5
WAS (Steph) Roberts	21	1	–	–	–	5	55	3	–	–	–	15
HL (Hendrik) Roodt	2	–	–	–	–	0	2	–	–	–	–	0
MR (Matthew) Rosslee	7	1	–	–	–	5	7	1	–	–	–	5
Z (Zahier) Ryland	7	3	–	–	–	15	7	3	–	–	–	15
DB (Burger) Schoeman	13	3	–	–	–	15	13	3	–	–	–	15
FA (Frikkie) Spies	16	3	–	–	–	15	16	3	–	–	–	15
JH (Jean) Stemmet	5	2	–	–	–	10	5	2	–	–	–	10
DG (Donald) Stevens	5	–	6	1	–	15	7	–	6	1	–	15
JC (Johan) van Deventer	6	1	–	–	–	5	6	1	–	–	–	5
CG (Coenie) van Wyk	3	2	7	1	–	27	3	2	7	1	–	27
D (Divan) van Zyl	6	–	1	–	–	2	6	–	1	–	–	2
BCG (Ben) Venter	1	–	–	–	–	0	1	–	–	–	–	0
C (Frik) Venter	4	2	–	–	–	10	4	2	–	–	–	10
R (Riaan) Viljoen	16	6	4	6	–	56	60	11	42	41	6	280
R (Rudi) Vogt	8	2	6	–	–	22	8	2	6	–	–	22
S (Simon) Westraadt	17	5	–	–	–	25	25	5	–	–	–	25
WA (Wesley) Wilkins	13	6	–	–	–	30	15	6	–	–	–	30
49 players	**482**	**111**	**77**	**34**	**1**	**814**	**964**	**224**	**178**	**105**	**7**	**1812**

PROVINCIAL ROUND-UP

APPEARANCES AND POINTS IN VODACOM CUP 2010

	Blue Bulls	Griffons	Welwitchias	Pumas	Golden Lions	Leopards	Valke	Sharks XV	Matches	Tries	Conversions	Penalties	Drop Goals	Points
Herman Pretorius	15	10R	18R	–	–	x	x	–	3	1	–	–	–	5
Dewald Pretorius	14	14	14	14	14	14	14	14	8	3	–	–	–	15
Wilmaure Louw	13	13	13	13	–	–	–	–	4	–	–	–	–	0
Barry Geel	12	12	12	12	12	–	–	–	5	1	–	–	–	5
Bjorn Basson	11	15	15	15	–	15	15	15	7	6	–	–	–	30
Coenie van Wyk	10	10	–	x	10	–	–	x	3	2	7	1	–	27
Warren Malgas	9	–	–	9R	15R	9R	9R	9R	6	–	1	–	–	2
Leon Karemaker	8	8	8	8	x	8	8	8	7	5	–	–	–	25
Davon Raubenheimer	7	–	7	6	8	–	–	–	4	–	–	–	–	0
Wesley Wilkins	6	6	4R	–	–	6	6	6	6	3	–	–	–	15
Jaco Nepgen	5c	5c	5c	7	7	7	7	7	8	–	–	–	–	0
Frikkie Spies	4	4	4	5	–	5	–	–	5	–	–	–	–	0
Jacobie Adriaanse	3	1R	–	3	3R	3	1R	3	7	–	–	–	–	0
Simon Westraadt	2	2	2	–	–	2R	3R	2R	6	5	–	–	–	25
Albertus Buckle	1	3	1	1c	1c	1c	3c	1c	8	6	–	–	–	30
Andries Kruger	2R	2R	–	2R	–	2	2	2	6	2	–	–	–	10
Frik Venter	3R	–	1R	2	1R	–	–	–	4	2	–	–	–	10
Michael Passaportis	4R	–	–	5R	5	5R	5	5	6	–	–	–	–	0
Rohan Kitshoff	6R	8R	6	8R	6	8R	6R	6R	8	2	–	–	–	10
Donald Stevens	9R	9R	9	–	9R	–	–	9	5	–	6	1	–	15
Divan van Zyl	10R	–	10	–	10R	12	12	12	6	–	1	–	–	2
Danwill Erasmus	x	x	–	x	13	–	–	–	1	–	–	–	–	0
Zhahier Ryland	–	11	11	11	11	11	11	11	7	3	–	–	–	15
Marnus Hugo	–	9	9R	9	9	9	9	–	6	–	–	–	–	0
Burger Schoeman	–	7	8R	–	–	–	5R	7R	4	1	–	–	–	5
Steph Roberts	–	1	3R	1R	–	3R	1	1R	6	–	–	–	–	0
Cecil Kemp	–	4R	–	4	4	4	4	4	6	–	–	–	–	0
Ruaan du Preez	–	–	3	–	3	–	–	–	2	–	–	–	–	0
Richard Lawson	–	–	14R	–	15	–	–	–	2	–	–	–	–	0
Riaan Viljoen	–	–	–	10		–	–	–	1	–	4	3	–	17
Ryno Barnes	–	–	–	–	2	–	–	–	1	–	–	–	–	0
Ben Venter	–	–	–	–	5R	–	–	–	1	–	–	–	–	0
Rocco Jansen	–	–	–	–	–	13	13	13	3	1	–	–	–	5
Logan Basson	–	–	–	–	–	10	10	10	3	–	8	1	–	19
Hanno Coetzee	–	–	–	–	–	10R	10R	10R	3	–	–	–	–	0
35 players									**168**	**43**	**27**	**6**	**0**	**287**

APPEARANCES AND POINTS IN ABSA CURRIE CUP 2010

	Sharks	Free State	Lions	Leopards	WP	Pumas	Blue Bulls	Sharks	Free State	Lions	Leopards	WP	Pumas	Blue Bulls	Matches	Tries	Conversions	Penalties	Drop Goals	Points
Riaan Viljoen	15	15	15	15	15	15	15	15	15	15	15	15	15	15	14	5	–	3	–	34
Rocco Jansen	14	14	14	x	14R	11	15R	14R	14	14	14	14	14	14	13	3	–	–	–	15
Wilmaure Louw	13	13	13	13	13	13	13	13	13	13	13	13	13R	13R	14	–	–	–	–	0
Matthew Rosslee	12	12R	x	12R	12R	12	12	–	–	–	–	–	–	x	6	–	–	–	–	0
Bjorn Basson	11	11	11	11	11		11	11	11	11	11	11	11	11	13	21	–	–	–	105
Naas Olivier	10c	10c	10c	10c	10c	10c	10c	10c	10c	10c	10c	10c	10c	10c	14	3	40	25	1	173
Sarel Pretorius	9	9	9	9	9	9	9	9	9	9R	9	9	9	9	14	6	–	–	–	30
Leon Karemaker	8	8	8	–	–	8	–	–	–	–	–	–	8	8	6	–	–	–	–	0
Davon Raubenheimer	7	7	7	8	7	7	7	7		8	6R	7	–	–	11	–	–	–	–	0
Wesley Wilkins	6	6	6	7	–	–	–	–	–	–	–	–	7R	7	6	2	–	–	–	10
Cecil Kemp	5	5	5	5	5	5	5	4	5	5	5	5	5R	5	14	2	–	–	–	10
Hendrik Roodt	4	–	–	–	–	–	–	–	–	–	–	–	–	–	1	–	–	–	–	0
Albertus Buckle	3	3	3R	–	–	–	–	–	–	–	–	–	–	–	3	–	–	–	–	0
Ryno Barnes	2	2	2	2	2	2	2	2	2	2R	2	2	2	2	14	2	–	–	–	10
Steph Roberts	1	1	1	1	1	1	1	1	1	1	1	1R	1	1	14	1	–	–	–	5
Simon Westraadt	x	x	x	6R	2R	2R	2R	x	2R	2	2R	2R	2R	2R	10	–	–	–	–	0
Jacobie Adriaanse	3R	3R	3	3	3R	3	3	–	1R	3R	1R	3	3	3R	13	1	–	–	–	5
Frikkie Spies	4R	4	4	4	4	4	4	–	–	–	–	5R	5	4	10	2	–	–	–	10
Gerhard Human	7R	7R	8R	5R	6R	–	–	5R	–	–	–	x	–	5R	7	–	–	–	–	0
Marnus Hugo	x	–	x	9R	9R	9R	9R	9R	9R	9	x	x	9R	–	8	–	–	–	–	0
Barry Geel	12R	12	12	12	12	12R	12R	12	12	12	12	12	12	12	14	2	–	–	–	10
Richard Lawson	x	14R	14R	14	14	14	14	14	–	–	–	–	–	–	7	1	–	–	–	5
Zane Kilian	–	1R	–	–	–	–	–	–	–	–	–	–	–	–	1	–	–	–	–	0
Rohan Kitshoff	–	6R	–	6	–	6	6	6	6	–	–	–	–	–	6	–	–	–	–	0
Michael Passaportis	–	–	4R	8R	5R		4R	5	–	–	–	–	–	–	5	–	–	–	–	0
Jean Botha	–	–	–	3R	3	1R	1R	3	3	3	3	1	–	3	10	1	–	–	–	5
Burger Schoeman	–	–	–	–	8	8R	8	8	8	6R	8	8	7	–	9	2	–	–	–	10
Johan van Deventer	–	–	–	–	6	6R	x	6R	6R	6	6	–	–	–	6	1	–	–	–	5
Rudi Vogt	–	–	–	–	–	15R	–	15R	x	10R	10R	10R	10R	10R	7	2	5	–	–	20
Ivann Espag	–	–	–	–	–	–	–	3R	–	–	–	–	3R	–	2	–	–	–	–	0
Justin Downey	–	–	–	–	–	–	–	7	7	7	6	6	6	6	6	1	–	–	–	5
Luvyuiso Lusaseni	–	–	–	–	–	–	–	4	4	4	–	–	–	–	3	–	–	–	–	0
Jean Stemmet	–	–	–	–	–	–	–	x	12R	13R	13R	13	13	–	5	2	–	–	–	10
Edwin Hewitt	–	–	–	–	–	–	–	4R	4R	4R	4	4	4R	–	6	–	–	–	–	0
34 players															**292**	**60**	**45**	**28**	**1**	**477**

PROVINCIAL ROUND-UP

Barry Geel with ball in hand as the Griquas kicked off their ABSA Currie Cup campaign with a win over the Sharks.

ABSA UNDER-21 CHAMPIONSHIP (6th, Section B)

Played	Won	Drawn	Lost	Points for	Points against	Tries for	Tries against	Winning %
6	2	0	4	152	199	19	25	78.00%

RESULTS Lost Border (a) 11-15. Lost Griffons (a) 10-29. Bt SWD (a) 43-27. Lost Valke (h) 26-51. Bt Mpumalanga (h) 27-29. Lost EP (h) 25-48.

SCORERS 64 Kevin Plaatjies (3t, 8c, 11p). 20 Lundi Ralarala (4t). 11 Sarel Pretorius (1t, 3c). 10 Etienne Swarts, Lwandile Makibi (2t each). 7 Irlon April (1t, 1c). 5 Rudolph Britz, Hendrik Beets, David Strauss, Schalk van der Merwe, George Tzorvas, Russell van Wyk (1t each).

ABSA U19 CHAMPIONSHIP (5th, Section B)

Played	Won	Drawn	Lost	Points for	Points against	Tries for	Tries against	Winning %
6	2	1	3	141	129	22	17	17.00%

RESULTS Bt Border (a) 45-10. Lost Boland (a) 22-27. Lost SWD (a) 12-22. Drew Valke (h) 15-15. Beat Mpumalanga (h) 27-26. Lost EP (h) 20-29.

SCORERS 33 Junior Cornelissen (2t, 10c, 1p). 20 Werner Badenhorst (4t). 15 Tiaan le Roux (2t, 1c, 1p), Visser Vermaas, Mason Vermeulen (3t each). 10 Pieter Martinson, Leonard du Raan (2t each). 8 Noel Marx (1t, 1p). 5 Strip Cornelissen, Herman van Niekerk, Jasper Marais (1t each).

AMATEUR CHAMPIONSHIP

Griquas (5th Central Section)

Played	Won	Drawn	Lost	Points for	Points against	Tries for	Tries against	Winning %
6	2	0	4	166	270	24	40	33.00%

RESULTS Lost KZN Rural (a) 27-36. Bt Valke Rural (h) 33-19. Bt Free State Rural (h) 45-31. Lost Free State (a) 12-76. Lost Griffons (a) 34-59. Lost Griffons Rural (h) 15-49.

Griquas Rural (7th, South Section)

Played	Won	Drawn	Lost	Points for	Points against	Tries for	Tries against	Winning %
7	2	0	5	154	218	20	30	29.00%

RESULTS Lost WP (h) 19-42. Bt EP Rural (h) 20-17. Bt Border Rural (a) 24-14. Lost SWD (a) 15-26. Lost Boland (h) 27-30. Lost Border (h) 18-41. Lost EP (a) 31-48.

GRIQUAS RECORDS

MATCH RECORDS

Biggest win	94-0	vs. South Western Districts Federation	1978
Biggest win (Currie Cup)	87-14	vs. Border	1998
	80-07	vs Cavaliers	2009
Heaviest defeat	3-75	vs. Western Province	1985
Heaviest defeat (Currie Cup)	7-78	vs. Natal Sharks	2002
Highest score	94	vs. South Western Districts Federation (94-0)	1978
Highest score (Currie Cup)	87	vs. Border (87-14)	1998
Moist points conceded	75	vs. Western Province	1985
Moist points conceded (Currie Cup)	78	vs. Natal Sharks (7-78)	2002
	78	vs. Western Province (31-78)	2004
Most tries	18	vs. South Western Districts Federation	1978
Most tries (Currie Cup)	14	vs. Griffons (84-12)	2002
Most points by a player	42	IP Olivier vs. Griffons	2009
Most points by a player (Currie Cup)	33	PJ Visagie vs. Rhodesia	1968
Most tries by a player	7	J Jonker vs. Namibia	1996
Most tries by a player (Currie Cup)	4	D Prins vs. Eastern Province	1978
	4	J Nicholas vs. North West	1998
	4	BA Basson vs. Sharks	2010
Most conversions by a player (Currie Cup)	11	JC Wessels vs. Border	1998

SEASON RECORDS

Most team points	1428	32 matches	1998
Most team points (Currie Cup)	489	14 matches	1998
Most points by a player	361	GS du Toit	1998
Most points by a player (Currie Cup)	173	IP Olivier	2010
Most team tries	210	32 matches	1998
Most team tries (Currie Cup)	86	21 matches	2003
Most tries by a player	29	BA Basson	2010
Most tries by a player (Currie Cup)	21	BA Basson	2010
Most conversions by a player	98	GS du Toit	1998
Most drop goals by a player	7	GS du Toit	1998

CAREER RECORDS

Most appearances	161	AWA van Wyk	1984-1995
Most appearances (Currie Cup)	69	D Prins	1979-1987
Most consecutive games	97	P Smith	1963-1973
Most matches as captain	66	AWA van Wyk	1989-1994
Most points	719	JMF Lubbe	1995-2001
Most points (Currie Cup)	440	CS Erasmus	1977-1985
Most tries	61	J Nicholas	1998-2002
Most tries (Currie Cup)	37	D Prins	1979-1987
Most conversions by a player	133	JMF Lubbe	1995-2001
Most penalties by a player	91	JMF Lubbe	1995-2001
Most drop goals by a player	15	PJ Visagie	1964-1974
Most drop goals by a player (Currie Cup)	8	PJ Visagie	1964-1974

HONOURS

Absa Currie Cup	1899, 1911, 1970
Vodacom Cup	1998, 2005, 2007, 2009

PROVINCIAL ROUND-UP

KWAZULU-NATAL RUGBY UNION

FOUNDED 1890 (as Natal Rugby Union) **GROUND** ABSA Stadium **CAPACITY** 53 000
ADDRESS Jacko Jackson Drive, Stamford Hill, Durban
POSTAL ADDRESS PO Box 307, Durban, 4000
TELEPHONE NUMBER 031-308 8400 **WEBSITE** www.sharksrugby.co.za
COLOURS Black and white jersey and socks, white shorts
CURRIE CUP COACH John Plumtree **VODACOM CUP COACH** Swys de Bruin
CAPTAIN Stefan Terblanche **PRESIDENT** Peter Hassard
COMPANY CEO Brian van Zyl **UNION CEO** Peter Smith

Sharks surge to top of heap

COACH John Plumtree transformed a Vodacom Super 14 nightmare into a dream Absa Currie Cup campaign as the Sharks took take the premier domestic title for the second time in three years.

The Sharks' year started with five successive Super 14 losses but ended in triumph as they topped the Currie Cup log and then downed first the Blue Bulls (16-12) and then Western Province (30-10) on their way to the title.

Plumtree's flyhalf woes in the Super 14 hurt him tactically but he had no such problems in the Currie Cup with the skilful teenager Pat Lambie switched from fullback to flyhalf providing attacking nous. And so he and the Sharks were able to embrace an ambitious, modern, high-tempo, ball-in-the-hand approach.

It paid rich dividends as the Sharks won all their home games, scored the most tries in the league competition (62) and, crucially, earned home play-offs against first the Bulls and then Province, the Super 14 finalists. And, as Plumtree was quick to concede, the energy of the home crowd was significant and galvanised the Sharks in their strong defensive efforts in both play-offs.

The Sharks started with a defeat (40-34) at the hands of Griquas in Kimberley, but they then found their attacking rhythm and reeled off seven wins in a row including home wins over the Blue Bulls (34-28), Lions (48-19), Province (27-16) and Griquas (48-30).

They did, worryingly, struggle at altitude, going down to the Blue Bulls (34-40) and the Lions (20-22), but they were in an unassailable position at the top of the log by the last round when Plumtree's much-changed team went down 33-21 to Province at Newlands.

Strong attack in the first half against the Bulls (in the semi-final) and Province, in the final, was followed by remarkable defence to ensure victory and the title.

The Sharks' title win was a team effort, built on a solid tight five, but prominent were flanks Keegan Daniel and the burly Willem Alberts, the slick halfback pairing of the snappy Charl McLeod and Lambie, the hard-tackling Andries Strauss in midfield and their leading try-scorer (12) on the wing, Lwazi Mvovo.

And providing grunt when it was needed most – against the Bulls and Province – were returning Springbok front-rowers Beast Mtawarira and the Du Plessis brothers, Bismarck and Jannie.

The senior Sharks are all returning to Durban next year but there are regrets that Strauss' resurgence came after he had signed for Free State, while two fringe players, prop Patric Cilliers and flank Michael Rhodes, now have Lions contracts. New Sharks signings include Free State centre Meyer Bosman, WP scrumhalf Conrad Hoffmann and Bulls flyhalf Jacques-Louis Potgieter.

The successful Sharks U19 and U21 teams narrowly failed to reach the finals, after both were pipped by the Blue Bulls in Pretoria semi-finals. College Rovers won the SAA National Club Championships for the first time, upsetting Maties 24-15 in the Stellenbosch final.

But it was the emphatic 20-point win by Stefan Terblanche's team in the Currie Cup final which will be long remembered in Sharks country as early gloom of the Super 14 campaign turned into late-season cheer.

Winger Lwazi Mvovo was one of the standout players for the Sharks in 2010, so much so that he earned himself a Springbok call-up for the end-of-year tour.

SHARKS LOG POSITIONS

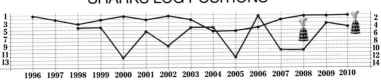

1996 1997 1998 1999 2000 2001 2002 2003 2004 2005 2006 2007 2008 2009 2010

SHARKS XV RESULTS AND SCORERS IN 2010

VODACOM CUP Played **9** Won **6** Drawn **0** Lost **3** Points for **245** Points against **188** Tries for **26** Tries against **20**

Date	Venue	Opponent	Result	Score	Scorers
Feb 26	Durban	BULLDOGS	WON	69-8	T: Stemmet (2), Ludik, Vulindlu, Lusaseni, Groenewald, Hargreaves, Cronje, Pretorius, Jordaan. C: Dumond (8). P: Dumond.
Mar 06	Cape Town	WP	LOST	23-26	T: Downey, Pretorius. C: Venter, Cronje. P: Venter (3).
Mar 13	Empangeni	FREE STATE	WON	26-17	T: Cooper, McLeod. C: Dumond (2). P: Dumond (3), Venter.
Mar 20	George	EAGLES	LOST	10-16	T: Pretorius (2).
Mar 26	Pietermaritzburg	CAVALIERS	WON	35-20	T: Strauss, Cilliers. C: Dumond (2). P: Dumond (6). DG: Dumond.
April 09	Port Elizabeth	ELEPHANTS	WON	27-25	T: Jordaan, Stemmet, Ndlovu. C: Dumond (3). P: Dumond (2)
April 16	Durban	PAMPAS XV	WON	24-19	T: McLeod, Cilliers. C: Dumond. P: Dumond (4).
Quarter-final					
April 24	Durban	GRIQUAS	WON	28-24	T: McLeod (2), Cilliers. C: Dumond (2). P: Dumond (3).
Semi-final					
May 1	Pretoria[1]	BLUE BULLS	LOST	03-33	P: Dumond.

[1]Loftus Versfeld C-field

ABSA Currie Cup Played **16** Won **12** Lost **4** Drawn **0** Points for **538** Points against **322** Tries for **66** Tries against **31**

Date	Venue	Opponent	Result	Score	Scorers
July 10	Kimberley	GRIQUAS	LOST	34-40	T: Mvovo (2), Meyer, Rhodes, Cilliers. C: Kockott (2), Dumond. P: Kockott.
July 17	Durban	BLUE BULLS	WON	34-28	T: Mvovo (2), Daniel (2), Burden. C: Lambie (3). P: Lambie.
July 23	Durban	PUMAS	WON	27-17	T: Daniel (3), McLeod. C: Lambie (2). P: Lambie.
July 31	Bloemfontein	CHEETAHS	WON	25-13	T: Lambie (2), Van Staden. C: Lambie (2). P: Lambie (2).
Aug 7	Durban	GOLDEN LIONS	WON	48-19	T: Mvovo (2), Lambie, Burden, Botes. C: Lambie (4). P: Lambie (5).
Aug 13	Phokeng	LEOPARDS	WON	51-6	T: Terblanche (2), Ludik, Mvovo, Kockott, Alberts, Cilliers. C: Lambie (3), Kockott (2). P: Lambie (2).
Aug 21	Durban	WP	WON	27-16	T: Ndungane, Kankowski. C: Lambie. P: Lambie (4). D: Terblanche.
Aug 27	Durban	GRIQUAS	WON	48-30	T: Dumond, Ndungane, Terblanche, Mtawarira, Burden. C: Lambie (4). P: Lambie (5).
Sept 4	Pretoria	BLUE BULLS	LOST	34-40	T: Terblanche, Mvovo, Hargreaves. C: Lambie (2). P: Lambie (5).
Sept 10	Witbank	PUMAS	WON	30-14	T: Ndungane, Mvovo, Botes, Burden. C: Lambie (2). P: Lambie (2).
Sept 18	Durban	CHEETAHS	WON	30-16	T: Ndungane, McLeod, Alberts, Kockott. C: Lambie (2). P: Lambie (2).
Sept 25	Johannesburg	GOLDEN LIONS	LOST	20-22	T: Mvovo (2), Ndungane. C: Lambie. P: Lambie.
Oct 1	Durban	LEOPARDS	WON	63-6	T: Ndungane, Daniel (2), J du Plessis (2), Ludik, Mvovo, Van Staden. C: Pretorius (6), Lambie (3).
Oct 9	Cape Town	WP	LOST	21-33	T: Kankowski, Jacobs, Ludik. C: Lambie (3).
Semi-final					
Oct 16	Durban	BLUE BULLS	WON	16-12	T: Daniel. C: Lambie. P: Lambie (3)
Final					
Oct 30	Durban	WP	WON	30-10	T: Lambie (2), McLeod. C: Lambie (3). P: Lambie (3).

SHARKS INVITATIONAL XV

Date	Venue	Opponent	Result	Score	Scorers
June 25	Nigel	VALKE	WON	80-03	T: Botes (3), Daniel (2), McLeod, Jenner, Cooper, Richards, Rhodes, Terblanche, Mtawarira. C: Kockott (6), Dumond (2), Daniel, Botes.

Team: Terblanche (c), Richards, Lindeque, Strauss (Jenner), Ludik, Meyer (Dumond), Kockott (McLeod), Daniel, Rhodes, Botes, Hargreaves, Bresler (Downey), Herbst (Van Staden), Burden (Cooper), Mtwawarira (Cilliers).

APPEARANCES AND POINTS FOR SHARKS IN 2010   CAREER

PLAYER	Appearances	Tries	Conversions	Penalties	Drop Goals	Points	Career Matches	Career Tries	Conversions	Penalties	Drop Goals	Points
WS (Willem) Alberts	13	2	–	–	–	10	13	2	–	–	–	10
LJ (Jacques) Botes	16	2	–	–	–	10	86	27	–	–	–	135
A (Anton) Bresler	4	–	–	–	–	0	4	–	–	–	–	0
CB (Craig) Burden	15	4	–	–	–	20	48	18	–	–	–	90
PM (Patric) Cilliers	9	2	–	–	–	10	34	5	–	–	–	25
KL (Kyle) Cooper	8	–	–	–	–	0	8	–	–	–	–	0
KR (Keegan) Daniel	14	8	–	–	–	40	69	27	–	–	–	135
JR (Jean) Deysel	2	–	–	–	–	0	30	1	–	–	–	5
G (Monty) Dumond	8	1	1	–	–	7	34	7	22	15	–	124
BW (Bismarck) du Plessis	8	–	–	–	–	0	33	10	–	–	–	50
JN (Jannie) du Plessis	5	2	–	–	–	10	27	3	–	–	–	15
AJ (Alistair) Hargreaves	13	1	–	–	–	5	36	1	–	–	–	5
WJ (Wiehahn) Herbst	10	–	–	–	–	0	15	–	–	–	–	0
AA (Adi) Jacobs	1	1	–	–	–	5	61	22	3	–	–	116
R (Ryan) Kankowski	8	2	–	–	–	10	52	14	–	–	–	70
RM (Rory) Kockott	14	2	4	1	–	21	47	3	40	50	1	248
P (Patrick) Lambie	16	5	36	36	–	205	17	5	36	36	–	205
L (Louis) Ludik	13	3	–	–	–	15	13	3	–	–	–	15
C (Charl) McLeod	16	3	–	–	–	15	31	7	–	–	–	35
SD (Steve) Meyer	4	1	–	–	–	5	6	1	4	1	–	16
G (Gerhard) Mostert	2	–	–	–	–	0	2	–	–	–	–	0
T (Beast) Mtawarira	9	1	–	–	–	5	31	2	–	–	–	10
LN (Lwazi) Mvovo	16	12	–	–	–	60	30	15	–	–	–	75
S (Skholiwe) Ndlovu	3	–	–	–	–	0	12	1	–	–	–	5
OM (Odwa) Ndungane	11	7	–	–	–	35	53	19	1	–	–	97
R (Ruan) Pienaar	1	–	–	–	–	0	33	7	59	36	–	261
J-PR (JP) Pietersen	5	–	–	–	–	0	35	16	–	–	–	80
AS (Andre) Pretorius	8	–	6	–	–	12	8	–	6	–	–	12
MK (Michael) Rhodes	11	1	–	–	–	5	19	1	–	–	–	5
RC (Ross) Skeate	6	–	–	–	–	0	6	–	–	–	–	0
AJ (Andries) Strauss	16	–	–	–	–	0	55	6	3	–	–	36
R (Riaan) Swanepoel	11	–	–	–	–	0	30	3	1	–	1	20
SR (Steven) Sykes	16	–	–	–	–	0	80	5	–	–	–	25
CS (Stefan) Terblanche	15	4	–	–	1	23	88	38	2	1	5	212
E (Eugene) van Staden	15	2	–	–	–	10	15	2	–	–	–	10
L (Luzuko) Vulindlu	2	–	–	–	–	0	6	1	–	–	–	5
36 players	**344**	**66**	**47**	**37**	**1**	**538**	**1167**	**273**	**177**	**139**	**7**	**2157**

PROVINCIAL ROUND-UP

APPEARANCES AND POINTS FOR SHARKS IN ABSA CURRIE CUP 2010

	Griquas	Blue Bulls	Pumas	Cheetahs	Golden Lions	Leopards	WP	Griquas	Blue Bulls	Pumas	Cheetahs	Golden Lions	Leopards	WP	Blue Bulls	WP	Matches	Tries	Conversions	Penalties	Drop Goals	Points
Lambie	15	12	12	12	10	10	10	10	10	10	10	10	10R	15	10	10	16	5	36	36	–	205
Ludik	14	15	15	15	15	15	15	–	–	–	15	15	15	11R	15	15	13	3	–	–	–	15
Terblanche	13c	13c	13c	13c	13c	13c	13c	13c	13c	15c	13c	13c	–	13c	13c	13c	15	4	–	–	1	23
Swanepoel	12	–	–	–	12R	15R	12R	12R	12R	12	12R	13R	12	–	–	12R	11	–	–	–	–	–
Mvovo	11	11	11	11	11	11	11	11	11	11	11	11	11	11	11	11	16	12	–	–	–	60
Meyer	10	10	10R	10	–	–	–	–	–	–	–	–	–	–	–	–	4	1	–	–	–	5
Kockott	9	9R	9R	–	9R	9	9R	9R	9R	9R	9R	9R	9R	9	x	9R	14	2	4	1	–	21
Daniel	8	8	8	7	6	7	6	8	8	–	6	6	8c	x	6	6	14	8	–	–	–	40
Rhodes	7	7	7	–	–	8R	–	5	7R	6R	7R	5R	7R	7	–	–	11	1	–	–	–	5
Botes	6	6	6	6	7R	6	6R	6	6	6	4R	4R	6	6	5R	5R	16	2	–	–	–	10
Hargreaves	5	5	5	–	5	5	5	–	5	5	5	5	–	5	5	5	13	1	–	–	–	5
Sykes	4	4	4	4	4	5R	4	4	4	4	4	4	4	5R	4	4	16	–	–	–	–	–
Herbst	3	3	3	3	–	–	3	3	3	3R	3R	3R	–	–	–	–	10	–	–	–	–	–
Burden	2	2	2	2	2	2	7R	2R	2R	2	2	2	2	2R	x	2R	15	4	–	–	–	20
Cilliers	1	1	1	1	–	1	–	–	–	1	1	1	3R	–	–	–	9	2	–	–	–	10
Cooper	2R	2R	2R	2R	–	–	–	–	–	2R	2R	2R	8R	–	–	–	8	–	–	–	–	–
van Staden	3R	3R	x	3R	3R	3	3R	3R	3R	3	3	3	1	3R	1R	1R	15	2	–	–	–	10
Bresler	4R	–	–	–	–	–	–	5R	x	–	–	–	5R	–	x	4R	4	–	–	–	–	–
Ndlovu	7R	7R	–	–	–	–	–	x	–	7R	–	–	–	–	–	–	3	–	–	–	–	–
McLeod	9R	9	9	9	9	9R	9	9	9	9	9	9	9	9R	9	9	16	3	–	–	–	15
Dumond	10R	10R	10	–	10R	10R	15R	15	15	–	–	–	–	–	–	–	8	1	1	–	–	7
Strauss	12R	15R	12R	15R	12	12	12	12	12	13	12	12	13	12	12	12	16	–	–	–	–	–
JP Pietersen	–	14	14	14	14	–	–	–	–	–	–	–	–	14	–	–	5	–	–	–	–	–
Skeate	–	4R	5R	5	4R	4	5R	–	–	–	–	–	–	–	–	–	6	–	–	–	–	–
Alberts	–	–	7R	6R	8	8	7	7	7	7	7	7	–	7	7	7	13	2	–	–	–	10
Kankowski	–	–	–	8	–	–	8	–	–	8	8	8	–	8	8	8	8	2	–	–	–	10
Mtawarira	–	–	–	1R	1	1R	1	1	1	–	–	–	1	1	1	–	9	1	–	–	–	5
Deysel	–	–	–	5R	7	–	–	–	–	–	–	–	–	–	–	–	2	–	–	–	–	–
Pienaar	–	–	–	10R	–	–	–	–	–	–	–	–	–	–	–	–	1	–	–	–	–	–
J du Plessis	–	–	–	–	3	–	–	–	–	–	–	–	3	3	3	3	5	2	–	–	–	10
B du Plessis	–	–	–	–	2R	2R	2	2	2	–	–	–	–	2	2	2	8	–	–	–	–	–
Ndungane	–	–	–	–	–	14	14	14	14	14	14	14	14	14	14R	14	11	7	–	–	–	35
Pretorius	–	–	–	–	–	–	x	15R	10R	15R	15R	10	10	–	15R	15R	8	–	6	–	–	12
Vulindlu	–	–	–	–	–	–	–	11R	–	–	–	13R	–	–	–	–	2	–	–	–	–	–
Mostert	–	–	–	–	–	–	–	–	–	–	–	–	–	5	4	–	2	–	–	–	–	–
Jacobs	–	–	–	–	–	–	–	–	–	–	–	–	–	11R	–	–	1	1	–	–	–	5
36 Players																	344	66	47	37	1	538

ABSA UNDER-21 CHAMPIONSHIP (3rd, Section A)

Played	Won	Drawn	Lost	Points for	Points against	Tries for	Tries against	Winning %
13	9	0	4	578	313	77	36	69%

RESULTS: Bt Boland (h) 106-3. Lost Blue Bulls (h) 16-20. Bt Free State (a) 27-23. Bt Golden Lions (h) 49-25. Bt Leopards (a) 45-25. Bt WP (h) 41-14. Bt Boland (a) 85-5. Lost Blue Bulls (h) 31-51. Bt Free State (h) 51-25. Bt Lions (a) 26-20. Bt Leopards (h) 57-27. Lost WP (a) 9-36. SEMI FINAL Lost Blue Bulls (a) 35-39.

SCORERS: 111 Guy Cronje (3t,27c,14p); 93 Willem du Plessis (2t,31c,7p); 50 Mark Richards (10t); 32 Ross Cronje (5t,2c,1p); 30 Lubabalo Mtembu, Xolane Mnisi, Meyer Swanepoel (6t each); 20 Jaco Reinach, Johannes Prinsloo, Jacobus Otto (4t each); 15 Kyle Cooper, Quinton Dormehl, Sibusiso Sithole, Wynand Pienaar, Rosko Specman (3t each); 10 Daniel Ojiambo, Jan Marais, Dale Chadwick (2t each); 9 Dwayne Jenner (1t,2c); 5 Lambert Groenewald, Arno van Zyl, Cameron Dunlop, Johannes Snyman, Penalty try (1t each).

FOR SHARKS XV IN 2010 VODACOM CUP   CAREER

PLAYER	Appearances	Tries	Conversions	Penalties	Drop Goals	Points	Career Matches	Career Tries	Conversions	Penalties	Drop Goals	Points
A (Anton) Bresler	9	–	–	–	–	0	9	–	–	–	–	0
CB (Craig) Burden	1	–	–	–	–	0	22	9	–	–	–	45
DM (Dale) Chadwick	4	–	–	–	–	0	4	–	–	–	–	0
PM (Patrick) Cilliers	9	3	–	–	–	15	18	3	–	–	–	15
KL (Kyle) Cooper	9	1	–	–	–	5	9	1	–	–	–	5
R (Ross) Cronje	9	1	1	–	–	7	13	1	11	1	0	30
J (Justin) Downey	9	1	–	–	–	5	18	3	–	–	–	15
G (Monty) Dumond	8	–	18	20	1	99	18	2	29	42	1	197
LS (Lambert) Groenewald	6	1	–	–	–	5	6	1	–	–	–	5
AJ (Alistair) Hargreaves	2	1	–	–	–	5	19	2	–	–	–	10
WJ (Wiehann) Herbst	5	–	–	–	–	0	11	–	–	–	–	0
CM (Chris) Jordaan	6	2	–	–	–	10	13	6	–	–	–	30
L (Louis) Ludik	3	1	–	–	–	5	3	1	–	–	–	5
L (Luvuyiso) Lusaseni	8	1	–	–	–	5	11	1	–	–	–	5
JA (Jandre) Marais	8	–	–	–	–	0	14	–	–	–	–	0
C (Charl) McLeod	9	4	–	–	–	20	19	7	–	–	–	35
WM (Waylon) Murray	3	–	–	–	–	0	8	–	–	–	–	0
LN (Lwazi) Mvovo	1	–	–	–	–	0	20	9	–	–	–	45
S (Sikholiwe) Ndlovu	8	1	–	–	–	5	15	3	–	–	–	15
S (Sabelo) Nhlapo	4	–	–	–	–	0	11	–	–	–	–	0
J (Jerome) Pretorius	8	4	–	–	–	20	8	4	–	–	–	20
J (Julian) Redelinghuys	7	–	–	–	–	0	7	–	–	–	–	0
MK (Michael) Rhodes	7	–	–	–	–	0	18	5	–	–	–	25
M (Mark) Richards	9	–	–	–	–	0	9	–	–	–	–	0
SCT (Sibusiso) Sithole	3	–	–	–	–	0	3	–	–	–	–	0
JJ (Hannes) Snyman	3	–	–	–	–	0	3	–	–	–	–	0
RS (Rosko) Specman	2	–	–	–	–	0	2	–	–	–	–	0
JH (Jean) Stemmet	9	3	–	–	–	15	9	3	–	–	–	15
AJ (Andries) Strauss	4	1	–	–	–	5	22	4	4	2	–	29
M (Meyer) Swanepoel	3	–	–	–	–	0	3	–	–	–	–	0
LR (Lee) Thompson	3	–	–	–	–	0	3	–	–	–	–	0
AC (Arno) van Zyl	3	–	–	–	–	0	3	–	–	–	–	0
JL (Jacques) Venter	6	–	1	4	–	14	6	–	1	4	–	14
L (Luzuko) Vulindlu	6	1	–	–	–	5	12	2	–	–	–	10
34 players	**194**	**26**	**20**	**24**	**1**	**245**	**369**	**67**	**45**	**49**	**1**	**570**

ABSA U19 CHAMPIONSHIP (3rd, Section A)

Played	Won	Drawn	Lost	Points for	Points against	Tries for	Tries against	Winning %
13	8	0	5	408	269	54	28	62%

RESULTS: Lost Blue Bulls (h) 15-25. Bt Griffons (h) 73-6. Bt Free State (a) 33-13. Lost Golden Lions (h) 24-26. Lost Leopards (a) 24-29. Lost WP (h) 25-28. Bt Blue Bulls (a) 19-15. Bt Griffons (a) 28-11. Bt Free State (h) 37-28. Bt Lions (a) 39-15. Bt Leopards (h) 34-17. Bt WP (a) 36-32. SEMI FINAL Lost Blue Bulls (a) 21-24.

SCORERS: 103 Ryno Olivier (1t,25c,15p,1d); 63 Piet Lindeque (7t,8c,4p); 33 Jaco van Tonder (5t,1c,2p); 25 Helmar Williams, Francois Kleinhans (5t each); 20 Kieran Goss, Orefile Nakin, Marcell Coetzee (4t each); 15 Jacques Lombard, Siseko Jafta, Mandla Dube (3t each); 10 Kyle Wilkinson, Adrian de la Rey, Gideon Bruwer (2t each); 5 Rynardt van Wyk, Nicholas Schonert, Nicolas Dodgen, Wayne Lemley (1t each); 4 Stefan Ungerer (2c).

PROVINCIAL ROUND-UP

APPEARANCES AND POINTS IN VODACOM CUP 2010

	Bulldogs	WP	Free State	Eagles	Cavaliers	Elephants	Pampas XV	Griquas	Blue Bulls	Matches	Tries	Conversions	Penalties	Drop Goals	Points
Ludik	15	15	–	–	–	–	–	–	14R	3	1	–	–	–	5
Richards	14	14	14	14	14	14R	14	15	15	9	–	–	–	–	0
Stemmet	13	13	13	13	13	13	13	13	13	9	3	–	–	–	15
Strauss	12c	12c	12c	–	12c	–	–	–	–	4	1	–	–	–	5
Vulindlu	11	11	11	13R	14R	–	x	14	–	6	1	–	–	–	5
Dumond	10	–	10	10	10	10	15	10	10	8	–	18	20	1	99
Mcleod	9	9	9	9R	9	9	9	9	9	9	4	–	–	–	20
Lusaseni	8	8	–	8	8	8	5R	8	7R	8	1	–	–	–	5
Groenewald	7	8R	–	–	6R	6R	6R	6R	–	6	1	–	–	–	5
Downey	6	6	7	6R	7	7	8	7	8	9	1	–	–	–	5
Hargreaves	5	5	–	–	–	–	–	–	–	2	1	–	–	–	5
Bresler	4	4	5	5	5	5	5	5	5	9	–	–	–	–	0
Herbst	3	3	3	–	–	3	–	3	–	5	–	–	–	–	0
Cooper	2	2	2	2	2	2R	2	2	2	9	1	–	–	–	5
Cilliers	1	1	1	1c	1	1c	1c	1c	1c	9	3	–	–	–	15
Snyman	2R	2R	–	–	x	–	x	–	2R	3	–	–	–	–	0
Nhlapo	3R	3R	1R	3R	–	–	–	–	–	4	–	–	–	–	0
Rhodes	7R	7	8	7	–	8R	7	–	7	7	–	–	–	–	0
Ndlovu	4R	–	6	6	6	6	6	6	6	8	1	–	–	–	5
Cronje	9R	9R	9R	9	9R	9R	9R	9R	9R	9	1	1	–	–	7
Pretorius	12R	10R	12R	12	15R	12	12	–	12R	8	4	–	–	–	20
Jordaan	15R	15R	15	15	15	15	–	–	–	6	2	–	–	–	10
Venter	–	10	10R	10R	–	15R	10	11R	–	6	–	1	4	–	14
Marais	–	4R	4	4	4	4	4	4	4	8	–	–	–	–	0
Redelinghuys	–	–	3R	3	3	3R	3	3R	3	7	–	–	–	–	0
Thompson	–	–	5R	–	–	–	–	7R	4R	3	–	–	–	–	0
Swanepoel	–	–	5R	5R	8R	–	–	–	–	3	–	–	–	–	0
Sithole	–	–	–	11	11	–	–	–	14	3	–	–	–	–	0
Chadwick	–	–	–	8R	3R	–	3R	x	3R	4	–	–	–	–	0
Murray	–	–	–	–	–	14	11	12	–	3	–	–	–	–	0
Mvovo	–	–	–	–	–	11	–	–	–	1	–	–	–	–	0
Burden	–	–	–	–	–	2	–	–	–	1	–	–	–	–	0
van Zyl	–	–	–	–	–	–	10R	12R	12	3	–	–	–	–	0
Specman	–	–	–	–	–	–	–	11	11	2	–	–	–	–	0
34 Players										**194**	**26**	**20**	**24**	**1**	**245**

AMATEUR CHAMPIONSHIP
KZN RURAL (4th, Central Section)

Played	Won	Drawn	Lost	Points for	Points against	Tries for	Tries against
6	3	1	2	199	165	31	22

RESULTS: Bt Griquas (h) 36-27. Lost Griffons (a) 24-34. Drew Griffons Rural (h) 19-19. Lost Free State (h) 24-48. Bt Valke Rural (a) 39-20. Bt Free State Rural (a) 57-17. *

SHARKS RECORDS

MATCH RECORDS

Biggest win	90-9	vs. South Eastern Transvaal (Currie Cup)	1996
Heaviest defeat	6-62	vs. Northern Transvaal	1991
Heaviest Currie Cup defeat	0-52	vs. Western Province	1932
Highest score	90	vs. South Eastern Transvaal (Currie Cup) (90-9)	1996
Most points conceded	62	vs. Northern Transvaal (6-62)	1991
Most tries	15	vs. Northern Natal (78-0)	1990
Most Currie Cup tries	13	vs. South Eastern Transvaal (90-9)	1996
Most points by a player	50	GK Lawless vs. Otago Highlanders	1997
Most Currie Cup points by a player	38	HW Honiball vs. Boland	1996
Most tries by a player	4	By 11 players - most recently by JP Pietersen vs. Leopards	2005
Most conversions by a player	11	HW Honiball vs. South Eastern Transvaal (Currie Cup)	1996
Most penalties by a player	8	GS du Toit vs. Western Province (Currie Cup)	2001
Most drop goals by a player	4	WJdeW Ras vs. Western Province (Currie Cup)	1979

SEASON RECORDS

Most team points	1348	30 matches	1996
Most Currie Cup points by team	792	15 matches	1996
Most points by a player	304	JT Stransky	1990
Most Currie Cup points by a player	195	JT Stransky	1990
Most team tries	184	30 matches	1996
Most Currie Cup tries by team	112	15 matches	1996
Most tries by a player	28	JF van der Westhuizen	1993
Most Currie Cup tries by a player	13	JF van der Westhuizen	1996
	13	J Joubert	1996
	13	H Mentz	2005

CAREER RECORDS

Most appearances	165	HM Reece-Edwards	1982-1995
	165	S Atherton	1988-2000
Most points	1114	HM Reece-Edwards	1982-1995
Most tries	90	JF van der Westhuizen	1992-1998

HONOURS

ABSA Currie Cup   1990, 1992, 1995, 1996, 2008, 2010

The Natal side celebrates only its second ABSA Currie Cup in 1992, after defeating Transvaal at Ellis Park to follow up their epic 1990 victory.

PROVINCIAL ROUND-UP

LEOPARDS RUGBY UNION

FOUNDED 1920 (as Western Transvaal) **GROUND** Profert Olën Park
CAPACITY 15 000 **ADDRESS** Lombard Street, Potchefstroom
POSTAL ADDRESS PO Box 422, Potchefstroom 2520
TELEPHONE NUMBER 018 297 5304/5 **EMAIL** nwr-unie@iafrica.com
COLOURS Green & red jersey, white shorts
CURRIE CUP COACH Chaka Willemse **VODACOM CUP COACH** Chaka Willemse
CAPTAIN Wilhelm Koch **PRESIDENT** James Stoffberg (resigned and replaced by
Adv André May **COMPANY CEO** Dr Eugene Hare

Leopards grab Premier lifeline

THE lucky Leopards survived the relegation axe yet again, scraping through in their two-legged playoff against the SWD Eagles for the second year in a row.

Like the previous year, points difference decided the fate of the two sides. The Leopards finished 11 points to the good – an 'improvement' of seven points compared to their 2009 tussle against the same team.

In the first of the matches, played in Potchefstroom, the home side recorded their first victory (37-22) since the start of the Absa Currie Cup but then lost the return game in George (28-32). Both teams finished the two-match series with six log points, which meant that those 11 points became the Leopards' lifeline.

Not that coach Chaka Willemse was around to see it: after a winless Currie Cup, he received his marching orders with round and the promotion/relegation matches remaining.

Replacement Leon Boshoff is a former Western Transvaal hooker who played 99 matches for the former Mielieboere before notching 88 games for the Lions. He is known as a disciplinarian with a no-nonsense attitude, and only time will tell whether he can spark an improvement in 2011.

The Leopards enjoyed a fairly good Vodacom Cup and progressed to the quarterfinals after wins over the Welwitchias, Valke, Griffons and Pumas. Although they lost narrowly (25-30) to Boland, the team looked set to do well in the Currie Cup.

But what a disaster! Thirteen losses in a row, 654 points conceded and only 164 put on the board in reply. That's an average loss of 50-12! Early in the campaign there was a promising effort against the Blue Bulls, when the Leopards lost 43-38, but towards the end the wheels well and truly came off. Their last two results, 63-6 against the Sharks and 78-7 against the Cheetahs, said it all.

"All is not lost," said Leopards CEO Eugene Hare, who is confident that the province will do better next season under Boshoff.

Hare revealed that the following players were not offered contracts for 2011: Russell Jeacocks, Ghafoer Luckan, Bom Samaai, Japie Nel, Brendt Theisinger, Basil de Doncker, Nardus Lombaard and Bennie Adams. In addition, stalwarts Jan van Zyl, Philip Lemmer and Draad Linde all hung up their boots.

The Leopards have also lost an number of players to other unions, the biggest of those being that of scrumhalf Michael Bondesio to the Lions. Captain Wilhelm Koch will join the SWD Eagles, hooker Pellow van der Westhuizen moves to the Pumas and promising prop forward Aranos Coetzee joins Racing Metro. Under-21 utility back Sarel Marais, who as a replacement saved the Leopards with decisive tries in both playoff matches, is set to join the EP Kings.

On the positive side, Hare announced that wing Vainon Willis, scrumhalf Wesley Moolman, prop Peet Vorster (all Blue Bulls), flanker Robert Kruger (Lions) and lock Brendon Snyman (EP Kings) had signed Leopards contracts. Pukke stars Stoffel Duvenhage and Joubert Engelbrecht have also been contracted, but the club as a whole did not enjoy a good season. They were knocked out of both the Varsity Cup and the SAA National Club Championships and also lost their Golden Lions when the University of Johannesburg beat them in the Predator League final.

Leon Boshoff was appointed new head coach during the Currie Cup

PROVINCIAL ROUND-UP

LEOPARDS LOG POSITIONS

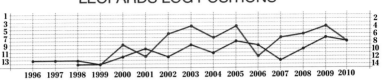

1996 1997 1998 1999 2000 2001 2002 2003 2004 2005 2006 2007 2008 2009 2010

LEOPARDS RESULTS AND SCORERS IN 2010

Played	Won	Drawn	Lost	Points for	Points against	Tries for	Tries against	Winning %
24	5	0	19	598	902	72	127	21%

VODACOM CUP Played **8** Won **4** Drawn **0** Lost **4** Points For **270** Points Against **194** Tries For **35** Tries Against **24** Winning Percentage **50%**

Date	Venue	Referee	Opponent	Result	Score	Scorers
Feb 27	Johannesburg[1]	Mlungiselele Mdashe	GOLDEN LIONS	LOST	22-27	T: Van Zyl (2), Scholtz, Samaai. C: Du Toit
Mar 05	Potchefstroom	Pro Legoete	WELWITCHIAS	WON	52-11	T: Scholtz (2), Williamson (2), Bowles (2), Bondesio (2). C: Du Toit (4), Durand (2).
Mar 12	Rustenburg[2]	Jason Jaftha	VALKE	WON	59-08	T: Samaai (2), Gronum, Van Niekerk, Scholtz, Matyeshana, Van der Westhuizen, Penalty try. C: Durand (4), Dumond. P: Durand (3)
Mar 19	Pretoria	Stuart Berry	BLUE BULLS	LOST	15-25	P: Durand (5)
Mar 26	Potchefstroom	Archie Sehlako	GRIFFONS	WON	43-13	T: Matyeshana (2), Koch (2), Tiedt, Van der Westhuizen, Lemmer. C: Dumond (3), Tiedt.
April 09	Kimberley[3]	Tiaan Jonker	GRIQUAS	LOST	21-51	T: Bowles, Jeacocks, Landman. C: Tiedt (3).
April 16	Potchefstroom	Mlugiseleli Mdashe	PUMAS	WON	33-29	T: Samaai (2), Scholtz. P: Dumond (5). DG: Dumond.
Quarter-final						
April 24	Wellington	Mlugiseleli Mdashe	CAVALIERS	LOST	25-30	T: Scholtz, Jeacocks. P: Dumond (5).

[1] Jhbg Stadium, [2] Royal Bafokeng Stadium, Phokeng, [3] AR Abass Stadium.

ABSA CURRIE CUP Played **14** Won **0** Lost **14** Drawn **0** Points For **263** Points Against **654** Tries For **30** Tries Against **94** Winning Percentage **0%**

Date	Venue	Referee	Opponent	Result	Score	Scorers
July 09	Rustenburg[1]	Lourens van der Merwe	LIONS	LOST	13-43	T: Scholtz, Koch. P: Dumond.
July 17	Witbank	Joey Salmans	PUMAS	LOST	32-37	T: Scholtz (2), Matyeshana, Bowles, Bondesio. C: Durand (2). P: Durand.
July 23	Potchefstroom	Sandile Mayende	WP	LOST	23-42	T: Matyeshana, Bowles, Schoitz. C: Tiedt. P: Tiedt. DG: Jacobs.
July 30	Potchefstroom	Jason Jaftha	GRIQUAS	LOST	27-41	T: Bondesio (2), Koch. C: Durand (2), Jacobs. P: Jacobs, Durand.
Aug 06	Pretoria	Stuart Berry	BLUE BULLS	LOST	38-43	T: Bondesio (2), Venter, Matyeshana, Landman. C: Jacobs (4), Durand. P: Jacobs.
Aug 13	Rustenburg[1]	Jaco Peyper	SHARKS	LOST	06-51	P: Jacobs (2).
Aug 20	Bloemfontein	Jason Jaftha	FREE STATE	LOST	00-57	
Aug 27	Johannesburg	Craig Joubert	LIONS	LOST	22-45	T: Van Zyl, Bondesio, Kember. C: Durand (2). P: Jacobs (3).
Sep 03	Potchefstroom	Pro Legoete	PUMAS	LOST	26-27	T: Mateyshana, Van Wyk. C: Durand (20. P: Durand (4).
Sep 11	Cape Town	Sandile Mayende	WP	LOST	17-59	T: Kember, Van Wyk. C: Durand (2). P: Durand.
Sep 17	Kimberley	Jason Jaftha	GRIQUAS	LOST	20-29	T: Venter (2). C: Durand (2). P: Durand (2).
Sep 25	Potchefstroom	Nathan Pearce	BLUE BULLS	LOST	26-39	T: Dumond, Matyeshana. C: Dumond (2). P: Durand (4).
Oct 01	Durban	Jaco Peyper	SHARKS	LOST	06-63	P: Durand (2).
Oct 08	Rustenburg[1]	Marius Jonker	FREE STATE	LOST	07-78	T: Van Niekerk. C: Durand.

[1] Royal Bafokeng Sports Palace, Phokeng

PROMOTION AND RELEGATION PLAY-OFF

Played **2** Won **1** Lost **1** Drawn **0** Points For **65** Points Against **54** Tries For **7** Tries Against **9** Winning Percentage **50%**

Date	Venue	Referee	Opponent	Result	Score	Scorers
Oct 23	Potchefstroom	Craig Joubert	SWD EAGLES	WON	37-22	T: Dames (2), Marais (2). C: Durand (4). P: Durand (3).
Oct 29	George	Jaco Peyper	SWD EAGLES	LOST	28-32	T: Kember, Marais, Venter. C: Durand, Marais. P: Durand (3)

nwr-unie@iafrica.com

APPEARANCES AND POINTS FOR LEOPARDS IN 2010   CAREER

PLAYER	Appearances	Tries	Conversions	Penalties	Drop Goals	Points	Career Matches	Career Tries	Conversions	Penalties	Drop Goals	Points
BI (Bennie) Adams	3	–	–	–	–	0	74	3	–	–	–	15
M (Michael) Bondesio	17	8	–	–	–	40	52	10	–	–	–	50
AH (Andries) Botha	1	–	–	–	–	0	1	–	–	–	–	0
JJ (Jovan) Bowles	21	5	–	–	–	25	41	13	–	–	–	65
JG (Gys) Briedenhann	8	–	–	–	–	0	8	–	–	–	–	0
EM (Eric) Coetzee	6	–	–	–	–	0	6	–	–	–	–	0
JV (Johan) Coetzee	11	–	–	–	–	0	11	–	–	–	–	0
DJ (Danie) Crous	6	–	–	–	–	0	6	–	–	–	–	0
HDP (Danie) Dames	13	2	–	–	–	10	24	6	–	–	–	30
BJ (Basil) de Doncker	5	–	–	–	–	0	36	6	–	–	–	30
TA (Tiaan) Dorfling	2	–	–	–	–	0	2	–	–	–	–	0
C (Cecil) Dumond	12	1	4	11	1	49	24	2	18	29	2	139
C (Clayton) Durand	17	–	27	29	–	141	72	2	119	115	5	608
CJ (Stoffel) Duvenage	2	–	–	–	–	0	2	–	–	–	–	0
M (Marcel) du Toit	2	–	5	–	–	10	2	–	5	–	–	0
GJ (Joubert) Engelbrecht	1	–	–	–	–	0	1	–	–	–	–	0
AJ (Anthonie) Gronum	21	1	–	–	–	5	55	2	–	–	–	10
N (Neill) Jacobs	11	–	5	5	1	28	13	–	6	5	1	30
RA (Russel) Jeacocks	9	2	–	–	–	10	25	9	–	–	–	45
VH (Victor) Joubert	9	–	–	–	–	0	9	–	–	–	–	0
WJ (Wilhelm) Koch	22	4	–	–		20	56	6	–	–	1	33
D (Divan) Kotze	11	–	–	–	–	0	41	–	–	–	–	0
TAW (Theuns) Kotze	3	–	–	–	–	0	3	–	–	–	–	0
RW (RW) Kember	21	3	–	–	–	15	49	7	–	–	–	35
C (Charlie) King	3	–	–	–	–	0	3	–	–	–	–	0
RJ (Rynard) Landman	12	2	–	–	–	10	39	2	–	–	–	10
PA (Philip) Lemmer	7	1	–	–	–	5	21	1	–	–	–	5
E (Edrich) Linde	13	–	–	–	–	0	83	2	–	–	–	10
CR (Colin) Lloyd	3	–	–	–	–	0	90	48	14	11	–	301
GJ (Nardus) Lombaard	7	–	–	–	–	0	51	–	–	–	–	0
G (Ghafoer) Luckan	2	–	–	–	–	0	2	–	–	–	–	0
SP (SP) Marais	2	3	1	–	–	17	2	3	1	–	–	17
D (Dumisani) Matyeshana	23	8	–	–	–	40	23	8	–	–	–	40
BP (Bradley) Mockford	12	–	–	–	–	0	16	–	–	–	–	0
J (Japie) Nel	5	–	–	–	–	0	35	4	–	–	–	20
JC (JC) Oberholzer	1	–	–	–	–	0	1	–	–	–	–	0
CJ (Kempie) Rautenbach	9	–	–	–	–	0	9	–	–	–	–	0
MS (Shuaib) Samaai	9	5	–	–	–	25	40	17	–	–	–	85
D (Deon) Scholtz	21	10	–	–	–	50	21	10	–	–	–	50
JAJ (Riaan) Swanepoel	21	–	–	–	–	0	51	7	–	–	–	35
B (Bernd) Theisinger	2	–	–	–	–	0	10	–	–	–	–	0
J (Jean) Tiedt	9	1	5	1	–	18	46	5	7	4	–	51
BG (BG) Uys	10	–	–	–	–	0	10	–	–	–	–	0
BC (Os) van der Walt	19	–	–	–	–	0	39	–	–	–	–	0
MRS (Pellow) van der Westhuizen	20	2	–	–	–	10	85	7	–	–	–	34
C (Christo) van Niekerk	16	2	–	–	–	10	39	5	–	–	–	25
TC (Theo) van Wyk	10	2	–	–	–	10	81	9	–	–	–	45
JHA (Jan) van Zyl	8	3	–	–	–	15	53	23	–	–	–	115
W (Walter) Venter	11	4	–	–	–	20	11	4	–	–	–	20
G (Gavin) Williamson	23	2	–	–	–	10	67	2	–	–	–	10
Penalty try	–	1	–	–	–	5	–	1	–	–	–	5
50 players	**512**	**72**	**47**	**46**	**2**	**598**	**1541**	**224**	**170**	**164**	**9**	**1968**

PROVINCIAL ROUND-UP

APPEARANCES AND POINTS IN VODACOM CUP 2010

	Golden Lions	Welwitchias	Valke	Blue Bulls	Griffons	Griquas	Pumas	Cavaliers	Matches	Tries	Conversions	Penalties	Drop Goals	Points
Jan van Zyl	15	15	–	11	–	–	–	–	3	2	–	–	–	10
Deon Scholtz	14	14	14	14	14	14	14	14	8	6	–	–	–	30
Jovan Bowles	13	13	13	13	13	13	13	13	8	3	–	–	–	15
Japie Nel	12	–	12	12	12	12	–	–	5	–	–	–	–	–
Shuaib Samaai	11	–	11R	–	–	14R	11	11	5	5	–	–	–	25
Marcel du Toit	10	10	–	–	–	–	–	–	2	–	5	–	–	10
Jean Tiedt	9	9R	9R	–	9	9	–	–	5	1	4	–	–	13
Riaan Swanepoel	8	8	8c	8c	8c	8c	–	x	6	–	–	–	–	–
Wilhelm Koch	7c	7c	–	6R	7	7	7c	7c	7	2	–	–	–	10
Christo van Niekerk	6	6	6	6	6	6	–	–	6	1	–	–	–	5
Anthonie Gronum	5	5	5	5	5	5	4R	4R	8	1	–	–	–	5
Rynard Landman	4	4	–	5R	4	4	5	5	7	1	–	–	–	5
Os van der Walt	3	3	3	3	3R	3	3	3	8	–	–	–	–	–
Gavin Williamson	2	2	2R	2	2R	2R	2	2	8	2	–	–	–	10
Divan Kotze	1	1	–	1	–	–	1	1	5	–	–	–	–	–
P van der Westhuizen	2R	2R	2	2R	2	2	2R	x	7	2	–	–	–	10
Nardus Lombaard	3R	1R	1	1R	1	1	–	–	6	–	–	–	–	–
Gys Briedenhann	5R	4R	4	4	5R	5R	4	4	8	–	–	–	–	–
RW Kember	6R	8R	7	7	–	6R	8	8	7	–	–	–	–	–
Michael Bondesio	9R	9	9	9R	–	–	9	9	6	2	–	–	–	10
Neil Jacobs	x	–	–	–	–	10	x	x	1	–	–	–	–	–
Dumisani Matyeshane	12R	11	11	15R	11	11	11R	11R	8	3	–	–	–	15
Basil de Doncker	–	12	–	–	12R	12R	12	12	5	–	–	–	–	–
Clayton Durand	–	10R	10	10	–	–	–	–	3	–	6	8	–	36
Russel Jeacocks	–	11R	15	15	15	15	15	15	7	2	–	–	–	10
Philip Lemmer	–	–	3R	–	3	3R	3R	3R	5	1	–	–	–	5
Bradley Mockford	–	–	4R	–	–	–	–	–	1	–	–	–	–	–
Danie Crous	–	–	6R	–	–	–	6	6	3	–	–	–	–	–
Cecil Dumond	–	–	10R	10R	10	–	10	10	5	–	4	10	1	41
Theo van Wyk	–	–	–	9	10R	10R	x	9R	4	–	–	–	–	–
Bennie Adams	–	–	–	–	8R	–	–	–	1	–	–	–	–	–
Colin Lloyd	–	–	–	–	9R	–	–	–	1	–	–	–	–	–
Victor Joubert	–	–	–	–	–	–	6R	–	1	–	–	–	–	–
Penalty try	–	–	–	–	–	–	–	–	0	1	–	–	–	5
									170	35	19	18	1	270

nwr-unie@iafrica.com

APPEARANCES AND POINTS IN ABSA CURRIE CUP 2010

	Golden Lions	Pumas	WP	Griquas	Blue Bulls	Sharks	Free State	Golden Lions	Pumas	WP	Griquas	Blue Bulls	Sharks	Free State	SWD Eagles	SWD Eagles	Matches	Tries	Conversions	Penalties	Drop Goals	Points
Jeacocks	15	15	–	–	–	–	–	–	–	–	–	–	–	–	–	–	2	–	–	–	–	0
Scholtz	14	14	14	14	14	14	14	14	14	14	14	15R	–	14	–	–	13	4	–	–	–	20
Bowles	13	13	13	13	13	13	13	13	13	13	13R	14	13	–	–	–	13	2	–	–	–	10
Jacobs	12	12	10	10	10	10	10	10	–	12R	–	–	–	12R	x	–	10	–	5	5	1	28
Matyeshana	11	11	11	11	11	11	11	–	11	11	11	11	11	11	14	14	15	5	–	–	–	25
Dumond	10	–	–	–	–	–	–	–	12R	12	13R	13R	15	12	–	–	7	1	–	1	–	8
Bondesio	9	9	9	9	9	9	9	9	–	–	–	–	–	9	9	9	11	6	–	–	–	30
RW Kember	8	6R	8R	–	–	6R	6R	7	7	7	7	7	7	8R	7	8	14	3	–	–	–	15
Koch	7c	7c	7c	7c	7c	7c	7c	6c	6c	6c	–	8R	7	6	7c	7c	15	2	–	–	–	10
Joubert	6	6	–	–	–	–	–	–	–	–	6R	4R	6	8R	6	6	8	–	–	–	–	0
Landman	5	5	5	–	5	5	–	–	–	–	–	–	–	–	–	–	5	1	–	–	–	5
Gronum	4	4	4	4	4	–	5R	4	4	4	4	4	4R	5R	–	–	13	–	–	–	–	0
Lemmer	3	3	–	–	–	–	–	–	–	–	–	–	–	–	–	–	2	–	–	–	–	0
Williamson	2	2	2	2	2R	2R	2	2	2	2R	–	2R	2	2	2	2	15	–	–	–	–	0
Kotze	1	1	1	1	–	–	–	–	–	–	–	–	–	1	3R	x	6	–	–	–	–	0
v/d Westhuizen	2R	2R	2R	2R	2	2	2R	2R	2R	2	2	2	–	–	–	–	12	–	–	–	–	0
Coetzee	3R	3R	3R	3R	3R	3R	3R	3R	–	3	3R	3	–	–	–	–	11	–	–	–	–	0
Linde	4R	4R	5R	5	4R	4R	5	x	x	4R	5R	–	5	5	5R	5	13	–	–	–	–	0
Swanepoel	8R	8	8	8	8	8	8	8	8	8	8c	8c	8c	8c	–	–	14	–	–	–	–	0
Tiedt	12R	–	15	–	9R	15R	–	–	–	–	–	–	–	–	–	–	4	–	1	1	–	5
Rautenbach	13R	–	–	–	–	–	–	11R	13R	13	13	14	13	13	13	–	9	–	–	–	–	0
Dames	14R	11R	15R	15	15	15	–	11R	15	15	15	15	–	–	15	15	13	2	–	–	–	10
Durand	–	10	x	12R	10R	10R	10R	10R	10	10	10	10	10	10	10	10	14	–	21	21	–	105
Theisinger	–	12R	–	–	–	–	–	–	12	–	–	–	–	–	–	–	2	–	–	–	–	0
van Wyk	–	x	–	9R	–	–	9R	9R	9	9	–	–	–	–	x	10R	6	2	–	–	–	10
Venter	–	–	12	12	12	12	12	12	–	–	12	12	12	–	12	12	11	4	–	–	–	20
Crous	–	–	6	6	6	–	–	–	–	–	–	–	–	–	–	–	3	–	–	–	–	0
van der Walt	–	–	3	3	3	3	3	3	3	3R	3		3	3	–	–	11	–	–	–	–	0
Samaai	–	–	11R	14R	–	–	11R	11	–	–	–	–	–	–	–	–	4	–	–	–	–	0
Mockford	–	–	–	5R	4	4	5	5	5	5	5	4	–	5	5R	–	11	–	–	–	–	0
Van Niekerk	–	–	–	6R	6R	6	6	x	x	8R	6	6	–	4	4	4	10	1	–	–	–	5
Uys	–	–	–	–	1	1	1	1	–	1	1	1	1	–	1	1	10	–	–	–	–	0
Van Zyl	–	–	–	–	15R	11R	15	15	–	–	–	–	12R	–	–	–	5	1	–	–	–	5
Lombaard	–	–	–	–	–	–	–	–	1	–	–	–	–	–	–	–	1	–	–	–	–	0
E Coetzee	–	–	–	–	–	–	–	1R	–	–	3R	1R	3R	3	–	3	6	–	–	–	–	0
Kotze	–	–	–	–	–	–	–	x	14R	–	–	–	9	15	–	–	3	–	–	–	–	0
Dorfling	–	–	–	–	–	–	–	–	9	9	–	–	–	–	–	–	2	–	–	–	–	0
JC Oberholzer	–	–	–	–	–	–	–	–	x	–	2R	–	–	–	–	–	1	–	–	–	–	0
King	–	–	–	–	–	–	–	–	12R	9R	–	9R	–	–	–	–	3	–	–	–	–	0
Luckan	–	–	–	–	–	–	–	–	–	–	22R	13R	–	–	–	–	2	–	–	–	–	0
Botha	–	–	–	–	–	–	–	–	–	–	13R	–	–	–	–	–	1	–	–	–	–	0
Duvenage	–	–	–	–	–	–	–	–	–	–	–	–	–	2R	x	2R	2	–	–	–	–	0
Lloyd	–	–	–	–	–	–	–	–	–	–	–	–	–	–	11	11	2	–	–	–	–	0
SP Marais	–	–	–	–	–	–	–	–	–	–	–	–	–	–	14R	14R	2	3	1	–	–	17
Adams	–	–	–	–	–	–	–	–	–	–	–	–	–	–	7R	7R	2	–	–	–	–	0
Engelbrecht	–	–	–	–	–	–	–	–	–	–	–	–	–	–	–	13R	1	–	–	–	–	0
46 players																	**340**	**37**	**28**	**28**	**1**	**328**

Totals include performance in the relegation play-offs

PROVINCIAL ROUND-UP

Michael Bondesio on the break during their Promotion/Relegation match against the SWD Eagles.

ABSA UNDER-21 CHAMPIONSHIP (5th, Section A)

Played	Won	Drawn	Lost	Points for	Points against	Tries for	Tries against	Winning %
12	4	0	8	370	406	45	52	33.00%

RESULTS Bt Golden Lions (h) 36-16. Bt Boland (h) 36-17. Lost WP (h) 19-20. Bt Boland (a) 34-18. Lost Blue Bulls (a) 30-43. Lost KZN (h) 25-45. Lost Free State (a) 24-30. Lost Golden Lions (a) 14-33. Lost WP (a) 17-59. Lost Blue Bulls (h) 36-41. Lost KZN (a) 27-57. Bt Free State (h) 62-20.

SCORERS 137 Louis Fouche (3t, 25c, 22p, 2dg). 35 Gabriel Engelbrecht (7t). 34 Sarel Marais (6t, 2c). 30 Tiaan Dorfling, Andrew van Wyk (6t each). 20 André Barnard (4t). 19 Francois Nel (5c, 2p, 1dg). 15 Leighton Bezuidenhout (3t). 10 Christiaan Botha (2t). 5 Gabriel Strydom, Jan Joubert, Armandt Joubert, Jaice Terblanche, Philip de Wet, Danie van der Merwe, Juandré Williams, Penalty try (1t each).

ABSA U19 CHAMPIONSHIP (4th, Section A)

Played	Won	Drawn	Lost	Points for	Points against	Tries for	Tries against	Winning %
13	7	0	6	377	383	48	52	54.00%

RESULTS Bt Griffons (h) 42-03. Lost Golden Lions (h) 22-25. Lost WP (h) 11-29. Lost Blue Bulls (a) 10-33. Bt KZN (h) 29-24. Bt Free State (a) 31-22. Bt Golden Lions (a) 37-36. Bt Griffons (a) 47-29. Bt WP (a) 37-36. Lost Blue Bulls (h) 31-40. Lost KZN (a) 17-34. Bt Free State (h) 50-23. SEMI-FINAL Lost WP (a) 13-49.

SCORERS 150 Jaco Lourens (3t, 33c, 23p). 35 Gerhard Fouche (7t). 30 Rowell Fielding (6t), Anton Kruger (5t). 20 Lucian Cupido, Armand van der Merwe (4t each). 17 John Welthagen (3t, 1c). 15 Rowayne Beukman, John-Roy Jenkinson (3t each). 10 Sidney Labuschagne (2t). 5 Erens Strydom, Matheus Schuurman, Albertus van Vuuren, Gideon Blignault, Rudolph Muller, Herman Basson, Cornell du Preez, Frederick Schnetler (1t each).

AMATEUR CHAMPIONSHIP

Leopards (3rd, North Section)

Played	Won	Drawn	Lost	Points for	Points against	Tries for	Tries against	Winning %
6	3	0	3	219	210	30	28	50.00%

RESULTS Lost Valke (h) 27-32. Bt Mpumalanga Rural (h) 56-22. Bt Blue Bulls (a) 34-30. Lost Mpumalanga (a) 18-32. Bt Blue Bulls Limpopo (h) 49-47. Lost Golden Lions (a) 35-47.

Leopards Rural (5th, North Section)

Played	Won	Drawn	Lost	Points for	Points against	Tries for	Tries against	Winning %
7	3	0	4	173	205	27	24	43.00%

RESULTS Lost Golden Lions (a) 10-30. Bt Leopards (a) 29-12. Lost Valke (h) 19-29. Lost Blue Bulls (a) 5-71. Bt Mpumalanga (h) 38-19. Lost Blue Bulls Limpopo (h) 12-23. Bt Mpumalanga Rural (a) 60-21.

nwr-unie@iafrica.com

LEOPARDS RECORDS

MATCH RECORDS

Biggest win	80-3	vs Niteroi, Brazilia	1993
Biggest win (Currie Cup)	103-9	vs Eastern Orange Free State	1988
Heaviest defeat	12-98	vs Transvaal	1996
Heaviest defeat (Currie Cup)	25-89	vs Free State Cheetahs	1998
Highest score	83	vs Uruguay (83-10)	1994
Highest score (Currie Cup)	103	vs Eastern Orange Free State (103-9)	1988
Moist points conceded	98	vs Transvaal (12-98)	1996
Moist points conceded (Currie Cup)	89	vs Free State Cheetahs	1998
Most tries (Currie Cup)	18	vs Eastern Orange Free State	1988
Most points by a player	41	D Basson vs Namibia	1994
Most points by a player (Currie Cup)	31	T Marais vs Eastern Orange Free State	1988
	31	IP Olivier vs Pumas	2005
Most tries by a player	5	T Van Niekerk vs Eastern Transvaal	1965
Most tries by a player (Currie Cup)	3	K Meyer vs Griffons	2000
	3	**H Mentz vs Mighty Elephants**	**2003**

SEASON RECORDS

Most points by a player	368	D Basson	1994
Most points by a player (Currie Cup)	204	C Durand	2008
Most tries by a player	25	CR Lloyd	2006
Most tries by a player (Currie Cup)	19	CR Lloyd	2006

CAREER RECORDS

Most appearances	191	WH (Werner) Lessing	1998-2007
Most matches as captain	129	E Hare	1989-1996
Most points	1183	D Basson	1991-1998
Most points (Currie Cup)	703	T Marais	1980-1988
Most tries	48	CR (Colin) Lloyd	2004-2010

PROVINCIAL ROUND-UP

MPUMALANGA RUGBY UNION

FOUNDED 1969 (as South Eastern Transvaal) **GROUND** Puma Stadium
CAPACITY 20 000 **ADDRESS** Lukin Street, Witbank
POSTAL ADDRESS PO Box 1574, Witbank 1035
TELEPHONE NUMBER 013 656 2647 **EMAIL** mru@mweb.co.za
COLOURS Dove grey & red jersey, black shorts
CURRIE CUP COACH Jimmy Stonehouse
VODACOM CUP COACH Jimmy Stonehouse **CAPTAIN** Hannes Franklin
PRESIDENT Hein Mentz **COMPANY CEO** Koos Kruger

Pumas bare fangs in Premiership fight

MEMORABLE wins over their big-brother unions, the Vodacom Blue Bulls and the Xerox Golden Lions, headlined a memorable year for the cash-strapped Pumas as they celebrated their return to the Absa Currie Cup Premier Division in style.

But whereas those two victories would've counted for little more than some exclusive bragging rights, it was their victory over the Eastern Province Kings in a promotion/relegation series in late October that really mattered.

The Pumas needed victory in Port Elizabeth in the second leg of the playoff games after they failed to deliver in the home leg in Witbank – drawing the first game 36-36.

But inspired by some typically robust forward play they crushed the Kings' hopes of replacing them in the Premier Division with a convincing 46-28 win in the decider.

So another year among the big boys awaits coaches Jimmy Stonehouse and Johan du Toit, whose troops now know that they can indeed muscle it up with the larger unions.

Their 23 log points was the most gathered by a team in their first year after promotion in the modern Currie Cup format.

And in 2010 the Pumas certainly put daylight between themselves and the other so-called smaller unions, although they still ended some way behind sixth-placed Griquas.

The victory over the Blue Bulls will be remembered for a long time in these parts though, coming as it did in the first-ever rugby match played at Nelspruit's FIFA World Cup ground, the Mbombela Stadium.

They beat the defending champions 22-21, but faltered in their second game at the same ground, crashing to a 62-10 defeat to Western Province.

Inconsistency and the odd error-ridden performance troubled their progress at times, but Stonehouse's men managed to pick themselves up right at the very end of the season.

Not only did they do this by winning that most important of games in Port Elizabeth, but they also earlier ended the Currie Cup league phase by beating the Lions at Coca-Cola Park 34-27 – a match that included a memorable individual try by centre Shaun Venter.

Earlier in the year the side did fail to make the quarterfinals of the Vodacom Cup, but admittedly that tournament was much used very much as preparation for the Currie Cup.

When the latter competition came round the team fired well with a pack of forwards that included action-packed flanker Corné Steenkamp and hard-running eighthman Doppies le Roux.

Their huge front row, with oversized props Ronnie Uys and Ashley Buys enjoying near-cult status, were a joy to watch, as was lineout kingpin Marius Coetzer. At the back, flyhalf Elgar Watts shone on his way to a personal tally of nine tries in the competition.

Unfortunately the Pumas' lack of depth was often exposed as injuries took their toll, and they eventually had to revert to loan deals with players from the Lions.

And with the lack of major sponsorship the Pumas were always likely to lose players, and this was proven as Watts, Jacques Coetzee, Alistair Kettledas and Junior Bester had all signed deals to play elsewhere by the end of 2010.

Leopards hooker Pellow van der Westhuizen is joining the Pumas in 2011 and, most importantly, the union was on the verge of securing a meaningful sponsorship deal.

Former Matie Elgar Watts was a constant threat, scoring nine tries in the Absa Currie Cup.

PUMAS LOG POSITIONS

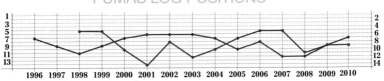

1996 1997 1998 1999 2000 2001 2002 2003 2004 2005 2006 2007 2008 2009 2010

PUMAS RESULTS AND SCORERS IN 2010

Played	Won	Drawn	Lost	Points for	Points against	Tries for	Tries against	Winning %
23	9	1	13	651	800	89	102	39%

VODACOM CUP PLAYED **7** WON **4** DRAWN **0** LOST **3** POINTS FOR **240** POINTS AGAINST **163** TRIES FOR **32** TRIES AGAINST **17**

Date	Venue	Opponent	Result	Score	
Feb 26	Witbank	VALKE	WON	52-17	T: Pretorius (2), Kettledas (2), Bouwer (2), Van der Nest, Coetzer. C: Pretorius (6).
Mar 05	Pretoria	BLUE BULLS	LOST	15-29	T: Van der Walt, Bouwer. C: Pretorius. P: Pretorius.
Mar 12	Witbank	GRIFFONS	WON	66-14	T: Kettledas (2), T Meyer (2), Kritzinger, Marx, Bouwer, Serfontein, Van Jaarsveld, Uys. C: Croy (8).
Mar 19	Kimberley[1]	GRIQUAS	LOST	26-42	T: Kettledas, Kritzinger, Marx, Bouwer. C: Croy (3).
Mar 27	Nelspruit[2]	WELWITCHIAS	WON	30-10	T: Kettledas, Kritzinger, R Steyn, Bouwer, Coetzer. C: Pretorius. P: Pretorius.
April 09	Secunda[3]	GOLDEN LIONS	WON	22-18	T: Bouwer. C: Croy. P: Croy (5).
April 16	Potch	LEOPARDS	LOST	29-33	T: Bouwer, Pretorius. C: Croy (2). P: Croy (4). DG: Croy.

[1]AR Abass Stadium, [2] Nelspruit RC, [3] Lillian Ngoyi Stadium.

ABSA CURRIE CUP PLAYED **16** WON **5** LOST **10** DRAWN **1** POINTS FOR **411** POINTS AGAINST **637** TRIES FOR **57** TRIES AGAINST **85** WINNING PERCENTAGE **34%**

Date	Venue	Opponent	Result	Score	
July 9	Pretoria	BLUE BULLS	LOST	15-38	T: Meyer, Kettledas. C: Croy. P: Croy.
July 17	Witbank	LEOPARDS	WON	37-32	T: Watts (3), Venter, Kettledas. C: Watts (3). P: Watts (2).
July 23	Durban	SHARKS	LOST	17-27	T: Le Roux, Uys. C: Croy (2). D: Croy.
July 30	Cape Town	WP	LOST	13-54	T: Van Jaarsveld, Venter. P: Watts.
Aug 7	Witbank	CHEETAHS	LOST	30-45	T: Venter, Coetzee, Bezuidenhout. C: Watt (2), Croy. P: Croy (3).
Aug 13	Kimberley	GRIQUAS	LOST	25-58	T: Venter, Watts, Bester. C: Watts (2). P: Watts (2).
Aug 20	Witbank	GOLDEN LIONS	LOST	30-33	T: Kritzinger, Watts, Le Roux, Penalty try. C: Watts (2). P: Watts, Croy.
Aug 27	Nelspruit	BLUE BULLS	WON	22-21	T: Meyer, Watts, Le Roux, Scott. C: Watts.
Sept 3	Potchefstroom	LEOPARDS	WON	27-26	T: Venter, Meyer, Jackson, Pretorius. C: Pretorius (2). P: Pretorius.
Sept 10	Witbank	SHARKS	LOST	14-30	T: Steenkamp, Watts. C: Pretorius (2).
Sept 17	Witbank	WP	LOST	10-62	T: Watts. C: Watts. P: Watts.
Sept 24	Bloemfontein	CHEETAHS	LOST	24-59	T: Venter, Van Dyk, Croy. C: Croy (3). P: Watts.
Oct 2	Witbank	GRIQUAS	LOST	31-61	T: Steenkamp (2), Venter, Van der Nest, Watts. C: Watts (2), Croy.
Oct 8	Johannesburg	GOLDEN LIONS	WON	34-27	T: Steenkamp (2), Jackson, Venter, Van der Nest. C: Watts (3). P: Watts.

PROMOTION/RELEGATION:

Date	Venue	Opponent	Result	Score	
Oct 22	Witbank	EP KINGS	DREW	36-36	T: Willis, Meyer, Kettledas, Watts, Steenkamp, Uys. C: Bezuidenhout (2), Watts.
Oct 29	Port Elizabeth	EP KINGS	WON	46-28	T: Le Roux (2), Willis, Steenkamp, Kruger, D Steyn. C: Bezuidenhout (5). P: Bezuidenhout (2).

mru@mweb.co.za

APPEARANCES AND POINTS FOR PUMAS IN 2010   CAREER

PLAYER	Appearances	Tries	Conversions	Penalties	Drop Goals	Points	Career Matches	Career Tries	Conversions	Penalties	Drop Goals	Points
A (Alwyn) Bester	7	1	–	–	–	5	7	1	–	–	–	5
C (Carl) Bezuidenhout	11	1	7	2	–	25	11	1	7	2	–	25
JL (Jovan) Botha	5	–	–	–	–	0	42	7	–	–	–	35
WJ (Jaco) Bouwer	21	8	–	–	–	40	37	12	–	–	–	60
AS (Ashley) Buys	23	–	–	–	–	0	44	–	–	–	–	0
J (Jacques) Coetzee	11	1	–	–	–	5	71	16	14	5	–	123
M (Marius) Coetzer	20	2	–	–	–	10	36	5	–	–	–	25
R (Ricardo) Croy	19	1	22	14	2	97	19	1	22	14	2	97
J (Hannes) Franklin	16	–	–	–	–	0	53	11	–	–	–	55
J (Johan) Jackson	7	2	–	–	–	10	7	2	–	–	–	10
A (Allister) Kettledas	19	9	–	–	–	45	40	33	–	–	–	165
N (Nicky) Kritzinger	12	4	–	–	–	20	12	4	–	–	–	20
AG (Andries) Kruger	11	1	–	–	–	5	11	1	–	–	–	5
C (Christo) le Roux	23	5	–	–	–	25	43	8	–	–	–	40
SW (Siviwe) Magaba	13	–	–	–	–	0	13	–	–	–	–	0
C (Conrad) Marais	2	–	–	–	–	0	2	–	–	–	–	0
T (Tiaan) Marx	13	2	–	–	–	10	40	12	7	8	1	101
PGJ (Pieter) Meyer	2	–	–	–	–	0	10	1	–	–	–	5
TC (Tian) Meyer	19	6	–	–	–	30	19	6	–	–	–	30
N (Nicol) Mostert	2	–	–	–	–	0	26	2	–	–	–	10
BA (Brett) Nel	3	–	–	–	–	0	7	1	–	–	–	5
B (Braam) Pretorius	7	4	12	3	–	53	21	7	68	37	–	282
AR (Ashwin) Scott	12	1	–	–	–	5	27	3	–	–	–	15
WJ (Willem) Serfontein	23	1	–	–	–	5	23	1	–	–	–	5
SM (Martin) Sithole	2	–	–	–	–	0	33	6	–	–	–	30
DE (Duwayne) Smart	2	–	–	–	–	0	7	2	–	–	–	10
CJ (Corne) Steenkamp	22	7	–	–	–	35	98	15	–	–	–	75
D (Dawie) Steyn	21	1	–	–	–	5	57	3	–	–	–	15
RP (Roelof) Steyn	4	1	–	–	–	5	4	1	–	–	–	5
JE (Jarrod) Taylor	2	–	–	–	–	0	2	–	–	–	–	0
DJ (De-Jay) Terblanche	16	–	–	–	–	0	39	3	–	–	–	15
PR (Ronnie) Uys	22	3	–	–	–	15	32	4	–	–	–	20
AH (Hendrik) van der Nest	8	3	–	–	–	15	17	4	–	–	–	20
ER (Eduan) van der Walt	13	1	–	–	–	5	36	6	–	–	–	30
RR (Roche) van der Westhuizen	1	–	–	–	–	0	1	–	–	–	–	0
HJ (Hans) van Dyk	5	1	–	–	–	5	5	1	–	–	–	5
JP (Johan) van Heerden	1	–	–	–	–	0	32	4	–	–	–	20
TG (Torsten) van Jaarsveld	17	2	–	–	–	10	34	5	–	–	–	25
JM (Luan) Velthuizen	10	–	–	–	–	0	30	0	–	–	–	0
S (Shaun) Venter	15	8	–	–	–	40	57	21	–	–	–	105
CH (Harry) Vermaas	2	–	–	–	–	0	2	–	–	–	–	0
J (Juan) Visser	2	–	–	–	–	0	12	1	–	–	–	5
EG (Elgar) Watts	22	10	17	9	–	111	22	10	17	9	–	111
V (Vainon) Willis	9	2	–	–	–	10	9	2	–	–	–	10
Penalty try	–	1	–	–	–	5	–	–	–	–	–	–
44 players	**479**	**87**	**51**	**26**	**2**	**651**	**1132**	**221**	**128**	**73**	**3**	**1589**

APPEARANCES AND POINTS IN VODACOM CUP 2010

vodacom CUP	Valke	Blue Bulls	Griffons	Griquas	Welwitchias	Golden Lions	Leopards	Matches	Tries	Conversions	Penalties	Drop Goals	Points
Nicky Kritzinger	15	15	14	14	15	15	15	7	3	–	–	–	15
Braam Pretorius	14	14	–	–	14	14R	14	5	3	8	2	–	37
Tiaan Marx	13	13	13	13	13	13	13	7	2	–	–	–	10
Ricardo Croy	12	12	10	10	10	10	10	7	–	14	9	1	58
Allister Kettledas	11	11	11	11	11R	11	11	7	6	–	–	–	30
Elgar Watts	10	10	14R	14R	10R	x	10R	6	–	–	–	–	0
Hendrik van der Nest	9	9	–	–	–	–	–	2	1	–	–	–	5
Christo le Roux	8	8	8	8	8	8	8	7	–	–	–	–	0
Jaco Bouwer	7	5R	7	7	7	7R	7	7	8	–	–	–	40
Pieter Meyer	6	–	–	–	–	–	–	1	–	–	–	–	0
Marius Coetzer	5	5	–	5	5	5	5	6	2	–	–	–	10
Luhan Velthuizen	4	4R	–	–	4	4	4	5	–	–	–	–	0
Ashley Buys	3	3	3	3	3R	3	3	7	–	–	–	–	0
Brett Nel	2	2	2R	–	–	–	–	3	–	–	–	–	0
Ronnie Uys	1c	1	1	1	1R	1	1	7	1	–	–	–	5
Jarrod Taylor	2R	–	–	2R	–	–	–	2	–	–	–	–	0
Roche van der Westhuizen	3R	–	–	–	–	–	–	1	–	–	–	–	0
Eduan van der Walt	6R	7	5	–	–	7	–	4	1	–	–	–	5
Willem Serfontein	4R	4	4	4	4R	4R	4R	7	1	–	–	–	5
Tian Meyer	9R	9R	9	9	9	9	9	7	2	–	–	–	10
Siviwe Magaba	10R	10R	12	12	12	12	12	7	–	–	–	–	0
Roelof Steyn	14R	–	–	–	11	14	–	3	1	–	–	–	5
Corne Steenkamp	–	6c	6c	6c	6c	6c	6c	6	–	–	–	–	0
Dawie Steyn	–	1R	1R	1R	1	1R	1R	6	–	–	–	–	0
Torsten van Jaarsveld	–	2R	2	2	2	2	2	6	1	–	–	–	5
Dee-Jay Terblanche	–	3R	3R	3R	3	–	–	4	–	–	–	–	0
Carl Bezuidenhout	–	–	15	15	–	–	–	2	–	–	–	–	0
Andries Kruger	–	–	4R	4R	–	–	–	2	–	–	–	–	0
Nicol Mostert	–	–	7R	–	–	–	–	1	–	–	–	–	0
Jovan Botha	–	–	13R	15R	12R	x	12R	4	–	–	–	–	0
Martin Sithole	–	–	–	7R	–	–	–	1	–	–	–	–	0
Harry Vermaas	–	–	–	–	2R	x	2R	2	–	–	–	–	0
Johan van Heerden	–	–	–	–	–	–	7R	1	–	–	–	–	0
Jacques Coetzee	–	–	–	–	–	–	9R	1	–	–	–	–	0
34 Players								**151**	**32**	**22**	**11**	**1**	**240**

mru@mweb.co.za

APPEARANCES AND POINTS IN ABSA CURRIE CUP 2010

	Blue Bulls	Leopards	Sharks	WP	Cheetahs	Griquas	Golden Lions	Blue Bulls	Leopards	Sharks	WP	Cheetahs	Griquas	Golden Lions	EP Kings	EP Kings	Matches	Tries	Conversions	Penalties	Drop Goals	Points
Bezuidenhout	15	15	15	15	10R	15	–	–	–	–	–	–	–	14R	15	15	9	1	7	2	–	25
Smart	14	–	–	–	–	14	x	–	–	–	–	–	–	–	–	–	2	–	–	–	–	–
Scott	13	13	14	14	14	–	9R	9R	12	12	9R	–	12R	–	9R	–	12	1	–	–	–	5
Botha	12	–	–	–	–	–	–	–	–	–	–	–	–	–	–	–	1	–	–	–	–	–
Venter	11	14	13	9R	11	11	13	13	13	–	13	13	13	13	13	13	15	8	–	–	–	40
Croy	10	10R	10	15R	10	13R	10R	x	x	9R	12	10R	10	x	x	10R	12	1	8	5	1	39
Meyer	9	9R	9R	–	22R	12	12	12	9	9	–	–	–	12	12	12	12	4	–	–	–	20
Bester	8	7	7	7	7	7	–	–	–	–	–	–	7	–	–	–	7	1	–	–	–	5
van der Walt	7	4	4	–	–	–	–	5R	–	–	5	4	–	7	7R	7	9	–	–	–	–	–
Steenkamp	6	6	6	6	6c	6c	6	6	6	6	6c	6	6	6	6	6	16	7	–	–	–	35
Coetzer	5	5	5	5	5	7R	5	5	5	5	–	–	5	5	5	5	14	–	–	–	–	–
Veldhuizen	4	–	–	–	–	–	–	–	–	–	–	5	4	4	4	–	5	–	–	–	–	–
Buys	3	3	3	3	3	3	3	3	3	3	3	3	3	3	3	3	16	–	–	–	–	–
Franklin	2c	2c	2c	2c	2R	2R	2c	2c	2c	2c	2R	2c	2c	2c	2c	2c	16	–	–	–	–	–
Steyn	1	1R	–	1R	1	1R	1R	1R	1R	1R	1R	1	1R	1R	1R	1R	15	1	–	–	–	5
van Jaarsveld	6R	2R	2R	2R	2	2	7	7	7	7	2	–	–	–	–	–	11	1	–	–	–	5
Uys	1R	1	1	1	–	1	1	1	1	1	1	1R	1	1	1	1	15	2	–	–	–	10
Serfontein	4R	5R	4R	4	5R	5	4R	4R	4R	5R	4R	5R	5R	5R	4R	5R	16	–	–	–	–	–
le Roux	8R	8	8	8	8	8	8	8	8	8	8	8	8	8	8	8	16	5	–	–	–	25
Coetzee	9R	9	9	9	9	9	9	9	–	–	–	9R	9	–	–	–	10	1	–	–	–	5
Watts	14R	10	10R	10	15	10	10	10	10	10	10	10	10R	10	10	10	16	10	17	9	–	111
Kettledas	12R	11	11	11	–	–	11	11	11	11	11	–	–	11	11	11R	12	3	–	–	–	15
Magaba	–	12	12	12	12	–	–	–	–	12R	–	12	–	–	–	–	6	–	–	–	–	–
Bouwer	–	8R	8R	–	6R	8R	7R	2R	6R	2R	7	7	6R	7R	7	7R	14	–	–	–	–	–
Marx	–	12R	12R	13	13	13	–	–	–	13	–	–	–	–	–	–	6	–	–	–	–	–
Terblanche	–	–	1R	3R	3R	3R	3R	3R	3R	3R	3R	–	–	3R	3R	3R	12	–	–	–	–	–
Kruger	–	–	–	5R	4	4	4	4	4	4	4	–	–	–	–	4	9	1	–	–	–	5
P Meyer	–	–	–	8R	–	–	–	–	–	–	–	–	–	–	–	–	1	–	–	–	–	–
R Steyn	–	–	–	–	12R	–	–	–	–	–	–	–	–	–	–	–	1	–	–	–	–	–
Willis	–	–	–	–	–	9R	14	14	x	–	11R	11	14	14	14	14	9	2	–	–	–	10
Kritzinger	–	–	–	–	–	–	15	15	15	–	–	14R	11	–	–	–	5	1	–	–	–	5
Jackson	–	–	–	–	–	–	–	15R	15	15	15	15	15	–	11	–	7	2	–	–	–	10
Pretorius	–	–	–	–	–	–	–	14	14	–	–	–	–	–	–	–	2	1	4	1	–	16
Sithole	–	–	–	–	–	–	–	R8	–	–	–	–	–	–	–	–	1	–	–	–	–	–
Marais	–	–	–	–	–	–	–	–	–	–	14	14	–	–	–	–	2	–	–	–	–	–
van der Nest	–	–	–	–	–	–	–	–	–	–	9	9	9R	9	9	9	6	2	–	–	–	10
Visser	–	–	–	–	–	–	–	–	–	–	12R	–	12	–	–	–	2	–	–	–	–	–
van Dyk	–	–	–	–	–	–	–	–	–	–	–	2R	2R	2R	2R	2R	5	1	–	–	–	5
Mostert	–	–	–	–	–	–	–	–	–	–	–	8R	–	–	–	–	1	–	–	–	–	–
Penalty try	–	–	–	–	–	–	–	–	–	–	–	–	–	–	–	–	0	1	–	–	–	5
40 Players																	**346**	**57**	**36**	**17**	**1**	**411**

Totals include performances in the relegation play-offs

PROVINCIAL ROUND-UP

Corne Steenkamp scores a try as the Pumas defeat the Xerox Lions in their final ABSA Currie Cup match in Johannesburg.

ABSA UNDER-21 CHAMPIONSHIP (4th, Section B)

Played	Won	Drawn	Lost	Points for	Points against	Tries for	Tries against	Winning %
7	3	0	4	235	209	25	27	43.000%

RESULTS: Lost EP (a) 21-23. Bt SWD (h) 40-10. Bt Valke (h) 44-35. Lost Griquas (a) 29-37. Bt Border (a) 53-28. Lost Griffons (h) 28-33. SEMI FINAL Lost EP (a) 20-43

SCORERS: 111 Neil Janse van Rensburg (1t,20c,18p,4d); 25 Zane Sloane (5t); 20 Johannes Tromp, Dewald Pieters (4t each); 10 Lambertus Potgieter, Quintin Posthumus (2t each); 5 Neels Pienaar, Quintin Posthumus, Raymond van Niekerk, Ruan Grobler, Theunis Kruger, Wayne Dreyer, Jean-Di Oosthuizen, Pieter Strydom (1t each); 2 Riaan Vosloo, Gerhard Pretorius (1c).

ABSA U19 CHAMPIONSHIP (2nd, Section B)

Played	Won	Drawn	Lost	Points for	Points against	Tries for	Tries against	Winning %
7	3	0	4	204	167	28	21	43%

RESULTS: Lost EP (a) 5-25. Lost SWD (h) 21-28. Bt Valke (h) 26-13. Lost Griquas (a) 26-27. Bt Border (a) 61-9. Bt Boland (h) 36-28. SEMI FINAL Lost SWD (h) 29-37.

SCORERS: 69 Christian Schoeman (1t,23c,6p); 20 Dirk Boshoff, Rasmus Engelbrecht, Adriaan Nel (4t each); 15 Michael Killian, Jacobus Bezuidenhout, Jacques-Louw Badenhorst (3t each); 10 Bruce Zeelie, Neil Manley (2t each); 5 Lourens du Preez, Roelf Fritz (1t each).

AMATEUR CHAMPIONSHIP – Mpumalanga (6th, North Section)

Played	Won	Drawn	Lost	Points for	Points against	Tries for	Tries against
6	1	0	5	136	236	18	33

RESULTS: Lost Lowveld (a) 19-36. Bt Limpopo (h) 53-38. Lost Leopards (h) 18-32. Lost Lions (a) 19-42. Lost Valke (h) 9-47. Lost Blue Bulls (a) 18-41. *

AMATEUR CHAMPIONSHIP - Lowveld (7th, North Section)

Played	Won	Drawn	Lost	Points for	Points against	Tries for	Tries against
6	1	0	5	134	285	20	39

RESULTS: Bt Pumas (h) 36-19. Lost Leopards (a) 22-56. Lost Valke (h) 12-38. Lost Lions (a) 23-64. Lost Blue Bulls (h) 68-19. Lost Limpopo (a) 22-40. *Bt Leopards (h) 27-26. Lost Valke (a) 17-82. Lost Lions (h) 10-73. Lost Leopards Rural (h) 21-60.

      mru@mweb.co.za

SWD EAGLES RECORDS

MATCH RECORDS

Biggest win	104-3	vs. South Western Districts Federation	1978
Biggest Currie Cup win	111-14	vs. Vodacom Eagles	2001
Heaviest defeat	10-116	vs. Transvaal	1993
Heaviest Currie Cup defeat	9-90	vs. Natal	1996
Highest score	111	vs. Vodacom Eagles (111-14)	2001
Most points conceded	116	vs. Transvaal (10-116)	1993
Most tries	20	vs. South Western Districts Federation (104-3)	1978
Most Currie Cup tries	16	vs. Vodacom Eagles (111-14)	2001
Most points by a player	37	J Benade vs. Lowveld	1995
	37	CP Steyn vs. Vodacom Cheetahs (Currie Cup)	2003
Most tries by a player	5	D Pretorius vs. South Western Districts Federation	1978
Most Currie Cup tries by a player	4	A Fourie vs. North West	1998

SEASON RECORDS

Most team points	852	28 matches	1999
Most Currie Cup points by team	631	14 matches	2009
Most points by a player	294	J Benade	1995
Most Currie Cup points by a player	202	B Pretorius	2009
Most team tries	114	28 matches	1999
Most Currie Cup tries by team	82	14 matches	2009
Most tries by a player	24	A Kettledas	2009
Most Currie Cup tries by a player	**18**	**A Kettledas**	**2009**

CAREER RECORDS

Most appearances	183	
FJ Rossouw	1991-2000	
Most points	869	
JH Muller	1973-1985	
Most tries	57	
K Grobler	1979-1990	

HONOURS

ABSA Currie Cup (First Division)	2005, 2009

rugby@swdeagles.co.za

SOUTH WESTERN DISTRICTS RUGBY UNION

FOUNDED 1899 **GROUND** Outeniqua Park **CAPACITY** 10 000
ADDRESS CJ Langenhoven Street, George
POSTAL ADDRESS PO Box 10471, George 6530
TELEPHONE NUMBER 044 873 0137 **EMAIL** rugby@swdeagles.co.za
COLOURS White & green jersey, white shorts and green socks
CURRIE CUP COACH Johann Lerm **VODACOM CUP COACH** Johann Lerm
CAPTAIN Bevin Fortuin **PRESIDENT** Hennie Bartmann
UNION CEO Willem Small

Heartbreak for Eagles yet again

THE sense of déjà vu was palpable at Outeniqua Park in George on the last Friday in October after the SWD Eagles missed out on promotion to the Absa Currie Cup Premier Division by the narrowest of margins yet again.

The Eagles must have wondered what they had done to anger the rugby gods when, for the second year in a row, the Leopards somehow hung onto their top-flight status in the Southern Cape city, after it had seemed certain that they would be relegated.

The face of Walter Venter is sure to occupy centre-stage in Eagles coach Johann Lerm's worst nightmares until the 2011 season – should he stick around, that is – after the former Lions centre scored a dramatic try with two minutes remaining, which gave the Leopards the bonus point they required to stay up.

Over the two-legged playoff, the both sides accumulated six log points (the Leopards five for a 37-22 win in the first leg, and one losing bonus point in the 32-28 second-leg defeat; the Eagles one for scoring four tries in the first leg, and five points for a win in the second), which made it a straight points-difference shootout.

It was a painful scenario reminiscent of the movie Groundhog Day, in which the lead character is forced to relive the same day over and over again until he's able to prove he's learnt from past mistakes. A year earlier, the two sides played out a virtually identical script, with the Leopards winning the first leg 47-42 in Potch and losing 18-17 in George, with points difference again being the deciding factor.

Never mind that the Eagles had completely dominated the game until just before Venter's try – they led 32-16 with six minutes remaining – or that Bevin Fortuin's brave troops had overturned a 37-22 first-leg defeat in Potchefstroom to stand on the brink of what would have been an amazing accomplishment.

The Eagles won the match, but the bonus point that Venter's try brought, against a tired defence visibly hanging on for the final whistle, made it the most bittersweet of victories.

The Eagles have been consistent performers in the First Division over the past five years, finishing third, first, third, second and first on the log. But they have just not been able to close out the matches that really counted, as evidenced in 2010 by their 16-12 home defeat in the First Division final to the Eastern Province Kings.

That said, the Eagles did shock the Kings 25-8 in their final round-robin match in Port Elizabeth to secure top spot – which gave them a shot at the winless Leopards instead of the Pumas, who had beaten the Blue Bulls and Lions and who would go on to also retain their Premier status by dominating the Kings.

Despite not reaching their goal, the Eagles can be proud of their season, coming as it did against the backdrop of union infighting and the threat of not being paid their salaries.

Flyhalf Ambrose Barends finished as the competition's top point-scorer with 133, while the likes of Fortuin, Henry Grimes, Sinethemba Zweni, Shaun Raubenheimer, Jandré Blom and Baldwin McBean can be proud of their individual efforts in a gutsy and determined side who added up to far more than the sum of its parts.

Sinethemba Zweni enjoyed an outstanding season for the Eagles at centre.

PROVINCIAL ROUND-UP

SWD EAGLES LOG POSITIONS

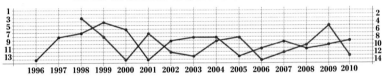

1996 1997 1998 1999 2000 2001 2002 2003 2004 2005 2006 2007 2008 2009 2010

EAGLES RESULTS AND SCORERS IN 2009

Played	Won	Drawn	Lost	Points for	Points against	Tries for	Tries against	Winning %
22	12	0	10	603	580	73	74	55%

VODACOM CUP Played **7** Won **2** Drawn **0** Lost **5** Points For **151** Points Against **176** Tries For **17** Tries Against **26** Winning Percentage **29%**

Date	Venue	Referee	Opponent	Result	Score	Scorers
Feb 27	George[1]	Francois Veldsman	FREE STATE	LOST	13-22	T: Penalty try. C: Zana. P: Zana (2).
Mar 13	Saldanha	Lourens van der Merwe	CAVALIERS	LOST	24-25	T: Raubenheimer, Bennett. C: Blom. P: Blom (3), Zana.
Mar 20	Oudtshoorn[2]	Bongani Maloni	SHARKS XV	WON	16-10	T: McBean, Bennett. P: Blom, Zana.
Mar 26	Port Elizabeth	Matt Kemp	ELEPHANTS	LOST	19-24	T: Bennett. C: Rhoode. P: Zana (4).
April 7	Stellenbosch[3]	Joey Salmans	PAMPAS XV	LOST	17-36	T: Fortuin, Saayman. C: Rhoode, Blom. P: Rhoode.
April 10	Parow	Sandile Mayende	WESTERN PROVINCE	LOST	23-29	T: Mtyanda, Raubenheimer, Bennett. C: Barends. P: Barends (2).
April 17	Beaufort West	Rasta Rashivenge	BULLDOGS	WON	39-30	T: McBean (2), Fortuin, Ewerts, Du Plessis, Bennett. C: Barends (3). P: Barends.

1 Saasveld, 2 Bridgton, 3 Van der Stel RC

ABSA CURRIE CUP Played **14** Won **10** Drawn **0** Lost **4** Points For **440** Points Against **354** Tries For **54** Tries Against **40** Winning Percentage **71.4%**

Date	Venue	Referee	Opponent	Result	Score	Scorers
July 23	George	Craig Joubert	BORDER	WON	33-12	T: Barends, Potts, Raubenheimer, Zweni. C: Barends, Blom. P: Barends (3).
July 31	Welkom	Sandile Mayende	GRIFFONS	WON	18-14	T: Breytenbach, Zweni. C: Barends. P: Barends (2).
Aug 6	George	Marius Jonker	BOLAND	WON	45-36	T: Joubert, Breytenbach, Raubenheimer, Harmse. C: Barends (3), Blom. P: Barends (3), Blom.
Aug 14	Kempton Park	Craig Joubert	VALKE	WON	55-47	T: Van der Westhuizen, Fortuin, Joubert, Manuel, Engelbrecht, Blom, Mtyanda, Raubenheimer. C: Barends (3), Blom (3). P: Barends.
Aug 20	George	Jaco Peyper	EP KINGS	LOST	17-19	T: McBean. P: Barends (4).
Sep 3	East London	Craig Joubert	BORDER	WON	17-07	T: Fortuin, Raubenheimer. C: Barends (2). P: Barends.
Sep 10	George	Stuart Berry	GRIFFONS	WON	42-27	T: Zweni (2), Barends, Joubert, Breytenbach. C: Barends (4). P: Barends (2), Blom.
Sep 17	Wellington	Mark Lawrence	BOLAND	LOST	33-38	T: McBean, Joubert, Raubenheimer. C: Blom (3). P: Barends (3).
Sep 24	George	Andrew Lees	VALKE	WON	57-35	T: McBean (3), Scott (2), Joubert, Breytenbach, Raubenheimer, Terblanche. C: Barends (4), Blom (2).
Oct 1	Port Elizabeth	Sandile Mayende	EP KINGS	WON	25-08	T: McBean, Hellmuth. P: Barends (2), Blom. DG: Barends
Semi-final						
Oct 8	George	Sandile Mayende	GRIFFONS	WON	32-30	T: Breytenbach (2), McBean, Engelbrecht. C: Barends (3). P: Barends (2).
Final						
Oct 15	George	Pro Legoete	EP KINGS	LOST	12-16	P: Blom (2), Barends (2).
Promotion & Relegation play-off						
Oct 23	Potchefstroom	Craig Joubert	LEOPARDS	LOST	22-37	T: Raubenheimer, Hartnick, Hellmuth, Manuel. C: Barends.
Oct 29	George	Jaco Peyper	LEOPARDS	WON	32-28	T: Grimes, Grobler, Raubenheimer, Terblanche, Engelbrecht. C: Barends (2).P: Barends.

COMPULSORY FRIENDLY

July 2	Oudtshoorn	Stuart Berry	Griquas	LOST	12-50	T: McBean, Potts. C: Blom.

Team: B Joubert, B McBean, S Zweni (M Potts), B Fortuin (c), J Breytenbach, A Barends (J Blom), D Hellmuth, J Engelbrecht, C du Plessis (J de Beer), D Manuel (L Hartnick), H Grimes, L Mtyanda (P Spies), T de Kock (B Bekker), W Bennett, J Terblanche. Unused sub: C Ryneveldt.

rugby@swdeagles.co.za

APPEARANCES AND POINTS FOR SWD EAGLES IN 2010   CAREER

PLAYER	Appearances	Tries	Conversions	Penalties	Drop Goals	Points	Career Matches	Career Tries	Conversions	Penalties	Drop Goals	Points
HCH (Herzon) Amill	3	–	–	–	–	0	3	–	–	–	–	0
AR (Ambrose) Barends	18	2	28	30	1	159	72	12	89	73	2	463
RL (Raynor) Becker	1	–	–	–	–	0	1	–	–	–	–	0
B (Beyers) Bekker	7	–	–	–	–	0	7	–	–	–	–	0
WA (Wayne) Bennett	8	5	–	–	–	25	50	9	–	–	–	45
J (Jandré) Blom	21	1	15	10	–	61	33	4	26	23	–	137
RD (Ronald) Bratz	5	–	–	–	–	0	5	–	–	–	–	0
JC (Joe) Breytenbach	21	6	–	–	–	30	36	7	–	–	–	35
JF (Jandre) de Beer	14	–	–	–	–	0	14	–	–	–	–	0
T (Tiaan) de Kock	1	–	–	–	–	0	56	–	–	–	–	0
LA (Layle) Delo	0	–	–	–	–	0	0	–	–	–	–	0
T (Theunis) Dercksen	3	–	–	–	–	0	3	–	–	–	–	0
CJ (Christo) du Plessis	9	1	–	–	–	5	14	–	–	–	–	0
EA (Edwin) du Preez	0	–	–	–	–	0	4	2	–	–	–	10
M (Mzo) Dyantyi	0	–	–	–	–	0	13	–	–	–	–	0
JJ (Jacques) Engelbrecht	21	3	–	–	–	15	48	3	–	–	–	15
HO (Henk) Eksteen	7	–	–	–	–	0	7	–	–	–	–	15
CD (Charlie) Ewerts	3	1	–	–	–	5	3	1	–	–	–	5
BA (Bevin) Fortuin	22	4	–	–	–	20	122	29	7	4	2	177
H (Henry) Grimes	21	1	–	–	–	5	103	11	–	–	–	55
JH (Hans) Grobler	12	1	–	–	–	5	12	1	–	–	–	5
WJ (Wikus) Harmse	13	1	–	–	–	5	68	2	–	–	–	15
LL (Lyndon) Hartnick	13	1	–	–	–	5	13	1	–	–	–	5
JU (Dougie) Hellmuth	22	2	–	–	–	10	29	4	–	–	–	20
MG (Bobby) Joubert	19	5	–	–	–	25	50	16	–	–	–	80
B (Barry) Landman	2	–	–	–	–	0	2	–	–	–	–	0
PL (Vickus) Liebenberg	6	–	–	–	–	0	20	–	–	–	–	0
VJP (Vogan) Lourens	1	–	–	–	–	0	1	–	–	–	–	0
DBJ (Danzel) Manuel	16	2	–	–	–	10	23	3	–	–	–	15
BJH (Baldwin) McBean	21	11	–	–	–	55	47	16	–	–	–	80
L (Lubabalo) Mtyanda	16	3	–	–	–	15	31	4	–	–	–	20
MCL (Marchell) Potts	8	2	–	–	–	10	8	2	–	–	–	10
S (Shaun) Raubenheimer	20	10	–	–	–	50	28	12	–	–	–	60
DE (Deroy) Rhoode	8	–	2	1	–	7	9	–	2	1	–	7
C (Cedrick) Ryneveldt	0	–	–	–	–	0	0	–	–	–	–	0
JIA (Izak) Saayman	2	1	–	–	–	5	97	30	4	–	–	158
WS (Wentsley) Scott	5	2	–	–	–	10	5	2	–	–	–	10
P (Philip) Spies	3	–	–	–	–	0	3	–	–	–	–	0
RP (Roelof) Steyn	1	–	–	–	–	0	1	–	–	–	–	0
JK (Jaco) Terblanche	18	2	–	–	–	10	66	2	–	–	–	10
A (Anton) van der Westhuizen	20	1	–	–	–	5	41	2	–	–	–	10
JF (Jan) Volschenk	7	–	–	–	–	0	7	–	–	–	–	0
AP (Algernon) Waarts	3	–	–	–	–	0	34	–	–	–	–	0
ES (Eric) Zana	17	–	1	8	–	26	17	–	1	8	–	26
S (Sinethemba) Zweni	18	4	–	–	–	20	34	4	–	–	–	20
Penalty try	–	1	–	–	–	5	–	1	–	–	–	5
45 players	**456**	**73**	**46**	**49**	**1**	**603**	**976**	**135**	**62**	**62**	**4**	**997**

APPEARANCES AND POINTS IN VODACOM CUP 2010

	Free State	Cavaliers	Sharks XV	Elephants	Pampas XV	WP	Bulldogs	Matches	Tries	Conversions	Penalties	Drop Goals	Points
Bobby Joubert	15c	15	15	15	–	–	–	4	–	–	–	–	0
Baldwin McBean	14	14	14	14	14	14	14	7	3	–	–	–	15
Joe Breytenbach	13	11	11	11	11	12	12R	7	–	–	–	–	0
Izak Saayman	12	–	–	–	12	–	–	2	1	–	–	–	5
Charlie Ewerts	11	–	–	–	–	11	11R	3	1	–	–	–	5
Eric Zana	10	10	10	10	–	–	–	4	–	1	8	–	26
Dougie Hellmuth	9	9R	9R	9	9	9	9R	7	–	–	–	–	0
Jacques Engelbrecht	8	8	–	8	8	8	8	6	–	–	–	–	0
Shaun Raubenheimer	7	7	7	7	7	7	–	6	2	–	–	–	10
Barry Landman	6	–	–	6R	–	–	–	2	–	–	–	–	0
Henry Grimes	5	5	5	5	5	5	5	7	–	–	–	–	0
Vickus Liebenberg	4	4	4	4	4	4R	–	6	–	–	–	–	0
Jan Volschenk	3	3	3	3	3	3	3R	7	–	–	–	–	0
Jandré de Beer	2	–	x	–	2R	2R	–	3	–	–	–	–	0
Jaco Terblanche	1	1		3R	1R	3R	1	6	–	–	–	–	0
Wayne Bennett	2R	2	2	2	2	2	2	7	5	–	–	–	25
Anton van der Westhuizen	1R	1R	1	1	1	1	1R	7	–	–	–	–	0
Wikus Harmse	3R	3R	–	–	3R	–	3	4	–	–	–	–	0
Jandré Blom	9R	9	9	–	9R	9R	9	6	–	2	4	–	16
Bevin Fortuin	11R	12c	12c	12c	10c	15c	12c	7	2	–	–	–	10
Deroy Rhoode	13R	13R	x	15R	15	x	15	5	–	2	1	–	7
Christo du Plessis	x	6R	–	–	–	–	4R	2	1	–	–	–	5
Sinethemba Zweni	–	13	13	13	13	13	13	6	–	–	–	–	0
Danzel Manuel	–	6	8	–	13R	6	6	5	–	–	–	–	0
Layle Delo	–	x	–	x	–	–	x	0	–	–	–	–	0
Edwin du Preez	–	x	–	–	–	–	–	0	–	–	–	–	0
Ronald Bratz	–	–	6	6	6	6R	7	5	–	–	–	–	0
Herzon Amill	–	–	x	–	–	–	–	0	–	–	–	–	0
Theunis Dercksen	–	–	x	–	–	–	–	0	–	–	–	–	0
Algernon Waarts	–	–	6R	7R	6R	–	–	3	–	–	–	–	0
Raynor Becker	–	–	11R	–	–	–	–	1	–	–	–	–	0
Marchell Potts	–	–	–	10R	–	–	11	2	–	–	–	–	0
Mzo Dyantyi	–	–	–	x	–	–	–	0	–	–	–	–	0
Ambrose Barends	–	–	–	–	12R	10	10	3	–	4	3	–	17
Lubabalo Mtyanda	–	–	–	–	–	4	4	2	1	–	–	–	5
Vogan Lourens	–	–	–	–	–	14R	–	1	–	–	–	–	0
Penalty try	–	–	–	–	–	–	–	0	1	–	–	–	5
36 players								**143**	**17**	**9**	**16**	**0**	**151**

rugby@swdeagles.co.za

APPEARANCES AND POINTS IN ABSA CURRIE CUP 2010

	Border	Griffons	Boland	Valke	EP Kings	Border	Griffons	Pumas	Valke	EP Kings	Griffons	EP Kings	Leopards	Leopards	Matches	Tries	Conversions	Penalties	Drop Goals	Points
Joubert	15	15	15	13	15	15	15	15	15	15	15	15	15	14	14	5	–	–	–	25
McBean	14	14	14	14	14	14	14	14	14	14	14	14	14	–	13	7	–	–	–	35
Zweni	13	13	–	–	13	13	13	13	–	13	13	13	13	13	11	4	–	–	–	20
Fortuin	12c	12c	12c	12c	12c	12c	12c	12c	12c	12c	12c	12c	12c	12c	14	2	–	–	–	10
Breytenbach	11	11	13	11	11	11	11	–	11	11	11	11	11	11	13	6	–	–	–	30
Barends	10	10	10	10	10	10	10	10	10	10	10	10	10	10	14	2	24	27	1	142
Hellmuth	9	9	9	9	9R	12R	15R	11R	13R	9R	15R	9R	11R	9	14	2	–	–	–	10
Engelbrecht	8	8	8	8	8	4R	8	8	8	8	8	8	8	8	14	3	–	–	–	15
Raubenheimer	7	7	7	7	7	7	7	7	7	7	7	7	7	7	14	8	–	–	–	40
Hartnick	6	6	–	–	4R	8	6	4R	6	6	6	6	6	6	12	1	–	–	–	5
Grimes	5	5	5	5	5	5	–	5	5	5	5	5	5	5	13	1	–	–	–	5
Mtyanda	4	4	4	4	4	4	4	4	4R	4R	4R	4R	5R	x	13	2	–	–	–	10
Harmse	3	3	3	–	3	3	–	–	–	–	3	3	3	3	9	1	–	–	–	5
Grobler	2	2	2	2	2	2	2	–	2	2	–	2	2	2	12	1	–	–	–	5
van der Westhuizen	1	1	1	3	1R	3R	3	3	3	3	1	3R	3R	–	13	1	–	–	–	5
de Beer	2R	2R	x	2R	x	–	2R	2	2R	2R	2	x	2R	2R	10	–	–	–	–	0
Bekker	3R	3R	–	3R	–	–	3R	3R	–	–	1R	–	–	–	6	–	–	–	–	0
du Plessis	6R	6R	6R	4R	x	–	7R	–	–	–	–	7R	–	–	6	–	–	–	–	0
Manuel	4R	4R	6	6	6	6	5	6	–	–	–		7R	6R	10	2	–	–	–	10
Blom	9R	9R	11R	15	9	9	9	9	9	9	9	9	9	15	14	1	12	6	–	43
Zana	10R	10R	10R	10R	10R	10R	10R	10R	10R	15R	10R	x	10R	10R	13	–	–	–	–	0
Potts	14R	11R	11	14R	x	–	–	–	6R	–	–	–	–	x	5	1	–	–	–	5
Terblanche	–	–	1R	1	1	1	1	1	1	1	–	1	1	1	11	2	–	–	–	10
Scott	–	–	15R	9R	–	–	11R	13R	13	x	x	x	–	–	5	2	–	–	–	10
Spies	–	–	4R	7R	–	–	–	–	–	–	–	–	–	–	2	–	–	–	–	0
Amill	–	–	–	–	–	x	–	6R	3R	3R	x	–	–	–	3	–	–	–	–	0
Dercksen	–	–	–	–	–	6R	4R	–	8R	x	x	–	–	–	3	–	–	–	–	0
Rhoode	–	–	–	–	–	14R	–	–	–	–	–	–	12R	12R	3	–	–	–	–	0
Steyn	–	–	–	–	–	–	–	–	11	–	–	–	–	–	1	–	–	–	–	0
Eksteen	–	–	–	–	–	–	–	7R	4	4	4	4	4	4	7	–	–	–	–	0
30 players															**292**	**54**	**36**	**33**	**1**	**440**

*Totals include performance in the relegation play-offs

Shaun Raubenheimer driving the ball up during the second leg of the ABSA Promotion and Relegation match against the Leopards.

ABSA UNDER-21 CHAMPIONSHIP (7th, Section B)

Played	Won	Drawn	Lost	Points for	Points against	Tries for	Tries against	Winning %
6	1	0	5	92	219	12	31	17.00%

RESULTS Lost Griquas (h) 27-43. Lost Mpumalanga (a) 10-40. Bt Border (a) 18-10. Lost Griffons (h) 12-20. Lost Valke (h) 13-33. Lost EP (a) 12-73.

SCORERS 21 Henn-Lin Botha (6c, 3p). 16 Raynor Becker (2t, 2p). 15 Antonio Delo (3t). 5 Cedrick Ryneveldt (1c, 1p), Johan van Wyk, Reginald Kleinbooi, Stephan Engelbrecht, Anton Beswick, Arden-Lee Wesso, Enrico Treurnicht, Francois Kemp (1t each).

ABSA U19 CHAMPIONSHIP (Champions, 3rd, Section B)

Played	Won	Drawn	Lost	Points for	Points against	Tries for	Tries against	Winning %
9	7	0	2	209	188	29	23	78.00%

RESULTS Bt Griquas (h) 22-12. Bt Mpumalanga (a) 28-21. Lost Border (a) 08-16. Bt Boland (h) 34-28. Bt Valke (h) 14-12. Lost EP (a) 15-29. SEMI-FINAL Bt Mpumalanga (a) 37-29. FINAL Bt Valke (h) 27-20. PROMOTION-RELEGATION Bt Griffons (a) 24-21.

SCORERS 30 Karl-Hein Schuld (6t). 28 Gaybrin Smith (5t, 1p). 25 Justin Moos (1t, 7c, 2p), Frederick Eksteen (5t). 23 Danie Roberts (7c, 3p). 15 Charlton Afrika, Emile Temperman (3t each). 11 Gerhard de Jager (1c, 3p). 10 Charlton Adrika, Granville Jansen (2t each). 7 Jac du Preez (2c, 1p). 5 Heinrich Leslie, Carlos Da Silva (1t each).

AMATEUR CHAMPIONSHIP

SWD (5th, South Section)

Played	Won	Drawn	Lost	Points for	Points against	Tries for	Tries against	Winning %
7	2	0	5	184	271	26	39	29.00%

RESULTS Lost Boland (h) 30-56. Lost Border (a) 37-50. Lost EP (a) 08-63. Bt Griquas Rural (h) 26-15. Lost EP Rural (a) 17-36. Bt Border Rural (h) 37-07. Lost WP (h) 29-44.

rugby@swdeagles.co.za

SWD EAGLES RECORDS

MATCH RECORDS

Biggest win	102-0	vs. Transkei	1995
Biggest win (Currie Cup)	102-0	vs. Griffons	1999
Heaviest defeat	0-97	vs. British Lions	1974
Heaviest defeat (Currie Cup)	8-147	vs. Northern Transvaal	1996
Highest score	105	vs. Transkei (105-8)	1994
Highest score (Currie Cup)	102	vs. Griffons (102-0)	1999
Moist points conceded	97	vs. British Lions (0-97)	1974
Moist points conceded (Currie Cup)	147	vs. Northern Transvaal (8-147)	1996
Most tries	16	vs. Transkei (102-0)	1995
Most tries (Currie Cup)	16	vs. Griffons (102-0)	1999
Most points by a player	28	AJJ Van Straaten	1997
Most points by a player (Currie Cup)	29	CR Van As vs. Leopards	2002
Most tries by a player	4	G Cilliers vs. North Eastern Districts	1965
	4	F Amsterdam vs. Northern Natal	1992
Most tries by a player (Currie Cup)	4	MG Joubert vs. Valke	2009

SEASON RECORDS

Most team points	943	29 matches	1998
Most team points (Currie Cup)	471	14 matches	1997
Most points by a player	252	AJJ Van Straaten	1997
Most points by a player (Currie Cup)	173	CR Van As	2002
Most team tries	132	29 matches	1998
Most team tries (Currie Cup)	79	21 matches	2003
Most tries by a player	18	B Vorster	1997
	18	L Floors	2003
Most tries by a player (Currie Cup)	**14**	**L Floors**	**2003**

CAREER RECORDS

Most appearances	177	C Botha	1993-2005
Most points	638	CR Van As	2000-2004
Most points (Currie Cup)	480	CR Van As	2000-2004
Most tries	53	DB Coeries	1998-2005
Most conversions by a player	134	CR Van As	2000-2004
Most penalties by a player	105	CR Van As	2000-2004

HONOURS

Bankfin Cup	2002
ABSA Cup	2007

PROVINCIAL ROUND-UP

valke@global.co.za

VALKE RUGBY UNION

FOUNDED 1947 (as Eastern Transvaal) **GROUND** Barnard Stadium, Kempton Park
CAPACITY 7 000 **ADDRESS** CR Swart Avenue, Kempton Park
POSTAL ADDRESS PO Box 27, Brakpan 1540
TELEPHONE NUMBER 011 975 2822/2487 **EMAIL** valke@global.co.za
COLOURS Red jersey, white shorts and red socks
CURRIE CUP COACH John Williams
VODACOM CUP COACH John Williams
CAPTAIN Warren Perkins **PRESIDENT** SJ de Beer **CEO** Jurie Coetzee

Flightless Valke grounded again

PERHAPS the saddest thing about the Valke team's freefall from grace is that one doesn't have to page back very far into the history books for evidence of better days.

As recently as two seasons ago, the then-Brakpan-based union not only had Absa Currie Cup Premier Division status, but also beat Western Province at their Bosman Stadium fortress.

Without the benefits of hindsight, it's always difficult to pinpoint the exact moment – be it in rugby or in real life – when things go wrong. But it's safe to say that 3 October 2008 will be remembered as a major turning point in the history of a proud East Rand province that had largely succeeded in punching above its weight.

On that day, the Blue Bulls squeezed home 22-20 at Loftus Versfeld in the final match of the regular season – a result that condemned the former Red Devils to rugby's version of hell: promotion-relegation matches, followed by the wilderness of the First Division.

Had Piet Krause's men prevailed on that Pretoria afternoon, who knows what might have happened? But the hard truth is that, two years on, the Valke are a provincial team in name only.

The jubilation of 20 May 2006, when Krause and the likes of Louis Strydom, Clinton van Rensburg and Riaan Viljoen romped to a famous win over Natal to lift the Vodacom Cup, now seems like a distant memory.

The statistics make for frightening reading: in the three seasons from 2006 to 2008, the Valke lost 37 of their 42 Premier Division matches. They have since lost 19 of their 20 First Division games, conceding 148 tries and 1039 points (at an average of xx per match) in the process. Sadly, those figures look posi-

tively rosy when you look at 2006-2008 and wonder, as any reasonable person would, just how a team could possibly leak 1942 points?

Any hopes of a revival in fortunes in 2010 were put on ice as early as the last week in February when the side was hammered 52-17 by the Pumas. Six more defeats followed to ensure that, once again, the team's Currie Cup campaign was stillborn.

Their only victory – the first in the competition since their 38-32 win over WP on 18 July 2008 – came in last August, when they held out for a 38-37 win over the Border Bulldogs in East London.

The Valke hero on the night was their tireless eighthman Reg Muller, who weighed in with two tries while popping up everywhere in general play. Muller epitomised the team's spirit during yet another disastrous season, but sadly guts gets you only so far in professional rugby.

For a team whose defence has become more porous than a shower sponge, the Valke's final match of the season, against the self-same Bulldogs, summed up their predicament perfectly.

A diehard crowd of 1,000 traipsed down to Barnard Stadium to watch their team score seven converted tries en route to racking up 49 points – only to witness the Bulldogs score 56 in reply!

And so another season in the doldrums looms for a team on the edge of the precipice – but with no sponsors and very few quality players willing to commit to the red shirt, president SJ de Beer's prediction last year of a turnaround in 2011 may need updating.

Any hopes of a Valke revival were dashed as early as the last week of February, when they were hammered 52-17 by the Pumas.

PROVINCIAL ROUND-UP

VALKE LOG POSITIONS

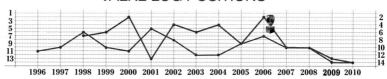

| 1996 | 1997 | 1998 | 1999 | 2000 | 2001 | 2002 | 2003 | 2004 | 2005 | 2006 | 2007 | 2008 | **2009** | 2010 |

VALKE RESULTS AND SCORERS IN 2010

Played	Won	Drawn	Lost	Points for	Points against	Tries for	Tries against	Winning %
18	1	0	17	395	936	54	138	6%

VODACOM CUP Played **7** Won **0** Lost **7** Drawn **0** Points For **116** Points Against **357** Tries For **15** Tries Against **55**

Date	Venue	Opponent	Result	Score	Scorers
Febr 26	Witbank	PUMAS	LOST	17-52	T: Claassen, De la Porte. C: Anderson (2). P: Anderson.
Mrch 6	Nigel	GOLDEN LIONS	LOST	13-34	T: Engelbrecht. C: George. P: Anderson (2).
Mrch 12	Rustenburg[1]	LEOPARDS	LOST	08-59	T: W Perkins. P: Anderson.
Mrch 19	Windhoek	WELWITCHIAS	LOST	35-66	T: Kotze (2), Anderson, George. C: George (3). P: George (3).
Mrch 27	Kempton Park	BLUE BULLS	LOST	07-50	T: Palm. C: Anderson.
April 9	Welkom	GRIFFONS	LOST	24-36	T: Rhodes, De Bruin, Gauche, Horn. C: George (2).
April 17	Kempton Park	GRIQUAS	LOST	12-60	T: Hendricks (2). C: George.

[1]Royal Bafokeng Stadium, Phokeng

ABSA CURRIE CUP Played **10** Won **1** Lost **9** Drawn **0** Points For **276** Points Against **499** Tries For **39** Tries Against **71**

Date	Venue	Opponent	Result	Score	Scorers
July 17	Welkom	GRIFFONS	LOST	08-43	T: Gauche. P: Botha.
July 24	Kempton Park	CAVALIERS	LOST	10-53	T: Cronje. C: George. P: Botha.
Aug 7	Port Elizabeth	EP KINGS	LOST	03-38	P: Botha.
Aug 14	Kempton Park	EAGLES	LOST	47-55	T: Cronje (3), Botha, Van Lill, Van der Walt, Booysen. C: Horn (2), Thomsen. P: Horn (2).
Aug 20	East London	BULLDOGS	WON	38-37	T: Muller (2), Hendricks, Cronje, Fortuin, Perkins. C: Horn (3), Naude.
Aug 28	Kempton Park	GRIFFONS	LOST	30-69	T: Hendricks (2), Snyman, Van der Walt. C: Thomsen (2). P: George (2)
Sept 3	Wellington	CAVALIERS	LOST	21-41	T: Fortuin (2), Gauche. C: Thomsen (2), Naude.
Sept 17	Kempton Park	EP KINGS	LOST	35-50	T: Hendricks, Snyman, Gauche, Van der Walt, Hefer. C: Thomsen (2). P: Thomsen (2).
Sept 24	George	EAGLES	LOST	35-57	T: Botha (2), Hendricks, Cronje, Klonaridis. C: Thomsen (4), Naude.
Oct 2	Kempton Park	BULLDOGS	LOST	49-56	T: Cronje (3), Hendricks (2), Thomsen, Snyman. C: Thomsen (5), Naude (2).

COMPULSORY FRIENDLY

June 25	Nigel	Sharks Inv XV	LOST	03-80	P: Naude.

Valke: Kyle Hendriks (Chrysander Botha), Coert Cronjé, Ernie Kruger, Clinton Kayser (Carel van Lill), Theo Rhodes (Llewellyn Winkler), Japie Naudé , Jaco Snyman (Willie Odendaal), Marco Kotzé, Reg Muller, Warren Perkins (c), Johan de Bruin, Eddie Gauche (Chris Ehlers), Thulani Ngidi (Jacques George), Shone van der Walt (BB Hefer), Sean Johnson.

valke@global.co.za

APPEARANCES AND POINTS FOR VALKE IN 2010 — CAREER

PLAYER	Appearances	Tries	Conversions	Penalties	Drop Goals	Points	Career Matches	Career Tries	Conversions	Penalties	Drop Goals	Points
D (Deon) Anderson	7	1	3	4	–	23	7	1	3	4	–	23
CA (Chrysander) Botha	11	3	–	3	–	24	11	3	–	3	–	24
YMT (Yves) Bashiya	2	–	–	–	–	0	14	2	–	–	–	10
T (Theo) Bekker	9	–	–	–	–	0	15	1	–	–	–	5
F (Franco) Booysen	7	1	–	–	–	5	21	4	–	–	–	20
RK (Rowan) Campher	3	–	–	–	–	0	3	–	–	–	–	0
N (Nico) Claassen	5	1	–	–	–	5	5	1	–	–	–	5
J (Jacques) Coetzee	1	–	–	–	–	0	14	1	–	–	–	5
CF (Coert) Cronje	11	9	–	–	–	45	11	9	–	–	–	45
JM (Johan) de Bruin	13	1	–	–	–	5	25	2	–	–	–	10
DC (Dieter) de la Port	6	1	–	–	–	5	10	2	–	–	–	10
V (Vernon) du Preez	2	–	–	–	–	0	2	–	–	–	–	0
CE (Chris) Ehlers	13	–	–	–	–	0	13	–	–	–	–	0
NJE (Nico) Engelbrecht	10	1	–	–	–	5	10	1	–	–	–	5
B (Bradley) Fortuin	9	3	–	–	–	15	14	3	–	–	–	15
E (Eddie) Gauche	18	4	–	–	–	20	18	4	–	–	–	20
JN (Jacques) George	17	1	8	5	–	36	26	1	8	5	–	36
WR (Wayne) Havenga	3	–	–	–	–	0	3	–	–	–	–	0
AC (BB) Hefer	16	1	–	–	–	5	26	2	–	–	–	10
K (Kyle) Hendricks	13	9	–	–	–	45	15	9	–	–	–	45
RS (Ryno) Hendrikz	3	–	–	–	–	0	7	–	–	–	–	0
G (Gido) Horn	8	1	5	2	–	21	17	2	11	5	–	47
M (Morne) Hyman	2	–	–	–	–	0	2	–	–	–	–	0
S (Sean) Johnson	13	–	–	–	–	0	16	–	–	–	–	0
C (Clinton) Kayser	9	–	–	–	–	0	16	–	–	–	–	0
AE (Andonis) Klonaridis	9	1	–	–	–	5	12	3	–	–	–	15
M (Marco) Kotze	9	2	–	–	–	10	9	2	–	–	–	10
GD (Gerhard) Kotzee	5	–	–	–	–	0	12	–	–	–	–	0
JE (Ernie) Kruger	6	–	–	–	–	0	26	12	–	–	–	60
AG (Alvandre) Maart	3	–	–	–	–	0	12	1	–	–	–	5
R-H (Reg) Muller	12	2	–	–	–	10	40	13	–	–	–	65
JJ (Japie) Naude	7	–	5	1	–	13	7	–	5	1	–	13
TS (Thulani) Ngidi	11	–	–	–	–	0	11	–	–	–	–	0
WA (Willie) Odendaal	9	–	–	–	–	0	9	–	–	–	–	0
J (Juan) Palm	2	1	–	–	–	5	2	1	–	–	–	5
G (George) Perkins	2	–	–	–	–	0	6	–	–	–	–	0
W (Warren) Perkins	17	2	–	–	–	10	35	3	–	–	–	15
JH (Herman) Rens	1	–	–	–	–	0	2	–	–	–	–	0
TM (Theo) Rhodes	11	1	–	–	–	5	21	2	–	–	–	10
JP (Jaco) Snyman	9	3	–	–	–	15	12	3	–	–	–	15
JJ (Jaco) Swart	3	–	–	–	–	0	3	–	–	–	–	0
M (Martin) Thomsen	6	1	16	2	–	43	8	2	20	2	–	56
WJ (Willy) van den Berg	4	–	–	–	–	0	4	–	–	–	–	0
LJ (Johan) van der Merwe	2	–	–	–	–	0	2	–	–	–	–	0
S (Shone) van der Walt	15	3	–	–	–	15	24	3	–	–	–	15
CP (Carel) van Lill	7	1	–	–	–	5	7	1	–	–	–	5
JJ (Johan) van Rooyen	7	–	–	–	–	0	7	–	–	–	–	0
CJ (Chris) van Tonder	2	–	–	–	–	0	2	–	–	–	–	0
G (Grant) Victor	2	–	–	–	–	0	3	–	–	–	–	0
LP (Llewellyn) Winkler	1	–	–	–	–	0	1	–	–	–	–	0
DN (Duncan) Witbooi	5	–	–	–	–	0	5	–	–	–	–	0
CW (Christopher) Yearsley	9	–	–	–	–	0	9	–	–	–	–	0
52 players	**387**	**54**	**37**	**17**	**0**	**395**	**612**	**94**	**47**	**20**	**0**	**624**

APPEARANCES AND POINTS IN VODACOM CUP 2010

	Pumas	Golden Lions	Leopards	Welwitchias	Blue Bulls	Griffons	Griquas	Matches	Tries	Conversions	Penalties	Drop Goals	Points
Dieter de la Porte	15	15	15	15	15	–	11R	6	1	–	–	–	5
Kyle Hendricks	14	–	–	–	11	15	15	4	2	–	–	–	10
Duncan Witbooi	13	13	12	12	12	–	–	5	–	–	–	–	0
George Perkins	12	12	–	–	–	–	–	2	–	–	–	–	0
Nico Claasen	11	11	11	11	–	6	–	5	1	–	–	–	5
Deon Anderson	10	10	10	10	12R	10	10R	7	1	3	4	–	23
Johan van Rooyen	9	9	9	13R	9R	9R	9	7	–	–	–	–	0
Reg Muller	8	8	8	8	–	8	8	6	–	–	–	–	0
Johan de Bruin	7	5	5	5	8c	5	5	7	1	–	–	–	5
Warren Perkins	6c	7c	6c	6c	–	7c	7c	6	1	–	–	–	5
Chris Ehlers	5	5R	5R	5R	5	5R	5R	7	–	–	–	–	0
Eddie Gauche	4	4	4	4	4	4	4	7	1	–	–	–	5
Sean Johnson	3	3	–	–	–	3R	3R	4	–	–	–	–	0
BB Hefer	2	2	2	2	2	x	–	5	–	–	–	–	0
Jacques George	1	1	1	1	1	1	1	7	1	7	3	–	28
Morne Hyman	2R	x	–	–	16R	–	–	2	–	–	–	–	0
Jacques Coetzee	1R	–	–	–	–	–	–	1	–	–	–	–	0
Marco Kotze	5R	6	7	7	7	–	8R	6	2	–	–	–	10
Theo Bekker	6R	8R	–	–	–	7R	6	4	–	–	–	–	0
Johan van der Merwe	11R	9R	–	–	–	–	–	2	–	–	–	–	0
Chris van Tonder	14R	–	10R	–	–	–	–	2	–	–	–	–	0
Rowan Campher	13R	10R	14	–	–	–	–	3	–	–	–	–	0
Nico Engelbrecht	–	3R	3	3	3	3	3	6	1	–	–	–	5
Theo Rhodes	–	14	13	14	14	14	14	6	1	–	–	–	5
Juan Palm	–	x	7R	x	6R	–	–	2	1	–	–	–	5
Shone van der Walt	–	–	2R	2R	1R	2	2	5	–	–	–	–	0
Grant Victor	–	–	3R	3R	–	–	–	2	–	–	–	–	0
Willy van den Berg	–	–	13R	9R	9	9	–	4	–	–	–	–	0
GD Kotzee	–	–	14R	13	13	11	11	5	–	–	–	–	0
Ryno Hendrikz	–	–	–	9	13R	–	9R	3	–	–	–	–	0
Clinton Kayser	–	–	–	12R	10	12	12	4	–	–	–	–	0
Herman Rens	–	–	–	–	6	–	–	1	–	–	–	–	0
Wayne Havenga	–	–	–	–	7R	6R	7R	3	–	–	–	–	0
Gido Horn	–	–	–	–	–	10R	10	2	1	–	–	–	5
Carel van Lill	–	–	–	–	–	13	13	2	–	–	–	–	0
35 Players								**150**	**15**	**10**	**7**	**0**	**116**

valke@global.co.za

APPEARANCES AND POINTS IN ABSA CURRIE CUP 2010

	Griffons	Cavaliers	EP Kings	Eagles	Bulldogs	Griffons	Cavaliers	EP Kings	Eagles	Bulldogs	Matches	Tries	Conversions	Penalties	Drop Goals	Points
Chrysander Botha	15	15	15	15	15R	11R	15	15	15	15	10	3	–	3	–	24
Theo Rhodes	14	11	–	–	–	–	11	–	–	12R	4	–	–	–	–	–
Ernie Kruger	13	14	14	–	–	–	–	15R	11	–	5	–	–	–	–	–
Andonis Klonaridis	12	12	12	14	14	14	11R	–	11R	11	9	1	–	–	–	5
Coert Cronje	11	13	13	13	13	13	13	13	13	13	10	9	–	–	–	45
Gido Horn	10	10R	12R	10R	10	10R	–	–	–	–	6	–	5	2	–	16
Willie Odendaal	9	9	x	12R	x	9R	14R	14	9R	R 9	8	–	–	–	–	–
Reg Muller	8	6R	–	8	8	8	–	–	–	–	5	2	–	–	–	10
Bradley Fortuin	7	7	7	7	7	–	7	7	7	7	9	3	–	–	–	15
Warren Perkins	6c	6c	6c	6c	6c	6c	8c	8c	8c	8c	10	1	–	–	–	5
Bovril de Bruin	5	4R	8R	5	5	–	–	–	–	–	5	–	–	–	–	–
Eddie Gauche	4	5	5	4	4	5	5	5	5	5	10	3	–	–	–	15
Thulani Ngidi	3	3	3	3	3	3	3	3R	3R	3R	10	–	–	–	–	–
Shone van der Walt	2	2	2	2R	–	2R	2	2	2	2	9	3	–	–	–	15
Jacques George	1	1	1	1R	1R	1	1	1	1	–	9	–	1	2	–	8
BB Hefer	2R	2R	2R	2	2	2	1R	2R	2R	1R	10	1	–	–	–	5
Sean Johnson	1R	3R	3R	1	1	8R	–	1R	–	1	8	–	–	–	–	–
Chris Ehlers	5R	–	4R	4R	8R	7R	–	–	–	–	5	–	–	–	–	–
Christopher Yearsley	6R	4	4	–	5R	4	4	4	4	5R	9	–	–	–	–	–
Alvandre Maart	9R	11R	–	–	–	–	–	9R	–	–	3	–	–	–	–	–
Japie Naude	10R	–	–	–	10R	–	10R	11R	10R	10R	6	–	5	–	–	10
Clinton Kayser	x	10	10	–	–	–	–	–	12R	12	4	–	–	–	–	–
Marco Kotze	–	8	8	–	–	–	–	–	–	–	2	–	–	–	–	–
Carel van Lill	–	12R	–	12	11	11	–	–	–	–	4	1	–	–	–	5
Kyle Hendricks	–	–	11	11	15	15	14	11	14	14	8	7	–	–	–	35
Haas Snyman	–	–	9	9	9	9	9	9	9	9	8	3	–	–	–	15
Franco Booysen	–	–	10R	15R	12	12	12	12	12	–	7	1	–	–	–	5
Martin Thomsen	–	–	–	10	–	10	10	10	10	10	6	1	16	2	–	43
Theo Bekker	–	–	–	6R	–	–	6	6	6	6	5	–	–	–	–	–
Vernon du Preez	–	–	–	–	x	3R	2R	–	–	–	2	–	–	–	–	–
Yves Bashiya	–	–	–	–	–	7	–	–	–	7R	2	–	–	–	–	–
Nico Engelbrecht	–	–	–	–	–	–	3R	3	3	3	4	–	–	–	–	–
Jaco Swart	–	–	–	–	–	–	4R	4R	x	4	3	–	–	–	–	–
33 Players											**215**	**39**	**27**	**9**	**0**	**276**

PROVINCIAL ROUND-UP

Bradley Fortuin during the Absa First Division match between Valke and Border in Brakpan.

ABSA UNDER-21 CHAMPIONSHIP (Champions, 3rd, Section B)

Played	Won	Drawn	Lost	Points for	Points against	Tries for	Tries against	Winning %
8	5	1	2	338	204	42	28	69%

RESULTS: Drew Griffons (h) 25-25. Bt Griquas (a) 51-26. Lost Pumas (a) 35-44. Lost EP (h) 22-26. Bt SWD (a) 33-13. Bt Border (h) 83-12. SEMI FINAL Bt Griffons (a) 36-22. FINAL Bt EP (a) 53-36.

SCORERS: 66 Charl Nieuwenhuis (9c,14p,2d); 60 Dillan Laubscher (18c,8p); 52 Roland Syphus (10t,1c); 45 Michael Nienaber (9t); 10 Bruce Miller, Johan Nel, Johannes Radebe, Paseka Moloi, Anton van Deventer, Ruan Coetzee (2t each); 5 Jurgens Lambrecht, Bertus van der Merwe, Felix Gondo, Frederick Kalp, Willem Meyer, Gerhard Venter, Johnny van Niekerk, Franco Marais, Hannes Ludik, Pieter Lubbe, Sihle Mtwa (1t each).

ABSA U19 CHAMPIONSHIP (Runner-up, 4th, Section B)

Played	Won	Drawn	Lost	Points for	Points against	Tries for	Tries against	Winning %
8	2	2	4	212	200	31	27	38%

RESULTS: Bt Boland (h) 29-24. Drew Griquas (a) 15-15. Lost Pumas (a) 13-26. Lost EP (h) 34-37. Lost SWD (a) 12-14. Bt Border (h) 53-21. SEMI FINAL Drew EP (a) 36-36. FINAL Lost SWD (a) 20-27.

SCORERS: 49 Arno Poley (1t,13c,6p); 38 Anrich Richter (5t,5c,1p); 30 Morne Erasmus, Johan Greyling (6t each); 15 Jacques Alberts (3t); 10 Jean-Pierre Bezuidenhout, Tshepo Manaka, Marno Kotzee (2t each); 5 Daniel Jordaan, Thato Marobeki, Wikus Coetzer, Duan Pekeur (1t each).

AMATEUR CHAMPIONSHIP
Valke (Runner-up, 1st, North Section)

Played	Won	Drawn	Lost	Points for	Points against	Tries for	Tries against	Winning %
7	5	0	2	264	183	36	24	71%

RESULTS: Bt Leopards (a) 32-27. Bt Lions (h) 41-36. Bt Pumas Rural (a) 38-12. Bt Blue Bulls (h) 56-34. Bt Pumas (a) 47-9. Lost Limpopo (h) 24-26. FINAL Lost WP (h) 26-39.

AMATEUR CHAMPIONSHIP
Valke Rural (7th, Central Section)

Played	Won	Drawn	Lost	Points for	Points against	Tries for	Tries against	Winning %
6	1	0	5	120	271	17	42	

RESULTS: Lost Griquas (a) 19-33. Bt Griffons (h) 25-21. Lost Griffons Rural (a) 22-62. Lost KZN Rural (h) 20-39. Lost Free State (h) 20-62. Lost Free State Rural (a) 14-54. *

VALKE RECORDS

MATCH RECORDS

Biggest win	109-0	vs. Vagabonds	1998
Biggest Currie Cup win	65-15	vs. North West	1999
Heaviest defeat	3-151	vs. Western Province	1995
Heaviest Currie Cup defeat	14-95	vs. Pumas	2009
Highest score	109	vs. Vagabonds (109-0)	1998
Most points conceded	151	vs. Western Province (3-151)	1995
Most points conceded (CC)	95	vs. Pumas (14-95)	2009
Most tries	17	vs. Vagabonds	1998
Most Currie Cup tries	11	vs. Griquas	2001
	11	vs. Griffons	2003
Most points by a player	33	A de Kock vs. Eastern Orange Free State	1994
	33	A de Kock vs. Namibia	1995
Most Currie Cup points by a player	27	G Peens vs. Border	1997
Most tries by a player	4	C van Zyl vs. North West Cape	1980
	4	P Hiten vs. Curda	1986
	4	D Nortje vs. Eastern Orange Free State	1989
	4	W Geyer vs. Northern Free State	1998
	4	W Geyer vs. Blue Bulls	1998
	4	J Houtsamer vs. Mighty Elephants	2001
	4	LD Lubbe vs. Griffons	2003
	4	G Mbangeni vs. Leopards	2004

SEASON RECORDS

Most team points	884	35 matches	1998
Most Currie Cup points by team	381	13 matches	1998
Most points by a player	277	J Viljoen	1996
Most Currie Cup points by a player	**158**	**Louis Strydom**	**2005**
Most team tries	118	35 matches	1998
Most Currie Cup tries by team	50	10 matches	2001
Most tries by a player	22	W Geyer	1998
Most Currie Cup tries by a player	10	LD Lubbe	1989
	10	E Botha	2001

CAREER RECORDS

Most appearances	158	E Rossouw 1997-2004
Most points	732	H Labuschagne
Most tries	55	L Lubbe

HONOURS

Vodacom Cup	2006

BY JON CARDINELLI,
SA Rugby Magazine

WESTERN PROVINCE RUGBY UNION

FOUNDED 1883 **GROUND** Newlands **CAPACITY** 49 000
ADDRESS 11 Boundary Road, Newlands **POSTAL ADDRESS** PO Box 66, Newlands 7725
TELEPHONE NUMBER 021 659 4500 **WEBSITE** www.wprugby.com
COLOURS Royal blue & white hoops, black shorts & socks
CURRIE CUP COACH Allister Coetzee
VODACOM CUP COACH Jerome Paarwater
CAPTAIN Schalk Burger **PRESIDENT** Tobie Titus
COMPANY MD Rob Wagner **UNION CEO** Theuns Roodman

Province's long wait continues

I N 2010, Vodacom Western Province lived up to their reputation. At times they played an attacking brand that was innovative and inspired, but there was to be no climax to their domestic journey. South Africa's beautiful letdowns were undone by inconsistency in the league phase, which robbed them of a magnificent opportunity to stage a home final.

Province began their campaign strongly, winning six games in succession even though eight key players were on Springbok duty. Fullback Joe Pietersen had also decided to further his career at Bayonne in France, while flyhalf Peter Grant opted for a six-month stint in Japan with the Kobelco Steelers.

Nevertheless, WP's second-stringers finished the first round at the top of the table. It was this early success that allowed Province to qualify for the play-offs, as the second half of the campaign was a comparative disappointment. They lost to the Cheetahs, Lions and Blue Bulls, and going into the final league game against the Sharks, they were in danger of relinquishing an opportunity to host a semi-final.

Injuries played their part in WP's dip in form. They lost two key front-row components when loosehead prop Wicus Blaauw and hooker Tiaan Liebenberg suffered season-ending injuries. Andries Bekker's back ailment precluded the Bok lock from domestic rugby, while Jaque Fourie's provincial debut ended in disappointment when he was ruled out after the final league match. While WP had an able centre replacement in Juan de Jongh, the lineout suffered without Liebenberg and Bekker.

It was up to the domestic heroes to guarantee Province's progression. No 8 Duane Vermeulen (right) was named the WP players' player of the year for his hard-nosed performances. His ball-carrying prowess and brutal tackling style contributed to WP's reputation as a fearsome defensive unit (they topped the defensive stats with just 28 tries conceded in 14 league games), and it surprised a lot of people when he was overlooked for Springbok selection on the Grand Slam tour.

Playing his last season for WP before joining Italian club Treviso, flyhalf Willem de Waal contributed 220 points to the Cape union's cause. 'Die Generaal' was justifiably criticised for his attacking and defensive limitations, but his coaches argued that every team needs a reliable kicker. De Waal's accurate goal-kicking in the final league match against the Sharks ensured WP banked a home play-off.

After signing a new deal with the union, Jean de Villiers showed how a season with Irish giants Munster had improved his skills. Gio Aplon and De Jongh returned from the Boks with plenty of confidence, and consistently delivered linebreaking and scoring performances. WP smashed the Cheetahs 31-7 in the semi-final, and many felt that the Bok-laden backline would be the difference in the final, against the Sharks in Durban.

But Province were outmuscled at the collisions and outplayed tactically, slipping behind 20-3 in the first 15 minutes. They underperformed in the final, but if not for their lacklustre showing in the second round that final might have been staged at Newlands, a venue where the Stormers and WP combined conceded just two defeats in 2010.

There was much to suggest that this season was an improvement, but ultimately it was another year that could have been monumental rather than memorable.

WESTERN PROVINCE LOG POSITIONS

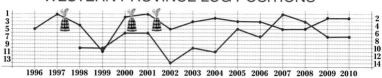

1996 1997 1998 1999 2000 2001 2002 2003 2004 2005 2006 2007 2008 2009 2010

WESTERN PROVINCE RESULTS AND SCORERS IN 2010

Played	Won	Drawn	Lost	Points for	Points against	Tries for	Tries against
25	17	0	8	767	481	85	49

VODACOM CUP Played **8** Won **5** Drawn **0** Lost **3** Points For **177** Points Against **159** Tries For **18** Tries Against **16** Winning Percentage **63%**

Date	Venue	Referee	Opponent	Result	Score	Scorers
Feb 27	Bredasdorp	Archie Sehlako	CAVALIERS	LOST	28-37	T: Fortuin, Marais, Hartzenberg. C: De Waal (2). P: De Waal (3)
Mar 06	Cape Town	Jaco Peyper	SHARKS XV	WON	26-23	T: Visser, Hartzenberg. C: De Waal (2). P: De Waal (4).
Mar 13	Port Elizabeth	Francois Veldsman	EP	WON	28-23	T: Des Fountain, De Waal, Hartzenberg. C: De Waal (2). P: De Waal (3)
Mar 20	Cape Town	Pro Legoete	BORDER	WON	29-00	T: Welsh (2), Shimange, Sadie, Van der Walt. C: Hoffmann, Jinka.
Mar 27	Cape Town¹	Pro Legoete	PAMPAS XV	WON	19-16	T: Sadie. C: Hoffmann. P: Hoffman (2), Visser (2).
April 10	Parow	Sandile Mayende	SWD EAGLES	WON	29-23	T: Jinka, Des Fountain, Myburgh, Hartzenberg. C: Hoffmann (2), Visser. P: Hoffmann.
April 17	Petrusburg	Luke Burger	FREE STATE	LOST	12-20	P: Hoffmann (3). DG: Visser.
Quarter-final						
April 24	Pretoria²	Tiaan Jonker	BLUE BULLS	LOST	06-17	P: Hoffmann (2).

¹ Away game for WP. Home game for the Pampas XV, ² Loftus Versfeld B-Field

CURRIE CUP Played **16** Won **11** Drawn **0** Lost **5** Points For **561** Points Against **317** Tries For **63** Tries Against **32** Winning Percentage **69%**

Date	Venue	Referee	Opponent	Result	Score	Scorers
July 10	Bloemfontein	Marius Jonker	FREE STATE	WON	25-11	T: Fondse. C: De Waal. P: De Waal (6).
July 17	Cape Town	Jaco Peyper	GOLDEN LIONS	WON	32-00	T: Jantjes, P Louw, Myburgh. C: De Waal. P: De Waal (5).
July 23	Potchefstroom	Sandile Mayende	LEOPARDS	WON	42-23	T: Harris, Hoffmann, Welsh, Bosch, P Louw, Myburgh. C: De Waal (3). P: De Waal (2).
July 30	Cape Town	Pro Legoete	PUMAS	WON	54-13	T: Aplon (2), P Louw (2), Van Zyl, Engelbrecht, Cronje. C: De Waal (3), Cronje (2). P: De Waal (3)
Aug 07	Kimberley	Sandile Mayende	GRIQUAS	WON	50-03	T: Jantjes, Aplon, De Jongh, P Louw, D Fourie, Cronje. C: De Waal (3), Cronje. P: De Waal (4).
Aug 14	Cape Town	Marius Jonker	BLUE BULLS	WON	15-12	P: De Waal (5)
Aug 21	Durban	Lourens van der Merwe	SHARKS	LOST	16-27	T: Koster. C: Cronje. P: De Waal (3).
Aug 27	Cape Town	Pro Legoete	FREE STATE	LOST	24-29	T: Fondse, Vermeulen, Aplon. C: De Waal (3). P: De Waal.
Sep 03	Johannesburg	Mark Lawrence	GOLDEN LIONS	LOST	28-46	T: Hoffmann, Vermeulen, Engelbrecht. C: De Waal (2). P: De Waal (3).
Sep 11	Cape Town	Sandile Mayende	LEOPARDS	WON	59-17	T: F Louw (2), Van Zyl, Harris, D Fourie, Duvenage, De Jongh, Koster, Hartzenberg. C: Cronje (4), De Waal (3).
Sep 17	Nelspruit	Andrew Lees	PUMAS	WON	62-10	T: F Louw (2), Aplon (2), De Villiers, Engelbrecht, De Jongh, Bosch. C: De Waal (5), Van Aswegen (3). P: De Waal (2).
Sep 24	Cape Town	Marius Jonker	GRIQUAS	WON	48-32	T: Engelbrecht (3), Fondse, D Fourie, Vermeulen, De Villiers. C: De Waal (4), Van Aswegen. P: De Waal.
Oct 02	Pretoria	Craig Joubert	BLUE BULLS	LOST	32-36	T: Aplon, De Jongh. C: De Waal (2). P: De Waal (6).
Oct 09	Cape Town	Mark Lawrence	SHARKS	WON	33-21	T: Vermeulen, Aplon, De Villiers. C: De Waal (2), Cronje. P: De Waal (4).
Semi-final						
Oct 16	Cape Town	Mark Lawrence	FREE STATE	WON	31-07	T: Habana, F Louw, Aplon. C: De Waal (2). P: De Waal (4).
Final						
Oct 30	Durban	Craig Joubert	SHARKS	LOST	10-30	T: Burger. C: De Waal. P: De Waal.

COMPULSORY FRIENDLY

Date	Venue	Referee	Opponent	Result	Score	Scorers
July 2	Welkom	Lourens van der Merwe	GRIFFONS	WON	29-05	T: P Louw (3), Fondse. C: De Waal (3). P: De Waal.

Team: C Jantjes, F Juries, T Whitehead, P Bosch, M Brache, W de Waal (L Cronje), D Duvenage (C Hoffmann), D Vermeulen (P Myburgh), R Elstadt, P Louw, A van Zyl (c), A Fondse (M Muller), B Harris (W Blaauw), T Liebenberg (D Fourie), JD Moller (JC Kritzinger).

APPEARANCES AND POINTS FOR WP IN 2010   CAREER

PLAYER	Appearances	Tries	Conversions	Penalties	Drop Goals	Points	Career Matches	Career Tries	Conversions	Penalties	Drop Goals	Points
GG (Gio) Aplon	10	9	–	–	–	45	70	27	2	–	–	139
L (Liam) Bax	1	–	–	–	–	0	5	1	–	–	–	5
JL (Wicus) Blaauw	10	–	–	–	–	0	41	–	–	–	–	0
PW (Paul) Bosch	18	2	–	–	–	10	28	3	–	–	–	15
M (Marcel) Brache	2	–	–	–	–	0	2	–	–	–	–	0
JD (Jody) Burch	6	–	–	–	–	0	13	4	–	–	–	20
SWP (Schalk) Burger	3	1	–	–	–	5	30	7	–	–	–	35
M (Marvin) Christians	4	–	–	–	–	0	4	–	–	–	–	0
RJ (Ruan) Combrink	1	–	–	–	–	0	1	–	–	–	–	0
L (Lionel) Cronje	14	2	9	–	–	28	14	2	9	–	–	28
JL (Juan) de Jongh	9	4	–	–	–	20	25	9	–	–	–	45
D (Dylan) des Fountain	8	2	–	–	–	10	24	4	–	–	–	20
MV (Mike) de Neuilly-Rice	4	–	–	–	–	0	16	1	–	–	–	5
J (Jean) de Villiers	7	3	–	–	–	15	44	28	–	–	–	140
W (Willem) de Waal	20	1	44	61	–	276	32	2	62	99	1	434
T (Tertius) Daniller	1	–	–	–	–	0	1	–	–	–	–	0
DO (Dewaldt) Duvenage	16	1	–	–	–	5	37	1	–	–	–	5
R (Rynhardt) Elstadt	13		–	–	–	0	13	–	–	–	–	0
JJ (JJ) Engelbrecht	9	6	–	–	–	30	13	6	–	–	–	30
AR (Adriaan) Fondse	19	4	–	–	–	20	34	6	–	–	–	30
B (Bradley) Fortuin	3	1	–	–	–	5	3	1	–	–	–	5
DA (Deon) Fourie	16	3	–	–	–	15	55	9	–	–	–	45
J (Jaque) Fourie	1	–	–	–	–	0	1	–	–	–	–	0
S (Stephan) Greeff	4	–	–	–	–	0	4	–	–	–	–	0
BG (Bryan) Habana	3	1	–	–	–	5	3	1	–	–	–	5
J (Brok) Harris	17	2	–	–	–	10	68	10	–	–	–	50
Y (Yaasir) Hartzenberg	11	5	–	–	–	25	17	5	–	–	–	25
CF (Conrad) Hoffmann	21	2	4	8		42	44	7	4	8	–	67
CA (Conrad) Jantjes	17	2	–	–	–	10	36	4	1	–	–	22
ER (Ricky) Januarie	3	–	–	–	–	0	11	3	–	–	–	15
D (Dustin) Jinka	5	1	1	–	–	7	5	1	1	–	–	7
FM (Fabian) Juries	9	–	–	–	–	0	9	–	–	–	–	0
PH (Hugo) Kloppers	4	–	–	–	–	0	4	–	–	–	–	0
RN (Nick) Koster	11	2	–	–	–	10	18	4	–	–	–	20
JC (JC) Kritzinger	12	–	–	–	–	0	29	1	–	–	–	5
CR (Tiaan) Liebenberg	9	–	–	–	–	0	40	2	–	–	–	10
L-FP (Francois) Louw	10	5	–	–	–	25	65	13	–	–	–	65
PJ (Pieter) Louw	12	8	–	–	–	40	64	17	–	–	–	70
C (Conrad) Marais	1	1	–	–	–	5	1	1	–	–	–	5
JD (JD) Moller	19	–	–	–	–	0	80	3	–	–	–	15
MD (Martin) Muller	12	–	–	–	–	0	22	1	–	–	–	5
PA (Pieter) Myburgh	13	3	–	–	–	15	42	6	–	–	–	30
B (Buhle) Mxunyelwa	8	–	–	–	–	0	8	–	–	–	–	0
MR (Morgan) Newman	7	–	–	–	–	0	59	11	11	5	–	92
DJG (Danie) Poolman	3	–	–	–	–	0	3	–	–	–	–	0
DB (Denzel) Riddles	2	–	–	–	–	0	6	–	–	–	–	0
J (Johann) Sadie	5	2	–	–	–	10	5	2	–	–	–	10
L (Louis) Schreuder	4	–	–	–	–	0	4	–	–	–	–	0
HM (Hanyani) Shimange	11	1	–	–	–	5	41	2	–	–	–	10
J-P (Jean-Pierre) Smith	5	–	–	–	–	0	5	–	–	–	–	0
R-H (Ruan) Smith	1	–	–	–	–	0	1	–	–	–	–	0
M de K (De Kock) Steenkamp	12	–	–	–	–	0	24	–	–	–	–	0
S (Sidney) Tobias	2	–	–	–	–	0	2	–	–	–	–	0
GJ (Gary) van Aswegen	2	–	4	–	–	8	2	–	4	–	–	8
PW (Wimpie) van der Walt	6	1	–	–	–	5	5	1	–	–	–	5
A (Anton) van Zyl	17	2	–	–	–	10	34	2	–	–	–	10
DJ (Duane) Vermeulen	17	4	–	–	–	20	30	6	–	–	–	30
C-T (Callie) Visagie	9	–	–	–	–	0	9	–	–	–	–	0
PJ (Jurgen) Visser	7	1	1	2	1	16	8	1	9	4	1	38
A (Ashley) Wells	2	–	–	–	–	0	2	–	–	–	–	0
BF (Frikkie) Welsh	13	3	–	–	–	15	26	6	–	–	–	30
TJ (Tim) Whitehead	10	–	–	–	–	0	10	–	–	–	–	0
61 players	**531**	**85**	**63**	**71**	**1**	**767**	**1350**	**275**	**137**	**138**	**7**	**2084**

PROVINCIAL ROUND-UP

APPEARANCES AND POINTS IN VODACOM CUP 2010

	Cavaliers	Sharks XV	Elephants	Bulldogs	Pampas XV	SWD Eagles	Free State	Blue Bulls	Matches	Tries	Conversions	Penalties	Drop Goals	Points
Jurgen Visser	15	15	15	–	15	15	15	15	7	1	1	2	1	16
Conrad Marais	14	–	–	–	–	–	–	–	1	1	–	–	–	5
Frikkie Welsh	13	13c	13	13	–	–	–	–	4	2	–	–	–	10
Dylan des Fountain	12	14	14	11	11	13	13	13	8	2	–	–	–	10
Fabian Juries	11	11	11	15	–	–	–	–	4	–	–	–	–	0
Willem de Waal	10	10	10	–	–	–	–	–	3	1	6	10	–	47
Conrad Hoffmann	9	9	9	10	10	9	9	9	8	–	4	8	–	32
Jody Burch	8	8R	–	8	x	8	8	8R	6	–	–	–	–	0
Yaasir Hartenberg	7	7	7	4R	8	7	7	7	8	4	–	–	–	20
Wimpie van der Walt	6	–	6R	6R	4R	–	7R	6	6	1	–	–	–	5
Martin Muller	5	5	–	5	5	5	5	5	7	–	–	–	–	0
Rynhardt Elstadt	4	4	4	7	7	–	4	4	7	–	–	–	–	0
JD Moller	3	3	1	1	–	–	–	–	4	–	–	–	–	0
Hanyani Shimange	2c	–	2c	2c	2c	2c	2c	2c	7	1	–	–	–	5
Denzel Riddles	1	1	–	–	–	–	–	–	2	–	–	–	–	0
Sidney Tobias	2R	3R	–	–	–	–	–	–	2	–	–	–	–	0
Jean-Pierre Smith	1R	1R	3R	3R	1	–	–	–	5	–	–	–	–	0
Stephan Greeff	5R	5R	5	–	–	4R	–	–	4	–	–	–	–	0
Bradley Fortuin	8R	8	8	–	–	–	–	–	3	1	–	–	–	5
Dustin Jinka	x	9R	x	9	9	9R	x	10R	5	1	1	–	–	7
Tim Whitehead	14R	12	12	–	–	–	–	–	3	–	–	–	–	0
Marvin Christians	15R	15R	15R	12R	–	–	–	–	4	–	–	–	–	0
Pieter Myburgh	–	6	6	6	6	6	6	–	6	1	–	–	–	5
Callie Visagie	–	2	2R	2R	2R	2R	2R	2R	7	–	–	–	–	0
Hannes Snyman	–	x	–	–	–	–	–	–	0	–	–	–	–	0
Buhle Mxunyelwa	–	–	3	3	3	3	3	3	6	–	–	–	–	0
Hugo Kloppers	–	–	8R	–	–	4	4R	6R	4	–	–	–	–	0
Michael de Neuilly-Rice	–	–	x	–	3R	1	1	1	4	–	–	–	–	0
JJ Engelbrecht	–	–	–	14	14	–	–	–	2	–	–	–	–	0
Morgan Newman	–	–	–	12	12	12	12	13R	5	–	–	–	–	0
Adriaan Fondse	–	–	–	4	4	–	–	–	2	–	–	–	–	0
Johann Sadie	–	–	–	13R	13	11	11	11	5	2	–	–	–	10
Louis Schreuder	–	–	–	14R	9R	–	–	–	2	–	–	–	–	0
Ruan Combrink	–	–	–	–	14R	–	–	–	1	–	–	–	–	0
Paul Bosch	–	–	–	–	10R	12R	12R	12	4	–	–	–	–	0
Nick Koster	–	–	–	–	–	14	14	8	3	–	–	–	–	0
Lionel Cronje	–	–	–	–	–	10	10	10	3	–	–	–	–	0
Tertius Daniller	–	–	–	–	–	8R	–	–	1	–	–	–	–	0
Ruan-Henry Smith	–	–	–	–	–	3R	–	–	1	–	–	–	–	0
Danie Poolman	–	–	–	–	–	14R	14R	14	3	–	–	–	–	0
Ashley Wells	–	–	–	–	–	–	8R	3R	2	–	–	–	–	0
Liam Bax	–	–	–	–	–	–	–	14R	1	–	–	–	–	0
42 players									**170**	**18**	**12**	**20**	**1**	**177**

APPEARANCES AND POINTS IN ABSA CURRIE CUP 2010

	Free State	Lions	Leopards	Pumas	Griquas	Blue Bulls	Sharks	Free State	Lions	Leopards	Pumas	Griquas	Blue Bulls	Sharks	Free State	Sharks	Matches	Tries	Conversions	Penalties	Drop Goals	Points
Jantjes	15	15	15	15	15	15	15	15	15	14	15	15	15	13R	15	15	16	2	–	–	–	10
Juries	14	14	14	–	–	14	–	–	–	–	–	–	–	–	–	–	4	–	–	–	–	0
Whitehead	13	13	13	–	–	13	13	–	13	–	–	–	–	–	–	–	6	–	–	–	–	0
Bosch	12	12	12	12	12	12	12	12	12	x	13R	12R	x	–	11R	13R	13	2	–	–	–	10
Welsh	11	11	11	11	11	11	11	13	11	–	–	–	–	–	–	–	9	1	–	–	–	5
de Waal	10	10	10	10	10	10	10	10	10	10R	10	10	10	10	10	10	16	–	35	50	–	220
Duvenage	9	9	9	–	9	9	9	9	9	9	9	9	9	9R	9R	9R	15	1	–	–	–	5
Vermeulen	8	8	8	8	8	8	8	8	8	8	8	8	8	8	8	8	16	4	–	–	–	20
Elstadt	7	7	7	7	–	–	7	–	–	–	–	–	–	–	–	–	5	–	–	–	–	0
P Louw	6	6	6	6	6	6	6	–	–	–	6	6	6	x	7R	x	11	5	–	–	–	25
van Zyl	5c	5c	5c	5c	5c	5c	5c	5c	5c	5c	5c	5c	5c	5	5	5	16	2	–	–	–	10
Fondse	4	4	4	4	4	4	4	4	4	4	4	5R	4	4	4	4	16	3	–	–	–	15
Harris	3	3	3	3	3	3	3	3	3	3	3	3	3	3	3	3	16	2	–	–	–	10
Liebenberg	2	2	2R	2	2	2	2	2	–	–	–	–	–	–	–	–	8	–	–	–	–	0
Blaauw	1	1	–	–	1R	1R	1	1	1R	1R	1	1	–	–	–	–	10	–	–	–	–	0
D Fourie	2R	2R	2	–	2R	2R	6R	2R	2	2	2	2	2	2	2	2	15	3	–	–	–	15
JD Moller	1R	1R	1	1	1	1	–	1R	1	1	–	–	1	1	1	1	13	–	–	–	–	0
JC Kritzinger	3R	3R	3R	1R	–	–	–	–	–	3R	3R	1R	3R	1R	1R	1R	11	–	–	–	–	0
Muller	8R	8R	4R	4R	–	–	–	–	–	–	–	–	–	–	–	–	4	–	–	–	–	0
Myburgh	7R	7R	8R	7R	–	x	–	6R	7	–	–	–	–	–	–	–	6	2	–	–	–	10
Hoffmann	9R	9R	15R	9	15R	14R	14R	14R	11R	15	15R	–	15R	–	–	–	12	2	–	–	–	10
Cronjé	10R	10R	10R	10R	10R	x	10R	x	–	10	–	–	x	10R	10R	22R	10	2	9	–	–	28
Hartzenberg	–	–	7R	–	–	–	–	–	7R	8R	–	–	–	–	–	–	3	1	–	–	–	5
Aplon	–	–	–	14	14	–	–	11	–	11	11	11	11	15	14	14	10	9	–	–	–	45
de Jongh	–	–	–	13	13	–	–	–	–	13	13	13	13	12	13	13	9	4	–	–	–	20
Shimange	–	–	–	2R	–	–	–	–	–	–	2R	x	x	2R	2R	x	4	–	–	–	–	0
Schreuder	–	–	–	15R	–	–	–	–	–	–	9R	–	–	–	–	–	2	–	–	–	–	0
Engelbrecht	–	–	–	14R	–	–	14	14	14	–	14	14	14	–	–	–	7	6	–	–	–	30
Koster	–	–	–	–	7R	7	7R	7	–	7	8R	8R	8R	–	–	–	8	2	–	–	–	10
Steenkamp	–	–	–	–	4R	4R	4R	4R	4R	4R	4R	4	4R	4R	4R	4R	12	–	–	–	–	0
Mxunyelwa	–	–	–	–	3R	x	1R	–	x	–	–	–	–	–	–	–	2	–	–	–	–	0
Newman	–	–	–	–	–	–	12R	13R	–	–	–	–	–	–	–	–	2	–	–	–	–	0
F Louw	–	–	–	–	7	–	–	6	6	6	7	7	7	7	7	7	10	5	–	–	–	25
Brasche	–	–	–	–	–	–	–	–	13R	–	–	–	–	–	–	–	1	–	–	–	–	0
Visagie	–	–	–	–	–	–	–	–	8R	2R	–	–	–	–	–	–	2	–	–	–	–	0
de Villiers	–	–	–	–	–	–	–	–	–	12	12	12	12	14	12	12	7	3	–	–	–	15
van Aswegen	–	–	–	–	–	–	–	–	–	10R	10R	–	–	–	–	–	2	–	4	–	–	8
J Fourie	–	–	–	–	–	–	–	–	–	–	–	–	–	13	–	–	1	–	–	–	–	0
Habana	–	–	–	–	–	–	–	–	–	–	–	–	–	11	11	11	3	1	–	–	–	5
Januarie	–	–	–	–	–	–	–	–	–	–	–	–	–	9	9	9	3	–	–	–	–	0
Burger	–	–	–	–	–	–	–	–	–	–	–	–	–	6c	6c	6c	3	1	–	–	–	5
41 players																	**339**	**63**	**48**	**50**	**0**	**561**

Gary van Aswegen top-scored for the U21 Western Province side with 207 points.

ABSA UNDER-21 CHAMPIONSHIP (Champions, 1st Section A)

Played	Won	Drawn	Lost	Points for	Points against	Tries for	Tries against	Winning %
14	12	1	1	625	345	79	38	86.00%

RESULTS Bt Free State (a) 42-40. Bt Golden Lions (h) 33-08. Bt Leopards (a) 20-19. Bt Boland (a) 54-00. Bt Blue Bulls (h) 27-16. Lost KZN (a) 14-41. Bt Free State (h) 40-39. Bt Golden Lions (a) 55-37. Bt Leopards (h) 59-17. Bt Boland (a) 111-00. Bt Blue Bulls (a) 42-38. Bt KZN (h) 36-09. SEMI-FINAL Drew Free State (h) 49-49. FINAL Bt Blue Bulls (a) 43-32.

SCORERS 207 Gary van Aswegen (1t, 44c, 37p, 1dg). 85 Danie Poolman (17t). 35 JJ Engelbrecht, Johann Sadie (7t each). 31 Kurt Coleman (1t, 13c). 20 Berton Klaasen, Tythan Adams, Nick Koster, Martin du Toit (4 tries each). 15 Tertius Daniller, Yaasir Hartzenberg, Sidney Tobias, Louis Screuder (3 tries each). 10 Daniel Hugo, Helmut Lehmann, Nicolaas Hanekom, Albertus de Swardt (2 tries each). 5 Nicholas Groom, Reuben Johannes, JP Smith, Siya Kolisi, Pieter van der Walt, Grant Hattingh, Quinn Roux, Ruan-Henry Smith, Stephan Greeff, Penalty try (1 try each). 2 Lionel Cronjé (1c).

ABSA U19 CHAMPIONSHIP (Champions, 1st Section A)

Played	Won	Drawn	Lost	Points for	Points against	Tries for	Tries against	Winning %
14	12	0	2	501	247	58	28	86.00%

RESULTS Bt Free State (a) 31-27. Bt Golden Lions (h) 47-07. Bt Leopards (a) 29-11. Bt Griffons (a) 63-03. Bt Blue Bulls (h) 22-17. Bt KZN (a) 28-25. Bt Free State (h) 35-13. Bt Golden Lions (a) 47-23. Lost Leopards (h) 36-37. Bt Griffons (h) 29-07. Bt Blue Bulls (a) 29-08. Lost KZN (h) 32-36. SEMI-FINAL Bt Leopards (h) 49-13. FINAL Bt Blue Bulls 26-20 (a).

SCORERS 181 Ulrich Beyers (2t, 42c, 29p). 80 William van Wyk (8t, 5c, 5p, 5dg). 35 Siya Kolisi (7t). 30 Michael van der Spuy (6t). 20 Bradley Mentoor, Damian de Allende, Clearance Khumalo (4t each). 15 Nizaam Carr, Christoff Fernhout, Sizo Maseko (3t each). 10 Eben Etzebeth, Jakobus Porter, André Kotze, Stephan Schoeman, Siyabonga Ntubeni (2t each). 5 Samuel Lane, Cameron Lindsay, Jacques-Pier Swanepoel, Rick Schroeder (1t each).

AMATEUR CHAMPIONSHIP

SWD (5th, South Section)

Played	Won	Drawn	Lost	Points for	Points against	Tries for	Tries against	Winning %
9	9	0	0	422	178	50	14	100.00%

RESULTS Bt Griquas Rural (a) 42-19. Bt Boland (h) 30-20. Bt EP Rural (a) 52-18. Bt Border (h) 69-00. Bt Border Rural (a) 57-20. Bt EP (h) 41-07. Bt SWD (a) 44-29. SEMI-FINAL Bt Free State (h) 48-39. FINAL Valke (a) 39-26.

WESTERN PROVINCE RECORDS

MATCH RECORDS

Biggest win	151-3	vs. Eastern Transvaal	1995
Biggest win (Currie Cup)	107-23	vs. South Western Districts	1996
Heaviest defeat	18-58	vs. Pumas	2002
Heaviest defeat (Currie Cup)	13-50	vs. Lions	2002
Highest score	151	vs. Eastern Transvaal (151-3)	1995
Highest score (Currie Cup)	107	vs. South Western Districts (107-23)	1996
Moist points conceded	62	vs. Griqualand West (26-62)	1998
Moist points conceded (Currie Cup)	66	vs. Transvaal	1992
Most tries	23	vs. Easten Transvaal (151-3)	1995
Most tries (Currie Cup)	17	vs. South Western Districts (107-23)	1996
Most points by a player	46	JT Stransky vs. Eastern Transvaal	1995
Most points by a player (Currie Cup)	33	C Rossouw vs. Blue Bulls	2003
Most tries by a player	6	S Berridge vs. Eastern Transvaal	1995
Most tries by a player (Currie Cup)	5	J Swart vs. Northern Free State	1996
	5	BJ Paulse vs. Falcons	1997
	5	ER Seconds vs. Griqus	2004
	5	A Bekker vs. Valke	2008
Most conversions by a player	18	JT Stransky vs. Eastern Transvaal	1995
Most conversions by a player (Currie Cup)	11	LJ Koen vs. South Western Districts	1996
Most penalties by a player (Currie Cup)	7	LR Sherrell vs. Northern Transvaal	1991
	7	NV Cilliers vs. Transvaal	1993
	7	C Rossouw vs. Falcons	2001
	7	AJJ van Straaten vs. Cheetahs	2001
Most drop goals by a player (Currie Cup)	4	L Rodriguez vs. Griqualand West	1950

SEASON RECORDS

Most team points	1357	31 matches	1997
Most team points (Currie Cup)	619	15 matches	1997
Most points by a player	391	NB Scholtz	1988
Most points by a player (Currie Cup)	227	NB Scholtz	1988
Most team tries	182	31 matches	1997
Most team tries (Currie Cup)	84	15 matches	1997
Most tries by a player	25	CJ du Plessis	1989
	25	J Swart	1997
Most tries by a player (Currie Cup)	19	CJ du Plessis	1989
Most conversions by a player	80	NB Scholtz	1989
Most penalties by a player	73	LR Sherrell	1991
Most drop goals by a player	5	NV Cilliers	1997

CAREER RECORDS

Most appearances	156	CP Strauss	1986-1995
Most points	1570	NB Scholtz (116 matches)	1982-1989
Most points (Currie Cup)	992	NB Scholtz	1982-1989
Most tries	95	NJ Burger	1982-1991
Most tries (Currie Cup)	70	BJ Paulse	1996-2007
Most conversions by a player	293	NB Scholtz	1982-1989
Most penalties by a player	256	NB Scholtz	1982-1989
Most drop goals by a player	12	NB Scholtz	1982-1989

HONOURS

Absa Currie Cup	1889, 1892, 1894, 1895, 1897, 1898, 1904, 1906, 1908, 1914, 1920, 1925, 1927, 1929, 1932 (shared), 1934 (shared), 1936, 1947, 1954, 1959, 1964, 1966, 1979 (shared), 1982, 1983, 1984, 1985, 1986, 1989 (shared), 1997, 2000, 2001
Lion Cup	1984, 1988, 1989
Bankfin Nite Series	1997

PROVINCIAL ROUND-UP

SECTION 7
AMATEUR RUGBY, SCHOOLS, REFEREES & OBITUARIES

SAA NATIONAL CLUB CHAMPIONSHIPS

Third time lucky for Rovers

Maties *(5)* 15 College Rovers *(11)* 24

September 24, Danie Craven Stadium, Stellenbosch. Referee: Sindile Mayende.
MATIES – TRIES: Arno White 2. CONVERSION: Coenie van Wyk. PENALTY: André Kemp.
COLLEGE ROVERS – TRIES: Jerome Pretorius 2. CONVERSION: Wesley Dunlop. PENALTIES: Dunlop 3. DROP GOAL: Dunlop.

COLLEGE Rovers provided ample proof that club rugby is not quite ready to go the way of the dodo when they soared to a maiden national club championship title at the Danie Craven Stadium in Stellenbosch.

The Durbanites, runners-up at the same venue in 2006 and 2008, became the first KZN team in 16 years to lift the trophy and in doing so condemned hosts and 12-time champions Maties to their first defeat in a final since 1980, when Morné du Plessis' Villagers, thanks to two tries from the late Chris Burger, won 14-3 at Newlands.

The tournament, in its 36th year, remains a penniless cousin of the glitzy Varsity Cup but for the second year running it was an open club (Hamiltons beat Pukke in 2009) who were left with the pleasant task of administering the last rites to student opponents.

Rovers' victory also sent out a timely reminder to those seduced by the dizzying razzmatazz of the Varsity Cup that, for all the latter tournament's cheerleaders, capacity crowds and cheap beer, it is with the country's cash-strapped open clubs that the balance of power, on the field at least, now lies.

Like an otherwise perfect cake missing a teaspoon of baking powder, club rugby however remains perpetually short of the one vital ingredient that would allow it to stand up and be counted in the professional era.

"We need the exposure," said Rovers' head coach Brad MacLeod-Henderson. "The Varsity Cup is getting a lot of television cover-

age and a lot of money is being thrown into it. The open clubs need to keep in touch with that."

MacLeod-Henderson, the 34-year-old former Sharks back-rower, was also concerned at a growing gulf developing between the big four of Rovers, Hamilton, Maties, Pukke and the rest of the field.

"There is a bit of a divide starting to happen," he said, in reference to the many one-sided contests that plagued the event. "The top varsity sides are quasi-professional. The facilities at Maties are unbelievable compared to what we've got, and we're one of the top clubs in KZN. But what you can't coach and can't measure is the size of people's hearts."

Rovers also had to overcome a schedule that would most likely spark a revolt in the professional ranks. "The guys played four games in seven days and two of those kicked off at 11.45am and 1pm," said MacLeod-Henderson. "They went out there, got smashed, then got one day's rest and did it all over again. I'd be interested to hear what Prof. Tim Noakes thought about it."

Rovers also proved that transformation in KZN club rugby is alive and well, with the likes of eighthman Eric Ngoie and prop Sabelo Nhlapo leading the charge against Maties in a pack that contained five black players. "Our club is completely transformed," said MacLeod-Henderson. "We don't have quotas or any of that rubbish, just numerous players of colour putting their bodies on the line and producing."

MATIES (15-1): Ruan Combrinck, Wilhelm Loock, Pieter Stoffberg, Dabeon Draghoender, Louw Schabort, Coenie van Wyk, Johan Herbst, Cameron Peverett, Jonathan Adendorff, Boetie Brits, Hugo Kloppers, Chris van Zyl, Lourens Adriaanse (c), Arno White, Gerrit Jacobs. *Replacements (from): Gareth Light, Johan Roets, Hein van der Merwe, JP Mostert, Sam Mabombo, Bennie Booysen, Johann Laker, André Kemp, Stefan van der Merwe, Jonathan Francke.*
COLLEGE ROVERS (15-1): Chris Jordaan (c), Matt de Beer, Jerome Pretorius, Rudi Keil, Anton Verster, Wesley Dunlop, Neil de Bruyn, Eric Ngoie, Jody Jenneker, Kosie Haarhof, Byron Egan, Anton Bressler, Ross Anderson, Monde Hadebe, Sabelo Nhlapo. *Replacements (from): Jono Lee, Siko Sinelizwe, Francois Robertse, Nico Claasen, Shannin Rick, Ncedo Koyana, Arno van Zyl, Stuart Hudson, Jim Agaba, Michael Rhodes.*

CLUB CHAMPIONSHIPS

2010 NATIONAL CLUB CHAMPIONSHIP REPRESENTATIVES

*denotes new champion – 9 of 16 teams did not play in 2009
**A successful High Court application brought against the Border RFU by Fort Hare University regarding the docking of points during the league season resulted in the province deciding to withdraw their representatives from the tournament. Officially, East London Police, despite winning their provincial title, took part in the Club Championships not as Border champions but as a team invited by SARU.

Defending champion: Hamilton (WP) **Blue Bulls:** Tukkies* **Boland:** Roses United* **Border**:** East London Police*
EP: Progress* **Free State:** Shimlas **Golden Lions:** University of Johannesburg (UJ)* **Griffons:** Bethlehem Old Boys*
Griquas: Kimberley Police* **KZN:** College Rovers **Leopards:** Pukke (play in Golden Lions league) **Mpumalanga:**
Middelburg **SWD:** Mossel Bay Barbarians* **Valke:** Springs **WP:** University of Stellenbosch (Maties)*
SARU invited team: Noordelikes (Limpopo Blue Bulls champions).

2009 NATIONAL CLUB CHAMPIONSHIPS RESULTS:

FIRST ROUND – SATURDAY 18 SEPTEMBER:
Springs 80 (40) **Mossel Bay Barbarians 12** (7)
Progress 44 (27) **SAPS East London 38** (0)
Roses United 23 (3) **Shimlas 22** (10)
UJ 33 (20) **Tuks 23** (10)
College Rovers 52 (26) **Bethlehem Oud-Skoliere 24** (10)
Pukke 83 (40) **Middelburg 17** (17)
Maties 99 (38) **Kimberley Police 12** (7)
Hamilton 83 (34) **Noordelike 25** (11)

QUARTERFINALS – MONDAY 20 SEPTEMBER:
PLATE: SAPS East London 31 Noordelike 27
Mossel Bay Barbarians 32 Kimberley Police 31
Shimlas 41 Middelburg 10
Tuks 52 Bethlehem Oud-Skoliere 19

CUP: Maties 49 (20) – TRIES: Jonathan Francke (2), Louis Jordaan, Bennie Booysen, Boetie Brits, Pieter Stoffberg. CONVERSIONS: André Kemp (5). PENALTIES: Kemp (3). **Springs 27** (13) – TRIES: Armand Steynvaart, Rudi Klopper (2). CONVERSIONS: Charl Nieuwenhuis (2), Niel Erasmus. PENALTIES: Nieuwenhuis (2).

Hamilton 76 (28) – TRIES: Elric van Vuuren (2), Jacques Rossouw, Alshaun Bock (2), Francois Prinsloo, JG Giliomee (3), Tiaan Fick, Jeffrey Williams. CONVERSIONS: Van Vuuren (9). PENALTY: Van Vuuren. **Progress 14** (14) – TRIES: Nolan Jacobs, Giovanni Fourie. CONVERSIONS: Curtis Sais (2).

Pukke 90 (68) – TRIES: SW Oosthuizen, Adriaan Engelbrecht, Johannes Seerane, Marcel du Toit (2), PJ van Zyl, Savvas Nel, Siya Mdaka (2), Dirco Rautenbach (2), Martin Dreyer, Jacques Moller, Jean Pretorius. CONVERSIONS: Kotze (10). **Roses United 14** (0) – TRIES: Ashton Constant (2). CONVERSIONS: Percival Williams, Ryan Jordaan.

College Rovers 26 (15) – TRIES: Michael Rhodes, Anton Verster, Wesley Dunlop. Conversion: Dunlop. PENALTIES: Dunlop (3). **UJ 20** (8) – TRIES: JP Jansen van Rensburg, Danny Botha, Earl Lewis. Penalty: Wesley Roberts. CONVERSION: Andre Smith.

SEMIFINALS – WEDNESDAY 22 SEPTEMBER:
PLATE: East London Police 40 Mossel Bay Barbarians 10
Shimlas 42 Tukkies 27
CUP: Pukke 14 (14) – TRIES: Jean Pretorius, Dirco Rautenbach. CONVERSIONS: Theuns Kotze (2). **College Rovers 33** (28) – TRIES: Anton Verster, Kosie Haarhof, Jerome Pretorius, Chris Jordaan, Rudi Keil. CONVERSIONS: Wesley Dunlop (4).

Hamilton 19 (7) – TRIES: Francois Prinsloo (2), Alshaun Bock. CONVERSIONS: Elric van Vuuren, Bock. **Maties 45** (28) – TRIES: Wilhelm Loock (2), Johan Herbst, Boetie Brits, Ruan Combrinck. CONVERSIONS: Coenie van Wyk (3), André Kemp. PENALTIES: Van Wyk (3), Kemp.

FINALS – FRIDAY 24 SEPTEMBER:
PLATE: Shimlas 35 East London Police 17
CUP: Maties 15 College Rovers 24

Wesley Dunlop

SAA NATIONAL CLUB CHAMPIONSHIP WINNERS 1975 – 2010

Year	Winner		Runner-up		Year	Winner		Runner-up	
2010	Maties	15	College Rovers	24	1991	Old Greys	36	Despatch	6
2009	Hamilton	36	Pukke	34	1990	Tukkies	22	Despatch	20
2008	Pukke	17	College Rovers	12	1989	Roodepoort	29	Goudstad	
2007	Maties	24	Tukkies	8				Onderwyskollege	22
2006	Pukke	33	College Rovers	21	1988	Despatch	13	Tukkies	12
2005	Maties	24	UJ	13	1987	Defence (Cape)	26	Despatch 8	
2004	Pukke	41	TUT	10	1986	Shimlas	14	Tukkies	6
2003	Tukkies	46	Pukke	25	1985	Despatch	28	Tukkies	6
2002	Shimlas	34	Pukke	26	1984	Maties	16	Tukkies	15
2001	Pirates	37	Tygerberg	13	1983	Harlequins	29	Tukkies	12
2000	Maties	54	Tukkies	37	1982	Maties	25	UJ	6
1999	Shimlas	45	Welkom Rovers	9	1981	Maties	32	Pretoria Police	9
1998	Maties	28	UJ	10	1980	Villager	14	Maties	3
1997	Maties	30	UJ	15	1979	Maties	27	Tukkies	11
1996	Pretoria Police	70	Old Greys	29	1978	Maties	15	Tukkies	9
1995	Pretoria Police	26	Crusaders	12	1977	Maties	12	Harlequins	10
1994	Crusaders	34	Oudstudente	3	1976	Tukkies	19	Maties	0
1993	Crusaders	8	Despatch	3	1975	Maties	28	Durban Collegians	20
1992	UJ	40	Harlequins	22					

CLUB CHAMPIONSHIPS

FNB VARSITY CUP

Hat-trick of titles for Maties

THE University of Stellenbosch surged to a hat-trick of FNB Varsity Cup titles when they beat arch-rivals the University of Cape Town 17-14 at a packed Danie Craven Stadium in Stellenbosch on the last Monday in March.

The full house of 20,000 watched on as the Stellenbosch students survived a late onslaught from the Ikeys to take the spoils once again in a tournament that has outstripped all expectations in the three years since its inception.

Such has been the impact – and the resultant re-emergence of student rugby culture as a result – that the organisers decided in mid-year to expand the tournament to include a second-tier competition from 2011.

The B-section Varsity Shield, which will benefit from the same sponsorship deals as currently enjoyed by teams in the A-section Varsity Cup, will pit five additional universities against each other in a double-round tournament, taking the amount of competing institutions to 13 in total. They are the University of KwaZulu-Natal (UKZN), the University of the Witwatersrand (Wits), the Central University of Technology (CUT – Free State), the University of the Western Cape (UWC) and Fort Hare University.

"It was inevitable for the Varsity Cup to take its involvement to more institutions," said outgoing Varsity Cup chairman Jurie Roux, who was appointed SARU CEO in October 2010. "Having now got 13 universities on board, the Varsity Cup will make an even more significant contribution to SA rugby from 2011 onwards."

The Varsity Shield will run at the same time as the Varsity Cup, whose fourth installment kicks off in February 2011.

A once-off promotion/relegation match will take place after the 2011 tournament between the bottom team in the 'A-Section' and the top Varsity Shield side, to decide the lineup for the 2012 Varsity Cup.

Maties coach Chean Roux celebrating.

Following the 2012 tournament, the Varsity Shield winner will be automatically promoted, while the bottom-placed Varsity Cup team will be automatically relegated.

In the 2010 Varsity Cup final, tries from Tythan Adams, Charl Weideman and Danie Poolman, as well as a conversion from André Kemp, was just enough to allow Maties, who had finished top of the log, to keep out the strong-finishing UCT, who had finished second on the table.

The Ikeys' points came via a try by Sam Peter and three penalties – two to late replacement Doug Mallett, and one to Marcel Brache.

FNB VARSITY CUP

FNB VARSITY CUP

PLAY-OFF RESULTS

SEMI-FINALS: MATIES beat PUKKE 47-11 (Stellenbosch), IKEYS beat SHIMLAS 27-21 (Cape Town)

FINAL RESULTS

Danie Craven Stadium, Stellenbosch, Monday 29 March. Referee: Tiaan Jonker

MATIES 17 (TRIES: Weideman, Poolman, Adams. CONVERSION: Kemp)

IKEYS 14 (TRY: Peter. PENALTIES: Mallet 2, Brache)

MATIES: Adriaan Osman, Wilhelm Loock (Hayden Groepes), Danie Poolman, Charl Weideman, Tythan Adams, Andr Kemp, Johan Herbst (Johan Laker), Josh Strauss (Cameron Peverett/Gareth Light), Jonathan Adendorf, Sam Mabombo, Hugo Kloppers, Andrew Prior (Marinus Pretorius), Lourens Adriaanse(c), Matthew Dobson (Andrew Crausaz), Johan Roets (Michael de Neuilly-Rice). *Unused sub: Jonathan Francke.* **Head coach:** Chean Roux

IKEYS: Therlow Pietersen (Mark Esterhuizen), Pete Haw, Marcel Brache, Sean van Tonder (Matthew Rosslee), Marcello Sampson, Douglas Mallett, Stuart Commins (Nicholas Groom), JJ Gagiano, Michael Morris, Nicholas Fenton-Wells(c) (Sam Peter), Donovan Armand, Levi Odendaal (Michael Ledwidge), Grant Kemp (Chris Heiberg), Mark Goosen (Matthew Page), Ashley Wells. *Unused sub: Wesley Chetty.* **Head coach:** John Dobson.

2010 FNB VARSITY CUP LOG & LEADING SCORERS

TEAM	P	W	L	D	PF	PA	PD	TF	TA	LB	TB	Pts
Maties	7	7	0	0	324	96	228	41	12	0	5	33
UCT	7	5	1	1	223	139	84	24	13	1	2	25
Shimlas	7	4	2	1	230	169	61	29	18	1	4	23
Pukke	7	4	3	0	184	155	29	23	14	2	3	21
UJ	7	3	3	1	247	208	39	32	25	1	4	19
Tuks	7	2	4	1	227	264	-37	29	30	1	3	14
TUT	7	1	6	0	156	285	-129	16	33	2	1	7
NMMU	7	0	7	0	148	423	-275	13	62	2	1	3

NOTE: LB = Lost bonus, TB = Try bonus

50 POINTS OR MORE

PLAYER	Team	Tries	Conversions	Penalties	Drop Goals	Points
Theuns Kotze	Pukke	2	14	13	0	77
Conrad Hoffmann	Maties	2	22	6	1	75
Justin van Staden	Tuks	3	12	10	0	69
Jaco Oosthuizen	TUT	2	10	13	0	69
Matthew Rosslee	UCT	0	12	15	0	69
Willem Laubscher	NMMU	0	7	15	3	68
André Kemp	Maties	0	17	9	1	64
André Smith	UJ	2	16	4	0	54

FOUR TRIES

Boom Prinsloo	Shimlas	7		Tythan Adams	Maties	5
Lolo Waka	UJ	7		Edgar Marutlulle	UJ	5
Dabeon Draghoender	Maties	6		Andrew Prior	Maties	5
Danie Poolman	Maties	6				

SPRINGBOK WOMEN

Team achieves 10th at World Cup

THE Springbok Women completed a landmark season with a best-ever record of six wins from nine internationals.

At the Women's Rugby World Cup in Guildford, England, South Africa performed admirably although the odds were stacked against them from the very start. The team shared the tournament's 'group of death' with the unbeatable New Zealand, 2009 Women's Rugby World Cup Sevens winners Australia and regular Six Nations campaigners Wales.

Eventually, the SA Women performed marginally better at the 2010 World Cup than four years previously to claim 10th spot after wins over the Welsh as well as over Kazakhstan.

The team began the year in splendid fashion. In April, they beat Kazakhstan in the glittering desert city of Dubai to record a first-ever away victory. They played even better in the second match to win by a comfortable margin and so clinch a historic series win.

A two-match series against Scotland in June resulted in another 2-0 win, which meant that the team would approach only their second appearance at a WRWC with some degree of confidence. In the first match, Scotland managed to restrict the SA Women to a halftime lead of 8-3, but they were no match in the second half for Mandisa Williams and her teammates, who finished the much stronger team and 27-8 winners.

In the first half of the second match, Scotland played some clever rugby to lead 14-7 at the break. However, the halftime talk from coach Denver Wannies did the trick as his team transformed themselves to score a comprehensive 41-17 win.

Stagefright and New Zealand's class resulted in a 53-3 victory for the Kiwis in the opening World Cup match at the world-class Surrey Sports Park. Next up Wales, and this time Williams and her team played much better to win their first-ever World Cup match 15-12.

Australia proved far too strong and won 62-0 – a massive disappointment for a team who were missing injured skipper Williams and suspended tighthead prop Cebisa Kula.

A 25-10 victory over Kazakhstan allowed SA to recover some lost pride, but they ended the WRWC on a low note when Wales won their rematch and play-off for ninth place.

Coach Wannies and his team deserved credit for their thorough preparation. The SA Women were considered to be the most improved team at the WRWC and all pundits were in agreement that the team would have fared better had it not been for their extremely tough group: New Zealand won the title again while Australia claimed third spot.

In domestic competition, Western Province won the interprovincial tournament after beating the Golden Lions 26-12 in the final, which was played after all the national squad players had been withdrawn to prepare for the World Cup.

SA WOMEN 2010 RESULTS
8 April, Al Ain, Dubai, United Arab Emirates
South Africa 22 Kazakhstan 17
South Africa – TRIES: Phumeza Gadu, Cebisa Kula, Namhla Nojoko. CONVERSION: Yolanda Meiring. PENALTY: Meiring.

11 April, Al Ain, Dubai, United Arab Emirates
South Africa 38 Kazakhstan 0
South Africa – TRIES: Ziyanda Tywaleni, Lamla Momoti, Zenay Jordaan, Phumeza Gadu. CONVERSIONS: Yolanda Meiring (3). PENALTY: Meiring.
South Africa won the series 2-0.

5 June, Lasswade, Scotland
Scotland 8 South Africa 27
Scotland – TRY: Lucy Millard. PENALTY: Nicola Halfpenny
South Africa – TRIES: Namhla Siyolo, Mandisa Williams, Lorinda Brown, Zenay Jordaan. PENALTY: Yolanda Meiring. CONVERSIONS: Meiring (2).

12 June, Lasswade, Scotland
Scotland 17 South Africa 41
Scotland – TRY: Heather Lockheart. PENALTIES: Nicola Halfpenny (4).
South Africa – TRIES: Mandisa Williams, Lorinda Brown (2), Zenay Jordaan (2), Lamla Momoti. PENALTY: Zandile Nojoko. CONVERSIONS: Nojoko (4).
South Africa won the series 2-0

WOMEN'S RUGBY

WOMEN'S RUGBY WORLD CUP LOG

Pool A	P	W	D	D	PF	PA	TF	TA	B	Pts
New Zealand	3	3	0	0	128	16	22	2	3	15
Australia	3	2	0	1	93	44	14	8	2	10
South Africa	3	1	0	2	18	127	3	19	0	4
Wales	3	0	0	3	30	82	4	14	1	1
Pool B	P	W	D	D	PF	PA	TF	TA	B	Pts
England	3	3	0	0	146	10	22	2	3	15
Ireland	3	2	0	1	59	42	11	6	2	10
USA	3	1	0	2	73	59	11	10	1	5
Kazakhstan	3	0	0	3	3	170	0	26	0	0
Pool C	P	W	D	D	PF	PA	TF	TA	B	Pts
France	3	3	0	0	55	24	10	2	1	13
Canada	3	2	0	1	85	43	12	7	2	10
Scotland	3	1	0	2	49	59	8	9	1	5
Sweden	3	0	0	3	24	87	2	14	1	1

FINAL STANDINGS

1 New Zealand
2 England
3 Australia
4 France
5 USA
6 Canada
7 Ireland
8 Scotland
9 Wales
10 South Africa
11 Kazakhstan
12 Sweden

SA WOMEN'S SQUAD

BACKS	Position	Date of birth	Height	Weight	Province
Aimee Barrett	Fullback	27/06/1987	1.68	74	Western Province
Yolanda Meiring	Fullback	14/08/1983	1.65	65	Blue Bulls
Zandile Nojoko	Fullback	01/07/1986	1.80	65	Eastern Province
Phumeza Gadu	Wing	21/06/1985	1.64	56	Eastern Province
Ziyanda Tywaleni	Wing	26/11/1987	1.61	70	Border
Lorinda Brown	Centre	16/12/1983	1.61	59	Eastern Province
Charmaine Kayser	Centre	27/02/1987	1.61	58	Eastern Province
Daphne Scheepers	Centre	02/02/1984	1.65	77	Eastern Province
Zenay Jordaan	Flyhalf	04/04/1991	1.56	54	Eastern Province
Cherne Roberts	Scrumhalf	08/08/1987	1.50	56	Western Province
Saloma Booysen	Scrumhalf	04/06/1987	1.51	52	Eastern Province
Fundiswa Plaatjie	Scrumhalf	12/04/1985	1.58	60	Border
FORWARDS					
Namhla Siyolo	No 8	23/07/1987	1.68	96	Eastern Province
Nombulelo Mayongo	Flanker	26/05/1985	1.58	69	Free State
Lamla Momoti	Flanker	27/03/1985	1.60	76	Eastern Province
Mandisa Williams(c)	Flanker	11/08/1984	1.69	84	Eastern Province
Pulane Motloung	Flanker	10/03/1985	1.63	72	Blue Bulls
Nolusindiso Booi	Lock	29/06/1985	1.78	74	Border
Dolly Mavumengwana	Lock	23/12/1976	1.80	79	KwaZulu-Natal
Onicca Moaga	Lock	20/02/1988	1.66	68	SANDF
Nedene Botha	Prop	19/02/1982	1.69	90	Western Province
Laurian Johannes	Prop	09/08/1984	1.67	99	Western Province
Portia Jonga	Prop	24/04/1973	1.66	90	Border
Cebisa Kula	Prop	19/05/1981	1.65	86	Eastern Province
Cynthia Poswa	Hooker	16/03/1984	1.62	74	Western Province
Donna Sidumbu	Hooker	18/12/1977	1.55	80	Eastern Province

26 Players

COACHES & MANAGEMENT

COACH: Denver Wannies
ASSISTANT COACHES: Rudolf Gerber & Kaya Malotana
TECHNICAL ANALYST: Anthony Heugh
MANAGER: Orna Prinsloo
CONDITIONING: Denzil van Heerden
PHYSIO: Tanushree Pillay
DOCTOR: Jacoba Lindeque
COMMUNICATIONS: Rayaan Adriaanse

SA WOMEN RUGBY WORLD CUP RESULTS

South Africa 3, New Zealand 55
August 20. Surrey Sports Park (Pitch 1), Guildford.
Referee: Andrew McMenemy (Scotland)
SOUTH AFRICA - PENALTY: Nojoko
Nojoko, Meiring, Brown, Scheepers, Gadu (Kayser), Jordaan, Booysen, Siyolo, Williams (c), Momoti, Mavumengwana, Booi, Kula, Sidumbu, Botha (Jonga). Unused subs: Poswa, Johannes, Mayongo, Plaatjie, Tywaleni.
NEW ZEALAND - TRIES: Hohepa (3), Manuel (2), Fa'amausili, Brazier, Wickcliffe, Robertson. CONS: Brazier (5) Grant, Hohepa (Hurring), Manuel, Brazier, Wickliffe, Richards (Mahoney), Jensen (Cocksedge), Robertson, Lavea (Sione), Ruscoe (c), Heighway (Codling), Robinson, Taufateau (Bosman), Fa'aumausili (Penetito), McKay.

South Africa 15, Wales 10
August 24, Surrey Sports Park (Pitch 2), Guildford.
Referee: Joyce Henry (Canada)
SOUTH AFRICA - TRIES: Siyolo, Kayser, Nojoko.
Nojoko, Meiring, Brown, Scheepers (Gadu), Kayser, Jordaan, Booysen, Siyolo, Williams (c), Momoti, Mavumengwana, Booi (Moaga), Kula, Sidumbu (Poswa), Botha (Johannes). Unused subs: Mayongo, Plaatjie, Tywaleni.
WALES - TRY: E Evans. CON: N Evans. P: N Evans.
N Evans, James (A Thomas), Berry, Redman, M Evans, N Thomas, Prosser (Day), Kift (c), S Harries (L Newton), Nicholas (E Evans), Taylor (Powell-Hughes), Hallett, Edwards, L Harries (Bowden), C Thomas. Unused sub: Flowers.

South Africa 00, Australia 62
August 28, Surrey Sports Park (Pitch 1), Guildford.
Referee: David Keane (Ireland)
SOUTH AFRICA - no points.
Nojoko (Barrett), Meiring (Tywaleni), Kayser, Brown (c), Gadu, Jordaan, Booysen (Plaatjie), Siyolo, Mayongo (Motloung), Momoti, Mavumengwana, Booi (Moaga), Johannes (Jonga), Sidumbu (Poswa), Botha.
AUSTRALIA - TRIES: L Morgan (2), Williams (2), Giteau,

Brown, Hodghinson, Hargreaves, C Morgan. CONS: Beck (7). Pen: Beck.
Brown, Giteau, Williams, Campbell, Beck, McGann, Soon (c), Hodgkinson, Hargreaves, Trethowan. Porter, Ross, L Morgan, watson, Vakalahi.

South Africa 25, Kazakhstan 10 (9th Place Semi-Final)
September 1, Surrey Sports Park (Pitch 2), Guildford. Referee: David Keane (Ireland)
SOUTH AFRICA - TRIES: Gadu, Jordaan, Roberts. C: Nojoko (2). P: Nojoko (2).
Nojoko, Tywaleni (Roberts), Brown (c), Scheepers (Barrett), Gadu, Jordaan, Booysen, Siyolo, Mayongo (Motloung), Momoti, Moaga, Johannes, Kula (Jonga), Poswa (Sidumbu), Botha. Unused subs: Meiring, Plaatjie.
KAZAKHSTAN - Tries: Amossova, Mustafina.
Daurembayeva, Sazanova (Adler), Sherer, Klyuchikova, Amossova, Tur, Baratova, Yaklovleva (c), Balashova (Radzivil), Mustafina (Khamova), Kumanikina, Karatygina, Rudoy (Zhamankulova), Ashikmina (Falen), Kamendrovskaya (Nuklich). Unused sub: Pshenicnaya.

South Africa 17, Wales 29 (9th Place Play-Off)
September 5, Surrey Sports Park (Pitch 2), Guildford. Referee: Andrew McMenemy (Scotland)
SOUTH AFRICA - TRIES: Jordaan, Kayser, Gadu. CON: Meiring.
Nojoko (Meiring), Tywaleni (Roberts), Kayser, Brown, Gadu, Jordaan, Booysen, Siyolo, Williams (c), Momoti, Mavumengwana, Moaga, Jonga (Johannes), Poswa (Sidumbu), Botha. Unused subs: Motloung, Plaatjie, Barrett.
WALES - TRIES: N Thomas (2), M Evans (2), Bowden. C: A Thomas (2)
N Thomas, E Evans (James), Redman, Flowers, M Evans (Taviner), A Thomas, Prosser (Day), Berry (c), Kift , S Harries Taylor, Hallett, Edwards (C Thomas), Bowden (L Harries), Davies. Unused sub: Powell-Hughes, Newton.

WOMEN'S RUGBY

APPEARANCES AND POINTS IN WOMEN'S RUGBY WORLD CUP

	New Zealand	Wales	Australia	Kazakhstan	Wales	Matches	Tries	Conversions	Penalties	Drop Goals	Points
Zandile Nojoko	15	15	15	15	15	5	1	2	3	–	18
Yolanda Meiring	14	14	14	x	15R	4	–	1	–	–	2
Lorinda Brown	13	13	12c	13c	–	3	–	–	–	–	0
Daphne Scheepers	12	12	–	12	12	4	–	–	–	–	0
Phumeza Gadu	11	12R	11	11	11	5	2	–	–	–	10
Zenay Jordaan	10	10	10	10	10	5	2	–	–	–	10
Saloma Booysemn	9	9	9	9	9	5	–	–	–	–	0
Namhla Siyolo	8	8	8	8	8	5	1	–	–	–	5
Mandisa Williams	7c	7c	–	–	7c	3	–	–	–	–	0
Lamla Momoti	6	6	6	6	6	5	–	–	–	–	0
Nolusindiso Booi	5	5	5	–	–	3	–	–	–	–	0
Dolly Navumengwana	4	4	4	5	5	5	–	–	–	–	0
Cebisa Kula	3	3	–	–	–	2	–	–	–	–	0
Donna Sidumbu	2	2	2	2R	2R	5	–	–	–	–	0
Nedene Botha	1	1	1	1	1	5	–	–	–	–	0
Nosipho Poswa	x	2R	2R	2	2	4	–	–	–	–	0
Portia Jonga	1R	–	3R	3R	3	4	–	–	–	–	0
Laurian Johannes	x	1R	3	3	3R	4	–	–	–	–	0
Nombulelo Mayongo	x	x	7	7	–	2	–	–	–	–	0
Fundiswa Plaatjie	x	x	9R	x	x	1	–	–	–	–	0
Charmaine Kayser	11R	11	13	–	13	4	2	–	–	–	10
Ziyanda Tywaleni	x	x	14R	14	14	3	–	–	–	–	0
Onicca Moaga	–	4R	4R	4	4	4	–	–	–	–	0
Aimee Barrett	–	–	15R	12R	x	3	–	–	–	–	0
Pulane Motloung	–	–	7R	7R	x	2	–	–	–	–	0
Cherne Roberts	–	–	–	14R	14R	2	1	–	–	–	5
26 players						**97**	**9**	**3**	**3**	**0**	**60**

LEADING POINTS SCORERS

Kelly Brazier	New Zealand	48
Anna Schnell	Canada	46
Christy Ringgenbeg	USA	44
Carla Hohepa	New Zealand	35
Katy McLean	England	35
Heather Moyse	Canada	35
Niamh Briggs	Ireland	34
Nicole Beck	Australia	30

LEADING TRY SCORERS

Carla Hohepa	New Zealand	7
Heather Moyse	Canada	7
Charlotte Barras	England	4
Kelly Brazier	New Zealand	4
Niamh Briggs	Ireland	4
Huriana Manuel	New Zealand	4
Mandy Marchak	Canada	4
Lucy Millard	Scotland	4
Cobie-Jane Morgan	Australia	4
Joy Neville	Ireland	4
Fiona Pocock	England	4

SA SCHOOLS

Schoolboys denied chance to show off talent

THE dominance which Free State and Western Province enjoyed at the 2010 Coca-Cola Under-18 Craven Week was reflected in the composition of the SA Schools team, with the two sides contributing nine players (Free State six, WP three) to the squad that beat Namibia in their only match of the year.

WP would have had four players but for the post-selection injury to Paul Roos fullback Craig Barry, while the Blue Bulls also contributed three players.

The dominance of a handful of schools, which some may argue constitutes an unhealthy state for South African schoolboy rugby, is further illustrated by the fact that these 12 players – more than 50% of the SA Schools squad – come from just three schools: six from Bloemfontein's Grey College and three each from Paul Roos Gymnasium in Stellenbosch and Pretoria's Afrikaans Hoër Seunskool.

A noteworthy name on the team sheet was that of Affies lock Schalk van Heerden, son of legendary 1970s Springbok lock Moaner and the younger brother of another Bok of more recent times, World Cup winner Wikus.

The class of 2010 was a particularly talented bunch but unfortunately they never got the chance to show it.

Whereas SARU's High Performance group (which consisted of Craven Week players as well as others identi-

fied as having potential) were involved in matches against France, England and a Namibian XV, the SA Schools team, supposedly the cream of the crop, had to settle for below-par opposition.

Lindsay Mould, chair of the South African Schools' Rugby Association, publicly echoed these sentiments while Mervin Green, SARU's Manager of Youth Rugby, in addressing the team, unveiled plans for an under-18 Tri-Nations tournament against Australia and New Zealand.

However, many members of the under-18 team are usually in grade 12, and an already over-full school and sport curriculum will be further taxed by any new overseas competition.

It remains to be seen whether these ambitious plans, which may involve long-haul travelling, will materialise.

The 2010 SA Schools team's only match saw them hammer their Namibian counterparts 92-21 in a match played at Raiders Rugby Club in Johannesburg on 29 August.

The team, marshalled by flyhalf Johan Goosen, scored 14 tries in a one-sided contest. Goosen, who scored 28 points, is the latest in a long line of excellent Bloem schoolboy flyhalves to have come off the conveyor belt in recent times, among them Morné and Francois Steyn.

SA Schools – 92: TRIES: Leroy Bitterhout (3), Johan Goosen (2), JP Lewis, William Small-Smith, Andile Jho, Nardus van der Walt, Rudi van Rooyen, Paul Jordaan, Kevin Luiters, Tsotsho Mbovane, Anrich Bitzi. **CONVERSIONS:** Goosen (9), Jordaan (2).
Namibia Under-19 – 21: TRIES: Ranthony Bekker, Nico de Jager, Jurie Loois. **CONVERSIONS:** Daniel Bock (2), Chase Diergaardt.

SA SCHOOLS SQUAD 2010:
Marinus van der Merwe (Pumas), Jean-Paul Lewis (WP), William Small-Smith (FS) (capt), Andile Jho (Border), Leroy Bitterhout (Boland), Johan Goosen (FS), Rudi van Rooyen (BB), Nardus van der Walt (BB), Sikhumbuzo Notshe (WP), Khaya Majola (KZN), Ruan Botha (Valke), Ruan Venter (GL), Allan Dell (Border), Jason Thomas (EP), Steven Kitshoff (WP). Replacements: Anrich Bitzi (FS), Neethling Fouché (FS), Schalk van Heerden (BB), Wiaan Liebenberg (Boland), Kevin Luiters (FS), Paul Jordaan (FS), Tshotso Mbovane (WP).

SA SCHOOLS

COCA-COLA CRAVEN WEEK

Welkom hat-trick Free State, WP

TWENTY teams participated in the 2010 Coca-Cola Under-18 Craven Week, which was held at the North West Stadium in Welkom. It was the 47th time that this national showcase of schools rugby took place but the first time since 1976 that the event had been hosted in the northern Free State region.

Apart from the 14 provinces, there were also teams from Namibia, Zimbabwe, Border Country Districts (previously Transkei), Limpopo Blue Bulls (previously Far North), Eastern Province Country Districts (previously North Eastern Cape) and Griquas Country Districts (previously North Western Cape).

For a third year in a row, Free State and Western Province were awarded the honour of competing in the main match of the Week. But they by no means had things all their own way en route to the 'final'.

Both teams could – and should – have lost early on in the tournament. Although WP beat the Lions 20-3 on the opening day, the Gauteng side came very close to ending their Cape counterparts' success Craven Week since 2007.

The Lions dominated for long periods and missed several scoring opportunities, but a spate of penalties and a decisive try by WP flanker Sikhumbuzo Notshe just before halftime sealed their fate.

Free State were also relatively fortunate to reach the 'final', after beating KZN 30-20 in a match in which Natal flyhalf Duncan Campbell missed four penalties.

WP followed up their win over the Lions with a 58-17 thrashing of EP, which installed them as favourites to retain their unofficial title against Free State.

In the 'final', WP drew first blood when fullback and captain Craig Barry dived over in the sec-ond minute. Flyhalf Gavin Hauptfleisch's penalty made it 8-0 but the Free State forwards then took complete control, allowing Grey College No 10 Johan Goosen to deliver a man-of-the-match performance. Goosen scored 22 points as his side ran out 42-21 winners to finish the Week as one of only two unbeaten teams – the other being Boland.

But the most sought-after signature for the provincial scouts was that of William Small-Smith, the Free State centre and skipper who was later appointed SA Schools captain. Perhaps unsurprisingly, Small-Smith will play his rugby in Pretoria in 2011, and in doing so he will follow in the footsteps of the late Ruben Kruger (Free State 1987-88), Dewald Potgieter (EP 2005) and CJ Stander (SWD 2008), who were also lured away to the capital at some stage of their careers.

Craig Barry enjoyed an excellent Craven Week but injury prevented him from taking his place in the SA Schools team.

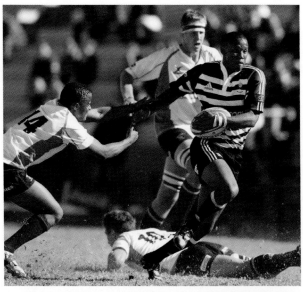

COCA-COLA U18 CRAVEN WEEK RESULTS

DAY ONE: June 27
WP 20 – T: Sikhumbuzo Notshet, Steven Kitshoff; **C:** Gavin Hauptfleisch (2); **P:** Hauptfleisch (2). **Lions 3** – P: Marais Schmidt.
Griffons 28 – T: Buran Parks, Barend Wessels, Rewaan Rodgers, Pierre Botes; **C:** Ryno Venter (4). **EP CD 25** – T: Jamion-Lewellyn Booysen, Charl Theron, Deswell van der Berg; **C:** Ntsikelelo Mlamleli (2); **P:** Mlamleli (2).
EP 19 – T: Jaco Grobler, Llwellyn Pieterse; **P:** Franz Botha (3). **BB 17** – T: Luan de Bruyn, Nardus van der Walt, Patrick Maponya; **C:** Rudi van Rooyen.
Boland 41 – T: Leroy Bitterhoutt (2), Wiaan Liebenberg, Robin Andrews, Ruan van Rooy, Maree Kotze; **C:** Gerbrand Roets (4); **P:** Roets.
Limpopo BB 11 – T: Roy-Ramon Auret; **P:** Lukas van Zyl (2).
Namibia 37 – T: Ian van Wyk (2), Gerhard Lotter, Eric Jordaan, Desiderius Sethie; **C:** Aurelio Plato (3); **P:** Plato (2). **Border CD 8** – T: Sakhi Notwala; **P:** Iwandile Dabele.

DAY TWO: June 28
FS 35 – T: William Small-Smith, Armandt Stoman, Kevin Luiters, Paul Jordaan; **C:** Johan Goosen (3); **P:** Goosen (3). **Border 13** – T: Andile Jho; **C:** Bongi Kobese; **P:** Kobese (2).
KZN 33 – T: Mbembe Payi, Meyrick Walker, Patrick Howard; **C:** Duncan Campbell (3); **P:** Campell (4). **Leopards 12** – T: Pieter Bornman, Louwrens Strydom; **C:** Divan Visser.
SWD 18 – T: Johannes Potgieter, Ruan Snyman; **C:** Hendri Rust; **P:** Rust (2). **Pumas 26** – T: Nkululeko Ngozo (2), Marthinus van der Merwe, Mark Pretorius; **C:** Van der Merwe (2), Clinton Swart.
Griquas 26 – T: Herman Groenewald, Hermanus van Niekerk; **C:** Jacobus du Plessis (2); **P:** Du Plessis (4). **Valke 24** – T: Wiehan Hay, Ruaan Stephen Lerm, Damian van Wyk; **C:** Ruan Barnard (3); **P:** Barnard.
Griquas CD 23 – T: Juan Booysen, Derek Botha, Johan Myburgh; **C:** Myburgh; **P:** Myburgh (2). **Zimbabwe 15** – T: Fakudzwa Chieza, Graham Logan; **C:** Corey van Rensburg; **P:** Van Rensburg.

Day Three: June 29
WP 58 – T: Devon Williams (2), Craig Barry (3), Sikumbuzo Notshe, Marvin Orie, Heinrich Arendse; **C:** Williams (6); **P:** Williams (2).
EP 19 – T: Marzuq Marman, Jacobus Swart, Duane Adams; **C:** Cleavan Laport (2).
Boland 36 – T: Ruan van Rooy (2), Jacques Rossouw, Ashlon Davids, Wiaan Liebenberg; **C:** Rossouw (4). **Griffons 34** – T: Niel Neethling, Jaco Enslin, Rene Eksteen (2), Ryno Venter; **C:** Venter (3); **P:** Venter.
Lions 23 – T: Gideon Muller, Fabian Booysen; **C:** Marius Schmidt (2); **P:** Schmidt (3). **Blue Bulls 20** – T: Rudi van Rooyen, Justin van Wyk ; **C:** Tony Jantjies (2); **P:** Jantjies; Drop goal: Jantjies.
Limpopo BB 50 – T: Roy-Ramon Auret (3), LC van Tonder, Cor Rautenbach, Lyvette Shikwambana, Lucas van Zyl, Juan Smit, Madala Ndinisa; **C:** Arno Venter (5). **Border CD 0**
EP CD 27 – T: Bart van der Vyver, Dylan Bon, Ryan Dugmore (2); **C:** Charl Theron (2); **P:** Willem Venter. **Namibia 18** – T: Berto Miller, Malcolm Moore; **C:** Aurelfo Plato (2).

Day Four: June 30
FS 30 – T: Anrich Bitzi (2), Marthinus Keyser, Gerhardus Olivier; **C:** Johan Goosen (2); **P:** Goosen (2). **KZN 20** – T: Pat Howard, Keelin Bastew, **C:** Duncan Campbell (2); **P:** Campbell (2).
Pumas 38 – T: Christoph Gouws, Jean-Pierre du Plessis, Marthinus van der Merwe, Mcebo Khumalo, Thembinkosi Nkosi; **C:** Clinton Swart, Van der Merwe; **P:** Swart (2), Van der Merwe. **Griquas 7** – T: Berne Bergh; **C:** Jacobus du Plessis.
SWD 21 – T: Percival Williams, Charlton Afrika, Carl Bowers; **P:** Hendri Rest (2). **Zimbabwe 3** – P: Corey Adam van Rensburg
Griquas CD 27 – T: Eswyn Heyns (2), Adolf du Plessis; **C:** Johan Myburgh (3); **P:** Johan Myburgh, Brendon Coetzer. **Leopards 25** – T: Franco Marais, Casper Badenhorst, Barend Swanepoel, Ando Booyens; **C:** Divan Visser; **P:** Visser.
Valke 26 – T: Ruaan Lerm, Jeandre Kotze; **C:** Ruan Barnard (2); **P:** Barnard (4). **Border 22** – T: Konke Maholwana (2), Thabo Sisusa, Andile Jho; **C:** Jason Germishuys.

Day Five: July 2
FS 42 – T: Johan Goosen, Paul Jordaan, Siphosethu Tom (2), Henco Greyling, Andreas Dercksen; **C:** Goosen (3). **WP 21** – T: Craig Barry, Andreas Dercksen; **C:** Devon Williams; **P:** Gavin Hauptfleisch (3)
Boland 49 T: Leroy Bitterhout (3), Andrew Van Wyk, Chevandre van Schoor, Willem Liebenberg, Ruan van Rooy; **C:** Jacques Rossouw (4); **P:** Rossouw (2). **Kwazulu Natal 23** – T: Wade Elliot, Jason Klaasen; **C:** Duncan Campbell (2); **P:** Campbell (3).
Blue Bulls 38 T: Rudi van Rooyen (2), Richmond Collins, Marcelle Smit, Justin Forwood, Brink Botha; **C:** Tony Jantjies (4). **Valke 15** P: Ruan Barnard (5).
Lions 28 T: Fabian Booysen, David Schmidt, Armandt Liebenberg; **C:** Schmidt (2); **P:** Schmidt (3). **Pumas 11** – T: Johan Haasbroek; P: Ryno Swart (2).
Griquas 29 – T: Herman van Niekerk, James Cloete, Johan du Plessis, Coenraad Cohn; **C:** Du Plessis (3); **P:** Du Plessis. **Griffons 7** – T: Buran Parks; Conversion: Ryno Venter.
EP 34 T: Francois Grobler (2), Marthinus du Toit, Justin Benn, Duane Adams; **C:** Franz Botha (2), Shane Gates; **P:** Botha. **Border 20** – T: Gert Meyer, Dean Hammond; **C:** Bongi Kobese (2); **P:** Kobese (2).
Platinum Leopards 65 – T: Zeann Lazenby, Sechaba Monyaki, Johan Bornman, Louwrens Strydom, Etienne Oosthuizen, Elvis Phalane, Divan Visser, Dean Basson, Christoffel Marais, Casper Badenhorst, Barend Swanepoel; **C:** Lazenby (4), Andries de Wet. **Border CD 5** – T: Siphesihle Bidli;
Zimbabwe 30 – T: Justin Coles, Cornelius Pieters, Ben Viljoen; **C:** Corey van Rensburg (2); **P:** Van Rensburg (2). **Namibia 19** – T: Nandivabu Karuuombe, Keff Lotter; **C:** Ailo-John Plato; **P:** John Plato.
Limpopo Blue Bulls 26 – T: Hencus van Wyk, Kefentse Mahlo; **C:** Lukas van Zyl (2); **P:** Van Zyl (4). **SWD Eagles 20** – T: Percival Williams, Sylvian Mahuza; Conversion: Hendri Rust (2); **P:** Rust (2).
Eastern Province CD 31 – T: Grant Prior (2), Dylan Bond, Ryan Dugmore, Deswell van der Berg; **C:** Willem Venter (3). **Griquas CD 20** – T: Frederick Botha, Gabriel Liebenberg, Johan Myburgh; **C:** Juan Booysen; **P:** Myburgh.

UNDER-18 COCA-COLA CRAVEN WEEK
27 June - 2 July 2010, Welkom

BLUE BULLS
J Forwood (Waterkloof), J van Wyk (Menlo Park), L de Bruin (Afrikaans HS), G Grobler (Afrikaans HS), S van Heerden (Afrikaans HS), D Meyer (Waterkloof), K Maake (Pretoria Boys' High), N vd Walt (Afrikaans HS), R van Rooyen (Afrikaans HS), T Jantjies (Menlo Park), L Africa (St Alban's College), T Smith (Waterkloof), B Botha (Afrikaans HS), R Collins (Pretoria Boys' High), S Robinson (Waterkloof), T Nhlapo (Zwartkops), J Rautenbach (Afrikaans HS), D Fielies (Waterkloof), E Wallis (Waterkloof), F Tredoux (Waterkloof), P Maponya (Waterkloof), X Nkosi (Hendrik Verwoerd).

BOLAND
Julian Swarts (Schoonspruit), Jaco Visagie (Augsburg), Visser Jonck (Lutzville), Carlon Carolissen (Klein Nederburg), Pieter-Stef du Toit (Swartland), Ancor van Wyk (Vredendal), Wiaan Liebenberg (Drostdy THS), Malherbe van Wyk (Hugenote), Robin Andrews (New Orleans), Gerbrand Roets (Drostdy THS), Leroy Bitterhout (Klein Nederburg), Bronvin Marais (Weston), Chevandre van Schoor (Klein Nederb), Ruan van Rooy (Dirkie Uys), Jacques Rossouw (Piketberg), Danie Cillie (Piketberg), Andrew Beerwinkel (Porterville), Eduan Coetzee (Vredenburg), Glenton du Plessis (New Orleans), Godlen Masimla (Hugenote), Ashlon Davids (Schoonspruit), Maree Kotze (Hugenote).

BORDER
Allan Dell (Queen's College), Sihle Gogela (Queen's College), Chase Morison (Selborne), Andrew Love (Selborne), Callan Venter (Selborne), Dean Hammond (Selborne), Roelof Smit (Hangklip), Johan Meyer (Queen's College), Banai Kobese (Dale), James Alderman (Selborne), Ofenze Boloko (Selborne), Andile Jho (Dale), Keegan Schalkwyk (Stirling), Achumile Mashalaba (Dale), Jason Germishuys (Selborne), Tyran Fagan (Hudson Park), Minlali Mpafi (Hudson Park), Kwezi Mona (Selborne), Sermaine Kleinsmith (Hangklip), Solanga Mahoulana (Queen's College), Sinjin Greyvenstein (Dale), Thabo Sisua (Hudson Park).

BORDER COUNTRY DISTRICTS
Christopher Keegan (Mthatha HS), Whity Jali (Zimele), Luzuko Tyali (Mthatha HS), Msawenkosi Tungela (Mthawelanga), Sakhe Notwala (Ugi HS), Sphathise Nyanda (Jamangile), Athi Ntshiba (Kokstad HS), Odwa Akhaula (Mtawelanga), Siphesihle Bidu (JS Skenja), Lizalise Maliwa (Ugi HS), Lunga Grangxa (Dalibaso), Aphiwe Makala (Dalibaso), Axole Beqezi (CHB-Nggeleni), Sibabalwe Msuthu (Mthatha), Thabo Dislokwe (Dalibaso), Manyano Ntshontsho

(Zimele), Wanda Mpulu (Dordrecht HS), Siphelele Jobeni (Indwe HS), Lwando Simunca (St John's), Aphiwe Doti (Dalibaso), Sandisile Poswa (Zimele), Buhle Mtyana (Zimele).

EASTERN PROVINCE
Brendon Olivier (Nico Malan), Jason Thomas (Muir), Asanda Modise (Newton THS), Ian Groenewald (Nico Malan), Lourens du Toit (Framesby), Justin Benn (Daniel Pienaar), Xolani Mate (Newton THS), JJ Swart (Grey), Jaco Grobler (Framesby), Franz Botha (Brandwag), Vaughan Casling (Grey), Shane Gates (Muir), Rossouw Prinsloo (Nico Malan), Nzuko Ndlela (Grey), Dwayne Adams (Despatch), Marzug Maarman (Muir), Arno Ebersohn (Framesby), Stephan Zaaiman (Framesby), Jaco Bernardo (Framesby), Clinton Felix (Framesby), Llwellyn Pieterse (Brandwag), Cleavan Laporte (Newton THS).

EASTERN PROVINCE COUNTRY DISTRICTS
Chad Bandfield (Graeme College), Wickus Deysel (Cradock), Chris Johan Steenkamp (Burgersdorp), Dean Moos (Volkskool), Grant Prior (St Andrew's College), Ricky van Straaten (Marlow), Roché Moss (HS Burgersdorp), Paul Schoeman (Marlow), Ryan Dugmore (St Andrew's College), Willem Venter (Aliwal-Noord), Deswell vd Berg (Marlow), Jamlon Booysen (Gill College), Bart vd Vyver (Gill College), Jaymo Lamont (Volkskool), Charl Theron (Volkskool), Waynver Reeners (Middellande), Andrew Kebble (St Andrew's College), Mark Prior (St Andrew's College), Luwellen George (Volkskool), Alsandro Davids (Union High), Dylan Bond (Alexandria High), Ntsikelelo Mlamleli (St Andrew's College).

GRIFFONS
Rewaan Rodgers (Hentie Cilliers), Rudi van Niekerk (Welkom Gym.), Pierre Botes (Vrede), Hanru vd Westhuizen (Welkom Gym.), Jason Bloemstein (Hentie Cilliers), Lilitha Kambula (Hentie Cilliers), Cloete Wessels (Afrikaans HS), Johntie Human (Kroonstad), Mario Noordman (Welkom Gym.), Ryno Venter (Hentie Cilliers), Luciano James (Hentie Cilliers), Jaco Enslin (Kroonstad), André Coetzee (Kroonstad), Jaco Arendse (Hentie Cilliers), Niel Neethling (Voortrekker), Carlyle Abrahams (Nobillis), Kubaan Laing (Afrikaans HS), Paul Lehoko (Harmony High), Buran Parks (Nobillis), René Eksteen (Kroonstad), Rian van Zyl (Voortrekker), Simon Marcus (Wessel Maree).

FREE STATE
Rudolf Fuls (Grey College), Anrich Bitzi (Grey College), Neethling Fouché (Grey College), Jacobus Nel (Grey College), Gerhardus Olivier (Grey College), Tyron Schultz (Grey College), Heinrich Douglas (Louis Botha THS), Neill Jordaan (Grey College), Kevin Luiters (Grey College), Johan Goosen (Grey

College), Ruwellyn Isbel (Grey College), Paul Jordaan (Grey College), William Small-Smith (Grey College), Jan Serfontein (Grey College), Raymond Rhule (Louis Botha THS), Armandt Stoman (Grey College), Rudolph Botha (Grey College), Thuso Chalatsi (Louis Botha THS), Leneve Damens (Grey College), Nhlanhla Hlongwane (Louis Botha THS), Siphosethu Tom (Grey College), Dylan Douglas (Louis Botha THS).

GOLDEN LIONS
Mauritz van Rooyen (Monument), Wian Fourie (Florida), Gideon Muller (Florida), Ruan Venter (Monument), Paul Willemse (Monument), Stefan Nel (Monument), Fabian Booysen (Florida), Ruan Steenkamp (Monument), Vian vd Watt (Florida), Marais Schmidt (Monument), Chad de Klerk (Monument), Sebastian v Heerden (Helpmekaar), Jako Viljoen (Monday), Tshepo Mooki (Florida), K Holtzhauzen (King Edward), Rikus van Niekerk (Monument), Siyotula (Jeppe), K Asiedu-Darkwah (King Edward), Tiaan MacDonald (Monument), Hanco Venter (Monument), S Shabangu (Jeppe), L Ntleki (King Edward).

GRIQUALAND WEST
Coenraad Cohn (Noord-Kaap), Nico vd Westhuizen (Diamantveld), Willem Bergh (Noord-Kaap), Francis Rooifontein (Prieska), Herman Groenewalt (Diamantveld), JJ Cloete (Noord-Kaap), Hendrik du Plessis (Noord-Kaap), Herman v Niekerk (Noord-Kaap), Renier Botha (Diamantveld), Noël Marx (Diamantveld), Valentino Meyers (Warrenvale), Petrus vd Merwe (Hartswater), Garneth Kock (Diamantveld), Richard-Dean Gorrah (Noord-Kaap), Hendrik Olivier (Noord-Kaap), Willem Botha (Noord-Kaap), Jean Maclean (Diamantveld), Andrick Keuler (Noord-Kaap), Leonardus Meyer (Pescodia), Darryl van Eck (Noord-Kaap), Elrico Fielies (Diamantveld), Thapelo Thupe (Noord-Kaap).

GRIQUAS COUNTRY DISTRICTS
Charles Thomas (Duineveld), Nigel Wentworth (Upington), Andre Esterhuyse (Upington), Johannes Maritz (Duineveld), Jacobus Hough (Duineveld), Werner Smit (Upington), Jacobus Alberts (Upington), Frederik Botha (Duineveld), Adolf du Plessis (Duineveld), Juan Booysen (Duineveld), Daphnul Booysen (Duineveld), John Goeieman (Upington), Eben Nel (Upington), Johannes Myburgh (Duineveld), Peter-John Walters (Upington), Abraham Jv Vuuren (Upington), Neo Masenge (Upington), Breyton du Plessis (Kalahari), Christiaan Steenkamp (Postmasburg), Brendon Coetzer (Kathu), Eswyn Heyns (Upington), Jacques Louw (Duineveld).

KWAZULU-NATAL
Niel Oelofse (Glenwood), Senzo Mtshali (Glenwood), Colin Richmond (Glenwood),

COCA-COLA CRAVEN WEEK

Wade Elliott (Glenwood), Alwyn Jv Vuuren (Glenwood), Meyrick Walker (Glenwood), Jason Klaasen (Maritzburg College), Guy Alexander (Hilton), Hilton Mudariki (Michaelhouse), Duncan Campbell (Westville), Emil Schwarz (Hilton), Patrick Howard (Michaelhouse), Andrew Holland (Kearsney), Mondli Ntshingila (Glenwood), Mbembe Payi (Durban HS), Zane van Greunen (Glenwood), Michael Tack (Hilton), Lungelo Chonco (Maritzburg College), Khaya Majola (Westville), Matthew Torrance (Glenwood), Edward Mongwambe (Durban HS), Bastew Keelin (Maritzburg College).

LEOPARDS
Koos Strauss (Volkskool Potch), Paballo Mohapi (Potch Boys' High), Louwrens Strydom (Vryburg), Etienne Oosthuizen (Bergsig Acad.), Etienne Smith (Schweizer-Reineke), Casper Badenhorst (Westvalia), Franco Marais (Rustenburg), Claude Tshidibi (Potch Boys' High), Divan Visser (Volkskool), Zeann Lazenby (HS Vryburg), Macdonal Monyaki (New Vision), Jacques van Staden (Schoonspruit), Khotso Leepile (Potch THS), Pieter Bomman (Klerksdorp), Fanie de Wet (Lichtenburg), Ando Booyens (Klerksdorp), Johan Jooste (Klerksdorp), Kyle Brook (Potch Boys' High), Barend Swanepoel (Westvalia), Elvis Phalane (Rustenburg THS), Dean Basson (Rustenburg), Stephan Kekana (Hartbeespoort).

LIMPOPO BLUE BULLS
Hencus van Wyk (Nylstroom), Mauritz Senekal (Hans Strijdom), Dewald Els (Ben Vorster), Jannie Stander (Frans du Toit), Lyvette Shikwambana (Ben Vorster), Madala Ndinisa (Ben Vorster), Roy-Ramon Auret (Ben Vorster), LC van Tonder (Pietersburg), Lucas van Zyl (Ben Vorster), Harold Vorster (Frans du Toit), Tovhi Nefale (Ben Vorster), Danie Ludick (Pietersburg), Marco Mason (Piet Potgieter), Maphuta Dolo (Ben Vorster),Kefentse Mahlo (Ben Vorster),Emmanuel Semeno (Pietersburg), Hermanus Swart (Hans Strijdom), Louis Uys (Pietersburg), Kiewiet Coetzee (Pietersburg), Cor Rautenbach (Hans Strijdom), Juan Smit (Ben Vorster), Don Mlondodozi (Ben Vorster).

NAMIBIA
Deserius Sethie (Walvis Bay), Meyer Moolman (Elnatan), Johan Steenkamp (Tsumeb Gym), Erik Jordaan (Windhoek Gym), Ian van Wyk (Windhoek Gym), Kevin Thuysema (Elnatan), Gerhard Jakobs (Otjiwarongo), Gerhard Lotter (Windhoek), Carel Thomas (Otjiwarongo), Aurelio Plato (Walvis Bay), Nandi Karuuombe (Jan Mohr), Walter Johr (MK Ger), Berto Miller (Windhoek), Malcolm Moor (Windhoek Gym), Daniel Bock (Walvis Bay), Hennie vd Westhuizen (Winhoek Gym), Kobus Mostert (Elnatan), Ethan Coetzee (Windhoek Gym), Simba Samson (Windhoek THS), Garth Ockhuisen (Windoek Gym), Kasper Esterhuizen (Windhoek Gym), Zian van Wyk (Jan Mohr).

JP du Plessis of the Pumas in action on the fith day of the Coca-Cola Craven Week.

PUMAS
Henri Boshoff (Nelspruit), Mark Pretorius (Nelspruit), Nico van Vuuren (Nelspruit), Vian Smit (Secunda), Christoph Gouws (Nelspruit), Hendrik Haasbroek (Nelspruit), Kwagga Smit (HTS Middleburg), CJ van der Schyff (Ligbron), Dillon Smit (HTS Middelburg), Clinton Swart (Standerton),Sanele Dlamini (Standerton), JP du Plessis (HTS Middelburg), Thabang Nkosi (Ligbron), Khumalo Mischak (Uplands College), Marinus van der Merwe (Standerton), Marais de Klerk (HTS Middelburg), Kudu Mhlanga (Gen. Hertzog), Chester Motha (Middelburg), Marchant van Aard (Nelspruit), Lourens Wild (Nelspruit), Henson Ngozo (Middelburg), Anele Blaauw (Middelburg).

SWD YOUNG EAGLES
Blaine James (Oudtshoorn), Conrad Estherhuizen (Sentraal), Nicol du Plessis (Oakdale), Ivan van Vuren (Outeniqua), Ruan Snyman (Oakdale), Leon Bredenhand (Oakdale), AJ du Toit (Oakdale), Rudi Boshoff (Outeniqua), Percy Williams (Oudtshoorn), Johannes Potgieter (Langenhoven), Doveno Bowers (Oudtshoorn), Tertius Kruger (Outeniqua), Lu-Wayne Meyer (Pacaltsdorp), Charlton Afrika (PW Botha), Jade Roelfse (York High), Lwando Maxeke (PW Botha), Ruan van Deventer (Outeniqua), Niel Hattingh (Outeniqua), Nigel Olieslager (Oudtshoorn), Ivan Ludick (Oakdale), Sylvian Mahuza (Outeniqua), Christian Rust (Oakdale).

VALKE
James Jackson (EG Jansen), Ruan de Bruto (EG Jansen), Wiehan Hay (Jeugland), P Matthee (EG Jansen), Ruan Botha (Jeugland), Isaac Nkosi (Oosterlig), S de Witt (Transvalia), Ruaan Lerm (EG Jansen), Wynand Venter (Jeugland), Michael Holtzhauzen (EG Jansen), Keanu Roman (Overvaal),

Gershan Helder (Jeugland), Damion van Wyk (Kempton Park), O Fortuin (Hans Moore), Ruan Barnard (EG Jansen), Ian Oosthuizen (Jeugland), Vincent Legae (Genl Smuts), Tiaan Benade (Kemptonp Park), T Pooe (Drie Riviere), Armand Erasmus (EG Jansen), Jeandre Kotze (EG Jansen), Katlego More (Hans Moore).

WESTERN PROVINCE
Steven Kitshoff (Paul Roos), Stephanus Coetzee (Paarl BH), Pieter Stemmet (Paul Roos), Rayn Smid (Rondebosch), Abraham Steyn (Paul Roos), Beyers de Villiers (Paarl BH), Sikhumbuzo Notshe (Wynberg), Jacobus Smit (Paarl Gym), Gerhard Jordaan (Boland Agric), Gavin Haupfleisch (Paarl BH), Heinrich Arendse (Scottsdene), Jacobus van Wyk (Paarl Gym), Tshotsho Mbovane (Paul Roos), Jean-Paul Lewis (Paul Roos), Craig Barry (Paul Roos), Jandré Conradie (Paarl Gym), Tshepo Motale (Bishops), Marvin Orie (Tygerberg), Andreas Dercksen (Paul Roos), Cheslin Kolbe (Brackenfell), Errol Jaggers (Paul Roos), Lionel Abrahams (Paarl BH).

ZIMBABWE
Kelvin Swan (St John's), Ben Viljoen (Lomagundi), Ian Muza (Prince Edward), Graham Logan (St John's), Matthew Lawson (St George's), Sir Farai Jijita (Prince Edward), Hopewell Tembo (St George's), Boris Fodoup-Mwambo (Falcon), MJ MacIntosh (St John's), Ulrich Kontchou (St John's), Justin Coles (St John's), Gareth Meikle (Lomagundi), Takudzwa Chieza (Prince Edward), Claude Bare (Prince Edward), Corey van Rensburg (Falcon), Kyle Lucas (St George's), Simon Kadirire (St George's), James Bruce (St George's), Murray Bryce-Rogers (Lomagundi), Jacobus Pieters (St John's), Takudzwa Chipumha (St John's), Victor Mushoriwa (Prince Edward).

OBITUARIES

GAWIE ACKERMAN

Gawie Ackerman played loosehead prop for Durban Wanderers and for Natal 29 times from 1960-65 though looking nothing like the bulky mastodons of modern times. He was a clever player at a time when Natal rugby was particularly strong under men like Brian Irvine, Tommy Bedford and Keith Oxlee, with the great Izak van Heerden as their coach. Ackerman was in Natal's unbeaten 1963 side that beat the Wallabies 14-13. For most of his working life Ackerman was a representative for Atlas Copco, a company specialising in industrial tools and equipment. He became a manager and went on pension in 2003. In 1966 he moved to Vryheid and played for Northern Natal, which was then a sub-union of Natal. In 1973 he moved to Ogies in Mpumalanga and played for South Eastern Transvaal.

Gabriel Joshua Ackermann was born in Port Elizabeth on 20 April 1938. After many months of ill health he died of a heart complaint on 8 March 2010.

DOROTHY BAISE

Dorothy Baise, wife of legendary referee Max Baise, died in Riversdale Hospital after a long battle against cancer. Dorothy and Max were always very close in their 56-year marriage and she supported him throughout his successful career in which he refereed seven Tests between 1967 and 1974 – in years when Tests were few. Dorothy was only 16 when she and Max, then 21, were married. She was born in Krugersdorp but her family moved to Odendaalsrus, where Max's father had a shop. When they met, Max was a chemist's assistant. Max says that Dorothy was his great support and his greatest critic.

Dorothy is survived by Max, their son Ronald and their daughter Bernice, and four grandchildren.

MARIUS BOSMAN

Marius Bosman was a player who achieved much in several countries during an itinerant career. He played rugby for teams in South Africa, New Zealand, Italy and Ireland. He was born in Johannesburg, educated at DF Malan High in Cape Town and showed early promise as a lock. He played for the Western Province Craven Week side and for South African Schools in 1988 and two years later started his provincial career, playing for Stellaland, a union based in Lichtenburg which no longer exists. The next year he played for the Pumas of Mpumalanga, whom he was to represent 107 times. In the middle of his Pumas career, in 1998 and 1999, he played for the South Western Districts Eagles 47 times. In 1999 he also had a match for the Stormers and in 2000 seven matches for the Bulls.

From the Pumas, Bosman went to Italy and played for Parma and then in 2004 went down to East London and played for the Border Bulldogs. The next year he was playing in New Zealand's National Provincial Championship for Marlborough. He ended his playing career playing for Westport in County Mayo, Ireland, as a player-coach. In reporting his death, the Westport club wrote: "Marius will be remembered as one of the most successful of Westport's coaches. His unique style and determination to succeed was a great inspiration to his teammates who are saddened by his unexpected death at such an early age." Higher honours came in 2003 when he played twice for an SA Development team and once for Central Unions. He went on tour to South America with the SA Development team. The Central Unions lost to an Irish Development team. Future Springbok Marius Hurter played for both teams.

Marius Bosman was born on 12 May 1969. He died of cancer on 21 October 2010.

DENNIS BRUTUS

Dennis Brutus was a political activist who channelled much of his activities into sport and did much to get South Africa excluded from the Olympic improvement because of apartheid. To some he was a nuisance, to others a hero. Brutus was born in Salisbury, as Harare then was, of South African parents. When he was four the family moved back to Port Elizabeth. A graduate of Fort Hare and a student at Wits, he would later hold professorships at three American universities, ending in Pittsburgh – a poet and a philosopher. Politically a Trotskyite, in 1959 he helped form the South African Sports Association that tried to get the establishment sports organisations to change of their own accord. That failed, and in 1962 he was a founding member of the South African Non-Racial Olympic Committee (SANROC) that sought the exclusion of South Africa from sport. He was also a patron of SACOS with its famous motto, 'no normal sport in an abnormal society'.

He suffered increasing persecution by the apartheid authorities – banned, arrested, condemned, shot escaping. He was sent to Robben Island where he was in the cell next door to Nelson Mandela and eventually went into exile, first in Britain and then in the USA. In 1991 he returned to South Africa. Rugby involvement? Obliviously the pressure he exerted on international bodies had an effect on rugby in South Africa. More directly, his non-racial stance opposed the playing of 'Tests' between the South African Coloured Rugby Board and the South African African Rugby Board. These had started in 1950. In 1961 Brutus loudly urged their discontinuance. At that time he also urged that the SA African Rugby Board disband and that the Wallaby tour be boycotted because there were no Aboriginals in their side. A few years later the SA Coloured Rugby Board was disbanded and instead the SA Rugby Union was founded as a non-racial body.

Dennis Vincent Brutus was born on 28 November 1924 and died at his home in Cape Town on 26 December 2009, survived by his wife, May, two sisters, nine grandchildren and four great-grandchildren.

RALPH CAWOOD

Ralph Cawood discovered his life's true actualisation, combining a passion for rugby coaching with his compassion for those

OBITUARIES

less privileged. Like all the best coaches, Cawood had an eye for spotting raw young talent; more specifically, those do who not stem from a community rugby culture. While a development officer with the KZN Rugby Union in Pietermaritzburg, Cawood trawled the sprawling townships, introducing youngsters to the game with such success that a healthy number were awarded bursaries to top rugby schools. And, in so doing, Cawood changed the lives of many children from deprived backgrounds, including those who didn't excel in the game, his humble example inspiring all those whose lives he touched, engendering in them the life skills and values inherent in the sport. At the time of his death he was the assistant manager of the Midlands Rugby Academy.

Cawood, a backline player just below the provincial radar, was an honourable, principled man who enjoyed life to the full while disliking pomp and ceremony. He could be said to have got it right: putting others before self, serving his fellow man, especially the downtrodden. He never judged, always seeing the good in others. Apart from rugby, his other interests included the family farm and herb cultivation. Ralph Cawood's unique qualities will be sorely missed by all. There are not many like him.

Ralph Cawood Cawood was born in Kimberley on 2 November 1957 and died near Pietermaritzburg on 9 March 2010 after suffering a heart attack. He is survived by sons Ralph-Marc and Guy, mother Yvonne, twin sisters Jeanne and Bridgette, and brothers Timothy and Nicholas. – By Jonathan Cook

- -

BRIAN CLARKE

When the new union of South Eastern Transvaal was formed out of Eastern Transvaal in 1969, Brian Clarke of the Witbank club was a founder member, playing prop in all eight matches that year. Playing days over, he coached South Eastern Transvaal (now the Mpumalanga Pumas) from 1971-75 and was for many years on the South Eastern Transvaal executive, part of the time as a vice-president of the union.

Brian Percy Clarke was born on 28 April 1938 and died on 12 February 2010.

ERNEST CLARKE

Ernest Clarke of Eastern Province appeared in the very first Test played by the South African Coloured Rugby Board when they played the South African Bantu Rugby Board's Springboks at the Showgrounds in Port Elizabeth. There was a crowd of 15,000 which included mayor Boet Erasmus. It was a great game for rugby in South Africa outside of white establishment rugby.

The Coloured side had just come off a week-long tournament and had had little chance to recover or prepare. The Bantu Springboks, captained by Grant Khomo, were beaten up front but were too good on the attack and won 14-3, their points including a penalty try awarded by referee Punky Davids. Clarke was also an outstanding cricketer.

- -

HARRY CONRADIE

Harry Conradie had an enormous appetite for rugby. He had already propped for Orange Free State B when he moved to Port Elizabeth and played for Crusaders. He went on to play for Park and Police as well, ending as the chairman of Police and still playing for them at the age of 60, after starting at the age of five. In fact, at that age he played two matches for the club – for the 2nd XV and for the Old Crocks. A tough man, his nickname was Ratel (Badger). He said of his rugby longevity: "I've not got a secret. I've just never stopped playing rugby."

Gavin Cowley, who was a team-mate describes Conradie as a versatile player, often a reserve. But in 1978 he twice propped for Eastern Province. He died in 2010.

- -

SKY DE BEER

Sky de Beer and his brother MC both played loose forward for Garrison and for Northern Transvaal – MC seven times on the flank and Sky 28 times at eighthman, MC from 1953-55, Sky from 1954-59. They go down in history as two of the hard men of the hard world of Northern Transvaal rugby. Sky was in the 1956 team which won the Currie Cup and in the combined Northern Transvaal-Western Transvaal team which beat the French 19-18 in 1958.

Richard de Beer died on 7 June 2010, aged 78.

ERNST DINKELMANN

Ernst Dinkelmann, a great Springbok lock of the 1950s and Northern Transvaal coach, was one of many locks who developed only after school, for at Ermelo High he was mainly a scrumhalf who played for the old South Eastern Transvaal Sub-union. His flyhalf was Lourens Stopforth, his school coach. On that tour he played in 19 matches, including the Tests against Scotland, when he scored a try in the 44-0 rout, Ireland, England and France when he scored a try as well. His

From Erries, Dinkelmann went off to the University of Pretoria to read medicine, played for the University and Northern Transvaal before becoming a Junior Springbok in 1950 and a Springbok on the 1951/52 tour to the UK, Ireland and France. On that tour he played in 19 matches, including the Tests against Scotland, when he scored a try in the 44-0 rout, Ireland, England and France when he scored a try as well. His other two Tests were against the Wallabies in 1953. He played 49 times (five times as captain) for Northern Transvaal between 1947 and 1955, never once dropped, at lock and eighthman. He was the first Tukkie to become a Springbok.

Doc Craven said of him: "He was one of the few players I knew who would play himself into total exhaustion in a match." In his book on the 1951/52 tour, Dick Stent wrote: "A nice character touch was the ready way in which he went to the help of anyone of either side who was hurt during play." He was dropped for the Welsh Test but in the week before the game Salty Durand, one of the other locks on tour and chosen for the Test, had a bout of flu. Dinkelmann looked after him and declared him fit to play – at his own expense.

After his playing days Dinkelmann remained involved in rugby. He was the chairman of Northern Transvaal's medical subcommittee as well as the selection committee. He coached Oostelikes, Defence and Tukkies as well as Northern Transvaal. He was also one of those who got mini rugby going in Northern Transvaal as the Blue Bulls were then known. He wrote a handbook on the development of handling skills in rugby. At one stage he helped Transvaal when Harry Viljoen was the coach. He had coached Viljoen when the scrumhalf was playing in the Northern Transvaal. Dinkelmann, who won a gold medal as the best student at the University of Pretoria in 1950, was a medical practitioner, first in Nelspruit and then in Pretoria for many years in partnership with Louis Wessels, well known as a referee and a doctor to the Springboks.

Ernst Erich Dinkelmann was born near Breyton in the Ermelo District on 14 May 1927. He married Lucia Schoeman and the couple had six children – a daughter Ingrid and five sons, Anton, Richard, Roland, Paul and Manfred. He and his wife went back to Nelspruit. He died in the Nelspruit Medi-Clinic on 22 October 2010.

His son Roland said after his father's death: "My father loved rugby so much he was on the field practically every day. He was probably the best role model a young man could ask for."

Dinkelmann is survived by Lucy, his six children and his grandchildren.

- -

MANNETJIES GERICKE

It may have been an old knee injury that contributed much to the death of Mannetjies Gericke, a Springbok scrumhalf of 1960. Gericke had trouble with his knee and was unable to walk when he went into hospital for a knee replacement in September 2010. He suffered greatly after the operation and died little more than a month afterwards. In the photograph of the 1960 Springbok side, his only Test, he was unable to kneel because he had so injured his knee playing against Scotland.

Born in Kimberley, Gericke was the first old boy of Diamantveld High to become a Springbok, a scrumhalf in the days of Richard Lockyear, Tommy Gentles, Dawie de Villiers, Nelie Smith and Piet Uys. He joined the railways after school and played for Griqualand West, including the match against the 1953 Wallabies. Later he moved to the Transvaal and a job at South African Breweries, for whom he was a representative. A particularly strong scrumhalf, he played for Western Transvaal and, 34 times between 1956 and 1961, for Transvaal. He scored two tries on debut against Orange Free State. He played for the Junior Springboks against the 1955 Lions while a Griqua player and was then the vice-captain of the Junior Springboks on their South American tour in 1959. He had three uncles who played for Griqualand West, one of them for the Junior Springboks in 1932

who also toured South America.

In 1960 Mannetjies played his only Test, the early one of the year against Scotland in Port Elizabeth when the Springboks won 18-10. Gericke also played provincial baseball and cricket and then when there were attempts to establish rugby league in South Africa in the early 1960s he went off to play rugby league and went on the ill-fated tour to Australia. In later years he coached the Transvaal Rooibokke and Roodepoort. His widow Wilna said he "lived for the game".

Frederick Wilhelm Gericke was born on 8 June 1933. He died in the Wilgeheuwel Hospital in Roodepoort on 22 October 2010, survived by Wilna, his sixth wife to whom he was married for 24 years, daughter Doris Brown, sons Fred (Frederick Wilhelm), Butch (Lucas) and Fanie (Stephanus), eight grandchildren and five great-grandchildren.

- -

RODNEY HARTMAN

Rodney Hartman was one of South Africa's top sports journalists, best known for his writings on boxing but also for his other involvement. Hartman had a long battle against cancer. One of the last people to see him was former South African cricket boss Ali Bacher, who told how Hartman's greatest regret had been the burden that he felt he had become to his family. His wife, journalist Carien Hartman, said it had been a relief for him. His dying words to her were: "This is my gift for you, finally a long holiday from me."

He died at the Linksfield Clinic on the night of 18 May 2010, on his 32nd wedding anniversary. He was 61. Bacher was with him the night of his death and before he died Hartman said to him: "Ali, you and I have run well between the wickets." Hartman had been Bacher's chief of communications during the 2003 Cricket World Cup in South Africa. Apart from his biography of Bacher, Hartman wrote Hansie and the Boys as well as a biography of Brian Mitchell. Two months before he died, Golden Gloves Promotions CEO Rodney Berman and Jeff Ellis organised a boxing event to help Hartman meet his medical bills. Hartman was there.

- -

ALLEN HIRSCHBERG

Allen Hirschberg was a most reliable

referee. The plea is often for consistency and Hirschberg was that from match to match throughout a long career that started in the early 1960s when he joined the Western Province Referees' Society.

Hirschberg had been a player - for False Bay and then for Union. His father had no appreciation of rugby at all and so Allen, being Jewish, was not allowed to play because rugby happened on a Saturday. But going for a walk on a Saturday was acceptable. Allen would throw his togs over the wall into Alf Greenblo's garden and go for a walk. Alf would pick him up around the corner and off they would go. This was fine till one Monday when Allen came to breakfast and there was his father with the Cape Times and a picture of Allen scoring a try at Newlands!

Hirschberg was for many years a first-league referee in the Western Province, reaching provincial honours. After refereeing he coached at Villagers for a while and stayed fit, attending their gym classes virtually up to the time of his last illness.

Allen David Hirschberg was born in Victoria West on 21 September 1929. He died at home in Wynberg of cancer on 17 October 2010, survived by wife Daphne and their three sons. Daphne tells of Allen's excitement before his first match. She was in the kitchen and in he came in his full regalia, whistle and all, to ask: "How do I look?"

- -

PEEWEE HOWE

Born in Port Nolloth on 30 August 1932, Howe switched coasts and grew up on the eastern side of South Africa. It was at Dale College that Bennett Frederick Howe became Peewee as the school already had a Shortie and a Stompie. Peewee stuck.

Howe was a wool buyer by occupation and travelled far and wide, to Europe, the USA and the Far East. Most of his life was spent in East London but he moved to Port Elizabeth in 1980. He was a talented sportsman, also playing cricket for Border – small but a great ball player and quick on his feet.

Howe played club rugby for Hamiltons in East London and played for Border as a flyhalf or a centre. In 1953, not yet 21, he twice played at centre when the Wallabies beat Border 9-6 and 24-13. In 1955 he was in the Border team that beat the great British Lions 14-12. In 1956 he

OBITUARIES

toured Australia and New Zealand on that tough Springbok tour. The Springboks won both Tests in Australia but then walked into New Zealand, which was on a war footing after the 4-0 whitewash of 1949. It was a tough tour and, for the first time, after four series between the two countries, the All Blacks won. Howe played centre in the first and flyhalf in the fourth Test, both won by the All Blacks. In the first Test he scored South Africa's only try in a 10-6 defeat. The tour started with a loss, and Howe was the flyhalf when Waikato – and Don Clarke – won 14-10. He played in the first five matches on the tour and in 18 of the 29 matches in all – eight times at flyhalf and 10 times in the centre.

In 1958 Howe was at centre for a combined Border, Eastern Province and North Eastern Districts side that lost to France and in 1960 was again at centre when the All Blacks gave Border a hiding. For his time, Howe had remarkable international experience on the rugby field.

Howe, who suffered from Alzheimer's in his later years, died in Port Elizabeth on 22 April 2010 at the age of 77, survived by wife Anne (nee Phelps), sons Michael, who played centre for Eastern Province, and Gareth, daughter Janet Meyer and grandchildren.

- -

KANON ISAACS

His real name was Yusuf Isaacs. His nickname was given him as a boy because of the sudden, urgent sounds that his bowel managed. "Daar poep kanon alweer." Kanon he stayed for the rest of his days.

Kanon gained much fame as a referee within the SA Coloured Rugby Board and SARU ranks. Three matches stand out. In 1965 he became a 'Test' referee when he refereed the match between the SA Coloureds and the SA Africans at Green Point Track, a match the Coloureds won 14-11. In 1966 Isaacs refereed the Rhodes Trophy Final at City Park and a woman ran onto the field to remonstrate with him. In 1978 Eastern Province, of SARU, played KWARU in the Adcock Stadium. Cheeky Watson seemed about to score a try when Desmond Booysen flew into him. Watson lost the ball and rioting ensued, enough to stop the match which SARU ordered replayed. To ensure fair play they flew

Kanon Isaacs up from Cape Town. He clamped down from the start, sending off Edgar Maree of Eastern Province and Temba Ludwaba of KWARU.

Yusuf Isaacs was born in Cape Town's Bo-Kaap on 28 January 1931. He went to Muir Street School and then to Trafalgar High. He became a tailor. Group Areas sent him to Lotus River, where he was living when he died in 2009.

- -

MENDEL KAPLAN

Mendel Kaplan, a seriously wealthy businessman with big interests in South Africa and Israel, was a great rugby lover. He played fullback for Wynberg in the same team as Doug Hopwood and Dave Stewart and then for Northerns RFC. In 2009 he instigated and funded a magnificent rugby exhibition at the Jewish Museum in Cape Town. He was a great philanthropist, a dollar billionaire. He had homes in Jerusalem, Caesarea, Cape Town and at Twickenham – just to be near to the rugby ground.

Kaplan, who was born in South Africa in 1936, had a stroke watching the Springboks lose to Saracens and died two days later, on 21 November 2009, and was buried in Cape Town. He was survived by his wife Jill and children David, Sharon, Romi and Oren and grandchildren.

- -

LIAAN KIRKHAM

Every year we record a rugby death in a motor accident. This time it's Liaan Kirkham, a mercurial wing/fullback in the Gio Aplon mould who came within an ace of becoming a Springbok. Kirkham had just dropped his son off and was on his way home when his car was hit by an oncoming vehicle. A case of culpable homicide is pending.

Kirkham had a full rugby career spanning 11 representative seasons, starting in 1978 when he was 19. He played provincial rugby for Stellaland (6 matches) while doing his military training, Transvaal (72 matches) between 1980 and 1987 and Natal (6 matches) in 1988. He had higher honours, playing for the Gazelles against the Jaguars in 1980, SA Country and the SA Barbarians. In 1984 he was on the bench for both Springbok Tests against England without getting onto the field. His brother Tobie also played provincial rugby.

William Henry Kirkham was born in Welkom on 18 November 1958. He was educated at CBC Welkom and the University of Natal. He died not far from his home in Johannesburg on 9 October 2010, survived by his ex-wife Ria, their daughter Liandi and their son Greg, who is a boarder at Pretoria Boys' High.

- -

JOHN KNOX

Sturdy, fast John Knox was an outstanding three-quarter in his time, a player who would surely have become a Springbok in more generous times. In 1975 he went on tour to South America with the Oribis (SA U21) and was a Springbok trialist but did not quite get there. Knox, a Pretorian, played his first provincial rugby for Northern Transvaal in 1973 when he was 19, then for Natal in 1975 and 1976 but then went home to Pretoria and again played for Northern Transvaal, for whom he played 67 times till he retired in 1980.

John Knox was born in Pretoria on 15 March 1954. He went to school at Wonderboom in Pretoria and played his club rugby in Pretoria for Oostelikes and then Pretoria Harlequins. He died in Pretoria of throat cancer on 8 September 2009, survived by daughter Jessica and son Jason. The funeral service was held in the NG Ooskerk just opposite Loftus Versfeld.

- -

RUBEN KRUGER

Ruben Kruger was a great Springbok – a great player and an exceptional gentleman, the epitome of brave selflessness on the field and even more so off it. His death at such a young age has been a blow to many even though he had fought a long battle with cancer. His end came so suddenly, driving his car when the disease overwhelmed him.

Kruger was a man of the Free State but played much of his rugby for Northern Transvaal, rewarded with great honours at all levels – Craven Week for Free State, SA Schools, SA U20, Springbok Sevens, Junior Springboks and then Springboks. Nobody played for South Africa with greater dedication – the silent assassin on the flank who gave his all and was never known to do anything out of place on the field. In 1995 he scored the try in the Durban wet that got the Springboks into the World Cup final. He was convinced that he scored a try in the final but, in the days before the TMO, it was not awarded. He was made Player of the Year in that World Cup-winning year when all the Springboks were heroes. In all Kruger played in 36 Tests from his debut against Argentina in 1993 to his health-enforced retirement after the disappointing 1999 Rugby World Cup, though he did sign off with a victory over the All Blacks in Cardiff. He also played in another 20 matches on tours.

In 1996 the Springboks led France 13-12 with time running out. The French won a great ball for their drop-goal specialist Christophe Lamaison. It seemed that he had time, but somehow, miraculously, straining every muscle in his powerful body, Kruger charged down the kick and the day was won for South Africa. He must have found it an exciting moment, though his expression just did not change. It never did.

Ruben Jacobus Kruger was born in Vrede on 30 March 1970. He spent the latter part of his schooling at Grey College. He first played club rugby for Collegians and provincial rugby for Free State, making his provincial debut in 1991 when the Free Staters beat Northern Transvaal in Bloemfontein. In 1995 he moved to Pretoria to join his brother-in-law, Springbok Drikus Hattingh, as a market agent. His illness first manifested itself in 1999 when he was diagnosed as having a brain tumor. The tumor was removed and he paid a visit to a faith-healer in Nigeria. In 2009 the trouble returned and he had an operation. He was well enough to be driving his car when he was overcome and died in Pretoria on 27 January 2010, survived by his wife Lize and daughters Zoe and Isabella.

- - - - - - - - - - - - - - - - -

TIGER LANCE

Tiger Lance was one of the greatest all-round sportsmen in South Africa's history. He was best known for his cricketing exploits but also played flyhalf for Northern Transvaal Under-19.

Herbert Roy Lance was born in Pretoria on 8 June 1940 and educated at CBC Pretoria. He died in a Johannesburg hospital on 10 November 2010 of complications following a motor accident nearly a month earlier. He is survived by wife Marlene and children Clinton, who played for Transvaal Schools at Craven Week, and Tracey.

BUTCH LOCHNER

Butch Lochner, Springbok loose forward of the 1950s, was much involved in rugby football all his life and at the highest level. He was a tough Springbok, a devastating tackler in the Ryk van Schoor mould, but mostly on the flank. Like Van Schoor he was not a big man but determined.

Lochner was born in Vredenburg, where he died, a Weskusklong, like his uncle Flappie Lochner who played for South Africa in the 1930s. Flappie was a centre and in later years Butch said that he too would be a centre in modern rugby because he would not have been big enough to be a forward. Uncle Flappie and Butch Lochner's father were brothers but Uncle Flappie and Butch shared the same names – George Philip, or, in Uncle Flappie's case, George Philippus. Like Uncle Flappie, Butch went to school at Dirkie Uys in Moorreesburg and then to university in Stellenbosch, as both his parents had done. Uncle Flappie qualified as a schoolmaster, Butch in the agricultural field.

While at Stellenbosch, Butch played for Western Province, but then he went off to Moorreesburg for a year and then on agricultural missions to the Eastern Cape, playing for Grootfontein and Eastern Province and for Hamilton in East London as well as for Border. He also played for Moorreesburg and, like Uncle Flappie, for Boland. Like Uncle Flappie, Butch became the chairman of selectors. In fact, from 1967 to 1981, the chairman of selectors was GP Lochner, except for one year when Johan Claassen held the position.

Uncle Flappie played for Western Province, Eastern Province and Boland, Butch for Western Province, Boland, Eastern Province and Border. Butch was nine when he played for Vredenburg High's Under-17s and 20 when he played for Maties and Western Province. In 1954 he was in Moorreesburg and played for Boland. In 1955 he returned to Maties and played eighthman for WP against the Lions and flank for Southern Universities, when he scored a try and the Lions won 20-17. In the third Test he was at eighthman in the place of the injured Daan Retief [see page 382].

The next year Butch went to Australasia, playing in both Tests in Australia and in all four against the All Blacks.

The French came in 1958 when Butch was at the agricultural College in Grootfontein. He played for Eastern Province and in both Tests against France. The Springboks drew the first 3-all when Butch scored a try, and lost the second 9-5, their first losing series at home since 1896. In 1971 Butch became a Western Province selector and then in 1977 the convener of the South African selection committee. That was the year when Springboks trials were opened to all races and Dougie Dyers became a national selector. Butch was a chicken farmer at Kuils River at one stage, then a colonel and sports director in the army at the invitation of Magnus Malan, and then as successor to Doc Craven as the director of sport at Stellenbosch University.

Always a fitness fanatic, Butch had his first health setback when he suffered a stroke walking on the mountains at Stellenbosch. He and wife Jean-Marie, whom he met when she was 16, moved to Mykonos on the West Coast. Heart troubles persisted and he suffered from Alzheimer's. Born in Vredenburg on 1 February 1931, he died in Vredenburg Hospital on 27 August 2010, survived by Jean-Marie, sons Dieter and Jan, daughters Tina and Margie, and nine grandchildren.

- - - - - - - - - - - - - - - - -

BOBBY MYBURGH

Bobby Myburgh loved rugby, loved Northern Transvaal and loved his club, Pretoria, the oldest club in Northern Transvaal. He was an eighthman and played 22 times for Northern Transvaal from 1959-62. A policeman, he played for Combined Services when they famously beat the All Blacks 8-3 at Loftus Versfeld in 1960. He also played against them when they beat Northern Transvaal 27-3 earlier in the tour. It was said of him that the Blue Bulls were his life. After his playing days Myburgh became a provincial selector and a coach, first of Pretoria, who won the Carlton Cup on his watch, then of Northern Transvaal and later Lowveld.

JL Myburgh was 75 when he died of natural causes in an old-age home in Pretoria on 22 December 2009. He was survived by his wife, five children and nine grandchildren. His son Johan said of him: "We will remember him best for his ability to make all of us laugh. He always had time for a joke."

OBITUARIES

DIRK NAUDE

Like his famous brother Tiny Naudé, Dirk Naudé played lock, a giant of a man and athletic to boot. He made his debut for Transvaal in 1975. He played for them that year before going off to Italy. He was revered at Rovigo where he played for six seasons, a man the Italians thought of as a Samson. In 1975 and 1979 Rovigo won the Italian championship. Back in South Africa Naudé played for Western Province from 1979-82. In 1983 he again played for Transvaal.

Dirk Frederick Naudé was born in Bothaville on 23 January 1953. He was educated at Volkskool in Potchefstroom and then at Stellenbosch University. He was walking with a friend when he had a sudden heart attack and died on 15 January 2010.

WILLIE ODENDAAL

Eighthman Willie Odendaal of Wasps-Wanderers in Durban played 38 times for Natal from 1946-53. In 1952 he was Natal's captain. He played against the 1949 All Blacks who beat Natal 8-0 and against the 1953 Wallabies whom Natal beat 15-14 in the opening match of their tour.

TOMMY PETERSEN

Big, strong, gentle Tommy Petersen had an interesting career during interesting times in South African rugby – a time of growing closer and growing further apart. There were four national bodies to run rugby in South Africa: the SA Rugby Board, the SA Rugby Union, the SA Rugby Football Federation and the SA African Rugby Board. There were several attempts to get the four to get closer to each other. Three managed it but SARU grew more distant.

Tours became a divisive issue, starting with the Federation's tour to Europe and England's 1971 tour to South Africa. The latter was the start of Petersen's international career. England played the Federation at Athlone Stadium. The Proteas were captained by the great Dougie Dyers. The Moerats of Paarl withdrew because of pressure on the Tuesday before the match and Dyers brought in Blue Birds club-mate Petersen, big and strong and in the front row. Petersen then played 17 successive 'Tests' for the Federation, either against the SA African side or against touring teams. Petersen was in the sides

that played England in that watershed match, the 1974 British & Irish Lions, France in 1975, New Zealand in 1976 and Rhodesia on tour in 1978.

In the late 1970s the SA Rugby Football Board, the Federation and the SA Rugby Association, as the SA African Rugby Board came to be known, joined forces. Western Province League, a Federation affiliate, played in the Sport Pienaar competition with Petersen as their captain and they beat Northern Free State. After his playing days he coached Northerns, a Western Province club based at Avonwood.

Thomas Petersen was born in Ravensmead, Cape Town, on 14 March 1947. He was educated at Glenlily School and played for Western Province schools.

Petersen died of lung cancer on 1 December 2009, survived by wife Pauline, sons Therlow and Eldron. Therlow is a nippy fullback who made a name for himself in the Varsity Cup.

JOHAN PIENAAR

Johan Pienaar played 41 times in the threequarters for Orange Free State, making his debut in 1948 when Free State beat Natal 22-8. What made his achievements more remarkable was that he played his rugby for the Bethlehem club, which was remote from Bloemfontein. In fact his debut was in Bethlehem when Natal came over the mountains. He played twice against the 1949 All Blacks – Free State drew 9-9 with them in Kroonstad but lost 14-9 in Bloemfontein. Pienaar was a Springbok trialist in 1949, a big, powerful centre who could also play flyhalf. Pienaar was born in Nylstroom in 1927 and went to Voortrekker High School in Boksburg before moving to Bethlehem. In 1947 he played for the town side and then for North Eastern Free State.

FJ Pienaar died on 4 March 2010. He was 83, the third oldest living Free State player at the time.

DAAN RETIEF

Daan Retief, great Springbok loose forward, first played top rugby as a wing for Northern Transvaal, for whom he played 45 times, but he was an eighthman when he played for South Africa and rose to be one of the best players in the world

in his time. He was 30 when he became a Springbok in 1955, playing in three of the four Tests against the British Lions and missing out the third only because he was injured. In that Test he was replaced by Butch Lochner [see page 381].

Retief played in all six Tests on the 1956 Australasian tour. He scored tries in both Tests against Australia and in the second Test against New Zealand, the one the Springboks won. The Australian press referred to him as Wild Man Retief.

Daniel Francois Retief was born in Lichtenburg on 28 June 1925. He went to Lichtenburg High and then the University of Pretoria. Finished with university he played for Harlequins. He was a market agent. He died at a clinic in Bedfordview on 22 September 2010 after an illness of two months. Retief is survived by wife Toetie, children Charl, Linda and Antoinette and seven grandchildren.

DAN SKINETTE

Dan Skinette, lock for Eastern Province and the SA Coloured side, was the biggest man of his time. He played twice for the Coloured side against the Bantu/African Springboks – winning 18-11 in 1957 and losing 8-5 in 1968, both in Port Elizabeth. At the time of the second match he was 41.

Daniel Daan Skinette was born in Graaff-Reinet on 27 September 1927, moved to Port Elizabeth when young and worked in a bakery. He died in Port Elizabeth on 6 October 2009. His wife predeceased him.

GERT SMIT

Gert Smit of the Garrison club played fullback for Northern Transvaal 17 times from 1956-57, scoring 90 points. Gert Albertus Smit died in 2010.

WELILE SPEELMAN

Welile Speelman was a founder member of Walmer Wallabies and hooked for KWARU. After playing he coached Wallabies. *Welile Joseph Speelman was born on 13 August 1940 and died in Zwide, Port Elizabeth, on 3 May 2010.*

DARRELL THOMSON

Sportswriter Darrell Thomson was very much a man of Natal. He was also much admired and loved for his dedication, skill and gentlemanliness. Thomson was sports editor of the Sunday Tribune for

25 years, from somewhere in the 1960s. He won many awards, including the SA Breweries Sports Journalist of the Year several times, covered especially rugby, cricket and tennis, and he did other things like the centenary publications of the Natal Rugby Union and the Natal Cricket Union. He loved Natal and its sport.

Thomson played for the Maritzburg College 1st XV when Skonk Nicholson was a young coach and Keith Oxlee was a young flyhalf just behind him at school. When Natal won the Currie Cup for the first time, at Loftus Versfeld in 1990, captain Craig Jamieson insisted that Thomson join in the team's celebration. He was so respected and trusted and delivered his last copy just a week before he died.

Darrell Aubrey Thomson was born in Pietermaritzburg on 7 October 1932 and died of a heart attack in Durban on 18 February 2010, survived by wife Brenda, sons Rodney and Barry, and grandchildren Wesley, Kyle, Blaire-Anne and Jessica.

BRUCE THORNE

Grahame Thorne was a famous All Black centre and later a member of the New Zealand parliament. After the 1970 tour to South Africa he settled here for some years, played for Tukkies and Northern Transvaal, married Jenny-Lynn and became the father of Bruce. Grahame and his family went to New Zealand but the marriage broke up and Jenny-Lynn and three-year-old Bruce returned to South Africa.

Thorne played lock or flank for Narbonne in France and then for the Golden Lions from 1996-2000, including the Currie Cup victory of 1999. He also played for the Cats and in 1998 for the Emerging Springboks when they beat Wales 35-13 in Secunda. In 1997 he played for the Lions against the British & Irish Lions. After his playing days he coached Pirates in Johannesburg.

Bruce Thorne was born on 24 September 1971. He died in a motor accident near Ventersburg in the Free State on his way back to Johannesburg on 23 December 2009. Apparently Thorne lost control of the car, which overturned. Thorne's wife and one-year-old son survived the crash and were taken to the Kroon Hospital in Kroonstad.

Thorne was survived by wife Siobhan, son Benjamin, his mother and his father.

PIET UYS

Piet Uys, the strong Northern Transvaal and Springbok scrumhalf, died in the early hours of Saturday 12 December 2009 in the Little Company of Mary Hospital in Pretoria after a long illness. He had been suffering with a heart complaint for some time.

In his playing days Uys was a first-choice scrumhalf, big for his time and a strong man who suited Northern Transvaal's playing style. He first became a Springbok on the 1960/61 tour of the UK, Ireland and France, playing in all the Tests against the Four Home Unions when for the fourth time the Springboks achieved a Grand Slam. He made his debut against Wales at the age of 22. He went on to play in 12 Tests all told, ending against the Wallabies in Durban in 1969 when Dawie de Villiers was injured. Perhaps his most famous Test was the second against the powerful Australian side of 1963. In the days before there were replacements for injury, he played for most of the second half with a dislocated shoulder.

Pieter de Waal Uys was born in Paarl. He was educated at Maitland High in Cape Town and then joined the police force, starting his long and happy relationship with Pretoria and Northern Transvaal in a period when their rugby was powerful. He played for one club, Police, and one province, Northern Transvaal. Uys formed part of a cheerful trio with Mof Myburgh, who was also a policeman, and Frik du Preez, who was in the air force.

On one occasion they were flying back to Johannesburg from Cape Town on a Sunday after playing Western Province. Those were days when Sunday flights did not serve alcohol, but suddenly Piet had a fit and started convulsions. Frik and Mof tried to hold him down and Frik said to the hostess: "We know what's going on. Bring ice." She hurried back with ice whereupon the trio took their seats. Mof produced glasses and Frik a bottle of whisky and the journey back was eased.

Uys left the police force and became a fertiliser representative, then a restaurateur and finally a farmer in Schoeman-skloof. He stayed involved in Blue Bulls rugby and was the chairman of the old players' committee.

Uys was survived by his second wife Jean and his three children: sons Pierre and Phillip and daughter Zahn Ann Viljoen.

ANDRE VAN WYK

André van Wyk was killed when the helicopter he was in crashed near Kenhardt in the Northern Cape on a jackal hunt at the request of farmers in the area. Twenty-year-old Jandré Pretorius died with him.

Van Wyk holds the record for having captained Griqualand West more than anybody else – 66 times in his 161 matches. But in his time he was part of the upliftment of Griqua rugby, an intensely loyal man who wore his Griquas blazer when he got married and had a Griquas jersey draped on his coffin at his burial. He played for the province from the age of 19 in 1984 until his injury in 1994. In 1995 he played for North West Cape. After his rugby career, he represented Griquas at cycling.

Abraham Willem Adriaan van Wyk was born in Postmasburg, went to school there and was farming sheep and cattle in the district on the farm Aucampsrus when he died. He was a fully-trained helicopter pilot with some 800 hours' flying time behind him. He was born on 19 February 1965 and died on 6 August 2010. He is survived by ex-wife Teresa and two daughters, Maritz (20) en Terre (13). At the time of his death he was engaged to marry Mrs Debbie Maritz on 30 October 2010.

There was a huge attendance at the funeral service in Postmasburg. Former Springbok and Griquas coach André Markgraaff praised him as a legend of South African rugby who never got the recognition he deserved, a colossus who would have been a Springbok in another era. Markgraaff said: "In the 124 years of its existence Griquas produced many Springboks but only one André van Wyk."

NOMTHA XAPE

Nomtha Xape played rugby for Hilltop Eagles in Port Elizabeth, South Africa Women's Sevens and in 2008 for South Africa when Scotland came on tour.

Nomtha Cleo Xape was born in Port Elizabeth on 17 August 1985.

SA REFEREES

Golden year for Joubert

ALTHOUGH Jonathan Kaplan finished 2010 as the number-one ranked referee in the country, it was the man ranked fourth on the SA Referees' National Panel, Craig Joubert, who leapfrogged not only Kaplan but also second-ranked Marius Jonker and third-placed Mark Lawrence to blow the Vodacom Super 14 and Absa Currie Cup finals for the first time in his career.

Joubert, the former Maritzburg College pupil, has gone from a nervous under-14 referee (when 14 himself) to a composed, world-class 32-year-old for whom 2010 will always stand out as his breakthrough year.

SANZAR decided in 2009 that referee appointments for Super 14 playoff matches would be done on merit, regardless of the referees' national affiliations. Kaplan blew the 2009 Super 14 final between the Bulls and Chiefs at Loftus Versfeld, and in 2010 it was Joubert who officiated in the historic final between the Bulls and Stormers at Orlando Stadium in Soweto. It was his 39th Super Rugby game and was followed up by four Test matches and seven Currie Cup games, including the final in Durban between the Sharks and Western Province.

It was on this occasion that Joubert became, at 32 years and 356 days, the youngest referee to blow a Currie Cup final. Interestingly, Joubert's father, Des, was also a provincial referee.

Kaplan meanwhile took charge of 27 first-class matches in 2010 – including seven Tests (the most by any referee in

one year), nine Super Rugby matches and eight Currie Cup games – to take his career first-class tally to 359, comprising 62 Tests (a world record), 75 Super Rugby matches (the second most by any referee), 134 Currie Cup games (a South African record) as well as 88 other first-class fixtures.

In addition, Kaplan, who was SA referee of the year from 2003-07, has refereed more Six Nations matches (16) more Tests (17) involving New Zealand and more Bledisloe Cup matches (7) between the All Blacks and Wallabies than anyone. His nine Rugby World Cup matches are more than any other South African referee while he is also the only referee to officiate in matches during four separate British & Irish Lions tours – from 1997 to 2009.

Four South Africans – namely Kaplan, Joubert, Jonker and Lawrence – have been included in the IRB's 2011 panel comprising the world's 20 best referees. Only Ireland have as many representatives.

The list, in alphabetical order, is: Wayne Barnes (Eng), Christophe Berdos (Fra), Keith Brown (NZ), George Clanzy (Ire), Stuart Dickinson (Aus), Peter Fitzgibbon (Ire), Jérôme Garces (Fra), Marius Jonker (SA), Craig Joubert (SA), Jonathan Kaplan (SA), Bryce Lawrence (NZ), Mark Lawrence (SA), Alan Lewis (Ire), Nigel Owens (Wal), Dave Pearson (Eng), Romain Poite (Fra), Chris Pollock (NZ), Alain Rolland (Ire), Andrew Smasll (Eng) and Steve Walsh (Aus).

Most Tests (+10) 62 Jonathan Kaplan (1996-2010 – World Record). 28 Mark Lawrence (2000-2010). 27 André Watson (1996-2004). 21 Marius Jonker (2005-2010). 20 Craig Jouber (2003-2010). 14 Tappe Henning (1995-2004). 11 Steve Strydom (1979-1986). 10 Freek Burger (1989-1994), Ian Rogers (1993-1998), Louis Mzomba (2001-2007).

TEST REFEREES – MEN

1 **Griffin, John** - 1 Test 1891: SA vs BI (1).

2 **Frames, Percy Ross** - 1 Test 1891: SA vs BI (2).

3 **Castens, Herbert Hayton** (HH or Fatty) - 1 Test 1891: SA vs BI (3).

4 **Kemsley, Henry Rickon** - 1 Test 1896: SA vs BI (1).

5 **Beves, Gordon** - 1 Test 1896: SA vs BI (2).

6 **Bisset, William Molteno** (Bill) - 1 Test 1896: SA vs BI (3).

7 **Richards, Alfred Renfrew** (Alf) - 1 Test 1896: SA vs BI (4).

8 **Donaldson, William Patrick** (Bill) - 1

Test 1903: SA vs BI (1).

9 **Day, Percy Ware** - 1 Test 1903: SA vs BI (2).

10 **Anderson, John Henry** (Biddy) - 1 Test 1903: SA vs BI (3).

11 **Stanton, Reginald William** (Reg) - 3 Tests 1910: SA vs BI (1,2,3).

12 **Oakley, Lionel David** - 1 Test 1924: SA vs BI (1).

13 **Neser, Vivian Herbert** (Boet or Knoppies) - 9 Tests 1924: SA vs BI (2). 1928: SA vs NZ (1,2,3,4). 1933: SA vs A (1,2,3,5).

14 **Millar, William Alexander** (Billy) - 2 Tests 1924: SA vs BI (3,4)

15 **Van der Horst, Alexander Wilhelm Archibald** (Alex) - 1 Test 1933: SA vs A (4).

16 **Horak, Adriaan Marthinus** (Att) - 1 Test 1938: SA vs BI (1).

17 **Strasheim, Johannes Jacobus** (Johnny) - 1 Test 1938: SA vs BI (2).

18 **Pretorius, Nicolaas Francois** (Nic) - 1 Test 1938: SA vs BI (3).

19 **Hofmeyr, Edwin William Neilson** (Eddie) - 4 Tests 1949: SA vs NZ (1,3).

REFEREES

1961: SA vs A (2). 1963: SA vs A (1).

20 **Burmeister, Ralph Douglas** - 8 Tests 1949: SA vs NZ (2,4). 1953: SA vs A (1). 1955: SA vs BI (1,3). 1960: SA vs NZ (3,4). 1961: SA vs A (1).

21 **Ackermann, Chrisman Joël** (Chris) - 4 Tests 1953: SA vs A (2,3). 1955: SA vs BI (4). 1958: F (2).

22 **Louw, Lambertus Petrus Johannes** (Lammie) - 1 Test 1953: SA vs A (4).

23 **Slabber, Michael John** (Mike) - 2 Tests 1955: SA vs BI (2). 1960: SA vs NZ (2).

24 **Strasheim, Erdam Albert** (Bertie) - 7 Tests 1958: SA vs F (1). 1960: SA vs S; SA vs NZ (1). 1962: SA vs BI (1,3). 1964: SA vs F. 1967: SA vs F (1). 1968: SA vs BI (4).

25 **Calitz, Pieter Melt Hertzog** (Piet) - 1 Test 1961: SA vs I.

26 **Carlson, Kenneth Robert Victor** (Ken) - 1 Test 1962: SA vs BI (2).

27 **Myburgh, Pieter Abraham** (Toy) - 4 Tests 1962: SA vs BI (4). 1963: SA vs A (2,3,4).

28 **Engelbrecht, Gert Kotzé** (Kallie) - 1 Test 1964: SA vs W.

29 **Baise, Max** - 7 Tests 1967: SA vs F (2,3). 1968: SA vs BI (1,3). 1969: SA vs A (2). 1974: SA vs BI (1,4).

30 **Robbertse, Pieter** (Piet) - 4 Tests 1967: SA vs F (4). 1969: SA vs A (1). 1970: SA vs NZ (1,3).

31 **Schoeman, Johannes Petrus Jacobus** (Hansie) - 1 Test 1968: SA vs BI (2).

32 **Baise, Solomon Louis** (Solly) - 1 Test 1969: SA vs A (3).

33 **De Bruyn, Casparus Johannes** (Cas) - 3 Tests 1969: SA vs A (4). 1974: SA vs BI (2,3).

34 **Malan, Wynand Charl** - 3 Tests 1970: SA vs NZ (2). 1971: SA vs F (1,2).

35 **Woolley, Thomas Herbert** (Bert) - 1 Test 1970: SA vs NZ (4).

36 **Moolman, Justus de Jager** (Justus) - 1 Test 1972: SA vs E.

37 **Gourlay, Ian Watson** (Ian) - 1 Test 1976: SA vs NZ (1).

38 **Bezuidenhout, Gert Peter** (Gert) - 3 Tests 1976: SA vs NZ (2,3,4).

39 **Gouws, Johannes Stephanus** (Johan) - 1 Test 1977: SA vs World XV.

40 **Strydom, Stefanus** (Steve) - 11 Tests 1979: Arg vs A (1,2). 1980: Arg vs WT; U vs Par; Braz vs Par; U vs Chile; 1982: SA vs S Am (1). 1985: S vs I; F vs W. 1986: F vs NZ (2,3).

41 **Muller, Frans** (Fransie) - 3 Tests 1982: SA vs S Am (2). 1988: S vs F; F vs I.

42 **Coetzer, Gerrit** (Gerrit) - 1 Test 1988: U vs Arg.

43 **Burger, Frederick** (Freek) - 10 Tests 1989: F vs A (1,2). 1990: S vs Arg. 1992: S vs F; F vs I; Arg vs F (1,2). 1993: S vs NZ; E vs NZ. 1994: HK vs PNG.

44 **Adams, Albert Louie** (Albert) - 4 Tests 1991: US vs F (1,2); Nam vs Z (1,2).

45 **Rogers, Ian** (Ian) - 10 Tests 1993: Z vs W (1); Arab Gulf vs Ken; Ken vs Nam. 1994: C vs F; C vs W; A vs It (1,2). 1995: E vs WS (2); [I vs W (2)]. 1997: Arg vs E (1). 1998 Tun vs Z.

46 **Anderson, Ian Charles** (Ian) - 3 Tests 1993: Z vs W (2); Nam vs Arab Gulf; Z vs Arab Gulf.

47 **Neethling, Stefanus Johannes** (Stef) - 3 Tests 1993: IC vs Mor. 1994: E vs R. 1995: [I vs J].

48 **Henning, Willem Taljaardt Stopforth** (Tappe) - 14 Tests 1995: S vs WS. 1996: NZ vs WS; E vs Arg. 1997: S vs A. 1998: T vs Sam. 1999: U vs P. 2000: Sam vs It. 2001: E vs F; A vs NZ (2). 2002: NZ vs I (2); W vs NZ. 2004: Fiji vs Sam;

49 **Watson, André Jacobus** (André) - 27 Tests 1996: A vs C. 1997: I vs F; E vs A (2). 1998: I vs S; A vs E (1); A vs S (1); F vs A. 1999: W vs E; A vs I (1,2); [E vs It; A vs US; A vs F]. 2000: Arg vs I; A vs NZ (1); E vs A. 2001: A vs BI (1); I vs NZ. 2002: F vs E; A vs NZ (2). 2003: I vs F; NZ vs F (1); [I vs Arg; NZ vs W; E vs A (2)]. 2004: A vs PI; Andorra vs Nor.

50 **Spannenberg, Carl Moses** (Carl) - 6 Tests 1996: It vs W (2). 1997: T vs Z; Ken vs Arab Gulf. 1998: Nam vs Z; U vs US. 2000: Z vs Nam.

51 **Kaplan, Jonathan Isaac** (Jonathan) - 62 Tests 1996: Z vs Nam. 1997: Bots vs Arab Gulf; Arg vs E (2). 1998: Fiji vs T; G vs R. 2000: It vs S; NZ vs A (2); F vs NZ. 2001: It vs I; A vs BI (2); W vs I. 2002: NZ vs A (1); E vs NZ; Russ vs Sp. 2003: I vs E; NZ vs A (2); [I vs R; S vs US; E vs Sam; F vs I]. 2004: NZ vs E (1); A vs NZ (2); F vs Arg. 2005: I vs E; S vs W; T vs Fiji; NZ vs BI (3); I vs NZ. 2006: NZ vs I; NZ vs A; I vs W; S vs F. 2007: E vs F; It vs I; A vs W; SA vs Nam; E vs USA; Sam vs T: C vs J; S vs It; F vs E. 2008: I vs It; S vs E; NZ vs E; Ken vs Uga; A vs NZ; Fr vs Arg; W vs NZ. 2009: W vs E, S vs I, Fj vs Sam; Fj vs J; A vs NZ (1); I vs A; E vs NZ. 2010: W vs F; I vs S; NZ vs Wal; Z vs Bots; Z vs Mad; NZ vs A; F vs Arg.

52 **Schoonwinkel, Arnold Jacobus** (Arrie) -

1 Test 1997: T vs Nam.

53 **Meuwesen, Johannes Coenraad** (Johann) - 5 Tests 1994: Neth vs Czech Rep. 1995: SA vs WS. 1996: SA vs Fj. 1997: Tun vs Ken. 1998: Z vs W.

54 **Lawrence, Steven Mark** (Mark) - 28 Tests 2000: Fiji vs It. 2001: It vs Nam; F vs Fiji. 2002: It vs E; US vs Chile; S vs Fiji. 2003: A vs W; F vs E (2). 2004: W vs It; A vs S (2); SA vs NZ (2R); 2005: E vs It; E vs Sam. 2007: Ug vs Nam. 2008: E vs I; F vs W; A vs NZ; NZ vs A; I vs NZ. 2009: E vs It; F vs W; A vs NZ (3); Tun vs Nam. 2010: E vs I; Ken vs Ug; A vs NZ; U vs Rom; I vs Arg.

55 **Turner, Daniel Andrew** (Andy) - 9 Tests 2000: Nam vs Z. 2001: US vs E; It vs Fiji. 2002: Nam vs Tun; S vs R. 2003: Kor vs T; W vs R. 2004: It vs E; C vs F.

56 **Daniels, Eugene Clive** (Eugene) - 5 Tests 2001: Nam vs Z; Mad vs Ken; Ug vs Bots. 2004: Bots vs Swazi; Nam vs Mor.

57 **Mzomba, Louis** (Louis) - 10 Tests 2001: Swazi vs Mad. 2002: Ug vs Z; Ug vs Cam. 2003: Ug vs Zam; Ug vs Ken; Mad vs Z; Swazi vs Bots; Bots vs Ken. 2006: Ken vs Tun. 2007: IC v Ken.

58 **Katzenellenbogen, Michael Labe** (Michael) - 2 Tests 2002: Nam vs Mad. 2003: Ug vs Z.

59 **Joubert, Craig** (Craig) - 20 Tests 2003: Nam vs Ug. 2005: US vs W; T vs Sam. 2006: T vs Fiji; Ur vs Chile, It vs Arg. 2007: F vs S; NZ vs F. 2008: E vs W; A vs NZ, F vs A. 2009: I vs E; Nam vs IC; NZ vs A (1); NZ vs A (3); W vs NZ. 2010: I vs W; Z vs Ken; A vs NZ; E vs A.

60 **Veldsman, Shaun Ivan** (Shaun) - 3 Tests 2003: Nam vs Sam; Arg vs C. 2004: Nam vs Ken.

61 **Roos, Hendrik Willem** (Willie) - 9 Tests 2004: Bots vs Tanz. 2005: Zam vs Senegal. 2006: Nam vs Ken; Ug vs Mad. 2007: Sam vs T; Mad vs IC; Ug vs Mad. 2008: Jap vs Ton; Ug vs Ken.

62 **Fortuin, Jerome Christopher** (JC) - 3 Tests 2005: Ken vs Mad; Z vs Ug. 2006: Ug vs IC.

63 **Jonker, Marius** (Marius) - 21 Tests 2005: Ug vs Z; Mauritius vs Burkina Faso. 2006: Fiji vs It; It vs Can; I vs Aus. 2007: E vs S; A vs NZ; It vs P; Fj vs J; S vs NZ. 2008: W vs F; A vs F; E vs A. 2009: E vs S; NZ vs F; Ug vs Ken; I vs Fj; Nam vs Tun. 2010: S vs E; Z vs Ug; I vs NZ.

64 **Legoete, Lesego** (Pro) - 3 Tests 2008: R vs U; Nam vs Zim. 2009: Ug vs Tun.

PRE-UNITY REFEREES

In days before the 1992 unification of rugby in South Africa there were five national bodies – the SA Rugby Board; the SA Coloured Rugby Board (SACRB); the SA Bantu Rugby Board (SABRB), which later became the SA African Rugby Board (SAARB) and then the SA Rugby Association (SARA); the SA Rugby Football Federation (SARFF) and the SA Rugby Union (SARU).

Of these bodies only the SA Rugby Board was recognised by the International Rugby Board and could play Tests against other International Rugby Board countries. In 1950 the national bodies not recoignised by the International Rugby Board begane playing Tests, first amongst themselves and later against touring teams. These matches had referees.

1 Davids, Gamatdien (Punky) - 3 Tests 1950: SACRB vs SABRB; 1951 SACRB vs SABRB; 1952: SACRB vs SABRB
2 May, T - 1 Test 1951: SACRB vs SABRB
3 Cossie, Byram Patrick Badirella (Pat) - 2 Tests 1952: SACRB vs SABRB; 1959: SACRB vs SAARB
4 Basardien, Mohammed Salie (Doewe) - 1 Test 1957: SACRB vs SAARB
5 Daniels, Hassiem Magmoed (Heneke, Baard) - 1 Test 1961: SACRB vs SABRB
6 Mbatyoti, Alvin Njokweni - 1 Test 1963: SACRB vs SABRB
7 Khan, Gamat Noor (Noortjie) - 1 Test 1964: SACRB vs SARFF
8 Isaacs, Yusuf (Kanon) - 1*Test 1965: SACRB vs SAARB

9 Smith, Ebrahim (Hima) - 1 Test 1965: SARFF vs SAARB
10 Mbelekana, Gladman Vuyisile - 1 Test 1965: SACRB vs SAARB
11 Gordon, Ronald Albert (Ronnie) - 1 Test 1966: SARFF vs SAARB
12 Dlala, Richard Totosi - 2 Tests 1966: SARFF vs SAARB; 1968: SARU vs SAARB
13 Kulsen, John Fortuin - 1 Test 1967: SARFF vs SAARB
14 Sizani, Norman Thembile - 3 Tests 1967: SARFF vs SAARB; 1968: SARFF vs SAARB;1970: SARFF vs SAARB
15 Hardenberg, Theophilus Cornelius (TC) - 1 Test 1967: SARU vs SAARB
16 Schroeder, Ismail (Miley) - 2 Tests 1969: SARU vs SAARB; 1970: SARU vs SAARB
17 Rhoxo, Nono William - 1 Test 1969: SARFF vs SAARB
18 Ncunyana, Richard Brice - 1 Test 1969: SARFF vs SAARB
19 Abrahams, Harry Francis - 1 Test 1971: SARFF vs SAARB
(*Visser, Dirk - 1 Test 1971: SARFF vs Holland)
20 Smith-Belton, James Walter (Jimmy) - 3 Tests 1972: SARFF vs SAARB; 1976: SARFF vs SAARB; 1980 SARA vs British Isles & Ireland
21 Abels, Suleiman - 2 Tests 1972: SARFF vs SAARB; SARFF vs England
22 Baise, Max - 1 Test 1972: SAARB vs England
23 Rabie, Denzil John - 3 Tests 1973: SARFF vs SAARB; 1976: SARFF vs

SAARB; 1977: SARFF vs SAARB
24. Moolman, Justus de Jager - 1 Test 1973: Italy vs SAARB
25 May, James - 1 Test 1973: SARFF vs SAARB
26 Jekwa, Hubert Mfana - 1 Test 1974: SARFF vs SAARB
27 Swart, Edmund Hubert (Eppie) - 2 Tests 1974: SARFF vs SAARB; 1976: SARFF vs SAARB
28 Katzenellenbogen, Deon - 1 Test 1974: SARFF vs British Isles & Ireland
29 Strydom, Stefanus (Steve) - 2 Tests 1974: SAARB vs British Isles & Ireland; 1975: SAARB vs France
30 Bezuidenhout, Gert Peter - 1 Test 1975: SARFF vs SAARB
31 Caga, William Mzwandile - 1 Test 1975: SARFF vs SAARB
32 Gourlay, Ian Watson - 1 Test 1976: SARFF vs New Zealand,
33 Steenkamp, Johannes Jurgens Antonie (Stoney) - 1 Test 1976: SAARB vs New Zealand
34 Muller, Frans - 2 Tests 1976: SARFF vs SAARB; 1984: SARA vs England,
35 Kulsen, Edward Geoff (Eddie) - 1 Test 1977: SARFF vs SAARB
36 Gouws, Johannes Stefanus (Johan) - 1 Test 1980: SARFF vs SAARB
37 Carstens, Nicholaas Johannes Petrus (Cassie) - 1 Test 1984: SARFF vs England
38 Mans, Wynand Jacobus - 1 Test 1987: SARFF vs South Pacific Barbarians
Dirk Visser, a South African, was resident in Holland at the time and not a South African appointment.

PANELS FOR 2010

National Panel 11 (in merit order): 1. Jonathan Kaplan, 2. Marius Jonker, 3. Mark Lawrence, 4. Craig Joubert, 5. Pro Legoete, 6. Jaco Peyper, 7. Jason Jaftha, 8. Stuart Berry, 9. Sindile Mayende, 10. Joey Salmans, 11. Lourens van der Merwe. **Provincial Panel 14 (in merit order):** 1. Ben Crouse (BB), 2. Archie Sehlako (Natal), 3. Mlungiseli Mdashe (Natal), 4. Matt Kemp (WP), 5. Tiaan Jonker (Golden Lions), 6. François Veldsman (Boland), 7 Bongani Maloni (Border), 8. Luke Burger (BB), 9. Dilbert November (South Western Districts), 10. Quinton Immelman (WP), 11. Pieter de Villiers (Golden Lions), 12. Rasta Rashivenga (Golden Lions), 13. François Groenewald (WP), 14. Lusanda Jam (Border). **Contenders Squad (Top 2 ranked):** 1. Sewes Terblanche (BB), 2. François De Bruin (Griquas). Alphabetical: Jimmy Aphane (BB), Rodney Bonaparte (EP), Petri Bosch (Griquas), André Botha (BB), Martin Lekhanye (Free State), Willie Killian (Leopards), François Pretorius (WP), Andries Retief (Pumas), Jocelyn Tucker (BB), Marius van der Westhuizen (WP), Jan Venter (BB). **Primary School Panel (alphabetical):** Sakkie Meyer (Free State), Mtheleli Msileni (Eastern Province). **Women's Panel (Merit order):** 1. Roslyn Fortuin (Boland), 2. Madel Herselman (Golden Lions), 3. Eugenia Daniels (WP), 4. Kim Smit (Golden Lions), 5 Sipokazi Njani (Border), 6. Marlize Jordaan (Free State), 7. Eska Claasen (South Western Districts), 8. Magda van der Heever (Pumas), 9. Sanet Ludick (Leopards). **Women's Contender's/ Academy Squad (alphabetical):** Renee Daniell (BB), Duthie Melany

(Boland), Henchalla Hoffman (SWD), Ilana Scholtz (Golden Lions), Lize van Biljon (Golden Lions). **Specialised National Assistant Referees panel (alphabetical):** 1. Phillip Bosch (EP), 2. Stefan Breytenbach (Pumas), 3. Christie du Preez (EP), 4. Linston Manuels (Boland), 5. Reuben Rossouw (Sharks), 6. Cobus Wessels (SWD), 7. Fumanekile Yamile (EP), 8. Marc van Zyl (WP). **National Women's Match Reviewers (alphabetical):** Eugene de Villiers (Lions), Keith Hendricks (Boland). **Specialised Assistant referees – Nominees for Regional Squad:** 1. Jannie Oosthuizen (Golden Lions), 2. Gert Stander (Free State), 3. Johan Wasserman (Free State), 4. Sieg van Staden (Valke), 5. Attie Buitenbach (Limpopo), 6. Basie Ferreira (Griffons), 7. Gerhard Marais (Griffons). **National Panel of Television Match Officials (alphabetical):** 1. Gerrie Coetzee (Free State), 2. Michael Cupido (Golden Lions), 3. JC Fortuin (WP), 4. Johann Meuwesen (EP), 5. Shaun Veldsman (Boland). **National Selectors (alphabetical):** 1. Hulet Billett (SWD), 2. Dennis Immelman (WP), 3. Thuso Mngqibisa (WP), 4. Arrie Schoonwinkel (Free State), 5. Yantolo Banks (Border), 6. Balie Swart (SARU - coach/player representative). **National Coaches (alphabetical):** 1. Hendrik Greyvenstein (WP), 2. Tappe Henning (SARU), 3. Theuns Naudé (SARU), 4. Hulet Billett (SWD). **National Match Reviewers (alphabetical):** Dries Breytenbach (Pumas), Gerrit Coetzer (Free State - Converting from PR to MR - Trial), Jacques Hugo (EP), Theuns Janse van Vuuren (Lions - Converting from PR to MR - Trial), Lusanda Menze (EP), Allan O'Connell (Natal), Pierre Oelofse (Lions - Converting from PR to MR - Trial).

REFEREES

SECTION 8
RECORDS

SOUTH AFRICAN FIRST-CLASS RECORDS

MATCH RECORDS

Scores of 150 points

163	Lowveld vs Transkei	1994
151	Western Province vs Eastern Transvaal	1995

Wins by 130 points

153	Lowveld vs Transkei (163-10)	1994
148	WP vs Eastern Transvaal (151-3)	1995
139	Northern Transvaal vs SWD (147-8)	1996

Twenty-five tries

26	Lowveld vs Transkei	1994

Forty-eight points by a player

50	GE Lawless, Sharks vs Highlanders	1997
48	WJ de W Ras, OFS vs EOFS	1977
48	JH de Beer, SA Students vs Taiwan	1992
48	J Nel, Lowveld vs Transkei	1994

Seven tries by a player

8	M Watson, Lowveld vs Transkei	1994
7	C Fourie, Gazelles vs Neuquen (Arg.)	1972
7	J Olivier, N.Transvaal vs SWD	1996
7	J Jonker, Griquas vs Namibia	1996

Twenty conversions by a player

20	WJ de W Ras, OFS vs EOFS	1977

Nine penalty goals by a player

9	JH Kruger, N.Transvaal vs WP	1996
9	E Herbert, NFS vs Falcons	1997
9	E Herbert, Griffons vs Pumas	2001
9	DJ Hougaard, Blue Bulls vs WP	2002

SEASON RECORDS

Five drop goals by a player

5	HE Botha, N.Transvaal vs Natal	1992
5	JH de Beer, SA vs England	1999

Most points by a team

1434	Free State	1996
1390	Lions	1999
1348	Natal Sharks	1996

Most tries by a team

191	Free State	1996
184	Natal Sharks	1996
181	Lions	1999

400 points by a player

528	NB Scholtz, Western Province	1988
471	M Steyn, Bulls, Blue Bulls, SA	2010
460	MJ Smith, Free State	1996
456	J Engelbrecht, Lions	1999
444	DJB Basson, Western Transvaal	1994
443	E Herbert, NFS & Free State	1994
434	M Steyn, Bulls, Blue Bulls, SA	2009
427	JT Stransky, Western Province	1994
424	CP Steyn, Blue Bulls	1999
406	K Tsimba, Vodacom Cheetahs	2002
401	HE Botha, Northern Transvaal	1987

30 tries by a player

35	P Hendriks, Transvaal	1992
34	BA Basson, Cheetahs, GW, SA	2010
34	C Fourie, North East Cape & Gazelles	1972
32	BJ Paulse, Western Province	2000
30	AJ Joubert, Natal	1996

CAREER RECORDS

1 500 points

3781	HE Botha (NTvl & SA)	1977-95
3525	E Herbert (NFS & OFS)	1986-01
2358	WJ de W Ras (OFS, Natal & SA)	1974-86
2303	AJ Joubert (OFS, Natal & SA)	1986-99
2140	JT Stransky (NTvl, Natal, WP & SA)	1987-96
1972	M Steyn (Bulls, Blue Bulls, SA)	2002-10
1914	AJJ van Straaten	1994-05
	(NTvl, SWD, Falcons, WP, Griquas, Stormers, SA)	
1853	W de Waal, Leop, FS, WP	2002-10
1862	NB Scholtz (Boland, WP, Gazelles)	1980-88
1880	PC Montgomery (WP, Stormers, KZN, Sharks, SA)	1994-09
1789	LJ Koen (WP, Stormers, Lions, Cats, Bulls, SA)	1996-03
1766	JF van Wyk (EOFS)	1985-95
1753	JH de Beer (Tvl, FS, Bulls, Cats, SA)	1990-00
1671	CP Steyn (Far North, Blue Bulls, Pumas)	1993-06
1658	LR Sherrell (Natal, WP, Tvl, NTvl & SA)	1986-98
1569	R Blair (WP, Tvl & SA)	1974-84
1515	KC Tsimba (FS, BB, Pumas, NFS)	2000-09

100 tries

173	C Badenhorst (OFS, SA)	1986-99
159	BJ Paulse (WP, Stormers, SA)	1997-07
158	DM Gerber (EP, OFS, WP, SA)	1978-95
157	JT Small (Tvl, Natal, WP, SA)	1988-99
156	JS Germishuys (OFS, Tvl, SA)	1971-85
156	JI Daniels (Boland, Lions, Cats, Bulls)	1998-08
151	CS Terblanche (Boland, Natal, Sharks, SA)	1994-09
139	JH van der Westhuizen (Blue Bulls, SA)	1992-03
135	AJ Joubert (OFS, Natal & SA)	1986-99
128	PWG Rossouw (WP, Stormers, SA)	1991-04
119	P Hendriks (Tvl, SA)	1989-97
116	RH Mordt (Zimbabwe, NTvl, Tvl, SA)	1977-85
115	BG Habana (Lions, Blue Bulls, WP, SA)	2004-10
113	CJ du Plessis (WP, Tvl, SA)	1980-89
113	D Oosthuysen (WTvl, NTvl, SA)	1986-94
109	JF van der Westhuizen (Natal, WP, Tvl, SA)	1989-97
106	NJ Burger (WP)	1982-91
105	S Brink (FS, Natal, Sharks)	1993-04

450 conversions

669	HE Botha (NTvl, SA)	1977-95
484	WJ de W Ras (OFS, Natal, SA)	1974-86
478	E Herbert (NFS & OFS)	1986-01
346	W de Waal (Leopards, FS, WP)	2002-10
316	LJ Koen (WP, Lions, Boland)	1996-10
306	M Steyn (Blue Bulls, Bulls, SA)	2002-10

300 penalty goals

710	E Herbert (NFS, OFS)	1986-01
545	HE Botha (NTvl, SA)	1977-95
328	WJ de W Ras (OFS, Natal, SA)	1974-86

75 drop goals

210	HE Botha (NTvl, SA)	1977-95
90	WJ de W Ras (OFS, Natal, SA)	1974-86
83	E Herbert (NFS, OFS)	1986-01

Most appearances in a single position for a province

159	Fullback	HM Reece-Edwards
221	Wing	C Badenhorst
225	Centre	HL Müller
205	Flyhalf	E Herbert
162	Scrumhalf	E Hare
154	No. 8	AWA van Wyk
183	Flank	SB Geldenhuys
191	Lock	WH Lessing
177	Prop	CJ Botha
157	Hooker	T van der Walt

100 matches as a provincial captain

129	E Hare (WTvl)	1989-96
128	HE Botha (NTvl)	1980-92
103	M du Plessis (WP)	1972-80
102	JC Breedt (Tvl)	1986-92
101	M Reitz (Boland)	1989-94
100	JR van Rensburg (Vaal Triangle)	1983-89

Fastest to 100 games

CJ Kapp (SWD) 3 years 240 days	1997-00

Youngest player to 100 games

P Hendriks (Tvl)	24 years 339 days on 18/03/1995

Played for seven provinces

J-P Joubert	NFS, SWD, Bol, GW, BB, FS, GL

Played for six provinces

St E Wilken	EP, FS, Tvl, NTvl, Griquas, Natal
J Nel	WTvl, EP, WP, Boland, Tvl, FS
H Rheeders	Blue Bulls, EP, FS, Pumas, Griffons, SWD
JN Van der Walt	Blue Bulls, Valke, Sharks, Griquas, Griffons, SWD Eagles
TC Kokoali	GL, FS, NFS, KZN, BB, Valke
PH Myburgh	KZN, Valke, BB, Bol, FS, NFS

More than 300 first-class matches*

397	Stefan Terblanche (Bol, KZN, SA, Ospreys)
357	A-H le Roux (FS, KZN, SA, Leinster)
338	PA van den Berg (GW, KZN, SA)
337	V Matfield (BB, GW, SA, Toulon)
323	JW Smit (KZN, SA, Clermont)
315	AE Drotske (FS, BB, Pumas, SA, London Irish)

*including overseas games

FIRST-CLASS RECORDS

100 APPEARANCES FOR A PROVINCE

A

Alcock, C.D (Chad) Eastern Province 113. Allan, J (John) Natal 126. Andrews, K.S (Keith) Western Province 147. Andrews, M.G (Mark) Natal 122. Appelgryn, J (Kobie) NFS 103. Atherton, S (Steve) Natal 165.

B

Badenhorst, C (Chris) Free State 221. Badenhorst, M.J.L (Thys) NFS 103. Bedford, T.P (Tommy) Natal 119. Bekker, H.J (Hennie) Western Province 108. Bekker, I.A (Sakkie) EOFS 100. Berry, D.P (Don) Western Transvaal 104. Bester, H (Hennie) NFS 100. Beukes, J (Joe) OFS 121. Beukes, J.A (Boela) Vaal Triangle 115. Blakeway, A.D (Andrew) Natal 111. Blom, L.F (Louis) Western Province 125. Booysen, J (Jaco) Eastern Transvaal 134. Bosman, M (Marius) South Eastern Transvaal 107. Botha, A (Anton) Border 119. Botha, A.A (André) Natal 137. Botha, C.J (Connie) SWD 177. Botha, H.E (Naas) Northern Transvaal 179. Botha, J.N (Taai) Eastern Transvaal 122. Brandt, F (Fabian) Boland Cavaliers 132. Breedt, J.C (Jannie) Transvaal 118. Breedt, J.P.F (Jan) NFS 148. Bucholz, A.P (Pierre) Vaal Triangle 152. Burger, N.J (Niel) Western Province 126. Burke, JC (Conrad) Boland Cavaliers 113.

C

Campher, L (Lourens) Northern Transvaal 106. Claasen, A.D (André) Border 141. Claassen, J.T (Johan) Western Transvaal 105. Claassens, J.P (Jannie) Northern Transvaal 102. Cloete, A. (André) OFS 152. Cockrell, R.J (Robert) Western Province 102. Coeries, D.B (Darryll) SWD Eagles 118. Coetzee, H (Harry) SWD 108. Coetzee, J (Jaco) OFS 141. Coetzee, J (Jannie) Boland 140. Coetzee, J (Japie) Namibia 119 Coetzee, J.H.H (Boland) Western Province 127. Cooke, R.E (Richard) South Eastern Transvaal 112.

D

De Jager, J.J (Jakkie) Northern Natal 122. De Klerk, K.B.H (Kevin) Transvaal 107. De Lange, P (Draadkar) South Eastern Transvaal 114. De Villiers, T.T.C.R (Tielman) Griqualand West

101. De Villiers, A (André) EOFS 106 De Villiers, F (Frikkie) Griqualand West 112. De Wet, F.P (Eric) NWC 124. Dixon, T (Tommy) Boland Cavaliers 103. Domoney, W (Wayne) Border 111. Douw, T.J (Turtius) Falcons 108. Drotské, A.E (Naka) FS Cheetahs 127. Du Plessis, C.J (Carel) Western Province 108. Du Plessis, H (Henley) Boland Cavaliers 133. Du Plessis, M (Morné) Western Province 112. Du Plessis, T.D (Tommy) Northern Transvaal 126. Du Plooy, A.J.J (Amos) Eastern Province 102. Du Preez, GJD (Delarey) Border Bulldogs 103. Du Preez, F.C.H (Frik) Northern Transvaal 109. Du Preez, J (Kosie) Vaal Triangle 100. Du Preez, WH (Wian) FS Cheetahs 105. Du Randt, J.P (Os) FS Cheetahs 105. Du Toit, H.B (Manie) SWD Eagles 109. Du Toit, H.J (Hein) Boland 104. Du Toit, P.A (Fonnie) Northern Transvaal 102. Durrheim, E.A (Ertjies) Eastern Transvaal 152.

E

Edwards, W (Bull) Border 103. Els, J.C.W (Jannie) Eastern Transvaal 117. Els, W.W (Braam) OFS 155. Engelbrecht, H (Herklaas) NWC 126. Erasmus, F.S (Frans) Eastern Province 119. Erasmus, J (Johan/Rassie) FS Cheetahs 117.

F

Ferreira, C.F (Freddie) Western Province 104. Fihlani, I.Z (Ian) Border Bulldogs 129. Fortuin, BA (Bevin) SWD Eagles 122. Fourie, M.J (Pote) Northern Transvaal 105. Fourie, P.D (Kleinboet) Eastern Transvaal 109. Fredericks, E.R (Eddie) Free State 105. Froneman, P (Philip) Border 117.

G

Garvey, A.C (Adrian) Natal 109. Geldenhuys, A (Adri) Eastern Province 110. Geldenhuys, S.B (Burger) Northern Transvaal 184. Gelderbloom, G (Glen) Border 115. Gerber, A (André) NFS 111. Gerber, D.M (Danie) Eastern Province 116. Geyser, F.M (Frikkie)

NFS 118. Greeff, J (Jacques) Eastern Province 101. Greyling, M (Tienie) EOFS 171. Grimes, H (Henry) SWD Eagles 103. Grobler, G (Gerbrand) Northern Transvaal 108.

H

Hankinson, R.G (Rob) Natal 110. Hare, E (Eugene) Western Transvaal 176. Harrison, J (Julian) NFS 102. Hendriks, P (Pieter) Transvaal 138. Herbert, E (Eric) NFS 205. Heunis, D.F (Danie) Eastern Transvaal 124. Heunis, J.W (Johan) Northern Transvaal 109. Heymans, J.H (Dougie) OFS 154. Honiball, H.W (Henry) Natal 111. Hugo, D.P (Niel) Western Province 146. Human, J (Hannes) Leopards 125. Human, P.G (Pote) Eastern Province 116.

J

Jacobs, B.J (Bennie) Border 179. Jamieson, C.M (Craig) Natal 123. Jansen, E (Eben) OFS 125. Jerling, J.J (Jurie) NFS 174. Johnson, A.M (Andrew) Eastern Province 123. Jonck, C (Chris) Mighty Elephants 121. Joubert, A (Alex) NWC 108. Joubert, B (Bobby) Border 101. Joubert, P.C (Piet) South Eastern Transvaal 112. Julies, R (Randile) Boland Cavaliers 104.

K

Kahts, W.J.H (Willie) Northern Transvaal 110. Kapp, C.J (Johan) SWD 124. Karg, D.H (Deon) Namibia 102. Knoetze, F (Faffa) Western Province 110. Koch, A.C (Chris) Boland 112. Koch, W (Willem) Boland 101. Kruger, CR (Chris) FS Cheetahs 100.

L

Labuschagne, H.J (Hendrik) Eastern Transvaal 107. Labuschagne, J.J (Jannes) Lions 103. Lamprecht, J.C (Johann) Northern Transvaal 101. Le Roux, A-H (Ollie) Natal Sharks/Wildebeest 101*. Le Roux, H.P (Hennie) Transvaal 153. Le Roux, J.H.S (Johan) Transvaal 100. Le Roux, M (Martiens) OFS 162. Lessing, W.H (Werner) Leopards 191. Ligman, EJ (Elroy) Eastern Province 101. Linee, M (Tinus) Western Province 112.

Lock, J.L (Jan) Northern Transvaal 106.
Lombard, JR (Nardi) Mighty Elephants
104. Loots, P (Pietie) Border Bulldogs
121. Losper, S.J (Sarel) Namibia 116.
Lötter, J.G (Deon) Griqualand West
104. Lotz, J.W (Jan) Transvaal 114.
Lourens, M.J (Thys) Northern Transvaal
168. Louw, SJ (Sarel) Griffons 104.
Lubbe, J.M.F (Edrich) Griqualand West
114. Lubbe, L (Leon) Eastern Transvaal
119. Luus, NJ (Nico) Valke 134.
M
Macdonald, I (Ian) Transvaal 145.
Malan, A.W (Adolf) Northern Transvaal
159. Mametsa, SJ (John) Blue Bulls 136.
Marais, F.S (Frans) Boland 101. Maritz,
A (Dries) Transvaal 141. Maritz, W
(Willem) Namibia 103. Matthys, P
(Piet) Eastern Transvaal 110. Mbulali,
V (Vusumzi) Border 100. Meintjes,
J (Kobus) Boland 102. Meiring, F.A
(FA) Northern Transvaal 105. Meyer,
E (Eugene) Eastern Transvaal 110.
Meyer, J (Nico) Eastern Province 107.
Meyer, W (Willie) Eastern Province
105. Moolman, J.H (Jannie) NEC
100. Moolman, L.C (Louis) Northern
Transvaal 171. Mortassagne, A.M
(Mort) Natal 100. Mtimka, LJJ (Black)
Border Bulldogs 109. Muir, D.J (Dick)
Natal 108. Mulder, J.C (Japie) Transvaal
113. Müller, H.L (Helgard) OFS 245.
Muller, J.H (Harry) South Eastern
Transvaal 126. Myburgh, J.L (Mof)
Northern Transvaal 109.
N
Nel, D (Donie) Far North 140.
Nicholas, J (Jearus) Griqualand West
116. Nieuwenhuyzen, S.L (Stephen)
NFS 151.
O
Olivier, J (Jacques) Northern Transvaal
137. Oosthuysen, D.E (Deon) Northern
Transvaal 140. Opperman, R.J (Ryno)
OFS 137. Oxlee, K (Keith) Natal 102.
P
Papier, N (Neil) Boland Cavaliers 126.
Patterson, A.C (Andrew) Western
Province 131. Pienaar, J.F (Francois)
Transvaal 100. Pienaar, Z.M.J (Gysie)
OFS 165. Pinnock, B.C (Barry) Eastern
Province 173. Potgieter, CJ (Chris)
Boland Cavaliers 115. Potgieter, R
(Riaan) Eastern Province 108. Potgieter,
R (Riaan) South Eastern Transvaal 109.
Povey, S.A (Shaun) Western Province

103. Pretorius, A.J (Attie) Stellaland
124. Pretorius, D.B (Dawie) EOFS 117.
Prins, D.R (Dave) Griqualand West 107.
Putt, K.B (Kevin) Natal 118.
R
Rademeyer, H.N (Hempas) Transvaal
105. Ras, W.J.de W (De Wet) OFS
141. Reece-Edwards, H.M (Hugh)
Natal 165. Reitz, M (Takkies) Boland
101. Richter, A.J (Adriaan) Northern
Transvaal 137. Rodgers, P.H (Heinrich)
Northern Transvaal 115. Roets, J (Jo-
han) Blue Bulls 105. Rossouw, E (Naas)
Falcons 158. Rossouw, F.J (Francois)
South Eastern Transvaal 183. Rossouw,
P.W.G (Pieter) Western Province 126.
Roux, J.P (Johan) Transvaal 111. Roux,
WG (Wessel) Blue Bulls 114. Ryan,
M.W (Mike) NFS 115.
S
Santon, D (Dale) Boland Cavaliers 120.
Schmidt, U.L (Uli) Northern Transvaal
136. Schoeman, M (Matthys) Stellaland
112. Scholtz, H (Hendro) FS Cheetahs
140. Scholtz, N.B (Calla) Western Prov-
ince 116. Senekal, C (Chris) Namibia
101. Serfontein, D.J (Divan) Western
Province 100. Serfontein, J.L (Jan) East-
ern Province 117. Slade, J (John) Natal
101. Smit, F.C (FC) Western Province
104. Smit, J (Koos) Vaal Triangle 101.
Smith, J.D (Tos) Griqualand West 137.
Smith, M.J (MJ) OFS 117. Sonnekus,
G.H.H (Gerrie) OFS 160. Stewart,
J.C (Christian) Western Province 136.
Stoop, L (Leon) Namibia 105. Strauss,
C.P (Tiaan) Western Province 156.
Strauss, J.H.P (Johan) Transvaal 105.
Strydom, J.J (Hannes) Transvaal 115.
Swart, D.P (DP) Western
Transvaal 117. Swart, EJ
(Eddie) Border 111.
Swart, G.J (Hakkies)
South Eastern Transvaal
158. Swart, I. S. De
V (Balie) Transvaal
108. Swart, M (Marius)
Border 131.
T
Teichmann, G.H (Gary) Natal
144. Theron, D.F (Dawie) Griqualand
West 108. Thomson, J.R.D (Jeremy)
Natal 152. Treu, P.M (Paul) SWD 105.
V
Van der Linde, A (Toks) Western Prov-
ince 133. Van der Merwe, C.A (Chris)

Boland 137. Van der Merwe, D (Danie)
Namibia 106. Van der Merwe, L (Le-
onard) Griffons 111. Van der Merwe,
W.J (Wessel) Western Transvaal 122.
Van der Walt, J.A (Jannie) Transvaal
116. Van der Walt, T (Tjaart) Eastern
Transvaal 157. Van der Westhuizen, J.F
(Cabous) Natal 128. Van der Westhui-
zen, J.H (Joost) Northern Transvaal 144.
Van Greunen, M (Markus) Leopards
111. Van Rensburg, J.R (James) Vaal
Triangle 101. Van Rooyen, J.C.O
(Kobus) Eastern Transvaal 134. Van
Schouwenburg, FJ (Francois) Blue
Bulls 112. Van Tonder, H.V (Hendry)
South Eastern Transvaal 103. Van Wyk,
A.W.A (André) Griqualand West 161.
Van Wyk, J.F (Japie) EOFS 150. Van
Zyl, C.A.A (Carlo) Border 115. Van
Zyl, C.G.P (Sakkie) OFS 121. Van Zyl,
G.C (Giepie) Eastern Province 109. Van
Zyl, WP (Piet) Boland Cavaliers 144.
Venter, A.G (André) OFS 115. Venter,
B (Brendan) OFS 122. Venter, De W
(De Waal) Griqualand West 106. Venter,
J.A (Barabas) Transvaal 106. Verhoeven,
A (Antonius) Boland Cavaliers 124.
Vermeulen, A (André) Griqualand West
121. Vermeulen, R (Ruan) Blue Bulls
115. Visagie, R (Richard) Boland 105.
Visagie, R.G (Rudi) OFS 109. Visagie,
R.G (Rudi) Natal 109. Visser, J. de
V (Div) Western Province 106. Vos, J
(Johnny) Border 104.
W
Wagener, O (Otto) NFS 128. Watson,
A.C (Tony) Natal 144. Webb, T.C
(Tommie) SWD Eagles 119. Wessels, H
(Hedley) Western Transvaal 131. Wessels,
H.J (Japie) OFS 145. Wessels,
J.C (Boeta) Griqualand West
111. Weyer, W.A (Wayne)
Border 183. Wiese, J.J
(Kobus) Transvaal 128.
Willemse, C (Chaka)
South Eastern Transvaal
101. Williamson, G
(Gunder) Falcons 139.
Wolfaardt, E.P (Elmo) Boland
117. Wolfaardt, J (Jacques) SWD
121. Wolmarans, B.J. (Barry) OFS 116.

*Ollie le Roux played 100 games for
the KZN Sharks and one for the KZN
Wildebeest*

FIRST-CLASS RECORDS

VODACOM SUPER RUGBY RECORDS

CHAMPIONS

1996	Blues	1999	Crusaders	2003	Blues	2007	Vodacom Bulls
1997	Blues	2000	Crusaders	2004	ACT Brumbies	2008	Crusaders
1998	Crusaders	2001	ACT Brumbies	2005	Crusaders	2009	Vodacom Bulls
		2002	Crusaders	2006	Crusaders	2010	Vodacom Bulls

RESULTS OF FINALS

1996	Blues	45	Sharks	21	Auckland
1997	Blues	23	ACT Brumbies	7	Auckland
1998	Blues	13	Crusaders	20	Auckland
1999	Highlanders	19	Crusaders	24	Dunedin
2000	ACT Brumbies	19	Crusaders	20	Canberra
2001	ACT Brumbies	36	Sharks	6	Canberra
2002	Crusaders	31	ACT Brumbies	13	Christchurch
2003	Blues	21	Crusaders	17	Auckland
2004	ACT Brumbies	47	Crusaders	38	Canberra
2005	Crusaders	35	NSW Waratahs	25	Christchurch
2006	Crusaders	19	Hurricanes	12	Christchurch
2007	Sharks	19	Vodacom Bulls	20	Durban
2008	Crusaders	20	Waratahs	12	Christchurch
2009	Vodacom Bulls	61	Chiefs	17	Pretoria
2010	Vodacom Bulls	25	Vodacom Stormers	17	Soweto

MATCH RECORDS

75 points

96-19	Crusaders vs. NSW Waratahs	Christchurch	2002
92-3	Vodacom Bulls vs. Queensland Reds	Pretoria	2007
77-34	Crusaders vs. Sharks	Christchurch	2005
75-43	Natal vs. Highlanders	Durban	1997
75-27	Crusaders vs. Bulls	Christchurch	2000
75-14	Bulls vs. Stormers	Pretoria	2005

Wins by 50 points

89	Vodacom Bulls vs. Queensland Reds (92-3)	Pretoria	2007
77	Crusaders vs. Waratahs (96-19)	Christchurch	2002
64	ACT Brumbies vs. Bulls (73-9)	Canberra	1999
64	ACT Brumbies vs. Cats (64-0)	Canberra	2000
61	Bulls vs. Stormers (75-14)	Pretoria	2005
53	Blues vs. Hurricanes (60-7)	Wellington	2002
53	Crusaders vs. Western Force	Christchurch	2007
50	Cats vs. Chiefs (53-3)	Bloemfontein	2000

Eleven tries

14	Crusaders vs. Waratahs (96-19)	Christchurch	2002
13	Vodacom Bulls vs. Queensland Reds (92-3)	Pretoria	2007
11	Blues vs. Stormers (74-28)	Auckland	1998
11	Crusaders vs. Bulls (75-27)	Christchurch	2000
11	Crusaders vs. Sharks (77-34)	Christchurch	2005

Three drop goals by a player

4	M Steyn, Bulls vs. Crusaders	2009
3	AP Mehrtens, Crusaders vs. Highlanders	1998
3	LJ Koen, Bulls vs. Cats	2003

Thirty-fve points by a player

50	GE Lawless (4t, 9c, 4p) Natal vs. Highlanders	1997
39	JH Kruger (1t, 5c, 8p) NTvl vs. Highlanders	1996
35	M Steyn (1t, 9c, 4p) Bulls vs. Stormers	2005
35	M Steyn (2t, 5c, 5p) Bulls vs. Brumbies	2010

Four tries by a player

4	JWC Roff, ACT Brumbies vs. Natal	1996
4	GE Lawless, Natal vs. Highlanders	1997
4	CS Terblanche, Sharks vs. Chiefs	1998
4	J Vidiri, Blues vs. Bulls	2000
4	DC Howlett, Blues vs. Hurricanes	2002
4	M Muliaina, Blues vs. Bulls	2002
4	CS Ralph, Crusaders vs. NSW Waratahs	2002
4	SW Sivivatu, Chiefs vs. Blues	2009
4	DA Mitchell, Waratahs vs Lions	2010

Ten conversions by a player

13	AP Mehrtens, Crusaders vs. Waratahs	2002
11	DJ Hougaard, Vodacom Bulls vs. Queensland Reds	2007

Eight penalty goals by a player

8	JH Kruger, N.Transvaal vs. Highlanders	1996
8	WC Walker, Highlanders vs. Chiefs	2003
8	HM Bosman, Cheetahs vs. Stormers	2006
8	DJ Hougaard, Vodacom Bulls vs. Crusaders	2007

SEASON RECORDS

160 POINTS OR MORE

	PLAYER	Province	Season	Tries	Conversions	Penalties	Drop Goals
263	M Steyn	Bulls	2010	5	38	51	3
221	DW Carter	Crusaders	2006	5	38	37	3
206	AP Mehrtens	Crusaders	1998	5	23	41	4
201	DW Carter	Crusaders	2004	6	27	39	–
194	SA Mortlock	ACT Brumbies	2000	4	39	32	–
192	AP Mehrtens	Crusaders	1999	1	23	43	4
191	P Hewat	NSW Waratahs	2006	5	29	36	–
191	M Steyn	Bulls	2009	1	33	29	11
182	AP Mehrtens	Crusaders	2002	1	30	35	4
182	JWC Roff	ACT Brumbies	2004	7	51	15	–
180	AR Cashmore	Blues	1998	5	34	28	1
173	P Hewat	NSW Waratahs	2005	10	18	29	–
171	DW Carter	Crusaders	2005	5	37	24	–
171	QS Cooper	Reds	2010	5	31	27	1
170	GE Lawless	Sharks	1997	6	25	30	–
164	SR Donald	Chiefs	2007	2	26	34	–
161	DJ Hougaard	Vodacom Bulls	2007	–	28	32	3
160	AP Mehrtens	Crusaders	2000	–	23	36	2

12 Tries

15	JWC Roff	ACT Brumbies	1997
15	RL Gear	Crusaders	2005
13	JT Small	Natal	1996
13	AM Walker	ACT Brumbies	2000
12	AJ Joubert	Natal	1996
12	JF Umaga	Hurricanes	1997
12	RQ Randle	Chiefs	2002
12	DC Howlett	Blues	2003
12	JP Pietersen	Sharks	2007

35 or more conversions

51	JWC Roff	ACT Brumbies	2004
39	SA Mortlock	ACT Brumbies	2000
38	DW Carter	Crusaders	2006
38	M Steyn	Bulls	2010
37	DW Carter	Crusaders	2005
36	SR Donald	Crusaders	2009
35	JWC Roff	ACT Brumbies	2003

40 or more penalty goals

51	M Steyn	Bulls	2010
43	AP Mehrtens	Crusaders	1999
41	AP Mehrtens	Crusaders	1998
40	NR Spooner	Queensland Reds	1999

Five or more drop goals

11	M Steyn	Bulls	2009
7	LJ Koen	Bulls	2003
6	AS Pretorius	Lions	2009

MATCH RECORDS

Most points in a log season
469	Crusaders	2002

Most points in all matches
541	Crusaders (13 matches)	2005

Most points conceded
585	Lions	2010
500	Bulls	2002

Most log points
52	Crusaders	2008

Fewest log points
4	Bulls	2002

Fewest log points to reach semi-finals
30	Sharks	1997

Most tries in a log season
61	Crusaders	2005

Most tries in all matches
71	Crusaders	2005

Fewest tries scored
13	Lions	2007
15	Blues	1999
15	Queensland Reds	2007

MOST tries conceded
72	Lions	2010
67	Bulls	2002

Most wins in a log season
11	Crusaders	2002

Fewest wins in a season
0	Lions	2010
0	Bulls	2002

SUPER RUGBY RECORDS

CAREER RECORDS

500 POINTS OR MORE

	PLAYER	Province	Matches	Tries	Conversions	Penalties	Drop Goals
1078	DW Carter	Crusaders	82	26	183	187	7
1019	SA Mortlock	ACT Brumbies	123	53	161	144	–
990	AP Mehrtens	Crusaders	87	13	134	202	17
959	MC Burke	NSW Waratahs	79	24	160	173	–
902	TE Brown	Highlanders	99	5	143	190	7
757	M Steyn	Bulls	73	10	139	126	17
738	SR Donald	Chiefs	72	18	132	127	1
700	DE Holwell	Hurricanes/Blues	82	8	123	138	–
645	AS Pretorius	Cats/Lions	69	11	106	115	11
629	EJ Flatley	Queensland Reds	87	11	92	130	–
619	AR Cashmore	Blues	47	13	106	113	1
645	AS Pretorius	Cats/Lions	69	11	100	117	13
625	CJ Spencer	Blues/Lions	108	28	121	78	3
588	JWC Roff	ACT Brumbies	83	57	99	34	1
580	MJ Giteau	Brumbies/Force	89	29	93	81	2
555	LJ Koen	Stormers/Bulls/Cats	51	5	79	113	11
533	PJ Grant	Stormers	62	8	86	107	–
520	PG Hewat	NSW Waratahs	40	17	66	101	–

40 tries
59	DC Howlett	Hurr/Highl/Blues	104 matches
58	CS Ralph	Chiefs/Crusaders	135 matches
57	JWC Roff	ACT Brumbies	83 matches
56	CM Cullen	Hurricanes	85 matches
53	SA Mortlock	ACT Brumbies	123 matches
47	JF Umaga	Hurricanes	122 matches
44	BG Habana	Bulls/Stormers	76 matches
43	J Vidiri	Blues	61 matches
42	LR MacDonald	Crusaders	127 matches
41	CE Latham	Reds	109 matches
41	SNG Staniforth	Waratahs/Western Force	106 matches
40	RL Gear	Crusaders	79 matches
40	MA Nonu	Hurricanes	98 matches

100 conversions
183	DW Carter	Crusaders	82 matches
161	SA Mortlock	ACT Brumbies	123 matches
160	MC Burke	NSW Waratahs	79 matches
143	TE Brown	Highlanders & Sharks	91 matches
139	M Steyn	Bulls	73 matches
134	AP Mehrtens	Crusaders	87 matches
132	SR Donald	Chiefs	72 matches
123	DE Holwell	Hurricanes/Blues	82 matches
121	CS Spencer	Blues/Lions	108 matches
106	AR Cashmore	Blues	57 matches
100	AS Pretorius	Cats/Lions	69 matches

100 penalty goals
202	AP Mehrtens	Crusaders	87 matches
187	DW Carter	Crusaders	82 matches
186	TE Brown	Highlanders & Sharks	91 matches
173	MC Burke	NSW Waratahs	71 matches
144	SA Mortlock	ACT Brumbies	123 matches
138	DE Holwell	Hurricanes/Blues	82 matches
130	EJ Flatley	Reds	87 matches
127	SR Donald	Chiefs	72 matches
126	M Steyn	Bulls	73 matches
117	AS Pretorius	Cats/Lions	69 matches
113	AR Cashmore	Blues	57 matches
113	LJ Koen	Stormers/Bulls/Cats	51 matches
108	AJJ van Straaten	Bulls/Stormers	45 matches
107	PJ Grant	Stormers	62 matches
101	P Hewat	NSW Waratahs	40 matches

10 drop goals
17	AP Mehrtens	Crusaders	87 matches
17	M Steyn	Bulls	73 matches
11	LJ Koen	Bulls	51 matches
11	AS Pretorius	Cats/Lions	69 matches
10	DJ Hougaard	Bulls	51 matches

100 appearances
136	GM Gregan	ACT Brumbies
135	CS Ralph	Chiefs/Crusaders
132	NC Sharpe	Reds/Force
129	RD Thorne	Crusaders
128	GB Smith	ACT Brumbies
127	AD Oliver	Highlanders
127	LR MacDonald	Crusaders/Chiefs
125	AJ Venter	Cats/Sharks/Stormers
123	SA Mortlock	ACT Brumbies
123	SP Hardman	Reds
123	PR Waugh	NSW Waratahs
122	JF Umaga	Hurricanes
117	KF Mealamu	Blues/Chiefs
116	SJ Larkham	ACT Brumbies
116	GM Somerville	Crusaders
113	JA Paul	ACT Brumbies
113	PJ Wannenburg	Bulls
111	JW Smith	Sharks
109	CE Latham	Waratahs/Reds
109	V Matfield	Cats/Bulls
108	A-H Le Roux	Sharks/Cheetahs
108	CJ Spencer	Blues/Lions
107	CJ Whitaker	NSW Waratahs
106	BJ Cannon	Waratahs/Force
106	AKE Baxter	NSW Waratahs
106	SNG Staniforth	Waratahs/Force
105	JW Marshall	Crusaders
105	CS Terblanche	Sharks
104	DC Howlett	Highlanders/Blues
103	JA Collins	Blues/Chiefs
103	RH McCaw	Crusaders
102	PA van den Berg	Cats/Sharks
102	BJ Botha	Bulls
101	R So'oialo	Hurricanes
101	MJ Dunning	Waratahs/Force
100	DJ Lyons	Waratahs
100	WK Young	ACT Brumbies

VODACOM TRI-NATIONS RECORDS

CHAMPIONS							
		1999	New Zealand	2003	New Zealand	2007	New Zealand
1996	New Zealand	2000	Australia	2004	South Africa	2008	New Zealand
1997	New Zealand	2001	Australia	2005	New Zealand	2009	South Africa
1998	South Africa	2002	New Zealand	2006	New Zealand	2010	New Zealand

MATCH RECORDS

Fifty points

61-22	South Africa vs. Australia	Pretoria	1997
55-35	New Zealand vs. South Africa	Auckland	1997
53-8	South Africa vs. Australia	Johannesburg	2008
52-16	New Zealand vs. South Africa	Pretoria	2003
50-21	New Zealand vs. Australia	Sydney	2003

Wins by 35 pints

49	Australia vs. South Africa (49-0)	Brisbane	2006
45	South Africa vs. Australia (53-8)	Johannesburg	2008
39	South Africa vs. Australia (61-22)	Pretoria	1997
37	New Zealand vs. Australia (43-6)	Wellington	1996
36	New Zealand vs. South Africa (52-16)	Pretoria	2003

Fifty points away from home

52	New Zealand vs. South Africa	Pretoria	2003
50	New Zealand vs. Australia	Sydney	2003

Most by SA is 35 vs. NZ, Auckland, 1997.
Most by Australia is 31 vs. SA, Johannesburg, 2002.

Six tries

8	South Africa vs. Australia	Pretoria	1997
8	South Africa vs. Australia	Johannesburg	2008
7	New Zealand vs. South Africa	Auckland	1997
7	New Zealand vs. South Africa	Pretoria	2003
7	New Zealand vs. Australia	Sydney	2003
7	New Zealand vs. Australia	Melbourne	2010
6	New Zealand vs. Australia	Wellington	1996
6	South Africa vs. New Zealand	Johannesburg	2000
6	Australia vs. South Africa	Brisbane	2006

Twenty-five points by a player

31	M Steyn (1t, 1c, 8p), SA vs. NZ	Durban	2009
29	AP Mehrtens (1c, 9p), NZ vs. Australia	Auckland	1999
26	JH de Beer (1t, 6c, 3p), SA vs. Australia	Pretoria	1997
25	CJ Spencer (1t, 4c, 4p), NZ vs. SA	Auckland	1997
25	JT Stransky (1t, 1c, 6p), SA vs. Aus.	Bloemfontein	1996
25	DW Carter (2c, 7p), NZ vs. SA	Wellington	2006

Most by an Australian: 24 by MC Burke (2t, 1c, 4p) vs. NZ in Melbourne, 1998.

Three tries by a player

4	JL Nokwe, SA vs. Australia	Johannesburg	2008
3	JT Rokocoko, NZ vs. Australia	Sydney	2003
3	MC Joubert, SA vs. NZ	Johannesburg	2004
3	DC Howlett, NZ vs. Australia	Auckland	2005

Most by an Australian is two by eight players

Five conversions by a player

6	JH de Beer, SA vs. Australia	Pretoria	1997
5	AJJ van Straaten, SA vs. NZ	Johannesburg	2000
5	SA Mortlock, Australia vs. SA	Brisbane	2006

Seven penalty goals by a player

9	AP Mehrtens, NZ vs. Australia	Auckland	1999
8	M Steyn, SA vs NZ	Durban	2009
7	MC Burke, Australia vs. NZ	Sydney	1999
7	AP Mehrtens, NZ vs. Australia	Pretoria	1999
7	DW Carter, NZ vs. SA	Wellington	2006
7	DW Carter, NZ vs. Australia	Auckland	2007
7	M Steyn, SA vs Australia	Cape Town	2009

Two drop goals by a player

2	JH de Beer, SA vs. NZ	Johannesburg	1997
2	FPL Steyn, SA vs. Australia	Cape Town	2007

SEASON RECORDS BY TEAM

One hundred and fifty points		
184	New Zealand	2010
179	New Zealand	2006
162	Australia	2010
159	New Zealand	1997
158	South Africa	2009
152	New Zealand	2008

One hundred and fifty points conceded		
194	South Africa	2010
188	Australia	2010
185	South Africa	2006
163	Australia	2008
150	Australia	1997

Most by New Zealand - 131 in 2009

Sixty or fewer points conceded		
54	South Africa	1998
57	Australia	1999
59	New Zealand	2007

Fifteen tries		
22	New Zealand	2010
18	South Africa	1997
17	New Zealand	1997
17	New Zealand	2003
17	New Zealand	2006
17	Australia	2010
16	New Zealand	2008

Fifteen tries conceded		
22	South Africa	2010
21	Australia	2008
21	Australia	2010
18	South Africa	1997
18	South Africa	2006
17	Australia	1997

Most conceded by New Zealand - 13 in 1997 & 2000

Three tries or fewer conceded		
3	Australia	1999
3	South Africa	2001

Fewest tries conceded by New Zealand - 4 in 2001

Eighteen or more log points		
27	New Zealand	2010
23	New Zealand	2006
21	South Africa	2009
19	New Zealand	2008
18	New Zealand	1997
18	New Zealand	2003

Most by Australia is 14 (2000 & 2008)

SEASON RECORDS BY A PLAYER

Sixty points			
99	DW Carter	New Zealand	2006
95	M Steyn	South Africa	2009
84	CJ Spencer	New Zealand	1997
82	DW Carter	New Zealand	2008
77	M Steyn	South Africa	2010
72	MJ Giteau	Australia	2009
71	SA Mortlock	Australia	2000
69	AP Mehrtens	New Zealand	1996
68	AP Mehrtens	New Zealand	1999
64	JH de Beer	South Africa	1997
64	MJ Giteau	Australia	2010
63	DW Carter	New Zealand	2010
62	DW Carter	New Zealand	2007
60	CJ Spencer	New Zealand	2003
60	SA Mortlock	Australia	2006

Four tries			
7	CM Cullen	New Zealand	2000
6	JT Rokocoko	New Zealand	2003
5	DC Howlett	New Zealand	2003
4	CM Cullen	New Zealand	1997
4	SA Mortlock	Australia	2000
4	JL Nokwe	South Africa	2008
4	JD O'Connor	Australia	2010
4	JM Muliaina	New Zealand	2010

Ten conversions			
14	DW Carter	New Zealand	2006
13	CJ Spencer	New Zealand	1997
12	JH de Beer	South Africa	1997
12	SA Mortlock	Australia	2006
12	DW Carter	New Zealand	2008
11	MJ Giteau	Australia	2008
11	MJ Giteau	Australia	2010
11	DW Carter	New Zealand	2010
10	M Steyn	South Africa	2010

Fifteen penalty goals			
23	M Steyn	South Africa	2009
21	DW Carter	New Zealand	2006
19	AP Mehrtens	New Zealand	1996
19	AP Mehrtens	New Zealand	1999
19	M Steyn	South Africa	2010
16	CJ Spencer	New Zealand	1997
15	DW Carter	New Zealand	2007
15	DW Carter	New Zealand	2008

Two drop goals			
3	M Steyn	South Africa	2009
2	JH de Beer	South Africa	1997
2	AP Mehrtens	New Zealand	2000
2	PC Montgomery	South Africa	2005
2	AS Pretorius	South Africa	2005
2	FPL Steyn	South Africa	2007
2	BS Barnes	Australia	2009

CAREER RECORDS

80 POINTS OR MORE

PLAYER	Country	Tries	Conversions	Penalties	Drop Goals	Points
DW Carter	New Zealand	6	54	94	2	426
AP Mehrtens	New Zealand	1	34	82	3	328
MC Burke	Australia	7	19	65	1	271
MJ Giteau	Australia	7	36	47	3	257
PC Montgomery	South Africa	4	26	43	3	210
SA Mortlock	Australia	9	21	37	0	198
M Steyn	South Africa	1	16	42	3	172
CJ Spencer	New Zealand	3	21	32	0	153
AJJ van Straaten	South Africa	0	5	28	0	94
CM Cullen	New Zealand	16	0	0	0	80

Nine tries
16	CM Cullen	New Zealand
15	JT Rokocoko	New Zealand
13	DC Howlett	New Zealand
11	RH McCaw	New Zealand
9	JW Marshall	New Zealand
9	SA Mortlock	Australia
9	LD Tuqiri	Australia
9	J Fourie	South Africa

Eighteen conversions
54	DW Carter	New Zealand
36	MJ Giteau	Australia
34	AP Mehrtens	New Zealand
26	PC Montgomery	South Africa
21	CJ Spencer	New Zealand
21	SA Mortlock	Australia
19	MC Burke	Australia

Thirty penalty goals
94	DW Carter	New Zealand
82	AP Mehrtens	New Zealand
65	MC Burke	Australia
47	MJ Giteau	Australia
43	PC Montgomery	South Africa
42	M Steyn	South Africa
37	SA Mortlock	Australia
32	CJ Spencer	New Zealand

Three drop goals
4	AS Pretorius	South Africa
3	AP Mehrtens	New Zealand
3	PC Montgomery	South Africa
3	MJ Giteau	Australia
3	M Steyn	South Africa
3	BS Barnes	Australia

Thirty appearances
48	GM Gregan	Australia
42	V Matfield	South Africa
41	GB Smith	Australia
40	JM Muliaina	New Zealand
39	NC Sharpe	Australia
38	SJ Larkham	Australia
37	MJ Giteau	Australia
36	JW Smit	South Africa
36	RH McCaw	New Zealand
35	JW Marshall	New Zealand
35	KF Mealamu	New Zealand
34	PC Montgomery	South Africa
31	SA Mortlock	Australia
31	TD Woodcock	New Zealand
30	PR Waugh	Australia
30	GM Somerville	New Zealand
30	DW Carter	New Zealand
30	J de Villiers	South Africa

ABSA CURRIE CUP RECORDS

CHAMPIONS					
1892[1]	Western Province	1952	Transvaal	1986	Western Province
1894	Western Province	1954	Western Province	1987	Northern Transvaal
1895	Western Province	1956	Northern Transvaal	1988	Northern Transvaal
1897	Western Province	1957-59[3]	Western Province	1989	Northern Transvaal
1898	Western Province	1964	Western Province		& Western Province
1899[2]	Griqualand West	1966	Western Province	1990	Natal
1904	Western Province	1968	Northern Transvaal	1991	Northern Transvaal
1906	Western Province	1969	Northern Transvaal	1992	Natal
1908	Western Province	1970	Griqualand West	1993	Transvaal
1911	Griqualand West	1971	Northern Transvaal	1994	Transvaal
1914	Western Province		& Transvaal	1995	Natal
1920	Western Province	1972	Transvaal	1996	Natal
1922	Transvaal	1973	Northern Transvaal	1997	Western Province
1925	Western Province	1974	Northern Transvaal	1998	Blue Bulls
1927	Western Province	1975	Northern Transvaal	1999	The Lions
1929	Western Province	1976	Orange Free State	2000	Western Province
1932	Western Province	1977	Northern Transvaal	2001	Western Province
	& Border	1978	Northern Transvaal	2002	Blue Bulls
1934	Western Province	1979	Northern Transvaal	2003	Blue Bulls
	& Border		& Western Province	2004	Blue Bulls
1936	Western Province	1980	Northern Transvaal	2005	Free State
1939	Transvaal	1981	Northern Transvaal	2006	Free State & Blue Bulls
1946	Northern Transvaal	1982	Western Province	2007	Free State
1947	Western Province	1983	Western Province	2008	Natal Sharks
1950	Transvaal	1984	Western Province	2009	Blue Bulls
		1985	Western Province	2010	Natal Sharks

[1] The Currie Cup was first presented to the South African inter-provincial champions in 1892. It had been given by Sir Donald Currie (owner of the Castle Shipping Line) to WE Maclagan, captain of the first British Isles team on their departure for South Africa, with instructions that it should be awarded to the first side to beat the tourists and thereafter become a floating trophy for the South African inter-provincial champions. In the event they won all 19 of their games and the cup was presented to Griqualand West who lost only 3-0. Griquas in turn handed over the trophy to the South African Rugby Board as per Currie's instructions.
[2] Western Province and Transvaal did not compete due to the impending Anglo-Boer war.
[3] Contested over two seasons (suspended in 1958 due to tour by France).
Note: Western Province won the SA Rugby Board Trophy at the tournament in Kimberley in 1889.

RESULTS OF FINALS

1939[1]	Western Province	6	Transvaal	17	Cape Town
1946	Northern Transvaal	11	Western Province	9	Pretoria
1947	Western Province	16	Transvaal	12	Cape Town
1950	Transvaal	22	Western Province	11	Johannesburg
1952	Boland	9	Transvaal	11	Wellington
1954	Western Province	11	Northern Transvaal	8	Cape Town
1956	Natal	8	Northern Transvaal	9	Durban
1968	Northern Transvaal	16	Transvaal	3	Pretoria
1969	Northern Transvaal	28	Western Province	13	Pretoria
1970	Griqualand West	11	Northern Transvaal	9	Kimberley
1971	Transvaal	14	Northern Transvaal	14	Johannesburg
1972	Eastern Transvaal	19	Transvaal	25	Springs
1973	Northern Transvaal	30	Orange Free State	22	Pretoria
1974	Northern Transvaal	17	Transvaal	15	Pretoria
1975	Orange Free State	6	Northern Transvaal	12	Bloemfontein
1976	Orange Free State	33	Western Province	16	Bloemfontein
1977	Northern Transvaal	27	Orange Free State	12	Pretoria

1978	Orange Free State	9	Northern Transvaal	13	Bloemfontein
1979	Western Province	15	Northern Transvaal	15	Cape Town
1980	Northern Transvaal	39	Western Province	9	Pretoria
1981	Northern Transvaal	23	Orange Free State	6	Pretoria
1982	Western Province	24	Northern Transvaal	7	Cape Town
1983	Northern Transvaal	3	Western Province	9	Pretoria
1984	Western Province	19	Natal	9	Cape Town
1985	Western Province	22	Northern Transvaal	15	Cape Town
1986	Western Province	22	Transvaal	9	Cape Town
1987	Transvaal	18	Northern Transvaal	24	Johannesburg
1988	Northern Transvaal	19	Western Province	18	Pretoria
1989	Western Province	16	Northern Transvaal	16	Cape Town
1990	Northern Transvaal	12	Natal	18	Pretoria
1991	Northern Transvaal	27	Transvaal	15	Pretoria
1992	Transvaal	13	Natal	14	Johannesburg
1993	Natal	15	Transvaal	21	Durban
1994	Orange Free State	33	Transvaal	56	Bloemfontein
1995	Natal	25	Western Province	17	Durban
1996	Transvaal	15	Natal	33	Johannesburg
1997	Western Province	14	Free State	12	Cape Town
1998	Blue Bulls	24	Western Province	20	Pretoria
1999	Natal	9	Lions	32	Durban
2000	Natal	15	Western Province	25	Durban
2001	Western Province	29	Natal	24	Cape Town
2002	Lions	7	Blue Bulls	31	Johannesburg
2003	Blue Bulls	40	Natal Sharks	19	Pretoria
2004	Blue Bulls	42	Free State Cheetahs	33	Pretoria
2005	Blue Bulls	25	Free State Cheetahs	29	Pretoria
2006	Free State	28	Blue Bulls	28	Bloemfontein
2007	Free State	20	Lions	18	Bloemfontein
2008	Natal	14	Blue Bulls	9	Durban
2009	Blue Bulls	36	Free State Cheetahs	24	Pretoria
2010	Natal Sharks	30	Vodacom Western Province	10	Durban

[1] A final has decided the winner in every competition since 1939 except 1957-59, 1964 & 1966.

MOST TITLES

31	Western Province (four times shared)	last	2001	6	Natal	last	2010
23	Blue Bulls (four times shared)	last	2006	4	Free State (once shared)	last	2007
9	Lions (once shared)	last	1999	3	Griqualand West	last	1970
				2	Border (twice shared)	last	1934

ABSA CURRIE CUP RECORDS

FINAL RECORDS

Won by 30 points

56	Transvaal vs Free State, 1994 final score 56-33*	
42	Blue Bulls vs FS Cheetahs, 2004 final score 42-33	
40	Blue Bulls vs Sharks , 2003 final score 40-19	
39	Northern Transvaal vs WP, 1980 final score 39-9	
36	Blue Bulls vs FS Cheetahs, 2009 final score 36-24	
33	Free State vs WP, 1976 final score 33-16	
33	Free State vs Lions, 1994 final score 33-56	
33	Natal vs Lions, 1996 final score 33-15	
33	FS Cheetahs vs Blue Bulls, 2004 final score 33-42	

The match aggregate of 89 points is also a finals record

Five tries

7	Lions vs Free State	1 October 1994
6	Blue Bulls vs Cheetahs	23 October 2004
5	Blue Bulls vs WP	4 October 1980
5	Lions vs Sharks	11 September 1999
5	Blue Bulls vs Sharks	1 November 2003

Twenty points by a player

26	Derick Hougaard Blue Bulls vs Lions, 2002
	(1try,5 penalties, 2 drop goals)
25	Patrick Lambie Sharks vs Western Province, 2010
	(2 tries, 3 conversions, 3 penalties)
24	Naas Botha Blue Bulls vs Lions, 1987
	(4 penalties, 4 drop goals)
	Braam van Straaten vs Sharks, 2001
	(1try,2 conversions, 5 penalties)
21	Gavin Johnson Lions vs Free State ,1994
	(6 conversions,3 penalties)
	Morné Steyn Blue Bulls vs FS Cheetahs, 2009
	(3 conversions, 4 penalties, 1 drop goal)
20	Thierry Lacroix Natal vs WP, 1995
	(6 penalties, 1 conversion)

Six conversions by a player

6	Gavin Johnson Lions vs Cheetahs	1994

Six penalty goals by a player

6	Thierry Lacroix Natal vs WP	1995

Four drop goals by a player

4	Naas Botha Northern Transvaal vs Transvaal	1987

Most appearances in finals

11	Burger Geldenhuys	Northern Transvaal	1977-1989
	Naas Botha	Northern Transvaal	1977-1991
9	Louis Moolman	Northern Transvaal	1975-1986

Forty points in finals

138	Naas Botha	1t, 10c, 20p, 18dg	1977-1991
62	Willem de Waal	7c, 16p	2004-2010
54	Morné Steyn	6c, 12p, 2dg	2005-2009
53	Willem de Waal	7c, 13p	2004-2007
45	Calla Scholtz	1t, 4c, 9p, 2dg	1983-1988
44	Derick Hougaard	1t, 3c, 8p, 3dg	2002-2006
41	Joel Stransky	1c, 13p	1990-1995

Three tries in final

4	Ettienne Botha	Blue Bulls	2003-2004
3	Neil Burger	WP	1982-1985
3	Edrich Krantz	FS & N Tvl	1976-1980

Oldest and youngest winning captains

35 years 138 days	Thys Lourens	Northern Transvaal	1978
22 years 217 days	Naas Botha	Northern Transvaal	1980

Most wins as Coach

11*	Brigadier Buurman van Zyl (and two draws)		
	Northern transvaal		1968-1981

Including two draws

MATCH RECORDS

One hundred and ten points

147	Blue Bulls vs SWD (147-8)	Pietersburg	1996
113	Cheetahs vs SWD (113-11)	Bloemfontein	1996
111	Pumas vs SWD (111-14)	Witbank	2001

Wins by 100 points

139	Blue Bulls vsSWD (147-8)	Pietersburg	1996
106	Cheetahs vs NFS (106-0)	Bloemfontein	1997
102	Cheetahs vs SWD (113-11)	Bloemfontein	1996
102	SWD Eagles vs NFS (102-0)	George	1999

Sixteen tries

23	Blue Bulls vs SWD (147-8)	1996
18	Western Transvaal vs EOFS (103-9)	1988
16	Transvaal vs Far North (99-9)	1973
16	SWD Eagles vs NFS (102-0)	1999
16	Pumas vs SWD Eagles (111-14)	2001

Thirty-five points by a player

46	Jannie de Beer (3t, 14c, 1p)	FS vs NFS	1997
40	Casper Steyn (2t, 3c, 8p)	BB vs SWD	2000
38	Henry Honiball (4t, 6c, 2p)	Natal vs Bol	1996
38	Lance Sherrell (2t, 14c)	BB vs SWD	1996
37	Casper Steyn (2t, 3c, 7p)	Pumas vs FS	2003
36	Gerald Bosch (1t, 13c, 2dg)	Tvl vs FN	1973
36	Eric Herbert (3c, 9p, 1dg)	NFS vs Valke	1997
36	Casper Steyn (1t, 7c, 7p)	BB vs Pumas	2000
35	Jacques Olivier (7t)	BB vs SWD	1996
	Kennedy Tsimba (1t, 9c, 4p)	FS vs GW	2003
	Braam Pretorius (2t, 11c, 1p)	Pumas vs Valke	2009

Six tries by a player

7	Jacques Olivier	Blue Bulls vs SWD (147-8)	1996
6	Buks Marais	Boland vs NED (33-3)	1952

Fourteen conversions by a player

14	Lance Sherrell	Blue Bulls vs SWD	1996

MATCH RECORDS

| 14 | Jannie de Beer | FS vs NFS | 1997 |
| 14 | Nel Fourie | Pumas vs SWD Eagles | 2001 |

Nine penalty goals by a player

| 9 | Eric Herbert | NFS vs Valke | 1997 |
| 9 | Derick Hougaard | BB vs WP | 2002 |

Five drop goals by a player

| 5 | Naas Botha | N Transvaal vs Natal | 1992 |

SEASON RECORDS

Seven hundred and fifty points

| 792 | Natal | 15 matches | 1996 |
| 783 | Northern Transvaal | 13 matches | 1996 |

One hundred tries by a team

| 112 | Natal | 15 matches | 1996 |
| 102 | Northern Transvaal | 13 matches | 1996 |

Two hundred and fifty points by a player

268	Johan Heunis	N Transvaal	1989
263	Gavin Lawless	Transvaal	1996
252	Casper Steyn	Blue Bulls	1999

Fifteen tries

21	Bjorn Basson	Griquas	2010
19	Carel du Plessis	WP	1989
19	Colin Lloyd	Leopards	2006
18	Ettienne Botha	Blue Bulls	2004
18	Allister Kettledas	Pumas	2009
16	Jan-Harm van Wyk	FS	1997

| 16 | Ryno Benjamin | Boland | 2006 |
| 15 | Philip Burger | FS | 2006 |

Fifty conversions

62	Louis Koen	WP	1997
55	Jannie de Beer	FS	1997
54	Braam Pretorius	Pumas	2009

Forty penalties

50	Willem de Waal	WP	2010
48	Gavin Lawless	Transvaal	1996
47	Willem de Waal	FS	2005
45	Lance Sherrell	WP	1991
	Johan Heunis	N Transvaal	1987
	Cameron Oliver	Transvaal	1989
42	Cameron Oliver	Transvaal	1990
	Andre Joubert	FS	1989

Twenty drop goals

| 20 | Naas Botha | N Transvaal | 1985 |

CAREER RECORDS

One hundred matches

142	Helgard Muller	FS	1983-1998
141	Rudi Visagie	FS, Ntl & SE-TVL	1980-1996
136	Chris Badenhorst	FS, Ntl & SE-TVL	1986-1999
128	Burger Geldenhuys	N Tvl	1977-1989
	Ollie le Roux	FS & Natal	1993-2007
126	Andre Joubert	FS & Natal	1986-1999
125	Eric Herbert	NFS & FS	1986-2001
123	Naas Botha	N Tvl	1977-1992
118	Willie Meyer	EP, FS & Lions	1989-2002
115	AJ Venter	FS, Lions & Sharks	1997-2008
115	Eddie Fredericks	Leop, FS, NFS	1998-2010
114	Piet Krause	Lions, GW, BB, Valke	1996-2007
114	Bevin Fortuin	SWD/FS	2000-2010
114	Louis Strydom	Griff,BB,Valke,Lions,FS	2001-2010
113	Skipper Badenhorst	Valke,Pumas,Sharks,FS	2000-2010
112	Louis Moolman	N Tvl	1974-1986
112	Stefan Terblanche	Boland & Sharks	1996-2010
111	Jacques Botes	Pumas & Sharks	2002-2010
111	Willem de Waal	Leop, FS, WP	2002-2010
110	Justin Peach	EP & Boland	2001-2010
108	Willem Stoltz	Lions, Leop, EP	1998-2010
106	Martiens le Roux	FS	1973-1986
106	De Wet Ras	FS & Natal	1974-1986
106	Gavin Passens	Griff, Pumas, BB, FS, GW	1999-2010
105	Kabamba Floors	SWD & FS	2003-2010
104	Gerrie Sonnekus	FS	1974-1985
103	Uli Schmidt	N Tvl & Tvl	1983-1994

103	Albert van den Berg	GW & Natal	1996-2009
102	Adolf Malan	N Tvl	1983-1992
102	John Daniels	Boland & Lions	1998-2008
102	Adi Jacobs	Valke/Natal	2001-2010
101	Gysie Pienaar	FS	1974-1987
101	Hendro Scholtz	FS	1999-2010

One thousand points

1699	Naas Botha	N Transvaal	1977-1992
1433	Willem de Waal	FS & WP	2002-2010
1402	Eric Herbert	NFS & FS	1986-2001
1210	De Wet Ras	FS & Natal	1974-1986
1165	Andre Joubert	FS & Natal	1986-1999
1017	Calla Scholtz	Boland & WP	1980-1989

Fifty tries

77	John Daniels	Boland & Lions	1998-2008
70	Breyton Paulse	WP	1996-2007
65	Chris Badenhorst	FS	1986-1999
58	Andre Joubert	FS & Natal	1986-1999
56	Stefan Terblanche	Boland & Natal	1994-2010
52	Egon Seconds	WP & Griquas	2001-2009
53	Eddie Fredericks	WP, NFS, Leop, FS	1998-2010
51	Gerrie Germishuys	FS & Transvaal	1971-1985
	Carel du Plessis	WP & Transvaal	1980-1989
	Neil Burger	WP	1982-1991
	Jan-Harm van Wyk	FS & Pumas	1996-2001
50	Fabian Juries	EP, FS & NFS	2001-2009

ABSA CURRIE CUP RECORDS

VODACOM CUP RECORDS

CHAMPIONS		2002	Lions	2007	Griquas
1998	Griquas	2003	Lions	2008	Blue Bulls
1999	Lions	2004	Lions	2009	Griquas
2000	Cheetahs	2005	Griquas	2010	Blue Bulls
2001	Blue Bulls	2006	Falcons		

RESULTS OF FINALS

1998	Griquas	57	Lions	0	Kimberley
1999	Lions	73	Griquas	7	Johannesburg
2000	Cheethas	44	Griquas	24	Bloemfontein
2001	Blue Bulls	42	Boland Cavaliers	24	Pretoria
2002	Lions	54	Blue Bulls	38	Johannesburg
2003	Blue Bulls	17	Lions	26	Pretoria
2004	Lions	35	Blue Bulls	16	Johannesburg
2005	Wildeklawer Griquas	27	Leopards	25	Kimberley
2006	Falcons	25	Natal	17	Brakpan
2007	Griquas	33	Blue Bulls	29	Kimberley
2008	Blue Bulls	25	Free State	21	Pretoria
2009	Blue Bulls	19	Griquas	28	Pretoria
2010	Blue Bulls	31	Free State	29	Pretoria

MATCH RECORDS

90 or more points

110-17	EP vs Welwits. (Namibia)	Port Elizabeth	2001
101-20	Lions vs Welwits.	Johannesburg	2001
92-8	Natal vs North West	Durban	1998
92-25	Blue Bulls vs Welwits.	Pretoria	2000

Won by 80 or more

93	EP vs Welwits. (110-17)	Port Elizabeth	2001
84	Natal vs North West (92-8)	Durban	1998
81	Lions vs Welwits. (101-20)	Johannesburg	2001

15 or more tries

16	EP vs Welwits. (110-17)	Port Elizabeth	2001
15	Lions vs Welwits. (101-20)	Johannesburg	2001

35 or more points by a player

42	IP Olivier (4t, 11c) Griquas vs Griffons	2009
38	RG Jordaan (2t, 11c, 2p) Elephants vs Welwits.	2001
36	C Barnard (2t, 10c, 2p) Cheetahs vs Falcons	2004
36	J Peach (2t, 7c, 4p) Boland vs Eagles	2006
35	GS du Toit (3t, 10c) Griquas vs EP	1998

4 or more tries by a player

5	S Brink, Natal vs Griffons	1998
5	JA van der Walt, Lions vs Welwits.	2001
4	C Manuel, Natal vs North West	1998
4	W Geyer, Falcons vs Griffons	1998
4	S Marot, Griffons vs SWD	2002
4	G Mbangeni, Falcons vs Leopards	2004
4	E Seconds, WP vs SWD	2006
4	IP Olivier, Griquas vs Griffons	2009

Ten or more conversions by a player

11	RG Jordaan, Elephants vs Welwits.	2001
11	IP Olivier, Griquas vs Griffons	2009
10	GS du Toit, Griquas vs EP	1998
10	C Barnard, Cheetahs vs Falcons	2004

Nine penalty goals by a player

9	E Herbert, Griffons vs Pumas	2001

Two drop goals by a player

2	GS du Toit, Griquas vs Cheetahs	1998
2	J Benade, Pumas vs Falcons	1999
2	A Hough, Griffons vs Border	2006

SEASON RECORDS

700 or more points

731	Griquas	1998

150 or more points by a player

236	GS du Toit	Griquas	1998
193	E Herbert	Griffons	2001
186	J Engelbrecht	Lions	1999
166	KC Tsimba	Cheetahs	2000
163	KC Tsimba	Cheetahs	2002
163	A Hough	Griffons	2006
158	F Brummer	Blue Bulls	2009
150	JD du Toit	Falcons	1999

100 or more team tries

109	Griquas	1998

12 or more tries by a player

15	J Daniels	Boland Cavaliers	1998
14	JNB van der Westhuyzen	Natal	1998
	RR Jansen	Blue Bulls	2008
12	PA van den Berg	Griquas	1998
12	DB Hall	Lions	1999
12	RF Smith	Griquas	1999
12	J Daniels	Lions	2006

50 or more conversions

72	GS du Toit	Griquas	1998

40 or more penalties

44	E Herbert	Griffons	2001

Four or more drop goals

6	BK Francis	Blue Bulls	2008
6	F Brummer	Blue Bulls	2010
4	GS du Toit	Griquas	1998
4	J Kotze	Welwitchias	2001

CAREER RECORDS

300 or more points

682	J Peach	EP, Boland
476	C Barnard	Cheetahs, KZN, Griquas
449	K Tsimba	Cheetahs, Pumas
425	QJ van Tonder	Griquas, Lions
373	G Goosen	Border, Boland, Leopards, WP
367	K Engelbrecht	Lions
344	C April	WP,Blue Bulls,Boland & SWD
334	R de Marigny	KZN, Leopards, Blue Bulls
326	R van As	Falcons, Eagles
307	E Herbert	Griffons
301	C Steyn	Blue Bulls, Pumas
300	PB Petersen	Boland,Griquas, Leopards, WP

20 or more tries

63	J Daniels	Boland, Lions
34	J Booysen	Lions
32	J Nicholas	Griquas
24	JA Juries	SWD, Pumas
23	AC Rafferty	Cheetahs
22	JNB van der Westhuyzen	KZN, Pumas, Blue Bulls
22	RF Smith	Griquas, WP, KZN, Cheetahs
21	J Peach	EP/Boland
20	T Douw	Falcons

80 or more conversions

110	J Peach	EP/Boland
99	K Tsimba	Cheetahs, Pumas
83	J Engelbrecht	Lions
80	C April	WP, Blue Bulls, Boland, SWD

60 or more penalty goals

119	J Peach	EP
69	E Herbert	Griffons
67	G Goosen	Border, Boland, Leopards, WP
64	R de Marigny	KZN, Leopards, Blue Bulls

Five or more drop goals

12	J Schutte	KZN, Pumas, Blue Bulls
12	F Brummer	Blue Bulls
7	QJ van Tonder	Griquas, Lions

VODACOM CUP RECORDS

SPRINGBOK RECORDS

SOUTH AFRICA TEST RESULTS SUMMARY - 1891 TO 2010

OPPONENTS	Played	Won	Lost	Drawn	% Won	Points For	Points Against	Tries	Conversions	Penalties	Drop goal	Tries	Conversions	Penalties	Drop goal
									SOUTH AFRICA				OPPONENTS		
Argentina	13	13	0	0	100%	544	272	70	52	29	1	26	20	33	1
Australia	71	41	29	1	58%	1347	1239	164	94	148	17	128	81	152	12
British Isles	46	23	17	6	50%	600	516	95	48	52	7	68	30	59	14
Canada	2	2	0	0	100%	71	18	10	6	3	0	2	1	2	0
England	32	19	12	1	59%	661	491	61	44	84	12	34	22	89	7
Fiji	2	2	0	0	100%	80	38	10	6	6	0	4	3	4	0
France	38	21	11	6	55%	764	568	88	59	89	7	50	27	80	19
Georgia	1	1	0	0	100%	46	19	7	4	1	0	1	1	4	0
Ireland	20	15	4	1	75%	401	236	59	31	30	5	24	14	32	3
Italy	10	10	0	0	100%	533	129	74	59	15	0	11	7	19	1
Namibia	1	1	0	0	100%	105	13	15	12	2	0	1	1	2	0
New Zealand	81	33	45	3	41%	1261	1514	124	81	161	27	155	92	195	19
NZ Cavaliers	4	3	1	0	75%	96	62	7	7	15	3	5	3	11	1
Pacific Islands	1	1	0	0	100%	38	24	4	3	4	0	4	2	0	0
Romania	1	1	0	0	100%	21	8	2	1	3	0	1	0	1	0
Scotland	21	16	5	0	76%	518	237	66	44	43	5	24	17	30	3
South America	6	5	1	0	83%	156	86	22	16	6	6	7	5	13	3
S America & Spain	2	2	0	0	100%	54	28	9	3	4	0	3	2	4	0
Spain	1	1	0	0	100%	47	3	7	6	0	0	0	0	1	0
Tonga	2	2	0	0	100%	104	35	16	9	2	0	4	3	3	0
USA	3	3	0	0	100%	145	42	23	16	2	0	4	1	6	1
Uruguay	3	3	0	0	100%	245	12	38	23	3	0	0	0	4	0
Wales	25	23	1	1	92%	698	351	87	56	55	2	31	17	54	2
W Samoa/Samoa	6	6	0	0	100%	316	65	44	30	11	1	9	4	4	0
World Teams	3	3	0	0	100%	87	59	11	5	10	1	9	7	3	0
	395	**250**	**126**	**19**	**63.3%**	**8938**	**6065**	**1113**	**715**	**778**	**94**	**605**	**360**	**805**	**86**

COMPARITIVE WIN PERCENTAGE WITH SOUTH AFRICA'S MAJOR RIVALS*

TEAM	Played	Won	% Won
New Zealand	472	354	75.0%
South Africa	395	250	63.3%
France	663	366	55.2%
England	633	334	52.8%
Wales	616	315	51.1%
Australia	520	262	50.4%
Scotland	594	252	42.4%
Ireland	596	251	42.1%

*As at 29 November, 2010.

TEST MATCHES BY DECADE

DECADE	Played	Won	Lost	Drawn	Win %	Prog. win %
1891-1900	7	1	6	0	14.3%	14.3%
1901-1910	10	5	2	3	50.0%	35.3%
1911-1920	5	5	0	0	100.0%	50.0%
1921-1930	11	6	3	2	54.5%	51.5%
1931-1940	17	13	4	0	76.5%	60.0%
1941-1950	4	4	0	0	100.0%	63.0%
1951-1960	28	18	8	2	64.3%	63.4%
1961-1970	46	26	14	6	56.5%	60.9%
1971-1980	28	20	6	2	71.4%	62.8%
1981-1990	18	14	4	0	77.8%	64.4%
1991-2000	94	60	32	2	63.8%	64.2%
2001-2010	127	78	47	2	61.4%	63.3%
395	**250**	**126**	**19**			

SOUTH AFRICA'S SEASONAL TEST RECORD

YEAR	Played	Won	Drawn	Lost	Points For	Points Against	% Won Season	Overall	Total Wins	Total Matches
1891	3	0	0	3	0	11	0.00	0.00	0	3
1896	4	1	0	3	16	34	25.00	14.29	1	7
1903	3	1	2	0	18	10	33.33	20.00	2	10
1906	4	2	1	1	29	21	50.00	28.57	4	14
1910	3	2	0	1	38	23	66.67	35.29	6	17
1912-13	5	5	0	0	104	8	100.00	50.00	11	22
1921	3	1	1	1	14	18	33.33	48.00	12	25
1924	4	3	1	0	43	15	75.00	51.72	15	29
1928	4	2	0	2	39	26	50.00	51.52	17	33
1931-32	4	4	0	0	29	9	100.00	56.76	21	37
1933	5	3	0	2	50	42	60.00	57.14	24	42
1937	5	4	0	1	72	47	80.00	59.57	28	47
1938	3	2	0	1	61	36	66.67	60.00	30	50
1949	4	4	0	0	47	28	100.00	62.96	34	54
1951-52	5	5	0	0	100	14	100.00	66.10	39	59
1953	4	3	0	1	79	38	75.00	66.67	42	63
1955	4	2	0	2	75	49	50.00	65.67	44	67
1956	6	3	0	3	47	41	50.00	64.38	47	73
1958	2	0	1	1	8	12	0.00	62.67	47	75
1960-61	10	7	2	1	81	43	70.00	63.53	54	85
1961	3	3	0	0	75	22	100.00	64.77	57	88
1962	4	3	1	0	48	20	75.00	65.22	60	92
1963	4	2	0	2	50	29	50.00	64.58	62	96
1964	2	1	0	1	30	11	50.00	64.29	63	98
1965	8	1	0	7	55	102	12.50	60.38	64	106
1967	4	2	1	1	62	31	50.00	60.00	66	110
1968	6	5	1	0	89	58	83.33	61.21	71	116
1969-70	8	4	2	2	101	62	50.00	60.48	75	124
1970	4	3	0	1	59	35	75.00	60.94	78	128
1971	5	4	1	0	81	40	80.00	61.65	82	133
1972	1	0	0	1	9	18	0.00	61.19	82	134
1974	6	2	1	3	57	91	33.33	60.00	84	140
1975	2	2	0	0	71	43	100.00	60.56	86	142
1976	4	3	0	1	55	46	75.00	60.96	89	146

SPRINGBOK RECORDS

SOUTH AFRICA'S SEASONAL TEST RECORD

YEAR	Played	Won	Drawn	Lost	Points For	Points Against	% Won Season	% Won Overall	Total Wins	Total Matches
1977	1	1	0	0	45	24	100.00	61.22	90	147
1980	9	8	0	1	208	130	88.89	62.82	98	156
1981	6	4	0	2	128	83	66.67	62.96	102	162
1982	2	1	0	1	62	39	50.00	62.80	103	164
1984	4	4	0	0	122	52	100.00	63.69	107	168
1986	4	3	0	1	96	62	75.00	63.95	110	172
1989	2	2	0	0	42	35	100.00	64.37	112	174
1992	5	1	0	4	79	130	20.00	63.13	113	179
1993	7	3	1	3	169	146	42.86	62.37	116	186
1994	9	5	1	3	225	164	55.56	62.05	121	195
1995	10	10	0	0	308	121	100.00	63.90	131	205
1996	13	8	0	5	352	260	61.54	63.76	139	218
1997	13	8	0	5	535	307	61.54	63.64	147	231
1998	12	11	0	1	361	136	91.67	65.02	158	243
1999	13	8	0	5	447	236	61.54	64.84	166	256
2000	12	6	0	6	301	301	50.00	64.18	172	268
2001	11	5	1	5	271	223	45.45	63.44	177	279
2002	11	5	0	6	284	318	45.45	62.76	182	290
2003	12	7	0	5	338	280	58.33	62.58	189	302
2004	13	9	0	4	408	276	69.23	62.86	198	315
2005	12	8	1	3	416	243	66.67	63.00	206	327
2006	12	5	0	7	258	321	41.67	62.24	211	339
2007	17	14	0	3	658	257	82.35	63.20	225	356
2008	13	9	0	4	360	195	69.23	63.41	234	369
2009	12	8	0	4	276	249	66.67	63.51	242	381
2010	14	8	0	6	397	344	57.14	63.29	250	395
Totals	**395**	**250**	**19**	**126**	**8938**	**6065**				

SOUTH AFRICA'S INTERNATIONAL TESTS AND TOUR MATCHES

TEST NO.	TOUR MATCH	Date	Venue	Opponent	Captain	Results	Points For	Points against
1		30/07/1891	Port Elizabeth	BRITISH ISLES	HH Castens	Lost	0	4
2		29/08/1891	Kimberley	BRITISH ISLES	RCD Snedden	Lost	0	3
3		05/09/1891	Cape Town	BRITISH ISLES	AR Richards	Lost	0	4
4		30/07/1896	Port Elizabeth	BRITISH ISLES	FTD Aston	Lost	0	8
5		22/08/1896	Johannesburg	BRITISH ISLES	FTD Aston	Lost	8	17
6		29/08/1896	Kimberley	BRITISH ISLES	FTD Aston	Lost	3	9
7		05/09/1896	Cape Town	BRITISH ISLES	BH Heatlie	Won	5	0
8		26/08/1903	Johannesburg	BRITISH ISLES	A Frew	Drew	10	10
9		05/09/1903	Kimberley	BRITISH ISLES	JM Powell	Drew	0	0
10		12/09/1903	Cape Town	BRITISH ISLES	BH Heatlie	Won	8	0
	1	27/09/1906	Northampton	East Midlands	PJ Roos	Won	37	0
	2	29/09/1906	Leicester	Midland Counties	PJ Roos	Won	29	0
	3	03/10/1906	Blackheath	Kent	PJ Roos	Won	21	0
	4	06/10/1906	West Hartlepool	Durham	PJ Roos	Won	22	4
	5	10/10/1906	Newcastle	Northumberland	PJ Roos	Won	44	0
	6	13/10/1906	Leeds	Yorkshire	PJ Roos	Won	34	0
	7	17/10/1906	Plymouth	Devon	PJ Roos	Won	22	6
	8	20/10/1906	Taunton	Somerset	WAG Burger	Won	14	0
	9	24/10/1906	Richmond	Middlesex	PJ Roos	Won	9	0
	10	27/10/1906	Newport	Newport	PJ Roos	Won	8	0
	11	31/10/1906	Cardiff	Glamorgan	PJ Roos	Won	6	3
	12	03/11/1906	Gloucester	Gloucestershire	HW Carolin	Won	23	0

SOUTH AFRICA'S INTERNATIONAL TESTS AND TOUR MATCHES

TEST NO.	TOUR MATCH	Date	Venue	Opponent	Captain	Results	Points For	Points against
	13	07/11/1906	Oxford	Oxford University	PJ Roos	Won	24	3
	14	10/11/1906	Cambridge	Cambridge University	FJ Dobbin	Won	29	0
	15	13/11/1906	Hawick	South of Scotland	HW Carolin	Won	32	5
11		17/11/1906	Glasgow	SCOTLAND	HW Carolin	Lost	0	6
	16	20/11/1906	Aberdeen	North of Scotland	FJ Dobbin	Won	35	3
12		24/11/1906	Belfast	IRELAND	PJ Roos	Won	15	12
	17	27/11/1906	Dublin	Dublin University	HW Carolin	Won	28	3
13		01/12/1906	Swansea	WALES	PJ Roos	Won	11	0
14		08/12/1906	London	ENGLAND	PJ Roos	Drew	3	3
	18	12/12/1906	Manchester	Lancashire	PJ Roos	Won	11	8
	19	15/12/1906	Carlisle	Cumberland	PJ Roos	Won	21	0
	20	19/12/1906	Richmond	Surrey	PJ Roos	Won	33	0
	21	22/12/1906	Redruth	Cornwall	PJ Roos	Won	9	3
	22	26/12/1906	Newport	Monmouthshire	PJ Roos	Won	17	0
	23	29/12/1906	Llanelli	Llanelli	PJ Roos	Won	16	3
	24	01/01/1907	Cardiff	Cardiff	PJ Roos	Lost	0	17
15		06/08/1910	Johannesburg	BRITISH ISLES	DFT Morkel	Won	14	10
16		27/08/1910	Port Elizabeth	BRITISH ISLES	WA Millar	Lost	3	8
17		03/09/1910	Cape Town	BRITISH ISLES	WA Millar	Won	21	5
	25	03/10/1912	Bath	Somerset	WA Millar	Won	24	3
	26	05/10/1912	Exeter	Devon	WA Millar	Won	8	0
	27	10/10/1912	Redruth	Cornwall	DFT Morkel	Won	15	6
	28	12/10/1912	Newport	Monmouthshire	WA Millar	Won	16	0
	29	17/10/1912	Cardiff	Glamorgan	WA Millar	Won	35	3
	30	19/10/1912	Llanelli	Llanelli	FJ Dobbin	Won	8	7
	31	24/10/1912	Newport	Newport	WA Millar	Lost	3	9
	32	26/10/1912	Blackheath	London	WA Millar	Won	12	8
	33	30/10/1912	Portsmouth	United Services	WA Millar	Won	18	16
	34	02/11/1912	Northampton	East Midlands	WA Millar	Won	14	5
	35	06/11/1912	Oxford	Oxford University	WA Millar	Won	6	0
	36	09/11/1912	Leicester	Midland Counties	WA Millar	Won	25	3
	37	14/11/1912	Cambridge	Cambridge University	DFT Morkel	Won	24	0
	38	16/11/1912	Twickenham	London	WA Millar	Lost	8	10
	39	20/11/1912	Newcastle	North of England	DFT Morkel	Won	17	0
18		23/11/1912	Edinburgh	SCOTLAND	FJ Dobbin	Won	16	0
	40	27/11/1912	Glasgow	West of Scotland	WA Millar	Won	38	3
19		30/11/1912	Dublin	IRELAND	WA Millar	Won	38	0
	41	04/12/1912	Belfast	Ulster	WA Millar	Won	19	0
	42	07/12/1912	Birkenhead	North of England	DFT Morkel	Won	21	8
20		14/12/1912	Cardiff	WALES	WA Millar	Won	3	0
	43	19/12/1912	Neath	Neath	WA Millar	Won	8	3
	44	21/12/1912	Cardiff	Cardiff	WA Millar	Won	7	6
	45	26/12/1912	Swansea	Swansea	WA Millar	Lost	0	3
	46	28/12/1912	Bristol	Gloucestershire	DFT Morkel	Won	11	0
21		04/01/1913	Twickenham	ENGLAND	DFT Morkel	Won	9	3
22		11/01/1913	Bordeaux	FRANCE	WA Millar	Won	38	5
	47	25/06/1921	Sydney	New South Wales	TB Pienaar	Won	25	10
	48	27/06/1921	Sydney	New South Wales	TB Pienaar	Won	16	11
	49	02/07/1921	Sydney	New South Wales	WH Morkel	Won	28	9
	50	06/07/1921	Sydney	Metropolitan	WH Morkel	Won	14	8
	51	13/07/1921	Wanganui	Wanganui	TB Pienaar	Won	11	6
	52	16/07/1921	New Plymouth	Taranaki	WH Morkel	Drew	0	0
	53	20/07/1921	Masterton	Wairarapa-Bush	TB Pienaar	Won	18	3
	54	23/07/1921	Wellington	Wellington	TB Pienaar	Won	8	3
	55	27/07/1921	Greymouth	West Coast - Buller	HJL Morkel	Won	33	3
	56	30/07/1921	Christchurch	Canterbury	TB Pienaar	Lost	4	6

SOUTH AFRICA'S INTERNATIONAL TESTS AND TOUR MATCHES

TEST NO.	TOUR MATCH No.	Date	Venue	Opponent	Captain	Results	Points For	Points against
	57	03/08/1921	Timaru	South Canterbury	WH Morkel	Won	34	3
	58	06/08/1921	Invercargill	Southland	TB Pienaar	Won	12	0
	59	10/08/1921	Dunedin	Otago	WH Morkel	Won	11	3
23		13/08/1921	Dunedin	NEW ZEALAND	WH Morkel	Lost	5	13
	60	17/08/1921	Palmerston N.	Manawatu-Horowhenua	TB Pienaar	Won	3	0
	61	20/08/1921	Auckland	Auckland - North Auckland	TL Krüger	Won	24	8
	62	24/08/1921	Rotorua	Bay of Plenty	TL Krüger	Won	17	9
24		27/08/1921	Auckland	NEW ZEALAND	WH Morkel	Won	9	5
	63	31/08/1921	Hamilton	Waikato	TB Pienaar	Won	6	0
	64	03/09/1921	Napier	Hawkes Bay - Poverty Bay	TB Pienaar	Won	14	8
	65	07/09/1921	Napier	New Zealand Maoris	WH Morkel	Won	9	8
	66	10/09/1921	Nelson	Nelson, Marlborough & Golden Bay - Motueka	JP Michau	Won	26	3
25		17/09/1921	Wellington	NEW ZEALAND	WH Morkel	Drew	0	0
26		16/08/1924	Durban	BRITISH ISLES	PK Albertyn	Won	7	3
27		23/08/1924	Johannesburg	BRITISH ISLES	PK Albertyn	Won	17	0
28		13/09/1924	Port Elizabeth	BRITISH ISLES	PK Albertyn	Drew	3	3
29		20/09/1924	Cape Town	BRITISH ISLES	PK Albertyn	Won	16	9
30		30/06/1928	Durban	NEW ZEALAND	PJ Mostert	Won	17	0
31		21/07/1928	Johannesburg	NEW ZEALAND	PJ Mostert	Lost	6	7
32		18/08/1928	Port Elizabeth	NEW ZEALAND	PJ Mostert	Won	11	6
33		01/09/1928	Cape Town	NEW ZEALAND	PJ Mostert	Lost	5	13
	67	03/10/1931	Bristol	Gloucestershire & Somerset	BL Osler	Won	14	3
	68	08/10/1931	Newport	Newport	BL Osler	Won	15	3
	69	10/10/1931	Swansea	Swansea	JC van der Westhuizen	Won	10	3
	70	14/10/1931	Abertillery	Abertillery & Cross Keys	BL Osler	Won	10	9
	71	17/10/1931	Twickenham	London	BL Osler	Won	30	3
	72	21/10/1931	Birmingham	Midland Counties	Unknown	Won	13	3
	73	24/10/1931	Sunderland	Durham & Northumberland	JC van der Westhuizen	Won	41	0
	74	28/10/1931	Glasgow	Glasgow	JC van der Westhuizen	Won	21	13
	75	31/10/1931	Melrose	South of Scotland	MM Louw	Drew	0	0
	76	04/11/1931	Cambridge	Cambridge University	BL Osler	Won	21	9
	77	07/11/1931	Twickenham	Combined Services	BL Osler	Won	23	0
	78	12/11/1931	Oxford	Oxford University	BL Osler	Won	24	3
	79	14/11/1931	Leicester	Midland Counties	JC van der Westhuizen	Lost	21	30
	80	18/11/1931	Devonport	Devon & Cornwall	BL Osler	Drew	3	3
	81	21/11/1931	Cardiff	Cardiff	BL Osler	Won	13	5
	82	24/11/1931	Llanelli	Llanelli	MM Louw	Won	9	0
	83	28/11/1931	Neath	Neath & Aberavon	BL Osler	Won	8	3
34		05/12/1931	Swansea	WALES	BL Osler	Won	8	3
	84	09/12/1931	Liverpool	Lancashire & Cheshire	BL Osler	Won	20	9
	85	12/12/1931	Belfast	Ulster	Unknown	Won	30	3
35		19/12/1931	Dublin	IRELAND	BL Osler	Won	8	3
	86	26/12/1931	Twickenham	London	BL Osler	Won	16	8
36		02/01/1932	Twickenham	ENGLAND	BL Osler	Won	7	0
	87	06/01/1932	Workington	Yorkshire & Cumberland	BL Osler	Won	27	5
	88	09/01/1932	Aberdeen	North of Scotland	JC van der Westhuizen	Won	9	0
37		16/01/1932	Edinburgh	SCOTLAND	BL Osler	Won	6	3
38		08/07/1933	Cape Town	AUSTRALIA	PJ Nel	Won	17	3
39		22/07/1933	Durban	AUSTRALIA	BL Osler	Lost	6	21
40		12/08/1933	Johannesburg	AUSTRALIA	PJ Nel	Won	12	3
41		26/08/1933	Port Elizabeth	AUSTRALIA	PJ Nel	Won	11	0
42		02/09/1933	Bloemfontein	AUSTRALIA	PJ Nel	Lost	4	15
	89	12/06/1937	Melbourne	Victoria	PJ Nel	Won	45	11
	90	16/06/1937	Orange	Combined Western Districts	GH Brand	Won	63	0

SOUTH AFRICA'S INTERNATIONAL TESTS AND TOUR MATCHES

TEST NO.	TOUR MATCH No.	Date	Venue	Opponent	Captain	Results	Points For	Points against
	91	19/06/1937	Sydney	New South Wales	PJ Nel	Lost	6	17
43		26/06/1937	Sydney	AUSTRALIA	PJ Nel	Won	9	5
	92	30/06/1937	Newcastle	Newcastle	PJ Nel	Won	58	8
	93	03/07/1937	Brisbane	Australian XV	PJ Nel	Won	36	3
	94	07/07/1937	Toowoomba	Toowoomba	PJ Nel	Won	60	0
	95	10/07/1937	Brisbane	Queensland	PJ Nel	Won	39	4
44		17/07/1937	Sydney	AUSTRALIA	PJ Nel	Won	26	17
	96	24/07/1937	Auckland	Auckland	PJ Nel	Won	19	5
	97	28/07/1937	Hamilton	Waikato-King Country-Thames Valley	PJ Nel	Won	6	3
	98	31/07/1937	New Plymouth	Taranaki	PJ Nel	Won	17	3
	99	04/08/1937	Palmerston N.	Manawatu	PJ Nel	Won	39	3
	100	07/08/1937	Wellington	Wellington	GH Brand	Won	29	0
45		14/08/1937	Wellington	NEW ZEALAND	DH Craven	Lost	7	13
	101	18/08/1937	Blenheim	Nelson-Golden Bay-Motueka-Marlborough	PJ Nel	Won	22	0
	102	21/08/1937	Christchurch	Canterbury	PJ Nel	Won	23	8
	103	25/08/1937	Greymouth	West Coast-Buller	PJ Nel	Won	31	6
	104	28/08/1937	Timaru	South Canterbury	PJ Nel	Won	43	6
46		04/09/1937	Christchurch	NEW ZEALAND	PJ Nel	Won	13	6
	105	08/09/1937	Invercargill	Southland	PJ Nel	Won	30	17
	106	11/09/1937	Dunedin	Otago	DH Craven	Won	47	7
	107	15/09/1937	Napier	Hawke's Bay	PJ Nel	Won	21	12
	108	18/09/1937	Gisborne	Poverty Bay-Bay of Plenty-East Coast	PJ Nel	Won	33	3
47		25/09/1937	Auckland	NEW ZEALAND	PJ Nel	Won	17	6
	109	29/09/1937	Whangarei	North Auckland	PJ Nel	Won	14	6
48		06/08/1938	Johannesburg	BRITISH ISLES	DH Craven	Won	26	12
49		03/09/1938	Port Elizabeth	BRITISH ISLES	DH Craven	Won	19	3
50		10/09/1938	Cape Town	BRITISH ISLES	DH Craven	Lost	16	21
51		16/07/1949	Cape Town	NEW ZEALAND	F du Plessis	Won	15	11
52		13/08/1949	Johannesburg	NEW ZEALAND	F du Plessis	Won	12	6
53		03/09/1949	Durban	NEW ZEALAND	F du Plessis	Won	9	3
54		17/09/1949	Port Elizabeth	NEW ZEALAND	BJ Kenyon	Won	11	8
	110	10/10/1951	Bournemouth	South Eastern Counties	BJ Kenyon	Won	31	6
	111	13/10/1951	Plymouth	South Western Counties	HSV Muller	Won	17	8
	112	18/10/1951	Pontypool	Pontypool & Newbridge	BJ Kenyon	Won	15	6
	113	20/10/1951	Cardiff	Cardiff	HSV Muller	Won	11	9
	114	23/10/1951	Llanelli	Llanelli	BJ Kenyon	Won	20	11
	115	27/10/1951	Liverpool	North Western Counties	BJ Kenyon	Won	16	9
	116	31/10/1951	Glasgow	Glasgow & Edinburgh	HSV Muller	Won	43	11
	117	03/11/1951	Newcastle	North Eastern Counties	BJ Kenyon	Won	19	8
	118	08/11/1951	Cambridge	Cambridge University	HSV Muller	Won	30	0
	119	10/11/1951	Twickenham	London Counties	HSV Muller	Lost	9	11
	120	15/11/1951	Oxford	Oxford University	HSV Muller	Won	24	3
	121	17/11/1951	Port Talbot	Neath & Aberavon	HSV Muller	Won	22	0
55		24/11/1951	Edinburgh	SCOTLAND	HSV Muller	Won	44	0
	122	28/11/1951	Aberdeen	North of Scotland	JA du Rand	Won	14	3
	123	01/12/1951	Belfast	Ulster	HSV Muller	Won	27	5
56		08/12/1951	Dublin	IRELAND	HSV Muller	Won	17	5
	124	11/12/1951	Limerick	Munster	PA du Toit	Won	11	6
	125	15/12/1951	Swansea	Swansea	HSV Muller	Won	11	3
57		22/12/1951	Cardiff	WALES	HSV Muller	Won	6	3
	126	26/12/1951	Twickenham	Combined Services	SP Fry	Won	24	8
	127	29/12/1951	Leicester	Midland Counties	B Myburgh	Won	3	0
58		05/01/1952	Twickenham	ENGLAND	HSV Muller	Won	8	3

SPRINGBOK RECORDS

SOUTH AFRICA'S INTERNATIONAL TESTS AND TOUR MATCHES

TEST NO.	TOUR MATCH No.	Date	Venue	Opponent	Captain	Results	Points For	Points against
	128	10/01/1952	Newport	Newport	HSV Muller	Won	12	6
	129	12/01/1952	Bristol	Western Counties	PA du Toit	Won	16	5
	130	16/01/1952	Coventry	Midland Counties	PA du Toit	Won	19	8
	131	19/01/1952	Hawick	South of Scotland	HSV Muller	Won	13	3
	132	26/01/1952	Cardiff	Barbarians	HSV Muller	Won	17	3
	133	02/02/1952	Lyon	South Eastern France	HSV Muller	Won	9	3
	134	07/02/1952	Bordeaux	South Western France	SP Fry	Won	20	12
	135	09/02/1952	Toulouse	France 'B'	HSV Muller	Won	9	6
59		16/02/1952	Paris	**FRANCE**	HSV Muller	Won	25	3
60		22/08/1953	Johannesburg	**AUSTRALIA**	HSV Muller	Won	25	3
61		05/09/1953	Cape Town	**AUSTRALIA**	HSV Muller	Lost	14	18
62		19/09/1953	Durban	**AUSTRALIA**	HSV Muller	Won	18	8
63		26/09/1953	Port Elizabeth	**AUSTRALIA**	HSV Muller	Won	22	9
64		06/08/1955	Johannesburg	**BRITISH ISLES**	SP Fry	Lost	22	23
65		20/08/1955	Cape Town	**BRITISH ISLES**	SP Fry	Won	25	9
66		03/09/1955	Pretoria	**BRITISH ISLES**	SP Fry	Lost	6	9
67		24/09/1955	Port Elizabeth	**BRITISH ISLES**	SP Fry	Won	22	8
	136	15/05/1956	Canberra	Australian Capital Territories	SS Vivier	Won	41	6
	137	19/05/1956	Sydney	New South Wales	SS Vivier	Won	29	9
	138	22/05/1956	Tamworth	New South Wales Country	JAJ Pickard	Won	15	8
68		26/05/1956	Sydney	**AUSTRALIA**	SS Vivier	Won	9	0
	139	29/05/1956	Brisbane	Queensland	SS Vivier	Won	47	3
69		02/06/1956	Brisbane	**AUSTRALIA**	SS Vivier	Won	9	0
	140	09/06/1956	Hamilton	Waikato	JAJ Pickard	Lost	10	14
	141	13/06/1956	Whangarei	North Auckland	SS Vivier	Won	3	0
	142	16/06/1956	Auckland	Auckland	SS Vivier	Won	6	3
	143	20/06/1956	Palmerston N.	Manawatu-Horowhenua	AC Koch	Won	14	3
	144	23/06/1956	Wellington	Wellington	JA du Rand	Won	8	6
	145	27/06/1956	Gisborne	Poverty Bay-East Coast	JA du Rand	Won	22	0
	146	30/06/1956	Napier	Hawke's Bay	JA du Rand	Won	20	8
	147	04/07/1956	Nelson	Nelson, Marlborough & Golden Bay - Motueka	JA du Rand	Won	41	3
	148	07/07/1956	Dunedin	Otago	JA du Rand	Won	14	9
70		14/07/1956	Dunedin	**NEW ZEALAND**	JA du Rand	Lost	6	10
	149	18/07/1956	Timaru	S Canterbury, Mid Canterbury & North Otago	JAJ Pickard	Won	20	8
	150	21/07/1956	Christchurch	Canterbury	JA du Rand	Lost	6	9
	151	25/07/1956	Westport	West Coast-Buller	SS Vivier	Won	27	6
	152	28/07/1956	Invercargill	Southland	JA du Rand	Won	23	12
	153	31/07/1956	Masterton	Wairarapa-Bush	SS Vivier	Won	19	8
71		04/08/1956	Wellington	**NEW ZEALAND**	SS Vivier	Won	8	3
	154	08/08/1956	Wanganui	Wanganui-King Country	SS Vivier	Won	36	16
	155	11/08/1956	New Plymouth	Taranaki	SS Vivier	Drew	3	3
72		18/08/1956	Christchurch	**NEW ZEALAND**	SS Vivier	Lost	10	17
	156	22/08/1956	Wellington	New Zealand Universities	SS Vivier	Lost	15	22
	157	25/08/1956	Auckland	New Zealand Maoris	SS Vivier	Won	37	0
	158	28/08/1956	Rotorua	Bay of Plenty-Thames Valley-Counties	SS Vivier	Won	17	6
73		01/09/1956	Auckland	**NEW ZEALAND**	SS Vivier	Lost	5	11
74		26/07/1958	Cape Town	**FRANCE**	JT Claasen	Drew	3	3
75		16/08/1958	Johannesburg	**FRANCE**	JT Claasen	Lost	5	9
76		30/04/1960	Port Elizabeth	**SCOTLAND**	DC van Jaarsveld	Won	18	10
77		25/06/1960	Johannesburg	**NEW ZEALAND**	RG Dryburgh	Won	13	0
78		23/07/1960	Cape Town	**NEW ZEALAND**	RG Dryburgh	Lost	3	11
79		13/08/1960	Bloemfontein	**NEW ZEALAND**	AS Malan	Drew	11	11
80		27/08/1960	Port Elizabeth	**NEW ZEALAND**	AS Malan	Won	8	3

SOUTH AFRICA'S INTERNATIONAL TESTS AND TOUR MATCHES

TEST NO.	TOUR MATCH No.	Date	Venue	Opponent	Captain	Results	Points For	Points against
	159	22/10/1960	Hove	Southern Counties	AS Malan	Won	29	9
	160	26/10/1960	Oxford	Oxford University	RJ Lockyear	Won	24	5
	161	29/10/1960	Cardiff	Cardiff	AS Malan	Won	13	0
	162	02/11/1960	Pontypool	Pontypool & Cross Keys	JT Claasen	Won	30	3
	163	05/11/1960	Leicester	Midland Counties	RJ Lockyear	Drew	3	3
	164	09/11/1960	Cambridge	Cambridge University	AS Malan	Won	12	0
	165	12/11/1960	Twickenham	London Counties	AS Malan	Won	20	3
	166	16/11/1960	Glasgow	Glasgow & Edinburgh	JT Claasen	Won	16	11
	167	19/11/1960	Hawick	South of Scotland	AS Malan	Won	19	3
	168	23/11/1960	Manchester	North Western Counties	JT Claasen	Won	11	0
	169	26/11/1960	Swansea	Swansea	RJ Lockyear	Won	19	3
	170	29/11/1960	Ebbw Vale	Ebbw Vale & Abertillery	AS Malan	Won	3	0
81		03/12/1960	Cardiff	WALES	AS Malan	Won	3	0
	171	07/12/1960	Camborne	South Western Counties	AS Malan	Won	21	9
	172	10/12/1960	Gloucester	Western Counties	AS Malan	Won	42	0
	173	13/12/1960	Llanelli	Llanelli	AS Malan	Won	21	0
82		17/12/1960	Dublin	IRELAND	AS Malan	Won	8	3
	174	21/12/1960	Cork	Munster	JT Claasen	Won	9	3
	175	26/12/1960	Twickenham	Combined Services	AS Malan	Won	14	5
	176	28/12/1960	Birmingham	Midland Couties	AS Malan	Won	16	5
	177	31/12/1960	Gosforth	North Eastern Counties	JT Claasen	Won	21	9
	178	03/01/1961	Bournemouth	South Eastern Counties	AS Malan	Won	24	0
83		07/01/1961	Twickenham	ENGLAND	AS Malan	Won	5	0
	179	11/01/1961	Newport	Newport	AS Malan	Won	3	0
	180	14/01/1961	Neath	Neath & Aberavon	AS Malan	Won	25	5
84		21/01/1961	Edinburgh	SCOTLAND	AS Malan	Won	12	5
	181	25/01/1961	Aberdeen	North of Scotland	AS Malan	Won	22	9
	182	28/01/1961	Belfast	Ulster	JT Claasen	Won	19	6
	183	01/02/1961	Dublin	Leinster	AS Malan	Won	12	5
	184	04/02/1961	Cardiff	Barbarians	AS Malan	Lost	0	6
	185	08/02/1961	Bordeaux	South Western France	RJ Lockyear	Won	29	3
	186	11/02/1961	Toulouse	France 'B'	RJ Lockyear	Won	26	10
	187	14/02/1961	Bayonne	Coast of Basque	AS Malan	Won	36	9
85		18/02/1961	Paris	FRANCE	AS Malan	Drew	0	0
86		13/05/1961	Cape Town	IRELAND	JT Claasen	Won	24	8
87		05/08/1961	Johannesburg	AUSTRALIA	JT Claasen	Won	28	3
88		12/08/1961	Port Elizabeth	AUSTRALIA	JT Claasen	Won	23	11
89		23/06/1962	Johannesburg	BRITISH ISLES	JT Claasen	Drew	3	3
90		21/07/1962	Durban	BRITISH ISLES	JT Claasen	Won	3	0
91		04/08/1962	Cape Town	BRITISH ISLES	JT Claasen	Won	8	3
92		25/08/1962	Bloemfontein	BRITISH ISLES	JT Claasen	Won	34	14
93		13/07/1963	Pretoria	AUSTRALIA	GF Malan	Won	14	3
94		10/08/1963	Cape Town	AUSTRALIA	GF Malan	Lost	5	9
95		24/08/1963	Johannesburg	AUSTRALIA	AS Malan	Lost	9	11
96		07/09/1963	Port Elizabeth	AUSTRALIA	GF Malan	Won	22	6
97		23/05/1964	Durban	WALES	GF Malan	Won	24	3
98		25/07/1964	Springs	FRANCE	CM Smith	Lost	6	8
	188	03/04/1965	Belfast	Combined Provinces (Ireland)	AS Malan	Drew	8	8
	189	06/04/1965	Limerick	Combined Universities, Past & Present	AS Malan	Lost	10	12
99		10/04/1965	Dublin	IRELAND	AS Malan	Lost	6	9
	190	13/04/1965	Hawick	Scottish Districts XV	DJ de Villiers	Lost	8	16
100		17/04/1965	Edinburgh	SCOTLAND	AS Malan	Lost	5	8
	191	10/06/1965	Perth	Western Australia	DJ de Villiers	Won	60	0
	192	12/06/1965	Melbourne	Victoria	CM Smith	Won	52	6
	193	14/06/1965	Sydney	New South Wales	DJ de Villiers	Lost	3	12

SOUTH AFRICA'S INTERNATIONAL TESTS AND TOUR MATCHES

TEST NO.	TOUR MATCH No.	Date	Venue	Opponent	Captain	Results	Points For	Points against
101		19/06/1965	Sydney	AUSTRALIA	CM Smith	Lost	11	18
	194	22/06/1965	Brisbane	Queensland	CM Smith	Won	50	5
102		26/06/1965	Brisbane	AUSTRALIA	CM Smith	Lost	8	12
	195	30/06/1965	Gisborne	Poverty Bay - East Coast	CM Smith	Won	32	3
	196	03/07/1965	Wellington	Wellington	CM Smith	Lost	6	23
	197	07/07/1965	Palmerston N.	Manawatu-Horowhenua	DJ de Villiers	Won	30	8
	198	10/07/1965	Dunedin	Otago	DJ de Villiers	Won	8	6
	199	14/07/1965	Christchurch	New Zealand Juniors	CM Smith	Won	23	3
	200	17/07/1965	New Plymouth	Taranaki	DJ de Villiers	Won	11	3
	201	21/07/1965	Invercargill	Southland	CM Smith	Won	19	6
	202	24/07/1965	Christchurch	Canterbury	DJ de Villiers	Won	6	5
	203	27/07/1965	Greymouth	West Coast-Buller	CM Smith	Won	11	0
103		31/07/1965	Wellington	NEW ZEALAND	DJ de Villiers	Lost	3	6
	204	04/08/1965	Wanganui	Wanganui-King Country	DJ de Villiers	Won	24	19
	205	07/08/1965	Hamilton	Waikato	CM Smith	Won	26	13
	206	11/08/1965	Whangarei	North Auckland	CM Smith	Won	14	11
	207	14/08/1965	Auckland	Auckland	DJ de Villiers	Lost	14	15
	208	17/08/1965	Blenheim	Marlborough, Nelson & Golden Bay- Motueka	CM Smith	Won	45	6
104		21/08/1965	Dunedin	NEW ZEALAND	CM Smith	Lost	0	13
	209	25/08/1965	Timaru	S Canterbury, Mid Canterbury & North Otago	DJ de Villiers	Won	28	13
	210	28/08/1965	Wellington	New Zealand Maoris	DJ de Villiers	Won	9	3
	211	31/08/1965	Masterton	Wairarapa-Bush	CM Smith	Won	36	0
105		04/09/1965	Christchurch	NEW ZEALAND	DJ de Villiers	Won	19	16
	212	08/09/1965	Auckland	New Zealand Universities	CM Smith	Won	55	11
	213	11/09/1965	Napier	Hawke's Bay	DJ de Villiers	Won	30	12
	214	14/09/1965	Rotorua	Bay of Plenty-Counties-Thames Valley	DJ de Villiers	Won	33	17
106		18/09/1965	Auckland	NEW ZEALAND	DJ de Villiers	Lost	3	20
107		15/07/1967	Durban	FRANCE	DJ de Villiers	Won	26	3
108		22/07/1967	Bloemfontein	FRANCE	DJ de Villiers	Won	16	3
109		29/07/1967	Johannesburg	FRANCE	DJ de Villiers	Lost	14	19
110		12/08/1967	Cape Town	FRANCE	DJ de Villiers	Drew	6	6
111		08/06/1968	Pretoria	BRITISH ISLES	DJ de Villiers	Won	25	20
112		22/06/1968	Port Elizabeth	BRITISH ISLES	DJ de Villiers	Drew	6	6
113		13/07/1968	Cape Town	BRITISH ISLES	DJ de Villiers	Won	11	6
114		27/07/1968	Johannesburg	BRITISH ISLES	DJ de Villiers	Won	19	6
	215	29/10/1968	Toulon	Littoral-Provence	DJ de Villiers	Won	24	3
	216	02/11/1968	Lyon	South Eastern France	TP Bedford	Won	3	0
	217	05/11/1968	Clermont-Ferrand	Auvergne-Limousin	DJ de Villiers	Won	26	9
115		09/11/1968	Bordeaux	FRANCE	DJ de Villiers	Won	12	9
	218	11/11/1968	Toulouse	South Western France	TP Bedford	Lost	3	11
116		16/11/1968	Paris	FRANCE	DJ de Villiers	Won	16	11
117		02/08/1969	Johannesburg	AUSTRALIA	DJ de Villiers	Won	30	11
118		16/08/1969	Durban	AUSTRALIA	TP Bedford	Won	16	9
119		06/09/1969	Cape Town	AUSTRALIA	TP Bedford	Won	11	3
120		20/09/1969	Bloemfontein	AUSTRALIA	DJ de Villiers	Won	19	8
	219	05/11/1969	Twickenham	Oxford University	DJ de Villiers	Lost	3	6
	220	08/11/1969	Leicester	Midland Counties (E)	TP Bedford	Won	11	9
	221	12/11/1969	Newport	Newport	DJ de Villiers	Lost	6	11
	222	15/11/1969	Swansea	Swansea	DJ de Villiers	Won	12	0
	223	19/11/1969	Ebbw Vale	Gwent	JFK Marais	Lost	8	14
	224	22/11/1969	Twickenham	London Counties	DJ de Villiers	Won	22	6
	225	26/11/1969	Manchester	North Western Counties	DJ de Villiers	Won	12	3
	226	02/12/1969	Aberdeen	North & Midlands				

SOUTH AFRICA'S INTERNATIONAL TESTS AND TOUR MATCHES

TEST NO.	TOUR MATCH No.	Date	Venue	Opponent	Captain	Results	Points For	Points against
				of Scotland	DJ de Villiers	Won	37	3
121		06/12/1969	Edinburgh	SCOTLAND	TP Bedford	Lost	3	6
	227	10/12/1969	Aberavon	Aberavon & Neath	TP Bedford	Won	27	0
	228	13/12/1969	Cardiff	Cardiff	DJ de Villiers	Won	17	3
	229	16/12/1969	Aldershot	Combined Services	JFK Marais	Won	14	6
122		20/12/1969	Twickenham	ENGLAND	DJ de Villiers	Lost	8	11
	230	27/12/1969	Exeter	South Western Counties	DJ de Villiers	Won	9	6
	231	31/12/1969	Bristol	Western Counties	TP Bedford	Drew	3	3
	232	03/01/1970	Gosforth	North Eastern Counties	DJ de Villiers	Won	24	11
	233	06/01/1970	Coventry	Midland Counties (W)	TP Bedford	Won	21	6
123		10/01/1970	Dublin	IRELAND	DJ de Villiers	Drew	8	8
	234	14/01/1970	Limerick	Munster	DJ de Villiers	Won	25	9
	235	17/01/1970	Galashiels	South of Scotland	TP Bedford	Drew	3	3
	236	20/01/1970	Llanelli	Llanelli	DJ de Villiers	Won	10	9
124		24/01/1970	Cardiff	WALES	DJ de Villiers	Drew	6	6
	237	28/01/1970	Gloucester	Southern Counties	TP Bedford	Won	13	0
	238	31/01/1970	Twickenham	Barbarians	DJ de Villiers	Won	21	12
125		25/07/1970	Pretoria	NEW ZEALAND	DJ de Villiers	Won	17	6
126		08/08/1970	Cape Town	NEW ZEALAND	DJ de Villiers	Lost	8	9
127		29/08/1970	Port Elizabeth	NEW ZEALAND	DJ de Villiers	Won	14	3
128		12/09/1970	Johannesburg	NEW ZEALAND	DJ de Villiers	Won	20	17
129		12/06/1971	Bloemfontein	FRANCE	JFK Marais	Won	22	9
130		19/06/1971	Durban	FRANCE	JFK Marais	Drew	8	8
	239	26/06/1971	Perth	Western Australia	JFK Marais	Won	44	18
	240	30/06/1971	Adelaide	South Australia	TP Bedford	Won	43	0
	241	03/07/1971	Melbourne	Victoria	JFK Marais	Won	50	0
	242	06/07/1971	Sydney	Sydney	JFK Marais	Won	21	12
	243	10/07/1971	Sydney	New South Wales	JFK Marais	Won	25	3
	244	13/07/1971	Orange	New South Wales Country	PJF Greyling	Won	19	3
131		17/07/1971	Sydney	AUSTRALIA	JFK Marais	Won	19	11
	245	21/07/1971	Canberra	Australian Capital Territories	JFK Marais	Won	34	3
	246	24/07/1971	Brisbane	Queensland	JFK Marais	Won	33	14
	247	27/07/1971	Brisbane	Junior Wallabies	JFK Marais	Won	31	12
132		31/07/1971	Brisbane	AUSTRALIA	JFK Marais	Won	14	6
	248	03/08/1971	Toowoomba	Queensland Country	PJF Greyling	Won	45	14
133		07/08/1971	Sydney	AUSTRALIA	JFK Marais	Won	18	6
134		03/06/1972	Johannesburg	ENGLAND	PJF Greyling	Lost	9	18
135		08/06/1974	Cape Town	BRITISH ISLES	JFK Marais	Lost	3	12
136		22/06/1974	Pretoria	BRITISH ISLES	JFK Marais	Lost	9	28
137		13/07/1974	Port Elizabeth	BRITISH ISLES	JFK Marais	Lost	9	26
138		27/07/1974	Johannesburg	BRITISH ISLES	JFK Marais	Drew	13	13
	249	06/11/1974	Nice	South Eastern France	JFK Marais	Won	10	7
	250	09/11/1974	Lyon	North Eastern France	DSL Snyman	Won	25	12
	251	13/11/1974	Agen	South Western France	JFK Marais	Won	16	3
	252	16/11/1974	Tarbes	Second Division Clubs	JFK Marais	Won	36	4
	253	20/11/1974	Clermont-Ferrand	Central France	DSL Snyman	Won	29	10
139		23/11/1974	Toulouse	FRANCE	JFK Marais	Won	13	4
	254	27/11/1974	Angoulême	Western France	JCP Snyman	Lost	4	7
140		30/11/1974	Paris	FRANCE	JFK Marais	Won	10	8
	255	04/12/1974	Reims	Northern France	JFK Marais	Won	27	19
141		21/06/1975	Bloemfontein	FRANCE	M du Plessis	Won	38	25
142		28/06/1975	Pretoria	FRANCE	M du Plessis	Won	33	18
143		24/07/1976	Durban	NEW ZEALAND	M du Plessis	Won	16	7
144		14/08/1976	Bloemfontein	NEW ZEALAND	M du Plessis	Lost	9	15
145		04/09/1976	Cape Town	NEW ZEALAND	M du Plessis	Won	15	10
146		18/09/1976	Johannesburg	NEW ZEALAND	M du Plessis	Won	15	14

SPRINGBOK RECORDS

SOUTH AFRICA'S INTERNATIONAL TESTS AND TOUR MATCHES

TEST NO.	TOUR MATCH No.	Date	Venue	Opponent	Captain	Results	Points For	Points against
147		27/08/1977	Pretoria	WORLD TEAM	M du Plessis	Won	45	24
148		26/04/1980	Johannesburg	SOUTH AMERICA	M du Plessis	Won	24	9
149		03/05/1980	Durban	SOUTH AMERICA	M du Plessis	Won	18	9
150		31/05/1980	Cape Town	BRITISH ISLES	M du Plessis	Won	26	22
151		14/06/1980	Bloemfontein	BRITISH ISLES	M du Plessis	Won	26	19
152		28/06/1980	Port Elizabeth	BRITISH ISLES	M du Plessis	Won	12	10
153		12/07/1980	Pretoria	BRITISH ISLES	M du Plessis	Lost	13	17
	256	09/10/1980	Asunción	Paraguay Invitation XV	RB Prentiss	Won	84	6
	257	11/10/1980	Asunción	South America Invitation XV	MTS Stofberg	Won	79	18
	258	14/10/1980	Montevideo	British Schools Old Boys	MTS Stofberg	Won	83	13
154		18/10/1980	Montevideo	SOUTH AMERICA	MTS Stofberg	Won	22	13
	259	21/10/1980	Santiago	Chile Invitation XV	M du Plessis	Won	78	12
155		25/10/1980	Santiago	SOUTH AMERICA	M du Plessis	Won	30	16
156		08/11/1980	Pretoria	FRANCE	M du Plessis	Won	37	15
157		30/05/1981	Cape Town	IRELAND	W Claasen	Won	23	15
158		06/06/1981	Durban	IRELAND	W Claasen	Won	12	10
	260	22/07/1981	Gisborne	Poverty Bay	E Jansen	Won	24	6
	261	29/07/1981	New Plymouth	Taranaki	W Claasen	Won	34	9
	262	01/08/1981	Palmerston N.	Manawatu	MTS Stofberg	Won	31	19
	263	05/08/1981	Wanganui	Wanganui	W Claasen	Won	45	9
	264	08/08/1981	Invercargill	Southland	MTS Stofberg	Won	22	6
	265	11/08/1981	Dunedin	Otago	W Claasen	Won	17	13
159		15/08/1981	Christchurch	NEW ZEALAND	MTS Stofberg	Lost	9	14
	266	22/08/1981	Nelson	Nelson Bays	W Claasen	Won	83	0
	267	25/08/1981	Napier	New Zealand Maoris	DJ Serfontein	Drew	12	12
160		29/08/1981	Wellington	NEW ZEALAND	W Claasen	Won	24	12
	268	02/09/1981	Rotorua	Bay of Plenty	MTS Stofberg	Won	29	24
	269	05/09/1981	Auckland	Auckland	W Claasen	Won	39	12
	270	08/09/1981	Whangarei	North Auckland	E Jansen	Won	19	10
161		12/09/1981	Auckland	NEW ZEALAND	W Claasen	Lost	22	25
	271	19/09/1981	Wisconsin	Midwest	MTS Stofberg	Won	46	12
	272	22/09/1981	New York	Eastern	W Claasen	Won	41	0
162		25/09/1981	New York	USA	W Claasen	Won	38	7
163		27/03/1982	Pretoria	SOUTH AMERICA	W Claasen	Won	50	18
164		03/04/1982	Bloemfontein	SOUTH AMERICA	W Claasen	Lost	12	21
165		02/06/1984	Port Elizabeth	ENGLAND	MTS Stofberg	Won	33	15
166		09/06/1984	Johannesburg	ENGLAND	MTS Stofberg	Won	35	9
167		20/10/1984	Pretoria	S AMERICA & SPAIN	DJ Serfontein	Won	32	15
168		27/10/1984	Cape Town	S AMERICA & SPAIN	DJ Serfontein	Won	22	13
169		10/05/1986	Cape Town	NZ CAVALIERS	HE Botha	Won	21	15
170		17/05/1986	Durban	NZ CAVALIERS	HE Botha	Lost	18	19
171		24/05/1986	Pretoria	NZ CAVALIERS	HE Botha	Won	33	18
172		31/05/1986	Johannesburg	NZ CAVALIERS	HE Botha	Won	24	10
173		26/08/1989	Cape Town	WORLD TEAM	JC Breedt	Won	20	19
174		02/09/1989	Johannesburg	WORLD TEAM	JC Breedt	Won	22	16
175		15/08/1992	Johannesburg	NEW ZEALAND	HE Botha	Lost	24	27
176		22/08/1992	Cape Town	AUSTRALIA	HE Botha	Lost	3	26
	273	03/10/1992	Bordeaux	French Selection	HE Botha	Lost	17	24
	274	07/10/1992	Pau	Aquitaine XV	WJ Bartmann	Won	29	22
	275	10/10/1992	Toulouse	Midi-Pyrenées XV	HE Botha	Won	18	15
	276	13/10/1992	Marseilles	Provence-Côte D'Azur XV	RJ du Preez	Won	41	12
177		17/10/1992	Lyon	FRANCE	HE Botha	Won	20	15
	277	20/10/1992	Béziers	Languedoc XV	RJ du Preez	Won	36	15
178		24/10/1992	Paris	FRANCE	HE Botha	Lost	16	29
	278	28/10/1992	Tours	French Universities	RJ du Preez	Lost	13	18
	279	31/10/1992	Lille	French Barbarians	HE Botha	Lost	20	25

SOUTH AFRICA'S INTERNATIONAL TESTS AND TOUR MATCHES

TEST NO.	TOUR MATCH No.	Date	Venue	Opponent	Captain	Results	Points For	Points against
	280	04/11/1992	Leicester	Midland Division	HE Botha	Won	32	9
	281	07/11/1992	Bristol	England 'B'	HE Botha	Won	20	16
	282	10/11/1992	Leeds	Northern Division	RJ du Preez	Won	19	3
179		14/11/1992	Twickenham	ENGLAND	HE Botha	Lost	16	33
180		26/06/1993	Durban	FRANCE	JF Pienaar	Drew	20	20
181		03/07/1993	Johannesburg	FRANCE	JF Pienaar	Lost	17	18
	283	14/07/1993	Perth	Western Australia	JF Pienaar	Won	71	8
	284	17/07/1993	Adelaide	South Australian Invitation XV	CP Strauss	Won	90	3
	285	21/07/1993	Melbourne	Victoria	AH Richter	Won	78	3
	286	24/07/1993	Sydney	New South Wales	JF Pienaar	Lost	28	29
	287	27/07/1993	Orange	New South Wales Country	AH Richter	Won	41	7
182		31/07/1993	Sydney	AUSTRALIA	JF Pienaar	Won	19	12
	288	04/08/1993	Canberra	Australian Capital Territories	AH Richter	Won	57	10
	289	08/08/1993	Brisbane	Queensland	JF Pienaar	Won	17	3
	290	11/08/1993	Mackay	Queensland Country	AH Richter	Won	63	5
183		14/08/1993	Brisbane	AUSTRALIA	JF Pienaar	Lost	20	28
	291	18/08/1993	Sydney	Sydney	AH Richter	Won	31	20
184		21/08/1993	Sydney	AUSTRALIA	JF Pienaar	Lost	12	19
	292	27/10/1993	Cordoba	Provincial XV	CP Strauss	Won	55	37
	293	30/10/1993	Buenos Aires	Buenos Aires XV	WJ Bartmann	Lost	27	28
	294	03/11/1993	Tucumán	Tucumán	CP Strauss	Won	40	12
185		06/11/1993	Buenos Aires	ARGENTINA	JF Pienaar	Won	29	26
	295	09/11/1993	Rosario	Provincial XV	WJ Bartmann	Won	40	26
186		13/11/1993	Buenos Aires	ARGENTINA	JF Pienaar	Won	52	23
187		04/06/1994	Pretoria	ENGLAND	JF Pienaar	Lost	15	32
188		11/06/1994	Cape Town	ENGLAND	JF Pienaar	Won	27	9
	296	23/06/1994	Taupo	King Country	JF Pienaar	Won	46	10
	297	25/06/1994	Pukekohe	Counties	WJ Bartmann	Won	37	26
	298	28/06/1994	Wellington	Wellington	JF Pienaar	Won	36	26
	299	02/07/1994	Invercargill	Southland	AH Richter	Won	51	15
	300	05/07/1994	Timaru	Hanan Shield Districts	CP Strauss	Won	67	19
189		09/07/1994	Dunedin	NEW ZEALAND	CP Strauss	Lost	14	22
	301	13/07/1994	New Plymouth	Taranaki	RAW Straeuli	Won	16	12
	302	16/07/1994	Hamilton	Waikato	CP Strauss	Won	38	17
	303	19/07/1994	Palmerston N.	Manawatu	JF Pienaar	Won	47	21
190		23/07/1994	Wellington	NEW ZEALAND	JF Pienaar	Lost	9	13
	304	27/07/1994	Dunedin	Otago	CP Strauss	Lost	12	19
	305	30/07/1994	Christchurch	Canterbury	JF Pienaar	Won	21	11
	306	02/08/1994	Rotorua	Bay of Plenty	CP Strauss	Won	33	12
191		06/08/1994	Auckland	NEW ZEALAND	JF Pienaar	Drew	18	18
192		08/10/1994	Port Elizabeth	ARGENTINA	JF Pienaar	Won	42	22
193		15/10/1994	Johannesburg	ARGENTINA	JF Pienaar	Won	46	26
	307	22/10/1994	Cardiff	Cardiff	RAW Straeuli	Won	11	6
	308	26/10/1994	Newport	Wales 'A'	RAW Straeuli	Won	25	13
	309	29/10/1994	Llanelli	Llanelli	JF Pienaar	Won	30	12
	310	02/11/1994	Neath	Neath	CP Strauss	Won	16	13
	311	05/11/1994	Swansea	Swansea	JF Pienaar	Won	78	7
	312	09/11/1994	Melrose	Scotland 'A'	CP Strauss	Lost	15	17
	313	12/11/1994	Glasgow	Scottish Combined Districts	JF Pienaar	Won	33	6
	314	15/11/1994	Aberdeen	Scottish Select	CP Strauss	Won	35	10
194		19/11/1994	Edinburgh	SCOTLAND	JF Pienaar	Won	34	10
	315	22/11/1994	Pontypridd	Pontypridd	CP Strauss	Won	9	3
195		26/11/1994	Cardiff	WALES	JF Pienaar	Won	20	12
	316	29/11/1994	Belfast	Combined Provinces	RAW Straeuli	Won	54	19
	317	03/12/1994	Dublin	Barbarians	JF Pienaar	Lost	15	23
196		13/04/1995	Johannesburg	WESTERN SAMOA	JF Pienaar	Won	60	8

SOUTH AFRICA'S INTERNATIONAL TESTS AND TOUR MATCHES

TEST NO.	TOUR MATCH No.	Date	Venue	Opponent	Captain	Results	Points For	Points against
197		25/05/1995	Cape Town	AUSTRALIA	JF Pienaar	Won	27	18
198		30/05/1995	Cape Town	ROMANIA	AJ Richter	Won	21	8
199		03/06/1995	Port Elizabeth	CANADA	JF Pienaar	Won	20	0
200		10/06/1995	Johannesburg	WESTERN SAMOA	JF Pienaar	Won	42	14
201		17/06/1995	Durban	FRANCE	JF Pienaar	Won	19	15
202		24/06/1995	Johannesburg	NEW ZEALAND	JF Pienaar	Won	15	12
203		02/09/1995	Johannesburg	WALES	JF Pienaar	Won	40	11
204		12/11/1995	Rome	ITALY	JF Pienaar	Won	40	21
205		18/11/1995	Twickenham	ENGLAND	JF Pienaar	Won	24	14
206		02/07/1996	Pretoria	FIJI	JF Pienaar	Won	43	18
207		13/07/1996	Sydney	AUSTRALIA	JF Pienaar	Lost	16	21
208		20/07/1996	Christchurch	NEW ZEALAND	JF Pienaar	Lost	11	15
209		03/08/1996	Bloemfontein	AUSTRALIA	JF Pienaar	Won	25	19
210		10/08/1996	Cape Town	NEW ZEALAND	JF Pienaar	Lost	18	29
211		17/08/1996	Durban	NEW ZEALAND	GH Teichmann	Lost	19	23
212		24/08/1996	Pretoria	NEW ZEALAND	GH Teichmann	Lost	26	33
213		31/08/1996	Johannesburg	NEW ZEALAND	GH Teichmann	Won	32	22
	318	05/11/1996	Rosario	Rosario	WS Fyvie	Won	45	36
214		09/11/1996	Buenos Aires	ARGENTINA	GH Teichmann	Won	46	15
	319	12/11/1996	Mendoza	Mendoza	WS Fyvie	Won	89	19
215		16/11/1996	Buenos Aires	ARGENTINA	GH Teichmann	Won	44	21
	320	23/11/1996	Brive	French Barbarians	WS Fyvie	Lost	22	30
	321	26/11/1996	Lyon	South East Selection	WS Fyvie	Won	36	20
216		30/11/1996	Bordeaux	FRANCE	GH Teichmann	Won	22	12
	322	03/12/1996	Lille	French Universities	WS Fyvie	Lost	13	20
217		07/12/1996	Paris	FRANCE	GH Teichmann	Won	13	12
218		15/12/1996	Cardiff	WALES	GH Teichmann	Won	37	20
219		10/06/1997	Cape Town	TONGA	GH Teichmann	Won	74	10
220		21/06/1997	Cape Town	BRITISH ISLES	GH Teichmann	Lost	16	25
221		28/06/1997	Durban	BRITISH ISLES	GH Teichmann	Lost	15	18
222		05/07/1997	Johannesburg	BRITISH ISLES	GH Teichmann	Won	35	16
223		19/07/1997	Johannesburg	NEW ZEALAND	GH Teichmann	Lost	32	35
224		02/08/1997	Brisbane	AUSTRALIA	GH Teichmann	Lost	20	32
225		09/08/1997	Auckland	NEW ZEALAND	GH Teichmann	Lost	35	55
226		23/08/1997	Pretoria	AUSTRALIA	GH Teichmann	Won	61	22
227		08/11/1997	Bologna	ITALY	GH Teichmann	Won	62	31
	323	11/11/1997	Biarritz	French Barbarians	AD Aitken	Lost	22	40
228		15/11/1997	Lyon	FRANCE	GH Teichmann	Won	36	32
	324	18/11/1997	Toulon	France 'A'	AD Aitken	Lost	7	21
229		22/11/1997	Paris	FRANCE	GH Teichmann	Won	52	10
230		29/11/1997	Twickenham	ENGLAND	GH Teichmann	Won	29	11
231		06/12/1997	Edinburgh	SCOTLAND	GH Teichmann	Won	68	10
232		13/06/1998	Bloemfontein	IRELAND	GH Teichmann	Won	37	13
233		20/06/1998	Pretoria	IRELAND	GH Teichmann	Won	33	0
234		27/06/1998	Pretoria	WALES	GH Teichmann	Won	96	13
235		04/07/1998	Cape Town	ENGLAND	GH Teichmann	Won	18	0
236		18/07/1998	Perth	AUSTRALIA	GH Teichmann	Won	14	13
237		25/07/1998	Wellington	NEW ZEALAND	GH Teichmann	Won	13	3
238		15/08/1998	Durban	NEW ZEALAND	GH Teichmann	Won	24	23
239		22/08/1998	Johannesburg	AUSTRALIA	GH Teichmann	Won	29	15
	325	10/11/1998	Firhill	Glasgow Caledonians	RB Skinstad	Won	62	9
240		14/11/1998	London	WALES	GH Teichmann	Won	28	20
	326	17/11/1998	Edinburgh	Edinburgh Reivers	RB Skinstad	Won	49	3
241		21/11/1998	Edinburgh	SCOTLAND	GH Teichmann	Won	35	10
	327	24/11/1998	Cork	Combined Provinces	AN Vos	Won	32	5
242		28/11/1998	Dublin	IRELAND	GH Teichmann	Won	27	13

SOUTH AFRICA'S INTERNATIONAL TESTS AND TOUR MATCHES

TEST NO.	TOUR MATCH No.	Date	Venue	Opponent	Captain	Results	Points For	Points against
	328	01/12/1998	Belfast	Ireland 'A'	AN Vos	Won	50	19
243		05/12/1998	Twickenham	ENGLAND	GH Teichmann	Lost	7	13
244		12/06/1999	Port Elizabeth	ITALY	GH Teichmann	Won	74	3
245		19/06/1999	Durban	ITALY	CPJ Krige	Won	101	0
246		26/06/1999	Cardiff	WALES	GH Teichmann	Lost	19	29
247		10/07/1999	Dunedin	NEW ZEALAND	GH Teichmann	Lost	0	28
248		17/07/1999	Brisbane	AUSTRALIA	J Erasmus	Lost	6	32
249		07/08/1999	Pretoria	NEW ZEALAND	JH van der Westhuizen	Lost	18	34
250		14/08/1999	Cape Town	AUSTRALIA	JH van der Westhuizen	Won	10	9
251		03/10/1999	Edinburgh	SCOTLAND	JH van der Westhuizen	Won	46	29
252		10/10/1999	Edinburgh	SPAIN	AN Vos	Won	47	3
253		15/10/1999	Glasgow	URUGUAY	JH van der Westhuizen	Won	39	3
254		24/10/1999	Paris	ENGLAND	JH van der Westhuizen	Won	44	21
255		30/10/1999	London	AUSTRALIA	JH van der Westhuizen	Lost	21	27
256		04/11/1999	Cardiff	NEW ZEALAND	JH van der Westhuizen	Won	22	18
257		10/06/2000	East London	CANADA	AN Vos	Won	51	18
258		17/06/2000	Pretoria	ENGLAND	AN Vos	Won	18	13
259		24/06/2000	Bloemfontein	ENGLAND	AN Vos	Lost	22	27
260		08/07/2000	Melbourne	AUSTRALIA	AN Vos	Lost	23	44
261		22/07/2000	Christchurch	NEW ZEALAND	AN Vos	Lost	12	25
262		29/07/2000	Sydney	AUSTRALIA	AN Vos	Lost	6	26
263		19/08/2000	Johannesburg	NEW ZEALAND	AN Vos	Won	46	40
264		26/08/2000	Durban	AUSTRALIA	AN Vos	Lost	18	19
	329	08/11/2000	Tucuman	Argentina 'A'	DJ van Zyl	Won	32	21
265		12/11/2000	Buenos Aires	ARGENTINA	AN Vos	Won	37	33
	330	15/11/2000	Limerick	Ireland 'A'	A-H le Roux	Lost	11	28
266		19/11/2000	Dublin	IRELAND	AN Vos	Won	28	18
	331	22/11/2000	Cardiff	Wales 'A'	DJ van Zyl	Won	34	15
267		26/11/2000	Cardiff	WALES	AN Vos	Won	23	13
	332	28/11/2000	Worcester	England National Divisions XV	V Matfield	Lost	30	35
268		02/12/2000	Twickenham	ENGLAND	AN Vos	Lost	17	25
	333	09/12/2000	Cardiff	Barbarians	AN Vos	Won	41	31
269		16/06/2001	Johannesburg	FRANCE	AN Vos	Lost	23	32
270		23/06/2001	Durban	FRANCE	AN Vos	Won	20	15
271		30/06/2001	Port Elizabeth	ITALY	RB Skinstad	Won	60	14
272		21/07/2001	Cape Town	NEW ZEALAND	RB Skinstad	Lost	3	12
273		28/07/2001	Pretoria	AUSTRALIA	RB Skinstad	Won	20	15
274		18/08/2001	Perth	AUSTRALIA	RB Skinstad	Drew	14	14
275		25/08/2001	Auckland	NEW ZEALAND	RB Skinstad	Lost	15	26
276		10/11/2001	Paris	FRANCE	RB Skinstad	Lost	10	20
277		17/11/2001	Genoa	ITALY	RB Skinstad	Won	54	26
278		24/11/2001	London	ENGLAND	RB Skinstad	Lost	9	29
279		01/12/2001	Houston	USA	AN Vos	Won	43	20
280		08/06/2002	Bloemfontein	WALES	RB Skinstad	Won	34	19
281		15/06/2002	Cape Town	WALES	RB Skinstad	Won	19	8
282		29/06/2002	Springs	ARGENTINA	CPJ Krige	Won	49	29
283		06/07/2002	Pretoria	SAMOA	CPJ Krige	Won	60	18
284		20/07/2002	Wellington	NEW ZEALAND	CPJ Krige	Lost	20	41
285		27/07/2002	Brisbane	AUSTRALIA	CPJ Krige	Lost	27	38
286		10/08/2002	Durban	NEW ZEALAND	CPJ Krige	Lost	23	30
287		17/08/2002	Johannesburg	AUSTRALIA	CPJ Krige	Won	33	31
288		09/11/2002	Marseilles	FRANCE	CPJ Krige	Lost	10	30
289		16/11/2002	Edinburgh	SCOTLAND	CPJ Krige	Lost	6	21
290		23/11/2002	London	ENGLAND	CPJ Krige	Lost	3	53
291		07/06/2003	Durban	SCOTLAND	JH van der Westhuizen	Won	29	25
292		14/06/2003	Johannesburg	SCOTLAND	JH van der Westhuizen	Won	28	19

SOUTH AFRICA'S INTERNATIONAL TESTS AND TOUR MATCHES

TEST NO.	TOUR MATCH No.	Date	Venue	Opponent	Captain	Results	Points For	Points against
293		28/06/2003	Port Elizabeth	ARGENTINA	CPJ Krige	Won	26	25
294		12/07/2003	Cape Town	AUSTRALIA	CPJ Krige	Won	26	22
295		19/07/2003	Pretoria	NEW ZEALAND	CPJ Krige	Lost	16	52
296		02/08/2003	Brisbane	AUSTRALIA	CPJ Krige	Lost	9	29
297		09/08/2003	Dunedin	NEW ZEALAND	CPJ Krige	Lost	11	19
298		11/10/2003	Perth	URUGUAY	JH van der Westhuizen	Won	72	6
299		18/10/2003	Perth	ENGLAND	CPJ Krige	Lost	6	25
300		24/10/2003	Sydney	GEORGIA	JW Smit	Won	46	19
301		01/11/2003	Brisbane	SAMOA	CPJ Krige	Won	60	10
302		08/11/2003	Melbourne	NEW ZEALAND	CPJ Krige	Lost	9	29
303		12/06/2004	Bloemfontein	IRELAND	JW Smit	Won	31	17
304		19/06/2004	Cape Town	IRELAND	JW Smit	Won	26	17
305		26/06/2004	Pretoria	WALES	JW Smit	Won	53	18
306		17/07/2004	Gosford	PACIFIC ISLANDS	JW Smit	Won	38	24
307		24/07/2004	Christchurch	NEW ZEALAND	JW Smit	Lost	21	23
308		31/07/2004	Perth	AUSTRALIA	JW Smit	Lost	26	30
309		14/08/2004	Johannesburg	NEW ZEALAND	JW Smit	Won	40	26
310		21/08/2004	Durban	AUSTRALIA	JW Smit	Won	23	19
311		06/11/2004	Cardiff	WALES	JW Smit	Won	38	36
312		13/11/2004	Dublin	IRELAND	JW Smit	Lost	12	17
313		20/11/2004	London	ENGLAND	JW Smit	Lost	16	32
314		27/11/2004	Edinburgh	SCOTLAND	JW Smit	Won	45	10
315		04/12/2004	Buenos Aires	ARGENTINA	JW Smit	Won	39	7
316		11/06/2005	East London	URUGUAY	JW Smit	Won	134	3
317		18/06/2005	Durban	FRANCE	JW Smit	Drew	30	30
318		25/06/2005	Port Elizabeth	FRANCE	JW Smit	Won	27	13
319		09/07/2005	Sydney	AUSTRALIA	JW Smit	Lost	12	30
320		23/07/2005	Johannesburg	AUSTRALIA	JW Smit	Won	33	20
321		30/07/2005	Pretoria	AUSTRALIA	JW Smit	Won	22	16
322		06/08/2005	Cape Town	NEW ZEALAND	JW Smit	Won	22	16
323		20/08/2005	Perth	AUSTRALIA	JW Smit	Won	22	19
324		27/08/2005	Dunedin	NEW ZEALAND	JW Smit	Lost	27	31
325		05/11/2005	Buenos Aires	ARGENTINA	JW Smit	Won	34	23
326		19/11/2005	Cardiff	WALES	JW Smit	Won	33	16
327		26/11/2005	Paris	FRANCE	JW Smit	Lost	20	26
328		10/06/2006	Durban	SCOTLAND	JW Smit	Won	36	16
329		17/06/2006	Port Elizabeth	SCOTLAND	JW Smit	Won	29	15
330		24/06/2006	Cape Town	FRANCE	JW Smit	Lost	26	36
331		15/07/2006	Brisbane	AUSTRALIA	JW Smit	Lost	0	49
332		22/07/2006	Wellington	NEW ZEALAND	JW Smit	Lost	17	35
333		05/08/2006	Sydney	AUSTRALIA	JW Smit	Lost	18	20
334		26/08/2006	Pretoria	NEW ZEALAND	JW Smit	Lost	26	45
335		02/09/2006	Rustenburg	NEW ZEALAND	JW Smit	Won	21	20
336		09/09/2006	Johannesburg	AUSTRALIA	JW Smit	Won	24	16
337		11/11/2006	Dublin	IRELAND	JW Smit	Lost	15	32
338		18/11/2006	London	ENGLAND	JW Smit	Lost	21	23
339		25/11/2006	London	ENGLAND	JW Smit	Won	25	14
	334	03/12/2006	Leicester	World XV	GvG Botha	Won	32	7
340		26/05/2007	Bloemfontein	ENGLAND	JW Smit	Won	58	10
341		02/06/2007	Pretoria	ENGLAND	JW Smit	Won	55	22
342		09/06/2007	Johannesburg	SAMOA	JW Smit	Won	35	8
343		16/06/2007	Cape Town	AUSTRALIA	JW Smit	Won	22	19
344		23/06/2007	Durban	NEW ZEALAND	V Matfield	Lost	21	26
345		07/07/2007	Sydney	AUSTRALIA	RB Skinstad	Lost	17	25
346		14/07/2007	Christchurch	NEW ZEALAND	GJ Muller	Lost	6	33
347		15/08/2007	Cape Town	NAMIBIA	V Matfield	Won	105	13

SOUTH AFRICA'S INTERNATIONAL TESTS AND TOUR MATCHES

TEST NO.	TOUR MATCH No.	Date	Venue	Opponent	Captain	Results	Points For	Points against
	335	21/08/2007	Galway	Connacht	RB Skinstad	Won	18	3
348		25/08/2007	Edinburgh	SCOTLAND	V Matfield	Won	27	3
349		09/09/2007	Paris	SAMOA	JW Smit	Won	59	7
350		14/09/2007	St Denis	ENGLAND	JW Smit	Won	36	0
351		22/09/2007	Lens	TONGA	RB Skinstad	Won	30	25
352		30/09/2007	Montpellier	USA	JW Smit	Won	64	15
353		07/10/2007	Marseilles	FIJI	JW Smit	Won	37	20
354		14/10/2007	St Denis	ARGENTINA	JW Smit	Won	37	13
355		20/10/2007	St Denis	ENGLAND	JW Smit	Won	15	6
356		24/11/2007	Cardiff	WALES	JW Smit	Won	34	12
	336	01/12/2007	London	Barbarians	GJ Muller	Lost	5	22
357		07/06/2008	Bloemfontein	WALES	JW Smit	Won	43	17
358		14/06/2008	Pretoria	WALES	JW Smit	Won	37	21
359		21/06/2008	Cape Town	ITALY	V Matfield	Won	26	0
360		05/07/2008	Wellington	NEW ZEALAND	JW Smit	Lost	8	19
361		12/07/2008	Dunedin	NEW ZEALAND	V Matfield	Won	30	28
362		19/07/2008	Perth	AUSTRALIA	V Matfield	Lost	9	16
363		09/08/2008	Johannesburg	ARGENTINA	V Matfield	Won	63	9
364		16/08/2008	Cape Town	NEW ZEALAND	V Matfield	Lost	0	19
365		23/08/2008	Durban	AUSTRALIA	V Matfield	Lost	15	27
366		30/08/2008	Johannesburg	AUSTRALIA	V Matfield	Won	53	8
367		08/11/2008	Cardiff	WALES	JW Smit	Won	20	15
368		15/11/2008	Edinburgh	SCOTLAND	JW Smit	Won	14	10
369		22/11/2008	London	ENGLAND	JW Smit	Won	42	6
370		20/06/2009	Durban	BRITISH ISLES	JW Smit	Won	26	21
371		27/06/2009	Pretoria	BRITISH ISLES	JW Smit	Won	28	25
372		04/07/2009	Johannesburg	BRITISH ISLES	JW Smit	Lost	9	28
373		25/07/2009	Bloemfontein	NEW ZEALAND	JW Smit	Won	28	19
374		01/08/2009	Durban	NEW ZEALAND	JW Smit	Won	31	19
375		08/08/2009	Cape Town	AUSTRALIA	JW Smit	Won	29	17
376		29/08/2009	Perth	AUSTRALIA	JW Smit	Won	32	25
377		05/09/2009	Brisbane	AUSTRALIA	JW Smit	Lost	6	21
378		12/09/2009	Hamilton	NEW ZEALAND	JW Smit	Won	32	29
	337	06/11/2009	Leicester	Leicester Tigers	MC Ralepelle	Lost	17	22
379		13/11/2009	Toulouse	FRANCE	JW Smit	Lost	13	20
	338	17/11/2009	London	Saracens	DJ Potgieter	Lost	23	24
380		21/11/2009	Florence	ITALY	JW Smit	Won	32	10
381		28/11/2009	Dublin	IRELAND	JW Smit	Lost	10	15
382		05/06/2010	Cardiff	WALES	JW Smit	Won	34	31
383		12/06/2010	Cape Town	FRANCE	JW Smit	Won	42	17
384		19/06/2010	Witbank	ITALY	V Matfield	Won	29	13
385		26/06/2010	East London	ITALY	JW Smit	Won	55	11
386		10/07/2010	Auckland	NEW ZEALAND	JW Smit	Lost	12	32
387		17/07/2010	Wellington	NEW ZEALAND	JW Smit	Lost	17	31
388		24/07/2010	Brisbane	AUSTRALIA	JW Smit	Lost	13	30
389		21/08/2010	Soweto	NEW ZEALAND	JW Smit	Lost	22	29
390		28/08/2010	Pretoria	AUSTRALIA	JW Smit	Won	44	31
391		04/09/2010	Bloemfontein	AUSTRALIA	JW Smit	Lost	39	41
392		06/11/2010	Dublin	IRELAND	V Matfield	Won	23	21
393		13/11/2010	Cardiff	WALES	V Matfield	Won	29	25
394		20/11/2010	Edinburgh	SCOTLAND	V Matfield	Lost	17	21
395		27/11/2010	London	ENGLAND	V Matfield	Won	21	11
	339	04/12/2010	London	Barbarians	JH Smith	Lost	20	26

TEST	**8938**	**6065**
TOUR	8268	2758

SPRINGBOK RECORDS

SOUTH AFRICA'S TEST RESULTS BY OPPONENT

ARGENTINA
Played 13 - Won 13 - Lost 0 - Drawn 0 - PF 544 - PA 272

Year	Winner	Score	Venue
1993	South Africa	29-26	Buenos Aires
1993	South Africa	52-23	Buenos Aires
1994	South Africa	42-22	Port Elizabeth
1994	South Africa	46-26	Johannesburg
1996	South Africa	46-15	Buenos Aires
1996	South Africa	44-21	Buenos Aires
2000	South Africa	37-33	Buenos Aires
2002	South Africa	49-29	Springs
2003	South Africa	26-25	Port Elizabeth
2004	South Africa	39-7	Buenos Aires
2005	South Africa	34-23	Buenos Aires
2007	South Africa	37-13	Paris
2008	South Africa	63-9	Johannesburg

AUSTRALIA
Played 71 - Won 41 - Lost 29 - Draw 1 - PF 1347 - PA 1239

Year	Winner	Score	Venue
1933	South Africa	17-3	Cape Town
1933	Australia	6-21	Durban
1933	South Africa	12-3	Johannesburg
1933	South Africa	11-0	Port Elizabeth
1933	Australia	4-15	Bloemfontein
1937	South Africa	9-5	Sydney
1937	South Africa	26-17	Sydney
1953	South Africa	25-3	Johannesburg
1953	Australia	14-18	Cape Town
1953	South Africa	18-8	Durban
1953	South Africa	22-9	Port Elizabeth
1956	South Africa	9-0	Sydney
1956	South Africa	9-0	Brisbane
1961	South Africa	28-3	Johannesburg
1961	South Africa	23-11	Port Elizabeth
1963	South Africa	14-3	Pretoria
1963	Australia	5-9	Cape Town
1963	Australia	9-11	Johannesburg
1963	South Africa	22-6	Port Elizabeth
1965	Australia	11-18	Sydney
1965	Australia	8-12	Brisbane
1969	South Africa	30-11	Johannesburg
1969	South Africa	16-9	Durban
1969	South Africa	11-3	Cape Town
1969	South Africa	19-8	Bloemfontein
1971	South Africa	19-11	Sydney
1971	South Africa	14-6	Brisbane
1971	South Africa	18-6	Sydney
1992	Australia	3-26	Cape Town
1993	South Africa	19-12	Sydney
1993	Australia	20-28	Brisbane
1993	Australia	12-19	Sydney
1995	South Africa	27-18	Cape Town
1996	Australia	16-21	Sydney
1996	South Africa	25-19	Bloemfontein
1997	Australia	20-32	Brisbane
1997	South Africa	61-22	Pretoria
1998	South Africa	14-13	Perth
1998	South Africa	29-15	Johannesburg
1999	Australia	6-32	Brisbane
1999	South Africa	10-9	Cape Town
1999	Australia	21-27	London
2000	Australia	23-44	Melbourne
2000	Australia	6-26	Sydney
2000	Australia	18-19	Durban
2001	South Africa	20-15	Pretoria
2001	Drawn	14-14	Perth
2002	Australia	27-38	Brisbane
2002	South Africa	33-31	Johannesburg
2003	South Africa	26-22	Cape Town
2003	Australia	9-29	Brisbane
2004	Australia	26-30	Perth
2004	South Africa	23-19	Durban
2005	Australia	12-30	Sydney
2005	South Africa	33-20	Johannesburg
2005	South Africa	22-16	Pretoria
2005	South Africa	22-19	Perth
2006	Australia	0-49	Brisbane
2006	Australia	18-20	Sydney
2006	South Africa	24-16	Johannesburg
2007	South Africa	22-19	Cape Town
2007	Australia	17-25	Sydney
2008	Australia	9-16	Perth
2008	Australia	15-27	Durban
2008	South Africa	53-8	Johannesburg
2009	South Africa	29-17	Cape Town
2009	South Africa	32-25	Perth
2009	Australia	6-21	Brisbane
2010	Australia	13-30	Brisbane
2010	Australia	44-31	Pretoria
2010	Australia	39-41	Bloemfontein

BRITISH ISLES
Played 46 - Won 23 - Lost 17 - Drawn 6 - PF 600 - PA 516

Year	Winner	Score	Venue
1891	British Isles	0-4	Port Elizabeth
1891	British Isles	0-3	Kimberley
1891	British Isles	0-4	Cape Town
1896	British Isles	0-8	Port Elizabeth
1896	British Isles	8-17	Johannesburg
1896	British Isles	3-9	Kimberley
1896	South Africa	5-0	Cape Town
1903	Drawn	10-10	Johannesburg
1903	Drawn	0-0	Kimberley
1903	South Africa	8-0	Cape Town
1910	South Africa	14-10	Johannesburg
1910	British Isles	3-8	Port Elizabeth
1910	South Africa	21-5	Cape Town

1924	South Africa	7-3	Durban
1924	South Africa	17-0	Johannesburg
1924	Drawn	3-3	Port Elizabeth
1924	South Africa	16-9	Cape Town
1938	South Africa	26-12	Johannesburg
1938	South Africa	19-3	Port Elizabeth
1938	British Isles	16-21	Cape Town
1955	British Isles	22-23	Johannesburg
1955	South Africa	25-9	Cape Town
1955	British Isles	6-9	Pretoria
1955	South Africa	22-8	Port Elizabeth
1962	Drawn	3-3	Johannesburg
1962	South Africa	3-0	Durban
1962	South Africa	8-3	Cape Town
1962	South Africa	34-14	Bloemfontein
1968	South Africa	25-20	Pretoria
1968	Drawn	6-6	Port Elizabeth
1968	South Africa	11-6	Cape Town
1968	South Africa	19-6	Johannesburg
1974	British Isles	3-12	Cape Town
1974	British Isles	9-28	Pretoria
1974	British Isles	9-26	Port Elizabeth
1974	Drawn	13-13	Johannesburg
1980	South Africa	26-22	Cape Town
1980	South Africa	26-19	Bloemfontein
1980	South Africa	12-10	Port Elizabeth
1980	British Isles	13-17	Pretoria
1997	British Isles	16-25	Cape Town
1997	British Isles	15-18	Durban
1997	South Africa	35-16	Johannesburg
2009	South Africa	26-21	Durban
2009	South Africa	28-25	Pretoria
2009	British Isles	9-28	Johannesburg

CANADA
Played 2 - Won 2 - Lost 0 - Drawn 0 - PF 71 - PA 18

Year	Winner	Score	Venue
1995	South Africa	20-0	Port Elizabeth
2000	South Africa	51-18	East London

ENGLAND
Played 32 - Won 19 - Lost 12 - Drawn 1 - PF 661 - PA 491

Year	Winner	Score	Venue
1906	Drawn	3-3	Crystal Palace
1913	South Africa	9-3	Twickenham
1932	South Africa	7-0	Twickenham
1952	South Africa	8-3	Twickenham
1961	South Africa	5-0	Twickenham
1969	England	8-11	Twickenham
1972	England	9-18	Johannesburg
1984	South Africa	33-15	Port Elizabeth
1984	South Africa	35-9	Johannesburg
1992	England	16-33	Twickenham
1994	England	15-32	Pretoria
1994	South Africa	27-9	Cape Town
1995	South Africa	24-14	Twickenham
1997	South Africa	29-11	Twickenham
1998	South Africa	18-0	Cape Town
1998	England	7-13	Twickenham
1999	South Africa	44-21	Paris
2000	South Africa	18-13	Pretoria
2000	England	22-27	Bloemfontein
2000	England	17-25	Twickenham
2001	England	9-29	Twickenham
2002	England	3-53	Twickenham
2003	England	6-25	Perth
2004	England	16-32	Twickenham
2006	England	21-23	Twickenham
2006	South Africa	25-14	Twickenham
2007	South Africa	58-10	Bloemfontein
2007	South Africa	55-22	Pretoria
2007	South Africa	36-0	Paris
2007	South Africa	15-6	Paris
2008	South Africa	42-6	Twickenham
2010	South Africa	21-11	Twickenham

FIJI
Played 2 - Won 2 - Lost 0 - Drawn 0 - PF 80 - PA 38

Year	Winner	Score	Venue
1996	South Africa	43-18	Pretoria
2007	South Africa	37-20	Marseille

FRANCE
Played 38 - Won 21 - Lost 11 - Drawn 6 - PF 764 - PA 568

Year	Winner	Score	Venue
1913	South Africa	38-5	Bordeaux
1952	South Africa	25-3	Paris
1958	Drawn	3-3	Cape Town
1958	France	5-9	Johannesburg
1961	Drawn	0-0	Paris
1964	France	6-8	Springs
1967	South Africa	26-3	Durban
1967	South Africa	16-3	Bloemfontein
1967	France	14-19	Johannesburg
1967	Drawn	6-6	Cape Town
1968	South Africa	12-9	Bordeaux
1968	South Africa	16-11	Paris
1971	South Africa	22-9	Bloemfontein
1971	Drawn	8-8	Durban
1974	South Africa	13-4	Toulouse
1974	South Africa	10-8	Paris
1975	South Africa	38-25	Bloemfontein
1975	South Africa	33-18	Pretoria
1980	South Africa	37-15	Pretoria
1992	South Africa	20-15	Lyon
1992	France	16-29	Paris
1993	Drawn	20-20	Durban
1993	France	17-18	Johannesburg
1995	South Africa	19-15	Durban
1996	South Africa	22-12	Bordeaux
1996	South Africa	13-12	Paris
1997	South Africa	36-32	Lyon

SPRINGBOK RECORDS

1997	South Africa	52-10	Paris
2001	France	23-32	Johannesburg
2001	South Africa	20-15	Durban
2001	France	10-20	Paris
2002	France	10-30	Marseilles
2005	Drawn	30-30	Durban
2005	South Africa	27-13	Port Elizabeth
2005	France	20-26	Paris
2006	France	26-36	Cape Town
2009	France	13-20	Toulouse
2010	South Africa	42-17	Cape Town

GEORGIA
Played 1 - Won 1 - Lost 0 - Drawn 0 - PF 46 - PA 19

Year	Winner	Score	Venue
2003	South Africa	46-19	Sydney

IRELAND
Played 20 - Won 15 - Lost 4 - Drawn 1 - PF 401 - PA 236

Year	Winner	Score	Venue
1906	South Africa	15-12	Belfast
1912	South Africa	38-0	Dublin
1931	South Africa	8-3	Dublin
1951	South Africa	17-5	Dublin
1960	South Africa	8-3	Dublin
1961	South Africa	24-8	Cape Town
1965	Ireland	6-9	Dublin
1970	Drawn	8-8	Dublin
1981	South Africa	23-15	Cape Town
1981	South Africa	12-10	Durban
1998	South Africa	37-13	Bloemfontein
1998	South Africa	33-0	Pretoria
1998	South Africa	27-13	Dublin
2000	South Africa	28-18	Dublin
2004	South Africa	31-17	Bloemfontein
2004	South Africa	26-17	Cape Town
2004	Ireland	12-17	Dublin
2006	Ireland	15-32	Dublin
2009	Ireland	10-15	Dublin
2010	South Africa	23-21	Dublin

ITALY
Played 10 - Won 10 - Lost 0 - Drawn 0 - PF 533 - PA 129

Year	Winner	Score	Venue
1995	South Africa	40-21	Rome
1997	South Africa	62-31	Bologna
1999	South Africa	74-3	Port Elizabeth
1999	South Africa	101-0	Durban
2001	South Africa	60-14	Port Elizabeth
2001	South Africa	54-26	Genoa
2008	South Africa	26-0	Cape Town
2009	South Africa	32-10	Udine
2010	South Africa	29-13	Witbank
2010	South Africa	55-11	East London

NAMIBIA
Played 1 - Won 1 - Lost 0 - Drawn 0 - PF 105 - PA 13

Year	Winner	Score	Venue
2007	South Africa	105-13	Cape Town

NEW ZEALAND
Played 81 - Won 33 - Lost 45 - Draw 3 - PF 1261 - PA 1514

Year	Winner	Score	Venue
1921	New Zealand	5-13	Dunedin
1921	South Africa	9-5	Auckland
1921	Drawn	0-0	Wellington
1928	South Africa	17-0	Durban
1928	New Zealand	6-7	Johannesburg
1928	South Africa	11-6	Port Elizabeth
1928	New Zealand	5-13	Cape Town
1937	New Zealand	7-13	Wellington
1937	South Africa	13-6	Christchurch
1937	South Africa	17-6	Auckland
1949	South Africa	15-11	Cape Town
1949	South Africa	12-6	Johannesburg
1949	South Africa	9-3	Durban
1949	South Africa	11-8	Port Elizabeth
1956	New Zealand	6-10	Dunedin
1956	New Zealand	8-3	Wellington
1956	New Zealand	10-17	Christchurch
1956	New Zealand	5-11	Auckland
1960	South Africa	13-0	Johannesburg
1960	New Zealand	3-11	Cape Town
1960	Drawn	11-11	Bloemfontein
1960	South Africa	8-3	Port Elizabeth
1965	New Zealand	3-6	Wellington
1965	New Zealand	0-13	Dunedin
1965	South Africa	19-16	Christchurch
1965	New Zealand	3-20	Auckland
1970	South Africa	17-6	Pretoria
1970	New Zealand	8-9	Cape Town
1970	South Africa	14-3	Port Elizabeth
1970	South Africa	20-17	Johannesburg
1976	South Africa	16-7	Durban
1976	New Zealand	9-15	Bloemfontein
1976	South Africa	15-10	Cape Town
1976	South Africa	15-14	Johannesburg
1981	New Zealand	9-14	Christchurch
1981	South Africa	24-12	Wellington
1981	New Zealand	22-25	Auckland
1992	New Zealand	24-27	Johannesburg
1994	New Zealand	14-22	Dunedin
1994	New Zealand	9-13	Wellington
1994	Drawn	18-18	Auckland
1995	South Africa	15-12	Johannesburg
1996	New Zealand	11-15	Christchurch
1996	New Zealand	18-29	Cape Town
1996	New Zealand	19-23	Durban
1996	New Zealand	26-33	Pretoria
1996	South Africa	32-22	Johannesburg
1997	New Zealand	32-35	Johannesburg

1997	New Zealand	35-55	Auckland
1998	South Africa	13-3	Wellington
1998	South Africa	24-23	Durban
1999	New Zealand	0-28	Dunedin
1999	New Zealand	18-34	Pretoria
1999	South Africa	22-18	Cardiff
2000	New Zealand	12-25	Christchurch
2000	South Africa	46-40	Johannesburg
2001	New Zealand	3-12	Cape Town
2001	New Zealand	15-26	Auckland
2002	New Zealand	20-41	Wellington
2002	New Zealand	23-30	Durban
2003	New Zealand	16-52	Pretoria
2003	New Zealand	11-19	Dunedin
2003	New Zealand	9-29	Melbourne
2004	New Zealand	21-23	Christchurch
2004	South Africa	40-26	Johannesburg
2005	South Africa	22-16	Cape Town
2005	New Zealand	27-31	Dunedin
2006	New Zealand	17-35	Wellington
2006	New Zealand	26-45	Pretoria
2006	South Africa	21-20	Rustenburg
2007	New Zealand	21-26	Durban
2007	New Zealand	6-33	Christchurch
2008	New Zealand	8-19	Wellington
2008	South Africa	30-28	Dunedin
2008	New Zealand	0-19	Cape Town
2009	South Africa	28-19	Bloemfontein
2009	South Africa	31-19	Durban
2009	South Africa	32-29	Hamilton
2010	New Zealand	12-32	Auckland
2010	New Zealand	17-31	Wellington
2010	New Zealand	22-29	Soweto

NEW ZEALAND CAVALIERS

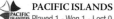

Played 4 - Won 3 - Lost 1 - Drawn 0 - PF 96 - PA 62

Year	Winner	Score	Venue
1986	South Africa	21-15	Cape Town
1986	NZ Cavaliers	18-19	Durban
1986	South Africa	33-18	Pretoria
1986	South Africa	24-10	Johannesburg

PACIFIC ISLANDS

Played 1 - Won 1 - Lost 0 - Drawn 0 - PF 38 - PA 24

Year	Winner	Score	Venue
2004	South Africa	38-24	Gosford

ROMANIA

Played 1 - Won 1 - Lost 0 - Drawn 0 - PF 21 - PA 8

Year	Winner	Score	Venue
1995	South Africa	21-8	Cape Town

SAMOA

Played 6 - Won 6 - Lost 0 - Drawn 0 - PF 316 - PA 65

Year	Winner	Score	Venue
1995	South Africa	60-8	Johannesburg
1995	South Africa	42-14	Johannesburg
2002	South Africa	60-18	Pretoria
2003	South Africa	60-10	Brisbane
2007	South Africa	35-8	Johannesburg
2007	South Africa	59-7	Paris

SCOTLAND

Played 21 - Won 16 - Lost 5 - Drawn 0 - PF 518 - PA 237

Year	Winner	Score	Venue
1906	Scotland	0-6	Glasgow
1912	South Africa	16-0	Edinburgh
1932	South Africa	6-3	Edinburgh
1951	South Africa	44-0	Edinburgh
1960	South Africa	18-10	Port Elizabeth
1961	South Africa	12-5	Edinburgh
1965	Scotland	5-8	Edinburgh
1969	Scotland	3-6	Edinburgh
1994	South Africa	34-10	Edinburgh
1997	South Africa	68-10	Edinburgh
1998	South Africa	35-10	Edinburgh
1999	South Africa	46-29	Edinburgh
2002	Scotland	6-21	Edinburgh
2003	South Africa	29-25	Durban
2003	South Africa	28-19	Johannesburg
2004	South Africa	45-10	Edinburgh
2006	South Africa	36-16	Durban
2006	South Africa	29-15	Port Elizabeth
2007	South Africa	27-3	Edinburgh
2008	South Africa	14-10	Edinburgh
2010	Scotland	17-21	Edinburgh

SOUTH AMERICA (*indicates includes Spain)

Played 8 - Won 7 - Lost 1 - Drawn 0 - PF 210 - PA 114

Year	Winner	Score	Venue
1980	South Africa	24-9	Johannesburg
1980	South Africa	18-9	Durban
1980	South Africa	22-13	Montevideo
1980	South Africa	30-16	Santiago
1982	South Africa	50-18	Pretoria
1982	South America	12-21	Bloemfontein
1984*	South Africa	32-15	Pretoria
1984*	South Africa	22-13	Cape Town

SPAIN

Played 1 - Won 1 - Lost 0 - Drawn 0 - PF 47 - PA 3

Year	Winner	Score	Venue
1999	South Africa	47-3	Edinburgh

SPRINGBOK RECORDS

TONGA
Played 2 - Won 2 - Lost 0 - Drawn 0 - PF 104 - PA 35

Year	Winner	Score	Venue
1997	South Africa	74-10	Cape Town
2007	South Africa	30-25	Lens

UNITED STATES OF AMERICA
Played 3 - Won 3 - Lost 0 - Drawn 0 - PF 145 - PA 42

Year	Winner	Score	Venue
1981	South Africa	38-7	Glenville
2001	South Africa	43-20	Houston
2007	South Africa	64-15	Montpellier

URUGUAY
Played 3 - Won 3 - Lost 0 - Drawn 0 - PF 245 - PA 12

Year	Winner	Score	Venue
1999	South Africa	39-3	Glasgow
2003	South Africa	72-6	Perth
2005	South Africa	134-3	East London

WALES
Played 25 - Won 23 - Lost 1 - Drawn 1 - PF 698 - PA 351

Year	Winner	Score	Venue
1906	South Africa	11-0	Swansea
1912	South Africa	3-0	Cardiff
1931	South Africa	8-3	Swansea
1951	South Africa	6-3	Cardiff
1960	South Africa	3-0	Cardiff
1964	South Africa	24-3	Durban
1970	Drawn	6-6	Cardiff
1994	South Africa	20-12	Cardiff
1995	South Africa	40-11	Johannesburg
1996	South Africa	37-20	Cardiff
1998	South Africa	96-13	Pretoria
1998	South Africa	28-20	Wembley
1999	Wales	19-29	Cardiff
2000	South Africa	23-13	Cardiff
2002	South Africa	34-19	Bloemfontein
2002	South Africa	19-8	Cape Town
2004	South Africa	53-18	Pretoria
2004	South Africa	38-36	Cardiff
2005	South Africa	33-16	Cardiff
2007	South Africa	34-12	Cardiff
2008	South Africa	43-17	Bloemfontein
2008	South Africa	37-21	Pretoria
2008	South Africa	20-15	Cardiff
2010	South Africa	34-31	Cardiff
2010	South Africa	29-25	Cardiff

WORLD TEAMS
Played 3 - Won 3 - Lost 0 - Drawn 0 - PF 87 - PA 59

Year	Winner	Score	Venue
1977	South Africa	45-24	Pretoria
1989	South Africa	20-19	Cape Town
1989	South Africa	22-16	Johannesburg

SPRINGBOK TOURS 1906-2010 *(Excludes tours where only Test matches were played)*

Year	Tour	Captain	Tour Matches	Tests	Tot Matches	Won	Lost	Drawn	Points for	Pts against	Tries for	Tries against
1906/07	British Isles, Ireland & France	PJ Roos	24	4	28	25	2	1	553	79	130	19
1912/13	British Isles, Ireland & France	WA Millar	22	5	27	24	3	0	441	101	103	22
1921	Australia & New Zealand	TB Pienaar	20	3	23	19	2	2	327	119	74	21
1931/32	British Isles & Ireland	BL Osler	22	4	26	23	1	2	407	124	86	23
1937	Australia & New Zealand	PJ Nel	21	5	26	24	2	0	753	169	161	29
1951/52	British Isles, Ireland & France	BJ Kenyon	26	5	31	30	1	0	562	167	120	26
1956	Australia & New Zealand	SS Vivier	23	6	29	22	6	1	520	203	108	31
1960/61	British Isles, Ireland & France	AS Malan	29	5	34	31	1	2	567	132	132	25
1965	Ireland & Scotland	AS Malan	3	2	5	0	4	1	37	53	7	8
1965	Australia & New Zealand	DJ de Villiers	24	6	30	22	8	0	669	285	144	42
1968	France	DJ de Villiers	4	2	6	5	1	0	84	43	12	5
1969/70	British Isles & Ireland	DJ de Villiers	20	4	24	15	5	4	323	157	59	23
1971	Australia	JFK Marais	10	3	13	13	0	0	396	102	76	11
1974	France	JFK Marais	7	2	9	8	1	0	170	74	23	10
1980	South America	M du Plessis	4	2	6	6	0	0	376	78	66	8
1981	New Zealand & USA	W Claassen	13	4	17	14	2	1	535	190	81	16
1992	France & England	HE Botha	10	3	13	8	5	0	297	236	30	16
1993	Australia	JF Pienaar	9	3	12	9	3	0	527	147	75	15
1993	Argentina	JF Pienaar	4	2	6	5	1	0	243	152	32	11
1994	New Zealand	JF Pienaar	11	3	14	10	3	1	445	241	58	22
1994	Wales, Scotland & Ireland	JF Pienaar	11	2	13	11	2	0	375	151	50	12
1996	Argentina, France & Wales	GH Teichmann	5	5	10	8	2	0	367	205	53	19
1997	Italy, France, England & Scotland	GH Teichmann	2	5	7	5	2	0	276	155	40	16
1998	British Isles & Ireland	GH Teichmann	4	4	8	7	1	0	290	92	42	6

SPRINGBOK TOURS 1906-2010 *(Excludes tours where only Test matches were played)*

Year	Tour	Captain	Tour Matches	Tests	Tot Matches	Won	Lost	Drawn	Points for	Pts against	Tries for	Tries against
2000	Argentina, Ireland, Wales & England	AN Vos	5	4	9	6	3	0	253	219	30	20
2006	Ireland & England	JW Smit	1	3	4	2	2	0	93	76	9	8
2007	Ireland & Scotland	JW Smit	1	1	2	2	0	0	18	3	2	0
2007	Wales & England	JW Smit	1	1	2	1	1	0	39	34	6	5
2009	France, Italy, Ireland & England	JW Smit	2	3	5	1	4	0	95	91	10	5
2010	British Isles & Ireland	V Matfield	1	4	5	3	2	0	110	104	10	10
			339	105	444	359	70	15	10148	3982	1829	484

INTERNATIONAL TOURS TO SOUTH AFRICA 1891-2010
(Exclude tours where only test matches were played)

Year	Tour	Captain	Tour Matches	Tests	Total Matches	Won	Lost	Drawn	Points for	Points against	Tries for	Tries against
1891	British Isles	WE Maclagan (Scotland)	16	3	19	19	0	0	224	1	89	1
1896	British Isles	JF Hammond (Cambridge University)	17	4	21	19	1	1	310	45	64	10
1903	British Isles	MC Morrison (Scotland)	19	3	22	11	8	3	231	138	49	29
1910	British Isles	T Smyth (Ireland)	21	3	24	13	8	3	290	236	68	54
1924	British Isles	R Cove-Smith (England)	17	4	21	9	9	3	175	155	45	26
1928	New Zealand	MJ Brownlie (Hawke's Bay)	18	4	22	16	5	1	339	144	70	23
1933	Australia	AW Ross (New South Wales)	18	5	23	12	10	1	299	195	67	29
1938	British Isles	S Walker (Ireland)	20	3	23	17	6	0	407	272	79	43
1949	New Zealand	FR Allen (Auckland)	20	4	24	14	7	3	230	146	43	8
1953	Australia	HJ Solomon (New South Wales)	23	4	27	16	10	1	450	413	92	68
1955	British Isles	RH Thompson (Ireland)	20	4	24	18	5	1	418	271	94	39
1958	France	M Celaya (Biarritz)	8	2	10	5	3	2	137	124	26	17
1960	Scotland	GH Waddell (Cambridge University)	2	1	3	2	1	0	61	45	13	9
1960	New Zealand	WJ Whineray (Auckland)	22	4	26	20	4	2	441	164	75	23
1961	Ireland	AR Dawson (Wanderers)	3	1	4	3	1	0	59	36	8	6
1961	Australia	KW Catchpole (New South Wales)	4	2	6	3	2	1	90	80	15	16
1962	British Isles	AR Smith (Scotland)	20	4	24	15	5	4	351	208	62	37
1963	Australia	JE Thornett (New South Wales)	20	4	24	15	8	1	303	233	46	28
1964	Wales	DCT Rowlands (Pontypool)	3	1	4	2	2	0	43	58	5	6
1964	France	M Crauste (Lourdes)	5	1	6	5	1	0	117	55	18	4
1967	France	C Darrouy (Mont-de-Marsan)	9	4	13	8	4	1	209	161	30	23
1968	British Isles	TJ Kiernan (Ireland)	16	4	20	15	4	1	377	181	55	21
1969	Australia	GV Davis (New South Wales)	22	4	26	15	11	0	465	353	78	54
1970	New Zealand	BJ Lochore (Wairarapa)	20	4	24	21	3	0	687	228	135	23
1971	France	C Carrère (Toulon)	7	2	9	7	1	1	228	92	42	9
1972	England	JV Pullin (Bristol)	6	1	7	6	0	1	166	58	23	4
1974	British Isles	WJ McBride (Ireland)	18	4	22	21	0	1	729	207	107	16
1975	France	J Fouroux (La Voulte) & R Astre (Béziers)	9	2	11	6	4	1	282	190	41	20
1976	New Zealand	AR Leslie (Wellington)	20	4	24	18	6	0	610	291	89	27
1977	World Team	WJ McBride (Ireland)	2	1	3	0	3	0	76	142	13	23
1980	South America	H Porta (Argentina)	5	2	7	4	3	0	174	134	23	16
1980	British Isles	WB Beaumont (England)	14	4	18	15	3	0	401	244	47	27
1980	France	J-P Rives (Toulouse)	3	1	4	3	1	0	90	95	13	12
1981	Ireland	JF Slattery (Blackrock College)	5	2	7	3	4	0	207	90	30	10
1982	South America	H Porta (Argentina)	12	2	14	12	1	1	448	179	62	25
1984	England	JP Scott (Cardiff)	5	2	7	4	2	1	156	145	19	18
1984	South America & Spain	H Porta (Argentina)	5	2	7	4	3	0	146	140	17	20
1986	New Zealand Cavaliers	AG Dalton (Counties)	8	4	12	8	4	0	275	229	33	16
1989	World Team	P Berbizier (France)	3	2	5	1	4	0	100	130	14	20
1992	New Zealand	SBT Fitzpatrick (Auckland)	4	1	5	5	0	0	167	79	20	6

SPRINGBOK RECORDS

INTERNATIONAL TOURS TO SOUTH AFRICA 1891-2010 *(Continued)*

Year	Tour	Captain	Tour Matches	Tests	Tot Matches	Won	Lost	Drawn	Points for	Pts against	Tries for	Tries against
1992	Australia	NC Farr-Jones (New South Wales)	3	1	4	4	0	0	130	41	15	4
1993	France	J-F Tordo (Nice)	6	2	8	4	2	2	169	159	14	12
1994	England	WDC Carling (Harlequins)	6	2	8	3	5	0	152	165	11	13
1994	Argentina	MH Lofreda (Buenos Aires)	4	2	6	3	3	0	216	216	27	28
1995	Western Samoa	P Fatialofa (Auckland, New Zealand)	2	1	3	0	3	0	38	104	4	12
1995	Wales	JM Humphreys (Cardiff)	1	1	2	0	2	0	17	87	1	10
1996	Fiji	J Veitayaki (King Country, New Zealand)	1	1	2	1	1	0	62	80	7	9
1996	New Zealand	SBT Fitzpatrick (Auckland)	4	3	7	5	1	1	190	139	24	14
1997	British Isles	MO Johnson (England)	10	3	13	11	2	0	480	278	56	32
1997	Tonga	L Katoa (Siutaka)	3	1	4	2	2	0	77	149	9	23
1998	Ireland	PS Johns (Saracens, England)	5	2	7	2	5	0	126	214	11	26
1998	Wales	R Howley (Cardiff)	4	1	5	0	5	0	94	224	9	32
1999	Italy	M Giovanelli (Narbonne, France)	2	2	4	0	4	0	30	267	3	40
2000	England	MO Johnson (Leicester)	3	2	5	4	1	0	183	105	20	6
2001	Italy	A Moscardi (Benetton Treviso)	1	1	2	0	2	0	25	102	2	14
2002	Argentina	A Pichot (Bristol, England)	1	1	2	0	2	0	65	91	7	11
2002	Samoa	S Sititi (Borders, Scotland)	2	1	3	1	2	0	75	117	9	15
2003	Argentina	G Longo (Narbonne, France)	1	1	2	0	1	1	55	56	6	5
2009	British Isles	PJ O'Connell (Ireland)	7	3	10	7	2	1	309	169	34	15
			555	144	699	457	202	40	13461	9150	2188	1187

MATCH RECORDS

Highest scores

134-3	vs. Uruguay	East London	2005
105-13	vs. Namibia	Cape Town	2007
101-0	vs. Italy	Durban	1999
96-13	vs. Wales	Pretoria	1998
74-10	vs. Tonga	Cape Town	1997
74-3	vs. Italy	Port Elizabeth	1999
72-6	vs. Uruguay	Perth	2003
68-10	vs. Scotland	Edinburgh	1997
64-15	vs. USA	Montpellier	2007
63-9	vs. Argentina	Johannesburg	2008
62-31	vs. Italy	Bologna	1997
61-22	vs. Australia	Pretoria	1997
60-8	vs. Western Samoa	Johannesburg	1995
60-14	vs. Italy	Port Elizabeth	2001
60-18	vs. Samoa	Pretoria	2002
60-10	vs. Samoa	Brisbane	2003
52	vs. Western Samoa (60-8)	Johannesburg	1995
52	vs. Samoa (59-7)	Paris	2007
50	vs. Samoa (60-10)	Brisbane	2003

Biggest wins

131	vs. Uruguay (134-3)	East London	2005
101	vs. Italy (101-0)	Durban	1999
92	vs. Namibia (105-13)	Cape Town	2007
83	vs. Wales (96-13)	Pretoria	1998
71	vs. Italy (74-3)	Port Elizabeth	1999
66	vs. Uruguay (72-6)	Perth	2003
64	vs. Tonga (74-10)	Cape Town	1997
58	vs. Scotland (68-10)	Edinburgh	1997
54	vs. Argentina (63-9)	Johannesburg	2008

Most tries scored

21	vs. Uruguay	East London	2005
15	vs. Italy	Durban	1999
15	vs. Wales	Pretoria	1998
15	vs. Namibia	Cape Town	2007
12	vs. Uruguay	Perth	2003
12	vs. Tonga	Cape Town	1997
11	vs. Italy	Port Elizabeth	1999
10	vs. Scotland	Edinburgh	1997
10	vs. Ireland	Dublin	1912

Most points conceded

55-35	vs. New Zealand	Auckland	1997
53-3	vs. England	Twickenham	2002
52-16	vs. New Zealand	Pretoria	2003
49-0	vs. Australia	Brisbane	2006
45-26	vs. New Zealand	Pretoria	2006
44-23	vs. Australia	Melbourne	2000
41-20	vs. New Zealand	Wellington	2002
41-39	vs. Australia	Bloemfontein	2010
40-46	vs. New Zealand	Johannesburg	2000
38-27	vs. Australia	Brisbane	2002
36-38	vs. Wales	Cardiff	2004
36-26	vs. France	Cape Town	2006

SPRINGBOK.

| 35-32 | vs. New Zealand | Johannesburg | 1997 |
| 35-17 | vs. New Zealand | Wellington | 2006 |

Biggest defeats

50	England (3-53)	Twickenham	2002
49	Australia (0-49)	Brisbane	2006
36	New Zealand (16-52)	Pretoria	2003
28	New Zealand (0-28)	Dunedin	1999
27	New Zealand (6-33)	Christchurch	2007
26	Australia (6-32)	Brisbane	1999
23	Australia (3-26)	Cape Town	1992
21	Australia (23-44)	Melbourne	2000
21	New Zealand (20-41)	Wellington	2002
20	New Zealand (35-55)	Auckland	1997
20	Australia (6-26)	Sydney	2000
20	England (9-29)	Twickenham	2001
20	France (10-30)	Marseilles	2002
20	Australia (9-29)	Brisbane	2003
20	New Zealand (9-29)	Melbourne	2003
20	New Zealand (12-32)	Auckland	2010

Most points by a player

35	PC Montgomery vs. Namibia (1t, 12c, 2p)	Cape Town	2007
34	JH de Beer vs. England (2c, 5p, 5dg)	Paris	1999
31	PC Montgomery vs. Wales (2t, 9c, 1p)	Pretoria	1998
31	M Steyn vs. New Zealand (1t, 1c, 8p)	Durban	2009
30	T Chavhanga vs. Uruguay (6t)	East London	2005
29	GS du Toit vs. Italy (2t, 8c, 1p)	Port Elizabeth	1999
29	PC Montgomery vs. Samoa (2t, 5c, 3p)	Paris	2007
28	GK Johnson vs. W Samoa (3t, 5c, 1p)	Johannesburg	1995
26	JH de Beer vs. Australia (1t, 6c, 3p)	Pretoria	1997
26	PC Montgomery vs. Scotland (2t, 8c)	Edinburgh	1997
26	M Steyn vs. Italy (2t, 5c, 2p)	East London	2010
25	JT Stransky vs. Australia (1t, 1c, 6p)	Bloemfontein	1996
25	CS Terblanche vs. Italy (5t)	Durban	1999

Most tries by a player

6	T Chavhanga vs. Uruguay	East London	2005
5	CS Terblanche vs. Italy	Durban	1999
4	CM Williams vs. W Samoa	Johannesburg	1995
4	PWG Rossouw vs. France	Paris	1997
4	CS Terblanche vs. Ireland	Bloemfontein	1998
4	BG Habana vs. Samoa	Paris	2007
4	JL Nokwe vs. Australia	Johannesburg	2008
3	EE McHardy vs. Ireland	Dublin	1912
3	JA Stegmann vs. Ireland	Dublin	1912
3	KT van Vollenhoven vs. B. Isles	Cape Town	1955
3	HJ van Zyl vs. Australia	Johannesburg	1961
3	RH Mordt vs. New Zealand	Auckland	1981
3	RH Mordt vs. USA	New York	1981
3	DM Gerber vs. South America	Pretoria	1982
3	DM Gerber vs. England	Johannesburg	1984
3	GK Johnson vs. W Samoa	Johannesburg	1995
3	JH van der Westhuizen vs. Wales	Cardiff	1996
3	AH Snyman vs. Tonga	Cape Town	1997
3	PWG Rossouw vs. Wales	Pretoria	1998

3	BJ Paulse vs. Italy	Port Elizabeth	1999
3	DJ Kayser vs. Italy	Durban	1999
3	JH van der Westhuizen vs. Uruguay	Perth	2003
3	MC Joubert vs. New Zealand	Johannesburg	2004
3	JH Smith vs. Namibia	Cape Town	2007
3	SWP Burger vs. Namibia	Cape Town	2007

Most conversions by a player

12	PC Montgomery vs. Namibia	Cape Town	2007
9	PC Montgomery vs. Wales	Pretoria	1998
9	AD James vs. Argentina	Johannesburg	2008
8	PC Montgomery vs. Scotland	Edinburgh	1997
8	GS du Toit vs. Italy	Port Elizabeth	1999
8	GS du Toit vs. Italy	Durban	1999

Most penalty goals by a player

8	M Steyn vs. New Zealand	Durban	2009
7	PC Montgomery vs. Scotland	Port Elizabeth	2006
7	PC Montgomery vs. France	Cape Town	2006
7	M Steyn vs. Australia	Cape Town	2009
6	GR Bosch vs. France	Pretoria	1975
6	JT Stransky vs. Australia	Bloemfontein	1996
6	JH de Beer vs. Australia	Twickenham	1999
6	AJJ van Straaten vs. England	Pretoria	2000
6	AJJ van Straaten vs. Australia	Durban	2000
6	PC Montgomery vs. France	Johannesburg	2001
6	LJ Koen vs. Scotland	Johannesburg	2003
6	M Steyn vs. Australia	Bloemfontein	2010

Most drop goals by a player

5	JH de Beer vs. England	Paris	1999
4	AS Pretorius vs. England	Twickenham	2006
3	HE Botha vs. South America	Durban	1980
3	HE Botha vs. Ireland	Durban	1981
3	JNB van der Westhuyzen vs. Scotland	Edinburgh	2004

Scored all points in a test (>15)

31*	M Steyn vs. New Zealand	Durban	2009
25	JT Stransky vs. Australia	Bloemfontein	1996
21	JH de Beer vs. Australia	Twickenham	1999
18	AJJ van Straaten vs. England	Pretoria	2000
18	AJJ van Straaten vs. Australia	Durban	2000
17	AJJ van Straaten vs. England	Twickenham	2000

*World record

Scored in all four ways in a test

22	JT Stransky (22 pts - 1t, 1c, 4p, 1dg) vs. Australia	1995
18	AS Pretorius (18 pts - 1t, 2c, 2p, 1dg) vs. New Zealand	2002
21	DJ Hougaard (21 pts - 1t, 5c, 1p, 1dg) vs. Samoa	2003

Most points by a player against SA

29	SA Mortlock, Australia (2t, 2c, 5p)	Melbourne	2000
27	CR Andrew, England (1t, 2c, 5p, 1d)	Pretoria	1994
27	JP Wilkinson, England (8p, 1d)	Bloemfontein	2000
27	G Merceron, France (1t, 2c, 6p)	Johannesburg	2001
27	CC Hodgson, England (1t, 2c, 5p, 1d)	Twickenham	2004

SPRINGBOK RECORDS

25	CJ Spencer, New Zealand (1t, 4c, 4p)	Auckland	1997
25	DW Carter, New Zealand (2c, 7p)	Wellington	2006
24	MC Burke, Australia (8p)	Twickenham	1999
23	DW Carter, New Zealand (1t, 3c, 4p)	Christchurch	2007
23	DW Carter, New Zealand (1c, 6p, 1d)	Dunedin	2008
22	CJ Spencer, New Zealand (1t, 4c, 3p)	Pretoria	2003
21	H Porta, S America (1t, 1c, 4p, 1d)	Bloemfontein	1982
21	SE Meson, Argentina (1t, 2c, 4p)	Buenos Aires	1993
21	J-L Cilley, Argentina (1t, 2c, 4p)	Johannesburg	1994
21	D Dominguez, Italy (1t, 2c, 4p)	Bologna	1997
21	AP Mehrtens, New Zealand (7p)	Pretoria	1999
21	SA Mortlock, Australia (1t, 2c, 4p)	Sydney	2000
21	JP Wilkinson, England (7p)	Twickenham	2001
21	SM Jones, Wales (3c, 5p)	Cardiff	2004
21	DA Parks, Scotland (6p, 1d)	Edinburgh	2010
20	CJ Spencer, New Zealand (1t, 3c, 3p)	Johannesburg	1997
20	AP Mehrtens, New Zealand (4c, 3p, 1d)	Johannesburg	2000
20	JP Wilkinson, England (1c, 6p)	Twickenham	2000
20	JP Wilkinson, England (1c, 4p, 2d)	Perth	2003
20	DW Carter, New Zealand (4c, 4p)	Pretoria	2006
20	SM Jones, British Isles (1c, 5p, 1d)	Pretoria	2009
20	MJ Giteau, Australia (2t, 2c, 2p)	Perth	2009

Most tries by a player against SA

2	HS Sugars (Ireland)	Belfast	1906
2	JL Sullivan (New Zealand)	Christchurch	1937
2	IST Smith (New Zealand)	Auckland	1965
2	B Dauga (France)	Bordeaux	1968
2	JJ Williams (British Isles)	Pretoria	1974
2	JJ Williams (British Isles)	Port Elizabeth	1974
2	J-L Averous (France)	Pretoria	1977
2	PV Carozza (Australia)	Cape Town	1992
2	A Penaud (France)	Lyon	1992
2	JS Little (Australia)	Brisbane	1993
2	JW Wilson (New Zealand)	Pretoria	1996
2	FE Bunce (New Zealand)	Johannesburg	1997
2	BN Tune (Australia)	Brisbane	1997
2	CM Cullen (New Zealand)	Auckland	1997
2	JW Roff (Australia)	Brisbane	1999
2	CM Cullen (New Zealand)	Pretoria	1999
2	SA Mortlock (Australia)	Melbourne	2000
2	CM Cullen (New Zealand)	Christchurch	2000

2	CM Cullen (New Zealand)	Johannesburg	2000
2	JF Umaga (New Zealand)	Johannesburg	2000
2	CE Latham (Australia)	Brisbane	2000
2	WJH Greenwood (England)	Twickenham	2000
2	JT Rokocoko (New Zealand)	Pretoria	2003
2	DC Howlett (New Zealand)	Pretoria	2003
2	S Sivivatu (Pacific Islands)	Gosford	2004
2	GL Henson (Wales)	Cardiff	2004
2	MJ Giteau (Australia)	Sydney	2005
2	JT Rokocoko (New Zealand)	Dunedin	2005
2	V Clerc (France)	Cape Town	2006
2	MJ Giteau (Australia)	Brisbane	2006
2	T Croft (British Isles)	Durban	2009
2	SM Williams (British Isles)	Johannesburg	2009
2	MJ Giteau (Australia)	Perth	2009
2	JD O'Connor (Australia)	Pretoria	2010
2	G North (Wales)	Cardiff	2010

Most conversions by a player against SA

5	SA Mortlock (Australia)	Brisbane	2006
4	A Cameron (British Isles)	Johannesburg	1955
4	PE McLean (World Team)	Pretoria	1977
4	CJ Spencer (New Zealand)	Auckland	1997
4	AP Mehrtens (New Zealand)	Johannesburg	2000
4	CJ Spencer (New Zealand)	Pretoria	2003
4	DW Carter (New Zealand)	Pretoria	2006
4	MJ Giteau (Australia)	Pretoria	2010
4	MJ Giteau (Australia)	Bloemfontein	2010

Most penalty goals by a player against SA

8	MC Burke (Australia)	Twickenham	1999
8	JP Wilkinson (England)	Bloemfontein	2000
7	AP Mehrtens (New Zealand)	Pretoria	1999
6	JP Wilkinson (England)	Twickenham	2000
6	G Merceron (France)	Johannesburg	2001
6	DW Carter (New Zealand)	Dunedin	2008
6	DA Parks (Scotland)	Edinburgh	2010

Most drop goals by a player against SA

2	G Camberabero (France)	Johannesburg	1967
2	P Bennett (British Isles)	Port Elizabeth	1974
2	JP Wilkinson (England)	Perth	2003

SEASON RECORDS

BY THE TEAM

Most points

658	17 tests	38.7 per game	2007
535	13 tests	41.2 per game	1997
447	13 tests	34.4 per game	1999
416	12 tests	34.7 per game	2005
408	13 tests	31.4 per game	2004
397	14 tests	28.4 per game	2010
361	12 tests	30.1 per game	1998
360	13 tests	27.7 per game	2008
352	13 tests	27.1 per game	1996
338	12 tests	28.2 per game	2003
308	10 tests	30.8 per game	1995
301	12 tests	25.1 per game	2000

Most tries

81	17 tests	4.8 per game	2007
74	13 tests	5.7 per game	1997
52	13 tests	4.0 per game	1999

Most conversions

62	17 tests	3.7 per game	2007
54	13 tests	4.2 per game	1997

Most penalty goals

46	14 tests	3.3 per game	2010
42	12 tests	3.5 per game	2009
41	17 tests	2.4 per game	2007
40	13 tests	3.1 per game	1996

Most drop goals

8	13 tests		1999

Most consecutive wins

17	August 1997 to November 1998

Most consecutive defeats

7	July 1964 to August 1965

Most consecutive matches without conceding a try

5	1999

Most consecutive matches without scoring a try

4	1891 to 1896 & 1972 to 1974

BY A PLAYER
Most points

219	PC Montgomery in 14 tests (5t, 52c, 30p)	2007
185	M Steyn in 13 tests (3t, 25c, 40p)	2010
158	PC Montgomery in 12 tests (1t, 24c, 32p, 3d)	2005
154	PC Montgomery in 11 tests (1t, 28c, 31p)	2004
137	M Steyn in 12 tests (1t, 12c, 31p, 5d)	2009
136	AJJ van Straaten in 11 tests (2t, 12c, 34p)	2000
120	LJ Koen in 11 tests (15c, 28p, 2d)	2003
112	JT Stransky in 9 tests (2t, 12c, 23p, 3d)	1995
111	PC Montgomery in 12 tests (2t, 25c, 17p)	1998
102	JH de Beer in 6 tests (18c, 16p, 6d)	1999
102	AS Pretorius in 10 tests (2t, 22c, 15p, 1d)	2002

Most tries

13	BG Habana in 11 tests	2007
12	BG Habana in 12 tests	2005
10	PWG Rossouw in 11 tests	1997
9	CS Terblanche in 12 tests	1998
9	J Fourie in 12 tests	2007
8	JT Small in 7 tests	1993
8	CM Williams in 6 tests	1995
8	PC Montgomery in 10 tests	1997
8	JH van der Westhuizen in 12 tests	1998
8	JH Smith in 13 tests	2007

Most conversions

52	PC Montgomery in 14 tests	2007
28	PC Montgomery in 11 tests	2004
25	PC Montgomery in 12 tests	1998
25	M Steyn in 13 tests	2010
24	PC Montgomery in 12 tests	2005
23	HW Honiball in 12 tests	1997
22	AS Pretorius in 10 tests	2002

Most penalty goals

40	M Steyn in 13 tests	2010
34	AJJ van Straaten in 11 tests	2000
32	PC Montgomery in 12 tests	2005
31	PC Montgomery in 11 tests	2004
31	M Steyn in 12 tests	2009
30	PC Montgomery in 14 tests	2007

Most drop goals

6	HE Botha in 9 tests	1980
6	JH de Beer in 6 tests	1999
5	HE Botha in 6 tests	1981
5	AS Pretorius in 6 tests	2006
5	M Steyn in 12 tests	2009

CAREER RECORDS

Most test match appearances

105	V Matfield	2001-2010
102	PC Montgomery	1997-2008
102	JW Smit	2000-2010
89	JH van der Westhuizen	1993-2003
80	JP du Randt	1994-2007
77	MG Andrews	1994-2001
72	JP Botha	2002-2010
69	JH Smith	2003-2010
69	CJ van der Linde	2002-2010
68	BG Habana	2004-2010
67	J de Villiers	2002-2010
66	AG Venter	1996-2001
64	BJ Paulse	1999-2007
63	SWP Burger	2003-2010

62	J Fourie	2003-2010
55	PF du Preez	2004-2009
54	A-H le Roux	1994-2002
54	DJ Rossouw	2003-2010
52	JC van Niekerk	2001-2010
51	PA van den Berg	1999-2007

Most appearances in all Springbok matches

111	JH van der Westhuizen	1993-2003
109	V Matfield	2001-2010
104	PC Montgomery	1997-2008
103	JW Smit	2000-2010
90	MG Andrews	1994-2001
87	FCH du Preez	1961-1971
85	JP du Randt	1994-2007

75	JFK Marais	1963-1974
74	JH Ellis	1965-1976
74	BJ Paulse	1999-2007
74	CJ van der Linde	2002-2010
73	JP Botha	2002-2010
71	JL Gainsford	1960-1967
70	AG Venter	1996-2001
70	BG Habana	2004-2010

Most points in test matches

893	PC Montgomery (102 tests)	1997-2008
322	M Steyn (25 tests)	2009-2010
312	HE Botha (28 tests)	1980-1992
240	JT Stransky (22 tests)	1993-1996
221	AJJ van Straaten (21 tests)	1999-2001
190	JH van der Westhuizen (89 tests)	1993-2003
190	BG Habana (68 tests)	2004-2010
181	JH de Beer (13 tests)	1997-1999
171	AS Pretorius (31 tests)	2002-2007
156	HW Honiball (35 tests)	1993-1999
150	J Fourie (62 tests)	2003-2010

Most points in all Springbok matches

906	PC Montgomery (104 matches)	1997-2008
485	HE Botha (40 matches)	1980-1992
329	JT Stransky (36 matches)	1993-1996
322	M Steyn (25 matches)	2009-2010
294	AJJ van Straaten (27 matches)	1999-2001
293	GH Brand (46 matches)	1928-1938
280	JH van der Westhuizen (111 matches)	1993-2003
258	AJ Joubert (49 matches)	1989-1997
240	PJ Visagie (44 matches)	1967-1971
201	K Oxlee (48 matches)	1960-1965

Most tries in test matches

38	JH van der Westhuizen (89 tests)	1993-2003
38	BG Habana (68 tests)	2004-2010
30	J Fourie (62 tests)	2003-2010
26	BJ Paulse (64 tests)	1999-2007
25	PC Montgomery (102 tests)	1997-2008
21	PWG Rossouw (43 tests)	1997-2003
20	JT Small (47 tests)	1992-1997
19	DM Gerber (24 tests)	1980-1992
19	CS Terblanche (37 tests)	1998-2003
19	J de Villiers (67 tests)	2002-2010

Most tries in all Springbok matches

56	JH van der Westhuizen (111 matches)	1993-2003
44	JP Engelbrecht (67 matches)	1960-1969
39	BJ Paulse (74 matches)	1999-2007
38	BG Habana (70 matches)	2004-2010
32	JH Ellis (74 matches)	1965-1976
31	JL Gainsford (71 matches)	1960-1967
30	J Fourie (64 matches)	2003-2010

Most conversions in test matches

153	PC Montgomery (102 tests)	1997-2008
50	HE Botha (28 tests)	1980-1992
38	HW Honiball (35 tests)	1993-1999
37	M Steyn (25 tests)	2009-2010
33	JH de Beer (13 tests)	1997-1999
31	AS Pretorius (31 tests)	2002-2007
30	JT Stransky (22 tests)	1993-1996

Most conversions in all Springbok matches

157	PC Montgomery (104 matches)	1997-2008
100	GH Brand (46 matches)	1928-1938
91	HE Botha (40 matches)	1980-1992
55	JT Stransky (36 matches)	1993-1996

Most penalty goals in test matches

148	PC Montgomery (102 tests)	1997-2008
71	M Steyn (25 tests)	2009-2010
55	AJJ van Straaten (21 tests)	1999-2001
50	HE Botha (28 tests)	1980-1992
47	JT Stransky (22 tests)	1993-1996
31	LJ Koen (15 tests)	2000-2003
27	JH de Beer (13 tests)	1997-1999
26	AD James (39 tests)	2001-2010
25	HW Honiball (35 tests)	1993-1999
25	AS Pretorius (31 tests)	2002-2007

Most penalty goals in all Springbok matches

148	PC Montgomery (104 matches)	1997-2008
71	M Steyn (25 matches)	2009-2010
66	HE Botha (40 matches)	1980-1992
59	AJJ van Straaten (27 matches)	1999-2001
55	JT Stransky (36 matches)	1993-1996

Most drop goals in test matches

18	HE Botha (28 tests)	1980-1992
8	JH de Beer (13 tests)	1997-1999
8	AS Pretorius (31 tests)	2002-2007
6	PC Montgomery (102 tests)	1997-2008
5	JD Brewis (10 tests)	1949-1953
5	PJ Visagie (25 tests)	1967-1971
5	M Steyn (25 tests)	2009-2010

Most drop goals in all Springbok matches

27	HE Botha (40 matches)	1980-1992
8	BL Osler (30 matches)	1924-1933
8	PJ Visagie (44 matches)	1967-1971
8	JH de Beer (14 matches)	1997-1999
8	AS Pretorius (33 matches)	2002-2007

Most test match appearances against SA

30	GM Gregan (Australia)	1994-2007
23	SJ Larkham (Australia)	1996-2007
22	JW Marshall (New Zealand)	1995-2005
22	GB Smith (Australia)	2000-2009
21	JM Muliaina (New Zealand)	2003-2010

| 21 | MJ Giteau (Australia) | 2002-2010 |
| 20 | NC Sharpe (Australia) | 2002-2010 |

Most points in tests against SA

221	DW Carter (New Zealand) (15 tests)	2003-2010
209	AP Mehrtens (New Zealand) (16 tests)	1995-2004
150	SA Mortlock (Australia) (18 tests)	2000-2009
159	MJ Giteau (Australia) (21 tests)	2002-2010
140	MC Burke (Australia) (16 tests)	1993-2004
127	JP Wilkinson (England) (9 tests)	1998-2007
113	NR Jenkins (Wales & BI) (11 tests)	1994-2002

Most tries in tests against SA

10	CM Cullen (New Zealand) (15 tests)	1996-2002
9	JT Rokocoko (New Zealand) (15 tests)	2003-2010
9	MJ Giteau (Australia) (21 Tests)	2002-2010
7	SA Mortlock (Australia) (18 tests)	2000-2009
6	SJ Larkham (Australia) (23 tests)	1996-2007
5	JW Wilson (New Zealand) (15 tests)	1993-2001
5	JW Roff (Australia) (15 tests)	1995-2004
5	JW Marshall (New Zealand) (22 tests)	1995-2005
5	BN Tune (Australia) (13 tests)	1996-2002
5	CE Latham (Australia) (15 tests)	1998-2007
5	DC Howlett (New Zealand) (11 tests)	2000-2007

Most conversions in tests against SA

25	DW Carter (New Zealand) (15 tests)	2003-2010
21	MJ Giteau (Australia) (21 tests)	2002-2010
19	AP Mehrtens (New Zealand) (16 tests)	1995-2004
17	SA Mortlock (Australia) (18 tests)	2000-2009
16	SM Jones (Wales & BI) (13 tests)	1998-2010
12	MC Burke (Australia) (16 tests)	1993-2004
12	CJ Spencer (New Zealand) (7 tests)	1997-2004

Most penalty goals in tests against SA

53	AP Mehrtens (New Zealand) (16 tests)	1995-2004
51	DW Carter (New Zealand) (15 tests)	2003-2010
36	MC Burke (Australia) (16 tests)	1993-2004
36	JP Wilkinson (England) (9 tests)	1998-2007
35	NR Jenkins (Wales & BI) (11 tests)	1994-2002
28	SM Jones (Wales & BI) (13 tests)	1998-2010
27	SA Mortlock (Australia) (18 tests)	2000-2009

Most drop goals in tests against SA

4	AP Mehrtens (New Zealand) (16 tests)	1995-2004
3	JP Wilkinson (England) (9 tests)	1998-2007
3	RJR O'Gara (Ireland) (6 tests)	2000-2010

MISCELLANEOUS RECORDS

Most test match appearances in each position

Fullback	PC Montgomery [1]	87
Wing	BG Habana [2]	67
Centre	J de Villiers [3]	53
Flyhalf	AD James [4]	36
Scrumhalf	JH van der Westhuizen [5]	87
Prop	JP du Randt	80
Hooker	JW Smit [6]	87
Lock	V Matfield	105
Flank	SWP Burger [7]	61
Eighthman	GH Teichmann	42
Captain	JW Smit	76*

[1] Also made nine appearances as a centre, five as flyhalf and one as wing. [2] Also made one appearance as a centre. [3] Also made fourteen appearances as a wing. [4] Also made three appearances as a centre and one as a fullback. [5] Also made two appearances as a replacement wing. [6] Also made two appearances as a replacement prop and thirteen as a prop in the starting 15. [7] Also made two appearances as a No 8.
* World record

Most consecutive test match appearances by position

Fullback	PC Montgomery (1997-1999)	24
Wing	PWG Rossouw (1997-1999)	24
Centre	JL Gainsford (1961-1967)	23
Flyhalf	BL Osler (1924-1933)	17
	HE Botha (1980-1982)	17
	JNB van der Westhuyzen (2004-2005)	17

Scrumhalf	PF du Preez (2004-2006)	21
Prop	A-H le Roux (1998-1999)	25
Hooker	JW Smit (2003-2007)	46
Lock	V Matfield (2008-2010)	28
Flank	RJ Kruger (1995-1997)	22
Eighthman	GH Teichmann (1996-1999)	39
Captain	JW Smit (2004-2007)	43

Most consecutive test match appearances

46	JW Smit (hooker)	2003-2007
39	GH Teichmann (eighthman)	1996-1999
28	V Matfield (lock)	2008-2010
26	AH Snyman (centre/wing)	1996-1998
26	AN Vos (eighthman/flank)	1999-2001

Most test match tries in each position

Fullback	18	PC Montgomery	*87 tests
Wing	38	BG Habana	*67 tests
Centre	26	J Fourie	*51 tests
Flyhalf	6	PJ Visagie	25 tests
	6	JT Stransky	*21 tests
Scrumhalf	38	JH van der Westhuizen	*87 tests
Prop	5	AC Koch	22 tests
	5	JP du Randt	80 tests
	5	GG Steenkamp	31 tests
Hooker	5	J Dalton	43 tests
	5	BW du Plessis	*35 tests
Lock	12	MG Andrews	*75 tests
Flank	11	SWP Burger	*61 tests

SPRINGBOK RECORDS

11	JH Smith	*59 tests
Eighthman	7 PJ Spies	*35 tests

*Excludes tests played in other positions

Longest international career

14 seasons	JP du Randt (1994-2007)	13 years, 12 days
13 seasons	HE Botha (1980-1992)	12 years, 202 days
13 seasons	DM Gerber (1980-1992)	12 years, 27 days
13 seasons	BH Heatlie (1891-1903)	12 years, 14 days
13 seasons	JM Powell (1891-1903)	12 years, 7 days

Most test matches as a replacement *Total tests*

43	A-H le Roux	54
31	CJ van der Linde	69
28	PA van den Berg	51
28	R Pienaar	47
19	DJ Rossouw	54
18	JC van Niekerk	52

Oldest living Springboks*

P Malan	b 13/02/1919	91 years, 321 days
WHM Barnard	b 07/08/1923	87 years, 146 days
C Moss	b 12/02/1925	85 years, 322 days
MT Lategan	b 29/09/1925	85 years, 93 days
RP Bekker	b 15/12/1926	84 years, 16 days

*Age as at 31/12/2010

Most appearances as a test match combination

Fullback/wings	PC Montgomery, CS Terblanche & PWG Rossouw (1998-1999)	13
Centre pair	J de Villiers & J Fourie (2005-2010)	22
Halfbacks	JH van der Westhuizen & HW Honiball (1993-1999)	24
Locks	V Matfield & JP Botha (2003-2010)	60*
Front row	EP Andrews, JP du Randt & JW Smit (2004-2006)	14
Loose forwards	AG Venter, RJ Kruger & GH Teichmann (1996-1997)	14
	AG Venter, J Erasmus & GH Teichmann (1997-1999)	14

*World record

Springboks sent off in tests (7)

Player	Opponent	Referee	Venue	Date
JT Small	vs. Australia	EF Morrison (England)	Brisbane	1993
J Dalton	vs. Canada	DTM McHugh (Ireland)	Port Elizabeth	1995
AG Venter	vs. New Zealand	WD Bevan (Wales)	Auckland	1997
B Venter	vs. Uruguay	PL Marshall (Australia)	Glasgow	1999
MC Joubert	vs. Australia	PD O'Brien (New Zealand)	Johannesburg	2002
JJ Labuschagne	vs. England	PD O'Brien (New Zealand)	Twickenham	2002
PC Montgomery*	vs Wales	SJ Dickinson (Australia)	Cardiff	2005

Montgomery's first yellow card was subsequently dismissed by a disciplinary commission and his red card rescinded.

Springboks yellow carded in tests (70)

Player	Opponent	Referee	Venue	Date
RF Fleck	vs. Canada	A Lewis (Ireland)	East London	2000
W Meyer	vs. England	CJ Hawke (New Zealand)	Pretoria	2000
JH van der Westhuizen	vs. England	SJ Dickinson (Australia)	Bloemfontein	2000
CPJ Krige	vs. New Zealand	C White (England)	Christchurch	2000
RB Kempson	vs. Ireland	SJD Lander (England)	Dublin	2000
GM Delport	vs. Ireland	SJD Lander (England)	Dublin	2000
RF Fleck	vs. Wales	SR Walsh (New Zealand)	Cardiff	2000
MG Andrews	vs. France	C White (England)	Durban	2001
D Barry	vs. France	C White (England)	Durban	2001
AD James	vs. Australia	SR Walsh (New Zealand)	Perth	2001
RB Skinstad	vs. Australia	SR Walsh (New Zealand)	Perth	2001
AJJ van Straaten	vs. Italy	WD Erickson (Australia)	Genoa	2001
IJ Visagie	vs. USA	D Méné (France)	Houston	2001
W Meyer	vs. Wales	AJ Spreadbury (England)	Cape Town	2002
MC Joubert	vs. New Zealand	SJ Dickinson (Australia)	Wellington	2002
WW Greeff	vs. Australia	SJD Lander (England)	Brisbane	2002
SJ Rautenbach	vs. Australia	Retrospectively	Brisbane	2002
D Barry	vs. Australia	PD O'Brien (New Zealand)	Johannesburg	2002
JP Botha	vs. France	AC Rolland (Ireland)	Marseilles	2002
V Matfield	vs. Scotland	J Jutge (France)	Durban	2003

JH van der Westhuizen	vs. Scotland	J Jutge (France)	Durban	2003
RB Kempson	vs. Scotland	S Young (Australia)	Johannesburg	2003
D Barry	vs. Australia	SR Walsh (New Zealand)	Cape Town	2003
D Coetzee	vs. Australia	PD O'Brien (New Zealand)	Brisbane	2003
RB Kempson	vs. Australia	PD O'Brien (New Zealand)	Brisbane	2003
H Scholtz	vs. Georgia	SJ Dickinson (Australia)	Sydney	2003
SWP Burger	vs. Ireland	AJ Spreadbury (England)	Bloemfontein	2004
W Julies	vs. Ireland	J Jutge (France)	Cape Town	2004
PC Montgomery	vs. Australia	PD O'Brien (New Zealand)	Durban	2004
BJ Paulse	vs. Australia	PD O'Brien (New Zealand)	Durban	2004
SWP Burger	vs. Wales	PD O'Brien (New Zealand)	Cardiff	2004
SWP Burger	vs. Ireland	PG Honiss (New Zealand)	Dublin	2004
V Matfield	vs. Scotland	N Williams (Wales)	Edinburgh	2004
JP Botha	vs. Scotland	N Williams (Wales)	Edinburgh	2004
SWP Burger	vs. France	D Courtney (Ireland)	Port Elizabeth	2005
BJ Paulse	vs. Australia	SR Walsh (New Zealand)	Johannesburg	2005
SWP Burger	vs. Australia	SR Walsh (New Zealand)	Johannesburg	2005
BJ Paulse	vs. Australia	AC Rolland (Ireland)	Perth	2005
J de Villiers	vs. Argentina	AJ Spreadbury (England)	Buenos Aires	2005
PC Montgomery	vs. Wales	SJ Dickinson (Australia)	Cardiff	2005
V Matfield	vs. Australia	PG Honiss (New Zealand)	Brisbane	2006
J de Villiers	vs. England	SR Walsh (New Zealand)	Twickenham	2006
BG Habana	vs. England	J Jutge (France)	Pretoria	2007
RB Skinstad	vs. Samoa	M Changleng (Scotland)	Johannesburg	2007
PJ Spies	vs. Australia	W Barnes (England)	Cape Town	2007
PJ Wannenburg	vs. New Zealand	AC Rolland (Ireland)	Durban	2007
GvG Botha	vs. Australia	PG Honiss (New Zealand)	Sydney	2007
GJ Muller	vs. Australia	PG Honiss (New Zealand)	Sydney	2007
PJ Wannenburg	vs. New Zealand	SJ Dickinson (Australia)	Christchurch	2007
FPL Steyn	vs. Tonga	W Barnes (England)	Lens	2007
BG Habana	vs. Tonga	W Barnes (England)	Lens	2007
JH Smith	vs. Argentina	SR Walsh (New Zealand)	Paris	2007
PA van den Berg	vs. Wales	CR White (England)	Cardiff	2007
BW du Plessis	vs. Wales	CR White (England)	Cardiff	2007
CJ van der Linde	vs. Wales	D Pearson (England)	Bloemfontein	2008
V Matfield	vs. New Zealand	M Goddard (Australia)	Dunedin	2008
J Fourie	vs. Wales	AC Rolland (Ireland)	Cardiff	2008
T Mtawarira	vs. England	N Owens (Wales)	Twickenham	2008
CA Jantjes	vs. England	N Owens (Wales)	Twickenham	2008
SWP Burger	vs. British Isles	C Berdos (France)	Pretoria	2009
J-PR Pietersen	vs. New Zealand	N Owens (Wales)	Durban	2009
JP Botha	vs. New Zealand	N Owens (Wales)	Durban	2009
M Steyn	vs. France	W Barnes (England)	Toulouse	2009
R Kankowski	vs. France	W Barnes (England)	Toulouse	2009
PR van der Merwe	vs France	BJ Lawrence (New Zealand)	Cape Town	2010
JP Botha	vs New Zealand	DA Lewis (Ireland)	Auckland	2010
DJ Rossouw	vs New Zealand	AC Rolland (Ireland)	Wellington	2010
J Fourie	vs Australia	G Clancy (Ireland)	Brisbane	2010
BJ Botha	vs Australia	G Clancy (Ireland)	Brisbane	2010
BG Habana	vs Ireland	N Owens (Wales)	Dublin	2010

Players sent off in tests against South Africa (3)

Player	Team	Referee	Venue	Date
R Snow	Canada	DTM McHugh (Ireland)	Port Elizabeth	1995
GL Rees	Canada	DTM McHugh (Ireland)	Port Elizabeth	1995
GR Jenkins	Wales	J Dumé (France)	Johannesburg	1995

SPRINGBOK RECORDS

Players yellow carded in tests against South Africa (33)

Player	Team	Referee	Venue	Date
PBT Greening	England	CJ Hawke (New Zealand)	Pretoria	2000
J Leonard	England	SJ Dickinson (Australia)	Bloemfontein	2000
LBN Dallaglio	England	SJ Dickinson (Australia)	Bloemfontein	2000
MJ Cockbain	Australia	PG Honiss (New Zealand)	Durban	2000
PM Clohessy	Ireland	SJD Lander (England)	Dublin	2000
O Magne	France	C White (England)	Durban	2001
A Lo Cicero	Italy	WD Erickson (Australia)	Genoa	2001
E Reed	USA	D Méné (France)	Houston	2001
T Leota	Samoa	AJ Cole (Australia)	Pretoria	2002
JBG Harrison	Australia	SJD Lander (England)	Brisbane	2002
JA Paul	Australia	SJD Lander (England)	Brisbane	2002
R Alvarez	Argentina	N Williams (Wales)	Port Elizabeth	2003
LD Tuqiri	Australia	Retrospectively	Cape Town	2003
KJ Meeuws	New Zealand	AC Rolland (Ireland)	Pretoria	2003
M Kvirikashvili	Georgia	SJ Dickinson (Australia)	Sydney	2003
R Corrigan	Ireland	J Jutge (France)	Cape Town	2004
CL Horsman	Wales	SJ Dickinson (Australia)	Cardiff	2005
S So'oalo	Samoa	M Changleng (Scotland)	Johannesburg	2007
JH Va'a	Samoa	M Changleng (Scotland)	Johannesburg	2007
J Vaka	Tonga	W Barnes (England)	Lens	2007
S Rabeni	Fiji	PG Honiss (New Zealand)	Marseille	2007
F Contepomi	Argentina	SR Walsh (New Zealand)	Paris	2007
R Hibbard	Wales	D Pearson (England)	Bloemfontein	2008
C-A Del Fava	Italy	G Clancey (Ireland)	Cape Town	2008
SD Shaw	British Isles	SJ Dickinson (Australia)	Johannesburg	2009
IB Ross	New Zealand	N Owens (Wales)	Durban	2009
MJ Giteau	Australia	AC Rolland (Ireland)	Cape Town	2009
RN Brown	Australia	AC Rolland (Ireland)	Cape Town	2009
GB Smith	Australia	AC Rolland (Ireland)	Cape Town	2009
S Favaro	Italy	AC Rolland (Ireland)	Udine	2009
D Yachvili	France	BJ Lawrence (New Zealand)	Cape Town	2010
QS Cooper	Australia	G Clancy (Ireland)	Brisbane	2010
SM Fainga'a	Australia	W Barnes (England)	Bloemfontein	2010

International referees in South African test matches

Tests	Referee	Country	SA Won	SA Lost	Drawn	% Wins
12	PD O'Brien	New Zealand	7	5	-	58%
12	AC Rolland	Ireland	7	5	-	58%
11	SJ Dickinson	Australia	3	8	-	27%
10	CJ Hawke	New Zealand	7	3	-	70%
10	SR Walsh	New Zealand	8	1	1	80%
9	WD Bevan	Wales	7	2	-	78%
9	EF Morrison	England	3	6	-	33%
8	PG Honiss	New Zealand	3	5	-	38%
8	PL Marshall	Australia	3	5	-	38%
8	CR White	England	6	2	-	75%

Highest winning percentage as a Springbok (20 or more tests)

	Played	Won	Lost	Drawn	% Wins
AC Garvey	28	24	4	0	86%
M du Plessis	22	18	4	0	82%
J Dalton	43	35	8	0	81%
MTS Stofberg	21	17	4	0	81%
JS Germishuys	20	16	4	0	80%

Lowest winning percentage as a Springbok (20 or more tests)

	Played	Won	Lost	Drawn	% Wins
AJJ van Straaten	21	9	11	1	43%
D Barry	39	18	20	1	46%
CPJ Krige	39	18	21	0	46%
EP Andrews	23	11	11	1	48%
IJ Visagie	29	14	14	1	48%

SPRINGBOK CAPTAINS AND COACHES

SPRINGBOK TEST CAPTAINS 1891-2010

	CAPTAIN	TESTS AS CAPTAIN (TOTAL TESTS)	DEBUT AS CAPTAIN	DEBUT MATCH
1	HH Castens - Prop, Western Province	1 (1)	1891	British Isles 1st test
2	RCD Snedden - Prop, Griqualand West	1 (1)	1891	British Isles 2nd test
3	AR Richards - Flyhalf, Western Province	1 (3)	1891	British Isles 3rd test
4	FTD Aston - Centre & wing, Transvaal	3 (4)	1896	British Isles 1st test
5	BH Heatlie - Prop & lock, Western Province	2 (6)	1896	British Isles 4th test
6	A Frew - Prop, Transvaal	1 (1)	1903	British Isles 1st test
7	JM Powell - Flyhalf, Griqualand West	1 (4)	1903	British Isles 2nd test
8	HW Carolin - Flyhalf, Western Province	1 (3)	1906	Scotland
9	PJ Roos - Prop, Western Province	3 (4)	1906	Ireland
10	DFT Morkel - Prop, Transvaal	2 (9)	1910	British Isles 1st test
11	WA Millar - No. 8 & flank, Western Province	5 (6)	1910	British Isles 2nd test
12	FJ Dobbin - Scrumhalf, Griqualand West	1 (9)	1912	Scotland
13	TB Pienaar - Prop, Western Province	0 (0)	1921	Did not play in tests
14	WH Morkel - No. 8, Transvaal	3 (9)	1921	New Zealand 1st test
15	PK Albertyn - Centre, South Western Districts	4 (4)	1924	British Isles 1st test
16	PJ Mostert - Prop & hooker, Western Province	4 (14)	1928	New Zealand 1st test
17	BL Osler - Flyhalf, Western Province	5 (17)	1931	Wales
18	PJ Nel - Lock & prop, Natal	8 (16)	1933	Australia 1st test
19	DH Craven - Flyhalf & scrumhalf, Eastern Province	4 (16)	1937	New Zealand 1st test
20	F du Plessis - Lock, Transvaal	3 (3)	1949	New Zealand 1st test
21	BJ Kenyon - Flank, Border	1 (1)	1949	New Zealand 4th test
22	HSV Muller - No. 8, Transvaal	9 (13)	1951	Scotland
23	SP Fry - Flank, Western Province	4 (13)	1955	British Isles 1st test
24	SS Viviers - Fullback & flyhalf	5 (5)	1956	Australia 1st test
25	JA du Rand - Lock, Northern Transvaal	1 (21)	1956	New Zealand 1st test
26	JT Claassen - Lock, Western Transvaal	9 (28)	1958	France 1st test
27	DC van Jaarsveldt - Flank, Rhodesia	1 (1)	1960	Scotland
28	RG Dryburgh - Fullback, Natal	2 (8)	1960	New Zealand 1st test
29	AS Malan - Lock, Transvaal	10 (16)	1960	New Zealand 3rd test
30	GF Malan - Hooker, Transvaal	4 (18)	1963	Australia 1st test
31	CM Smith - Scrumhalf, Orange Free State	4 (7)	1964	France
32	DJ de Villiers - Scrumhalf, Western Province	22 (25)	1965	New Zealand 1st test
33	TP Bedford - No. 8, Natal	3 (25)	1969	Australia 2nd test
34	JFK Marais - Prop, Eastern Province	11 (35)	1971	France 1st test
35	PJF Greyling - Flank, Transvaal	1 (25)	1972	England
36	M du Plessis - No. 8, Western Province	15 (22)	1975	France 1st test
37	MTS Stofberg - Flank, Northern Transvaal	4 (21)	1980	South America 1st test
38	W Claassen - No. 8, Natal	7 (7)	1981	Ireland 1st test
39	DJ Serfontein - Scrumhalf, Western Province	2 (19)	1984	South America & Sp. 1st test
40	HE Botha - Flyhalf, Northern Transvaal	9 (28)	1986	NZ Cavaliers 1st test
41	JC Breedt - No. 8, Transvaal	2 (8)	1989	World Team 1st test
42	JF Pienaar - Flank & No. 8, Transvaal	29 (29)	1993	France 1st test
43	CP Strauss - Flank, Western Province	1 (15)	1994	New Zealand 1st test
44	AJ Richter - No. 8, Northern Transvaal	1 (10)	1995	Romania
45	GH Teichmann - No. 8, Natal	36 (42)	1996	New Zealand 1st test

SPRINGBOK RECORDS

SPRINGBOK TEST CAPTAINS 1891-2010

	CAPTAIN	TESTS AS CAPTAIN (TOTAL TESTS)	DEBUT AS CAPTAIN	DEBUT MATCH
46	CPJ Krige - Flank, Western Province	18 (39)	1999	Italy 2nd test
47	J Erasmus - Flank, Golden Lions	1 (36)	1999	Australia 1st test
48	JH van der Westhuizen - Scrumhalf, Blue Bulls	10 (89)	1999	New Zealand 2nd test
49	AN Vos - No. 8, Golden Lions	16 (33)	1999	Spain
50	RB Skinstad - No. 8, Western Province	12 (42)	2001	Italy
51	JW Smit - Hooker, Natal	76 (102)	2003	Georgia
52	V Matfield - Lock, Blue Bulls	15 (105)	2007	New Zealand 1st test
53	GJ Muller - Lock, Natal	1 (22)	2007	New Zealand 2nd test

WINNING PERCENTAGES OF SPRINGBOK CAPTAINS (10 or more tests)

	PLAYER	Matches	Won	Drawn	Lost	Points For	Points Against
86.67%	M du Plessis	15	13	0	2	357	230
80.00%	JH van der Westhuizen	10	8	0	2	329	191
72.22%	GH Teichmann	36	26	0	10	1228	661
67.11%	JW Smit	76	51	1	24	2238	1545
66.67%	V Matfield	15	10	0	5	468	240
65.52%	JF Pienaar	29	19	2	8	780	503
59.09%	DJ de Villiers	22	13	4	5	306	210
56.25%	AN Vos	16	9	0	7	434	371
54.55%	JFK Marais	11	6	2	3	138	131
50.00%	AS Malan	10	5	2	3	67	50
50.00%	RB Skinstad	12	6	1	5	285	233
38.89%	CPJ Krige	18	7	0	11	495	502

Percentage of Springbok points scored during a test career

	Player	Player points	Springbok points
50.73%	HE Botha	312	615
50.23%	M Steyn	322	641
42.02%	AJJ van Straaten	221	526
39.47%	JT Stransky	240	608
38.68%	LJ Koen	135	349
35.46%	JH de Beer	181	510
34.39%	PJ Visagie	130	378
27.00%	PC Montgomery	893	3307

Percentage of Springbok tries scored during a test career

	Player	Tries	Springbok tries
26.76%	DM Gerber	19	71
18.45%	BG Habana	38	206
13.97%	CS Terblanche	19	136
13.83%	BJ Paulse	26	188
13.45%	J Fourie	30	223
12.80%	PWG Rossouw	21	164
12.75%	JH van der Westhuizen	38	298
12.42%	JT Small	20	161

BIOGRAPHICAL FEATURES

Springbok relationships

Farther & son	TEN SETS	
Last PR van der Merwe & PR van der Merwe	1981-1989 & 2010	
Three brothers	THREE SETS	
Last W, CJ & MJ du Plessis 1980-1982, 1981-1989 & 1984-1989		
Two brothers	THIRTY TWO SETS	
Last AK & OM Ndungane		2008

Brothers in tests (since World War II)

Twice	HPJ & RP Bekker	1953
Once	ID & RJ McCallum	1974
Once	DSL & JCP Snyman	1974
Once	HE & DS Botha	1981
Twice	CJ & W du Plessis	1982
Eight times	CJ & MJ du Plessis	1984-1989
Twice	G & J Cronjé	2004
Fourteen times	JN & BW du Plessis	2007-2010

Tallest, shortest, heaviest, lightest

Tallest	A Bekker	2.08m (6ft 10in)
Shortest	TA Gentles	1.60m (5ft 3in)
Heaviest	RG Visagie	138kgs (21st 8lbs)
Lightest	WD Sendin	60kgs (9st 6lbs)

Youngest Springboks on test debut

18 Years, 18 days	AJ Hartley	British Isles (3rd test) 1891
19 Years, 8 days	DG Cope	British Isles (2nd test) 1896
19 Years, 37 days	JA Loubser	British Isles (3rd test) 1903
19 Years, 51 days	RCB van Ryneveld	British Isles (2nd test) 1910
19 Years, 72 days	WJ Mills	British Isles (2nd test) 1910
19 Years, 112 days	FG Turner	Australia (1st test) 1933
19 Years, 126 days	BH Heatlie	British Isles (2nd test) 1891
19 Years, 158 days	SC de Melker	British Isles (2nd test) 1903

Oldest Springboks in final test

37 Years, 34 days	JN Ackermann	Australia (2nd test) 2007
36 Years, 258 days	WH Morkel	New Zealand (3rd test) 1921
35 Years, 277 days	D Lötter	Australia (2nd test) 1993
35 Years, 252 days	FCH du Preez	Australia (3rd test) 1971
35 Years, 208 days	PJ Geel	New Zealand (3rd test) 1949
35 Years, 130 days	LC Moolman	NZ Cavaliers (4th test) 1986

Least and Most experienced Springbok starting XV since 1992

115 Caps - vs. Italy, Durban, 1999: PC Montgomery (23); BJ Paulse (1), RF Fleck (1), JC Mulder (26), CS Terblanche (13); GS du Toit (2), DNB von Hoesslin (1); AN Vos (1), J Erasmus (18), CPJ Krige (0), CS Boome (1), PA van den Berg (1), W Meyer (1), AE Drotské (14), RB Kempson (12).

750 Caps - vs. Australia, Bloemfontein, 2010: FPL Steyn (38); J-PR Pietersen (35), J Fourie (61), J de Villiers (62), BG Habana (65); M Steyn (20), F Hougaard (4); PJ Spies (36), JH Smith (64), SWP Burger (62), V Matfield (100), DJ Rossouw (53), JN du Plessis (19), JW Smit (101), GG Steenkamp (30).

(This is the most experienced side of all time)

SPRINGBOK COACHES SINCE 1992

	First & Last Test	P	W	L	D	PF	PA	Diff	TF	TA	Win%
JG Williams	Aug 92 - Nov 92	5	1	4	0	79	130	-51	7	14	20.00%
GHH Sonnekus	Did not take up appointment										
IB McIntosh	June 93 - Aug 94	12	4	6	2	252	240	12	25	14	33.33%
GM Christie	Oct 94 - Nov 95	14	14	0	0	450	191	259	54	16	100.00%
AT Markgraaff	July 96 - Dec 96	13	8	5	0	352	260	92	38	21	61.54%
CJ du Plessis	June 97 - Aug 97	8	3	5	0	288	213	75	39	22	37.50%
NVH Mallett	Nov 97 - Aug 00	38	27	11	0	1251	678	573	152	49	71.05%
HJ Viljoen	Nov 00 - Dec 01	15	8	6	1	376	312	64	38	18	53.33%
RAW Straeuli	Jun 02 - Nov 03	23	12	11	0	622	598	24	71	61	52.17%
JA White	Jun 04 -Dec 07	54	36	17	1	1740	1097	643	194	110	66.67%
P de Villiers	Jun 08-	39	25	14	0	1033	788	245	102	71	64.10%
South Africa's record since 1992		**221**	**138**	**79**	**4**	**6443**	**4507**	**1936**	**720**	**396**	**62.44%**

STADIUMS

SPRINGBOKS BY STADIUM - HOME

		P	W	L	D	PF	PA	TF	TA	Ave.score	%Win
Rustenburg	Royal Bafokeng Sports Palace	1	1	0	0	21	20	2	2	21-20	100%
East London	Border Rugby Stadium	3	3	0	0	240	32	36	3	80-11	100%
Johannesburg	Wanderers (New)	1	1	0	0	24	9	3	1	24-9	100%
Witbank	Puma Stadium	1	1	0	0	29	13	4	1	29-13	100%
Port Elizabeth	EPRFU Stadium	16	14	1	1	423	182	49	17	26-11	88%
Durban	Kingsmead	5	4	1	0	57	35	7	7	11-7	80%
Pretoria	Loftus Versfeld	30	22	8	0	985	619	117	62	33-21	73%
Bloemfontein	Vodacom Stadium	18	13	4	1	504	307	57	28	28-17	72%
Johannesburg	Ellis Park	43	30	11	2	1121	654	140	58	26-15	70%
Port Elizabeth	Crusader Ground	9	6	2	1	102	53	18	13	11-6	67%
Cape Town	Newlands	48	32	14	2	911	587	119	63	19-12	67%
Durban	ABSA Stadium	26	16	7	3	611	414	62	37	24-16	62%
Johannesburg	Wanderers (Old)	4	2	1	1	49	37	12	7	12-9	50%
Springs	PAM Brink Stadium	2	1	1	0	55	37	7	3	28-19	50%
Bloemfontein	Springbok Park	1	0	1	0	4	15	0	3	4-15	0%
Kimberley	Eclectic Ground	1	0	1	0	0	3	0	0	0-3	0%
Kimberley	KAC Ground	2	0	1	1	3	9	1	1	2-5	0%
Port Elizabeth	Cricket Club Ground	1	0	1	0	0	4	0	2	0-4	0%
Soweto	FNB Stadium	1	0	1	0	22	29	1	3	22-29	0%
		213	**146**	**55**	**12**	**5161**	**3059**	**635**	**311**		**69%**

SPRINGBOK RECORDS

SPRINGBOKS BY STADIUM - AWAY

		P	W	L	D	PF	PA	TF	TA	Ave.score	%Win
Gosford, Australia	Advocate Express	1	1	0	0	38	24	4	4	38-24	100%
Belfast	Balmoral Ground	1	1	0	0	15	12	4	3	15-12	100%
Bologna	Stadio Dall 'Ara	1	1	0	0	62	31	9	3	62-31	100%
Bordeaux	Route de Médoc, Le Bouscat	1	1	0	0	38	5	9	1	38-5	100%
Bordeaux	Municipal Stadium	1	1	0	0	12	9	0	3	12-9	100%
Bordeaux	Parc Lescure	1	1	0	0	22	12	2	0	22-12	100%
Brisbane	Exhibition Ground	2	2	0	0	23	6	5	0	12-3	100%
Buenos Aires	Ferro Carril Oeste Stadium	4	4	0	0	171	85	24	8	43-22	100%
Buenos Aires	River Plate Stadium	1	1	0	0	37	33	5	3	37-33	100%
Buenos Aires	Velez Sarsfield Stadium	2	2	0	0	73	30	8	4	37-15	100%
Edinburgh	Inverleith	1	1	0	0	16	0	4	0	16-0	100%
Genoa	Luigi Ferraris Stadium	1	1	0	0	54	26	8	2	54-26	100%
Glenville, New York	Owl Creek Polo Field	1	1	0	0	38	7	8	1	38-7	100%
Houston, Texas	Robertson Stadium	1	1	0	0	43	20	6	1	43-20	100%
Lens	Stade Felix Bollaert	1	1	0	0	30	25	4	3	30-25	100%
London	Wembley Stadium	1	1	0	0	28	20	3	1	28-20	100%
Lyon	Stade Gerland	2	2	0	0	56	47	7	5	28-24	100%
Montevideo	Wanderers Club	1	1	0	0	22	13	3	2	22-13	100%
Montpellier	Stade de la Mosson	1	1	0	0	64	15	9	2	64-15	100%
Rome	Olympic Stadium	1	1	0	0	40	21	4	2	40-21	100%
Santiago	Prince of Wales Country Club	1	1	0	0	30	16	6	2	30-16	100%
Swansea	St Helen's	2	2	0	0	19	3	5	1	10-2	100%
Hamilton	Waikato Stadium	1	1	0	0	32	29	2	2	32-29	100%
Udine	Stadio Friuli	1	1	0	0	32	10	4	1	32-10	100%
Cardiff[1]	Millennium Stadium	15	13	1	1	327	236	35	18	22-16	87%
Sydney	Sydney Cricket Ground	6	5	1	0	92	57	18	8	15-10	83%
Paris	Parc des Princes	5	4	1	0	150	66	18	6	30-13	80%
Edinburgh	Murrayfield	15	11	4	0	409	149	57	13	27-10	73%
Paris	Colombes Stadium	3	2	0	1	41	14	9	1	14-5	67%
Paris	Stade de France	6	4	2	0	162	86	12	5	27-14	67%
Dublin	Lansdowne Road/Aviva Stadium	11	7	3	1	190	129	30	13	17-12	64%
Toulouse	Municipal Stadium	2	1	1	0	26	24	2	2	13-12	50%
Sydney	Aussie Stadium	4	2	2	0	93	71	13	4	23-18	50%
Marseille	Stade Velodrome	2	1	1	0	47	50	6	4	24-25	50%
Glasgow	Hampden Park	2	1	1	0	39	9	5	2	20-5	50%
Perth	Subiaco Oval	8	4	3	1	195	148	23	14	24-19	50%
London	Twickenham	18	9	9	0	288	308	26	26	16-17	50%
Wellington	Athletic Park	7	3	3	1	64	50	5	6	9-7	43%
Christchurch	Jade Stadium	8	2	6	0	101	149	13	17	13-19	25%
Auckland	Eden Park	9	2	6	1	136	198	17	22	15-22	22%
Brisbane[2]	Suncorp Stadium	8	1	7	0	122	215	15	21	15-29	13%
Dunedin	Carisbrook	8	1	7	0	93	164	9	18	12-21	13%
Wellington	Westpac Stadium	4	0	4	0	62	126	7	12	16-32	0%
Brisbane	Ballymore	1	0	1	0	20	28	2	3	20-28	0%
Brisbane	The Gabba	1	0	1	0	27	38	4	4	27-38	0%
Melbourne	Telstra Dome	2	0	2	0	32	73	3	8	16-37	0%
Sydney	Telstra Stadium	4	0	4	0	53	101	4	12	13-25	0%
London	Crystal Palace	1	0	0	1	3	3	1	1	3-3	0%
Dublin	Croke Park	1	0	1	0	10	15	1	0	10-15	0%
AWAY RECORD		**182**	**104**	**71**	**7**	**3777**	**3006**	**478**	**294**		**57%**
OVERALL RECORD		**395**	**250**	**126**	**19**	**8938**	**6065**	**1113**	**605**		**63%**

[1] Includes records of the original Cardiff Arms Park on the Millennium Stadium site.
[2] Includes one match at Lang Park on which site the Suncorp Stadium was developed.

SOUTH AFRICA'S 828 INTERNATIONALS 1891-2010

A

Springbok No. 324 **Ackermann, DSP** (Dawie) b 03/06/1930 d 01/01/1970 - WP - 8 Tests (3 - 1T) 19 matches (27 - 9T) 1955: BI2, 3, 4. 1956: A1, 2, NZ1, 3. 1958: F2.

632 **Ackermann, JN** (Johan) b 03/06/1970 - NTvl - 13 Tests (-) 15 matches (-) 1996: Fj, A1, NZ1, A2. 2001: F2(R), It1, NZ1(R), A1. 2006: I, E1, 2. 2007: Sm1, A2.

805 **Adams, HJ** (Heinie) b 29/05/1980 - BB - No Tests - 2 matches (-) Toured F, It, I & E. 2009.

658 **Aitken, AD** (Andrew) b 10/06/1968 - WP - 7 Tests (-) 9 matches (-) 1997: F2(R), E. 1998: I2(R), W1(R), NZ1, 2(R), A2(R).

822 **Alberts, WS** (Willem) b 05/11/1984 - KZN - 3 Tests (15 - 3T) 4 matches (15 - 3T) 2010: W2(R), S(t+R), E(R).

179 **Albertyn, PK** (Pierre) b 27/05/1897 d 07/03/1973 - SWD - 4 Tests (3 - 1T) 4 matches (3 - 1T) 1924: BI1*, 2*, 3*, 4*.

673 **Alcock, CD** (Chad) b 09/01/1973 - EP - No Tests - 4 matches (5 - 1T) Toured BI & I. 1998.

13 **Alexander, FA** (Fred) b 30/12/1870 d 20/04/1937 - GW - 2 Tests (-) 2 matches (-) 1891: BI1, 2.

594 **Allan, J** (John) b 25/11/1963 - Natal - 13 Tests (-) 25 matches (30 - 6T) 1993: A1(R), Arg1, 2(R). 1994: E1, 2, NZ1, 2, 3. 1996: Fj, A1, NZ1, A2, NZ2.

355 **Allen, PB** (Peter) b 10/04/1930 d 22/01/1998 - EP - 1 Test (-) 1 match (-) 1960: S.

121 **Allport, PH** (Percy) b 24/03/1885 d 01/01/1959 - WP - 2 Tests (3 - 1T) 2 matches (3 - 1T) 1910: BI2, 3.

31 **Anderson, JH** (Biddy) b 26/04/1874 d 11/03/1926 - WP - 3 Tests (-) 3 matches (-) 1896: BI1, 3, 4.

89 **Anderson, JW** (Joe) b 31/12/1881 d 02/11/1953 - WP - 1 Test (-) 1 match (-) 1903: BI3.

47 **Andrew, JB** (Ben) b 15/05/1870 d 09/04/1911 - Tvl - 1 Test (-) 1 match (-) 1896: BI2.

759 **Andrews, EP** (Eddie) b 18/03/1977 - WP - 23 Tests (-) 23 matches (-) 2004: I1, 2, W1(t+R), PI, NZ1, A1, NZ2, A2, W2, I3, E. 2005: F1, A2, NZ2(t), Arg(R), F3(R). 2006: S1, 2, F, A1(R), NZ1(t). 2007: A2(R), NZ2(R).

574 **Andrews, KS** (Keith) b 03/05/1962 - WP - 9 Tests (-) 31 matches (-) 1992: E. 1993: F1, 2, A1(R), 2, 3, Arg1(R), 2. 1994: NZ3.

602 **Andrews, MG** (Mark) b 21/02/1972 - Natal - 77 Tests (60 - 12T) 90 matches (60 - 12T) 1994: E2, NZ1, 2, 3, Arg1, 2, S, W. 1995: WS1, [A, WS2, F, NZ], W, It, E. 1996: Fj, A1, NZ1, A2, NZ2, 3, 4, 5, Arg1, 2, F1, 2, W. 1997: T(R), BI1, 2, NZ1, A1, NZ2, A2, It, F1, 2, E, S. 1998: I1, 2, W1, E1, A1, NZ1, 2, A2, W2, S, I3, E2. 1999: NZ1, 2(R), A2(R), [S, U, E, A3, NZ3]. 2000: A2, NZ2, A3, Arg, I, W, E3. 2001: F1, 2, It1, NZ1, A1, 2, NZ2, F3, E.

358 **Antelme, JGM** (Mike) b 23/04/1934 - Tvl - 5 Tests (-) 25 matches (45 - 15T) 1960: NZ1, 2, 3, 4. 1961: F.

816 **Aplon, GG** (Gio) b 06/10/1982 - WP - 13 Tests (15 - 3T) 14 matches (15 - 3T) 2010: W1, F, It1, 2, NZ1(R), 2(R), A1, NZ3, A3(R), I, W2, S, E.

243 **Apsey, JT** (John) b 16/04/1911 d 12/11/1987 - WP - 3 Tests (-) 3 matches (-) 1933: A4, 5. 1938: BI2.

76 **Ashley, S** (Syd) b 23/02/1880 d 20/01/1959 - WP - 1 Test (-) 1 match (-) 1903: BI2.

32 **Aston, FTD** (Ferdy) b 18/09/1871 d 15/10/1926 - Tvl - 4 Tests (-) 4 matches (-) 1896: BI1*, 2*, 3*, 4.

576 **Atherton, S** (Steve) b 17/03/1965 - Natal - 8 Tests (-) 23 matches (5 - 1T) 1993: Arg1, 2. 1994: E1, 2, NZ1, 2, 3. 1996: NZ2.

178 **Aucamp, J** (Hans) b 27/10/1898 d 14/03/1970 - WTvl - 2 Tests (3 - 1T) 2 matches (3 - 1T) 1924: BI1, 2.

B

376 **Baard, AP** (Attie) b 17/05/1933 d 01/05/2009 - WP - 1 Test (-) 13 matches (9 - 3T) 1960: I.

246 **Babrow, L** (Louis) b 24/04/1915 d 26/01/2004 - WP - 5 Tests (9 - 3T) 16 matches (42 - 14T) 1937: A1, 2, NZ1, 2, 3.

712 **Badenhorst, AJ** (Adri) b 18/07/1978 - WP - No Tests - 1 match (-) Toured E. 2000.

610 **Badenhorst, C** (Chris) b 12/12/1965 - OFS - 2 Tests (10 - 2T) 12 matches (45 - 9T) 1994: Arg2. 1995: WS1(R).

745 **Bands, RE** (Richard) b 25/03/1974 - BB - 11 Tests (10 - 2T) 11 matches (10 - 2T) 2003: S1, 2, Arg(R), A1, NZ1, A2, NZ2, [U, E, Sm(R), NZ3(R)].

538 **Barnard, AS** (Anton) b 07/04/1958 - EP - 4 Tests (-) 4 matches (-) 1984: S. Am&Sp1, 2. 1986: NZC1, 2.

399 **Barnard, JH** (Jannie) b 29/01/1945 d 21/02/1985 - Tvl - 5 Tests (-) 18 matches (21 - 7T) 1965: S, A1, 2, NZ3, 4.

442 **Barnard, RW** (Robbie) b 26/11/1941 - Tvl - 1 Test (-) 10 matches (9 - 3T) 1970: NZ2(R).

285 **Barnard, WHM** (Willem) b 07/08/1923 - NTvl - 2 Tests (-) 14 matches (3 - 1T) 1949: NZ4. 1951: W.

690 **Barry, D** (De Wet) b 24/06/1978 - WP - 39 Tests (15 - 3T) 41 matches (20 - 4T) 2000: C, E1, 2, A1(R), NZ1, A2. 2001: F1, 2, US(R). 2002: W2, Arg, Sm, NZ1, A1, NZ2, A2. 2003: A1, NZ1, A2, [U, E, Sm, NZ3]. 2004: PI, NZ1, A1, NZ2, A2, W2, I3, E, Arg(t). 2005: F1, 2, A1, NZ2, W(R), F3(R). 2006: F.

63 **Barry, J** (Joe) b 16/03/1876 d 29/03/1961 - WP - 3 Tests (3 - 1T) 3 matches (3 - 1T) 1903: BI1, 2, 3.

545 **Bartmann, WJ** (Wahl) b 13/06/1963 - Tvl - 8 Tests (-) 15 matches (5 - 1T) 1986: NZC1, 2, 3, 4. 1992: NZ, A, F1, 2.

817 **Basson, BA** (Bjorn) b 11/02/1987 - GW - 4 Tests (-) 4 matches (-) 2010: W1(R), It1(R), I, W2.

661 **Basson, WW** (Wium) b 23/10/1975 d 22/04/2001 - BB - No Tests - 2 matches (-) Toured It, F, E & S. 1997.

252 **Bastard, WE** (Ebbo) b 10/12/1912 d 14/02/1949 - Natal - 6 Tests (6 - 2T) 18 matches (15 - 5T) 1937: A1, NZ1, 2, 3. 1938: BI1, 3.

438 **Bates, AJ** (Albie) b 18/04/1941 - WTvl - 4 Tests (-) 18 matches (3 - 1T) 1969: E.

Notes: *Number preceding name is player's Springbok number. Figures in brackets following the number of tests or matches are points scored, followed by a breakdown of the method of scoring. A figure following a test appearance indicates which match of a sequence against any one opponent it may have been in that year and does not always refer to a test in a rubber (i.e. the Springboks played five matches against New Zealand in 1996 but only three were officially part of the series). Birth and death dates are in the order of day/month/year. A player's province is the one for which he was appearing on his Springbok debut.*

Key: *b > born; d > died; * captain; (R) replacement appearance; (t) indicates a temporary replacement; [Square brackets] enclose Rugby World Cup matches; ?? Indicates date unknown. Dm > Drop goal from a mark.*

SPRINGBOK RECORDS

1970: NZ1, 2. 1972: E.

468 Bayvel, PCR (Paul) b 28/03/1949 - Tvl - 10 Tests (-) 13 matches (-) 1974: BI2, 4, F1, 2. 1975: F1, 2. 1976: NZ1, 2, 3, 4.

524 Beck, JJ (Colin) b 27/03/1959 - WP - 3 Tests (4 - 1T) 12 matches (35 - 5T, 3C, 2P, 1D) 1981: NZ2(R), 3(R), US.

387 Bedford, TP (Tommy) b 08/02/1942 - Natal - 25 Tests (3 - 1T) 48 matches (12 - 4T) 1963: A1, 2, 3, 4. 1964: W, F. 1965: I, A1, 2. 1968: BI1, 2, 3, 4, F1, 2. 1969: A1, 2*, 3*, 4, S*, E. 1970: I, W. 1971: F1, 2.

795 Bekker, A (Andries) b 05/12/1983 - WP - 24 Tests (5 - 1T) 26 matches (5 - 1T) 2008: W1, 2(R), It(R), NZ1(R), 2(t+R), A1(t+R), Arg(R), NZ3, A2, 3, W3(R), S(R), E(R). 2009: BI1(R), 2(R), NZ2(R), A1(R), 2(R), F(t+R), It, I. 2010: It2, NZ1(R), 2(R).

527 Bekker, HJ (Hennie) b 12/09/1952 - WP - 2 Tests (4 - 1T) 10 matches (16 - 4T) 1981: NZ1, 3.

298 Bekker, HPJ (Jaap) b 11/02/1925 d 06/08/1999 - NTvl - 15 Tests (3 - 1T) 39 matches (12 - 4T) 1952: E, F. 1953: A1, 2, 3, 4. 1955: BI2, 3, 4. 1956: A1, 2, NZ1, 2, 3, 4.

353 Bekker, MJ (Martiens) b 03/05/1930 d 10/11/1971 - NTvl - 1 Test (-) 1 match (-) 1960: S.

308 Bekker, RP (Dolf) b 15/12/1926 - NTvl - 2 Tests (3 - 1T) 2 matches (3 - 1T) 1953: A3, 4.

639 Bekker, S (Schutte) b 21/10/1971 - NTvl - 1 Test (-) 3 matches (15 - 3T) 1997: A2(t).

640 Bennett, RG (Russell) b 27/11/1971 - Border - 6 Tests (10 - 2T) 10 matches (25 - 5T) 1997: T(R), BI1(R), 3, NZ1, A1, NZ2.

228 Bergh, WF v R v O (Ferdie) b 02/11/1906 d 28/05/1973 - SWD - 17 Tests (21 - 7T) 41 matches (42 - 14T) 1931: W, I. 1932: E, S. 1933: A1, 2, 3, 4, 5. 1937: A1, 2, NZ1, 2, 3. 1938: BI1, 2, 3.

485 Bestbier, A (André) b 31/03/1946 - OFS - 1 Test (-) 5 matches (-) 1974: F2(R).

186 Bester, JJN (Jack) b 02/03/1898 d 27/10/1943 - WP - 2 Tests (3 - 1T) 2 matches (3 - 1T) 1924: BI2, 4.

247 Bester, JLA (Johnny) b 25/12/1917 d 14/05/1977 - WP - 2 Tests (6 - 2T) 14 matches (30 - 10T) 1938: BI2, 3.

49 Beswick, AM (Allan) b 30/06/1870 d 06/09/1908 - Border - 3 Tests (-) 3 matches (-) 1896: BI2, 3, 4.

383 Bezuidenhout, CE (Chris) b 13/10/1937 d ??/??/2002 - NTvl - 3 Tests (-) 3 matches (-) 1962: BI2, 3, 4.

751 Bezuidenhout, CJ (Christo) b 14/05/1970 - Mpu - 4 Tests (-) 4 matches (-) 2003: NZ2(R), [E, Sm, NZ3].

457 Bezuidenhout, NSE (Niek) b 04/08/1950 - NTvl - 9 Tests (-) 13 matches (-) 1972: E. 1974: BI2, 3, 4, F1, 2. 1975: F1, 2. 1977: WT.

225 Bierman, JN (Nic) b 13/02/1910 d 08/06/1977 - Tvl - 1 Test (-) 14 matches (18 - 6T) 1931: I.

8 Bisset, WM (William) b 11/09/1867 d 23/02/1958 - WP - 2 Tests (-) 2 matches (-) 1891: BI1, 3.

494 Blair, R (Robbie) b 03/06/1953 - WP - 1 Test (21 - 3C, 5P) 1 match (21 - 3C, 5P) 1977: WT.

747 Bobo, G (Gcobani) b 12/09/1979 - GL - 6 Tests (-) 6 matches (-) 2003: S2(R), Arg, A1(R), NZ2. 2004: S(R). 2008: It.

670 Boome, CS (Selborne) b 16/05/1975 - WP - 20 Tests (10 - 2T) 25 matches (15 - 3T) 1999: It1, 2, W, NZ1(R), A1, NZ2, A2. 2000: C, E1, 2. 2003: S1(R), 2(R), Arg(R), A1(R), NZ1(R), A2, NZ2(R), [U(R), G, NZ3(R)].

467 Bosch, GR (Gerald) b 12/05/1949 - Tvl - 9 Tests (89 - 7C, 23P, 2D) 14 matches (132 - 15C, 31P, 3D) 1974: BI2, F1, 2. 1975: F1, 2. 1976: NZ1, 2, 3, 4.

771 Bosman, HM (Meyer) b 19/04/1985 - FS - 3 Tests (7 - 2C, 1P) 6 matches (7 - 2C, 1P) 2005: W, F3. 2006: A1(R).

185 Bosman, NJS (Nico) b 06/10/1902 d ??/??/1990 - Tvl - 3 Tests (-) 3 matches (-) 1924: BI2, 3, 4.

778 Botha, BJ (BJ) b 04/01/1980 - KZN - 25 Tests (5 - 1T) 26 matches (5 - 1T) 2006: NZ2(R), 3, A3, I(R), E1, 2. 2007: E1, Sm1, A1, NZ1, N(R), S(t+R), [Sm(R), E3, T(R), US.]. 2008: W2. 2009: It(R), NZ1(R), 2(R), A1. It2(R), NZ1(R), 2(R), A1.

522 Botha, DS (Darius) b 26/06/1955 - NTvl - 1 Test (-) 8 matches (12 - 3T) 1981: NZ1.

770 Botha, GvG (Gary) b 12/10/1981 - BB - 12 Tests (-) 14 matches (-) 2005: A3(R), F3(R). 2007: E1(R), 2(R), Sm1(R), A1(R), NZ1, A2, NZ2(R), N, S, [T.].

502 Botha, HE (Naas) b 27/02/1958 - NTvl - 28 Tests (312 - 2T, 50C, 50P, 18D) 40

matches (485 - 6T, 91C, 66P, 27D) 1980: S. Am1, 2, BI1, 2, 3, 4, S. Am3, 4, F. 1981: I1, 2, NZ1, 2, 3, US. 1982: S. Am1, 2. 1986: NZC1*, 2*, 3*, 4*. 1989: WT1, 2. 1992: NZ*, A*, F1*, 2*, E*.

90 Botha, JA (John) b 19/11/1879 d 08/12/1920 - Tvl - 1 Test (-) 1 match (-) 1903: BI3.

733 Botha, JP (Bakkies) b 22/09/1979 - BB - 72 Tests (35 - 7T) 73 matches (40 - 8T) 2002: F. 2003: S1, 2, A1, NZ1, A2(R), [U, E, G, Sm, NZ3]. 2004: I1, PI, NZ1, A1, NZ2, A2, W2, I3, E, S, Arg. 2005: A1, 2, 3, NZ1, A4, NZ2, Arg, W, F3. 2007: E1, 2, A1, NZ1, N, S. [Sm, E3, T, US(R), Fiji, Arg, E4.], W. 2008: W1, 2, It, NZ1, 2, A1, Arg, W3, S, E. 2009: BI1, 2, NZ1, 2, A1, 2, 3, NZ3, F, It. 2010: It1, 2, NZ1, I, W2, S, E.

374 Botha, JPF (Hannes) b 11/05/1937 - NTvl - 3 Tests (-) 10 matches (9 - 3T) 1962: BI2, 3, 4.

412 Botha, PH (Piet) b 13/11/1935 - Tvl - 2 Tests (-) 11 matches (3 - 1T) 1965: A1, 2.

4 Boyes, HC (Harry) b 12/03/1868 d 26/10/1892 - GW - 2 Tests (-) 2 matches (-) 1891: BI1, 2.

149 Braine, JS (Jack) b 01/05/1891 d 25/10/1940 - GW - No Tests - 11 matches (-) Toured BI, I & F. 1912/13.

204 Brand, GH (Gerry) b 08/10/1906 d 04/02/1996 - WP - 16 Tests (55 - 13 C, 7P, 2D) 46 matches (293 - 27, 100C, 25P, 3D) 1928: NZ2, 3. 1931: W, I. 1932: E, S. 1933: A1, 2, 3, 4, 5. 1937: A1, 2, NZ2, 3. 1938: BI1.

39 Bredenkamp, MJ (Mike) b 02/05/1873 d 22/12/1940 - GW - 2 Tests (-) 2 matches (-) 1896: BI1, 3.

547 Breedt, JC (Jannie) b 04/06/1959 - Tvl - 8 Tests (-) 8 matches (-) 1986: NZC1, 2, 3, 4. 1989: WT1*, 2*. 1992: NZ, A.

268 Brewis, JD (Hannes) b 15/06/1920 d 09/09/2007 - NTvl - 10 Tests (18 - 1T, 5D) 19 matches (36 - 6T, 6D) 1949: NZ1, 2, 3, 4. 1951: S, I, W. 1952: E, F. 1953: A1.

313 Briers, TPD (Theuns) b 11/07/1929 - WP - 7 Tests (15 - 5T) 12 matches (27 - 9T) 1955: BI1, 2, 3, 4. 1956: NZ2, 3, 4.

104 Brink, DJ (Koei) b 07/11/1882 d 29/10/1970 - WP - 3 Tests (-) 18 matches (9 - 3T) 1906: S, W, E.

626 Brink, RA (Robby) b 21/07/1971 - WP - 2 Tests (-) 2 matches (-) 1995: [R, C].

799 Brits, SB (Schalk) b 16/05/1981 -

Team abbreviations: A > Australia; Arg > Argentina; BB > Blue Bulls; BI > British Isles; C > Canada; E > England; EP > Eastern Province; ETvl > Eastern Transvaal; F > Falcons (if province); France (if opponent); FS > Free State; G > Georgia; GF > Gauteng Falcons; GL > Golden Lions; GW > Griqualand West; I > Ireland; It > Italy; Mpu > Mpumalanga; NTvl > Northern Transvaal; NZ > New Zealand; NZC > New Zealand Cavaliers; OFS > Orange Free State; PI > Pacific Islanders; R > Romania; S > Scotland; Sam > Samoa; SAm > South America; SETvl > South Eastern Transvaal; Sp > Spain; SWA > South West Africa; SWD > South Western Districts; T > Tonga; Tvl > Transvaal; U > Uruguay; W > Wales; WP > Western Province; WS > Western Samoa; WT > World Team; WTvl > Western Transvaal.

WP - 3 Tests (-) 3 matches (-) 2008: It(R), NZ2(R), A1.

760 Britz, GJJ (Gerrie) b 14/04/1978 - FS - 13 Tests (-) 14 matches (-) 2004: I1(R), 2(R), W1(R), PI, A1, NZ2, A2(R), I3(t), S(t+R), Arg(R). 2005: U. 2006: E2(R). 2007: NZ2(R).

725 Britz, WK (Warren) b 07/11/1973 - Natal - 1 Test (-) 1 match (-) 2002: W1.

244 Broodryk, JA (Tallie) b 11/04/1910 d 22/10/1993 - Tvl - No Tests - 6 matches (22 - 6T, 1D) Toured A & NZ. 1937.

100 Brooks, D (Cocky) b 22/09/1881 d 14/11/1962 - Border - 1 Test (-) 11 matches (3 - 1T) 1906: S.

655 Brosnihan, WG (Warren) b 28/12/1971 - GL - 6 Tests (5 - 1T) 10 matches (10 - 2T) 1997: A2. 2000: NZ1(t+R), A2(t+R), NZ2(R), A3(R), E3(R).

74 Brown, CB (Charlie) b 29/01/1878 d 18/06/1944 - WP - 3 Tests (-) 3 matches (-) 1903: BI1, 2, 3.

801 Brüssow, HW (Heinrich) b 21/07/1986 - FS - 13 Tests (5 - 1T) 13 matches (5 - 1T) 2008: E(R). 2009: BI1, 2(R), 3, NZ1, 2, A1, 2, 3, NZ3, F, It, I.

407 Brynard, GS (Gertjie) b 21/10/1938 - WP - 7 Tests (6 - 2T) 21 matches (42 - 14T) 1965: A1, NZ1, 2, 3, 4. 1968: BI3, 4.

287 Buchler, JU (Johnny) b 07/04/1930 - Tvl - 10 Tests (8 - 1C, 1P, 1D) 26 matches (26 - 4C, 5P, 1D) 1951: S, I, W. 1952: E, F. 1953: A1, 2, 3, 4. 1956: A2.

108 Burdett, AF (Adam) b 20/08/1882 d 04/11/1918 - WP - 2 Tests (-) 11 matches (6 - 2T) 1906: S, I.

552 Burger, JM (Kobus) b 31/03/1964 - WP - 2 Tests (-) 2 matches (-) 1989: WT1, 2.

511 Burger, MB (Thys) b 10/11/1954 - NTvl - 3 Tests (8 - 2T) 13 matches (52 - 13 T) 1980: BI2(R), S. Am3. 1981: US(R).

535 Burger, SWP (Schalk) b 06/10/1955 - WP - 6 Tests (-) 6 matches (-) 1984: E1, 2. 1986: NZC1, 2, 3, 4.

754 Burger, SWP (Schalk) b 13/04/1983 - WP - 63 Tests (65 - 13T) 65 matches (65 - 13T) 2003: [G(R), Sm(R), NZ3(R)]. 2004: I1, 2, W1, PI, NZ1, A1, NZ2, A2, W2, I3, E. 2005: F1, 2, A1, 2(R), 3(R), NZ1, A4, NZ2, Arg(R), W, F3. 2006: S1, 2. 2007: E1, 2, A1, NZ1, N, S, [Sm, US, Fiji, Arg, E4.], W. 2008: It(R), NZ1, 2, A1, NZ3, A2, 3, W3, S, E. 2009: BI2, A2(R), 2(R), NZ3, F, I. 2010: F, It2, NZ1, 2, A1, NZ3, A2, 3.

99 Burger, WAG (Bingo) b 12/08/1883 d 08/08/1963 - Border - 4 Tests (-) 23 matches (3 - 1T) 1906: S, I, W. 1910: BI2.

91 Burmeister, ARD (Arthur) b 01/05/1885 d 25/05/1952 - WP - No Tests

- 10 matches (-) Toured BI, I & F. 1906/07.

C

395 Carelse, G (Gawie) b 21/07/1941 d 03/08/2002 - EP - 14 Tests (-) 30 matches (5 - 1T, 1C) 1964: W, F. 1965: I, S. 1967: F1, 2, 3. 1968: F1, 2. 1969: A1, 2, 3, 4, S.

456 Carlson, RA (Ray) b 02/10/1948 - WP - 1 Test (-) 1 match (-) 1972: E.

83 Carolin, HW (Paddy) b 10/04/1881 d 15/03/1967 - WP - 3 Tests (-) 18 matches (73 - 6T, 15C, 3P, 4D) 1903: BI3. 1906: S*, I.

734 Carstens, PD (Deon) b 03/06/1979 - Natal - 9 Tests (-) 10 matches (-) 2002: S, E. 2006: E1(t+R), 2(R). 2007: E1, 2(t+R), Sm1(R). 2009: BI1(R), 3(t).

9 Castens, HH (Herbert) b 23/11/1864 d 18/10/1929 - WP - 1 Test (-) 1 match (-) 1891: BI1*.

768 Chavhanga, T (Tonderai) b 24/12/1983 - WP - 4 Tests (30 - 6T) 4 matches (30 - 6T) 2005: U. 2007: NZ2(R). 2008: W1, 2.

28 Chignell, TW (Charlie) b 28/04/1866 d 17/10/1952 - WP - 1 Test (-) 1 match (-) 1891: BI3.

384 Cilliers, GD (Gert) b 28/07/1940 d 26/01/1986 - OFS - 3 Tests (3 - 1T) 6 matches (3 - 1T) 1963: A1, 3, 4.

637 Cilliers, NV (Vlok) b 26/03/1968 - WP - 1 Test (-) 1 match (-) 1996: NZ3(t).

319 Claassen, JT (Johan) b 23/09/1929 - WTvl - 28 Tests (10 - 2T, 2C) 56 matches (16 - 4T, 2C) 1955: BI1, 2, 3, 4. 1956: A1, 2, NZ1, 2, 3, 4. 1958: F1*, 2*. 1960: S, NZ1, 2, 3, W, I. 1961: E, S, F, I*, A1*, 2*. 1962: BI1*, 2*, 3*, 4*.

519 Claassen, W (Wynand) b 16/01/1951 - Natal - 7 Tests (-) 13 matches (8 - 2T) 1981: I1*, 2*, NZ2*, 3*, US*. 1982: S. Am 1*, 2*.

611 Claassens, JP (Jannie) b 30/06/1969 - NTvl - No Tests - 8 matches (15 - 3T) Toured NZ. 1994 and W, S & I. 1994.

765 Claassens, M (Michael) b 28/10/1982 - FS - 8 Tests (-) 8 matches (-) 2004: W2(R), S(R), Arg(R). 2005: Arg(R), W, F3. 2007: A2(R), NZ2(R).

240 Clark, WHG (Ginger) b 22/09/1906 d 20/09/1999 - Tvl - 1 Test (-) 1 match (-) 1933: A3.

157 Clarkson, WA (Wally) b 08/07/1896 d 03/06/1973 - Natal - 3 Tests (-) 11 matches (9 - 3T) 1921: NZ1, 2. 1924: BI1.

61 Cloete, HA (Patats) b 15/06/1873 d 29/03/1959 - WP - 1 Test (-) 1 match (-) 1896: BI4.

441 Cockrell, CH (Charlie) b 10/01/1939 - WP - 3 Tests (-) 10 matches (-) 1969: S. 1970: I, W.

486 Cockrell, RJ (Robert) b 04/04/1950 d 26/05/2000 - WP - 11 Tests (4 - 1T) 25 matches (8 - 2T) 1974: F1, 2. 1975: F1, 2.

1976: NZ1, 2. 1977: WT. 1981: NZ1, 2(R), 3, US.

513 Cocks, TMD (Tim) b 29/09/1952 - Natal - No Tests - 3 matches (8 - 2T) Toured S. Am. 1980.

730 Coetzee, D (Danie) b 02/09/1977 - BB - 15 Tests (5 - 1T) 15 matches (5 - 1T) 2002: Sm. 2003: S1, 2, Arg, A1, NZ1, A2, NZ2, [U, E, Sm(R), NZ3(R)]. 2004: S(R), Arg(R). 2006: A1(R).

463 Coetzee, JHH (Boland) b 20/01/1945 - WP - 6 Tests (-) 6 matches (-) 1974: BI1. 1975: F2(R). 1976: NZ1, 2, 3, 4.

724 Conradie, JHJ (Bolla) b 24/02/1978 - WP - 18 Tests (13 - 2T, 1D) 18 matches (13 - 2T, 1D) 2002: W1, 2, Arg(R), Sm, NZ1, A1, NZ2(R), A2(R), S, E. 2004: W1(R), PI, NZ2, A2. 2005: Arg. 2008: W1, 2(R), NZ1(R).

404 Conradie, SC (Faan) b 27/06/1942 d 21/10/1992 - WP - No Tests - No matches Toured I & S. 1965.

41 Cope, DG (Davie) b 14/08/1877 d 16/08/1898 - Tvl - 1 Test (2 - 1C) 1 match (2 - 1C) 1896: BI2.

53 Cotty, WAH (Bill) b 24/02/1875 d 06/09/1928 - GW - 1 Test (-) 1 match (-) 1896: BI3.

81 Crampton, G (George) b 30/03/1875 d 27/12/1946 - GW - 1 Test (-) 1 match (-) 1903: BI2.

219 Craven, DH (Danie) b 11/10/1910 d 04/01/1993 - WP - 16 Tests (6 - 2T) 38 matches (24 - 8T) 1931: W, I. 1932: S. 1933: A1, 2, 3, 4, 5. 1937: A1, 2, NZ1*, 2, 3. 1938: BI1*, 2*, 3*.

406 Cronjé, CJC (Kerneels) b 16/04/1940 d 13/05/2009 - ETvl - No Tests - No matches Toured A & NZ. 1965.

750 Cronjé, G (Geo) b 23/07/1980 - BB - 3 Tests (-) 3 matches (-) 2003: NZ. 2004: I2(R), W1(R).

758 Cronjé, J (Jacques) b 04/08/1982 - BB - 32 Tests (20 - 4T) 33 matches (25 - 5T) 2004: I1, 2, W1, PI, NZ1, A1, NZ2(R), A2(t+R), S(t+R), Arg. 2005: U, F1, 2, A1, 3, NZ1(R), 2(t), Arg, W, F3. 2006: S2(R), F(R), A1(t+R), NZ2, A2, A3(R), I(R), E1. 2007: A2(R), NZ2, N.

447 Cronje, PA (Peter) b 21/09/1949 - Tvl - 7 Tests (10 - 3T) 15 matches (16 - 5T) 1971: F1, 2, A1, 2, 3. 1974: BI3, 4.

144 Cronjé, SN (Fanie) b 24/04/1886 d 20/09/1972 - Tvl - No Tests - 7 matches (3 - 1T) Toured BI, I & F. 1912/13.

51 Crosby, JH (Jim) b 03/07/1873 d 25/02/1960 - Tvl - 1 Test (-) 1 match (-) 1896: BI2.

116 Crosby, NJ (Nic) b 21/08/1883 d 14/07/1938 - Tvl - 2 Tests (-) 2 matches (-)

SPRINGBOK RECORDS

1910: BI1, 3.

78 **Currie, C** (Clem) b 21/10/1880 d 12/10/1937 - GW - 1 Test (-) 1 match (-) 1903: BI2.

D

235 **D'Alton, G** (George) b 17/08/1908 d 22/11/1975 - WP - 1 Test (-) 1 match (-) 1933: A1.

614 **Dalton, J** (James) b 16/08/1972 - Tvl - 43 Tests (25 - 5T) 58 matches (25 - 5T) 1994: Arg1(R). 1995: [A, C], W, It, E. 1996: NZ2(R), 3, Arg1, 2, F1, 2, W. 1997: T(R), BI3, NZ2, A2, It, F1, 2, E, S. 1998: I1, 2, W1, E1, A1, NZ1, 2, A2, W2, S, I3, E2. 2002: W1, 2, Arg, NZ1, A1, NZ2, A2, F, E.

197 **Daneel, GM** (George) b 29/08/1904 d 19/10/2004 - WP - 8 Tests (6 - 2T) 20 matches (9 - 3T) 1928: NZ1, 2, 3, 4. 1931: W, I. 1932: E, S.

102 **Daneel, HJ** (Pinkie) b 04/05/1882 d 07/01/1947 - WP - 4 Tests (-) 15 matches (3 - 1T) 1906: S, I, W, E.

823 **Daniel, KR** (Keegan) b 05/03/1985 - KZN - 1 Test (-) 2 matches (-) 2010: I(R).

302 **Dannhauser, G** (Gert) b 16/04/1918 d 07/10/1983 - Tvl - No Tests - 12 matches (-) Toured BI, I & F. 1951/52.

706 **Davids, Q** (Quinton) b 17/08/1975 - WP - 9 Tests (-) 13 matches (-) 2002: W2, Arg(R), Sm(R). 2003: Arg. 2004: I1(R), 2, W1, PI(t+R), NZ1(R).

700 **Davidson, CD** (Craig) b 23/02/1977 - Natal - 5 Tests (10 - 2T) 8 matches (10 - 2T) 2002: W2(R), Arg. 2003: Arg, NZ1(R), A2.

119 **Davison, PM** (Max) b 05/06/1885 d 14/11/1931 - EP - 1 Test (-) 1 match (-) 1910: BI1.

653 **De Beer, JH** (Jannie) b 22/04/1971 - FS - 13 Tests (181 - 2T, 33C, 27P, 8D) 14 matches (188 - 3T, 34C, 27P, 8D) 1997: BI3, NZ1, A1, NZ2, A2, F2(R), S. 1999: A2, [S, Sp, U, E, A3].

475 **De Bruyn, J** (Johan) b 12/10/1948 - OFS - 1 Test (-) 4 matches (-) 1974: BI3.

205 **De Jongh, HPK** (Manus) b 10/10/1902 d 05/09/1974 - WP - 1 Test (3 - 1T) 1 match (3 - 1T) 1928: NZ3.

806 **De Jongh, JL** (Juan) b 15/04/1988 - WP - 6 Tests (5 - 1T) 8 matches (10 - 2T) 2010: W1, F(R), It1(R), 2, A1(R), NZ3.

440 **De Klerk, IJ** (Sakkie) b 28/10/1938 - Tvl - 3 Tests (-) 9 matches (-) 1969: E. 1970: I, W.

464 **De Klerk, KBH** (Kevin) b 06/06/1950 - Tvl - 13 Tests (-) 18 matches (4 - 1T) 1974: BI1, 2, 3(R). 1975: F1, 2. 1976: NZ2(R), 3, 4. 1980: S. Am1, 2, BI2. 1981: I1, 2.

16 **De Kock, AN** (Arthur) b 11/01/1866 d 06/07/1957 - GW - 1 Test (-) 1 match (-) 1891: BI2.

722 **De Kock, D** (Deon) b 11/05/1975 - GF - 2 Tests (-) 2 matches (-) 2001: It2(R), US.

160 **De Kock, JS** (Sas) b 17/08/1896 d 04/11/1972 - WP - 2 Tests (-) 7 matches (6 - 2T) 1921: NZ3. 1924: BI3.

717 **De Kock, NA** (Neil) b 20/11/1978 - WP - 10 Tests (10 - 2T) 10 matches (10 - 2T) 2001: It1. 2002: Sm(R), NZ1(R), 2, A2, F. 2003: [U(R), G, Sm(R), NZ3(R)].

75 **De Melker, SC** (Syd) b 31/03/1884 d 01/11/1953 - GW - 2 Tests (-) 14 matches (9 - 3T) 1903: BI2. 1906: E.

334 **De Nysschen, CJ** (Chris) b 31/01/1936 - Natal - No Tests - 10 matches (3 - 1T) Toured A & NZ. 1956.

112 **De Villiers, DI** (Dirkie) b 20/07/1889 d 01/10/1958 - Tvl - 3 Tests (3 - 1T) 3 matches (3 - 1T) 1910: BI1, 2, 3.

382 **De Villiers, DJ** (Dawie) b 10/07/1940 - WP - 25 Tests (9 - 3T) 53 matches (29 - 5T, 4C, 2P) 1962: BI2, 3. 1965: I, NZ1*, 3*, 4*. 1967: F1*, 2*, 3*, 4*. 1968: BI1*, 2*, 3*, 4*, F1*, 2*. 1969: A1*, 4*, E*. 1970: I*, W*, NZ1*, 2*, 3*, 4*.

95 **De Villiers, HA** (Boy) b 05/01/1883 d 09/11/1944 - WP - 3 Tests (-) 18 matches (22 - 6T, 1D) 1906: S, W, E.

418 **De Villiers, HO** (HO) b 10/03/1945 - WP - 14 Tests (26 - 7C, 4P) 29 matches (80 - 2T, 22C, 10P) 1967: F1, 2, 3, 4. 1968: F1, 2. 1969: A1, 2, 3, 4, S, E. 1970: I, W.

151 **De Villiers, IB** (IB) b 10/03/1892 d 09/01/1966 - Tvl - No Tests - 10 matches (35 - 10C, 5P) Toured A & NZ. 1921.

735 **De Villiers, J** (Jean) b 24/02/1981 - WP - 67 Tests (95 - 19T) 67 matches (95 - 19T) 2002: F. 2004: PI, NZ1, A1, NZ2, A2, W2(R), E. 2005: U, F1, 2, A1, 2, 3, NZ1, A4, NZ2, Arg, W, F3. 2006: S1, NZ2, 3, A3, I, E1, 2. 2007: E1, 2, A1, NZ1, N, [Sm,]. 2008: W1, 2, It, NZ1, 2, A1Arg, NZ3, A2, 3, W3, S, E. 2009: BI1, 2, NZ1, 2, A1, 2, 3, NZ1, A4. 2010: F(t+R), It1, 2, NZ1, 2, 3, A2, 3, I, W2, S, E.

195 **De Villiers, P du P** (Pierie) b 14/06/1905 d 14/11/1975 - WP - 8 Tests (-) 28 matches (6 - 2T) 1928: NZ1, 3, 4. 1932: E. 1933: A4. 1937: A1, 2, NZ1.

400 **De Vos, DJJ** (Dirkie) b 08/04/1941 - WP - 3 Tests (-) 18 matches (9 - 3T) 1965: S. 1969: A3, S.

423 **De Waal, AN** (Albie) b 04/02/1942 - WP - 4 Tests (-) 4 matches (-) 1967: F1, 2, 3, 4.

60 **De Waal, PJ** (Paul) b 02/06/1875 d 18/05/1945 - WP - 1 Test (-) 1 match (-) 1896: BI4.

429 **De Wet, AE** (André) b 01/08/1946 - WP - 3 Tests (-) 11 matches (-) 1969: A3, 4, E.

261 **De Wet, PJ** (Piet) b 12/03/1917 d

18/10/1968 - WP - 3 Tests (-) 3 matches (-) 1938: BI1, 2, 3.

335 **De Wilzem, CJ** (Chris) b 14/10/1932 d 02/03/2006 - OFS - No Tests - 16 matches (3 - 1T) Toured A & NZ. 1956.

145 **Delaney, ETA** (Ned) b 12/06/1892 d 18/10/1918 - GW - No Tests - 13 matches (-) Toured BI, I & F. 1912/13.

662 **Delport, GM** (Thinus) b 02/02/1975 - GL - 18 Tests (15 - 3T) 20 matches (15 - 3T) 2000: C(R), E1(t+R), A1, NZ1, A2, NZ2, A3, Arg, I, W. 2001: F2, It1. 2003: A1, NZ2, [U, E, Sm, NZ3].

297 **Delport, WH** (Willa) b 05/11/1920 d 14/10/1984 - EP - 9 Tests (6 - 2T) 21 matches (12 - 4T) 1951: S, I, W. 1952: E, F. 1953: A1, 2, 3, 4.

50 **Devenish, CE** (Charles) b 13/01/1874 d 11/01/1922 - GW - 1 Test (-) 1 match (-) 1896: BI2.

10 **Devenish, GE** (Tiger) b 27/07/1870 d 23/03/1930 - Tvl - 1 Test (-) 1 match (-) 1891: BI1.

45 **Devenish, G St L** (Long George) b 11/05/1871 d 01/02/1943 - Tvl - 1 Test (-) 1 match (-) 1896: BI2.

189 **Devine, D** (Dauncie) b 20/03/1904 d 22/09/1965 - Tvl - 2 Tests (-) 2 matches (-) 1924: BI3. 1928: NZ2.

814 **Deysel, JR** (Jean) b 05/03/1985 - KZN - 1 Test (-) - 3 matches (-) 2009: It(R).

300 **Dinkelmann, EE** (Ernst) b 14/05/1927 d 22/10/2010 - NTvl - 6 Tests (6 - 2T) 21 matches (9 - 3T) 1951: S, I. 1952: E, F. 1953: A1, 2.

597 **Dirks, CA** (Chris) b 23/05/1967 - Tvl - No Tests - 2 matches (10 - 2T) Toured Arg. 1993.

393 **Dirksen, CW** (Corra) b 22/01/1938 - NTvl - 10 Tests (9 - 3T) 11 matches (9 - 3T) 1963: A4. 1964: W. 1965: I, S. 1967: F1, 2, 3, 4. 1968: BI1, 2.

713 **Dixon, PJ** (Pieter) b 17/10/1977 - WP - No Tests - 1 match (-) Toured E. 2000.

762 **Dlulane, VT** (Tim) b 05/06/1981 - Mpu - 1 Test (-) 1 match (-) 2004: W2(R).

67 **Dobbin, FJ** (Uncle) b 10/10/1879 d 05/02/1950 - GW - 9 Tests (3 - 1T) 36 matches (21 - 7T) 1903: BI1, 2. 1906: S, W, E. 1910: BI1. 1912: S*, I, W.

202 **Dobie, JAR** (John) b 04/08/1905 d 12/08/1989 - Tvl - 1 Test (-) 1 match (-) 1928: NZ2.

230 **Dold, JB** (Jack) b 03/01/1902 d 17/09/1968 - EP - No Tests - 10 matches (3 - 1T) Toured BI & I. 1931/32.

54 **Dormehl, PJ** (Pieter) b 04/11/1872 d 01/09/1958 - WP - 2 Tests (-) 2 matches (-) 1896: BI3, 4.

40 **Douglass, FW** (Frank) b 15/07/1875

SPRINGBOK.

d Post 1920 - EP - 1 Test (-) 1 match (-) 1896: BI1.

601 Drotské, AE (Naka) b 15/03/1971 - OFS - 26 Tests (15 - 3T) 34 matches (20 - 4T) 1993: Arg(2). 1995: [WS2(R)]. 1996: A1(R). 1997: T, BI1, 2, 3(R), NZ1, A1, NZ2(R). 1998: I2(R), W1(R), I3(R). 1999: It1, 2, W, NZ1, A1, NZ2, A2, [S, Sp(R), U, E, A3, NZ3].

321 Dryburgh, RG (Roy) b 01/11/1929 d 10/05/2000 - WP - 8 Tests (28 - 3T, 5C, 3P) 20 matches (116 - 15T, 13C, 15P) 1955: BI2, 3, 4. 1956: A2, NZ1, 4. 1960: NZ1*, 2*.

787 Du Plessis, BW (Bismarck) b 22/05/1984 - KZN - 36 Tests (25 - 5T) 38 matches (25 - 5T) 2007: A2(t+R), NZ2, N(R), S(R), [Sm(R), E3(R), US(R), Arg(R), E4(t).], W(R). 2008: W1(R), 2(R), It, NZ1(R), 2, Arg, NZ3, A2, 3, W3, S. 2009: BI1, 2, 3(R), NZ1, 2, A1, 2, 3, NZ3, F, I(R). 2010: I, W2, S, E.

523 Du Plessis, CJ (Carel) b 24/06/1960 - WP - 12 Tests (16 - 4T) 22 matches (40 - 10T) 1982: S. Am1, 2. 1984: E1, 2, S. Am&Sp1, 2. 1986: NZC1, 2, 3, 4. 1989: WT1, 2.

496 Du Plessis, DC (Daan) b 09/08/1948 - NTvl - 2 Tests (-) 2 matches (-) 1977: WT. 1980: S. Am2.

275 Du Plessis, F (Felix) b 24/11/1919 d 01/05/1978 - Tvl - 3 Tests (-) 3 matches (-) 1949: NZ1*, 2*, 3*.

788 Du Plessis, JN (Jannie) b 16/11/1982 - FS - 24 Tests (5 - 1T) 26 matches (5 - 1T) 2007: A2, NZ2, [Fiji, Arg(t+R).], W. 2008: A3(R), E. 2009: NZ1(t), 2(R), A1(R), 2(R), NZ3(R). 2010: W1(R), F(R), It1, 2, NZ1, 3, A2, 3, I, W2, S, E.

455 Du Plessis, M (Morné) b 21/10/1949 - WP - 22 Tests (12 - 3T) 32 matches (18 - 5T) 1971: A1, 2, 3. 1974: BI1, 2, F1, 2. 1975: F1*, 2*. 1976: NZ1*, 2*, 3*, 4*. 1977: WT*. 1980: S. Am1*, 2*, BI1*, 2*, 3*, 4*, S. Am4*, F*.

537 Du Plessis, MJ (Michael) b 04/11/1958 - WP - 8 Tests (7 - 1T, 1D) 8 matches (7 - 1T, 1D) 1984: S. Am&Sp1, 2. 1986: NZC1, 2, 3, 4. 1989: WT1, 2.

166 Du Plessis, NJ (Nic) b 04/12/1894 d 10/08/1949 - WTvl - 5 Tests (-) 20 matches (-) 1921: NZ2, 3. 1924: BI1, 2, 3.

458 Du Plessis, PG (Piet) b 23/07/1947 - NTvl - 1 Test (-) 1 match (-) 1972: E.

503 Du Plessis, TD (Tommy) b 29/06/1953 - NTvl - 2 Tests (4 - 1T) 5 matches (12 - 3T) 1980: S. Am1, 2.

500 Du Plessis, W (Willie) b 04/09/1955 - WP - 14 Tests (12 - 3T) 20 matches (28 - 7T) 1980: S. Am1, 2, BI1, 2, 3, 4, S. Am3, 4, F. 1981: NZ1, 2, 3. 1982: S. Am1, 2.

317 Du Plooy, AJJ (Amos) b 31/05/1921 d 17/05/1980 - EP - 1 Test (-) 1 match (-) 1955: BI1.

375 Du Preez, FCH (Frik) b 28/11/1935 - NTvl - 38 Tests (11 - 1T, 1C, 2P) 87 matches (87 - 12T, 15C, 7P) 1961: E, S, A1, 2. 1962: BI1, 2, 3, 4. 1963: A1. 1964: W, F. 1965: A1, 2, NZ1, 2, 3, 4. 1967: F4. 1968: BI1, 2, 3, 4, F1, 2. 1969: A1, 2, S. 1970: I, W, NZ1, 2, 3, 4. 1971: F1, 2, A1, 2, 3.

701 Du Preez, GJD (De 12/06/1975 - GL - 2 Tests (5 - 1T) 5 matches (10 - 2T) 2002: Sm(R), A1(R).

327 Du Preez, JGH (Jan) b 06/10/1930 - WP - 1 Test (-) 6 matches (15 - 5T) 1956: NZ1.

757 Du Preez, PF (Fourie) b 24/03/1982 - BB - 55 Tests (65 - 13T) 55 matches (65 - 13T) 2004: I1, 2, W1, PI(R), NZ1, A1, NZ2(R), A2(R), W2, I3, E, S, Arg. 2005: U(R), F1, 2(R), A1(R)2(R), 3, NZ1(R), A4(R). 2006: S1, 2, F, A1(R), NZ1, A2, NZ2, 3, A3. 2007: N, S, [Sm, E3, US, Fiji, Arg, E4.]. 2008: Arg(R), NZ3, A2, 3, W3. 2009: BI1, 2, 3, NZ1, 2, A1, 2, 3, NZ3, F, It, I.

562 Du Preez, RJ (Robert) b 19/07/1963 - Natal - 7 Tests (-) 15 matches (45 - 9T) 1992: NZ, A. 1993: F1, 2, A1, 2, 3.

792 Du Preez, WH (Wian) b 30/10/1982 - FS - 1 Test (-) 2 matches (-) 2009: It.

281 Du Rand, JA (Salty) b 16/01/1926 d 27/02/1979 - Rhodesia - 21 Tests (12 - 4T) 47 matches (27 - 9T) 1949: NZ2, 3. 1951: S, I, W. 1952: E, F. 1953: A1, 2, 3, 4. 1955: BI1, 2, 3, 4. 1956: A1, 2, NZ1*, 2, 3, 4.

619 Du Randt, JP (Os) b 08/09/1972 - OFS - 80 Tests (25 - 5T) 85 matches (25 - 5T) 1994: Arg1, 2, S, W. 1995: WS1, [A, WS2, F, NZ]. 1996: Fj, A1, NZ1, A2, NZ2, 3, 4. 1997: T, BI1, 2, 3, NZ1, A1, NZ2, A2, It, F1, 2, E, S. 1999: NZ1, A1, NZ2, A2, [S, Sp(R), U, E, A3, NZ3]. 2004: I1, 2, W1, PI, NZ1, A1, NZ2, A2, W2, I3, E, S(R), Arg(R). 2005: U(R), F1, A1, NZ1, A4, NZ2, Arg, W(R), F3. 2006: S1, 2, F, A1, NZ1, A2, NZ2, 3, A3. 2007: Sm1, NZ1, N, S, [Sm, E3, US, Fiji, Arg, E4.].

208 Du Toit, AF (AF) b 12/05/1899 d 09/09/1988 - WP - 2 Tests (-) 2 matches (-) 1928: NZ3, 4.

253 Du Toit, BA (Ben) b 10/11/1912 d 25/01/1989 - Tvl - 3 Tests (3 - 1T) 10 matches (9 - 3T) 1938: BI1, 2, 3.

667 Du Toit, GS (Gaffie) b 24/03/1976 - GW - 14 Tests (108 - 5T, 25C, 11P) 23 matches (153 - 10T, 29C, 15P) 1998: I1. 1999: It1, 2, W(R), NZ1, 2. 2004: I1, W1(R), A1(R), S(R), Arg. 2006: S1(R), 2(R), F(R).

279 Du Toit, PA (Fonnie) b 13/03/1920 d 21/07/2001 - NTvl - 8 Tests (6 - 2T) 25

matches (9 - 3T) 1949: NZ2, 3, 4. 1951: S, I, W. 1952: E, F.

516 Du Toit, PG (Hempies) b 23/08/1953 - WP - 5 Tests (-) 16 matches (8 - 2T) 1981: NZ1. 1982: S. Am1, 2. 1984: E1, 2.

332 Du Toit, PS (Piet) b 09/10/1935 d 26/02/1997 - WP - 14 Tests (-) 49 matches (9 - 3T) 1958: F1, 2. 1960: NZ1, 2, 3, 4, W, I. 1961: E, S, F, I, A1, 2.

220 Du Toit, SR (Schalk) b 08/08/1902 d 18/11/1965 - WP - No Tests - 12 matches (3 - 1T) Toured BI & I. 1931/32.

1 Duff, BR (Ben) b 16/10/1867 d 25/06/1943 - WP - 3 Tests (-) 3 matches (-) 1891: BI1, 2, 3.

194 Duffy, BAA (Bernie) b 17/11/1905 d 16/03/1958 - Border - 1 Test (-) 1 match (-) 1928: NZ1.

430 Durand, PJ (Paul) b 21/01/1946 d ??/??/?? - WTvl - No Tests - 2 matches (-) Toured BI & I. 1969/70.

265 Duvenage, FP (Floors) b 06/11/1917 d 16/09/1999 - GW - 2 Tests (-) 2 matches (-) 1949: NZ1, 3.

E

499 Edwards, P (Pierre) b 23/05/1953 - NTvl - 2 Tests (-) 2 matches (-) 1980: S. Am1, 2.

415 Ellis, JH (Jan) b 05/01/1942 - SWA - 38 Tests (21 - 7T) 74 matches (97 - 32T) 1965: NZ1, 2, 3, 4. 1967: F1, 2, 3, 4. 1968: BI1, 2, 3, 4, F1, 2. 1969: A1, 2, 3, 4, S. 1970: I, W, NZ1, 2, 3, 4. 1971: F1, 2, A1, 2, 3. 1972: E. 1974: BI1, 2, 3, 4, F1, 2. 1976: NZ1.

165 Ellis, MC (Mervyn) b 16/09/1892 d 24/03/1959 - Tvl - 6 Tests (-) 20 matches (3 - 1T) 1921: NZ2, 3. 1924: BI1, 2, 3, 4.

656 Els, WW (Braam) b 01/11/1971 - FS - 1 Test (-) 3 matches (-) 1997: A2(R).

347 Engelbrecht, JP (Jannie) b 10/11/1938 - WP - 33 Tests (24 - 8T) 67 matches (132 - 44T) 1960: S, W, I. 1961: E, S, F, A1, 2. 1962: BI2, 3, 4. 1963: A2, 3. 1964: W, F. 1965: I, S, A1, 2, NZ1, 2, 3, 4. 1967: F1, 2, 3, 4. 1968: BI1, 2, F1, 2. 1969: A1, 2.

549 Erasmus, FS (Frans) b 19/06/1959 d 07/03/1998 - NTvl - 3 Tests (-) 3 matches (-) 1986: NZC3, 4. 1989: WT2.

649 Erasmus, J (Rassie) b 05/11/1972 - FS - 36 Tests (35 - 7T) 39 matches (35 - 7T) 1997: BI3, A2, It, F1, 2, S. 1998: I1, 2, W1, E1, A1, NZ2, A2, W2, S, I3, E2. 1999: It1, 2, W, A1*, NZ2, A2, [S, U, E, A3, NZ3]. 2000: C, E1, A1, NZ1, 2, A3. 2001: F1, 2.

692 Esterhuizen, G (Grant) b 28/04/1976 - GL - 7 Tests (-) 7 matches (-) 2000: NZ1(R), 2, A3, Arg, I, W(R), E3(t).

58 Etlinger, TE (Tommy) b 07/09/1872 d 23/02/1953 - WP - 1 Test (-) 1 match (-) 1896: BI4.

F

543 **Ferreira, C** (Christo) b 28/08/1960 - OFS - 2 Tests (-) 2 matches (-) 1986: NZC1, 2.

540 **Ferreira, PS** (Kulu) b 17/03/1959 - WP - 2 Tests (4 - 1T) 2 matches (4 - 1T) 1984: S. Am & Sp1, 2.

84 **Ferris, HH** (Hugh) b 06/12/1877 d 17/07/1929 - Tvl - 1 Test (-) 1 match (-) 1903: BI3.

674 **Fleck, RF** (Robbie) b 17/07/1975 - WP - 31 Tests (50 - 10T) 36 matches (65 - 13T) 1999: It1, 2, NZ1(R), A1, NZ2(R), A2, [S, U, E, A3, NZ3]. 2000: C, E1, 2, A1, NZ1, A2, NZ2, A3, Arg, I, W, E3. 2001: F1(R), 2, It1, NZ1, A1, 2. 2002: S, E.

784 **Floors, L** (Kabamba) b 15/11/1980 - FS - 1 Test (-) 1 match (-) 2006: E2.

42 **Forbes, HH** (Spanner) b 02/01/1873 d 17/09/1955 - Tvl - 1 Test (-) 1 match (-) 1896: BI2.

229 **Forrest, HM** (Skaap) b 17/11/1907 d 26/01/1989 - Tvl - No Tests - 7 matches (-) Toured BI & I. 1931/32.

780 **Fortuin, BA** (Bevin) b 06/02/1979 - FS - 2 Tests (-) 3 matches (-) 2006: I. 2007: A2.

481 **Fourie, C** (Tossie) b 01/08/1950 - d 05/05/1997 - EP - 4 Tests (10 - 1T, 2P) 9 matches (14 - 2T, 2P) 1974: F1, 2. 1975: F1, 2.

752 **Fourie, J** (Jaque) b 04/03/1983 - GL - 62 Tests (150 - 30T) 64 matches (150 - 30T) 2003: [U, G, Sm(R), NZ3(R)]. 2004: I2, E(R), S, Arg. 2005: U(R), F2(R), A1(R), 2, 3, NZ1, A4, NZ2, Arg, W, F3. 2006: S1, A1, NZ1, A2, NZ2, 3, A3. 2007: Sm1(R), A1, NZ1, N, S, [Sm, E3, US, Fiji, Arg, E4.], W. 2008: Arg(R), W3(R), S(R), E(R). 2009: BI1(R), 2(R), 3, NZ1, 2, A1, 2, 3, NZ3, F, It, I. 2010: W1, F, It2, NZ1, 2, A1, 2, 3.

476 **Fourie, TT** (Polla) b 10/07/1945 - SETvl - 1 Test (-) 5 matches (12 - 3T) 1974: BI3.

339 **Fourie, WL** (Loftie) b 23/07/1936 d 23/07/2001 - SWA - 2 Tests (3 - 1T) 2 matches (3 - 1T) 1958: F1, 2.

148 **Francis, JAJ** (Joe) b 24/01/1889 d 20/12/1924 - Tvl - 5 Tests (6 - 2T) 19 matches (9 - 3T) 1912: S, I, W. 1913: E, F.

218 **Francis, MG** (Tiny) b 26/08/1907 d 02/08/1961 - OFS - No Tests - 8 matches (18 - 1T, 4C, 1P, 1D) Toured BI & I. 1931/32.

469 **Frederickson, CA** (Dave) b 17/08/1950 - Tvl - 3 Tests (-) 3 matches (-) 1974: BI2. 1980: S. Am1, 2.

68 **Frew, A** (Alex) b 24/10/1877 d 29/04/1947 - Tvl - 1 Test (3 - 1T) 1 match (3 - 1T) 1903: BI1*.

492 **Froneman, DC** (Dirk) b 14/04/1954 - OFS - 1 Test (-) 1 match (-) 1977: WT.

234 **Froneman, IL** (Fronie) b 18/12/1907 d 11/08/1984 - Border - 1 Test (-) 1 match (-) 1933: A1.

294 **Fry, DJ** (Dennis) b 25/02/1926 d 25/02/2003 - WP - No Tests - 17 matches (12 - 4T) Toured BI, I & F. 1951/52.

303 **Fry, SP** (Stephen) b 14/07/1924 d 29/06/2002 - WP - 13 Tests (-) 28 matches (9 - 3T) 1951: S, I, W. 1952: E, F. 1953: A1, 2, 3, 4. 1955: BI1*, 2*, 3*, 4*.

567 **Fuls, HT** (Heinrich) b 08/03/1971 - Tvl - 8 Tests (-) 21 matches (5 - 1T) 1992: NZ(R). 1993: F1, 2, A1, 2, 3, Arg1, 2.

710 **Fynn, EE** (Etienne) b 14/12/1972 - Natal - 2 Tests (-) 4 matches (-) 2001: F1, It1(R).

638 **Fyvie, WS** (Wayne) b 28/03/1972 - Natal - 3 Tests (-) 8 matches (10 - 2T) 1996: NZ4(t), 5(R), Arg2(R).

233 **Gage, JH** (Jack) b 02/04/1907 d 30/06/1989 - OFS - 1 Test (-) 1 match (-) 1933: A1.

G

348 **Gainsford, JL** (John) b 04/08/1938 - WP - 33 Tests (24 - 8T) 71 matches (93 - 31T) 1960: S, NZ1, 2, 3, 4, W, I. 1961: E, S, F, A1, 2. 1962: BI1, 2, 3, 4. 1963: A1, 2, 3, 4. 1964: W, F. 1965: I, S, A1, 2, NZ1, 2, 3, 4. 1967: F1, 2, 3.

645 **Garvey, AC** (Adrian) b 25/06/1968 - Natal - 28 Tests (20 - 4T) 28 matches (20 - 4T) 1996: Arg1, 2, F1, 2, W. 1997: T, BI1, 2, 3(R), A1(t), It, F1, 2, E, S. 1998: I1, 2, W1, E1, A1, NZ1, 2, A2, W2, S, I3, E2. 1999: [Sp].

282 **Geel, PJ** (Flip) b 07/02/1914 d 12/06/1971 - OFS - 1 Test (-) 1 match (-) 1949: NZ3.

227 **Geere, V** (Manie) b 09/09/1905 d 25/10/1989 - Tvl - 5 Tests (-) 17 matches (-) 1933: A1, 2, 3, 4, 5.

270 **Geffin, AO** (Okey) b 28/05/1921 d 16/10/2004 - Tvl - 7 Tests (48 - 9C, 10P) 17 matches (121 - 1T, 26C, 22P) 1949: NZ1, 2, 3, 4. 1951: S, I, W.

564 **Geldenhuys, A** (Adri) b 11/07/1964 - EP - 4 Tests (-) 11 matches (-) 1992: NZ, A, F1, 2.

528 **Geldenhuys, SB** (Burger) b 18/05/1956 - NTvl - 7 Tests (4 - 1T) 15 matches (20 - 5T) 1981: NZ2, 3, US. 1982: S. Am1, 2. 1989: WT1, 2.

316 **Gentles, TA** (Tommy) b 31/05/1934 - WP - 6 Tests (-) 18 matches (9 - 3T) 1955: BI1, 2, 4. 1956: NZ2, 3. 1958: F2.

283 **Geraghty, EM** (Carrots) b 20/04/1927 - Border - 1 Test (-) 1 match (-) 1949: NZ4.

514 **Gerber, DM** (Danie) b 14/04/1958 - EP - 24 Tests (82 - 19T, 1C) 35 matches (120 - 28T, 1C) 1980: S. Am3, 4, F. 1981: I1, 2, NZ1, 2, 3, US. 1982: S. Am1, 2. 1984: E1,

2, S. Am&Sp1, 2. 1986: NZC1, 2, 3, 4. 1992: NZ, A, F1, 2, E.

709 **Gerber, HJ** (Hendrik) b 12/04/1976 - WP - 2 Tests (-) 6 matches (-) 2003: S1, 2.

337 **Gerber, MC** (Mickey) b 12/10/1935 d 07/10/2005 - EP - 3 Tests (8 - 4C) 3 matches (8 - 4C) 1958: F1, 2. 1960: S.

351 **Gericke, FW** (Mannetjies) b 08/06/1933 d 21/10/2010 - Tvl - 1 Test (3 - 1T) 1 match (3 - 1T) 1960: S.

465 **Germishuys, JS** (Gerrie) b 29/10/1949 - OFS - 20 Tests (48 - 12T) 29 matches (76 - 19T) 1974: BI2. 1976: NZ1, 2, 3, 4. 1977: WT. 1980: S. Am1, 2, BI1, 2, 3, 4, S. Am3, 4, F. 1981: I1, 2, NZ2, 3, US.

77 **Gibbs, EAH** (Bertie) b 25/08/1878 d 29/12/1952 - GW - 1 Test (-) 1 match (-) 1903: BI2.

641 **Gillingham, JW** (Joe) b 27/02/1974 - GL - No Tests - 7 matches (5 - 1T) Toured Arg, F & W. 1996 and It, F, E & S. 1997.

413 **Goosen, CP** (Piet) b 03/02/1937 - d 06/06/1991 - OFS - 1 Test (-) 13 matches (3 - 1T) 1965: NZ2.

37 **Gorton, HC** (Hubert) b 28/10/1871 d 11/01/1900 - Tvl - 1 Test (-) 1 match (-) 1896: BI1.

424 **Gould, RL** (Rodney) b 10/08/1942 - Natal - 4 Tests (3 - 1D) 7 matches (3 - 1D) 1968: BI1, 2, 3, 4.

789 **Grant, PJ** (Peter) b 15/08/1984 - WP - 5 Tests (-) 5 matches (-) 2007: A2(R), NZ2(R). 2008: W1(t+R), It(R), A1(R).

215 **Gray, BG** (Geoff) b 28/07/1909 d 04/08/1989 - WP - 4 Tests (-) 13 matches (12 - 4T) 1931: W. 1932: E, S. 1933: A5.

729 **Greeff, WW** (Werner) b 14/07/1977 - WP - 11 Tests (31 - 4T, 4C, 1D) 11 matches (31 - 4T, 4C, 1D) 2002: Arg(R), Sm, NZ1, A1, NZ2, A2, F, S, E. 2003: [U, G].

379 **Greenwood, CM** (Colin) b 25/01/1936 d 03/10/1999 - WP - 1 Test (6 - 2T) 1 match (6 - 2T) 1961: I.

422 **Greyling, PJF** (Piet) b 16/05/1942 - OFS - 25 Tests (15 - 5T) 43 matches (18 - 6T) 1967: F1, 2, 3, 4. 1968: BI1, F1, 2. 1969: A1, 2, 3, 4, NZ1. 1970: I, W, NZ1, 2, 3, 4. 1971: F1, 2, A1, 2, 3. 1972: E*.

478 **Grobler, CJ** (Kleintjie) b 24/08/1944 d 29/09/1999 - OFS - 3 Tests (4 - 1T) 7 matches (12 - 3T) 1974: BI4. 1975: F1, 2.

431 **Grobler, RN** (Rysmier) b 14/11/1946 d 26/05/1971 - NTvl - No Tests - 10 matches (9 - 3T) Toured BI & I. 1969/70.

5 **Guthrie, FEH** (Frank) b 03/11/1869 d 19/06/1954 - WP - 3 Tests (-) 3 matches (-) 1891: BI1, 3. 1896: BI1.

H

766 **Habana, BG** (Bryan) b 12/06/1983 - GL - 68 Tests (190 - 38T) 70 matches (190

SPRINGBOK.

- 38T) 2004: E(R), S, Arg. 2005: U, F1, 2, A1, 2, 3, NZ1, A4, NZ2, Arg, W, F3. 2006: S2, F, A1, NZ1, A2, NZ2, 3, I, E1, 2. 2007: E1, 2, S, [Sm, E3, T(R), US, Fiji, Arg, E4.], W. 2008: W1, 2, It, NZ1, 2, A1, NZ3, W3, S, E. 2009: BI1, 2, NZ1, 2, A1, 2, 3, NZ3, F, It, I. 2010: F, It1, 2, NZ1, 2, A1, NZ3, A2, 3, I, W2.

113 **Hahn, CHL** (Cocky) b 07/01/1886 - d 27/09/1948 - Tvl - 3 Tests (3 - 1T) 3 matches (3 - 1T) 1910: BI1, 2, 3.

714 **Hall, DB** (Dean) b 02/09/1977 - GL - 13 Tests (20 - 4T) 13 matches (20 - 4T) 2001: F1, 2, NZ1, A1, 2, NZ2, It2, E, US. 2002: Sm, NZ1, 2, A2.

720 **Halstead, TM** (Trevor) b 17/06/1976 - Natal - 6 Tests (15 - 3T) 6 matches (15 - 3T) 2001: F3, It2, E, US(R). 2003: S1, 2.

15 **Hamilton, GH** (George) b 30/04/1863 d 07/08/1901 - EP - 1 Test (-) 1 match (-) 1891: BI1.

333 **Hanekom, M v d S** (Melt) b 27/07/1931 d 1997/1998 - Boland - No Tests - 9 matches (9 - 3T) Toured A & NZ. 1956.

809 **Hargreaves, AJ** (Alistair) b 29/04/1986 - KZN - 2 Tests (-) 5 matches (-) 2010: W1(R), It1(R).

251 **Harris, TA** (Tony) b 27/08/1916 d 07/03/1993 - Tvl - 5 Tests (3 - 1T) 13 matches (16 - 4T, 1D) 1937: NZ2, 3. 1938: BI1, 2, 3.

24 **Hartley, AJ** (Jack) b 18/08/1873 d 15/05/1923 - WP - 1 Test (-) 1 match (-) 1891: BI3.

568 **Hattingh, H** (Drikus) b 21/02/1968 - NTvl - 5 Tests (-) 17 matches (20 - 4T) 1992: A(R), F2(R), E. 1994: Arg1, 2.

239 **Hattingh, LB** (Lappies) b 01/09/1903 d 16/10/1974 - OFS - 1 Test (-) 1 match (-) 1933: A2.

623 **Hattingh, SJ** (Ian) b 31/10/1964 - Tvl - No Tests - 7 matches (10 - 2T) Toured W, S & I. 1994.

22 **Heatlie, BH** (Fairy) b 25/04/1872 d 19/08/1951 - WP - 6 Tests (6 - 3C) 6 matches (6 - 3C) 1891: BI2, 3. 1896: BI1, 4*. 1903: BI1, 3*.

657 **Hendricks, M** (McNeil) b 10/07/1973 - Boland - 2 Tests (5 - 1T) 4 matches (5 - 1T) 1998: I2(R), W1(R).

559 **Hendriks, P** (Pieter) b 13/04/1970 - Tvl - 14 Tests (10 - 2T) 23 matches (30 - 6T) 1992: NZ, A. 1994: S, W. 1995: [A, R, C]. 1996: A1, NZ1, A2, NZ2, 3, 4, 5.

57 **Hepburn, TB** (Tommy) b 14/02/1872 d 13/09/1933 - WP - 1 Test (2 - 1C) 1 match (2 - 1C) 1896: BI4.

521 **Heunis, JW** (Johan) b 26/01/1958 - NTvl - 14 Tests (72 - 3T, 6C, 7P) 24 matches (72 - 3T, 9C, 14P) 1981: NZ3(R), US. 1982: S. Am1, 2. 1984: E1, 2, S. Am&Sp1, 2. 1986:

NZC1, 2, 3, 4. 1989: WT1, 2.

372 **Hill, RA** (Ronnie) b 20/12/1934 - Rhodesia - 7 Tests (-) 21 matches (18 - 6T) 1960: W, I. 1961: I, A1, 2. 1962: BI4. 1963: A3.

575 **Hills, WG** (Willie) b 26/01/1962 - NTvl - 6 Tests (-) 13 matches (-) 1992: F1, 2, E. 1993: F1, 2, A1.

96 **Hirsch, JG** (Jack) b 20/02/1883 d 26/02/1958 - EP - 2 Tests (-) 18 matches (37 - 11T, 1D) 1906: I. 1910: BI1.

86 **Hobson, TEC** (Tommy) b 26/03/1881 d 02/09/1937 - WP - 1 Test (-) 1 match (-) 1903: BI3.

307 **Hoffman, RS** (Steve) b 02/12/1931 d 15/05/1986 - Boland - 1 Test (-) 1 match (-) 1953: A3.

248 **Hofmeyr, SR** (Koffie) b 23/08/1912 d 06/01/1975 - WP - No Tests - 11 matches (17 - 3T, 2D) Toured A & NZ. 1937.

352 **Holton, DN** (Dougie) b 28/09/1932 d 12/04/1994 - EP - 1 Test (-) 4 matches (-) 1960: S.

590 **Honiball, HW** (Henry) b 01/12/1965 - Natal - 35 Tests (156 - 1T, 38C, 25P) 45 matches (191 - 1T, 45C, 32P) 1993: A3(R), Arg2. 1995: WS1(R). 1996: Fj, A1, NZ5, Arg1, 2, F1, 2, W. 1997: T, BI1, 2, 3(R), NZ1(R), A1(R), NZ2, A2, It, F1, 2, E. 1998: W1(R), E1, A1, NZ1, 2, A2, W2, S, I3, E2. 1999: [A3(R), NZ3].

356 **Hopwood, DJ** (Doug) b 03/06/1934 d 10/01/2002 - WP - 22 Tests (-) 53 matches (45 - 15T) 1960: S, NZ3, 4, W. 1961: E, S, F, I, A1, 2. 1962: BI1, 2, 3, 4. 1963: A1, 2, 4. 1964: W, F. 1965: S, NZ3, 4.

753 **Hougaard, DJ** (Derick) b 04/01/1983 - BB - 8 Tests (69 - 2T, 13C, 10P, 1D) 8 matches (69 - 2T, 13C, 10P, 1D) 2003: [U(R), E(R), G, Sm, NZ3]. 2007: Sm1, A2, NZ2.

807 **Hougaard, F** (Francois) b 06/04/1988 - BB - 8 Tests (-) 11 matches (-) 2009: It(R). 2010: A1(R), NZ3, A2, 3, W2(R), S, E(t).

330 **Howe, BF** (Pee-Wee) b 30/08/1932 - Border - 2 Tests (3 - 1T) 18 matches (9 - 3T) 1956: NZ1, 4.

118 **Howe-Browne, NRFG** (Noel) b 24/12/1884 d 03/04/1943 - WP - 3 Tests (-) 3 matches (-) 1910: BI1, 2, 3.

555 **Hugo, DP** (Niel) b 11/11/1958 - WP - 2 Tests (-) 2 matches (-) 1989: WT1, 2.

726 **Human, DCF** (Daan) b 03/04/1976 - WP - 4 Tests (-) 4 matches (-) 2002: W1, 2, Arg(R), Sm(R).

627 **Hurter, MH** (Marius) b 08/10/1970 - NTvl - 13 Tests (-) 18 matches (5 - 1T) 1995: [R, C], W. 1996: Fj, A1, NZ1, 2, 3, 4, 5. 1997: NZ1, 2, A2.

I

139 **Immelman, JH** (Jack) b 02/08/1888 d 21/07/1960 - WP - 1 Test (-) 13 match-

es (3 - 1T) 1913: F.

J

97 **Jackson, DC** (Mary) b 21/04/1885 d 17/09/1976 - WP - 3 Tests (-) 17 matches (29 - 7T, 4C) 1906: I, W, E.

80 **Jackson, JS** (Jack) b 01/10/1878 d 30/06/1954 - WP - 1 Test (-) 1 match (-) 1903: BI2.

721 **Jacobs, AA** (Adrian) b 14/08/1980 - GF - 32 Tests (35 - 7T) 33 matches (35 - 7T) 2001: It2(R), US. 2002: W1(R), Arg, Sm(R), NZ1(t+R), A1(R), F, S, E(R). 2008: W1, 2, NZ1, 2, Arg, NZ3, A2, 3, W3, S, E. 2009: BI1, 2, NZ2(R), A1(R), 2(R), 3(R), NZ3(R), F, It. 2010: I(R), E(R).

715 **James, AD** (Butch) b 08/01/1979 - Natal - 40 Tests (148 - 3T, 26C, 26P, 1D) 41 matches (153 - 3T, 27C, 27P, 1D) 2001: F1, 2, NZ1, A1, 2, NZ2. 2002: F(R), S, E. 2006: NZ1, A2, NZ2, 3(R), E1. 2007: E1, 2, A1, NZ1, N, S, [Sm, E3, US, Fiji, Arg, E4.]. 2008: W1, 2, NZ1, 2, A1, Arg, NZ3, A2, 3. 2010: It1, 2(R), NZ1(R), A1(R), 2(R).

436 **Janse van Rensburg, MC** (Martin) b . 29/12/1944 - Natal - No Tests - 6 matches (10 - 2C, 2P) Toured BI & I. 1969/70.

518 **Jansen, E** (Eben) b 05/06/1954 - OFS - 1 Test (-) 11 matches (16 - 4T) 1981: NZ1.

444 **Jansen, JS** (Joggie) b 05/02/1948 - OFS - 10 Tests (3 - 1T) 15 matches (18 - 6T) 1970: NZ1, 2, 3, 4. 1971: F1, 2, A1, 2, 3. 1972: E.

414 **Janson, A** (Andrew) b 29/05/1935 - WP - No Tests - 11 matches (24 - 8T) Toured A & NZ. 1965.

716 **Jantjes, CA** (Conrad) b 24/03/1980 - GL - 24 Tests (22 - 4T, C) 25 matches (22 - 4T, C) 2001: It1, A1, 2, NZ2, F3, It2, E, US. 2005: Arg, W. 2007: W(R). 2008: W1, 2, It, NZ1, 2(R), A1, Arg, NZ3(R), A2(R), 3(R), W3(R), S, E. 2009: BI1(R), NZ1(R), 2(R), A1(R), 2(R), NZ3(R). 2010: W1, F, It1, 2, NZ1, 2, 3(R).

819 **Jantjies, ET** (Elton) b 01/08/1990 - GL - No Tests - 1 match (5 - 1C,1P) Toured BI & I. 2010.

769 **Januarie, ER** (Ricky) b 01/02/1982 - GL - 47 Tests (25 - 5T) 50 matches (25 - 5T) 2005: U, F2, A1, 2, 3(R), NZ1, A4, NZ2. 2006: S1(R), 2(R), F(R), A1, I, E1, 2(R). E1, 2, Sm1, N(R), [Sm(R), T.], W. 2008: W2, It, NZ1, 2, A1, Arg, NZ3(R), A2(R), 3(R), W3(R), S, E. 2009: BI1(R), NZ1(R), 2(R), A1(R), 2(R), NZ3(R). 2010: W1, F, It1, 2, NZ1, 2, 3(R).

254 **Jennings, CB** (CB) b 16/08/1914 d 02/10/1989 - Border - 1 Test (-) 11 matches (9 - 3T) 1937: NZ1.

439 **Jennings, MW** (Mike) b 21/12/1946 - Boland - No Tests - 10 matches (6 - 2T) Toured BI & I. 1969/70.

377 **Johns, RG** (Bobby) b 21/02/1934 d

SPRINGBOK RECORDS

01/07/1990 - WP - No Tests - 1 match (-) Toured BI, I & F. 1960/61.

810 **Johnson, AF** (Ashley) b 16/05/1986 - FS - No Tests - 2 matches (-)˙ Toured F, It, I & E. 2009.

604 **Johnson, GK** (Gavin) b 17/10/1966 - Tvl - 7 Tests (86 - 5T, 14C, 11P) 17 matches (173 - 9T, 25C, 26P) 1993: Arg2. 1994: NZ3, Arg1. 1995: WS1, [R, C, WS2].

291 **Johnstone, PGA** (Paul) b 30/06/1930 d 22/04/1996 - WP - 9 Tests (11 - 2T, 1C, 1P) 35 matches (68 - 14T, 7C, 4P) 1951: S, I, W. 1952: E, F. 1956: A1, NZ1, 2, 4.

62 **Jones, CH** (Charlie) b 24/03/1880 d 06/03/1908 - Tvl - 2 Tests (-) 2 matches (-) 1903: BI1, 2.

30 **Jones, PST** (Percy) b 13/09/1876 d 08/03/1954 - WP - 3 Tests (3 - 1T) 3 matches (3 - 1T) 1896: BI1, 3, 4.

742 **Jordaan, N** (Norman) b 03/04/1975 - BB - 1 Test (-) 1 match (-) 2002: E(R).

271 **Jordaan, RP** (Jorrie) b 13/07/1920 d 22/09/1998 - NTvl - 4 Tests (-) 4 matches (-) 1949: NZ1, 2, 3, 4.

557 **Joubert, AJ** (André) b 15/04/1964 - OFS - 34 Tests (115 - 10T, 7C, 17P) 49 matches (258 - 18T, 39C, 30P) 1989: WT1(R). 1993: A3, Arg1. 1994: E1, 2, NZ1, 2(R), 3, Arg2, S, W. 1995: [A, C, WS2, F, NZ], W, It, E. 1996: Fj, A1, NZ1, 3, 4, 5, Arg1, 2, F1, 2, W. 1997: T, BI1, 2, A2.

711 **Joubert, MC** (Marius) b 10/07/1979 - Boland - 30 Tests (45 - 9T) 31 matches (45 - 9T) 2001: NZ1. 2002: W1, 2, Arg(R), Sm, NZ1, A1, NZ2, A2, F(R). 2003: S2, Arg, A1. 2004: I1, 2, W1, PI, NZ1, A1, NZ2, A2, W2, I3, E, S, Arg. 2005: U, F1, 2, A1.

110 **Joubert, SJ** (Steve) b 08/04/1887 - d 27/03/1939 - WP - 3 Tests (8 - 1T, 1C, 1P) 6 matches (20 - 1T, 4C, 2P, 1D) 1906: I, W, E.

689 **Julies, W** (Wayne) b 23/10/1978 - Boland - 11 Tests (10 - 2T) 12 matches (10 - 2T) 1999: [Sp]. 2004: I1, 2, W1, S, Arg. 2005: A2(R), 3(t). 2006: F(R). 2007: Sm1, [T.].

K

509 **Kahts, WJH** (Willie) b 20/02/1947 - NTvl - 11 Tests (4 - 1T) 15 matches (12 - 3T) 1980: BI1, 2, 3, S. Am3, 4, F. 1981: I1, 2, NZ2. 1982: S. Am1, 2.

344 **Kaminer, J** (Joe) b 25/01/1934 - Tvl - 1 Test (-) 1 match (-) 1958: F2.

791 **Kankowski, R** (Ryan) b 14/10/1985 - KZN - 17 Tests (5 - 1T) 19 matches (5 - 1T) 2007: W. 2008: W2(R), It, A1(R), W3(R), S(R), E(R). 2009: BI3, NZ3(R), F, It. 2010: W1(R), It1(R), NZ2(R), A1, 3(R), S.

675 **Kayser, DJ** (Deon) b 03/07/1970 - EP - 13 Tests (25 - 5T) 21 matches (30 - 6T) 1999: It2(R), A1(R), NZ2, A2, [S, Sp(R), U, E, A3]. 2001: It1(R), NZ1(R), A2(R),

NZ2(R).

599 **Kebble, GR** (Guy) b 02/05/1966 - Natal - 4 Tests (-) 12 matches (5 - 1T) 1993: Arg1, 2. 1994: NZ1(R), 2.

288 **Keevy, AC** (Jakkals) b 12/11/1917 d 09/02/1990 - ETvl - No Tests - 13 matches (10 - 2C, 2P) Toured BI, I & F. 1951/52.

55 **Kelly, EW** (Ted) b 23/10/1869 d 11/03/1949 - GW - 1 Test (-) 1 match (-) 1896: BI3.

669 **Kempson, RB** (Robbie) b 23/02/1974 - Natal - 37 Tests (5 - 1T) 38 matches (5 - 1T) 1998: I2(R), W1, E1, A1, NZ1, 2, A2, W2, S, I3, E2. 1999: It1, 2, W. 2000: C, E1, 2, A1, NZ1, A2, 3, Arg, I, W, E3. 2001: F1, 2(R), NZ1, A1, 2, NZ2. 2003: S1(R), 2(R), Arg, A1(R), NZ1(R), A2.

286 **Kenyon, BJ** (Basil) b 19/05/1918 d 09/05/1996 - Border - 1 Test (-) 6 matches (13 - 2T , 2C, 1P) 1949: NZ4*.

226 **Kipling, HG** (Bert) b 24/12/1903 d 13/09/1981 - GW - 9 Tests (-) 24 matches (-) 1931: W, I. 1932: E, S. 1933: A1, 2, 3, 4, 5.

804 **Kirchner, Z** (Zane) b 16/06/1984 - BB - 14 Tests (5 - 1T) 14 matches (5 - 1T) 2009: BI13, F, It, I. 2010: W1(R), F, It1, NZ1, 2, A1, I, W2(R), S, E.

306 **Kirkpatrick, AI** (Ian) b 25/07/1930 - GW - 13 Tests (-) 43 matches (18 - 6T) 1953: A2. 1956: NZ2. 1958: F1. 1960: S, NZ1, 2, 3, 4, W, I. 1961: E, S, F.

143 **Knight, AS** (Saturday) b 16/12/1885 d 01/07/1946 - Tvl - 5 Tests (-) 18 matches (3 - 1T) 1912: S, I, W. 1913: E, F.

553 **Knoetze, F** (Faffa) b 18/01/1963 - WP - 2 Tests (4 - 1T) 8 matches (14 - 3T) 1989: WT1, 2.

280 **Koch, AC** (Chris) b 21/09/1927 d 21/03/1986 - Boland - 22 Tests (15 - 5T) 46 matches (33 - 11T) 1949: NZ2, 3, 4. 1951: S, I, W. 1952: E, F. 1953: A1, 2, 4. 1955: BI1, 2, 3, 4. 1956: A1, NZ2, 3. 1958: F1, 2. 1960: NZ1, 2.

274 **Koch, HV** (Bubbles) b 13/06/1921 d 02/11/2003 - WP - 4 Tests (-) 4 matches (-) 1949: NZ1, 2, 3, 4.

693 **Koen, LJ** (Louis) b 07/07/1975 - GL - 15 Tests (145 - 23C, 31P, 2D) 15 matches (145 - 23C, 31P, 2D) 2000: A1. 2001: It2, E, US. 2003: S1, 2, Arg, A1, NZ1, A2, NZ2, [U, E, Sm(R), NZ3(R)].

420 **Kotzé, GJM** (Gert) b 12/08/1940 - WP - 4 Tests (-) 4 matches (-) 1967: F1, 2, 3, 4.

487 **Krantz, EFW** (Edrich) b 10/08/1954 - OFS - 2 Tests (4 - 1T) 11 matches (48 - 12T) 1976: NZ1. 1981: I1.

676 **Krige, CPJ** (Corné) b 21/03/1975 - WP - 39 Tests (10 - 2T) 43 matches (15 - 3T) 1999: It2*, W, NZ1. 2000: C(R), E1(R),

2, A1(R), NZ1, A2, NZ2, A3, Arg, I, W, E3. 2001: F1, 2, It1(R), A1(t+R), It2(R), E(R). 2002: W2, Arg*, Sm*, NZ1*, A1*, NZ2*, A2*, F*, S*, E*. 2003: Arg*, A1*, NZ1*, A2*, NZ2*. [E*, Sm*, NZ3*].

64 **Krige, JD** (Japie) b 05/07/1879 d 14/01/1961 - WP - 5 Tests (3 - 1T) 13 matches (12 - 4T) 1903: BI1, 3. 1906: S, I, W.

136 **Krige, WA** (Willie) b 02/12/1887 d 20/08/1961 - WP - No Tests - 9 matches (10 - 2T, 1D) Toured BI, I & F. 1912/13.

477 **Kritzinger, JL** (Klippies) b 01/03/1948 - Tvl - 7 Tests (4 - 1T) 12 matches (4 - 1T) 1974: BI3, 4, F1, 2. 1975: F1, 2. 1976: NZ4.

318 **Kroon, CM** (Colin) b 22/02/1931 d 13/11/1981 - EP - 1 Test (-) 1 match (-) 1955: BI1.

550 **Kruger, PE** (Piet) b 11/04/1958 - Tvl - 2 Tests (-) 2 matches (-) 1986: NZC3, 4.

596 **Kruger, RJ** (Ruben) b 30/03/1970 - OFS - 36 Tests (35 - 7T) 56 matches (105 - 21T) 1993: Arg1, 2. 1994: S, W. 1995: WS1, [A, R, WS2, F, NZ], W, It, E. 1996: Fj, A1, NZ1, A2, NZ2, 3, 4, 5, Arg1, 2, F1, 2, W. 1997: T, BI1, 2, NZ1, A1, NZ2. 1999: NZ2, A2(R), [Sp, NZ3(R)].

169 **Krüger, TL** (Theuns) b 17/06/1896 d 06/07/1957 - Tvl - 8 Tests (-) 21 matches (6 - 2T) 1921: NZ1, 2. 1924: BI1, 2, 3, 4. 1928: NZ1, 2.

828 **Kruger, W** (Werner) b 23/01/1985 - BB - No Tests - 1 match (-) Toured BI & I. 2010.

364 **Kuhn, SP** (Fanie) b 12/06/1935 - Tvl - 19 Tests (-) 37 matches (-) 1960: NZ3, 4, W, I. 1961: E, S, F, I, A1, 2. 1962: BI1, 2, 3, 4. 1963: A1, 2, 3. 1965: I, S.

191 **La Grange, JB** (Paul) b 25/05/1897 d 23/05/1971 - WP - 2 Tests (-) 2 matches (-) 1924: BI3, 4.

L

694 **Labuschagne, JJ** (Jannes) b 16/04/1976 - GL - 11 Tests (-) 11 matches (-) 2000: NZ1(R). 2002: W1, 2, Arg, NZ1, A1, NZ2, A2, F, S, E.

820 **Lambie, P** (Patrick) b 17/10/1990 -KZN - 4 Tests (2 - 1C) 5 matches (2 - 1C) 2010: I(R), W2(R), S(R), E(R).

46 **Larard, A** (Alf) b 30/12/1870 d 15/08/1936 - Tvl - 2 Tests (3 - 1T) 2 matches (3 - 1T) 1896: BI2, 4.

266 **Lategan, MT** (Tjol) b 29/09/1925 - WP - 11 Tests (9 - 3T) 26 matches (15 - 5T) 1949: NZ1, 2, 3, 4. 1951: S, I, W. 1952: E, F. 1953: A1, 2.

620 **Laubscher, TG** (Tommie) b 08/10/1963 d 26/05/2007 - WP - 6 Tests (-) 12 matches (-) 1994: Arg1, 2, S, W. 1995: It, E.

396 **Lawless, MJ** (Mike) b 17/09/1941 -

WP - 4 Tests (-) 15 matches (12 - 1T, 1P, 2D) 1964: F. 1969: E(R). 1970: I, W.

245 **Lawton, AD** (Dandy) b 21/08/1911 d 06/05/1967 - WP - No Tests - 5 matches (24 - 8T) Toured A & NZ. 1937.

600 **Le Roux, A-H** (Ollie) b 10/05/1973 - OFS - 54 Tests (5 - 1T) 68 matches (25 - 5T) 1994: E1. 1998: I1, 2, W1(R), E1(R), A1(R), NZ1(R), 2(R), A2(R), W2(R), S(R), I3(R), E2(t+R). 1999: Ir1(R), 2(R), W(R), NZ1(R), A1(R), NZ2(R), A2(R), [S(R), Sp, U(t+R), E(R), A3(R), NZ3(R)]. 2000: E1(t+R), 2(R), A1(R), 2(R), NZ2, A3(R), Arg(R), I(t), W(R), E3(R). 2001: F1(R), 2, It1, NZ1(R), A1(R), 2(R), NZ2(R), F3, It2, E, US(R). 2002: W1(R), 2(R), Arg, NZ1(R), A1(R), NZ2(R), A2(R).

572 **Le Roux, HP** (Hennie) b 10/07/1967 - Tvl - 27 Tests (34 - 4T, 1C, 4P) 51 matches (90 - 12T, 6C, 6P) 1993: F1, 2. 1994: E1, 2, NZ1, 2, 3, Arg2, S, W. 1995: WS1, [A, R, C(R), WS2, F, NZ], W, It, E. 1996: Fj, NZ2, Arg1, 2, F1, 2, W.

608 **Le Roux, JHS** (Johan) b 15/11/1961 - Tvl - 3 Tests (-) 7 matches (-) 1994: E2, NZ1, 2.

94 **Le Roux, JSR** (Japie) b 21/08/1882 d 04/03/1949 - WP - No Tests - 9 matches (30 - 10T) Toured BI, I & F. 1906/07.

510 **Le Roux, M** (Martiens) b 30/03/1951 d 14/10/2006 - OFS - 8 Tests (-) 12 matches (4 - 1T) 1980: BI1, 2, 3, 4, S. Am3, 4, F. 1981: I1.

103 **Le Roux, PA** (Pietie) b 22/01/1885 d 11/07/1954 - WP - 3 Tests (-) 16 matches (11 - 3T, 1C) 1906: I, W, E.

146 **Ledger, SH** (Sep) b 29/04/1889 d 30/01/1918 - GW - 4 Tests (3 - 1T) 15 matches (3 - 1T) 1912: S, I. 1913: E, F.

688 **Leonard, A** (Anton) b 31/05/1974 - SWD - 2 Tests (5 - 1T) 2 matches (5 - 1T) 1999: A1, [Sp].

794 **Liebenberg, CR** (Tiaan) b 18/12/1981 - WP - 0 Tests (-) 1 match (-) Toured I & E. 2007.

591 **Linee, M** (Tinus) b 23/08/1969 - WP - No Tests - 9 matches (10 - 2T) Toured A. 1993 and W, S & I. 1994.

12 **Little, EM** (Edward) b 01/11/1864 d ??/05/1945 - GW - 2 Tests (-) 2 matches (-) 1891: BI1, 3.

781 **Lobberts, H** (Hilton) b 11/06/1986 - BB - 2 Tests (-) 4 matches (-) 2006: E1(R). 2007: NZ2(R).

326 **Lochner, GP** (Butch) b 01/02/1931 d 27/08/2010 - WP - 9 Tests (6 - 2T) 22 matches (15 - 5T) 1955: BI3. 1956: A1, 2, NZ1, 2, 3, 4. 1958: F1, 2.

249 **Lochner, GP** (Flappie) b 11/01/1914 d 30/01/1996 - EP - 3 Tests (3 - 1T) 12 matches (27 - 9T) 1937: NZ3. 1938: BI1, 2, 3.

360 **Lockyear, RJ** (Dick) b 26/06/1931 d 03/03/1988 - GW - 6 Tests (20 - 4C, 4P) 20 matches (97 - 32C, 11P) 1960: NZ1, 2, 3, 4, I. 1961: F.

127 **Lombard, AC** (Antonie) b 06/12/1885 d 22/02/1960 - EP - 1 Test (-) 1 match (-) 1910: BI2.

736 **Lombard, F** (Friedrich) b 04/03/1979 - FS - 2 Tests (-) 2 matches (-) 2002: S, E.

588 **Lötter, D** (Deon) b 10/11/1957 - Tvl - 3 Tests (-) 7 matches (5 - 1T) 1993: F2, A1, 2.

255 **Lotz, JW** (Jan) b 26/08/1910 d 13/08/1986 - Tvl - 8 Tests (3 - 1T) 26 matches (6 - 2T) 1937: A1, 2, NZ1, 2, 3. 1938: BI1, 2, 3.

697 **Loubscher, RIP** (Ricardo) b 11/06/1974 - EP - 4 Tests (-) 7 matches (-) 2002: W1. 2003: S1, [U(R), G].

85 **Loubser, JA** (Bob) b 06/08/1884 b 07/12/1962 - WP - 7 Tests (9 - 3T) 23 matches (66 - 22T) 1903: BI3. 1906: S, I, W, E. 1910: BI1, 3.

425 **Lourens, MJ** (Thys) b 15/05/1943 - NTvl - 3 Tests (3 - 1T) 11 matches (12 - 4T) 1968: BI2, 3, 4.

704 **Louw, FH** (Hottie) b 02/03/1976 - WP - 3 Tests (-) 7 matches (-) 2002: W2(R), Arg, Sm.

11 **Louw, JS** (Japie) b 30/08/1867 b 17/08/1936 - Tvl - 3 Tests (-) 3 matches (-) 1891: BI1, 2, 3.

147 **Louw, LH** (Louis) b 23/06/1884 d 13/09/1968 - WP - No Tests - 12 matches (3 - 1T) Toured BI, I & F. 1912/13.

815 **Louw, L-FP** (Francois) b 15/06/1985 - WP - 7 Tests (10 - 2T) 7 matches (10 - 2T) 2010: W1, F, It1, 2, NZ1, 2, 3(R).

454 **Louw, MJ** (Martiens) b 20/04/1938 - Tvl - 2 Tests (-) 9 matches (-) 1971: A2, 3.

207 **Louw, MM** (Boy) b 21/02/1906 d 03/05/1988 - WP - 18 Tests (3 - 1T) 49 matches (18 - 6T) 1928: NZ3, 4. 1931: W, I. 1932: E, S. 1933: A1, 2, 3, 4, 5. 1937: A1, 2, NZ2, 3. 1938: BI1, 2, 3.

505 **Louw, RJ** (Rob) b 26/03/1955 - WP - 19 Tests (20 - 5T) 28 matches (44 - 11T) 1980: S. Am1, 2, BI1, 2, 3, 4, S. Am3, 4, F. 1981: I1, 2, NZ1, 3. 1982: S. Am1, 2. 1984: E1, 2, S. Am&Sp1, 2.

222 **Louw, SC** (Fanie) b 16/09/1909 d 13/07/1940 - WP - 12 Tests (6 - 2T) 30 matches (24 - 8T) 1933: A1, 2, 3, 4, 5. 1937: A1, NZ1, 2, 3. 1938: BI1, 2, 3.

650 **Lubbe, JMF** (Edrich) b 29/07/1969 - GW - 2 Tests (17 - 7C, 1P) 2 matches (17 - 7C, 1P) 1997: T, BI1.

114 **Luyt, FP** (Freddie) b 26/02/1888 d 06/06/1965 - WP - 7 Tests (8 - 2T, 1C) 21 matches (27 - 5T, 6C) 1910: BI1, 2, 3. 1912: S, I, W. 1913: E.

150 **Luyt, JD** (John) b 06/12/1884 d 03/10/1964 - EP - 4 Tests (-) 19 matches (3 - 1T) 1912: S, W. 1913: E, F.

122 **Luyt, RR** (Dick) b 16/04/1886 d 14/01/1967 - WP - 7 Tests (3 - 1T) 21 matches (28 - 8T, 1D) 1910: BI2, 3. 1912: S, I, W. 1913: E, F.

29 **Lyons, DJ** (Dykie) b 03/08/1873 d 01/05/1921 - EP - 1 Test (-) 1 match (-) 1896: BI1.

236 **Lyster, PJ** (Pat) b 31/05/1913 d 25/07/2002 - Natal - 3 Tests (-) 11 matches (39 - 13T) 1933: A2, 5. 1937: NZ1.

M

409 **MacDonald, AW** (Andy) b 27/08/1934 d 18/08/1987 - Rhodesia - 5 Tests (-) 17 matches (3 - 1T) 1965: A1, NZ1, 2, 3, 4.

470 **MacDonald, DA** (Dugald) b 20/01/1950 - WP - 1 Test (-) 1 match (-) 1974: BI2.

811 **Maku, BG** (Bandise) b 24/06/1986 - BB - 1 Test (-) 4 matches (5 - 1T) 2010: It1(R).

361 **Malan, AS** (Avril) b 09/04/1937 - Tvl - 16 Tests (-) 36 matches (3 - 1T) 1960: NZ1, 2, 3*, 4*, W*, I*. 1961: E*, S*, F*. 1962: BI1. 1963: A1, 2, 3*. 1964: W. 1965: I*, S*.

556 **Malan, AW** (Adolf) b 06/09/1961 - NTvl - 7 Tests (-) 11 matches (-) 1989: WT1, 2. 1992: NZ, A, F1, 2, E.

512 **Malan, E** (Ewoud) b 04/07/1953 - NTvl - 2 Tests (-) 2 matches (-) 1980: BI3(R), 4.

345 **Malan, GF** (Abie) b 18/11/1935 - WP - 18 Tests (3 - 1T) 44 matches (9 - 3T) 1958: F2. 1960: NZ1, 3, 4. 1961: E, S, F. 1962: BI1, 2, 3. 1963: A1*, 2*, 4*. 1964: W*. 1965: A1, 2, NZ1, 2.

284 **Malan, P** (Piet) b 13/02/1919 - Tvl - 1 Test (-) 1 match (-) 1949: NZ4.

541 **Mallett, NVH** (Nick) b 30/10/1956 - WP - 2 Tests (4 - 1T) 2 matches (4 - 1T) 1984: S. Am&Sp1, 2.

687 **Malotana, K** (Kaya) b 30/01/1976 - Border - 1 Test (-) 1 match (-) 1999: [Sp].

708 **Manana, TD** (Thando) b 16/10/1977 - GW - No Tests - 3 matches (-) Toured Arg, I, W & E. 2000.

398 **Mans, WJ** (Wynand) b 21/02/1942 - WP - 2 Tests (5 - 1T, 1C) 19 matches (123 - 14T, 30C, 6P, 1D) 1965: I, S.

685 **Marais, CF** (Charl) b 02/09/1970 - WP - 12 Tests (5 - 1T) 15 matches (5 - 1T) 1999: It1(R), 2(R). 2000: C, E1, 2, A1, NZ1, A2, NZ2, A3, Arg(R), W(R).

264 **Marais, FP** (Buks) b 13/12/1927 b 12/12/1996 - Boland - 5 Tests (10 - 1T, 2C, 1P) 18 matches (40 - 11T, 2C, 1P) 1949: NZ1, 2. 1951: S. 1953: A1, 2.

390 Marais, JFK (Hannes) b 21/09/1941 - WP - 35 Tests (3 - 1T) 75 matches (38 - 12T) 1963: A3. 1964: W, F. 1965: I, S, A2. 1968: BI1, 2, 3, 4, F1, 2. 1969: S, E, A1, 2, 3, 4. 1970: I, W, NZ1, 2, 3, 4. 1971: F1*, 2*, A1*, 2*, 3*. 1974: BI1*, 2*, 3*, 4*, F1*, 2*.

529 Marais, JH (Johan) b 28/05/1959 - NTvl - No Tests - 5 matches (4 - 1T) Toured NZ & USA. 1981.

98 Maré, DS (Dietlof) b 02/07/1885 d 14/10/1913 - Tvl - 1 Test (-) 11 matches (31 - 2T, 11C, 1P) 1906: S.

677 Markram, RL (Robert) b 15/09/1975 d 06/07/2001 - GW - No Tests - 4 matches (-) Toured BI & I. 1998.

92 Marsberg, AFW (Artie) b 24/09/1883 d 15/01/1942 - GW - 3 Tests (-) 18 matches (15 - 5T) 1906: S, W, E.

111 Marsberg, PA (Archie) b 01/10/1885 d 23/10/1962 - GW - 1 Test (-) 1 match (-) 1910: BI1.

598 Martens, HJ (Hentie) b 29/10/1971 - OFS - No Tests - 3 matches (5 - 1T) Toured Arg. 1993.

82 Martheze, WC (Rajah) b 29/11/1877 d 16/02/1912 - GW - 3 Tests (-) 16 matches (18 - 6T) 1903: BI2. 1906: I, W.

256 Martin, HJ (Kalfie) b 10/06/1910 d 20/10/2000 - Tvl - 1 Test (-) 16 matches (9 - 3T) 1937: A2.

705 Matfield, V (Victor) b 11/05/1977 - GW - 105 Tests (35 - 7T) 109 matches (35 - 7T) 2001: It1(R), NZ1, A2, NZ2, F3, It2, E, US. 2002: W1, Sm, NZ1, A1, NZ2(R). 2003: S1, 2, Arg, A1, NZ1, A2, NZ2, [U, E, Sm, NZ3]. 2004: I1, 2, W1, NZ2, A2, W2, I3, E, S, Arg. 2005: F1, 2, A1, 2, 3, NZ1, A4, NZ2, Arg, W, F3. 2006: S1, 2, F, A1, NZ1, A2, NZ2, 3, A3. 2007: E1, 2, A1, NZ1*, N*, S*, [Sm, E3, T(R), US, Fiji, Arg, E4.]. 2008: W1(R), 2, It*, NZ1, 2*, A1*, Arg*, NZ3*, A2*, 3*, W3, S, E. 2009: BI1, 2, 3, NZ1, 2, A1, 2, 3, NZ3, F, It(R), I. 2010: W1, F, It1*, NZ1, 2, A1, NZ3, A2, 3, I*, W2*, S*, E*.

443 McCallum, ID (Ian) b 30/07/1944 - WP - 11 Tests (62 - 10C, 14P) 17 matches (134 - 2T, 28C, 24P) 1970: NZ1, 2, 3, 4. 1971: F1, 2, A1, 2, 3. 1974: BI1, 2.

462 McCallum, RJ (Roy) b 12/04/1946 - WP - 1 Test (-) 5 matches (4 - 1T) 1974: BI1.

138 McCulloch, JD (John) b 11/04/1885 d 23/04/1953 - GW - 2 Tests (-) 11 matches (3 - 1T) 1913: E, F.

565 McDonald, I (Ian) b 22/02/1968 - Tvl - 6 Tests (-) 18 matches (25 - 5T) 1992: NZ, A. 1993: F1, A3. 1994: E2. 1995: WS1(R).

223 McDonald, JAJ (André) b 17/02/1909 - d 13/07/1991 - GW - No Tests - 15 matches (15 - 5T) 1931: W, I. 1932: E, S.

69 McEwan, WMC (Willie) b 24/10/1875

d 04/04/1934 - Tvl - 2 Tests (-) 2 matches (-) 1903: BI1, 3.

134 McHardy, EE (Boetie) b 11/06/1890 d 13/12/1959 - OFS - 5 Tests (18 - 6T) 17 matches (60 - 20T) 1912: S, I, W. 1913: E, F.

27 McKendrick, JA (Jim) b 27/07/1870 d 01/01/1895 - WP - 1 Test (-) 1 match (-) 1891: BI3.

826 McLeod, C (Charl) b 05/08/1983 - KZN - No Tests - 1 match (-) Toured BI & I. 2010.

131 Meintjes, JJ (Cooper) b 05/05/1887 d 30/01/1970 - GW - No Tests - 4 matches (-) Toured BI, I & F. 1912/13.

612 Meiring, FA (FA) b 24/08/1967 - NTvl - No Tests - 7 matches (10 - 2T) Toured NZ. 1994.

48 Mellet, TB (Tom) b 29/08/1871 d 29/07/1943 - GW - 1 Test (-) 1 match (-) 1896: BI2.

172 Mellish, FW (Frank) b 26/03/1897 d 21/08/1965 - WP - 6 Tests (-) 15 matches (-) 1921: NZ1, 3. 1924: BI1, 2, 3, 4.

427 Menter, MA (Alan) b 03/10/1941 - NTvl - No Tests - 2 matches (-) Toured F. 1968.

756 Mentz, H (Henno) b 25/09/1979 - Natal - 2 Tests (-) 2 matches (-) 2004: I1, W1(R).

14 Merry, GA (George) b 03/03/1869 d 02/05/1917 - EP - 1 Test (-) 1 match (-) 1891: BI1.

79 Metcalf, HD (Henry) b 20/04/1878 d 03/03/1966 - Border - 1 Test (-) 1 match (-) 1903: BI2.

159 Meyer, C du P (Charlie) b 14/01/1897 d 31/05/1980 - WP - 3 Tests (-) 15 matches (27 - 9T) 1921: NZ1, 2, 3.

38 Meyer, PJ (PJ) b ??/05/1873 d 27/07/1919 - GW - 1 Test (-) 1 match (-) 1896: BI1.

663 Meyer, W (Willie) b 06/11/1967 - FS - 26 Tests (5 - 1T) 31 matches (10 - 2T) 1997: S(R). 1999: It2, NZ1(R), A1(R). 2000: C(R), E1, NZ1(R), 2(R), Arg, I, W, E3. 2001: F1(R), 2, It1, F3(R), It2, E, US(t+R). 2002: W1, 2, Arg, NZ1, 2, A2, F.

168 Michau, JM (Baby) b 14/08/1890 d 20/06/1945 - Tvl - 1 Test (-) 10 matches (-) 1921: NZ1.

162 Michau, JP (Mannetjies) b 06/10/1900 d 22/05/1960 - WP - 3 Tests (-) 16 matches (6 - 2T) 1921: NZ1, 2, 3.

109 Millar, WA (Billy) b 06/11/1883 d 18/03/1949 - WP - 6 Tests (6 - 2T) 37 matches (15 - 5T) 1906: E. 1910: BI2*, 3*. 1912: I*, W*. 1913: F*.

123 Mills, WJ (Wally) b 16/06/1891 d 23/02/1975 - WP - 1 Test (3 - 1T) 13 matches (30 - 10T) 1910: BI2.

125 Moll, TM (Toby) b 20/07/1890 d 14/07/1916 - Tvl - 1 Test (-) 1 match (-) 1910: BI2.

651 Montgomery, PC (Percy) b 15/03/1974 - WP - 102 Tests (893 - 25T, 153C, 148P, 6D) 104 matches (906 - 26T, 157C, 148P, 6D) 1997: BI2, 3, NZ1, A1, NZ2, A2, F1, 2, E, S. 1998: I1, 2, W1, E1, A1, NZ1, 2, A2, W2, S, I3, E2. 1999: It1, 2, W, NZ1, A1, NZ2, A2, [S, U, E, A3, NZ3]. 2000: C, E1, 2, A1, NZ1, A2(R), Arg, I, W, E3. 2001: F1, 2(t), It1, NZ1, F3(R), It2(R). 2004: I2, W1, PI, NZ1, A1, NZ2, A2, W2, I3, E, S. 2005: U, F1, 2, A1, 2, 3, NZ1, A4, NZ2, Arg, W, F3. 2006: S1, 2, F, A1, NZ1, A2, NZ2. 2007: E1, 2, Sm1(R), A1, NZ1, N, S, [Sm, E3, T(R), US, Fiji, Arg, E4.]. 2008: W1(R), 2(R), NZ1(R), 2, Arg(R), NZ3, A2(R), 3(R).

328 Montini, PE (Pat) b 15/06/1929 d 26/08/2008 - WP - 2 Tests (-) 11 matches (6 - 1T, 1D) 1956: A1, 2.

498 Moolman, LC (Louis) b 21/01/1951 d 10/02/2006 - NTvl - 24 Tests (-) 31 matches (12 - 3T) 1977: W.T. 1980: S. Am1, 2, BI1, 2, 3, 4, S. Am3, 4, F. 1981: I1, 2, NZ1, 2, 3, US. 1982: S. Am1, 2. 1984: S. Am&Sp1, 2. 1986: NZC1, 2, 3, 4.

501 Mordt, RH (Ray) b 15/02/1957 - Zimbabwe - 18 Tests (48 - 12T) 25 matches (88 - 22T) 1980: S. Am1, 2, BI1, 2, 3, 4, S. Am3, 4, F. 1981: I2, NZ1, 2, 3, US. 1982: S. Am1, 2. 1984: S. Am&Sp1, 2.

106 Morkel, DFT (Dougie) b 26/10/1885 d 20/02/1950 - Tvl - 9 Tests (38 - 3T, 7C, 5P) 40 matches (137 - 8T, 37C, 13P) 1906: I, E. 1910: BI1*, 3. 1912: S, I, W. 1913: E*, F.

66 Morkel, DJA (Andrew) b 04/08/1882 d 14/06/1965 - Tvl - 1 Test (-) 2 matches (-) 1903: BI1.

173 Morkel, HJL (Harry) b 08/12/1888 d 16/07/1956 - WP - 1 Test (-) 13 matches (6 - 2T) 1921: NZ1.

155 Morkel, HW (Henry) b 14/07/1894 d 25/12/1969 - WP - 2 Tests (-) 9 matches (18 - 6T) 1921: NZ1, 2.

171 Morkel, JA (Royal) b 30/04/1894 d 22/10/1926 - WP - 2 Tests (-) 13 matches (9 - 2T, 1D) 1921: NZ2, 3.

137 Morkel, JWH (Jacky) b 13/11/1890 d 15/05/1916 - WP - 5 Tests (16 - 4T, 2C) 18 matches (34 - 6T, 4C, 2D) 1912: S, I, W. 1913: E, F.

130 Morkel, PG (Gerhard) b 15/10/1888 d 05/09/1963 - WP - 8 Tests (16 - 6C, 1D) 33 matches (79 - 33C, 3P, 1D) 1912: S, I, W. 1913: E, F. 1921: NZ1, 2, 3.

211 Morkel, PK (PK) b 01/07/1905 d 24/07/1993 - WP - 1 Test (-) 1 match (-) 1928: NZ4.

128 Morkel, WH (Boy) b 02/01/1885

d 06/02/1955 - WP - 9 Tests (6 - 2T) 31 matches (21 - 7T) 1910: BI3. 1912: S, I, W. 1913: E, F. 1921: NZ1*, 2*, 3*.

105 Morkel, WS (Sommie) b 26/09/1879 d 11/07/1921 - Tvl - 4 Tests (-) 16 matches (3 - 1T) 1906: S, I, W, E.

267 Moss, C (Cecil) b 12/02/1925 - Natal - 4 Tests (-) 4 matches (-) 1949: NZ1, 2, 3, 4.

176 Mostert, PJ (Phil) b 30/10/1898 d 03/10/1972 - WP - 14 Tests (6 - 1T, 1D) 40 matches (18 - 5T, 1D) 1921: NZ1, 2, 3. 1924: BI1, 2, 4. 1928: NZ1*, 2*, 3*, 4*. 1931: W, I. 1932: E, S.

682 Moyle, BS (Brent) b 31/03/1974 - GF - No Tests - 1 match (-) Toured BI & I. 1998.

797 Mtawarira, T (Tendai) b 01/08/1985 - KZN - 26 Tests (5 - 1T) 27 matches (5 - 1T) 2008: W2, It, A1(R), Arg, NZ3, A2, 3, W3, S, E. 2009: BI1, 2, 3, NZ1, 2, A1, 2, 3, NZ3, F, It(R), I. 2010: I, W2, S, E.

642 Muir, DJ (Dick) b 20/03/1965 - Natal - 5 Tests (10 - 2T) 10 matches (20 - 4T) 1997: It, F1, 2, E, S.

796 Mujati, BV (Brian) b 28/09/1984 - WP - 12 Tests (-) 12 matches (-) 2008: W1, It(R), NZ1(R), 2(t), A1(R), Arg(R), NZ3(R), A2(R), 3, W3(t), S(R), E(R).

405 Mulder, CG (Boet) b 21/05/1939 - ETvl - No Tests - 13 matches (20 - 7C, 2P) Toured A & NZ. 1965.

617 Mulder, JC (Japie) b 18/10/1969 - Tvl - 34 Tests (30 - 6T) 43 matches (45 - 9T) 1994: NZ2, 3, S, W. 1995: WS1, [A, WS2, F, NZ], W, It, E. 1996: Fj, A1, NZ1, A2, NZ2, 5, Arg1, 2, F1, 2, W. 1997: T, BI1. 1999: It1(R), 2, W, NZ1. 2000: C(R), A1, E3. 2001: F1, It1.

428 Müller, GH (Gert) b 10/05/1948 - WP - 14 Tests (12 - 4T) 20 matches (45 - 15T) 1969: A3, 4, S. 1970: W, NZ1, 2, 3, 4. 1971: F1, 2. 1972: E. 1974: BI1, 3, 4.

773 Muller, GJ (Johan) b 01/06/1980 - KZN - 23 Tests (-) 25 matches (-) 2006: S1(R), NZ1(R), A2, NZ2, 3, A3, I(R), E1, 2. 2007: E1(R), 2(R), Sm1(R), A1(R), NZ1(R), A2, NZ2*, N(R), [Sm(R), E3(R), Fiji(t+R), Arg(t+R).], W. 2009: BI3.

748 Müller, GP (Jorrie) b 03/01/1981 - GL - 6 Tests (5 - 1T) 6 matches (5 - 1T) 2003: A2, NZ2, [E, G(R), Sam, NZ3].

551 Müller, HL (Helgard) b 01/06/1963 - OFS - 2 Tests (-) 5 matches (-) 1986: NZC4(R). 1989: WT1(R).

277 Muller, HSV (Hennie) b 26/03/1922 d 26/04/1977 - Tvl - 13 Tests (16 - 3T, 2C, 1P) 28 matches (28 - 4T, 5C, 2P) 1949: NZ1, 2, 3, 4. 1951: S*, I*, W*. 1952: E*, F*. 1953: A1*, 2*, 3*, 4*.

563 Müller, LJJ (Lood) b 05/07/1959 - Natal - 2 Tests (-) 2 matches (-) 1992: NZ, A.

560 Müller, PG (Pieter) b 05/05/1969 - Natal - 33 Tests (15 - 3T) 52 matches (50 - 10T) 1992: NZ, A, F1, 2, E. 1993: F1, 2, A1, 2, 3, Arg1, 2. 1994: E1, 2, NZ1, S, W. 1998: I1, 2, W1, E1, A1, NZ1, 2, A2. 1999: It1, W, NZ1, A1, [Sp, E, A3, NZ3].

785 Murray, WM (Waylon) b 27/04/1986 - KZN - 3 Tests (-) 4 matches (-) 2007: Sm1, A2, NZ2.

821 Mvovo, LN (Lwazi) b 03/06/1986 - KZN - 2 Tests (5 - 1T) 3 matches (5 - 1T) 2010: S, E.

305 Myburgh, B (Ben) b 17/06/1919 d 30/10/1984 - ETvl - No Tests - 17 matches (12 - 4T) Toured BI, I & F. 1951/52.

34 Myburgh, FR (Francis) b 20/07/1871 d 30/11/1929 - EP - 1 Test (-) 1 match (-) 1896: BI1.

371 Myburgh, JL (Mof) b 24/08/1936 - NTvl - 18 Tests (-) 57 matches (9 - 3T) 1962: BI1. 1963: A4. 1964: W, F. 1968: BI1, 2, 3, F1, 2. 1969: A1, 2, 3, 4, E. 1970: I, W, NZ3, 4.

182 Myburgh, WH (Champion) b 10/10/1897 d ??/??/1978 - WTvl - 1 Test (-) 1 match (-) 1924: BI1.

N

394 Naudé, JP (Tiny) b 02/11/1936 d 28/12/2006 - WP - 14 Tests (47 - 2T, 4C, 11P) 28 matches (90 - 6T, 9C, 18P) 1963: A4. 1965: A1, 2, NZ1, 3, 4. 1967: F1, 2, 3, 4. 1968: BI1, 2, 3, 4.

774 Ndungane, AZ (Akona) b 20/02/1981 - BB - 11 Tests (5 - 1T) 13 matches (5 - 1T) 2006: A1, 2, NZ2, 3, A3, E1, 2. 2007: E2, N(R), [US.], W(R).

798 Ndungane, OM (Odwa) b 20/02/1981 - KZN - 7 Tests (10 - 2T) 10 matches (15 - 3T) 2008: It, NZ1, A3. 2009: BI3, A3, NZ3. 2010: W1.

401 Neethling, JB (Tiny) b 06/07/1939 d 03/04/2009 - WP - 8 Tests (-) 23 matches (3 - 1T) 1967: F1, 2, 3, 4. 1968: BI4. 1969: S. 1970: NZ1, 2.

101 Neill, WA (William) b 30/12/1882 d 03/02/1947 - Border - No Tests - 4 matches (-) Toured BI, I & F. 1906/07.

362 Nel, JA (Lofty) b 11/08/1935 - Tvl - 11 Tests (-) 24 matches (18 - 6T) 1960: NZ1, 2. 1963: A1, 2. 1965: A2, NZ1, 2, 3, 4. 1970: NZ3, 4.

329 Nel, JJ (Jeremy) b 21/09/1934 - WP - 8 Tests (3 - 1T) 23 matches (32 - 9T, 1C, 1P) 1956: A1, 2, NZ1, 2, 3, 4. 1958: F1, 2.

72 Nel, PARO (PO) b 17/04/1877 d 23/07/1928 - Tvl - 3 Tests (-) 3 matches (-) 1903: BI1, 2, 3.

199 Nel, PJ (Flip) b 17/06/1902 d 12/02/1984 - Natal - 16 Tests (3 - 1T) 46 matches (6 - 2T) 1928: NZ1, 2, 3, 4. 1931:

W, I. 1932: E, S. 1933: A1*, 3*, 4*, 5*. 1937: A1*, 2*, NZ2*, 3*.

238 Nijkamp, JL (Joe) b 16/10/1904 d 03/04/1969 - Tvl - 1 Test (-) 1 match (-) 1933: A2.

369 Nimb, CF (Charlie) b 06/09/1938 d 15/06/2004 - WP - 1 Test (9 - 3C, 1P) 6 matches (20 - 2T, 4C, 2P) 1961: I.

679 Nkumane, SO (Owen) b 10/08/1975 - GL - No Tests - 4 matches (-) Toured BI & I. 1998.

767 Nokwe, JL (Jongi) b 30/12/1981 - Boland - 4 Tests (25 - 5T) 7 matches (40 - 8T) 2008: Arg, A2, 3. 2009: BI3.

408 Nomis, SH (Syd) b 15/11/1941 - Tvl - 25 Tests (18 - 6T) 54 matches (45 - 15T) 1967: F4. 1968: BI1, 2, 3, 4, F1, 2. 1969: A1, 2, 3, 4, S, E. 1970: I, W, NZ1, 2, 3, 4. 1971: F1, 2, A1, 2, 3. 1972: E.

O

289 Ochse, JK (Chum) b 09/02/1925 d 13/07/1996 - WP - 7 Tests (9 - 3T) 22 matches (48 - 16T) 1951: I, W. 1952: E, F. 1953: A1, 2, 4.

295 Oelofse, JSA (Hansie) b 16/12/1926 d 31/05/1978 - Tvl - 4 Tests (6 - 2T) 13 matches (12 - 4T) 1953: A1, 2, 3, 4.

209 Oliver, JF (John) b 17/05/1917 d ??/??/1980 - Tvl - 2 Tests (-) 2 matches (-) 1928: NZ3, 4.

417 Olivier, E (Eben) b 10/04/1944 - WP - 16 Tests (15 - 5T) 34 matches (30 - 10T) 1967: F1, 2, 3, 4. 1968: BI1, 2, 3, 4, F1, 2. 1969: A1, 2, 3, 4, S, E.

570 Olivier, J (Jacques) b 13/11/1968 - NTvl - 17 Tests (15 - 3T) 34 matches (65 - 13T) 1992: F1, 2, E. 1993: F1, 2, A1, 2, 3, Arg1. 1995: W, It(R), E. 1996: Arg1, 2, F1, 2, W.

174 Olivier, JS (Fien) b 27/05/1897 d 08/06/1980 - WP - No Tests - 13 matches (2 - 1C) Toured A & NZ. 1921.

772 Olivier, W (Wynand) b 11/06/1983 - BB - 32 Tests (5 - 1T) 36 matches (5 - 1T) 2006: S1(R), 2, F, A1, NZ1, A2, NZ2(R), 3, A3, I(R), E1, 2. 2007: E1, E2, NZ1(R), A2, NZ1(R), A2, NZ2*, N(R), [Sm(R), E3(R), T, Arg(R).], W(R). 2009: BI3, NZ1(R), 2(R), F(R), It(R), I. 2010: F, It2(R), NZ1, 2, A1.

33 Olver, E (Ernest) b 27/07/1874 d 12/06/1943 - EP - 1 Test (-) 1 match (-) 1896: BI1.

824 Oosthuizen, CV (Coenie) b 22/03/1989 - FS - No Tests - 1 match (-) Toured BI & I. 2010.

460 Oosthuizen, JJ (Johan) b 04/07/1951 - WP - 9 Tests (8 - 2T) 14 matches (23 - 5T, 1D) 1974: BI1, F1, 2. 1975: F1, 2. 1976: NZ1, 2, 3, 4.

646 Oosthuizen, LT (Theo) b 24/02/1964 -

GW - No Tests - 4 matches (15 - 3T) Toured Arg, F & W. 1996.

520 Oosthuizen, OW (Okkie) b 01/04/1955 - NTvl - 9 Tests (4 - 1T) 14 matches (12 - 3T) 1981: I1(R), 2, NZ2, 3, US. 1982: S. Am1, 2. 1984: E1, 2.

571 Oosthuysen, DE (Deon) b 04/12/1963 - NTvl - No Tests - 12 matches (20 - 4T) Toured F & E. 1992 and A. 1993.

181 Osler, BL (Bennie) b 23/11/1901 d 24/04/1962 - WP - 17 Tests (46 - 2T, 6C, 4P, 4D) 30 matches (108 - 7T, 17C, 7P, 8D) 1924: BI1, 2, 3, 4. 1928: NZ1, 2, 3, 4. 1931: W*, I*. 1932: E*, S*. 1933: A1, 2*, 3, 4, 5.

193 Osler, SG (Sharkey) b 31/01/1907 d 16/04/1980 - WP - 1 Test (-) 1 match (-) 1928: NZ1.

615 Otto, K (Krynauw) b 08/10/1971 - NTvl - 38 Tests (5 - 1T) 51 matches (30 - 6T) 1995: [R, C(R), WS2(R)]. 1997: BI3, NZ1, A1, NZ2, It, F1, 2, E, S. 1998: I1, 2, W1, E1, A1, NZ1, 2, A2, W2, S, I3, E2. 1999: It1, W, NZ1, A1, [S(R), Sp, U, E, A3, NZ3]. 2000: C, E1, 2, A1.

359 Oxlee, K (Keith) b 17/12/1934 d 31/08/1998 - Natal - 19 Tests (88 - 5T, 14C, 14P, 1D) 48 matches (201 - 11T, 45C, 23P, 3D) 1960: NZ1, 2, 3, 4, W, I. 1961: S, A1, 2. 1962: BI1, 2, 3, 4. 1963: A1, 2, 4. 1964: W. 1965: NZ1, 2.

P

628 Pagel, GL (Garry) b 17/09/1966 - WP - 5 Tests (-) 8 matches (-) 1995: [A(R), R, C, NZ(R)]. 1996: NZ5(R).

411 Parker, WH (Hambly) b 13/04/1934 - EP - 2 Tests (-) 14 matches (-) 1965: A1, 2.

73 Partridge, JEC (Birdie) b 13/06/1879 d 01/07/1965 - Tvl - 1 Test (-) 1 match (-) 1903: BI1.

698 Passens, GA (Gavin) b 18/05/1976 - Mpu - No Tests - 3 matches (10 - 2T) Toured Arg, I, W & E. 2000.

647 Paulse, BJ (Breyton) b 25/04/1976 - WP - 64 Tests (130 - 26T) 74 matches (195 - 39T) 1999: It1, 2, NZ1, A1, 2(R), [S(R), Sp, NZ3]. 2000: C, E1, 2, A1, NZ1, A2, NZ2, A3, Arg, W, E3. 2001: F1, 2, It1, NZ1, A1, 2, NZ2, F3, It2, E. 2002: W1, 2, Arg, Sm(R), A1, NZ2, A2, F, S, E. 2003: [G]. 2004: I1, 2, W1, PI, NZ1, A1, NZ2, A2, W2, I3, E. 2005: A2, 3, NZ1, A4, F3. 2006: S1, 2, A1(R), NZ1, 3(R), A3(R). 2007: A2, NZ2.

183 Payn, C (Bill) b 09/08/1893 d 31/10/1959 - Natal - 2 Tests (-) 2 matches (-) 1924: BI1, 2.

341 Pelser, HJM (Martin) b 23/03/1934 - Tvl - 11 Tests (6 - 2T) 26 matches (18 - 6T) 1958: F1. 1960: NZ1, 2, 3, 4, W, I. 1961: F, I, A1, 2.

331 Pfaff, BD (Brian) b 02/03/1930 d

08/05/1998 - WP - 1 Test (-) 5 matches (6 - 2T) 1956: A1.

301 Pickard, JAJ (Jan) b 25/12/1927 d 30/05/1998 - WP - 4 Tests (-) 34 matches (19 - 5T, 2C) 1953: A3, 4. 1956: NZ2. 1958: F2.

584 Pienaar, JF (Francois) b 02/01/1967 - Tvl - 29 Tests (15 - 3T) 40 matches (20 - 4T) 1993: F1*, 2*, A1*, 2*, 3*, Arg1*, 2*. 1994: E1*, 2*, NZ2*, 3*, Arg1*, 2*, S*, W*. 1995: WS1*, [A*, C*, WS2*, F*, NZ*], W*, It*, E*. 1996: Fj*, A1*, NZ1*, A2*, NZ2*.

779 Pienaar, R (Ruan) b 10/03/1984 - KZN - 47 Tests (107 - 6T, 13C, 17P) 52 matches (130 - 6T, 14C, 24P) 2006: NZ2(R), 3(R), A3(R), I(t), E1(R). 2007: E1(R), 2(R), Sm1(R), A1, NZ1, A2, NZ2, N(R), S(R), [E3(t+R), T, US(R), Arg(R).], W. 2008: W1(R), It(R), NZ2(R), A1(R), 3(R), W3, S, E. 2009: BI1, 2, 3(R), NZ1, A1(R), 2, 3, It(R), I(R). 2010: W1, F(R), It1(R), 2(R), NZ1(R), 2(R), A1, I, W2, S(R), E.

164 Pienaar, TB (Theo) b 23/11/1888 d 14/11/1960 - WP - No Tests - 10 matches (-) Toured A & NZ. 1921.

506 Pienaar, ZMJ (Gysie) b 21/12/1954 - OFS - 13 Tests (14 - 2T, 2P) 21 matches (59 - 6T, 10C, 4P, 1D) 1980: S. Am2(R), BI1, 2, 3, 4, S. Am3, 4, F. 1981: I1, 2, NZ1, 2, 3.

793 Pieterse, BH (Barend) b 23/01/1979 - FS - 0 Tests (-) 1 match (5 - 1T) Toured I & E. 2007.

775 Pietersen, J-PR (JP) b 12/07/1986 - KZN - 36 Tests (60 - 12T) 38 matches (60 - 12T) 2006: A3. 2007: Sm1, A1, NZ1, A2, NZ2, N, S, [Sm, E3, T, US(R), Fiji, Arg, E4.], W. 2008: NZ2, A1, Arg, NZ3, A2, W3, S, E. 2009: BI1, 2, NZ1, 2, A1, 2, F, It, I. 2010: NZ3, A2, 3.

421 Pitzer, G (Gys) b 08/07/1939 - NTvl - 12 Tests (-) 16 matches (-) 1967: F1, 2, 3, 4. 1968: BI1, 2, 3, 4, F1, 2. 1969: A3, 4.

461 Pope, CF (Chris) b 30/09/1952 - WP - 9 Tests (4 - 1T) 13 matches (4 - 1T) 1974: BI1, 2, 3, 4. 1975: F1, 2. 1976: NZ2, 3, 4.

812 Potgieter, DJ (Dewald) b 22/02/1987 - BB - 6 Tests (5 - 1T) 8 matches (5 - 1T) 2009: I(t). 2010: W1, F(R), It1, 2(R), A1(R).

200 Potgieter, HJ (Hennie) b 24/10/1903 d 11/11/1957 - OFS - 2 Tests (-) 2 matches (-) 1928: NZ1, 2.

493 Potgieter, HL (Hermanus) b 11/01/1953 - OFS - 1 Test (4 - 1T) 1 match (4 - 1T) 1977: W.T.

435 Potgieter, R (Ronnie) b 18/11/1943 - NTvl - No Tests - 6 matches (-) Toured BI & I. 1969/70.

531 Povey, SA (Shaun) b 09/08/1954 - WP - No Tests - 2 matches (-) Toured NZ &

USA. 1981.

52 Powell, AW (Bertie) b 18/07/1873 d 11/09/1948 - GW - 1 Test (-) 1 match (-) 1896: BI3.

17 Powell, JM (Jackie) b 12/12/1871 d 19/12/1955 - GW - 4 Tests (-) 4 matches (-) 1891: BI2. 1896: BI3. 1903: BI1, 2*.

504 Prentis, RB (Richard) b 27/02/1947 - Tvl - 11 Tests (-) 14 matches (-) 1980: S. Am1, 2, BI1, 2, 3, 4, S. Am3, 4, F. 1981: I1, 2.

723 Pretorius, AS (André) b 29/12/1978 - GL - 31 Tests (171 - 2T, 31C, 25P, 8D) 33 matches (174 - 2T, 31C, 26P, 8D) 2002: W1, 2, Arg, Sm, NZ1, A1, NZ2, F, S(R), E. 2003: NZ1(R), A2. 2005: A2, 3, NZ1, A4, NZ2, Arg. 2006: NZ2(R), 3, A3, I, E1(t+R), 2. 2007: S(R), [Sm(R), E3(R), T, US(R), Arg(R).], W.

782 Pretorius, JC (Jaco) b 10/12/1979 - GL - 2 Tests (-) 3 matches (-) 2006: I. 2007: NZ2.

198 Pretorius, NF (Nick) b 10/12/1904 d 19/02/1990 - Tvl - 4 Tests (-) 4 matches (-) 1928: NZ1, 2, 3, 4.

577 Pretorius, PIL (Piet) b 17/08/1964 - NTvl - No Tests - 6 matches (-) Toured F & E. 1992.

392 Prinsloo, J (Poens) b 11/10/1935 - NTvl - 1 Test (-) 1 match (-) 1963: A3.

338 Prinsloo, JC (Jan) b 28/01/1935 d 28/07/1966 - Tvl - 2 Tests (-) 2 matches (-) 1958: F1, 2.

192 Prinsloo, JP (Boet) b 14/10/1905 d 04/10/1968 - Tvl - 1 Test (-) 1 match (-) 1928: NZ1.

622 Putt, KB (Kevin) b 28/07/1965 - Natal - No Tests - 11 matches (15 - 3T) Toured W, S & I. 1994 and Arg, F & W. 1996.

386 Putter, DJ (Dick) b 13/02/1937 d 31/10/2002 - WTvl - 3 Tests (-) 3 matches (-) 1963: A1, 2, 4.

R

71 Raaff, JWE (Klondyke) b 10/03/1879 d 13/07/1949 - GW - 6 Tests (3 - 1T) 20 matches (12 - 4T) 1903: BI1, 2. 1906: S, W, E. 1910: BI1.

776 Ralepelle, MC (Chiliboy) b 11/09/1986 - BB - 18 Tests (-) 20 matches (-) 2006: NZ2(R), E2(R). 2008: E(t+R). 2009: BI3, NZ1(R), 2(R), A2(R), NZ3(R). 2010: W1(R), F(R), It1, 2(R), NZ1(R), 2(R), A1(R), 2(R), 3(R), W2(R).

488 Ras, WJ de W (De Wet) b 28/01/1954 - OFS - 2 Tests (-) 5 matches (69 - 4T, 25C, 1P) 1976: NZ1(R). 1980: S. Am2(R).

813 Raubenheimer, D (Davon) b 16/07/1984 - GW - No Tests - 2 matches (-) Toured F, It, I & E. 2009.

728 Rautenbach, SJ (Faan) b 22/02/1976 - WP - 14 Tests (5 - 1T) 14 matches (5 - 1T)

2002: W1(R), 2(t+R), Arg(R), Sm, NZ1(R), A1, NZ2(R), A2(R). 2003: [U(R), G, Sm, NZ3]. 2004: W1, NZ1(R).

569 Reece-Edwards, HM (Hugh) b 05/01/1961 - Natal - 3 Tests (-) 12 matches (103 - 3T, 23C, 14P) 1992: F1, 2. 1993: A2.

87 Reid, A (Oupa) b 23/11/1878 d 18/05/1952 - WP - 1 Test (3 - 1T) 1 match (3 - 1T) 1903: BI3.

242 Reid, BC (Bunny) b 12/07/1910 d 11/09/1976 - Border - 1 Test (-) 1 match (-) 1933: A4.

107 Reid, HG (Bert) b 19/12/1881 - d 30/05/1944 - Tvl - No Tests - 14 matches (6 - 2T) Toured BI, I & F. 1906/07.

542 Reinach, J (Jaco) b 01/01/1962 d 21/01/1997 - OFS - 4 Tests (8 - 2T) 4 matches (8 - 2T) 1986: NZC1, 2, 3, 4.

310 Rens, IJ (Natie) b 19/07/1929 d 19/12/1989 - Tvl - 2 Tests (19 - 5C, 2P, 1D) 2 matches (19 - 5C, 2P, 1D) 1953: A3, 4.

320 Retief, DF (Daan) b 28/06/1925 - NTvl - 9 Tests (12 - 4T) 21 matches (36 - 12T) 1955: BI1, 2, 4. 1956: A1, 2, NZ1, 2, 3, 4.

129 Reyneke, HJ (Koot) b 19/01/1882 d 22/03/1970 - WP - 1 Test (3 - 1T) 1 match (3 - 1T) 1910: BI3.

6 Richards, AR (Alf) b 14/12/1867 d 09/01/1904 - WP - 3 Tests (-) 3 matches (-) 1891: BI1, 2, 3*.

580 Richter, AJ (Adriaan) b 10/05/1966 - NTvl - 10 Tests (20 - 4T) 29 matches (55 - 11T) 1992: F1, 2, E. 1994: E2, NZ1, 2, 3. 1995: [R*, C, WS2(R)].

388 Riley, NM (Norman) b 25/02/1939 - ETvl - 1 Test (-) 1 match (-) 1963: A3.

117 Riordan, CA (Cliff) b 24/12/1885 d 07/02/1958 - Tvl - 2 Tests (-) 2 matches (-) 1910: BI1, 2.

573 Roberts, H (Harry) b 03/12/1960 - Tvl - No Tests - 6 matches (5 - 1T) Toured F & E. 1992.

480 Robertson, IW (Ian) b 28/04/1950 - Rhodesia - 5 Tests (3 - 1D) 10 matches (21 - 3T, 1P, 2D) 1974: F1, 2. 1976: NZ1, 2, 4.

554 Rodgers, PH (Heinrich) b 23/06/1962 - NTvl - 5 Tests (-) 12 matches (-) 1989: WT1, 2. 1992: NZ, F1, 2.

534 Rogers, CD (Chris) b 10/10/1956 - Tvl - 4 Tests (-) 4 matches (-) 1984: E1, 2, S. Am&Sp1, 2.

126 Roos, GD (Gideon) b 20/07/1890 d 08/03/1920 - WP - 2 Tests (3 - 1T) 2 matches (3 - 1T) 1910: BI2, 3.

88 Roos, PJ (Paul) b 30/10/1880 d 22/09/1948 - WP - 4 Tests (-) 22 matches (5 - 1T, 1C) 1903: BI3. 1906: I*, W*, E*.

802 Rose, EE (Earl) b 12/01/1984 - GL - No Tests - 4 matches (-) Toured BI, 2008 and E, F, It & I, 2009.

322 Rosenberg, W (Wilf) b 18/06/1934 - Tvl - 5 Tests (6 - 2T) 9 matches (6 - 2T) 1955: BI2, 3, 4. 1956: NZ3. 1958: F1.

699 Rossouw, C (Chris) b 14/11/1976 - WP - No Tests - 4 matches (-) Toured Arg, I, W & E. 2000.

624 Rossouw, C le C (Chris) b 14/09/1969 - Tvl - 9 Tests (10 - 2T) 10 matches (10 - 2T) 1995: WS1, [R, WS2, F, NZ]. 1999: NZ2(R), A2(R), [Sp, NZ3(R)].

309 Rossouw, DH (Daantjie) b 05/09/1930 d 28/01/2010 - WP - 2 Tests (3 - 1T) 2 matches (3 - 1T) 1953: A3, 4.

755 Rossouw, DJ (Danie) b 05/06/1978 - BB - 54 Tests (40 - 8T) 58 matches (45 - 9T) 2003: [U, G, Sm(R), NZ3]. 2004: E(R), S, Arg. 2005: U, F1, 2, A1, W(R), F3(R). 2006: S1, 2, F, A1, I, E1, 2. 2007: E1, Sm1, A1(R), NZ1, S, [Sm, E3, T, Fiji, Arg, E4.]. 2008: W1(t+R), NZ3(R), A3(R), S(R), E. 2009: BI1(R), 2(R), NZ1(R), 2(R), A1(R), 3(R), F(R), It, I. 2010: W1, F, NZ1(R), 2, A1, NZ3(t+R), A2(R), 3.

578 Rossouw, PB (Botha) b 03/11/1969 - WTvl - No Tests - 2 matches (5 - 1T) Toured F & E. 1992.

652 Rossouw, PWG (Pieter) b 03/12/1971 - WP - 43 Tests (105 - 21T) 43 matches (105 - 21T) 1997: BI2, 3, NZ1, A1, NZ2(R), A2(R), It, F1, 2, E, S. 1998: I1, 2, W1, E1, A1, NZ1, 2, A2, W2, S, I3, E2. 1999: It1, W, NZ1, A1(R), NZ2, A2, [S, U, E, A3]. 2000: C, E1, 2, A2, Arg(R), I, W. 2001: F3, US. 2003: Arg.

206 Rousseau, WP (Willie) b 11/08/1906 d 28/12/1996 - WP - 2 Tests (-) 2 matches (-) 1928: NZ3, 4.

367 Roux, F du T (Mannetjies) b 12/04/1939 - WP - 27 Tests (18 - 6T) 56 matches (39 - 13T) 1960: W. 1961: A1, 2. 1962: BI1, 2, 3, 4. 1963: A2. 1965: A1, 2, NZ1, 2, 3, 4. 1968: BI3, 4, F1, 2. 1969: A1, 2, 3, 4. 1970: I, NZ1, 2, 3, 4.

607 Roux, JP (Johan) b 25/02/1969 - Tvl - 12 Tests (10 - 2T) 17 matches (20 - 4T) 1994: E2, NZ1, 2, 3, Arg1. 1995: [R, C, F(R)]. 1996: A1(R), NZ1, A2, NZ3.

426 Roux, OA (Tonie) b 22/02/1947 - NTvl - 7 Tests (-) 31 matches (15 - 4T, 1D) 1969: S, E. 1970: I, W. 1972: E. 1974: BI3, 4.

737 Roux, WG (Wessel) b 01/10/1976 - Blue Bulls - 3 Tests (-) 3 matches (-) 2002: F(R), S, E.

727 Russell, RB (Brent) b 05/03/1980 - Mpu - 23 Tests (40 - 8T) 23 matches (40 - 8T) 2002: W1(R), 2, Arg, A1(R), NZ2(R), A2, F, E(R). 2003: Arg(R), A1(R), NZ1, A2(R). 2004: I2(t+R), W1, NZ1(R), W2(R), Arg(R). 2005: U(R), F2(R), A1(t), Arg(R), W(R). 2006: F.

44 Samuels, TA (Theo) b 21/07/1873 d 16/11/1896 - GW - 3 Tests (6 - 2T) 3 matches (6 - 2T) 1896: BI2, 3, 4.

S

666 Santon, D (Dale) b 18/08/1969 - Boland - 4 Tests (-) 5 matches (-) 2003: A1(R), NZ1(R), A2(t), [G(R)].

449 Sauermann, JT (Theo) b 16/11/1944 - Tvl - 5 Tests (-) 11 matches (-) 1971: F1, 2, A1. 1972: E. 1974: BI1.

290 Saunders, MJ (Cowboy) b 26/11/1927 d 17/05/2006 - Border - No Tests - 14 matches (33 - 11T) Toured BI, I & F. 1951/52.

472 Schlebusch, JJJ (Jan) b 05/05/1949 - OFS - 3 Tests (-) 3 matches (-) 1974: BI3, 4. 1975: F2.

346 Schmidt, LU (Louis) b 06/02/1936 d 23/01/1999 - NTvl - 2 Tests (-) 2 matches (-) 1958: F2. 1962: BI2.

544 Schmidt, UL (Uli) b 10/07/1961 - NTvl - 17 Tests (9 - 2T) 25 matches (29 - 6T) 1986: NZC1, 2, 3, 4. 1989: WT1, 2. 1992: NZ, A. 1993: F1, 2, A1, 2, 3. 1994: Arg1, 2, S, W.

391 Schoeman, J (Haas) b 15/03/1940 d 01/01/2006 - WP - 7 Tests (-) 23 matches (15 - 5T) 1963: A3, 4. 1965: I, S, A1, NZ1, 2.

618 Scholtz, CP (Christiaan) b 22/10/1970 - Tvl - 4 Tests (-) 4 matches (-) 1994: Arg1. 1995: [R, C, WS2].

732 Scholtz, H (Hendro) b 22/03/1979 - FS - 5 Tests (5 - 1T) 5 matches (5 - 1T) 2002: A1(R), NZ2(R), A2(R). 2003: [U(R), G].

177 Scholtz, H (Tokkie) b 29/08/1892 d 08/04/1959 - WP - 2 Tests (-) 15 matches (-) 1921: NZ1, 2.

582 Schutte, PJW (Phillip) b 07/10/1969 - NTvl - 2 Tests (-) 8 matches (-) 1994: S, W.

36 Scott, PA (Paul) b 26/10/1872 d (unknown) - Tvl - 4 Tests (-) 4 matches (-) 1896: BI1, 2, 3, 4.

156 Sendin, WD (Billy) b 04/10/1895 d 16/07/1977 - GW - 1 Test (3 - 1T) 9 matches (18 - 6T) 1921: NZ2.

702 Sephaka, LD (Lawrence) b 08/08/1978 - GF - 24 Tests (-) 29 matches (-) 2001: US. 2002: Sm, NZ1, A1, NZ2, A2, F. 2003: S1, 2, A1, NZ1, A2(t+R), NZ2, [U, E(t+R), G]. 2005: F2, A1, 2(R), W. 2006: S1(R), NZ3(t+R), A3(R), I.

508 Serfontein, DJ (Divan) b 03/08/1954 - WP - 19 Tests (12 - 3T) 26 matches (16 - 4T) 1980: BI1, 2, 3, 4, S. Am3, 4, F. 1981: I1, 2, NZ1, 2, 3, US. 1982: S. Am1, 2. 1984: E1, 2, S. Am&Sp1*, 2*.

19 Shand, R (Bob) b 27/08/1866 d 01/03/1934 - GW - 2 Tests (-) 2 matches (-) 1891: BI2, 3.

613 Sherrell, LR (Lance) b 09/02/1966 -

N Tvl - No Tests - 6 matches (31 - 3T, 5C, 2P) Toured NZ. 1994.

257 Sherriff, AR (Roger) b 17/03/1913 d 04/12/1951 - Tvl - 3 Tests (-) 6 matches (3 - 1T) 1938: BI1, 2, 3.

761 Shimange, MH (Hanyani) b 17/04/1978 - FS - 9 Tests (-) 9 matches (-) 2004: W1(R), NZ2(R), A2(R), W2(R). 2005: U(R), A1(R), 2(R), Arg(R). 2006: S1(R).

140 Shum, EH (Baby) b 17/08/1886 d 27/06/1952 - Tvl - 1 Test (-) 15 matches (6 - 2T) 1913: E.

175 Siedle, LB (Jack) b 01/07/1891 d 07/11/1962 - Natal - No Tests - 1 match (-) Toured A & NZ. 1921.

292 Sinclair, DJ (Des) b 14/07/1927 d 29/04/1996 - Tvl - 4 Tests (-) 17 matches (15 - 5T) 1955: BI1, 2, 3, 4.

70 Sinclair, JH (Jimmy) b 16/10/1876 d 23/02/1913 - Tvl - 1 Test (-) 1 match (-) 1903: BI1.

343 Skene, AL (Alan) b 02/10/1932 d 13/08/2001 - WP - 1 Test (-) 1 match (-) 1958: F2.

659 Skinstad, RB (Bob) b 03/07/1976 - WP - 42 Tests (55 - 11T) 47 matches (70 - 14T) 1997: E(t). 1998: W1(R), E1(t), NZ1(R), 2(R), A2(R), W2(R), S, I3, E2. 1999: [S, Sp(R), U, E, A3]. 2007: E2(t+R), Sm1, NZ1. 2001: F1(R), 2(R), It1*, NZ1*, A1*, 2*, NZ2*, F3*, It2*, E*. 2002: W1*, 2*, Arg, Sm, NZ1, A1, NZ2, A2. 2003: Arg(R). 2007: A2*[E3(R), T*, US(R), Arg(R).].

416 Slabber, LJ (Louis) b 05/03/1935 d 11/05/2003 - OFS - No Tests - 7 matches (9 - 3T) Toured A & NZ. 1965.

188 Slater, JT (Jack) b 16/04/1901 d 16/02/1986 - EP - 3 Tests (6 - 2T) 3 matches (6 - 2T) 1924: BI3, 4. 1928: NZ1.

546 Smal, GP (Gert) b 27/12/1961 - WP - 6 Tests (4 - 1T) 6 matches (4 - 1T) 1986: NZC1, 2, 3, 4. 1989: WT1, 2.

561 Small, JT (James) b 10/02/1969 - Tvl - 47 Tests (100 - 20T) 60 matches (135 - 27T) 1992: NZ, A, F1, 2, E. 1993: F1, 2, A1, 2, 3, Arg1, 2. 1994: E1, 2, NZ1, 2, 3(t), Arg1. 1995: WS1, [A, R, F, NZ], W, It, E(R). 1996: Fj, A1, NZ1, A2, NZ2, Arg1, 2, F1, 2, W. 1997: T, BI1, NZ1(R), A1(R), NZ2, A2, It, F1, 2, E, S.

583 Smit, FC (FC) b 13/08/1966 - WP - 1 Test (-) 4 matches (-) 1992: E.

691 Smit, JW (John) b 03/04/1978 - Natal - 102 Tests (30 - 6T) 103 matches (30 - 6T) 2000: C(t), A1(R), NZ1(t+R), A2(R), NZ2(R), A3(R), Arg, I, W, E3. 2001: F1, 2, It1, NZ1(R), A1(R), 2(R), NZ2(R), F3(R), It2, E, US(R). 2003: [U(R), E(t+R), G*, Sm, NZ3]. 2004: I1*, 2*, W1*, PI*, NZ1*, A1*,

NZ2*, A2*, W2*, I3*, E*, S*, Arg*. 2005: U*, F1*, 2*, A1*, 2*, 3*, NZ1*, A4*, NZ2*, Arg*, W*, F3*. 2006: S1*, 2*, F*, A1*, NZ1*, A2*, NZ2*, 3*, A3*, I*, E1*, 2*. 2007: E1*, 2*, Sm1*, A1*, [Sm*, E3*, T(R), US*, Fiji*, Arg*, E4*.], W*. 2008: W1*, 2*, NZ1*, W3*, S*, E*. 2009: BI1*, 2*, 3*, NZ1*, 2*, A1*, A2*, A3*, NZ3*, F*, It*, I*. 2010: W1*, F*, It2*, NZ1*, 2*, A1*, NZ3*, A2*, 3*.

660 Smit, PL (Philip) b 27/07/1973 - GW - No Tests - 5 matches (-) Toured It, F, E & S. 1997 and BI & I. 1998.

389 Smith, CM (Nelie) b 08/05/1934 - OFS - 7 Tests (12 - 1T, 3P) 19 matches (21 - 4T, 3P) 1963: A3, 4. 1964: W, F*. 1965: A1*, 2*, NZ2*.

23 Smith, CW (Toski) b 09/04/1871 d 28/02/1934 - GW - 3 Tests (-) 3 matches (-) 1891: BI2. 1896: BI2, 3.

507 Smith, DJ (David) b 09/11/1957 - Zimbabwe - 4 Tests (-) 4 matches (-) 1980: BI1, 2, 3, 4.

21 Smith, DW (Dan) b 08/04/1869 d 27/02/1926 - GW - 1 Test (-) 1 match (-) 1891: BI2.

262 Smith, GAC (George) b 31/08/1916 d 23/03/1978 - EP - 1 Test (-) 1 match (-) 1938: BI3.

746 Smith, JH (Juan) b 30/07/1981 - FS - 69 Tests (60 - 12T) 71 matches (60 - 12T) 2003: S1(R), 2(R), A1, NZ1, A2, NZ2, [U, E, Sm, NZ3]. 2004: W2. 2005: U(R), F2(R), A2, 3, NZ1(R), A4, NZ2, Arg, W, F3. 2006: S1, 2, F, A1, NZ1, A2, I, E2. 2007: E1, 2, A1, N, S, [Sm, E3, T(R), US, Fiji, Arg, E4.], W. 2008: W1, 2, It, NZ1, 2, A1, Arg, NZ3, A2, 3, W3, S. 2009: BI1, 2, 3, NZ1, 2, A1, 2, 3. 2010: NZ3, A2, 3, I, W2, S, E.

643 Smith, PF (Franco) b 29/07/1972 - GW - 9 Tests (23 - 2T, 2C, 3P) 18 matches (85 - 5T, 21C, 6P) 1997: S(R). 1998: I1(t), 2, W1, NZ1(R), 2(R), A2(R), W2. 1999: NZ2.

241 Smollan, FC (Fred) b 20/08/1908 d 02/08/1998 - Tvl - 3 Tests (-) 3 matches (-) 1933: A3, 4, 5.

18 Snedden, RCD (Bob) b 20/03/1867 d 03/04/1931 - GW - 1 Test (-) 1 match (-) 1891: BI2*.

636 Snyman, AH (André) b 02/02/1974 - N Tvl - 38 Tests (50 - 10T) 42 matches (60 - 12T) 1996: NZ3, 4, Arg2(R), W(R). 1997: T, BI1, 2, 3, NZ1, A1, NZ2, A2, It, F1, 2, E, S. 1998: I1, 2, W1, E1, A1, NZ1, 2, A2, W2, S, I3, E2. 1999: NZ2. 2001: NZ2, F3, US. 2002: W1. 2003: S1, NZ1. 2006: S1, 2.

453 Snyman, DSL (Dawie) b 05/07/1949 - WP - 10 Tests (24 - 1T, 1C, 4P, 2D) 22 matches (86 - 7T, 13C, 8P, 4D) 1972: E. 1974: BI1, 2(R), F1, 2. 1975: F1, 2. 1976:

NZ2, 3. 1977: WT.

466 Snyman, JCP (Jackie) b 14/04/1948 - OFS - 3 Tests (18 - 6P) 7 matches (29 - 4C, 6P, 1D) 1974: BI2, 3, 4.

473 Sonnekus, GHH (Gerrie) b 01/02/1953 - OFS - 3 Tests (4 - 1T) 3 matches (4 - 1T) 1974: BI3. 1984: E1, 2.

731 Sowerby, RS (Shaun) b 01/07/1978 - Natal - 1 Test (-) 1 match (-) 2002: Sm(R).

446 Spies, JJ (Johan) b 08/05/1945 - N Tvl - 4 Tests (-) 11 matches (-) 1970: NZ1, 2, 3, 4.

777 Spies, PJ (Pierre) b 08/06/1985 - BB - 40 Tests (35 - 7T) 40 matches (35 - 7T) 2006: A1, NZ2, 3, A3, I, E1. 2007: E1(R), 2, A1. 2008: W1, 2, A1, Arg, NZ2, A2, 3, W3, S, E. 2009: BI1, 2, 3(R), NZ1, 2, A1, 2, 3, NZ3. 2010: F, It1, 2, NZ1, 2, A1, NZ3, A2, 3, I, W2, E.

479 Stander, JCJ (Rampie) b 25/12/1944 d 28/08/1980 - OFS - 5 Tests (-) 8 matches (4 - 1T) 1974: BI4(R). 1976: NZ1, 2, 3, 4.

482 Stapelberg, WP (Willem) b 29/01/1947 - N Tvl - 2 Tests (8 - 2T) 6 matches (12 - 3T) 1974: F1, 2.

336 Starke, JJ (James) b 16/05/1931 - WP - 1 Test (-) 8 matches (3 - 1T) 1956: NZ4.

180 Starke, KT (Kenny) b 18/06/1900 d 03/01/1982 - WP - 4 Tests (13 - 3T, 1D) 4 matches (13 - 3T, 1D) 1924: BI1, 2, 3, 4.

342 Steenekamp, J (Johan) b 02/09/1935 d 16/08/2007 - Tvl - 1 Test (-) 1 match (-) 1958: F1.

764 Steenkamp, GG (Gurthro) b 12/06/1981 - FS - 31 Tests (25 - 5T) 33 matches (25 - 5T) 2004: S, Arg. 2005: U, F2(R), A2, 3, NZ1(R), A4(R). 2007: E1(R), 2, A1, [T, Fiji(R).]. 2008: W1, 2(R), NZ1, 2, A1, W3(R), S(R). 2009: BI1(R), 3(R). 2010: F, It1, 2, NZ1, 2, A1, NZ3, A2, 3.

93 Stegmann, AC (Anton) b 25/08/1883 d 23/01/1972 - WP - 2 Tests (3 - 1T) 16 matches (54 - 18T) 1906: S, I.

825 Stegmann, GJ (Deon) b 22/03/1986 - BB - 4 Tests (-) 4 matches (-) 2010: I, W2, S, E.

132 Stegmann, JA (Jan) b 21/06/1887 d 07/12/1984 - Tvl - 5 Tests (15 - 5T) 16 matches (39 - 13T) 1912: S, I, W. 1913: E, F.

350 Stewart, DA (Dave) b 14/07/1935 - WP - 11 Tests (9 - 1T, 2P) 30 matches (25 - 5T, 2C, 2P) 1960: S. 1961: E, S, F, I. 1963: A1, 3, 4. 1964: W, F. 1965: I.

678 Stewart, JC (Christian) b 17/10/1966 - WP - 3 Tests (-) 5 matches (-) 1998: S, I3, E2.

783 Steyn, FPL (Francois) b 14/05/1987 - KZN - 42 Tests (97 - 6T, 5C, 16P, 3D) 44 matches (106 - 6T, 8C, 17P, 3D) 2006: I, E1, 2. 2007: E1(R), 2(R), Sm1, A1(R),

NZ1(R), S, [Sm(R), E3, T(R), US, Fiji, Arg, E4.], W. 2008: W2(R), It, NZ1(R), 2(R), A1NZ3(R), A2(R), W3(R), S(R), E(R). 2009: BI1, 2, 3(R), NZ1, 2, A1, 2(R), 3(R), NZ3. 2010: W1, A2, 3, W2, S, E.

803 Steyn, M (Morné) b 11/07/1984 - BB - 25 Tests (322 - 4T, 37C, 71P, 5D) 25 matches (322 - 4T, 37C, 71P, 5D) 2009: BI1(t+R), 2(R), 3, NZ1(R), 2, A1, 2, 3, NZ3, F, It, I. 2010: F, It1, 2, NZ1, 2, A1, NZ3, A2, 3, I, W2, S, E.

489 Stofberg, MTS (Theuns) b 06/06/1955 - OFS - 21 Tests (24 - 6T) 29 matches (36 - 9T) 1976: NZ2, 3. 1977: W.T. 1980: S.Am1, 2, BI1, 2, 3, 4, S. Am3*, 4, F. 1981: I1, 2, NZ1*, 2, US. 1982: S. Am1, 2. 1984: E1*, 2*.

224 Strachan, LC (Louis) b 12/09/1907 d 04/03/1985 - Tvl - 10 Tests (-) 38 matches (18 - 6T) 1932: E, S. 1937: A1, 2, NZ1, 2, 3. 1938: BI1, 2, 3.

616 Straeuli, RAW (Rudolf) b 20/08/1963 - Tvl - 10 Tests (20 - 4T) 23 matches (45 - 9T) 1994: NZ1, Arg1, 2, S, W. 1995: WS1, [A, WS2, NZ(R)], E(R).

592 Stransky, JT (Joel) b 16/07/1967 - Natal - 22 Tests (240 - 6T, 30C, 47P, 3D) 36 matches (329 - 9T, 55C, 55P, 3D) 1993: A1, 2, 3, Arg1. 1994: Arg1, 2. 1995: WS1, [A, R(t), C, F, NZ], W, It, E. 1996: Fj(R), NZ1, A2, NZ2, 3, 4, 5(R).

827 Strauss, AJ (Andries) b 05/03/1984 - FS - No Tests - 1 match (-) Toured BI & I. 2010.

579 Strauss, CP (Tiaan) b 28/06/1965 - WP - 15 Tests (20 - 4T) 37 matches (55 - 11T) 1992: F1, 2, E. 1993: F1, 2, A1, 2, 3, Arg1, 2. 1994: E1, NZ1*, 2, Arg1, 2.

539 Strauss, JA (Attie) b 02/09/1959 - WP - 2 Tests (-) 2 matches (-) 1984: S. Am&Sp1, 2.

800 Strauss, JA (Adriaan) b 18/11/1985 - FS - 9 Tests (-) 11 matches (-) 2008: A1(R), Arg(R), NZ3(R), A2(R), 3(R). 2009: F(R), It. 2010: S(R), E(R).

490 Strauss, JHP (Johan) b 27/09/1951 - Tvl - 3 Tests (-) 3 matches (-) 1976: NZ3, 4. 1980: S. Am1.

158 Strauss, SSF (Sarel) b 24/11/1891 d 06/02/1946 - GW - 1 Test (-) 12 matches (23 - 5T, 2D) 1921: NZ3.

325 Strydom, CF (Popeye) b 20/01/1932 d 31/03/2001 - OFS - 6 Tests (-) 17 matches (3 - 1T) 1955: BI3. 1956: A1, 2, NZ1, 4. 1958: F1.

586 Strydom, JJ (Hannes) b 13/07/1965 - Tvl - 21 Tests (5 - 1T) 30 matches (10 - 2T) 1993: F2, A1, 2, 3, Arg1, 2. 1994: E. 1995: [A, C, F, NZ]. 1996: A2(R), NZ2(R), 3, 4, W(R). 1997: T, BI1, 2, 3, A2.

276 Strydom, LJ (Ou-Boet) b 27/10/1921

d 11/05/2003 - NTvl - 2 Tests (-) 2 matches (-) 1949: NZ1, 2.

566 Styger, JJ (Johan) b 31/01/1962 - OFS - 7 Tests (-) 18 matches (-) 1992: NZ(R), A, F1, 2, E. 1993: F2(R), A3(R).

403 Suter, MR (Snowy) b 14/12/1939 - Natal - 2 Tests (-) 4 matches (3 - 1T) 1965: I, S.

654 Swanepoel, W (Werner) b 15/04/1973 - FS - 20 Tests (25 - 5T) 25 matches (30 - 6T) 1997: BI3(R), A2(R), F1(R), 2, E, S. 1998: I2(R), W1(R), E2(R). 1999: It1, 2(R), W, A1, [Sp, NZ3(t)]. 2000: A1, NZ1, A2, NZ2, A3.

452 Swanson, PS (Peter) b 26/12/1946 d 26/10/2003 - Tvl - No Tests - 4 matches (5 - 1T, 1C) Toured A. 1971.

595 Swart, IS de V (Balie) b 18/05/1964 - Tvl - 16 Tests (-) 31 matches (-) 1993: A1, 2, 3, Arg1. 1994: E1, 2, NZ1, 3, Arg2(R). 1995: WS1, [A, WS2, F, NZ], W. 1996: A2.

630 Swart, J (Justin) b 23/07/1972 - WP - 10 Tests (5 - 1T) 13 matches (15 - 3T) 1996: Fj, NZ1(R), A2, NZ2, 3, 4, 5. 1997: BI3(R), It, S(R).

312 Swart, JJN (Sias) b 29/07/1934 d 18/01/1993 - SWA - 1 Test (3 - 1T) 1 match (3 - 1T) 1955: BI1.

T

43 Taberer, WS (Bill) b 11/04/1872 d 10/02/1938 - GW - 1 Test (-) 1 match (-) 1896: BI2.

380 Taylor, OB (Ormy) b 05/06/1937 - Natal - 1 Test (-) 1 match (-) 1962: BI1.

603 Teichmann, GH (Gary) b 09/01/1967 - Natal - 42 Tests (30 - 6T) 52 matches (35 - 7T) 1995: W. 1996: Fj, A1, NZ1, A2, NZ2, 3*, 4*, 5*, Arg1*, 2*, F1*, 2*, W*. 1997: T*, BI1*, 2*, 3*, NZ1*, A1*, NZ2*, A2*, It*, F1*, 2*, E*, S*. 1998: I1*, 2*, W1*, E1*, A1*, NZ1*, 2*, A2*, W2*, S*, I3*, E2*. 1999: It1*, W*, NZ1*.

668 Terblanche, CS (Stefan) b 02/07/1975 - Boland - 37 Tests (95 - 19T) 41 matches (115 - 23T) 1998: I1, 2, W1, E1, A1, NZ1, 2, A2, W2, S, I3, E2. 1999: It1(R), 2, W, A1, NZ2(R), [Sp, E(t), A3(R), NZ3]. 2000: E3. 2002: W1, 2, Arg, Sm, NZ1, A1, 2(R). 2003: S1, 2, Arg, A1, NZ1, A2, NZ2, [G].

633 Theron, DF (Dawie) b 15/09/1966 - GW - 13 Tests (-) 15 matches (-) 1996: A2(R), NZ2(R), 5, Arg1, 2, F1, 2, W. 1997: BI2(R), 3, NZ1(R), A1, NZ2(R).

749 Theron, JT (Gus) b 10/01/1975 - WP - No Tests - No matches Toured Aus & NZ. 2003.

56 Theunissen, DJ (Danie) b 12/07/1869 d 19/03/1964 - GW - 1 Test (-) 1 match (-) 1896: BI3.

142 Thompson, G (Tommy) b 04/10/1886 d 20/06/1916 - WP - 3 Tests (-) 15 matches

(-) 1912: S, I, W.

648 Thomson, JRD (Jeremy) b 24/06/1967 - Natal - No Tests - 4 matches (5 - 1T) Toured Arg, F & W. 1996.

161 Tindall, JC (Jackie) b 26/03/1900 d 03/05/1946 - WP - 5 Tests (-) 27 matches (3 - 1T) 1924: BI1. 1928: NZ1, 2, 3, 4.

515 Tobias, EG (Errol) b 18/03/1950 - Boland - 6 Tests (22 - 1T, 3C, 4P) 15 matches (65 - 5T, 15C, 5P) 1981: I1, 2. 1984: E1, 2, S. Am&Sp1, 2.

201 Tod, NS (Jacko) b 11/03/1904 d 01/05/1965 - Natal - 1 Test (-) 1 match (-) 1928: NZ2.

163 Townsend, WH (Taffy) b 12/03/1896 d 27/01/1943 - Natal - 1 Test (-) 11 matches (3 - 1T) 1921: NZ1.

20 Trenery, WE (Wilfred) b 21/09/1867 d 23/08/1905 - GW - 1 Test (-) 1 match (-) 1891: BI2.

635 Tromp, H (Henry) b 29/12/1966 - NTvl - 4 Tests (-) 8 matches (5 - 1T) 1996: NZ3, 4, Arg2(R), F1(R).

581 Truscott, JA (Andries) b 22/07/1968 - NTvl - No Tests - 4 matches (-) Toured F & E. 1992.

187 Truter, DR (Pally) b 19/04/1897 d 21/11/1962 - WP - 2 Tests (-) 2 matches (-) 1924: BI2, 4.

385 Truter, JT (Trix) b 05/06/1939 - Natal - 3 Tests (3 - 1T) 16 matches (33 - 11T) 1963: A1. 1964: F. 1965: A2.

680 Trytsman, JW (Johnny) b 29/07/1971 - WP - No Tests - 4 matches (-) Toured BI & I. 1998.

232 Turner, FG (Freddy) b 18/03/1914 d 12/09/2003 - EP - 11 Tests (29 - 4T, 4C, 3P) 24 matches (131 - 18T, 26C, 7P, 1D) 1933: A1, 2, 3. 1937: A1, 2, NZ1, 2, 3. 1938: BI1, 2, 3.

349 Twigge, RJ (Robert) b 24/07/1936 - NTvl - 1 Test (-) 1 match (-) 1960: S.

763 Tyibilika, S (Solly) b 23/06/1979 - KZN - 8 Tests (15 - 3T) 8 matches (15 - 3T) 2004: S, Arg. 2005: U, A2, Arg. 2006: NZ1, A2, NZ2.

U

315 Ulyate, CA (Clive) b 11/12/1933 - Tvl - 7 Tests (6 - 1T, 1D) 16 matches (12 - 2T, 2D) 1955: BI1, 2, 3, 4. 1956: NZ1, 2, 3.

370 Uys, P de W (Piet) b 10/12/1937 d 12/12/2009 - NTvl - 12 Tests (-) 29 matches (12 - 4T) 1960: W. 1961: E, S, I, A1, 2. 1962: BI1, 4. 1963: A1, 2. 1969: A1(R), 2.

738 Uys, PJ (Pierre) b 05/02/1976 - Mpu - 1 Test (-) 1 match (-) 2002: S.

V

525 Van Aswegen, HJ (Henning) b 11/02/1955 - WP - 2 Tests (-) 10 matches (-) 1981: NZ1. 1982: S. Am2(R).

718 **Van Biljon, L** (Lukas) b 16/03/1976 - Natal - 13 Tests (5 - 1T) 13 matches (5 - 1T) 2001: It1(R), NZ1, A1, 2, NZ2, F3, It2(R), E(R), US. 2002: F(R), S, E(R). 2003: NZ2(R).

59 **Van Broekhuizen, HD** (Broekie) b 17/06/1872 d 04/08/1953 - WP - 1 Test (-) 1 match (-) 1896: BI4.

2 **Van Buuren, MCWE** (Mosey) b 12/08/1865 d 03/10/1951 - Tvl - 1 Test (-) 1 match (-) 1891: BI1.

250 **Van de Vyver, DF** (Vandie) b 14/12/1909 d 18/03/1977 - WP - 1 Test (-) 14 matches (12 - 4T) 1937: A2.

484 **Van den Berg, DS** (Derek) b 02/01/1946 - Natal - 4 Tests (-) 7 matches (-) 1975: F1, 2. 1976: NZ1, 2.

258 **Van den Berg, MA** (Mauritz) b 09/05/1909 d 09/04/1948 - WP - 4 Tests (-) 18 matches (15 - 5T) 1937: A1, NZ1, 2, 3.

684 **Van den Berg, PA** (Albert) b 26/01/1974 - GW - 51 Tests (20 - 4T) 55 matches (30 - 6T) 1999: It1(R), 2, NZ2, A2, [S, U(R), E(R), A3(R), NZ3(R)]. 2000: E1(t+R), A1, NZ1, A2, NZ2(R), A3(t+R), Arg, I, W, E3. 2001: F1(R), 2, A2(R), NZ2(R), US. 2004: NZ1. 2005: U, F1, 2, A1(R), 2(R), 3(R), 4(R), Arg(R), F3(R). 2006: S2(R), A1(R), NZ1, A2(R), NZ2(R), A3(R), I, E1(R), 2(R). 2007: Sm1, A2(R), NZ2, N(t+R), S(R), [T, US.], W(R).

621 **Van den Bergh, E** (Elandré) b 09/12/1966 - EP - 1 Test (-) 8 matches (5 - 1T) 1994: Arg2(t+R).

133 **Van der Hoff, AD** (Apie) b 24/09/1888 d 09/03/1970 - Tvl - No Tests - 9 matches (30 - 10T) Toured BI, I & F. 1912/13.

629 **Van der Linde, A** (Toks) b 30/12/1969 - WP - 7 Tests (-) 18 matches (10 - 2T) 1995: It, E. 1996: Arg1(R), 2(R), F1(R), W(R). 2001: F3(R).

741 **Van der Linde, CJ** (CJ) b 27/08/1980 - FS - 69 Tests (20 - 4T) 74 matches (20 - 4T) 2002: S(R), E(R). 2004: I1(R), 2(R), PI(R), A1(R), NZ2(t+R), A2(R), W2(R), I3(R), E(t+R), S, Arg. 2005: U, F1(R), 2, A1(R), 3, NZ1, A4, NZ2, Arg, W, F3. 2006: S2(R), F(R), A1, NZ1, A2, NZ2, I, E1, 2. 2007: E1(R), 2, A1(R), NZ1(R), A2, NZ2, N, S, [Sm, E3(R), T, US(R), Arg, E4.], W. 2008: W1(t+R), It, NZ1, 2, A1, Arg, NZ3, A2. 2009: F(R), I(t). 2010: W1, It1(R), NZ2, A1(t+R), NZ3(R), A2(R), 3(R), I(R), W2(R), S(R), E(R).

323 **Van der Merwe, AJ** (Bertus) b 14/07/1929 d 23/11/1971 - Boland - 12 Tests (-) 26 matches (3 - 1T) 1955: BI2, 3, 4. 1956: A1, 2, NZ1, 2, 3, 4. 1958: F1. 1960: S, NZ2.

221 **Van der Merwe, AV** (Alvi) b

14/09/1908 d 18/09/1986 - WP - 1 Test (-) 13 matches (6 - 2T) 1931: W.

273 Van der Merwe, BS (Fiks) b 02/01/1917 d 11/07/2005 - NTvl - 1 Test (-) 1 match (-) 1949: NZ1.

703 **Van der Merwe, CP** (Carel) b 05/10/1971 - Boland - No Tests - 4 matches (-) Toured Arg, I, W & E. 2000.

365 **Van der Merwe, HS** (Stompie) b 24/08/1936 d 04/06/1988 - NTvl - 5 Tests (-) 17 matches (6 - 2T) 1960: NZ4. 1963: A2, 3, 4. 1964: F.

790 **Van der Merwe, HS** (Heinke) b 03/05/1985 - GL - 1 Test (-) 2 matches (-) 2007: W(t+R).

433 **Van der Merwe, JP** (JP) b 07/12/1947 - WP - 1 Test (-) 12 matches (9 - 3T) 1970: W.

526 **Van der Merwe, PR** (Flippie) b 08/07/1957 - SWD - 6 Tests (-) 12 matches (-) 1981: NZ2, 3, US. 1986: NZC1, 2. 1989: WT1.

818 **Van der Merwe, PR** (Flip) b 03/06/1985 - BB - 10 Tests (5 - 1T) 11 matches (5 - 1T) 2010: F(R), It2(R), A1(R), NZ3, A2, 3(R), I(R), W2(R), S(R), E(R).

299 Van der Ryst, FE (Franz) b 17/10/1920 d 21/02/1981 - Tvl - No Tests - 14 matches (-) Toured BI, I & F. 1951/52.

263 **Van der Schyff, JH** (Jack) b 11/06/1928 d 02/12/2001 - GW - 5 Tests (10 - 2C, 2P) 5 matches (10 - 2C, 2P) 1949: NZ1, 2, 3, 4. 1955: BI1.

434 **Van der Schyff, PJ** (Johan) b 19/01/1942 - WTvl - No Tests - 2 matches (-) Toured BI & I. 1969/70.

432 **Van der Watt, AE** (Andy) b 10/10/1946 - WP - 3 Tests (-) 22 matches (42 - 14T) 1969: S(R), E. 1970: I.

203 **Van der Westhuizen, JC** (JC) b 22/11/1905 d 08/07/2003 - WP - 4 Tests (3 - 1T) 19 matches (25 - 7T, 1D) 1928: NZ2, 3, 4. 1931: I.

609 **Van der Westhuizen, JF** (Cabous) b 11/01/1965 - Natal - No Tests - 11 matches (10 - 2T) Toured NZ 1994 and W, S & I. 1994.

593 **Van der Westhuizen, JH** (Joost) b 20/02/1971 - NTvl - 89 Tests (190 - 38T) 111 matches (280 - 56T) 1993: Arg1, 2. 1994: E1, 2(R), Arg2, S, W. 1995: WS1, [A, C(R), WS2, F, NZ], W, It, E. 1996: Fj, A1, 2(R), NZ2, 3, (R), 4, 5, Arg1, 2, F1, 2, W. 1997: T, BI1, 2, 3, NZ1, A1, NZ2, A2, It, F1. 1998: I1, 2, W1, E1, A1, NZ1, 2, A2, W2, S, I3, E2. 1999: NZ2*, A2*, [S*, Sp(R), U*, E*, A3*, NZ3*]. 2000: C, E1, 2, A1(R), NZ1(R), A2(R), Arg, I, W, E3. 2001: F1, 2, It1(R), NZ1, A1, 2, NZ2, F3, It2, E, US(R). 2003: S1*, S2*, A1, NZ1, A2(R), NZ2, [U*, E, Sm, NZ3].

213 **Van der Westhuizen, JH** (Ponie) b 04/11/1909 d 05/03/1995 - WP - 3 Tests (-) 16 matches (45 - 12T, 1C, 2D) 1931: I. 1932: E, S.

696 **Van der Westhuyzen, JNB** (Jaco) b 06/04/1978 - Mpu - 32 Tests (51 - 5T, 7C, 1P, 3D) 32 matches (51 - 5T, 7C, 1P, 3D) 2000: NZ2(R). 2001: It1(R). 2003: S1(R), 2, Arg, A1, [E, Sm, NZ3]. 2004: I1, 2, W1, PI, NZ1, A1, NZ2, A2, W2, I3, E, S, Arg. 2005: U, F1, 2, A1, 4(R), NZ2(R). 2006: S1, 2, F, A1.

437 **Van Deventer, PI** (Piet) b 06/06/1946 - GW - No Tests - 12 matches (12 - 4T) Toured BI & I. 1969/70.

184 **Van Druten, NJV** (Jack) b 12/06/1898 d 16/01/1989 - Tvl - 8 Tests (6 - 2T) 8 matches (6 - 2T) 1924: BI1, 2, 3, 4. 1928: NZ1, 2, 3, 4.

152 **Van Heerden, AJ** (Attie) b 10/03/1898 d 14/10/1965 - Tvl - 2 Tests (3 - 1T) 17 matches (42 - 14T) 1921: NZ1, 3.

606 **Van Heerden, FJ** (Fritz) b 29/06/1970 - WP - 14 Tests (5 - 1T) 26 matches (5 - 1T) 1994: E1, 2(R), NZ3. 1995: It, E. 1996: NZ5(R), Arg1(R), 2(R). 1997: T, BI2(t+R), 3(R), NZ1(R), 2(R). 1999: [Sp].

474 **Van Heerden, JL** (Moaner) b 18/07/1951 - NTvl - 17 Tests (4 - 1T) 23 matches (4 - 1T) 1974: BI3, 4, F1, 2. 1975: F1, 2. 1976: NZ1, 2, 3, 4. 1977: WT. 1980: BI1, 3, 4, S. Am3, 4, F.

744 **Van Heerden, JL** (Wikus) b 25/02/1979 - GL - 14 Tests (5 - 1T) 16 matches (10 - 2T) 2003: S1, 2, A1, NZ1, A2(t). 2007: A2, NZ2, S(R), [Sm(R), E3, T, US, Fiji(R), E4(R).].

272 **Van Jaarsveld, CJ** (Hoppy) b 21/02/1917 d 08/12/1980 - Tvl - 1 Test (-) 1 match (-) 1949: NZ1.

354 **Van Jaarsveldt, DC** (Des) b 31/03/1929 - Rhodesia - 1 Test (3 - 1T) 1 match (3 - 1T) 1960: S*.

368 **Van Niekerk, BB** (Bennie) b 01/12/1937 d 21/08/2000 - OFS - No Tests - 5 matches (3 - 1T) Toured BI, I & F. 1960/61.

210 **Van Niekerk, JA** (Jock) b 01/06/1907 d 19/04/1983 - WP - 1 Test (-) 2 matches (-) 1928: NZ4.

719 **Van Niekerk, JC** (Joe) b 14/05/1980 - GL - 52 Tests (50 - 10T) 52 matches (50 - 10T) 2001: NZ1(R), A1(R), NZ2(t+R), F3(R), It2, US. 2002: W1(R), 2(R), Arg(R), Sm, NZ1, A1, NZ2, A2, F, S, E. 2003: A2, NZ2, [U, E, G, Sm]. 2004: NZ1(R), A1(t), NZ2, A2, W2, I3, E, S, Arg(R). 2005: U(R), F2(R), A1(R), 2, 3, NZ1, A4, NZ2. 2006: S1, 2, F, A1, NZ1(R), A2(R). 2008: It(R), NZ1, 2, Arg(R), A2(R). 2010: W1.

259 **Van Reenen, GL** (George) b 29/03/1914 d 12/11/1967 - WP - 2 Tests (6 - 2T) 11 matches (24 - 8T) 1937: A2, NZ1.

26 **Van Renen, CG** (Charlie) b 23/08/1868 d 20/07/1942 - WP - 3 Tests (-) 3 matches (-) 1891: BI3. 1896: BI1, 4.

65 **Van Renen, WA** (Willie) b 29/08/1880 d 17/02/1942 - WP - 2 Tests (-) 2 matches (-) 1903: BI1, 3.

558 **Van Rensburg, JTJ** (Theo) b 26/05/1967 - Tvl - 6 Tests (40 - 2C, 12P) 22 matches (182 - 7T, 21C, 34P, 1D) 1992: NZ, A, E. 1993: F1, 2, A1. 1994: NZ2.

167 **Van Rooyen, GW** (Tank) b 09/12/1892 d 21/09/1942 - Tvl - 2 Tests (-) 13 matches (3 - 1T) 1921: NZ2, 3.

124 **Van Ryneveld, RCB** (Clive) b 07/07/1891 d 25/08/1969 - WP - 2 Tests (-) 2 matches (-) 1910: BI2, 3.

631 **Van Schalkwyk, D** (Danie) b 01/02/1975 - NTvl - 8 Tests (10 - 2T) 8 matches (10 - 2T) 1996: Fj(R), NZ1, 2, 3. 1997: BI2, 3, NZ1, A1.

278 **Van Schoor, RAM** (Ryk) b 03/12/1921 d 22/03/2009 - Rhodesia - 12 Tests (6 - 2T) 23 matches (21 - 7T) 1949: NZ2, 3, 4. 1951: S, I, W. 1952: E, F. 1953: A1, 2, 3, 4.

483 **Van Staden, JA** (André) b 15/12/1945 - NTvl - No Tests - 3 matches (-) Toured F. 1974.

671 **Van Straaten, AJJ** (Braam) b 28/09/1971 - GF - 21 Tests (221 - 2T, 23C, 55P) 27 matches (294 - 5T, 46C, 59P) 1999: It2(R), W, NZ1(R), A1. 2000: C, E1, 2, NZ1, A2, NZ2, A3, Arg(R), I(R), W, E3. 2001: A1, 2, NZ2, F3, It2, E.

314 **Van Vollenhoven, KT** (Tom) b 29/04/1935 - NTvl - 7 Tests (15 - 4T, 1D) 23 matches (63 - 20T, 1D) 1955: BI1, 2, 3, 4. 1956: A1, 2, NZ3.

141 **Van Vuuren, TFJ** (Tom) b 09/07/1889 d 07/07/1947 - EP - 5 Tests (-) 17 matches (6 - 2T) 1912: S, I, W. 1913: E, F.

304 **Van Wyk, CJ** (Basie) b 05/11/1923 d 29/08/2002 - Tvl - 10 Tests (18 - 6T) 23 matches (24 - 8T) 1951: S, I, W. 1952: E, F. 1953: A1, 2, 3, 4. 1955: BI1.

445 **Van Wyk, JFB** (Piston) b 21/12/1943 - NTvl - 15 Tests (-) 19 matches (-) 1970: NZ1, 2, 3, 4. 1971: F1, 2, A1, 2, 3. 1972: E. 1974: BI1, 3, 4. 1976: NZ3, 4.

196 **Van Wyk, SP** (SP) b 12/01/1901 d 22/01/1978 - WP - 2 Tests (-) 2 matches (-) 1928: NZ1, 2.

378 **Van Zyl, BP** (Ben-Piet) b 01/08/1935 d 10/03/1973 - WP - 1 Test (6 - 2T) 5 matches (12 - 4T) 1961: I.

410 **Van Zyl, CGP** (Sakkie) b 01/07/1932 - OFS - 4 Tests (-) 16 matches (6 - 2T) 1965: NZ1, 2, 3, 4.

665 **Van Zyl, DJ** (Dan) b 08/01/1971 - Mpu - 1 Test (-) 7 matches (10 - 2C, 2P) 2000: E(R).

340 **Van Zyl, GH** (Hugo) b 20/08/1932 d 08/05/2007 - WP - 17 Tests (12 - 4T) 35 matches (27 - 9T) 1958: F1. 1960: S, NZ1, 2, 3, 4, W, I. 1961: E, S, F, I, A1, 2. 1962: BI1, 3, 4.

357 **Van Zyl, HJ** (Hennie) b 31/01/1936 - Tvl - 10 Tests (18 - 6T) 24 matches (54 - 18T) 1960: NZ1, 2, 3, 4, I. 1961: E, S, I, A1, 2.

373 **Van Zyl, PJ** (Piet) b 23/07/1933 d 28/05/1988 - Boland - 1 Test (-) 17 matches (3 - 1T) 1961: I.

190 **Vanderplank, BE** (BV) b 29/04/1894 d 22/12/1990 - Natal - 2 Tests (-) 2 matches (-) 1924: BI3, 4.

497 **Veldsman, PE** (Piet) b 11/03/1952 - WP - 1 Test (-) 1 match (-) 1977: WT.

634 **Venter, AG** (André) b 14/11/1970 - FS - 66 Tests (45 - 9T) 70 matches (50 - 10T) 1996: NZ3, 4, 5, Arg1, 2, F1, 2, W. 1997: T, BI1, 2, 3, NZ1, A1, NZ2, It, F1, 2, E, S. 1998: I1, 2, W1, E1, A1, NZ1, 2, A2, W2, S(R), I3(R), E2(R). 1999: It1, 2(R), W(R), NZ1, A1, NZ2, A2, [S, U, E, A3, NZ3]. 2000: C, E1, 2, A1, NZ1, A2, NZ2, A3, Arg, I, W, E3. 2001: F1, It1, NZ1, A1, 2, NZ2, F3(R), It2(R), E(t+R), US(R).

695 **Venter, AJ** (AJ) b 29/07/1973 - Natal - 25 Tests (-) 28 matches (-) 2000: W(R), E3(R). 2001: F3, It2, E, US. 2002: W1, 2, Arg, NZ1(R), 2, A2, F, S(R), E. 2003: Arg. 2004: PI, NZ1, A1, NZ2(R), A2, I3, E. 2006: NZ3, A3.

605 **Venter, B** (Brendan) b 29/12/1969 - OFS - 17 Tests (10 - 2T) 26 matches (30 - 6T) 1994: E1, 2, NZ1, 2, 3, Arg1, 2. 1995: [R, C, WS2(R), NZ(R)]. 1996: A1, NZ1, A2. 1999: A2, [S, U].

214 **Venter, FD** (Floors) b 13/04/1909 d ??/??/1992 - Tvl - 3 Tests (-) 14 matches (24 - 8T) 1931: W. 1932: S. 1933: A3.

672 **Venter, SL** (Lourens) b 25/06/1976 - GW - No Tests - 4 matches (15 - 3T) Toured BI & I. 1998.

25 **Versfeld, C** (Hasie) b 24/09/1866 d 06/01/1942 - WP - 1 Test (-) 1 match (-) 1891: BI3.

7 **Versfeld, M** (Oupa) b 15/05/1860 d 01/09/1931 - WP - 3 Tests (-) 3 matches (-) 1891: BI1, 2, 3.

3 **Vigne, JT** (Chubb) b 23/12/1868 d 09/04/1955 - Tvl - 3 Tests (-) 3 matches (-) 1891: BI1, 2, 3.

448 **Viljoen, JF** (Joggie) b 14/05/1945 - GW - 6 Tests (6 - 2T) 10 matches (12 - 4T) 1971: F1, 2, A1, 2, 3. 1972: E.

644 **Viljoen, J** (Joggie) b 22/07/1976 - WP - No Tests - 3 matches (-) Toured Arg, F & W. 1996.

808 **Viljoen, R** (Riaan) b 04/01/1983 - GW - No Tests - 2 matches (-) Toured F, It, I & E. 2009.

451 **Viljoen. JT** (Hannes) b 21/04/1943 - Natal - 3 Tests (6 - 2T) 10 matches (48 - 16T) 1971: A1, 2, 3.

532 **Villet, JV** (John) b 03/11/1954 - WP - 2 Tests (-) 2 matches (-) 1984: E1, 2.

530 **Visagie, GP** (Gawie) b 31/03/1955 - Natal - No Tests - 3 matches (8 - 2T) Toured NZ & USA. 1981.

683 **Visagie, IJ** (Cobus) b 31/10/1973 - WP - 29 Tests (-) 29 matches (-) 1999: It1, W, NZ1, A1, NZ2, A2, [S, U, E, A3, NZ3]. 2000: C, E2, A1, NZ1, A2, NZ2, A3. 2001: NZ1, A1, 2, NZ2, F3, It2(R), E(t+R), US. 2003: S1(R), 2(R), Arg.

419 **Visagie, PJ** (Piet) b 16/04/1943 - GW - 25 Tests (130 - 6T, 20C, 19P, 5D) 44 matches (240 - 8T, 36C, 40P, 8D) 1967: F1, 2, 3, 4. 1968: BI1, 2, 3, 4, F1, 2. 1969: A1, 2, 3, 4, S, E. 1970: NZ1, 2, 3, 4. 1971: F1, 2, A1, 2, 3.

536 **Visagie, RG** (Rudi) b 27/06/1959 - OFS - 5 Tests (-) 9 matches (5 - 1T) 1984: E1, 2, S. Am&Sp1, 2. 1993: F1.

517 **Visser, J de V** (De Villiers) b 26/11/1958 - WP - 2 Tests (-) 12 matches (16 - 4T) 1981: NZ2, US.

625 **Visser, M** (Mornay) b 30/03/1969 - WP - 1 Test (-) 1 match (-) 1995: WS1(R).

237 **Visser, PJ** (Paul) b 25/12/1903 d 25/04/1963 - Tvl - 1 Test (-) 1 match (-) 1933: A2.

293 **Vivier, SS** (Basie) b 01/03/1927 d 18/10/2009 - OFS - 5 Tests (11 - 4C, 1P) 31 matches (165 - 5T, 45C, 17P, 3D) 1956: A1*, 2*, NZ2*, 3*, 4*.

471 **Vogel, ML** (Leon) b 22/10/1949 - OFS - 1 Test (-) 1 match (-) 1974: BI2(R).

686 **Von Hoesslin, DJB** (Dave) b 10/05/1975 - GW - 5 Tests (10 - 2T) 5 matches (10 - 2T) 1999: It1(R), 2, W(R), NZ1, A1(R).

681 **Vos, AN** (André) b 09/01/1975 - GL - 33 Tests (25 - 5T) 38 matches (30 - 6T) 1999: It1(t+R), 2, NZ1(R), 2(R), A2, [S(R), Sp*, E(R), A3(R), NZ3]. 2000: C*, E1*, 2*, A1*, NZ1*, A2*, NZ2*, A3*, Arg*, I*, W*, E3*. 2001: F1*, 2*, It1, NZ1, A1, 2, NZ2, F3, It2, E, US*.

W

491 **Wagenaar, C** (Christo) b 11/03/1952 - NTvl - 1 Test (-) 1 match (-) 1977: WT.

269 **Wahl, JJ** (Ballie) b 10/07/1920 d 25/06/1978 - WP - 1 Test (-) 1 match (-) 1949: NZ1.

170 **Walker, AP** (Alf) b 08/05/1893 d 17/07/1971 - Natal - 6 Tests (-) 14 matches (-) 1921: NZ1, 3. 1924: BI1, 2, 3, 4.

311 **Walker, HN** (Harry) b 01/07/1928 d

05/08/2008 - OFS - 4 Tests (-) 19 matches (-) 1953: A3. 1956: A2, NZ1, 4.

115 **Walker, HW** (Henry) b 22/02/1884 d 21/08/1951 - Tvl - 3 Tests (-) 3 matches (-) 1910: BI1, 2, 3.

397 **Walton, DC** (Don) b 05/04/1939 - Natal - 8 Tests (-) 31 matches (12 - 4T) 1964: F. 1965: I, S, NZ3, 4. 1969: A1, 2, E.

739 **Wannenburg, PJ** (Pedrie) b 02/01/1981 - BB - 20 Tests (15 - 3T) 20 matches (15 - 3T) 2002: F(R), E. 2003: S1, 2, Arg, A1(t+R), NZ1(R). 2004: I1, 2, W1, PI(R). 2006: S1(R), F, NZ2(R), 3, A3. 2007: Sm1(R), NZ1(R), A2, NZ2.

216 **Waring, FW** (Franky) b 07/11/1908 d 24/01/2000 - WP - 7 Tests (6 - 2T) 19 matches (12 - 4T) 1931: I. 1932: E. 1933: A1, 2, 3, 4, 5.

707 **Wasserman, JG** (Johan) b 29/07/1977 - SWD - No Tests - 4 matches (5 - 1T) Toured Arg, I, W & E. 2000

786 **Watson, LA** (Luke) b 26/10/1983 - WP - 10 Tests (-) 10 matches (-) 2007: Sm1. 2008: W1, 2, It, NZ1(R), 2(R), Arg, NZ3(R), A2(R), 3(t+R).

260 **Watt, HH** (Howard) b 01/03/1911 d 18/08/2005 - WP - No Tests - 7 matches (9 - 3T) Toured A & NZ. 1937.

154 **Weepner, JS** (Jackie) b 16/01/1896 d 14/12/1965 - WP - No Tests - 9 matches (6 - 2T) Toured A & NZ. 1921.

587 **Wegner, GN** (Nico) b 03/12/1968 - WP - 4 Tests (-) 12 matches (-) 1993: F2, A1, 2, 3.

366 **Wentzel, GJ** (Giepie) b 28/02/1938 d 01/07/1996 - EP - No Tests - 12 matches (37 - 2T, 14C, 1P) Toured BI, I & F. 1960/61.

740 **Wentzel, M v Z** (Marco) b 05/05/1979

- Mpu - 2 Tests (-) 2 matches (-) 2002: F(R), S.

664 **Wessels, JC** (Boeta) b 30/06/1973 - GW - No Tests - 1 match (-) Toured It, F, E & S. 1997.

35 **Wessels, JJ** (Scraps) b 13/09/1874 d 06/04/1929 - WP - 3 Tests (-) 3 matches (-) 1896: BI1, 2, 3.

402 **Wessels, JW** (John) b 14/05/1935 d 22/01/2006 - OFS - No Tests - 2 matches (-) Toured I & S. 1965.

296 **Wessels, PW** (Piet) b 11/02/1926 d 24/08/1997 - OFS - No Tests - 14 matches (-) Toured BI, I & F. 1951/52.

459 **Whipp, PJM** (Peter) b 22/09/1950 - WP - 8 Tests (4 - 1T) 10 matches (4 - 1T) 1974: BI1, 2. 1975: F1. 1976: NZ1, 3, 4. 1980: S. Am1, 2.

217 **White, J** (Jimmy) b 20/05/1911 d 03/07/1997 - Border - 10 Tests (10 - 2T, 1D) 26 matches (23 - 5T, 2D) 1931: W. 1933: A1, 2, 3, 4, 5. 1937: A1, 2, NZ1, 2.

585 **Wiese, JJ** (Kobus) b 16/05/1964 - Tvl - 18 Tests (5 - 1T) 32 matches (15 - 3T) 1993: F1. 1995: WS1, [R, C, WS2, F, NZ], W, It, E. 1996: NZ3(R), 4(R), 5, Arg1, 2, F1, 2, W.

743 **Willemse, AK** (Ashwin) b 08/09/1981 - GL - 19 Tests (20 - 4T) 20 matches (25 - 5T) 2003: S1, 2, NZ1, A2, NZ2, [U, E, Sm, NZ3]. 2004: W2, I3. 2007: E1, 2(R), Sm1, A1, NZ1, N, S(R), [T.].

120 **Williams, AE** (Arthur) b 01/07/1879 d 21/07/1930 - GW - 1 Test (-) 1 match (-) 1910: BI1.

533 **Williams, AP** (Avril) b 10/02/1961 - WP - 2 Tests (-) 2 matches (-) 1984: E1, 2.

589 **Williams, CM** (Chester) b 08/08/1970 - WP - 27 Tests (70 - 14T) 47 matches (135

- 27T) 1993: Arg2. 1994: E1, 2, NZ1, 2, 3, Arg1, 2, S, W. 1995: WS1, [WS2, F, NZ], It, E. 1998: A1(t), NZ1(t). 2000: C(R), E1(t), 2(R), A1(R), NZ2, A3, Arg, I, W(R).

231 **Williams, DO** (Dai) b 16/06/1913 d 24/12/1975 - WP - 8 Tests (15 - 5T) 18 matches (51 - 17T) 1937: A1, 2, NZ1, 2, 3. 1938: BI1, 2, 3.

450 **Williams, JG** (John) b 29/10/1946 - NTvl - 13 Tests (-) 24 matches (3 - 1T) 1971: F1, 2, A1, 2, 3. 1972: E. 1974: BI1, 2, 4, F1, 2. 1976: NZ1, 2.

363 **Wilson, LG** (Lionel) b 25/05/1933 - WP - 27 Tests (6 - 2D) 58 matches (19 - 3T, 2C, 2D) 1960: NZ3, 4, W, I. 1961: E, F, I, A1, 2. 1962: BI1, 2, 3, 4. 1963: A1, 2, 3, 4. 1964: W, F. 1965: I, S, A1, 2, NZ1, 2, 3, 4.

495 **Wolmarans, BJ** (Barry) b 22/02/1953 - OFS - 1 Test (4 - 1T) 7 matches (4 - 1T) 1977: WT.

135 **Wrentmore, GM** (Bai) b 20/02/1893 d 16/08/1953 - WP - No Tests - 9 matches (27 - 3T, 5C, 2D) Toured BI, I & F. 1912/13.

548 **Wright, GD** (Garth) b 09/09/1963 - EP - 7 Tests (4 - 1T) 12 matches (4 - 1T) 1986: NZC3, 4. 1989: WT1, 2. 1992: F1, 2, E.

381 **Wyness, MRK** (Wang) b 23/01/1937 - WP - 5 Tests (3 - 1T) 5 matches (3 - 1T) 1962: BI1, 2, 3, 4. 1963: A2.

Z

153 **Zeller, WC** (Bill) b 18/07/1894 d 27/07/1969 - Natal - 2 Tests (-) 14 matches (39 - 13T) 1921: NZ2, 3.

212 **Zimerman, M** (Morris) b 08/06/1911 - d 09/01/1992 - WP - 4 Tests (3 - 1T) 18 matches (42 - 14T) 1931: W, I. 1932: E, S.

PROVINCIAL REPRESENTATION

South Africa's 828 International Players have come from 15 provincial unions as follows:

Western Province	254
Golden Lions (previously Transvaal)	156
Blue Bulls (previously Northern Transvaal)	100
Free State (previously Orange Free State)	76
KwaZulu Natal (previously Natal)	72
Griqualand West	61
Eastern Province	34
Border	16
Boland	15
Falcons (previously Eastern Transvaal)	10
Leopards (previously North West, Western Transvaal)	9
Mpumalanga (previously South Eastern Transvaal)	9
Zimbabwe (previously Rhodesia)	8
South Western Districts	5
Namibia (previously South West Africa)	3
TOTAL	**828**

SOUTH AFRICANS CAPPED OVERSEAS 1896-2010

† Indicates also played for South Africa at rugby.

A

Abbott, SR (Stuart) - England - 9 Tests - 2003-2006
Abendanon, NJ (Nick) - England - 2 tests - 2007
†Allan, J (John) - Scotland - 9 Tests - 1990-1991
Alexander, M (Matt) - USA - 25 Tests - 1995-1998
Anderson HJ (Henry) - Ireland - 4 Tests - 1903-1906
Antoni, JA (Giovani) - Italy - 2 Tests - 2001
Appleford, GN (Geoff) - England - 1 Test - 2002

B

Bell, PJD (Patrick) - USA - 7 Tests - 2006
Black, BH (Brian) - England - 10 Tests - 1930-1933
Blom, A (André) - USA - 13 Tests - 1998-2000
Botes, L-W (Lu-Wayne) - Namibia - 9 Tests 2006-2007
Brooks, FG (Freddie) - England - 1 Test - 1906
Buchanan, JCR (John) - Scotland - 16 Tests - 1921-1925

C

Catt, MJ (Mike) - England (75 Tests), Lions (1 Test) - 1994-2007
Constable R (Ryan) - Australia - 1 Test - 1994
Cuttitta, M (Marcello) - Italy - 54 Tests - 1987-1999
Cuttitta, M (Massimo) - Italy - 69 Tests - 1990-2000

D

Davey, J (Jas) - England - 2 Tests - 1908-1909
Davies, MJ (Mickey) - Wales - 2 Tests - 1939
De Jager, B (Benjamin) - Italy - 1 Test - 2006
De Jong, MG (Mike) - USA - 9 Tests - 1990-1991
De Marigny, JR (Roland).- Italy - 19 Tests - 2004-2007
De Villiers, P (Pieter) - France - 69 Tests - 1999-2007
Del Fava, CA (Carlo) - Italy - 49 Tests - 2004-2010
Dickson, WM (Walter) - Scotland - 7 Tests - 1912-1913
Downes, GT (Graham) - USA - 1 Test - 1992
Duncan, DD (Denoon) - Scotland - 4 Tests - 1920

E

Elgie, MK (Kim) - Scotland - 8 Tests - 1954-1955
Eloff, PT (Phillip) - USA - 35 Tests - 2000-2007
Erasmus, DJ (Danie) - Australia - 2 Tests - 1923
Erasmus, J (Jaco) - Italy - 3 Tests - 2008
Erskine, CE (Chad) - USA - 10 tests - 2007-2008
Evans, I (Ian) - Wales - 16 Tests - 2006-2008

F

Francis, TES (Tim) - England - 4 Tests - 1926
Fourie, CH (Hendré) - England - 4 Tests - 2010
Freakes, HD (Trilby) - England - 3 Tests - 1938-1939

G

†Gage, JH (Jack) - Ireland - 4 Tests - 1926-1927
Gagiano, JR (JJ) - USA - 11 Tests - 2008-2010
Geldenhuys, Q (Quintin) - Italy - 16 Tests - 2008-2010
Gouws, J (Jurie) - USA - 8 Tests - 2003-2004
Grobler, J (Juan) - USA - 33 Tests - 1996-2002

H

Hall, S (Steven) - France - 2 Tests - 2002
Hands, RHM (Reg) - England - 2 Tests - 1910
Harris, SW (Stan) - England (2 Tests) Lions (2 Tests) - 1920-1924
Hauck, A (Alexander) - Germany - 6 Tests - 2009-2010
Hawkins, M (Matt) - USA - 1 Test - 2010
Heatlie, BH (Fairy) - Argentina - 1 Test - 1910
Henderson, JH (Chick) - Scotland - 9 Tests - 1953-1954
Hendriks, JHF (Tenk) - Russia - 2 Tests - 2002
Hindson, RE (Ro) - Canada - 31 Tests - 1973-1990
Hofmeyr, MB (Murray) - England - 3 Tests - 1950
Hopley, FJV (John) - England - 3 Tests - 1907-1908
Horak, MJ (Michael) - England - 1 Test - 2002

J

Jones IC (Ian) - Wales - 1 Test - 1968

K

Keyter, JC (Jason) - USA - 17 Tests - 2000-2003
Klerck, GS (Gerhard) - USA - 8 Tests - 2003-2004
Krige, JA (Jan) - England - 1 Test - 1920

L

Labuschagne, NA (Nick) - England - 5 Tests - 1953-1955

Lentz, O (Owen) - USA - 8 Tests - 2006-2007
Liebenberg, B (Brian) - France - 12 Tests - 2003-2005
Lipman, S (Sean) - USA - 9 Tests - 1988-1991
Lupini, E (Tito) - Italy - 11 Tests - 1987-1989
Luscombe, HN (Hal) - Wales - 16 Tests - 2003-2007

M

Macdonald, DSM (Donald) - Scotland - 7 Tests - 1977-1978
MacDonald, JS (Jimmy) - Scotland - 5 Tests - 1903-1905
Marinos, AWN (Andy) - Wales - 8 Tests - 2002-2003
Marshall, KW (Kenneth) - Scotland - 8 Tests - 1934-1937
McCowat, RH (Harold) - Scotland - 1 Test - 1905
McMillan, KHD (Keith) - Scotland - 4 Tests - 1953
Mehrtens, AP (Andrew) - New Zealand - 70 Tests - 1995-2004
†Mellish, FW (Frank) - England - 6 Tests - 1920-1921
Melville, E (Eric) - France - 6 Tests - 1990-1991
Meyer, JM (Johannes) - Namibia - 16 Tests - 2003-2007
Milton, JG (Jumbo) - England - 5 Tests - 1904-1907
Mulligan, PJ (Patrick) - Australia - 1 Test - 1925
Mullins, RC (Cuthbert) - British Isles - 2 Tests - 1896

N

Newman, SC (Sid) - England - 3 Tests - 1947-1948
Newton-Thompson, JO (Ossie) - England - 2 Tests - 1947
Nieuwenhuis, J (Jacques) - Namibia - 17 Tests 2006-2010

O

O'Cuinneagain, D (Dion) - Ireland - 19 Tests - 1998-2000
Osler, FN (Frank) - Scotland - 2 Tests - 1911
Owen-Smith, HG (Tuppy) - England - 10 Tests - 1934-1937

P

Peens, G (Gert) - Italy - 23 Tests - 2002-2006
Pieters, W (Werner) - Russia - 2 Tests - 2002
Pocock, DW (David) - Australia - 30 Tests - 2008-2010
Poppmeier, M (Michael) - Germany - 6 Tests - 2009-2010
Proudfoot, MC (Matthew) - Scotland - 4 Tests - 1998-2003

R

Rathbone, C (Clyde) - Australia - 26 Tests - 2004-2006
Rawlinson, GP (Greg) - New Zealand - 4 Tests 2006-2007
Reid, RE (Roland) - Scotland - 2 Tests - 2001
Robertsen, JR (John) - Canada - 9 Tests - 1985-1991
Rosenblum, ME (Myer) - Australia - 4 Tests - 1928
Roxburgh, JR (James) - Australia - 9 Tests - 1968-1970

S

Small, HD (Harry) - England - 4 Tests - 1950
Stevens, MJH (Matt) - England - 32 Tests - 2004-2008
†Stewart, JC (Christian) - Canada - 14 Tests - 1991-1995
Steyn, SSL (Stephen) - Scotland - 2 Tests - 1911-1912
Stickling, C (Conrad) - Portugal - 5 Tests - 2010
†Strauss, CP (Tiaan) - Australia - 11 Tests - 1999

T

Theron, JP (Diumpie) - Namibia - 8 Tests - 1997-1999
Thomas, RM (Rhys) - Wales - 7 Tests - 2006-2009
Trenkel, N (Nick) - Canada - 1 Test - 2007

V

Van der Merwe, DTH - Canada - 15 Tests - 2006-2010
Van Heerden, A (Andries) - France - 2 Tests - 1992
Van Ryneveld, CB (Clive) - England - 4 Tests - 1949
Van Zyl, WP (Piet) - Namibia - 14 Tests - 2007-2010
Van Zyl, R (Riaan) - USA - 13 Tests - 2003-2004
Vickerman, DJ (Dan) - Australia - 54 Tests - 2002-2008
Viljoen, F (Francois) - USA - 16 Tests - 2004-2006
Visser, W (Wim) - Italy - 22 Tests - 1999-2002
Volschenk, R (Bloues) - Russia - 2 Tests - 2002

W

Waters, FHH (Fraser) - England - 3 Tests - 2001-2004
White-Cooper, WRS (Steve) - England - 2 Tests - 2001
Williamson, RH (Rupert) - England - 5 Tests - 1908-1909
Wilson, AW (Andrew) - Scotland - 1 Test - 2005
Wilson, DS (Tug) - England - 8 Tests - 1952-1955

Z

Zaayman, C (Christian) - Namibia - 13 Tests - 1997-1999

SPRINGBOK RECORDS

SA SEVENS INTERNATIONALS 1993-2010

† indicates 15-a-side Springbok

A

Adams, BI (Bennie) (WP) – 04 HK, Sing, Bor, Lon, Dub, SA.

Afrika, CS (Cecil) (Griffons) 09 WG, 09 Dub, SA, 10 NZ, USA, Aus, HK, Lon, Sco, CG.

Alberts, N (Nico) (WP) - 01 Wel.

†**Aplon, GG** (Gio) (WP) 06 Wel, LA, Par, Lon 07 Lon, Sco 08 Lon, Sco, 08 Dub, SA, 09 NZ, USA, Lon, Sco, RWC.

April, C (Chelton) (WP) - 96 HK.

Arnold, P (Peet) (N Tvl) - 96 Dub; 98 Arg, Ur, Viña.

B

†**Badenhorst, C** (Chris) (FS)* - 93 HK, RWC; 96 Ur.

Basson, S (Stefan) (WP) – 04 HK, Sing, Bor, Lon. 05 Sing, Lon, Par, RWC, WG, Dub, SA, 06 Wel, LA, Par, Lon, CG, Dub, SA, 07 HK, Aus, 08 lon, Sco.

Benjamin, RS (Ryno) (Boland) 05 Sing, Lon, Par, WG, 06 Par, Lon, Dub, SA, 07 HK, Aus, 08 Dub, SA, 09 NZ, USA, HK, Aus, Lon, Sco, RWC, WG,)(Dub, 10 NZ, USA, Aus, HK, Lon, Sco, CG.

Blom, J (Jandré) (FS) 05 Dub, SA, 06 HK, Sing 07 Wel, USA.

†**Bobo, G** (Gcobani) (Lions) - 99 SA; 01 Lon, Car, Jap, 07 Wel, USA, HK, Aus, Lon(c), Sco(c).

Bock, AG (Alshaun) (Bol) - 03 HK.

†**Boome, CS** (Selborne) (WP) - 98 Arg, Ur, Viña .

Botha, BC (Bernardo) (Golden Lions) 10 CG.

Bouwer, G (Graeme) (NTvl) - 96 Dub; 97 RWC; 98 HK; 99 Fiji*, HK.

Bowles, JJ (Jovan) (Sharks) 06 Dub, SA, 07 Lon, Sco.

Brand, J (Janneman) (WP) - 96 Ur, HK.

Breytenbach, CL (Conrad) (NTvl) - 96 HK.

Brink, HM (Helgard) (FS) - 99 Par, Dub, SA; 00 NZ, Fiji, Aus, HK, Jap, Fr, Dur,

Dub; 01 RWC, HK, Sha, KL, Tok, Lon, Car, Jap, Dub, Dur; 02 San, Arg, Bris, Wel, Sing, KL, Bris.

Brink, S (Stephen) (FS) - 96 Ur, HK, Dub(c); 97 RWC; 98 Arg(c), Ur(c), Viña(c).

†**Britz, GJJ** (Gerrie) (FS) - 01 Dub, Dur, San, Arg.

†**Britz, WK** (Warren) (Sharks) - 99 Par, Dub, SA; 00 Ur, Arg, NZ, Fiji, Aus, HK, Jap, Fr, Dur, Dub; 01 RWC.

Brown, K (Kyle) (WP) 08 Dub, SA, 09 NZ, USA, HK, Aus, Lon, Sco, RWC, WG, 09 Dub, SA, 10 NZ, USA, Aus(c), HK(c).

†**Brüssow, HW** (Heinrich) (FS) 06 HK, Sing.

Burger, PB (Phillip) (FS) 06 Wel, LA, Par, Lon, CG, Dub, SA.

C

Calitz, JP (Johan) (Leopards) - 99 Arg, San, Fiji, HK, Tok, Par; 00 HK, Tok*, Dur, Dub; 01 Wel, HK, Sha, KL, Tok, Lon, Car, Jap.

†**Chavhanga, T** (Tonderai) (Free State) – 03 Dub, SA

†**Cilliers, NV** (Vlok) (WP) – 93 HK; 94 HK; 96 Dub; 98 HK.

†**Claassens, JP** (Jannie) (NTvl)* - 93 HK, RWC; 96 HK, Dub.

Coeries, DB (Darryl) (SWD Eagles) - 02 Dub, SA; 03 Bris, NZ, HK.

Coetzee, F (Fielies) (Falcons) - 99 Arg, San.

Coetzee, R (Rudi) (Lions) - 02 Dub, SA; 03 Car, Lon.

†**Conradie , JHJ** (Bolla) (WP) - 99 Dub, SA; 00 NZ, Fiji, Aus.

D

Dames, A (Archer) (Pumas) - 99 Par.

Damons, O (Ossie) (Griffons) 05 Lon, Par.

Dazel, RL (Renfred) (Boland) 05 WG,

Dub, SA, 06 Wel, LA, HK, Sing, CG, SA, 07 Wel, USA , 07 Dub, SA, 08 Wel, USA, HK, Aus 08 Dub, SA, 09 Nz, USA, HK, Aus, Lon, Sco, RWC, WG, 10 lon, Sco, CG.

†**De Jongh, JL** (Juan) (WP) 08 Wel.

Delport, PS (Paul) (WP) – 03 Dub, 04 Wel, LA 06 Par, Lon, 08 Dub, Sa, 09 Nz, USA, Sco, RWC, WG, 09 Dub(c), SA(c), CG(c).

De Marigny, MRD (Marc) (Sharks) - 03 Bris, NZ, HK, Car, Lon, Dub (c), SA(c),04 Wel, LA, HK(c), Sing(c), Bor(c), Lon(c) Dub.

Demas, JP (Danwel) (WP) – 03 Dub, SA, 04 Wel, LA, HK, Sing, Bor ,Lon, 05 Sing, Lon, Par, RWC, WG, Dub, SA, 06 Par, CG, Dub, SA, 07 Dub, SA, 08 Lon, Sco.

†**De Villiers, J** (Jean) (WP) - 02 San, Arg, Bris, Wel, Bei, HK, Sing, KL, Lon, Car, CG.

†**Dirks, CA** (Chris) (Tvl)* - 94 HK.

Dry, CA (Chris) (SARU contracted) 10 Aus, HK, Lon, Sco.

Du Plessis, M (Malan) (Bol) - 03 HK.

Du Plooy, JP (JP) (Lions) - 98 Arg, Ur, Viña .

Du Preez, BWN (Branco) (Blue Bulls) 10 NZ, USA, Aus, HK.

†**Du Toit, GS** (Gaffie) (GW) - 98 CG; 02 CG.

E

Ebersohn, RT (Robert) (Free State) 08 HK, Aus, 08 Dub, SA, 09 NZ, USA, HK, Aus, Lon, RWC

Engelbrecht, G (Gerrie) (Griffons) - 00 Ur, Arg, NZ, Fiji, Aus, HK, Jap; 01 Wel.

†**Esterhuizen, G** (Grant) (Lions) - 03 NZ.

Eyre, NJ (Nicolas) (Lions) - 03 NZ, 04 bor, Lon.

F

Fihlani, IZ (Ian) (Bulldogs) - 01 Wel; 02

Key: Arg > Argentina (Mar del Plata). Aus > Australia. Bei > Beijing. Bol > Boland. Bor > Bordeaux. Bris > Brisbane. Car > Cardiff, Wales. CG > Commonwealth Games. Dub > Dubai. Dur > Durban. Fr > France. Fs > Free State. GL > Golden Lions. HK > Hong Kong. Jap > Japan. KL > Kuala Lumpur. Lon > London. NZ > New Zealand. Par > Paris. Punte > Punte del Este, Uruguay. RWC > Rugby World Cup. SA > South Africa. San > Santiago, Chile. Sha > Shangai. Sing > Singapore. Ur > Uruguay. Tok > Tokyo. Viña > Viña del Mar, Chile. Wel > Wellington, NZ. WG > World Games (Duisburg, Germany). A player's province is at his first selection for a tournament. Captains are indicated by (c).

Bei, HK, Sing, KL, Lon, Car, Dub, SA; 03 HK, Car, Lon.

†**Floors, L** (Lucas) (SWD Eagles) – 03 Dub, SA, 04 HK, Sing, Bor 05 Dub 06 Dub(c), SA 07 SA, 08 Lon, Sco.

Foote, KW (Kevin) (Natal) - 02 Dub; 03 Bris, NZ, HK, Car, Lon, 04 Wel(c), LA(c).

Fourie, AJ (Andries) (EP) - 99 Arg, San, Fiji, HK, Par(c), Dub, SA; 00 Ur, Arg, NZ(c), Fiji(c), Aus(c), HK(c), Jap(c), Fr(c), Dur, Dub; 01 Wel, HK, Sha, KL, Tok, Lon, Car.

Fourie, DA (Deon) (Western Province) 07 Lon, Sco.

Fowles, JJ (Josh) (Bulldogs) - 02 Sing, KL.

Francis, E (Eugene) (WP) - 02 Bris, Wel, Bei, HK, Sing, KL, Lon, Car; 03 Bris, NZ, HK, Car, Lon 03 Dub, SA, 04 Wel, LA,

Fredericks, ER (Eddie) (NW) - 99 Par; 00 NZ, Fiji, Aus.04 Dub, SA, 05 Wel, LA, Lon, Par, RWC.

Frolick, S (Shandre) (WP) 05 Wel, LA 06 Dub.

G

†**Gerber, HJ** (Hendrik) (WP) - 98 Arg, Ur, Viña .

†**Gillingham, JW** (Joe) (Lions) - 98 Arg, Ur, Viña , CG.

Grobler, D (??) - 99 Fiji, HK.*

H

†**Habana, BG** (Bryan) (Lions) – 04 Wel, LA.

Haupt, PJ (Hannru) (FS) - 03 Bris, NZ.

Heidtmann, DM (Dale) (Bulldogs) - 01 Wel, Dub, Dur; 02 San, Arg, Bris, Wel, Bei, HK, Sing, KL, Lon, Car, CG, 03 Dub, SA, 04 Wel, LA, HK, Sing, Bor, Lon, SA

Helberg, GG (Deon) (Blue Bulls) 09 Dub, SA.

†**Honiball, HW** (Henry) (Natal) 94 HK.

Horne, FH (Frankie) (SARU contract) 07 Dub, SA, 08 Wel, USA, HK, Aus, Lon, Sco, 08 Dub, SA, 09 NZ, USA, HK, Aus, Lon, Sco, RWC, WG, 09 Dub, SA, 10 NZ, USA, Aus,HK, Lon, Sco.

Houtshamer, J (Juan) (Falcons) - 00 HK, Jap.

Hulme, A (Alten) (BB) - 03 HK.

Human, WA (Wylie) (FS) - 00 HK, Jap, Fr.

Hunt, SM (Steven) (WP) 10 NZ, USA, Aus.

J

Jackson, KL (Lesley) (Boland) 04 Dub, SA 04 RWC 05 SA,06 HK, Sing.

†**Jacobs, AA** (Adi) (Falcons) - 00 HK, Tok.*

Jacobsz, SPE (Barry) (SWD Eagles) - 01 Jap.

†**Jantjes, CA** (Conrad) (Lions) - 99 Dub, SA; 00 Ur, Arg, NZ, Fiji, Aus, HK, Jap, Fr; 01 HK, Sha; 02 CG, Dub; 03 Car, Lon.

Joka, W (Wonga) (Elephants) - 00 NZ, Fiji, Aus.

Jonker, J (Jacques) (FS) - 95 HK.

Jonker, JW ("JW") (SARU contracted) 09 Dub, SA, 10 Aus, HK.

†**Joubert, AJ** (André) (Natal) - 93 HK(c), RWC(c); 94 HK(c).

Juries, FM (Fabian) (EP) - 00 Dur, Dub; 01 Wel, HK, Sha, KL, Tok, Lon, Car, Jap, Dub, Dur; 02 San, Arg, Bris, Wel, CG; 03 Car, Lon, 03 Dub, Sa, 04 Wel, LA, HK, Sing, Bor, Lon, 05 Wel, LA, Sing, Lon, Par, RWC, WG, SA, 06 Wel(c), LA(c), HK, Sing, CG, 07 Dub, SA, 08 Wel, USA, HK, Aus, Lon, Sco, 10 Lon, Sco.

K

†**Kankowski, R** (Ryan) (KZNl) 06 Wel, LA, HK, Sing, CG.

†**Kayser, DJ** (Deon) (EP) - 98 HK, CG.

Krause, GE (Gareth) (GW) 04 Dub, SA, 05 Wel, LA, RWC.

Kriese, D (Dieter) (Natal) - 93 HK, RWC; 95 HK.

Kruger, CR (Chris) (FS) - 98 Arg; 99 San.

†**Kruger, RJ** (Ruben) (FS) - 93 HK, RWC; 94 HK.

Kruger, HJ (Jorrie) (FS) - 96 Dub; 98 Arg, Ur, Viña .

Kruger, OC (Okkie) (Blue Bulls) 10 CG

Kuün, GWF (Derick) (Blue Bulls) 05 Wel, LA,

L

†**Loubscher, RIP** (Ricardo) (EP) - 99 Arg, San; 00 Fr; 01 RWC.

M

Mapoe, LG (Lionel) (FS Cheetahs) 09 USA, HK, Aus, RWC.

Maritz, H (Hoffman) (FS Cheetahs) 10 Nz, USA, Aus, HK, Lon, Sco.

Markow, A (Tony) (EP) - 95 HK.

Masina, M (Mac) (Lions) - 99 Dub; 00 Ur, Arg, Dur, Dub; 02 Bris, Wel.

Mastriet, S (SAmpie) (Blue Bulls) 10 Aus, HK.

Mbiyozo, MM (Mpho) (Western Province) 06 Dub, 07 Wel, USA, HK, Aus, Lon, Sco, 07 Dub, 07 SA, 08 Wel, USA, HK,Aus, Lon, Sco 08 Dub, SA, 09 NZ,

USA(c), HK, Aus, lon, Sco, RWC(c), WG; 09 Dub; Sa; 10 NZ; USA; Aus; HK; Lon; Sco;

McBean, BJH (Baldwin) (Griquas) 07 Wel, USA, 07 Dub, SA.

Mdaka, TLP (Thobela) (Border) - 00 NZ, Fiji, Aus, HK, Jap, Fr, Dur, Dub; 01 Wel, Dub 05 Wel, LA, Sing, Lon, Par, RWC, WG, Dub,06 Wel, LA, HK, Sing, Par, Lon, CG, Dub, SA 07 HK, Aus 08 Wel, USA.

Mentz, M J ("MJ") (Griquas) 07 Lon, Sco 07 Dub, SA, 08 Wel, USA, HK, Aus, Lon, Sco, 09 Dub, SA, 10 HK, Lon, Sco, CG.

Minnaar, CD (Chase) (SARU contract) 09 HK, Aus, Lon, WG; 09 Dub; SA; 10 NZ, USa, Aus, HK, Lon, Sc, CG.

Mofu, Z (Zolani) 05 WG, Dub, SA, 06 Wel, LA, CG.

Mokuena, J (Jonathan) (Leopards) 05 Lon, Par, WG, Dub, SA, 06 Wel, LA, HK, Sing, Par, Lon, CG, Dub(c), SA(c) 07 Wel(c), USA(c), HK(c), Aus(c) 07 Dub, 08 Wel, USA, HK, Aus, Sco.

Mostert, H (Herman) (WP) - 99 Fiji, HK, Par; 00 NZ, Fiji, Aus, HK, Jap, Fr, Dur, Dub; 01 Wel, HK, Sha, KL, Tok, Lon, Car.

Mtembu, LS (Lubabalo) (Sharks) 10 CG.

†**Müller, GP** (Jorrie) (Lions) - 01 HK, Sha, KL, Tok, Dub, Dur; 02 San, Arg, Bris, Wel, Lon, Car, CG, SA.

Munn, W (Wayne) (SWD Eagles) - 99 Fiji*, 99 HK.

†**Muir, DJ** (Dick) (Natal) - 93 RWC; 95 HK.

N

†**Ndungane, AZ** (Akona) (Bulldogs) – 04 Hk, Sing, Bor, Lon

Nelson, NT (Norman) (SARU contract) 08 Lon, Sco.

Noble, DC (Dusty) (Sharks) 06 Dub, SA, 07 HK, Aus, Lon, Sco.

Noble, HG (Howard) (Sharks) 07 wel, USA, HK, Aus, 09 NZ, USA, Aus.

†**Nokwe, JL** (Jongi) (Boland) 04 SA, 05 Sing.

Nqoro, M (Milo) (Sharks) 08 SA.

O

O'Cuinneagan, D (Dion) (WP) - 93 HK, 93 RWC; 95 HK(c); 96 Ur(c), 96HK(c).

† **Olivier, J** (Jacques) (NTvl) - 93 HK, RWC; 97 RWC; 99 Arg(c), San(c), Dub(c); 00 Ur(c), Arg(c), Dur, Dub; 01 HK, Sha, KL, Tok, Lon, Car, Jap.

†**Oosthuysen, DE** (Deon) (Lions) - 99 San.

P

†**Paulse, BJ** (Breyton) (WP)* - 96 Ur, HK; 98 Arg, Ur, Viña; 01 RWC.

Payne, L (Shaun) (Natal) - 95 HK; 97 RWC; 98 Ur, Viña .

Penrose, N (Neil) (WP) - 98 HK.

Petersen, PB (Patrick) (WP) - 00 Fr.

Philander, D (Daniel) (WP) - 01 Jap.

Pietersen, JC (Johan) (WP) 04 Dub, SA.

Pietersen, WJ (Wilton) (WP) 08 HK, Aus.

Pitout, AC (Anton) (FS) - 01 Dub, Dur; 02 San, Arg, Bris, Wel, Bei, HK, Sing, KL, Lon, Car, CG, 04 Dub.

Plumtree, J (John) (Natal) - 94 HK; 95 HK.

Potgieter, R (Riaan) (EP) - 95 HK.

Potgieter, SP (Sarel) (WP) 06 HK, Sing, Par, Lon.

Powell, JD (Neil) (FS) - 01 Dur; 02 San, Arg, Bei, HK, Lon, Car, CG, Dub, SA, 07 Dub(c), SA(c), 08 Wel(c), USA(c), HK(c), Aus(c), Lon(c), Sco(c), 09 HK, Aus, Lon, Sco, RWC, WG, 09 Dub, 10 Lon, Sco, CG.

Pretorius, A (Abrie) (GW) - 96 Ur.

†**Pretorius, AS** (André) (Lions) - 00 Dur, Dub; 01 RWC, Wel, KL, Tok, Lon, Car.

†**Pretorius, JC** (Jaco) (Lions) - 02 Dub, 02 SA; 03 Bris(c), NZ(c), HK(c), Car, Lon 04 Dub, SA(c), 05 Wel(c), LA(c),Sing(c), Lon(c), Par(c), RWC(c), Dub(c), SA(c) 06 HK(c), Sing(c), Par(c), Lon(c), CG(c).

Prinsloo, JG (Boom) (FS) 10 CG.

†**Putt, KB** (Kevin) (Natal) - 95 HK

R

Raats, W (Wemer) (WP) - 98 HK, CG.

Rafferty, AC (Ashwell) (FS) - 99 Par.

Rees, G (Grant) (Sharks) 07 Wel, USA.

†**Richter, AH** (Adriaan) (NTvl) - 94 HK.

†**Rose, EE** (Earl) (WP) - 03 Bris, NZ, Car, Lon, Dub, SA, 04 Wel, LA.

†**Rossouw, PWG** (Pieter) (WP) - 96 Dub; 97 RWC; 98 CG.

†**Russell, RB** (Brent) (Pumas) - 01 Dur; 02 San, Arg, Bris, Wel, Bei, HK, Sing, KL, SA. 03 SA.

S

Saayman, JIA (Izak) (Eagles) 05 SA.

Schoeman, MW (Marius) (Pumas) - 01 HK, Sha, KL, Tok, Lon, Car, Jap; 02 Bei, HK, Sing, KL, Lon, Car, CG, Dub, SA; 03 Bris, NZ, HK, Car, Lon, Dub, SA, 04 Wel, LA, Lon, 05 Sing, Lon, Par, RWC,

WG(c) 06 SA, 07 Wel, USA, HK, Aus, Lon, Sco. 07 SA, 08 Wel, USA, 08 Dub, 09 Sco, WG, 09 SA, 10 NZ, USA.

Seconds, ER (Egon) (WP) - 01 Dub, Dur; 02 Bei, HK, Sing, KL, Lon, Car, CG 05 Dub.

Sithole, SCT (Sibusiso) (Sharks) 10 CG.

Siwundla, O (Oginga) (Golden Lions) 04 Dub, SA

†**Skinstad, RB** (Bob) (WP) - 96 Dub, 97 RWC, 98 CG, 01 RWC.

Smith, LA (Luke) (Natal) - 95 HK.

†**Smit, PL** (Philip) (GW) - 98 Ur, Viña .

Smith, RF (Rodger) (GW) - 98 HK; 99 Mar, San, Fiji (c), HK (c), Dub, SA; 00 Ur, Arg, Par; 01 RWC; 02 Dub, SA; 03 Bris.

†**Snyman, AH** (André) (NTvl) - 97 RWC.

Snyman, PAB (Phillip) (Cheetahs) 08 Dub, Sa, 09 Nz, USA, HK, Lon, Sco, RWC, WG.

Stevens, J (Jeffrey) (Boland) - 96 Dub; 97 RWC; 98 CG; 99 Arg, San, Fiji, HK, Tok, Par, Dub, SA; 00 Ur, Arg, NZ, Fiji, Aus, HK, Jap, Fr.

Stick, M (Mzwandile) (Elephants) – 04 HK, Sing, Bor, Lon. Dub, 05 Wel, LA,Sing, RWC, WG, Dub, SA, 06 Wel, LA, HK, Sing, CG, 07 Wel, USA, HK, Aus, Lon, Sco 07 Dub, 08 USA, HK, Aus, 08 Dub(c), SA(c), 09 NZ(c), HK(c), Aus(c), lon(c), Sco(c), WG(c), 09 Dub, SA, 10 NZ(c), USA(c), Lon(c), Sco(c)

Strauss, AJ (Andries) (Sharks) 07 Lon, Sco.

Strydom, DH (Dirkie) (NTvl) - 96 Dub; 98 HK; 99 Arg, San, Fiji, Tok, Dub, SA; 00 Ur, Arg, NZ, Fiji, Aus, Fr, Dur, Dub

Treu, PM (Paul) (SWD Eagles) - 99 Fiji*, HK, Dub, SA; 00 Ur, Arg, Dur, Dub; 01 RWC, Wel, HK, Sha, KL, Tok, Lon, Car, Jap, Dub, Dur; 02 San, Arg, Bris, Wel, Bei, HK, Sing, KL, Lon, Car, CG, Dub(c), SA(c).

T

Truter, HJ (Hendrik) (FS) - 94 HK.

Van den Heever, LM (Leon) (Bol) - 02 Dub, SA, 03 Bris, NZ

V

Van der Merwe, SM (Schalk) (Golden Lions) 05 Wel, LA, Sing, Lon, Par, RWC, WG, Dub, SA, 06 Wel, LA, Par, Lon, CG, Dub, SA, 07 Wel, USA, HK, Aus, Lon, Sco, 07 Dub, SA, 08 Wel, USA, HK, Aus, Lon, Sco.

Van der Walt, CP (Phillip) (FS Cheetahs) 10 NZ, USA.

†**Van der Westhuizen, JH** (Joost) (NTvl) - 93 HK, RWC; 94 HK; 97 RWC(c).

Van Heerden, W (Wayne) (EP) - 01 RWC, Wel, HK, Sha, KL, Tok, Lon, Car, Dub, Dur; 02 Lon, Car, CG, 03 Dub, SA, 04 Wel, LA, HK, Sing, Bor, Lon Dub, SA, 05 Wel, LA.

†**Van Niekerk, JC** (Joe) (Lions) - 01 HK, Sha, KL, Tok, Lon, Car.

Van Rensburg, JM (José) (GW) - 02 Dub, SA; 03 Bris, NZ, HK, Car, Lon, Dub, SA, 04 Wel, LA, HK, Sing, Bor, Lon. Dub, SA, 05 Wel, LA, Sing, Lon, Par.

Van Schalkwyk, J (Jaco) (FS) - 03 HK, Car, Lon, SA, 04 HK, Sing, 04 Dub,SA.

Van Wyk, JH (Jan-Harm) (FS) - 98 Arg, Ur, Viña; 01 Dub; 02 San, Arg, Bris, Wel, Beij, HK.

Van Zyl, R (Riaan) (WP) - 96 Ur, HK.

†**Venter AG** (André) (FS) - 96 Ur, HK; 97 RWC; 98 CG.

†**Venter, AJ** (AJ) (FS) - 98 Arg, Ur, Viña .

Venter, J (Hannes) (Blue Bulls) - 99 Arg, San, Dub, SA; 00 Ur, Arg.

Venter, N (Nico) (Bor) - 98 HK.

Venter, S (Shaun) (SARU contracted) 09 SA.

Verhoeven, AG (Antonius) (Bol) - 02 San, Arg, Bris, Wel, 06 Wel, LA, HK, Sing, Par, Lon, CG, 07 Wel, USA.

Vermaak, J (Jano) (Golden Lions) 05 Wel, LA, RWC.

Verster, E (Eben) (WP) - 99 Par.

W

†**Watson, LA** (Luke) (Elephants) - 02 CG.

†**Willemse, AK** (Ashwin) (Bol) - 01 Dub, Dur.

†**Williams, CM** (Chester) (WP) - 93 RWC; 94 HK; 98 Arg, Ur, Viña , HK(c), CG(c); 99 SA; 00 Ur, Arg; 01 RWC.

Winter, RG (Russell) (Lions) - 98 HK, CG.

Witbooi, N (Nigel) (WP) - 96 Ur, HK.

Z

Zangqa, V (Vuyo) (Border) 07 HK, Aus, Lon, Sco, 07 Dub, SA, 08 Wel, USA, HK, Aus, Lon, Sco, 08 Dub, SA, 09 Nz, USA, HK, Aus, Lon, Sco, RWC.

* unconfirmed

SA UNDER-21 1974-2006

† Indicates those who also became senior Springboks

A

Adams, B (Bennie) - WP - 2003

Avenant, C (Corrie) - GW - 2001

B

Baadjies, C (Chrisjan) - FS - 1998

Badenhorst, D (Derick) - NTvl - 1995, 1994

Badenhorst, RS (Skipper) - BB - 1999

Barnard, JJ (Jaco) - BB - 1998

Barnard, PC (Patrick) - WP - 2002

Barritt, BM (Brad) - Natal - 2006

†Barry, D (De Wet) - WP - 1999, 1998

†Basson, WW (Wium) - WP - 1996, 1995

†Bekker, A (Andries) - WP - 2004, 2003

Bekker, JC (JC) - 2004

Bernard, R (Roland) - GL - 2002

Blakely, SP (Simon-Peter) - WP - 2004

Blignaut, N (Nikolaai) - Natal - 2005, 2006

Blom, CA (Charl) - WP - 1998

Bock, AG (Alshaun) - Boland - 2003

Booi, C (Chumani) - Border - 2001

†Boome, CS (Selborne) - WP - 1995, 1994

Bosch, T (Tommy) - Tvl - 1975

†Botha, BJ (Brendon) - Natal - 2001

†Botha, GvG (Gary) - BB - 2002, 2001

Bowles, MF (Maso) - FS - 1998

Brinkhuis, GE (Germaine) - WP - 1998

Britz, D (David) - FS - 2003

†Britz, GJJ (Gerrie) - FS - 1999

Britz, L (Lodie) - FS - 2001, 2000

Bronkhorst, S (Stefan) - Tvl - 1995

†Burger, SWP (Schalk) - WP - 1975

†Burger, SWP (Schalk) jnr - WP - 2003, 2002

Buys, BO (Bronwen) - Leopards - 2003

C

Campbell-McGeachy, N (Neil) - WTvl - 1995, 1994

Carshagen, E (Erich) - FS - 1998

†Carstens, PD (Deon) - WP - 2000

†Chavhanga, T (Tonderai) - FS - 2003

†Claassens, M (Michael) - FS - 2003

†Coetzee, D (Danie) - FS - 1998

Coetzee, EL (Eduard) - BB - 2000, 1999, 1998

†Conradie, JHJ (Bolla) - WP - 1998

Constant, A (Ashton) - WP - 2004

Cooke, RJ (Ronnie) - Leopards - 2005

Cooper, JC (John) - SWD - 2000

†Cronjé, G (Geo) - GW - 2001, 2000

†Cronjé, J (Jacques) - BB - 2003, 2002

D

Daniel, KR (Keegan) - Natal - 2006

Daniller, HJ (Hennie) - BB - 2004, 2005

De Kock, J (Hannes) - WP - 1994

†De Kock, NA (Neil) - WP - 1999

De Marigny, M (Marc) - Natal - 2001

De Sa, N (Nelio) - FS - 1995

†De Villiers, J (Jean) - WP - 2001, 2002

De Waal, D (Danie) - NW - 1997

De Wet, L (Louis) - OFS - 1975

[1]Del Fava, C (Carlo) - Natal - 2001

Delport, M (Marius) - BB - 2004, 2005, 2006

Delport, PS (Paul) - WP - 2004, 2005

Dercksen, C (Chris) - WP - 1996

Diedericks, H (Henk) - NTvl - 1996

†Dixon, PJ (Pieter) - Natal - 1998

Dollie, I (Isma-eel) - Southern Spears - 2006

Doubell, HB (Rabie) - NEC - 1975

†Du Plessis, BW (Bismarck) - Natal - 2005

†Du Plessis, JN (Jannie) - FS - 2003

Du Plessis, N (Neil) - Leopards - 2000

Du Plooy J (Johan) - OFS - 1975

Du Plooy, TJ (Boela) - FS - 1998

†Du Preez, PF (Fourie) - BB - 2003, 2002

Du Toit, JD (Dawie) - NTvl - 1995

Du Toit, JPA (Jaco) - SWD - 2002

E

Eloff, SJ (Sarel) - GL - 1998

Els, C (Christiaan) - Leopards - 2002

Engelbrecht, J (Kobus) - Tvl - 1995

†Esterhuizen, G (Grant) - BB - 1997, 1996

Everitt, DG (Donovan) - WP - 1999

F

Faure, CL (Chris) - NTvl - 1975

Ferreira, BT (Braden) - Natal - 2003

Ferreira, SJP (Schalk) - WP - 2004

Fondse, A (Adriaan) - BB - 2004

Ford, K (Ken) - GL - 1997

†Fortuin, BA (Bevin) - SWD - 2000

Fourie, D (Danie) - OFS - 1975

Fowles, JJ (Josh) - Border - 2001

Franck, MEJ (Matt) - Natal - 1996

Frederiks, ER (Eddie) - NW - 1997

Fredericks, JJ (JJ) - WP - 1996, 1995

†Froneman, DC (Dirk) - OFS - 1975

Fullard, N (Neil) - WP - 2003

G

Geldenhuys, Q (Quintin) - Natal - 2002

Gerber, R (Rayno) - FS - 2002

Gilfillan, GJ (Gordon) - WP - 2003, 2002

†Gillingham, JW (Joe) - Tvl - 1995, 1994

Goosen, M (Marius) - WP - 1994

Groenewald, CA (Coenraad) - BB - 1999, 1998

H

†Habana BG (Bryan) - GL - 2004

Hargreaves, AJ (Alistair) - Natal - 2006

Hattingh, LJ (Lood) - FS - 1995

Haupt, PJ (Hanro) - FS - 2003

Hector, T (Tino) - WP - 1995

Henderson, AJ (Grant) - Natal - 1999

Heunis, AF (Bertus) - FS - 1997

Hoffman, D (Dirk) - WP - 1975

Hopp, DJL (Dean) - SWD - 2002

†Hougaard, DJ (Derick) - BB - 2004, 2003

†Human, DCF (Daan) - FS - 1997

Human, WA (Wylie) - FS - 2000, 1999, 1998

Hume, G (Gavin) - Natal - 2001

J

†Jacobs, AA (Adi) - Falcons - 2000

Jacobs, PH (Heinre) - FS - 1995

Jacobs, RW (Ryan) - SWD - 1998

†James, AD (Butch) - Natal - 2000, 1999

†Jantjes, CA (Conrad) - GL - 2000, 1998

†Januarie, ER (Ricky) - Boland - 2003, 2002

Japhta, GX (Gustav) - WP - 1996

Jelliman, R (Reg) - Griffons - 1975

Johnson, AF (Ashley) - Southern Spears - 2006

†Jordaan, N (Norman) - WP - 1996

Joubert, CHB (Tiaan) - Tvl - 1994

†Joubert, MC (Marius) - Boland - 2000

Key: [1] *Appeared for Italy at full international level.* [2] *Appeared for Australia at full international level.* [3] *Appeared for Scotland at full international level.* [4] *Appeared for the USA at full international level.*

DIRECTORIES

Julies, RF (Randile) - Boland - 1997
†Julies, W (Wayne) - Boland - 1999, 1998
Juries, FM (Fabian) - EP - 2000
K
Karemaker, L (Leon) - WP - 2004
Keil, RR (Rudi) - GL - 1998
†Kempson, RB (Robbie) - Natal - 1995, 1994
Kennedy, CJ (Charlton) - Border - 1996, 1995
Kiva, O (Ondela) - Border - 2000
Knox, J (John) - Natal - 1975
†Koen, LJ (Louis) - WP - 1996
Kok, HC (Heinrich) - WP - 1995, 1994
Kokoali, TC (Tsepo) - GL - 2002
†Krantz, EFW (Edrich) - OFS - 1975
†Krige, CPJ (Corné) - WP - 1996
Kruger, CR (Chris) - FS - 1996
Kruger, D (Diaan) - Tvl - 1994
Kruger, W (Werner) - BB - 2005, 2006
Kuün, GWF (Derick) - BB - 2004, 2005
L
Laufs, GH (Gerhard) - WTvl - 1995
Le Roux, C (Chris) - BB - 1998
⁴Lentz, O (Owen) - EP - 2001
Linee, B (Bernard) - WP - 1995
†Lobberts, H (HIlton) - BB - 2005, 2006
Lombard, D (Deon) - FS - 1997
†Lombard, F (Friedrich) - FS - 2000, 1998
Louw, PJ (Pieter) - WP - 2005, 2006
†Louw, RJ (Rob) - WP - 1975
Louw, C (Chris) - FS - 1995
†Louw, FH (Hottie) - WP - 1997, 1996
Loxton, (Morné) - EP - 1997
M
Maku, B (Bandise) - Blue Bulls - 2006
Malgas, W (Warren) - Southern Spears - 2006
†Malotana, K (Khaya) - Border - 1997, 1996
Manuel, DJ (David) - BB - 2001
Manuel, Y (Yazeed) - WP - 1996
Maqwelena, E (Eugene) - Boland - 2001
Marais, D (Dawie) - NTvl - 1975
Marx, E (Eugene) - GL - 1999
†Matfield, V (Victor) - BB - 1998, 1997
McDonald, B (Barry) - Natal - 1999, 1998
McKenzie, KF (Kenny) - GL - 2003
Mdyesha, MC (Monwabisi) - EP - 2000
Melck, RJ (Justin) - WP - 2004
Mentz, MJ (MJ) - Leopards - 2003
Methula, PM (Petros) - Natal - 2004
Meyer, W (Wim) - NTvl - 1995

Milton, JC (Cliffie) - BB - 2004, 2005
Mkhize, C (Cedric) - Natal - 2005, 2006
Moerat, EM (Ebrahim) - WP - 2003
Mokuena, J (Jonathan) - WP - 2001
Molefe, T (Thabang) - BB - 2005
Moller, JD (Jan) - WP - 2003
Moore, W (Wouter) - FS - 2004
Mostert, G (Gerhard) - Leopards - 2005
†Moyle, BS (Brent) - Tvl - 1995
†Müller, GP (Jorrie) - GL - 2001, 2002
Muller, L (Lourens) - NTvl - 1996
†Murray, WM (Waylon) - Natal - 2006
Mxoli, SM (Sangoni) - Natal - 2004, 2005, 2006
Myburgh, PH (Piet) - Natal - 1999
N
Ncunyana, B (Bandile) - Border - 2000
†Ndungane, OM (Odwa) - Border - 2002
Nel, JP (JP) - BB - 2002
Newman, MR (Morgan) - WP - 2006
†Nkumane, SO (Owen) - Tvl - 1996
Nontshinga, L (Trompie) - FS - 2004
O
Oelschig, NH (Noël) - FS - 2000
Olivier, DJ (Danie) - WP - 1975
†Olivier, W (Wynand) - BB - 2004
P
Pangeti, GX (Gordon) - WP - 2003
†Paulse, BJ (Breyton) - WP - 1995, 1996, 1997
Petersen, PB (Patrick) - WP - 1997, 1996
Philander, D (Daniel) - WP - 2001
†Pienaar, R (Ruan) - FS - 2004, 2005
†Pienaar, ZMJ (Gysie) - OFS - 1975
†Pieterse, BH (Barend) - GL - 2000
†Pietersen, J-PR (JP) - Natal - 2006
Plaatjii, JJ (Jeremy) - SWD - 2004
Plaatjies, SR (Sean) - EP - 1999, 1998, 1997
Potgieter, JH (Jan) - Tvl - 1975
†Povey, SA (Shaun) - WP - 1975
Powell, JD (Neil) - FS - 1999
Powell, WJ (Jimmy) - FS - 1997
†Pretorius, AS (André) - GL - 1998
R
Raats, W (Wemar) - WP - 1998
†Ralepelle, MC (Chiliboy) - BB - 2005, 2006
Ralo, K (Kholekile) - BB - 1998
†Ras, WJDeW (De Wet) - OFS - 1975
²Rathbone, C (Clyde) - Natal - 2002
Raubenheimer, D (Davon) - SWD - 2005
Reid, MO (Maurice) - Boland - 2002

³Reid, RE (Roland) - GL - 1998
Robertson, B (Bruce) - Natal - 1975
Roets, J (Johan) - BB - 1999, 1998
Röhrs, NP (Nico) - NW - 1997
†Rose, EE (Earl) - WP - 2004, 2005
S
Scholtz, AW (Dries) - GW - 2000
†Scholtz, H (Hendro) - FS - 2000, 1999
Schräder Kevin - NTvl - 1994
Schutte, J (Jacques) - BB - 2001
†Sephaka, LD (Lawrence) - GL - 1999, 1998
†Serfontein, DJ (Divan) - WP - 1975
†Shimange, MH (Hanyani) - BB - 1999
Sithole, M (Martin) - Leopards - 2005
Skeate, R (Ross) - WP - 2003
†Skinstad, RB (Bob) - WP - 1997, 1996
†Smit, JW (John) - Natal - 1997, 1998, 1999
†Smith, JH (Juan) - FS - 2002
Smith, MJ (MJ) - FS - 1996
Smith, RF (Rodger) - WP - 1995
†Snyman, AH (André) - NTvl - 1995
Sogidashe, L (Luvo) - BB - 2004, 2005
†Sowerby, RS (Shaun) - Natal - 1998, 1999
Spannenberg, F (Frikkie) - NTvl - 1994
Spedding, S (Scott) - Natal - 2006
†Spies, PJ (Pierre) - BB - 2006
†Steenkamp, GG (Gurthro) - FS - 2001, 2002
Steenkamp, JWA (Wilhelm) - BB - 2006
Steenkamp, W (Willie) - Leopards - 2003
Stevens, J (Jeffrey) - Boland - 1998
Steyn, CP (Casper) - FN - 1994
Steyn, M (Morné) - BB - 2005
Stick, M (Mzwandile) - Natal - 2005
†Stofberg, MTS (Theuns) - OFS - 1975
Strachan, J (Jaco) - GL - 2001
Strauss, AJ (Andries) - FS - 2004
†Strauss, JA (Adriaan) - BB - 2005, 2006
Strauss, JC (JC) - NTvl - 1975
†Swanepoel, W (Werner) - NTvl - 1994
Swart, FJ (Swys) - WP - 2003, 2002
Swartbooi, DF (Dewey) - BB - 2003, 2002
T
†Terblanche, CS (Stefan) - Boland - 1996
Thiart, C (Chris) - Boland - 1998
Thiart, D (Danie) - WP - 2001
U
Uys, PF (Lafras) - BB - 2003
V
Van der Bergh, RJ (Renier) - FS - 1997

†Van der Linde, CJ (CJ) - FS - 2001, 2000

Van der Merwe, F (Franco) - Leopards - 2004

†Van der Merwe, HS (Heinke) - Lions - 2005, 2006

Van der Walt, GJ (George) - NTvl - 1994

Van der Walt, J (James) - FS - 2000, 1998

Van der Walt, JN (Nicky) - NTvl - 1995

Van der Westhuizen, MRS (Thinus) - Leopards - 2004

†Van der Westhuyzen, JNB (Jaco) - Natal - 1999, 1998

Van Eck, D (Dewald) - EP - 1994

†Van Heerden, JL (Wickus) - GL - 2000

Van Heerden, W (Wayne) - EP - 2000

Van Niekerk, D (Dirk) - GL - 1997

†Van Niekerk, JC (Joe) - GL - 2001, 2000

Van Niekerk, P (Pietman) - GL - 1998

Van Rensburg, N (Noel) - FS - 1975

Van Rensburg, L (Louis) - Tvl - 1995

Van Rensburg, P (Pierre) - WP - 2001

Van Rooyen, S (Windpomp) - Leopards - 2002

Van Vuuren, H (Hein) - FS - 1998

Van Vuuren, JJJ (Kosie) - BB - 1997

Van Wijk, F (Frans) - NTvl - 1975

Van Wyk, J (Johan) - WP - 1994

Venter, J (Hannes) - NTvl - 1994

Vermaak, J (Jano) - Lions - 2006

Venter, L (Wickus) - GL - 1998, 1997

Vermaas, CH (Harry) - BB - 2005

Vermeulen, A (André) - Natal - 1996

²Vickerman, DJ (Daniel) - WP - 1999, 1998

†Viljoen, R (Joggie) - WP - 1997, 1996

†Visagie, IJ (Cobus) - WP - 1994

Vlok, W (Wilnad) - Tvl - 1994

†Vos, AN (André) - EP - 1996

W

Wagenstroom, FJ (Frank) - WP - 2005, 2006

†Wannenburg, PJ (Pedrie) - Natal - 2001, 2002

†Watson, LA (Luke) - Natal - 2004

Welsh, BF (Frikkie) - Natal - 1999, 1998

†Willemse, AK (Ashwin) - Boland - 2001, 2002

Williams, KJ (Kevin) - Boland - 2001

Wimble, TE (Tim) - Natal - 2003

Winter, AAA (Attie) - FS - 2000

Wise, A (Ashieq) - WP - 2001

Wium, V (Vion) - WP - 1994

Wright, GJT (Gareth) - Lions - 2000

SA UNDER-20 2008-2010

A

Afrika, CS (Cecil) - Grif - 2008

B

Badenhorst, WHB (Brummer) - WP - 2010

Bali, M (Mlungisi) - BB - 2010

Bantjes, HJ (Henri) - BB - 2008

Blommetjies, C (Clayton) - BB - 2009

Botha, ZW (Zane) - BB - 2009

Brummer, F (Francois) - BB - 2008, 2009

Bullbring, DJ (David) - GL - 2009

C

Chikukwa, TA (Tendayi) - BB - 2009

Cooper, KL (Kyle) - KZN - 2009

Cronjé, L (Lionel) - FS - 2009

Cronjé, R (Ross) - KZN - 2009

D

De Chaves, SJ (Sebastian) - GL - 2010

Dippenaar, SC (Stephan) - BB - 2008

Dreyer, RM (Ruan) - GL - 2010

Du Rand, CW (Wessel) - GL - 2010

Du Toit, F (Francois) - GL - 2010

Duvenage, DO (Dewaldt) - Bol - 2008

Du Preez, BBN (Branco) - BB - 2010

E

Ebersohn, JM (Sias) - FS -2008, 2009

Ebersohn, RT (Robert) - FS - 2008, 2009

Elstadt, R (Rynhardt) - WP - 2009

F

Fourie, C (Corné) - BB - 2008

H

Hadebe, MS (Monde) - KZN - 2010

Hanekom, NJ (Nicolaas) - WP - 2009

Hartzenberg, Y (Yaasir) - WP - 2009

Herbst, WJ (Wiehan) - Leop - 2008

Hess, CN (Cornell) - BB - 2008

Hougaard, F (Francois) - BB - 2008

J

Jacobs, AJ (Adri) - BB - 2010

Jacobs, WJ (Lohan) - BB - 2010

Jantjies, ET (Elton) - GL - 2010

K

Kirsten, FBC (Frik) - BB - 2008

Kolisi, S (Siya) - WP - 2010

Koster, RN (Nick) - WP - 2008

L

Lambie, P (Patrick) - KZN - 2010

Lusaseni, L (Luyvuyiso) - KZN - 2008

M

Mapoe, LG (Lionel) - FS - 2008

Marais, JA (Jandré) - KZN - 2009

Marais, PC (Peet) - KZN - 2010

Marole, T (Thiliphatu) - KZN - 2008

Mastriet, S (Sampie) - BB - 2009, 2010

Mellett, MM (Morné) BB - 2009

Mjekevu, WG (Wandile) - GL - 2010

Mtembu, LS (Lubabalo) - KZN - 2010

Muller, FJ (Freddie) - WP - 2010

Muller, MD (Martin) - WP - 2008

N

Nhlapo, S (Sabelo) - KZN - 2008

O

Okafor, K (Kene) - KZN - 2009, 2010

Oosthuizen, CR (Caylib) - GL - 2009

Oosthuizen, CV (Coenie) - FS - 2009

P

Paige, R (Rudy) - GL - 2009

Pietersen, WJ (Wilton) - FS 2008

R

Redelinghuys, J (Julian) - KZN - 2009

Rossouw, JJ (Jean-Jacques) - WP - 2008

S

Sadie, J (Johann) - WP - 2009

Scheepers, JN (Nico) - FS - 2010

Schoeman, M (Marnus) - BB - 2009

Schreuder, L (Louis) - WP - 2010

Seabela OT (Omphile) - BB - 2008, 2009

Sithole, ST (Sibusiso) - KZN - 2010

Stander, CJ (CJ) - BB - 2009, 2010

T

Taute, JJ (Jaco) - GL - 2010

V

Van den Heever, GJ (Gerhard) - BB - 2009

Van der Merwe, M (Marcel) - FS - 2010

Van der Walt, HS (Fanie) - FS - 2010

Van Deventer, JC (Johan) - GL - 2008

Van Velze, G-J (Gerrit-Jan) - BB - 2008

Van Vuuren, P-W (PW) - FS - 2008

Venter, JF (Francois) - BB - 2010

W

Watermeyer, S (Stefan) - BB - 2008

Willis, VS (Vainon) Willis - BB - 2008

DIRECTORIES

SA SCHOOLS PLAYERS 1974-2010

† Became senior Springbok (15-man code).

* SA Schools captain (in second year if played for two years)

A

Adams, Tythan (Paul Roos Gymnasium) WP 2008

Afrika, Cecil (Harmony Sport) Griffons 2006

Alberts, Nicolaas (AHS, Pretoria) BB 1996

†Alcock, Chad (Alexander Road) EP 1991

Alexander, Enwill (Stellenberg) WP 2002

Anderson, Severin (Westering) EP 1978

April, Garth (Bergrivier) Boland 2008

April, Randall (Bergrivier) Boland 2004

Arends, Neil (McCarthy, Uitenhage) EP 1999

Arendse, Riaan (Brandwag, Uitenhage) EP 2007

Arlow, Wium (Nelspruit) Mpu 2002

B

Bakkes, Luther (Diamantveld) GW 1989

Bali, Mlungisi (St Alban's) BB 2008

Bangihlonbe, Kobese (Dale College) Bor 2009

Bannink, Wimpie (Hans Strijdom) Far North 1992

Barker, Michael (DHS) Natal 1978

Barnard, JanHendrik (Menlopark) BB 1988

Barnard, Kierie (Volkskool Potch.) Leopards 1981

Barnard, Lee (King Edward VII) GL 1974-75

Barnies, Francois (Parow) WP 2000

Baronet, Dennis (Glenwood) Natal 1985

Barrett, Brett (Kingswood College) EP 1991

Barritt, Bradley (Kearsney College) Natal 2004

Bartle, Grant (Middelburg THS) Mpu 1995

†Bartmann, Wahl (Florida) GL 1981

Bartmann, Leon (Florida) GL 1978

Basson, JP (Boland Agric..) WP 1994-95

Basson, Stefan (Boland Agric.) WP 2000

Bennett, Richard (Dale College.) Bor 1992

Beukes, Chris (DHS) Natal 1990

Bezuidenhout, Riaan (Framesby) EP 1984

Bitterhout, Leroy (Klein Nederb) Boland 2010

Bitzi, Anrich (Grey Coll) FS 2010

Blignaut, Robert (Muir College) EP 1978

†Bobo, Gcobani (Dale College) Bor 1996

Böhmer, Manfred (Ermelo) Mpu 1998

Bolofo, Moeka (Louis Botha) FS 2007

Bolus, Robert (Bishops) WP 1974-75

Bonthuys, John (Abbots College) WP 1974-75

Bosch, Jan (Helpmekaar) GL 1991

Boshoff, Marnitz (Nelspruit) Mpu 2007

Botes, Bennie (AHS, Pretoria) BB 1991

Botha, Calla (DF Malan) GL 1979

Botha, Ettienne (John Vorster, Nigel) Falcons 1997

†Botha, Gary (Overkruin) BB 199899

†Botha, Bakkies (Vereeniging THS) Falcons 1998

Botha, Justin (Monument) GL 2006

Botha, Leon (Grey College) FS 1981

Botha, Ruan (Jeugland) Valke 2010

Botha, Wimpie (Queen's College) Bor 1998

Breedt, Johan (Wonderboom) BB 1993

Breedt, Nico (Kearsney College) Natal 1998

Brink, Stephen (Sentraal) FS 1991-92

†Brits, Schalk (Paul Roos Gymnasium) WP 1999

Britz, Conraad (Oakdale Agric.) SWD 2005

Britz, Riaan (Grey College) FS 2009

Bronkhorst, Stephan (Randburg) GL 1992

Brown, Dick (Pearson) EP 1986

Brown, John (Hentie Cilliers) NFS 1999

†Brüssow, Heinrich (Grey College) FS 2004

Buckle, Albertus (Boland Agric.) Boland 2001

†Burger, Kobus (Paarl Gymnasium) WP 1980-81

Burger, Altus (Ermelo) Mpu 198283

BurtonMoore, Mark (Bishops) WP 1978

Bushney, Marais (Roodepoort) GL 1989

C

Caldo, Kobus (Oakdale Agric.) SWD 1998-99

Campbell-McGeachy, Walter (Pietersburg) Far North 1994-95

Campher, Connie (Potchefstroom THS) Leopards 1985

Campher, Fanie (THS Wolmaransstad)

Stellaland 1974-75

Carr, Nizaam (Bishops) WP 2009

†Carstens, Deon (Boland Agric.) WP 1997

Carswell, Michael (Grey) EP 1984

Carty, Shane (King Edward VII) GL 1974-75

Cattrell,* Brenton (Maritzburg College) Natal 1987

Cawood, Mark (Wynberg BH) WP 1974-75

Celliers,* Norman (Ermelo) Mpu 1991

Chadwick, Dale (Westville) KwaZulu Natal 2007

Claassen, Andrew (Andrew Rabie) EP 1988

Clancy, Sean (Selborne College) Bor 1995

Cloete, Chris (Selborne College) Bor 2009

Cloete, Hannes (Jim Fouché) FS 1995

Cloete, Jan (Waterkloof) BB 1996

Coetzee, Deon (Helpmekaar) GL 1979

Coetzee, Eduard (AHS, Pretoria) BB 1997

Coetzee, Jaco (Ellisras) Far North 1988

Coetzee, Jannie (Bloemfontein THS) FS 1982

Coetzer, Jacques (Middelburg THS) Mpu 1996

†Conradie, Bolla (Kasselsvlei) WP 1996-97

Cook, Jean (Grey College) FS 2009

Cooper, Barney (Paarl Gymnasium) WP 1986

Cooper, John (Soa Bras, Mosselbaai) SWD 1998

Coyle-Meybery,* Craig (Dale College) Bor 1983-84

Craven, Jean (Grey College) FS 1990

Cronjé, Frans (Grey College) FS 1985

†Cronjé, Jacques (John Vorster THS) BB 2000

Croy, Ricardo (Paarl Gymnasium) WP 2004

D

Daffue, Hendrik (Grey College) FS 1980

Daffue, Willem (Grey College) FS 1977

Dames, Arno (Framesby) EP 1990

Dames, Rudi (Vereeniging THS) Falcons 1999

Daniller, Hennie (Paarl Gymnasium) WP 2002

Key: [1] Appeared for Ireland at full international level. [2] Appeared for Australia at full international level. [3] Appeared for France at full international level. [4] & [5] Earned SA Schools caps from two different provinces. Three SA Schools players gained senior national colours in other sports than rugby: Warren McCann, Jaco Reinach, Herman Venske (athletics); Herschelle Gibbs, Errol Stewart (cricket). Two SA Schools players later coached the Springbok team: Harry Viljoen, Nick Mallett.

Davel, Chris (Ermelo) Mpu 1985
De Beer,* Conrad (Grey College) FS 1981
De Bruin, Michael (Nelspruit) Mpu 2001
De Bruyn, Corné (Worcester) Boland 1994
De Coning,* Basil (Kingswood College) EP 1990
De Haas, Pieter (Grey College) FS 1986
De Jager, Bruce (Bishops) WP 1994
De Jager, Wilhelm (Ermelo) Mpu 2002
De Kock, Jason (Hugenote HS) Falcons 1996
De Kock, Zander (Vereeniging THS) Falcons 2005
De Nobrega, Paul (Worcester) Boland 1984
De Ru, Ian (Marais Viljoen THS) GL 1989
†De Villiers, Jean (Paarl Gymnasium) WP Acad. 1999
De Waal, Adriaan (Paarl BH) WP Acad. 1995
Dell, Allan (Queens Coll) Border 2010
Delport,* Paul (SACS) WP 200102
Delport, Marius (Zwartkop) BB 2003
Dercksen, Chris (Grey College) FS 1993
Diedericks, Ernest (Scottsville) WP 1994
†Dixon,* Pieter (Maritzburg College) Natal 1995
Dreyer, Hano (Winterberg Agric.) NEC 1995
†Drotské, Naka (Grey College) FS 1989
†Du Plessis, Carel (Paarl BH) WP 1978
†Du Plessis, Bismarck (Grey College) FS 2001-02
Du Plessis, Charl (Kroonstad Agric.) NFS 1978
Du Plessis, Johan (Sand du Plessis) FS 1985
Du Plessis, JP (Paul Roos Gymnasium) WP 2009
Du Plessis, Neil (Selborne College) Bor 1984
Du Plessis, Pierre (Port Natal) Natal 1987
†Du Preez, Delarey (Hangklip) Bor 1994
Du Preez, André (Oudtshoorn THS) SWD 1974
Du Preez, Fransie (EG Jansen) GL 1985
†Du Preez, Wian (Grey College) FS 1999-2000
†Du Randt, Os (Piet Retief) NEC 1990
Du Toit, Dawie (Vereeniging THS) GL 1974-75
Du Toit, Dawie (Monument) GL 1992-93
Du Toit, Franna (Grey College) FS 2008
Du Toit, Jaco (Paarl Gymnasium) WP 1999
Duvenhage, Braam (HSS Hugenote) Falcons 1982
Duvenhage, Stoffel (Middelburg THS) Mpu 2004

E
Ebersöhn, Robert (Grey College) FS 2007

Edgar, David (Michaelhouse) Natal 2001
Ehrentraut,* Michael (Bishops) WP 1989
Ellerd, Rialoo (Jacobsdal) Griquas 2005
†Els, Braam (AHS, Kroonstad) NFS 1990
Els,* Anton (DHS du Plessis) EP 1975
Engelbrecht, Andries (Volkskool) Leopards 1981
Engelbrecht,* Fanus (R Ferreira Witrivier) Mpu 1983
Engelbrecht,* Frankel (Paarl Gymnasium) WP 1986
Engelbrecht, Johan (Paul Roos Gymnasium) WP 1986
Engelbrecht, Morné (Rustenburg) Leopards 1994
Erasmus, Greyling (Ermelo) Mpu 2000
Erasmus, Kerneels (Frikkie Meyer) Far North 1982
Erlank, Karel (Klerksdorp) Leopards 1979
Erwee,* Jurie (Grey College) FS 1980
Espag,* Jaco (Witbank THS) Mpu 1984-85

F
Faas, Chuma (Grey HS) EP 2008
Faku, Zolani (Grey HS) SA Acad (EP) 2009
Farmer, Steven (Kasselsvlei) WP 2001
Fenwick, Alex (Grey College) FS 1990-91
Fenwick, Kobie (Grey College) FS 1975
Ferreira, Andries (AHS, Pretoria) BB 2008
†Ferreira, Christo (Welkom Gymnasium) NFS 1978
Ferreira, Freddie (Brandwag) EP 1980
Ferreira, Marthinus (Florida) GL 2000
Ferreira, Schalk (Paul Roos Gymnasium) WP 2002
Feurer, Lee (Bishops) WP 1988
Fitchet, Christo (Kirkwood) EP 1975
Flanagan, Sean (Westville) Natal 1999
Forslara, Vuyani (Grens HS) Bor 1999
Fortuin, Sean (Bellville South HS) WP 1999
Fouche, Neethling (Grey Coll) FS 2010
Fourie, Andries (Framesby) EP 1990
Fourie, Dawie (Kroonstad Agric.) NFS 197879
Fourie, Kenneth (Port Shepstone) Natal 1994
Fourie, Nel (Ermelo) Mpu 2000
Fourie, Stompie (Grey College) FS 1984
Frolick, Shandré (Worcester Gymnasium) Boland 2004
Froneman, Stephan (Montana) BB 1995
Fullard, Neil (Paarl BH) WP 2000
†Fynn, Etienne (St Charles) Natal 1990

G
Gage, Shaun (DHS) Natal 1985
Geldenhuys, Jan (Grey College) FS 1974-75

Genis, James (DF Malan) WP 1977
†Gerber,* Danie (Despatch) EP 1975-77
†Gerber, Hendrik (Nico Malan) EP 1993-94
Gericke, Jaco (Port Elizabeth THS) EP 1988
Gericke, Neethling (Oakdale Agric.) SWD 2008
Gibbs, Herschelle (Bishops) WP 1992
Giezing, Kalf (Grey College) FS 1983
†Gillingham, Joe (Alberton) GL 1992
Glover, Shaun (Maritzburg College) Natal 1985
Goedeke, Frank (Carter) Natal 1990
Goedeke, Udo (Maritzburg College) Natal 1987
Goosen, Johan (Grey Coll) FS 2010
Goosen, Niel (Waterkloof) BB 1997
Goosen, Gregory (Kearsney College) Natal 2001
Gouws, Scheepers (Grey College) FS 1981
Gqoba, Andisa (Hudson Park) Bor 2003
†Grant, Peter (Maritzburg College) Natal 2002
Greyling, Gert (Sand du Plessis) FS 2003
Griesel, Jannie (Verwoerdburg) BB 1987
Gronum, Antonie (Oakdale Agric.) SWD 2003
Grobler, Gerbrand (Grey College) FS 1981
Grobler, Jacques (FH Odendaal) BB 1990
Grobler, Lukas (Hugenote HS) Falcons 1981
Gwavu, Vincent (Daniël Pienaar, Uitenhage) EP 2005

H
[3] Hall, Stephen (Dale College) Bor 1991
Hammer, Ernst (Fakkel) GL 1993
Hancke, Wim (Linden) GL 1974-75
Hankinson, Rob (Michaelhouse) Natal 1974-75
Hargreaves,* Alistair (Durban HS) Natal 2004
Hartzenberg, Vaasir (Paarl BHS) WP 2006
Hearne, Ashlyn (Hottentots Holland) WP 2000
†Hendriks, Pieter (Standerton) Mpu 1988
Hendriks, Braam (Sandveld) NFS 1993
Hess, Cornel (AHS Pretoria) BB 2006-07
Heuer, Merrick (Queen's College) Bor 1988
Heunis, Nico (Dirkie Uys) Boland 1994
Heydenrich,* Johan (Standerton) Mpu 1982
Hickson, André (Bosmansdam) WP 1985
Hill, Jaydon (Glenwood) Natal 2002
Hollenbach, Alwyn (Grey College) FS 2003
Hopkins, Clifford (Kearsney College) Natal 1979

DIRECTORIES

Hopp, Dean (Kairos SS) SWD 2000
†Hougaard, Derick (Boland Agric.) Boland 2001
Hough, André (Framesby) EP 1988
Hugo, JanHarm (Ermelo) Mpu 1997
Hugo, Werner (Paarl BH) WP 1993
Hulme,* Altenstädt (Voortrekker, CT) WP 1999
Human, Gerhard (Despatch) EP 1977

I

Ingles, Warren (Alexander Road) EP 1987

J

†Jacobs, Adrian (Scottsville) WP 1998
Jacobs, Divan (Ermelo) Mpu 2001
Jacobs, Jaco (Grey College) FS 1987
Jamieson, Craig (Maritzburg College) Natal 1979
Jankowitz, Anton (Hilton College) Natal 1989
†Jantjes, Conrad (CBS Boksburg) Falcons 1997
Jantjes, Elton (Florida HS) GL 2008
Jantjies, Tony (Menlo Park) BB 2009
†Januarie, Enrico (Weston HS) Boland 2000
Jho, Andile (Dale Coll) Border 2009-10
Job, Izak (Pres. Steyn, Bloemfontein) FS 1998
Johnson, Ashley (Paarl Gymnasium) WP 2004
Johnson, Nicolas (Selborne College) Bor 1998
Johnston, Gordon (Paarl BH) WP 1999
Jooste, Morné (The Settlers) WP 2005
Jordaan, Hennie (Menlopark) BB 1980
Jordaan, Paul (Grey Coll) FS 2010
Joubert, JanHendrik (Oakdale Agric.) SWD 2001
Joubert, Riaan (Grey College) FS 1978
Joubert, Wilhelm (Overkruin) BB 1982
Juries, Christopher (Kingswood College) EP 2005

K

Kalonji, Kadima (Pretoria THS) BB 1998
Kankowski, Tino (PJ Olivier) EP 1977
Kaplan, Kevin (Kimberley THS) GW 1980
Kapp, Divan (Middelburg THS) Mpu 2005
Kapp, Neil (Outeniqua) SWD 2008
Karemaker, Leon (Bellville) WP 2003
Kasselman, Chris (Sandveld) NFS 1979-80
Kelly, Richard (Maritzburg College) Natal 1996
Kemp,* Scott (Hudson Park) Bor 1991-92
†Kempson, Rob (Queen's College) Bor 1992
King, Kelvano (Alexandria) Eastern Province 2007

Kirsten, Frik (AHS Pretoria) BB 2006
Kitshoff, Steven (Paul Roos) WP 2010
Kleinenberg, Mark (Selborne College) Bor 1974-75
Klopper, Chris (Die Burger) GL 1978
Knoetze, Frederick (Framesby) EP 1982
Koch, Agie (Paul Roos Gymnasium) WP 1974-75
Koch, Hendrik (Rustenburg) Leopards 1978
†Koen, Louis (Paarl Gymnasium) WP 1993-94
Koen, Barabas (Ermelo) Mpu 1991
Kolisi, Siyamthanda (Grey) EP 2008-09
Köster, Nick (Bishops) WP 2006-07
Kotze, Christo (Dirkie Uys) Boland 1977-78
Kotze, Divan (Waterkloof) BB 2006
Kotze, Stephanus (Grey College) FS 2009
Koyana, Ncedo (Selborne College) Bor 2003
Krause, Piet (Sasolburg THS) Vaal Triangle 1991
†Krige,* Corné (Paarl BH) WP 1993
†Kruger,* Ruben (Grey College) FS 1987-88
Kruger, Bertus (Die Burger) GL 1989
Kruger, Ernst (Jeugland) GL 1974-75
Kruger, Kobus (Middelburg THS) Mpu 1996
Kruger, Morné (Monument) GL 2001
Kruger, Warren (SACS) WP 1974-75
Kuttel, Peter (Bishops) WP 1983
Kuün, Derick (AHS, Pretoria) BB 2002

L

Lambie, Patrick (Michaelhouse) Natal 2007-08
Lanning, Andrew (Bishops) WP 1989
Laubscher, Michael (Tygerberg) WP 1974-75
Laufs, Gerhard (Alberton) GL 1992
Le Grange, Anton (Despatch) EP 1975
Le Marque,* Derek (Glenwood) Natal 1979
†Le Roux, Ollie (Grey College) FS 1991
Le Roux,* Chris (Waterkloof) BB 1996-97
Le Roux, Kobus (Boland Agric.) WP 1995
Le Roux, Stephan (Brits/Waterkloof) BB 1993-94
Lehmann, Helmut (Paarl Gymnasium) WP 2008
Lewis, Marlon (Bertram) EP 2004-05
Lewis, Jean-Paul (Paul Roos) WP 2010
Liebenberg, Christo (Roodepoort) GL 1986
Liebenberg, Wiaan (Drostdy THS) Boland 2010

Lightfoot, Wessel (Diamantveld) GW 1981
Linde, Nico (Grey College) FS 1990
Linde, Rob (Maritzburg College) Natal 1997
Lindeque, Piet (Grey College) FS 2009
Lindsay, Paul (Maritzburg College) Natal 1975-77
†Lobberts, Hilton (New Orleans, Paarl) Boland 2004
Loest, Gary (Queen's College) Bor 1985-86
†Lombard, Frederich (Frankfort) NFS 1997
Luiters, Kevin (Grey Coll) FS 2010
Loubser, Pieter (Paarl BH/Bishops) WP 1975-76
Louw, Coenie (Dirkie Uys) Boland 1995
†Louw, Hottie (Boland Agric.) WP 1994
Louw,* Pieter (Paarl BH) WP 2003
Lusaseni, Luvuyo (Selborne College) Bor 2006

M

Maherry, Chet (Grey College) FS 1985-86
Mahlangu, Daniel (Oosterland Secunda) Mpu 1999
Majola, Khaya (Westville) KZN 2010
Malgas, Warren (PW Botha) SWD 2003
Malherbe, Frans (Paarl BH) WP 2009
†Mallett, Nick (St Andrew's) EP 1974-75
Malton, Shaun (Glenwood) KZN 2008
Manuel, David (Waterkloof) BB 1997-98
Manuel, Rodrique (Ben. Heights) WP 1996
Marais, Abrie (Grey College) FS 1977
Marais, Gert (Grey College) FS 1983
Marothodi, Ompile (Pretoria BHS) BB 2007
Martyn, Angus (Michaelhouse) Natal 1998
Marutlulle, Edgar (Potch. BHS) Leopards 2004-05
Maseko, Sizo (Ermelo) Mpu 2009
Mashele, Ntokozo (Nelspruit) Mpu 2006
Masina, Sibi (Standerton) Mpu 2007
Masuga, Tshepo (Monument) GL 2006
Matthysen, John (Sand du Plessis) FS 1974-75
Mbonambi, Bongi (St Alban's) BB 2009
Mbovane, Tshotso (Paul Roos) WP 2010
McAlister, Daniel (Selborne College) Bor 1991
McCann, Warren (Jeppe BH) GL 1985
4 McDonald, Aubrey (Winterberg HS, Fort Beaufort) EP 2005
4 McDonald, Aubrey (Waterkloof HS) BB 2006
5 McDonald, Barry (Adelaide Gymnasium) NEC 1996
5 McDonald, Barry (Waterkloof) BB 1997
McIntyre, Mark (Grey College) FS 1989

†Meiring, FA (Gill College) NEC 1986

Mentz, Kosie (Paarl Gymnasium) WP 1988

Mentz, MJ (Ermelo) Mpu 2000

Meyer, Altus (Vredenburg HS) Boland 1997

Meyer, Clinton (Maritzburg College) Natal 1989

Meyer, Pieter (Waterkloof) BB 2005

Meyer, Renier (Wessel Maree) NFS 1998

Mhlobiso, Luvuyo (Daniel Pienaar) EP 2004

Michaels, Devan (Kasselsvlei) WP 2001

Micklewood, Christopher (Westville) Natal 2005

Miller, Greg (Grey) EP 1991

Mills, David (Maritzburg College) Natal 1978

Milton, Cliff (AHS, Pretoria) BB 200102

Mjekevu, Wandile (King Edward VII) GL 2008

Mkize, Njabula (Westville) KZN 2008

Mkokeli, Tembani (Msobomvu) Bor 2001-02

Moller, JD (Paarl BH) WP 2000

†Montgomery, Percy (SACS) WP 1992-93

Moolman, Hansie (Ermelo) Mpu 2005

Morotothe, Omphile (Pretoria BHS) BB 2007

Mostert, Juan-Pierre (Brits) Leopards 2006

Methula, Petros (Glenwood) Natal 2001

†Müller, Helgard (Grey College) FS 1981-82

†Müller, Pieter (Grey College) FS 1987-88

†Müller, Jorrie (Monument) GL 1999

Muller, Lourens (Hartbeespoort) BB 1993

Muller, Rudi (Potch. Gymnasium) Leopards 1993

Munn, Wayne (Maritzburg College) Natal 1994

Mxoli, Sangoni (DHS) Natal 2003

Myburgh, Jaco (Paarl BH) WP 1996

Myburgh, Pieter (Paul Roos Gymnasium) WP 2004

Myburgh, Stefaan (Paul Roos Gymnasium) WP 1996

N

Naudé, Dawie (David Ross) NEC 1986

Neethling, Sydwhill (Worcester Gymnasium) Boland 2000

Nel, Boeta (Bloemfontein THS) FS 1979-80

Nel, Johan (Wolmaranstad) Stellaland 1987

Nel, Leon (Nelspruit) Mpu 1982

Nel, Pieter (Patriot, Witbank) Mpu 1983

Nell, Jacques (Grey College) FS 1977

Ngoro, Mlindazwe (St John's) Bor CD 2006

Nieuwenhuys, Jacques (Monument) GL

1984

Ngonyoza, Mtobeli (Oscar Mpetha) WP 2003

Nkosi, Malungisa (Giant) (St Stithians) GL 2005

Notshe, Sikhumbuzo (Wynberg BH) WP 2010

North, Andrew (Bishops) WP 1989

Nortjé, Danie (Jan Viljoen) GL 1976

Ntubeni, Siyabonga (King Edward VII) GL 2009

Ntunja,* Kaunda (Dale College) Bor 1999-2000

Nyoka, Sinovuyo (Dale College) Bor 2008

O

¹ O'Cuinneagain, Dion (Rondebosch BH) WP 1989-90

O'Neill, Pieter (Despatch) EP 1988-89

Oberholster, Johan (Vereeniging THS) Falcons 1998

Oberholzer, Johan (Jan Viljoen) GL 2007

Oberholzer, Lourens (Linden) GL 1982

Ockafor, Kene (Kearsney College) Natal 2007

Oelschig, Noël (Grey College) FS 1997

Olckers, Riaan (AHS, Pretoria) BB 1995

Olivier, HJ (Kroonstad) NFS 1995

Oosthuizen, Coenraad (Grey College) FS 2007

Oosthuizen, Josephus (Grey College) FS 2005

Oosthuizen, JR (Grey College) FS 1992

Oosthuizen,* Willie (Helpmekaar) GL 1976

P

Paige,* Rudy (Bastion) GL 2007

Palmer, Shaun (Middelburg THS) Mpu 1986

Penzhorn, Adrian (Maritzburg College) Natal 2002

Petersen, Patrick (Florida) WP 1995

†Pienaar, Francois (Patriot, Witbank) Mpu 1985

Pienaar, Andries (Paarl BH) WP 1975

Pienaar,* Bernard (Paarl Gymnasium) WP 1974-75

Pienaar, Pieter (Paarl BH) Boland 2001

Pienaar, Roelof (Grey College) Free State 2007

†Pienaar, Ruan (Grey College) FS 2002

Pieterse, Koen (Grey College) FS 1980

Pietersen, Ricardo (Groot Brak) SWD 1999

Plaatjies, Jeremy (Outeniqua) SWD 2001

Plaatjies,* Sean (Brandwag, Uitenhage) EP 1996

Poni, Onke (Selborne College) Bor 2002

Potgieter,* Dewald (Daniël Pienaar, Uiten-

hage) EP 2005

Pretorius, Christo (Paarl Gymnasium) WP 1996

Pretorius, Herman (Grey College) FS 2004

Pretorius, Flippie (De Wet Nel THS) NFS 1979

Pretorius, Johannes (Hentie Cilliers) NFS 1984

Pretorius, Riaan (Ben Viljoen, Groblersdal) Mpu 1994

Pretorius, Wynand (Sand du Plessis) FS 1975-76

Prinsloo, Carlo (Paarl Gymnasium) WP 2004

Prinsloo, Jamie (John Vorster THS) BB 1975

Prinsloo, Michael (Ficksburg THS) EFS 1977

R

Radebe, Colin (Secunda HS) Mpu 2000

Rademan, Pieter* (Grey College) FS 2009

†Ralepelle, Chilliboy (Pretoria BHS) BB 2002-03

² Rathbone, Clyde (Kingsway, Amanzimtoti) Natal 1999

†Rautenbach, Faan (Kroonstad Agric.) NFS 1993-94

Rautenbach, George (Paul Roos Gymnasium) WP 1974-75

Redelinghuys, Julian (Monument) GL 2006-07

Reid, Grant (Maritzburg College) Natal 1987

†Reinach, Jaco (Grey College) FS 1979-80

Reingold, Jeremy (Constantia) WP 1985

Rich, Rockey (Kearsney College) Natal 1975

Richardson, Craig (Despatch) EP 1986

Richardson, Michael (Despatch) EP 1989

Richter, Jan (Grey College) FS 1977

Richter, Toppie (Grey College) FS 1977

Ries, Alfred (Monument) GL 2006

Robberts, Steph (Grey College) FS 2003

Roodt, Hendrik (Lichtenburg HS) Leopards 2005

†Rose, Earl (Strand) WP 2002

Rose, Jody (Paul Roos Gymnasium) WP 2003

†Rossouw, Chris (Hugenote HS) Falcons 1987

Rossouw, Francois (Middelburg) Mpu 1986

Rossouw,* Jean-Jacques (Paarl Gymnasium) BB 2006

Rossouw, Johan (Durbanville) WP 1977

Roux, Daan (Lichtenburg) Stellaland 1974-75

Roux, Paul (Paul Roos Gymnasium) WP

DIRECTORIES

2000

Ruiters, Marlin (Grey College) EP 2006

S

Saaiman, Willem (Menlopark) BB 1991

Saayman, Daniel (Daniel Pienaar THS) EP 1992

Sadie, Ian (Grey College) FS 1979

Scheepers, Eben (Grey College) FS 1983

Schnetler, Fredrick (Glenwood) KZN 2009

Schickerling, Adriaan (Boland Agric.) Boland 1984

Schoeman, Barry (Verwoerdburg) BB 1975

Schoeman, Marnus (Waterkloof) BB 2006-07

†Scholtz, Hendro (Voortrekker, Bethlehem) NFS 1997

Schurmann, Deon (Eldoraigne) BB 1984

Schwartz, Lean (Waterkloof) BB 2009

Scott, Ashwin (Parkdene) SWD 2003

Scriba, Hans (Outeniqua) SWD 1983

Searson, Paul (Bishops) WP 1989

Senekal, Dawie (Abbots College) WP 1988

Serfontein,* Jan (Otto du Plessis) EP 1976-78

Siegelaar, Alastair (Paul Roos Gymnasium) WP 2004

Sitole, Martin (Embalenthele) Mpu 2001-02

Sithole, Sibusiso (Queen's College) Bor 2008

Skeate, Ross (SACS) WP 2000

†Skinstad, Bob (Hilton College) Natal 1994

Skosana, Brian (St Andrew's) EP CD 2009

Slabbert, Henk (Potch. Gymnasium) Leopards 1980

†Small, James (Greenside) GL 1987

Small-Smith*, William (Grey Coll) FS 2010

†Smit, John (Pretoria BHS) BB 1996

Smit, Chris (Grey College) FS 1979

Smith, André (Paarl Gymnasium) WP 2005

†Smith, David (Hamilton, Rhodesia) Rhodesia 1974-75

Smith, Headley (Grey College) FS

Smith, Philip (Hangklip) Bor 1975

Smith, Ruan (Paarl Gymnasium) WP 2008

Snyman, Earl (Outeniqua) SWD 2007

Snyman, Johan (Outeniqua) SWD 2004

Snyman, Tiaan (AHS, Pretoria) BB 1997-98

Sofoko, Jerry (Pretoria THS) BB 2002

Sogidashe, Luvo (Kama) Bor 2002

Sonnekus, Pieter (Bloemfontein THS) FS 1980

†Sowerby, Shaun (Sasolburg) Vaal Triangle

1996

Spamer, Pieter (Pietersburg) Limpopo BB 2003

Sparks, Bradley (Selborne College) Bor 1998

Squires, Brandon (Maritzburg College) Natal 2002

Stampu, Yondela (St Alban's) BB 2007

Stander,* Chris (Oakdale Agric.) SWD 2008

Steenkamp, Buks (Grey College) FS 1985-86

Steenkamp, Corrie (Vereeniging THS) Falcons 1997

Steenkamp, Jabez (Paarl BH) WP 2003

Steenkamp, Pieta (Grey College) FS 1990

Steenkamp, Virgulle (Excelsior Belhar) WP 1997

Steenkamp, Willie (Grey College) FS 2000

Stegmann, Deon (Grey College) FS 2004

Stevens, Jeffrey (Breërivier) Boland 1995-96

Stevens, Kees (Grey College) FS 1983

Stevenson, Jacques (Ermelo) Mpu 1989

Stewart, Clayton (Strand HS) WP 2006

Stewart, Errol (Westville) Natal 1987

Steyn, Christo (Bloemfontein THS) FS 1976

Steyn, Jacques (Andrew Rabie) EP 1995

Stoop, Ockert (John Vorster, Nigel) Falcons 1974-75

†Stransky, Joel (Maritzburg College) Natal 1984

†Strauss, Adriaan (Grey College) FS 2003

Strauss, Johan (Kearsney College) Natal 2004

Strauss, Richardt (Grey College) FS 2003

Strydom, Emil-Jan (Grey College) FS 1986

†Swanepoel, Werner (Grey College) FS 1991

†Swart, Justin (Paul Roos Gymnasium) WP 1991

Swart, Hakkies (Drostdy THS) Boland 1988

Swart, Johan (Paarl Gymnasium) WP 1982

†Swart, Balie (Paarl Gymnasium) WP 1983

Swartbooi, Dewey (Worcester Gymnasium) Boland 2000

Swiegers, Gielie (Monument) GL 1984

T

Taute, Jaco (Klerksdorp) Leopards 1989

Temple, Stephan (Pretoria Boys' High) BB 1993

Theron, Danie (Kimberley THS) GW 1980

Theron, Gerrie (Rustenburg) Leopards 1994-95

Theron, Jannie (Sand du Plessis) FS 1987

Theron, Pieter (Grey College) FS 1975

Thomas, Gray (Volkskool) Leopards 1984

Thomas, Jason – (Muir Coll) – EP – 2010

†Thompson, Jeremy (Maritzburg College) Natal 1986

Thompson, Malcolm (Maritzburg College) Natal 1974-75

Tile, Mandilakhe (Dale College) Bor 2005

Topkin, Gareth (Rondebosch) WP 2008

†Truscott, Andries (Grey College) FS 1986

U

Uys, Petrus (Monument) GL 2008

V

Van Buuren, Albertus (Hoopstad) NFS 1992

Van Collegeer, Stephan (Volkskool) Leopards 1981

†Van der Linde, CJ (Grey College) FS 1998

Van der Linden, Lallie (Pretoria Noord) BB 1974-75

Van der Merwe, Bennie (Paarl BH) WP 1979-80

Van der Merwe, Danie (Mariental) SWA 1980

Van der Merwe, Gert (DF Malan) WP 1976

Van der Merwe, Jaco (Bishops) WP 1983

Van der Merwe, Joepie (Grey College) FS 1979-80

Van de Merwe, Marinus (Standerton) Pumas 2010

Van der Merwe, Phillip (Grey College) FS 2003

Van der Merwe, Pikkie (Helpmekaar) GL 1978

Van der Mescht, JP (Daniel Pienaar) EP 1993

Van der Schyff, Jonathan (Monument) GL 2001

Van der Walt, CP (Piet Potgieter) Far North 1981

Van der Walt, Danie (Ermelo) Mpu 1989

Van der Walt, James (Ermelo) Mpu 1997

Van der Walt, Kobus (AHS, Pretoria) BB 1999

Van der Walt, Nardus (AHS, Pretoria) BB 2010

Van der Walt, Nicky (Ermelo) Mpu 1993

Vd Westhuizen, Chrisjan (Menlopark) BB 1995

Vd Westhuizen, Richard (Vryburger) GL 1976

Vd Westhuizen, Roedolf (AHS, Pretoria) BB 2000

†Vd Westhuyzen, Jaco (Ben Viljoen) Mpu 1996

Van Genderen, Jan (Monument) GL 1978

Van Genderen, Kolie (Monument) GL

1980
Van Heerden, Frans (Langenhoven) BB
1975
Van Heerden, Schalk (AHS, Pretoria) BB
2010
Van Heerden, Wayne (Brandwag, Uit.) EP
1997-98
Van Heerden, Wickus (Voortrekkerhoogte)
BB 1982
†Van Niekerk, Joe (King Edward VII) GL
1997-98
Van Niekerk, Ernst (Paul Roos Gymnasium) WP 1986
Van Niekerk, Niekie (De Wet Nel THS)
NFS 1985
Van Rensburg, Charl (Queen's College)
Bor 1992
Van Rensburg, Robbie (AHS, Pretoria)
BB 1998
Van Rooyen, Leon (Estcourt) Natal 1987
Van Rooyen, Nico (Rustenburg) Leopards
1981
Van Rooyen, Rudi (AHS, Pretoria) BB
2010
Van Vuuren, Kosie (AHS, Kroonstad)
NFS 1994
Van Rooyen, Marchand (Jan Viljoen) GL
2007
Van Vuuren, Pieter-Willem (Grey College)
FS 2006
Van Vuuren, Rodney (AHS, Kroonstad)
NFS 1983
Van Westing, Carl (Marais Viljoen THS)
GL 1992
Van Wyk, Cobus (Schoonspruit) Leopards
1976
Van Wyk, William (Paarl Gymnasium)
WP 2009
Van Zyl, Jaco (JG Meiring) WP 1994

Van Zyl, Willem Petrus (Paarl BH) WP
1997
Venske, Herman (Vanderbijlpark) GL 1979
†Venter, Brendan (Monument) GL 1989-91
⁴ Venter, André (Grey College) FS 1990-91
⁴ Venter, André (Monument) GL 1989
Venter, Deon (AHS, Pretoria) BB 2001
Venter, Francois (Grey College) FS 2008
Venter, Hugo (Grey College) FS 1991
Venter, Ruan (Monument) GL 2010
Verhoeven, Antonius (Charlie Hofmeyer)
Boland 1995
Vermaak, Jano (Vereeniging THS) Falcons
2003
Vermeulen, Gielie (Paul Roos Gymnasium)
WP 1983
Vermeulen, PJ (Noordkaap HS) Griquas
2005
Vermeulen, Riaan (Grey College) FS 2002
Viljoen, Gert (De Wet Nel THS) NFS
1980
Viljoen, Harry (Florida) GL 1976-77
†Viljoen, Roelof (Joggie) (Framesby) EP
1993-94
Visagie, Johan (Potchefstroom THS) Leopards 1974
Visagie, Ronnie (Rob Ferreira, Witrivier)
Mpu 1983-84
†Visser, De Villiers (Voortrekker, CT) WP
1976
†Visser, Mornay (Paarl Gymnasium) WP
1988
Visser, Jacques (Paarl Gymnasium) WP
1982
Volschenk, Johan (Oakdale Agric.) SWD
2004
†Von Hoesslin, David (Bishops) WP 1993
Vundla, Tshipiso (St Alban's) BB 2000

W
Wagenstroom, Frank (Tygerberg) WP
2003
Wait, Clayton (Pearson) EP 1989
Walker, Robert (St John's) GL 1981
Walters, Clint (Woodridge) EP 1993
Walters, Rowan (Upington HS) Griquas
2005
Wannenburg, Callie (Oakdale Agric.)
SWD 2001
†Wannenburg, Pedrie (Oakdale Agric.)
SWD 1999
Watermeyer, Stefan (Waterkloof) BB
2005-06
†Watson,* Luke (Grey) EP 2001
Weideman, Greyling (Drostdy THS)
Boland 1996
Weitz, Gerhard (Grey College) FS 1974-75
Wenger, Charl (Grey College) FS 2009
White, Bruce (Maritzburg College) Natal
1974-75
Whitfield, Brendon (Selborne College) Bor
1994
Wiese, Cornel (Paarl Gymnasium) WP
League 1988
Wiggins, Deon (Hugenote) Boland 1988
Willemse, Coenie (Hendrik Verwoerd) BB
1982
Willemse, Martin (Sandveld) NFS 1993
Williams, Jerome (Middelande Sec.) EP
2004
Willis, Vainon (Waterkloof) BB 2006
Wilson, Warren (Maritzburg College) Natal 1987
Wolmarans, Jan (Wonderboom) BB 1982
Z
Zaltsman, Neil (Northlands) Natal 1985

Provincial Representation (642 players)

Western Province	111	Eastern Transvaal / Valke	14
Free State	96	Griqualand West	7
Northern Transvaal / Blue Bulls	65	Far North / Limpopo BB	6
Natal / KwaZulu-Natal	58	North Eastern Cape / EP CD	6
Transvaal / Golden Lions	55	Stellaland	3
Eastern Province	52	Vaal Triangle	2
South Eastern Transvaal / Mpumalanga	43	WP Academy	2
Border	34	WP League	1
Boland	24	Border Country Districts	1
Northern Free State / Griffons	21	Zimbabwe (Rhodesia)	1
South Western Districts	20	Namibia (South West Africa)	1
Western Transvaal / Leopards	18	SA Academy (EP)	1

DIRECTORIES

SECTION 9
RUGBY WORLD CUP RECORDS

FIXTURES

NO	DATE	POOL	TEAM A		TEAM B	VENUE	STADIUM	CAPACITY
1	09/09/2011	A	New Zealand (1)	vs	Tonga (17)	Auckland	Eden Park	60,000
2	10/09/2011	B	Scotland (7)	vs	Romania (19)	Invercargill	Rugby Park Stadium	16,500
3	10/09/2011	D	Fiji (10)	vs	Namibia (22)	Rotorua	Rotorua International Stadium	34,000
4	10/09/2011	A	France (6)	vs	Japan (13)	Albany	North Harbour Stadium	30,000
5	10/09/2011	B	Argentina (8)	vs	England (4)	Christchurch	Stadium Christchurch	45,000
6	11/09/2011	C	Australia (2)	vs	Italy (12)	Christchurch	Stadium Christchurch	45,000
7	11/09/2011	C	Ireland (5)	vs	USA (16)	New Plymouth	Stadium Taranaki	25,500
8	11/09/2011	D	South Africa (3)	vs	Wales (9)	Wellington	Wellington Regional Stadium	40,000
9	14/09/2011	D	Samoa (11)	vs	Namibia (22)	Rotorua	Rotorua International Stadium	34,000
10	14/09/2011	A	Tonga (17)	vs	Canada (14)	Whangarei	Northland Events Centre	20,000
11	14/09/2011	B	Scotland (7)	vs	Georgia (15)	Dunedin	Carisbrook	29,000
12	15/09/2011	C	Russia (18)	vs	USA (16)	New Plymouth	Stadium Taranaki	25,500
13	16/09/2011	A	New Zealand (1)	vs	Japan (13)	Hamilton	Waikato Stadium	30,800
14	17/09/2011	B	Argentina (8)	vs	Romania (19)	Invercargill	Rugby Park Stadium	16,500
15	17/09/2011	D	South Africa (3)	vs	Fiji (10)	Wellington	Wellington Regional Stadium	40,000
16	17/09/2011	C	Australia (2)	vs	Ireland (5)	Auckland	Eden Park	60,000
17	18/09/2011	D	Wales (9)	vs	Samoa (11)	Hamilton	Waikato Stadium	30,800
18	18/09/2011	B	England (4)	vs	Georgia (15)	Christchurch	Stadium Christchurch	45,000
19	18/09/2011	A	France (6)	vs	Canada (14)	Napier	McLean Park	16,000
20	20/09/2011	C	Italy (12)	vs	Russia (18)	Nelson	Trafalgar Park	20,080
21	21/09/2011	A	Tonga (17)	vs	Japan (13)	Whangarei	Northland Events Centre	20,000
22	22/09/2011	D	South Africa (3)	vs	Namibia (22)	Albany	North Harbour Stadium	30,000
23	23/09/2011	C	Australia (2)	vs	USA (16)	Wellington	Wellington Regional Stadium	40,000
24	24/09/2011	B	England (4)	vs	Romania (19)	Dunedin	Carisbrook	29,000
25	24/09/2011	A	New Zealand (1)	vs	France (6)	Auckland	Eden Park	60,000
26	25/09/2011	D	Fiji (10)	vs	Samoa (11)	Auckland	Eden Park	60,000
27	25/09/2011	C	Ireland (5)	vs	Russia (18)	Rotorua	Rotorua International Stadium	34,000
28	25/09/2011	B	Argentina (8)	vs	Scotland (7)	Christchurch	Stadium Christchurch	45,000
29	26/09/2011	D	Wales (9)	vs	Namibia (22)	New Plymouth	Stadium Taranaki	25,500
30	27/09/2011	A	Canada (14)	vs	Japan (13)	Napier	McLean Park	16,000
31	27/09/2011	C	Italy (12)	vs	USA (16)	Nelson	Trafalgar Park	20,080
32	28/09/2011	B	Georgia (15)	vs	Romania (19)	Palmerston North	Arena Manawatu	18,300
33	30/09/2011	D	South Africa (3)	vs	Samoa (11)	Albany	North Harbour Stadium	30,000
34	01/10/2011	C	Australia (2)	vs	Russia (18)	Christchurch	Stadium Christchurch	45,000
35	01/10/2011	A	France (6)	vs	Tonga (17)	Wellington	Wellington Regional Stadium	40,000
36	01/10/2011	B	England (4)	vs	Scotland (7)	Auckland	Eden Park	60,000
37	02/10/2011	B	Argentina (8)	vs	Georgia (15)	Palmerston North	Arena Manawatu	18,300
38	02/10/2011	A	New Zealand (1)	vs	Canada (14)	Wellington	Wellington Regional Stadium	40,000
39	02/10/2011	D	Wales (9)	vs	Fiji (10)	Hamilton	Waikato Stadium	30,800
40	02/10/2011	C	Ireland (5)	vs	Italy (12)	Dunedin	Carisbrook	29,000
41	08/10/2011	QF 1	W C	vs	RU D	Wellington	Wellington Regional Stadium	40,000
42	08/10/2011	QF 2	W B	vs	RU A	Christchurch	Stadium Christchurch	45,000
43	09/10/2011	QF 3	W D	vs	RU C	Wellington	Wellington Regional Stadium	40,000
44	09/10/2011	QF 4	W A	vs	RU B	Christchurch	Stadium Christchurch	45,000
45	15/10/2011	SF 1	W QF 1	vs	W QF 2	Auckland	Eden Park	60,000
46	16/10/2011	SF 2	W QF 3	vs	W QF 4	Auckland	Eden Park	60,000
47	21/10/2011		L SF 1	vs	L SF 2	Auckland	Eden Park	60,000
48	23/10/2011		W SF 1	vs	W SF 2	Auckland	Eden Park	60,000

IRB World Rankings as at 29 November, 2010

IRB RUGBY WORLD CUP RECORDS

RWC TEAM RECORDS

Best performance		**AUSTRALIA** - Winners in 1991 and 1999
		SOUTH AFRICA - Winners in 1995 and 2007
Biggest win	142	**Australia** vs. Namibia, 2003 (142-0)
Biggest defeat	142	**Namibia** vs. Australia, 2003 (0-142)
Most points in a match	145	**New Zealand** vs. Japan, 1995 (145-17)
Most points conceded in a match	145	**Japan** vs. New Zealand, 1995 (17-145)
Most tries in a match	22	**Australia** vs. Namibia, 2003 (22-0)
Most tries conceded in a match	22	**Namibia** vs. Australia, 2003 (0-22)
Most conversions in a match	20	**New Zealand** vs. Japan, 1995
Most penalty goals in a match	8	**Argentina** vs. Samoa, 1999
	8	**Australia** vs. South Africa, 1999
	8	**France** vs. Ireland, 1995
	8	**Scotland** vs. Tonga, 1995
Most drop goals in a match	5	**South Africa** vs. England, 1999
Most points in a tournament	361	**New Zealand** in 2003 (7 matches)
Most points conceded in a tournament	310	**Namibia** in 2003 (4 matches)
Most tries in a tournament	52	**New Zealand** in 2003 (7 matches)
Most tries conceded in a tournament	47	**Namibia** in 2003 (4 matches)
Most conversions in a tournament	40	**New Zealand** in 2003 (7 matches)
Most penalty goals in a tournament	32	**Argentina** in 1999 (5 matches)
Most drop goals in a tournament	8	**South Africa** in 1999 (6 matches)
	8	**England** in 2003 (7 matches)
Penalty tries for	6	**Argentina**
Penalty tries against	6	**Samoa**
Yellow cards in previous tournaments	7	**France**
	7	**Tonga**
Red cards in previous tournaments	3	**Canada**

RWC INDIVIDUAL RECORDS

Most points in a match	45	SD Culhane (New Zealand) vs. Japan, 1995
Most tries in a match	6	MCG Ellis (New Zealand) vs. Japan, 1995
Most conversions in a match	20	SD Culhane (New Zealand) vs. Japan, 1995
Most penalty goals in a match	8	G Quesada (Argentina) vs. Samoa, 1999
	8	MC Burke (Australia) vs. South Africa, 1999
	8	T Lacroix (France) vs. Ireland, 1995
	8	AG Hastings (Scotland) vs. Tonga, 1995
Most drop goals in a match	5	JH de Beer (South Africa) vs. England, 1999
Most points in a tournament	126	GJ Fox (New Zealand) in 1987 (6 matches)
Most tries in a tournament	8	JT Lomu (New Zealand) in 1999 (6 matches)
	8	BG Habana (South Africa) in 2007 (7 matches)
Most conversions in a tournament	30	GJ Fox (New Zealand) in 1987 (6 matches)
Most penalty goals in a tournament	31	G Quesada (Argentina) in 1999 (5 matches)
Most drop goals in a tournament	8	JP Wilkinson (England) in 2003 (6 matches)
Most appearances	22	J Leonard (England) between 1991 and 2003
Most points in a career	249	JP Wilkinson (England) (15 matches)
Most tries in a career	15	JT Lomu (New Zealand) (11 matches)
Most conversions in a career	39	AG Hastings (Scotland) (13 matches)
Most penalty goals in a career	53	JP Wilkinson (England) (15 matches)
Most drop goals in a career	13	JP Wilkinson (England) (15 matches)

SOUTH AFRICA IN THE 1995 RUGBY WORLD CUP (Winner)

Date	Venue	OPPONENT	Points For	Points Against	Difference	Aggregate	Tries For	Conversions For	Penalties For	Drop Goals For	Tries Against	Conversions Against	Penalties Against	Drop Goals Against
25/05/1995	Cape Town	Australia	27	18	9	45	2	1	4	1	2	1	2	0
30/05/1995	Cape Town	Romania	21	8	13	29	2	1	3	0	1	0	1	0
03/06/1995	Port Elizabeth	Canada	20	0	20	20	2	2	2	0	0	0	0	0
10/06/1995	Johannesburg (Q/F)	W Samoa	42	14	28	56	6	3	2	0	2	2	0	0
17/06/1995	Durban (S/F)	France	19	15	4	34	1	1	4	0	0	0	5	0
24/06/1995	Johannesburg (F)	New Zealand	15	12	3	27	0	0	3	2	0	0	3	1
			144	**67**	**77**	**211**	**13**	**8**	**18**	**3**	**5**	**3**	**11**	**1**

Played 6. Won 6. Points for: 144. Points against: 67. Tries for: 13. Tries against: 5.

SOUTH AFRICA IN THE 1999 RUGBY WORLD CUP (Third)

Date	Venue	OPPONENT	Points For	Points Against	Difference	Aggregate	Tries For	Conversions For	Penalties For	Drop Goals For	Tries Against	Conversions Against	Penalties Against	Drop Goals Against
03/10/1999	Edinburgh	Scotland	46	29	17	75	6	5	2	0	2	2	4	1
10/10/1999	Edinburgh	Spain	47	3	44	50	7	6	0	0	0	0	1	0
15/10/1999	Glasgow	Uruguay	39	3	36	42	5	4	2	0	0	0	1	0
24/10/1999	Paris (Q/F)	England	44	21	23	65	2	2	5	5	0	0	7	0
30/10/1999	London (S/F)	Australia	21	27	-6	48	0	0	6	1	0	0	8	1
04/11/1999	Cardiff (3rd/4th)	New Zealand	22	18	4	40	1	1	3	2	0	0	6	0
			219	**101**	**118**	**320**	**21**	**18**	**18**	**8**	**2**	**2**	**27**	**2**

Played 6. Won 5. Lost 1. Points for: 219. Points against: 101. Tries for: 21. Tries against: 2.

SOUTH AFRICA IN THE 2003 RUGBY WORLD CUP (Losing Quarter-finalist)

Date	Venue	OPPONENT	Points For	Points Against	Difference	Aggregate	Tries For	Conversions For	Penalties For	Drop Goals For	Tries Against	Conversions Against	Penalties Against	Drop Goals Against
11/10/2003	Perth	Uruguay	72	6	66	78	12	6	0	0	0	0	2	0
18/10/2003	Perth	England	6	25	-19	31	0	0	2	0	1	1	4	2
24/10/2003	Sydney	Georgia	46	19	27	65	7	4	1	0	1	1	4	0
01/11/2003	Brisbane	Samoa	60	10	50	70	8	7	1	1	1	1	1	0
08/11/2003	Melbourne (Q/F)	New Zealand	9	29	-20	38	0	0	3	0	3	1	3	1
			193	**89**	**104**	**282**	**27**	**17**	**7**	**1**	**6**	**4**	**14**	**3**

Played 5. Won 3. Lost 2. Points for: 193. Points against: 89. Tries for: 27. Tries against: 6.

SOUTH AFRICA IN THE 2007 RUGBY WORLD CUP (Winner)

Date	Venue	OPPONENT	Points For	Points Against	Difference	Aggregate	Tries For	Conversions For	Penalties For	Drop Goals For	Tries Against	Conversions Against	Penalties Against	Drop Goals Against
09/09/2007	Paris	Samoa	59	7	52	66	8	5	3	0	1	1	0	0
14/09/2007	Paris	England	36	0	36	36	3	3	5	0	0	0	0	0
22/09/2007	Lens	Tonga	30	25	5	55	4	2	2	0	3	2	2	0
30/09/2007	Montpellier	USA	64	15	49	79	9	8	1	0	2	1	1	0
10/07/2007	Marseilles (Q/F)	Fiji	37	20	17	57	5	3	2	0	2	2	2	0
14/10/2007	Paris (S/F)	Argentina	37	13	24	50	4	4	3	0	1	1	2	0
20/10/2007	Paris (F)	England	15	6	9	21	0	0	5	0	0	0	2	0
			278	**86**	**192**	**364**	**33**	**25**	**21**	**0**	**9**	**7**	**9**	**0**

Played 7. Won 7. Points for: 278. Points against: 86. Tries for: 33. Tries against: 9.

WORLD CUP RECORDS

TEAM RECORDS FOR SOUTH AFRICA

Best performance		**WINNER**: 1995 & 2007
Biggest win	66	Against **Uruguay**, 2003 (72-6)
Biggest defeat	20	Against **New Zealand**, 2003 (9-29)
Most points in a match	72	Against **Uruguay**, 2003 (72-6)
Most points conceded in a match	29	Against **Scotland**, 1999 (46-29)
	29	Against **New Zealand**, 2003 (9-29)
Most tries in a match	12	Against **Uruguay**, 2003 (12-0)
Most tries conceded in a match	3	Against **New Zealand**, 2003 (0-3)
	3	Against **Tonga**, 2007 (4-3)
Most conversions in a match	8	Against **USA**, 2007
Most penalty goals in a match	6	Against **Australia**, 1999
Most drop goals in a match	5	Against **England**, 1999 *(RWC Record)*
Most points in a tournament	278	2007 (7 matches)
Most points conceded in a tournament	101	1999 (6 matches)
Most tries in a tournament	33	2007 (7 matches)
Most tries conceded in a tournament	9	2007 (7 matches)
Most conversions in a tournament	25	2007 (7 matches)
Most penalty goals in a tournament	21	2007 (7 matches)
Most drop goals in a tournament	8	1999 (6 matches) *(RWC Record)*
Penalty tries for	1	Against **Spain**, 1999
Penalty tries against	-	

INDIVIDUAL RECORDS FOR SOUTH AFRICA

Most points in a match	34	**JH de Beer** vs. England, 1999
Most tries in a match	4	**CM Williams** vs. Western Samoa, 1995
	4	**BG Habana** vs. Samoa, 2007
Most conversions in a match	6	**JH de Beer** vs. Spain, 1999
	6	**PC Montgomery** vs. USA, 2007
Most penalty goals in a match	6	**JH de Beer** vs. Australia, 1999
Most drop goals in a match	5	**JH de Beer** vs. England, 1999 *(RWC Record)*
Most points in a tournament	105	**PC Montgomery**, 2007 (7 matches)
Most tries in a tournament	8	**BG Habana**, 2007 (7 matches)
Most conversions in a tournament	22	**PC Montgomery**, 2007 (7 matches)
Most penalty goals in a tournament	17	**PC Montgomery**, 2007 (7 matches)
Most drop goals in a tournament	6	**JH de Beer**, 1999 (5 matches)
Most appearances	16	**JP du Randt** (1995-2007)
Most points in a career	111	**PC Montgomery** (12 matches)
Most tries in a career	8	**BG Habana** (7 matches)
Most conversions in a career	22	**PC Montgomery** (12 matches)
Most penalty goals in a career	17	**PC Montgomery** (12 matches)
Most drop goals in a career	6	**JH de Beer** (5 matches)
Yellow cards in previous tournaments	4	**H Scholtz** vs. Georgia, 2003
		FPL Steyn vs. Tonga, 2007
		BG Habana vs. Tonga, 2007
		JH Smith vs. Argentina, 2007
Red cards in previous tournaments	2	**J Dalton** vs. Canada, 1995
		B Venter vs. Uruguay, 1999

BEST PERFORMANCE OF PARTICIPATING COUNTRIES

Argentina	Third in 2007
Australia	Winners in 1991 and 1999
Canada	Losing Quarter-finalist in 1991
England	Winner in 2003
Fiji	Losing Quarter-finalist in 1987 and 2007
France	Second in 1987 and 1999
Georgia	Winning first match at RWC against Namibia, 2007 (30-0)
Ireland	Losing quarter-finalist in 1987, 1991, 1995 and 2003
Italy	Won two pool matches in 2003 and 2007
Japan	Won one pool match in 1991
Namibia	A negative points difference of 144 in 1999
New Zealand	Winner in 1987
Romania	A negative points difference of 33 in 1991
Russia	RWC 2011 will be Russia's first tournament
Samoa	Losing quarter-finalist in 1991 and 1995
Scotland	Fourth in 1991
South Africa	Winners in 1995 and 2007
Tonga	A negative points difference of 7 in 2007
USA	A negative points difference of 39 in 2003
Wales	Third in 1987

WORLD CUP RECORDS